CONCISE ENCYCLOPEDIA OF
INFORMATION PROCESSING IN SYSTEMS & ORGANIZATIONS

ADVANCES IN SYSTEMS, CONTROL AND INFORMATION ENGINEERING

This is a new series of Pergamon Scientific reference works, each volume providing comprehensive, self-contained and up-to-date coverage of a selected area in the field of systems, control and information engineering. The series is being developed primarily from the highly acclaimed *Systems & Control Encyclopedia* published in 1987. Other titles in the series are listed below.

ATHERTON & BORNE (eds.)
Concise Encyclopedia of Modelling & Simulation

FINKELSTEIN & GRATTAN (eds.)
Concise Encyclopedia of Measurement & Instrumentation

MORRIS & TAMM (eds.)
Concise Encyclopedia of Software Engineering

PAPAGEORGIOU (ed.)
Concise Encyclopedia of Traffic & Transportation Systems

PAYNE (ed.)
Concise Encyclopedia of Biological & Biomedical Measurement Systems

PELEGRIN & HOLLISTER (eds.)
Concise Encyclopedia of Aeronautics & Space Systems

YOUNG (ed.)
Concise Encyclopedia of Environmental Systems

NOTICE TO READERS

Dear Reader
If your library is not already a standing order/continuation order customer to the series **Advances in Systems, Control and Information Engineering**, may we recommend that you place a standing order/continuation order to receive immediately upon publication all new volumes. Should you find that these volumes no longer serve your needs, your order can be cancelled at any time without notice.

ROBERT MAXWELL
Publisher at Pergamon Press

CONCISE ENCYCLOPEDIA OF INFORMATION PROCESSING IN SYSTEMS & ORGANIZATIONS

Editor
ANDREW P SAGE
*George Mason University
Fairfax, VA, USA*

Series Editor-in-Chief
MADAN G SINGH
UMIST, Manchester, UK

PERGAMON PRESS
Member of Maxwell Macmillan Pergamon Publishing Corporation
OXFORD • NEW YORK • BEIJING • FRANKFURT
SÃO PAULO • SYDNEY • TOKYO • TORONTO

U.K.	Pergamon Press plc, Headington Hill Hall, Oxford OX3 0BW, England
U.S.A.	Pergamon Press, Inc., Maxwell House, Fairview Park, Elmsford, New York 10523, U.S.A.
PEOPLE'S REPUBLIC OF CHINA	Pergamon Press, Room 4037, Qianmen Hotel, Beijing, People's Republic of China
FEDERAL REPUBLIC OF GERMANY	Pergamon Press GmbH, Hammerweg 6, D-6242 Kronberg, Federal Republic of Germany
BRAZIL	Pergamon Editora Ltda, Rua Eça de Queiros, 346, CEP 04011, Paraiso, São Paulo, Brazil
AUSTRALIA	Pergamon Press Australia Pty Ltd., P.O. Box 544, Potts Point, N.S.W. 2011, Australia
JAPAN	Pergamon Press, 5th Floor, Matsuoka Central Building, 1-7-1 Nishishinjuku, Shinjuku-ku, Tokyo 160, Japan
CANADA	Pergamon Press Canada Ltd., Suite No. 241, 253 College Street, Toronto, Ontario, Canada M5T 1R5

Copyright © 1990 Pergamon Press plc

All rights reserved. No part of this publication may be reproduced, stored in any retrieval system or transmitted in any form or by any means: electronic, electrostatic, magnetic tape, mechanical, photocopying, recording or otherwise, without permission in writing from the publishers.

First edition 1990

Library of Congress Cataloging in Publication Data
Concise Encyclopedia of information processing in systems & organizations / editor, Andrew P. Sage; executive editor, Madan G. Singh — 1st ed.
  p. cm. — (Advances in systems, control & information engineering)
  Includes index.
  1. Electronic data processing — Dictionaries. I. Sage, Andrew P. II. Singh, Madan G. III. Series
QA76.15. C655 1989
004'.03—dc20   89-8818

British Library Cataloguing in Publication Data
Concise encyclopaedia of information processing in systems & organizations. — (Advances in systems, control & information engineering)
1. Information processing
I. Sage, Andrew P. (Andrew Patrick) II. Series
001.5

ISBN 0-08-035954-X

Printed in Great Britain by BPCC Wheatons Ltd, Exeter

CONTENTS

Honorary Editorial Advisory Board	vi
Foreword	vii
Preface	ix
Guide to Use of the Encyclopedia	xi
Alphabetical List of Articles	xiii
An Introduction to Information Processing in Systems and Organizations	xv
Articles	1
List of Contributors	519
Subject Index	525

HONORARY EDITORIAL ADVISORY BOARD

Chairman
John F Coales CBE, FRS
Cambridge, UK

Editor-in-Chief
Madan G Singh
UMIST, Manchester, UK

D Aspinall
UMIST, Manchester, UK

K J Åström
*Lund Institute of Technology
Sweden*

A Bensoussan
INRIA, Le Chesnay, France

P Borne
*Institut Industriel du Nord
Villeneuve D'Ascq, France*

A W Goldsworthy OBE
*Jennings Industries Ltd
Victoria, Australia*

J Lesourne
*Conservatoire National
des Arts et Métiers,
Paris, France*

P A Payne
UMIST, Manchester, UK

A P Sage
*George Mason University
Fairfax, VA, USA*

Y Sawaragi
*Japan Institute for Systems
Research, Kyoto, Japan*

G Schmidt
*Technische Universität München
Federal Republic of Germany*

B Tamm
*Tallinn Technical University
USSR*

M Thoma
*Universität Hannover
Federal Republic of Germany*

R Vichnevetsky
*Rutgers University
New Brunswick, NJ, USA*

FOREWORD

With the publication of the eight-volume *Systems & Control Encyclopedia* in September 1987, Pergamon Press was very keen to ensure that the scholarship embodied in the Encyclopedia was both kept up to date and was disseminated to as wide an audience as possible. For these purposes, an Honorary Editorial Advisory Board was set up under the chairmanship of Professor John F Coales FRS, and I was invited to continue as Editor-in-Chief of both the Systems & Control Encyclopedia Series of Supplementary Volumes and the Advances in Systems, Control and Information Engineering Series of Concise Encyclopedias. This involved me personally editing a series of Supplementary Volumes updating the original Encyclopedia and also arranging for the editing of a series of Concise Encyclopedias being developed from it on specific subject areas. The Honorary Editorial Advisory Board helped to select a series of subject areas which were perceived to be appropriate for the publication of Concise Encyclopedias and chose the most distinguished experts in those areas to edit them. The Concise Encyclopedias contain some updated and revised articles from the Main Encyclopedia and many that are totally new, reflecting recent advances in the subject and gaps in the original Encyclopedia.

It is a great pleasure to commend the reader to the first of these Concise Encyclopedias which is edited by one of the most innovative thinkers in the field of information processing in systems and organizations: Dean Andrew P Sage. This Concise Encyclopedia provides a comprehensive and up-to-date view of this important field.

Madan G Singh
Series Editor-in-Chief

PREFACE

The primary purpose of this Concise Encyclopedia is to describe the state-of-the-art and recent advances in the general area of information processing. In this volume we are concerned with information in the broad sense of collections of data important for decisionmaking. For information to be processed satisfactorily, it must be acquired, represented, transmitted, stored, transmitted and used. The current research reviewed in this Encyclopedia addresses these concerns and also looks at enhancing information processing in humans, in technological systems and in organizations of humans and technological systems.

There are many specialty areas that have interests in this broad subject. Among them are systems engineering, human factors engineering, cognitive science and psychology, judgement and choice, management science, information systems and computer science. The contributors to the 68 articles in this volume come from an equally diverse background. The intended audience is also diverse and includes individual scientists and engineers, including advanced undergraduates, graduate students and industrial practitioners.

There are at least two approaches to using this volume. The alphabetical list of articles can be examined and articles of interest consulted directly or, alternatively, the lengthy introduction can be consulted. This introduction provides a systematic overview and taxonomy of the whole field of information processing in systems and organizations as presented in this volume: from reading this introduction it should be possible to select specific topics that are of interest. Whichever route is taken, each article contains extensive cross references to further related articles within the Encyclopedia, as well as reference to key works in the literature of the field.

This Concise Encyclopedia would not have been possible without the very able contributions of the numerous authors who agreed to write for it. Their names appear at the foot of the articles they wrote as well as in the alphabetical List of Contributors found on p. 519. It was Madan Singh who suggested that I undertake this work and he made many helpful suggestions that supported it. At Pergamon Press, Colin Drayton and Michael Mabe did much to steer the project to a timely completion, while Sarah Warbrick and Christopher Tighe had the unenviable task of reading the initial draft material and contributed much to its editing. Their vigilant support is much appreciated.

Andrew P Sage
Editor

GUIDE TO USE OF THE ENCYCLOPEDIA

This Concise Encyclopedia is a comprehensive reference work covering all aspects of information processing in systems and organizations. Information is presented in a series of alphabetically arranged articles which deal concisely with individual topics in a self-contained manner. This guide outlines the main features and organization of the Encyclopedia, and is intended to help the reader to locate the maximum amount of information on a given topic.

Accessibility of material is of vital importance in a reference work of this kind and article titles have therefore been selected, not only on the basis of article content, but also with the most probable needs of the reader in mind. An alphabetical list of all the articles contained in this Encyclopedia is to be found on p. xiii.

Articles are linked by an extensive cross-referencing system. Cross-references to other articles in the Encyclopedia are of two types: in-text and end-of-text. Those in the body of the text are designed to refer the reader to articles that present in greater detail material on the specific topic under discussion. They generally take one of the following forms:

...as fully described in the article *Expert Systems for Managers: Design Issues*

...or on simulation (see *Simulation Methodology and Model Manipulation*)

The cross-references listed at the end of an article serve to identify broad background reading and to direct the reader to articles that cover different aspects of the same topic.

The nature of an encyclopedia demands a higher degree of uniformity in terminology and notation than many other scientific works. The widespread use of the International System of Units has determined that such units be used in this Encyclopedia. It has been recognized, however, that in some fields Imperial units are more generally used. Where this is the case, Imperial units are given with their SI equivalent quantity and unit following in parentheses. Where possible the symbols defined in *Quantities, Units, and Symbols*, published by the Royal Society of London, have been used.

All articles in the Encyclopedia include a bibliography giving sources of further information. Each bibliography consists of general items for further reading and/or references which cover specific aspects of the text. Where appropriate, authors are cited in the text using a name/date system as follows:

...as was recently reported (Smith 1988).

Jones (1984) describes...

The contributor's name and the organization to which they are affiliated appear at the end of each article. All contributors can be found in the alphabetical List of Contributors, along with their full postal address and the titles of the articles of which they are authors or co-authors.

The Introduction to this Concise Encyclopedia provides an overview of information processing in systems and organizations and directs the reader to many of the key articles in this work.

The most important information source for locating a particular topic in the Encyclopedia is the multilevel Subject Index, which has been made as complete and fully self-consistent as possible.

ALPHABETICAL LIST OF ARTICLES

Analogical Reasoning
Artificial Intelligence
Automated Planning
Automation: Social Effects
Cognitive Management and Models of Judgement and Choice Processes
Cognitive Science, Human Information Processing and Artificial Intelligence
Collective Enquiry
Command and Control Information Systems
Computer-Aided Systems Engineering
Computer-Based Instruction: Costs and Effectiveness
Decision Analysis
Decision Making: Information Processing and Organizational Models
Decision-Problem Structuring
Decision Support Systems
Design and Evaluation of Systems
Distributed Decision Making: Information Systems
Distributed Information and Organizational Decision-Making Models
Dynamic Decision Making
Evidentiary Reasoning and Human Information Processing
Expert Database Systems
Expert Systems
Expert Systems for Managers: Design Issues
Fuzzy Reasoning Methods
Group Decision Making and Voting
Group Decision Support Systems
Group Decision Support Systems: Software Architecture
Human Factors Engineering
Human Factors Engineering: Information-Processing Concerns
Human Information Processing
Human Judgement and Decision Rules
Human–System Interaction: Information-Presentation Requirements
Hypothesis Testing
Inference and Impact Analysis

Information Laws of Systems
Information Requirements Determination
Information Systems
Information Systems and Software Productivity
Information Systems Design in Industrial Practice
Information Theory
Intuitive and Analytical Cognition: Information Models
Knowledge Acquisition: Storyboarding and Computer-Based System Decision Research
Knowledge-Based Simulation
Knowledge Representation
Knowledge Support Systems: Uncertain Information Processing
Multiattribute Utility Theory
Multicriteria Decision Problem
Office Automation
Organizational Information Structures: Quantitative Models
Problem Formulation
Program Evaluation: A Systems and Model-Based Approach
Prototyping as Information in Systems Design
Real-Time Software Design: Information Concerns
Recognitional Decision Making: Information Requirements
Simulation Methodology and Model Manipulation
Simulation Methodology: Top-Down Approach
Simulation: Model-Base Organization and Utilization
Software Development: Human Information Processing
Supervisory Control: Philosophical Considerations in Manufacturing Systems
Support-System Design: Behavioral Concerns
System Acquisition and Procurement
System-Acquisition Information: Knowledge-Based Representation
System-Integration Fundamentals
Systems Analysis and Modelling: Time Series
Systems Concepts: History
Systems Knowledge: Philosophical Perspectives
Systems Management: Conflict Analysis
Systems Methodology

AN INTRODUCTION TO INFORMATION PROCESSING IN SYSTEMS AND ORGANIZATIONS
by Andrew P Sage

This Concise Encyclopedia provides a state-of-the-art report on the important area of human and machine information processing in systems and organizations. The scope of this subject is extraordinarily broad and there is no way in which complete coverage could be provided. Of primary importance are the general areas of

(a) Methodological Issues

(b) Information and Knowledge Organization, and Characterization in Humans and Machines

(c) Individual and Organizational Decisions

(d) Technological Systems to Aid Information Processing

and these have been further disaggregated into 11 different topic headings and further decomposed into the 68 articles found in the body of this work.

1. Methodological Issues in the Study of Systems

Systems concepts and history are important concerns in information science and information technology. A system can be regarded as a well-defined group of related elements organized to satisfy some purpose and having some well-defined boundaries. We must be aware of its purpose, and define the level of abstraction at which any analysis is to be carried out. Systems may contain recognizable subsystems, sub-subsystems and so on: such arrangements are sometimes depicted and investigated as hierarchies. One of the discoveries made by the systems approach, is the extent to which attempts to improve the performance of a subsystem by its own criteria may actually be detrimental to the total system and may even defeat its objectives. So, an optimal set of subsystems does not necessarily imply an optimal system.

The basic processes involved in the hypothetically deductive method associated with systems are:

(a) hypotheses, laws, assumptions or generalizations;

(b) deduction, including both formal and informal, or default, logic;

(c) observation, confirmation, experiment; and

(d) induction and abduction, which lead back to generalizations.

These processes are discussed by Frank H. George in the article *Systems Concepts: History*. They have evolved over the history of the systems movement and are very much in evidence in this work on information processing in systems and organizations.

Systems methodology, and the associated selection of appropriate tools and techniques of systems engineering to assist in the resolution of complicated issues, is one of the major results of systems research. These methods are equally appropriate in either the public or the private sector, as complicated issue resolution in all these areas displays many common characteristics. While systems methodology may be ubiquitous across these areas, the specific methods that are most appropriate for a given task will generally be very task dependent, and dependent upon the experiential familiarity of the problem solver with the task and the environment.

Typically, the identification of alternatives and the subsequent acts of judgement and choice that lead to selection of an alternative for implementation involve considerations of many who often have conflicting or competing desires. Resources are generally insufficient to satisfy the needs of everyone. Trade-offs have to be made, generally among incommensurate attributes of proposed alternative courses of action. The impacts to be traded off are often poorly known. There are, typically, large amounts of information imperfection associated with knowledge of future impacts. Many future developments are beyond the control of the decisionmaker. The values or needs of the individual or group to be satisfied may change in an often unpredictable way before a policy comes into effect. Institution and organizational factors play an important, sometimes even critical part.

Because there is often a mismatch between problem and method, and because many analysts are likely to overstate the potential power of their approach and raise higher expectations than is justified, analytical efforts often produce unsatisfactory results. Many of these prior experiences are characterized by frustration that results from often different, sometimes even conflicting, conclusions concerning the same issue that may be obtained by different analyses. This has added to the feeling that analysis results can be manipulated, and has generated mistrust among managers and decisionmakers towards the objectivity of analysts, and the utility of analytical methods.

Systems engineering involves the application of a general set of guidelines and methods useful to assist clients in the resolution of issues and problems which are often of large scale and scope. Three fundamental steps may be distinguished:

(a) problem or issue formulation,

(b) problem or issue analysis,

(c) interpretation of analysis results, including evaluation and selection of alternatives, and implementation of the chosen alternatives.

These steps are conducted at a number of phases throughout a system's lifecycle. This lifecycle begins with the determination of requirements for a system through system design, development, installation, ultimate maintenance and replacement. The article *Systems Methodology* provides a discussion of systems methodology. It includes presentation of the material just discussed as well as an overview of some methods appropriate for the practice of information systems engineering.

Most models of planning and design, problem solving and decisionmaking begin with a problem formulation step. This step, sometimes labelled "problem definition," "problem identification" or "problem diagnosis," is concerned with gathering information about the problem and classifying or describing the problem in sufficient detail that the uncertainty and risk of subsequent action is reduced.

Because it is one of the first phases in a larger process, problem formulation can determine the direction of the succeeding phases in the systems lifecycle. A problem that is formulated as a technical problem, for example, when it is better understood as a personnel problem, can lead to planning ineffectiveness and loss of confidence in the planners or the process. Determining which formulation of a situation is preferable is not easy. It is unlikely that an individual can tell from the semantics of a problem statement whether it is appropriate, without further study, for use in problem solving. For this reason, and because many complex problems require that multiple actions be taken to address multiple issues, a thorough exploration of the situation is often needed.

The article *Problem Formulation* by Roger J. Volkema is concerned with the problem formulation process, the factors that affect this process, and how problem formulation can be better managed to avoid committing Type III errors of solving the "wrong" problem. While the term used here is "problem," the concepts developed apply equally to opportunities as well, as a problem is, often, just an opportunity in disguise.

Topics relevant to the article *Design and Evaluation of Systems* are very important for information systems engineering. Some historical perspectives are first discussed that soon lead to consideration of the purpose and objectives of contemporary systems design engineering. A discussion of general objectives for quality system design is then followed by a presentation of a five phase design methodology for system design. Leadership and training requirements for use of the resulting system and the impact of these requirements upon design considerations are important and these are discussed as well. It is doubtlessly true that not every design process should, could, or would precisely follow each component in the detailed phases of system design outlined. However, the approach to system design is sufficiently robust and generic that it can be used as a normative model of the design process, including information concerns for design, and as a guide to the structuring and implementation of appropriate system evaluation practices.

It is the purpose of evaluation to provide answers to questions such as: Does the program work? Is it worth the cost? Can and should it be implemented elsewhere? Unfortunately, program evaluation has not lived up to its expectations. The field of evaluation contains many efforts which do not adequately address the important issues or objectives that follow from the questions just posed. Potential problems with an evaluation are:

(a) they do not employ valid controls for comparison purposes;

(b) they rely on inadequate measures or include expensive collection of data on measure that are in fact never used in the evaluation;

(c) they rely on inappropriate measurement methods; and

(d) they employ inadequate analytic techniques.

Most of these difficulties could be mitigated by developing a valid and comprehensive evaluation design prior to the start of an evaluation effort.

There is no stock evaluation design that can be taken off-the-shelf and implemented without revision in a specific evaluation. There is an approach or process by which designs can be developed, however. In the article *Program Evaluation: A Systems and Model-Based Approach*, Jim Tien discusses a method for developing valid and comprehensive evaluation designs. It also highlights a practical application of the systems and model-based approach to program evaluation.

There are many possible conflicts that arise among humans and organizations. In *Systems Management: Conflict Analysis*, the methodology of Neil Fraser and Keith Hipel is a comprehensive and flexible procedure that can be employed to study real-world conflict. The systematic examination of a conflict consists of two main stages of modelling and analysis:

(a) the particular conflict being studied is modelled by putting available information about the dispute into a proper perspective and then logically structuring the problem; and

(b) this conflict model is employed in an analytical effort to predict possible compromise resolutions to the dispute.

By appropriately varying the parameters in the conflict model, one can use sensitivity analyses to ascertain how robust or sensitive the predictions are to meaningful changes in the model. Based upon the results of a conflict study, a given decisionmaker can behave in an optimal manner within the social and political constraints of the conflict.

There are many distinct advantages for employing conflict analysis in systems management.

(a) Conflict analysis can handle general multiple participant decisionmaking problems in which each participant can have multiple objectives.

(b) Documented applications for both current and historical disputes confirm that conflict analysis produces realistic and useful results.

Fraser and Hipel's approach to conflict analysis represents

a reformulation and extension of metagame analysis, which in turn has some connections with classical game theory. In a conflict or game, two or more participants are in dispute over some resource or issue. Each participant in a conflict model is called a player and is considered to be an entity who has actions he or she can take which have significance to other players in the conflict. The possible actions of each player are called options. Any set of options that can be taken by a player is called a strategy, and the situation where each player selects a strategy is called an outcome. Each player has his or her own preference ordering of all the outcomes in the conflict. A game or conflict model consists of the players, their options and their preferences among the possible feasible outcomes. The analysis of the game is carried out by determining the stability of each outcome for every player. If an outcome is stable for a given strategy, it does not benefit the player to move unilaterally to any other outcome by changing his or her own strategy. An outcome that is stable for all players in the game model is an equilibrium and constitutes a possible resolution to the conflict.

Decisions often affect groups of people instead of isolated individuals. In such cases, managers, planners and decisionmakers are usually expected to consider the preferences of individuals concerned. Voting is one very common form of group decisionmaking and is emphasized in the article *Group Decision Making and Voting*. Some of the methods that may be used to determine social or group preference include dictatorship, widely encompassing sets of traditional rules or customs, market mechanisms and voting. With the possible exception of voting, it is reasonably clear that these methods do not necessarily use any "fair" scheme to determine group preferences for making decisions. As indicated in the article, voting is not nearly as perfect for determining group preferences as one might intuitively think. Thus we come to the question explored in this article: just how do, or how should we amalgamate individual preference structures into a group preference structure? An overview of various voting strategies is presented.

2. Knowledge, and its Gathering by Humans and Organizations

Rapid advances in the electronic transfer of information have produced a massive industry as well as large scale societal changes. Our understanding of the cognitive processes that transform information into knowledge and action remains incomplete. It is the subject of considerable research by scientists from a wide variety of disciplines. Much of the research is directed toward understanding what appears to be two antithetical types of information processing—analytical and intuitive cognition.

The meaning of analytical cognition in ordinary language is clear; it signifies a step-by-step, conscious, logically defensible process.

Analysis has usually had an advantage over intuition in clarity of meaning. This is because the associated interpretations can be exhausted by reference to logical and/or mathematical arguments or models. Analytical cognition is the basis of rationality, and a rational argument calls for an overt, step-by-step, systematic and defensible process. Thus analytical cognition and overt definition are part of the same system of thought.

Throughout history intuition has acquired a mysterious, ineffable, undefinable character and a mixed reputation as well. As a result there are numerous models for analytical cognition to which information system engineers may turn, but no fully worked-out models of intuitive cognition. In his definitive article *Intuitive and Analytical Cognition: Information Models*, Kenneth Hammond discusses important contemporary research in this area.

The designer of information systems must be concerned both with normative models of decision and choice processes and with descriptive models of how people perform, and can perform, in given situations. The article *Cognitive Management and Models of Judgement and Choice Processes* is especially concerned with describing cognitive processes as they are influenced by the contingency structural elements of task, environment and the human problem solver's experience with these. The contingency task structure model first described is related to Piaget's theory of intellectual development.

Decision tasks often are dynamic decisionmaking tasks in that they share the following characteristics.

(a) A series of decisions are required.

(b) These decisions are interdependent.

(c) The decision problem changes, both autonomously and as a consequence of the decisionmaker's actions.

(d) The decisions are made in real time.

Dynamic decision tasks differ from static tasks in that a series of interdependent decisions are required to reach the goal. They differ from sequential decision tasks in that the time aspect is very important. These tasks require a different conception of decisionmaking than the usual formulation of discrete choice options prevalent in traditional research on decisionmaking. Berndt Brehmer suggests that they also require a new conception of decision tasks and that the traditional conception, which is based upon gambles and sees a decision task in terms of a list of action alternatives connected to outcomes by means of probabilities, will not suffice.

In his article *Dynamic Decision Making*, Brehmer suggests that decisionmaking in dynamic tasks should be seen as a matter of trying to achieve control, instead of an attempt to resolve discrete choice dilemmas. He proposes a conceptualization of dynamic decision tasks in terms of six basic characteristics:

(a) complexity,

(b) feedback quality,

(c) feedback delay,

(d) possibilities for decentralization,

(e) rate of change, and

(f) prerequisites for control.

The article discusses these six characteristics and the review of results from empirical studies on dynamic decisionmaking.

The roles of information, feedback, and individual and organizational learning in determining choice, and the organizational objectives that lead to choice and that are responsive to choice, are very important in any discussion of information processing and organizational models for decisionmaking.

Sound design and implementation of information and knowledge-based support to organizational decisionmaking requires knowledge of the ways in which organizations can acquire and process information, how organizations adapt to their internal and external environment, how they cope with conflict, how organizational cultures result from decisions as well as being determined by them, and how organizations learn and fail to learn. Each of these provides a perspective of information processing in systems and organizations. The article *Decision Making: Information Processing and Organizational Models* presents a discussion and interpretation of critical factors relevant to the design of information support systems to enhance the quality of organizational decisionmaking.

It is very important that the structure of a decision problem be specified prior to subsequent formal analysis and evaluation of the alternative action options. The process of decision-problem structuring is dynamic and cyclical, in the sense that, as additional problem elements and their interactions continue to be discovered, the preliminary structure is repeatedly modified. A fully-structured decision problem contains:

(a) a list of possible action options,

(b) identification of associated attributes, or metrics, of these for use in evaluating the suitability of the options, and

(c) identification of possible states of nature which may have an impact on the outcome of the options.

The way a person processes decision-relevant information will have a large effect on the contents of the problem structure, the problem solving process used, and the ultimate solution of the problem. A number of methods of aiding a person to access relevant items in memory and structure a decision problem creatively are presented in *Decision-Problem Structuring* by Robin Keller and Joanna Ho.

There are several ways that might be used to describe how individuals and groups acquire, represent, and use information with which to describe their perceptions of the world around them and issues that are of importance. *Systems Knowledge: Philosophical Perspectives* discusses some of these perspectives on knowledge since they are of such considerable importance to the subject of information processing in systems and organizations. First described is Churchman's concept of an enquiry system. Then, the multiple perspectives concept of Linstone is discussed followed by a brief discussion of rationality concepts which serves to provide a natural transition to group situations. Several models of organizational choice are reviewed in the concluding portion of this article.

The concept of recognitional decisionmaking is one which claims that proficient decisionmakers can generate and implement options by judging situations as familiar. This enables the decisionmaker to recognize the typical response to those situations. The process avoids the analytical strategy of generating a set of options and then evaluating them to select the best one. Under conditions such as time pressure, such analytical decisionmaking may be impossible.

Skilled personnel rely on recognitional decisionmaking to handle naturalistic tasks. These may include such tasks as commanding teams of urban firefighters, commanding crews that combat forest fires, leading tank platoons, playing high-level chess, and performing battle management functions. The article *Recognitional Decision Making: Information Requirements* by Gary Klein discusses how people with sufficient experiential familiarity with the task at hand can and do identify information requirements and function competently without performing analyses.

The importance of information and knowledge in problem-solving tasks is well recognized. A meta-theory of knowledge is very important in enabling development and use of knowledge-based decision support systems by people with diverse experiential familiarity with a particular task. This experiential familiarity will strongly influence the method of knowledge representation, cognitive operations on the knowledge base as well as the memory, control, and user–system interfaces that are most appropriate for a given task. *Knowledge Representation* presents a description and interpretation of several approaches for knowledge representation and knowledge aggregation that support holistic, heuristic, and wholistic reasoning in systems and organizations.

System engineering is concerned with the synthesis of discrete elements or components into an organized entity to satisfy some specific purpose. The focus of system engineering is on *what* is to be built. To this end, system acquisition information is very important.

The term system acquisition generally refers to large scale, complex, high technology development projects that require extended periods on the order of several years to develop and place into operation. During the extended period, laws and regulations may be revised, new technological solutions may present themselves, and the initially perceived system requirements may undergo change.

System acquisition management is concerned with the business strategy by which a system is built or otherwise acquired for use. Its focus is on how a system is to be acquired. The information needed to make informed business decisions relative to acquiring complex systems

Introduction

and technologies is referred to as system acquisition information. This includes:

(a) system objectives—which represent the high level technical, performance, cost and delivery or time parameters that characterize a system;

(b) resources—or the amount of time and money actually or potentially available for the acquisition of the system, and

(c) acquisition methods—which refers to the set of techniques or business practices for acquiring desired systems or technologies.

The system acquisition problem can be viewed as one of searching for the set of acquisition methods that best achieve the system objectives within the resource constraints. For the acquisition manager, the problem is to strike a balance between system objectives and resources in a business and technological environment that evolves over an extended time horizon.

System acquisition is concerned with high-level business strategy. In particular, its main focus is not with the administrative and legal details of preparing procurement documents, selecting a contract type, monitoring and evaluating contractor performance, or generally any of the multitude of tactical details that are necessary in any organization to execute the business plan. Rather, the fundamental purpose of systems acquisition is to produce the business plan itself. This activity is an example of design problem solving; design itself has been categorized as problem solving involving object synthesis through constraint satisfaction, and it is this paradigm that underlies the discussion in *System-Acquisition Information: Knowledge-Based Representation* by Franz Hatfield and Dona Madalon.

Judgements, at least prudent judgements, are seldom made without information. For it is only through information that one becomes aware of the need for judgement and choice activities and the result of these, a decision. Information is often defined as data of value in decisionmaking. The activities of data acquisition, representation, storage, distribution and use are generally involved in information processing. The task of information requirements determination is necessarily involved with all of these, although formally it is concerned with determination of what information is to be acquired. This cannot be done, however, without some perceptions concerning what will be done with the information after its acquisition in order to convert it to useful knowledge. The objectives of human information processing for decisionmaking include acquiring the information that is most relevant to the task at hand and obtaining a relatively full and complete interpretation of the information that is obtained.

Distributed decisionmaking refers to the process of organizational decisionmaking that occurs when the information, and responsibility for the decision, are distributed across time, space, and decisionmaking units. In order to make correct, efficient, salient, and timely decisions, the effort of the decisionmaking units must be coordinated. Each decisionmaking unit may take part in the coordination process by attempting to negotiate its own role in the information gathering, processing, and decisionmaking process. Each decisionmaking unit has access to somewhat different information, has different criteria or goals for evaluating that information, has access to different technology for evaluating and gathering information, etc. These differences affect the decisionmaking units' ability to acquire new information, negotiation behavior, and decisionmaking behavior.

From an organizational standpoint it is important that the decision be correct given the information available, efficiently made, salient, and timely. From an information processing standpoint the factors affecting the organization's decisionmaking capability can be roughly divided into three categories:

(a) the organizational structure,

(b) the event theater, and

(c) the information gathering, processing, and decisionmaking capabilities of the decisionmaking units.

The organizational structure is a description of the modifiable characteristics of the organization and involves such characteristics as:

(a) size,

(b) the command, control and communication system structure

(c) distribution of information,

(d) procedures for making decisions, and

(e) procedures for redistributing decisionmaking units.

While the command structure may be hierarchical, the communication structure may be uniform in that everyone talks to everyone. Organizational procedures tend to be volatile in terms of:

(a) the person or unit which makes a given decision,

(b) the number of decisionmaking units involved,

(c) the relation of information to the problems and decision, and

(d) the procedures used to coordinate the decisionmaking units from one decision to another.

Further, the characteristics of the information available to the organization may continually change. The information gathering, processing and decisionmaking capabilities of decisionmaking units depend on their composition. If the decisionmaking unit is a single individual or machine then these capabilities are determined by the human cognitive or machine architecture and the information used to process other information. If the decisionmaking unit is a collection of individuals or individuals and machines then these capabilities are determined by the architecture, the information used to process other information, and the coordination and negotiation processes within the decisionmaking unit. Characteristics of the architecture such as the way the decisionmaking unit teams new information, stores information, plans and reasons about others are generally treated as similar across decisionmaking units and unchanging with time. Characteristics of the information that the decisionmaking unit uses to process other information will differ across decisionmaking units. These characteristics are contingency structure based and include:

(a) the goals or objectives;

(b) the salience which the decisionmaking unit attributes to different problems;

(c) the decisionmaking unit's level of expertise with this problem; and

(d) heuristics used by decisionmaking units to solve problems.

An organization is generally modelled as being composed of a set of decisionmaking units who will function identically, provided they are given identical information and information for processing information. When the organization is faced with a crisis, the factors affecting the organization's decisionmaking capability become more volatile. Crises are characterized by increasing unclearness of the procedures for making decisions, rapid event theaters and volatile information flows. As the clarity of the decision procedures decreases the decisionmaking unit's participation becomes volatile as the number of decisionmaking units decrease, coordination decreases, and communication channels become unreliable. In a rapid event theater the number of problems increase and the time available to make decisions decreases. And with a volatile information flow the amount of incoming information increases or decreases rapidly, and the information becomes less reliable.

In an effort to understand how to increase the organization's decisionmaking capability given the complexity of organizational decisionmaking in a distributed environment, researchers have turned to model building and simulation, generally of two types:

(a) those emphasizing characteristics of the organization structure, and

(b) those based on models of individual cognition.

Simulation is turned to as the nature of the problem involves feedback, effort allocation decisions, heuristic-based behavior, a large number of decisionmaking units, vast amounts of information and large numbers of problems. Analytical results obtained when dealing with two or three decisionmaking units and two or three problems are simply not generalizable to organizations of realistic size, in part, because patterns of negotiation and coordination are qualitatively different for extremely small and simple organizations. Further, in order to understand crises, short term consequences or changes in the event theater, rather than equilibrium or long run behavior, must be observed. The definitive article *Distributed Information and Organizational Decision-Making Models* by Kathleen Carley discusses each of these factors in a salient way that has much relevance for information processing in systems and organizations.

Identification or formulation of an issue or problem is a very necessary first step in any problem solving process. A problem statement should always be identified prior to the application of solution methods. Often, there is considerable merit in identifying the problem in terms of a number of interdependent elements that can be characterized as one or more of the issue formulation elements. These include:

(a) problem definition elements (needs, constraints, alterables);

(b) value system design elements (objectives or objectives measures); and

(c) system synthesis elements (activities or controls and activity measures).

All too often a notion of a problem is attacked with a large outpouring of energy only to end up back at the starting point, because an immature issue formulation effort has led to the solution of the wrong problem. The first section of the article *Collective Enquiry* discusses four generating or issue formulation methods which may be used to aid a decision group in beginning to formulate the problem or issue chosen for study. Collective enquiry methods are by no means a panacea and should be called upon only after simple conversational exchange of thoughts and ideas becomes inadequate, or is impossible. Each technique described utilizes a group of persons to generate ideas. After describing the three methods, some concerns regarding their use and associated evaluation issues are discussed. This article is a natural companion article to *Problem Formulation*, although it is relevant to our discussions of information and knowledge acquisitions as well.

3. Information Characterization and Use

Problem solving, judgement, and decisionmaking imply both thought and action. Hence, decisionmaking can be defined as the processes of thought and action involving an irrevocable allocation of resources that culminates in choice behavior. In making a decision, the human decisionmaker is dealing, more often than not, with environments that are characterized by risks, hazards, uncertainty, complexity, changes over time and conflict. Further, the quality of a decision depends upon how well the decisionmaker is able to acquire, analyze, evaluate and interpret information. Decision quality also depends upon how well the decisionmaker may arrive at a good problem solution, decision, or judgement. A number of models of human information processing are presented in the article *Human Information Processing*.

Almost all information is subject to uncertainties of various types. It may arise from inaccurate or incomplete data due to linguistic imprecision, from difficulties in

Introduction

prediction, or from disagreement between information sources. Even where we have complete information, uncertainty may arise from the unavoidable approximations required to make quantitative models computationally tractable. As well as being uncertain about what is the case in the external world, we may be uncertain about our preferences and about what actions to take. Very possibly we may even be uncertain about our degree of uncertainty and this imprecision is an item of major current interest.

A variety of approaches has been developed to formalize various notions of uncertainty, to quantify degrees of belief, and to mechanize reasoning under uncertainty. The best-known formalism is probability. However, practical difficulties in applying probabilistic schemes to model complex bodies of uncertain knowledge have given rise to the development of a variety of alternatives:

(a) interval representations, such as Demster–Shafer belief-functions;

(b) heuristic approximations to probability used in rule-based expert systems, such as the uncertainty factors;

(c) fuzzy set theory designed to handle linguistic imprecision; and

(d) several non-numerical approaches, including non-monotonic logic and default reasoning.

There has been quite a bit of controversy about the underlying assumptions, as well as the relative appropriateness and practicality of these various techniques. Meanwhile, recent developments in applied probability and decision analysis, notably belief nets and influence diagrams, have provided more flexible tools for encoding complex uncertain knowledge. These appear to resolve many of the earlier practical difficulties of the probabilistic approach.

In the article *Knowledge Support Systems: Uncertain Information Processing* by Max Henrion, the author examines two critical issues for the acceptance of any scheme for uncertain information processing. The design of acceptable systems requires some understanding of the psychology of human reasoning under uncertainty. Each of these is examined, for a number of contemporary methods, in this article.

In much of human reasoning, the form of reasoning is approximate rather than exact. The statement "If a tomato is red then the tomato is ripe" appears to be precise. "This tomato is more or less ripe" might be appropriate in that it suggests the imprecise conclusion that follows from the two previous ones. Such reasoning cannot, however, be made sufficient by the inference rules of classical two-valued logic and many-valued logic.

To make such reasoning with fuzzy concepts, Lotfi Zadeh first suggested the "compositional rule of inference" and proposed translation rules for translating the fuzzy conditional proposition "if x is A then y is B" into a fuzzy relation. Since then, several alternative approaches for fuzzy reasoning have been presented by several researchers. The article *Fuzzy Reasoning Methods* by M. Mizumoto provides a discussion of various forms of fuzzy reasoning.

In many application contexts we find ready examples of the necessity for drawing defensible conclusions from a mass of evidence having three general characteristics.

(a) No matter how massive is the collection of evidence, it is incomplete in its coverage of matters judged relevant on the possible conclusions or hypotheses being entertained.

(b) The items of evidence, taken separately or in the aggregate, are inconclusive in supporting the hypotheses being considered.

(c) The evidence is unreliable.

The available methods for drawing conclusions from information are not many, in the opinion of David Schum. We are simply much more adept at collecting information than we are in using it for inferential purposes. If we are close to this particular technology gap, we must know more than we presently do about evidence and its inferential uses. The acquisition of such knowledge is an enterprise now shared by persons in may different disciplines. In *Evidentiary Reasoning and Human Information Processing*, David Schum provides a truly definitive discussion of this very important area for information processing in systems and organizations.

Analogical reasoning is a paradigm for human problem-solving that has been adapted within the field of artificial intelligence. A system which employs analogical reasoning operates by transferring knowledge from past problem-solving cases to new problems that are similar to the past cases. The past cases known to the system are referred to as analogs. The design of an analogical reasoning system must:

(a) define what it means for a problem to be "similar" to a stored analog, and specify a means of computing similarity;

(b) specify how similar analogs are to be retrieved from a potentially huge memory of analogs; and

(c) specify how knowledge is transferred from analogs to a new problem.

In the article *Analogical Reasoning*, Stephen Pimentel, Barry G. Silverman, Walter Truszkowski, Robert Dominy, and Troy Ames define several approaches to analogical reasoning: associative, distributed, and connectionist or neural net. They conclude with an integrative discussion of these computer-based approaches to analogical reasoning.

To select an alternative plan or course of action for ultimate implementation, a decisionmaker applies one or more decision rules which enable comparison, prioritization and, ultimately, selection of a single policy from a set of choice alternatives. The purpose of a decision rule is to specify the most preferred alternative; generally from a partial or total ordering, or a prioritization of alternatives. To use a decision rule, we must have a set of alternatives, a set of objectives to be accomplished by the alternatives, a knowledge of the impacts of the alternatives, evaluation of these impacts and associated preference information. Decision rules may be explicit or implicit in terms of the way in which they are used in the decision process.

Each single policy alternative may represent a complex portfolio of individual alternatives and that set of choice alternatives contains mutually exclusive components. This formulation can always be accomplished but may result in a very large set of policy alternatives, since n individual alternatives can be combined into $2n$ possible portfolios of alternatives. Failure to consider a combination of alternatives may result in significant errors in decisionmaking unless the individual alternatives are independent or mutually exclusive.

It is assumed, at the interpretation step of the decision process, that formulation and analysis have been accomplished such that there exists a decision situation structural model. Thus objectives, relevant constraints, some bounds on the issue, possible policy alternatives, impacts of policy alternatives, and so on, are assumed to be known. The choice of a decision rule will depend, in large measure, upon the decision situation structural model as reflected in the contingency task structure. In the article *Human Judgement and Decision Rules,* which concludes the section on information characterization and use, a variety of models for human judgement and decisionmaking are discussed.

4. Quantitative Methods for Information Handling

Information theory was one of the first formal methods for information handling, and was first developed as the mathematical theory of communication. It combines various mathematical methods, including those of probability, statistics, analysis, functional equations, functional analysis, Fourier analysis, and some parts of algebra. A mathematical overview of information theory is presented by J. Aczél and B. Forte.

The article *Inference and Impact Analysis* presents an overview of contemporary efforts associated with impact assessment and forecasting. Here we are especially concerned with the use of cross-impact analysis and hierarchical inference analysis for the design of knowledge-based systems, typically based on Bayesian approaches that assist individuals and groups in the pro-cessing of inferential information of a causal or diagnostic nature.

Inferential activities based on imprecise, incomplete, inconsistent, or otherwise imperfect knowledge is becoming very important in the design, implementation, and operation of systems that support enhanced human information processing. Inference is concerned with the generation of theories and hypotheses beyond those originally given. In planning and decisionmaking activities the information that is usually available initially is limited as to allow satisfactory performance of judgement and choice. Hence, inference is an essential activity for humans, as well as systems intended to aid humans in information processing activities.

The two major areas of statistical inference are the testing of hypotheses and the estimation of system states and parameters. In *Hypothesis Testing*, some aspects of classical decision theory are discussed, and simple applications to communication and control sciences are described. There are many situations in which hypothesis testing, which is often called detection theory in the literature of communication theory, is applicable. A radar return is observed, and the presence or absence of a target is to be determined; from a smear of human tissue we attempt to determine whether a patient has cancer; from fluctuations in activity of a particular stock on one of the exchanges, we decide whether or not to buy some shares of the stock.

In each case we choose an answer yes or no, and we refer to these two choices (yes or no) as hypotheses H_0 and H_1. It is possible, of course, to have more than two hypotheses and to attempt to decide which one of N hypotheses to accept. The basic problem in hypotheses testing is to determine appropriate tests for situations such as these.

The concepts of system and of information are both very rich, and it is impossible to mention all that is noteworthy about their intersection. The article *Information Laws of Systems* by Roger Conant concentrates on systems understood abstractly as collections of interacting parts or variables, on information as understood in the context of mathematical information theory and information laws which can be expressed in mathematical form.

5. Information in Simulation and Modelling

Modelling and simulation is an emerging field whose boundaries are not well defined. Model building can be traced back at least as far as the Newtonian era but the tremendous enhancement it received with the advent of the electronic computer is a relatively recent phenomenon. There are two primary sources of simulation methods: the physical sciences and operations research. These are currently in a state of unification. In the article *Simulation Methodology and Model Manipulation,* Bernard Ziegler provides a discussion of the origin of computer simulation and shows how this has led to the many successful approaches that are available today.

One of the very successful approaches involves a systemic top-down view of the objects and relations that are to be simulated. In *Simulation Methodology: Top-Down Approach,* Tuncer Ören describes how this important approach to representing model systems on a computer can be undertaken.

A related article by Bernard Zeigler, *Simulation Methodology and Model Manipulation,* reviews the organization of models and data for storage and retrieval. The author indicates that recognition of the importance of such repositories of information and knowledge in the modelling and simulation enterprise is relatively recent. The article begins with the role of the model base in simulation methodology and then goes on to discuss principles for model base organization and to sketch a methodology for model construction that is based on this.

There are numerous occasions when humans wish to

make a forecast of possible future states and events. There are several methods that might be used to accomplish this. Some of these are very crude and some are sophisticated. Some are based upon the information that constitutes the expert judgement of an individual or a group. Others are based upon mathematical approaches and formal reasoning. The article *Systems Analysis and Modelling: Time Series* is concerned with quantitative forecasting approaches based on ordered time series of observations.

Knowledge-based simulation is a relatively new technology that permits the simulation of processes and systems in which there is a significant amount of noncausal knowledge that determines the behavior and performance of the system. Since it is a type of simulation, it facilitates the construction of models that endeavor to portray and delineate the behavior of an evolving process or system over time. It is the replication of process behavior over time that distinguishes it from other knowledge-based systems and expert systems. The latter systems have little or no interest in the characterization of how processes perform and change over time. Beyond the consideration of time that is common to all of simulation, knowledge-based simulation supports explicit representation of and reasoning from judgemental, declarative, associative and other forms of knowledge, in addition to causal and procedural knowledge that have always been inherent within simulation. Conventional simulation models have always been concerned with the representation of causal and procedural knowledge and the extraction of useful information from that knowledge.

Potential advantages of this approach over conventional simulation are many. They include:

(a) improved intelligibility, including increased descriptive power, explicit rules, and assumptions;

(b) improved modifiability;

(c) improved credibility, including greater explanation facilities; and

(d) rapid prototyping capability that enables us to get a model up and running rapidly.

Because knowledge-based simulation provides a representation and reasoning capability for additional knowledge forms beyond causal and procedural knowledge, it is possible to build within these systems intelligent facilities for aiding the user in formulation of these models and for interpretation of the results produced by such models. The article *Knowledge-Based Simulation* by James R. Burns and Dwight Haworth provides a discussion of these perspectives on simulation.

Modern decisionmaking organizations process large amounts of information that has been obtained from a variety of external sources or sensors, as well as from internal databases. The latter can be centralized or decentralized, depending on the architecture of the communications system that connects the members of the organization. The manner in which information is processed and distributed within an organization affects the process of decisionmaking and, consequently, the organization's performance as measured by the accuracy and the timeliness of the output, whether a decision or an action.

There are many approaches to organization design. Three are initially considered for modelling purposes in the article *Organizational Information Structures: Quantitative Models* by Alex Levis. These include

(a) classical management theory, in which the key concept is that of division of labor;

(b) the functional decomposition of tasks and their subsequent allocation to the organization members so that some objective function is maximized;

(c) viewing the organization as an information processing and decisionmaking system, whereby the cognitive limitations of humans (or the memory and information processing limitations of machines) determine the organizational form.

One of the several purposes of modelling and simulation is to forecast the future. A forecast predicts likely future states — as derived by a systematic and reproducible method. A technological forecast predicts the timing, degree, or nature of change of specific technical parameters, or developments, of concern. Technological forecasting is based on the observation that the processes of technological innovation are sufficiently orderly at some level of aggregation to allow a meaningful projection into the future. Innovation involves socioeconomic processes as well as technological development; therefore the developmental context must be well understood to make a viable technological forecast. Effective management of technology depends on awareness of likely changes, and it also entails consideration of the impacts of technology. Thus an effective forecast should be accompanied by a reasonable assessment of the full range of impacts of new technology, generally called "Technology Assessment," to help manage the development process. In an era of rapidly changing technology, technological forecasting and assessment are required in order that we be able to "look before we leap." The article *Technological Forecasting* by Alan Porter and Fred Rossini emphasizes five families of technological forecasting techniques that have proved effective: monitoring, expert opinion, trend extrapolation, modelling, and scenario construction.

6. Individual and Organizational Decisions

We make decisions every day. Our decisions range from very simple to very complex in difficulty and from very narrow to very broad in scope. We make very simple decisions without much consideration of the factors affecting and affected by the decision, at least we often think that this is what we do. In reality, a decision is often simple because it concerns an issue with which we are experientially familiar and where we understand the ingredients that go into the decision very well. Intuition or other affective forms of reasoning are perfectly acceptable in these situations. We normally give more complex decisions much more thought and consider more of the factors involved. Depending on the complexity and scope involved, the thought given may be a brief mental comparison of alternatives, or it may be a thorough analysis appropriate to a complex situation in which there are significant differences in the impacts of various alternative courses of action. The article *Decision Analysis* is concerned with an overview of this important topic. In this encyclopedia, we generally mean *formal* decision analysis when we use only the term decision analysis.

Decision problems involving multiple and conflicting objectives, goals, or attributes are generally referred to as multiple criteria decision problems. In many situations, it is useful to establish the hierarchy of objectives. For instance, an overall objective would be the broad and general statement about the desirable future state of the organization and is not often adequate for any operational purpose. The general statement is translated into more specific subobjectives. Subobjectives may be further broken down into lower-level objectives so as to identify attributes scales that can be objectively assessed. *Multicriteria Decision Problem* by Eiji Takeda provides a perspective on this important area.

One reason for decision support is the provision of tools for improving human performance in the resolution of complex decision problems. One class of aiding technique is decision analysis based on multiattribute utility theory (MAUT). One of the most useful features of the MAUT-based approach is that it provides guidelines and a framework for selecting relevant alternatives by means of identification and analysis of many aspects of the outcomes that may result from the selection of alternative courses of action, and the probabilities of these outcomes occurring. Decomposition is essential for the analysis of complex decision problems due to the multiple noncommensurate nature of the attributes of the outcomes that follow from alternative courses of action. The multiple attribute utility theory approach presumes that candidate alternatives can be studied in terms of different dimensions and offers a prescriptive procedure for alternative selection on the basis of normative behavior for rational choice.

In the existing formal decision analysis methodology, the analyst first develops a model that is based upon the decisionmaker's supplied information about the problem. An analysis is then performed using this model and, finally, a decision based on model-supplied information is recommended to the decisionmaker.

Information requirements for multiple attribute analysis are primarily determined by the functional form of the decision situation model used. Consequently, the coordination of the information assessment step would be a straightforward process once the decision situation structural model has been identified. This is the case only if all relevant information is precise and readily available. However, difficulties in obtaining consistent, numerically scaled utility functions, even for a single dimensional attribute or utility space, and related difficulties in the assessment of probabilities and risk attitude coefficients, often impose barriers to obtaining the precise, consistent and complete information that is needed for easy and direct use of the process. The article *Multiattribute Utility Theory* reviews several operational and behavioral issues in the use of multiattribute-based decision sup- port models.

In very general terms, a decision support system is a system that supports managerial decisionmaking by assisting in the organization of knowledge about ill structured issues. The primary components of a decision support system are a database management system, a model based management system, and a dialogue generation and management system. The emphasis is upon effectiveness of decisionmaking as this involves formulation of alternatives, analysis of their impacts, and interpretation and selection of appropriate options for implementation. Efficiency in terms of time required to evolve the decision, while important, is secondary to effectiveness in terms of the utility or value of the decision to the decisionmaker. The article *Decision Support Systems* discusses a conceptual framework for this important class of support systems that aid information processing in systems and organizations.

The goal of most knowledge support systems is to enhance human information processing and decision behavior. Yet many support systems do not effectively meet that goal. One of the reasons is that support system designers often utilize decision theoretical models and statistical principles that are inconsistent with how humans formulate problems, process information, and make choices. The article *Support-System Design: Behavioral Concerns* by Len Adelman overviews two areas of research which demonstrate these inconsistencies. A conceptual framework is then presented for simultaneously representing the task and both the support system user and designer. This supports designers in appreciating how human decision behavior is guided through the application of mental representations and processing heuristics that help people understand and efficiently deal with a complex world given significant limitations in information processing power.

As evident from the discussions in this Encyclopedia, there have been many definitions of an organization. A large number of them infer a group of individuals, established on a relatively continuous and stable basis, in an environment with changing characteristics. The organization contains relatively fixed boundaries, a normative order for management and authority, a communication system and a set of incentives that encourage engagement in activities that are the general pursuit of a common and accepted set of goals. From this definition of an organization, it follows that there are four top level attributes or success factors that are critical to the functionality of an organization. These are efficiency, effectiveness, adaptability to external environmental changes and job satisfaction. Each of these contributes to the primary goals of organizational management: to improve the products and the services of the organization. Four organizational needs and characteristics follow from these: complexity of tasks and the resulting specialization, centralization of authority into hierarchical levels, formalization and standardization of job duties, and a system with which to process organization information. The article *Group Decision Support Systems* is primarily concerned with the development of information systems to support the decisionmaking functions by organizations and groups of individuals.

7. Artificial Intelligence and Expert Systems

Artificial intelligence is a field of study that encompasses computational techniques for performing tasks that apparently require intelligence when performed by humans. A robust artificially intelligent system must be able to store knowledge, to apply that knowledge to the solution of problems and to acquire new knowledge through experience. Applications, particularly thorough expert systems, to business, medicine and education help illustrate the impact that artificial intelligence has on the skilled professions. The article *Artificial Intelligence* by Roy Rada discusses history, basic concepts and some applications.

An expert system is an intelligent system that is able to use expert knowledge, stored in the form of inference procedures, in order to resolve complex problems. The goal of the designer of an expert system is, somehow, to capture the knowledge of a human expert relative to some specific knowledge domain and code this in a computer in such a way that the knowledge of the expert is available to a less experienced user.

The knowledge of an expert will consist, in part, of fact files and knowledge sources. A fact file will consist of data and information that is generally agreed upon by a number of experts to characterize the domain under consideration. For the most part, a fact file is capable of being represented in a database. Knowledge sources consist of a typically large number of skill- and rule-based forms of knowledge that an expert may be expected to bring to bear upon a particular familiar issue in a given domain with which the expert is familiar. There are many ways in which this knowledge can be represented as, for the most part, knowledge sources are heuristic in nature as they are based upon the wisdom accumulated through experience. There will also exist a control structure or system, also known as an inference or cognitive engine, that organizes and directs the steps that are actually taken to resolve a problem. The principal task of the cognitive engine is to act as an intelligent interpreter in the selection of those portions of the knowledge base, consisting of fact files and knowledge sources, which are most applicable to resolution of a given issue. Finally, there must be interfaces between the two principal components of an expert system, the knowledge base and the cognitive engine, and between these subsystems and, the expert whose knowledge is captured in the system and the ultimate users. The article *Expert Systems* discusses the essential ingredients of this type of artificially intelligent system.

A major research topic in artificial intelligence is the development of systems that can autonomously generate and reason about plans. Within this research community, a plan is defined as a specified ordering of actions over time. Automated planning is the autonomous specification of a plan to achieve a goal.

As with many other artificially intelligent research topics, automated planning research is principally focused on domains involving ill-defined, open-ended problems. This includes many problems which are not easily modelled by well-defined mathematical optimization procedures, such as developing robots with enough "common sense" that they can function and maneuver in everyday environments. In *Automated Planning*, Paul Lehner discusses the role of these systems in information systems engineering.

One of the most important intellectual developments of the past few decades has been the birth of an exciting new interdisciplinary field called cognitive science. Researchers in psychology, linguistics, information science, philosophy, and neuroscience realized that they were asking many of the same questions about the nature of the human mind and that they had developed complementary and potentially synergistic methods of investigation. The word cognitive refers to perceiving and knowing. Thus, cognitive science is the science of mind. Cognitive scientists seek to understand perceiving, thinking, remembering, understanding language, learning, and other mental phenomena. All of these could potentially qualify as human information processing behaviors. Cognitive scientists' research is remarkably diverse, ranging from observing children, through programming computers to do complex problem solving, to analyzing the nature of meaning. The article *Cognitive Science, Human Information Processing and Artificial Intelligence* by Michael Donnell discusses the many interesting interrelationships in these important areas of endeavor.

8. Information Systems

The nucleus of the information society hinges on the easy acquisition, processing, production, and dissemination of information. But, what is information? Basically, information is intellectual knowledge and generally viewed as different from the data we often deal with in our daily lives. In common sense, data are the raw materials of information. They are mostly unrelated bare facts, such as measurements or statistics, that are used as a basis for discussion, decision, and calculation. When we start manipulating them to increase either value or utility, they become sources of information. Thus, data generate information through manipulation. The article *Information Systems* by Louis R. Chow expands on this broad perspective.

Expert database systems represent a new class of system architectures that support knowledge-based applications requiring access to large, shared databases. The article *Expert Database Systems* by Larry Kerschberg explores the concepts, tools, techniques and architectures that comprise this new and dynamic field. The major thrust of this important article is that expert database systems allow the specification, prototyping and implementation of knowledge-based information systems that represent a vertical extension beyond the well-defined, predictable, transaction-oriented systems to those with knowledge-directed reasoning and interpretation under very general conditions of uncertainty.

In the article *Distributed Decision Making: Information Systems*, a framework for information systems design for distributed decisionmaking is discussed that is composed of three principal integrated and interrelated components.

(a) Knowledge acquisition and representation, such as to enable effective and efficient understanding of the decision situation, and to model how people actually use information when solving a problem or making a decision.

(b) Information presentation of these representatives in a distributed multi-agent situation such as to enable evaluation of alternatives from perspectives that are commensurate with experiential familiarity with the task at hand.

(c) Organizational structure or architecture, which results in a network of communication channels in which distributed multi-agent decisionmaking takes place.

A purpose for this framework is to guide the design of distributed information systems, including resource distribution across nodes in the communication network, and associated information presentation and decision support aids.

9. Human Interfaces and Interactions in Information Processing

The design of systems that allow more effective human interaction is very important to the success of information processing in humans and organizations. *Human Factors Engineering* by Tom Sheridan, considers the science and art of interfacing people with machines, such as the displays, controls and computer hardware which send, receive and process information. Another type of interface is the computer software and administrative procedures which determine how people allocate their effort, make decisions and take actions. A third relevant interface is ergonomic and involves people and their seating, and environmental factors which determine their ability to function, such as temperature, humidity, lighting, sound, etc. Finally, there is the selection and training of people for their machine interactive tasks.

All living creatures process information. This activity is so vital that it may serve as a definition of life itself. The more advanced the creature, the more complex the physiological apparatus for information processing. The often debated opinion that the human animal stands at the pinnacle of evolution is at least corroborated by the fact that the human central nervous system is the most complex structure in the known universe. Comprehending the manner in which this amazing structure processes sensory information in the pursuit of goals is of no small consequence in the successful design of systems which are intended for human use. The discipline most often associated with the design of such systems is that of human factors engineering. A review of some of the paradigms which researchers in this and related fields employ to facilitate understanding of human information processing is the subject of *Human Factors Engineering: Information-Processing Concerns* by Ronald Hess.

Human factors research has also concentrated on the interactions between users and information systems. Screen formats, data entry and display methods, menu structures and graphical interfaces designed for human interaction and recognizing the cognitive abilities of the user, can significantly improve the user—system interface. Developers of guidelines governing interface design for information storage, manipulation, and retrieval are discussed in the article *Human–System Interaction: Information-Presentation Requirements* by Linda Weldon. Computerized databases present unique problems and these are given special emphasis.

Instruction is one of our oldest forms of information transmission, concerning the transmission primarily of skills and knowledge, but also attitudes, expectations and standards, from instructors or, more generally, from "the culture" to students or initiates into the culture. Instruction involves not only the transmission of information at a single point in time but also the transmission of information across generations of people and across time. Books made it possible to capture the content of great instruction and supply it at reasonable cost to nearly all segments of society. Dexter Fletcher in *Computer-Based Instruction: Costs and Effectiveness* believes that a second major technological advance in instruction may have occurred with the development of the digital computer. He discusses the costs and effectiveness of computer-based instruction in his article. Through use of the principles presented there, there is now the potential to capture the interactions as well as the content of outstanding pedagogy in a medium that is rapidly becoming both inexpensive and widely accessible.

System integration fundamentals are especially important in ensuring that it is possible to embed efficiently and effectively new systems together with existing systems such that the overall product is functionally useful. Theodore Kornreich discusses salient aspects of this subject in his article *System-Integration Fundamentals*.

10. Software Issues in Information Processing and Decision Support

Computer-aided systems engineering is, according to Howard Eisner, the systematic application of computer technology and software to the tasks and activities, or elements of systems engineering. Thus, CASE involves the application of software tools to the elements of systems engineering.

The efficient and effective development of information systems is greatly influenced by approaches used to construct the software that underlies the information system.

Introduction

Information systems may be developed using a variety of methods and approaches. Each of these has its own attributes and deficiencies, some take longer to produce results, and the quality of software construction is definitively influenced by the approach. In *Information Systems and Software Productivity*, Jim Palmer discusses information systems from the perspective of software development and examines the way that software productivity affects the construction of information systems.

Real time software systems have several information processing functions which distinguish them from other software systems. These are often associated with real time control, the sort of control in which human supervisory efforts are often needed. That is, the computer makes control decisions based on data received without any low level human intervention but with the possibility of human supervisory overrides at a higher level. Hassan Gomaa discusses many information concerns in the design of real time software in *Real-Time Software Design: Information Concerns*.

Software development is a human activity, and one would expect to find guidelines that direct the process. This is the goal of a design methodology. However, the human information processing aspect of software development is very complex. It involves a firm understanding of the application domain, knowledge of the technological domain, an ability to communicate and observe and a talent for invention and integration. Because software development requires many skills and varieties of knowledge, it is difficult to separate the cognitive activities that direct the problem solving from the other processes that affect designers and users during the development period. That is, the design methodology must address the details of problem solving within the context of human information processing capabilities. As a result, all methods will be imperfect and subject to personal biases and environmental variations.

Bruce Blum indicates that to comprehend how designers process information during the implementation of a software product, a foundation in two basic areas is required: how humans process information and how software is developed. Once this has been established, the cognitive aspects of development can be considered. The features of the development methodologies then can be classified with respect to how they approach the human information processing challenge. In the article *Software Development: Human Information Processing*, Bruce Blum presents a definitive discussion of how people design systems and discusses the tools that are of value for this activity.

Knowledge acquisition, in systems engineering sometimes also known as requirements analysis, is generally a critical bottleneck in the design and development process. Knowledge acquisition is typically tedious, time consuming and exceedingly difficult to do well. There are multiple techniques for extracting knowledge from domain experts. However, none of them guarantees the acquisition of reliable, valid, comprehensive knowledge. The task is made more complex in the case of advanced cognitive computer-based problem solving systems. These include increasingly ubiquitous classes of decision support systems, knowledge-based systems in artificial intelligence and the intelligent decision support hybrids of expert and decision support systems.

The knowledge engineer, or requirements analysis specialist, needs to be able to elicit many kinds of information from users, show users reconstructed versions of the decision, or problem solving process, and iterate on the reconstructed portrait until the user is satisfied that the "real" process has been captured adequately. The strategy for doing this entails an increasingly refined transition from generic decisionmaking process/task templates to storyboarding and then system prototyping. Appropriate tactics to enable this are discussed in the article by Gerald Hopple, *Knowledge Acquisition: Storyboarding and Computer-Based System Decision Research*.

Over the years systems designers have discovered just how difficult it can be to capture user requirements. A variety of tools and techniques have been developed to assist systems analysts, but they have often proven inadequate. This is especially the case when requirements are complex and analytical. Often systems design and development "life cycle" models fail to recognize the inherent requirements dilemma. Consequently, systems engineers have developed a new design perspective, one that assumes that requirements cannot be captured the first time through and that several iterations may be necessary to define requirements accurately.

This new perspective is termed requirements prototyping. It "informs" the design process by levering increasingly specific and verifiable information in the requirements analysis process. The usual objective of prototyping is to demonstrate a system concept before expensive programming begins. Successful prototyping can be traced to iterative requirements analysis, user involvement and the use of one of several tools for converting requirements hypotheses into a tangible system concept, preferably in software. Steve Andriole provides a thought provoking perspective on these concerns in *Prototyping as Information in Systems Design*.

The development of software systems to support groups of people who are responsible for decisionmaking represents an extension of supporting individual decisionmakers through appropriate computer software. Spreadsheet software, word processing and database packages that operate on the microcomputer have become a standard part of the modern office. As desktop computer systems are linked together to connect managers located throughout an office building or across the world, and as computers become increasingly used in the conference room as well as the office, there is corresponding interest in the development of software to support group work in organizations. Considerable commercial and research effort is being devoted to software systems that support collaborative work activities, such as idea creation, message exchange, project planning, document preparation, mutual product creation and joint decisionmaking. Particular attention is being given to development of meeting software, or systems that aim to support dispersed and face-to-face meetings within organizations. Technical advances, such as the development of high speed data communications networks and easy-to-use software interfaces, have contributed to the emergence of these systems.

Development of group decision support systems (GDSS) typifies new technology developments in that a variety of approaches are being taken to software design, with little standardization. Lack of standardization is in part due to the early stage of knowledge regarding the appropriate design of shared office systems, including operating system configuration and data management approaches. But there is also limited knowledge of the nature of collaborative work itself, or work sharing, in organizations. As a consequence, research in universities and corporate laboratories is proceeding along both of these fronts as software design in the GDSS area evolves. Geraldine DeSanctis reviews the status of GDSS as it currently exists in *Group Decision Support Systems: Software Architecture* and identifies apparent software directions.

11. Application Issues

During the past twenty-five years computer-based systems have been developed to simulate the behavior of knowledgeable and experienced specialists in various highly specialized areas. The resulting systems, which are now called expert systems, have been used to assist novices in performing specialized tasks and to understand more fully how experienced specialists perform these tasks.

The growing success of expert systems in technical areas have stimulated the development of such systems to assist managers in making decisions and in performing analyses and making recommendations leading to a decision. As with the early technical expert systems, many of the management expert systems now being developed are experimental. Developed primarily at universities, they are being used to determine the potential usefulness of these systems and the issues that will arise in their design and implementation. The article *Expert Systems for Managers: Design Issues* by Robert Blanning examines some of these systems and issues.

Although development of large information systems has been a difficult, expensive and failure-prone adventure for so many organizations, this experience is by no means universal. Large information systems are being developed successfully, using strategies borrowed from architecture and other engineering disciplines.

Milton Hess, in his article *Information Systems Design in Industrial Practice*, indicates that few other ubiquitous large systems are developed the way information systems have traditionally been developed. An information system project usually starts with the detailed specification of all the system's functions and features — the 'requirements'. Only after this specification process is complete is a software development effort generally continued through to completion. Dr Hess encourages us to imagine the outcome if a builder tried to detail every tenant's unique specifications before starting the design of an office building or to imagine the situation that would result if an aerospace firm had to define every payload's specifications before designing a space vehicle.

For such systems, a total system design is created early in the project that will satisfy the requirements of a whole class of intended users. For example, a commercial building is designed for a class of tenant — offices, or light manufacturing, or warehousing — but not for specific tenants. Common requirements for all prospective tenants are incorporated into the design. Tailoring the space to each tenant occurs later, perhaps even after the building is completed. This article describes how some organizations are applying a comparable strategy to develop successful, large information systems.

The overall process of specifying the "requirements" for a major system, through its design, development, production and subsequent deployment and support, is known as the "system acquisition process." The process which generates the binding paperwork tying together the buyer and the seller of this new system is called the "procurement process." It is in the implementation of these combined processes that the system engineers, component design engineers, procurement professionals, project or program managers, financial analysts, schedule and cost controllers, production experts and lawyers all come together.

The problem they are addressing, namely the development and production of a complex new system, is essentially one of multivariable, constrained optimization. However, it is normally split into its various functions, such as cost analysis, scheduling, system and subsystem design, production planning, risk analysis and subcontract management, with each of these being separately analyzed as part of some overall system's acquisition and procurement master plan.

In order to see how the overall acquisition process fits together, it is best to visualize it in terms of the major phases through which a new system evolves. While there is no standard categorization, most of the representations tend to fit into four categories:

phase zero	definition,
phase one	demonstration,
phase two	full-scale development, and
phase three	production and deployment.

The article *System Acquisition and Procurement* by Jacques Gansler explores these phases and the relevant aspects of this important problem area.

Most research on manufacturing automation in general, and flexible manufacturing system scheduling and control in particular, focuses on the derivation of fully automated control and scheduling techniques. Usually they involve optimal or heuristic analytical models or knowledge-based systems. An alternative and more realistic paradigm to "lights out" automation is presented in *Supervisory Control: Philosophical Considerations in Manufacturing*

Systems by Christine Mitchell. The alternative paradigm, supervisory control of manufacturing processes, entails the design of control and scheduling systems that explicitly integrate human decisionmakers with the underlying automation.

Supervisory control is a design philosophy that explicitly addresses the roles and functions of both human and automatic components of the control process. Supervisory control systems make use of capabilities and compensate for the limitations of both human decisionmakers and automatic components. More specifically, supervisory control designs the human—computer interaction in order to augment and to extend the human's role and decision-making effectiveness. This article describes some of the limitations of automated control systems in manufacturing, in particular why "full automation" is not possible. It also reviews some of the limitations in the typical use of emerging computer technology to provide decision support to the human decisionmaker.

The term "office automation" refers to the use of technology to increase the productivity of white collar workers. This automation of office work is made possible as a result of the merging of computer and communication technologies. The initial applications were to improve the routine typing tasks associated with secretarial work. As the technology has developed, it has been applied to all levels of office work, from the simple creation and dissemination of routine letters and memoranda, to meetings among senior executives. In the article *Office Automation* by Paul Gray, several examples of office automation are discussed together with related human factor considerations. These include: word processing, electronic mail, voice mail, facsimile, executive work stations, information retrieval systems, natural language software, telecommuting, computer conferences, video conferences, decision rooms, and local area networks.

An information system for command, control and communications (C3) system is a military decision support system. It is an extension of the sensing, processing and communicating capabilities of the military commanders whose activities it supports. These activities include the basic command and control functions of information gathering, situation assessment, action selection, and response planning and execution. The supporting system consists of radar and other sensors, and intelligence sources for gathering information about an enemy; computers for information processing, storage and display; and communications equipment and networks for transferring information among various commanders and command and staff levels. Finally, both the system and the people function within the context of a military organization and mission. In his definitive article *Command and Control Information Systems*, the late Joe Wohl describes the context, functions and supporting technology of modern military command and control, and identifies major analytical and systems engineering issues which must be addressed to design effective and efficient systems.

It is difficult to separate social effects of automation from those of other technologies. What distinguishes automation technology is the intended and explicit use of feedback within the technology itself. However, the interaction of any technology with people or society involves feedback loops which encompass people and society in some form. Thus automation ideas are ways of characterizing the social effects of any technology. This includes not only the automation technology's effect on workers, but also models of automation and control as applied to government institutions.

To anticipate all the social effects of any specific technology is clearly impossible. This is partly because those effects are complex and indirect, and partly because the effects may not be manifest until long after the introduction of the technology. Nevertheless, it is ethically obligatory that those responsible for the introduction of new technology try to anticipate as many as possible of the social effects, negative as well as positive.

The article by Tom Sheridan, *Automation: Social Effects*, presents some general approaches relating to this and provides a fitting conclusion to this introduction to information processing in systems and organizations.

A

Analogical Reasoning

Analogical reasoning (sometimes called analogous reasoning) is a paradigm for problem solving within the field of artificial intelligence (AI). A system which employs analogical reasoning operates by transferring knowledge from past problem-solving cases to new problems that are similar to the past cases. The past cases known to the system are referred to as analogs. The design of an analogical reasoning system must:

(a) define what it means for a problem to be "similar" to a stored analog and specify a means of computing similarity,

(b) specify how similar analogs are to be retrieved from a (potentially huge) memory of analogs, and

(c) specify how knowledge is transferred from analogs to a new problem.

In this article several approaches to analogical reasoning are defined—associative in Sect. 2, distributed in Sect. 3 and connectionist or neural network in Sect. 4. An integrative discussion is presented in Sect. 5.

1. Analogical Research Trends of the 1970s and 1980s

Analogical reasoning has been a relatively sparsely studied topic in AI, although some progress has been made in the design of analogical reasoning models during the 1970s and 1980s (Winston 1980, Silverman 1983, Nakamura et al. 1983, Eliot 1987). Nevertheless, it is safe to say that no general analogical reasoning systems of significant power have been constructed to date. In part, this is simply because the problem of analogical reasoning is thoroughly entangled with the more general problem of knowledge representation. However, even assuming a solution to this problem, analogical reasoning would still be very difficult for "real-world" problems, since it involves performing expensive pattern-matching operations on very large amounts of data.

Recently, there have been a number of developments in the fields of distributed and parallel processing that have the potential to yield solutions to this latter difficulty. First, the commercial development of massively parallel machines, has given rise to methods for performing the matching and retrieval operations necessary for analogical reasoning in real time. This has made possible the construction of large associative memories. Second, techniques developed for distributed artificial intelligence (DAI) promise to provide an organizational methodology by which the functions necessary for analogical reasoning can be coordinated in a distributed processing environment. In the distributed agent paradigm, the process of analogical reasoning is divided into its major functions and each function is assigned to a separate agent; these agents are then allowed to operate opportunistically in parallel (see Sect. 3). Finally, various of network memory models have been developed, the most prominent of which stem from the the paradigm of connectionism. Using the technique of spreading activation, these models promise a degree of robustness and efficiency not found elsewhere, however, they lack the explanation capabilities of the other approaches.

1.1 Integration of Diverse Techniques for the 1990s

Ultimately, research in analogical reasoning is heading toward the creation of an analogical reasoning shell or environment in which the best techniques drawn from the three areas outlined above can be integrated. Work towards this goal has begun in the form of an analogical reasoning integration and extension language (ARIEL) (Silverman and Murray 1986, Silverman et al. 1986, Silverman and Moustakis 1987). The strategy adopted in ARIEL is to use a blackboard as an integration tool for multiple models with complementary strengths. A common knowledge-representation language has been defined, and all analogs are represented on the blackboard in this language. Agents may be implemented by using different models internally, some of them massively parallel, and communication between agents takes place through the blackboard. A prototype ARIEL has been constructed using the blackboard shell blackboard system generator (BSG) (Silverman and Chang 1988).

2. Models of Associative Memory

One of the key components of an analogical reasoning system is the associative memory. In order for analogical reasoning to be effective, the system must store a large amount of domain knowledge in the form of analogs. Effectively accessing these analogs then becomes a major problem. Associative memories provide a means of retrieving analogs in an efficient manner.

The concept of associative memory is very general and has been studied in many different fields. The models of associative memory used in each of these fields differ from each other slightly, but they are all based on the core idea of associative retrieval. In the fields of computer architecture and AI, the definitions of associative memory require that the retrieval takes place within certain time constraints.

In the context of computer architecture, the data items to be retrieved are binary words all containing the same number of bits. If there are N words stored in the memory, the retrieval must take place in $O(1)$ time; that is, within some constant time, independent of N. Obviously, this requires that the words be examined in parallel; the best time that could possibly be achieved on a conventional machine is $O(N)$. In the context of AI, the data items to be retrieved are typically more complex structures, such as semantic networks, and may be of variable size. If there are N items stored in the memory, and the largest item is of size M, then the retrieval must take place in $O(M)$ time. Again, this requires that the items be examined in parallel; the shortest time to carry out this operation on a conventional machine is $O(M \times N)$. Of course, an associative memory can always be simulated on a conventional machine without regard to time constraints; one method of doing so is discussed in Sect. 2.3.

2.1 Associative Retrieval

In order to describe the range of features and uses of associative memory, the concept of an abstract, which is a greatly simplified model of associative memory, is introduced, and then its use in analogical reasoning is discussed. In this model, an associative memory consists of a set of items, called bases, each consisting of a number of named slots containing values. A base can be visualized as being similar to a frame with slots, although the exact representation of the bases is unimportant. The input to an associative memory, the target, is just like a base except that some of its slots may be empty. The empty slots of a target are called goals, while the slots containing data are called predictors. Note that nothing has been said about how the bases are arranged in associative memory. In practice, they may be arranged in a network, in which case the slots will correspond to links, and the values to other objects in the network, possibly bases. This possibility is explored in Sect. 4. For the present discussion, however, it is assumed that the associative memory is "unstructured".

The fundamental operation performed by the associative memory is associative retrieval. In terms of the model given above, this means that each predictor of the target is compared with the corresponding slot (if any) in each of the bases, and those bases judged sufficiently similar to the target are returned. The comparison is done according to a similarity metric, which assesses a numeric penalty for each mismatch between the value of a predictor and that of the corresponding base slot.

2.2 Analogical Pattern Completion

The exact method of associative retrieval can vary along several dimensions, such as the allowable format of the target slots and the type of similarity metric used. Typically, associative retrieval is used to construct values for the goals of the target. In other words, after the bases similar to the target have been retrieved, some algorithm is used to derive values for the goals of the target from the values of the corresponding slots in the retrieved bases. In this case, associative retrieval can be employed in the following fashions.

If the division of the target slots into predictors and goals is fixed, associative retrieval can be used to perform an input–output mapping (with the predictors as an input "vector" and the goals as an output "vector"). If the division of the target slots is variable, associative retrieval can be used to perform pattern completion (with the goals as the pattern "variables").

Likewise, if the similarity metric is a Boolean function, indicating only "perfect match" or "no match," then associative retrieval can be viewed as performing content addressing of the memory elements (bases). On the other hand, if the similarity metric is a real-valued function, indicating degrees of similarity, then associative retrieval can be used to perform generalization, deriving values for the goals even of targets which do not perfectly match any base.

Because an "unstructured" associative memory has been assumed, the similarity metrics only take into account the immediate value of a slot in a base. Note, however, that if the memory were arranged as a network with slots corresponding to links, the matching algorithm could well involve a recursive search procedure which traverses the links of the network. The exact form of such a similarity metric would, of course, be dependent on the network representation employed.

2.3 Associative Memory as a Taxonomic Hierarchy

Before describing various parallel implementations of associative memory, one way of organizing such a memory on a serial machine is examined. As a starting point, the organization of the analog knowledge base in the ARIEL prototype is described. In this prototype, each base analog is represented as a single object in an object-representation language. Note that this representation of associative memory is completely unstructured in the sense that the analogs are in no way related to each other. The analogs are in turn arranged in a classification hierarchy which is used to facilitate their retrieval. The classification hierarchy is necessary because, with the serial machine for which the prototype was developed, it is not feasible to similarity-match every stored analog in the knowledge base during each retrieval. The hierarchy makes it possible to examine only the analogs in a particular partition of the knowledge base, making a serial implementation feasible.

Section 2.4 examines the use of massive parallelism in implementing a more advanced associative memory for analogical reasoning. There are two basic ways in which massive parallelism can be used. The first is to maintain an unstructured associative memory (as described above for the prototype) and apply parallelism to the retrieval process, thereby removing the need for a classification hierarchy. The second is to devise a more complex, network representation of associative memory (see Sect. 4).

2.4 Parallel Retrieval from an Unstructured Associative Memory

Suppose the analogs are not arranged in any particular fashion, but simply exist in an unstructured associative memory. In this case, the retrieval process can be parallelized by assigning one processor to each analog, as in the active memory architecture. During associative retrieval, each analog is examined and matched against the target by its own processor. This allows as many analogs to be simultaneously processed as there are processors in the system, making it feasible to retrieve analogs from huge memories in real time without any classification hierarchy. In order to illustrate this point, the "memory-based reasoning" paradigm is examined together with a massively parallel text retrieval system, both of which have been developed for the connection machine. (The connection machine is a general-purpose, massively parallel architecture which can be used to implement a wide variety of paradigms. However, the only connection machine applications examined in this article are unstructured associative memory models. These should not be confused with the connectionist models examined in Sect. 4.)

Memory-based reasoning (MBR) is a paradigm which attempts to capture the human facility for reasoning from experience, rather than by the application of rules (Stanfill and Waltz 1986). The strategy of MBR is to rely almost entirely on associative retrieval from an associative memory of past cases as an inference mechanism. In order for good performance to be produced in such a fashion, it is necessary to have a sufficiently large database so that almost any new case will be "covered," in the sense of having a high similarity to a number of past cases. Naturally, parallel retrieval of the bases is required for a memory of this size.

The first MBR system to be implemented was a medical expert system called Quack (Waltz 1987). The associative memory in Quack contains a large number of medical histories of past patients, each in the form of a base, exactly as described in Sect. 2.1. Each base contains the patient's personal attributes, medical symptoms, test results and eventual diagnosis. A new patient (the target) contains only the patient's personal attributes and medical symptoms. The first phase of Quack's operation is to perform an associative retrieval using a simple, generic similarity metric. The initial bases retrieved are then used to form hypotheses concerning the patient's diagnosis. The second phase involves computing a new similarity metric specially tailored to the chosen hypotheses.

The new similarity metric is computed by weighting the slots of the bases according to their statistical correlation with the hypotheses. (The values of a slot with a high statistical correlation tend to strongly confirm or disconfirm a hypothesis, and therefore that slot will be given a high weight. Note that this computation involves examining every slot of every base in the associative memory and hence would require a tremendous amount of time on a serial machine.) Associative retrieval is performed again, this time with new similarity metric. The newly retrieved bases are used to strengthen or weaken belief in the existing hypotheses, and perhaps to form new ones. The process is repeated with the updated set of hypotheses, until only one to three hypotheses remain. Finally, in the third phase, Quack orders a number of tests to be performed. As might be suspected, the tests are selected by computing the statistical correlation of each test with the hypothesized diagnoses. On the basis of the test results, a final diagnosis is made.

With an associative memory containing 4096 bases, a typical example required 8.9 s to arrive at the correct diagnosis. With an associative memory of 32 768 bases, the same example required 10.7 s to arrive at the diagnosis, but generated fewer false hypotheses along the way. This behavior is very encouraging, as it shows that Quack "gets smarter" when more knowledge is added without incurring a significant time penalty. It should be emphasized that Quack contains no rule base: all inference is performed using purely statistical operations upon memory.

The second MBR system implemented was a word pronunciation system called MBRtalk. Given the spelling of a word, MBRtalk produces a string of phonemes corresponding to the word's pronunciation. The associative memory in MBRtalk contains a "pronunciation dictionary" of English words, represented so that each letter in each word corresponds to a single base, the slots of which contain the letter itself, the previous four letters, the succeeding four letters, the phoneme corresponding to the letter and the stress assigned to the phoneme. In a target, the letter to be pronounced and the four letters on either side are predictors, while the phoneme and stress are goals. The similarity metric works by computing how "tightly" a given slot–value pair in a predictor constrains the value of a goal. As in Quack, this involves a statistical computation over the entire database. Unlike Quack, however, a similarity metric is only computed once in MBRtalk and a single associative retrieval is used to produce an output. With an associative memory containing 131 072 bases, representing 18 098 words, MBRtalk produced exactly the correct phoneme 88% of the time, and a plausible output in the remaining cases.

The last unstructured associative memory system to be examined is a text-retrieval system called the connection machine document retrieval system (CMDRS) (Waltz 1987). A text-retrieval system can be viewed as an associative memory specialized to deal with analogs in the form of files containing free text. Typically, the system will contain a large number of text files (perhaps 10 000–20 000) and provide facilities which allow the user to retrieve all pieces of text on a subject of interest. The CMDRS is implemented on a 16K-processor connection machine in which each processor is used to store one document. The search algorithm used by this system is relevance search, which has the advantage that it requires no query language since no Boolean pattern is used. Instead, retrieval takes place according to the following two-phase process. In the first phase, the user simply specifies one or more keywords which are broadcast to all of the processors. Each processor computes a numeric score for its document based on the number of broadcast words which appear in the document. (In addition, each word is weighted in importance according to its frequency of appearance in the entire database. The less common the word, the more it will influence the score.) The documents with the largest scores are then presented to the user. In the second phase, the user can examine the retrieved documents and mark them as "good" or "bad," depending on their relevance. The search is then repeated, this time using all the words in all the documents marked good (called seed documents). This algorithm has been shown to have excellent properties of precision and recall.

The really astounding thing about the CMDRS, however, is its speed. Given 15 000 documents (with an average of 400 words per document, representing 40 Mbytes of free text) and a seed document of 200 words, the system takes 40 ms to assign scores to each document. In another 20 ms, the system has sorted all the documents by score and returned the best 20 to the user. Note that no classification hierarchy is used to arrange or speed access to the documents. The system's excellent performance rests entirely on the fact that all of the 15 000 documents are scored and sorted in parallel. Such performance vividly illustrates the potential of massively parallel systems, configured as active memories, to process very large knowledge bases in real time.

Of course, it must be recognized that massively parallel machines like the connection machine are very expensive at present and are likely to remain so for the foreseeable future. For this reason, the unstructured associative memory models discussed in this section will almost certainly not be feasible for most AI applications for some time to come.

3. Distributed Agent Architecture

One approach to the design of an analogical reasoning system is to draw upon techniques from the field of distributed AI. Using this paradigm, the process of analogical reasoning is divided into its major functions (e.g., similarity matching, analog retrieval, analog generalization, etc.) and each function is assigned to a separate agent. These agents are then allowed to operate in parallel with each other to perform opportunistic problem solving. One design for such a system is described below.

3.1 Problem–Solution Pairs

Most work on analogical reasoning within the distributed agent paradigm has used a model in which the slots of each base are partitioned into a problem set and a solution set, and the base is said to represent a "problem–solution pair" (Silverman 1985a,b). The problem slots are used to represent the functional requirements of some task, while the solution slots represent the components of a design or plan that satisfies those requirements.

Analogical problem solving within this model takes place in an interactive fashion. The user provides the system with a (possibly incomplete) specification of the target problem which is currently being worked upon. The system then retrieves all those problem–solution pairs whose problem component is similar to the current problem. After examining the solution to the most similar problem, the user may choose to accept or reject that solution and repeat the retrieval process. A CRAFTSMAN algorithm is then executed upon the solution components of the most recently retrieved bases to create a new solution to the target problem.

Clearly, this style of analogical reasoning maps very well onto the description of associative memory given in this article. The user's problem specification is used to form a target containing goals for those parts of the specification left incomplete and for the solution. (This presupposes that the system has a predefined format for problems and solutions in the user's domain). The retrieval of problem–solution pairs with similar problem components corresponds exactly to associative retrieval. Note that since the predictors of the target all come from the problem specification, the similarity metric will automatically examine only the problem components of bases. It can be seen that analogical reasoning should perform pattern completion and generalization, since the user can leave parts of the target problem unspecified, and there may be no bases that perfectly match. Therefore, the associative retrieval should allow a variable format for the target and use a real-valued similarity metric.

3.2 Current Blackboard Agent Design

A prototype using the analogical reasoning model described above has been implemented. Essentially, this version of ARIEL simulates the associative retrieval of an associative memory through a blackboard architecture. In the serial environment for which the prototype was constructed, it is not feasible to actually examine all the base analogs stored in the analog knowledge base. Therefore, the analog knowledge base is partitioned into a taxonomic classification hierarchy. Each target problem is classified within the hierarchy by the user during problem elicitation, and only the bases in the corresponding partition are examined during associative retrieval.

The operation of ARIEL's blackboard agents can be briefly described as follows. The entering of the target problem is handled by the WRITER, which performs all input–output for the user, and the CRITIC, which guides the actual elicitation process. The LIBRARIAN, which serves as the interface to the analog knowledge base, then copies all base analogs from the correct partition to the blackboard. The IDEA MAN, which contains the algorithm for the similarity metric, then ranks the bases on the blackboard according to their similarity with the target. Finally, the CRAFTSMAN produces the target solution from the similarity-sorted bases by "cutting and pasting" components of the relevant base solutions and by learning new possibilities with the aid of heuristic feedback from the CRITIC.

Note that in this prototype, the analog knowledge base is completely static, in the sense that it does not know how to perform associative retrieval on its own contents. Rather, a brute-force method is used whereby the LIBRARIAN retrieves all possibly relevant bases and the IDEA MAN applies the similarity metric after the bases have been copied to the blackboard. This means that the analog knowledge base by itself does not constitute an associative memory; instead, the ARIEL agents are doing all the work.

3.3 Role of Associative Memory in ARIEL

A new version of ARIEL is currently being designed. The key difference between this design and the earlier one is the absence of a similarity-matching function external to the associative memory. Here, the similarity matching is performed within the associative memory itself, before any bases are sent to the blackboard. The only bases copied to the blackboard from the associative memory are those that are already known to have a similarity with the target above some threshold. Of course, this is simply another way of saying that the associative memory is itself responsible for associative retrieval; it does not need some external function to do its work for it. This rearrangement of functionality makes it possible to parallelize the associative retrieval process by performing multiple similarity matches at once as discussed in Sect. 2.

3.4 Genetic Algorithms in Analogical Learning

An advanced technique for implementing the CRAFTSMAN is via genetic algorithms (GAs), which are a class of adaptive and general-purpose learning algorithms based on the mechanics of natural genetics. It has been shown, theoretically and empirically, that GAs are robust and effective in various task domains (Grefenstette 1987). GAs maintain a "population" which consists of a subset of candidate solutions. During each iteration, called a generation, the current population is evaluated. Associated with each candidate solution is a performance measure assigned and adjusted by the CRITIC. Candidate solutions with higher performance measures receive a greater number of copies in the next generation. In the reproduction phase the genetic operators, namely crossover and mutation, are applied. The crossover operator selects two good candidate solutions from the current population and swaps some of their parts. The mutation operator randomly flips some bits in the selected candidate solution at a prespecified rate. By doing so, new candidate solutions are generated is such a way that they still resemble, but are not identical to, their parents. The effect of this process is to transform the solutions from the current population into new, hopefully better, solutions. Within a finite population, candidate solutions with above-average performance survive, while other solutions are likely to be displaced owing to their low performance measures. This search is conducted iteratively over repeated generations until an acceptable solution is found or some conditions are met.

The robustness of the GAs is accomplished by incorporating, but not relying upon, a type of random search to ensure that all areas of the solution space are explored, not just the subspaces that appear promising during the early stages of the search. The effectiveness of the GAs is achieved by propagating the best partial solutions from one generation to another, and by sampling many combinations of partial solutions simultaneously. Aiming at better efficiency, it is important to provide the solutions of past problems closely related to the current situation for the GA to start with. It has been shown that by injecting similar past experience from the analog knowledge base to the initial population, the time needed for problem solving can be significantly reduced (Zhou 1987). Based on related knowledge and some randomly generated rules, the genetic operators, acting as the CRAFTSMAN, heuristically combine and construct new solutions using the useful building blocks brought in from the analog knowledge base or created in previous learning.

Another nice property of GAs is their intrinsic parallelism with respect to the ability to search many areas of the search space simultaneously. With an appropriate knowledge representation, it is feasible to parallelize the implementation of a GA by allowing several processors to work on the same set of candidate solutions, each processor manipulating a portion of the population and communicating through the blackboard. Overall, GAs provide a promising approach in machine learning and analogical reasoning.

4. Connectionist Models

A second direction for improving the associative memory model is to arrange the analogs in a manner which can be exploited to facilitate associative retrieval. The most obvious fashion in which to arrange the analogs in memory is in a network of relations. Among traditional AI paradigms, the most familiar example of such a representation is the semantic network. In the present case, the goal is to find network representations that have a natural parallel implementation. This problem has been studied extensively within the paradigm of connectionism (Rumelhart *et al.* 1986).

In the following discussion, it is assumed that the reader is already familiar with the basic concepts of connectionism. If this is not the case, the references should be consulted. Here only brief descriptions of the connectionist paradigm and the way in which connectionist representation techniques relate to associative memory are given. A connectionist system is a network of a very large number of simple processors, usually called units, which are highly interconnected and operate in parallel. Each unit has a numeric activation value which is communicated to other units along connections of varying strengths. As the network operates, the activation value of each unit continuously changes in response to the activity of the units to which it is connected. This process is called spreading activation and is the fundamental mechanism underlying the operation of all connectionist networks. All the knowledge held by such a network is stored in the numerical strengths of the connections between units. There are two major types of connectionist representations, localist and distributed.

4.1 Localist Representations

Localist representations are in some ways more intuitive than distributed ones. In a localist representation, each unit corresponds to exactly one concept and is connected to related concepts. Knowledge is captured in the network in an explicit, easily visualized fashion which makes it possible to design localist representations "by hand." The localist representations which are most appropriate for associative memory are called parallel semantic networks.

Semantic networks are a well-known class of knowledge representation formalisms in AI. In its simplest form, a semantic network consists of a number of objects representing concepts or domain entities interconnected in a network by links representing various relations between the objects. A very common form of semantic network is an inheritance lattice. In such a network, the links represent a subclass relation and are constrained to form a lattice or a directed acyclic graph. Inheritance lattices are intended to support two fundamental operations: (a) inheritance, in which properties of an object are inferred from properties of its ancestors in the lattice; and (b) categorization, in which the system infers the identity of an object from a partial description of its properties.

In recent years, connectionist researchers have worked on developing massively parallel implementations of semantic networks. The first attempt to do this was the NETL system, proposed by Fahlman (1979). In NETL, each object and link in the semantic network was implemented by a separate hardware processor. Up to a million processors were envisioned in the design. Objects could communicate by sending simple one-bit messages, called markers, across the links. This operation of marker passing, which is actually a discrete form of spreading activation, was used to implement inheritance and categorization. NETL was highly influential in subsequent work, serving, for example, as the primary inspiration behind the design of the connection machine.

Unfortunately, NETL had several serious limitations in its design. First, the inheritance mechanism did not always work correctly in the presence of exceptions and multiple ancestors. (Specifically, it was subject to race conditions in the network.) Second, because of the simple on/off nature of the markers, the system could only find objects that perfectly matched a description during categorization. The system had no notion of "best match" or "partial match." This made NETL inappropriate for implementing associative memory.

More recently, Shastri (1988) has designed a massively parallel implementation of semantic networks that avoids these problems and has many other advantages as well. As in NETL, Shastri's system implements each object in the semantic network with a separate processor, and processors communicate over hardware links. Also as in NETL, the basic operations supported are inheritance and categorization. Here, however, the similarity ends. Shastri's system is based on a mathematical theory of evidential reasoning, allowing evidence from multiple sources to be combined in a mathematically rigorous fashion. This theory is related to both Bayes' rule and the Dempster–Shafer rule, but is demonstrably superior to both in the context of semantic networks. (Given that it has a highly efficient parallel implementation, it could also provide an elegant solution to the problem of real-time data fusion.)

The network in Shastri's system works by spreading activation, rather than simple marker passing. In other words, the objects communicate real-valued activation levels to each other, rather than single-bit markers. The activation level of an object is used to represent the strength of evidence for the object computed so far. By means of spreading activation, the network is able to correctly compute inheritance, even in the presence of exceptions and multiple ancestors. Even better, the network is able to perform categorization by finding the "best match" to a partial description of an object, even if there is no perfect match. The system does this by computing a similarity metric, precisely defined in terms of the evidential reasoning theory, which takes into account information from the entire semantic network. The similarity metric is computed for all objects in the network in parallel, and the "best-matching" object is returned. As a result, categorization in Shastri's system could be used as the basis for associative retrieval in an associative memory.

4.2 Distributed Representations

Connectionist systems with distributed representations encode concepts as patterns of activity over many hidden units, and they use each hidden unit in the representation of multiple concepts (Rumelhart et al. 1986). Informally, each analog that the network learns is encoded on top of the same set of hidden units. This style of representation can be highly counterintuitive to persons trained in traditional symbolic AI, because it is often difficult or impossible to look at any single unit in the network and say exactly what it is doing. As a result, the internal representations are often not "human readable." A closely related issue is the fact that these representations are for the most part not explictly designed by the human builder of the system, but rather are automatically generated by means of a learning algorithm. This can be viewed either as an advantage or disadvantage, depending on the importance one places on learning. Note that similarity matching, analog retrieval and construction of the output are not separate steps in this model, but rather all take place in parallel via spreading activation.

There are already several known learning algorithms which produce the kind of distributed representations described above. The best known of these are the back-propagation algorithm and the Boltzmann learning algorithm. Although the details of these algorithms differ considerably, they all work by attempting to discover how best to use the network's hidden units to capture statistical regularities in the stored analogs. Conceptually, the algorithms try to use each hidden unit to detect some microfeature of the analogs which serves as a (possibly weak) predictor of the output or completed pattern. Implementationally, this is done by adjusting the weights on the connections between units. The algorithms discover the microfeatures by searching for a set of microfeatures that make it easy to express the statistical associations between components of the analogs. Once these microfeatures are discovered, the internal representation of an analog is a distributed pattern over the hidden units indicating which microfeatures that analog possesses. Since two analogs are exactly similar when they share most of the same microfeatures, similar analogs will be represented by similar patterns. In effect, the network constructs its own internal similarity metric. This is a significant advantage over paradigms in which a good generalization can only be achieved when the designer, using domain-specific knowledge, explicitly designs a representation to have an appropriate similarity metric.

An important limitation of these learning algorithms for distributed representations is their performance on large problems. For large problems, the network must have a large number of weights, and the learning time of algorithms does not scale well with the number of weights. For example, the back-propagation algorithm has been shown empirically to have a learning time on a serial machine of around $O(N^3)$, where N is the number of weights. This means that for any large-scale problem, the learning time will be astronomical. On a parallel machine, the time would be reduced only to $O(N^2)$ which is still unacceptable. The learning time for the Boltzmann algorithm scales in an even worse fashion.

4.3 Coarse-Coded Representations

Coarse-coded representations (Hinton and Anderson 1981) fall somewhere between the fully distributed representations of Sect. 4.2 and the localist representations of Sect. 4.1; accordingly, they might be described as "slightly distributed." The basic idea behind coarse coding is to allow each concept to be represented by a small number of units (i.e. small in relation to the total number of units in the network). Ideally, this scheme would make it possible to achieve the generalization capabilities of distributed representations, while preserving the structure and understandability of localist representations.

To see how analogs in an associative memory could be represented in a coarse-coded fashion, consider the discussion of analog structure given in Sect. 2, where an analog was described as a simple collection of slots and slot values. In a coarse-coded network, there is a small subnetwork corresponding to each possible slot of an analog. In addition, there is a larger "constraint" network to which each of the slot networks is connected. The value of a slot for any given analog is represented as a distributed pattern over the corresponding slot network. The pattern in one slot constrains the patterns in other slots through the constraint network, so that only one analog can be fully instantiated at a time. Associative retrieval can be performed by supplying the values for a subset of the slots, making analogs content-addressable.

4.4 Advantages and Disadvantages by Type

The advantages and disadvantages of the three types of connectionist systems can be summarized according to the following four criteria.

(a) Are there learning algorithms which allow the system to automatically incorporate information from a body of training examples?

(b) Can the system support the automatic generation of explanations of its behavior?

(c) Can the system generalize from its internal knowledge to examples it has not seen before?

(d) Can the system represent relations between concepts stored in the network (à la links in a semantic network)?

Localist representations have the disadvantage that there are presently no known learning algorithms for them, although the subject is under active research. They are capable of supporting explanation and can perform some generalization in the form of finding a "best-match" during categorization. Their strongest advantage is their ability to represent a rich set of relations between concepts stored in the network.

Distributed representations are best suited to domains requiring learning, since there already exist a number of well-tested learning algorithms for them, such as the Boltzmann learning algorithm and back-propagation. They are not able to support explanation, but have excellent properties of generalization. Their greatest weakness is that they cannot support precise well-defined relations between the concepts stored in the network.

Coarse-coded representations, as one might expect, share some of the advantages and disadvantages of both localist and "more fully" distributed representations. They are able to make use of the known learning algorithms, but may run into difficulties owing to constraints on the network architecture. Explanation can be supported, but not as conveniently as in a localist system. Generalization can be performed well and relations between concepts can be expressed, though in a more constrained fashion than in a localist system.

5. Conclusions: Toward an Analogical Reasoning Integration and Extension Language

Current research indicates that the future of analogical reasoning systems lies in the ability to exploit a high degree of parallelism to implement the fundamental analogical reasoning functions. Recent advances in the parallel processing of knowledge bases offer several models by which these tasks could be performed. Massively parallel similarity matching and analog retrieval turn out to be surprisingly straightforward to implement; parallel generalization, while requiring more sophisticated models, is feasible as well.

5.1 Summary of the Three Models

Three models which may prove integral to the future development of analogical reasoning systems have been discussed. First, the paradigm of MBR, exploiting massively parallel hardware such as the connection machine, makes possible the construction of fast associative memories supporting retrieval from unstructured knowledge bases. Similarity matching and retrieval are handled in a simple, elegant and efficient manner. Second, the field of DAI, and in particular the blackboard paradigm, offers a means of integrating the key analogical reasoning components into a hybrid system. Third, connectionist models, based on the mechanism of spreading activation, offer more sophisticated means of representing analogs that support not only similarity matching and retrieval, but strong properties of generalization as well.

5.2 The Integrated Concept

The challenge for future analogical reasoning systems is to integrate in some manner the necessary parallel techniques, including those discussed above, into a cooperative, problem-solving system. One method currently being explored is to use a blackboard shell with an ability to ascribe semantics to subsymbolic representations as an integration tool. Since a single representation language would be employed to represent analog knowledge on the blackboard, agents would be able to cooperatively make use of the same analog knowledge even if they internally incorporated computational techniques from different paradigms.

Bibliography

Ackley D H, Hinton G E, Sejnowski T J 1985 A learning algorithm for Boltzmann machines. *Cognit. Sci.* **9**, 147–69

Collins A M, Loftus E F 1972 A spreading-activation theory of semantic processing. *Psychol. Rev.* **6**, 407–28

Eliot L B 1987 Automated analogical problem solving and expert systems. In: Silverman B G (ed.) *Expert Systems for Business.* Addison–Wesley, Reading, Massachusetts

Fahlman S E 1979 *NETL: A System for Representing and Using Real-World Knowledge.* MIT Press, Cambridge, Massachusetts

Grefenstette J J (ed.) 1987 Genetic algorithms and their applications. *Proc. Int. Conf. Genetic Algorithms.* MIT Press, Cambridge, Massachusetts

Hinton G E, Anderson J A (eds.) 1981 *Parallel Models of Associative Memory.* Erlbaum, Hillsdale, New Jersey

Holland J H 1975 *Adaptation in Natural and Artificial Systems.* MIT Press, Cambridge, Massachusetts

Nakamura K, Sage A P, Iwai S 1983 An intelligent database interface using psychological similarity between data. *IEEE Trans. Syst., Man Cybern.* **13**, 558–68

Quillian M R 1968 Semantic memory. In: Minsky M (ed.) *Semantic Information Processing.* MIT Press, Cambridge, Massachusetts, pp. 216–70

Rumelhart D E, Feldman A, Hayes J (eds.) 1986 *Parallel Distributed Processing: Explorations in the Microstructure of Cognition.* Bradford Books, Cambridge, Massachusetts

Shastri L 1988 *Semantic Networks: An Evidential Formalization and its Connectionist Realization.* Morgan Kaufmann, Los Altos, California

Silverman B G 1983 Analogy in systems management: A theoretical inquiry. *IEEE Trans. Syst., Man Cybern.* **13**, 1049–75

Silverman B G 1984 INNOVATOR: An expert system for management of modeling and simulation. *Proc. Int. Conf. Test and Evaluation.* International Test and Evaluation Association, Springfield, Virginia

Silverman B G 1985a The use of analogs in the innovation process: A software engineering protocol analysis. *IEEE Trans. Syst., Man Cybern.* **15**, 30–44

Silverman B G 1985b Toward an integrated cognitive model of the inventor engineer. *R&D Manage.* **15**, 151–58

Silverman B G, Chang J 1988 *BSG: Toward A Blackboard Shell with Semantic Understanding.* George Washington

University Institute for Artificial Intelligence, Washington, DC

Silverman B G, Moustakis V S 1987 INNOVATOR: Representations and heuristics, In: Silverman B G (ed.) *Expert Systems for Business.* Addison–Wesley, Reading, Massachusetts, pp. 402–39

Silverman B G, Murray A J 1986 *Toward an Expert Project Management System.* George Washington University Institute for Artificial Intelligence, Washington, DC

Silverman B G, Murray A J, Feggos K 1986 *Analogical Reasoning Integration and Extension Language (ARIEL).* George Washington University Institute for Artificial Intelligence, Washington, DC

Stanfill C W, Waltz D L 1986 Toward memory-based reasoning. *Commun. ACM* **29**, 1213–28

Waltz D L 1987 Applications of the connection machine. *IEEE Trans. Comput.* **36**, 85–97

Winston P H 1980 Learning and reasoning by analogy. *Commun. ACM* **23**, 689–703

Zhou H H 1987 CSM: A genetic classifier system with memory for learning by analogy. Ph. D. thesis, Vanderbilt University, Nashville, Tennessee

B. G. Silverman
[George Washington University, Washington, DC, USA]

S. Pimental
[Intellitek, Rockville, Maryland, USA]

W. Truszkowski, R. Dominy and T. Ames
[Goddard Space Flight Center, Greenbelt, Maryland, USA]

Artificial Intelligence

Artificial intelligence (AI) is a field of study that encompasses computational techniques for performing tasks that apparently require intelligence when performed by humans. A robust AI system must be able to store knowledge, to apply that knowledge to the solution of problems and to acquire new knowledge through experience. Applications of AI, particularly through expert systems, to business, medicine and education help to illustrate the impact that AI is having on the skilled professions.

1. History and Goal

Babbage and Boole, who lived in early nineteenth-century England, are the intellectual grandfathers of AI. Babbage designed the analytical engine which was intended, among other things, to play championship chess, and Boole developed a calculus of logic. The modern history of AI begins with digital electronic computers and such geniuses as von Neumann and Turing. The 1980s have witnessed an enormous burgeoning of academic and industrial interest worldwide in the development of AI.

According to the Turing test, a machine is intelligent when a human observer who communicates with the machine via a teletypewriter cannot correctly determine whether the responses are being generated by a human or a machine. In general, AI researchers have two goals: first, to make computers more useful; and second, to understand the principles of intelligence. The latter goal assumes that intelligence has principles and that those principles can be understood. Thus, work in AI often involves the selection of an intelligent trait, analysis of its principles and construction of a machine which manifests that trait.

In order to handle the burgeoning information of the electronic age, AI is needed. The cornerstones of this work are representation, reasoning and learning (Forsyth and Rada 1986). More sophisticated information processing is needed (see Fig. 1) for:

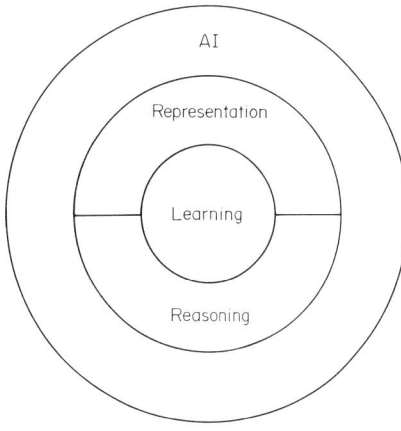

Figure 1
The key components of an AI system: representation, reasoning and learning

(a) storing many terms that are intricately related—machine representation of a knowledge base (KB);

(b) getting information from the KB—machine reasoning; and

(c) augmenting the KB—machine learning.

Both the structure and content of the KB are concerned with knowledge representation; how this knowledge is used is machine reasoning. Through time, intelligent systems have to change and adapt. The transition is controlled by learning and takes a form of representation and reasoning at time t and moves it to another more adapted form for the environment at time $t+1$:

$$\text{representation}_t + \text{reasoning}_t$$
$$\rightarrow \text{representation}_{t+1} + \text{reasoning}_{t+1}$$

Without adaptability in the machine, the ability of the machine to help solve information problems would be severely limited. Ultimately, systems must be designed whose learning component is itself modifiable through time.

2. Representation

For the computer programmer, what AI researchers call knowledge is just another word for data. Computer programs that manipulate knowledge use the same data structures as other programs: arrays, linked lists, binary trees, and so on. At the level of implementation (programming), knowledge and data appear to be identical. However, AI researchers do make a valid distinction between knowledge and data, based on what a program does with its data. If a program uses the meaning of some data, then that data is termed knowledge. For example, suppose a program accesses a file of names and addresses, as in a telephone directory. If the program was written to print the address of each name a user enters, then the file would be termed data. However, if the program was written to print directions on how to travel to the address of each name entered by the user, then the file could be termed knowledge. An intelligent program is one that uses knowledge as defined above. Knowledge is stored in knowledge bases similar to the way in which data are stored in databases. Not surprisingly though, knowledge bases tend to have a more complex structure and organization than databases.

Knowledge may be declarative or procedural. In a declarative representation most of the knowledge is represented as a static collection of facts accompanied by a small set of general procedures for manipulating the facts. Procedural representations embody knowledge in an executable code that acts out the meaning of the knowledge. In most domains both kinds of information are needed.

The first-order predicate calculus (FOPC) is an adequate system for representing any knowledge which people know how to formalize. Furthermore, FOPC is the standard language of logicians. Algorithms exist for converting any FOPC expression into a canonical form, such as the conjunctive normal form. Methods of performing deduction with FOPC have been thoroughly characterized, and a number of amendments to FOPC have been made to facilitate the storage of information. Some of these amendments permit inconsistent deductions or probabilistic deductions to be made. PROLOG is a popular AI programming language which has many features in common with FOPC.

Semantic nets were originally designed as a way to represent the meanings of English words. In a semantic net, information is represented as a set of nodes connected to each other by a set of labelled arcs, which represent relationships among the nodes. For instance, one might have the three nodes "boy," "person" and "arm," and connect "boy" to "person" with the arc "is-a" and connect "arm" to "person" with the arc "part-of" (see Fig. 2). It would be possible to create arbitrarily complex semantic nets, but for practical reasons the set of possible nodes and arcs should be circumscribed. Conceptual dependency diagrams are one variant of semantic nets that include a small set of arc types, such as "ingest" and "grasp." Conceptual dependency diagrams have been principally used in programs for natural-language processing.

In one extension of semantic nets, each node is represented as a frame with links to other nodes occurring as values in the slots of the frame. For instance, to indicate that "boy is-a person" the "boy" frame might have a slot called "is-a" which would be filled with the value "person." Inheritance occurs when the values of a slot for a frame x can be assumed to be the same values as those of that slot in the frame y when the value of the "is-a" slot for x is y (Tanimoto 1987). In frames, the value of a slot may also be a procedure. The "boy" frame might include a slot called "hobbies" whose value is a procedure, such as "inherit the hobbies of person, except those hobbies which are specific to girls."

Many knowledge-based programs are written in the LISP programming language. LISP and AI have a close association because LISP is designed to manipulate data as symbols—few assumptions are made by the LISP interpreter as to the meaning of the data. In contrast, programming languages like PASCAL require the programmer to declare each symbol as an integer, character or pointer. LISP is a cross between a procedural and a declarative language. It is specifically designed to operate on lists and is formally based on the lambda calculus, which is an applicative or functional language. A LISP program consists of several function definitions together with other statements which work together to perform the desired task. When modern AI application languages are tailored to a task, such as manipulating frames, these languages are often developed atop LISP.

3. Reasoning

Problem solving can be viewed as searching. One common way to deal with search uses rules, data and control (Nilsson 1980). The rules operate on the data, and the control operates on the rules. In the "travelling salesman problem," for instance, the data is the set of tours and their costs in a weighted graph, the rules are ways to proceed from tour to tour, and the control decides what rules to apply and when. Such rules, data and control systems are called a production system.

A very simple production-rule system has two rules: "if a then b" and "if b then c." Given the fact a, an

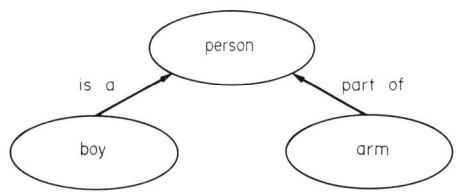

Figure 2
Example of a semantic net

algorithm can chain forward to b and then to c. If c is the solution, the algorithm halts. Conversely, in a backward chain a goal such as c is given, and the search goes backward to b and then a. If a is known to be true, then the backward search halts. The appropriateness of forward or backward chaining depends, of course, on the problem. Matching techniques are frequently an important part of a problem-solving strategy. In forward chaining, for instance, an "if a then b" rule is activated only if a exists in the data. The match between the a in the data and the a in the rule may not have to be exact, and various deductive and inductive methods may be used to try to ascertain whether or not an adequate match exists.

In the generate-and-test approach to problem solving, the problem is viewed as a set of states, including a start state and a goal state. The problem solver generates a state and then tests whether it is the goal state. Based on the results of the test, another state is generated and then tested, and so on. Depending on the constraints that the generate mechanism employs, various categories of generate-and-test algorithms arise. In practice, heuristics or problem-specific "rules of thumb" must be found to expedite the search process. In fact, some researchers (Rich 1983) would define the discipline of AI as: "The study of techniques for solving exponentially hard problems in polynomial time by exploiting knowledge about the problem domain." This exploitation involves characterizing the problem or search space. In general, a problem is solvable to the extent that examination of part of its search space gives significant information about the nature of the remainder of the search space. A variety of questions can be asked about a search space in the effort to characterize it. Is the problem neatly decomposable into smaller problems; does consistent, exact information about the problem exist; and should a human be expected to interact with the computer in the process of solving the problem?

One of the earliest investigations in AI was a study of automatic deduction using problem-solving heuristics. The objective was to develop a program that could prove simple theorems with a human-like approach. The program achieved the objective by breaking problems into subproblems and solving each one in turn. Another method for proving theorems makes use of the resolution principle. Resolution takes two parent clauses that share a complementary literal and obtain a new resolvent clause. Traditionally, proof by resolution first negates the desired conclusion and then adds it to the list of premises with the aim of deriving a contradiction.

The propositional and predicate calculi are monotonic. Suppose that S is the set of formulas provable from some set A of axioms. If A' is a larger set of axioms that includes A, then S', the set of formulas provable from A', is either a superset of S or is equivalent to S. In other words, the set of theorems is monotonically nondecreasing as one adds to the set of axioms. In everyday life, however, people often use nonmonotonic reasoning. To make plans, people often need to make assumptions which may need later to be retracted. A number of methods have been proposed to alter or extend traditional logics so that nonmonotonic reasoning can be accommodated.

In many situations, such as medical diagnosis, the available knowledge is incomplete or inexact. Probabilistic reasoning methods allow AI systems to use uncertain knowledge in ways that take the uncertainty into account.

The probability that a patient has a disease D given that he has a symptom S, represented by $P(D|S)$, is related to the probability that given disease D he has symptom S, represented by $P(S|D)$. More precisely.

$$P(D|S) = \frac{P(S|D) \times P(D)}{P(S|D) \times P(D) + P(S|\text{not } D) \times P(\text{not } D)}$$

$P(D)$ is the frequency of D in the population, and $P(S|\text{not } D)$ is the frequency of symptom S in the population without disease D. The above formula, called Bayes formula, may be readily extended to the case of many symptoms $S_1, \ldots, S_n$. The validity of Bayes formula depends on the mutual independence of the symptoms $S_1, \ldots, S_n$. This requirement is the Achilles heel of Bayesian analysis, as the symptoms are rarely mutually independent.

4. Learning

Shortly after electronic computers became available, experimentation began with computers that learn. By the 1950s a computer program had already been developed which "learned" to play checkers by adjusting coefficients on a polynomial that evaluated checkerboard situations. The perception-learning algorithm was a major focus of interest in the 1960s and was thought to simulate, in part, what happens in neural networks. The advent of inexpensive, highly parallel computers in the late 1980s has again stimulated interest in learning through neural-network simulation. Because of the many connections among processors, work in this field now often goes under the heading of connectionism.

In a simple model of a learning system, the environment supplies some information to the learning element, the learning element uses this information to make improvements in an explicit knowledge base, and the performance element uses the knowledge base to perform its task (see Fig. 3). The most important factor affecting the design of learning systems is the kind of information supplied to the system by the environment—particularly the level and quality of this information. Since its knowledge is imperfect, the learning element does not know in advance how to fill in missing details or ignore unimportant details. After guessing, the system must receive some feedback that

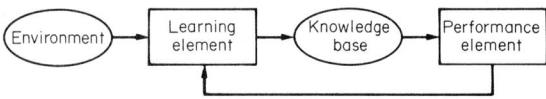

Figure 3
A simple model of learning systems

allows it to evaluate its hypotheses and revise them if necessary.

The learning element often tries to discover correct generalizations. Generalizations can be made by learning a single generalization from many instances. Alternatively, by applying substantial domain knowledge, a program can generalize from one example. In either case there has been substantial interest in the development of hierarchies of generalizations because hierarchies are both natural to people and lend themselves to computer manipulation.

In similarity-based learning, a program takes a number of instances, compares them in terms of similarities and differences, and creates a generalized description based on this structural analysis. Much of the similarity work has been based on comparing instances syntactically. An explanation-based learning program takes a single instance, builds an explanation of how the various components relate to each other using domain-dependent understanding or planning methods, and then generalizes the properties of various components of the instance. This generalized description of the instance can then be applied in understanding further instances. An explanation-based learning system constructs an explanation in terms of a domain theory that proves how a training example satisfies a goal concept definition. Then a set of conditions under which the explanation structure holds is stated in terms that satisfy an operationality criterion.

Machine learning may involve two rather different kinds of information processing: inductive and deductive. Induction is concerned with determining general patterns and rules from raw data or experience. Alternatively, deductive information processing is the determination of specific facts using general rules. The proof of a theorem is a deduction from the axioms and other existing theorems. Similarity-based learning uses induction, while explanation-based learning depends on both induction and deduction.

The importance of knowledge bases and the difficulties of learning have led to the development of various interactive methods for augmenting knowledge bases. If there are experts in a given field, it is usually easier to obtain the compiled experience of the experts than to try to duplicate the direct experience that gave rise to the expertise. Some of the knowledge-acquisition systems guide experts through an existing knowledge base and ask the expert to make modifications as appropriate.

5. Computer Vision

The goal of a computer vision system is to interpret a visual scene so that meaningful action can be based on that interpretation. The vision analysis process begins with sensing the image which is then preprocessed by digitizing and filtering. Next, lines and shapes are determined with a variety of techniques such as region growing. The three-dimensional characteristics of the image must be determined from various two-dimensional manifestations. To detect motion a chronological sequence of images is studied. Finally, the image is interpreted in terms of high-level semantic and pragmatic units.

Significant success has been obtained with scenes that are highly constrained. A general-purpose scene interpreter will not be built before it is possible to give the machine knowledge about the world for which the interpretation needs to be made. In vision work, as elsewhere in AI, the challenge is to find the constraints on real-world situations that allow an algorithm to efficiently handle that situation. A "constraint-propagation program" has been developed which recognizes objects in a line drawing by noting that in the real world only certain edge intersections are possible.

In a strict sense, computer vision would be concerned only with images analogous to the images formed within the eyes of natural vision systems. However, there are many kinds of nonvisual images, obtainable in computer readable form, which pose similar problems in their interpretation. Not only may the raw input to a computer vision system differ from that available to a natural vision system, but some systems may already exceed the performance of natural systems for a small subset of tasks.

6. Natural-Language Processing

The vision problem is related to the natural-language problem because both must ultimately share a set of primitives for describing the world. Automated natural-language processing may, however, be easier to achieve than automated visual processing because humans are the originators of language and can introspect about language. In one view, language is a complex system of rules which connect meanings to particular choices of signals. In this view there is a hierarchy of levels of analysis, from the signals to the words to the syntactic structures to the meaning. An alternative view is that language processing is part of a general relationship between mental and physical states, and any aspect of the cognitive system which is relevant to a communication is part of the language-processing system.

At the lexical level, words and components of words, including prefixes, suffixes, and other morphological forms and inflections, are studied. At the syntactic level, a grammar is used to parse a sentence. The semantic interpretation depends on a large body of knowledge, in addition to that provided by the lexical and syntactic analysis, to assess what an utterance means. Finally, to interpret the pragmatic significance of a conversation, the computer needs a detailed understanding of the goals and resources of the participants in the conversation.

Computational linguists have produced powerful syntactic and semantic analyzers. These analyzers have been able to resolve some of the simple ambiguities in language such as those which occur with anaphoric reference. An anaphoric reference occurs when a pronoun refers to a noun. For instance, if someone said, "He hit the ball with the bat: it sailed high," then the natural-language processor needs to determine that in such a situation the word "it" is likely to refer to the ball.

Various complex issues of space, time and belief are being addressed by those developing the semantics of natural-language processors. To deal with the pragmatics, a program has to understand the modes and phases of a dialog. For small domains of discourse, domain knowledge has been modelled well enough so that a computer can converse with a human about the domain.

One of the most successful areas of natural-language processing has occurred with front-ends to databases. If the processing system can assume that the user of the database will restrict his concerns to those which the database is likely to be able to handle, then the structure and content of the database can provide powerful constraints to guide the interpretation of queries to the database. In this way, programs have been developed which include a large lexicon, a grammar, and an ability to adapt to a database and begin to do sophisticated handling of natural-language queries to the database.

7. General Applications

Two of the oldest and most famous expert programs in AI are DENDRAL and MACSYMA (Barr and Feigenbaum 1982). DENDRAL accepts a mass spectrogram of a chemical and determines the molecular structure of the chemical. MACSYMA assists scientists in solving mathematical problems. Both DENDRAL and MACSYMA are often used by professionals in the field for whom the programs were intended to be helpful. The design principles behind both projects are rather complicated, because at the time of the inception of the projects the appropriate AI principles were only just beginning to be developed.

Robotics is the intelligent connection of perception to action. The software of modern, commercially available robot systems includes a wide variety of functions: it performs trajectory calculation, interprets sense data, executes adaptive control, and interfaces to databases of geometric models (Yazdani 1986). Robotics challenges AI by forcing it to deal with real objects in real time, particularly with rich three-dimensional geometric situations.

Expert systems strive to imitate the advice of a human expert in a given domain. Knowledge engineering is the part of AI which is specialized in the building of expert systems. Most expert systems are rule based, which means their knowledge is in the form of if–then rules:

> Rule: if   condition 1
>   condition 2
>   ⋮
>   then   action 1
>   action 2
>   ⋮

Such rules can be chained together in various ways to arrive at rules which are not explicitly contained in the knowledge base. This is a form of reasoning.

Since the 1970s, numerous programs have been written to incorporate a skilled professional's expertise into software. One program diagnoses a patient's infectious disease as well as, if not better than, a physician. Another program looks for signs of important minerals in seismic data, and a third provides intelligent computer instruction in a variety of courses. The conclusion has been reached that only a few hundred rules are typically adequate to represent the knowledge that is crucial to an expert's successful performance within a narrow range of his expertise. Such an expert system is, however, not typically good at a variety of secondary tasks which an expert is expected to perform.

One of the early stimulants of the expert-systems explosion was the work with MYCIN (Clancey and Shortliffe 1984). MYCIN employed a few hundred if–then rules about meningitis and bacteremia in order to deduce the proper treatment for a patient who presented with signs of either of those diseases. Claims were made that the rule-based approach to encoding knowledge was ideal for many problems, and the Japanese initiated massive AI experiments based, in part, on production-rule representations. Many extensions have been made to MYCIN and one, in particular, has focused on learning or knowledge acquisition.

MYCIN was originally thought by many to incorporate knowledge in a form similar to that used by physicians; however, it was subsequently seen as too arbitrary and difficult to extend. NEOMYCIN was heralded as the "cognitively realistic" successor to MYCIN. NEOMYCIN separates strategy and domain knowledge. The MYCIN group has directed much of its efforts of the past few years to work on an oncology ward information-management system. The system is called ONCOCIN. The oncologist would not want to seek advice from the computer about therapy, if he or she had to first type into the computer large amounts of previously collected and recorded data about the patient. Accordingly, ONCOCIN includes software for maintenance and attractive display of patient records. When the physician comes to the terminal, the information available is similar to that in the standard paper medical record.

8. Intelligent Information Systems

In the publishing field there is an explosive growth of machine readable output. Simultaneously, computer hardware is becoming better able to deal with large amounts of textual and graphical material. This is a result of the development of compact disks, graphic displays, powerful micro and parallel processors, and networks. Software is also improving along all the fronts that are important for improved information access, User interfaces make it easier for novices to communicate with the machine, because information-retrieval systems help hone the users' request into forms that the machine understands. The end user is now targeted by information providers. This is the result and the cause of societal changes which are stimulating the development of progressively better information systems.

The idea of applying the concepts and techniques of AI's knowledge-based systems to build information-system interfaces is attractive for a variety of reasons. As online search systems tend to rely on specialized-access mechanisms, it is natural to seek effective automatic ways of mapping the user's request onto a search query, both because assistance by human intermediaries is costly and because it would be nice to offer the end user direct access to the search system. However, there is also the important business of establishing the user's real need, so a more significant function of an intelligent interface could be to help the user explicitly formulate a statement of his need.

The standard paradigm of a document system shows documents and queries as the input to a system which must be able to translate new documents and new queries into some canonical form in order that documents relevant to the query can be returned to the user (see Fig. 4). As one imagines a distributed version of such a system, many possibilities come to mind. The documents could be distributed across different systems; there could be many searchers who come one after the other to the system; or all the users could simultaneously be interacting through many workstations with many document bases.

The process of making these systems more intelligent or expert involves placing a variety of sources of knowledge or expertise into the system that can help the searcher gain access to information. This leads to a type of distributed system where a single workstation interacting with a single user who wants a document from a single document base has distributed expertise within itself. The distribution here is among the kinds of expertise that the information system must have in order to operate so as to best satisfy the user. In some cases the functional modules embodying that expertise can be distributed among several workstations or larger computers.

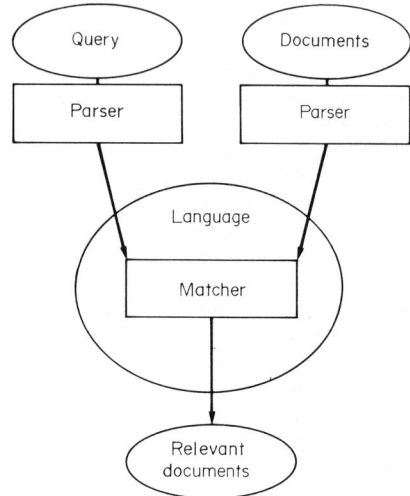

Figure 4
Flowchart of an information retrieval system which emphasizes the role of language for representing documents and queries

9. Future

Surprisingly, the areas of human activity which depend most on common sense are the areas where AI research has been least successful. There is active research into such areas as qualitative physics, which is expected to provide new insights into how everyday situations are handled. One of the principle conclusions of the work on common sense is that people base their everyday decisions on a vast amount of everyday knowledge. Efforts are underway to build knowledge bases that are encyclopedic in their coverage and which could support a wide variety of intelligent activity.

The history of AI is marked by some successes and many failures. If the number of AI projects which are described in the literature as eminently useful for health-care-delivery are called TRIALS and the number of AI projects which achieve acceptance in the health-care-community are called SUCCESS, then the ratio of SUCCESS to TRIALS was reported in the 1970s to be close to 0 (Friedman and Gustafson 1977).

$$\frac{\text{SUCCESS}}{\text{TRIALS}} \approx 0$$

The reasons given for this failure tend to take one of two forms:

(a) the user community is hostile, or

(b) the AI program is too shallow.

As to a hostile user community, both education and a general cultural–technological shift is making the computer more acceptable in the workplace. As to a shallow AI program, enormous effort has been and is being expended toward the development of systems that can explain their behavior, and that can be easily modified and improved by the user.

As the automobile replaced the horse-drawn carriage, stable attendants and carriage drivers were replaced by automobile mechanics and motorcar chauffeurs. Robots are replacing assembly-line laborers in factories. Book knowledge is being transformed into interactive-system knowledge. AI poses a kind of psychological threat to people whose sense of identity is based on their perception of the difference between a mind and a machine. Perhaps the greatest danger of any new technology is that we may lose control of it, or that its power may fall into the hands of those who will use it against human interests. AI technology is information technology and it is capable of being transmitted relatively rapidly; there may thus be a greater potential for it to move into irresponsible hands than, say, nuclear-power technology. This puts an extra responsibility on the society for the proper use of AI.

The wide availability of personal computers is accelerating the move towards an information age. The development of intelligent interfaces to information systems will allow more information to be available to more people. The computer will store progressively more knowledge which people will interactively modify. The possible benefits of AI are both dramatic and seemingly unlimited.

See also: Expert Systems; Knowledge Representation

Bibliography

Barr A, Feigenbaum E 1982 *Handbook of Artificial Intelligence*, Vol. 2. Pitman, London
Clancey W, Shortliffe E 1984 Introduction: Medical artificial intelligence programs. In: Shortliffe E (ed.) *Readings in Medical Artificial Intelligence.* Addison–Wesley, Reading, Massachusetts
Forsyth R, Rada R 1986 *Machine Learning: Expert Systems and Information Retrieval.* Horwood, London
Friedman R, Gustafson D 1977 Computers in clinical medicine, a critical review. *Comput. Biomed. Res.* **10**, 199–204
Nilsson N 1980 *Principles of Artificial Intelligence.* Springer-Verlag, Berlin
Rich E 1983 *Artificial Intelligence.* McGraw–Hill, Singapore
Tanimoto S L 1987 *The Elements of Artificial Intelligence.* Computer Science Press, Rockville, Maryland
Yazdani M 1986 *Artificial Intelligence: Principles and Applications.* Chapman and Hall, London

R. Rada
[University of Liverpool, Liverpool, UK]

Automated Planning

A major research topic in artificial intelligence (AI) is the development of systems that can autonomously generate and reason about plans. Within this research community, a plan is defined as a specified ordering of actions over time; automated planning is the autonomous specification of a plan to achieve a goal. As with many other AI research topics, automated-planning research is principally focused on domains involving ill-defined open-ended problems. This includes many problems which are not easily modelled by well-defined mathematical optimization procedures (e.g., developing robots with enough "common sense" so that they can function and maneuver in everyday environments).

1. Fundamental Issues

There are some fundamental problems with trying to develop autonomous systems for planning, and automated-planning systems are often characterized by how they address these fundamental problems.

The qualification problem is the problem of enumerating all the conditions that must be true before an action can be performed (McCarthy and Hayes 1969). For instance, suppose a robotic system proposes the action Pickup(B). (A class of actions such as Pickup( ) is called an operator.) Typically, the principal preconditions for this action are that the robot "hand" is empty (HANDEMPTY) and that object B has nothing on top of it (CLEAR(B)). However, there are also an infinite number of other possible qualifiers on the feasibility of this action: B could be too heavy, the robot's "arm" may be broken, B may be glued to the table, B may crumble, etc. Clearly, an automated-reasoning system should not be required to examine all possible qualifiers before performing an action. Yet in an individual circumstance, any single qualifier may be important.

The frame problem is the problem of predicting all consequences of an action, or at least all relevant consequences (McCarthy and Hayes 1969). Common sense tells us that if object A is leaning on object B, and we pick up B, then A will fall. The fact that object A will fall is a side effect of the action Pickup(B). Developing formal models of this type of common-sense reasoning is a difficult problem. For instance, some systems (see Sect. 2.2) address this problem by specifying, for each operator, logical axioms that identify all things that will *not* change as a result of executing an operator.

The relevancy problem is the problem of identifying all relevant effects of an action. In principle, any action can have an infinite number of enumerable effects but in order to make a planning problem tractable, it is necessary to identify, prior to planning, the domain of effects that need to be reasoned about. Unfortunately, classes of effects that initially appear irrelevant may turn out to be critical after examining the plan that was generated. In many contexts it is impossible to determine, prior to having generated a plan, which classes of effects are going to be relevant to evaluating the plan.

Consequently, even if the frame problem were solved and a real-world planning system was capable of enumerating all effects, there would still be no guarantee that the planner would in fact account for all effects relevant to a given problem.

The persistence problem is the problem of determining how long something will last (Shoham 1987). Many actions (e.g., feed cat) achieve effects (e.g., cat not hungry) for only a limited duration. Furthermore, the persistence over time of these effects may be dependent on other events (e.g., run around and build up an appetite).

Finally, there is the general problem of reasoning about the knowledge, beliefs and intentions of other agents. Many planning problems involve multiple agents where the automated-planning system (often representing one of the agents) must take into account what other agents (people, robots, etc.) might do. This requires an ability to reason about the beliefs and intended actions of these other agents.

2. Single-Agent Planning

2.1 STRIPS

One of the earliest automated planners was a system called the general problem solver (GPS). GPS used a search procedure called means–ends analysis. As applied to planning problems, means–ends analysis begins with a description of the initial state, the desired goal state and a set of state-change operators. The principal operation of GPS is to iterate through the following steps. Beginning with the initial state, GPS:

(a) compares the present state with the goal state to generate a list of differences,

(b) identifies a state-change operator that will reduce one or more of these differences, and

(c) applies this operator to the present state to generate a new state, and goes to (a).

Whenever step (a) finds no differences between the present and goal state, then GPS terminates and returns the sequence of state-change operators it applied; that is, the plan. When step (b) fails to find an operator, or step (c) generates a previously explored state, then GPS will backtrack on the sequence of operators to an earlier state, find a new state-change operator to apply, and continue processing.

STRIPS (Stanford Research Institute Problem Solver) operates in a similar manner to GPS, but makes some additional assumptions about how states and state-change operators are represented (Fikes and Nilsson 1971). States must be described as a list of propositions which are statements of the form Block(A), ON(A,B), etc. (see Fig. 1). State-change operators define different types of actions. Each operator is composed of:

(a) a *precondition list* that lists all propositions that must be contained in the state description before the operator can be executed in that state,

(b) an *add list* which is a list of propositions that are added to the state description if the operator is applied, and

(c) a *delete list* which lists all propositions that must be deleted from the state description.

Figure 2 gives several examples of state-change operators.

In STRIPS, a planning problem is defined by a state description of the initial state, a list of propositions that must be true of the goal state, and a list of STRIPS state-change operators. (Planning problems defined in this way will be referred to as STRIPS problems.) STRIPS plans by searching for a sequence of state-change operations (actions) that will transform the initial state into the goal state (see Fig. 3, for example). Note that in STRIPS each new state is calculated by simply adding and deleting the nodes in the state-change operators' "add" and "delete" list; nothing else changes. In effect, STRIPS assumes that the only consequences of an action are those that are always associated with that type of action. There are no side effects. This approach to the frame problem is usually referred to as the STRIPS assumption.

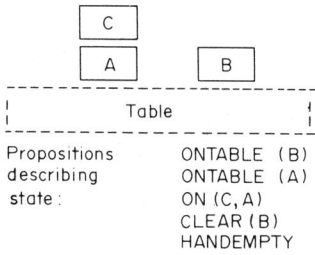

Figure 1
Propositional statement of a blocks-world state

```
Pickup (X)
    Preconditions: HANDEMPTY, CLEAR (X), ONTABLE (X)
    Add list: HOLDING (X)
    Delete list: HANDEMPTY, CLEAR (X), ONTABLE (X)

Putdown (X)
    Preconditions: HOLDING (X)
    Add list: HANDEMPTY, CLEAR (X), ONTABLE (X)
    Delete list: HOLDING (X)

Stack (X,Y)
    Preconditions: HOLDING (X), CLEAR (Y)
    Add list: ON (X,Y), CLEAR (X), HANDEMPTY
    Delete list: HOLDING (X), CLEAR (Y)

Unstack (X,Y)
    Preconditions: ON (X,Y), CLEAR (X), HANDEMPTY
    Add list: HOLDING (X), CLEAR (Y)
    Delete list: ON (X,Y), CLEAR (X), HANDEMPTY
```

Figure 2
Sample STRIPS operators for blocks-world domain

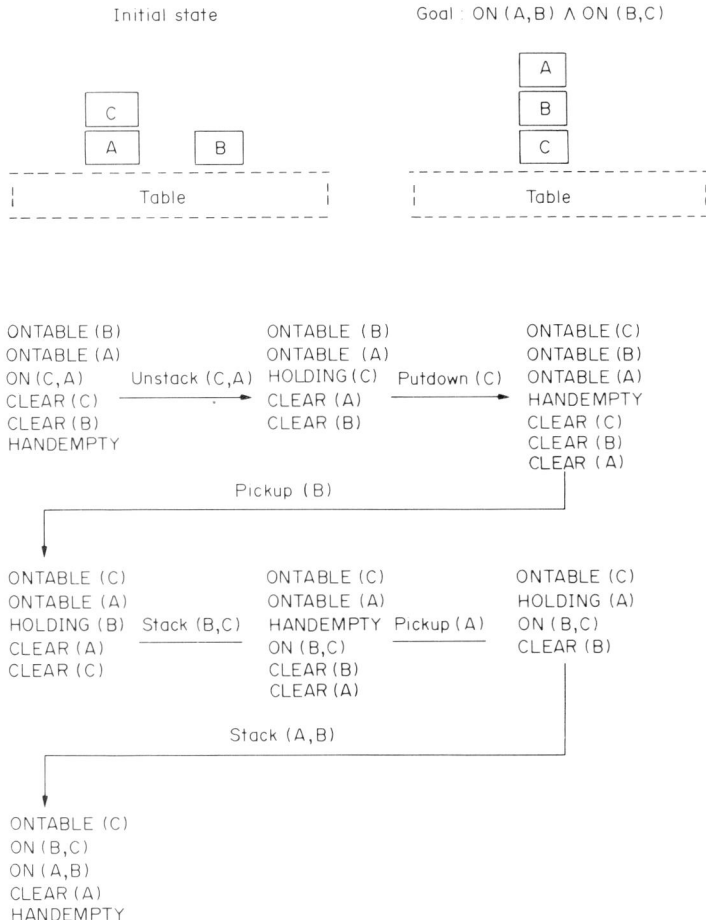

Figure 3
Examples of STRIPS plan with corresponding sequence of state descriptions

A series of planners enhancing the STRIPS approach have been developed. Virtually all these planners use STRIPS-like state-change operators and assume the STRIPS assumption. Waldinger (1977) introduced the technique of regression. Regression allows a planner to deduce whether or not a proposition will be true after a series of actions without actually calculating the state sequence. Using regression, it becomes possible to generate and revise plans without the added computational burden of calculating the new state that will result from each action.

Sacerdotti (1974, 1977) introduced the concept of nonlinear planning. A linear plan is a fully ordered sequence of actions. A nonlinear plan is a partial order of actions; for some pairs of actions, temporal order is irrelevant to success. STRIPS considers only linear plans. In Sacerdotti's NOAH system, actions remain unordered until NOAH finds a reason to impose an order. Sacerdotti also introduced the concept of hierarchical planning, where the planner generates an initial plan by considering only the most important propositions. It then fills in the details of a plan by successively considering layers of less important propositions. The differing importance levels that propositions may be decomposed into are sometimes referred to as levels of abstraction.

Stefik (1981b) introduced the concepts of skeletal planning and variable constraint satisfaction. A skeletal plan is a predefined sequence of operators that can be instantiated as a specific plan by specifying values for the variables in the skeletal plan. For instance, one may have the skeletal plan of flying from Washington, DC to New York in the morning and returning in the evening. This skeletal plan is instantiated by identifying specific flights that satisfy the constraints of there being morning and evening flights, respectively.

Wilkins (1984) expanded the notion of constraint satisfaction to problems involving reasoning about limited resources.

To some extent, the planning system described by Chapman (1987) is the culmination of this line of research. Chapman's planner, TWEAK, begins with an empty plan (does not require any specific actions) and proceeds to add constraints to the plan sequentially. These constraints are of three types: inserting a state-change operation into the plan, imposing a temporal order on two state-change operations, or adding a variable constraint. At each step in this constraint-posting process, there will be several constraints that could be added to the system. If a particular sequence of constraints leads to a contradiction, then the planner backtracks to a previous step and picks a different constraint. The most important feature of Chapman's approach is that it is provably complete. That is, if there exists a solution to a STRIPS problem, then TWEAK will find it in a finite time. If no solution exists, then TWEAK will either return that result or continue processing. Furthermore, STRIPS problems are semi-decidable; there cannot exist a procedure which is guaranteed to prove, in a finite time, that no solution exists. Consequently, for STRIPS problems, fundamental improvements to TWEAK's capabilities are not possible.

2.2 Situation Calculus

Within AI there is a strong tradition of logic-based approaches to automated reasoning. Within single-agent automated-planning research this tradition manifests itself in two ways. The first is the use of predicate calculus as a state-description language, and the second is the use of automated theorem proving techniques for automatic-plan generation.

Virtually all automated-planning systems use predicate calculus as the basic state-description language. Planners in the STRIPS approach, for instance, generally utilize propositional calculus, a subset of predicate calculus, as the state-description language. For instance, to express the fact that block A is on top of B, a propositional statement such as ON(A,B) is used. One limitation of this approach is that there is no way to express, within these propositional statements, the relationship between states. For instance, state s_1 may contain ON(A,B), but the next state, s_2, obtained after Pickup(A) is performed, contains ¬ON(A,B).

Situation calculus (McCarthy and Hayes 1969) is a predicate calculus that includes state indentifiers as objects in the language. For instance, a general HOLDS predicate can be defined that specifies a certain state in which a proposition is true. For instance, HOLDS[ON(A,B),s_1] and ¬HOLDS[ON(A,B),s_2].

In situation calculus, actions are defined as functions on states. For instance, do (Pickup(A),s) is defined as the state that results from performing the action Pickup(A) in s. This allows us to write proper axioms such as

HOLDS[ON(A,B),s] ∧ POSS[Pickup(A),s] →

¬HOLDS[ON(A,B), do (Pickup(A),s)]

∧HOLDS[CLEAR(B), do (Pickup(A),s)]

which is intended to mean that if in state s ON(A,B) is true and it is possible to Pickup(A), then in the state resulting from executing Pickup(A) in state s, ON(A,B) will be false and CLEAR(B) will be true.

Planning is performed by giving an automated theorem prover a set of axioms describing the initial state, a second set of axioms that describe the effects of actions and a target theorem to prove. For instance, the target theorem may be:

∃s:HOLDS[CLEAR(A),s]

which is intended to mean that there exists a state where CLEAR(A) is true. To prove this theorem, the theorem prover would need to find a specific state in which CLEAR(A) is true. For instance, for the problem shown in Fig. 2, it might deduce

HOLDS[CLEAR(A),do(Pickup(B), do(Putdown(C),

do(Unstack(C,A),s_0)))]

which is intended to mean that CLEAR(A) will be true in the situation resulting from the sequence of actions Unstack(C,A), Putdown(C) and Pickup(B).

The principal advantage of the situation-calculus approach is that it allows the use of existing automatic theorem proving techniques (e.g., Kowalski 1979). Most of these techniques are complete in the sense that if a solution exists, then they will find a solution in finite time. If no solution exists, they will either return that result or continue processing. The major disadvantage is their approach to the frame problem. In situation calculus, proper specification of an operator's effects must include a set of frame axioms that describe everything that does not change as a result of performing an action. Usually this requirement leads to a proliferation of axioms that are difficult to engineer and are time-consuming for the theorem prover to process.

2.3 Recent Trends

Historically, the STRIPS approach and the use of situation calculus have dominated research in automated planning. As can be seen from the above discussion, however, both of these research traditions have to some extent reached their culmination. That is, if a problem can be properly represented as either a STRIPS problem or as a set of situation-calculus axioms, then procedures exist which will find a plan if one exists. Unfortunately, both of these approaches are very limited in the range of problems they can properly represent. The STRIPS approach, for instance, cannot easily represent effects that require more than one action to produce. For instance, it may take two people to pick up a heavy object, yet the proposition ¬ON(Object, Y) could not be on the add list of either Pickup action.

Another problem is that both the STRIPS and situation-calculus approach fail to handle the frame problem effectively. In both cases, all consequences of an action must be definitively stated and it is assumed (implicitly or as axioms) that nothing else changes. This is in contrast to the commonsense notion of an action, where unusual consequences sometimes occur. It is in fact never truly safe to assume that an action, such as Pickup(A), will not affect the status of an apparently unrelated proposition, say ONTABLE(B). (The table may be unstable and tip when Pickup(A) is performed.) A more reasonable approach is to assume that ONTABLE(B) will be unaffected, *unless* there is reason to believe otherwise. That is, to assume that ONTABLE(B) will be unaffected, but to allow for the possibility that one might expect otherwise.

Nonmonotonic reasoning is a general term denoting an ability to reason and draw conclusions in the context of assumptions that can later be retracted. For instance, assuming that Pickup(A) will not affect the status of ONTABLE(B) but later realizing that it might. Nonmonotonic logic is a general term for extensions of predicate logic that allow for non-monotonic reasoning (see McCarthy 1980; McDermott and Doyle 1980; Reiter 1980, for examples of conceptualizations of nonmonotonic logics). In a non-monotonic logic there may be an axiom such as

HOLD(ONTABLE(B),s)∧MHold[ONTABLE(B),

do(Pickup(A),s)] →

Hold[ONTABLE(B), do(Pickup(A),s)]

which is intended to mean that if ONTABLE(B) is true in s, and there is no reason to conclude otherwise, then ONTABLE(B) will be true of the situation that results from the action Pickup(A). A statement such as Ma is loosely intended to mean "if ¬a cannot be deduced."

There is considerable interest in the application of nonmonotonic logic to automated planning (e.g., Hanks and McDermott 1987), although few planning systems have been developed that effectively incorporate nonmonotonic logic-based reasoning capabilities. The work of Ginsburg (1987) is something of an exception to this. Ginsburg's "possible worlds" planning system is a variant of the STRIPS approach. The system describes operators in terms of precondition and add lists, but no delete list. The planner then applies a set of domain-constraint axioms and some automatic theorem-proving techniques to derive all propositions that must be deleted in the state that results from applying the operator. This makes it easier to define state-change operations, while also allowing the system to automatically deduce some side effects. In effect, this approach assumes that all propositions are unaffected by an action unless proven otherwise.

Another weakness of both STRIPS and the situation-calculus approach is their treatment of time as a series of discrete states, where nothing changes unless an action is performed. In reality, situations evolve continuously and many changes occur *unless* some action intervenes. For instance, a moving vehicle will continue to move on its present course (and probably run into something) unless an action is taken to change its course. A discrete state representation cannot easily represent this type of temporal evolution. As a result, several researchers (e.g., McDermott 1982; Allen 1984, Shoham 1987) are pursuing the development of temporal logics for reasoning about the impact of actions and events over time. A number of planners are being developed that incorporate temporal reasoning into their planning systems (e.g., Lansky 1987; Dean and Kanazawa 1989).

Finally, some researchers are beginning to move away from the "traditional" logic-based problem-solving orientation to planning. The case-based approach to planning argues that planning is largely a matter of remembering and modifying plans that have worked in previous similar situations. Relatively little actual problem solving is done. The opportunistic planning approach suggests the use of blackboard architectures to support a piecewise incremental development of plans. In addition, there is a growing recognition that the inherently unpredictable nature of the world requires that any attempt to execute the plan will involve a considerable amount of replanning. New paradigms are emerging that emphasize procedures for interleaving planning and execution (e.g., Kaelbling 1987).

3. Multiagent Planning

Research in automated planning evolved out of research in robot problem solving. As a result, much of planning research has been focused on topics relevant to helping a robot maneuver in and around the everyday world. However, there are many planning problems that involve more than simply the planning of a sequence of robot maneuvers. Most planning problems involve multiagent environments, where the planner must reason about the intentions and possible actions of other agents (human or machine).

In problems involving cooperative agents, a primary problem that the planner (who may represent one of the cooperative agents) must address is that of determining the intentions of other agents. Once an assessment is made about how the other agents will behave, then the planner can formulate its own plan which may involve appropriate communications with other agents. Consequently, research in cooperative planning is being addressed by the development of formal logics for reasoning about the intentions and beliefs of other agents (Halpern 1986).

Domains involving simultaneous activities by multiple agents are especially difficult to represent using a discrete state space representation (although Georgeff (1987) has made significant progress in this area). Actions vary in their duration, and the actions of different agents will partially overlap in time. Consequently, temporal rather than situation logics are often used to represent multiagent problems. This makes it possible for the planner to reason about how the actions of one agent must be interleaved with those of others (e.g., Lansky 1987).

At the other extreme is the problem of adversarial planning. An adversarial-planning problem involves an agent and (at least one) adversary, where both the agent and adversary are trying to achieve competitive goals in a common environment. Unlike single-agent and cooperative multiagent problems, adversarial planning requires a considerable amount of contingency planning. It is rarely the case that a single plan of action can be developed that will achieve a goal no matter what the adversary does. However, like any multiagent planning problem, the planner needs to have (a) an ability to simulate the environment and predict the environmental consequences of actions; (b) an ability to reason about the beliefs and intentions of other agents, and how they will change as the environment changes; and (c) a planning knowledge base for proposing goals, subgoals and actions.

For many adversarial-planning problems where (a)–(c) above have been specified, Lehner (1989) defines a set of provably complete search procedures that will find a winning set of contingency plans (for either side), or determine that there is no way to guarantee a win, or continue processing.

Finally, it should be noted that many planning problems involve multiple agents, none of whom can be considered to be strictly cooperative or competitive. Depending on the circumstances, two agents may cooperate, compete or simply "work around" each other. Carbonell's counterplanning system (Carbonell 1982) examines some alternative skeletal plans for dealing with problems of this type.

4. Applications

Automated planning remains largely a research topic in AI. Since the early 1980s, however, a number of efforts have been initiated which attempt to apply this technology (see Lehner (1990) for a review of many of these applications).

The most promising applications involve the development of autonomous robots that can operate in complex environments. For instance, automated-planning techniques will be embedded in the Mars Rover, an autonomous robot designed to maneuver on the surface of Mars. Similar types of autonomous-planning capabilities are expected to be part of many space-based systems where human direction is infeasible or undesirable (e.g., control of distant satellites). Another important example is the autonomous land vehicle (ALV), an ambitious effort sponsored by the Defense Advanced Research Projects Agency Strategic Computing Program (SCP) to develop a vehicle that can autonomously navigate roads and cross-country terrain.

A second class of efforts involves the development of automated-planning systems that can support human operators of dynamic systems. For instance, the "Pilot's Associate" portion of the SCP is an attempt to develop a cockpit advisory system that will recommend various plans (e.g., navigational plans, tactical plans, etc.) that a pilot may pursue.

A third area is the development of decision support systems for high-level strategic-planning problems. Wilkins (1984) describes an interactive planning system that could support a variety of scheduling problems. The SCP is promoting the development of several systems that will support tactical military planning. For instance, the Air Land Battle Management component of the SCP is attempting to develop a system that will recommend various maneuver and fire support plans to military commanders. Similar kinds of applications are being pursued to support resource allocation and mission-planning problems in a tactical air force.

5. Conclusion

Automated planning is an important area in AI that is beginning to emerge from the pure research domain. At present, most efforts to exploit automated-planning techniques are exploratory. It is unclear whether they will succeed in developing practical planning systems. However, in the long run, automated-planning techniques are sure to emerge as an important element of any system that must operate autonomously in a real-world environment, and may emerge as a key technology in the development of organizational decision support systems designed to support planning problems.

See also: Artificial Intelligence; Decision Support Systems

Bibliography

Allen J 1984 Towards a general theory of action and time. *Artif. Intell.* **23**(2), 123–54

Carbonell J 1982 Counterplanning: A computational approach to planning under adversity. *Artif. Intell.* **22**, 293–329

Chapman D 1987 Planning for conjunctive goals. *Artif. Intell.* **32**(3), 333–77

Dean T, Kanazawa K 1989 Persistence and probabilistic projection. *IEEE Trans. Syst., Man Cybern.* (in press)

Fikes R, Hart P, Nilsson N 1972 Learning and executing generalized robot plans. *Artif. Intell.* **3**(4), 251–88

Fikes R, Nilsson N 1971 STRIPS: A new approach to the application of theorem proving to problem solving. *Artif. Intell.* **2**(3–4): 189–208

Georgeff M 1987 Actions, processes and causality. In: Georgeff and Lansky 1987, pp. 99–122

Georgeff M, Lansky A (eds.) 1987 *Reasoning About Actions and Plans*. Kaufman, Los Altos, California

Ginsberg M 1987 Possible worlds planning. In: Georgeff and Lansky 1987, pp. 213–44

Halpern J (ed.) 1986 *Theoretical Aspects of Reasoning About Knowledge*. Kaufmann, Los Altos, California

Hanks S, McDermott D 1987 Nonmonotonic logic and temporal projection. *Artif. Intell.* **33**(3), 379–412

Hobbs J, Moore R (eds.) 1985 *Formal Theories of the Commonsense World*. Ablex, Norwood, New Jersey

Kaelbling L 1987 An architecture for intelligent reactive systems. In: Georgeff and Lansky 1987, pp. 395–410

Kowalski R 1979 *Logic for Problem Solving*. North-Holland, New York

Lansky A 1987 A representation of parallel activity based on events, structure, and causality. In: Georgeff and Lansky 1987, pp. 123–60

Lehner P 1986 On the role of artificial intelligence in command and control. *IEEE Trans. Syst., Man Cybern.* **16**(6), 824–33

Lehner P 1989 *Artificial Intelligence and National Defense: Opportunity and Challenge*. Petrocelli, Princeton, New Jersey (in press)

Lehner P 1990 Automated adversarial planning search procedures with provable properties. In: Andriole S (ed.) *Advanced Technology for C^2 Systems Engineering*. AFCEA International

McCarthy J 1980 Circumscription—A form of nonmonotonic reasoning. *Artif. Intell.* **13**(1–2), 27–39

McCarthy J, Hayes P 1969 Some philosophical problems from the standpoint of artificial intelligence. In: Meltzer B, Michie D (eds.) *Machine Intelligence 4*. Edinburgh University Press, Edinburgh, pp. 463–502

McDermott D 1982 A temporal logic for reasoning about processes and plans. *Cognit. Sci.* **6**(2), 101–55

McDermott D, Doyle J 1980 Non-monotonic logic I. *Artif. Intell.* **13**(1–2), 41–72

Reiter R 1980 A logic for default reasoning. *Artif. Intell.* **13**(1–2), 81–132

Sacerdotti E 1974 Planning in a hierarchy of abstraction spaces. *Artif. Intell.* **5**(2), 115–35

Sacerdotti E 1977 *A Structure for Plans and Behavior*. Elsevier, New York

Shoham Y 1987 What is the frame problem? In: Georgeff and Lansky 1987, pp. 83–98

Stefik M 1981a Planning and meta-planning (MOLGEN: Part 2). *Artif. Intell.* **16**(2), 141–70

Stefik M 1981b Planning with constraints (MOLGEN: Part 1). *Artif. Intell.* **16**(2), 111–40

Waldinger R 1977 Achieving several goals simultaneously. In: Elcock E, Michie D (eds.) *Machine Intelligence 8: Machine Representations of Knowledge*. Horwood, Chichester

Wilkins D 1984 Domain-indpendent planning: Representation and plan generation. *Artif. Intell.* **22**(3), 269–301

P. E. Lehner
[George Mason University, Fairfax, Virginia, USA]

Automation: Social Effects

It is difficult to separate the social effects of automation from those of other technologies. What distinguishes automation technology is the intended and explicit use of feedback within the technology itself. However, the interaction of any technology with other people or society involves feedback loops which encompass people and society in some form. Thus, automation ideas are ways of characterizing the social effects of any technology. This includes not only the effect of automation technology on workers, as characterized, for example, by the president of Volvo in describing new work arrangements between people and production machinery (Gyllenhammer 1977), but also models of automation and control as applied to government institutions (Deutsch 1966, Licklider 1979). However, while both automation technology itself and the ideas of feedback control have spread very widely, to analyze thoroughly the control of technology over people, people's control over technology, and people's control over themselves and each other is much too great a task for this article.

To anticipate all the social effects of any specific technology is also clearly impossible. This is partly because the effects are complex and indirect, and partly because they may not be manifest until long after the introduction of the technology (e.g., cultural changes brought on by the automobile or the telephone, or carcinogenic effects of asbestos products). Nevertheless, it is ethically obligatory that those responsible for the introduction of new technology try to anticipate as many as possible of the social effects, negative as well as positive.

1. Concurrence of Positive and Negative Effects

Technology is introduced to derive the benefits which it promises—otherwise there would be no reason for it to be introduced. These positive effects are naturally the ones the inventor, developer, merchant or other proponent of the technology thinks most about and refers to in communicating with others.

Besides the direct monetary costs, there are often no other effects presented to the potential buyer or user. The latter, attracted by the promise and novelty of the new technology, may commit themselves to using it without awareness of any or very many negative effects—only a vague concern over "will it work?" or "will it be liked?". Furthermore, these persons may be unaware that those who suffer at least some of the negative effects may be different individuals from those who reap the benefits. Of course this is accepted in many applications as appropriate (e.g., all the taxpayers pay for the schooling of children in a community, even though they themselves may have no prospect of ever receiving those services). In other situations this would be regarded as grossly unjust.

Both positive and negative effects can be direct or indirect. Because the indirect effects, by definition, are not obvious and immediate they deserve special attention, for they can be just as, or more, important when integrated over time. Examples of indirect effects of automation are an increase of opportunity for some classes of skilled workers, loss of dignity because of the nature of new assignments for other skilled workers, and a general decrease of opportunity for unskilled workers. These factors are discussed more fully below.

2. *Technology Forecasting and Assessment*

Society's assessment of the social effects of technology, and indeed the very development of that technology which produces the effects, is studied by technology forecasting and assessment. For this reason a very brief review of this subject is provided here.

Conscious of the need to assess the social and economic implications of new technology, various governments and private companies have begun specialized activities in technology assessment. This usually begins with a technology forecast of some kind. The forecast involves:

(a) selection of the variables of interest;

(b) consultation with the affected persons or organizations;

(c) development and execution of a model to project into the future; and

(d) assessment of those projections in terms of what is wanted.

With regard to development and execution of forecasting models, three types of approach may be distinguished:

(a) extrapolation of trends based upon present state plus derivatives of present values of the appropriate output variables (in this case the "model" is simply the time history of the variables with no equations relating them to each other or to other variables);

(b) extrapolation based on some assumed model about how those output variables are affected by some input variables; and

(c) using the latter approach to determine either what the input variables must do or what the model form of parameters must be in order that the output variables attain given values at given times.

(a) and (b) are called "descriptive forecasts" and (c) a "normative forecast." A fourth type of forecast, sometimes called a "retrospective forecast," is where one goes back in history, tries to put oneself in the place of a forecaster at some earlier time, executes steps (a)–(d) described above, then compares the resulting "forecast" to what actually happened, thereby (presumably) learning in the process.

The forecasting of trends in objective and measurable technical, economic, demographic or political variables is difficult enough. What is even more difficult is the assessment—the evaluation in terms of good and bad impacts of these trends on the various affected parties. Whoever does this evaluation, whether it be the analyst, outside experts in the subject areas, or the affected parties, can themselves be expected to affect the outcome. So, too, may the particular assessment techniques which are used, whether they are the more qualitative type, such as group "brainstorming," morphological analysis, scenario writing, gaming or the Delphi method (Linstone and Turoff 1975), or whether instead they involve some formal quantitative techniques.

Quantitative assessment techniques are so named because they are based upon formal mathematical theories. However, to be used for actual preference assessment by real people in real situations, there is necessarily much that is subjective. Subjective judgements should be gleaned from individuals in an orderly way, and the data then processed by an objective procedure to produce a model capable of predicting preferences among alternatives.

Some such theories or techniques seek primarily to model individual preferences. One example is multi-attribute utility (Keeney and Raiffa 1976), which produces an analytical model of an individual's utility (relative subjective evaluation of worth for all points in a space of several measurable attributes or variables). This is derived by having that person make a series of equivalence judgements among lotteries which include different probablities of the occurrence of different consequences (points in attribute space). A second example makes use of fuzzy sets (Zadeh and Fu 1975) and requires the judge to specify a set of rules for choosing alternatives in terms of "fuzzy" variables (linguistic terms like large, fast, expensive). In association with this, the judge must also specify "membership functions" (how "true" each fuzzy variable is with respect to an associated attribute (such as length, velocity, dollars). Again a multivariable input space is mapped into an output—a decision among discrete or continuous policy alternatives.

Other theories or techniques for assessment would seem to allow for the aggregation of an individual's subjective preferences into the group's preferences. One such technique is policy capturing (Hammond *et al.* 1980), based upon multiple regression. Another is multidimensional scaling (Carroll 1969) which involves similar least-squares fits of data for different multiattribute objects of judgement as well as different judges. A third is interpretive structural modelling (Warfield 1976), which makes use of the discrete mathematics of graph theory to define hierarchical preference structures from individual paired comparisons.

One specific form of technology assessment is probabilistic risk assessment (PRA). It attempts to assign probability numbers to specific failure events and catastrophic outcomes in large-scale technological systems. It has been particularly popular in the field of nuclear power, and many millions of dollars have been spent in recent years to perform PRAs for many different failures for many different nuclear plants. The problems of PRA epitomize, in a sense, the problems of technology assessment generally; namely the social aspects of obtaining requisite inputs from human "experts" and the social aspects of convincing the nontechnical public that the analytical results are meaningful and useful. Perrow (1984), for example, is highly critical of PRA efforts, and asserts that one simply cannot anticipate all the ways in which complex technology can fail: "abnormal" becomes "normal."

3. Effects of Automation on Employment

The history of automation has been closely coupled with the history of economic development and improved standard of living. From automatic mechanical irrigation pumps in primitive rural areas to advanced air traffic control systems for commercial aviation, the introduction of automation has produced more and better goods and services and has enhanced employment opportunities. Few persons would wish to turn back the clock.

The first major demonstration of concern for the potentially negative social impacts of labor-saving machinery was the Luddite movement in the early 1800s, where English workmen attempted to prevent the use of knitting machinery by destroying it. The technology prevailed, however, and—except in less-developed countries—machinery has extensively replaced human muscle both on the farm and in the factory. In the USA, for example, the agricultural sector is reduced to only a few percent of the workforce, and even in the manufacturing sector the in-factory workforce is less than 10% by most counts. In Hungary, since the 1960s, the working population on the farm has changed from well over half to less than 20% of the workforce. In Japan, the percentage of the workforce in agriculture is much higher than in the USA, but the number of industrial employees is currently increasing and continued expansion is expected, especially in knowledge-intensive industries.

Up to the present time many trade unions and worker organizations around the world have welcomed automation because both productivity and worker safety can be increased. Although the requirements of the actual production phase, as a percentage of total effort, decline with automation, the phases of preparation (e.g., research, design) and product support (e.g., distribution, sales, installation, maintenance) require more effort. While preparation and support activities are likely to require higher skill levels than are required by production, insistent workers have demanded that they be retrained for these new jobs and participate in decisions about how automation will be introduced.

This works well as markets expand and productivity grows. It may not work when markets stabilize, and especially now that computer technology is being introduced to the preparation and support phases (in the form of computer-aided design, communications, inspection and accounting, and repair). There is a real danger that increasingly larger segments of the unskilled labor force may be left without meaningful work. This phenomenon has already appeared in some countries. Significant minority groups (for example, gypsies in Hungary, blacks in the USA) have much higher unemployment rates than the norm for their societies.

A concomitant occurrence is an increasing number of well-educated but nontechnical people who find no economic demand for their talents. On the other hand the demand for well-educated technical people has continued to increase in developed countries, especially Japan, and in some less-developed countries. Automation may not be the only cause of this disparity of demand between the nontechnical and technically educated, but it is seen as a principal factor.

Probably the most extensive recent consideration of the effects of technology on employment was that of a US National Research Council panel (Cyert and Mowery 1987). They concluded that there was certainly no immediate concern for mass unemployment caused by high technology. If anything, they concluded, there may be more unemployment resulting from failure to adopt new technology. However, they evidenced a serious concern over problems of job training and skill updating; that is, problems of early training for a workforce adequate for the new technologies.

4. Effects on Culture

History records many overzealous efforts to "civilize the natives," where developed nations have pushed their sophisticated technology on primitive agrarian peoples who had neither the knowledge required to use and maintain it, nor the infrastructure to provide proper power, transportation, spare parts and so on. In such cases rubber-tired ox carts may function better and longer than the latest diesel trucks; also, shrewd governors may work better than computer controllers.

Unfortunately, distinctions between societies where increased automation is appropriate and where it is not are always clear. Such distinctions do not fall easily into categories like developed versus underdeveloped, or socialist versus capitalist countries. An approach for introducing automation that is highly successful in one culture may fail dismally in another. Sometimes the reasons for such failure are obvious. For example, in Arabic and Hebrew, words are read from right to left, and in Japanese from top to bottom. In these cultures, electronic displays may need to be designed to conform to the style of the written language. Ethnic variables must be accommodated to properly "human engineer" the automation to particular cultures (Chapanis 1975).

Other cultural differences are much more subtle. Western engineers are often amazed at the productivity of Japanese workers and the quality of their products. What these engineers fail to see are the societal values encouraging productivity and quality, such as the long time-horizons the Japanese are willing to give to returns on investment, or the loyalty and devotion which binds the workers in many firms to the management. Furthermore, Westerners are only beginning to understand the decision-by-consensus method which governs much of group behavior in Japan and which plays a significant role in production-process changes and quality control in Japanese industry. Thus, if technical cooperation across' international boundaries is to succeed, it is critical that we approach others with a desire to understand their practices, rather than a contempt that they are different from ourselves.

In the developed nations, technology is undergoing what Toffler (1980) has called "demassification"—the production of unique technological goods and services which are adapted to the particular needs or expressed desires of individual customers or clients—a trend away from the mass production used by Henry Ford. Automation technology is at the core of this adaptivity. For example, automatic design and manufacture of a single pair of shoes for a given wearer is now possible (Dertouzos 1979). There are limits on simply getting whatever we want when we want it, but we are moving surely in that direction. But then it must be asked: "Is automation technology simply making us a more and more consumptive society? What does that do to us as individuals? Is the Protestant work ethnic dead? Is this trend really to the net benefit of the ordinary person, or only to the corporate supplier of those goods and services, and the people in power?"

Conventional Marxist ideas of class struggle seem to be relevant, and many writers have pointed to the gap (some assert a widening gap) between the technological "have" and "have not" individuals and groups within society. Some writers put the technological elite into the "have" group. Noble (1977), however, in reviewing the history or the introduction of computer-controlled production machinery in the USA, takes the more classical Marxist stance, namely, that engineers and technologists themselves have ended up as servants of the capitalists (those with corporate money and power).

Taking a long-term historical perspective it must also be asked whether automation technology has resulted in "progress." The contemporary critic Marx (1987) points out that there are really two views of "progress": a technocratic one and a social one. By any standard we have made great technocratic progress; that is by the measures of control system performance (rms error, speed, energy efficiency, reliability). In terms of social progress, we are obliged to ask "progress toward what social ends?"

5. Individual Productivity and Alienation

The trends in modern automation mean that the worker in the factory, farm or office is having less direct bodily contact with the product being manufactured or processed. His sensing and motor actions are becoming mediated by computing and electronic communication devices, and his supervisory duties are being made more remote from the physical processes he controls. The operator is not only becoming separated in space, but also desynchronized in time from such processes, and is now performing different physical actions than he would in the traditional factory, farm or office tasks. There are promises of greater product quality, better energy and economic efficiency, and improved worker safety which motivate these changes. Nevertheless, the potential negative impacts which need to be reduced to achieve a satisfactory adoption of automation by a society must also be assessed.

In the following subsections, several factors which might degrade the job and alienate the worker are enumerated.

5.1 Erratic Mental Workload and Work Dissatisfaction

Automation greatly affects not only the nature but also the pace of work, and makes it vary between extremes. Airline pilots and nuclear-plant operators refer to their work as "hours of boredom punctuated by moments of terror." Unfortunately, satisfactory objective measures have not yet been developed for mental workload (stress) or job satisfaction. Although automation has eliminated many mundane tasks from work and has produced long periods of relatively little required effort, it has not relieved the stress induced by sudden unpredictable crises, particularly when sytems fail. For example, airline and government authorities often believe that with the automation currently present in cockpits two pilots are sufficient to cope with the physical and mental workload of a flight. Many pilots, however, feel that in times of emergency or high stress, the automation is not sufficient to ensure safety and that three pilots are needed. Additionally, while workers are often glad that automation has broken the dull monotony of repetitive manual work, they may not get as much satisfaction from their new, supervisory monitoring role (Shepard 1971). The satisfaction derived from putting in a hard day's work and producing something with their own wits and efforts may be gone.

5.2 Atrophy of Skill and Loss of Dignity

A skill such as machining or inspection of products, developed over a long time period, provides the worker with a sense of dignity and self-respect. If the worker becomes a button-pushing supervisor and monitor, that skill may atrophy and may not be available when called upon, with consequent loss of dignity and self-respect.

5.3 Centralization of Management Control and Loss of Worker Control

One result of automation and the introduction of electronic technology often feared by workers is the possibility of secret centralized monitoring of their work through the equipment. Rarely does management engage in such activities, but the mere possibility is often sufficient to produce worker anxiety. This anxiety occurs not only in production employees but can include office workers who are fearful that private data stored electronically may be accessed by others. Apart from this fear of workers is the question of whether centralization of control, so easy with advanced automation, is really synonymous with efficiency. While in some cases centralization may enhance productivity, in other cases it will surely prove detrimental because of added bureaucracy.

The pressures are for "high-tech" companies to diminish the power of unions, since the traditional union procedures call for well-defined work rules and a clean separation between union and management. "High-tech" fosters flexibility in both rules and organization. Unions, operating in traditional ways, simply become impediments. Innovative strategies are needed to surmount formidable pressures of organizing and providing effective protection for workers (Early and Wilson 1986).

5.4 Diffusion and Abandonment of Responsibility

A worker is usually regarded as having the primary responsibility for use and maintenance of his tools or machine, though he may try to place the blame for difficulties elsewhere. The worker is accountable for what is produced. When a worker's actions in using a machine are mediated by a powerful control system (e.g., a computer), however, the lines of responsibility are not so clear, and the worker may not be sure which should get the credit or the blame for a situation—the computer or himself. As a result the worker may, in effect, abandon his responsibility for the task performed or the good produced, believing instead that it is in the "hands" of the computer. This can be the case even when computers are installed to aid information flow from one worker to another. Although in this situation the computer may act primarily as a processor or storer of data, individuals using the system may feel that the machine is in complete control, disclaiming personal accountability for any error or performance degradation.

5.5 Mysticism and Misplaced Trust

One danger apparent as computers become increasingly common is the phenomenon of misplaced trust. This was particularly well articulated by Wiener (1964) and later by Weizenbaum (1976). To a naïve user the computer can be simultaneously so wonderful and intimidating as to seem faultless, and if the computer produces other than what its user expects, that can be attributed to its superior wisdom. Such discrepancies are usually harmless, but if allowed to continue can, in some complex and highly interconnected systems, endanger lives. It is therefore crucial as new computer-controlled technology is introduced that it comes to be accepted by users for what it is—a tool meant to serve and ultimately be controlled by human beings.

5.6 Human–Machine Symbiosis or Bliss of Enslavement?

Many engineers spend a significant fraction of their professional lives trying to make the relation between human and computer closer—presumably for the purpose of achieving better control over some variables of interest. Occasionally it must be asked: "Can the human–computer relation become too close? Would it be better to maintain some distance?"

It is well known that computer jargon has become fashionable for describing human behavior, and that human behavioral properties are often ascribed to computers. Turkle (1984) describes her study of children and fledgling "computer hackers" who take delight in coming to "think like the machine." "To this community and increasingly for all of us" she claims, "the question of mind in relation to machine . . . is becoming for us what sex was to the Victorians—threat and obsession, taboo and fascination."

For those who design such systems, automation is challenging and fun. Yet to many writers the worst form of alienation, the worst tragedy, occurs if the worker is happy to accept a role in which he is made to feel powerful while in actuality he is enslaved. Engelberger in an IFAC newsletter (March 1981 p. 4) reminded us that "it will always be far easier to make a robot of a man rather than to make a robot like a man."

6. Extending the Control Loop—How Far to Go

The threat of future energy shortages inhibits our plans to travel freely, to build and to process resources. Microelectronic advances create further opportunities for communication in many ways. Both factors mean that we must evaluate seriously the new capability to do much of our work, our shopping, and our leisure and social activities without leaving our homes. It is difficult to predict the benefits and hazards of such radical changes in living style.

The use of modern communication technology can provide not only "feed forward" of information from those in power down to the masses of citizens, but also can provide "feedback" from the masses to the powerful. The technology is already available in developed countries to talk back to one's home television, and optical fibers and synchronous satellite communications greatly expand the limited bandwidth available on telephone circuits. In both western and eastern societies there have been studies of "electronic citizen participation" and "transparent administration," where both decisions and decision rules are made available on the home television screens of citizens along with electronic means for feedback from citizens to political decision makers. This is a way to lengthen the control loop which necessarily takes a different form in different societies. Initial experiments are encouraging, but the process will require much "human factors engineering."

In contrast to legitimate political feedback, extending the control loop may also lead to exploitation of the powerless by the powerful. The powerless can rightly fear this possibility. Automation technology can just as easily be used to exploit them as to enrich their lives. Thus, feedback control in the political sector is deserving of continuous reflection and debate.

The great concern about "limits to growth" has ceased. To planners of future automation systems it is especially important that the "technological imperative"—that we build automatic systems because we can—be restrained with respect to use of energy and other precious natural resources. Many nations of the world are lucky enough to have many such resources. Others are not so lucky.

Proper use of automation will produce the same or greater benefits for people while reducing demands on energy and other, especially nonrenewable, resources. Many assessors of technology point out that it would be criminal to employ automation which, for the sake of short-term productivity, gluttonously exhausts these resources and leaves none for less-developed nations and for future generations. Recovering resources from the sea is an example often cited. The Law of the Sea treaty was an attempt to prevent such exploitation by the rich and powerful nations. Regrettably some such nations refused to sign.

It has become popular to ask what is the proper extent of automation. Is there a reasonable limit? For any given task, large or small, it is helpful to consider an ordered scale of "degrees of assistance" that a computer might provide (Sheridan et al. 1983). Each succeeding level of the scale below assumes some previous ones (when ANDed) or imposes more constraints (when ORed).

(a) The computer offers no assistance.

(b) The computer offers a complete set of alternatives, and

(c) narrows the selection down to a restricted set, or

(d) suggests one alternative, and

(e) executes that suggestion if the human approves, or

(f) allows the human to veto before automatic execution, or

(g) necessarily informs the human after execution, or

(h) informs the human after execution if asked, or

(i) informs the human after execution if it decides to.

(j) The computer decides everything autonomously.

Clearly for some tasks we are happy to let the computer go to the limit, while for others we would prefer to stop well up in the list. One reason to stop is the decision that systems are more safely operated with people in charge at some point. In the nuclear-power industry this is a critical issue today, and many studies, with somewhat limited success, are trying to determine numerical reliability for the human operator. The problem is difficult because people fail in ways different from machines, and people can correct their own errors. For complex systems it is felt that greatest reliability is achieved by some combination of human and automatic control, but we have yet to know the best methods of interaction. Perhaps what is best is always a function of particular circumstances.

The most acute problem of reliability results from adapting automation to weapons of war. Greater sophistication or complexity in the automation of weapon systems may result in greater possible destruction combined with potentially lowered reliability, because of the impossibility of fully testing these systems. This can produce uncertainty and fear about what an adversary might do, resulting in a net destabilizing influence and arms escalation. The much heralded Aegis radar surveillance system (Adam 1988) is a case in point. In one much publicized incident this system provided signals which, in time of war, might have been entirely appropriate, but under circumstances of "civilian protective" actions in the Persian Gulf resulted in fallacious human decisions and the tragic shooting down of a civilian airliner. Because weapons are becoming more remote (e.g., in outer space), more "robotic" or "artificially intelligent," and more complex generally (e.g., software reliability of systems such as the proposed US Strategic Defense Initiative (SDI) has been seriously challenged (Enfield 1987)), they may become less inclined to take timely orders from their human programmers or supervisors. Thus there is the possibility of humans losing control–where gaining control was the anticipated social effect motivating the development of automation.

Bibliography

Adam J A 1988 Pinning defence hopes on Aegis. *IEEE Spectrum* **25**(6), 24

Carroll J 1969 *How to Use INDSCAL, A Computer Program for Canonical Decomposition of N-way Tables and Individual Differences in Multi-Dimensional Scaling*. Bell Laboratories, Murray Hill, New Jersey

Chapanis A (ed.) 1975 *Ethnic Variables in Human Factors Engineering*. John Hopkins University Press, Baltimore, Maryland

Cyert R M, Mowery D C (eds.) 1987 *Technology and Employment*. National Academy Press, New York

Dertouzos M L 1979 Individualized automation. In: Dertouzos M L (ed.) *The Computer Age, A Twenty Year View*. MIT Press, Cambridge, Massachusetts

Deutsch K W 1966 *The Nerves of Government*. Macmillan Free Press, New York

Early S, Wilson R 1986 Do unions have a future in high technology? *Technol. Rev.* **88**(10), 56

Enfield R L 1987 The limits of software reliability. *Technol. Rev.* **89**(4), 36

Gyllenhammer P G 1977 *People at Work*. Addison–Wesley, New York

Hammond K, McClelland G H, Mumpower J 1980 *Human Judgement and Decision Making*. Praeger, New York

Keeney R L, Raffia H 1976 *Decisions with Multiple Objectives*. Wiley, New York

Licklider J C L 1979 Computers and governments. In: Dertouzos M L (ed.) *The Computer Age, A Twenty Year View*. MIT Press, Cambridge, Massachusetts

Linstone H, Turoff M 1975 *The Delphi Method, Techniques and Applications*. Addison–Wesley, Reading, Massachusetts

Marx L 1987 Does improved technology mean progress? *Technol. Rev.*. **89**(1), 33

Noble D F 1977 *America by Design*. Knopf, New York

Perrow C 1984 *Normal Accidents*. Basic Books, New York

Shepard J M 1971 *Automation and Alienation*. MIT Press, Cambridge, Massachusetts

Sheridan T B, Vamos T, Aida S 1983 Adapting automation to man, culture and society. *Automatica* **19**(6), 605–12

Toffler A 1980 *The Third Wave*. Morrow, New York

Turkle S 1984 *The Second Self*. Simon and Schuster, New York

Warfield J 1976 *Societal Systems*. Wiley, New York

Weizenbaum J 1976 *Computer Power and Human Reason*. Freeman, San Francisco, California

Wiener N 1964 *God and Golem Incorporated*. MIT Press, Cambridge, Massachusetts

Zadeh L, Fu K-S 1975 *Fuzzy Sets and their Applications to Cognitive and Decision Processes*. Academic Press, New York

T. B. Sheridan
[Massachusetts Institute of Technology,
Cambridge, Massachusetts, USA]

C

Cognitive Management and Models of Judgement and Choice Processes

The designer of an information system must be concerned both with normative models of decision and choice processes and with descriptive models of how people perform, and can perform, in given situations. This article is especially concerned with describing cognitive processes as they are influenced by the contingency structural elements of task, environment and the experience of the human problem solver with these. The contingency task structure model first described is related to Piaget's theory of intellectual development (Flavell 1977, Brainerd 1978, Ginsberg and Opper 1979, Stone and Day 1980). After a description of this model (Sage 1981a), its implications for information system design are explored. Finally, a number of more recent models are described that attempt to explain how we decide how to process information and exercise judgement.

1. Motivations for the Study of Metalevel Models

The motivation for the study of metalevel decision processes involved in the judgement concerning how to process information and exercise judgement is very pragmatic. This can be seen from a brief examination of the use of information in organizational management efforts. Management is vitally concerned with the processing (broadly defined to include acquisition, representation, transmission and use) of information in the organization. Generally, information is recognized as a vital strategic resource. A simple three-step reasoning process leads to this conclusion:

(a) organizational success depends upon management quality,

(b) management quality depends upon decision quality, and

(c) decision quality depends upon information quality.

Of course, there are many factors other than quality information that influence organizational success. One of the major tasks of management is that of minimizing the equivocality or ambiguity of the information that results from the interaction of the organization with the external environment. This is accomplished in order to enable the organization to understand its environment more efficiently, to detect or identify problems in need of resolution, to diagnose their causes, to identify alternative courses of action or policies to correct or resolve problems, to evaluate the potential efficacy of these policies, to select an appropriate priority order for problem resolution, to select appropriate policies for implementation and to augment existing knowledge with the new knowledge obtained in this implementation such that organizational learning occurs. Figure 1 illustrates the flow of these cognitive activities for the particular case of formal learning.

As learning about a task increases, the task becomes experientially familiar, and the type of approach or style that is used in approaching the task is modified. A person who is familiar with a given issue and the environment in which the issue occurs will approach problem solving in a much different way, typically, than a person who is experientially unfamiliar with the problem and/or the environment in which it is occurring. This occurs on an individual level as well as an organizational level.

There are a number of human information processing capabilities and limitations that interact with organizational arrangements and task requirements to strongly influence resource allocations for organizational problem solving. The concepts of *information sharing* and *shared concept models* then become especially important: These concepts involve many factors. Some involve the perceptions that the different members of a group have regarding the internal and

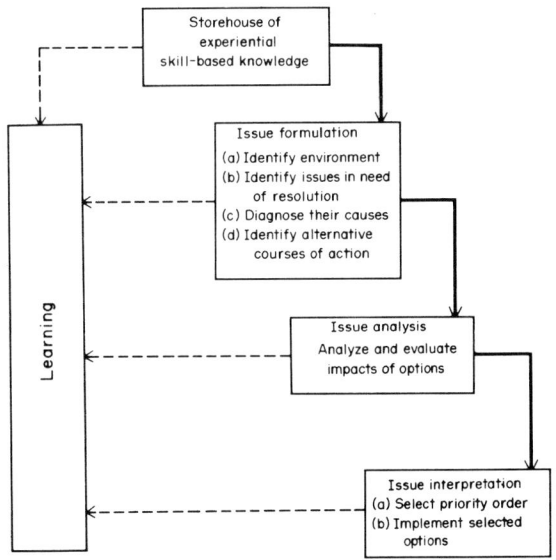

Figure 1
Illustration of the three formal steps in problem solving and decision making with learning

external environment, and the situation assessment and decision-making needs and styles of the different agents or actors. A central need relative to these is that of translation of thoughts and ideas into some more-or-less common language so that these can be shared. To do this effectively requires an awareness of the different ways in which individuals will go about problem solving, and judgement and choice problems.

Essentially the same maladies that affect individual decision making and problem-solving behavior, as well as many others, can result from group and organizational limitations. There exists a considerable body of knowledge, generally qualitative, relative to organizational structure, effectiveness and decision making in organizations. The majority of these studies suggest that a bounded rationality or "satisficing" perspective, often heavily influenced by bureaucratic political considerations, will generally be the decision perspective adopted in actual decision-making practice in organizations. To cope with this effectively requires the ability to concurrently deal with technological, organizational and cognitive structural concerns as they each, separately and collectively, motivate individual and group problem-solving issues.

2. Models Based on the Intellectual Development Stages of Piaget

Insights into the nature of cognitive development and insights into a conceptual model of cognitive activity are contained in the works of Piaget, the founder of "genetic epistemology." According to Piaget, there are four stages of intellectual development: sensory motor, preoperational, concrete operational and formal operation. The last two of these are of particular importance to this article. In the writings of Piaget, intellectual development is seen as a function of four variables: maturation, experience, education and self-regulation—a process of mental struggle with discomforting information until identification of a satisfactory mental construct allows intellectual growth or learning. In Piaget's model of intellectual development, concrete operational thinkers can deal logically with empirical data, manipulate symbols and organize facts towards the solution of well-structured and personally familiar problems. Formal operational thinkers can also cope in this fashion. A major difference, however, is that those concrete thinkers who are not also capable of formal thought lack the capacity to reason hypothetically and to consider the effect of different variables or possibilities outside of personal experience. Concrete operational *only* thinkers, for instance, will often have difficulty in responding "true" or "false" to the statement, "six is not equal to three plus four." As another example: "A card has a number on one side and a letter on the other; test the hypothesis that a card with a vowel on one side will have an even number on the other side." Concrete operational thinkers will have difficulty selecting cards for bottom-side examination if the top sides of four cards are a,b,2,3. However, failure to pick the cards with "a" and 3 on top may not indicate inability as a formal operational thinker but, rather, failure to properly diagnose the task and determine the need for formal operational thought.

We wish to develop a model of higher-order cognitive processing that describes the mature adult decision maker. Such a decision maker will typically be capable of both formal and concrete operational thought. As will be argued, selection of a formal or concrete cognitive process will depend upon the decision maker's diagnosis of need with respect to a particular task. This need will depend upon a decision maker's maturity, experience and education with respect to a particular problem. Each of these influence cognitive strain or stress, a subject that is discussed later in this section. Ordinarily, a decision maker will prefer a concrete operational thought process and will make use of a formal operational thought process only when concrete operational thought is perceived to be inappropriate. In general, a concrete operational thought process involves less stress and may well involve repetitive and previously learned behavioral patterns. Familiarity and experience, with the issue at hand or with issues perceived to be similar or analogous, play a vital role in concrete operational thought. In novel situations, which are unstructured and where new learning is required, formal operational thought is typically more appropriate than concrete operational thought.

In concrete operational thought, people use concepts which:

(a) are drawn directly from their personal experiences;

(b) involve elementary classification and generalization concerning tangible and familiar objects;

(c) involve direct cause-and-effect relationships, typically in simple two-variable situations;

(d) can be taught or understood by analogy, algorithms, affect, standard operating procedures or recipes; and

(e) are "closed" in the sense of not demanding exploration of possibilities outside the known environment of the person and the given observed data.

In formal operational thought, people use concepts which may:

(a) be imagined, hypothetical, based on alternative scenarios and/or which may be contrary to fact;

(b) be "open ended" in the sense of requiring speculation about unstated possibilities;

(c) require deductive reasoning using unverified and perhaps flawed hypotheses;

(d) require definition by means of other concepts or abstractions that may have little or no obvious correlation with contemporary reality; and

(e) require the identification and structuring of intermediate concepts not initially specified.

Formal operational thought involves three principal stages as shown in Fig. 2: reversal of realities and possibilities, hypotheticodeductive reasoning and operations on operations. These are accomplished through reflective observation, abstract conceptualization and the testing of the resulting concept implications in new situations. It is in this way that the divergence produced by discomforting new experiences allows the learning of new developments and concepts to be "stored" in memory as part of one's concrete operational experiences. Before discussing this model, see Sect. 7, some contemporary related models of human judgement and choice must be introduced.

3. The Rasmussen Model

One particularly useful taxonomy due to Rasmussen (1983, 1986) conceptualizes three distinct types of problem-solving behavior, or reasoning: formal knowledge-based behavior, rule-based behavior and skill-based behavior. The choice of which type of reasoning to employ is made by the problem solver on the basis of experiential familiarity with the task at hand, and the environment into which this task is embedded. Figure 3 presents an interpretation of the Rasmussen model which was initially devised to describe the judgement and choice processes of process control operators. This illustration does not explicitly show the dynamic learning over time which enables a person to transfer formal rule-based reasoning results

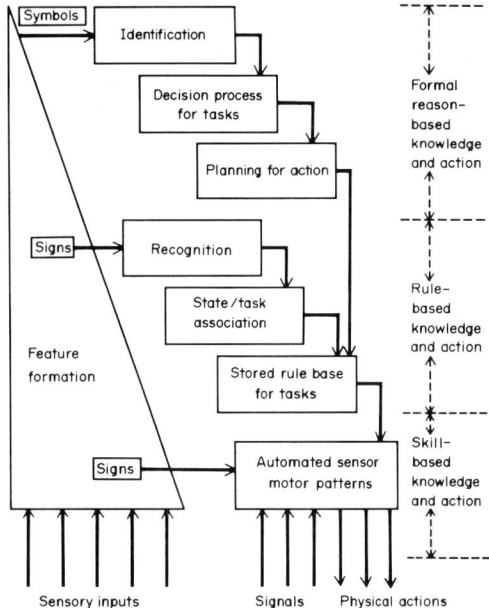

Figure 3
Three-level decision-style model of Rasmussen (the metalevel systems management for choice of style is not shown)

to a set of rule-based judgements and then, in turn, to skill-based reasoning. These notions are heavily present in the works of Rasmussen.

Often, there is a mismatch between the problem-solving behavior that a particular human might wish to use in a given situation, and the behavior that a machine designed to support a human in judgement and choice activities might be programmed to emulate. Expert systems often attempt, for example, to use rule-based representations of skill-based knowledge, or alternatively to use rules when an experienced expert would use a more skill-based representation of knowledge. This knowledge may initially be expressed in any of several affective or intuitive forms that have been learned by the expert on the basis of much relevant experience. Although the expert may well have learned how to be an expert through formal means that require an absorbed and alert monitoring of the task components, experts may no longer be formally aware of all of their monitoring actions, and may therefore give incomplete information concerning their activities. This simply reflects the view that expertise develops through perceptual learning and through the acquisition of a large number of rules. Experts are not just faster and more accurate with their use of a large number of rules, but can perceive situations, similarities and task objectives with considerable clarity. Dreyfus (1982), Dreyfus and Dreyfus (1986) and Klein (1980) have stated very useful

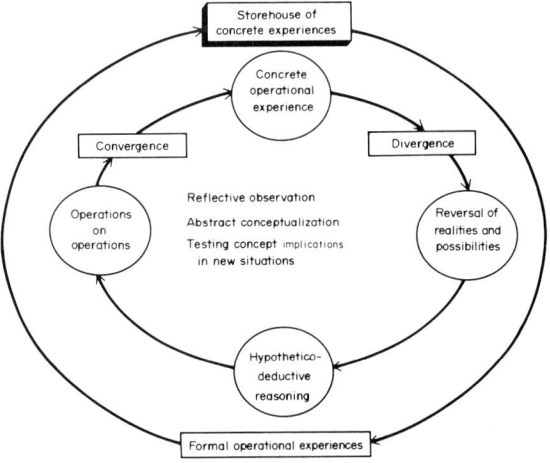

Figure 2
Learning through formal operational experiences

models of human problem-solving activity based on these observations.

4. The Klein Model

Studies of information support for US Air Force command and communication systems accomplished by Klein (Klein and Weitzenfeld 1978, Klein 1980) express a number of concerns regarding artificial intelligence (AI) and information-processing approaches for aiding decision making. These reservations concern potential inabilities of humans to disaggregate situations into components and to analyze these discrete components. He indicates that the proficient performance of experts may well be based more on reasoning by analog than by representations in terms of step-by-step descriptions capable of (discrete) digital computer processing. Further, expert proficient performers may not follow explicit conscious rules. Requiring them to do so may reduce performance quality and they will be unable to accurately describe the rules that they do follow. Klein views expertise as arising from perceptual abilities including recognitional capacity in terms of analogous situations, sensitivity to environmental context in the sense of appreciation of the significance of subtle variations, and sensitivity to intentional context by viewing the relevance and importance of task components as a whole by anticipating what has to occur to achieve a goal rather than just what will occur at the next time instant or step. He presents a comparison-guided model of proficient decision-making, In this model, which is illustrated in Fig. 4:

(a) a current decision situation is perceived in terms of objectives;

(b) the decision maker's experience allows recognition of a comparison situation;

(c) similarities and differences between the comparison situation and the current situation are noted;

(d) options are suggested, including evaluation of options, and a preferred option is selected based on what worked in the comparison option; and

(e) the way the objectives and the decision are perceived, possible further adjustments of options, generation of new options and combination of options, follow from this.

Klein strongly encourages the development of decision aids to support the recognitional capacity of the experts; aids that will assist the expert in recognizing new situations in terms of analogous comparison cases and using these to define options or alternatives. This adjuvant would also keep track of options, assist in the generation of new ones and perform computations to assess the impacts of various options. It certainly appears that this is a necessary role for information systems adjuvants for planning and decision support. However, it must be remembered that not all users of such a system will be proficient and expert in all of the tasks they are to perform. There will generally also exist a need for provisions for formal operational thought type processes for those contingency task situations that have not been sufficiently cognized, so that appropriate use of concrete operational thought necessarily leads to efficient and effective performance.

5. The Dreyfus Model

Dreyfus (1982) and Dreyfus and Dreyfus (1986) also argue that experienced and expert human decision makers solve new problems primarily by seeing similarities to previously experienced situations. They argue strongly that since similarity-based processes used by experienced and expert humans lead to better performance than formal approaches practised by beginners, decision making based on proven expertise should not be replaced by formal models. Dreyfus and Dreyfus pose a model which contains five developmental stages through which a person passes in acquiring a skill in order to become a proficient expert. Their basic tenet is that people depend less and less on abstract principles and more and more on concrete experience as they become proficient. The models proposed have evolved over time and as a function of the specific purpose to which the model is to be put. A total of six stages of development have been identified: these six stages and suggested judge-

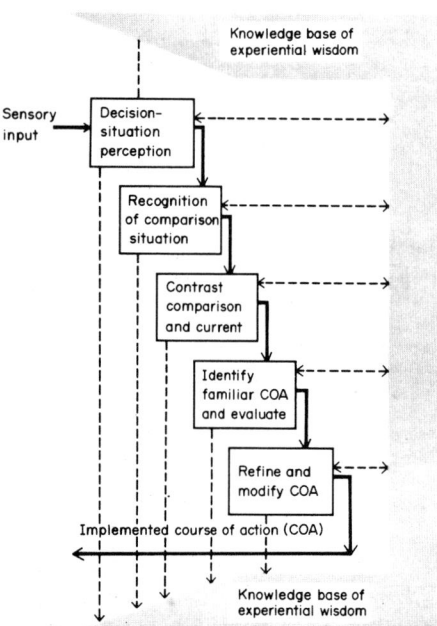

Figure 4
Interpretation of the Klein proficient decision style

ment characteristics or instructions at each stage are as follows.

(a) *Novice.* Decompose the task environment into context-free nonsituational features which the beginner can recognize without experience. Give the beginner rules for determining action, and provide monitoring and feedback to improve rule following. Expect the beginner to be consciously aware of monitoring their performance of the task, to have no perspective from which to judge their efforts, and to be detached relative to their commitment to the task.

(b) *Advanced beginner.* Decompose the task environment into context-free situationally dependent features. Except for now being able to view features from a situational perspective, other judgement features are those of a beginner or novice.

(c) *Competent.* Encourage aspect recognition not by calling attention to recurrent sets of features but rather by singling out perspicuous examples. Encourage recognition of dangerous aspects and knowledge of guidelines to correct these conditions. Equal importance weights are typically associated with aspects at this stage. The competent person is also consciously aware of personal monitoring of their performance and is beginning to develop a perspective relative to the task at hand. There is still a detached commitment relative to understanding of the situation and deciding, but the competent person has become involved in the outcome of the decision.

(d) *Proficient.* A proficient skill level comes with increased practice that exposes one to a variety of whole situations. Aspects appear more or less important depending upon relevance to goal achievement. Contextual identification of similar features and aspects of the task is now possible and memorized principles (maxims) are used to determine action. There is still a detached commitment relative to deciding, but the competent person has become involved in the outcome of the decision and understanding of the features and aspects of the task. The proficient person has developed an experienced perspective of the task.

(e) *Expert.* The repertoire of experienced situations is now vast, so that the occurrence of a specific situation triggers an intuitively appropriate action. The expert is consciously aware of monitoring of performance and has an involved commitment to all facets of the task.

(f) *Master.* The master is absorbed and no longer needs to devote constant attention to performance. There is no need for self-monitoring of performance and energy is devoted only to identifying the appropriate perspectives and appropriate alternative actions.

Dreyfus and Dreyfus associate the development of these six skill categories with successive transformation of four mental functions. Figure 5 indicates how these transformations occur with increased stages of proficiency. While developed initially for training, this model contains much of importance with

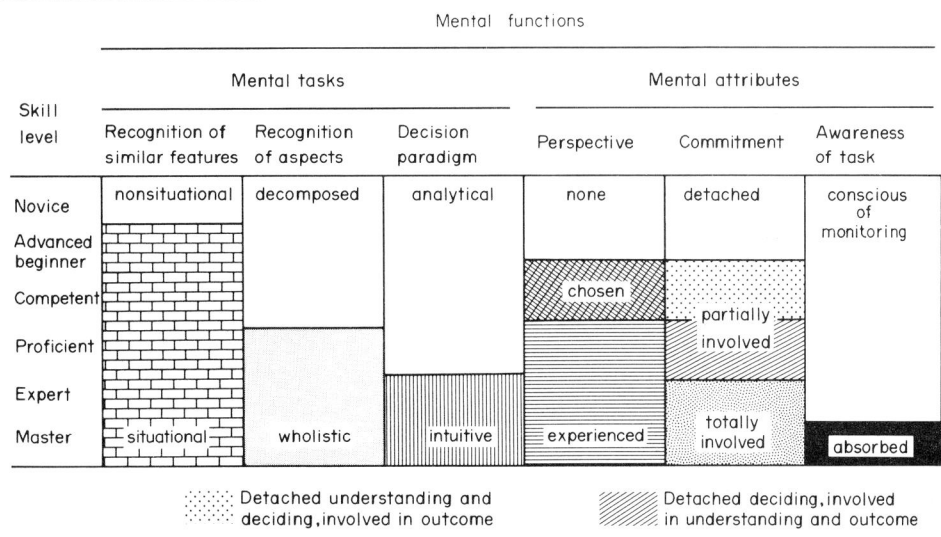

Figure 5
Interpretation of the Dreyfus decision-style model

respect to information system design and general automated knowledge support as well. There are three mental tasks that occur in the judgement and choice process.

(a) Recollection of similar features. This describes the way in which a person is able to sense environmental characteristics and task needs. A novice can only view these in a nonsituational way as the novice is, by definition, unfamiliar with the task at hand and the environment into which it is embedded.

(b) Recognition of aspects. This refers to the way in which the activities to resolve the task requirements are cognized. A novice and competent person must decompose these into component parts, such as the rules needed to make a left-hand turn when driving an automobile. Above the level of competence, a person is able to perceive necessary activities in a wholistic or *gestalt* fashion without the necessity of decomposition of the activities that will constitute potential solutions to the identified problem or task.

(c) Decision paradigm. This refers to how one decides how to decide. Up to the level of expertise, people will generally use an analytical decision style. At and above the level of expertise, intuitive judgement will be the decision style of choice.

There are also three mental attributes that vary across the six levels of capability.

(d) *Perspective.* A novice or advanced beginner will have no perspective relative to the unfamiliar task at hand. A person at the competent level will have a "chosen" perspective, and above the level of competent, an experienced perspective is developed.

(e) *Commitment.* Novices and advanced beginners are detached relative to all mental functions. They can perform only by being given instructions from others. At the level of competence, a person becomes involved in the outcome to be achieved from a decision or task solution, but is detached in commitment to all other mental functions. The commitment increases with increasing mastery of the task and experts and masters are involved in all facets of a task.

(f) *Monitoring.* Up to the level of mastery, people are aware of some conscious task monitoring efforts. At the level of mastery, a person becomes totally absorbed in the performance of the task and is not consciously aware of monitoring efforts.

A key issue in this model would appear to be the development of concrete situational experience which first occurs when a person is able to recognize aspects. The concrete operational thought of experienced decision makers would appear to be much the same as the thought of the expert and the master. Of course in all of these models, "expert" is a relative term, with the environment and the contingency task structure of a specific situation needed to determine whether a decision maker is familiar and experienced with it. Some differences in the models are doubtless present as well, some of which depend upon precisely what is meant by "processing information." The definition given here is rather broad and certainly not restricted to quantitative processing. Generally, information processing includes the formulation or acquisition, analysis and interpretation of data of value for decision making. This can be accomplished holistically, heuristically or wholistically, as noted here and especially in the article *Human Judgement and Decision Rules*.

It should be noted here that the identification of six levels of capability is somewhat arbitrary. Clearly a larger or smaller number could be identified and the model presented here is something of a composite of the evolving Dreyfus models. In the view of Dreyfus and Dreyfus, computers can, often with ease, emulate the performance of novices through capable levels of functionality. They are very strong in their arguments that the higher-level capabilities of the expert and the master will not be so easily emulated.

Very important concerns exist, in the author's view, with respect to possible cognitive bias and value incoherencies in the concrete operational decision making of experts or masters. Questions related to the effects of changing environments upon judgement and decision quality of masters and novices alike are very important in all of these models, because intuitive experience may not be a good guide for judgements and decisions in uncertain, unfamiliar and/or rapidly changing environments. However, quantitative or qualitative analysis-based efforts may well not be very good either, due to changed decision situation and contingency task structural models. In the author's view it is possible to become a "master," but unfortunately possible to become a master of the art of self-deception as well as of a specific task. The external behavior of the two "masters" may well be the same; situational, wholistic, intuitive and absorbed. What was an appropriate style for one "master" may well be inappropriate for another.

Behavior in familiar but uncertain environments is of much interest. Studies of failure, situations in which experts and masters fail or misdiagnose their degree of expertise or mastery, could yield exceptionally useful results and would also serve to incorporate and integrate much of the experimental work involving biases, poor heuristics and value coherences into a more-real decision situation. The author hypothesizes that the dynamic models of decision styles presented in this section, and others presented in the article on this topic, will be useful vehicles to these ends.

6. The Janis and Mann Model

Judgement and decision-making efforts are often characterized by intense emotion, stress and conflict, especially when there are significant consequences likely to follow from decisions. As the decision maker becomes aware of various risks and uncertainties that may be associated with a course of action, this stress becomes all the more acute. Janis and Mann (1977) have developed a conflict model of decision making. Conflict here refers to "simultaneous and opposing tendencies within the individual to accept and reject a given course of action." Symptoms of conflicts may be hesitation, feelings of uncertainty, vacillation and acute emotional stress with an unpleasant feeling of distress being, typically, the most prevalent of all characteristics associated with decision making (Broadbent 1971). The major elements associated with the conflict model are the concept of vigilant information processing, the distinction between "hot" and "cold" cognitions, and several coping patterns associated with judgements.

Cold cognitions are those made in a calm detached environmental state. The changes in utility possible due to different decisions are small and easy to determine. Hot cognitions are those associated with vital issues and concerns, and are associated with a high level of stress. Whether a cognition is, or should be, hot or cold is dependent upon the task at hand and the experiential familiarity and expertness of the decision maker with respect to the task. The symptoms of stress include feelings of apprehensiveness, a desire to escape from the distressing choice dilemma and self-blame for having allowed oneself to get into a predicament where one is forced to choose between unsatisfactory alternatives. Janis and Mann (1977) state that "psychological stress" is used as a generic term to designate unpleasant emotional states evoked by threatening environmental events or stimuli. They define a "stressful" event as "any change in the environment that typically induces a high degree of unpleasant emotion, such as anxiety, guilt or shame, and which affects normal patterns of information processing." Janis and Mann describe five functional relationships between psychological stress and decision conflict.

(a) The degree of stress generated by decision conflict is a function of those objectives which the decision maker expects to remain unsatisfied after implementing a decision.

(b) Often a person encounters new threats or opportunities that motivate consideration of a new course of action. The degree of decision stress is a function of the degree of commitment to adhere to the present course of action.

(c) When decision conflict is severe because all identified alternatives pose serious risks, failure to identify a better decision than the least objectionable one will lead to defensive avoidance.

(d) In severe decision conflict when the decision maker anticipates having insufficient time to identify an adequate alternative that will avoid serious losses, the level of stress remains extremely high. The likelihood that the dominant pattern of response will be hypervigilance, or panic, increases.

(e) A moderate degree of stress, which results when there is sufficient time to identify acceptable alternatives in response to a challenging situation, induces a vigilant effort to carefully scrutinize all identified alternative courses of action and to select a good decision.

Based upon these five functional relation propositions, Janis and Mann present five coping patterns which a decision maker would use as a function of the level of stress: unconflicted adherence or inertia, unconflicted change to a new course of action, defensive avoidance, hypervigilance or panic, and vigilance. These five coping patterns, in conjunction with the five functional relation propositions of psychological stress, were used by Janis and Mann to devise their conflict model of decision making. This model postulates that each pattern of decision stress and associated coping strategy is associated with a characteristic mode of information processing. It is this mode of information processing which governs the type and amount of information the decision maker will prefer. Figure 6 presents an interpretation of this conflict model of decision making in terms of the systems engineering contingency models discussed in this section. This model points a number of markedly different tendencies which become dominant under particular conditions of stress. These include open-mindedness, indifference, active evasion of disconfirming information, failure to assimilate new information, and all of the other cognitive information processing biases identified in the article *Human Information Processing*. There are a number of information processing preferences and decision styles generated by this conflict mode (Janis and Mann 1977, Sage 1981a). Particularly evident is the striking complexity entailed by the vigilant information-processing pattern in comparison to the other coping patterns. This vigilance pattern is characterized by seven key steps which require somewhat prolonged deliberation. The other four coping patterns require that only a few key steps be addressed. Selection of a coping pattern may be made properly or unwisely, just as selection of a decision style may be proper or improper. The seven steps of vigilant information processing appear quite

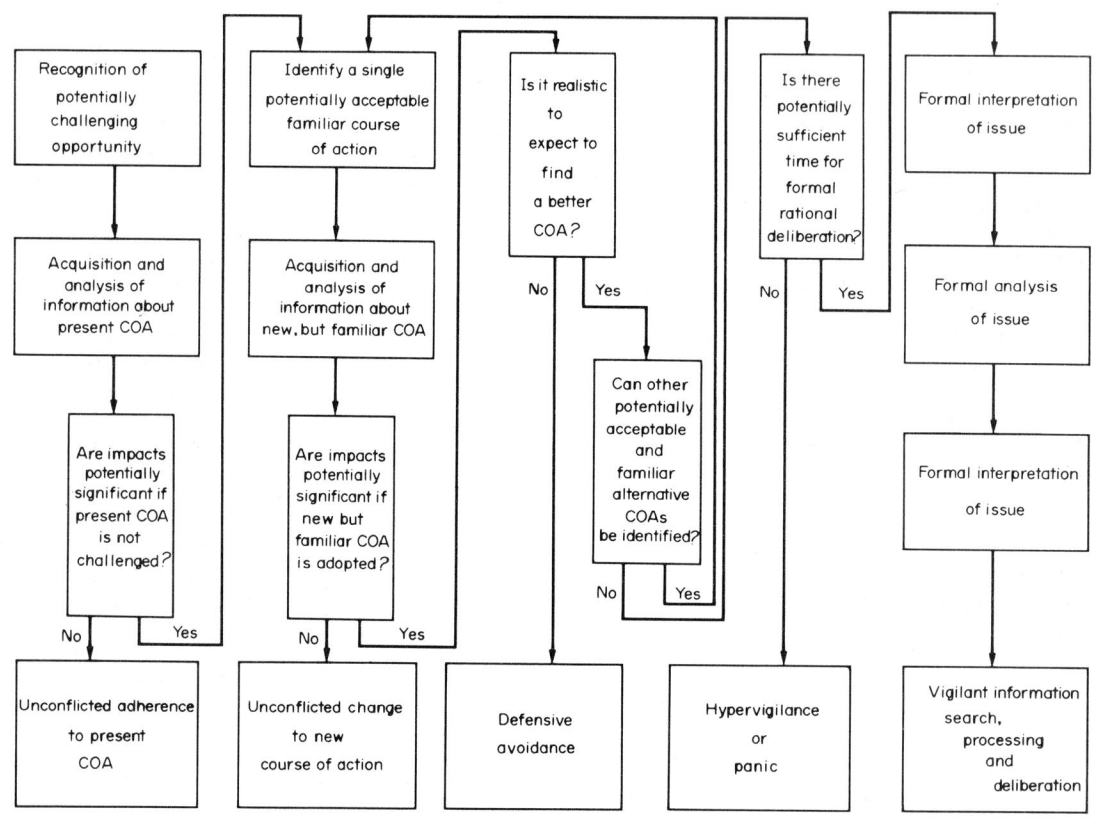

Figure 6
The Janis and Mann contingency model of judgement and choice

equivalent to the formal problem-solving steps of systems engineering that are discussed in the article *Systems Methodology*.

Janis and Mann (1977) combine the hypotheses they present concerning the four stages of decision making, the five functional relation propositions of psychological stress, and the five stress-coping patterns. Also they present a decision balance sheet, an adaptation of the moral algebra of Banjamin Franklin, on which to construct a profile of the identified options together with various cost and benefit attributes of possible decision outcomes. They have shown that decision-regret reduction and increased adherence to the adopted decision results from use of this balance sheet. Strategies for challenging outworn decisions and improving decisions quality are also developed in this seminal work.

7. Interpretation of the Models of Judgement and Choice

Each of the models described in this article is believed to be appropriate, portraying similar, but still somewhat different, relevant aspects and features of task evaluation, information-processing preference and decision-rule selection in terms of contingency elements associated with the environment and the experiences of the decision maker. It is beneficial and of considerable interest to indicate the typical interactions between the decision-style models.

The "concrete" operational thinker does not necessarily have limited abilities to process or integrate information in a formal sense. In a similar way, the "formal" operational thinker is not necessarily incapable of concrete operational thought, which is seen to be of a rule-based or skill-based nature. The contingency task structural model given here for the mature, perhaps expert, adult decision maker is one in which the decision maker may use formal or concrete operational thought based primarily on diagnosis of the contingency structure of the decision situation, and the stress that is perceived to be associated with the decision situation. This election of a formal or concrete operational mode of thought may be appropriate or inappropriate.

Information systems design must be responsive to the observation that there are two fundamentally different thought or cognition processes. These are often and correctly associated physiologically with different halves of the brain (Fishbein and Azjin 1975, Craik 1979, Blakeslee 1980, Gregory 1987). One type of thought process is typically described by adjectives or attributes such as verbal, logical, sequenced, thinking and analytical. The second type is described as nonverbal, intuitive, wholistic, feeling and heuristic. The verbal process is typically viewed as superior in engineering and natural science, and the affective process is more often associated with the arts. However, this viewpoint on the nature of thought appears to be wrong and should be discouraged as positively harmful, for the two processes are complementary and compatible; they are not competitive and incompatible in any meaningful way. One thought process may be deficient, in fact, if it is not supported by the other. The nonverbal supports the verbal by suggesting ideas, alternatives and so on. The verbal supports the nonverbal by expressing, structuring, analyzing and validating the creative ideas that occur in the nonverbal process. Appropriate information support for judgement and choice processes must provide for verbal and nonverbal support.

An appropriate support process must be tolerant and supportive of the cognitive (thought) processes of an individual or a group. These will typically vary across individuals and within the same individual as a function of the environment, the previous experience of the individual with the environment, and those associated factors which introduce varying amounts of stress. Thus, a contingency task structural view of individuals and organizations in decision situations is needed, as contrasted with a stereotypical view in which individuals are assumed to process fixed, static and unchanging cognitive characteristics which are uninfluenced by environmental and experiential considerations. This view will encourage us not only to consider the evolution of future events over time as inherently uncertain and associated with much information imperfection, but also to consider value change over time. It is especially important that we consider values as containing noncommensurate, ambiguous and uncertain components, rather than as being absolute, consistent, precise and exogenous with respect to choice (Mason and Mitroff 1973, March 1978).

We are most likely to have coherent value preferences and be able to develop and utilize appropriate evaluation heuristics in well-structured situations with which we are familiar. Learning by trial and error, and development of judgement based on either reasoning by analogy, standard operating procedures or organizational rules typically results from these "concrete operational" situations and experiences. Longstanding use of these "rules" results in purely affective judgement and decision responses. In a familiar and simple world, a "concrete operational" world, these judgement guides and judgement heuristics might well be, and in fact often are, quite acceptable. In a changing and uncertain environment, an environment that is different from the one with which we are familiar, we may well err considerably by using those judgement heuristics that are appropriate to the concrete operational world. If we do not have a developed set of coherent values relative to a changing environment, we may respond affectively with the first alternative option that comes to mind. We may well adopt post-decision behavior to support and maintain a chosen response and employ cognitive biases and heuristics to justify this potentially ill-chosen response. This results in an affective response appropriate for a "concrete operational" situation when an analytical response, appropriate for a "formal operational" situation, is needed. In the terminology used by Janis and Mann (1977), a coping pattern is adopted which is based on unconflicted adherence or unconflicted change, whereas vigilance is called for by the task and environment extant.

A particularly important role for a knowledge support system is to assist the user in minimizing errors between the perceived knowledge level relative to a particular task, and the environment into which the task requirements are embedded, and their actual knowledge level relative to the task and environment. When both perceived and actual knowledge level are at the level of "master," for example, then skill-based knowledge is generally appropriate for judgement and choice tasks. When the perceived and actual knowledge level is that of "novice," then the knowledge support system user is generally aware of the need for support. When the perceived knowledge level is that of "master" and the actual knowledge is that of "novice," perhaps due to an unrecognized change in environment, then it is very likely that acts of judgement and choice will be associated with self-deception. The task for a knowledge support system, in this regard, would be to alert the decision maker to the potential difficulties of skill-based behavior in an appropriate manner. A very important role for a knowledge support system is, therefore, that of alerting decision makers to the information requirements appropriate to the task at hand, and the environment surrounding the task and task requirements.

An appropriate conceptual framework for human information processing and judgement must be set within the context of real decisions made by real people in real decision situations. The terms judgement and choice refer to human cognition over a continuum of perspectives that range from formal analytical thought at one end of the spectrum to wholistic intuitive thought based on concrete operational experiences at the other. The differences between analytical and perceptual thought processes are rooted in the writings of many authors. Piaget's theory of intellectual development, which was briefly described in Sect. 2 was among the first to identify relevant variables that influence the selection of judgement and choice style: maturation, experience, education and "self-regulation." Brunswick (1952, 1956) describes perception as an intuitive, continuous and rapid process, as contrasted with analytical reasoning, which is typically deterministic, discontinuous and slow. Cyert and Simon (1983) describe "behavioral rules" as modes of behavior that an individual or an organization develop as guidelines for decision making in complex environments characterized by uncertainty and incomplete information. These rules incorporate the decision maker's assumptions about both the nature of the internal environment of the organization and the external environment of the world surrounding the environment. In this model, judgement is an entity that is capable of being decomposed into a set of behavioral rules that change and move closer to those described by simple known situations as uncertainties give way to certainty and knowledge increases.

A major conclusion from this is that it would be very desirable to develop predictable interrelations between human cognitive processes for human information processing and associated judgement and choice, and environmental characteristics. While these will be dependent upon the contingency task structure of the decision task, surrounding environment, and the experiential familiarity of the decision maker with these, it should be expected that most knowledge support processes will tend to encourage use of formal analytical thought processes by both novices and experts. Two observations support this.

(a) The use of support systems generally encourages people to justify their judgements and this has been shown to encourage formal analytical reasoning (Hagafors and Brehmer 1983).

(b) People tend to test and potentially change their initially favored hypotheses when provided with relevant information feedback (Chaiken 1980, Huber 1980, Hagafors and Brehmer 1983). Without information feedback, it is possible for alternatives to be selected without feeling a need to justify this selection. Thus, information feedback is highly desirable and provision of this through the use of most current approaches will encourage formal analytical thought.

It will be very important to determine the extent to which judgement and choice are improved through the use of support systems owing to the likely encouragement to use formal operational thought processes. One role for a knowledge support system is to assist the user in minimizing errors between their perceived knowledge level relative to a particular task and their actual knowledge level, as described earlier in this section. Such a situation is shown in Fig. 7. If the use of a support system will encourage people in quadrants 1 and 2 to use formal reasoning-based knowledge, then the change from quadrant 2 is appropriate,

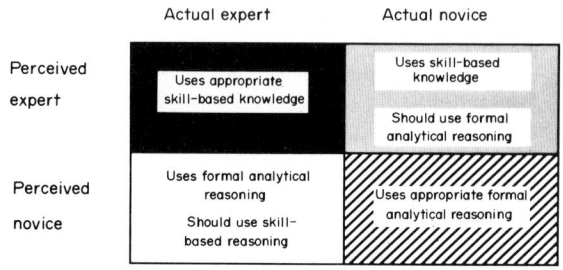

Figure 7
Actual knowledge perspective versus appropriate knowledge level

whereas that from quadrant 1 is not necessarily appropriate. This suggests the addition of a third dimension to Fig. 3, which is necessary to reflect the influence of a support system.

Styles or modes of information processing, which include information acquisition and information analysis, are of much importance in the design of information systems for the interpretation of the impacts of proposed policy. Information acquisition refers to the perceptual process by which the mind organizes the verbal and visual stimuli that it encounters. McKeeney and Keen (1974) discuss two modes of information acquisition, a preceptive mode and a receptive mode.

(a) In preceptive acquisition and analysis, individuals use existing experiential concepts and precepts in order to filter data. They focus on structural relations between items and look for deviations from their expectations. They then use formal precepts as cues for acquisition, analysis and associated structuring of data.

(b) In receptive acquisition and analysis, individuals focus on contextual detail rather than presumed structural relationships. They infer structure and impacts from direct and detailed examination of information, generally including potentially disconfirming information, rather than from fitting it to their precepts.

There is nothing inherently good or bad in either mode of information acquisition, analysis and associated structuring. The same individual may use different modes depending on the contingency task structure. Most people will have preferences for one mode or the other in a particular situation, depending upon their diagnosis of the contingency task structure and perceived needs to accomplish effective information interpretation and associated decision making. It is the author's hypothesis that cognitive biases often arise, or are initiated, by the use of a situationally incorrect mode of information acquisition and structuring. To use preceptive acquisition when receptive acquisition is more appropriate would appear to invite one or more of the many biases associated with selective perception. To use receptive acquisition when preceptive acquisition is appropriate would appear to introduce much stress associated with a low likelihood of being able to resolve an issue in the time available.

Information evaluation and interpretation refers to the decision-rule portion of the problem solution. The model given here for this is based on the use of Piaget's theory of concrete and formal operational thinking as a useful precept for information evaluation and interpretation. These thought process models may be summarized as follows.

(a) In concrete operational thought, individuals approach problems through intuitive affect, analogical reasoning or through following a standard operating policy or organizational processes, or some related process.

(b) In formal operational thought, individuals approach problems through structuring in terms of embedding realities into possibility scenarios, hypotheticodeductive reasoning and interpretation in terms of operations on operations.

Figure 2 has presented some of the dynamic learning experiences which link the concrete operational and formal operational thought processes. Again it must be noted that no style is inherently appropriate or inappropriate independent of the experiential familiarity of an individual with task and environment. Appropriateness of a particular style, as has been mentioned earlier in this section, is very much dependent on the task, environment and experience. That most decision makers function as concrete operational thinkers is doubtless correct. A principal task of a well-designed information system is to assist in aiding the decision maker to detect the appropriate style for a given task, environment and decision-maker experience level. Another task is to enhance the transfer of formal operational experiences to concrete operational experiences, through conceptualization and evolution of appropriate heuristics, wholistic thought, analogous reasoning guides, standard operating procedures, other forms of affective thought and perhaps even precognitive responses. It is posited here that both types of information acquisition and analysis may occur with either concrete or formal thought although the appropriate balance of receptive and preceptive acquisition and analysis will vary from situation to situation.

The discussions given here have indicated the strong environmental dependence of the formulation, analysis and interpretation steps necessary for problem resolution. These steps are necessary steps in the resolution of any issue using systematic means, regardless of the "style" adopted for problem solution. Environments, organizations and technologies are three dominant concerns of systems engineering in general and for the design of systems for information support in particular. It is the interaction of the environment with an organization and a technology that results in a management technology. Systems management is the term that has been used here to denote the interaction of human judgement with methodological concerns (Sage 1980, 1981a,b). Systems management therefore, denotes concerns at the cognitive process level that involve the contingency task structure and its role in influencing the selection of performance objectives and decision rules for the evaluation of options associated with issue resolution. There are many influences which act on the contingency task structure. Basically, as has been noted several times, the contingency task structure and the environment which influences it act to specify and direct problem-solving efforts through the selection of performance objectives and associated information processing and decision-rule paradigms. This is the metalevel function that is described as systems management of cognition.

The dynamic cognitive style models of Figs. 2–6 can be used as guides to illustrate both those modes of information acquisition and information evaluation that should be used and that will be used on a given issue. It must be stressed that the particular cognitive style most appropriate for a given issue will depend upon the decision maker's familiarity with a given issue, the issue itself and the environment in which the issue is embedded. Thus a receptive or preceptive information acquisition style will be appropriate in a formal operational setting if the issue at hand is an unfamiliar and unstructured one. The appropriate balance between preceptive and receptive information acquisition will be dependent upon the type of issue and the experience or familiarity the decision maker has with possible information sources and their likely reliability. It will, also, of course, be influenced by the "personal" style of the decision maker and the type, if any, of interaction with the systems analyst as well as upon other characteristics of the decision situation. The view is accepted here that systems methodologies, especially as implemented through the use of human judgement to form a systematic process, are highly value dependent. Different systems methodologies allow one to define issues in different ways and are responsive in differing amounts to value concerns, such as equity. Some methodologies explicitly encourage, for example, detection of the use of deficient heuristics and encourage correction. The "transparency" and communicability of a decision process, for example, is very much a function of the methodologies used in process aiding for the formulation of issues, the analysis of alternatives and associative interpretation efforts. This value dependence of systems methodologies is, therefore, an important aspect of information system design and is related to performance objectives for the task at hand.

There have been a number of studies which focus upon the critical importance of task description and the decision maker's interaction with the task through environment. Dawes(1975, 1979) stresses the critical interaction among the mind and the task, and integrated models of the mind and the task requirements. He discusses the "even-number–vowel" experiment described in Sect. 2 as does Anderson (1980). Anderson indicates that the failure (and a majority of educated adults do fail) to correctly resolve this task is a result of difficulties in applying the *modus tollens* concept of conditional deductive reasoning, a concept which requires thinking about what is not the case. Anderson also discusses a slight variation of this task in which almost all subjects performed correctly. The task involved looking at four pictures of ordinary letter envelopes with the possibility of a stamp on them and picking the letters which should be turned over to test the hypothesis: "if a letter is sealed, it has an 18 cent stamp on it." The critical difference between the two tasks is the fact that most people have experiences similar to the second task. It is relatively familiar compared to the first task, concerning which people do not have significant experience.

We should be rather cautious, however, in the apparently reasonable inference that we learn correctly from experience. A number of important studies by Brehmer (1978, 1980) have shown that by no means do people always improve their judgement and decision-making ability on the basis of increased experience. Biases, such as the tendency to use confirming evidence to the neglect of disconfirming evidence, are the key culprits. Brehmer (1980) indicates how these biases can be understood in terms of available information. He concludes that truth is not manifest. It needs to be inferred in order to extract from experiential information those components that will truly lead to better judgements and decisions. The definitive discussion of judgement and choice processes by Einhorn and Hogarth (1981) emphasizes the importance and the interdependence of attention, memory, cognitive representations, learning, conflict and feedback. It provides a valuable perspective concerning the importance of these topics for judgement and decision making.

Carroll (1980) is much concerned also with understanding decision behavior, especially through the process-tracing techniques that have been emphasized by Payne (1976, 1980, Payne et al. 1978, 1980). Carroll proposes that the decision maker might better be portrayed as possesing a rich store of knowledge organized around a variety of evoked schemas, complex units of organized knowledge which guide the acquisition and use of case information, rather than exclusively considering the decision maker as exhaustively following the prescriptions of normative models. Many of the chapters in the edited works of Estes (1975–1979), Howell and Fleishman (1980), Shweder (1980), Wallsten (1980a,b), Hamilton (1981), Howell (1981) discuss issues related to cognitive factors in judgement processes, including task descriptions for scripts, stereotypical sequences of actions and event schemas which are often very useful in explaining judgement. In addition, the articles *Dynamic Decision Making* and *Intuitive and Analytical Cognition: Information Models* provide much needed expansion concerning these notions.

See also: Human Information Processing; Human Judgement and Decision Rules.

Bibliography

Anderson J R 1980 *Cognitive Psychology and its Implications*. Freeman, San Francisco, California

Anderson J R 1983 *The Architecture of Cognition*. Harvard University Press, Cambridge, Massachusetts

Beach L R, Mitchell T R 1978 A contingency model for the selection of decision strategies. *Acad. Manage. Rev.* **3**, 439–48

Blakeslee T R 1980 *The Right Brain*. Anchor, New York

Borgida E, Nisbett R E 1977 Differential impact of abstract versus concrete information decisions *J.Appl. Soc. Psychol.* **7**(3), 258–71

Brainerd C J 1978 *Piaget's Theory of Intelligence*. Prentice–Hall, Englewood Cliffs, New Jersey

Brehmer B 1978 Response consisting in probabilistic inference tasks. *Organ. Behav. Hum. Perform.* **22**, 103–15

Brehmer B 1980 In one word: Not from experience. *Acta. Psychol.* **45**, 223–41

Broadbent D W 1971 *Decision and Stress*. Academic Press, London

Brunswick E 1952 The conceptual framework of psychology. In: *International Encyclopedia of Unified Science*, Vol. 1, No. 10, University of Chicago Press, Chicago, Illinois

Brunswick E 1956 *Perception and the Representative Design of Psychological Experiments*. University of California Press, Berkeley, California

Carroll J S 1980 Analyzing decision behavior: The magician's audience. In: Wallsten 1980a, pp. 69–76

Chaiken S 1980 Heuristic versus systematic information processing and the use of source versus message cues in persuasion. *J. Pers. Soc. Psychol.* **39**, 752–66

Craik F I M 1979 Human memory. *Annu. Rev. Psychol.* **30**, 63–102

Crocker J, Fiske S T, Taylor S E 1984 Schematic basis for belief change. In: Eiser J R (ed.) *Attitudinal Judgement*. Springer, Berlin

Cyert R M, Simon H A 1983 The behavioral approach: With emphasis on economics. *Behav. Sci.* **28**, 95–108

Dawes R M 1975 The mind, the model, and the task. In: Restle I F (ed.) *Cognitive Theory*. Erlbaum, Hillsdale, New Jersey, pp.119–30

Dawes R M 1979 The robust beauty of improper linear models in decision making. *Am. Psychol.* **34**(7), 571–82

Dreyfus H L, Dreyfus S E 1986 *Mind over Machine: The Power of Human Intuition and Expertise in the Era of the Computer*. Free Press, New York

Dreyfus S E 1982 Formal models versus human situational understanding: Inherent limitations in the modeling of business expertise. *Off., Technol. People* **1**, 133–65

Einhorn H J 1980a Learning from experience and suboptimal rules in decision making. In: Wallsten 1980a, pp. 1–20

Einhorn H J 1980b Overconfidence in judgement. In: Shweder 1980, pp. 1–16

Einhorn H J, Hogarth R M 1981 Behavioral decision theory: Processes of judgement and choice. *Annu. Rev. Psychol.* **32,** 53–88

Estes R M 1975–1979 *Handbook of Learning and Cognitive Processes*, Vols. 1–6. Erlbaum, Hillsdale, New Jersey

Fischhoff B 1981 No man is a discipline. In: Harvey J (ed.) *Cognition, Social Behavior and the Environment.* Erlbaum, Hillsdale, New Jersey

Fischhoff B, Goitein B, Shipira Z 1981a The experienced utility of expected utility approaches. In: Feather N (ed.) *Expectancy, Incentive, and Action.* Erlbaum, Hillsdale, New Jersey

Fischhoff B, Slovic P, Lichtenstein S 1981b Knowing what you want: Measuring labile values. In: Wallsten 1980a

Fishbein M, Azjin I 1975 *Belief, Attitude, Intention, and Behavior.* Addison–Wesley, Reading, Massachusetts

Flavell J H 1977 *Cognitive Development.* Prentice–Hall, Englewood Cliffs, New Jersey

Fleishman E A, Quaintance M K 1984 *Taxonomies of Human Performance.* Academic Press, New York

Ginsburg H, Opper S 1979 *Piaget's Theory of Intellectual Development.* Prentice–Hall, Englewood Cliffs, New Jersey

Gregory R L (ed.) 1987 *The Oxford Companion to the Mind.* Oxford University Press, Oxford

Hagafors R, Brehmer B 1983 Does having to justify one's judgements change the nature of the judgement process. *Organ. Behav. Hum. Perform.* **31,** 223–32

Hakathorn R, Keen P 1981 Organizational strategies for personal computing in decision support systems. *MIS. Q.* **5**(3)

Hamilton D (ed.) 1981 *Cognitive Processes in Stereotyping and Intergroup Perception.* Erlbaum, Hillsdale, New Jersey

Howell S C, Fleishman E A 1980 *Information Processing and Decision Making.* Scott, Foresman and Co., Glenview, Illinois

Howell W 1981 *Human Performance and Productivity.* Erlbaum, Hillsdale, New Jersey

Huber G P 1983 Cognitive style as a basis for MIS and DSS designs: Much ado about nothing. *Manage. Sci.* **29**(5), 567–79

Huber O 1980 The influence of some task variables on cognitive operations in an information processing decision model. *Acta. Psychol.* **45**(1–3), 187–96

Janis I L, Mann L 1977 *Decision Making: A Psychological Analysis of Conflict, Choice, and Commitment.* Free Press, New York

Klein G A 1980 Automated aids for the proficient decision maker. In: *Proc. 1980 IEEE Conf. Cybernetics Society.* IEEE Press, New York, pp. 301–4

Klein G A, Weitzenfeld J 1978 Improvement of skills for solving ill-defined problems. *Educ. Psychol.* **13,** 31–41

McKeeney J L, Keen P G W 1974 How managers' 'minds work'. *Harv. Bus. Rev.* **52**(3), 79–90

March J G 1978 Bounded rationality, ambiguity and the engineering of choice. *Bell J. Econ.* **10,** 587–608

Mason R O, Mitroff I I 1973 A program for research on management information systems. *Manage. Sci.* **19**(5), 475–85

Mintzberg H 1976 Planning on the left and managing on the right. *Harv. Bus. Rev.* **54,** 49–58

Mintzberg H 1980 Structure in 5's: A synthesis of the research on organizational design processes. *Manage. Sci.* **26,** 322–41

Mintzberg H, Raisinghani D, Theoret A 1976 The structure of unstructured decision processes. *Adm. Sci. Q.* **21,** 246–75

Payne J W 1976 Task complexity and contingent processing in decision making: An information search and protocol analysis. *Organ. Behav. Hum. Perform.* **16,** 366–87

Payne J W 1980 Information processing theory: Some concepts and methods applied to decision research. In: Wallsten 1980a, pp. 95–116

Payne J W, Braunstein M L, Carroll J S 1978 Exploring predecisional behavior: An alternative approach to decision research. *Organ. Behav. Hum. Perform.* **22,** 17–44

Payne J W, Laughhunn D J, Crum R 1980 Translation of gambler and aspiration level effects in risky choice behavior. *Manage. Sci.* **26**(10), 1039–60

Rasmussen J 1983 Skills, rules, knowledge; signals, signs, and symbols; and other distinctions in human performance models. *IEEE Trans. Syst., Man Cybern.* **13**(3)

Rasmussen J 1986 *On Information Processing and Human–Machine Interaction: An Approach to Cognitive Engineering.* North-Holland, Amsterdam

Sage A P 1977 *Methodology for Large Scale Systems.* McGraw–Hill, New York

Sage A P 1980 Desiderata for systems engineering education. *IEEE Trans. Syst., Man Cybern.* **10**(12), 777–80

Sage A P 1981a A methodological framework for systematic design and evaluation of computer aids for planning and decision support. *Comput. Electr. Eng.* **8**(2), 87–102

Sage A P 1981b Behavioral and organizational considerations in the design of information systems and processes for planning and decision support. *IEEE Trans. Syst., Man Cybern.* **11**(9), 640–78

Sage A P 1982 Methodological considerations in the design of large scale systems engineering processes. In: Haimes Y Y (ed.) *Large Scale Systems.* North-Holland, Amsterdam, pp. 99–141

Sage A P 1987a Knowledge, skills, and information requirements for systems design. In: Rouse W B, Boff K (eds.) *The Psychology of System Design.* Elsevier, Amsterdam

Sage A P (ed.) 1987b *System Design for Human Interaction.* IEEE Press, New York

Sage A P, Rouse W B 1986 Aiding the human decision maker through the knowledge-based sciences. *IEEE Trans. Syst., Man Cybern.* **16**(4)

Shweder R A (ed.) 1980 *Fallible Judgment in Behavioral Research.* Jossey-Bass, San Francisco, California

Stone C A, Day M C 1980 Competence and performance models and the characterization of formal operational skills. *Hum. Dev.* **28,** 323–53

Wallsten T S (ed.) 1980a *Cognitive Processes in Choice and Decision Behavior.* Erlbaum, Hillsdale, New Jersey

Wallsten T S 1980b Processing information for decisions. In: Castellan N J, Pisconi D B, Potts G (eds.) *Cognitive Theory*, Vol. 2. Erlbaum, Hillsdale, New Jersey

A. P. Sage
[George Mason University, Fairfax, Virginia, USA]

Cognitive Science, Human Information Processing and Artificial Intelligence

What exactly is the relationship of cognitive science and human information processing to artificial intelligence? In order to begin to answer this question, explicit answers to the following three questions must first be provided.

(a) What is cognitive science?
(b) What is human information processing?
(c) What is artificial intelligence?

1. Definitions

1.1 Cognitive Science

One of the most important intellectual developments since the 1940s has been the birth of an exciting new interdisciplinary field called cognitive science. Researchers in psychology, linguistics, computer science, philosophy and neuroscience realized that they were asking many of the same questions about the nature of the human mind and that they had developed complementary and potentially synergistic methods of investigation. The word "cognitive" refers to perceiving and knowing; thus, cognitive science is the science of mind. Cognitive scientists seek to understand perceiving, thinking, remembering, understanding language, learning and other mental phenomena. All of these could potentially qualify as human information processing behaviors. The research of cognitive scientists is remarkably diverse, ranging from observing children, through programming computers to perform complex problem solving, to analyzing the nature of meaning. A more restrictive definition of cognitive science limits it to the study of understanding human information processing.

1.2 Human Information Processing

Cognitive scientists perceive the human mind as a complex system that receives, stores, retrieves, transforms and transmits information—a human information processing (HIP) system. According to Stillings et al. (1987) there are four important corollary assumptions to this information-processing view.

(a) Formal information processes: information and information processes can be studied as patterns and the manipulation of patterns. The formal approach divorces symbols from their meanings in order to get a scientific grasp on information processing.

(b) HIP approaches symbolic significance through the notion of representation; symbols and formal processes are said to represent what they stand for. In order to function correctly, a representation must have the same structure as the part of the world that it represents. The strongest form of sameness of structure is called isomorphism. Two aspects of sameness of structure are:

(1) the symbols in a representation must have a well-defined mapping to the objects in the world that they represent; and

(2) a formal information process must operate in the same way as the process in the world that it represents.

(c) Separating formal processes from their physical basis: information processes can and in part must be studied without reference to the physics or biology of the system which is carrying them out.

(d) The study of HIP is a basic science: a basic science of information processing is possible. HIP scientists seek to discover highly general and explanatory fundamental principles of information processing.

1.3 Artificial Intelligence

Artificial intelligence (AI) is a part of computer science which overlaps considerably with cognitive science in general and the study of HIP in particular. Marvin Minsky, one of the founders of the field of AI, has said that AI is the science of making machines perform tasks that would require intelligence if done by humans (Minsky 1968). Cognitive scientists stress the relationship between human and machine intelligence. They are interested in using AI techniques to enlighten them about how human beings perform intelligent tasks and in using knowledge about human intelligence gathered in other disciplines to provide information for AI research.

2. The Relationship of Cognitive Science and HIP to AI

The relationship of cognitive science and HIP to AI may be explained in the following manner. Many researchers in AI attempt to model their computer programs on human intelligence, and they derive inspiration from insights into HIP that come from other disciplines in cognitive science, such as psychology and linguistics. The insights also flow in the other direction. Attempts by AI researchers to program systems that can understnd language, perceive or solve problems have led to new testable hypotheses about human cognition. In its interplay with the other cognitive-science disciplines, AI provides a powerful alternative methodology for exploring and testing theories of cognition and HIP that supplements the empirical methods of psychology and linguistics.

The author of this article adopts the view that the topic of the relationship of cognitive science and HIP to AI is best answered by taking an historical perspective on the evolution of this relationship. Over time, the relationship and respective roles that each science has played have changed often and, one might argue, continuously.

3. Machine Intelligence and HIP

As noted by Cohen and Feigenbaum (1982), anthropomorphism is a powerful tendency in human thinking—we ascribe personalities and emotions to all kinds of animate and inanimate objects. Cohen and Feigenbaum go on to write: "Thus, it is not surprising that we should do the same with computers, or even that we should reverse the terms of the equation and describe ourselves in terms reserved for the machine. This is not a new trend—it certainly predates the electronic computer (e.g., the Futurists around 1910 extolled the virtues of the machine in their manifestos)—but the comparison between man and machine is particularly compelling in the case of the computer."

Cohen and Feigenbaum note, however, that there is no science and no subtlety in the broad unqualified claim that we behave like computers or vice versa; they write, "the trick is to know enough about how humans and computers think to say exactly what they have in common, and, when we lack this knowledge, to use the comparison to suggest theories of human thinking or computer thinking." Thus, as previously noted, psychology and AI have a reciprocal relationship: what we learn about human intelligence suggests extensions to the theory of machine intelligence, and vice versa.

Cohen and Feigenbaum believe that this reciprocal relationship was most evident during the early years of the development of AI. As they point out, in 1956, Allen Newell and Herbert Simon developed a theory of problem solving called Logic Theorist (LT), which they implemented as a computer program. Cohen and Feigenbaum relate the story as follows: "Because the theory was formalized, Newell and Simon could specify exactly the problem-solving behaviors they expected to find in human problem-solvers. But when they tested their theory, they found that it failed in one respect: Humans did not use the same control process (working backward from theorem to axioms) as the program. Thus, they revised the theory, and wrote a new program, to incorporate what they had learned about human control processes during problem solving. They called the new program the General Problem Solver (GPS), and the new control process means–end analysis, and found that this process was much more efficient (in terms of computer time) than its predecessor. Means–ends analysis is now an established problem-solving technique in AI."

This example used by Cohen and Feigenbaum illustrates how, by exploiting the comparison between human and machine problem solving, it is possible to develop theories of both areas from a relative ignorance of either. As they note, the first step was LT, a preliminary theory. The next step was to test LT against human problem solvers, and the third step was to derive a new theory, GPS, from differences between the old one and the experimental data. This theory was tested again and was more successful, both as a theory of human problem solving and as a technique for AI. Cohen and Feigenbaum note, however, that this development succeeded not by simply asserting that human problem solving is like machine problem solving but, rather, by precisely describing the similarities of the two processes and, more importantly for the development of the theory, their differences. To quote Cohen and Feigenbaum: "Computer programs are precise descriptions of behavior and so are the results of experiments with humans; by using each to complement the other, a theory of behavior develops quickly."

This approach to psychological research is called information-processing psychology. The theories that are developed—computer models of human thinking—are called models of cognition. The central idea of information-processing psychology is to bring precision to the seductive comparison between human intelligence and AI to benefit our understanding of human cognition.

4. A History of AI and HIP Psychology

As noted by Cohen and Feigenbaum (1982), information-processing psychology has played an important part in the development of psychology in the USA since 1950. To quote them: "It has helped to reinstate the concept of mind, which had been abolished by behavioral psychologists because it was unobservable except by introspection." Methodological behaviorism condemned introspection as a psychological method because there was no guarantee that the words used by one person to describe his mental events would mean the same thing to another person. Cohen and Feigenbaum use the following example: If a person says, "I can't quite think of the word—it is on the tip of my tongue," you may know what he/she is thinking and feeling, but, in fact, regardless of the detail with which he/she describes his/her state, you cannot guarantee that your knowledge of the person's state is completely accurate. A stronger position on introspection is taken by radical behaviorism, which holds that knowledge obtained by introspection not only cannot be communicated accurately, but is not even perceived accurately by the introspector: "An organism behaves as it does because of its current structure, but most of this is out of the reach of introspection" (Skinner 1976 p. 19). Mental events are viewed as side effects, not causes, of the interaction between an organism and its environment and are thus not explanations of behavior.

These positions—radical and methodological behaviorism—were objective but resulted in a psychology that, according to Cohen and Feigenbaum, did not admit the mind. Theoretically, it was possible to explain behavior in terms of stimulus–response pairs, denying any mediating mental structures or processes

(Skinner 1976 pp. 93–94):

> A person is changed by the contingencies of reinforcement under which he behaves; he does not store the contingencies. In particular, he does not store copies of the stimuli which have played a part in the contingencies. There are no "iconic representations" in his mind; there are no "data structures stored in his memory"; he has no "cognitive map" of the world in which he has lived. He has simply been changed in such a way that stimuli now control particular kinds of perceptual behavior.

In contrast, all the research described in the *Handbook of AI* (Cohen and Feigenbaum 1982) is concerned with structures and processes that mediate intelligent responses to stimuli. Cohen and Feigenbaum believe that this fundamental change in theoretical positions took place between 1950 and 1960, during which time behaviorism was largely displaced by cognitive psychology. Quoting these authors, "The key to the change was the concept of information. Following the publication, in 1949, of Shannon and Weaver's 'The Mathematical Theory of Communication' information became a concrete, measurable quantity (see Shannon and Weaver 1963). Initially, the strict mathematical conception of information was explored; theorists tried to fit many aspects of human communication into the general model proposed by Shannon and Weaver (see, e.g., Cherry 1970). But the model was best suited to communication over electrical channels, and so, by the mid-1950s, a more relaxed, and more appropriate, conception of information was emerging."

Cohen and Feigenbaum identify the paper by Miller (1956) as being extremely influential. In this paper, Miller proposed that the information capacity of mental processes, particularly short-term memory, is best measured in terms of semantic chunks—meaningful units of information—and not in terms of abstract bits. For example, words from a sentence and nonsense syllables are considered to be chunks of information and place approximately equal demands on memory, despite the fact that the words contain more information, in the mathematical sense, than the syllables. In the years following Miller's paper, information structures such as discrimination nets, associative semantic nets and frames were developed to represent the information used in cognition. The original, mathematical formulation of information has been largely abandoned (Anderson and Bower 1973 p. 136).

> The problem was that the bit gave a very poorly articulated characterization of the information ... As descriptions of the information have become more articulated, the theories composed out of them have become more successful.

Cohen and Feigenbaum believe that the increasing sophistication of computers and computer science was the most important factor in the development of information-processing ideas. During the late 1950s, there was the realization in information-processing psychology that the computer was not simply a device for shifting bits or "crunching numbers," but was more generally capable of any kind of symbol manipulation, of any kind of information process. As Newell and Simon (1963 p. 366) write:

> An entirely different use of computers in psychology ... has emerged. This ... stems from the fact that a computer is a device for manipulating symbols of any kind, not just numerical symbols. Thus a computer becomes a way of specifying arbitrary symbolic processes. Theories of this type, which can be called information processing theories, are essentially nonquantitative (they may involve no numbers at all), although neither less precise nor less rigorous than classical mathematical theories.

Cohen and Feigenbaum also note that in cognitive psychology, the computer and the emergence of programs like LT had a profound effect, even though cognitive psychology does not share the enthusiasm of information-processing psychology for computer models. In the words of Neisser (1976 pp. 5–6):

> The activities of the computer itself seemed in some ways akin to cognitive processes. Computers accept information, manipulate symbols, store items in "memory" and retrieve them again, classify inputs, recognize patterns, and so on. Whether they do these things just like people was less important than that they do them at all. The coming of the computer provided a much-needed reassurance that cognitive processes were real ... Some theorists even maintained that all psychological theories should be explicitly written in the form of computer programs.

Cohen and Feigenbaum identify these theorists as Newell, Simon and Shaw. Cohen and Feigenbaum believe that these theorists' position that computer programs can be psychological theories is the point at which cognitive psychology and information-processing psychology part company. For most cognitive psychologists, information processing is a metaphor for human thought, a means of focusing attention on new and interesting questions about the mind. Cohen and Feigenbaum note that very few cognitive psychologists have implemented information-processing models—programs—of their theories. Even among those who have implemented such models, the strong position that the program is itself a theory is not universally accepted; for example, Anderson and Bower (1973 pp. 142–43) explicitly limit the sense in which their model of human associative memory (HAM) is a theory:

> It is important to be clear about the relationship between the theory and this simulation program. We make no claim that there is any careful correspondence between the step-by-step information processing in the simulation program and in the psychological theory... The claim is sometimes made...that the program is the theory. This is not the case for HAM, and we wish to make this denial explicit. HAM represents a very complicated set of speculations about human memory. Only some of these are

represented in the simulation program. Moreover, the simulation program does not serve as an embodiment of this subset of the theory; rather, it is but one test of the adequacy of that subset.

(The relationship between cognitive psychology and information-processing psychology is discussed in more detail in Newell and Simon (1970) and Miller (1978).)

To complete their historical overview, Cohen and Feigenbaum note the relationship between AI and information-processing psychology. For them, it was summed up nicely by Minsky in his own historical discussion in which he identified three extensions to early work in cybernetics (Minsky 1968 p. 9):

> The first was the continuation of the search for simple basic principles... The second important avenue was an attempt to build working models of human behavior incorporating, or developing as needed, specific psychological theories... The third approach, the one we call *Artificial Intelligence*, was an attempt to build intelligent machines without any prejudice toward making the system simple, biological, or humanoid.

In the words of Cohen and Feigenbaum, AI does not require that an intelligent program should demonstrate human intelligence, but information-processing psychologists insist that the correspondence be proved.

This brief history derived from Cohen and Feigenbaum is almost current; they discuss the common roots of AI, information-processing psychology and cognitive psychology, and the points at which they part company. However, they note that they present the strongest version of the information-processing approach, that advocated by Newell and Simon. The position of the latter is so strong that it defines information-processing psychology almost by exclusion: it is the field that uses methods alien to cognitive psychology to explore questions alien to AI. This is an exaggeration, but it serves to illustrate why there are thousands of cognitive psychologists, hundreds of AI researchers and very few information-processing psychologists. Recently, Cohen and Feigenbaum note, the strong position has been relaxed to admit research that does not necessarily prove the correspondence between programs and human behavior but that has some avowed concern for understanding human behavior. This research is called cognitive science by its practitioners.

5. *Models of Cognition*

Cohen and Feigenbaum (1982) identify a number of models of cognition that, for the most part, have been the basis for cognitive science. Of the eight models they discuss, five are devoted to models of human memory, two to problem solving and one to belief systems. Historically, cognitive psychology has concerned itself almost exclusively with memory, so it is not surprising that it should be a major topic in information-processing psychology. Here, each of these historically significant models are briefly discussed.

The first model discussed by Cohen and Feigenbaum is, appropriately, Newell and Simon's general problem solver (GPS) program. It represents some of the earliest research in information-processing psychology. The program introduces means–ends analysis, which constrains a problem solver to the task of reducing the differences between the current state of a problem and the goal state, or solution. The problem solver often cannot derive a solution immediately from the problem, so it is necessary to transform the problem into some intermediate state from which the solution might be derived. GPS was tested extensively as a theory of human problem solving.

The next model addressed by Cohen and Feigenbaum concerns problem solving; it is a model of opportunistic planning designed by Hayes-Roth and Hayes-Roth (1978). Opportunistic processing involves a flexible control strategy (implemented with a blackboard control structure) that permits planning decisions to be made when the opportunity arises, rather than in a strict order. Hayes-Roth and Hayes-Roth suggest that opportunistic processing is necessary for complex problem solving. Their model was developed specifically as a model of human planning abilities.

About the time that GPS was being implemented, Feigenbaum (1963) was designing the Elementary Perceiver and Memorizer (EPAM) program, the first of the memory models to be considered. This program learns paired-associate nonsense syllables, which have been used in experiments since the end of the nineteenth century, to reduce the effect on memory of the meaning of the material being remembered. Paired associates allow probing: one of a pair of syllables serves as a cue to invoke the memory of the other syllable. Many things can be learned about memory by varying the speed at which syllables are presented, the number that must be remembered or the similarity between the syllables. Feigenbaum modelled learning of the syllables as a process of storing just enough information about a syllable to distinguish it from the other syllables in memory at the time it was stored. Often, this did not require storing the whole syllable; this results in performance on a recall test that is less than perfect and strikingly similar to that of humans on similar tests.

Quillian (1968) developed a model of semantic memory. Conceptually, semantic-memory models are very simple. They can be thought of as graphs, where the points (called nodes) represent concepts and the lines represent relations between the points. The meaning of a concept in a semantic net is represented by its connections (or associations) with other concepts. Cohen and Feigenbaum note that Quillian's model was not developed as a psychological theory originally, but it was the first information-processing model that appeared to be capable of explaining recently discovered and curious effects of meaning on memory; for example, the category-size effect, whereby it takes longer to classify objects that are members of small classes.

Cohen and Feigenbaum see the MEMOD model developed by Rumelhart et al. (1972) as much more ambitious than Quillian's model. In the first place, it is intended to be a model of human memory that captures some of the richness of language. This requires three types of nodes, instead of just the one "concept" node of Quillian. Nodes represent concepts, but also episodes and events. Episode nodes can be the superordinate nodes of complex events like stories; moreover, MEMODs interpreter can "run" these events to simulate them. Episode nodes can designate arbitrary procedures that the interpreter can execute. The MEMOD model also permits a large number of relations between nodes, whereas Quillian had only about half a dozen. Furthermore, relations in this model have a case structure which is similar to that of Fillmore. Cohen and Feigenbaum believe that another improvement over Quillian's model was the introduction of more powerful interpretive procedures; semantic-net models only represent information. Interpretive procedures are required to manipulate this information.

The HAM model of Anderson and Bower (1973) is also a model of human long-term memory, but Cohen and Feigenbaum note that it differs in a number of important respects from MEMOD. Although it has a network knowledge base, relations in the network are much simpler than those in MEMOD. They are based on the syntactic categories of a simplified grammar of English that is used to interact with the system. Another difference between the two systems is that in HAM, arbitrary procedures cannot be written and the simple procedures that are used reside outside of the network. Anderson and Bower take the position that experimental data from the memory literature can be explained by a relatively simple strategy-free process.

Later work performed by Anderson (1980) on his ACT system is next discussed by Cohen and Feigenbaum. The ACT model uses a propositional semantic-network knowledge base, similar to that of HAM. It has, in addition, a procedural component to operate on the knowledge base. Procedures, represented by a production system, are written by the user of ACT. This feature makes ACT rather like the MEMOD system in that both provide a language for their users to build computer models of psychological processes. The major differences between the systems arise from the way in which procedures are represented and from the interpreter which controls the flow of computation in the systems.

Finally, belief systems are considered by Cohen and Feigenbaum; in particular, the model of ideological oversimplification designed by Abelson (1973). This model has a representation of beliefs that affect the interpretation of sentences. Cohen and Feigenbaum use the following example: a "typical liberal" would interpret a national event, like Congress appropriating money for urban redevelopment, in a different way than would a "typical conservative." Abelson was the first to discuss differences between belief systems and the knowledge-based expert systems that are current in AI.

Abelson (1979) outlined a number of peculiarities that set beliefs apart from facts and that distinguish belief systems from other systems in AI:

(a) Belief systems are not consensual. Different beliefs may result in different interpretations of the same phenomena.

(b) Beliefs deal with conceptual entities such as the generation gap, the supernatural and extrasensory perception.

(c) Sometimes belief systems represent alternative "worlds," typically, "the world as it should be."

(d) Beliefs have an evaluative or affective component. Events tend to be good or bad, and evoke pleasure or displeasure, etc.

6. Research at the Boundary of HIP and AI

Five research areas are overviewed in three clusters by Cohen and Feigenbaum (1982). These research areas are those that sit on the boundary of AI and cognitive psychology, the study of HIP. As such, these areas have contributed to progress in both fields specifically, as well as in cognitive science and computer science in general. For much more detailed reviews of these research areas, see Cohen and Feigenbaum (1982 Chaps. 12, 14, 15)

6.1 Automatic Deduction

Much of human thought involves manipulating knowledge structures to draw conclusions of various kinds. We decide what to do next, we predict what is likely to happen, we figure out why a certain event occurred, and so on. The general knowledge structures hypothesized by the various researchers identified in Sect. 5 give a reasonably good account of much of this reasoning. General concepts and schemas allow us to predict the properties of particular objects and to plan our actions during everyday activities. Much of the knowledge that we need is stored directly and activated by cues present in relevant contexts.

Cohen and Feigenbaum (1982) identify a central problem in AI research: how can it be made possible for computers to draw conclusions automatically from bodies of facts? Any attempt to address this problem requires choosing an application, a representation for bodies of facts and methods for deriving conclusions. This section provides an overview of the issues involved in drawing conclusions by means of deductive inference from bodies of commonsense knowledge represented by logical formulas. The history of automatic deduction is briefly reviewed—its origins, its fall into disfavor and its recent revival.

Automatic deduction, or mechanical theorem proving, has been a major concern of AI since its earliest days. Cohen and Feigenbaum (1982) note that at the first formal conference on AI, held at Dartmouth College in the summer of 1956, Newell and Simon (1956) discussed LT, a deduction system for propositional logic. Minsky was concurrently developing the ideas that were later embodied in Gelernter's theorem prover for elementary geometry (see Gelernter 1963, McCorduck 1979 p. 106). Shortly after this, Wang (1960) produced the first implementation of a reasonably efficient, complete algorithm for proving theorems in propositional logic.

Following these early efforts, the next important step identified by Cohen and Feigenbaum in the development of automatic-deduction techniques was Robinson's description of a relatively simple, logically complete method for proving theorems in first-order predicate calculus (Robinson 1965). Robinson's procedure and those derived from it are usually referred to as resolution procedures because the basic rule of inference they use is the resolution principle:

From $(A \vee B)$ and $(\neg A \vee C)$, infer $(B \vee C)$

According to Cohen and Feigenbaum, Robinson's work had a major influence on two somewhat distinct lines of research. One of these was mathematical theorem proving, which aims to provide practical tools for discovering new results in mathematics. Cohen and Feigenbaum write: "But Robinson's work also had a major impact on research into commonsense reasoning and problem solving. His ideas in this area brought about a rather dramatic shift in attitudes toward automatic deduction. The early attempts at automatic theorem-proving were generally thought of as exercises in expert problem solving: the Logic Theorist was regarded as an expert in propositional logic and Gelernter's program was considered an expert in geometry. However, the resolution method seemed powerful enough to make it possible to build a completely general problem-solver by describing problems in first-order logic and deducing solution by a general proof procedure."

Cohen and Feigenbaum believe that the idea of using formal logic as a representation scheme and deductive inference as a reasoning method was first suggested as an approach to commonsense reasoning and problem solving by McCarthy in 1959, in his "advice taker" proposal (McCarthy 1968). Black (1968) made the first serious attempt to implement McCarthy's idea in 1964. Cohen and Feigenbaum note that Robinson's work provided encouragement for this approach, and that a few years later Green (1969) carried out extensive experiments with a question-answering and problem-solving system based on resolution.

The results of Green's experiments and several similar projects were disappointing, however. Cohen and Feigenbaum believe that the difficulty was that, in the general case, the search space generated by the resolution method grows exponentially with the number of formulas used to describe a problem; hence, problems of even moderate complexity cannot be solved in a reasonable time. Several domain-independent heuristics (e.g., set of support) were proposed to deal with this issue, but they proved too weak to produce satisfactory results.

Cohen and Feigenbaum attempt to explain these difficulties: "It appears that these failures resulted principally from two constraints the researchers had imposed upon themselves. They attempted to use only uniform, domain-independent proof procedures, and they tried to force all reasoning and problem-solving behavior into the framework of logical deduction. Like a number of earlier ideas such as self-organizing systems and heuristic search, automatic theorem-proving turned out not to be the magic formula that would solve all AI problems at once." In the reaction that followed, however, not only was there a turning away from attempts to use deduction to create general problem solvers, but there was also widespread condemnation of any use of logic or deduction in commonsense reasoning or problem solving. Cohen and Feigenbaum note that arguments made by Minsky (1980 Appendix) and Hewitt (Hewitt 1975, Hewitt *et al.* 1973) seem to have been particularly influential in this regard.

Despite the disappointments of the late 1960s and early 1970s, there has recently been a revival of interest in deduction-based approaches to commonsense reasoning. This is apparent in the work of McDermott (1978), Doyle (1979, 1980) and Moore (1980a,b); in the current work on nonmonotonic reasoning (Bobrow 1980); and in recent textbooks by Nilsson (1980) and Kowalski (1979). Cohen and Feigenbaum explain this resurgence in the following manner: "To a large extent, this renewed interest seems to stem from the recognition of an important class of problems that resist solution by any other method."

6.2 Learning and Inductive Inference

Learning is a very general term denoting the way in which people (and computers) increase their knowledge and improve their skills. From the very beginnings of AI, researchers have sought to understand the process of learning and to create computer programs that can learn.

Learning is one of the most difficult issues known to researchers in AI and cognitive science. Stillings *et al.* (1987) believe this is so for two reasons. First, learning subsumes some of the most difficult problems from the other areas of representation, search and control.

A learning system cannot be designed without addressing issues in these areas even if only in the minimal sense of selecting an "off the shelf" method. Second, they note that it is fairly easy to achieve some initial successes with a learning system, but exceedingly difficult to sustain the learning. Stillings *et al.* (1987) elaborate on this problem: "The immediately learned first results are often a direct result of good choices concerning representation, search, and control. This phenomenon can lead to the criticism that the results were "built in" or implicitly already known to the system. Though no one would seriously advocate a program starting with absolutely no knowledge, what counts as too much or just enough is a matter of controversy. In fact, this debate is fundamentally unresolvable in general since one person's (or machine's) learned result can be another's basic fact."

Cohen and Feigenbaum (1982) note two fundamental reasons for studying learning. One is to understand the process itself. By developing computer models of learning, psychologists have attempted to gain an understanding of the way humans learn. Cohen and Feigenbaum note that philosophers since Plato have also been interested in learning research, because it may help them understand what knowledge is and how it grows. The second reason they propose for conducting learning research is to provide computers with the ability to learn. They write: "It has long been a goal of AI to develop computer systems that could be taught rather than programmed. Many other applications of computers, such as intelligent programs for assisting scientists, involve the acquisition of new knowledge. Thus, learning research has potential for extending the range of problems to which computers can be applied."

(a) *A brief history of AI research on learning.* Machine learning has long been a topic of interest. In the 1940s researchers focused on self-organizing systems, stimuli and feedback. Cohen and Feigenbaum (1982) write: "Their hope was that somehow out of an unknowing system possessing some general capabilities would arise knowledge; in this, however, they were disappointed." Cohen and Feigenbaum note that AI research on learning has evolved through three stages. The first, and most optimistic, stage they identify centered on self-organizing systems that modified themselves to adapt to their environments (see Yovits *et al.* 1962). According to Cohen and Feigenbaum, "The hope was that if a system were given a set of stimuli, a source of feedback, and enough degrees of freedom to modify its own organization, it would adapt itself toward an optimum organization." Attempts were made, for example, to simulate evolution in the hope that intelligent programs would result from the processes of random mutation and natural selection (Friedberg 1958, Friedberg *et al.* 1959, Fogel *et al.* 1966). Various computational analogs of neurons were developed and tested; foremost of these was the perceptron (Rosenblatt 1957). Unfortunately, most of these attempts failed to produce systems of any complexity or intelligence.

Stillings *et al.* (1987) note that in the early 1960s there was a transition to using certain AI ideas about memory, search and retrieval for learning. Selfridge's PANDEMONIUM program was one of the earliest efforts; it combined the older technique of adaptive control with newer ideas on learning to tackle the pattern-recognition problem of recognizing letters (Selfridge 1959). This program improved its performance by tuning numerical parameters. It introduced the new idea of an independent knowledge source, called a demon, which "shouts" when it sees something of interest about which it knows something (for instance, A-ness or W-ness). The demon is really a forerunner of the type of knowledge source built into the HEARSAY-II control architecture.

Stillings *et al.* (1987) discuss Samuel's CHECKER-PLAYER which achieved championship-level checker-playing performance and represents another early landmark in research on machine learning (Samuel 1959). The system could learn in two ways: (1) by acquiring knowledge through being told about specific board positions and moves, and then storing them in memory; and (2) by improving its ability to evaluate board positions through tuning of certain parameters. A larger store of memorized positions and better evaluation skill improved system performance because the system could both look up more book moves and look down deeper and more accurately into its game tree. CHECKER-PLAYER emphasized search, rote memorization and adaptive tuning of certain evaluation functions (which could also be viewed as a search through the space of all such functions).

Stillings *et al.* note that theoretical limitations were discovered that dampened the optimism of these early AI researchers (see Minsky and Papert 1969). In the 1960s, attention moved away from learning and toward knowledge-based problem solving and natural-language understanding (Minsky 1968). Those people who continued to work with adaptive systems ceased to consider themselves AI researchers; their research branched off to become a subarea of linear systems theory. Adaptive-systems techniques are presently applied to problems in pattern recognition and control theory.

The beginning of the 1970s saw a renewal of interest in learning with the publication of Winston's influential thesis (Winston 1970). In the second stage of learning research (as identified by Cohen and Feigenbaum), workers adopted the view that learning is a complex and difficult process and that, consequently, a learning system cannot be expected to learn high-level concepts by starting without any knowledge at all. This view has led researchers, on the one hand, to study simple learning problems in depth (such as learning single concepts) and, on the other hand, to incorporate large amounts of domain knowledge into learning systems (such as the META-DENDRAL and AM) programs so that they could discover high-level concepts.

In the 1970s, Winston developed the ARCH-LEARNER which made use of semantic nets. This program was based not on heavy search or numerical tuning but on representation and use of domain knowledge; it heralded the start of a new era in machine learning. Cohen and Feigenbaum observe that this shift in emphasis towards representation was also apparent in the field of AI as a whole. ARCH-LEARNER was instrumental in providing impetus for work in machine learning to focus on issues of concept acquisition and representation, particularly of a symbolic nature as opposed to a numerical nature.

Cohen and Feigenbaum believe that a third stage of learning research, motivated by the need to acquire knowledge for expert systems, is now under way. They write: "Unlike the first two phases of learning research, which focused on rote learning and learning from examples, the current work looks at all forms of learning, including advice-taking and learning from analogies." Stillings *et al.* (1987) provide more details on this stage of learning research. They note that more recently the emphasis in machine learning has been on knowledge-intensive learning and the study of learning algorithms. They perceive that this new era in learning research began with the work of Lenat on the program AM and Mitchell on the program LES. They write: "As we have seen, AM is a program that performs concept discovery in mathematics. Among the key elements of learning, AM emphasizes knowledge acquisition more than improvement in task performance. It never gets better at discovering (and is not supposed to); in fact, its ability to discover interesting new concepts flattens out after its initial rush of successes. (Lenat tried to address this problem in his EURISKO program whose task was to discover the kind of heuristics that made AM successful (Lenat 1983)). LEX is a program that learns how to improve its ability to solve problems in integral calculus by actually working problems. Both programs combine well-explicated search and control schemes with a rich, well-represented base of domain knowledge. LEX also uses a very explicit learning algorithm . . . "

Although they do not consider them all in detail, several other interesting machine-learning programs are mentioned by Stillings *et al.* (1987).

(1) POKER PLAYER (Waterman 1970) learned how to play draw poker; specifically, it learned heuristics for evaluating hands and taking action.

(2) HACKER (Sussman (1975) modelled the acquisition of programming skills, particularly concerning generalizing and debugging subroutines.

(3) META-DENDRAL (Buchanan and Mitchell 1978) worked as a learning element for DENDRAL, a program that inferred the chemical structure of a substance from its chemical formula and mass spectrogram, to discover cleavage rules for molecules.

(4) BASEBALL (Soloway 1978) learned concepts like "base hit" and "double play" by interpreting noise-free snapshots of baseball games showing the location of the players, the location of the ball, the score and so forth.

Today the field of machine learning is extremely active. Much of the work investigates different algorithms and control structures for learning, and relies on already understood search and representation techniques. The ideas of numerical adaptation and small independent knowledge sources or agents have also enjoyed renewed attention in what is now called connectionist learning. Below, four perspectives on learning are briefly presented.

(*b*) *Four perspectives on learning.* Cohen and Feigenbaum (1982) first note that Herbert Simon defines learning as any process by which a system improves its performance. His definition assumes that the system has a task that it is attempting to perform. It may improve its performance by applying new methods and knowledge or by improving existing methods and knowledge to make them faster, more accurate or more robust.

A more constrained view of learning, according to Cohen and Feigenbaum, which is adopted by many people who work on expert systems, is that learning is the acquisition of explicit knowledge. Many expert systems represent their expertise as large collections of rules that need to be acquired, organized and extended. This view emphasizes the importance of making the acquired knowledge explicit, so that it can be easily verified, modified and explained. Researchers are presently working on knowledge-acquisition systems that discover new rules from examples or accept new rules from experts and integrate them into the knowledge base of the system.

The third view that Cohen and Feigenbaum present is that learning is skill acquisition. Psychologists have pointed out that long after people are told how to do a task, such as touch typing or computer programming, their performance on that task continues to improve through practice (Norman 1980). Cohen and Feigenbaum write: "It appears that although people can easily understand verbal instructions on how to perform a task, much work remains to be done to turn that verbal knowledge into efficient mental or muscular operations. Researchers in AI and cognitive psychology have sought to understand the kinds of knowledge that are needed to perform skillfully. The processes by which people acquire this knowledge through practice are little understood."

The collective enterprise of science is usually considered to be one of the most effective ways that our culture learns about the world. Thus, Cohen and Feigenbaum's fourth view of learning is that it comprises theory formation, hypothesis formation and inductive inference. They write: "Work on theory formation has centered on understanding how scientists build theories to describe and explain complex phenomena. A necessary part of theory formation is hypothesis formation—the activity of finding one or more plausible hypotheses to explain a particular set of data in the context of a more general theory. Another aspect of theory formation is inductive inference—the process of inferring general laws from particular examples."

(c) Key questions about learning. According to Stillings *et al.* (1987), learning concerns how a system gets "better" in the sense of knowing more and being able to do more. To them, sometimes this means "merely" acquiring new facts; sometimes it entails reorganizing the knowledge base or the structure of the program itself. Most frequently it means performing a task better. Learning is a very rich and exceedingly important topic that touches on important issues from psychology and epistemology. According to Stillings *et al.* (1987), some of the key questions about learning from the AI point of view are as follows.

(1) What primitive capabilities and knowledge does the learning system possess?

(2) How are new knowledge and capabilities acquired and molded into those already known to the learning system?

(3) What is the role of the teacher (for instance, as critic) in the system's learning?

(4) What is the role of examples or experiences presented to the learning system?

Stillings *et al.* (1987) elaborate on these questions:

> Question 1 addresses the baseline of performance that the learning system is to start with. It clearly cannot start with nothing—but how much is enough, and how much is too much? This issue is often the focus of attacks on learning systems ("The system knew it all along"), and there is no simple analysis of it, as any philosopher or AI researcher will attest. Question 2 addresses issues of acquisition and improvement. Once the base for the learning system has been established, how should it go about acquiring new capabilities and improving its performance? Some learning is inductive and based on examples; some proceed by criticizing a problem-solving performance and then refining. Question 2 also addresses the integration of the new knowledge and performance capabilities into the existing system. Questions 1 and 2 therefore address what could be called the basic learning cycle: start, acquire, revise, improve. Questions 3 and 4 single out two other important issues. Question 3, on the role of the teacher in (or when absent, the self-direction of) the system, has long been recognized, as it has been in psychological studies of learning. Question 4, on the role of examples, has been too long overlooked but is now more consciously addressed. Examples provide grist for the mill of learning, and without them almost all learning systems could not function.

(d) General issues in learning. Stillings *et al.* (1987) identify a slightly different set of key general issues in learning. According to them, in discussing a learning system, several clusters of questions are relevant.

(1) *What is the computational architecture of the learning system?* Which component actually does the learning? What component critiques the performance so that the learning component can improve it? What knowledge does the system possess?

(2) *What is the role and source of examples?* How are examples, or "training instances," used to drive the learning system? Who provides them: an external or an internal teacher? What properties do or should they have? What kinds are there? How are they organized? How are they generated? How is their order of presentation determined?

(3) *What types of learning is the system capable of?* Does the system learn by rote memorization or by being told exactly what to do? Can it fill in missing details or handle unreliable data? Can it use analogy? Can it take advice? Does it learn incrementally from one example at a time or does it proceed by induction from a set of examples taken all at once?

(4) *What is the influence of the initial knowledge?* What conceptual and representational primitives does the system start with? At what level and in what detail is the knowledge represented? Is the domain knowledge hierarchical? Is there an inherent bias in the concept-description language and can it be shifted when appropriate?

(5) *What learning algorithms are used?* How does the learning system generalize or specialize, carry out induction, or otherwise modify or improve itself?

Even this handful of questions raises an abundance of interesting learning issues. In addition, there is the issue always present with AI systems of how to judge the success of the effort: how do we know if a system has successfully learned? As usual, various approaches are possible.

The key questions and general issues in learning which are identified above obviously focus on both how the HIP system functions and how we might best construct AI machine-learning systems. Research in both HIP and AI is focused on providing the answers to these and other key questions. The problem of learning stands out as a core issue for both cognitive and computer science.

6.3 Planning and Problem Solving

Cohen and Feigenbaum (1982) offer an excellent summary of research on planning and problem solving. According to them, problem solving is the process of developing a sequence of actions to achieve a goal. Their broad definition admits all goal-directed AI programs to the ranks of problem solvers; examples that Cohen and Feigenbaum provide include MYCIN which solves the problem of determining a bacteremia infection, HARPY which solves the problem of understanding speech signals and AM which solves the problem of filling in slots in its representations of concepts.

According to Cohen and Feigenbaum, planning means deciding on a course of action before acting. They believe that this definition accurately describes most planning systems. To them a plan is, thus, a representation of a course of action. It can be an unordered list of goals, such as a grocery list, but usually a plan has an implicit ordering of its goals; for example, most people plan to get dressed to go to the theater, not the other way around. Many plans include steps that are vague and require further specification. These serve as place holders in a plan; for example, a daily plan includes the goal "eat lunch," although the details—where to eat, what to eat, when to leave—are not specified. The detailed plan associated with eating lunch is a subplan of the overall daily plan. Cohen and Feigenbaum note that most plans have a rich subplan structure; each goal in a plan can be replaced by a more detailed subplan to achieve it. Although a finished plan is a linear or partial ordering of problem-solving operators, the goals achieved by the operators often have a hierarchical structure (see Fig. 1). This aspect of plans prompted one of the earliest definitions (Miller et al. 1960 p. 16):

> A Plan is any hierarchical process in the organism that can control the order in which a sequence of operations is to be performed.

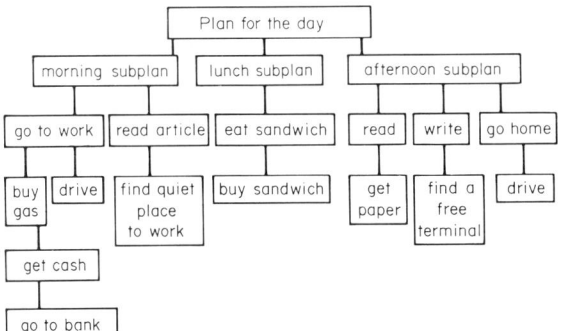

Figure 1
Plan for a day illustrating the hierarchical structure of subplans (after Cohen and Feigenbaum (1982).
© Kaufmann, Los Altos, California. Reproduced with permission)

Stillings et al. (1987) note that reasoning (deductive and nondeductive) and problem solving overlap considerably, and some researchers have attempted to combine theories of the two processes (see, for example, Stillings 1975; Newell 1980). They write: "Researchers typically speak of problem solving, as opposed to reasoning, when the needed principles are more specific to a domain (such as chess, sewing, or physics) and when the information processing needed to reach the desired goal takes place over an extended period of time. Some of the most interesting findings concern the contrast between novice and expert problem solving. The general theory of the acquisition of cognitive skills gives a good account of the striking improvements that occur when a person practises solving problems in a particular domain."

(a) *Overview of planning and problem solving.* Cohen and Feigenbaum (1982) observe that failure to plan can result in less than optimal problem solving; one may go to the library twice, for example, having failed to plan to borrow a book and return another at the same time. Moreover, in cases where goals are not independent, these authors note that failing to plan before acting may actually preclude a solution to the problem. They provide the following example: the goal of building a house includes the subgoals of installing a dry wall and installing electrical wiring, but these goals are not independent. The wiring must be installed first; otherwise, the dry wall will be in the way.

Cohen and Feigenbaum write: "Plans can be used to monitor progress during problem solving and to catch errors before they do too much harm. This is especially important if the problem solver is not the only actor in the problem solver's environment and if the environment can change in unpredictable ways. Consider the example of a roving vehicle on a distant planet: It must be able to plan a route and then replan if it finds that the state of the world is not as it expected. Feedback about the state of the world is compared with what is predicted by the plan, which can then be modified in the event of discrepancies." This topic is discussed more fully in Sacerdoti (1975). The benefits of planning can be summarized as reducing search, resolving goal conflicts and providing a basis for error recovery.

(b) *Approaches to Planning.* Four distinct approaches to planning are discussed by Cohen and Feigenbaum (1982): nonhierarchical planning, hierarchical planning, script-based planning and opportunistic planning. Cohen and Feigenbaum resolve a confusing ambiguity in the word hierarchical. The vast majority of plans have nested subgoal structures —hierarchical structures—as shown in Fig. 1. However, the word has another interpretation, one that provides the basis for distinguishing hierarchical from nonhierarchical planning. The distinction is that hierarchical planners generate a hierarchy of representations of a plan in which the highest is a simplification, or abstraction, of the plan and the lowest is a detailed plan, sufficient to solve the problem. In contrast, nonhierarchical planners have only one representation of a plan. Cohen and Feigenbaum note that both kinds of planners generate plans with hierarchical subgoal structures, but only hierarchical planners utilize a hierarchy of representations of the plan. This distinction is discussed further by Cohen and Feigenbaum in an article in which STRIPS (a nonhierarchical planner) and ABSTRIPS (the hierarchical extension of STRIPS) are compared.

Cohen and Feigenbaum explain: "Nonhierarchical planning corresponds roughly to the colloquial meaning of planning; that is, a nonhierarchical planner develops a sequence of problem-solving actions to achieve each of its goals. It may reduce goals to simpler ones, or it may use means–ends analysis to reduce the differences between the current state of the world and that would hold after the problem has been solved. Examples of nonhierarchical planners are STRIPS, HACKER, and INTERPLAN."

Cohen and Feigenbaum believe that the major disadvantage of nonhierarchical planning is that it does not distinguish between problem-solving actions that are critical to the success of a plan and those that are simple details. As a result, plans developed by nonhierarchical planners get bogged down in unimportant details. In any plan there are levels of detail that are too specific or too vague and a level of detail that is appropriate for the problem; for example, a too-detailed plan for dinner starts with "Go to the table, sit down, unfold the napkin, pour a glass of water, find matches, light the candles . . ." A too-vague plan is "Sit down somewhere, have food." According to Cohen and Feigenbaum, planning with too many details is a waste of effort, but plans that are too vague do not specify which problem-solving operators should be used: "A balance between these extremes is necessary for efficient planning." To this end, the method of hierarchical planning has been implemented in a number of planning systems. The method is first to sketch a plan that is complete but too vague and then to refine the vague parts of the plan into more detailed subplans until finally the plan has been refined to a complete sequence of detailed problem-solving operators. Cohen and Feigenbaum believe that the advantage of this approach is that the plan is first developed at a level at which the details are not computationally overwhelming.

Cohen and Feigenbaum observe that hierarchical planning also takes several forms in these systems. One approach they identify, typified by the ABSTRIPS program, is to determine which subgoals are critical to the success of the plan and to ignore, at least initially, all others. (In ABSTRIPS, a detail is a subgoal for which a subplan can be found if plans have been found to accomplish goals that are not details.) They provide the following example. The problem of buying a piano cannot be solved unless two subgoals are accomplished; namely, "locate piano" and "get money." Thus, an intimal plan for buying a piano might simply be "locate piano, get money, buy piano." Subsequently, this plan can be refined with inessential details, such as "drive to the store and select piano." As Cohen and Feigenbaum note, ABSTRIPS plans in a hierarchy of abstraction spaces, the highest of which contains a plan which is devoid of all unimportant details and the lowest of which contains a complete and detailed sequence of problem-solving operators. They believe that the advantage of considering the critical subgoals before the details is that it reduces search: "By ignoring details, one effectively reduces the number of subgoals to be accomplished in any given abstraction space."

Cohen and Feigenbaum note that hierarchical planning was implemented in its earliest form by Newell and Simon (1972 pp. 429–35) in their GPS model of theorem proving in logic. They write: "The GPS approach was slightly different from that of ABSTRIPS. In ABSTRIPS, a hierarchy of abstraction spaces is defined by treating some goals as more important than others, while in GPS there was a single abstraction space defined by treating one representation of the problem as more general than others. GPS planned in an abstraction space defined by replacing all logical connectives by a single abstract symbol. The original problem space defined four logical connectives, but many problem-solving operators were applicable to any connective. Thus, it could be treated as a detail and abstracted out of the formulation for the problem. A problem could be solved in the abstraction space, the space with only one connective, and the solution could be mapped back into the original four-connective space."

Subsequent implementations of the hierarchical planning approach such as NOAH and MOLGEN are, according to Cohen and Feigenbaum, slightly different from either ABSTRIPS or GPS. They write: "ABSTRIPS abstracted critical goals, and GPS abstracted a more general representation of an aspect of its problem space. NOAH abstracts problem-solving operators; it plans initially with generalized operators that it later refines to problem-solving operators given in its problem space. MOLGEN goes one step further, abstracting both the operators and the objects in its problem space." In all cases, however, they note that hierarchical planning involves defining and planning in one or more abstraction spaces. A plan is first generated in the highest, most abstract space; this constitutes the skeleton onto which details are fleshed out in lower abstraction spaces. Hierarchical planning provides a means of ignoring the details that obscure or complicate a solution to a problem.

A third approach to planning identified by Cohen and Feigenbaum also makes use of skeleton plans but, unlike hierarchical planning, these skeletons are recalled from a store of plans rather than being generated. This approach was adopted in one of the MOLGEN systems. The stored plans contain the outlines for solving many different kinds of problems. They range in detail from extremely specific plans for common problems to very general plans for broad classes of problems. The planning process is explained by Cohen and Feigenbaum in two steps: first, a skeleton plan is found that is applicable to the given problem and second, the abstract steps in the plan are filled in with problem-solving operators from the particular problem context. This instantiation process involves large amounts of domain-specific knowledge, often working through several levels of generality until a problem-solving operator is found to accomplish each skeleton-plan step. If a suitable instantiation is found for each abstracted step, the plan as a whole will be successful. Cohen and Feigenbaum point out that this approach has much in common with that of Schank and Abelson (1977). Their approach to natural-language understanding is to use stored scripts (and other more sophisticated structures) to provide top-down expectations about the course of a story.

Cohen and Feigenbaum discuss a fourth approach to planning which has been found by Hayes-Roth and Hayes-Roth (1978) in human planning. It is described as opportunistic and is characterized by a more flexible control strategy than is found in the other approaches. The Hayes-Roths have adopted a blackboard control structure to model human planning. The blackboard is a "clearinghouse" for suggestions about plan steps, suggestions that are made by planning specialists. Cohen and Feigenbaum explain the blackboard as follows: "Each specialist is designed to make a particular kind of planning decision. Specialists do not operate in any particular order; the asynchrony of planning decisions that are made only when there is reason to do so gives rise to the term opportunistic. In the Hayes-Roths' model, and apparently in human planning, the ordering of operators that characterizes a plan is developed piecewise—the plan "grows out" from concrete clusters of problem-solving operators."

Opportunistic planning includes a bottom-up component; it is driven by opportunities to include detailed problem-solving actions in the developing plan. It contrasts with the top-down refinement process which is characteristic of hierarchical planning, where detailed problem-solving actions are not decided until the last possible moment in developing the plan. Another difference between opportunistic planning and other forms noted by Cohen and Feigenbaum (1982) is that it can develop islands of planning actions—parts of a plan—independently, while hierarchical planners try to develop an entire plan at each level of abstraction. The Hayes-Roths' model is intended as a model of human planning abilities.

See also: Artificial Intelligence; Human Information Processing

Bibliography

Abelson R P 1973 The structure of belief systems. In: Schank R C, Colby K M (eds.) *Computer Models of Thought and Language.* Freeman, San Francisco, California

Abelson R P 1979 Differences between belief and knowledge systems. *Cognit. Sci.* **3**, 355–66

Anderson J R 1980 On the merits of ACT and information-processing psychology: A response to Wexler's review. *Cognition* **8**, 73–88

Anderson J R, Bower G H 1973 *Human Associative Memory.* Winston, Washington, DC

Black F 1968 A deductive question-answering system. In: Minsky M (ed.) *Semantic Information Processing.* MIT Press, Cambridge, Massachusetts, pp. 354–402

Bobrow D G (ed.) 1980 Special issue on non-monotonic logic. *Artif. Intell.* **13**(1,2)

Buchanan B G, Mitchell T M 1978 Model-directed learning of production rules. In: Waterman D A, Hayes-Roth F (eds.) *Pattern-Directed Inference Systems.* Academic Press, New York, pp. 297–312

Cherry C 1970 *On Human Communication.* MIT Press, Cambridge, Massachusetts

Cohen P R, Feigenbaum E A 1982 *The Handbook of AI.* Kaufmann, Los Altos, California

Doyle J 1979 A truth maintenance system. *Artif. Intell.* **12**, 231–72

Doyle J 1980 A model for deliberation, action, and introspection, Doctoral dissertation, Technical Report No. A1-TR-581. Massachusetts Institute of Technology, Cambridge, Massachusetts

Feigenbaum E A 1963 The simulation of verbal learning behavior. In: Feigenbaum E A, Feldman J (eds.) *Computers and Thought.* McGraw–Hill, New York, pp. 297–309

Fogel L J, Owens A J, Walsh M J 1966 *Artificial Intelligence Through Simulated Evolution.* Wiley, New York

Friedberg R M 1958 A learning machine: Part 1. *IBM J. Res. Dev.* **2**, 2–13

Friedberg R M, Dunham B, North J H 1959 A learning machine: Part 11. *IBM J. Res. Dev.* **3**, 282–87

Gelernter H 1963 Realization of a geometry theorem-proving machine. In: Feigenbaum E A, Feldman J (eds.) *Computers and Thought.* McGraw–Hill, New York, pp. 134–52

Green C 1969 Theorem-proving by resolution as a basis for question-answering systems. In: Meltzer, B, Michie D (eds.) *Machine Intelligence 4.* Elsevier, New York, pp. 183–205

Hayes-Roth B, Hayes-Roth F 1978 Cognitive processes in planning, Report No. R-2366-ONR. Rand Corporation, Santa Monica, California

Hewitt C 1975 How to use what you know. *IJCAI* **4**, 189–98

Hewitt C et al. 1973 A universal modular actor formalism for artificial intelligence. *IJCAI* **3**, 235–45

Kowalski R 1979 *Logic for Problem Solving.* Elsevier, New York

Lenat D B 1983 EURISKO: A program that learns new heuristics and domain concepts. The nature of heuristics III: Program design and results. *Artif. Intell.* **21**, 61–98

McCarthy J 1968 Programs with common sense. In: Minsky M (ed.) *Semantic Information Processing*. MIT Press, Cambridge, Massachusetts, pp. 403–9

McCorduck P 1979 *Machines who Think*. Freeman, San Francisco, California

McDermott D 1978 Planning and acting. *Cognit. Sci.* **2**, 71–109

Miller G A 1956 The magical number seven, plus or minus two: Some limits of our capacity for processing information. *Psychol. Rev.* **63**, 81–97

Miller G A, Galanter E, Pribram K H 1960 *Plans and the Structure of Behavior*. Holt, New York

Miller L 1978 Has artificial intelligence contributed to an understanding of the human mind? A critique of arguments for and against. *Cognit. Sci.* **2**, 111–27

Minsky M L (ed.) 1968 *Semantic Information Processing*. MIT Press, Cambridge, Massachusetts

Minsky M L 1980 A framework for representing knowledge. In: Haugeland J (ed.) *Mind Design: Philosophy, Psychology, and Artificial Intelligence*. Bradford Books, Montgomery, Vermont

Minsky M L, Papert S 1969 *Perceptions: An Introduction to Computational Geometry*. MIT Press, Cambridge, Massachusetts

Moore R C 1980a Reasoning about knowledge and action, Technical Note 191. AI Center, SRI International, Menlo Park, California

Moore R C 1980b *Reasoning from Incomplete Knowledge in a Procedural Deduction System*. Farland, New York

Neisser U 1976 *Cognition and Reality*. Freeman, San Francisco, California

Newell A 1980 Reasoning, problem solving, and decision processes: The problem space as a fundamental category. In: Nickerson R S (ed.) *Attention and Performance VIII*. Erlbaum, Hillsdale, New Jersey

Newell A, Simon H A 1956 The logic theory machine. *IRE Trans. Inf. Theory* **2**, 61–79

Newell A, Simon H A 1963 Computers in psychology. In: Luce R D, Bush R R, Galanter E (eds.) *Handbook of Mathematical Psychology*, Vol. 1. Wiley, New York, pp. 361–428

Newell A, Simon H A 1970 Remarks on the relationship between artificial intelligence and cognitive psychology. In: Banerji R B, Mearovic M D (eds.) *Theoretical Approaches to Non-Numerical Problem Solving*. Springer-Verlag, Berlin

Newell A, Simon H A 1972 *Human Problem Solving*. Prentice–Hall, Englewood Cliffs, New Jersey

Nilsson N J 1980 *Principles of Artificial Intelligence*. Tioga, Palo Alto, California

Norman D A 1980 Twelve issues for cognitive science. *Cognit. Sci.* **4**, 1–32

Quillian M R 1968 Semantic memory. In: Minsky M (ed.) *Semantic Information Processing*. MIT Press, Cambridge, Massachusetts, pp. 216–70

Robinson J A 1965 A machine-oriented logic based on the resolution principle. *J. Assoc. Comput. Mach.* **12**, 23–41

Rosenblatt F 1957 The perception: A perceiving and recognizing automaton, Report No. 85-460-1, Project PARA. Cornell Aeronautical Laboratory, Ithaca, New York.

Rumelhart D E, Lindsay P H, Norman D A 1972 A process model for long-term memory. In: Tulving E, Donaldson W (eds.) *Organization and Memory*. Academic Press, New York, pp. 198–246

Sacerdoti E D 1975 A structure for plans and behavior, Doctoral dissertation, Technical Note 109, AI Center, SRI International, Menlo Park, California

Samuel A L 1959 Some studies in machine learning using the game of checkers. *IBM J. Res. Dev.* **3**: 210–29 (reprinted in: Feigenbaum E A, Feldman J (eds.) 1963 *Computers and Thought*. McGraw–Hill, New York, pp. 71–105)

Schank R C, Abelson R P 1977 *Scripts, Plans, Goals, and Understanding*. Erlbaum, Hillsdale, New Jersey

Selfridge O G 1959 PANDEMONIUM: A paradigm for learning. In: *Proc. Symp. Mechanisation of Thought Processes*, National Physical Laboratory, Teddington, UK

Shannon C E, Weaver W 1963 *The Mathematical Theory of Communication*. University of Illinois Press, Urbana, Illinois

Skinner B F 1976 *About Behaviorism*. Vintage Books, New York

Soloway E M 1978 Learning interpretation generalization: A case study in knowledge-directed learning, Report No. COINS-TR-78-13. University of Massachusetts, Amherst, Massachusetts

Stillings N A 1975 Meaning rules and systems of inference for verbs of transfer and possession. *J. Verbal Learn. Verbal Behav.* **14**, 453–70

Stillings N A, Neil A, Feinstein M H, Garfield J, Rissland E L, Rosenbaum D A, Weisler S E, Baker-Ward L 1987 *Cognitive Science—An Introduction*. MIT Press, Cambridge, Massachusetts

Sussman G J 1975 *A Model of Skill Acquisition*. Elsevier, New York

Wang H 1960 Toward mechanical mathematics. *IBM J. Res. Dev.* **4**, 2–22

Waterman D A 1970 Generalization learning techniques for automating the learning of heuristics. *Artif. Intell.* **1**, 121–70

Winston P H 1970 Learning structural descriptions from examples, Report No. TR-231. Massachusetts Institute of Technology, Cambridge, Massachusetts (reprinted in: Winston P H (ed.) 1975 *The Psychology of Computer Vision*. McGraw–Hill, New York, pp. 157–209)

Yovits M C, Jacobi G T, Goldstein G D (eds.) 1962 *Self-Organizing Systems 1962*. Spartan Books, Washington, DC

M. L. Donnell
[Donnell and Associates Inc., McLean, Virginia, USA]

Collective Enquiry

The identification or formulation of an issue or problem is a very necessary first step in any problem-solving process. A problem statement should always be identified prior to the application of solution methods. Often, there is considerable merit in identifying the problem in terms of a number of interdependent elements that can be characterized as one or more of the issue formulation elements. These include: problem definition elements (needs, constraints, alterables); value system design elements (objectives or objective measures); or system-synthesis elements (activities or controls and activity measures). Frequently a problem is energetically attacked only for it to be found that an immature issue formulation effort has led to solution of the wrong problem.

The first section of this article discusses four generating or issue formulation methods which may be used to aid a decision group in beginning to formulate the problem or issue chosen for study. These methods are known as collective enquiry methods. They are by no means a panacea and should be called upon only after simple conversational exchange of thoughts and ideas becomes inadequate, or is not possible. Each technique involves a group of persons and leads to the generation of ideas. After describing the four methods, some concerns regarding their use and associated evaluation issues are discussed.

1. Motivation for Collective Enquiry

One of the difficulties in coping with a complex situation is that often there is no individual with sufficient knowledge of the situation to develop a set of elements which describes it. Usually a most difficult problem area concerns the unsatisfactory nature of available information, since data are often incomplete, imprecise, or otherwise imperfect or faulty. Each of these suggests the use of group judgements.

It has often been assumed that "two heads are better than one." It would follow that "n heads are better than $n-1$ heads." Committees, juries, boards of advisors, boards of directors, citizens' groups and the like represent the many mechanisms for pooling the product of wisdom and mental activity to generate ideas and hopefully display either expert knowledge or collective opinion, with each group judgement hopefully having a high probability of being correct.

There are both advantages and disadvantages of relying upon group judgement. A group will interact to balance the bias of individual members of the group, and knowledge of one member of the group may well compensate for ignorance or speculation on the part of other members. It is unfortunately true, however, that "a camel is a horse designed by a committee." Furthermore, opinion can be highly influenced by the individual who talks the loudest and most often. This influence of one or more dominant individuals can be most upsetting to a group, as there is little necessary correlation between loudness or frequency of speech and knowledge. Also, unless the group activity is well organized, a "bull session" may well result in which much more discussion deals with matters of individual and group interest than with the problem at hand. This type of difficulty could well be called "noise." Also, there is often strong pressure for group conformity and avoidance of unpopular or minority viewpoints. Martino (1972) has indicated the following disadvantages to the use of committees to evolve expert opinion.

(a) There is at least as much misinformation available to the committee as there is available to any of its members. Hopefully, the misinformation held by one group member is cancelled out by information held by other group members. However, there is no *a priori* guarantee that this will occur.

(b) A group may exert strong social pressure on its members and encourage all members to agree with the majority even when various individuals feel strongly that the majority view is wrong.

(c) Often, the number and volume of comments and arguments for and against a position will be more influential in determining results than their validity. Again, a strong, loud and vocal majority may overwhelm the group.

(d) The group could be more concerned with reaching agreement than with reaching well-thought-out and useful conclusions. The result is usually very highly axiological views which can offend no one rather than concrete, specific suggestions which may well be unacceptable to some members of the group.

(e) The dominant individual will often have an undue impact on the final results of the group unless there is strong and impartial group leadership. This dominance may be due to active and loud participation, a persuasive personality or extreme persistence.

(f) Hidden intents and vested interests on the part of some group members may lead to a game in which the objective to convince the group of their view, rather than to strive for what might possibly be a better group decision.

(g) The entire group may possess a common bias for a particular culture or technology.

Each of these disadvantages provides much motivation for a search for methods that will result in an emphasis being placed on the meritorious features of group effort and, at the same time, will reduce the potentially damaging aspects of group efforts to the greatest extent.

2. Brainwriting

The brainwriting, or ideawriting, technique of idea generation is based on the premise that group effort toward the generation of ideas may be more effective than individual effort. In a group, the possibility of cross-fertilization of ideas exists because of the creative stimuli provided by the group environment. A unique aspect of brainwriting is that the generation of ideas is conducted separately from the analysis and evaluation of ideas. A brainwriting session is complete when the final list of ideas is compiled. Brainwriting is useful in situations where the following conditions are met:

(a) there is a need and willingness to collect many ideas on some issue,

(b) appropriate participants can be easily brought together to take part in the process, and

(c) it is desirable to eliminate the inhibiting influence of dominant personalities.

The brainwriting method is most often used in the issue formulation step of the systems process. However, it may be useful in any of the systems steps where idea generation is needed. The method is applicable in situations where ideas, in the form of elements, need to be generated and recorded for later evaluation and possible use. For example, at a gathering of experts such as might occur naturally at a workshop or a conference, a side activity might be a brainwriting session. The participants are already together in one location and the opportunity to bring them together again may not present itself or may be quite expensive.

Participants are selected for their motivation, creativity and background knowledge with respect to the issue. It is important to select participants with some stake in the issue, so that motivation to examine ideas concerning alternatives and other issue formulation elements will be high. Also, this generally ensures that a group is knowledgeable about the issue under consideration. The size of the group is typically six to ten people. If more people are available, several parallel sessions might be held. A group leader familiar with the brainwriting method is designated for the instruction and coordination of each group.

Initially, participants are gathered around a table. Each person has paper and writing instruments for recording ideas. The session begins with an explanation of the rules of brainwriting, generally by the facilitator or leader of the effort. Then, a trigger question is posed to the group by the facilitator. The trigger question is a clear, concise, simple question which is stated in such a fashion as to elicit ideas from the panel. It may be productive to hold separate sessions to generate ideas that are responsive to several trigger questions rather than holding one session with a very broad trigger question. In response to the trigger question, each member of the group records several thoughts. After writing a few ideas, the papers are placed in the center of the table in a "kitty," and each member draws out another paper from the kitty. That paper is read by the member, one or two ideas are added to it, the sheet is then put back into the kitty, and another paper is withdrawn. Once an "idea paper" is drawn out of the kitty, the stimulus to write another idea generally comes from the last ideas written on that page. The trigger question is used primarily to initiate the process; however, it is referred back to if a participant loses track of the principal ideas that are contained on the paper.

No talking is allowed. The emphasis is on the silent generation of ideas. This constraint effectively eliminates the interference that can be caused by dominating individuals or personalities. Unfortunately, it may also lead to a very unnatural situation in which open discussion of ideas might be very helpful. The session ends when no new ideas are forthcoming or when an established time constraint is exceeded. Ordinarily, 15–30 min are sufficient to write down the principal ideas which occur in response to a specific trigger question.

Following the formal idea-writing portion of the session, discussion is generally needed to clarify the meaning of some of the ideas. No evaluation or criticism of ideas is appropriate. The discussion is mostly for the purpose of eliminating duplication of ideas, and for providing a preliminary, clarifying analysis of the ideas that have been captured.

There are a number of attributes, or advantages, and also limitations of brainwriting that should be noted. First, brainwriting is especially useful for generating a relatively large quantity of ideas in a short time. Any number of people (preferably placed into groups of not more than six) can generate ideas simultaneously. Ideally, each person's creativity and insight will be stimulated by reading the ideas of other group members. Furthermore, this method encourages everyone to participate simultaneously, hence it may be very efficient. It is, therefore, a good approach when there are time constraints. The brainwriting approach may help to avoid the problem of having certain people dominate the meeting. Moreover, the leader can easily participate in the generation of ideas, because he or she does not need to serve as moderator. Once the process begins, the leader only needs to watch the time and see that each paper is circulated to each person. The leader does not control the generation of ideas, and is anonymous with respect to idea generation.

The limitations of brainwriting are mostly matters of inappropriate use. For example, the process is most effective if one type of idea is generated at a time. This focuses each person's attention. Brainwriting is generally not particularly useful for analysis, evaluation or interpretation; however, it is often an efficient and effective way of identifying and beginning to formulate an issue. This simply means that the process must be followed with, and supported by, efforts to analyze, evaluate and decide how the ideas generated by brainwriting should be used. It is also essential that the preparation of the session be well planned and executed. The trigger question must be carefully formulated, and the participants must understand the process. Finally, it should be noted that anonymity is not always maintained with this method, especially during the discussion phase. While this is not necessarily a problem, special care must be taken if it is important to avoid difficulties due to social pressure and dominant personalities.

Brainwriting produces concrete, specific ideas and suggestions while minimizing the effect of digressions and individual domination that often occur in group discussions. These problems, however, may become manifest in postsession idea analysis, editing and evaluating.

The measures of success in the brainwriting process are straightforward. They relate to the following questions. (a) Were many ideas generated? (b) Were the ideas new or innovative? (c) Did all participants contribute freely to the process?

These can, in turn, be related to three more general questions.

(a) Was each group meeting well structured such that it was competitive, creative, effective, efficient, exciting, organized and participative?
(b) Were the functional components of formulation, analysis and interpretation well executed?
(c) Were the purposes of the meeting achieved in terms of outcome commitment, quality of ideas and preparation of activity for the next meeting?

3. Brainstorming

Brainstorming is a method for stimulating the generation of ideas in a group meeting. Before the meeting, a trigger question is provided to the brainstorming panel, often by means of a brief memo. In the meeting, ideas are expressed verbally and recorded. New ideas are stimulated by previously stated ones. Combination and extension of ideas are encouraged, but criticisms of expressed ideas are not allowed by the leader of the group effort. The result of the session is a long list of ideas or suggestions in direct response to the initial trigger question.

The classical brainstorming exercise involves a small group, a well-defined problem, prior awareness of the problem by the group, a leader, a secretary, and a blackboard. Rules for the exercise, which normally would not last for more than 60–90 min, are that the leader should remind the group of the problem at hand and the rules for brainstorming. He or she will ensure that all participants join in the discussion and will suppress his or her own ideas as long as the group is generating their own; the leader will inject new ideas only when the group does not. No criticism of ideas expressed is allowed. This group is encouraged not to concentrate primarily on thorough presentation of an idea but to keep the ideas short and to develop full details later. The leader writes short, two-word descriptions of all ideas on the blackboard, and the secretary keeps more detailed records. The leader may, if appropriate, reread the ideas and elements described as a means of stimulating new ideas and problem elements.

Many minor variations of this brainstorming exercise may occur. In particular, the participants may supply ideas in writing to the leader prior to the meeting. These ideas would then be presented to the group without necessarily presenting the source of the ideas. The classical brainstorming approach, if conducted by an adroit leader, can minimize disadvantages (a), (e) and (f) in the listing in Sect. 1. Anonymous brainstorming, as just described, should minimize disadvantages (b) and (d) as well. Furthermore, it is possible to modify the exercise by not announcing the problem to the group prior to the meeting. The brainstorming exercise can also be altered by holding a series of meetings. In the first meeting, ideas and elements should be presented and criticized in all possible ways. In later meetings, solutions to difficulties generated in the first meeting could be presented. It is apparent that while this approach could further expose the problem elements, it may well emphasize some of the committee disadvantages noted above. Several other modifications are clearly also possible.

There are advantages and disadvantages to this method. Brainstorming does generate a substantial amount of ideas in a short period of time. It is often more productive, effective and creative than individual idea generation. Furthermore, the resulting list of ideas should reflect the variety of perspectives held by the group members; unfortunately, this does not always occur. Group opinion is likely to be dominated by dominant personal opinions. Group members may also intentionally or unintentionally stray from the main issue of discussion, thereby making the final result less fruitful than it might have been with respect to its original purpose. The group leader's role is, therefore, very important in a brainstorming effort because a carefully formulated trigger question and a well-run meeting can minimize this disadvantage. The quality of ideas generated is the primary indicator of the meeting's value. Hence, the success of a brainstorming session is always dependent on the group members' careful consideration of ideas.

4. Nominal Group Technique

The nominal group technique (NGT) is a structured group approach for the purpose of element or idea generation. In addition to idea generation, NGT is designed to provide for initial screening of ideas. The screening phase consists of a section of the meeting for discussion and clarification, followed by an optimal prioritization of ideas.

Like brainwriting, NGT emphasizes independent or silent idea generation in a group environment. A trigger question which concisely and clearly describes the issue is posed to the group in order to elicit responses in the form of ideas. The process is designed to overcome some of the problems associated with interacting groups, such as unbalanced participation among members or reduced creativity in element generation due to interference from other group members.

The process begins with the six to ten participants, selected on the basis of their background with regard to the issue and their motivation, sitting around a table in plain view of each other. Each participant has writing instruments and paper. The trigger question is posed by the group leader. The group leader is a person selected on the basis of familiarity with NGT and general leadership ability. After hearing the trigger question the group members record a list of ideas on their papers. At the end of a specified time, usually 5–15 min, the "screening" of the generated phase of the NGT process begins. Initially, a structured sharing of ideas takes place in order to clarify, and possibly combine, ideas. This structured sharing of ideas is conducted in a "round robin" fashion, with each member presenting a single idea from their "private list." Ideas are recorded on a flip chart or board by a scribe. This continues until all the ideas are recorded. Each idea is then discussed and clarified. It is possible to record ideas for greater clarity, or to combine very similar ideas. In essence, this discussion step is the first group interface with each individual's private list of ideas and is thus quite different from the efforts in brainwriting.

Evaluation and criticism of ideas are not appropriate during the discussion, or subsequent voting, sections of this exercise. Rank ordering is itself a limited evaluation of the ideas with relation to each other. However, the primary purpose of NGT is to generate a list of ideas for evaluation and not primarily to decide among alternative courses of action. The prioritized list, therefore, indicates the order in which the group feels the ideas ought to be addressed. The list is generally not an indicator of the worth of ideas or elements in resolving the issue under consideration unless the process is specifically guided in that direction by the leader. Generally, this is not an appropriate use of NGT.

A most important step in NGT is the formulation of the trigger question. Unless carefully conceived, problems of interpretation of the question may defeat the intended purpose of the effort. After the trigger question is posed, ideas will be silently generated, and then discussed. Discussion and even preliminary evaluation of these ideas should be postponed until the entire list is compiled. Any discussion or evaluation prior to that stage can lead to intimidation or fear that an idea would be unpopular, and to minimization of combining new ideas with previously stated ones. As a consequence of this, there would be fewer ideas generated than if discussion and evaluation are postponed.

The final step of NGT is one of clarification, amplification and prioritization of generated (and combined) ideas. This phase can very easily enter into an infinite circular loop where discussion of minor points or wording can erode available time. The NGT follows a regulated systemic approach until priority and weights are applied. Members may be inclined to retain "pet" ideas and exclude unpopular ones from further consideration even though further analysis might otherwise prove their worth. Owing to the subjectivity of this final stage, it may be appropriate to terminate the nominal group process after generation of ideas. The measures of success in NGT are similar to those in brainwriting.

5. Delphi

Delphi is a method for systematically developing, gathering and expressing the views of a panel of individuals, generally experts, who interact in an anonymous fashion. This method of idea or opinion gathering is most useful when individuals cannot be easily brought together for a meeting. Participants do not meet and are not known to each other during the course of the exercise. An advantage to the anonymity provided by this method is that it eliminates the overbearing effect of dominant personalities which typically affects a group meeting. Also, members of the panel are more likely to provide true feedback to questions when there is no fear of embarrassment for providing unpopular responses or minority views. The Delphi method may be conducted by mail to eliminate geographical limitations, but since the ideas gathered are in the form of responses to questionnaires, any method of delivering the questionnaires is a potential method for the execution of Delphi. A control and monitor group collects the results of the questionnaires and feeds them back to the panel members along with the next questionnaire. The Delphi technique is applicable whenever expert forecasts, opinions or judgements are needed.

The Delphi process begins with the selection of a group leader and a control and monitoring group. Both are selected based on their genuine interests in the process and its results as well as on the basis of their knowledge of the issue, and perhaps also in their written communication abilities. Each member of the control and monitoring group must have considerable time available to devote to the process. It is this group which develops the questionnaires and formulates the responses to feed back to the panel. Although the control and monitoring group members may not be experts on the issue, each of them must have the ability to write questions which elicit responses useful for the process.

Prior to selecting the participants for the Delphi exercise, the basic issue or question to be resolved must be formulated. This is done by the control and monitoring group and is a particularly crucial step because participant selection is determined by it. In the Delphi method, as with other idea generating methods, the clarity and conciseness of the problem statement is the pivotal element around which the rest of the process revolves.

Selection of panel members is based on their expertise in the issue. It is valuable, because the process is rather lengthy and high motivation is essential, to select stakeholders to the result of the process. Typically, a group of ten to one hundred or so respondents are selected. Each must possess skill in written communication and must have adequate time to participate. A supporting staff to type and mail questionnaires as well as to receive and process results is necessary.

The Delphi process has three fundamental elements: questionnaire writing, response writing, and analysis and compilation of responses. The process occurs iteratively and all responses must be received, tabulated and analyzed before the next questionnaire is written.

In the first iteration, the questionnaire is totally unstructured. The basic issue is provided to the respondent group and a request to discuss elements or make a forecast in connection with the specific issue is made. If the group is very knowledgeable concerning the subject under discussion, this approach to "round one" is most useful in that it allows the group to utilize their expertise to maximum advantage. If the questionnaire is too structured, then the experts might be led to overlook or discount the importance of some aspect of the issue. Once all the respondents have returned their questionnaires, the control group must identify events, elements, forecasts or opinions, and consolidate common items. Responses which are unimportant for the particular purpose of the Delphi process are eliminated at the conclusion of round one.

Round two begins with a questionnaire which asks the group to review the items identified and summarized from the results of round one, and to argue in favor of or against them and possibly to clarify individual issues. The respondents may be asked to establish a priority among items in the questionnaire and to provide estimates of the dates on which events will occur. The primary purpose of round two is to identify agreement and disagreement as well as to initiate an understanding of the priorities. Once all responses are gathered the results must be processed. Specific estimates or priorities may be statistically analyzed. Preparation for the third-round questionnaire is primarily an editing drill in which responses are sorted out and unimportant ones eliminated. The analysis phase of round two must provide a basis for a questionnaire which addresses aggregated group responses.

Round three begins with a questionnaire which asks the group to review their positions from the preceding round in light of the group responses. Questions on which agreement was established in round two may be eliminated from this round and new, more specific questions inserted.

Analysis of the third-round returns usually reveals some convergence toward agreement on the elements remaining in the questionnaire. Iterations are terminated when a sufficient level of convergence is reached. This will depend on the nature of the issue and the statement of each element. Normally, total agreement will not be reached, and in some instances such as when a "policy Delphi" is used, there will be some disagreement based on fundamental beliefs of the respondents with regard to the issue. It is up to the control group to identify the nature of the divergence among group members and correctly terminate the process when the potential for further agreement drops below a certain level.

Portions of the Delphi process are very similar to other idea gathering methods. It is possible to utilize other idea generation methods in conjunction with Delphi to provide such elements as the initial list of ideas from which the problem statement is formulated. Delphi could be used simultaneously with other methods, such as NGT, when certain experts whose opinion is highly valued cannot be present at the nominal group meeting.

In a very real sense, the Delphi exercise is a modification of brainstorming and brainwriting. However, there are two primary variations in Delphi which distinguish it from classical versions of these two techniques.

(a) There are simultaneous individual contributions from each participant at every step, without participants having knowledge of inputs supplied by others for the particular step.

(b) The sources of all inputs are anonymous. This anonymity of input is maintained through the entire group dialogue. Often, it is also desirable to maintain anonymity of the participants throughout the group dialogue.

Three essential features of the Delphi technique make it a generally successful method of soliciting and refining group opinion. These features are the following.

(a) Anonymous response: the use of a formal questionnaire will result in a response from members of the group participating.

(b) Iteration and controlled feedback: Delphi is a systematic exercise which is conducted in several iterations. There is carefully controlled feedback between each of the steps.

(c) Statistical group response: group opinion is defined as an appropriate combination or aggregation of individual opinions at the conclusion of the final iteration.

All of these features are specifically suggested for incorporation into the Delphi approach in an attempt to minimize the biasing effect of irrelevant dialogue between individuals and of group pressure toward conformity. Fundamental to all this is the notion that group interactions concerning the problem of interest will compensate for bias of individual members, and that the knowledge of one or more members of the group will compensate for ignorance on the part of others.

The general outcome, as well as the procedure for using, a Delphi exercise may be summarized as follows.

(a) The first round typically results in a rather wide distribution of individual responses to the questionnaire.
(b) With iteration and feedback provided by each additional round, the distribution of individual responses generally converges.
(c) Generally, the group response becomes more accurate from round to round (accuracy must be defined here as the median of the final individuals' responses). Since we are often talking about future events, there is no way at the present time of reducing inaccuracy to zero.

Dalkey (1969) and Martino (1972) and their references discuss the large number of case studies that have been conducted using the Delphi exercise.

Many variations on the original Delphi approach have been suggested by a number of authors, especially during the period when this was a very active research area. Some of these variations preserve the three fundamental characteristics of a Delphi exercise; anonymity, iteration and statistical response. Other variations result in the modifications of one or more of these characteristics. Some of these variations are as follows.

(a) *Begin with a blank sheet of paper.* The group is now completely unstructured, and no precise guidelines are given concerning how or where to start. The disadvantage of this approach is that the elements, events or forecasts produced by the group may be totally irrelevant to the director and the needs of the director. Also, there is the distinct possibility that an element, event or forecast suggested during the first round may be such that one or more members of the group are relatively inexpert with respect to it and may be, relatively speaking, a lay person with respect to other members of their knowledge of some particular topic on which the individual may be expected to give expert advice. It is possible to start with a list of events, elements or forecasts generated by external processes prior to the Delphi exercise and use this to initiate the Delphi sequence. This is effectively the same as accomplishing round one with one group and then transferring the results from round one to another group to start round two. Of course there are both advantages and disadvantages to using this modification, which will depend upon the particular problem under consideration. If indeed there is more than one group conducting a given Delphi exercise, there is no reason why the same individuals cannot be members of more than one group.

(b) *Individual rating of expertise.* If the problem under consideration is such that the individuals in a group vary considerably in expertise, they may be asked to indicate, according to some agreed scale, their degree of expertise on each question asked of them. Estimates obtained from the individuals would then be combined in a weighted average using this self-rating of expertise as the weights.

(c) *Considerable background material.* Material concerning the problem that members are being asked to discuss, as well as information concerning related problems, may be provided to the group. This will often be advantageous when highly technical sub-problems greatly influence the outcome of the Delphi exercise and when these subproblems are outside the scope of the principal expertise of the individuals constituting the group. For example, in determining futures for oil supply and demand, it might be quite advantageous to inform the group of likely developments in solar energy, particularly if the group is not expert in solar energy development.

(d) *Anonymity can be eliminated.* The purpose of anonymous responses is to allow arguments to be judged solely on their merits. Thus, the influence or position of the originator of an idea is not of material significance in swaying others in a Delphi exercise. In some exercises, however, we may have the unfortunate choice of eliminating some of the anonymity or abandoning the Delphi approach entirely.

(e) *Feedback may be eliminated.* Total elimination of feedback would have the unfortunate result that individual opinion on the second and subsequent rounds might merely represent a repetition of the first response without re-examination of that response. Thus, erroneous responses may well be reinforced through repetition. Sometimes, however, feedback may result in overconvergence to a given median. This will sometimes occur when an individual wishes to avoid providing an argument for not shifting to the median. A possible way of eliminating a portion of the feedback is not to indicate the previous group median to the individual, but only the upper and lower quartile information.

Martino (1972) presents several guidelines for successfully conducting a Delphi exercise. These include:

(a) obtaining from a few individuals willing agreement to serve on the Delphi group;
(b) explaining the Delphi procedure completely to the group;
(c) stating events, elements and forecasts in their simplest form, and avoiding statements involving compound events that are difficult to understand;
(d) avoiding ambiguous statements of events, elements and forecasts;

(e) making the questionnaire as easy as possible;
(f) using no more questions than an individual can adequately consider; and
(g) explaining the reason for inclusion of contradictory events, elements and forecasts so that individuals will not be left feeling that the director includes these for the purpose of trapping them.

In addition, the following must be satisfied.

(h) under no circumstances should the director or facilitator of the Delphi process inject personal opinions into group feedback. The facilitator must not meddle in the deliberation of the group. If the facilitator is convinced that the group overlooks areas of significance or problem areas, then the group output should be discarded and the group considered unqualified. The Delphi exercise should then be repeated with a more qualified group.
(i) compensation of group members for work load involved in a Delphi exercise should be appropriate to the service rendered as well as the type of organization (a profit-making business concern or a nonprofit-making professional society, for example) requesting the Delphi exercise.

6. Benefits of Collective Enquiry Approaches

There exist many routes that may be followed to derive the issue formulation elements (needs, alterables, constraints, objectives and alternatives) of a particular issue. No one individual typically has the necessary or complete knowledge and insight needed for resolution of a large-scale issue. The complexity and interrelatedness of an issue, and the involvement of different groups or sectors may well create a situation where n heads are better than $n-1$ heads (for all n not too large). Therefore, collective enquiry techniques seem to be an appropriate methodology for generating high-quality issue formulation elements.

There are many advantages and disadvantages of group techniques. An optimal group technique would result from a maximization of the advantages and a minimization of the disadvantages of several approaches. This is quantitatively impracticable, but we must nonetheless accept trade-offs or compromises to reach a feasible approach for collective enquiry.

The dynamics of a group will ideally produce more ideas, lessen or eliminate bias (in both questions and answers), and provide open and agreeable interaction processes. Some of the advantages of a group are: a greater sum total of knowledge and information; a greater number of approaches to the problem (participation in decision making increases general acceptance of the final choice), and better comprehension of the decision. Conversely, some disadvantages may be social pressure, individual domination, "winning" the decision, and excessive amiability and *esprit de corps*, all of which may result in the replacement of critical, independent thought by irrational and dehumanizing actions against outgroups. This is known as "groupthink."

7. Evaluation of Collective Enquiry Methods

The success of a group process is evaluated by comparing the end results with the original desires or purposes that led to conduction of the process. The most appropriate of the four methods—brainwriting, brainstorming, NGT or Delphi method—is chosen according to the needs of the situation. Then the members and the group leader are selected. It is important at this stage to choose a leader with the appropriate skills and experience, and to choose a group which can bring a variety of perspectives to the problem or issue. It is not at all necessary, and sometimes it is not even especially desirable, that the leader be extraordinarily knowledgeable in the specific knowledge domain under consideration. However, it is very important that the leader be quite able to work with people who are knowledgeable to assist them in expressing this knowledge. The role of the leader is to assist the group in developing a number of helpful behavioral attributes that will result in a balanced approach to idea generation. Figure 1 indicates some of these issues.

The success of a collective enquiry meeting (or series of anonymous iterations in the case of the Delphi approach) can be evaluated using the following criteria:

(a) Creative: was a summation of creative ideas for the issue compiled?
(b) Effective: were suggestions and conclusions feasible and understanding of the issue increased?
(c) Efficient: were the objectives accomplished within the optimal time span?
(d) Organized: did every member do their job? Together the "whole" team completed the task.
(e) Cooperative: did members work together constructively towards a group goal or did the meeting become an arena for individual competition?
(f) Participative: did every member contribute their knowledge and/or perspective?
(g) All encompassing: did the group overlook relevant items?

After concluding that these criteria were satisfactorily met, the appropriate fundamental components of idea generation (i.e., formulation, analysis and interpretation) also need to be examined to determine if they were well executed. Figure 1 illustrates a methodological framework for group meetings and success

Collective Enquiry

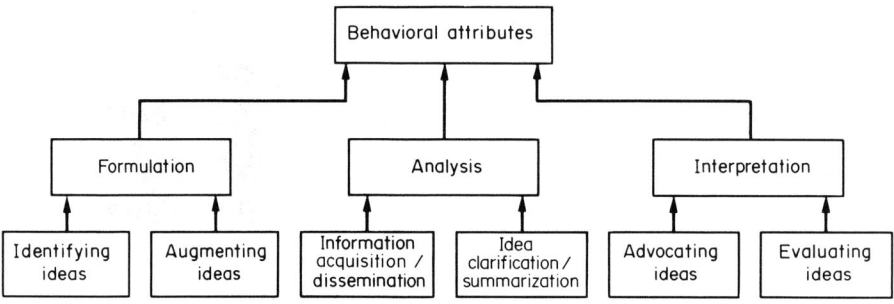

Figure 1
Characteristics of group idea (issue) formulation

may be discussed in terms of this framework. The components may be evaluated as follows.

(a) *Formulation.* Was a descriptive account of the problem attained? Does it seem to be relatively unbiased? Does it reflect input from the whole group? Does it identify sources of problems and needs rather than a simple listing of the symptoms? Are the ideas clearly identified and stated? Are the ideas responsive to the needs of the issue? Has enough information been gathered and disseminated?

(b) *Analysis.* Were forecasts of alternatives or assessment of impacts postulated? Have the ideas been clarified and examined for feasibility or linkages?

(c) *Interpretation.* Were alternatives carefully considered and ranked? Is it clear which activities aim at which objectives? Have utility, feasibility and normative values all been considered? Has a plan been designed for the implementation of chosen alternatives (i.e., has a clear report been made so that the decision maker can plan for action with full knowledge)?

Both the extremes of emphasis and de-emphasis on each of the fundamental components would cause ill effects on a group meeting as indicated in Fig. 2. Therefore, it is appropriate to assign a "weight" to each component of the meeting and each subcomponent as also shown in Fig. 2. According to the appropriate weight that is applied, we must then design the components of the meeting to obtain as high a score as possible for meeting effectiveness. Thus, we have presented a conceptual strategy that may be used both to design collective enquiry approaches and to evaluate the strategy of a specific collective enquiry activity.

Brainstorming, brainwriting and NGT are all appropriate approaches for small group meetings that aim to generate a list of ideas on some topic. They are all, therefore, most appropriately used for issue formulation. In each of these methods, group members respond to a carefully prepared trigger question and hopefully an increased understanding of the issue and a broad range of ideas result from the group interaction. Each method requires a relatively short amount of time. The primary differences result from the various styles of idea presentation utilized. Brainstorming is a verbal process, brainwriting is a written process, and NGT involves both written and oral components.

More specifically, the processes vary in the amounts and kinds of participation from the group members. Brainstorming is not too far removed from an unstructured debate. Participants volunteer ideas in response to the trigger question. This process is very vulnerable to dominant personalities and intimidation. Quiet or less-aggressive participants may not participate very much. The leader in this technique must therefore be a skilled moderator or facilitator rather than a participant. In contrast, brainwriting does not involve oral idea presentation, and this helps to reduce the likelihood of domination by certain people. Furthermore, in this process everyone must participate. Hence, even generally quiet or timid people will contribute. Also it is possible to make this method entirely anonymous by using typewriters and careful paper trading schemes. The NGT, like brainwriting, begins with each member writing out ideas thus ensuring that everyone will contribute. It is the most structured process of the three. The "round robin" presentation of ideas further helps to neutralize the effects of a dominant personality.

The method for augmenting ideas also varies. Criticism and evaluation are not allowed in brainstorming. Variants of alternatives to suggestions must be presented as separate suggestions. Brainwriting encourages direct responses to the ideas on a given paper, but once again responses are to be in the form of additional ideas rather than criticism or analysis. The NGT encourages spontaneous ideas by other members as individuals present their suggestions. This allows the greatest amount of free expression of opinion, but discussion or justification of ideas is not allowed at the initial stage.

All three techniques may simply be used to generate lists of ideas. The NGT also has a phase of prioritiz-

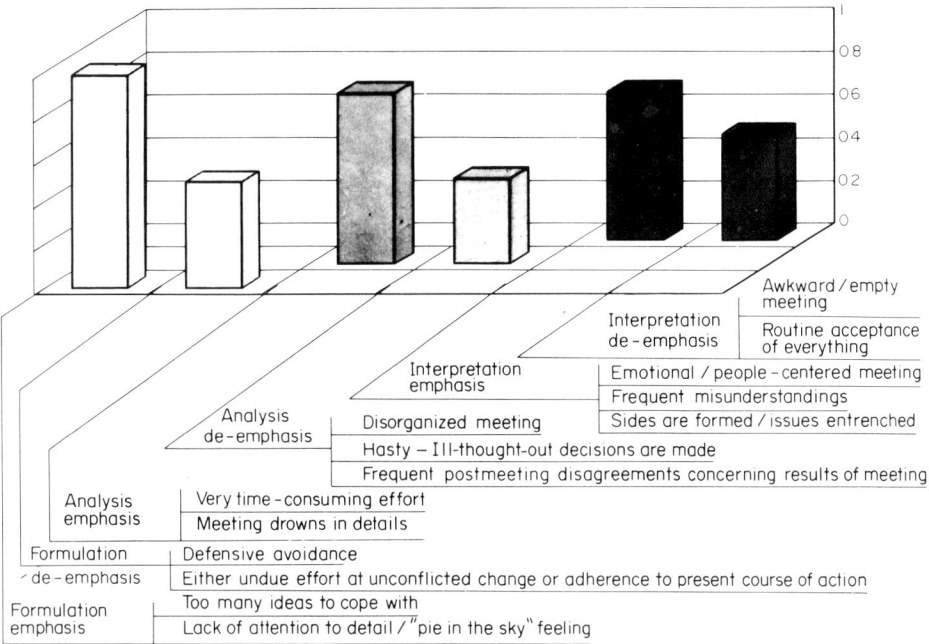

Figure 2
Attribute scores for collective enquiry

ation of ideas which may or may not be used. If it is used, then NGT differs substantively from brainstorming and brainwriting in that discussion, analysis and evaluation of the list of ideas follows its generation. This, of course, will accentuate problems of dominant personalities and social pressure. It also raises questions about the method of voting since the way the vote is counted can change the way the result is interpreted. However, ordering priorities may be very useful for value system design and system synthesis. Participating in prioritization may help group members to understand better the varied perspectives of other members.

The problem inherent in prioritization of ideas points out the fundamental importance of the way that the results of any of these processes are used. It would not help to have a very large number of suggestions that are closely related to one another, unless the whole range can in some way be considered during postmeeting evaluation stages. One of the aims of systems engineering is to extend and remove bias from information-processing abilities. These techniques can be used to that end. They can also help to involve clients, stakeholders and representatives of various sectors of society in the issue formulation process and to provide brokerage between various interested parties. Furthermore, brainstorming, brainwriting and NGT all provide structure and aid conceptual formulation. These methods are time efficient and can be extremely effective in identifying a variety of ideas on an issue. hence, all four of these methods—brainstorming, brainwriting, NGT and Delphi, are appropriate to the systems approach. They can provide the benefits of a rational and systemic approach from a systematic point of view.

See also: Group Decision Making and Voting; Human Information Processing; Knowledge Representation; Systems Methodology

Bibliography

Dalkey N C 1969 An experimental study of group opinion—The Delphi method. *Futures* Sept. issue, 408–26
Delbecq A L, Van de Van A H, Gustafson D H 1974 *Group Techniques for Program Planning.* Scott, Foresman and Co., Glenview, Illinois
Geschka H, Schaude G R, Schlincksupp H 1973 Modern techniques for solving problems. *Chem. Eng. (N.Y.)* **80**(8)
Linstone H A, Turoff M 1975 *The Delphi Method: Techniques and Applications.* Addison–Wesley, Reading, Massachusetts
Martino J 1972 *Technological Forecasting for Decision Making.* Elsevier, New York
Pillo J 1971 The Delphi method: Substance, content, a critique and an annotated bibliography. *Socio-Econ. Plann. Sci.* **5**, 57–71
Porter A L, Rossini F A, Carpenter S R, Roper A T 1980 *A Guidebook for Technology Assessment and Impact Analysis.* North-Holland, New York
Sage A P 1977a *Methodology for Large-Scale Systems.* McGraw-Hill, New York

Sage A P (ed.) 1977b *Systems Engineering: Methodology and Applications.* IEEE Press, New York

A. P. Sage
[George Mason University, Fairfax, Virginia, USA]

Command and Control Information Systems

A command and control information (C2I) system is a military decision support system. It is an extension of the sensing, processing and communicating capabilities of the military commanders whose activities it supports. These activities include the basic command and control (C2) functions of information gathering, situation assessment, action selection, and response planning and execution. The supporting system consists of radars and other sensors and intelligence sources for gathering information about an enemy; computers for information processing, storage and display; and communications equipment and networks for transferring information among various commanders and command and staff levels. Finally, both the system and the people function within the context of a military organization and mission. This article describes the context functions and supporting technology of modern military command and control, and identifies major analytical and system-engineering issues which must be addressed.

1. Background and Context

The basic functions of military command and control have remained relatively invariant since the beginning of recorded military history: *see* the battlefield, *decide* what to do and *act* accordingly. Prior to World War I a commander's effectiveness *vis-à-vis* his enemy counterpart, depended upon his ability to carry out these functions with accuracy and dispatch. Eyes, brains and legs were aided by field glasses, maps and horses.

The increasing ground, sea and air mobility between World War I and World War II resulted in an increase in both the complexity and the tempo of warfare. With high-speed ground and air movements coupled with radio communications, radar and sonar sensing, and radio direction-finding technologies, World War II exacerbated these trends, with the result that major changes were required in each military service to cope with the need for a quick-reaction capability. New concepts such as task force, task group and commando force, as well as special procedures such as the fragmentary order, were formalized and streamlined to cope with the increased tempo of operations. These changes in organization, procedures and doctrine proved more-or-less adequate throughout the Korean and Vietnam conflicts. However, by the beginning of the 1980s it was becoming increasingly clear that continued growth in the technology of modern land, sea, air and space warfare coupled with the urgent need for rapid and accurate situation assessment as well as positive control over the instruments of war had outrun the capabilities of the existing C2 structures, and major changes were needed again.

The requirements which must be met by current C2I systems are largely dictated by the military missions which those systems must support. For example, the US Strategic Forces (B-52s, ICBMs, and submarine-launched missiles) require a worldwide sensing, processing and communications system which is capable of surviving nuclear attack and of connecting a National Command Authority (e.g., the President of the USA and his designated deputies) with strategic force units wherever they may be located. With the exception of air- and space-borne components, much of a C2I system can be installed in fixed hardened installations. The C2 support for naval forces and for the tactical air and land battle forces must reflect the high degree of mobility inherent in such forces. In order to meet the special requirements of multinational forces such as those of NATO and SEATO, the separate C2I systems of several different countries must be made to operate together in a coordinated manner; West German radar data must appear on the radar displays of Dutch and US defensive units, and a coordinated tactical plan must be immediately disseminated in a language which is understood by all concerned. Finally, the inordinately severe response-time requirements for the US Strategic Defense Initiative (SDI) system dictate that many of its C2 functions be completely automated and physically located in Earth orbit (Yonas 1985).

The information trends associated with the evolution of warfare and its concomitant technology are depicted in Fig. 1. Based on these trends, three major interrelated problem areas for both current and future command and control can be anticipated.

(a) The mobility, speed and large numbers of potential enemy forces require a high degree of correlation capability in order to locate, identify and maintain track on important surface, air and space targets.

(b) This situation will create an extremely high unfiltered data rate coupled with a need for rapid response to real threats and equally rapid rejection of false alarms.

(c) Since there is a limit on unassisted human information handling capacity (Miller 1956), manual methods of information processing which were once relevant to C2 decision making have become inadequate, and new types of filtering and preplanning are required.

Thus, we see that the vastly increased information rate associated with both current and future warfare technology, when coupled with the need for accident-free,

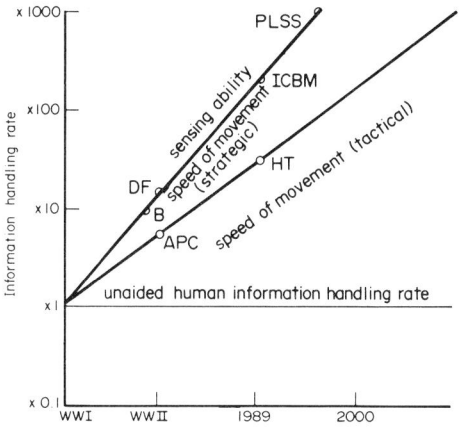

Figure 1
Battlefield information rate trends. APC, armored personnel carriers; B, bombers; DF, direction finder; HT, heliborne troops; ICBM, intercontinental ballistic missiles; PLSS, precision location and strike system

positive control over US forces and rapid response to real threats, presents a formidable challenge to the architects and designers of current and future C2I systems. In addition, the criticality, dimensionality, complexity and uncertainty of events and of information about them, in both crisis and war situations, is rapidly increasing. The effective management of forces increasingly requires the effective management of information; both require a deeper understanding of the interaction between the two domains. Design of effective C2I systems must also be based upon a deep understanding of the nature of the C2 decision processes which these systems must support.

2. Command and Control of Military Forces

The terms "command" and "control" can be used to distinguish between two separable categories of military-force-management decisions: those which are made long before forces are engaged in combat and those which are made when forces are on "ready alert" or are already engaged. These two categories are called *planning and commitment* and *control and coordination*, respectively. Planning and commitment is a command-oriented, broadly based decision category applicable prior to engagement, and control and coordination is a control-oriented, narrowly focused and time-critical decision category applicable when forces are engaged or are on alert.

2.1 Planning and Commitment

There are four basic planning and commitment decisions made by commanders at various levels. They are: the establishment of mission objectives; the allocation of resources to geographical area, time "window" and mission type; the tasking and scheduling of resources to perform specific military missions, and the selection of appropriate targets; and the detailed planning of each mission and its associated activities. The information required for these decisions includes: the status of enemy forces and its rate of change—from sensing and intelligence sources; the status of friendly forces and its rate of change—from reporting and communications sources; the environment (weather, terrain, darkness)—from local information sources; and command guidance (policy, rules of engagement, campaign priorities)—from sources in higher-level headquarters.

The major factors which differ in intensity among military command levels where planning and commitment decisions are made are time criticality, information aggregation and coordination. The time criticality of information required for planning and commitment decisions generally decreases with increases in the level of decision making; the higher-level commander deals with planning for "tomorrow's war," while the unit-level commander is concerned primarily with today's missions. Even at the highest levels of command, these factors can be critical. Such a condition is best illustrated by US strategic command and control, where (a) warning and assessment of missile attack on the continental USA must take place within minutes; (b) detailed information about the sources and targets of the attack is required; and (c) extensive coordination among command levels and forces is necessary. In contrast, the degree of information aggregation required generally increases with the decision-making level: the unit-level commander needs the latest information on location, characteristics and activity of specific enemy units and targets, while the higher-level commander needs only enough information about enemy forces to help allocate his own forces. Finally, decisions are not made by isolated decision makers; a decision at one level requires both inputs from, and coordination with, levels immediately above and below, as well as coordination with other commanders at the same level.

2.2 Control and Coordination

Control and coordination of alerted or engaged forces involves near-real-time activities. In the tactical air arena, mission aircraft will be assisted and sometimes redirected by a control and coordination hierarchy of airborne and ground- or sea-based C2I elements. Mission and flight plans will necessitate certain actions at critical times and locations, depending on the mission. Interdiction, close air support, defense suppression, offensive and defensive air counterattacks, surface strikes, antisubmarine and associated support missions may or may not have these actions defined in detail at takeoff. Ground, surface and subsurface targets appear and disappear as they move; support missions fail; priorities change; objectives and plans are superseded; new information is received; and mission plans with which a pilot took off must be modified accordingly, in flight if appropriate and possible. It is under these circumstances of high stress and severe time constraint that near-real-time decisions involving threat warning, rerouting, retargeting, rescheduling, and other types of dynamic reassignment and mission modification must be made. Especially critical are the areas of aircraft identification to minimize "fratricide," in-flight provision of surface and subsurface target updates, and threat warning and electronic warfare coordination to improve strike mission effectiveness and reduce the attrition of friendly forces.

In the strategic arena, control and coordination of surviving second-strike-capable forces is the paramount requirement; here, the role of survivable communications in a nuclear-exchange environment is one of the most critical factors. For an SDI system, the control and coordination of multiple, dispersed, space-based sensors and weapons for tracking, discriminating between targets and nontargets and destroying ballistic missiles in their boost, midcourse or terminal phases must be implemented by automated space-borne "battle managers" capable of near-instantaneous communication, coordination and data fusion.

2.3 Summary

Table 1 summarizes the critical C2 decisions and indicates how time constraints and information needs vary as the decision level descends. Note that the higher-level decisions take more time to execute or modify because of their strong dependence on coordination, material, maintenance and personnel resource scheduling and movement; and arbitrary changes will have little immediate effect because of the "inertia" of these supporting systems. When coupled with the increasing consequence and time criticality of military command and control, it is clear that decision-making procedures must somehow be significantly compressed (e.g., through more downward delegation, management by exception and increased automation where appropriate) in order to reduce both the number of hierarchical levels involved in a given C2 function and the impact of holding times and processing delays at each level. In addition, the lower-level decisions require more informational detail, while higher-level decisions require less detail and more aggregation. The impact of such changes on C2I system design requirements, especially in the area of decision support, needs to be carefully assessed.

3. Theory versus Reality in Military Decision Making

Discussions both with high-level military commanders and with people working in the fields of systems engineering and decision science indicate a divergence between theory and reality in decision making. Sage (1981) has summarized the extensive literature in the area of decision science, and Wohl (1981) has contrasted the reality of the military decision process with the normative constructs of decision theorists. Theorists have tended toward prescriptive definitions based on the concept of a decision as a selection from alternatives, while military commanders and corporate executives have tended toward descriptive definitions involving such statements as: "It seemed the best thing to do at the time" or "We had to act immediately based on whatever information we had at the time" or "The final course of action became obvious after a while." The qualitative difference between these two views is striking.

As noted by Wohl (1981), the preponderance of work in decision theory has concentrated on techniques for option selection, with little research on those portions of the process which are of greatest interest to military commanders; namely, the creation, evaluation and refinement of both hypotheses (i.e., what the situation is) and options (i.e., what can be done about the situation).

4. The Stimulus–Hypothesis–Option–Response Paradigm

To place this process in perspective, Table 2 and Fig. 2 have been adapted from Wohl (1981) to summarize the elements of force-management decision making along with their interactions. They represent a distillation from a number of sources, as well as from discussions

Table 1
Summary of critical C2 decisions and their relationship to decision time horizon and information aggregation

Relative time horizon	Type	Examples	Degree of information aggregation required
Long	Planning and commitment decisions	Resource allocation Tasking/targeting Detailed planning	More information, less detail
Short	Control and coordination decisions	Resource reallocation Reassignment/update Control and warning	Less information, more detail

Table 2
Anatomy of the C2 decision process—the SHOR paradigm (after Wohl 1981)

Generic elements	Functions required	Information processed
Stimulus (data) S	Gather/detect Filter/correlate Aggregate/display Store/recall	Capabilities, doctrine; position, velocity, type; mass, momentum, inertia relevance and trustworthiness of data
Hypothesis (perception alternatives) H	Create Evaluate Select	Commander's catechism Where am I? Where is the enemy? What is he doing? How can I thwart him? How can I do him in? Am I in balance?
Option (response alternatives) O	Create Evaluate Select	How long will it take me to . . . ? How long will it take him to . . . ? How will it look in . . . ? What is the most important thing to do right now? How do I get it done?
Response (action) R	Organize Execute	Who What When Where Why How How much

with high-ranking NATO and US Air Force, Army and Navy commanders.

Table 2 defines the elements themselves and relates them to decision information, while Fig. 2 indicates their complex dynamic relationships in terms of "triggering" events, feedforward and feedback loops. Wohl (1981) has termed this the stimulus–hypothesis–option–response (SHOR) paradigm, where "paradigm" represents a qualitative descriptive model as distinct from a quantitative predictive model. Basically, the paradigm is an attempt to provide explicitly for the necessity to deal with two realms of uncertainty in the decision-making process:

(a) information-input uncertainty, which creates the need for hypothesis generation and evaluation; and

(b) consequence-of-action uncertainty, which creates the need for option generation and evaluation.

In control-theory terms, these forms of uncertainty are recognizable as "measurement noise" and "process noise."

Some decision situations tend to short-circuit much of the hypothesis and option elements of Table 2 and Fig. 2 resulting in a classical stimulus–response "trigger" process ("if A then B"; or "if A and B and C, then D"). Such situations may range from simple push-button responses or discrimination tasks in which there is little or no information-input uncertainty and the hypotheses and options have been reduced to a minimum, to the single integrated operations plan (SIOP) of US strategic command and control, in which a large number of complex hypotheses and options have been carefully and painstakingly mapped out in detail beforehand, and a specific response awaits only an appropriate triggering pattern of information inputs to which specific sensors and processors have been "tuned."

As a rule, when options are clearly prescribed and input is of high quality, a system can be designed which directly maps input data into output or response data so that only key observables are considered in the mapping process (e.g., as with a highly trained pilot carrying out an emergency procedure). Where options are more-or-less clearly prescribed but input data is of low quality (e.g., as in intelligence analysis), a premium is placed upon the creation and testing of hypotheses (e.g., "What is the enemy attempting to do?"). Where input data is of high quality but options are open-ended (e.g., as in the Cuban missile crisis), a premium is placed upon the creation and analysis of

Command and Control Information Systems

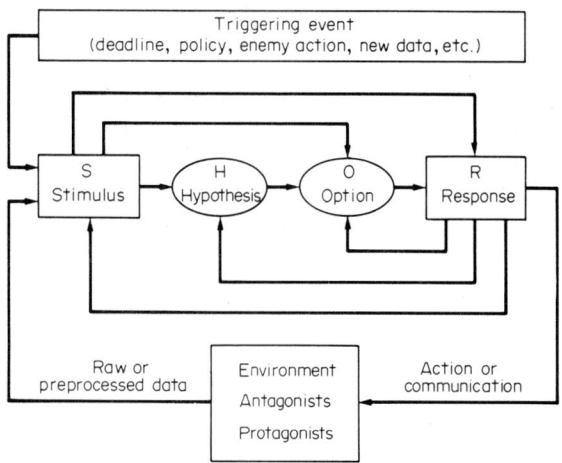

Figure 2
Dynamics of the C2 decision process—the SHOR paradigm (after Wohl 1981)

options and their potential consequences (e.g., "If we bomb the missile sites or if we establish a fully-fledged naval blockade, what will the Russians do?"). In contrast, tactical decision making in support of anti-submarine warfare and of combined air–land operations is generally characterized by both poor-quality input data and open-ended options; hence, there is a greater need than in other military situations for rapid hypothesis and option processing.

5. The Critical Role of Hypotheses in Military Decision Making

A military commander must deal with a wide diversity of input information from many sources. Some of it may be inaccurate, old, redundant, irrelevant, extremely important and/or of questionable credibility. Some of it may have been deliberately "planted" by a clever enemy with intent to mislead or confuse. Given a specified military objective, a commander faced with these uncertainties must nevertheless attempt to extract meaning from this morass and to use it in deciding upon his next move.

Uncertainty in physics and in information theory is a well-defined mathematical construct which is directly associated with the variance of a stochastic process and the resultant probability of occurrence of a given outcome at a given time. While this approach is satisfactory from a mathematical standpoint, the term itself is subject to confusion and argument when attempts are made to extend its application beyond physical systems. Shannon, for example, chose to eliminate the concept of "meaning" from his work, defining information as negative entropy (or uncertainty) in terms of discrete symbols and their probabilities of occurrence, or in terms of signal-to-noise ratio (Shannon 1948). This limited definition, while extremely powerful for communications systems engineering purposes, is of little use in designing C2I systems whose major functions, in addition to the obvious one of gathering and disseminating information, include extracting meaning and predicting outcomes.

5.1 Meaning Extraction

The key issue in extracting meaning from input information appears to be how military commanders construct hypotheses. For example, having an input set with no hypothesis about its meaning is tantamount to all possible hypotheses being equally likely—"anything could happen." At the other extreme, having a large and well-structured set of hypotheses tends to be overburdening in the opposite direction ("It could mean this or that or the other, or even ..."). Neither extreme serves to focus attention upon what new information is to be sought.

Given a plethora of information, the set of hypotheses under consideration can be further reduced to a subset of testable ones; this requires that new information be sought. As a case in point, modern military sensor and correlation equipment can provide simultaneous information on thousands of ground targets. The critical needs are those of blocking irrelevant information and cueing on selected sensors to obtain pertinent information on selected targets in real time. However, neither process can occur in the absence of hypotheses. A very few carefully constructed hypotheses will serve to eliminate irrelevant input information, and to direct attention to new and pertinent information which is required to further reduce the hypothesis set. Expert tacticians, strategists, diagnosticians, executives and commanders appear to possess this ability of hypothesis generation and testing (i.e., "gedanken" experiments) to a high degree.

A hypothesis is defined here, for C2 purposes, as a commander's mental model or assessment of the situation. The concept of a hypothesis as a blocking filter and as a stimulus to obtaining selected new information is central to assessing the effectiveness of C2I systems.

5.2 Outcome Prediction

Even though a commander's model of reality may not be mathematical, it is used in such a fashion. Based on data, a hypothesis is constructed which involves events, relationships and causality. The hypothesis is then tested by using it to predict the existence of other confirming observables and the course of events given a new set of conditions (i.e., "What would happen if ...?"), later observing the degree of concordance of the actual course with the predicted course and modifying the hypothesis accordingly. Thus, it can be seen that the hypothesis, as well as being a model of reality, can also act in a very real way as a generating function for future scenarios.

6. Example

An example of how this concept has been employed may be instructive here. In a recent study, the situation assessment activities of an antisubmarine warfare commander in a naval battle group have been modelled in a computer simulation (Wohl et al. 1987). These activities involved the estimation of possible enemy submarine tracks (both position and velocity) and their likelihoods, using information from multiple distributed, passive underwater acoustic sensors (sonars). As each sonar contact is reported, several alternative track hypotheses are constructed and tested, and previous ones which no longer meet the testing criteria (e.g., successive contacts within a one-hour time interval which are 100 miles apart) are dropped from consideration.

The simulation used was normative–descriptive in nature. A normative or optimal mathematical model was first developed using modern estimation and control theory (Van Trees 1968, Gelb 1974) and then applied in a range of battle scenarios. Experimental results involving 20 experienced naval subjects in the same scenarios indicated that the normative or optimal model always performed better than the human subjects across the entire range of scenarios. Known human cognitive limitations and biases, drawn from the cognitive and behavioral sciences and/or observed in the human subject performance, were then incorporated in the model to degrade its performance. These included:

(a) a working-memory limitation,

(b) a bias towards the overestimation of enemy submarine maneuverability (the major component of process noise in estimation theory), and

(c) a bias toward the overestimation of sonar accuracy (the major component of measurement noise in estimation theory).

Inclusion of these descriptive characteristics yielded a normative–descriptive model whose performance was within the intersubject error range.

7. Closing the Loop: C2I as both an Estimation and Control Problem

The literature on statistical analysis, estimation theory and experimental design is concerned almost entirely with hypothesis formulation and testing and, more specifically, the conditions under which and confidence with which hypotheses may be accepted or rejected. The literature on optimal control theory, on the other hand, is concerned almost entirely with the control of a set of variables to minimize a cost function subject to constraints. Since the purpose of command and control is to direct the application of military force in the pursuit of specified objectives, subject to estimatable constraints and costs, we must "close the loop" in representing the human aspect of military C2I by expanding the usual definition of hypothesis to include an expert commander's "mental model" of the "system" to be "controlled."

As an example, postulate an extension of Lanchester's equations as the system model, for which the mathematical development may be summarized briefly as follows.

Solving:
$$\dot{\mathbf{X}} = F(\mathbf{X}, \boldsymbol{\rho}, t) + \eta(\mathbf{X}, t) \qquad (1)$$

subject to the constraint
$$G(\mathbf{X}, t)|_{t=t_f} = 0 \qquad (2)$$

where $\boldsymbol{\rho}$ is selected such that
$$c(\mathbf{X}, t)|_{t=t_f} = \text{minimum} \qquad (3)$$

and X is a military-force vector; t is the time; F is a linear function of X, $\boldsymbol{\rho}$ and t; $\boldsymbol{\rho}$ is a control vector; η is a stochastic component (e.g., random variation in X due to inadequate measurement, weather factors, terrain factors, etc.); G is a final condition constraint (e.g., territory lost, attrition ratio reached); t_f is the final time associated with the final condition constraint; and c is the weighted attrition cost (e.g., i tanks $+j$ aircraft $+k$ platoons).

This formulation affords an ability to represent multicomponent forces, second echelon or second-wave effects, force-allocation decisions, (e.g., interdiction versus close air support) and stochastic variability. Uncertainty, represented by the stochastic term, corresponds to the inability of the Lanchester "hypothesis" or model to accurately estimate, other than on the average, future system states given the current one.

The example problem as posed can be analyzed in closed form to determine the cost of nonoptimal decision making (e.g., the additional attrition of ground and air units due to misallocation of close air support and interdiction sorties), and to trace the propagation of uncertainty through the model. In addition, it is possible to solve for the rate of change of uncertainty both in the absence and presence of measurements to correct the estimate of the state of the system. In this way, the effect of measurement errors (e.g., surveillance or intelligence input), time delays (e.g., due to processing or communications) and process errors (e.g., the unpredictability of enemy actions and weather effects) on net uncertainty reduction can be demonstrated.

8. Measurement of C2I Systems

The need for a quantitative assessment of the relative importance of proposed C2I technologies and system alternatives has become acute. Deficiencies in both strategic and tactical C2I systems, as well as the capabilities of systems still in development and of proposed new systems, make it imperative that methods be devised to quantify both their survivability in combat and their potential effects on mission outcomes. In addition, quantitative assessment tools are needed to provide a sound basis for C2I system-development planning. Proposed new C2I capabilities, sensors, decision aids and communication techniques must be considered in the light of their ultimate contributions to force-employment effectiveness. Finally, since communications-system needs tend to be driven by C2 system survivability and configuration (structural) characteristics, it has become especially important that analytical and simulation tools be developed which are useful in trade-off as well as effectiveness analyses. The potential utility of uncertainty reduction as a basis for developing such tools appears warranted.

One such tool involves the use of Petri nets (Peterson 1981). In particular, Andreadakis (1988) has developed a computational technique for the analysis and synthesis of distributed C2I organizations. Using the formalism of timed Petri nets, the interaction of, and coordination among, asynchronous C2 processes were modelled and performance-related measures such as accuracy, timeliness and throughput rate were computed. Andreadakis has also defined a measure of system survivability and is able to compute an overall measure of effectiveness, thus permitting a comparison of alternative C2I organizations and systems.

Additional background and approaches to the measurement of C2I systems can be found in Hwang et al. (1982).

9. Conclusion

In this brief article it was possible to touch upon only the more significant aspects of C2I systems-engineering concerns. Perhaps the most critical of these are the need to support, in near-real-time, the extraction of meaning from a morass of conflicting data by means of formulating and testing situation-assessment hypotheses, and the review and assessment of alternative courses of action. Providing the capability for a commander to perform these planning and decision-making functions in a dispersed system with distributed staff personnel and computing resources, and under severe time and communications constraints and a high degree of uncertainty, is the major challenge currently facing designers of large-scale C2I systems.

Bibliography

Andreadakis S 1988 Analysis and synthesis of decision-making organizations. Ph.D. thesis, Massachusetts Institute of Technology, Cambridge, Massachusetts
Gelb A 1974 *Applied Optimal Estimation.* MIT Press, Cambridge, Massachusetts
Hwang J, Schutzer D, Shere K, Vena P (eds.) 1982 *Selected Analytical Concepts in Command and Control.* Gordon and Breach, New York
Miller G 1956 The magical number seven, plus or minus two: Some limits on our capacity for processing information. *Psychol. Rev.* **63,** 81–97
Peterson J 1981 *Petri Net Theory and the Modeling of Systems.* Prentice–Hall, Englewood Cliffs, New Jersey
Sage A P 1981 Behavioral and organizational considerations in the design of information systems and processes for planning and decision support. *IEEE Trans. Syst., Man Cybern.* **11,** 640–78
Shannon C 1948 A mathematical theory of communication. *Bell Syst. Tech. J.* **27**
Van Trees H L 1968 *Detection Estimation, and Modulation Theory,* Part 1: *Detection, Estimation and Linear Modulation Theory.* Wiley, New York
Wohl J G 1981 Force management decision requirements for Air Force tactical command and control. *IEEE Trans. Syst., Man Cybern.* **11,** 618–39
Wohl J G, Serfaty D, Entin E 1987 Situation assessment in a naval environment: A normative–descriptive approach. *Proc. 1987 IEEE Int. Conf. Systems, Man and Cybernetics.* Institute of Electrical and Electronics Engineers, New York
Yonas J 1985 The Strategic Defense Initiative. *Proc. Am. Acad. Arts Sci.* **114**(2), 73–90
Zraket C A 1985 Strategic defense: A systems perspective. *Proc. Am. Acad. Arts Sci.* **114**(2), 109–26

J. G. Wohl
[Alphatech Inc., Burlington, Massachusetts, USA]

Computer-Aided Systems Engineering

Computer-aided systems engineering (CASE) is the systematic application of computer technology and software to the tasks and activities, or elements, of systems engineering. The elements of systems engineering are shown in Table 1 and the categories of computer tools that may be used to support systems engineering are listed in Table 2. Thus, CASE involves the application of the software tools given in Table 2 in relation to the elements of systems engineering, as cited in Table 1. Illustrative CASE examples therefore include the utilization of:

(a) a database management system (DBMS) to provide requirements analysis and traceability,

(b) project-management software to assist a system developer in defining and tracking schedules,

(c) a spreadsheet or integrated package to formulate a life-cycle cost model (LCCM),

(d) simulation software to evaluate system and subsystem performance,

(e) decision support software to assess alternative system architectures,

Table 1
A brief description of the elements of systems engineering

Element	Description
Definition of user needs	articulation by the user of specific operational requirements for the system
Requirements analysis	reviews of user requirements for completeness, consistency, accuracy and inter-relationships
Requirements allocation	distribution of requirement values from higher to lower levels of system indenture
Functional analysis	definition and verification of functional decomposition of the system
Functional allocation	distribution of functional elements and related values from higher to lower levels of system indenture
Specification development	conversion of user requirements and functional structure into levels of specific system and subsystem definition
Top-level (architecture) design	definition and selection of most promising overall design alternative
Trade-off/alternatives evaluation	assessing the effectiveness of various system designs
Subsystem design and analysis	definition, evaluation and configuration selection at the subsystem levels
Interface definition	articulation of interconnectivity between all subsystems that interoperate
Software definition and analysis	development of full life cycle software for the system
Schedule definition	development of appropriate system and subsystem activities with associated milestones
Life-cycle costing	assessment of the full costs of the system through the major phases of: (a) research, development, test and evaluation (RDT&E); (b) procurement; and (c) operations and maintenance (O&M)
Technical performance measurement	definition and tracking of measures of key system attributes and parameters (e.g., measures of merit and effectiveness)
Program and decision analysis	program and systems engineering management
Risk analysis	formal assessment of the potential operational hazards of the system as well as the possibilities of cost, schedule or performance variations from the plan
Integrated logistics support	full consideration and definition of means of maintaining operational readiness
Preplanned product improvement	early definition of future ways of enhancing system performance, beyond current specified levels
Reliability–maintainability–availability	specific analysis and trade-offs within an operational readiness context
Specialty engineering	consideration of particularized engineering factors (e.g., human engineering, safety, security, electromagnetic compatibility)
Integration	generic term for interconnection and intraconnection between system hardware, software and human resources
Test and evaluation	physical verification of actual system performance against performance defined by requirements and specifications
Configuration management	tracking, control and documentation of various versions of the system
Quality assurance	verification of the intended operation of all system elements over their full life cycles
Training	instruction in the operational use and maintenance of all system elements
Documentation	written descriptions of appropriate elements and products of the system developments and operations
Production	physical replication of one or more systems for operational deployment
Installation	formal initial replacement of at least one system in operation
Operation	a system working in a real-world environment
Operations evaluation/modification	assessments and changes made to a deployed system

Table 2
Categories of computer tools that support systems engineering, together with a brief description of selected application areas

Computer tool	Application area
Spreadsheet	row by column construction of a life-cycle cost model (LCCM); cost elements vs. time in years
DBMS	requirements traceability; configuration management
Word processor	writing of a systems engineering management plan (SEMP)
Graphics software	graphic comparison of major life-cycle cost elements; e.g., RDT&E vs. procurement vs. O&M
Integrated system	simultaneous tabulation and graphical output of life-cycle cost model
Multitask applications manager	preparation of key software documents (e.g., SDP, SCMP, SQEP, SSPM) and related graphics
Project management aid	master schedule for system and major subsystems
Alternatives and preference evaluator	assessment of the merits of alternative top-level system architectures
Decision support system	preparation of cost vs. performance trade-off curves
Toolchest/desk manager	daily calendar of chief engineer
Idea processor	organizer for preliminary design concepts, ideas and documentation
Management evaluator/aid	assessment of personnel aptitudes, skills and performance
Statistics software	statistical testing of reliability data for key components
Mathematics software	correlation analysis of signals embedded in noise
Engineering software (CAE)	performance analysis of an analog or digital circuit
Hardware reliability calculator	estimation of likelihood of successful operation of important subsystems
Mathematical programming tool	linear programming optimization of raw-materials usage
Simulation software	modelling and simulation of grade and speed of service in a telecommunications network; technical performance measurement
Curves and plotting package	scatter diagram for regression analysis to develop a cost estimating relationship (CER)
CAD/CAM software	three-dimensional views of a spaceborne platform
Requirements analyzer/language	traceability of requirements through specification and test and evaluation
Software estimator/evaluator	estimation of level of effort required to perform software development tasks
Workbench/structured analysis tool	construction of data-flow diagrams, data dictionary and minispec for software configuration item
Language	development of code for computer system component
General support tool/utility	easy manipulation of files within directory structure
Microcomputer-to-mainframe link	up- and down-loading of DBMS data between microcomputer and mainframe
Forecasting tool	preparation of demand for an intercity transportation system
Desktop publisher	preparation of operations and maintenance manuals
Expert system	development of microbased diagnostic tools for maintenance personnel
Specialized systems engineering tool	integrated logistics support or configuration management application

(f) a statistics package to analyze the failure characteristics of a particularly important component or subsystem,

(g) a workbench or structured analysis computer tool to assist a programmer in developing software, and

(h) a graphics package to construct and display charts and graphs.

Systems engineering may be defined as "an iterative process of top-down synthesis, development and operation of a real-world system that satisfies, in a near-optimal manner, the full range of requirements for the system" (Eisner 1988). In this context, a system is normally considered to be any combination of hardware, software and personnel that interoperate to serve some user-defined set of needs. Examples of large-scale systems include a national aviation system, a telecommunications system and a defense system. Elements of the above can also be considered as systems in their own right; for example, an air-traffic control system, the system that provides telephone services to our homes and a long-range radar, respectively.

The components of CASE can be described in terms of the following breakdown.

(a) systems engineering:

  (i) elements,

  (ii) top-level system (architecture) development,

  (iii) system life cycle, and

  (iv) systems engineering management.

(b) computer aids:

  (i) software,

  (ii) bases for computer tools,

  (iii) environments, and

  (iv) sources.

1. Systems Engineering

Significant formal investigators of systems engineering have included Goode and Machol (1957), Hall (1962), Chestnut (1965, 1967), Sage (1977a,b), and Blanchard and Fabrycky (1981), whose descriptions span 24 years. Although each investigator has approached this subject with a slightly different orientation, all have dealt with defining the elements of systems engineering and various methods of approaching the implementation of these elements.

In addition, the US government, through its development and acquisition of large-scale systems over the years, has addressed all aspects of systems engineering. These have been documented in government-sponsored texts (e.g., *System Engineering Management Guide* 1986) as well as numerous related standards, directives and handbooks, especially those published by the US Department of Defense (Eisner 1988 Appendix C)

1.1 Elements

The elements of systems engineering describe the tasks and activities of systems engineering that are normally required in most large-scale system developments and implementations. Each of these elements is briefly described in Table 1.

1.2 Top-Level System (Architecture) Development

Top-level systems engineering is often referred to as the formulation of an overall architecture for a system. Such an architecture represents the design of a baseline configuration of hardware, software and human-resource assets to satisfy the user's functional requirements. Fundamental ingredients in developing an architecture include:

(a) top-level requirements and specifications,

(b) design alternatives,

(c) measures of merit and effectiveness (MOM, MOE),

(d) evaluation criteria, and

(e) an evaluation framework.

As the starting point for top-level design or architecture definition, the requirements and specifications represent targets to be achieved by the design alternatives. The MOM and MOE are specific measurable parameters of the design for the assessment of how well the design satisfies the requirements and specifications. Additional and possibly subjective factors are added to this assessment to develop a comprehensive set of evaluation criteria. Design alternatives are then compared on the basis of these criteria in a formal evaluation framework (e.g., a weighting and rating formalism) to yield the preferred system design or architecture.

Top-level architectures represent fundamental design selections and approaches that are not significantly modified during the processes of detailed subsystem design. Examples include the selection of frequency as opposed to time-division multiplexing in a communications system, a distributed as opposed to a centralized database design and management, and a discrete rather than a continuous approach to the design of a large-scale system simulation.

1.3 System Life Cycle

A review of the elements in Table 1 reveals that the order of these tasks and activities as given generally follows the life cycle of a typical large-scale system; that is, the systems engineering process normally starts with a definition of user needs, follows through most if not all of the listed elements, and concludes with the evaluation and modification of the system in operation. This defines the total life cycle of the system and also reflects what is sometimes called the systems acquisition process. The life cycle or acquisition process of a system is often abbreviated by identifying the phases of the development cycle as:

(a) need development,

(b) concept definition,

(c) concept validation,

(d) engineering development,

(e) production, and

(f) operations.

Associated with these life-cycle phases are a variety of generally accepted program reviews, audits, milestones, tests, capabilities and documentation requirements. For example, program reviews that occur from concept definition through to engineering development include reviews of:

(a) systems requirements,

(b) system design,

(c) software specification,

(d) preliminary design,

(e) critical design, and

(f) test readiness.

In a similar context, formal milestone evaluations to be achieved by the customer, user or acquisition agent have been cited as program approval (to begin the concept definition phase), and approval of production by a system acquisition review council (SARC).

Documentation phases include specifications (A, B and C) that define the system in increasing levels of detail. Testing and related evaluation activities may constitute a phase following research and development; these are generally described as test and evaluation and the more formal activities of development test and evaluation, operational test and evaluation and production acceptance test and evaluation. Testing activities are often defined in a document known as the system test and evaluation master plan. Specific milestone capabilities both during and after completing the production phase include the interim operational capability and the final operational capability.

Similar life-cycle phases and related tasks and activities have been defined and accepted in the field of software development and engineering, an element that is regarded as a part of the overall process of systems engineering. For example, software life-cycle elements can be defined as:

(a) requirements analysis;

(b) preliminary design;

(c) detailed design;

(d) coding, unit testing and computer system component integration;

(e) computer software configuration item testing;

(f) system integration and testing;

(g) operational testing and evaluation; and

(h) production and deployment.

In addition, important planning documents that support the software development element include the Software Development Plan, the Software Standards and Procedures Manual, the Software Configuration Management Plan, and the Software Quality Evaluation Plan. Thus the phases of software development closely correspond to those of systems engineering but have been specialized for the software engineering process.

1.4 Systems Engineering Management

The elements of systems engineering, as listed in Table 1 and described in the above subsections, are intended to subsume the formal management of these same elements (sometimes known as systems engineering management). Some sources are available, however, that stress the management aspects of systems engineering (e.g., US Department of Defense 1974, *Systems Engineering Management Guide* 1986). As an example, the US Department of Defense (1974) defines three basic elements of systems engineering management:

(a) technical program planning and control,

(b) systems engineering process, and

(c) engineering specialty areas.

In addition, it establishes the requirement for a document that fully describes how systems engineering is to be managed; that is, a systems engineering management plan (SEMP). Acquisition agents for large-scale systems will often require a formal SEMP as a deliverable item and as documentation that defines and guides the systems engineering process.

2. Computer Aids

Computer tools that can be used to assist in carrying out the elements of systems engineering are listed, by categories, in Table 2. These tools or aids are all represented by specific software packages that operate on many machines, ranging from microcomputers to supercomputers.

2.1 Software

Within the categories of systems engineering, computer aids are found as a wide variety of specific commercial and noncommercial packages (Eisner 1988). To the extent that a particular computer aid is multifunctional or deals with several elements of systems engineering, it is advertised or represented as an integrated package. A brief description of a typical systems engineering application area for each of the categories of computer aids is shown in Table 2.

An item-by-item comparison between the categories of computer aids shown in this table and the elements of systems engineering (e.g., Eisner 1988) illustrates that there are areas in which a single category of computer aid applies to more than one engineering element; in addition, there are general gaps and overlaps in the application of tools to systems engineering.

2.2 Bases for Computer Tools

Each specific software package within the categories of computer aids has at least one basis for its underlying structure. For example, the packages are written in a language which is compatible with the specific computer and its operating system. In addition, some logic-based or mathematical set of algorithms may be dominant in the software package. Such underlying bases include procedures and computational routines from such fields as:

(a) computer programming,
(b) control systems theory,
(c) information theory,
(d) linear and dynamic programming,
(e) linear systems theory,
(f) multiattribute decision theory,
(g) nonlinear programming,
(h) operations research,
(i) optimization theory,
(j) probability theory,
(k) queuing theory,
(l) regression analysis,
(m) search theory,
(n) statistics, and
(o) utility theory.

Thus, the foundations upon which the various software tools are built may be drawn from a wide variety of fields in addition to the evident computer application bases such as type of language, operating system and database structure.

2.3 Environment

Availability of computer hardware and related operating systems represents the primary consideration for a computer-aided systems engineering environment. Five such environments are immediately identifiable: microcomputers, workstations, minicomputers, mainframes and supercomputers. Relatively inexpensive commercially available software is plentiful at the microcomputer level. Workstation computer manufacturers have made a significant amount of third-party software available to their users. Database management system vendors have made products available across the full range of computer capabilities. Increasingly, computer manufacturers have responded to the need for commercial software that is capable of supporting both systems and software engineering. Where such software has been needed and is not available commercially, many large systems-oriented companies have filled this gap by developing their own software.

Another aspect of a CASE environment is the degree to which the computer aids are integrated. A fully integrated set of tools that spans a broad range of systems engineering elements is a worthy goal since it provides maximum capability to a user. This is especially apparent in computer-aided software engineering. However, this normally requires more powerful computer resources as well as greater expense. Multiuser access to common data is also critically important in a large-scale systems engineering activity. Careful trade-offs are required to access a cost-effective set of tools for a multiuser systems engineering program. Continuing efforts in both systems and software engineering are devoted to establishing more effective "integrated project support environments."

2.4 Sources

Many sources are available to investigate further the scope and content of computer aids. Standard commercial information sources include computer-oriented magazines and newspapers as well as published catalogs. Several professional society journals and magazines encourage advertisements from various vendors. Some companies specialize in publishing lists of software which are available at all computer size levels and provide significant technical data on these packages.

The US government, notably through the National Institute of Standards and Technology (NIST), formerly the National Bureau of Standards (NBS), the National Technical Information Service (NTIS) and the Government Printing Office (GPO), also encourages the dissemination of computer software information. As examples, NBS publications (e.g., Houghton 1982, National Bureau of Standards 1984) are available through the GPO, and the US Department of Commerce, through the NTIS, publishes the *Directory of Computer Software* (US Department of Commerce 1986), as well as other significant materials. In this same context, many specialized computer tools have been developed and funded by US government programs. As government property in the public domain, several of these can be obtained through the above and other government channels and inquiries, despite the fact that they are not offered to the public as commercial products. Thus, both public and private sources of computer tools are plentiful and available to the systems engineer for CASE applications.

Bibliography

Blanchard B S, Fabrycky W J 1981 *Systems Engineering and Analysis*. Prentice–Hall, Englewood Cliffs, New Jersey

Chestnut H 1965 *Systems Engineering Tools*. Wiley, Chichester

Chestnut H 1967 *Systems Engineering Methods*. Wiley, Chichester

Eisner H 1988 *Computer-Aided Systems Engineering*. Prentice–Hall, Englewood Cliffs, New Jersey

Goode H H, Machol R E 1957 *System Engineering*. McGraw–Hill, New York

Hall A D 1962 *A Methodology for Systems Engineering.* Van Nostrand, New York

Houghton R C Jr 1982 *Software Development Tools.* National Bureau of Standards, Washington, DC

National Bureau of Standards 1984 *Introduction to Software Packages,* NBS Special Publication 500-114. NBS, Washington, DC

Sage, A P 1977a Introduction to systems engineering methodology and applications. In: Sage A P (ed.) *Systems Engineering: Methodology and Applications.* Wiley, Chichester

Sage A P 1977b *Methodology for Large Scale Systems.* McGraw–Hill, New York

System Engineering Management Guide, 2nd edn., 1986. Defense Systems Management College, Fort Belvoir, Virginia

US Department of Commerce 1986 *Directory of Computer Software, 1986,* PB86-135357, National Technical Information Service. US Department of Commerce, Washington, DC

US Department of Defense 1974 *Engineering Management,* Military Standard 499A. US Department of Defense, Washington, DC

H. Eisner
[Potomac, Maryland, USA]

Computer-Based Instruction: Costs and Effectiveness

Instruction is one of the oldest forms of information transmission, and primarily concerns the transmission of skills and knowledge, but also attitudes, expectations and standards, from instructors—or, more generally, from "the culture"—to students or initiates into the culture. Instruction involves not only the transmission of information at a single point in time but also the transmission of information across generations of people and across time.

A major technological advance in instruction occurred around 1456 AD with the publication of a book, Gutenberg's Bible, from movable type. Books made it possible to capture the content of great instruction and supply it at reasonable cost to nearly all segments of society. A second major technological advance in instruction may have occurred with the development of the digital computer. Computers have made it possible to capture the interactions as well as the content of great instruction in a medium that is becoming increasingly inexpensive and accessible to all segments of society.

It is not surprising, then, to find a relatively long history of attempts to apply computers to the problems and processes of instruction. Computers were first used in instruction in the mid-1950s (Fletcher 1986). Until recently, however, these applications were viewed by instructional decision makers as inventions and innovations outside the mainstream of institutionalized instructional technology. Computer applications were not included in the usual armamentarium of instructional approaches (classroom lecture, actual equipment experience, textbooks, etc.) which were ordinarily considered as alternatives from which decision makers would choose the appropriate approach for implementing instruction. Consequently, evaluations of the effectiveness of computer-based instruction (CBI) received less priority than they should have done. Resources were more likely to be allocated for developing and implementing successive generations of intuitively appealing approaches to CBI than for assessing those already in hand. Evaluations were not performed because decision makers did not demand them; decision makers did not demand them because there were too few evaluations to recommend CBI as a worthwhile alternative. Gradually, however, data on CBI effectiveness have accumulated, and attitudes have changed. Instructional administrators, managers, developers, students and instructors are now beginning to ask specifically if the costs of CBI repay its users with commensurately increased instructional effectiveness or, in other words, is CBI cost-effective?

Three issues naturally arise in pursuit of this question: "How do we measure costs and effectiveness in instruction?"; "How are computers applied in instruction?"; and "What do we know about the cost-effectiveness of these instructional applications?"

1. Measuring the Costs and Effectiveness

Most evaluations of new instructional approaches are performed by instructional researchers and are concerned only with effectiveness. These evaluations may be appropriate for researchers since they are mainly interested in whether or not their innovations "work." However, for instructional decision makers, effectiveness is only one factor involved. Superior effectiveness is important, but systems are closed and budgets are limited. Decisions about the allocation of scarce resources among competing alternatives in order to maximize given goals and objectives are a perennial necessity.

1.1 Economic Analysis

The problem of allocating instructional resources or expenditures can be aided to some extent by economic analysis. Economic analysis is a technique to help make resource allocation decisions attain maximum efficiency. The assumption here is that there is a combination of resources such that instructional productivity is maximized while utilizing the minimum amount of resources. Maximum instructional efficiency is attained when no other combination of resources can be found that will improve instructional productivity without increasing instructional costs. Economic analysis for instruction consists of the repertoire of approaches that helps us achieve maximum instructional efficiency.

The basic idea behind economic analysis is the well-established and straightforward notion that there is "no free lunch." The economic analyst looks for the opportunities which are sacrificed in selecting any alternative. This suggests that the economic analyst pursues a marginalist or incrementalist approach (Okun 1970). The economic analyst must insist on knowing how much would be gained and lost if an alternative approach were adopted.

Of course, economic analysis also has certain drawbacks. An incrementalist approach pursued rigidly can neglect major opportunities since it can only compare alternatives with identical or, at least, similar goals. It can also lead to the adoption of alternatives that are basically poor investments since it does not indicate if the benefits of any single alternative exceed its costs. An antidote for these problems is systems analysis, which is not the topic of this article, but is worth remembering in this context.

Economic analysis incorporates the concepts of both cost–benefit and cost-effectiveness analysis. Cost–benefit analysis is generally used to determine if the benefits of projects and policies outweigh their costs. The assumption underlying cost–benefit analysis is that both costs and benefits are measurable in the same units, which are usually monetary units such as dollars. This commensurability is a prerequisite for cost–benefit analysis. However, the full benefits of instruction may be impossible to assess in monetary units, despite heroic attempts by economists to do so by examining national productivity and individual earnings as a function of instruction. These measures are helpful, but we still study Shakespeare and Mozart and value what we learn even though we need to repair tractors. Commensurability that adequately reflects the benefits of instruction is very difficult to attain in comparisons of instructional alternatives and their outcomes.

When commensurability is lacking, cost-effectiveness analysis is used. Costs are usually expressed in monetary units such as dollars; benefits, such as information retention, productivity, job knowledge, motivation of workers, supervisor ratings, and the productivity and effectiveness of the client organization, are usually expressed in their own units, generally along as many dimensions as possible to reflect the full spectrum of instructional outcomes. In performing cost-effectiveness analyses for instruction, a common practice is to hold either the costs or effectiveness constant and observe variations in the other variable across the alternatives being considered. Often the variable is not actually held constant, it is simply assumed to be the same across the alternatives. There are evaluations in which costs of competing alternatives is explicitly assumed to be the same, and there are just as many evaluations in which effectiveness of competing alternatives are explicitly assumed to be the same. Frequently, no data or information is presented to support the assumptions of equal costs or equal effectiveness and decision makers must take it on faith that the assumptions are warranted.

There are other instances in which issues of either costs or effectiveness are simply ignored. If the object of the study is to study effectiveness or costs alone, then this approach is warranted. For example, early evaluations of research and development products may reasonably consider effectiveness alone; studies to verify accounting procedures may reasonably consider costs alone. Such studies are appropriate and may be invaluable.

The situation is different when operational choices must be made between instructional alternatives. Both costs and effectiveness must be considered in order to make these decisions properly. Studies that are intended to inform choices among instructional alternatives and that ignore either costs or effectiveness should not be submitted by evaluators nor accepted by administrators as adequate or even appropriate. On the other hand, current practice for cost-effectiveness analysis in instruction leaves much to be desired. With regard to cost, no standardized methodology for analysis of instructional costs has been developed, nor are cost data typically acquired in accordance with a common set of definitions. In most evaluation studies, the use of formal cost models is not documented nor evident, and available incidental cost data are usually fragmentary or otherwise unsuitable for comparisons. With regard to effectiveness, the objectives of the instruction are frequently not measured, immeasurable or inarticulated. In training, which is performed to effect a number of outcomes on the job, the effectiveness measures which are frequently considered are end-of-instruction test scores and not measures of job performance. These considerations lead directly to the question of what can actually be done in practice. This question is addressed in Sects. 1.2, 1.3 which discuss the measurement of costs effectiveness in instruction.

1.2 Measurement of Costs

Levin (1983) has provided an excellent "primer" on the measurement of costs in instruction, and Knapp and Orlansky (1983) have developed a detailed cost model for training that is applicable to all instruction. These contributions did not occur spontaneously or in a vacuum. They rely on and refer to numerous earlier efforts, but they represent fairly well the state-of-the-art. In measuring the costs of instruction, a practicable list or "structure" of well-defined cost components is required. These components have been termed "ingredients" by Levin and "elements" by Knapp and Orlansky. The list should, for any instructional alternative, capture all the components that are needed for cost-effectiveness comparisons regardless of the scope, complexity or technology of the alternative. It should also ensure a level of detail in the analysis that clearly identifies the "cost drivers"—the major contributors to the cost of the alternative. The list should be usable for selecting, planning, assessing and modifying instructional alternatives.

Conceptually, the cost of an alternative consists of those resources that must be sacrificed in order to implement it. Since these resources could be used for other things, costs are defined in terms of opportunities given up to secure the opportunities which have been chosen. This notion of opportunity costs is the basis for cost-effectiveness analysis.

Four general categories are found in most cost models: research and development, initial investment, operations and support, and disposal and salvage. Research and development costs consist of all hardware, software, other materials, people and facilities necessary to create, test and evaluate an instructional approach. Initial investment costs comprise the one-time costs of procuring and deploying resources in the quantities needed to satisfy anticipated requirements for an instructional approach. Operations and support costs include those which are needed for managing, operating and maintaining an instructional approach after it has been implemented. Disposal and salvage costs comprise the one-time costs of removing the instructional approach from operational use.

Levin has suggested that five classes of ingredients should be considered in a cost model: personnel, facilities, equipment and materials, other program inputs, and client inputs. Personnel costs include all the human resources required by the approach. Levin recommends that all personnel should be classified according to their roles (instructional, administration, clerical, etc.), qualifications (training, experience, specialized skill) and time commitments (full time, part time). Facilities costs include all resources required to provide physical space for the approach. Since we are concerned here with opportunity costs, these resources should be included whether or not they are paid for by the implementors of the approach. Equipment and materials include furnishings, instructional equipment and supplies—again, whether or not they are paid for by the implementors. Other inputs include components that cannot be categorized elsewhere. Examples of these are instructor training sessions and insurance costs. Client inputs include resources that must be contributed by the users (most commonly students and/or their employers) of the instructional approach. Client inputs are especially relevant in military and industrial training where student pay and allowances may be provided by the client.

A cost-element model for evaluating training systems was developed by Knapp and Orlansky (1983). It is intended to provide a common basis for cost evaluations and cost comparisons of all training programs in the US military. In an ideal world, this model would be a special instance of a more general cost model applicable to all instruction; in turn this would be a special case of an all-purpose cost model applicable everywhere. However, this is not the case.

The Knapp and Orlansky model is the only comprehensive cost model for instruction that has emerged from an extensive search of the literature, although an earlier effort by Seidel and Wagner (1979) to develop a cost specification for CBI should be noted. The Knapp and Orlansky model given in Table 1 is a large and comprehensive model involving 11 elements for research and development, 25 elements for initial investment, and 39 elements for operating and support: a total of 75 elements in all, including none for salvage and disposal. However, it will almost always be true that some of these elements can be eliminated in estimating the costs of specific alternatives because they will be irrelevant—airfield and carrier operations costs can probably be ignored in the training of cooks. Other elements can be eliminated from specific cost-effectiveness evaluations because the costs will be the same across all alternatives; for example, command support costs will probably be the same in a comparison of tank gunnery trainers. The Knapp and Orlansky model may be both comprehensive and practicable for most training applications. It may also be applicable elsewhere (for example, to industrial training or even education) but these possibilities await systematic analysis.

1.3 Measurement of Effectiveness

Just as there is a range of cost measures to be considered in instruction, there is also a range of effectiveness measures. The end-of-instruction test, typically used to evaluate the effectiveness of instruction, rarely reflects the full range of outcomes that instructional managers and other decision makers expect in return for their investment in the program. These outcomes include: speed of response, accuracy of response, short- and long-term retention of both performance and knowledge, ability to transfer performance and knowledge to new situations, insight and the ability to teach others what was learned, adherence to procedure, and motivation to pursue the development of performance and knowledge in the subject area. The subset of these objectives which ought to be measured depends on the intentions of the decision makers. Different measures could be used to evaluate the same instructional program depending on these intentions.

The ideal might be a full and comprehensive model of instructional outcomes, analogous to the Knapp and Orlansky cost-elements model. Just as cost analysts may choose from among the components in the cost model depending on the specific alternatives under consideration, effectiveness analysts could also choose among the components in the effectiveness model. This discussion is theoretical, however, because no such model exists. On the other hand, designers of many instructional programs use a method called "instructional system design," which is basically a systems approach (analysis through evaluation) guide to the design of instruction (Logan 1979). This

Table 1
A cost-element model for evaluating training systems (Knapp and Orlansky 1983)

Research and development	*Operating and support*
design	direct costs
component development	(1) instructional costs
producibility engineering and planning	(a) pay and allowances
tooling	(i) instructors
prototype manufacture	(ii) supervisors, administration, support personnel
data	(iii) maintenance personnel
(1) managerial	(b) other government personnel costs
(2) technical	(c) consumption
test and evaluation	(i) petrol, oil, lubricants
system/project management	(ii) training munitions
facilities	(iii) utilities: electric, etc.
other	(iv) instructional materials
	(v) other
Initial investment	(d) replenishments and spares
production	(e) modification material
(1) nonrecurring	(f) depot maintenance
(a) production planning	(i) labor and materials
(b) production tooling and equipment	(ii) second destination transportation
(c) industrial facilities	(iii) other
(d) others	(g) other purchased services
(2) recurring	(h) other
(a) manufacturing	(2) training activity costs
(b) sustaining engineering	(a) pay and allowances
(c) sustaining tooling	(b) other government personnel costs
(d) quality assurance	(c) other
(e) other	(3) airfield and carrier operations costs
(3) initial spares and repair parts	(a) pay and allowances
engineering changes	(b) other government personnel costs
purchased system-peculiar equipment	(c) other
common equipment	(4) student costs
data	(i) pay and allowances
(1) managerial	(ii) other student costs
(2) technical	(5) other
(3) instruction material	indirect costs
test and evaluation	(1) base operations
system/project management	(a) pay and allowances
rents	(b) other government personnel costs
operational/site activation	(c) other
initial training	(2) inventory and supply management
(1) instructors	(a) pay and allowances
(2) maintenance personnel	(b) other government personnel costs
transportation	(c) other
(1) first destination	(3) military family housing support
(2) second destination	(a) pay and allowances
other	(b) other government personnel costs
	(c) other
	(4) command support costs
	(a) pay and allowances
	(b) other government personnel costs
	(c) other
	(5) other

method is intended to ensure that instruction contains the information needed by students to accomplish objectives that instructional managers commissioned the instructional program for in the first place.

A guide, called the instructional quality profile (IQP), which ensures that effectiveness evaluations reflect both the objectives and content of instruction programs, and that the instructional content reflects the objectives, has been developed by Merrill *et al.* (1979). The IQP approach categorizes course content by its form, rather than by its subject matter. Content is classified according to type (facts, concepts, procedures and principles) and presentation mode (generality, generality practice, instance and instance practice). Effectiveness evaluations should be keyed to the type by presentation modes actually used in the instruction, and of course, the design of the instruction should be keyed to the type by presentation modes appropriate for accomplishing the instructional objectives.

A fairly comprehensive set of evaluation designs suitable for comparing the effectiveness of different instructional alternatives has been described by Campbell and Stanley (1963). It should be emphasized that although there are many excellent books and courses of instruction concerning the statistical manipulation of experimental data collected under proper conditions of tight control and measurement accuracy, there is much less help to be found concerning the methods of collecting adequate and proper data under the less-than-perfect conditions that characterize instructional settings. Campbell and Stanley deal with this latter problem in what has become a classic statement and guidebook, and this was extended somewhat by Cook and Campbell (1979). The set of evaluation designs discussed in these two publications makes up a model of evaluation, but it is keyed to the methodology of evaluation and not to the outcomes of instruction. A comprehensive and practicable model oriented to the varieties of instructional outcomes and their assessment has yet to be produced.

1.4 Measurement of Cost-Effectiveness

Kazanowski (1968) has developed a standardized, ten-step approach to cost-effectiveness evaluations. Although the approach was oriented toward the selection of weapon systems, it provides a foundation for developing a general approach for evaluating cost-effectiveness in instruction. Kazanowski's ten-step approach, adapted for instruction, is given below.

(a) *Define the objectives.* In any systematic approach to instruction, an analysis must be performed to identify and define what the instruction is supposed to do in order to establish the instructional objectives. These objectives are most often expressed in terms of what students can do or attributes they will possess once the instruction is completed. The objectives may be derived directly from the skills and knowledge required to perform a job, as they are in training, or they may be derived from national needs for a capable work-force and informed electorate, as they are in education. In the absence of these objectives, systematic design, development, implementation and evaluation of the instruction is impossible. It is, of course, possible to proceed nonsystematically, and unfortunately this is often done.

(b) *Identify the mission requirements.* It is fundamental that an instructional alternative should meet its objectives at a microlevel by bringing about the instructional outcomes we expect to see in its graduates. On a more macrolevel, the instructional alternative as a system must possess productivity, or "pipeline," characteristics defined by its mission—it must be able to produce a given number of graduates within a given amount of time. These pipeline requirements are determined by the instructional mission.

(c) *Develop the alternatives.* Once the instructional objectives in terms of student outcomes are defined, and once the pipeline requirements of the instructional program are established, it is then appropriate to locate or devise alternative approaches for satisfying these objectives and requirements. As in most analyses intended to support decisions, the generation of alternatives is a critical activity requiring considerable imagination and creativity. Although there are tools and aids, there are no effective procedures for developing comprehensive sets of instructional alternatives to subject to cost-effectiveness evaluation.

(d) *Design the effectiveness evaluation.* The measures to be examined by an effectiveness evaluation should be well-defined and evident. These measures should follow directly from the instructional objectives and pipeline requirements established for the program in steps (a) and (b). The omission of significant measures can invalidate the results of an evaluation, but the inclusion of too many measures (perhaps more than ten) could paralyze the final choice of an alternative. A test of the adequacy of the measures selected is to determine whether an instructional alternative could excel in most of the measures and still not be best on some intuitive level. If this is true, then some important measures are missing.

(e) *Select a fixed-cost or fixed-effectiveness approach.* A key distinction between education and training, which lie at opposite ends along the dimension of instruction, is that training is carried out to secure the threshold human performance needed to perform a job. In other words, training is a means to an end. Education may be viewed as a valuable end in its own right, rather than a means to an end. Its objectives are more general than those required to perform a single job, or even job group. The result is that in training we may hold effectiveness constant and try to minimize cost to achieve that level of effectiveness, whereas in education we may hold cost constant and try to maximize the effectiveness that can be obtained for that cost. The choice between fixed-cost and fixed-effectiveness approaches may depend on whether the client decision maker is a trainer or an educator. It is possible to avoid choosing between fixed-cost and fixed-effectiveness approaches by calculating and then comparing cost–effectiveness ratios or effectiveness–cost ratios for the various alternatives. If ratios are considered, the training ratio of interest may be cost–effectiveness, and we may be interested to see what a training alternative may cost per unit of effectiveness. The education ratio of interest may be effectiveness–cost, and we may be interested to see how much effectiveness an educational alternative may deliver per unit of cost. A ratio approach of this sort is appropriate only when cost and effectiveness that are increments to some baseline are being considered. Even when the cost and effectiveness measures are properly treated as incremental, methodological caution is still advisable (Hitch and McKean 1961).

(f) Determine the capabilities of the alternative systems. Once the measures and evaluation approach have been established, it is then appropriate to gather the data and proceed with the analysis.

(g) Tabulate the alternatives and measures. When the data are gathered, they should be tabulated in a form suitable for comparison. In a fixed-cost approach, the alternatives are usually tabulated in accordance with the "northwest" rule. That is to say, the measures are listed from left to right in decreasing priority and the alternatives are listed from top to bottom in order of decreasing apparent value.

(h) Analyze the merits of the alternative systems. The client decision makers may feel that a tabulated array of findings resembles raw data rather than useful information. Decision makers need information. Discussion of the findings, the strengths and weaknesses of the data-collection procedures and assessment of the alternatives in the light of the evaluation are advantageous and should be provided.

(i) Perform a sensitivity analysis. The outcome of a cost-effectiveness evaluation may or may not be sensitive to the assumptions on which it is based; the sensitivity analysis is intended to establish this. Cost-effectiveness evaluations in instruction may be sensitive to assumptions concerning personnel costs, software maintenance costs, costs of consumables (e.g., fuel and ammunition for the military and heating oil for public schools), mean times between failure for simulators and actual equipment, actual equipment operation costs and student–instructor ratios.

(j) Document the bases of the previous nine steps. No cost-effectiveness evaluation will be perfect. It is critical for decision makers to know its strengths and limitations. It is not a trivial task to identify the assumptions underlying an evaluation, and these assumptions should be identified and described as explicitly as possible. The underlying models of cost and effectiveness should be documented so that decision makers can see what has been excluded and therefore assumed either irrelevant or equivalent across alternatives.

2. Computer Uses in Instruction

Computer-based instruction (CBI) is a term which is commonly used to describe all the possible uses of computers in instruction. CBI activity may be categorized into three areas: instruction about computers, instruction by computers and instruction using computers. All three areas have become important to instructional decision makers. Most attention has been given to the first two, but the third may be the most important.

2.1 Instruction about Computers

Instruction about computers is usually called "computer literacy." What computer literacy should be in instructional practice remains to be determined. Luehrmann (1972) introduced the term when he suggested that computer programming was a form of literacy together with reading and writing spoken language. Hence, he proposed that future generations, as well as our own, ought to become computer literate. However, the term computer literacy took on a life of its own and there soon arose considerable resistance to the notion that computer literacy must involve computer programming. Today many CBI specialists argue that a working knowledge of electronic spreadsheets, database storage and retrieval, word processing, and electronic mail is more than sufficient for computer literacy. Others argue that abstract knowledge of effective procedures could be essential for a world in which microprocessors are embedded in every household appliance, and that learning a computer language may be the shortest path to learning about effective procedures. The issues concerning computer literacy will not be settled in the near future and instruction about computers will continue to attract controversy.

2.2 Instruction by Computers

Instruction by computers usually refers to the direct use of computers to teach and is commonly called computer assisted instruction (CAI). The techniques of CAI may be divided into four areas: drill and practice, tutorial, tutorial simulation, and tutorial dialog. This categorization was introduced by Suppes and Morningstar (1969) and remains appropriate today.

Drill and practice involves the presentation of relatively discrete items to students who have had some exposure to them or to the procedures required for their solution. Arithmetic calculation, spelling words, foreign language vocabulary, parts identification and weapons system characteristics have all been the object of drill-and-practice CAI. Drill and practice often evokes images of unimaginative and unsophisticated applications in which students plod through endless numbers of items. In fact, through the application of advanced quantitative models of memory and cognition and of sophisticated techniques for individualizing instructional content, sequences and pacing, genuinely (and provably) optimal approaches to instruction have been implemented in drill and practice. The students only become bored if the instructional sessions are over-long or the interactions are poorly designed.

Tutorial techniques appear to be both the most common and least effective approaches in CAI. These techniques treat the computer as a large, and sometimes intricate, programmed textbook. They are often used to present novel information to students rather than to provide them with practice on what they already know at some rudimentary level. Students receive pretests and posttests and are often "branched" to different sequences of instruction based on their responses to the items presented in the tests or instruction. This approach could probably be pursued in a book—although the book that incorporated a computer tutorial might be extremely large. The tutorial approach is the most common, easily produced and frequently implemented approach in CBI, and it is the approach which is best supported by CBI "authoring" languages designed to allow nonprogrammers to prepare instructional materials for computer presentation. The approach can be successful, but its success has been much less reliable than others. Reasonable intuitions about when to branch and what to branch to in instruction turn out to be poorly supported by effectiveness data. The unreliable success of this approach may be justified by its low cost, but this possibility awaits empirical verification.

Tutorial simulation is common in training applications of CAI, and it is becoming increasingly common in educational applications. In tutorial simulation, the computer emulates a device or situation, and the student is allowed a fairly free hand in solving problems concerning the device or situation. In CAI the simulation is usually tutorial in the sense that the computer will provide hints, midsolution corrections (coaching) and critiques of completed solutions. Tactical decision making, electronic troubleshooting and laboratory experimentation (without the laboratory or its expensive equipment) are instances in which tutorial simulation has been applied. The cost avoidances realized by substituting two-dimensional computer presentations and displays for hands-on experience with three-dimensional equipment are strong arguments for tutorial simulation as a cost-effective alternative to actual equipment experience in instruction.

Tutorial-dialog approaches evolved from the observation that the best instructional setting is a one-to-one situation involving a master teacher and a single student. Such a setting is simply too expensive to provide in most instructional practices. However, we are rapidly approaching the time when we can afford one computer for every student. If the capabilities of an expert tutor can be incorporated into the computer—an Aristotle for every Alexander as Suppes and Morningstar (1969) suggested—the ideal one-to-one instructional setting can be approximated. This is a basic objective of tutorial dialog. Instruction about rainfall patterns, geography and mathematical logic have all been the subject of tutorial dialogs in CAI.

Tutorial simulation and tutorial dialog may be supported by the application of techniques from artificial intelligence. Such approaches are usually called intelligent computer-assisted instruction (ICAI). These approaches reflect the current "cognitive revolution" in behavioral science which has emphasized that all human learning and perceptual process are overwhelmingly active and constructive, and that the information we transmit in instruction is not analogous to raw bits of data, but should be viewed as cues to sensory simulations being built, verified and modified by the receiver—the student. Generative inferencing procedures are needed to deal with these cues and simulations. Generative and not prestored models of the subject matter to be taught, the state of the student's understanding of the subject matter, and effective tutorial approaches and interactions must be maintained by the instructional program. These approaches fit well with tutorial simulations and are practically mandatory for tutorial dialog. A review of these approaches was documented by Fletcher (1985).

2.3 Instruction using Computers

Few notions about computers used in instruction have been as persistent as the idea that they should become tools for both instructors and students. This area includes the use of computers to help manage instructional resources, manage student progress, assist in administration, give tests and control simulations. These sorts of uses are frequently referred to as computer-managed instruction (CMI). In addition to these management functions, the area also includes the notion that word processors, spreadsheets, databases and other utility programs represent genuine opportunities for supporting and improving the effectiveness of classroom processes. As promising as these opportunities are, they have been pursued more slowly than CAI or computer literacy. This is the case because research, development and evaluation in this area requires cooperative efforts by instructors, students, administrators and researchers all working unobtrusively in operating instructional environments—schools. As might be expected, appropriate settings for research and development in this area have not been numerous, and progress has been slower than anyone—including, notably, classroom instructors—would like.

3. Cost and Effectiveness of Computer-Based Instruction

At this point we can consider what is currently known about the cost, the effectiveness and the cost-effectiveness of CBI.

3.1 Cost of Computer-Based Instruction

Little appears to be known about the determinants or composition of the costs of CBI. Budgets are available from contractors who propose to develop CBI materials. However, budgets are inadequate for cost estimation because they do not include all the components needed for an adequate cost accounting, they may distort the true costs of a component to accord with local accounting practices and they represent planned not actual expenditures.

The main problem with CBI costs is, as is generally true for instructional costs, the absence of a standard model upon which to base cost collection. The Seidel and Wagner (1979) cost specification for CBI was an important beginning, but more needs to be done. The reported cost of CBI per student or per instructional hour may vary widely from project to project simply because different assumptions and procedures were used in collecting the costs. Initial investment costs may be somewhat easier to estimate since the development of CBI is usually a labor-intensive process and the person-hours required to produce one student contact hour of CBI are documented in the literature. However, these vary widely. Orlansky and String (1979) report that 77–714 person-hours are required to produce one student contact hour of CBI, but the notion of student contact hour remains undefined for CBI—how, for instance, should the student contact hours be estimated for a simulation? In any case, a median value of about 200 person-hours to develop one student contact hour of CBI is a common finding.

It is not difficult to collect data on the cost of hardware for various computer systems used to support CBI and most existing cost analyses of CBI have focused primarily on the cost of procuring the necessary hardware. However, the costs of computer systems are among the most volatile of any commodity. Moreover, with rapid and continuing miniaturization of electronics, initial equipment costs are likely to be insignificant when compared with instructional program development costs and the life-cycle program costs associated with long-term use of CBI. These latter costs are rarely given serious consideration in cost evaluations of CBI. The problem will not be solved even when complete and reliable data on CBI system costs become available unless equivalent data are also available on the costs of the conventional instructional systems that form the baseline for comparison.

As cost models, such as the one developed by Knapp and Orlansky, find common use, reliable information will begin to emerge. In the interim, a number of studies report costs for CBI relative to some "baseline" instructional approach. These studies permit the calculation of ratios that estimate the cost of CBI compared to the more conventional approaches. Current research involving fixed-effectiveness evaluations and cost ratios calculated with the CBI costs in the numerators indicates that these ratios vary from 0.05 for CAI tutorial simulations for operators of expensive equipment to 1.11 for CMI compared to paper-based techniques of individualized instruction.

In considering any of these ratios, it is important to remember that some component(s) of cost that heavily favor one approach over the other could have been inadvertently excluded. Nevertheless, these ratios provide rough estimates of the relative costs of CBI and they allow us to consider, roughly, the cost-effectiveness of CBI.

3.2 Effectiveness of Computer-Based Instruction

More is known about the effectiveness of CBI than about the costs. About a dozen major reviews of research on CBI effectiveness have been completed and published. These all show CBI to be generally effective, but they also show considerable variability in its effectiveness—spectacular failures can be found as well as spectacular successes. Probably the earliest systematic review was published by Vinsonhaler and Bass (1972). This review covers 39 published empirical evaluations of CBI drill and practice involving over 10 000 students. For those who view CBI as a recent phenomenon, it should be emphasized that this review was completed in 1971 and published in 1972. The authors found positive or equal results in 30 of the 34 studies, a range in mean gain by the CBI students over students receiving conventional instruction of -0.80 to $+0.88$, and a median gain achieved by CBI students of 0.40.

The principal review of CBI effectiveness in training was published by Orlansky and String (1979). This study was concerned with skill training performed for the US military. The authors found 40 comparisons of student achievement under CBI and conventional instruction. Student achievement was the same in 24 of these studies. Of the 16 studies in which statistical significance was found, the CBI students performed better in 15 of them, leaving 1 study in which conventionally taught students performed better. The authors also found 8 comparisons of CMI and conventional instruction. No differences in student achievement were found in any of the 8 CMI studies. Finally, the authors considered the amount of student time required to finish the courses in all 48 comparisons. They found a range of -0.31 to 0.89 in student time savings under CBI, with a median time savings of 0.30.

The above studies relied on a "box-score" approach to synthesizing studies. These studies tally the number of studies favorable and unfavorable to the approach under consideration, tabulate them, and provide narrative explanations for the results. The statistical weaknesses of this approach were criticized by Hedges and Olkin (1980) who showed that the approach has unacceptably low power, in the statistical sense of avoiding false negatives, and that its power actually decreases as the number of studies considered increases. The response of reviewers has been to take a meta-analytic approach in which quantitative statistical methods are used to summarize findings and to discuss results of the empirical evaluations under consideration. Another notable characteristic of these newer approaches has been that reviewers now locate the evaluation studies to be summarized using more systematic and carefully defined collection methodologies than are found in most box-score studies.

Kulik et al. (Kulik et al. 1983, 1985; Kulik and Kulik 1986) (among others) have completed three meta-analyses of CBI, one each for elementary, secondary and college applications. In each case, a metric called "effect size" was used to measure the difference in achievement of students receiving CBI and students receiving conventional instruction. Effect size (Glass et al. 1981) is a normalized score obtained by dividing the difference of the group means (achievement of the CBI group minus achievement of the conventional instruction group) by the standard deviation of the conventional instruction group. A positive effect size in these studies indicates greater achievement by the CBI group.

In reviewing CBI in elementary schools, Kulik et al. (1985) found 32 evaluation studies suitable for their purposes—28 studies concerning CAI and 4 concerning CMI. The average effect size in the CAI studies was 0.47 standard deviations and the average effect size in the CMI studies was 0.07 standard deviations. The range in effect size was -0.08 to 1.31 standard deviations. In all 28 of the 32 studies that reported final examination scores, CBI students scored higher than the students receiving conventional instruction. In 23 of these 28 studies, the results were statistically significant.

In reviewing CBI in secondary schools, Kulik et al. (1983) found 51 evaluation studies suitable for their purposes. The average effect size across these studies was 0.32 standard deviations in favor of the students receiving CBI. The range was -0.5 to 1.5 standard deviations. In 39 of the 48 studies that reported final examination results, CBI students scored higher, and in 9 of these studies, students receiving conventional instruction scored higher. Of the 25 studies that resulted in a statistically significant difference, 23 favored the CBI students and 2 favored the students receiving conventional instruction.

In reviewing CBI in colleges, Kulik and Kulik (1986) found 101 evaluation studies suitable for their purposes. The average effect size across these studies was 0.26 standard deviations. The range was -1.20 to 1.94 standard deviations. In 77 of the 99 studies that reported final examination results, CBI students scored higher and in the remaining 22 studies, the students receiving conventional instruction scored higher. Of the 22 studies that reported statistically significant differences, 21 were in favor of the CBI students and 1 favored the students receiving conventional instruction. Fifteen studies compared instructional time. The CBI students generally needed only two thirds of the instructional time used by the conventionally taught students to finish the course.

In summary, existing studies provide substantial evidence for the general effectiveness of CBI. These results have been obtained from a wide variety of students, instructional effectiveness measures, instructional settings and instructional subject matters. The results also show that success is not automatic—some studies have found CBI to be less effective than conventional instruction.

3.3 Cost-Effectiveness of Computer-Based Instruction

If we cast caution aside and simply aggregate the results of reliably performed individual studies that consider only operating and support costs, and only end-of-instruction performance measures, the following conclusions can be drawn.

(a) CAI is generally more cost-effective than conventional instruction. Most studies of CAI—the direct use of computers to teach—that consider both cost and effectiveness report median values in the 20–30% range favoring CAI.

(b) CMI is generally more cost-effective than conventional instruction. Studies of CMI—the use of computers to manage student progress and instructional resources—that consider both cost and effectiveness report median values in the 5–20% range favoring CMI.

(c) CAI is generally more cost-effective than CMI. Simply by comparing results from the two types of studies mentioned above we find a 5–10% difference favoring the cost-effectiveness of CAI.

(d) CBI is generally more cost-effective than conventional instruction. By combining results from the CAI and CMI studies mentioned above, we find that instructional alternatives that use computers are more cost-effective than those that do not.

The cautions concerning these summary conclusions are notable, however; these are listed below.

(a) The costs considered here are known to be operating and support costs, but the specific set of cost components which were used in most of these studies is at best uncertain.

(b) The effectiveness measures considered here concern end-of-instruction performance. In training, which is the instructional setting of most of the findings, the effectiveness measure of interest is job performance; this is missing from these studies. Also, the impact of CBI on instructional outcomes not measured by these studies is unknown but is of potential interest to instructional decision makers.

(c) Few of these studies were performed by third-party evaluators. Most of them were performed by those who initially developed or implemented the CBI.

(d) Most of these results are based on prototype CBI applications. They do not evolve from stable-state well-established implementations in which the use of CBI is a routine matter.

Obviously, more work is needed. The cost-effectiveness of CBI is neither a mature nor settled issue, but the topic is growing and beginning to attract the attention of concerned and capable individuals.

Bibliography

Campbell, D T, Stanley J C 1963 *Experimental and Quasi-Experimental Designs for Research*. McNally, Chicago, Illinois

Cook T D, Campbell D T 1979 *Quasi-Experimentation: Design and Analysis for Field Settings*. McNally, Chicago, Illinois

Fletcher J D 1985 Intelligent instructional systems in training. In: Andriole S J (ed.) *Applications in Artificial Intelligence*. Petrocelli, Princeton, New Jersey, pp. 427–51

Fletcher J D 1986 Computer-based training in the military. In: Ellis J A (ed.) *Military Contributions to Instructional Technology*. Praeger, New York, pp. 171–222

Glass G V, McGaw B, Smith M L 1981 *Meta-Analysis in Social Research*. Sage, Beverly Hills, California

Hedges L V, Olkin I 1980 Vote-counting methods in research synthesis. *Psychol. Bull.* **88**, 359–69

Hitch C J, McKean R N 1961 *The Economics of Defense in the Nuclear Age*. Harvard University Press, Cambridge, Massachusetts

Kazanowski A D 1968 A standardized approach to cost-effectiveness evaluations. In: English J M (ed.) *Cost-Effectiveness: The Economic Evaluation of Engineered Systems*. Wiley, New York

Knapp M I, Orlansky J 1983 *A Cost Element Structure for Defense Training*, IDA Paper P-1709. Institute for Defense Analyses, Alexandria, Virginia

Kulik C-L C, Kulik J A 1986 Effectiveness of computer-based education in colleges. *AEDS J.* **19**, 81–108

Kulik J A, Bangert R L, Williams G W 1983 Effects of computer-based teaching on secondary school students. *J Educ. Psychol.* **75**, 19–26

Kulik J A, Kulik C-L C, Bangert-Drowns R L 1985 Effects of computer-based education in elementary schools. *Comput. Hum. Behav.* **1**, 59–74

Levin H A 1983 *Cost Effectiveness: A Primer*. Sage, Beverly Hills, California

Logan R S 1979 A state of the art assessment of instructional systems development. In: O'Neil H F (ed.) *Issues in Instructional Systems Development* Academic Press, New York

Luehrmann A 1972 Should the computer teach the student, or vice versa. In: *AFIPS Conf. Proc.: Spring Joint Computer Conf. 1972*. Prentice–Hall, Montvale, New Jersey

Merrill D M, Reigeluth C M, Faust G W 1979 The instructional quality profile: A curriculum evaluation and design tool. In: O'Neil H F (ed.) *Procedures for Instructional Systems Development*. Academic Press, New York

Okun A M 1970 *The Political Economy of Prosperity*. Norton, New York

Orlansky J, String J 1979 *Cost-Effectiveness of Computer Based Instruction in Military Training*, IDA Paper P-1375. Institute for Defense Analyses, Alexandria, Virginia

Seidel R J, Wagner H 1979 A cost-effectiveness specification. In: O'Neil H F (ed.) *Procedures for Instructional Systems Development*. Academic Press, New York, pp. 233–51

Suppes P, Morningstar M 1969 Computer assisted instruction. *Science* **166**, 343–50

Vinsonhaler J F, Bass R K 1972 A summary of ten major studies on CAI drill and practice. *Educ. Technol.* **12**, 29–32

J. D. Fletcher
[Institute for Defense Analyses, Alexandria, Virginia, USA]

D

Decision Analysis

We make decisions every day. Our decisions range in difficulty from the very simple to the very complex and in scope from the very narrow to the very broad. We make very simple decisions without much consideration of the factors affecting and affected by the decision, at least we often think that this is what we do. In reality, a decision is often *simple* because it concerns an issue with which we are experientially familiar and where we understand very well the components of the decision. Intuition or other affective forms of reasoning are perfectly acceptable in these situations. We normally give more complex decisions much more thought and consider more of the factors involved. Depending on the complexity and scope involved, the thought given may be a brief mental comparison of alternatives, or it may be a thorough analysis appropriate to a complex situation in which there are significant differences in the impacts of various alternative courses of action. This article will be more concerned with the latter situation. We generally imply *formal decision analysis* when we use the term *decision analysis* and this is the case here.

The decision-analysis problem may be described as follows. The decision maker is presented with a problem which requires a decision. Certain objectives are provided by those to whom the decision maker is responsible. Alternative courses of action are also provided, each of which satisfies the objectives in some way. The problem is to choose the course of action which best satisfies these objectives. If there is more than one factor which contributes to the satisfaction of the objectives, the decision maker must find some way of combining the contributions that satisfy the objectives in some "best" or most appropriate way. In large-scale public and private issues which involve technological choice there are many alternatives that may be implemented, many objectives to be satisfied, and diverse group opinions concerning the worth of various alternatives.

In considering decisions, a systems analyst must exercise great care to incorporate the values of those affected by the decision into the decision-making process. Incorporating these values into the process often results in making, either consciously or unconsciously, some very basic decisions. A decision analyst who has been called upon to help solve a problem must accept the fundamental decisions and values of those stakeholders whose brokerage has funded the problem study. It is essential that those fundamental values which act as constraints upon problem solution are explicitly enumerated as such when presenting the result of the decision analysis.

Normally, a decision analysis should result in the identification of the values of a client group, explicitly or implicitly, for use in the analysis. These values should not be altered. The primary objectives of a decision analysis are:

(a) to formulate the issue in terms of objectives to be attained, needs to be satisfied and the identification of potential alternative courses of action;

(b) to analyze the impacts of the alternatives upon the needs and objectives of the client; and

(c) to interpret these impacts in terms of the objectives of the client so that the selection of the best alternative course of action is possible.

These are just the formal steps of the systems engineering process and there is little difference between decision analysis and a general systems approach to problem resolution.

1. Elementary Decision Analysis

Decision analysis can be subdivided into four categories:

(a) decision under certainty, in which each action results in one and only one outcome;

(b) decision under risk, in which one of several outcomes can result from a given action depending on the state of nature, these states occurring with known probabilities;

(c) decision under uncertainty, in which one of several outcomes can result from a given action depending on the state of nature, these states occurring with unknown probabilities; and

(d) decision under conflict, in which nature is replaced by a not necessarily hostile opponent.

Problems in category (a) are problems to which deterministic theory may be applied. Problems in category (d) are game-theoretic problems. The domain for decision analysis is generally restricted to categories (b) and (c). The majority of decision-analysis efforts have been applied to issues in category (b), although current approaches to imperfect knowledge allows solution to problems in category (c) as well. We will initially concentrate on a description of problems in category (b), and will then provide an overview of solution methods for problems in category (c).

As a preliminary to the study of decision analysis in large-scale systems, an overview of the basic decision-analysis problem is presented here. Decision analysis provides us with a rational framework for choosing among alternative sources of action when the outcomes resulting from these alternatives are clouded by uncertainty. The theoretical foundations of decision analysis are probability theory and utility theory. Probability theory allows the decision maker to make maximum use of the information available, while utility theory guarantees that the choice will reflect the true preferences of the decision maker. While there are many introductory decision-analysis studies, those by Howard (1968, 1975), North (1968) Raiffa (1968), Brown (1974), Sage (1977) and Holloway (1979) are particularly pertinent to our efforts here.

A decision-analysis model contains the five elements listed below.

(a) the set of r alternative actions; e.g.
$$C = \{c(1), c(2), \ldots, c(r)\}.$$

(b) the set of m states of nature, e.g.,
$$N = \{n(1), n(2), \ldots, n(m)\}.$$

(c) the set of rm outcomes, e.g.,
$$Q = \{q(11), \ldots, q(ij), q(rm)\}$$
where $q(ij)$ corresponds to the pair of action–event possibilities $[a(i)e(j)]$.

(d) a utility function; e.g.,
$$U = \{u(11), u(ij), \ldots, u(rm)\}$$
where $u(ij) = U[q(ij)]$. expresses the decision maker's utility at having selected alternative i and receiving state of nature j as a result.

(e) the objective, a criterion or statement of what is desired.

It is necessary to consider in some detail what is meant by the concept of utility. Formally, a utility function is a transformation which maps the set of outcomes of a decision problem onto some interval of the real line. In other words, a utility function assigns a numerical value to each outcome of a decision problem. If the utility of outcome A is designated by $u(A)$, then the basic assumptions of utility theory may be described as follows.

Assumption 1. Any two outcomes resulting from a decision may be compared. If A and B are two such outcomes, then one must either prefer A to B ($A > B$), prefer B to A ($B > A$), or be indifferent between A and B ($A \sim B$). An extension of this assumption is the concept of transitivity, which states that if a rational decision maker prefers A to B and B to C, then the decision maker must also prefer A to C. If a decision maker is not transitive, various inconsistencies can result, as can easily be demonstrated. In the simple way posed here, every individual should normatively seek to be transitive relative to the preferential expressions. Unfortunately, what applies to individuals does not apply to groups, as indicated in the article *Group Decision Making and Voting*.

Assumption 2. Utilities may be assigned to lotteries involving outcomes as well as to the outcomes themselves. A lottery is a chance mechanism which yields outcomes $E_1, E_2, \ldots, E_n$ with probabilities $p_1, p_2, \ldots, p_n$, respectively, where each $p_i \geq 0$ and $\Sigma_{i=1}^n p_i = 1$. Such a lottery is denoted by: $L = (p_1, E_1; p_2, E_2; \ldots; p_n, E_n)$ and is illustrated in Fig. 1. From this it follows that if one prefers A to B then one should prefer A to the lottery $[p, A; (1-p), B]$, and one should prefer this lottery to B, where $0 < p < 1$. Further, if one prefers A to B then one should prefer the lottery $L = [p, A; (1-p), B]$ to the lottery $L' = [p', A; (1-p'), B]$ if and only if $p > p'$.

Assumption 3. There is no intrinsic reward in the lotteries themselves, or as it is more commonly expressed, there is "no fun in gambling." As an illustration of this assumption, consider the three outcomes A, B and C and a compound lottery in which one outcome is A with probability p and the other outcome is a lottery involving B and C $[p', B; (1-p'), C]$ with probability $(1-p)$. Such a lottery is given by $[p, A; (1-p), p', B; (1-p'), C]$ and is equivalent to the simple three-way lottery among A, B and C: $[p, A; (1-p)p', B; (1-p)(1-p'), C]$. In other words, the preferences of the decision maker should not be affected by the particular means chosen to resolve the uncertainty. If there is indeed "fun" in gambling, then this should be considered as one of the attributes of the alternative outcomes. This is easily accomplished and the result is a situation in which there is no reward associated with the lotteries themselves.

Assumption 4. This deals with the continuity of the utility function. If A is preferred to C and C is preferred to B, then for sufficiently large p, the lottery $[p, A; (1-p)B]$ is preferred to C. Similarly for sufficiently small p, C is preferred to the lottery $[p, A; (1-p), B]$. Thus there exists some p, $(0 < p < 1)$, such that one is indifferent between C and the lottery $[p, A; (1-p), B]$.

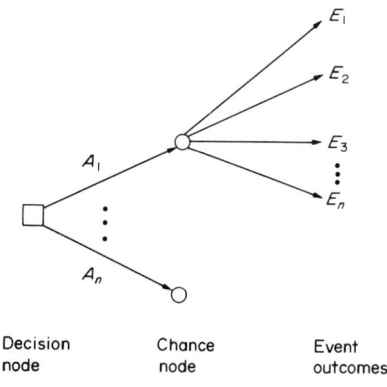

Figure 1
Decision-analysis tree structure for a lottery

Assumption 4 contains the key to resolving a decision-under-risk problem through the use of decision-analysis techniques. In actual practice, a situation like the one described in this assumption is used to measure the utility that a decision maker has for various outcomes.

It is important to keep in mind that the concept of preference precedes the concept of utility. In other words, A may be preferred to B but not because $u(A) > u(B)$; on the contrary, $u(A) > u(B)$ because A is preferred to B. Also, it is important to note that the numerical values assigned by the utility function are not unique. Given a utility function $u_1(x)$, it is possible to generate a new utility function $u_2(x) = au_1(x) + b$, where a is a positive constant and b is any constant, such that the preferences are not altered. Thus in a sense, a utility function may be viewed as a kind of "preference thermometer." The utility function must also be monotonically nondecreasing with the highest utility assigned to the most preferred outcome and the lowest utility assigned to the least preferred outcome.

As was mentioned earlier, decision analysis (or decision theory) attempts to combine probability theory with the concept of a utility function. A summary of how this is accomplished is presented here. Numerous excellent pedagogical examples of the basic decision problem are available in the literature. The "anniversary" problem discussed by North (1968) and the "wildcatter" problem described by Raiffa (1968) are especially good. The illustrative examples in Brown (1974) and Holloway (1979) are excellent. In order to keep the discussion relatively context free, the approach here will roughly parallel the treatment of the "ball–urn" type problems which are often used to illustrate decision-analysis concepts.

Assume a collection of urns each identical in external appearance and each containing a number of red balls and black balls. The decision maker knows in advance that there are n_1 urns, called type R_1, containing r_1 red balls and b_1 black balls, and there are n_2 urns, called type R_2, containing r_2 red balls and b_2 black balls. The decision maker is given an urn and must decide on the basis of the information given above, whether it is of type R_1 or of type R_2. The reward will be a certain gain or loss depending on both the choice of urn (R_1 or R_2) and the type of urn which the decision maker does in fact have. The reward matrix is given by Fig. 2 where W stands for win and L stands for lose. The decision maker is faced with two possible choices (three if the option of refusing to play is allowed): the decision maker may choose R_1 or R_2. Which choice should be made? According to the basic rules of decision theory, a rational decision maker will choose the urn which maximizes the expected reward. If the R_1 urn is chosen, the expected reward will be $E(R_1) = W_1 p(R_1) + L_1 p(R_2)$. If the R_2 urn is chosen, the expected reward will be $E(R_2) = L_2 p(R_1) + W_2 p(R_2)$ where $p(R_i)$ is the probability of being given an urn of type R_i. In this case, $p(R_1) = n_1/(n_1 + n_2)$ and $p(R_2)$

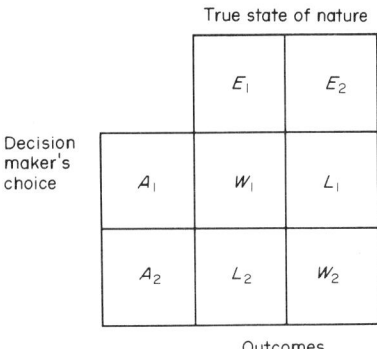

Figure 2
Pay-off matrix for simple decision options and outcomes

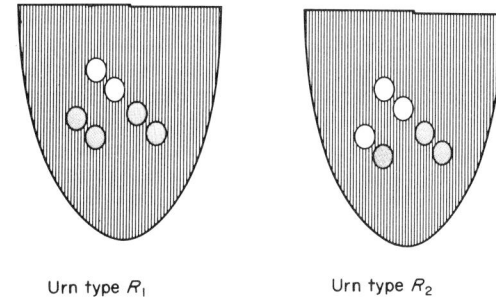

Figure 3
Generic urn model

$= n_2/(n_1 + n_2)$. Figure 3 illustrates some of the details concerning this urn model.

Now suppose the decision maker has the option of picking one ball out of the unknown urn and observing the color of the ball. Of course, a price must be paid for this privilege. There is generally always a cost associated with information acquisition. Note that previously, all the decision maker's knowledge of $p(R_1)$ and $p(R_2)$ came from the relative proportion of type R_1 and type R_2 urns. These are called *a priori* probabilities since they are known prior to sampling. Now the decision maker has picked a ball at random from the urn in question, has observed its color, and can use this knowledge, together with Bayes' rule, to update the assessment of $p(R_1)$ and $p(R_2)$. These are called *a posteriori* probabilities since they are determined after sampling. With these updated probabilities the decision maker again chooses the urn which maximizes the expected reward. Of course, the cost of the sample must be subtracted from the reward that might be obtained. Note that now the decision maker initially has four choices: (a) don't play, (b) pick R_1, (c) pick R_2, or (d) take a sample. If the decision maker chooses one of the first three of these options, then the outcome will be determined with no further action required by the decision maker. If the fourth alternative is chosen, then after sampling one ball from the urn and observing the color of the ball chosen, the decision maker will be faced with another decision: pick R_1 or pick R_2.

Thus, the problem now becomes a sequential decision problem. More complex examples may be constructed and displayed in the form of a decision tree with alternating decision nodes and chance nodes. The optimal policy is developed by starting at the terminal nodes and working back through the tree in a manner such that at each decision node the decision maker chooses the path which maximizes the expected reward from that point. This approach is known as "averaging out and folding back" and is analogous to the solution of a dynamic programming problem. While there are many situations where such an approach may be valid, there are also many cases where it is impossible since the decision maker must have all the information regarding probabilities of various outcomes and costs of sampling before it is possible to determine an optimal path through the decision tree.

The term decision analysis has come to be a generic term which refers to a wide variety of problems in systems engineering. The one common factor between all these problems is that they involve some kind of optimization. For example, in the model just described, the decision maker seeks to choose the alternative $a(i)$ which makes the resulting $u(ij)$ "best" in some sense. Often "best" will mean "maximum." However, the resulting $u(ij)$ will also depend upon the particular value of the random variable $e(j)$ so the best the decision maker can do here is to maximize some function such as the expected value of the random variable $u(ij)$:

$$\max_i E[a(i)] = \max_i \sum_{j=1}^{n} u(ij) p[e(j)] \quad (1)$$

where $p[e(j)]$ is the probability that the state of nature is $e(j)$, and we have used the abbreviated notation $E[a(i)]$ to mean the expected utility of taking action $a(i)$.

When choosing among alternatives, we must be able to indicate preferences among possible outcomes and resultant consequences.

Utility theory is needed for at least two reasons. First, we may have an aversion toward risk. We may not be willing to make a decision involving a risk unless the odds lean towards a favorable consequence. On the other hand, we may be risk-prone and make risky decisions simply for the "fun" of it or because of large rewards if we "win." Second, not all consequences are so easily quantified as money, and the decision maker has to clearly formulate preferences with that in mind. How do we compare apples and oranges? Or how much money is the life of a sick child worth? A utility function makes it possible to attempt to resolve very perplexing questions such as these.

However, before discussing utility theory, we need to define a lottery.

As stated earlier, a lottery is a chance mechanism which yields outcomes $E_1, E_2, \ldots, E_n$ with probabilities $p_1, p_2, \ldots, p_n$, respectively, where each $p_i \geq 0$ and $\sum_{i=1}^{n} p_i = 1$. The lottery is denoted by

$$L = (p_1 E_1, p_2 E_2, \ldots, p_n E_n) \quad (2)$$

We can now formally define a utility function as a transformation which maps the set of consequences onto an interval on the real line. We will denote the utility of a consequence $E(i)$ as $U[E(i)]$.

To establish a utility theory, several assumptions are made. The number of assumptions varies from four to six, depending on how they are presented. We have just described four assumptions or axioms, which enables establishment of subjective expected utility as the criterion of choice for rational decision making. The result of these assumptions is that the utility function $u(ij)$ of Eqn. (1) satisfies several properties. These utilities turn out to be indicators of preference and not absolute measurements. They are unique only up to a general linear transformation or, in other words, affine transformation.

A utility curve for money can be generated in the following manner. Arrange all the outcomes of a decision in order of preference. Call the most preferred outcome W and the least preferred outcome L. Arbitrarily assign utility $u(W) = 1$ and $u(L) = 0$. Next the decision maker asks, "Suppose I owned the rights to a lottery which pays W with probability $1/2$ and L with probability $1/2$. For what amount, say $X(0.5)$, would I be willing to sell the rights to this lottery?" Since the decision maker is indifferent between receiving $X(0.5)$ for certain and participating in the lottery $(0.5, W; 0.5, L)$, then $u(X(0.5)) = 0.5 u(W) + 0.5 u(L) = 0.5$. Figure 4 illustrates this in a decision-tree form.

Note that we could have picked any other lottery with outcomes W and L; for example, $(0.01, W; 0.99, L)$. There are several reasons, however, for choosing a

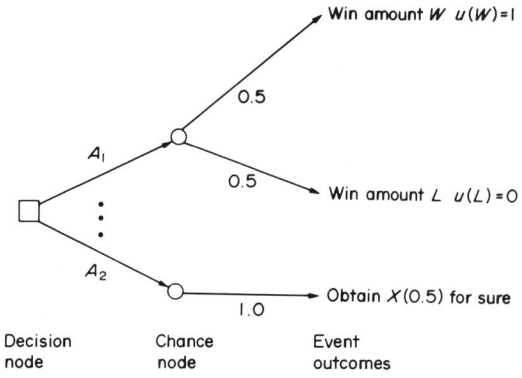

Figure 4
Decision-analysis tree structure to determine decision-maker utility

lottery which gives W or L with equal probability, or $L = (0.5, W; 0.5, L)$. First, it is often conceptually quite simple for the decision maker to imagine a lottery which gives W or L with equal probability. When W and L occur with equal probability, the decision maker need only be concerned with the relative preferences of W and L, since they are both weighted equally. Finally, the value of the lottery $(0.5, W; 0.5, L)$ occurs midway on the u axis between W and L and thus facilitates plotting the utility curve.

Next the decision maker must ask, "Suppose I owned the rights to a lottery which paid W with probability 1/2 and L with probability 1/2. For what amount, call it $X_{(0.75)}$, would I just be willing to sell the rights to this lottery?" Here, the decision maker is indifferent between receiving $X_{(0.75)}$ for certain and participating in the lottery $[0.5, W; 0.5 X_{(0.5)}]$. Therefore $u[X_{(0.75)}] = 0.5u[X_{(0.5)}] + 0.5u(L) = 0.75$. The lottery next considered is $[0.5, X(0.5); 0.5, L]$, and the amount to be determined is $X_{(0.25)}$. In this case $u[X_{(0.25)}] = 0.5u[X_{(0.5)}] + 0.5u(L) = 0.25$.

This process could be continued indefinitely; however, the three points generated here and the two end points are often sufficient to give an idea of the shape of the utility curve which will take on the general shapes shown in Fig. 5. It is rare that a decision maker is risk averse.

One of the major tasks in decision analysis is the process of specifying probabilities and associated utilities representing individual judgements concerning uncertain quantities. Spetzler and von Holstein (1975) discuss the subject of probability encoding in decision analysis and review examples of human bias and unconscious modes of judgement. They present a variety of encoding methods and discuss their applicability. Morris (1974) discusses a conceptual and methodological framework which allows the use of expert opinion in determining probabilities and utilities for decision making. Multiattribute utilities (Fishburn 1968; Raiffa 1968, Keeney and Raiffa 1976) are also of much importance. The seminal text by von Winterfeldt and Edwards (1986) is also of considerable value.

In dealing with any multiattributed decision problem, it is important to keep all the attributes in their proper perspective. One way of doing this is to arrange all the relevant attributes of the problem into a hierarchy. This can be done by asking questions to determine if one attribute is embedded within another, or if increasing the value of one attribute can be viewed as a means of increasing the value of another attribute. Once this has been done, the decision maker is provided with a graphical representation of how all the various attributes fit into the decision problem. Closely related to multiattributed utility theory is the concept of worth assessment and simple multiattribute utility theory (SMART). (Miller 1967, Farris and Sage 1975a,b, Edwards 1977, Sage 1977). This is a formal approach for evaluating complex alternatives under

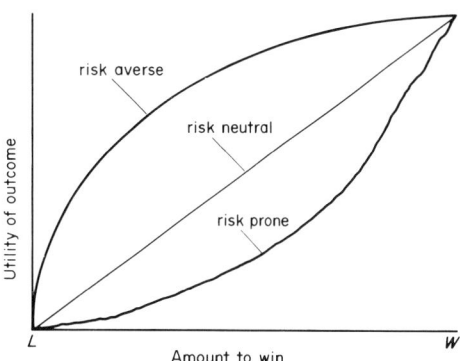

Figure 5
Hypothetical utility curve

certainty, and then later incorporating risk so that the resulting numbers can be used as utilities in a decision problem. The procedure here is to list all the relevant attributes and then arrange them in a criterion hierarchy. Worth assessment involves determining worth scores for single attributes and combining them into an overall worth score for a multiattributed consequence.

2. Steps Involved in Conducting a Decision Analysis

Decision analysis provides a formal rational, systematic framework for search, deliberation, evaluation and selection that facilitates the choice of a most preferred course of action for a decision maker in a complex decision situation. Typical activity steps in a decision analysis are listed below.

(a) structuring the relationship between decision alternatives and outcomes, typically in the form of a decision tree.

(b) encoding (extracting and quantifying) information known by the decision maker or others to describe the likelihood of occurrence of outcomes in uncertain situations.

(c) assessing decision-maker preferences for the various attributes characterizing the possible outcomes and then logically including decision-maker attitudes towards risk in uncertain situations. This will generally result in a utility or worth function.

(d) use of the utility function, the attribute measures of the outcomes and the probabilistic information to evaluate an overall utility score for the set of outcomes associated with each alternative.

(e) ranking of the outcomes, discussion of results with the decision maker, and iteration as necessary to enable final selection of a most preferred course of action.

The typical final products of a formal decision analysis are as follows.

(a) a decision tree which represents the real decision situation and which indicates probabilities assigned to outcomes thereby expressing their occurrence probabilities.

(b) a mathematical utility function describing the decision makers' preferences for the attributes that characterize the decision situation. This function might be useful for guiding future decisions of a similar nature.

(c) an evaluation and ranking of alternative courses of action according to their utility or value to the decision maker.

(d) a description of the decision situation and the utility function, how it was elicited, and how the overall evaluation of each alternative was derived.

(e) a sensitivity analysis of how the results might change for changes in uncertain inputs such as subjective probabilities, personal preferences and attribute measures.

A number of intermediate results that are also of value are typically obtained as a by-product of a decision analysis. These include the following.

(a) increased understanding of the decision situation through careful identification of alternatives, outcomes and their relationship.

(b) significant learning by the decision makers concerning their own preferences, and the logical consequences of those, resulting in more rational and consistent and less-stressful choicemaking.

(c) improved communication concerning perceptions, objectives and alternatives among the members of a decision-making group.

There are a number of information requirements for use of decision analysis. These include the following:

(a) a definition of the decision situation including an identification of the issue formulation elements of needs, constraints, objectives (and their structure) and measures of their achievement by which outcomes shall be evaluated;

(b) an identified list of all known alternatives available to the decision maker;

(c) a list of all known possible outcomes that may occur in the future due to implementation of each alternative: one and only one of these should occur when a decision is implemented;

(d) information about the relationship between these alternatives and the corresponding outcomes;

(e) information about the likelihood of occurrence of each outcome; and

(f) information about the attributes or objectives measures of all possible outcomes.

It is often difficult to obtain the information corresponding to the decision situation and alternative courses of action. In particular, the requirement that probabilities and utilities be known precisely is often not satisfied. There have been a number of recent developments to cope with these imperfect information situations. Some of these developments are covered here.

3. Decision Analysis with Multiattribute and Imperfect Information

In the decision-analysis paradigm, it is assumed that a set of feasible alternatives $A = [a(1), \ldots, a(m)]$ and a set $(X_1, \ldots, X_n)$ of attributes or evaluators of the alternatives can be identified. Associated with each alternative course of action a in A, there is a corresponding consequence $X_1(a), X_2(a), \ldots, X_n(a)$ in the n-dimensional consequence space $X = X_1 X_2 \ldots X_n$.

The problem of the decision maker is to choose an alternative a in A so that the maximum pleasure with the pay-off or consequence, $[X_1(a), \ldots, X_n(a)]$, results. It is always possible to compare the values of each $X_i(a)$ for different alternatives, but in most situations, the magnitudes of $X_i(a)$ and $X_j(a)$ for $i \neq j$ cannot be meaningfully compared since they may be measured in totally different units. Thus, a scalar-valued function defined on the attributes $(X_1, \ldots, X_n)$ is sought that will allow comparison of the alternatives across the attributes. The existence of the value function as a mechanism for representation and selection of alternatives in a utility space is based on the fundamental representation theorem of simple preferences which states that under certain conditions of rational behavior there exists a real-valued utility function U such that alternative $a(1)$ is preferred to alternative $a(2)$ if and only if the utility of $a(1)$, denoted by $U[a(1)]$, is greater than $U[a(2)]$, the utility of $a(2)$.

A primary interest in multiattribute utility theory (MAUT) is to structure and assess a utility function of the form

$$U[X_1(a), \ldots, X_n(a)] = f\{U_1[X_1(a)], \ldots, U_n[X_n(a)]\} \qquad (3)$$

where U_i is a utility function over the single attribute X_i and f aggregates the values of the single attribute utility functions hence enabling the computation of the scalar utility of the alternatives. The utility functions U and U_i are assumed to be continuous, monotonic and bounded. Usually, they are scaled by $U(x^*) = 1$, $U(x^o) = 0$, $U_i(x_i^*) = 1$ and $U_i(x_i^o) = 0$ for all i. Here $x^* = (x_1^*, x_2^*, \ldots, x_n^*)$ designates the most desirable consequence and the expression $x^o = (x_1^o, x_2^o, \ldots, x_n^o)$ denotes the least desirable consequence. The symbols x_i^* and x_i^o refer to the best and worst consequence, respectively, for each attribute X_i; i.e., $x_i^* = X_i(a^*)$ where a^* is the best alternative for attribute i, and $x_i^o = X_i(a^o)$ where a^o is the worst alternative for attribute i. In the simplest situation, additive independence of attributes (Keeney and Raiffa 1976) exists such that the MAUT function may be written as:

$$U(A_i) = w_1 U_1(A_i) + w_2 U_2(A_i) + \ldots + w_n U_n(A_i) \quad (4)$$

where w_j are the weights of the various attributes of the decision alternatives A_i and U_j are the attribute scores for the alternatives.

We have just described very briefly the case of certainty in a multiattribute decision-making framework. Associated with each alternative there is a known consequence that follows with certainty from implementation of the alternative. The foundations for decision making under risk are provided by the classical work of von Neumann and Morgenstern as discussed in Sects. 1, 2. The implications of this work are that probabilities and utilities can be used to calculate the expected utility of each alternative and that alternatives with higher expected utilities should be preferred over alternatives with lower ones. We simply calculate the scalar utility function of an outcome and use this scalar utility as was done in Sects. 1, 2.

Multiattribute utility theory provides representation theorems, based on some forms of independence across the attributes, that describe the functional form of the multiattribute utility U as an additive, multiplicative or multilinear function of the conditional single attribute utility functions U_i. The books by Keeney and Raiffa (1976), Krantz et al. (1971) and Fishburn (1964, 1970) are perhaps the most comprehensive works that deal with these representations.

The methodology of decision analysis, using MAUT is generally decomposed into the same generic steps we have outlined for the scalar utility case. The major difference is that it is, of course, necessary to elicit the multiattribute utility function.

Even though the theory and procedures of multiattribute decision analysis are conceptually straightforward, there are other circumstances that make its implementation very complex. Putting the methodology into practice is much more involved than might be believed. Each of the foregoing decision-analysis steps requires substantial interaction between the analyst and the decision maker. A very stressful thinking process is demanded of the decision maker while the analyst is in charge of coordinating a series of activities in order to facilitate this process. The analyst must obtain the minimum amount of relevant information about the decision problem to determine the various utility functions. Often, redundant information should also be obtained in order to check for consistency. It is rather interesting that in most of the literature on decision analysis, there is little or no mention of the information-system functions that need be accomplished in order to evolve a recommended decision. In effect, it is assumed that the decision maker is an expert with respect to knowledge of relevant information but is unable to aggregate this information in a proper fashion as needed for an effective judgement or decision.

In the exercise of an effective decision-aiding process, much is required of the analyst. The analyst must be sensitive to biases and flawed heuristics that the decision maker may utilize; the analyst must be able to structure the decision problem regardless of the degree of complexity; and the analyst must, above all, retain the confidence of the decision maker with respect to the belief that a formal analysis of the problem will result in a more intelligent and informed decision.

The large amount and complexity of information required for complete specification of multiattribute utility functions and probabilities leads, especially in practice, to the use of simplified heuristics. Often, these are flawed (Sage 1981). Even in prescriptive situations, screening procedures will often be needed to reduce the time, stress and effort demanded from decision makers. Screening methods are intended to identify and reduce the size of the nondominated set of alternatives (that is, those that are not bettered by at least one other alternative on each and every one of the attributes of importance) through the use of behaviorally relevant and easily available information. Fishburn (1965) was one of the first to develop a screening method for decision making with incomplete knowledge of probabilities. He was concerned with using incomplete information on probabilities to compare alternative strategies in a typical formulation of decision making under risk. The criterion of choice or strategy that should normatively be used is the principle of maximum expected utility, so that the decision maker seeks a strategy a^* which is the maximum over i of the expected utility of alternatives a_i. The utility function $U_i(a_i)$ is a precisely assessed multiattribute utility function defined on the set of possible strategies $\{a_i\}$, and $p_j(\cdot)$ is a measure of the likelihood of the possible state of nature j given that a particular strategy was selected. The imprecise forms of the measure of probability that Fishburn considered are as follows:

(a) no information about $p_j(\cdot)$;

(b) ordinal measure: an ordering of p_j (e.g., $p_1 \geq p_2 \geq p_3$);

(c) linear inequalities: an ordering of sums of p_j (e.g., $p_1 + p_2 \geq p_3$); and

(d) Bounded interval measure (e.g., $c_i \leq p_i \leq c_i + d_i$).

In this approach, the search for the best alternative is performed by pairwise comparisons of expected utility among candidate strategies. Because of the restricted form of the available information on the p_j, the search for the best alternative can be put, in general, into a straightforward linear-programming problem.

Sarin (1977) proposed a screening procedure similar to that of Fishburn with the additional assumption of additive independence for the set of attributes. This assumption simplifies the search for dominance structures and results in a procedure which can be formulated as a mathematical programming problem. The parameters of the mathematical programming formulation include probabilities, importance weights and single-attribute utility functions. A simple procedure is then developed for the case when the probabilities and the importance weights are precisely known and utilities are stated in the form of linear inequalities, thereby resulting in simple linear-programming formulations. Extensions to this research have been reported by Sage and White (1984) who have developed an alternative ranking interactive aid based on dominance structural elicitation (ARIADNE) concept. The general mathematical programming formulation of the search for dominance results in the interactive solution of a large number of relatively simple linear programs. Several cases have been considered:

(a) the probabilities p_j are known precisely, and the importance weights w_i and utilities U_i are described by linear inequalities;

(b) the importance weights w_i are known precisely, and the utilities u_i and probabilities p_j are described by linear inequalities; and

(c) the importance weigths w_i and utilities u_i are known precisely, and the probabilities p_j are described by linear inequalities.

In cases (a) and (b) the solution results in a set of hierarchically organized linear-programming problems. The simplest formulation is that of case (c), which is equivalent to the problems solved by Sarin and Fishburn, resulting in a set of simple linear-programming problems. Other approaches have been developed, but they all rely on the existence of additive independence conditions to facilitate the computations.

Decision-making problems in which there are several conflicting objectives have been formulated in terms of multiobjective programming problems. The mathematical programming formulation of the multiobjective decision problem is:

$$\max_a U[u_1(a), u_2(a), \ldots, u_n(a)] \quad (5)$$

where the u_i are the real-valued utility functions of the n objectives. The single-attribute utility functions u_i are assumed to be known; the overall utility function U is unknown. Generally, the solution to this problem is not a unique alternative but a set of nondominated alternatives. Multiobjective programming techniques operate under the notion of dominance for generating the set of nondominated alternatives. Interactive algorithms to gradually gain knowledge about U and solve the above problem uniquely have been proposed by many researchers. The books by Cohon (1978), Zeleny (1981) and Chankong and Haimes (1985) present a number of these.

Screening procedures can, in general, be made to be interactive. Interactive approaches of this type assume that the decision maker can provide preference information on simple, often hypothetical, alternatives. Initially, a reduction of the nondominated set is made with the available information. If the decision maker can select an alternative from the nondominated set, then the process is stopped; otherwise, further information is requested. Often, but not always, very little guidance is provided by these procedures about the information needed. The decision maker is asked to provide further information when a single nondominated alternative is not present. This information may be redundant, in that the decision model could have inferred it from previous information. In this case it could serve only as a check for consistency. The new information may be inconsistent with the existing information. Alternatively, the decision maker may never recognize and provide the information needed to reduce the nondominated set. All this may make decision support processes that are based on interactive multiobjective procedures which are ineffective and inefficient.

The flexibility that the interactive screening, or scanning, procedures provide can result in a more effective support process. However, this flexibility complicates, to a considerable extent, the task of the decision analyst as a facilitator. In order to make efficient use of these new screening procedures, it seems very necessary to provide the analyst with a suitable dialog generation and management system. Such a system must be designed with full knowledge of the particular database and model-based management system used to allow for the interactive dominance-based scanning. At the very least, it is necessary to provide assistance to the analyst in determining what information is most needed, in terms of relevancy to the task at hand and with due consideration being given to information that is both important and cognitively easy to assess. The analyst should be aided in the evaluation of acquired information for consistency and in ways to avoid and resolve inconsistencies that do result. Finally, the information that is acquired must be represented and used within a model-based management system that is valid and appropriate for decision making.

The foundations of multiattribute expected utility theory provides useful models of normative behavior for decision making under risk. The assessment of precise utility functions in these models is mathematically justified by the existence of a real-valued utility function. Whether it is behaviorally justified is another question. In addition to the several practical difficulties encountered in assessing precise utilities, there are a number of semantic issues involved with the precise representations of preference judgements.

One of the aims of contemporary research is to seek representations that incorporate incomplete measurements of preference and risk attitude, and to provide a behaviorally meaningful as well as rationally correct approach for decision support. Instead of assessing a real-valued utility function, various "fuzzy" kinds of imprecise and otherwise imperfect representations of utilities and probabilities are allowed.

4. Evaluation of Decision Analyses

There are a number of evaluation and validity concerns relative to a decision analysis. Among these, the following questions and observations appear critical.

(a) Were the attributes of the outcomes identified and clarified?

(b) Were the possible outcomes, or consequences, of the alternatives made explicit, and was knowledge about the likelihood of occurrence of each sufficient?

(c) Did the decision situation structural model capture satisfactorily the reality of the decision situation to give the decision maker confidence in the indicated results?

(d) Did the decision analysis produce decisions of sufficient quality to justify its costs?

(e) Did the decision maker have confidence in the decision model and the validity of the utility function?

(f) The quality of the output of a decision analysis is not better than the quality of the inputs provided by analyst, decision-maker(s) and experts.

(g) Quality and experience of the analyst are crucial to quality results.

(h) Subjective probabilities elicited from decision makers and/or experts are likely to be biased by a number of cognitive heuristics and biases.

(i) Decision makers may be inclined to avoid explicit exposure of personal or political motives in a formal decision analysis.

(j) The value of additional modelling or additional information should indicate a stopping point in the analysis.

(k) Decision-maker confidence in the decision situation structural model is essential to success of the effort.

(l) Since good decisions do not necessarily lead to good outcomes, there is no totally objective method of assessing the benefits of a decision analysis effort.

(m) Most decision-analysis methodology assumes an individual decision maker. In many real-world situations, decisions must be made by a group of people with interpersonal conflicts and different preference structures.

See also: Human Information Processing; Information Requirements Determination; Multiattribute Utility Theory; Systems Methodology

Bibliography

Brown R 1974 *Decision Analysis: An Overview.* Holt, Reinhart and Winston, New York

Brown R V, Lindley D V 1982 Improving judgement by reconciling incoherence. *Theory Decis.* **14**, 113–32

Chankong V, Haimes Y Y 1985 *Decision Making with Multiple Objectives.* Springer Verlag, Berlin

Charnetski J R, Soland R M 1978 Multiattribute decision making with partial information. *Nav. Res. Logistic Q.* **25**(2), 279–88

Charnetski J R, Soland R M 1979 Multiattribute decision making with partial information: The expected value criterion. *Nav. Res. Logistic Q.* **26**(2), 249–56

Cohon J L 1978 *Multiobjective Programming and Planning.* Academic Press, New York

DeWispelare A, Sage A P 1981 On combined multiple objective optimization theory and multiple attribute utility theory for evaluation and choice making. *Large Scale Syst.* **2**(1), 1–19

Edwards W 1977 How to use multiattribute utility measurement for social decisionmaking. *IEEE Trans. Syst., Man Cybern.* **7**, 326–40

Farris D, Sage A P 1975a Introduction and survey of group decision making with applications to worth assessment. *IEEE Trans. Syst., Man Cybern.* **5**(3), 346–58

Farris D, Sage A P 1975b On decision making and worth assessment. *Int. J. Syst. Sci.* **6**(12)

Fishburn P C 1964 *Decision and Value Theory.* Wiley, New York

Fishburn P C 1965 Analysis of decisions with incomplete knowledge of probabilities. *Oper. Res.* **13**(2), 217–37

Fishburn P C 1968 Utility theory. *Manage. Sci.* **14**(5), 335–78

Fishburn P C 1970 *Utility Theory for Decision Making.* Wiley, New York

Freeling A N S 1981 Reconciliation of multiple probability assessments. *Organ. Behav. Hum. Perform.* **28**, 395–414

Hammond K R, McClelland G H, Mumpower J 1980 *Human Judgement and Decision Making: Theories, Methods and Procedures.* Hemisphere/Praeger, New York

Holloway C A 1979 *Decision Making under Uncertainty: Models and Choice.* Prentice–Hall, Englewood Cliffs, New Jersey

Howard R A 1968 The foundations of decision analysis. *IEEE Trans. Syst., Sci. Cybern.* **4**(3), 211–19

Howard R A 1975 Social decision analysis. Special issue on social systems engineering. *IEEE Proc.* **63**(3), 359–71

Howard R A 1980 An assessment of decision analysis. *Oper. Res.* **28**(1), 4–27

Keeney R L 1982 Decision analysis: An overview. *Oper. Res.* **30**(5), 803–38

Keeney R L, Raiffa H 1976 *Decisions with Multiple Objectives, Preference and Value Trade-Offs.* Wiley, New York

Kmietowicz Z W, Pearman A D 1981 *Decision Theory and Incomplete Knowledge.* Gower, Aldershot

Krantz D H, Luce R D, Suppes P, Tversky A 1971 *Foundations of Measurement*, Vol. 1, *Additive and Polynomial Representations*. Academic Press, New York

Krzysztofowicz R, Duckstein L 1980 Assessment errors in multiattribute utility functions. *Organ. Behav. Hum. Perform.* **26**, 326–48

Lindley D V, Tversky A, Brown R V 1979 On the reconciliation of probability assessments. *J. R. Stat. Soc., Ser. A* **142** (2), 146–80

Miller J R III 1967 *A Systematic Procedure for Assessing the Worth of Complex Alternatives*, ESD TR 67 90 AD 662001. Air Force Systems Command, Washington, DC

Morris P A 1974 Decision analysis export use. *Manage. Sci.* **20**(9), 1233–41

North D W 1968 A tutorial introduction to decision theory. *IEEE Trans. Syst., Sci. Cybern.* **4**(3), 200–10

Raiffa H 1968 *Decision Analysis—Introductory Lectures on Choices under Uncertainty*. Addison–Wesley, Reading, Massachusetts

Rescher N, Manor R 1970 On inference from inconsistent premisses. *Theory Decis.* **1**, 179–217

Roberts F S 1979 *Measurement Theory with Application to Decision Making, Utility and Social Choice*. Addison–Wesley, Reading, Massachusetts

Sage A P 1977 *Methodology for Large Scale Systems*. McGraw–Hill, New York

Sage A P 1981 Behavioral and organizational considerations in the design of information systems and processes for planning and decision support. *IEEE Trans' Syst., Man Cybern.* **11**(9), 640–78

Sage A P, White C C 1984 ARIADNE: A knowledge based interactive system for planning and decision support. *IEEE Trans. Syst., Man Cybern.* **14**(1)

Sarin R K 1977 Screening of multiattribute alternatives. *OMEGA* **5**(4), 481–89

Spetzler C S, von Holstein C A 1975 Probability encoding in decision analysis. *Manage. Sci.* **22**(3), 340–58

von Winterfeldt D, Edwards W 1986 *Decision Analysis and Economic Behavior*, 3rd edn. Wiley, New York

von Winterfeldt D, Edwards W 1986 *Decision Analysis and Behavioral Research*. Cambridge University Press, Cambridge

Whitmore G A, Findlay N C (eds.) *Stochastic Dominance*. Lexington Books, Lexington, Massachusetts

Zeleny M 1981 *Multiple Criteria Decision Making*. McGraw–Hill, New York

A. P. Sage
[George Mason University, Fairfax,
Virginia, USA]

Decision Making: Information Processing and Organizational Models

This article presents a discussion and interpretation of those critical factors relevant to the design of information support systems which enhance the quality of organizational decision making. The roles of information, feedback, and individual and organizational learning in determining choice, and the organizational objectives that both lead to and are responsive to choice are emphasized.

Information-based technologies are major potential aids to organizational decision making. The sound design and implementation of information and knowledge-based support in organizational decision making require a knowledge of the ways in which organizations can acquire and process information, adapt to their internal and external environment and cope with conflict, knowledge is also needed of the ways in which organizational references result from decisions as well as being determined by them, and the ways in which organizations learn and fail to learn. These are discussed from the perspective of information processing in systems and organizations.

1. Organizational Realities

There are a variety of definitions of an organization, including:

(a) a system of consciously coordinated activities involving two or more people (Barnard 1938);

(b) social units deliberately constructed to seek specific goals (Etzioni 1964);

(c) collectives that have been established on a relatively continuous basis in an environment with relatively fixed boundaries, a normative order, authority ranks, communication systems and an incentive system designed to enable participants to engage in activities in the pursuit of a common set of goals (Hall 1977); and

(d) a set of individuals with bounded rationality engaged in the decision-making process (Mintzberg 1973).

A closed-system perspective can be adopted whereby an organization is perceived as an instrument designed to enable the pursuit of well-defined specified objectives. In this view an organization will be concerned primarily with four objectives (Hayre 1965): efficiency, effectiveness, flexibility or adaptability to external environmental influences, and job satisfaction. Four organizational means or activities follow from this: complexity and specialization of tasks, centralization or hierarchy of authority, formalization or standardization of jobs, and stratification of employment levels. From this viewpoint, every activity is functional and tuned so that all the resource inputs are optimum and the associated responses fit into a well-defined master plan.

March and Simon (1958), among others, discuss the inherent shortcomings associated with this closed-system model of humans as machines. Not only is the human-as-machine view inappropriate but there are pitfalls associated with viewing environmental influences as "noise."

In the open-system view, an organization is concerned not only with the achievement of objectives but also with making appropriate responses to a number of internal and external influences. Weick (1979, 1985) describes the organizational activities of enactment, selection and retention, which assist in the processing of the ambiguous information resulting from an organization's interactions with ecological changes in the environment. The overall result of this process is the minimization of information equivocality, enabling the organization to understand its environment, recognize problems, diagnose their causes, identify policies to potentially resolve problems, evaluate the efficacy of these policies and to select a priority order for problem resolution. Figure 1 presents a partial interpretation of Weick's social theory of organizing.

The enactment activities of the organization constitute the enacted environment of the organization. This enacted envrionment contains an external part, which represents the activities of the organization in product markets, and an internal part which is the result of organizing people into a structure to achieve organizational goals. Each of these environments is subject to uncontrollable ecological influences due to economic, social and other changes. Selection activities allow perception framing, and editing and interpretation of the effects of the organization's actions upon the external and internal environments, hence enabling the selection of a set of those relationships believed to be of importance. Retention activities allow the admission, rejection and modification of the set of selected knowledge in accordance with existing retained knowledge and the integration of previously retained organizational knowledge with new knowledge. A potentially large number of cycles may be associated with enactment, selection and retention. These cycles generally minimize informational equivocality and allow for organizational learning so that the organization is able to cope with very complex and changing environments.

A very important feature of many models of organizations is that of *organizational learning*. Much of the organizational learning that occurs in practice is not necessarily beneficial or appropriate in a descriptive sense. For example, there is much literature, referenced in the article *Human Information Processing*, which shows that organizations and individuals use improperly simplified and often distorted models of causal and diagnostic inferences, and improperly simplified and distorted models of the contingency structure of the environment and tasks in which these realities are embedded. This surely occurs in group situations, as well as in individual information processing and judgement situations. Individuals often join groups to enhance their survival possibilities and to enable the pursuit of their career and other objectives. These coalitions of like-minded people pursue interests that result in emotional and intellectual fulfillment and pleasure. Activities that are perceived to fulfill needs become objectives for the group. Group cohesion, conformity, and the reinforcement of beliefs often lead to what has been called "groupthink" (Janis and Mann 1977, Janis 1982) and to an information acquisition and analysis structure that only permits processing which is in accord with the belief structure of the group. The resulting selective perceptions and the neglect of potentially disconfirming information preclude a change of beliefs. A central purpose of knowledge support systems is to enhance both the knowledge base for decision making and the interpretation of this knowledge base to improve decision quality. To be able to discuss the full potential of decision making, an awareness of the ways in which decision making, and judgement and choice behavior are actually exercised is necessary.

2. Organizational Management

An important aspect of the study of organizations is the role of management and management decision making. In a work of extraordinary insight, Mintzberg (1973) identifies a three-dimensional taxonomy characterizing managerial paradigms. These paradigms are described in Table 1. The content roles, characteristic roles and contingencies which influence variations in managerial efforts are obtained from the interpretation of the results of the decision making and leadership schools of thought concerning managerial behavior. Mintzberg has identified six schools of thought concerning management, as indicated in Table 2; the information and decision roles of the manager are of particular relevance, as are the contingency-task-structure variables which influence these roles. Especially relevant is Mintzberg's discussion of several studies of managerial activities as a programmed system.

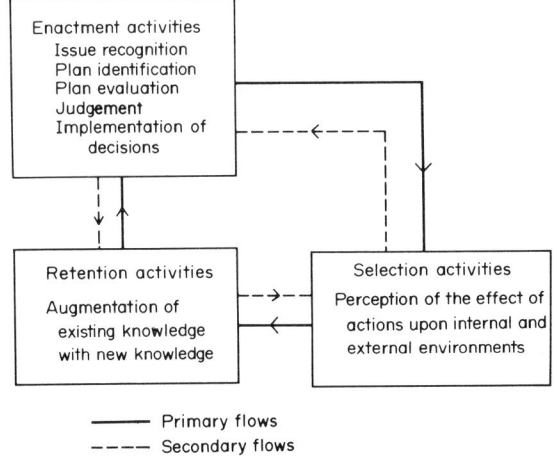

Figure 1
Interpretation of Weick's social theory of organizing

Decision Making: Information Processing and Organizational Models

Table 1
A taxonomy of management paradigms

Content roles of the manager	Contingency task variations of management effort
(a) Interpersonal roles:	(a) Environmental variables
figurehead	(b) Task variables
leader	(c) Person variables
liaison	(d) Situational (experiential) variables
(b) Informational roles:	
monitor	*Characteristic roles of the manager*
disseminator	(a) Much work at an unrelenting pace
spokesperson	(b) Activities characterized by brevity, variety and fragmentation
(c) Decisional roles:	(c) Preference for live action
entrepreneur	(d) Attraction to verbal media
disturbance handler	(e) Contacts with subordinates, superiors and external stakeholders
resource allocator	(f) Initial decisions define long-term commitments
negotiator	(g) Control of activities in which the manager must engage

Table 2
Management schools of thought

Classical	managerial functions: planning, organizing, staffing, directing, coordinating, reporting, budgeting (POSTDCORB)
Great managers	biographical and autobiographical literature
Entrepreneurship	innovation in structured situations and economic rationality
Decision theory	unprogrammed behavior in unstructured situations (satisficing and muddling through)
Leader effectiveness	interpersonal behavior—personality traits and managerial styles for effective performance
Work activity	inductive research and empirical studies of the characteristics of managerial work

3. Models of Organizational Decision Making

The organizational-science literature thoroughly discusses the development of conceptual models used in decision making by individuals and by organizations, based on various rationality conceptualizations. Among these are the (economic) rational-actor model; the satisficing or bounded-rationality model; the bureaucratic-politics, incremental or "muddling-through" model; the organizational-processes model; and the garbage-can model. These models are important to the discussion here and highlights of each of these models are presented in the article *Systems Knowledge: Philosophical Perspectives*.

3.1 Rational-Actor Model

Most formal decision-analytic efforts are based on the rational-actor model. In this model, the decision maker becomes aware of a problem, studies it, carefully weighs alternative means to a solution and makes a choice or decision based on an objective set of values. At first glance, the rational-actor model appears to contain much of value, being especially well matched to the entrepreneurship and decision-theory schools of thought as described by Mintzberg. However, it is a normative–substantive model. There may be any number of descriptive process realities which may make the realization of the rational-actor model infeasible. In rational planning or decision making one or more of the following may occur:

(a) the decision maker is confronted with an issue that can be meaningfully isolated from other issues;

(b) objectives, which will result in need satisfaction, are identified;

(c) possible alternative activities to resolve needs are identified;

(d) the impacts of action alternatives are determined;

(e) the utility of each alternative is evaluated in terms of its impacts upon needs; and

(f) the utilities of all alternatives are compared and the policy or activity with the highest utility is selected for action implementation.

Simon (1976, 1978, 1979a,b, 1980) was perhaps the first to observe, in the 1960s, that it may not be possible for unaided decision makers to make complete substantive use of the economic rational-actor model. In these situations, the concepts of bounded rationality and satisficing represent much more realistic substantive models of actual decision rules and practices. Argyris (1974) has presented a definitive discussion of the limits to rational-actor organizational theory. A variety of saftisficing heuristic rules have been described in Thorngate (1980); these rules are often used as "simple" substitutes for "difficult" rational behavior. Unless very carefully developed and applied, however, these heuristic rules may result in very inferior decisions; decisions which are re-inforced through feedback and repetition resulting in experiences (and learning) that are by no means necessarily the best or even a good teacher. Processes that are only economically rational may be neither desirable nor possible. Social, political or legal rationality concerns may well prevail; one of the other decision frameworks described here and in the article *Systems Knowledge: Philosophical Perspectives* may well be more appropriate if these concerns are dominant over economic rationality concerns.

3.2 Satisficing or Bounded-Rationality Model

Another often-used conceptual model is the satisficing or bounded-rationality model. According to this model, the decision maker looks for a course of action that can meet a minimum set of requirements. The goal is to "not shake the system" or to "play it safe" by making decisions primarily on the basis of short-term acceptability rather than seeking a long-term optimum. Simon introduced the concept of satisficing or bounded rationality as an effort to ". . . replace the global rationality of economic man with a kind of rational behavior that is compatible with the access to information and computational capabilities that are actually possessed by organisms, including man, in the kinds of environments in which such organisms exist." Simon suggested that decision makers compensate for their limited abilities by constructing a simplified representation of the problem and then behaving rationally within the constraints imposed by this simplified model. We may satisfice by finding either optimum solutions in a simplified world or satisfactory solutions in a more realistic world. As Simon (1979b) states, "neither approach dominates the other."

Satisficing can be described as searching for a "good enough" choice. Simon suggested that the threshold for satisfaction, or the aspiration level, may change according to the ease or difficulty of search. If many alternatives can be found, the conclusion is that the aspiration level is too low and needs to be increased; the converse is true if no satisfactory alternatives can be found. This may lead to a unique solution by iteration.

The principle of bounded rationality and the resulting satisficing model suggest that simple heuristics may well be adequate for complex problem-solving situations. While satisficing strategies may be excellent for repetitive problems by encouraging one to "do what we did last time if it worked last time and the opposite if it didn't," they may also lead to premature choices which result in unforeseen disastrous consequences; consequences which would have been foreseen by a more careful analysis.

3.3 Incremental or Muddling-Through Model

The bureaucratic-politics, incremental or muddling-through model represents another attempt to characterize individual and organizational behavior. When problems arise which require a change of policy, policy makers typically consider only a very narrow range of alternatives differing to a small degree from the existing policy. One alternative is selected and tried, with any unforeseen consequences treated by subsequent incremental policies when discovered. This is the incremental view.

In 1959, Lindblom postulated the approach called incrementalism, or muddling through (Lindblom 1959, 1965, 1980), to cope with perceived limitations in the economically rational approach. Only marginal values of change are considered—for only a few dimensions of value—whereas the rational approach calls for an exhaustive analysis of each identified alternative along all identified dimensions of value. A number of authors have shown incrementalism to be the typical, common and currently practised decision process of groups in pluralistic societies. Coalitions of special-interest groups make cumulative decisions and arrive at workable compromises through a give-and-take process that Lindblom calls "partisan mutual adjustment." Lindblom indicates that ideological and other value differences do not influence marginal decisions as much as they influence major changes and that, in fact, considering marginal values subject to practical constraints will lead to agreement on marginal programs. Further, incrementalism can result in agreement on decisions and plans even by those who are in fundamental disagreement on values. However, incrementalism appears to be based on keeping the masses marginally content and thus may not be able to do much to help the greatly underprivileged and unrepresented. There have been a number of studies which indicate that incrementalism is an often-used approach in practice. Without doubt, incrementalism is a realistic process-oriented descriptive model of judgement and choice, especially in political environments.

Lindblom rejects (economic) comprehensive rationality even as a normative model. He proposes incrementalism as a normative approach, and indicates that systems analysis and economic rationality will often lead to ill-considered, frequently accidental incompleteness. Lindblom indicates the following inevitable limitations to analysis: it is fallible and can be poorly informed, superficial, biased or mendacious. Analysis cannot wholly resolve conflicts of value and interest. Sustained analysis may be too slow and too costly compared with realistic needs. Issue-formulation questions call for acts of choice or will, and suggest that analysis must allow room for politics.

The main features of the model proposed by Lindblom are as follows. Ends and means are not viewed as being distinct; consequently, means–ends analysis is often considered inappropriate. The identification of values and goals is not distinct from the analysis of alternative actions. Rather, the two processes are interconnected. The test for a good policy is, typically, that various decision makers or analysts, agree that a policy is appropriate without necessarily agreeing that it is the most appropriate means to an end. Analysis is drastically limited, important policy options are neglected and important outcomes are not considered. By proceeding incrementally and comparing the results of each new policy with the old, decision makers reduce or eliminate reliance on theory. There is a greater preoccupation with ills to be remedied rather than positive goals to be sought. Incremental analysis is a good description of political decision making and is sometimes referred to as the "political process" model.

3.4 Organizational-Process Model

In practice, plans and decisions result from the interpretation of standard operating procedures. Improvements are obtained by careful identification of existing standard operating procedures and the associated organizational structures. The organizational-process model, originally due to Cyert and March (1963), functions by relying on standard operating procedures which constitute the memory or intelligence bank of the organization. Only if the standard operating procedures fail will the organization attempt to develop new standard procedures.

The organizational-process model may be viewed as an extension of the concept of bounded rationality to choice making in organizations. It is clearly an application of reasoning and rationality to cases (by the discovery and application of rules). Four main concepts of the behavioral theory of the firm have been suggested as descriptive models of actual choice making in organizations, as follows.

(a) *Quasiresolution of conflict.* Decision makers avoid conflicts arising from incommensurate and conflicting goals. Major problems are disaggregated and each subproblem is attacked locally by a department. An acceptable conflict resolution due to the efforts of different departments is reached by sequential attention to departmental goals and by the formulation of coalitions seeking power and status. When resources are scarce some objectives are unattainable and decisions concerning allocations are met largely on political grounds.

(b) *Uncertainty avoidance.* This is achieved by reacting to external feedback, by emphasizing short-term choices and by advocating negotiated futures. Generally, uncertainties about the future, uncertainties associated with the future impacts of alternatives and uncertainties associated with future preferences will exist. Generally, deficient information-processing heuristics and cognitive biases are used to avoid uncertainties. The effects are, of course, suboptimal.

(c) *Problem search.* This is stimulated when issues are encountered and not before issues surface. A form of satisficing is used as a decision rule. Search in the neighborhood of the status quo only is attempted and only incremental solutions are considered.

(d) *Organization learning.* Organizations adapt on the basis of experience. They often pay considerable attention to one part of their environment at the expense of another.

In the organizational-process model, decisions at time t may be forecasted with almost complete certainty from knowledge of decisions at time $t-T$, where T is planning or forecasting period. Standard operating procedures or "programs," and education, motivation and experience or "programming" of management are the critical determinants of behavior for the organizational-process model. Cyert and March (1963) recommend a strategy of management leadership to cope with organizational-process realities. Managers are encouraged to do the following: to become intimately involved in their organizations so that they will be able to strongly influence decisions, to become widely informed so that they will be highly valued in the information-poor organization, to be extraordinarily persistent since unmitigated chutzpah will often have entirely undeserved rewards, to encourage those with opposing views to participate, and to overload organizational systems to make themselves more necessary. In this view, the descriptive characteristics of the organization are seen as performance inhibiting factors. They are factors not to be overcome, but to be understood and used to the advantage of the manager.

4. Organizational Learning

Organizational learning results when members of the organization react to changes in the internal or external environment of the organization by the detection and correction of errors (Argyris 1982, Argyris and Schon 1974, 1978). An error is an aspect of knowledge making action ineffective. Individuals in an organization are agents of organizational action and organizational learning. Argyris cites two information-related factors inhibiting organizational learning: the degree to which information is distorted, which lessens its value in influencing quality decisions, and lack of receptivity to corrective feedback. Two types of organizational learning are defined. *Single-loop learning* does not question the fundamental objectives or actions of an organization. Members of the organization discover sources of error and identify new strategic activities which might correct the error. The activities are analyzed and evaluated and one or more selected for implementation. Environmental control and self-protection by control over others, primarily by the imposition of power, are typical strategies. The consequences of this approach include defensive group dynamics and low production of valid information. The lack of information does not disturb prevailing values. The resulting inefficiencies in decision making encourage frustration and an increase in secrecy and loyalty demands from decision makers. All of this is mutually self-reinforcing. It results in a stable autocratic state and a self-fulfilling prophecy of the need for organizational control. *Double-loop learning* involves the identification of potential changes in organizational goals and of the particular approach to inquiry which allows confrontation with, and resolution of conflict rather than the translation of incompatible objectives into intergroup conflict. Not all conflict resolution is the result of double-loop learning, however. A good example of this is a conflict settled through the imposition of power rather than inquiry. Thus, double-loop learning is seen to be the result of that organizational inquiry resolving organizational objectives, which are initially perceived to be incompatible through the restructuring and setting of new priorities and objectives. New understandings are developed which result in updated cognitive maps and scripts of organizational behavior. It is claimed that organizations learn primarily on the basis of single-loop learning and typically do not engage in double-loop learning.

Individuals act as agents of organizational learning by processing initially inaccessible and obscure information and by resolving those potential inadequacies associated with individual and organizational theories of action. All human action is said to be based on theories of action. There are two types:

(a) *espoused theories of action*, which are the "official" theories that people claim as a basis for action; and

(b) *theories in use*, which are descriptive theories of action inferable from actual behavior.

While people are often adept at identifying those discrepancies between espoused theories of action and theories in use that are associated with the behavior of others, they are not equally capable of self-diagnosis. Generally, people are "programmed" not to report inconsistent behavior, when they observe it in others, to the person they observed behaving inconsistently. This is another example of social exchanges and customs inhibiting double-loop learning.

There are several dilemmas associated with the theory of action building (Argyris and Schon 1974). Among these non-mutually-exclusive dilemmas, which aggregate to create conflicting and intolerable pressures, are:

(a) *incongruity* between an espoused theory and a theory in use which is recognized but not corrected,

(b) *inconsistency* between theories in use,

(c) *ineffectiveness* as objectives associated with theories in use become less and less achievable over time,

(d) *disutility* as theories in use become less valued over time, and

(e) *unobservability* as theories in use result in the suppression of information so that an evaluation of effectiveness becomes impossible.

The detection and correction of inappropriate espoused theories of action and theories in use may potentially lead to a reduction in those factors that inhibit double-loop learning. Of course, single-loop learning will often be appropriate, and is encouraged. The result of double-loop learning, however, is a *new* set of goals and standard operating policies that become part of the organization's knowledge base. It is when the environment changes, or more generally the contingency task structure changes, that double-loop learning is called for. An inability to accommodate double-loop learning is a flaw. The ability to successfully integrate and utilize the appropriate blend of single- and double-loop learning is called deutero, or dialectic, learning. Figure 2 presents systems engineering conceptualization of this model.

Several intervention models or approaches are suggested to encourage organizations to adopt a capability for double-loop learning. These approaches include comprehensive intervention; limited intervention through the structural mapping of the issue, internalization and validation of the map, simulation and analysis of impacts using the map, and use of the map to generate knowledge for future designs; and several partial models of intervention. Of particular interest in this seminal work are the several caveats given concerning difficulties in the design of management information and decision support systems so that they support double-loop learning rather than single-loop learning.

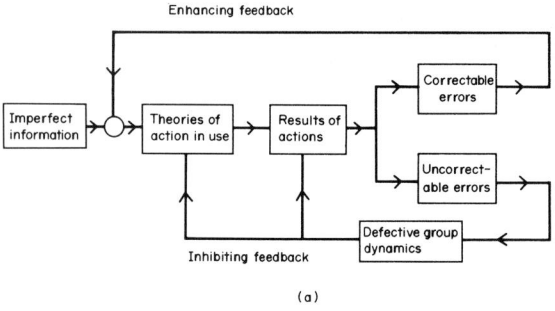

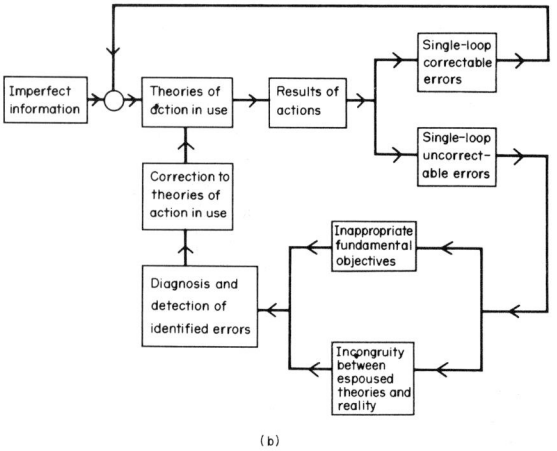

Figure 2
Interpretation of: (a) single-loop learning and (b) double-loop learning

5. Summary

A description and interpretation has been presented of some recent results in behavioral and organizational theory that have direct relevance to information processing in systems and organizations. The primary organizing principles in organizations include: the division of labor and task assignment, identifying standard operating principles, top-down flow of decisions, formal and informal channels of communication in all directions, the multiple uses of information, and organizational learning. These descriptive principles must be taken into account if normative aids are to be produced that are realistically grounded in the realities of human desires, capabilities for growth and self actualization.

Bibliography

Argyris C 1974 Some limits to rational-man organizational theory. In: *Systems and Management Science*. McGraw–Hill, New York, pp. 3333–47
Argyris C 1982 *Reasoning, Learning, and Action: Individual and Organizational*. Jossy–Bass, San Francisco, California
Argyris C, Schon D A 1974 *Theory in Practice: Increasing Professional Effectiveness*. Jossey–Bass, San Francisco, California
Argyris C, Schon D A 1978 *Organizational Learning: A Theory of Action Perspective*. Addison–Wesley, Reading, Massachusetts
Barnard C I 1938 *The Functions of the Executive*. Harvard University Press, Cambridge, Massachusetts
Baron J 1985 *Rationality and Intelligence*. Cambridge University Press, Cambridge
Cohen M D, March J B, Olsen J P 1972 A garbage can model of organizational choice. *Adm. Sci. Q.* **17**(1), 1–25
Cyert R M, March J G 1963 *A Behavioral Theory of the Firm*. Prentice–Hall, Englewood Cliffs, New Jersey
Etzioni A 1964 *Modern Organizations*. Prentice–Hall, Englewood Cliffs, New Jersey
Hall R H 1977 *Organizations: Structure and Process*. Prentice–Hall, Englewood Cliffs, New Jersey
Hayre J 1965 An axiomatic theory of organizations. *Adm. Sci. Q.* **10**(3), 289–320
Huber G P 1980 *Managerial Decision Making*. Scott, Foresman, Glenview, Illinois
Janis I L 1982 *Groupthink*. Free Press, New York
Janis I L, Mann L 1977 *Decision Making*. Free Press, New York
Lindblom C E 1959 The science of muddling through. *Publ. Adm. Rev.* **19**, 155–69
Lindblom C E 1965 *The Intelligence of Democracy: Decision Making Through Mutual Adjustment*. Free Press, New York
Lindblom C E 1980 *The Policy Making Process*. Prentice–Hall, Englewood Cliffs, New Jersey
March J G, Simon H A 1958 *Organizations*. Wiley, New York
Mintzberg H 1973 *The Nature of Managerial Work*. Harper and Row, New York
Mintzberg H 1979 *The Structuring of Organizations*. Prentice–Hall, Englewood Cliffs, New Jersey
Mintzberg H 1983 *Structure in Fives: Designing Effective Organizations*. Prentice–Hall, Englewood Cliffs, New Jersey
Sage A P 1985 Behavioral and organizational models for human decision making. *Policy Anal. Inf. Syst.* **7**(2), 1–17
Sage A P (ed.) 1987 *Systems Design for Human Interaction*. IEEE Press, New York
Shepard J M, Hougland T G Jr 1978 Contingency theory: 'Complexman' or complex organization. *Acad. Manage. Rev.* **3**(3), 413–27
Simon H A 1976 From substantive to procedural rationality. In: Latsis S J (ed.) *Method and Appraisal in Economics*. Cambridge University Press, New York, pp. 129–48
Simon H A 1978 On how to decide what to do. *Bell J. Econ.* **10**, 494–507
Simon H A 1979a *Models of Thought*. Yale University Press, New Haven, Connecticut
Simon H A 1979b Rational decision making in business organization. *Am. Econ. Rev.* **69**(4), 493–513
Simon H A 1980 The behavioral and social sciences. *Science* **209**, 72–78
Starbuck W H 1976 Organizations and their environments. In: Dunnette M (ed.) *Handbook of Industrial Psychology*. Rand McNally, Chicago, Illinois, pp. 1069–123

Thorngate W 1980 Efficient decision heuristics. *Behav. Sci.* **25**(3), 219–25
Vroom V H, Yetton P W 1973 *Leadership and Decision Making*. University of Pittsburgh Press, Pittsburgh, Pennsylvania
Weick K E 1979 *The Social Psychology of Organizing*. Addison–Wesley, Reading, Massachusetts
Weick K E 1985 Cosmos vs. chaos: Sense and nonsense in electronic contexts. *Organ. Dynam.* **14**(3), 50–64

A. P. Sage
[George Mason University, Fairfax,
Virginia, USA]

Table 1
Decision matrix containing two options, three states and four attributes; $k = 1\text{–}4$

Options	States		
	$j = 1$	$j = 2$	$j = 3$
$i = 1$	X_{11k}	X_{12k}	X_{13k}
$i = 2$	X_{21k}	X_{22k}	X_{23k}

Decision-Problem Structuring

The structure of a decision problem should be specified prior to formal evaluation of the alternative action options. The process of structuring a decision problem is dynamic and cyclical; as additional problem elements and their interactions continue to be discovered, the preliminary structure is repeatedly modified. A fully structured decision problem contains a list of possible action options, attributes for evaluating the suitability of the options, and possible states of nature which will have an impact on the outcome of the options. This is illustrated in the example decision matrix given in Table 1, which contains two options, three states and four attributes.

In general, each alternative option i results in j possible outcomes, represented by $X_{ij} = (X_{ij1}, X_{ij2}, X_{ij3}, \ldots, X_{ijk})$, where X_{ijk} is the level of attribute k which occurs in the outcome of option i being chosen and state j occurring. The set of all possible states of nature provides a mutually exclusive and exhaustive partition of the environment, so that each state consists of one specific level of each of the possible probabilistic variables in the problem (such as the bank prime rate and the strength of the US dollar). The probability of state j is p_j. Note that the action taken does not affect the probability of a state. Thus, the decision maker cannot control which state occurs (or the probability of its occurrence) by altering the action chosen. An event is a set of states. An example event is that the variable "Dow–Jones index level" is above 2000. In a formal decision analysis, one prevalent criterion for recommending a top choice is to take the alternative with the highest expected utility, where the expected utility of alternative action i is computed by taking the sum over all states of the utility $u(X_{ij})$ times the probability of the state p_j. When there are multiple attributes, $u(X_{ij})$ can be represented with a multiattribute utility function (Keeney and Raiffa 1976).

The way in which a person processes decision-relevant information will have a large effect on the contents of the problem structure, the problem-solving process used and the ultimate solution of the problem. A number of methods for aiding a person to access relevant items in memory to creatively structure a decision problem are presented here. It is important to note that there is very little research that has been done on these procedures, so they should not be seen as validated methods, but as suggestions, still to be subjected to laboratory and field testing. First, methods for generating options are given in Sect. 1; methods for generating states of nature are presented in Sect. 2 and means for identifying attributes are briefly presented in Sect. 3. Human long-term memory can be modelled as an associative network with nodes in the network being cognitive units (such as decision-problem options, states of nature or attributes.) Figure 1 contains a partial cognitive representation of the problem of deciding among possible options for personal investments. When diagramming a portion of a person's knowledge, option nodes for the current problem can be modelled as squares; states of nature nodes are circular; and attribute nodes are triangular. The methods described here are designed to stimulate creativity by accessing the different kinds of cognitive units within memory.

1. Methods for Generating Options

The methods for generating options are divided into five categories: attribute-based, state-based, composite, option-based and creativity procedures. Keller and Ho (1988) give a more complete description of the methods together with relevant research results and an extensive list of references. A number of criteria may be used to evaluate the sufficiency of a set of options for a specific problem. When possible, the criterion which a specific method is likely to satisfy is identified along with the method.

1.1 Attribute-Based Procedures

A principal strength of a person's information-processing system is the complex associative memory in which small cues or attributes can lead to retrieval of complex associations which stimulate the option-generating process. Hence, attention to different subsets of attributes can lead to different options. Seven versions of attribute-based procedures for generating options are identified. Attribute-based procedures

Decision-Problem Structuring

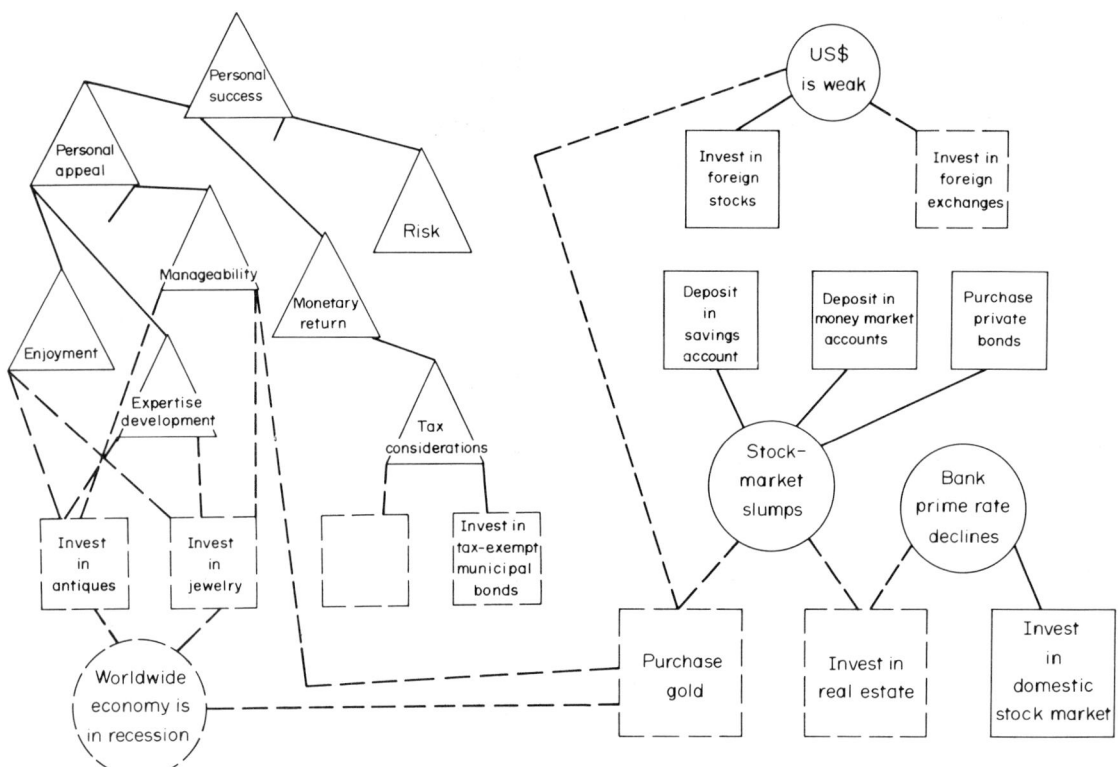

Figure 1
Partial cognitive representation containing some decision-problem elements: dotted lines indicate arcs and nodes that do not exist (or are weakly represented) in the associative network

provide stimulation from the environment by introducing nodes or stimulating existing nodes containing attributes or goals. Since a goal node serves as a relatively constant source of activation in a cognitive network, introducing an attribute should initiate a great deal of activation or search in the local region around that node.

One warning about attribute-based procedures should be given. In stimulating creativity, separation of idea generation from evaluation is recommended to avoid premature censoring of ideas before they are formally stated. In a cognitive network, premature evaluation might occur if a high threshold for activation level must be met before an idea would be added to the option set. Use of goals or attributes to prompt ideas may lead to immediate evaluation of options with respect to those attributes, and thus limit the number of options generated.

(a) *Present attributes one at a time. Elicit options which will help meet each individual attribute.* This method is likely to meet the criterion of maximizing the number of options in the choice set which are either perfect or good on at least one attribute. For instance, in the options for "personal investment"

example given in Fig. 1, an attribute "risk" can first be presented to the decision maker, then the attributes "risk" and "tax considerations" together, and so on, until all attributes are presented. Experimental subjects generated more options for solving personal dilemmas when the task was first to generate options to satisfy only one attribute, then to consider a different attribute, and so on, until all the attributes had been considered. These results provide empirical support for the GODDESS computer system developed by Pearl et al. (1982), which assesses goals and subgoals (attributes) before asking for possible options to lead to improvements in each subgoal.

(b) *Design options to do well on the heavily weighted attributes.* This approach is likely to meet the criterion of maximizing the number of options which are close to optimal. For example, when the Los Angeles Unified School District was legally ordered to develop and implement a desegregation plan, Ward Edwards helped the school board generate a complete value tree with 144 bottom-level attributes. Interested groups were encouraged to submit possible desegregation plans to the school board for evaluation via the value tree (von Winterfeldt and Edwards 1986). In addition, the school board developed a new plan after the value tree had been constructed and the attribute weights for an additive multiattribute value function were computed by averaging the attribute weights of five board members. Thus, it is possible that the new plan was creatively designed to satisfy the more heavily weighted attributes.

(*c*) *Be more detailed in partitioning the attributes prior to eliciting options.* Specifying the value tree of attributes in more detail is likely to identify more attribute nodes in the cognitive network which could potentially be connected to additional option nodes. This may lead to a number of reasonable options, which are feasible based on the person's values. More vacation package options were elicited from experimental subjects when a value tree was specified down to three levels with six attributes (such as mental relaxation) than when it was identified with only one or two level(s). However, if a value tree is specified in too much detail, viable options may be screened out. For example, when planning a vacation, the attribute "variety" might be partitioned into "number of towns visited" and "number of activities done." This may preclude the potentially attractive option of backpacking for a week in the mountains.

(*d*) *Deemphasize the personal nature of the attributes to increase the number of options generated upon consideration of goals. Emphasize the personal nature of the attributes to increase the quality of the options generated.* Rating the personal importance of vacation goals (attributes) prior to generating options led to experimental subjects generating fewer options than those who did not rate the goals first. However, the options generated by this "personally involved group" were rated higher on goal-achievement scales than the options generated by other subjects. Thus, fewer and "better" options were generated by emphasizing the personal nature of attributes. On the contrary, deemphasizing the personal nature of attributes is likely to lead to maximizing the number of novel options. This suggests that by varying the role perspective of the decision maker, a better option set may be achieved.

(*e*) *Completely enumerate all possible options by combining all possible levels of each attribute.* In designing creative options, a useful procedure is forcing morphological connections in which the attributes of the "standard" option are listed, then alternative levels of each attribute are generated. Finally, candidate options are created by forcing all possible connections across attributes. The commercially available DECISION AIDE II software first requires the user to list all the features of current options (such as low cost), then the user is prompted to supply a new option which matches a forced combination of three features. This approach is likely to meet the criterion of maximizing the fraction of total possible major option variants which are included in the option set.

(*f*) *Invent or temporarily replace an attribute.* Inventing a new attribute that has not been considered previously may suggest novel alternatives and may lead to maximizing the flexibility (i.e., responsiveness to unmodelled future changes) of the option set. For example, multiuse and convertibility are two attributes of a combined diaper tote bag and portable infant bed which were not factors in the standard tote bag, but introducing them as attributes readily suggests the attractiveness of having a padded bag convert into a portable bed.

Second, temporarily replacing an attribute with an isomorphic description may stimulate new ideas. The framing of the description of outcomes has been shown to alter choices, possibly by causing the accessing of different nodes in the cognitive network. For example, presenting outcomes in terms of number of lives saved or number dying can lead to opposite choices.

(*g*) *Expand the scope of the problem by examining higher-level attributes.* At the beginning of the modelling process, it is important to vary the scope of the problem by asking why the current attributes are important in order to discover higher-level attributes. For example, considering the problem of North Sea oil pollution from different institutional levels can introduce different sorts of options (von Winterfeldt and Edwards 1986 p. 522). Experimental subjects who expanded the scope of a problem via a "problem–purpose expansion" heuristic generated more ideas than the subjects who were warned that problem formulation and reformulation is important, but were not given a specific method. In the problem–purpose expansion method, the purpose is first stated in the form of action verb + object phrase + qualifying phrase (TO MAKE + A PROFIT OF $20 000 + WITHIN ONE YEAR), then it is expanded by repeatedly responding to the means–end question, "What am I trying to accomplish?" (TO ATTAIN BUSINESS SUCCESS WITHIN ONE YEAR). Altering the scope of the problem will also help meet the criterion of maximizing the flexibility of the option set by increasing responsiveness to future changes in problem structure which arise owing to expansion of the scope.

1.2 State-Based Procedures

Some procedures depend on prior determination of the states of nature or combination of probabilistic events which may impact on the outcomes of the decision options. Two procedures are presented here.

(*a*) *Present possible states of nature one at a time. Elicit options which will be effective in each individual state.* First, the possible future scenarios are generated (by combining different probabilistic events to determine alternative states of the world), and then options which would be effective in each scenario are elicited. For example, facing the scenario that both "the US dollar is weakening" and "the stock market slumps," the decision maker might generate the option of investing in foreign exchanges (e.g., the Japanese Yen). This approach can be especially useful in selecting strategic long-range plans. In addition, options for gathering more information about the probability of the state (e.g., through market research) should be considered. Note that the order in which states are presented may affect the option set. For example, if the first state is that "the worldwide economy is in a recession," then this "bad" state may induce a pessimistic mood and alter the pathways of spreading activation through the cognitive network.

(b) *Design options to do well in the more probable states of nature.* Identifying the few states of nature which are most probable, then designing options which will do well on that set of states of nature is another approach. For example, a stadium vendor might sell hats as rain hats or sun visors depending on the state of the weather. This procedure is likely to lead to the creation of options with expected utilities which are close to the expected utility of the best option, meeting the criterion of minimizing the number of options in the set which are close to optimal.

1.3 Composite (Attribute-Based and State-Based) Procedures

A procedure which relies on specification of both the attributes and the states of nature may be especially useful for generating an enlarged set of options once a preliminary model of the problem has been built.

Elicit a preliminary set of options that addresses the heavily weighted attributes. Then conduct a sensitivity analysis using a preliminary decision tree before eliciting more options. Arbel and Tong (1982) created an option-generation procedure that uses a preliminary decision tree with the initial options to conduct a sensitivity analysis. The sensitivity analysis highlights sensitive states, so that new options can be generated which reduce or circumvent this sensitivity. Sensitive states are defined as those which have greater differences in the payoffs for the different outcomes. For example, suppose the preliminary option which maximizes the expected utility results in utility u_1 if state 1 occurs (with probability p) and a lower utility of u_2 if it doesn't. Thus the expected utility of the option is $pu_1 + (1-p)u_2$. This best option will result in utility u_3 if state 2 (with probability q) occurs and a lower u_4 if it doesn't. Suppose $u_1 - u_2$ is greater than $u_3 - u_4$. Then state 1 is called more sensitive than state 2 because an "error" in assessing the probability p of state 1 (e.g., the actual p is found to be 0.1 more) will lead to a greater change in expected utility [0.1 $(u_1 - u_2)$] than if the same error were made with state 2. Arbel and Tong illustrated their procedure by generating alternative corporate strategic plans. The procedure is likely to lead to minimization of the number of options which are close to optimal.

1.4 Option-Based Procedures

(a) *Present examples of options and elicit more options.* Although presenting examples of options seems appropriate, experimental research results give mixed evidence about its effectiveness. Pitz et al. (1980) presented examples of possible vacation options to experimental subjects. This did not increase the number of options generated, but did lead to more options that related to the examples. Thus, providing examples seems to have caused subjects to anchor on those examples in the cognitive network, and to generate new options which were representative of the examples using the representativeness heuristic. Gettys *et al.* (1987) presented examples to encourage thinking prior to eliciting added options. Although the effectiveness of supplying examples was not directly tested, subjects only generated about 20–30% of the possible good options, so giving examples may have limited the quantity of generated options. This approach is likely to meet the criterion of maximizing the number of options related to examples.

(b) *Specify the characteristic or generic structure of options. Then select options which will meet the required structure.* For example, in a project to generate options for a psychology department's computer systems, the objectives were first decomposed into a tree. Then three requirements spaces (hardware, software and user) were mapped out. Finally, options for subsequent evaluation were designed which would span the requirements spaces. First options suitable in three small worlds (business, laboratory and statistics/simulation system) were identified, then they were combined as complete options.

Alternatively, the generic structure of example options can be used to identify goals or attributes which may be of interest. When experimental subjects were told to supply the goals which might be attained by example choices *and* the choices that could meet example goals, they generated more new options (and new goals). This method presumably aids a person in accessing problem prototypes or scripts in memory consisting of options linked with outcomes described in terms of attributes or goals. This should lead to maximizing the fraction of the total possible major option variations included in the option set.

(c) *Visualize the ideal option and design options which are close to it.* An ideal option which reaches the best level on each attribute can be imagined as an example option. This ideal option may be imagined with visual imagery and be represented as a spatial image in the cognitive network. Anchoring option generation on this option may activate search in the cognitive network locally about the node representing the ideal option and lead to maximizing the number of alternatives that are close to ideal. However, if a person is unable to imagine the ideal option, then it may also be hard to imagine options close to it.

(*d*) *Present examples of options framed in a different way.* The method of framing an attribute to stimulate new options has already been discussed. The framing of the reference point and sunk outcomes has also been shown to alter choices, perhaps because different frames lead to different node-activation patterns. The reference point, target level or neutral level on an attribute can greatly alter the perceptions of an option if changing the reference level leads to changing the perception of an outcome from being a gain or "good" to being a loss or "bad." For example, in a civil-defense problem of choosing between equal chances of losing 40 lives and 60 lives versus a sure loss of 50 lives, a different frame is achieved by setting the reference point at the 50 sure lives to be lost in the second option. Then the new frame for the first option leads to equal chances of saving 10 additional lives or losing 10 additional lives.

Sunk outcomes are costs or benefits of a problem situation which have already been experienced and which may or may not be perceived as relevant to the current decision problem. Presenting example options with and without sunk outcomes may lead to different new options. More generally, the time horizon (both backwards and forwards in time) which is spanned by the model must be specified.

1.5 General Creativity Methods

In addition to the specific techniques which are listed in the preceding subsections, some other general creativity techniques may be useful in generating novel options.

Examining the problem from the point of view of different experts, different interested parties and different levels of an organization may lead to more creative options. Similarly, an interdisciplinary team of analysts may generate a more complete set of options than a group of people from one shared background.

Methods for releasing self-imposed constraints can enhance creativity. For example, when confronted by the problem of an ostensibly broken doorbell, a person may think of the "creative" option of trying to open the door in case it isn't locked, but fail to relax the implicit constraint imposed by a written note (saying "please knock loudly, since the doorbell is broken") that ringing the doorbell wouldn't work.

The purpose of techniques such as brainstorming and synectics is to stimulate idea generation. Brainstorming involves the rapid generation of ideas, by building upon previously generated ideas or diverging onto new topics without concurrent evaluation of the ideas. A group of individuals separately brainstorming may lead to more breadth of options than if the same people do it in a group, which may lead to depth by following a specific idea with a related one. Synectics is a set of techniques which rely on metaphorical thinking and thinking with analogies to create new ideas. Training subjects to follow a diverging–converging two-step process called "ideation–evaluation" (in problem finding, solving and implementation) led to higher use of ideation in problem finding and solving and better performance in problem finding in a field experiment. Divergent thinkers have been shown to have a greater ability to generate alternative options. Inducing a good mood in experimental subjects (by having them watch a funny movie) helped to stimulate the creative generation of options for solving the problem of affixing a candle to a wall in a room with miscellaneous objects.

2. Methods for Generating States of Nature

This section contains four categories of methods for generating states of nature: probability-based, state-based, option-based and general creativity techniques. The methods prompt a person to search memory in a controlled fashion to stimulate creative generation of possible states by initiating activation of nodes in different parts of the cognitive network. There are many types of probabilistic variables which may be used to identify the state of the environment, including: technological advances, actions taken by competitors, "acts of God" and economic conditions. See Keller (1988) for a more complete description of the methods, experimental evidence and an extensive list of references.

Although the goal in state generation is to partition the environment with an exhaustive set of mutually exclusive states, this ideal will usually not be completely attainable. A general criterion (proposed in Keller 1988) for evaluating the sufficiency of the set of states is to continue searching for new states if the probability that these additional unmodelled states will occur exceeds a prespecified threshold p. The threshold will vary depending on the costs of suboptimality and of further search.

2.1 Probability-Based Procedures

(*a*) *Estimate the probability of "other" states.* A key necessity for computing the potential value of unadded states is an accurate assessment of their probability. Unfortunately, experimental subjects have been shown to underestimate this probability (Gettys *et al.* 1986). When Fischhoff *et al.* (1978) showed automobile mechanics and college students fault-tree structures hierarchically categorizing the reasons why a car might not start, their assessments of the probabilities of different causes varied systematically depending on how much detail was provided on the various branches of the tree. Branches on the fault tree included "battery charge insufficient," "fuel-system defective," and "all other problems." Although subjects consistently underestimated the probability of the "other" category, when asked to focus on what causes were grouped together in this miscellaneous branch, its probability increased. Also, the probability of a particular branch was increased by presenting it as two separate component branches. However, increasing the amount of detail for the tree as a whole or just for some of its branches produced small effects on perceptions.

Thus, based on this study, two methods for improving the estimate of the probability of unadded states are suggested. First, a decision maker should focus on what states have been omitted, prior to estimating the probability of unadded states. Thus, activation will be diffused throughout the cognitive network in the general regions near the already modelled states. Even if this mental simulation does not produce well-formed "visions" of additional future states, it should at least cause a person to anchor on some vague added states and lead to a higher and more accurate estimate of the probability. A by-product of this is that added future states may have been generated which can be formally included in the model if their joint probability exceeds the threshold. Second, a related method would be to ask the decision maker to partition the "other" category into two or more parts. Then the total probability estimate for both "other" state categories is likely to be higher and the partitioning process may also lead to the generation of added states.

(b) *Assess preliminary probabilities for the variables which have been already identified.* When a person is temporarily unable to think of additional states, the task can be switched to a preliminary elicitation of the probabilities of the events which have been already specified. It will sometimes be the case that the decision maker will be unable to easily supply a probability since the event E is dependent on another event S. Thus a new event which should be explicitly modelled is S.

2.2 State-Based Procedures

(a) *Consider the variables in an example state one at a time.* Once a preliminary set of states has been identified, one state can be used as an example to focus thinking. First, the variables in the example state (such as the competitor's price and the coupon redemption rate) would be listed and the person would be asked to generate different states suggested by each individual component or variable. Experimental subjects who generated more hypotheses (states) also generated more uses for an object when the attributes of the object were prespecified. This provides indirect evidence that prespecifying the variables in a state may lead to generation of more states.

(b) *Force morphological connections among components of a state.* A variation on the above method also begins with identifying the components of an example state of nature. Then variations of each component are listed and "forced" combinations between all possible variations are enumerated, to help identify other possible states. For example, in the terrorist-plagued Middle Eastern countries, a well-known state of nature is that a free-standing small bomb will be delivered in the mail to a US Embassy, and pressure and motion will detonate an explosion. Varying the delivery system from the mail to a suicide-committing driver in a Mercedes truck creates the unforeseen state of nature that occurred when a bomb-carrying truck crashed into a US Embassy in Beirut, Lebanon. This situation resulted in concrete barriers being erected at government building such as the US Capitol building in Washington, DC.

(c) *Decompose states into subjudgements.* When the states are different levels of a numerical quantity (such as sales volume by competitors), prompting a person to use a problem-specific algorithm eliciting appropriate subjudgements should lead to a better partition of the environment into possible states. For example, the aggregate sales volume by competitors could be estimated by first estimating the advertising expenses and the resulting sales volume of each competitor, then arithmetically combining these to get the aggregate estimate.

2.3 Option-Based Procedures

(a) *Focus on one example option and generate best- and worst-case scenarios.* Once one possible alternative action is known, it can be used as a focal point to think about the best possible state of the world if that option is chosen. It may help to think about the emotional good feeling that would result if this good outcome occurred. This should stimulate activation of the person's cognitive network in the region surrounding the option in the direction of "good" outcomes and surrounding the node containing the induced "good" emotional state. Then the same option can be used to think about the worst possible state of the world that could occur if that option is chosen. This should stimulate activation of nodes around the option in the direction of "bad" outcomes and "bad" emotional states.

(b) *Generate states which discriminate among options in terms of the range of outcomes.* In this method triples of example options are compared. The decision maker is asked to supply a state in which two options get the same outcome and the third option gets a different outcome. This approach is the reverse of the one by Arbel and Tong (1982) who discuss how to use such "sensitive states" to guide generation of options.

2.4 General Creativity Methods

The general creativity techniques for eliciting options listed in Sect. 1.5 are also useful for state generation. First, the problem should be examined from varied perspectives. The perspective of the current place in time can be manipulated by drawing a causal map of the problem, then mentally moving forward or backwards in time. Moving backwards in time to list possible causes of current states is likely to result in a more complex cognitive map than the parallel one for moving forward in time to list possible consequences of current states, since we may tend to report all factors that were noticed in past events, and not just the more valued factors which are selectively thought of when projecting the future.

Working on state generation with a group of people with different propensities and abilities to reason probabilistically and to abstract from concrete situations is likely to result in a more complete set of states. People from different organizational levels are likely to bring different perspectives to the problem and they may have different abilities to abstract from the concrete situation. Also, the team of state generators should contain people from cultural backgrounds differing in their worldview of causality.

One of the key requirements of the brainstorming creativity method is the prohibition of any censoring of ideas during idea generation. However, there is experimental evidence that peoples' generated hypotheses are censored prior to giving their responses. Thus, requiring that evaluation of possible states be deferred to a later stage should increase the number of states generated.

2.5 Modelling Structures to Aid Probabilistic Thought

In conjunction with the methods presented above for stimulating creative state generation, probabilistic modelling techniques can be used with the preliminary states and options to visually represent the problem structure and stimulate deeper thinking about the problem, leading to the generation of additional states. These methods include inference trees, fault trees, event trees, cognitive maps, influence diagrams, interpretive structural modelling and diagnostic questioning.

Once the relevant variables are identified, a formal procedure for forecasting the probability distribution of outcomes will be useful. Various formal forecasting and planning procedures are used in organizations to augment individual judgements about possible future states of the environment and the probability of those states. These procedures include computer simulation models (probabilistic system dynamics), trend extrapolation, the Delphi method, cross-impact analysis and scenario analysis.

3. Methods for Generating Attributes for Evaluating Options

The attributes (or objectives or criteria) by which options will be evaluated can be represented in a hierarchical value tree. Higher-level attributes (such as degree of personal success) will be subdivided into more specific characteristics of success (e.g., personal appeal, monetary return) (see Fig. 1). Keeney and Raiffa (1976) present value trees for many example problems and describe criteria for evaluating the sufficiency of the set of attributes (see also von Winterfeldt and Edwards 1986). The set of attributes should be complete, operational, decomposable, nonredundant and as small as possible.

The methods for generating attributes are divided into four categories: attribute-based, state-based, option-based and general creativity techniques. Examples of methods in each category are briefly mentioned below.

3.1 Attribute-Based Procedures

(a) Present examples of attributes and elicit more attributes. For example, the attribute of "monetary return" for evaluating personal investments may suggest the additional attribute of the "financial risk."

(b) Further partition attributes into subattributes. In choosing vacation options, one might divide "entertainment" into nighttime and daytime entertainment in a hierarchical value tree. The investment decision maker should ask the question "How will I attain the higher-level attribute (e.g., personal success)?", answering the question with a means to attain it, i.e., "increase monetary return."

(c) Generate higher-level attributes by answering why the lower-level attributes are important. The problem–purpose expansion method, which was described in Sect. 1.1(g) can be used to generate higher-level attributes.

3.2 State-Based Procedures

Present states one at a time. Elicit attributes which will characterize the possible outcomes of the preliminary options in each state. When choosing among possible investment options, the state that "the worldwide economy is in a recession" can be focused on first (see Fig. 1). Then the option of investing in antiques may suggest the attribute of the "ability to hold the commodity long enough for the economy to turn around," or the attribute of the "ability to use an investment in an alternative function (i.e., furniture to sit on or paintings to look at)."

3.3 Option-Based Procedures

Present options one at a time. Elicit attributes which will possibly evaluate each option. For example, the option of investing in foreign currency may suggest the attribute of the "stability of various countries' current governments."

3.4 General-Creativity Methods

In addition to the general creativity methods described in Sects. 1.5 and 2.4 the K-J method by Kawakita Jiro for creatively structuring problems may be useful (Hogarth 1987 p. 170). First, observations (i.e., decision-problem attributes) are recorded on separate cards. Then the cards are considered in random order to detect associations linking elements, and the cards are classified into groups with closely connected elements. Then these groups are arranged into meaningful patterns, such as a hierarchical value tree consisting of different groups of attributes.

4. Acknowledgments

This work was partially funded by a UCI Committee on Research grant and a UCI Faculty Career Development Award to Professor Keller.

See also: Collective Enquiry; Decision Analysis; Human Information Processing; Knowledge Representation

Bibliography

Arbel A, Tong R M 1982 On the generation of alternatives in decision analysis problems. *J. Oper. Res. Soc.* **33**, 377–87
Fischhoff B, Slovic P, Lichtenstein S 1978 Fault trees: sensitivity of estimated failure probabilities to problem representation. *J. Exp. Psychol.: Hum. Percept. Perform.* **4**, 330–44
Gettys C F, Mehle T, Fisher S 1986 Plausibility assessments in hypothesis generation. *Organ. Behav. Hum. Decis. Process.* **37**, 14–35
Gettys C F, Pliske R M, Manning C, Casey J T 1987 An evaluation of human act generation performance. *Organ. Behav. Hum. Decis. Process.* **39**, 23–51
Hogarth R 1987 *Judgement and Choice*. Wiley, New York
Keeney R L, Raiffa H 1976 *Decisions with Multiple Objectives: Preferences and Value Tradeoffs*. Wiley, New York
Keller L R 1988 Decision problem structuring: generating states of nature *IEEE Trans. Sys. Man. and Cybern.* **18**(5), 715–28
Keller L R, Ho J 1988 Decision problem structuring: Generating options, Working paper. University of California, Irvine, California
Pearl J, Leal A, Saleh J 1982 GODDESS: A goal-directed decision structuring system. *IEEE Trans. Pattern Anal. Mach. Intell.* **4**(3), 250–62
Pitz G F, Sachs N J, Heerboth J 1980 Procedures for eliciting choices in the analysis of individual decisions. *Organ. Behav. Hum. Perform.* **26**, 396–408
von Winterfeldt D, Edwards W 1986 *Decision Analysis and Behavioral Research*. Cambridge University Press, New York

L. R. Keller and J. L. Ho
[University of California, Irvine,
California, USA]

Decision Support Systems

In very general terms, a decision support system (DSS) is a system that supports managerial decision making by assisting in the organization of knowledge about ill-structured issues. The primary components of a DSS are a database management system (DBMS), a model-base management system (MBMS), and a dialog generation and management system (DGMS). The emphasis is upon effectiveness of decision making as this involves formulation of alternatives, analysis of their impacts, and interpretation and selection of appropriate options for implementation. Efficiency in terms of time required to evolve the decision, while important, is secondary to effectiveness in terms of the utility or value of the decision of the decision maker. There are many application areas where the use of a DSS is potentially promising. These include financial management and planning, command and control, health care, operations management, and essentially any area in which management has to cope with semistructured or unstructured decision situations.

1. Introduction and Taxonomies of Decision Problems

Numerous disciplinary areas have contributed to the development of the DSS. These include computer science which provides the hardware and software tools necessary to implement DSS design constructs. The field of management science and operations research has provided the theoretical framework in decision analysis that is necessary to design useful and relevant normative approaches to choice making. The area of management information systems has provided the database design tools that are needed. The areas of organizational behavior, and behavioral and cognitive science have provided rich sources of information concerning how humans and organizations process information and make judgements in a descriptive fashion.

There have been many attempts to classify different types of decisions. The articles *Human Judgement and Decision Rules* and *Knowledge Representation* discuss some of these. Among the classifications of particular interest is the decision type taxonomy of Anthony (1965). He describes four types of decisions as follows.

(a) *Strategic planning decisions.* These are decisions related to choosing highest-level policies and objectives, and associated resource allocations.

(b) *Management control decisions.* These are decisions made for the purpose of assuring effectiveness in the acquisition and use of resources.

(c) *Operational control decisions.* These are decisions made for the purpose of assuring effectiveness in the performance of operations.

(d) *Operational performance decisions.* These are the day-to-day decisions made while performing operations.

Figure 1 illustrates the way in which these decisions are related and the way in which they normatively influence organizational learning.

Simon (1960) has described decisions as structured or unstructured, depending on whether or not the decision-making process can be explicitly described prior to the time when it is necessary to make a decision. This taxonomy would seem to lead directly to that in which expert skills (wholistic reasoning), rules (heuristics) or formal reasoning (holistic evaluation) are normatively used for judgement. Generally, operational performance decisions are more likely to be prestructured than are strategic planning decisions. Thus, expert systems can usually be expected to be more appropriate for operational performance and operational control decisions than they are for strategic planning and management planning decisions. In a similar way, DSSs will often be more appropriate for strategic planning and management control than they are for operational control and operational performance. It is important to note that expertise is a relative term which depends on the familiarity with the task and the operational environment into which it is embedded. Since decision environments do change, and since novices become experts through learning and feedback, it is clear that there should exist many areas in which the proper form of knowledge-base support is a hybrid of an expert system and a decision support system. This suggests that there will be a variety of decision-making processes in practice and that an effective support system should support multiple decision processes. In a similar way, the information requirements for decision-making can be expected to be highly varied, and an effective support system should support a variety of database management needs.

There are a number of abilities that a DSS should support. It should support the decision maker in the formulation or framing of the decision situation in the sense of recognizing needs, identifying appropriate objectives by which to measure the successful resolution of an issue, and generating alternative courses of action that will resolve the needs and satisfy objectives. It should also provide support in enhancing the abilities of the decision maker to obtain the possible impacts on needs of the alternative courses of action. This analysis capability must be associated with the provision of a capability to enhance the ability of the decision maker to provide an interpretation of these impacts in terms of objectives. This interpretation capability will lead to the evaluation of the alternatives and the selection of a preferred alternative option. These three steps of formulation, analysis and interpretation are very fundamental for the formal analysis of difficult issues. They are the fundamental steps of systems engineering and are discussed at greater length in the article *Systems Methodology*.

Associated with these three steps must be the ability to acquire, represent and utilize information or knowledge, and the ability to implement the chosen alternative course of action. All of this must be accomplished with due consideration of the particular rationality perspective that is used for decision making. As noted in the article *Systems Knowledge: Philosophical Perspectives*, these include economic and technical rationality, satisficing rationality, organizational process rationality, incremental or bureaucratic politics rationality, and other forms of social, legal or organizational rationality.

There are many variables that will affect the information that is, or should be, obtained relative to any given decision situation. These variables are very clearly task dependent. Keen and Scott Morton (1978) identify eight variables.

(a) *Inherent accuracy of available information.* Operational control situations will often deal with information that is relatively certain and precise. The information in strategic planning situations is often uncertain, imprecise and incomplete.

(b) *Necessary level of detail.* Often, very detailed information is needed for operational-type decisions. Highly aggregated information is often described for strategic decisions, but there are many difficulties associated with information summarization that need attention (see *Human Information Processing*).

(c) *Time horizon for information needed.* Operational decisions are typically based on information over a short time horizon, and the nature of the control may be changed very frequently.

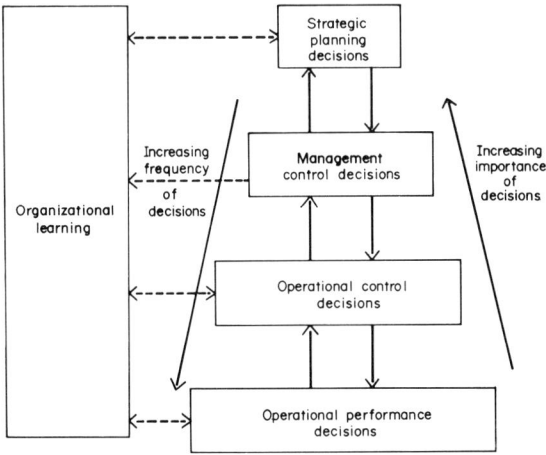

Figure 1
Organizational information and decision flows

Strategic decisions are based on information and predictions based on a long time horizon.

(d) *Frequency of use.* Strategic decisions are made infrequently, although they are perhaps refined fairly often. Operational decisions are made quite frequently and are relatively easily changed.

(e) *Internal or external information source.* Operational decisions are often based on information that is available internal to the organization, whereas strategic decisions are much more likely to be dependent on information content that can only be obtained external to the organization.

(f) *Information scope.* Generally, operational decisions are made on the basis of narrow-scope information related to well-defined events internal to the organization. Strategic decisions are based on broad-scope information and a wide range of factors that often cannot be fully anticipated prior to the need for the decision.

(g) *Information quantifiability.* In strategic planning, information is very likely to be highly qualitative, at least initially. For operational decisions, the available information is often highly quantified.

(h) *Information currency.* In strategic planning, information is often rather old, and it is often difficult to obtain current information. For operational control decisions, very current information is often needed.

The extent to which a support system possesses the capacity to formulate, analyze and interpret issues will depend on whether the resulting system should be called a management information system (MIS), a predictive management information system (PMIS) or a decision support system (DSS). In a classical MIS, the user inputs a request for a report concerning some question and the MIS supplies that report. When the user is able to pose a "what if?" type question and the system is able to respond with an "if then" type of response, then we have a PMIS. In each case there is some sort of formulation of the issue and this is accompanied by some capacity for analysis. The classic MIS need only be able to respond to queries with reports. Thus it would respond to a request for inputs concerning airline flights from Washington to Chicago on July 4 with a report of available flights on that date. Search of an electronic file cabinet, or perhaps a relational database, would provide information from which a report generator could construct the desired report. Alternatively, we might desire a response to a "what if?" type question such as "What will likely happen if we drill for oil at location x?" The computer might then respond with "Based on the physical characteristics of source x it is predicted that if you drill at this source then you should likely

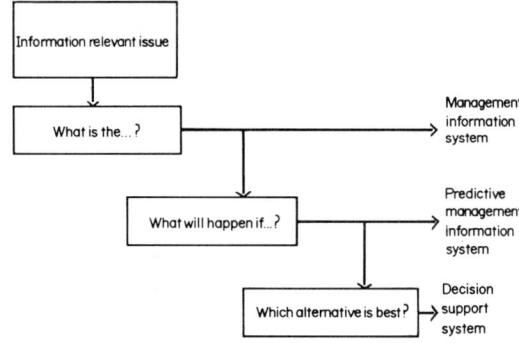

Figure 2
Conceptual differences between MIS, PMIS and DSS

expect . . . " In the first situation, the MIS would include the following capabilities: a focus on data processing and structured data flows at an operational level, and summary reports for the user. The PMIS would include an additional amount of analysis capability. This might require an intelligent database query system, or perhaps just the simple use of some sort of spreadsheet or macroeconomic model. It can be seen that the nature of the decision-making process is such that each of these questions needs to be asked. We can provide support to the decision-maker at any of several levels, as suggested by Fig. 2. Whether we have a MIS, a PMIS or a DSS depends on the type of support automated computer base that is provided to the decision maker in reaching the decision. Fundamental to the notion of a DSS is the assistance which is provided in identifying alternative courses of action and formulating the decision situation, structuring and analysis of the decision situation through the use of a model-base manager, and then interpretation of the analysis results of the alternatives in terms of the value system of the decision maker.

To obtain a DSS, we would need to add the capability of model-base management to an MIS. However, much more would be needed than just the simple addition of a set of decision trees and procedures to elicit decision-maker utilities, as might be believed from examination of the paradigms of decision analysis. We would also need a system that would be flexible and adaptable to changing user requirements so that support for the decision styles of the decision-maker can be provided as these change with task and environment, and also as experiential familiarity of the support system users fluctuate according to these variables. Most decision situations are fragmented in that there are multiple decision makers and groups of people working together, rather than just a single decision maker. In addition, there are temporal and spatial separation elements involved. Further, as Mintzberg (1973) has indicated, managers have many more activities than decision making to occupy themselves with, and it will be necessary for an appropriate

DSS to support many of these other information-related functions as well. Thus, the principal goal of a DSS, improving the effectiveness of organizational knowledge users through the use of information systems technology, is not a simple one to achieve.

2. Frameworks for Designing Decision Support Systems

As we have discussed, there are three principal components of a DSS: a database management system (DBMS), a model-base management system (MBMS), and a dialog generation and management system (DGMS). An appropriate DSS design framework will consider each of these three component systems and their interrelations and interactions. Figure 3 illustrates the interconnection of these three generic components and illustrates the interaction of the decision maker with the system through the DGMS. Sprague and Carlson (1982) have indicated that there are three technology levels at which a DSS may be considered. The first of these is the level of the DSS tools. This level would contain the hardware and software elements, and those system science and operations research methods that would be needed to design a specific DSS. The purpose of these DSS tools is to design a specific DSS that would be responsive to a particular task or issue.

Often the best designers of a DSS are not the specialists familiar with the DSS tools. The principal reason for this is that it is difficult for one person to be very familiar with a wide variety of tools and also the requirements needed for a specific DSS. This suggests an intermediate level, that of the decision support generator, as being a very useful level for DSS design. The DSS generator is a set of software, similar to a very-high-level programming language, that enables the construction of a specific DSS without the need to formally use the DSS tools. A DSS generator would contain an integrated set of features, such as inquiry capabilities, modelling language capabilities, financial and statistical (and perhaps other) analysis capabilities, and graphic display and report preparation capabilities. The major support provided by a DSS generator is that it allows the rapid construction of a prototype of the decision situation and allows the decision maker to experiment with this prototype. The prototype can then be refined, if necessary, so that it is more representative of the decision situation and more useful to the decision maker. This generally reduces, often to a considerable degree, the time required to design and build a DSS. It will often be the case that the process of constructing the prototype DSS through the use of the DSS generator leads to a set of requirements specifications for a DSS which are then realized in a more efficient form using DSS tools.

There are many actors who can become involved in the design and use of a DSS. At a minimum, these

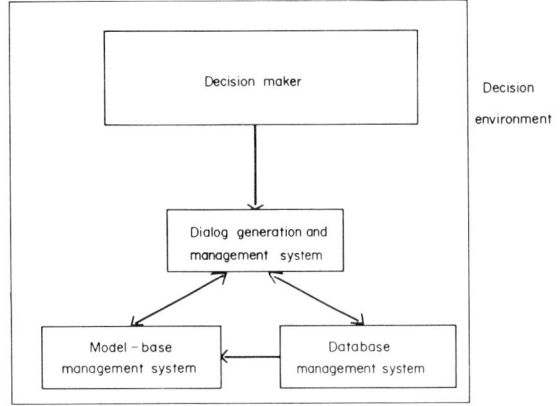

Figure 3
Generic components in a DSS

include the DSS users and their staff, the DSS designer, the technical support people who work with the DSS designer, and the specialists in computer and system science who develop the hardware, programming languages and operations research methods that ultimately become the components of a specific DSS. The advantage of the DSS generator is that it can be used by the DSS designer to directly interface the user group. This eliminates, or at least minimizes, the need for DSS user interaction with the content specialists in computer and system science. When it is recalled that the user will seldom be able to specify the requirements for a DSS initially, then the great advantage to having a DSS generator for use by the DSS designer in interacting with the DSS users becomes apparent.

The design and development of a DSS can be patterned after the stages of the design process discussed in the article *Design and Evaluation of Systems*. Since a DSS is intended to be used by decision makers with varying experiential familiarity and expertise with respect to a particular task, it is especially important that a DSS design should consider the variety of issue representations or frames that decision makers may use to describe issues, the operations that may be performed on these representations to enable formulation analysis and interpretation of the decision situation, the automated memory aids that support retention of the various results of operations on the representations, and the control mechanisms that assist decision makers in using these representations, operations and memory aids. A very useful control mechanism results in the construction of heuristic procedures, perhaps in the form of a set of production rules, to enable development of efficient and effective standard operating policies to be issued as staff directives. Other control mechanisms are intended to help the decision maker make direct use of the DSS and also acquire new skills and rules based on the formal-reasoning-based knowledge that is called forth through use of a DSS. This process-independent approach toward development of the necessary capabilities of a specific DSS is due to Sprague and Carlson (1982) and is known as the ROMC approach. It also serves to specify the capabilities that a useful DSS generator, or the specific DSS tools, must have in order to be potentially capable of building an effective DSS.

3. Database Management Systems

A DBMS is one of the three fundamental components of a DSS. An appropriate DBMS must be able to work with data that is both internal and external to the organization. In almost every instance in which there exists multiple decision makers, there will exist the need for personal databases, local databases and system-wide databases. Some of the desirable characteristics of a DBMS include the ability to cope with a variety of data structures that allow for probabilistic, incomplete and imprecise data, and data that is unofficial and personal, as contrasted with official and organizational. The DBMS should also be capable of informing the support-system user of the types of data that are available and how to gain access to them.

In order to construct a database, we must first identify a data model. A data model is a collection of data structures, operations that may be applied to the data structures, and integrity rules which are used to constrain or otherwise define permissible values of the data. There are at least five models that may be used to represent data. The most elementary of these is the individual record model. The relational model is a powerful generalization of the record model. A relation is the fundamental data structure in the relational model, and there may be a number of fields in any given relation. The relational model enables mathematical set operations on records in terms of the insertion of new records, updating fields within existing records, deleting existing records, creating relations that may be contained in records, deleting relations that may be contained in records, joining or combining two or more relations based on their containing common fields, selecting records by virtue of their containing certain specified relations, and projection such as to enable selection of a subset of the fields that exist in a relation.

The hierarchical or tree data model is a relatively efficient representation of data. In a hierarchical model, the structure represents the information that is contained in the fields of a relational model. In a hierarchical model, there will be certain records which must exist before other records can exist since every data structure must have a root record. Owing to this structured aspect of the model, it will be necessary to repeat some of the data that need be stored only once for a relational model. The network model is a generalization of the hierarchical model in that there are links between records which enable a given record to participate in several relationships. There are often major problems associated with insertions, deletions and updating in both the hierarchical and network models owing to the need to maintain a consistent database. These do not exist in the relational model since the same data is never entered more than once. Also there is additional search complexity since a search can start anywhere in the network structure. Searches are, however, generally more efficient than they are in a relational model.

Owing to the potential need to accommodate expert system type capabilities in a DSS, it is desirable to consider a production-rule model as a fifth data model. This will enable inferences to be made. Thus, this is a particularly desirable form of data model when we want to use many PMIS capabilities. The "if–then" type response to "what if?" queries is especially natural in this representation. For an additional discussion of production rules see *Knowledge Representation*. Much additional discussion of DBMS design approaches can be found in Sprague and Carlson (1982) and Date (1977, 1983).

4. Model-Base Management Systems

The desire to provide recommendation capability in a DSS leads us to a discussion of model-base management systems (MBMS). It is through the use of an MBMS that we are able to provide for sophisticated analysis and interpretation capability in a DSS. The single most important characteristic of an MBMS is that it should enable the decision maker to explore the decision situation through use of the database by a model base of algorithmic procedures and management protocols. This can occur through the use of modelling statements, in some procedural or nonprocedural language, through the use of model subroutines, such as mathematical programming packages, that are called by a management function, and through the use of data abstraction models. The latter approach is close to the expert system approach in that there will exist element, equation and solution procedures that together will form an inference engine. Advantages to this approach include ease of updating and use of the model for explanatory and explication purposes.

Typically, it will be desirable to allow for the use of multiple models in order to accommodate the requirement of the typical decision maker for flexibility. Thus a mixed scanning approach might be incorporated in which a conjunctive or disjunctive scanning mechanism is used to allow for an initial scan to eliminate grossly unacceptable alternatives. After this is accomplished, further evaluation of alternatives might be accomplished by a compensatory trade-off evaluation, or one based on a dominance search procedure (Sage and White 1984). The articles *Decision Analysis* and *Human Judgement and Decision Rules* provide much discussion concerning various aspects of MBMS design.

To provide flexibility, the MBMS should provide, on the request of the system user, a variety of prewritten models that have been found useful in the past, such as linear programming and multiattribute decision analysis models, and procedures to use the models. It should also allow for the development of user-built models and heuristics that are developed from established models that will either become permanent part of the MBMS or which will be considered as *ad hoc* models. It should also be possible to perform sensitivity tests of model outputs, and to run models with a range of data to obtain the response to a variety of "what if?" type questions.

5. *Dialog Generation and Management System*

The DGMS portion of a DSS is designed to satisfy the knowledge representation, and control and interface requirements of the DSS. The DGMS is responsible for the presentation of the outputs of the DSS to the decision makers and for acquiring and transmitting their inputs to the DBMS and the MBMS. Thus, the DGMS is responsible for producing DSS output representations, for obtaining the decision-maker inputs that result in the operations on the representations, for interfacing to the memory aids and for explicit provision of the control mechanisms that enable the dialog between user input and output and the DBMS and MBMS. Thus the DGMS is strongly involved in each of the ROMC approaches to systems analysis and design of decision support systems.

There are a number of possible dialogs. These are inherently linked to the representational forms that are used for the DBMS and MBMS. Menus, spreadsheets, trade-off graphs and production rules are some of the formats that may be used as a basis for dialog system design. Generally, several of these should be used as the user of the support system may wish to shift among these formats as the nature of issues and experiential familiarity with the DGMS changes. The DGMS should be sufficiently flexible such as to allow review and sensitivity analysis of past judgements, and to be able to provide partial judgements based on incomplete information. Of course the DGMS should be "user friendly" through provision of various HELP facilities, prompting the decision maker, and other abilities that support the knowledge of the support-system user. At all costs, it is necessary to avoid a system that destroys perspectives and to encourage a system that enhances them.

6. *Evaluation of Decision Support System Designs*

It is very important to obtain an evaluation of DSS designs. The article *Design and Evaluation of Systems* provides a discussion of typical evaluation procedures. There are a number of behavioral implications to DSS introduction that are very important. User involvement in the design process, management support for the DSS design effort, and the availability of user training activities are but a few of the many requisites for a successful DSS implementation. It is especially important that potential system users should not regard it as too difficult to learn to use, too hard or too time-consuming to actually use, or as producing inaccurate, incomplete or out-of-date results or recommendations. Perhaps the most damning charges of all that affect potential-user willingness to use the system are the feelings that it significantly interferes with the "normal" way of thinking about problems, or that it cannot adapt to changes in problem specifications, or that it does not produce intermediate results of value, or that it does not really address the actual problems that exist.

Implementation of a DSS can fail if it introduces significant conflict between the form of economic and technical rationality of the recommendations of the DSS and the politicosocial behavior of the organization and users of the system. The way in which groups interact in the decision-making process is also of importance. Hakathorn and Keen (1981) have identified three types of group decision activities. In an independent group activity, the decisions of the individual decision makers do not interact. Often there are interactions and dialog among the decision makers such that pooled interdependencies exist. There also exist situations where there are sequential interdependencies such that the decisions of one decision maker are passed as inputs to the efforts of other decision makers. These and other characteristics of organizational and group decision making need to be considered at all of the design phases for a DSS. The design requirements for a DSS and the implementation concerns will depend considerably on these organizational variables. All of this will also influence operational test and evaluation of the effects of DSS introduction.

See also: Group Decision Support Systems

Bibliography

Alter S L 1982 *Decision Support Systems: Current Practice and Continuing Challenges*. Addison–Wesley, Reading, Massachusetts

Andriole S J (ed.) 1986 *Microcomputer Decision Support Systems: Design, Implementation, and Evaluation*. QED, Wellesley, Massachusetts

Anthony R N 1965 *Planning and Control Systems: A Framework for Analysis*. Harvard University Press, Cambridge, Massachusetts

Bennet J L (ed.) 1983 *Building Decision Support Systems*. Addison–Wesley, Reading, Massachusetts

Bonczek R H, Holsapple C W, Whinston A B 1981 *Foundations of Decision Support Systems*. Academic Press, New York

Cats-Baril W L, Huber G P 1987 Decision support systems for ill-structured problems: An empirical study. *Decis. Sci.* **18,** 350–72

Date C J 1977 *An Introduction to Data Base Systems.* Addison–Wesley, Reading, Massachusetts
Date C J 1983 *Database: A Primer.* Addison–Wesley, Reading, Massachusetts
Hakathorn R, Keen P 1981 Organizational strategies for personal computing in decision support systems. *Manage. Inf. Syst. Q.* **5**(3)
Hogarth R M 1985 *Judgement and Choice.* Wiley, New York
House W C (ed.) 1984 *Decision Support Systems: A Data-Based, Model-Oriented, User-Developed Discipline.* Petrocelli, Princeton, New Jersey
Huber G P 1980 *Managerial Decision Making.* Scott Foresman, Glenview, Illinois
Janis I L, Mann L 1977 *Decision Making: A Psychological Analysis of Conflict, Choice, and Commitment.* Free Press, New York
Keen P G W, Scott Morton M S 1978 *Decision Support Systems: An Organizational Perspective.* Addison–Wesley, Reading, Massachusetts
Martin J 1983 *Managing the Data Base Environment.* Prentice–Hall, Englewood Cliffs, New Jersey
Mintzberg H 1973 *The Nature of Managerial Work.* Harper and Row, New York
Sage A P 1986 An overview of contemporary issues in the design and development of microcomputer decision support systems. In: Andriole S J (ed.) *Microcomputer Decision Support Systems: Design, Implementation, and Evaluation.* QED, Wellesley, Massachusetts
Sage A P (ed.) 1987 *System Design for Human Interaction.* IEEE Press, New York
Sage A P, White C C 1984 ARIADNE: A knowledge based interactive system for decision support. *IEEE Trans. Syst., Man Cybern.* **14**(1)
Simon H A 1960 *The New Science of Management Decision.* Harper and Row, New York
Sol H G 1983 *Processes and Tools for Decision Support.* North-Holland, Amsterdam
Sprague R H Jr, Carlson E D 1982 *Building Effective Decision Support Systems.* Prentice–Hall, Englewood Cliffs, New Jersey
Sprague R H Jr, McNurlin B C (eds.) 1986 *Information Systems Management in Practice.* Prentice–Hall, Englewood Cliffs, New Jersey
Zmud R W 1983 *Information Systems in Organizations.* Scott Foresman, Glenview, Illinois

A. P. Sage
[George Mason University, Fairfax, Virginia, USA]

Design and Evaluation of Systems

A successful system design typically passes through five distinct phases: requirements specifications identification; preliminary conceptual design; detailed design, testing and evaluation; evaluation; and operational design. It is doubtless true that not every design process should, could or would precisely follow each component in the detailed phases of system design outlined in this article. However, this approach to system design is considered to be sufficiently robust and generic for it to be used as a normative model of the design process, including information concerns for design, and as a guide to the structuring and implementation of appropriate system evaluation practices.

1. The Emergence of Systems Design Engineering

Throughout history, the development of increasingly sophisticated tools has invariably been associated with a decrease in our dependence on human physical energy as a source of effort. The industrial revolution of the late eighteenth century represented a major thrust in this direction. In most cases, a new tool or machine makes it possible to perform a familiar task in a somewhat new and different way. In a smaller number of cases, a new tool has made it possible to perform something entirely new and different that could not have been done previously. Profound social changes have often been associated with changes brought about by new tools. In the 1850s approximately 70% of the labor force in the USA was employed in agriculture. A little more than a century later, less than 3% is employed in this sector. This 3% is able to produce sufficient food to feed an entire country and to generally produce a large surplus as well. Occasionally, however, these tools have produced undesirable side effects; for example, pollution due to chemical plants, and potential depletion of fossil fuel sources. Furthermore, new tools sometimes have the potential for producing significantly harmful side effects, such as those which can occur owing to operational errors in nuclear power plant operation.

Concerns associated with the design of tools so that they can be used efficiently and effectively have always been addressed, but often on an implicit and "trial and error" basis. When tool designers were also tool users, which was more often than not the case for the simple tools and machines of the past, the resulting designs were often good initially, or soon evolved into good designs. When physical tools, machines and systems became so complex that it was no longer possible for them to be designed by a single individual, a design team became necessary. This led to the emergence of a host of new problems. To cope with this, a number of methodologies associated with systems design engineering have evolved. Through these, it has been possible to decompose large design issues into smaller-component subsystem design issues, design the subsystems and then build the complete system as a collection of these subsystems. Nevertheless, problems remain. Just simply connecting together the individual subsystems often did not result in a system that performed acceptably, either from perspectives of technological efficiency or effectiveness. This has led to the realization that systems integration engineering and systems management throughout an entire system life cycle will be necessary. Thus it is that contemporary efforts in systems engineering contain a focus on the tools and methods that support the application of the principles of the physical and material sciences

Design and Evaluation of Systems

for the betterment of humankind, as well as on systems methodology and management constructs that enable system design for more efficient and effective human interaction.

The information-technology revolution is having and will have major impacts on design. In the past, system designs have relied most heavily on the mathematics of optimization and the physical and material products that were being optimized. However, this can no longer be the case. Human behavioral and cognitive concerns now play a dominant role in the success or failure of system designs; these must be taken into consideration throughout all phases of the design process. System management and integration issues are also of major importance in determining effectiveness, efficiency and the overall functionality of system designs. To achieve a high measure of functionality, it must be possible for a system design to be produced, used, maintained, retrofitted and retired throughout all phases of a life cycle, from need conceptualization and identification, through specification of system requirements and architectural structures, to ultimate system installation and evaluation, and operational implementation.

Major improvements in system design evolve through the realization that there are knowledge practices, knowledge principles and knowledge perspectives that are associated with any potential product or service. Knowledge practices refer to the body of knowledge, typically in the form of skill- and rule-based knowledge, that is associated with how products and services result. Knowledge principles relate to formal and conceptual knowledge that ultimately might be related to design, often in a quantitative fashion to some standard of optimality. Finally, knowledge perspectives relate to the methodological and management perspectives that determine how a necessary product or service will, or should, be produced. This metalevel, or epistemological, perspective on knowledge determines the type and amount of knowledge practices and knowledge principles that are brought to bear on a given issue. The model of systems design given in this article is based on these three types of knowledge driving technological system design and management system design. Any product or service that results from purposeful effort is, necessarily, a blend of these two. There are desirable feedback loops that involve each of these elements. Figure 1 presents a conceptual view of this notion of the design process.

2. The Nature of Systems Design

Design is the creative process through which the products, processes or systems presumed to be responsive to client needs and requirements are conceptualized or specified. There are four primary components of this definition. The first is that design results in specifications or architecture for a product, process or system; the second is that design is a creative process; the third important idea is that design activity is conceptual in nature; and finally, there is the very important, and unfortunately often elusive, notion that a successful design must be responsive to client needs and requirements. Good design practice requires that the designer be responsive to each of these four ingredients for quality design effort. The latter stipulation results in the mandate to obtain, from the client for a design effort, a set of needs and

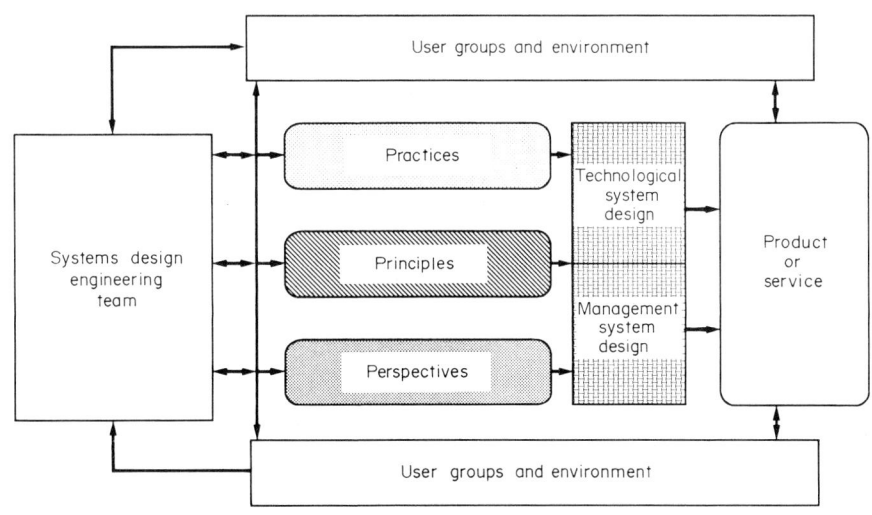

Figure 1
Multiple perspectives on systems design

requirements for the product, process or system that is to result from the design effort. This information requirement serves as the input to the design process. Design is creative and it is a process that is conceptual in nature. The result of this creative and conceptual process is information concerning the specifications or architecture for the product, process or service that will ultimately be manufactured, implemented, installed or brought to fruition in some other way. Information is the key word in this systems model of the design process; it is an essential feature in the input to the design process, the design process itself and the output of the design process. Consequently, design is an information technology and a fundamental goal of systems engineering. These are the perspectives that are taken in this article.

Systems design methodology is first discussed as a necessary element for design to be considered as a process. This leads to a consideration of the nature of design. Associated with this will be purposeful methodological approaches and resulting formalisms for design. These lead to theoretical and conceptual frameworks that are inherent in the nature of design as a process. It will be clear from the discussion of the nature of design that there are a variety of knowledge frameworks or perspectives which are necessary for design. We will be concerned with the characterization and understanding of the thought process of designers in organizing information about design, including the acquisition, representation and use of this information. Particular attention is paid to the requirements for successful knowledge-based support to designers, and aids that support design processes. This concern naturally turns to important issues relative to the knowledge base for design, and how this knowledge base might best be employed and exercised in a support system that assists in decision and design processes. To accomplish this, both analytical and perceptual capabilities are required. Also needed is a knowledge base and model base for support that allows a purposeful interplay of these characteristics of successful design.

Clients and designers have needs and requirements that should be satisfied by the results of a successful design process. Information requirements determination is, therefore, a multifaceted need for successful systems design. In a very real sense, this will often be the most important need for successful design. Without appropriate information, it is highly likely that functionality of the resulting design will be lacking and this may well be noticed only after expensive resources are allocated to a design that turns out to be immature.

3. Systems Design and Methodology

There are many ways in which we can characterize design. We could describe design as an activity involving the classic notions of hypothesis generation and the testing of alternatives or concepts. The hypothesis-generation step involves primarily inductive skills, generally based on experience, that enable the generation of design alternatives. These are evaluated through the primarily deductive activity of evaluation or testing. An initial hypothesis is often unacceptable. When it is rejected, generally through evaluation, iteration back through the hypothesis-generation step enables the modification of the identified alternative, and reevaluation which will hopefully lead to a successful design alternative. When a design is evaluated as successful, then design activity, as least the particular phase of design being undertaken, ceases. Effort then turns to the implementation of the acceptable design or initiation of the next phase in a design effort.

This design methodology is somewhat incomplete in that it does not formally recognize the stimulus that leads to hypothesis generation. There are at least two types of hypotheses generated in the typical design effort: those concerned with client needs, and those relating to the design alternatives or options that are available for choice. There is much uncertainty and information imprecision relative to each of these types of hypotheses. The first is information input imprecision; this creates the need for hypothesis generation regarding client needs. The second is a consequence of option implementation imprecision; this creates the need for generation of hypotheses relative to design alternatives. Similarly, we might talk about stimuli that lead to hypotheses about client needs, and to hypotheses about options and their impact. The first stimulus is generally the result of requirements identification or specifications for the design effort. The second is the result of imperfect knowledge of the environment and about the effect of implementing a given design option.

More often than not, the hypothesis-generation and option evaluation efforts are initially conducted in a preliminary way in order to obtain several concepts that might work. Several potential option alternatives are identified and the resulting options are subjected to at least a preliminary evaluation in order to eliminate clearly unacceptable alternatives. The surviving alternatives are then subjected to more detailed design efforts and more complete architectures or specifications are obtained. The result of this is a system that can then be subjected to detailed design, testing and at least preliminary operational implementation. Once this has occurred, operational evaluation and testing of the implemented system, product or process can occur. The system design may be modified as a result of this evaluation and this will hopefully lead to an ultimately improved system and operational implementation. This leads us to a system design methodology that consists of five phases (Sage 1981a):

(a) requirements specifications identification;
(b) preliminary conceptual design;

(c) detailed design, testing and implementation;
(d) evaluation; and
(e) operational deployment.

These are sequenced in an iterative manner as shown in Fig. 2. There are many descriptions of systems design methodology and associated frameworks (Sage 1977a,b, Nadler 1985), only one of these is described here.

The requirements specification phase of our system design methodology has as its goal the identification of client needs, activities and objectives to be achieved by implementation of the resulting design as a product, process or system. The effort in this phase should result in the identification and description of preliminary conceptual design considerations that are appropriate for the next phase. It is important to note that it is necessary to translate operational deployment needs into requirements specifications in order that these needs can be addressed by the system design efforts. Thus we see that information requirements specifications are affected by, and affect, each of the other design phases of the systemic framework for design.

As a result of the requirements specifications phase, there should exist a clear definition of design issues, hence facilitating a decision concerning whether or not to undertake preliminary conceptual design. If the result of the requirements specifications effort indicates that client needs can be satisfied in a functionally satisfactory manner, then documentation is typically prepared concerning specifications for the preliminary conceptual design phase. Initial specifications for the subsequent three phases of effort are typically also prepared and a concept design team is selected to implement the next phase of the design effort.

Preliminary conceptual design typically includes and results in specification of the content and associated architecture and general algorithms for the product, process or system that should result from this effort. The primary goal of this phase is to develop conceptualization of a prototype that is responsive to the requirements identified in the previous phase. Preliminary concept design according to the requirements specifications should be obtained. Rapid prototyping of the conceptual design is clearly desirable for many applications. The desired product of this phase of design activity is a set of detailed design and architectural specifications that should result in a useful product, process or system, and the result of the prototype design. There should exist a sufficiently high degree of user confidence that a useful product will result from detailed design, or the entire design effort should be repeated or possibly abandoned. Another product of this phase is a refined set of specifications for the evaluation and operational deployment phases of the design process.

A product, process or system is produced in the third phase of design. This is not the final design, but rather the result of implementation of the prototype design that resulted from the conceptual design effort of the last phase. User guides for the product should be produced, hence enabling realistic operational testing and evaluation.

Evaluation of the design and the resulting product, process or system is achieved in the fourth phase of the design process. Preliminary evaluation criteria are obtained as a part of requirements specifications and are subsequently modified during the following two phases of the design effort. The evaluation effort must be adapted to other phases of the design so that it becomes an integral and functional part of the overall design process. Generally, the critical issues for evaluation are adaptations of the elements present in the requirements specifications phase of the design process. A set of specific evaluation test requirements and tests are evolved from the objectives and needs determined in requirements specifications. These should be such that each objective measure and critical evaluation issue component can be measured from at least one evaluation test instrument.

If it is determined that the product, process or system cannot meet user needs, then the systemic design process reverts iteratively back to an earlier phase and effort continues. An important by-product of evaluation is the determination of ultimate performance limitations for an operationally attainable system and identification of those protocols and procedures for use of the result of the design effort that enable maximum user satisfaction. Often, operational evaluation is the only realistic way to establish meaningful information concerning functional effectiveness of the result of a design effort. Successful evaluation is dependent on explicit development of a plan for evaluation developed before initiation of the evaluation effort.

The last phase of a system design effort concerns final acceptance and operational deployment. This description of design methodology is heavily process-dependent. For our purposes, a process is the integration of a methodology with the behavioral concerns of

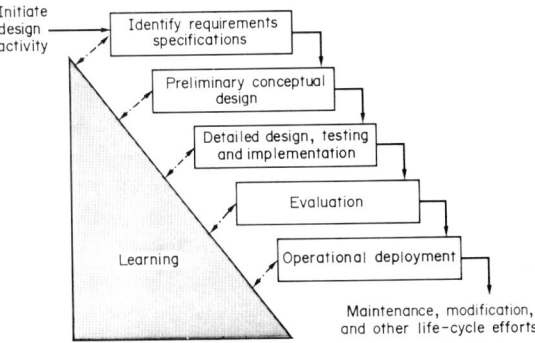

Figue 2
The systems design process

human judgement in a realistic operational environment. The description of systems design given in this section has emphasized the methodological concerns and, perhaps to a lesser extent, operational environment concerns. We now turn our attention to some of the human and behavioral concerns in design.

Regardless of the way in which the design process is characterized, all characterizations will necessarily involve a number of phases, such as the five just described, together with a number of steps within each phase. In a formal sense at least, there will be three principal steps (Sage 1977a,b, 1981a, 1982).

(a) *Formulation of the design problem.* In this step, the needs and objectives of a client group are identified and potentially acceptable design alternatives or options are identified or generated.

(b) *Analysis of the alternative designs.* At this stage, the impacts of the identified design options are evaluated.

(c) *Interpretation and selection.* In this step, the design options are compared by means of an evaluation of the impacts of the design alternatves; the needs and objectives of the client group are used as a basis for evaluation; and the most acceptable alternative is selected for implementation or further study in a subsequent phase of design.

Without question, this is a formal rational model of the way in which design is accomplished. Even within this formal framework, there is the need for much iteration from one step back to an earlier step when it is discovered that improvements in the results of an earlier step are needed in order to obtain a quality result at a later step of the design effort. Also, this description does not emphasize the key role of information and information requirements determination, which is concentrated in the formulation step but which exists throughout all steps of the design process (Sage et al. 1983). The article *Information Requirements Determination* provides an additional discussion on these points.

It is more important to emphasize here that this morphological framework, in terms of phases of the design process and steps within these phases, does not emphasize the different types of information and support that are needed at each step in the various phases. During the issue formulation step, the support that is needed tends to be of an affective, perceptive or gestalt nature. Intuition-based experiential wisdom plays a most important role in this. During the analysis step, there is typically a need for quantitative and algorithmic support, perhaps through the use of the formal models of operations research and management science. In the interpretation step, the necessary effort shifts to a blend of the perceptive and the analytical.

Even when these realities are associated with the morphological framework, it still represents an incomplete view of the way people do, could or should accomplish design, planning or other problem-solving activities. The most that can be argued is that this framework is correct in an "as if" manner. There are a variety of ways that might be used to describe how people seek information with which to describe their perceptions of the world around them, and then use this information in an effort to accomplish an identified task. The article *Systems Knowledge: Philosophical Perspectives* expands considerably on this topic.

The central result of the majority of these studies is that there is no unique judgement and decision style that can be adopted independently of the contingency task structural variables of issue, environment and problem-solver familiarity with the task and environment. Rather, the style of decision behavior which is adopted is a function of these three ingredients. This research appears to have strong descriptive, normative and prescriptive implications for design and computerized support systems that aid system designers.

4. Information Requirements for Design

Judgements concerning design, at least prudent judgements, are seldom made without information. Information is often defined as data which is of value for decision making. Activities associated with acquisition, representation, storage, transmission and use of pertinent data are generally associated with information processing. The task of information requirements determination is associated with each of these. Initially, it might appear that this would be associated only with information acquisition. However, since information acquisition is necessarily related to other activities associated with information processing, so also is information requirements determination.

There are many ways in which we can characterize information. Among attributes which we might use are: accuracy, precision, completeness, sufficiency, understandability, relevancy, reliability, redundancy, verifiability, consistency, freedom from bias, frequency of use, age, timeliness and uncertainty. It is also possible to define information at several levels. At the technical level, information and associated measures are concerned with transmission quality over a channel. At the semantic level, concern is with the meaning and efficiency of messages. At the pragmatic level, information is valued in terms of effectiveness in accomplishing an intended purpose. From the viewpoint of design, we are clearly concerned more with pragmatic and semantic issues than with technical-level issues. At the pragmatic and semantic levels, our concerns with information for design purposes are five-fold:

(a) information should be presented in very clear and familiar ways, hence facilitating rapid comprehension;

(b) information should improve the precision of understanding of the task situation;

(c) information that contains an advice or a decision recommendation component should contain an explication facility that enables the user to determine how and why results and advice are obtained;

(d) information needs should be based on identification of the information requirements for the particular situation; and

(e) information presentations and all other associated management control aspects of the design process should be such that the designer or decision maker, rather than a computerized support system, guides the process of judgement and choice.

Clearly, this relates directly to the concept of value of information and indicates that this concept is very dependent on the contingency task structure. The mix of task at hand, the environment in which the task is embedded and the problem solver's familiarity with these interact to determine both the perceptions and the intentions of the problem solver.

The concept of economic efficiency (Sage 1977a,b) is important and of value for design purposes. Effectiveness measures are of even greater importance, however. Yovitz *et al.* (1981) have expanded on the classical concept of value of information so that it includes effectiveness and efficiency measures. The value of a new item of information is dependent on the difference in decision-maker effectiveness before and after the information is received. There have been a number of other approaches to value-of-information concepts and to information requirements analysis; many of these are described by Sage *et al.* (1983).

There are at least three human limitations associated with information processing that may significantly affect the requirements for information that are likely to be identified and used in a design situation: limited information-processing capability, potential bias effects in the selection and use of information, and limited knowledge of appropriate problem-solving behavior that results in an incorrect assessment of the contingency task structure associated with a given issue.

The methodology of Davis (1982) is especially appropriate in that it is sufficiently comprehensive to address each of these concerns. Davis suggests four strategies for the determination of information requirements. The first of these is simply to ask people for their requirements. The appropriateness and completeness of the information needs determined by this approach will depend upon the extent to which the people questioned can define and structure their problem space, and can compensate for their biases. This approach can be further subdivided into the use of interacting and nominal group approaches to inquiry.

The second strategy is to elicit information requirements from existing systems that are similar in nature and purpose to the issue or design task under consideration. Properly executed anchoring and adjustment strategies or analogous-reasoning strategies are potentially useful here since a starting point can be determined from the existing system, and extrapolation subsequently can be performed. Examining existing plans or reports represents one approach to identifying information requirements from an existing or conceptualized system, or a previous design. The third approach consists of synthesizing information requirements from characteristics of the utilizing system or individuals. This permits the definition of an analytical structure for the problem space and will often allow use of formal analytical procedures, such as input-output analysis or decision analysis. The fourth strategy consists of determining information requirements through experimentation on an actual system, perhaps one which is specifically constructed for this purpose. Generally the former approaches are simpler and more economic than the latter approaches. The approaches can certainly be combined, and it would be desirable to be able to determine which of them is more appropriate in a given situation.

Information obtained from any, or a combination, of these approaches must be capable of representation in a support system to aid the designer. One purpose of a design support system should be to determine possibilities of insufficient and/or inappropriate information; that is, information that is sufficiently imperfect such as to make the likelihood of an acceptable design low. The support system should then be able to determine the nature of the missing or otherwise imperfect information, and suggest steps to the user to remedy this deficiency. This suggests that a design support system should be capable of detection, diagnosis and correction of faults in a set of information obtained for an issue. The type of information that the user of a particular support system will wish to, or should, use is highly dependent on the contingency task structure. Another information-associated requirement for a support system is that of identifying the information, and judgement and choice, perspectives that a designer will and should wish to use, and to be capable of coping with requirements for design support from this multiple-perspective viewpoint. Coping successfully with these needs should result in truly innovative and useful support systems for design processes.

5. The Environment for Systems Design and Characteristics of Successful Designs

There are many contemporary issues which may result in the need for system design; these issues are invariably complex. They typically involve a number of competing concerns, contain much uncertainty and require expertise from a number of different disciplines for resolution. One of the major challenges in system design is to develop processes that are appropriate for a variety of process users, some of whom may approach the design issue from a skill-based perspective, some from a rule-based perspective and some from a formal knowledge-based perspective.

A systems design procedure must be specifically related to the operational environment for which the final system is intended. Control-group testing and evaluation may serve many useful purposes with respect to determination of many aspects of algorithmic and behavioral efficacy of a system. Ultimate effectiveness involves user acceptability of the resulting system and evaluation of this process effectiveness will often involve testing and evaluation in the environment itself, or at least a closely simulated model of the environment in which the system would be potentially deployed.

The potential benefits of systems engineering approaches to design can be interpreted as attributes or criteria for evaluation of the design approach itself. Achievement of many of these attributes may often not be experimentally measured except by inference, anecdotal, or testimonial and case-study evidence taken in the operational environment for which the system is designed. Explicit evaluation of attribute achievement is a very important part of the overall systemic design process.

A number of characteristics of effective systems efforts are identifiable. These form the basis for determining the attributes of systems and systemic design procedures. Some of these attributes will be more important for a given environment than others. Effective design must typically include an operational evaluation component which will consider the strong interaction between the system and the situational issues that led to the system design requirement. This operational evaluation is needed to determine whether a system or a systemic process for incorporation into a physical system consisting of humans and machines fulfills the following criteria. It should:

(a) be logically sound;

(b) be matched to the extant operational and organizational situation and environment;

(c) support a variety of cognitive skills, styles and knowledge of those who must use the system;

(d) assist users of the system to develop and use their own cognitive skills, styles and knowledge;

(e) be sufficiently flexible to allow use and adaptation by users with differing experiential knowledge;

(f) encourage more effective solution of unstructured and unfamiliar issues allowing the application of job-specific experiences in a way which is compatible with various acceptability constraints; and

(g) promote effective long-term management.

A usable methodology that interrelates plans and/or designs, the values of those who will use the system, the design situation model and inferences about states of nature or the environment that surrounds the design situation are needed as a framework for systems design. To develop robust scenarios of planning and design situations in various operational environments, and specific instruments for evaluation, we first identify a mathematical and situational taxonomy of:

(a) algorithmic constructs used in systemic design,

(b) performance objectives for quality planning and design, and

(c) operational environments for planning and design

Planning, design and decision support, as ultimate goals of many systemic processes, are basically efforts which involve obtaining, interpreting, forecasting the consequences of, evaluating and prioritizing and thereby organizing actions or action recommendations based upon information, objectives and existing situations or needs. A system or systemic process that is used to aid the process of planning, design or decision making should assist in or support the evaluation of alternatives relative to some criteria. It is necessary that planning, design and decision-relevant information be condensed and described in ways which lead to effective analysis and problem structuring. Of equal importance is the need to be aware of the role of the affective in planning design and choice-making tasks so as to support different cognitive styles and needs, which vary from knowledge-based to rule-based to skill-based behavior.

Not all of the performance objectives for quality systems engineering will be, or need to be, fully attained in all design instances, but it is generally true that the quality of a system, or of a system design process, necessarily improves as an increasing number of these objectives are attained. Measures of quality of the resulting system, and therefore systemic process design quality, may be obtained by assessing the degree of achievement of these performance criteria by the resulting system, generally in an operational environment.

A taxonomy based on operational environments is necessary to describe particular situation models through which planning, design and decision support are achieved. We are able to describe a large number of situations using elements or features of the three-component taxonomy described earlier. With these, we are able to evolve test instruments to establish quantitative and qualitative evaluations of a system within an operational environment. The structural and functional properties of a system, or a systemic process, must be described so that a purposeful evaluation can be accomplished. This purposeful evaluation effort also allows iteration and feedback to ultimately improve the overall systems design process. The evaluation methodology to be described is useful, therefore, as a part or phase of the design process. Also it is useful, in and of itself, to evaluate and prioritize a set of systemic aids for planning, design and decision support. It is also useful for evaluation of resulting system designs and operational systems providing a methodological framework for both the design and evaluation of physical systems and systems that assist in the planning and design of systems.

As we have noted, there are five important phases in the design of systems and systemic process aids. These phases serve as a guide, not only for the sound design and development of systems and systemic aids for planning, design and decision support processes, but also for their evaluation and ultimate operational deployment. Although the five phases were described as if they are to be sequenced in a chronological fashion, sound design practice will generally necessitate iteration and feedback from a given phase to earlier phases.

5.1 Requirements Specifications

Among the many objectives of the requirements specifications phase of systems engineering are the following:

(a) to define the problem or range of problems to be solved, or issue to be resolved or ameliorated, including identification of needs, constraints, alterables and stakeholder groups associated with operational deployment of the system or the systemic process;

(b) to determine objectives for the operational system or the operational aids for planning, design and decision support;

(c) to obtain commitment for prototype design of a system or systemic process aid, from user group and management;

(d) to search the literature and seek other expert opinions concerning the approach that is most appropriate for the particular situation extant;

(e) to determine the estimated frequency and extent of need for the system or the systemic process;

(f) to determine the possible need to modify the system or the systemic process to meet changed requirements;

(g) to determine the degree and type of accuracy expected from the system or systemic process;

(h) to estimate expected effectiveness improvement or benefits due to the use of the system or systemic process;

(i) to estimate the expected costs of using the system or systemic process, including design and development costs, operational costs and maintenance costs;

(j) to determine typical planning horizons and periods over which the system or systemic process must be responsive;

(k) to determine the extent of tolerable operational environment alteration due to use of the system or systemic process;

(l) to determine what particular planning, design or decision process appears to be most appropriate;

(m) to determine the most appropriate roles for the system or systemic process to perform within the context of the planning, design or decision situation and operational environment under consideration;

(n) to estimate potential leadership requirements for use of the final system itself;

(o) to estimate user-group training requirements;

(p) to estimate the qualifications required of the design team;

(q) to determine preliminary operational evaluation plans and criteria;

(r) to determine political acceptability and institutional constraints affecting use of an aided support process and those of the system itself;

(s) to document analytical and behavioral specifications to be satisfied by the support process and the system itself;

(t) to determine the extent to which the user group can require changes during and after system development;

(u) to determine potential requirements for contractor availability after completion of development and operational tests for additional needs determined by the user group, perhaps as a result of the evaluation effort; and

(v) to develop requirements specifications for prototype design of a support process and the operational system itself.

As a result of this phase, there should exist a clear definition of typical planning, design and decision issues or problems requiring support and other requirements specifications, so that it is possible to make a decision concerning whether to undertake preliminary conceptual design. If the result of this phase indicates that the user group or client needs can potentially be satisfied in a cost-effective manner, then documentation should be prepared concerning detailed specifications for the next preliminary conceptual design phase. Initial specifications for the last three phases of effort are also prepared. A design team is then selected to implement the next phase of the system life cycle. This discussion emphasizes the inherently coupled nature of these phases of the system life cycle and illustrates why it is not reasonable to consider the phases as uncoupled.

5.2 Preliminary Conceptual Design

The preliminary conceptual design phase includes specification of the mathematical and behavioral content and associated algorithms for the system or process that should ultimately result from the effort, as well as the possible need for computer support to implement these. The primary goal of this phase is to develop conceptualization of a prototype system or process in response to the requirements specifications developed in the previous phase. Preliminary design according to the requirements specifications should be achieved. Some objectives for preliminary conceptual design are:

(a) to search the literature and seek expert opinion concerning the particular approach to design and implementation which is likely to be most responsive to requirements specifications;

(b) to determine the specific analytic algorithms to be implemented by the system or process;

(c) to determine the specific behavioral situation and operational environment in which the system or process is to operate;

(d) to determine the specific leadership requirements for use of the system in the operational environment;

(e) to determine specific hardware and software implementation requirements, including type of computer programming language and input devices;

(f) to determine specific information input requirements for the system or process;

(g) to determine the specific type of output, and interpretation of the output, to be obtained from the system or process that will result from the design procedure;

(h) to reevaluate objectives obtained in the previous phase, to provide documentation of minor changes, and to conduct an extensive reexamination of the effort if major changes are detected which could result in major modification and iteration through requirements specification or even termination of effort; and

(i) to develop a preliminary conceptual design of a prototype aid which is responsive to the requirements specification.

The expected product of this phase is a set of detailed design and testing specifications which, if followed, should result in a usable prototype system or process. User-group confidence that an ultimately useful product will result from detailed design should be above some threshold, or the entire design effort should be repeated. Another product of this phase is a refined set of specifications for the evaluation and operational deployment phases.

If the result of this phase is successful, the detailed design, testing and implementation phase is initiated. This phase is based on the products of the preliminary conceptual design phase and should result in a common understanding among all parties interested in the planning and decision support design effort concerning:

(a) who the user group of responsive stakeholders is;

(b) the structure of the operational environment in which plans, designs and decisions are made;

(c) what constitutes a plan, design or decision;

(d) how plans, designs and decisions are made without the process or system and how they will be made with it;

(e) what implementation, political acceptability and institutional constraints affect the use of the system or process; and

(f) what specific analysis algorithms will be used in the system or process, and how these algorithms will be interconnected to form the methodological construction of the system or process.

5.3 Detailed Design, Test and Implementation

In the third phase of design, a system or process which is presumably useful in the operational environment is produced. Among the objectives to be attained in this phase are:

(a) to obtain and design appropriate physical facilities (e.g. physical hardware, computer hardware, output device, room);

(b) to prepare computer software;

(c) to document computer software;

(d) to prepare a user's guide to the system and the process in which the system is embedded;

(e) to conduct control group or operational (simulated operational) tests of the system and make minor changes in the aid as a result of the tests;

(f) to complete detailed design and associated testing of a prototype system based on the results of the previous phase; and

(g) to implement the prototype system in the operational environment.

The products of this phase are detailed guides to use of the system as well as, of course, the prototype system itself. It is very important that the user's guide and the leader's guide address, at levels appropriate for the parties interested in the effort, the way in which the performance objectives for quality system design are satisfied. The description of system usage and leadership topics should be addressed in terms of the analytic and behavioral constructs of the system and the resulting process, as well as in terms of operational environment situation concerns. These concerns include:

(a) frequency of occurrence of need for the system;
(b) time available from recognition of need for a plan, design or decision to identification of an appropriate plan, design or decision;
(c) time available from determination of an appropriate plan, design or decision to implementation of the plan, design or decision;
(d) value of time;
(e) possible interactions with the plans, designs or decisions of others;
(f) information-base characteristics;
(g) organizational structure; and
(h) management support for the resulting system or process.

5.4 Evaluation

Evaluation of a design, or the system that results from a design, is accomplished in accordance with evaluation criteria that are intially determined in the requirements specification phase and potentially modified in subsequent phases. This evaluation should always be assisted to the greatest extent possible by all parties concerned with the systems design effort and the resulting system or process. The evaluation effort must be adapted to other phases of the design effort so that it becomes an integral functional part of the overall design process. It is, of course, necessary for there to be some evaluation of the efficacy of the requirements specifications themselves in terms of appropriate capturing of user requirements. As noted, evaluation may well be an effort distinct from design that is used to determine usefulness, or appropriateness for specified purposes, of one or more previously designed systems. Among the objectives of system evaluation are the following:

(a) to identify a methodology for evaluation;
(b) to identify criteria on which the success of the system or process may be judged;
(c) to determine the effectiveness of the system in terms of success criteria;
(d) to determine an appropriate balance between the operational environment evaluation and the control-group evaluation;
(e) to determine performance objective achievement of the system;
(f) to determine behavioral or human-factor effectiveness of the system;
(g) to determine the most useful strategy for employment of the existing system;
(h) to determine user-group acceptance of the system;
(i) to suggest refinements in existing systems for greater effectiveness of the process into which the new system has been embedded; and
(j) to evaluate the effectiveness of the resulting integrated system or process.

These objectives are obtained from a critical evaluation issue specification or evaluation need specification. This is the first, or issue formulation, step of the evaluation phase of the system life cycle. Generally, the critical issues for evaluation are minor adaptations of the elements which are present in the requirements specifications step of the design process. A set of specific evaluation test requirements and tests are evolved from these objectives and needs. These must be such that each objective measure and critical evaluation issue component can be determined from at least one evaluation test instrument.

If it is determined that the system and the resulting process support cannot meet user needs, the systems design process iterates to an earlier phase and development continues. An important by-product of evaluation is the determination of ultimate performance limitations and the establishment of a protocol and procedure for use of the system which results in maximum user-group satisfaction. A report is written concerning results of the evaluation process, especially those factors relating to user-group satisfaction with the designed system. The evaluation process should result in suggestions for improvement in design and in better methodologies for future evaluations.

Operational evaluation of a system or process that involves human interaction appears to be the only realistic way to extract truly meaningful information concerning process effectiveness of a given system design. This must necessarily include leadership and training requirements to use the system. There are necessary trade-offs associated with leadership and training for use of a system and these are addressed in operational evaluation.

Successful evaluation, especially operational evaluation, strongly depends on explicit development of a plan for evaluation developed before, and perhaps modified and improved during the course of, an actual evaluation. This section is concerned with the development of a methodological framework for system evaluation, especially for operational evaluation of systemic processes for planning, design and decision support.

Objectives for evaluation of a system include:

(a) identifying a methodology for operational evaluation;

(b) establishing criteria on which the success of the system may be judged;

(c) determining the effectiveness of the support in terms of these criteria; and

(d) determining the most useful strategy for employment of an existing system and potential improvements such that effectiveness of the newly implemented system and the overall process might be improved.

Evaluation of a system should be based on the performance objectives for the system identified as part of the requirements specification effort. These objectives form pertinent criteria for an operational evaluation of a system. They concern the algorithmic effectiveness or performance objective achievement of the system, the behavioral or human factor effectiveness of the system in the operational environment and system efficacy.

Many effectiveness questions are likely to arise as an evaluation of a system or system design proceeds. One of the important concerns in evaluation is that of those parts of the efficacy evaluation that deal with various "abilities" of a system. These include productibility, reliability, maintainability, and marketability. Questions specific to a given evaluation are determined after study of the particular situation and the system being evauated. It is, however, important to have an initial set of questions to guide the evaluation investigation and a purpose of this article is to provide a framework for accomplishing this.

5.5 Operational Deployment

The last phase of design is concerned with operational deployment and final implementation. This must be accomplished in such a way that all user groups obtain adequate instructions in the use of the system and complete operating and maintenance documentation and instructions. Specific objectives for the operational deployment phase of a system design effort are:

(a) to enhance operational deployment;

(b) to accomplish final design of the system;

(c) to provide for continuous monitoring of postimplementation effectiveness of the system and the process in which is imbedded;

(d) to provide for retrodesign of the system as indicated by effectiveness monitoring;

(e) to provide proper training and leadership for successful continued operational use of the system;

(f) to identify barriers to successful implementation of the final design product and strategies that will overcome these; and

(g) to provide for "maintenance" of the system.

6. *The Value of System Design*

The actual use of a system as contrasted with potential usefulness, is directly dependent on the value which the user group of stakeholders associates with use of the system and the resulting process in an operational environment. This depends, in part, on how well the system satisfies performance objectives, and on how well it is able to cope with one or more of the pathologies or pitfalls of planning, design and/or decision making under potentially stressful operational environment conditions.

Quality planning, design and decision support are very dependent on the ability to obtain relatively complete identification of pertinent factors which influence plans, designs and decisions. The careful comprehensive formulation of issues and associated requirements for issue resolution will lead to identification of pertinent critical factors for system design. These factors are ideally illuminated in a relatively easy-to-understand fashion which facilitates the interpretation necessary to evaluate and subsequently select plans, designs and decisions for implementation. However, success in this depends strongly on adroitness in use of the system. It is generally not fully meaningful to talk only of an algorithm or even a complete system, which is typically a piece of hardware and software but which may well be a carefully written set of protocols and procedures, as useful by itself. It is meaningful to talk of a particular systemic process as being useful. This process involves the interaction of a methodology with systems management at the cognitive process or human-judgement level. A systemic process depends upon the system, the operational environment and leadership associated with use of the system. A process involves design integration of a methodology with the behavioral concerns of human cognitive judgement in an operational environment. For all of these reasons, system design and evaluation must necessarily be concerned both with the algorithmic and the behavioral.

Bibliography

Davis G B 1982 Strategies for information requirements determination. *IBM Syst. J.* **21**(1), 4–30

Fischhoff B, Beyth-Marom R 1983 Hypothesis evaluation from a Bayesian perspective. *Psychol. Rev.* **90**(3), 239–60

Green T B, Lee S M, Newsom W B 1978 *The Decision Science Process*. Petrocelli, New York

Janis I L, Mann L 1977 *Decision Making: A Psychological Analysis of Conflict, Choice, and Commitment*. Free Press, New York

Linstone H A 1984 *Multiple Perspectives for Decision Making: Bridging the Gap Between Analysis and Action*. North-Holland, Amsterdam

Malhotra A, Thomas J C, Carroll J M, Miller L A 1980 Cognitive processes in design. *Int. J. Man-Mach. Stud.* **12**, 119–40

Nadler G 1985 Systems methodology and design. *IEEE Trans Syst., Man Cybern.* **15**(6), 685–97

Naumann J D, Davis G B, McKeen J D 1980 Determining information requirements: A contingency method for selection of a requirements assurance strategy. *J. Syst. Software* **1**, 273–81

Newell A, Simon H A 1972 *Human Problem Solving*. Prentice–Hall, Englewood Cliffs, New Jersey

Nystrom P C, Starbuck W H 1981 *Handbook of Organizational Design*, Vols. 1, 2, Oxford University Press, Oxford

Rasmussen J 1983 Skills, rules, knowledge; signals, signs, and symbols; and other distinctions in human performance models. *IEEE Trans. Syst., Man Cybern.* **13**(3)

Rasmussen J 1985 The role of hierarchical knowledge representation in decisionmaking and system management. *IEEE Trans. Syst., Man Cybern.* **15**(2), 234–43

Rasmussen J 1986 *On Information Processing and Human–Machine Interaction: An Approach to Cognitive Engineering*. North-Holland, Amsterdam

Rouse W B, Boff K R (eds.) 1987 *The Psychology of System Design*. North-Holland, New York

Sage A P 1977a *Methodology for Large Scale Systems*. McGraw–Hill, New York

Sage A P (ed.) 1977b *Systems Engineering: Methodology and Applications*. IEEE Press, New York

Sage A P 1981a A methodological framework for systemic design and evaluation of computer aids for planning and decision support. *Comput. Electr. Eng.* **8**(2), 87–102

Sage A P 1981b Behavioral and organizational concerns in the design of information systems and processes for planning and decision support. *IEEE Trans. Syst., Man Cybern.* **11**(9), 640–78

Sage A P 1981c Systems engineering: Fundamental limits and future prospects. *IEEE Proc.* **69**(2), 158–66

Sage A P 1982 Methodological considerations in the design of large scale systems engineering processes. In: Haimes Y Y (ed.) *Large Scale Systems*. North-Holland, Amsterdam

Sage A P (ed.) 1987 *System Design for Human Interaction*. IEEE Press, New York

Sage A P, Galing B, Lagomasino A 1983 Methodologies for the determination of information requirements for decision support systems. *Large Scale Syst.* **5**(2), 131–67

Simon H A 1983 Search and reasoning in problem solving. *Artif. Intell.* **21**, 7–29

Stevens R T 1979 *Operational Test and Evaluation*. Wiley, New York

Tien J M 1979 Towards a systematic approach to program evaluation design. *IEEE Trans. Syst., Man Cybern.* **9**(9), 494–515

Wallace R H, Stockenberg J E, Charette R N 1987 *A Unified Methodology for Developing Systems*. McGraw–Hill, New York

Whitten J L, Bentley L D, Ho T I M 1986 *Systems Analysis and Design Methods*. Times-Mirror/Mosby, St. Louis, Missouri

Yovitz M C, Foulk C R, Rose L L 1981 Information flow and analysis: Theory, simulation, and experiments, Parts 1–3. *J. Am. Soc. Inf. Sci.* **32**, 181–248

A. P. Sage
[George Mason University, Fairfax, Virginia, USA]

Distributed Decision Making: Information Systems

Much recent research on human judgement and choice suggests the need for the incorporation of behavioral perspectives in all aspects of system design. In this article a framework for information systems design for distributed decision making is discussed that consists of three principal integrated and interrelated components:

(a) Knowledge acquisition and representation, so as to enable effective and efficient understanding of the decision situation, and to model how people actually use information when solving a problem or making a decision;

(b) information presentation of these representations in a distributed multiagent situation so as to enable evaluation of alternatives from perspectives that are commensurate with experiential familiarity with the task at hand; and

(c) organizational structure or architecture, which results in a network of communication channels, in which distributed multiagent decision making takes place.

A purpose for this framework is to guide the design of distributed information systems, including resource distribution across nodes in the communication network, and associated information presentation and decision support aids, so that it becomes possible to:

(a) indicate the kinds of impeding interactions between people in distributed decision tasks that result in enhancing support for, or interference with or lack of support to, these distributed decision tasks;

(b) understand how one mode of information presentation, for both situation understanding and decision-making purposes, may be better than another mode in encouraging requests for other information that aids a better understanding of the decision situation;

(c) predict the characteristics of an information system that provides support for distributed multiagent decision making, so as to make information easy to understand, to relate to other relevant information presentations, and to encourage effective decision making;

(d) evaluate distributed information systems with respect to the extent to which they encourage "effective" decision making; and thereby

(e) to develop a methodology for the design of distributed information support systems that aid information processing in systems and organizations.

Among the many concerns that are important for a design theory for information systems engineering for distributed decision making, four are particularly important here:

(a) time sequencing of elements, such as activities and events;

(b) spatial separation between elements in the decision situation, such as cooperating decision makers;

(c) containment of elements within other elements of the decision situation, such as the incremental decisions of a person who must integrate, contain and coordinate the incremental decisions according to some strategic plan; and

(d) the inherent uncertainty and imprecision, and other forms of imperfection, that are associated with information inputs and knowledge of the consequences of actions that might be undertaken.

These concerns, especially (d), must be given particular attention in developing a design methodology for distributed information systems engineering. In such a development, careful consideration should be given to the needs imposed by the information and knowledge imperfections that arise in distributed communication environments. These imperfections, such as uncertainty and imprecision, are due to such realities as missing or erroneous data, incomplete rules for information analysis and interpretation, and erroneous guidelines for information analysis and interpretation. The effects of each of these sources of information imperfection can be potentially corrected by redundancy in the data and information, and redundancy in the guidelines or protocols used for information analysis and interpretation. Associated with this redundancy, however, is complexity. This complexity is due to both the potential number of communication nodes and the need for attention to contingencies associated with potential failures in part of the system. Redundancy, if properly exploited, enables improvements in information reliability and usefulness, and associated improvements in system survivability and response time.

1. Individual Information-Processing Realities

There are a number of human information-processing capabilities and limitations that interact with organizational arrangements and task requirements to strongly influence resource allocations in distributed multiagent environments. Among individual information-processing characteristics are those discussed below.

(*a*) *Humans have extensive wholistic information-processing abilities (intuitive affect, reasoning by analogy, etc.)* The judgements that follow from wholistic skill-based reasoning may well be very sound, but will often be very difficult to explain. Consequently there exists the need for decision and knowledge support efforts that will enable the construction of knowledge bases and judgement guidelines that follow from skill-based experiential reasoning. This is particularly needed in group situations in which all participants will not have the same level of expertise, but need to understand the rationale behind expert wholistic judgement. Policy capture and the social judgement theory due to Hammond *et al.* (1975) provide a regression-analysis-based approach to these ends. Recent research (Sage and White 1984) has developed an approach which, in part, uses linear programming to determine ranges of parameters over which a given judgement is invariant. This approach is considerably less data-intensive than the regression-analysis-based approaches. It has the potential to yield information that is directly suitable for incorporation into distributed information management structures.

Information sharing is one of the many features of a distributed multiagent system. An inherent advantage to knowledge support approaches which allow for the "blending" of formal reasoning, rule-based knowledge and skill-based expert knowledge is that explanations for judgements are potentially available from each knowledge perspective (Linstone 1984, Sage and Lagomasino 1987). This capability considerably enhances the potential contribution of all participants using the distributed multiagent information system for the issue under consideration, by enabling them to use the type of information and associated information presentation format most appropriate to the perspectives from which they approach the task at hand. To bring these potential advantages to fruition will require considerable additional research in dialog management and associated information presentation principles in distributed multiagent decision support situations.

(*b*) *Humans use potentially definable and identifiable judgemental guidelines, perspectives and rules that are more or less appropriate, depending on their applicability to the task at hand.* The judgemental perspectives that are actually used in a given situation will depend strongly on the format that is used to present various situation-assessment and decision-relevant information, and the experiential familiarity of an individual with respect to the task and the environment into which the task is "embedded." That it is possible to identify judgemental perspectives is more a desideratum than a present-day reality. It is very necessary that this identification can be accomplished for a variety of knowledge acquisition, representation and use tasks. It is well known that a diagram is worth many words (Larkin and Simon 1987), but we are only beginning to develop a theory of information presentation from which we will be able to design information presentation aids for purposes such as situation assessment. Although there is much more to learn, we do the following.

(i) When deemed appropriate, especially for unfamiliar and semistructured situations, when vigilant information processing is needed, humans will attempt to use approaches that stem from the formal-reasoning-based constructs of Janis and Mann (1977).

(ii) The particular blend of knowledge (skill based, rule based or formal-reasoning based in the typology of Rasmussen (1983, 1985, 1986)), used to reach judgements is a function of the contingency task structure. This structure consists of three elements: the internal and external environment in which the task need is embedded; the decision task requirements, including the stress associated with the decision and the "cost" to the decision maker of exercising various judgement strategies; and decision-maker experiential familiarity with the environment and the decision task requirements.

Both formal reasoning and rule-based reasoning approaches contribute to the accumulation of skill-based experiential knowledge through a learning process. The contingency task structure diagnosis leads to determination of the appropriate knowledge perspective. There is learning such that the contingency task structure, for a given individual, changes with experience. Thus, we envision a structure for knowledge acquisition, representation and use such as that shown in Fig. 1. In this figure we see a symbiotic relationship among three fundamental knowledge perspectives. A metalevel reasoning process results in a decision concerning the selection of a suitable decision-making strategy (Simon 1978). On the basis of this metalevel decision, a balance of skill-based, rule-based and formal-knowledge-based reasoning is used to determine a decision option or problem solution. This will often result in some sort of physical controlling action. Learning occurs, as both a direct and as a feedback process, through the observation of what results.

The identification of only three learning perspectives is simplistic. Many more can be identified, and a number of other taxonomies of problem-solving strategies can and have been developed. In an especially discerning analysis, Klein and Calderwood (1986) have identified no less than 38 problem-solving strategies. These 38 strategies have been aggregated to form eight upper-level perspectives. In turn these

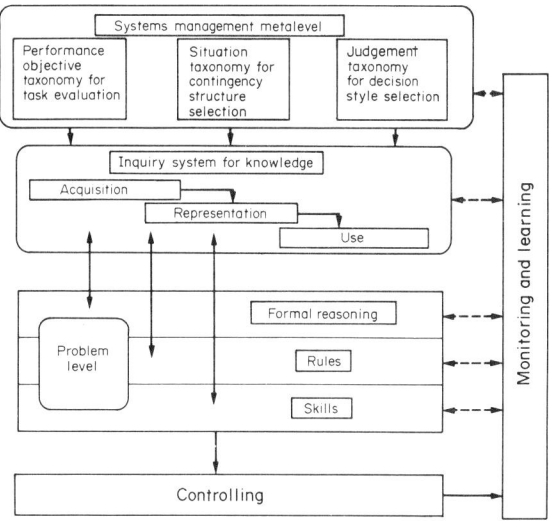

Figure 1
Reasoning perspectives and learning in decision making

could, with some trepidation, be aggregated into the trilogy identified here. A potential problem in doing this is that at no level are the identified knowledge perspectives mutually exclusive or collectively exhaustive. Also, in practice humans use a blend of these in realistic approaches to problem solving and decision making. The article *Recognitional Decision Making: Information Requirements* provides an additional discussion of these issues.

It is certainly now recognized that the mere insertion of a computerized aid for problem solving or decision making will in no way guarantee an increase in either the effectiveness, efficiency or explicability of the resulting problem-solving or decision-making task. Just the opposite may well occur. The complexity of tasks may increase due to technology infusion such that there is a reduction in the quality of the resulting information processing and judgements. Clearly, then, the amount and extent of technology infusion affects all the dimensions of the contingency task structure.

The complexity of a situation and the task requirements, together with the experiential familiarity of an individual with these, will influence how an issue under consideration is decomposed into aspects, elements or components believed to be tractable by that individual. High complexity will also encourage that this be done in such a way as to minimize the interaction among the elements, so that the human decision maker is able to cope with the resulting disaggregated issue. At least in a formal sense, this complexity will encourage modularization, the hierarchical structuring of issues and distributed processing of the subcomponents of these issues.

(c) *As the amount of information imperfection increases, there will exist a much greater need for cooperative interaction among the various human, technological and organizational elements that the task comprises.* This appears necessary because of the difficulty, especially when the available information about system behavior is of poor quality, of appropriately disaggregating task requirements. This need is particularly acute when expressed for the multiagent case (discussed in Sect. 2), since there will exist a large shared distributed data, information or knowledge base with sophisticated devices to obtain the sensory inputs that enable contributions from a number of individuals who each participate in various aspects of a problem-solving task.

Klein and Calderwood (1986) have made the observation that decision-making issues, in which the fundamental objective is to select a best course of action, are often sublimated into problem-solving issues. In these, the primary goals are situation understanding and immediate selection of a prescribed course of action once a situation is understood. Information imperfections are a primary cause of this lack of understanding and the resulting sublimation. They describe three types of ambiguities which determine whether a given issue is regarded as a decision-making issue or a problem-solving issue: problem situation ambiguities, appropriate goal ambiguities and ambiguities in relation to alternative options that will achieve goals. Thus, there exists a need for techniques to enable individuals and groups to deal with potentially competing and conflicting hypotheses so that they can resolve discordances due to uncertain, imprecise or otherwise imperfect information and knowledge. This suggests a relationship between the quality of information available in a given situation and the degree of expertise that a specific person will have about the situation. This does not in any way suggest that more information will lead to reduced information equivocality and, hence, better judgement. Just the opposite may well occur! It does suggest the major role of information and the value-of-information constructs as major determinants of situation understanding as well as of decision-making and problem-solving behavior.

This last observation is related to another one that pertains to the allocation of human resources to judgement and decision tasks.

(d) *The majority of studies of human decision making, especially in organizational settings, shows that people rarely concentrate on one problem at one time but generally consider, in a simultaneous, often nonsystematic and parallel manner, a diversity of problem-solving situations (Mintzberg 1973).* This leads to the following observation.

(e) *Human performance may suffer when the task requirements suggest the performance of several subtasks, often in diverse stages of completion, in parallel.* As has been noted, humans are limited in their cognitive ability to cope with many pieces of stimulus information. The effect of this is often selective perception in which only a portion, often that portion confirming a decision that the decision maker would like to make, of available information is used in the process of judgement and choice.

(f) *Humans are limited in their unaided ability to process aleatory, or statistical, information.* This is shown by studies such as those reprinted in Kahneman et al. (1982). For example, base rates or prior statistics will not be accorded the weight that they should be allocated as compared to individuating information. A large number of cognitive information-processing biases that degrade the quality of the resulting judgements have been identified and many of these are discussed in the article *Cognitive Management and Models of Judgement and Choice Processes*.

(g) *Humans often reason quite well based on epistemic and evidential information. Confirmation and denial rules, while potentially very flawed from the strict viewpoint of mathematical logic, often yield very acceptable judgements and often represent the only types of information available for judgement.* This has been noted by Cohen (1981), Baron (1985) and Kyburg (1983). At least two considerations suggest very real limits to the behavioral decision theory, or judgement and choice, viewpoint of humans as intellectual cripples who are very prone to the use of seriously flawed information-processing heuristics and the resulting cognitive biases. The first of these is that, on an individual basis, the continuous adaptive nature of operational judgemental processes acts in such a way as to overcome the discrete biases discovered in the laboratory (Hogarth 1981). The second is that there is the potential for group-based judgements to be of a higher quality than individual judgements.

Especially interesting concerns arise when these notions are considered in a distributed multiagent environment. The concepts of information sharing and shared concept models then become especially important. There are many ingredients in this environment including the communication nodes and links that exist; the perceptions of the different agents regarding the internal and external environment; and the situation assessment and decision-making needs of the different agents or actors. A central need in distributed multiagent situations is that of translation of thoughts and ideas into some more or less common language so that these can be shared. Thus, questions of dialogue generation and management, including information presentation, become especially important. Needs in this area have led to the development of group decision support systems (GDSS). The purpose of these computerized aids to planning, problem solving and decision making include (DeSanctis and Gallupe 1987):

(i) removing a number of common communication barriers;
(ii) providing techniques for structuring decisions; and
(iii) systematically directing group discussion, and associated problem solving and decision making, in terms of the patterns, timing and content of the information that influences these actions.

The article *Group Decision Support Systems* provides additional details concerning these points.

2. Distributed Multiagent Information-Processing Realities

Design of a distributed multiagent knowledge support system will incur all of the complexities of a non-distributed support system intended to be used by an individual. In addition to the distributed decision-making environment being prone to all of the errors of individuals in centralized single-agent situations, there will be added complexities due to the group nature of the support effort. The distributed nature of these systems, generally brought about because of the geographically dispersed sites, imposes at least three additional technological constraints that are generally not incurred in group information processing in a centralized location.

(h) *Communication*. Communication between sites will often, but not necessarily, be very much slower than communication within a single site.

(i) *Access time*. The access time to attach one network to another will often be longer than the time required for information transmission, especially in situations such as military conflict where jamming or other intentional message corruption is to be expected.

(j) *Communication channels and computers*. These will often, particularly in military situations, be subject to reliability and survivability concerns such that the knowledge-base system and the support system into which it is incorporated will be dependent, in effect, on continually changing topologies.

These message delays and associated potential conflicts and discrepancies in information available at various nodes in the communication network, as well as associated concerns relative to file allocation (i.e., location) strategies, result in a critical need for consideration of the architecture of a distributed information system. These technological realities, the finite rate of information flow, and the insufficiency and unreliability of information channels, each lead to a situation in which pertinent information is not available in the proper place at a suitable time. The effects of these technological information imperfections must be considered in determining resource-allocation strategies, as well as in the development of the resulting information-query strategies that are used to obtain information from and for the knowledge base.

Essentially the same maladies that affect individual decision-making and problem-solving behavior, as well as many others, can result from group and organizational limitations. There exists a considerable body of knowledge, generally qualitative, which relates to organizational structure and effectiveness, and decision making in organizations. Among the efforts pertinent to the discussion in this article are those by Argyris and Schon (1978), Argyris (1982), Cameron (1986), Lewin and Minton (1986), March and Olsen (1979), March and Weissinger-Baylon (1986) and Mintzberg (1979, 1983). The majority of these studies suggest that a bounded rationality or "satisficing" perspective, often heavily influenced by bureaucratic political considerations, will generally be the decision perspective adopted in actual decision-making practice in organizations. To cope with this effectively requires the ability to deal concurrently with technological, organizational, cognitive and other structural concerns as they each, separately and collectively, motivate systems engineering design issues, as noted by Carley (1986). The article *Distributed Information and Organizational Decision-Making Models* also discusses these concerns.

Satisficing, or bounded rationality (Simon 1979, 1983) results from a complex decision situation, for either an individual or a group, in which it is not possible to identify all alternative courses of action in advance of the time when an alternative must be selected, and it is not possible to predict to the necessary degree of precision all consequences of implementing a specified alternative. In situations like these, humans will typically attempt to satisfice; that is, pick a readily identifiable course of action that has been known to yield satisfactory performance in the past and perhaps make minor refinements to this alternative to render it more suitable for the given situation. Humans learn over time to adapt these past solutions to new problems more effectively so that they are able to raise their aspiration levels. This bounded rationality model of choice is roughly equivalent to the unconflicted adherence to an original course of action or unconflicted change to a new course of action in the stress-based model of judgement and choice due to Janis and Mann (1977) as also discussed in the article *Cognitive Management and Models of Judgement and Choice Processes*. In other words, bounded rationality often results in a sublimation of (large scale and scope) decision-making behavior for (microlevel) problem-solving behavior. The extent to which this is a desirable sublimation will be problem-dependent.

Organizational ambiguity is a major reason why this "bounded rationality" behavior is cited as being so pervasive by March and Oslen (1979), even in situations when formal rational thought or "vigilant information processing" might be thought to be a preferred decision style. There are at least four kinds of opaqueness or equivocality in organizations: ambiguity of intention, understanding, history and human participation. These four ambiguities relate to an organization's structure, function and purpose, as well as to the perception of these decision-making agents in an organization. They influence the information that is communicated in an organization, and generally introduce one or more forms of information imperfection. The notions of organizational management and organizational information processing are, indeed, inseparable. In the context of human information processing, it would not be incorrect to define the central purpose of management as the development of a consensual grammar to ameliorate the effects of equivocality or ambiguity. This is the perspective taken by Weick (1979a,b) in his noteworthy efforts concerning organizations.

Weick (1985) has studied five human activities that assist in their understanding of issues: enactment, triangulation, interaction, deliberation, and abstraction.

Enactment is the process through which people learn more about situations by probative and prodding efforts. Starbuck (1985) notes that such direct action is a form of deliberation. He indicates that action should often be introduced earlier in the process of deliberation than is usually the case and that action and thought should be integrated and interspersed with one another. The rationale behind this argument is that probative actions generate information and tangible results which modify potential thoughts. Of course, any approach that involves "act now, think later" type behavior should be applied with considerable caution.

Triangulation involves the systematic use of alternative sources of information. Weick uses the term "future perfect thinking" to characterize this. The benefits of triangularization include the use of potentially disconfirming information and multiple perspectives. There are trade-offs between triangularization and enactment in the sense that the time required for triangularization may inhibit enactment. Related to triangularization is the notion of *social interaction* which is the process of learning about situations by comparing various perceptions of them and then negotiating a communal view of the situation.

Deliberation involves slow, careful and formal systemic reasoning. This is a fundamental basis for most decision aids, of course. Weick suggests strong encouragement for deliberation under stress, including time pressure, since stress has such a major effect upon human and organizational information processing and often results in flawed decision making.

Abstraction leads to understanding of a situation by the process of building environmental contexts around situations and, through this, moving to higher levels of abstraction. As this involves studies of portfolios of similar situations, the process of abstraction would seem to be closely related to that of analogous reasoning in that both involve the use of larger, more comprehensive cases in which the special case at hand is embedded.

It is apparently Weick's view (Weick 1985) that a large number of conventional computerized decision aids often inhibit the use of these situation-understanding activities. Situation understanding and interpretation is, therefore, seen as a vital part of decision making and problem solving and one which is often neglected (Daft and Weick 1984, Daft and Lengel 1986, Sage and Rouse 1986) and that it needs to be a major determinant of the architecture of knowledge support systems.

Of course, an organization is also a mechanism for problem solving and decision making. When the realities of ambiguity are associated with organizational problem solving and decision making, the result is what is termed a "garbage-can model" of organizational choice by Cohen *et al.* (1972). In this model, which has generated much recent interest (March and Weissinger-Baylon 1986), there are five fundamental elements:

(a) issues or problems;

(b) organizational structure;

(c) participants, actors or agents;

(d) choice opportunities and actions; and

(e) solutions or products of the choice process.

The problems, solutions and choice opportunities are assumed to be quasi-independent, exogenous "streams" that are linked in a fashion that is determined by organizational structure constraints. There are several of these. The most important are *access structure*, or the access of problems to choice opportunities, *decision structure*, or the access of choice opportunities to solutions, and *energy structure*, which evolves in a dynamic fashion in terms of the number of problems or solutions that are linked to choice opportunities at a particular time. The participants in the process can also be regarded as variables since they "come and go" over time, and devote varying amounts of time and energy to problems, solutions and choice opportunities, due to other competing demands on their time.

In the garbage-can model, the problems, solutions and choice opportunities are mixed together in "garbage cans." The division of human effort among problems, solutions and choices is fuzzy and not fixed in any highly organized way. Problems, solutions and choice opportunities may not coalesce in the right way at the right time such as to lead to a "rational" solution to a problem.

There are many unanswered questions relative to descriptive and normative use of this interesting model, and there is much study in progress concerning extensions of this model. A book edited by March and Weissinger-Baylon (1986) describes an application of the garbage-can model to military decision making. There have been a considerable number of earlier studies in which university decision making, especially that of faculty search committees, is represented by a garbage-can model. Among the necessary and appropriate questions are the following.

(a) How is the number of "garbage cans" determined and what choice situations do they represent?
(b) Who participates and how do they participate in the various choices?
(c) What structures and flows represent the various problems, solutions and choice opportunities?
(d) How does this relative structure of the problems, solutions, choice opportunities and participants evolve over time?
(e) How is the interaction and information interchange among the various "garbage cans" determined?
(f) What influences situation assessment and variables that represent situation assessment in the various "garbage cans"?
(g) What is the appropriate role for models such as this in the normative design of information systems that support enhanced organizational efficiency and effectiveness?
(h) How can such designs be evaluated in an operational context, and the resulting information used to enhance system designs and organizational effectiveness?

There are several research needs that are suggested by the observations of this section. These are discussed below.

First the design of knowledge support systems that assist humans in cognitive tasks requires substantial comprehension of the human intellectual activities supporting judgement and choice on both an individual and an organizational basis. This comprises studies of skill-based, rule-based and formal-reasoning-based judgement, or the seemingly equivalent larger-dimensioned frameworks concerning judgemental perspectives. Importantly, it also involves the way in which the use of these types of knowledge depends on the contingency task structure. It also encompasses a study of ways in which humans process information, especially in distributed environments that are subject to considerable message delays, node failures and associated uncertainties and imprecision in the resulting database or knowledge base.

Second, the identification of appropriate ways to represent and use knowledge in a multiagent support system is a critical issue. This requires attention to studies that deal not only with the formal reasoning methods common to normative decision analysis, but also to studies of how humans can be aided in reasoning wholistically and affectively, such as reasoning by analogy. Perhaps more importantly, it requires studies of how holistic and wholistic knowledge can each normatively support one another to aid the decision-making processes of individuals and groups in distributed multiagent situations. It also requires knowledge of:

(a) how information queries are made, in terms of the number of requests and their distribution across communication nodes;
(b) the amount of information potentially available across network communication nodes;
(c) how much of this is used and unused; and
(d) the amount of information ambiguity and imperfection that is present in a given situation.

Research in this area should be, and typically is, very concerned with information-processing behaviors in organizational settings. Studies in this category are especially important since it has been shown that people in an organization will often ignore relevant information in their possession, simultaneously ask for more and then ignore that new information (Feldman and March 1981).

Third, information fusion studies and studies of the diverse interpretations that can result from the same knowledge presentation are important current issues. There exists the need to blend descriptive and prescriptive approaches in doing this such that the resulting knowledge support process is behaviorally acceptable.

Fourth, the acquisition and representation of knowledge from multiple perspectives are needed, as well as studies of how to accommodate this within the framework of specific-model-base and cognitive-engine constructs. This is needed in order to provide the input to the model management, cognitive engine and associated inference mechanisms that access the knowledge base of a support system. These must be designed in such a way as to consider the special needs that should be associated with a query language structure that may be used to elicit a knowledge base and the physical locations for various portions of the knowledge base.

Finally, there exist many needs relative to integration of the various knowledge bases, model bases and cognitive engines, such as to enable communication within a distributed multiagent knowledge environment by users of the system. In a representative distributed multiagent situation, it will typically not be possible, because of time constraints and other complexities, to evolve a "complete" set of potential action alternatives or plans, and possible ways to implement them. As has been already noted, this will generally lead to use of bounded rationality approaches to decision making, such as the use of a garbage-can model of organizational decision making. These realities must be considered in system conceptualization, and the resulting system architecture, so that the resulting designs are those which people may and will utilize in an efficient and effective way to develop appropriate and explicable policies and strategies.

3. Distributed Value-of-Information Concepts

If there is a single purpose for an overall information systems engineering design effort, it must be to enhance the value of information in distributed judgement and decision-making tasks. Information requirements analysis to enable choice of information requirements is discussed in a related article (see *Information Requirements Determination*). An auxiliary purpose of an appropriate information presentation framework should be to encourage the selection of effective and efficient information requirements. We see, therefore, that information requirements determination, and information presentation and use, are not independent concepts. They relate strongly to the notion of value of information and the vexing problem of making this determination, especially for normative and predictive purposes.

There have been many approaches suggested for the study of information value. These include empirical approaches, information theoretic approaches, information economics approaches and multiattribute utility theoretic approaches. Value of information is a multifaceted concept. It implies much more than the information theoretic notions concerning this might imply. One of the fundamental reasons for this is that much of the information that people request is requested for surveillance purposes in an effort to uncover potentially embarrassing "surprises" and not strictly for the purposes of decision making. There are also a number of factors, such as interpersonal conflicts and power struggles, that encourage intentional and unintentional misrepresentation of information. This again indicates that information is not "innocent" and must be suspected of many potential forms of bias. Also, information is a symbol that suggests rationality and there are many incentives to displaying what looks like, but which may not be, this symbol (Feldman and March 1981). It looks very bad not to display what can be regarded as this symbol! As a consequence, there will often be an expressed need for great quantities of information, but there may not be an equivalent desire to appropriately use the information that is requested. The information presentation system should encourage parsimonious requests for that information which is truly used for, and which will be appropriately used in, resolving the decision situation.

Thus, we see that information systems engineering design effort must be necessarily concerned with behavioral realities, such as with the potential incongruities schemata of individuals in a group or multiagent decentralized decision situation, as well as with the strictly technological issues. Thus, it is very desirable to be potentially able to examine possible approaches for constructing prototypical schemata of decision situations. Unfortunately, there does not seem to be a unique way to proceed from one knowledge representation perspective to another, and a number of interesting approaches may need to be examined further to determine appropriate architecture that encourages and enables efficient and effective knowledge acquisition, representation and use—and efficient and effective transitions from one form of knowledge representation to another. Some very general observations which may need to be addressed relative to this are noted below.

First, what happens when an individual decision maker discovers an incongruity between the knowledge representation that the information presentation system (somehow) constructs and the schema which the individual believes to be correct? These discrepancies may be of a structural, functional or purposeful nature. The implications of various discordances may be significantly different across different individuals.

Second, how do we deal with the three possible knowledge bases that may exist for a given decision situation? These are given below.

(a) A personal and private knowledge base which the individual may not wish to transmit over the system to others. This is not sinister in any way, necessarily. We all have hypotheses which we believe to be "half baked" and which we desire to explore personally before telling others about them.

(b) A personal knowledge base which an individual wishes to transmit openly to everyone on the system.

(c) A personal knowledge base which the individual possessing it wishes to transmit selectively to others, for any of a variety of reasons.

There exist, at least in principle, various sorts of "centralized" knowledge bases that might represent, in some way, group wisdom. Depending on the manner used to aggregate individual beliefs, or alternatively to use maps in a collective inquiry situation for judgement and choice, incongruities may or may not appear. Some of these concerns are of the old "paradox-of-voting" type that have led to Arrow's social choice theory. The article *Group Decision Making and Voting* discusses this. Other concerns, which relate to information representation and interpretation issues, are also quite important as they influence system architecture. It seems especially important to consider the principles affecting organization: division of labor and task assignment: standard operating principles for decisions; top-down versus bottom-up versus heterarchical flow of information and decisions; multiple uses for information; and group learning.

Much of the discussion to be found in the judgement, choice and decision literature concentrates on what may be called *formal reasoning and decision enactment* efforts that involve the six-issue resolution efforts that follow as part of the problem-solving efforts of issue formulation, analysis and interpretation that were discussed in a previous section. There are other decision-making activities as well. Very important among these are activities which allow perception, framing, editing and interpretation of the effects of actions upon the internal and external environments of a decentralized decision group. These might be called information selection activities. There will also exist information retention activities that allow admission, rejection and modification of the set of selected information or knowledge such as to result in short-term learning through reduction of incongruities, and long-term learning through the acquisition of new schemata that reflect enhanced understanding. Although the basic information system design effort may well be concerned with the short-term effects of various problem-solving, decision-making and information presentation formats, the actual knowledge that a person brings to bear on a given problem is a function of the accumulated experience that the person possesses, and thus long-term effects need to be considered, at least as a matter of secondary importance.

It was remarked earlier that a major purpose of the distributed information system design effort is to enhance the value of information. Three attributes of information appear dominant in this discussion and in the literature in general which are valuable for problem-solving purposes. These are listed below.

(*a*) *Equivocality reduction.* It is generally accepted that high-quality information may reduce imperfection or equivocality. This equivocality generally takes the form of uncertainty, imprecision, inconsistency or incompleteness. It is very important to note that it is neither necessary nor desirable to obtain decision information that is unequivocal or totally "perfect." Information need be only sufficiently unequivocal or unambiguous for the task at hand. For example, if we know that alternative *A* dominates alternative *B*, then the fact that there is imprecision among the weights of the attributes or among the utilities of the alternatives across the attributes is not bothersome. We should not be willing to pay anything to reduce this equivocality if we know that the information precision is sufficient to ensure that *A* dominates *B*.

(*b*) *Task relevance.* Of course, information must be relevant to the task at hand. It must allow the decision maker to know what needs to be known in order to make an effective and efficient decision. This is not as trivial a statement as might initially be suspected. Relevance varies considerably across individuals, as a function of the contingency task structure, and also over time.

(*c*) *Representational appropriateness.* In addition to the need that information be relevant to the task at hand, it must be represented in a form that is appropriate for use by the person who needs the information.

Each of these top-level attributes may be decomposed into attributes at a lower level. Each is needed as a fundamental metric for the evaluation of information quality. We have just indicated that the components of equivocality or imperfection are uncertainty, imprecision, inconsistency and incompleteness. Some of the attributes of representational appropriateness are naturalness, transformability to naturalness, and conciseness. These attributes of information presentation system effectiveness relate strongly to the overall value of information concerns and should be measured as a part of the information systems evaluation effort even though any one of them may appear to be a secondary theme.

4. Summary

This article has discussed contemporary research and a partial and preliminary framework and taxonomy for the design of information systems that support distributed decision making. An effort to interpret this concept in terms of contemporary literature has been made and some additional questions raised, the answers to which should enable a more precise specification of system architecture. Among these are questions concerning the robustness of knowledge representation frameworks relative to accommodating skill-, rule- and formal-reasoning-based knowledge, and questions concerning how the transformation from various representations and perspectives should be accomplished. A purpose of an information system for decision support is information selection and retention, and decision enactment based on this information in an interactive and adaptive fashion. An ancillary purpose is to enhance the value of information in terms of equivocality reduction, task relevance and appropriateness of form. An evaluation effort that encourages use and evaluation of the entire information presentation system concept, as contrasted with controlled experiments involving a portion of the system, is an essential part of the information system design effort.

See also: Distributed Information and Organizational Decision-Making Models; Group Decision Making and Voting

Bibliography

Applegate L M, Chen T T, Konsynski B R, Nunamaker J F 1987 Knowledge management in organizational planning. *J. Manage. Inf. Syst.* **3**(4), 20–38

Argyris C 1982 *Reasoning, Learning and Action: Individual and Organizational.* Jossey–Bass, San Francisco

Argyris C, Schon D 1978 *Organizational Learning: A Theory of Action Perspective.* Addison–Wesley, Reading, Massachusetts

Arkes H R, Hammond K R 1986 (eds.) *Judgement and Decision Making.* Cambridge University Press, Cambridge

Baron J 1985 *Rationality and Intelligence.* Cambridge University Press, Cambridge

Cameron K S 1986 Effectiveness as paradox: Concensus and conflict in conceptions of organizational effectiveness. *Manage. Sci.* **32**(5), 539–53

Carbonell J G 1983 Learning by analogy: Formulating and generalizing plans from past experience. In: Michalski R S, Carbonell J G, Mitchell T M (eds.) *Machine Learning: An Artificial Intelligence Approach.* Tioga, Palo Alto, California, pp. 137–62

Carley K M 1986 An approach for relating social structure to cognitive structure. *J. Math. Sociol.* **12**(2), 137–89

Cohen L J 1977 *The Probable and the Provable.* Oxford University Press, Oxford

Cohen L J 1981 Can human irrationality be experimentally demonstrated. *Behav. Brain Sci.* **4**, 317–31

Cohen M D, March J G, Olsen J P 1972 A garbage can model of organizational choice. *Adm. Sci. Q.* **17**(1), 1–25

Coulam R F, Fischer G W 1985 Problems of command and control in a major European war. *Adv. Inf. Process. Organ.* **2**, 211–68

Daft R L, Lengel R H 1986 Organizational information requirements, media richness, and structural design. *Manage. Sci.* **32**(5), 554–71

Daft R L, Weick K E 1984 Towards a model of organizations as interpretation systems. *Acad. Manage. Rev.* **9**, 284–95

Decker K S 1987 Distributed problem solving techniques: A survey. *IEEE Trans. Syst., Man Cybern.* **17**(5), 729–40

DeSanctis G, Gallupe R B 1987 A foundation for the study of group decision support systems. *Manage. Sci.* **33**(5), 547–88

Feldman M S, March J G 1981 Information in organizations as signal and symbol. *Adm. Sci. Q.* **26**, 171–86

Fox M S 1981 An organizational view of distributed systems. *IEEE Trans. Syst., Man. Cybern.* **11**(1), 70–80

Hammond K R, Stewart T R, Brehmer B, Steinmann D O 1975 Social judgement theory. In: Kaplin M F, Schwartz S (eds.) *Human Judgement and Decision Processes.* Academic Press, New York, pp. 271–312

Hogarth R M 1981 Beyond discrete biases: Functional and disfunctional aspects of judgmental heuristics. *Psychol. Bull.* **90**(2), 197–217

Huber G P, McDaniel R R 1986a Exploiting information systems to design more effective organizations. In: Jarke M (ed.) *Managers, Micros, and Mainframes.* Wiley, New York, pp. 221–36

Huber G P, McDaniel R R 1986b The decision making paradigm of organizational design. *Manage. Sci.* **32**(5), 572–89

Janis I L, Mann L 1977 *Decision Making: A Psychological Analysis of Conflict, Choice and Commitment.* Free Press, New York

Kahneman D, Slovic P, Tversky A (eds.) 1982 *Judgments under Uncertainty: Heuristics and Biases.* Cambridge University Press, New York

Klein G A, Calderwood R 1986 *A Preliminary Assessment of Factors Affecting Decision Complexity*, Report No. 96–86.1-F. Klein, Yellow Springs, Ohio

Kyburg H E 1983 Rational belief. *Behav. Brain Sci.* **6**(2), 231–74

Larkin J H, Simon H A 1987 Why a diagram is (sometimes) worth ten thousand words. *Cognit. Sci.* **11**(1), 65–99

Lewin A Y, Minton J W 1986 Determining organizational effectiveness: Another look and an agenda for research. *Manage. Sci.* **32**(5), 514–38

Linstone H A 1984 *Multiple Perspectives for Decision Making: Bridging the Gap Between Analysis and Action.* North-Holland, New York

March J G, Olsen 1979 *Ambiguity and Choice in Organization.* Universitelsforlaget Press, Bergen

March J G, Weissinger-Baylon R (eds.) 1986 *Ambiguity and Command: Organizational Perspectives on Military Decision Making.* Ballinger, Boston, Massachusetts

Mintzberg H 1973 *The Nature of Managerial Work.* Harper and Row, New York

Mintzberg H 1979 *The Structuring of Organizations.* Prentice–Hall, Englewood Cliffs, New Jersey

Mintzberg H 1983 *Structure in Fives: Designing Effective Organizations.* Prentice–Hall, Englewood Cliffs, New Jersey

Mumpower J, Phillips L, Renn O, Uppuluri V R R (eds.) 1987 *Expert Judgment and Expert Systems.* Springer-Verlag, Berlin

Rasmussen J 1983 Skills, rules, knowledge; Signals, signs, and symbols; and other distinctions in human performance models. *IEEE Trans. Syst., Man Cybern.* **13**(3), 257–66

Rasmussen J 1985 The role of hierarchical knowledge representation in decision making and system management. *IEEE Trans. Syst., Man Cybern.* **15**(2), 234–43

Rasmussen J 1986 *Information Processing and Human–Machine Interaction: An Approach to Cognitive Engineering.* North-Holland, Amsterdam

Rumelhart D E, McClelland J L 1985 *Parallel Distributed Processing: Explorations on the Microstructure of Cognition*, Vol. 1: *Foundations*. MIT Press, Cambridge, Massachusetts

Sage A P 1987a Information systems engineering for distributed decision making. *IEEE Trans. Syst., Man Cybern.* **17**(6), 920–36

Sage A P (ed.) 1987b *System Design for Human Interaction.* IEEE Press, New York

Sage A P, Lagomasino A 1987 Computer based intelligence support: An integrated expert system and decision support systems approach. In: Silverman B G (ed.) *Expert Systems for Managers*, TIMS series in Artificial Intelligence and Management Science. Addison–Wesley, Reading, Massachusetts, pp.338–57

Sage A P, Rouse W B 1986 Aiding the human decision maker through the knowledge based sciences. *IEEE Trans. Syst., Man Cybern.* **16**(2)

Sage A P, White C C 1984 ARIADNE: A knowledge based interactive system for planning and decision support. *IEEE Trans. Syst., Man Cybern.* **14**(1), 35–47

Simon H A 1978 On how to decide what to do. *Bell J. Econ.* **10**, 494–507

Simon H A 1979 Information processing models of cognition. *Annu. Rev. Psychol.* **30**, 363–96

Simon H A 1983 Search and reasoning in problem solving. *Artif. Intell.* **21**, 7–29

Smith R G 1981 *A framework for distributed problem solving.* UMI Research Press, Charlotte, North Carolina

Starbuck W E 1985 Acting first and thinking later. In: Pennings J (ed.) *Organizational Strategy and Change.* Jossey–Bass, San Francisco, California, pp. 336–72

Stefik M, Foster G, Bobrow D G, Kahn K, Lanning S, Suchman L 1987 Beyond the chalkboard: Computer support for collaboration and problem solving in meetings. *Commun. ACM* **30**(1), 32–47

Stephanou H, Sage A P 1987 Perspectives on imperfect information processing. *IEEE Trans. Syst., Man Cybern.* **17**(5)

Sternberg R J 1977 Component processes in analogical reasoning. *Psychol. Rev.* **84**(4), 353–78

Sternberg R J (ed.) 1982 *Handbook of Human Intelligence.* Cambridge University Press, New York

Sternberg R J, Turner M E 1981 Components of syllogistic reasoning. *Acta Psychol.* **47**, 245–65

Szewczak E J, King W R 1987 Organizational processes as determinants of information value. *OMEGA Int. J. Manage. Sci.* **15**(2), 103–11

Weick K E 1979a Cognitive processes in organizations. In: Staw B M (ed.) *Research in Organizational Behavior I.* JAI Press, Greenwich, Connecticut, pp. 41–74

Weick K E 1979b *The Social Psychology of Organizing.* Addison–Wesley, Reading, Massachusetts

Weick K E 1985 Cosmos vs chaos: Sense and nonsense in electronic contexts. *Organ. Dyn.* **14**, 50–64

A. P. Sage
[George Mason University, Fairfax, Virginia, USA]

Distributed Information and Organizational Decision-Making Models

The launch decision for the space shuttle is an organizational decision made in a distributed decision-making environment. Researchers and administrators at both NASA and outside contractors, such as Morton Thiokol, are involved. While the final launch decision is made by the mission management team, this decision is based on the decisions from readiness reviews conducted at multiple lower levels. The decisions of the lower levels, although not the information used to make those decisions, are communicated up to the next level; for example, the review decisions concerning the space shuttle main engine, solid rocket booster and external tank are all sent to the Marshall Space Flight Center for a flight readiness review decision. Researchers and administrators at each of these levels have access to different information, are concerned with different problems, have different goals and may be in different geographical locations. Today, many organizations operate in a distributed environment similar to that described above. Modelling organizational decision making when information, personnel and responsibility for parts of the decision are distributed makes it possible to explore the way in which the characteristics of the individuals involved, the information, the environment and the organization affect the timeliness and correctness of organizational decisions, and the efficiency with which they are made.

1. Distributed Decision Making

Distributed decision making refers to the process of organizational decision making that occurs when the information and responsibility for the decision are distributed across time, space and decision-making units (DMUs). A DMU can be an individual, group of individuals, a machine, or a collection of individuals and machines that is responsible for some component of the overall decision. Organizational decisions are a product of the information gathering, processing and decision making of multiple DMUs. In order to make correct, efficient, salient and timely decisions, the effort of the DMUs (which DMU collects what information and works on which aspect of the overall decision) must be coordinated. Each DMU may take part in the coordination process by attempting to negotiate its own role in the information gathering, processing and decision-making process. Each DMU has access to somewhat different information, has different criteria or goals for evaluating that information, has access to different technology for evaluating and gathering information, and so on. These differences affect both the ability of the DMUs to acquire new information, and their negotiation and decision-making behavior. Furthermore, these DMUs may be in different geographical locations and time zones.

From an organizational standpoint it is important that the decision be correct given the information available, and that the decision is efficiently made, salient and timely. From an information-processing perspective the factors affecting the decision-making capability of the organization can be roughly divided into three categories: the organizational structure, the event theater and the information gathering, processing and decision-making capabilities of the DMUs. The organizational structure is set of the modifiable characteristics that define the organization. These characteristics include size, the command, control and communication (C3) structure, distribution of information, procedures for making decisions and procedures for redistributing DMUs. DMUs can be redistributed by hiring, firing or redistributing personnel and by changing which DMUs have access to which computers or the power of those computers. The structure of an organization cannot be simply described as a hierarchy (Mintzberg 1979, 1983). While the command structure may be hierarchical, the communication structure may be uniform (everyone talks to everyone). Organizational procedures tend to be volatile. For example, for each decision, who makes the decision, the number of DMUs involved, the relation of information to the problems and decision, and the procedures to coordinate the DMUs may all be different. The event theater is the environment from which the organization draws information and which may dictate the schedule by which certain decisions must be made. Event theaters tend to be highly volatile. From day to day the flow of information, the number of problems faced by the organization, the number of decisions made and the rate at which decisions (at least certain decisions) must be made may all vary. Furthermore, the characteristics of the information available to the organization may continually change; for example, the level of completeness and reliability of the information relative to a problem change. The information gathering, processing and decision-making capabilities of the DMU depend on its composition. If the DMU is a single individual or machine then these capabilities are determined by the architecture (human cognitive or machine) and the information used to process other information. If the DMU is a collection of individuals or individuals and machines, then these capabilities are determined by the architecture, the information used to process other information, and the coordination and negotiation processes within the DMU. Characteristics of the architecture such as the way the DMU learns new information, stores information, plans and reasons about others are generally treated as similar across DMUs and constant over time. Characteristics of the information that the DMU uses to process other information (e.g., the goals or objectives, the salience which the DMU attributes to different problems, the DMU's level of expertise with this problem and heuristics used by the DMU to solve problems) are expected to differ across DMUs and to change over time for the DMU. Characteristics of the coordination and negotiation processes such as the degree of information loss and order of combining information are generally treated as similar across DMUs and constant over time. Thus, the organization is generally modelled as being composed of a set of DMUs which will function identically, provided they are given identical information and guidelines for processing information.

When the organization is faced with a crisis the factors affecting the decision-making capability of the organization become more volatile. Crises are characterized by increasing uncertainty about the procedures for making decisions, rapid event theaters and volatile information flows. As uncertainty about the decision procedures increases, the participation of the DMUs becomes volatile; as the number of DMUs decreases, coordination decreases and communication channels become unreliable. In a rapid event theater the number of problems increases and the time available to make decisions decreases. Furthermore, with a volatile information flow the amount of incoming information increases or decreases rapidly and the information becomes less reliable.

In an effort to understand how to increase the decision-making capability of the organization given the complexity of organizational decision making in a distributed environment, researchers have turned to model building and simulation. These models fall roughly into two categories—those emphasizing characteristics of the organizational structure and those based on models of individual cognition. In both cases, analyses tend to be done through simulation. Simulation is adopted since the nature of the problem involves feedback, effort allocation decisions, heuristic-based behavior, a large number of DMUs, vast amounts of information and large numbers of problems. Analytical results obtained when dealing with two or three DMUs and two or three problems are simply not generalizable to realistically sized organizations, in part because patterns of negotiation and coordination are qualitatively different for extremely small and simple organizations. Furthermore, in order to understand a crisis, the short-term consequences of changes in the event theater, rather than equilibrium or long-run behavior, must be observed (Carley 1986a).

2. Structure-Based Organizational Models

Predominant among the models that emphasize characteristics of the organizational structure are those following from the garbage-can theory of organizational choice (Cohen *et al.* 1972). According to the basic garbage-can model, organizations are anarchies characterized by severe ambiguity. There are three areas of ambiguity: problematic preferences (i.e., different DMUs have different goals and these goals change over time), unclear procedures for making decisions, and fluid participation (i.e., membership changes over time). People with their goals, problems and solutions flow through the organization and decisions happen by resolution (rationally solving a problem), by flight (ignoring the problem) and by oversight (owing to another related problem being solved). Public-sector organizations (e.g., city council and Red Cross), educational organizations (e.g., colleges) and any organization during crisis (e.g., joint task force) are typified by this model. Both educational (Cohen *et al.* 1972, Cohen and March 1974) and military (March and Weissinger-Baylon 1986) organizations have been analyzed using this model.

A variety of models based on the garbage-can concept have been proposed (Cohen *et al.* 1972, Padgett 1980, Anderson and Fischer 1986, Carley 1986a,b, for example). Using these models the researcher can explore the relationship between various characteristics of the organization's structure and its decision-making capability. Using their model, Cohen *et al.* (1972) found that regardless of organizational structure, as crisis approaches most decisions occur by flight and oversight, and that in organizations where the access structure is specialized (each DMU has access to different information and is responsible for different problems), more problems (50–65%) are solved by resolution. Alternatively, Padgett (1980) found that when the organization is modelled as a hierarchy with garbage-can properties, the chief executive officer (CEO) can most effectively get the organization to make decisions that meet the CEO's goals by exercising a hands-off policy and hiring liberal assistants for low-saliency programs and conservative assistants for high-saliency programs.

A very general model of this type is GARCORG (Carley 1986a,b). GARCORG is an interactive simulation model for exploring the relationship between organizational structure, the event theater and the decision-making capability of the organization. Unlike other models in the garbage-can tradition, GARCORG can be used to simulate organizations both with and without garbage-can-like features. The user specifies the organizational structure and some characteristics of the event theater. GARCORG then simulates the organization's behavior over time and reports on the results. The generic model used by GARCORG is portrayed in Fig. 1. In this model, the organization is set up as a four-level decision hierarchy (a) with four corresponding types of DMU: a CEO, an assistant executive officer (AEO), program chiefs (PC) and analysts (A). Each DMU occupies a particular slot in the organization (b). DMUs at higher levels may or may not have access to or consider salient the decisions that come out of slots at lower levels. Each time period, a certain amount of information comes into each slot (c), each piece of information having a different level of content (shown by different shading of the squares). Content can be thought of as the level of validity, reliability or completeness of the piece of information. Information in the form of decisions by DMUs from lower levels moves up the organizational hierarchy. For example, the decisions made by the analysts become the information available to the program chiefs.

In GARCORG, the user can describe the organizational structure by specifying the organization's size,

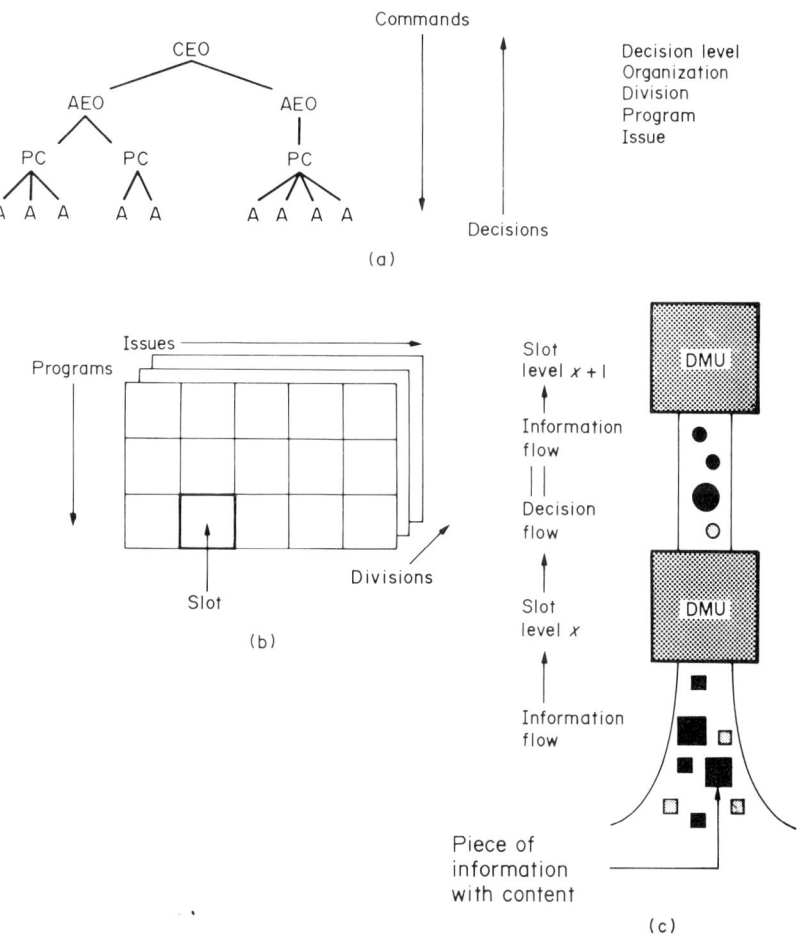

Figure 1
The generic model used by GARCORG

whether or not the organization is differentiated (the more differentiated, the larger the number of programs and the fewer people working on each program), the hiring and firing criteria (personnel transfer), the threshold for hiring or firing, the delay before hiring/firing decisions are made, who has access to what problems and hence information, the average level of saliency that the various problems have to the CEO and his assistants, and the level at which the CEO and assistants rubber-stamp the decisions of the lower echelons. The user can also characterize the event theater by specifying the amount and content (value or completeness) of new information per time period. Using this model the user can examine the impact of thousands of different organizational structures and nine event theaters on the organization's decision capability over time.

GARCORG can be used to simulate both crisis and normal operating conditions and response. Crisis can be simulated by setting up an event theater in which the amount of incoming information is high and the content low. Then, by observing the organization's behavior in the short run, the organization's response to crisis can be studied. In GARCORG the decision-making capability of the organization is measured in terms of the efficiency with which the decisions are made, and the percentage of decisions that are rubber-stamped by the CEO and assistants. Both structural and political efficiency are measured in terms of the fraction of bad slots in which analysts are working. A slot is a position in the organization. A slot is *structurally* bad if the CEO or assistants do not have access to the decisions made by the analyst in that slot. A slot is *politically* bad if the CEO or assistants do not consider salient the problem that the analyst in that slot is working on.

Using GARCORG, Carley (Carley 1986a) examined which organizational structures performed best during crisis. A total of 36 different organizational structures were simulated and the results statistically analyzed. It was found that: small organizations are more efficient than large organizations in the short run, especially structurally; differentiated organizations are more efficient overall; a hiring/firing criteria based on saliency does not guarantee political efficiency; and the criteria by which personnel are hired or fired has a more immediate and stronger impact on efficiency than do the other organizational structural features. This analysis also suggested that the organizations which must cope with crisis should be small and differentiated, with all managers having access to all problems, the hiring/firing criteria being based on information rather than saliency, and with the CEO not exerting direct control (high rubber-stamp level).

Collectively, the garbage-can models suggest that when information is distributed across DMUs, the best decisions (made by resolution) and the most efficiently made decisions occur when DMUs are responsible for making decsions about, and consider salient, those problems that need the information to which they have access. Thus, information, problem control and salience should be similarly distributed and segmented. Alternatively, all DMUs, should take part in all decisions or have access to all information; however, this distribution scheme may lower efficiency and the quality of the decisions. These conclusions are reached in part because these models do not allow communication of information (only decisions), negotiation or coordination among DMUs.

Recently, researchers have turned to models of parallel processing, rather than garbage-can models, to determine the impact of organizational structure and the event theater on the decision-making capability of an organization. For example, the petri net models (Hillion 1986, Remy and Levis 1986) and the effort allocation model (Carley *et al.* 1988) may be used. The effort allocation model is concerned with the impact of effort allocation schemes and coordination schemes on the timeliness and correctness of decisions. The effort allocation schemes are used to determine which DMU is responsible for working on which problem. The coordination schemes determine which DMU makes effort allocation decisions and what information it uses. Two effort allocation schemes have been explored: optimal allocation, determined analytically, and heuristic-based allocation. Coordination schemes explored include anarchy (each DMU acts independently, choosing which problems to attend to and making its decisions independently of the other DMUs in the organization), centralized (each DMU is arranged in a hierarchical structure and is coordinated by the CEO who makes all decisions) and decentralized (each DMU makes its own decisions, but these decisions are based on information received from other DMUs). These coordination schemes and resultant differences in information availability and the time it takes to make effort allocation decisions are shown in Fig. 2.

Using the effort allocation model it was found that any coordination scheme is better than none, heuristic-based allocation schemes are almost as effective in terms of number of correct decisions as optimal analytic schemes and they are less costly. In addition there is a trade-off between consistency and latency. This means the organizations with decentralized coordination schemes not only make more timely decisions, but also make incorrect decisions due to inconsistencies in the informaton available to them; centralized organizations make less timely but more correct decisions. In this model all information inconsistencies are due to lack of concurrency in the information.

Organizational decision making is not rational. Rather, because organizational decisions are the product, at least in part, of human decision making, such decisions are subject to limited rationality (March and Simon 1958). In the garbage-can models, limited rationality was achieved by affecting the infor-

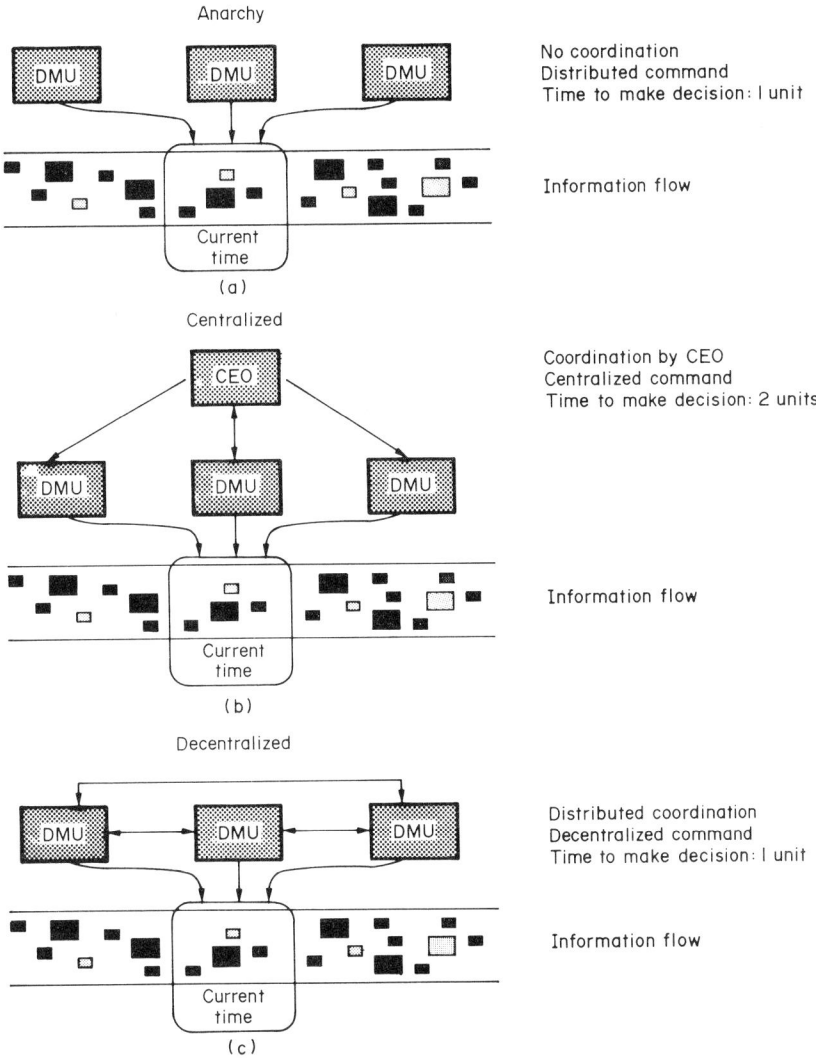

Figure 2
An illustration of three different coordination schemes: (a) anarchy, (b) centralized and (c) decentralized. In all three cases it is assumed that it takes one time unit for a DMU to acquire information from the external information flow and one time unit to communicate information to another DMU. In (a), as soon as the DMU acquires information (one time unit), it can make a decision. In (b), each DMU collects information (one time unit) and then communicates that information to the CEO (one time unit) who then makes a decision; hence it takes two time units before a decision can be made. In (c), each DMU can make a decision in one time unit after getting information from the external information flow and from the other DMUs. This decision, however, will rely on information about what the other DMUs are doing which is one time unit out of date

mation that the DMU used to process other information; for example, by giving the DMU goals that changed over time. In the effort allocation model, limited rationality was achieved by using heuristic-based allocation schemes. In neither case is there a model of the architecture of the DMU, nor of the coordination and negotiation processes within the DMU. It is expected that by basing the organizational model on more realistic models of the DMU it will be possible to explore how negotiation and planning are affected by different distributions of information and DMUs. It is further expected that such models will more accurately reflect organizational decision-making capability.

3. Cognitively-Based Organizational Models

Recently there has been growing interest in exploring the impact of the individual's cognitive architecture on organizational distributed decision making. In these models, the DMU is treated as a single individual. These models take into account features of the individual's cognitive architecture such as the information representation scheme, learning procedures, the ability to reason about others and planning procedures. Many of these models use techniques and ideas from artificial intelligence. Some of the organizational tasks that have been studied using this approach are tracking and surveillance (Drazovich et al. 1977–1979, Reid 1979, Lesser and Corkill 1981, Durfee et al. 1985), allocation of labor by bees (Reed and Lesser 1981), sensor data interpretation (Smith 1980), air traffic control (Steeb et al. 1980, Thorndyke et al. 1981) and general organizational management (Fox 1979, 1981).

A model of this type is CONSTRUCT (Carley 1987, 1988). CONSTRUCT is an interactive simulation model for exploring changes in the social or organizational structure that accrue as individuals communicate and gather information. CONSTRUCT, as a general social behavior simulator, can be used to simulate the learning and decision behavior of individuals in various group and organizational settings. CONSTRUCT utilizes a simplistic model of individual cognition based on a list-structured knowledge representation scheme and a series of learning mechanisms. CONSTRUCT is based on the premises that as individuals interact they acquire information, the more information that individuals share the more likely they are to interact given the opportunity to do so, and that the organizational structure is continually reconstructed as individuals acquire information and change their interaction patterns. Using CONSTRUCT, the researcher can explore the way in which different organizational structures are differentially useful for the storage and maintenance of information, development of shared knowledge and decisions consensus. CONSTRUCT can also be used to look at how different distributions of information and organizational structures alter as information flows through the organization. The use of CONSTRUCT suggests that when information is distributed across DMUs the organization's informal structure changes to become parallel to the information distribution scheme. Stability in the organization's structure can be maintained by segregating information across the DMUs according to the communication structure.

In CONSTRUCT the user can specify the organizational structure by specifying the size of the organization, the amount of information known to the organization, the rates at which DMUs enter and leave the organization, the initial command/communication structure (who interacts with whom) and the initial distribution of information across DMUs. The event theater is characterized by the rate of incoming information. To use CONSTRUCT the user first specifies the structure of the organization and the event theater, and then CONSTRUCT simulates the behavior of the organization for a series of time periods. CONSTRUCT can be used to simulate both crisis and normal operating conditions and response. Crises can be simulated by using a high rate of incoming information. As with GARCORG, crisis response can be studied by observing the behavior of the organization in the short run.

Organizational models which are cognitively based enable the exploration of issues such as the impact of information diffusion, planning and learning on organizational decision making. Currently, most of the cognitively-based models have only limited applications to organizational decision making as they do not allow the user to model the organizational structure. CONSTRUCT, on the other hand, can be used to model the organizational structure; however, the model of individual cognition and the facilities for modelling the event theater are limited.

4. Future Work

Organizational decision making when the information, DMUs and responsibility for parts of the decision are distributed is complex. Consequently, model building and simulation are viable approaches for studying this process. Among the factors affecting the decision-making capability of the organization are the organizational structure, the event theater and the information gathering, processing and decision-making capabilities of the DMUs. Future models of the organizational distributed decision-making process will combine these factors. The models discussed in this article indicate a variety of issues with which future models will need to contend. Three such issues are the impact of crisis, information characteristics, and the distribution and redistribution of DMUs on the decision-making capability of the organization.

A unique feature of the GARCORG and CONSTRUCT models is that they admit the study of organizational behavior during crisis. Crisis-related behavior can be studied by considering short-term behavior when the rate of incoming information increases. There are, however, many other characteristics of crisis. For example, during crisis it may become difficult for some DMUs to communicate with others and the number of decisions that need to be made may increase. Furthermore, crises last only a short time and the organization will then either recover, disintegrate or reorganize.

An important feature of all the models discussed in this article is that they deal with the relationship between various characteristics of information and the decision-making capabilities of the organization. The amount, content (completeness), distribution and the change over time in these information characteristics can all be explored. It is clear that information characteristics can affect organizational decision-making capabilities and that this relationship is complex. For example, the impact of the amount and content of the information may depend on the distribution of information across DMUs and the speed of communication between DMUs. Questions of information concurrency, information distortion, and the economics of transmission and storage still need to be explored.

Another important aspect of these models is that they begin to allow the user to study how policies which affect the role and placement of DMUs within the organization make impact on its decision-making capability. Policies which affect structural factors like the following can be studied: number of DMUs, movement of DMUs within the organization, coordination of DMUs, distribution of decision-making responsibility across DMUs and communication between the DMUs. In order to comprehend the impact of these policies on the organization's decision-making capability more fully, it will be necessary to examine issues such as the conditions under which useful heuristic strategies for coordination and communication evolve, changes in efficiency as DMUs enter, leave or move about in the organization, and information storage and loss as DMUs enter and leave the organization.

Even a brief consideration of organizational decision making shows that many organizational decisions are somewhat repetitive; for example, there were 25 shuttle launch decisions made between April 12, 1981 and January 28, 1986. It can also be seen that organizational decisions tend to be integrated decisions; that is, the final decision is the result of a plethora of previous decisions made by various DMUs. At a very primitive level, the models discussed in this article consider repeated and integrated decisions. There are, however, important aspects of repeated and integrated decisions that are not dealt with. For example, organizational learning from repeated decisions, and information loss and distortion when integrated decisions are made. Furthermore, it can also be seen that many DMUs are either a collection of individuals or a collection of individuals and machines. Up to the late 1980s, models of organizational decision making have not dealt with this complication, for example, the changes in communication speed, processing ability and storage capability when individuals can rely on machines are not explored in this framework.

Using models like those discussed here, it is possible to explore organizational decision making when information, personnel and responsibility for parts of the decision are distributed. As the concerns above illustrate, there are still many factors affecting organizational decision making that these models do not take into account. In order to understand and facilitate the decision-making capability of organizations such as joint task forces, NASA, Chrysler and the Red Cross, it will be necessary to develop not only new models but models which allow the user to examine empirical data drawn from studies of such organizations.

See also: Distributed Decision Making: Information Systems

Bibliography

Anderson P A, Fischer G W 1986 A Monte Carlo model of a garbage can decision process. In: March and Weissinger-Baylon (1986)

Carley K M 1986a Efficiency in a garbage can, implications for crisis management. In: March and Weissinger-Baylon (1986)

Carley K M 1986b Measuring efficiency in a garbage can hierarchy. In: March and Weissinger-Baylon (1986)

Carley K M 1987 *Increasing Consensus Through Interaction and Social Structure*, Social Decision Sciences Working Paper Series

Carley K M 1988 *Social Stability and Constructionalism*, Social and Decision Sciences Working Paper Series

Carley K M, LeHoczky J, Sha L, Tokuda H, Wang L, Rajkumar R 1988 Comparing approaches for achieving near optimal solutions in a distributed decision making environment, Annual Report to the ONR for Grant No. SFRC N00014-84-K-0734

Cohen M D, March J G 1974 *Leadership and Ambiguity*. McGraw–Hill, New York

Cohen M D, March J G, Olsen J P 1972 A garbage can model of organizational choice. *Admin. Sci. Q.* **17**(1), 1–25

Corkill D 1979 Hierarchical planning in a distributed environment. *Proc. 6th Int. Joint Conf. Artificial Intelligence*, Tokyo, Japan, pp. 168–75

Drazovich R, Brooks S, Payne J R, Lowerre B, Foster S 1977–1979 *Surveillance Integration Automation Project (SIAP)*, Technical Progress Report. Systems Control, Palo Alto, California

Durfee E, Lesser V, Corkill D 1985 Increasing coherence in distributed problem solving networks. *Proc. 9th Int. Conf. Artificial Intelligence.*

Fox M 1979 *Organization Structuring: Designing Large, Complex Software*, Technical Report No. CMU-CS-79-155. Carnegie-Mellon University, Pittsburgh, Pennsylvania

Fox M 1981 *The Intelligent Management System: An Overview*, Technical Report. Carnegie-Mellon University, Pittsburgh, Pennsylvania

Hillion H P 1986 Performance evaluation of decision making organizations using timed Petri nets, Technical Report. Massachusetts Institute of Technology, Cambridge, Massachusetts

Lesser V, Corkill D 1981 Functionally accurate, cooperative distributed systems. *IEEE Trans. Man. Syst. Cybern.* **1**, 81–96

March J G, Simon H A 1958 *Organizations*. Wiley, New York

March J, Weissinger-Baylon T (eds.) 1986 *Ambiguity and Command: Organizational Perspectives on Military Decision Making*. Pitman, Boston, Massachusetts

Mintzberg H 1979 *The Structure of Organizations*. Prentice–Hall, Englewood Cliffs, New Jersey

Mintzberg H 1983 *Structure in Fives: Designing Effective Organizations*. Prentice–Hall, Englewood Cliffs, New Jersey

Padgett J 1980 Managing garbage can hierarchies. *Admin. Sci. Q.* **25**(4), 583–604

Reed S, Lesser V 1981 *Division of Labor in Honey Bees and Distributed Focus of Attention*, Technical Report No. 80–17. University of Massachusetts, Amherst, Massachusetts

Reid D 1979 An algorithm for tracking multiple targets. *IEEE Trans. Autom. Control* **6**, 843–54

Remy P A, Levis A H 1986 On the generation of organizational architectures using Petri nets,Technical Report. Massachusetts Institute of Technology, Cambridge, Massachusetts

Smith R 1980 The contact net protocol: High-level communication and control in a distributed problem solver. *IEEE Trans. Comput.* **29**(12), 1104–13

Steeb R, Cammarata S, Hayes-Roth F, Wesson R 1980 Distributed intelligence for air fleet control, Technical Report No. WD-839-ARPA. Rand Corp.

Thorndyke, P, McArthur D, Cammarata S 1981 Autopilot: A distributed planner for air fleet control. *Proc. 7th IJCAI*. Vancouver, British Columbia, pp. 171–77

K. Carley
[Carnegie-Mellon University, Pittsburgh, Pennsylvania, USA]

Dynamic Decision Making

The tasks of process control in industry, treating a patient in an intensive-care ward, fighting a forest fire and managing a company are dynamic decision tasks in that they share the four following characteristics:

(a) a series of decisions are required;

(b) these decisions are interdependent;

(c) the decison problem changes, both autonomously and as a consequence of the decision maker's actions; and

(d) the decisions are made in real time.

Dynamic decision tasks differ from static tasks in that a series of interdependent decisions are required to reach the goal, and from sequential decision tasks in that the time aspect is important. Dynamic decision tasks require a different conception of decision making than the conception in terms of the resolution of discrete choice dilemmas prevalent in traditional research on decision making. They also require a new conception of decision tasks; the traditional conception, based on gambles, which sees a decision task in terms of a list of action alternatives connected to outcomes by means of probabilities is obviously unsatisfactory.

Brehmer and Allard (1988b) have suggested that decision making in dynamic tasks should be seen as an attempt to achieve control, instead of an attempt to resolve discrete choice dilemmas. They have also proposed a conceptualization of dynamic decision tasks in terms of six basic characteristics. We start with a discussion of these six characteristics, and move on to a brief review of results from empirical studies on dynamic decision making.

1. The Characteristics of Dynamic Decision Tasks

Brehmer and Allard (1988b) chose their six characteristics partly on the basis of systems theory in an attempt to capture what is needed to ascertain the possibilities for achieving control, and partly on the basis of psychological considerations to obtain a description that can be used to understand human performance in dynamic tasks.

1.1 Complexity

Although the meaning of the term complexity seems intuitively obvious, it is very hard to define. This is because complexity is a relative concept. Phenomena are not complex in general, they are complex in relation to something. In this article, we are interested in complexity in relation to control. We therefore follow Ashby (1956) and define the complexity of a system in relation to the capacity of the device that seeks to control the behavior of that system. Thus, a system is said to be too complex in relation to a given control structure if this structure cannot match the complexity of the system. The relative complexity of a task may then be defined as the extent to which it makes demands upon the resources of the control device.

In the present context, the control devices of interest are human decision makers. People are limited information processors in that they can only take a limited number of items into account at the same time. Hence, we may define complexity in terms of the number of elements and relations in the system that the decision maker seeks to control. However, from a psychological perspective, not all elements are the same, and we need to distinguish among at least four different kinds of elements:

(a) goals,

(b) control actions,

(c) processes that need to be controlled, and

(d) side effects.

Few, if any, dynamic decision tasks are so simple that the decision maker will have only one goal. Instead, there will often be many goals, with the attendant need to make trade-offs. In process control in a modern plant, for example, there is often a need to consider both productivity and safety, and to make a reasonable trade-off between them.

The number of control actions may vary in two different ways. First, there may simply be a number of different things that need to be done to acquire control. Second, there may be many alternative courses of action, and some of these may substitute for each other, so that there are different ways to achieve the same end. The former clearly increases the complexity of the task, while the latter might decrease complexity.

The number of processes that need to be controlled may also vary. For example, in fighting forest fires, there may not only be one, but many different forest fires that compete for resources. In a modern process plant, there is typically more than one process in operation at the same time, and the operators thus need to monitor many processes.

As the dynamic tasks constitute systems, they will not have a simple linear causal structure. Instead, they will exhibit a causal net structure. Consequently, when one control action is taken, there will often be various side effects, and these must also be considered in choosing an action. Alternatively, when the side effects cannot be avoided, as is the case in many forms of medical treatment, the side effects themselves need to be controlled, perhaps being made the subject of separate control actions.

It is an interesting question as to whether a variation in any of these four different aspects has the same effect on complexity. Unfortunately, the answer to this question is unknown; so far there are no studies that evaluate the relative effects of these different aspects. This evaluation is an important task for future studies on dynamic decision making. Only empirical studies on people's ability to control systems can clarify the concept of complexity; if we do not know the capacity of the control structure, we cannot decide whether the system to be controlled is complex or not. Thus, our understanding of human control of dynamic tasks and the definition of complexity will develop hand in hand.

1.2 Feedback Quality

Strictly speaking, all information in a dynamic decision task is feedback information. Such information may vary in quantity and quality. Thus, the feedback information may not give full information about the state of the system; it may only reveal selected aspects. This is often the case when an information system has been inserted between the decision maker and the system he seeks to control as, for example, in a modern process plant.

In dynamic decision tasks, part of the feedback cycle pertains to the actual process inherent in the task. In many tasks, however, this part is hidden from the decision maker. For example, in modern process plants, the operator tends to have no direct contact with the process he has to control, but has to infer the nature of the process from various measurements. Even if these measurements give complete and accurate information about the state of the process at any given moment in time, the fact that the operator has no direct perceptual information about the process may make it more difficult for him to form an adequate mental model of the process. This is indicated by results from a study by Brigham and Laios (1975). Consequently, it is important to distinguish between quality and quantity of feedback information, since the form in which information is provided may make it more or less useful for the decision maker.

1.3 Feedback Delay

In a complex system, feedback delays cannot be avoided. However, feedback delay is a complex factor, since such delays can occur anywhere in the feedback loop. There may be delays in the following processes:

(a) transmission of commands,

(b) response to commands,

(c) execution of commands,

(d) reports about the results, and

(e) transmission of the reports about the results.

From the mere fact that there are delays, it is, of course, impossible to decide what the source of the delays are.

The general implication of feedback delays is that the system cannot be controlled on the basis of feedback. This means that the decision maker has to shift from feedback control to feedforward control. This, in turn, requires a more complex model of the system than feedback control supplies. However, the need for such a well-developed model varies with the nature of the delay. If the delays are in the transmission of information, then there is an alternative to a more complex model: to decentralize control to local decision makers who have more up-to-date information about the state of the system.

Feedback delays are unavoidable; hence, the question of how such delays are dealt with is of central importance for understanding the capacity for achieving control in dynamic tasks. Feedback delays are also interesting in studies of dynamic decision making because the response to such delays gives information about the strategy employed by the subjects in their attempts to control the dynamic system. Specifically, the response to delays gives information about whether or not people are able to employ adequate forms of open-loop strategies or if they are limited to feedback control strategies.

1.4 Possibilities for Decentralization

As noted in Sect. 1.3, decentralization is an effective way to cope with delays due to the slow transmission of information. Slow transmission is likely to be the case in most complex systems, especially when the transmission is dependent on people who have many other things to do beside transmitting information. Decentralization is also one possible strategy for coping with complexity. To handle complex problems, a hierarchical structure is often imposed on a problem. When successful, the hierarchical structure regulates complexity in that it limits the number of elements that need to be considered at each level in the hierarchy. The primary example of such regulation of complexity by means of a hierarchical structure is the military organization in terms of units of different sizes (see Brehmer (1988) for a discussion of hierarchical control structures for decision making in complex systems).

1.5 Rate of Change

Humans cope with systems that vary greatly with respect to rate of change, from the case of making a low-level attack with a modern jet fighter at the one extreme to that of controlling the economy of a country at the other, with cases of fire fighting, process control and patient management in between. Rate of change is important at both extremes. At the fast end, there is the question of whether people are able to make decisions at the rate required to achieve control over the fast process. At the slow end, there is the question of whether the dynamics of the system will be detected, or whether what are really interdependent events will be treated independently.

1.6 Relation Between the Characteristics of the Process to be Controlled and the Characteristics of the Control Process

In a real-time dynamic task, it is not only the system that the decision maker seeks to control (be it a patient, a process plant or the economy of a country) that has process characteristics; control actions also have such characteristics. The actions will require time to take effect and their effects will develop over time. For example, medication given to a patient will not take effect immediately, but only after some time, and the substance will stay in the body for some period of time interacting with new doses or other substances. To control a dynamic system, the decision maker will therefore need to consider his control actions as processes to judge adequately whether a given course of action will achieve his ends and when to expect results so that he does not make new inputs that add to the inputs he has already made.

Hence, the problem in dynamic decision making can be defined as that of using one process to control another process. The relation between these two processes defines whether the system can be controlled at all, and what kind of strategy is needed. The fighting of forest fires illustrates this. In fire fighting, the process to be controlled (i.e., the fire) is an exponential process, while the fire-fighting process is a linear process. Thus, the problem is that of finding a way of controlling an exponential process by means of a linear one.

The case of a linear control process and an exponential process to be controlled is, of course, only a special case. Many other kinds of combinations are possible; the nature of the actual combination of these processes will determine whether the decision problem can be solved at all and if it can be solved, the strategy which would be applicable.

1.7 Prerequisites for Control

It may be useful at this point to relate the dimensions used in the Brehmer and Allard conception of dynamic tasks to the ordinary prerequisites for control. There are four such prerequisites:

(a) there must be a well-defined goal,

(b) there must be possibilities for ascertaining the state of the system,

(c) there must be a model of the system, and

(d) there must be possibilities for affecting the system.

As can be seen from this list, some of these characteristics pertain to the task, independent of the decision maker, while others specify properties that the decision maker needs to have. All the characteristics that pertain to the task can be found in the set of dimensions in the task model: the goal, the action alternatives (both of which form part of the complexity characteristic) and the possibility for ascertaining the state of the system (which is given as one aspect of feedback quality). The model is, of course, not part of the task, but specifies what the decision maker needs to be able to achieve control. In research on dynamic decision making, the model is thus the dependent variable, while the other three characteristics constitute independent variables which introduce limits of control.

2. Research on Dynamic Decision Making—A Brief Review

Research on dynamic decision making has followed different approaches. Although all approaches emphasize the first three defining characteristics of dynamic decision tasks as outlined in the introduction to this article (i.e., that a series of interdependent decisions is needed and that the decision problem changes), they differ in their treatment of the fourth characteristic: the real-time aspect. On one hand, we find approaches that have their origin in statistical decision theory (Edwards 1962, Rapoport 1975). These approaches consider the decision problem in terms of a series of "moves" but do not include time as such. On the other hand, we find approaches based on systems theory such as that of Brehmer and Allard (1988b) and that represented by studies of manual control based on engineering models (see, e.g., Baum and Drury (1976) for a review) which focus directly on decision making in real time. In between, we find a number of approaches that include time explicitly and describe their tasks as discrete time systems, but where decisions are not made in real time (e.g., Mackinnon and Wearing 1980, Dörner et al. 1983). Instead, the time dimension is cut up in a number of *trials*, and the task stops and waits for the subjects to make their decisions. Under these conditions, there is no time pressure on the decision maker as there will be in a real-time task, and the process characteristics of the task will presumably be less apparent. Whether the results obtained with such tasks will generalize to real-time tasks is unknown at the present time.

Studies on dynamic decision making also differ considerably with respect to the concrete experimental situation employed. Early studies on manual control often relied on concrete physical realizations of processes, while later studies have relied on computer simulations. Unfortunately, the research undertaken with each kind of experimental task is very limited and there have been no attempts to create a broader framework within which the results of these specific experiments can be judged. We therefore know very little about the specific characteristics which each of these tasks may have and it is therefore difficult to draw any general conclusions from the results.

In the following subsections, we will focus on results from real-time tasks, but also mention results from studies using a trial-by-trial presentation as they seem relevant. The six characteristics proposed by Brehmer and Allard are used to organize the results.

2.1 Complexity

Although complexity is often given as a prime characteristic of real-world dynamic tasks, especially in discussions of process control, there have not been any attempts to analyze the complexity of these tasks and to evaluate the importance of various sources of complexity.

There seem to be only two studies of complexity using real-time dynamic decision tasks. Brehmer and Allard (1988b) manipulated complexity by varying the relative effectiveness of different fire-fighting units in a computer-simulated forest fire-fighting task. They found no differences between a task which was more complex in the sense that there was a variation in effectiveness (thus requiring the subjects to keep track of specific units) and a task where all units were equally effective. These results were later replicated by Brehmer and Allard (1988a).

Bainbridge *et al.* (1974) compared experienced operators and students using a computer simulation of a process control task. They found little difference in overall performance on the task, but verbal protocols revealed that the experienced operators had a more complex goal structure and tried to take more aspects of the task into account, relying on their experience of what is important to the final product. These results show that the goal structure may not be what the experimenter thinks it is, and that complexity may vary in this respect in ways that are not controlled in the experiment. Thus, it is necessary to ascertain the subject's real goal structure before one draws any conclusions from studies where the number of goals is an important independent variable.

Kluwe and Reimann (1983) used a simulated process control task to study the effects of two kinds of causal structures: a net structure (where control actions directed at one goal variable also affected other goal variables) and a task with a linear causal structure (where there were no side effects but where control actions only affected one goal variable). They found that their subjects learned to control the task with the linear causal structure, but were unable to learn to control the task with the net structure. Mackinnon and Wearing (1980), on the other hand, failed to find differences in performance for a simple and a complex task, where the complex task had both more elements and a more complex net structure. One possible explanation for this is that the complex task may not really have required a more complex form of control strategy than the simple task. However, the actual requirements for achieving the level of control observed in the experiment by Mackinnon and Wearing were not analyzed.

While these results give some indications of what constitutes complexity for human decision making, it is clear that we are far from a general understanding of the nature of complexity in dynamic decision making.

2.2 Feedback Quality

As noted in Sect. 1.2, there are two ways in which feedback quality may be varied: the amount and form of the information about the state of the system may vary. So far, there seem to have been no studies which have varied the amount of information.

Brigham and Laios (1975) studied subjects' ability to maintain a target level in a leaking container in a simulation of an operator task in a process plant. They found that subjects were able to reach and maintain a high level of control if they were allowed to observe the flow from the various containers in the process, but they failed to do so if they were only given information about the level in different containers from instruments. These results are consistent with Johnson-Laird's hypothesis (Johnson-Laird 1983) that the source of mental models is perception, and it suggests that some ways of presenting information may be more effective than others. We will return to this result in subsequent subsections.

2.3 Feedback Delay

Using the simulated fire-fighting task, Brehmer and Allard have found in a series of studies (Brehmer and Allard 1988b, c, d) that their subjects were able to cope with the delays that are inherent in the physical process of fire fighting by open-loop control but that they were unable to cope with delays caused by slow information flows in this manner. Specifically, the subjects learned to cope with delays caused by the fact that it takes time to move fire-fighting units and to put out fires by means of a simple open-loop strategy involving rapid and massive responses to a fire, but that they failed to compensate for slow reporting of results. Consequently, slow reporting caused them to lag behind in their control actions. Brehmer (1989) has speculated that these results may be due to the fact that the delays caused by inherent features of the physical processes can be directly observed, while the delays caused by slow reporting must be inferred, and noted the similarity with the Brigham and Laios results. He also pointed to other results where subjects were unable to handle delays caused by processes that could not be observed; for example, experiments by Sterman (1988a, b) who used a simulated economic game to study the effects of delays illustrate this.

These results again underline the importance of not viewing these tasks merely in terms of systems concepts. Obviously, not all delays are equal. To a subject, delays that can be observed while they happen do not seem to have the same disastrous effect that delays that have to be inferred have. This is, of course, only a hypothesis based on inferences from a comparison of very different experiments, and it needs to be tested in more direct experiments.

2.4 Possibilities for Decentralized Control

Decentralizing control to local commanders is one way to compensate for delays caused by slow reporting. Brehmer and Allard (1988b, c, d) provided an opportunity for instituting such decentralized control in their fire-fighting task, but found that subjects were not willing to use it and furthermore that they used it no more frequently under conditions where there were delays in reporting than when there were no delays. Indeed, the use of decentralized control decreased with time in their experiment. Dörner (1980) points to such centralization of control as one symptom of dysfunctional thinking caused by what he called the "intellectual emergency reaction" in complex tasks.

2.5 Rate of Change

Brehmer and Allard (1988e) varied the rate of change in their fire-fighting task and found, not surprisingly, that a task with a high rate of change was harder to control than a task with a low rate of change. However, in a transfer test, they found that although there was positive transfer, subjects transferred to a task with a lower rate of change performed worse than subjects who had practised on a task with this particular rate of change from the start. Similarly, subjects who had practised with a low rate of change performed worse when transferred to a task with a higher rate of change than subjects who had practised on the high rate of change from the start. Brehmer and Allard interpreted these results to mean that the subjects had incorporated the actual rate of change in their control strategies and speculated that this may be part of the "process feel" that experienced operators exhibit.

Crossman and Cooke (1974), using a simulated process involving controlling the level in a container, found positive transfer only when subjects were transferred to a slower task.

The explanation for the differences between the Brehmer and Allard and Crossman and Cooke results is not clear. An important factor in this connection may be the relative role of open-loop and feedback control in the strategies employed by the subjects in these tasks, but no detailed evidence is available on this point. It is important to note that the actual rate of change was quite high in the slow conditions of both the Brehmer and Allard and Crossman and Cooke studies, and that neither of these studies can be said to have been concerned with very slow systems. So far, there have thus been no studies of very slow systems where subjects may have problems perceiving the dynamics of the system.

2.6 Relation between the Characteristics of the Process to be Controlled and the Characteristics of the Control Process

This is clearly one of the most important aspects of a dynamic task since it determines the kind of strategy required, but so far there are no studies on this topic. There is evidence from prediction experiments that subjects have considerable problems predicting exponential growth, and both Dörner *et al.* (1983) and Brehmer (1987) have commented on the possibility that the exponential processes to be controlled may be part of the difficulty in the tasks they employed. However, the process to be controlled is only half of the problem, and whether or not it is difficult to control an exponential process may be dependent on the nature of the control process. Perhaps it is particularly difficult to control exponential processes only when the control process is linear (as it was in the Brehmer and Allard experiments).

Mackinnon and Wearing (1985) present results relevant to the problem of whether subjects are able to cope with the process characteristics of their control actions. Using a simple abstract dynamic system they investigated subjects' ability to cope with systems that "remembered" their inputs for various periods of time. They found that subjects achieved a higher level of control for systems that retained their inputs for a long time than for systems that retained their inputs for a short time. These two kinds of systems differ with respect to their relative inertia. A system that retains previous inputs for a long time will, of course, be less affected by recent inputs than a system that retains a previous input for only a limited time.

The Mackinnon and Wearing results give a first hint that the subjects' understanding of the process characteristics of their actions may be important, but we are obviously far from a complete understanding of this important aspect of a dynamic decision task.

3. General Conclusions

As should be obvious even from the brief review above, we know very little about people's ability to control dynamic systems and the conditions that affect this ability. The main reason for this is, of course, that there has been very little research in the area. Nevertheless, the results available so far seem to have produced one important result: the nature of the feedback available is of crucial importance. Thus, subjects seem to learn to cope with those aspects about which they have direct and concrete feedback, but not with those that they need to infer from indirect information. This conclusion, if substantiated by future research, has wide implications for understanding human decision making in dynamic systems.

Clearly, the processes producing feedback information are not concrete and visible in very many cases. Consequently, we should expect that people will have considerable problems with many dynamic systems. The analyses by Sterman (1988a,b) substantiate this for one important class of systems, namely economical systems. Sterman shows how important dysfunctional aspects of the economic (mis)behavior of managers can be understood in terms of their inability to cope with feedback delays in systems where the processes producing these delays cannot be seen directly.

Bibliography

Ashby W R 1956 *Introduction to Cybernetics.* Chapman and Hall, London

Bainbridge L, Beishon J, Hemming J M, Splaine M 1974 A study of real-time human decision-making using a plant simulator. In: Edwards E, Lees F P (eds.) *The Human Operator in Process Control.* Taylor and Francis, London.

Baum A S, Drury C G 1976 Modelling the human process operator. *Int. J. Man–Mach. Stud.* **8,** 1–11

Brehmer B 1987 Systems design and the psychology of complex systems. In: Rasmussen J, Zunde P (eds.) *Empirical Foundations of Information and Software Science.* Plenum, New York

Brehmer B 1988 Organization for decision making in complex systems. In: Goodstein L, Andersen H B, Oleson S (eds.) *Tasks, Mental Models and Human Error.* Taylor and Francis, London

Brehmer B 1989 Strategies in real time dynamic decision making. In: Hogarth R (ed.) *Insights in Decision Making.* University of Chicago Press, Chicago, Illinois (in press)

Brehmer B, Allard R 1988a *Complexity in Dynamic Decision Making: Effects of a Variation in the Relative Effectiveness of Different Control Actions,* Technical Report No. 407. University of Uppsala, Uppsala

Brehmer B, Allard R 1988b *Dynamic Decision Making: Effects of Complexity and Feedback Delay,* Technical Report No. 405. University of Uppsala, Uppsala

Brehmer B, Allard R 1988c *Feedback Delays in Dynamic Decision Making,* Technical Report No. 406. University of Uppsala, Uppsala

Brehmer B, Allard R 1988d *Learning by Doing in Real Time Dynamic Decision Making.* Technical Report No. 409. University of Uppsala, Uppsala

Brehmer B, Allard R 1988e *Rate of Change in Real Time, Dynamic Decision Making,* Technical Report No. 401. Uppsala University, Uppsala

Brigham F R, Laios L 1975 Operator performance in the control of a laboratory process plant. *Ergonomics* **18,** 53–66

Crossman E R F W, Cooke J E 1974 Manual control of slow response systems. In: Edwards E, Lees F P (eds.) *The Human Operator in Process Control.* Taylor and Francis, London

Dörner D 1980 On the problems people have in dealing with complexity. *Simulation Games* **11,** 87–106

Dörner D, Kreuzig H, Reither, R, Stäudel T 1983 *Lohhausen: Vom Umgang mit Komplexität und Unbestimmtheit.* Huber, Berne

Edwards W 1962 Dynamic decision theory and probabilistic information processing. *Hum. Factors* **4,** 59–73

Johnson-Laird P N 1983 *Mental Models.* Cambridge University Press, Cambridge

Kluwe R, Reimann H 1983 *Problemlösen bei Vernetzten, Komplexen Problemen: Effekte der Verbalisierens auf die Problemlöseleistung,* Technical Report No. 1. Hochschule der Bundeswehr, Hamburg

Mackinnon A J, Wearing A J 1980 Complexity and decision making. *Behav. Sci.* **25,** 285–96

Mackinnon A J, Wearing A J 1985 Systems analysis and dynamic decision making. *Acta Psychol.* **58,** 159–72

Rapoport A 1975 Research paradigms for studying dynamic decision behavior. In: Wendt D, Vlek C (eds.) *Utility, Probability and Human Decision Making.* Reidel, Dordrecht

Sterman J D 1988a *Misperceptions of Feedback in Dynamic Decisionmaking,* Working Paper WP-1899-97. Massachusetts Institute of Technology, Cambridge, Massachusetts

Sterman J D 1988b *Modeling Managerial Behavior: Misperceptions of Feedback in a Dynamic Decisionmaking Experiment,* Working Paper WP-1933-87. Massachusetts Institute of Technology, Cambridge, Massachusetts

B. Brehmer
[Uppsala University, Uppsala, Sweden]

E

Evidentiary Reasoning and Human Information Processing

In legal, medical, business, military and other contexts we can find ready examples of the necessity for drawing defensible conclusions from a mass of evidence having the following general characteristics.

(a) However massive the collection of evidence, it is *incomplete* in its coverage of matters judged to be relevant to the possible conclusions or hypotheses being considered.

(b) The evidence items taken separately or on aggregate are *inconclusive* with regard to the hypotheses being considered; i.e., the evidence fails to make any particular conclusion necessary or certain.

(c) The evidence is *unreliable* to some extent, coming, as it does, from human or mechanical sources having any gradation of credibility.

We can also readily observe how our present methods for collecting, transmitting and storing information are far better, both in number and quality, than our methods for drawing conclusions from this information; we are simply much more adept at collecting information than we are in using it for inferential purposes. Quite obviously, if we are to close this particular technology gap, we must know more than we presently do about evidence and its inferential uses. The acquisition of such knowledge is an enterprise now shared by persons in many different disciplines.

The terms "evidentiary reasoning" and "human information processing" are, in fact, elements of a terminology that began to come into existence in the 1950s. At this time, developments in information theory (or statistical communications theory) as well as in computer science and technology led psychologists and others to adopt the metaphor of persons as information processors in the various tasks that they perform. Argument continues about whether or not this metaphor is useful in attempts to obtain a better understanding of human sensory, perceptual, motor, and cognitive or intellectual functions. The term evidentiary (or evidential) reasoning has recently become popularized and, in fact, covers matters that have been of concern for centuries among logicians, probabilists, scholars of evidence in jurisprudence, psychologists and others. The use of this term simply covers whatever matters are involved in the inferential use of evidence. The present coupling of these two terms has a purpose; some human information-processing tasks involve the use of evidence in order to draw conclusions from it. As we proceed, it becomes apparent that two natural questions arise: "How *should* we draw conclusions from evidence?" and "How *do* we draw conclusions from evidence?" One important and interesting question now at issue concerns the nature of the relationship between these two basic questions.

A person attempting to form a coherent view of contemporary research on evidential reasoning and human information processing faces something similar to the technology gap mentioned above. Many ideas have been generated on matters relevant to the inferential use of evidence, but what these ideas mean when taken together is far from obvious. With advances in computer science and technology came the hope that computers could assist persons facing difficult inference and decision tasks; with this hope came enormous enthusiasm in the study of ways of using computers to provide such assistance. Initially, much was promised by the designers of expert systems and other knowledge-based systems for assistance in inference and decision tasks; as a result, much is now expected of these designers by the public. However, human inferential reasoning is a very rich intellectual activity and involves many elements, some of which are only poorly understood. It is no idle matter to answer either of the questions posed above. Definitive answers to these questions, even in simple inferential exercises, have eluded some of the finest minds in history. When we have a mass of incomplete, inconclusive and unreliable evidence to contend with, the inferential issues we face have positively baroque complexity. Some of this complexity becomes apparent when we consider elements of actual human inference tasks performed in many different situations.

1. Characteristics of Evidential Reasoning

It would greatly simplify matters if the inferential tasks performed by medical diagnosticians, jurors, intelligence analysts, business forecasters, scientists and others all involved just one species of reasoning. Commonly, we are led to believe that there are just two species of reasoning: deductive reasoning as the task of showing that a conclusion is *necessary*, and inductive reasoning as the task of showing that a conclusion is *probable* to some degree. In recent years, however, attention has been paid to a third species, called abductive reasoning, in which some new conclusion is identified as *possible*. In a very informative and interesting collection of papers Eco and Sebeok (1983) relate how the US philosopher Charles Sanders Peirce was considering what he termed abductive reasoning as the basis for imaginative or creative thought, at the very same time that Sir Arthur Conan Doyle was "programming" Sherlock Holmes with abductive capabilities. Some philosophers such as Peirce have argued that there is more to imaginative or creative thought than can be accounted for in terms of deduction and induction. Others argue that abductive and inductive reasoning are very similar since they both proceed from evidence to hypotheses or conclusions.

The problem is that it is quite easy to discern various mixtures of all three of these forms of reasoning in most human inference tasks; "pure" deductive, inductive or abductive reasoning tasks seem to be encountered only in contrived exercises in the classroom. The reason for the lack of inferential purity seems quite obvious. In only a few inferential or diagnostic tasks are the essential ingredients of such tasks provided for us; very few human inference problems spring forth in a well-posed form in which all necessary ingredients are known. Hence, we have to generate or discover plausible conclusions as well as evidential tests of these possibilities. Furthermore, we are obliged to structure defensible arguments from our evidence for our conclusions. In constructing these arguments we encounter many difficulties: some are due to the intricate relationships we can readily discern among evidence and possible conclusions. Other difficulties arise because of the nonstationary nature of the world about us; with new evidence and/or corrected insight, we discern new possibilities and, in turn, identify new evidence and new lines of argument. These activities require various mixtures of the three identified forms of reasoning.

In some contexts (e.g., law and medicine) inference tasks form a necessary part of decision making; there is uncertainty about various possible consequence-producing states and we seek to remove at least some of this uncertainty, before a choice is necessary, by collecting and evaluating evidence judged to be relevant to the situation at hand. In other contexts such as science, inference tasks may not be associated with specific choices we have to make, but they are nevertheless associated with the basic process of knowledge acquisition. In all of these situations, whether choice-related or not, the discovery of hypotheses/possibilities and valid evidentiary tests of them are necessary. In at least one context, Anglo-American jurisprudence, some attempt is made to separate the process of discovery from other processes such as "proof" and choice. By "proof" here we mean the process of defending evidence-based arguments on possible conclusions in some forum such as a court trial. However, in most other contexts the process of discovery never ceases and one can easily observe various cycles of the processes of discovery, proof and choice. In such complex activity there may be several "actors," each having some distinguishable inferential role to play.

Thus, theories of evidentiary reasoning and human information processing have to acknowledge that people naturally perform inference tasks in which mixtures of these three species of reasoning are required. This adds considerable difficulty to any assessment of the suitability of formal or logical theories of inference; human inference seems rather too rich an activity to expect that all of this richness can be captured within the confines of a single axiom-based formal system. In addition, we should exercise care in interpreting the results of behavioral experiments on human reasoning skills; tasks given to persons in laboratory evaluations of their intellectual skills may bear little resemblance to the tasks these same persons encounter in their everyday lives.

2. Formal Issues in Evidentiary Reasoning

Canons or rules for valid deductive reasoning have been with us since antiquity, but similar canons for inductive reasoning have been much more difficult to identify. In addition, it is not easy to prescribe the behavior necessary to generate new ideas and valid evidentiary tests of them. In this brief survey of contemporary work on the logical or formal underpinnings of evidential reasoning, we confine attention to the substantial progress made during the past few years in understanding the process of inductive or probabilistic reasoning. In fact, this is quite an exciting time to have interest in such matters; for the very first time we have a variety of well-articulated views about the process of drawing conclusions from incomplete, inconclusive and unreliable evidence. Each of these views has something unique to say about probabilistic reasoning, but none has all there is to say.

2.1 Bayes' Rule

In the conventional view of probability as an additive set function defined on the interval [0, 1], a canon for inductive reasoning emerges from the manner in which a conditional probability is defined within this view; this canon is termed Bayes' rule after the putative discoverer of its essential properties (however, see Stigler (1983)). Using modern terminology, Bayes' rule tells us that the probability of some hypothesis or possibility H, upon observation of or after knowledge of evidence E, is the normalized product of the prior probability of H and the likelihood of evidence E, if H were true. Symbolically, $p(H|E) = p(H)p(E|H)/p(E)$. The normalizing term $p(E)$ simply ensures that $p(H|E) + p(\text{not-}H|E) = 1.0$, as required by the conventional view of probability. In its pristine form shown above, Bayes' rule tells us very little about probabilistic reasoning expect that it is a prior–posterior analysis; this rule tells us how to convert a prior belief in H, expressed by $p(H)$, into a posterior belief in H, upon observation of evidence E. The likelihood term $p(E|H)$ tells us something about the value of evidence E in a revision of our prior belief in H. With appropriate accounting for possible conditional nonindependence among evidence items, Bayes' rule can be applied sequentially in the process of belief revision as new evidence arrives.

Bayes' rule has been a subject of controversy ever since its first appearance in 1763; most of the controversy involves how we ever get the inferential process started in the first place. How should we express our *initial* belief in H before we have collected any evidence? How one answers this question depends on one's view of the basis for probability expressions. There are many logically distinguishable forms of evidence and various basic ways in which evidence items appear in combination; each of these forms and combinations of evidence reveals interesting and important subtleties that may be exploited in inference if they are recognized. In addition, the inferential linkage between evidence and hypotheses/possibilities may involve several reasoning stages; chains of reasoning are said to be cascaded, catenated or hierarchical in nature. Other important evidential subtleties, many involving the credibility of the sources of evidence, are revealed when the cascaded nature of most human inference is recognized. It is entirely fair to ask what Bayes' rule has to say about these evidential subtleties.

The richness and flexibility of conventional probability theory is quite apparent to anyone who samples the array of disciplinary areas in which this theory has been meaningfully and usefully applied. The simple formula known as Bayes' rule can be expanded so that it can incorporate the many recognized forms and combinations of evidence as well as the complex chains of reasoning occurring in cascaded inference. Such expansions show how we can expose for study and analysis a remarkable array of evidential and inferential subtleties (summarized in Schum (1987)). Among the subtleties that can be captured in Bayesian analyses are the following:

(a) conflicting and contradictory evidence from multiple sources,

(b) the various forms of redundant evidence,

(c) corroborative and convergent evidence as well as evidence that enhances the value of other evidence,

(d) second-hand or hearsay evidence,

(e) negative and missing evidence,

(f) a variety of matters associated with the credibility of the sources from which evidence comes,

(g) the temporal order of event occurrence; and

(h) inferential transitivity and other order-related effects in chains of reasoning.

In many contexts persons wish to know what questions they should be asking of their evidence; Bayesian analyses can supply such questions as well as some suggestions about what to do with answers that are obtained.

There are, however, some inferential matters that Bayesian analyses handle poorly, if at all; these matters become especially important when probabilistic expressions are construed in the epistemic sense of "degrees of belief." Questions about the general suitability of the conventional calculus of probability, when applied in epistemic situations, have been with us for quite some time (e.g., Hacking 1975). Some of these difficulties involve the additivity property of conventional probability; for some event F, if $p(F) = 0.8$, it must also be the case that $p(\text{not-F}) = 0.2$ in order to be consistent within this system. One alternative to the conventional view of probability is the nonadditive system of belief functions proposed by Shafer (1976). This system, rooted in the works of several early probabilists, has many remarkable properties, some of which concern the discovery-related issues mentioned above.

2.2 Shafer's Theory of Belief Systems

Discussion of probabilistic inference would be much simpler if agreement could be reached about what the inferential "weight" of evidence means. Shafer tells us that the weight of evidence is related to the support that the evidence provides for hypotheses being considered, and offers a numerical system for assigning evidential support that can result in nonadditive beliefs about these hypotheses. Many important credal or belief states find ready expression in Shafer's system; one of the most important concerns the distinction between disbelief and lack of belief. In assigning evidential support to our hypotheses according to Shafer's rules, we are free to withhold evidential support from any hypothesis or collection of hypotheses by leaving this support uncommitted in various ways. One result is that our belief in H and our belief in not-H need not sum to 1.0. Another result is that if, at the moment, we have no evidence supporting H, this does not mean that we necessarily disbelieve H; we simply lack any basis for believing H. Suppose, at the start of some inferential problem, we have no evidence at all and, therefore, no basis for belief in any H. If this is the case, we are justified in saying that we are in a state of ignorance as far as these hypotheses are concerned. In such an instance we would leave all of our belief uncommitted among H and not-H. Several other important credal states find ready expression in Shafer's system; for example, the credal state "doubt about H" is taken to be the degree to which we believe not-H.

One of the most important aspects of Shafer's work is his acknowledgement of the role of imagination in probabilistic inference and its bearing upon the process of discovery. Although Shafer's theory of belief functions is not a theory of the discovery process, it does acknowledge the various ways in which hypotheses or possible conclusions arise and may be revised in light of new evidence. New evidence may suggest new or revised hypotheses and, in turn, new or revised hypotheses may cause us to alter our interpretations of the weight of the evidence. At the start of some inferential problem the evidence we have may allow us to entertain only vague or undifferentiated hypotheses. Later evidence may be more specific in its focus, hence allowing us to refine or sharpen the hypotheses we consider. Thus, in a murder investigation, early evidence may bear only upon whether the person responsible was male or female, two quite vague possibilities. Later evidence may bear upon other characteristics of the appearance and behavior of this person and, ultimately, evidence may focus upon a particular person. In Shafer's terms, our "frames of discernment" of possibilities change over time and with the evidence we collect; new frames of discernment may cause us to make new assessments of the meaning of the evidence we have.

Within the system of belief functions, the algebraic rule for combining evidential support across items or bodies of evidence is called Dempster's rule; in common with Bayes' rule, Dempster's rule has controversial features. One concerns the manner in which beliefs based on dissonant or conflicting evidence are combined. Suppose we believe that body or item of evidence E_1 offers some support to H and that body or item E_2 offers some support for not-H. Apparently, we must then assign some positive degree of support to the empty intersection of H and not-H, in violation of Shafer's rules for assigning evidential support. Dempster's rule contains an adjustment process by which we simply discard whatever support is given to inconsistent possibilities. By such a process we at least identify the degree to which we hold inconsistent beliefs; but the discarding of such inconsistencies has not met with universal approval.

2.3 Baconian System of Probability

Bayes's rule asks us to consider the relative likeliness of hypotheses based on evidence we have and the Shafer–Dempster system asks us to consider the degree of support evidence provides for our hypotheses. In either case a particular item or body of evidence can make some hypothesis appear more or less probable. However, there is another commonly recognized form of inductive inference in which we use evidence, not to support hypotheses or make them seem more or less probable, but as a basis for eliminating them. In such a process some hypothesis becomes increasingly probable to the extent that it resists our best efforts to eliminate it. This eliminative form of induction can be traced back to the work of Francis Bacon and John Stuart Mill; owing to the work of Cohen (1977) we now have a "Baconian" system of probability that is quite congenial to the eliminative use of evidence. This system has many remarkable properties that add considerably to our understanding of probabilistic reasoning.

If we are entertaining some collection of hypotheses and wish to devise a sequence of evidentiary tests to eliminate some of them, we would certainly not perform the same test over and over again unless the reliability of the test was questionable; we would perform a variety of different tests thought to be relevant in discriminating among these hypotheses, since for a hypothesis to remain in serious contention it must hold under a variety of conditions. So, in this sense, eliminative induction is also variative in nature. It is certainly true that our confidence in some hypothesis is related to the number of relevant tests we perform; the more different tests a certain hypothesis passes the more we are justified in placing our confidence in it. Here we have the basis for Cohen's Baconian conception of the weight of evidence.

Cohen argues that the weight of evidence, in common with other things, can be measured in different ways, each of which may be useful. For example, we can price oranges by their number, weight or volume and each serves some useful purpose. Cohen tells us that the weight of evidence is usually measured in terms of the amount of evidence we have considered. The matter of basic concern here is the completeness of coverage of our evidence on matters judged to be relevant. According to Cohen, useful measures of probability should grade the extent or completeness of coverage of the evidence on matters judged to be relevant in the inference at hand and that part of our uncertainty about hypotheses is related to the number of evidential tests of them that we might have but did not perform. The more complete our evidentiary coverage of relevant matters, the more confidence we can place in any hypothesis that resists being disconfirmed by this evidence. Cohen argues that the conventional system of probability, to its great disadvantage, offers no way of grading completeness of evidential coverage.

The system of Baconian probabilities is a purely ordinal system for grading what Cohen terms the provability of hypotheses. However, this system has considerable power in spite of the fact that we cannot meaningfully combine Baconian probabilities by any algebraic means because of their purely ordinal properties. One of its most interesting properties bears resemblance to a property of Shafer's belief functions. A Baconian probability of zero for some hypothesis H simply indicates that we lack any proof for this hypothesis; it does not mean that we have disproved it. However, even though H may have a Baconian probability of zero at some stage, this does not mean that it must remain at zero forever (as would be the case if we assigned a conventional probability of zero to some hypothesis). We can go from lack of proof to some degree of proof, but we cannot go from disproof to any gradation of proof. Similarly, a belief function of zero for H means that we simply lack belief in H and *not* that we disbelieve it.

2.4 Fuzzy Reasoning

Together, Cohen and Shafer have compiled quite a list of anomalies and paradoxes that accompany the application of conventional probability in many inferential contexts. Both utterly reject the idea that Bayes' rule represents *the* canon for probabilistic reasoning. Yet another view critical of conventional probability involves an evidential characteristic we have not yet mentioned—imprecision. In many situations we find it natural to grade our uncertainty about events by means of verbal statements such as "very likely," "unlikely," "very improbable" and so on. These three verbal assessments are all examples of what have been termed fuzzy probabilities (Zadeh 1978). In a court trial, for example, you believe it "fairly probable" that the event reported by a certain witness did, in fact, occur. Asked to report a number to accompany this verbal statement, you might find it rather difficult to do so because of the fuzzy or imprecisely quantified evidence you have heard bearing upon the credibility of this witness. What you have heard is the following:

(a) this witness has "good character,"
(b) he "usually" tells the truth,
(c) he has "good eyesight," and
(d) he is "usually" objective in forming his beliefs based upon the sensory evidence he receives.

The best you can do is to be similarly imprecise in expressing your own beliefs, based on evidence of this sort.

The early work of Zadeh (1965) stimulated a continuously vigorous level of effort in research on fuzzy reasoning; the results of this research have found application in a variety of inferential situations. One of Zadeh's major contributions was the development of a calculus for combining fuzzy or inexact statements; he has given us some very precise methods for coping with imprecision. Zadeh has consistently argued that the two-valued logic forming the underpinnings of conventional probability theory cannot apply to the inexact reasoning tasks faced in so many situations; what is required is the multivalued logic that forms the basis for a calculus of fuzzy reasoning. Not surprisingly, this calculus has entirely different rules for handling event combinations than does the conventional probability calculus. However, the basic rules for fuzzy reasoning have two properties that also occur in Cohen's system of Baconian probability; these rules concern the operations of union and intersection and involve min–max operations rather than multiplication and addition.

All the formal probabilistic reasoning systems mentioned so far have found application in research on artificial intelligence. However, the developers of various knowledge-based systems have not been averse to developing various nonstandard logics for "approximate" or "inexact" inferential reasoning (see Turner 1984). Some expert systems result from the trapping of the heuristics or rules of thumb that alleged experts say they use in diagnostic or inferential reasoning. In some of these systems there have been attempts to develop heuristics for combining assessments of uncertainty rather than to use the rules from any formal reasoning system; one example involves the "certainty factors" and their combination in a system called MYCIN (Buchanan and Shortliffe 1984). The development of inexact or approximate methods for probabilistic reasoning arises not out of sloth on the part of developers of knowledge-based systems; formal analyses of the inference tasks of interest suggest that coping with all of the probabilistic ingredients such analyses identify would be inferentially paralytic.

3. Behavioral Issues in Human Information Processing

Highly skilled human performance is certainly not unheard of, even in very demanding tasks in which there is an enormous amount of information to be processed; the pilot of an aircraft must continually process information from nearly all of his/her senses in order to fly safely from A to B. Such skill is, of course, purchased with currency in the form of training and practice; we hear of no person who can pilot a Boeing 747 in the total absence of any kind of flight training. Since the late nineteenth century, psychologists and others have been concerned about various human performance capabilities and limitations. From much of the contemporary literature on human inferential reasoning skills, it appears that researchers in this area are more concerned about our limitations than about our capabilities.

It has appeared natural for behavioral researchers to ask how "good" human performance is in inferential reasoning and other decision-related tasks. The word good appears in quotes since its use presupposes some normative or prescriptive standard against which goodness can be measured. Presumably, inferential standards come from formal or logical representations of the inference tasks in which human performance is being assessed. Thus, for example, we might wish to compare probability assessments made by people with calculations made using some probability algorithm we believe represents the task and the evidential ingredients provided for the persons whose probabilistic reasoning capabilities are being evaluated. Consider the following probabilistic reasoning task: you are told that the probability of a "success" on any trial of a particular experiment, on which either a "success" or a "failure" can occur, remains constant over trials at $p = 0.37$. You are then asked to estimate the probability that there will be between 22 and 24 successes (inclusive) if 75 trials of this experiment were actually performed. How well you perform this task is to be measured by how close your estimate comes to a probability calculated using the Bernoulli probability distribution; the answer Bernoulli provides is 0.1544 (rounded).

Would you feel offended if your estimate was considerably smaller or larger than 0.1544 and you were then told, in either case, that you were "suboptimal" as a processor of probabilistic information? If you did know something about probability, you might have asked to have access to a calculator or to relevant tables in which probabilities of this sort are provided. However, if you knew nothing at all about Bernoulli's rule for determining such probabilities, you might easily believe there was an element of unfairness in your being branded as inferentially "suboptimal" simply because your estimate deviated from a calculation you had never heard of. You might be particularly offended if you were, say, a physician who had, on more than one occasion, evaluated substantial collections of inconclusive evidence and had then made diagnoses that were instrumental in the recovery of your patients.

Using a wide variety of contrived inferential reasoning problems, many behavioral researchers have concluded that the inferential judgements people make are typically suboptimal when they are compared with solutions to these problems provided by some formal expression taken to represent the problem at hand. On occasion the terms "irrational," "error-prone" and "biased" are used to describe human inferential behavior. Some of these studies have involved very simple reasoning tasks and some have involved quite complex matters involving ingredients such as the Bernoulli distribution mentioned above. In many person versus model studies, human judgements deviate from normative solutions in systematic ways. On some interpretations of these results, people are said to develop heuristics or rules of thumb that may serve various purposes but which also represent biases or systematic errors that can be very troublesome in inference and decision tasks. One very influential account of behavioral studies of human judgements under uncertainty concludes that these studies paint a "blemished portrait" of human inferential capabilities (Kahneman *et al.* 1982). The existence of various human inferential heuristics thought to be inappropriate is now accepted as orthodox by many persons in the behavioral sciences and elsewhere; efforts are now underway to develop methods for eliminating various suspected biases in human judgements.

The human inferential incompetence alleged in many behavioral studies, if taken seriously, cannot come as good news given the importance of human reasoning capability in law, medicine, science, government, business and elsewhere. In addition, the developers of expert systems that rest upon heuristic judgements cannot take comfort in the suggestion that these judgements are likely to be biased or erroneous in various ways. However, there are other possible interpretations that may be placed on the results of behavioral studies of inferential reasoning. Most behavioral studies of probabilistic reasoning assume that the conventional system of probability supplies all relevant rules for probabilistic reasoning. A person is said to be behaving coherently or rationally if his/her probability estimates have the same properties as those forming the basis for conventional probability. Thus, a person who estimates the probability of rain tomorrow as 0.6 and the probability of not-rain tomorrow as 0.2 might be said to be behaving irrationally. However, if, on available evidence, this person decided to withhold a portion of his/her beliefs, the above nonadditive expression of probabilistic beliefs would be entirely consistent within Shafer's system of belief functions. Similar examples can easily be constructed that illustrate how probabilistic responses inconsistent with Bayes' rule are not necessarily inconsistent when given a Baconian interpretation.

There is now a substantial level of reaction to the bleak assessments of human inferential competence offered by many behavioral scientists. In several works, Cohen (e.g., Cohen 1981, 1986) has argued that experimental evaluations of inferential reasoning capability are tests of the state of our education rather than tests of our intellectual competence and that they often represent either the application of inappropriate normative theory or the misapplication of appropriate normative theory. Cohen went on to argue that human irrationality could not be established in laboratory experiments of the sort behavioral scientists have been employing. Phillips (1982, 1983) has argued that instructions given to research subjects are often vague and that, as a consequence, subjects may perceive the structure of an inference problem in a different way from the experimenter. He also argues that behavioral research on human inference represents study of just the first impressions a person may have about an inference problem; these studies may say nothing at all about how a person would behave if given the opportunity to reflect upon the problem and the judgements it requires.

In most laboratory evaluations of human inferential behavior, the tasks given to a research subject are usually inferentially "pure" in the sense described earlier; that is, they are contrived to be instances of some particular reasoning form or step. On the view that most actual human inference tasks involve mixtures of deductive, inductive and abductive reasoning, it is difficult to accept indictments of general reasoning competence on the basis of studies that involve just one particular inferential form. The same person who fails to reason in exact accordance with a conventional probability prescription may be particularly adept at generating exciting new possibilities from evidence as well as valid evidential tests of them. Using the term suboptimal to describe this person seems not only unfair but foolish as well.

4. Prescriptions and Descriptions

In discussing some aspect of inferential reasoning a person will usually be asked to state whether he/she is speaking prescriptively or descriptively; that is, does this discussion involve how one ought to behave or how one actually does behave? There is certainly an accumulation of evidence suggesting that prescriptions from conventional probability theory fail to describe observed human behavior in making probabilistic judgements; what interpretation is to be placed on this evidence is now a matter of controversy. One might be tempted to ask what merit formal analyses have when they fail to be descriptive of actual human behavior; if human behavior deviates systematically from some inferential canon, may we not reasonably inquire about the legitimacy of the canon? Cohen, Shafer and others have argued that certain deviations from conventional canons for probabilistic reasoning are easily explicable using other views of such reasoning.

However, there is a third sense in which some formal or logical analysis of probabilistic reasoning can be interpreted; such analyses can at least tell us how we *might* behave, given some inferential task involving the assessment and combination of fallible evidence. Thus, for example, though both the prescriptive and descriptive status of Bayes' rule have been questioned, this rule suggests many questions that might be asked of evidence and it supplies possible ways of combining answers that are obtained when these questions are asked. The same applies to the other formal systems of probabilistic reasoning discussed in Sect. 2. In short, logical analyses of probabilistic inference can have distinct heuristic value even though they cannot be defended as prescriptions for ideal or rational behavior or as descriptions of actual behavior. Given the complexity of most human inferential reasoning tasks, it is far too much to ask of any single formal system that it give an account of all of the evidential and inferential subtleties observable when these tasks are examined in detail.

See also: Cognitive Science, Human Information Processing and Artificial Intelligence; Fuzzy Reasoning Methods; Human Information Processing; Hypothesis Testing

Bibliography

Buchanan B, Shortliffe E 1984 *Rule-Based Expert Systems*. Addison–Wesley, Reading, Massachusetts
Cohen L J 1977 *The Probable and the Provable*. Clarendon Press, Oxford
Cohen L J 1981 Can human irrationality be experimentally demonstrated. *Behav. Brain Sci.* **4**, 317–70
Cohen L J 1986 *The Dialogue of Reason*. Clarendon Press, Oxford
Eco U, Sebeok T 1983 *The Sign of Three: Dupin, Holmes, Peirce*. Indiana University Press, Bloomington, Indiana
Hacking I 1975 *The Emergence of Probability*. Cambridge University Press, Cambridge
Kahneman D, Slovic P, Tversky A 1982 *Judgment under Uncertainty: Heuristics and Biases*. Cambridge University Press, Cambridge
Phillips L 1982 Generation theory. In: *Choice Models for Buyer Behavior: Research in Marketing*. JAI Press, Greenwich, Connecticut
Phillips L 1983 Theoretical perspectives on heuristics and biases in probabilistic thinking. In: *Analyzing and Aiding Decision Processes*. North-Holland, Amsterdam
Schum D 1987 *Evidence and Inference for the Intelligence Analyst*. University Press of America, Lanham, Maryland
Shafer G 1976 *A Mathematical Theory of Evidence*. Princeton University Press, Princeton, New Jersey
Stigler S 1983 Who discovered Bayes' theorem? *Am. Stat.* **37**(4), 290–96
Turner R 1984 *Logics for Artificial Intelligence*. Ellis Horwood, Chichester
Zadeh L 1965 Fuzzy sets. *Inf. Control* **8**, 338–53
Zadeh L 1978 Fuzzy sets as a basis for a theory of possibility. *Fuzzy Sets Syst.* **1**, 3–28

D. A. Schum
[George Mason University, Fairfax, Virginia, USA]

Expert Database Systems

Expert database systems (EDSs) represent a new class of system architectures that support knowledge-based applications requiring access to large shared databases. This article explores the concepts, tools, techniques and architectures that make up this new and dynamic field.

Expert database systems allow the specification, prototyping and implementation of knowledge-based information systems that represent a vertical extension beyond the well-defined, predictable, transaction-oriented systems to those with knowledge-directed reasoning and interpretation under conditions of uncertainty.

During the past few years, expert database systems has emerged as a vibrant and productive field for research and development. Expert database systems represent the confluence of concepts, tools and techniques from diverse areas such as artificial intelligence (AI), database management (DB), logic programming (LP), information retrieval (IR) and fuzzy systems theory (FST). Three international forums have provided researchers and practitioners the opportunity to present and discuss their latest insights and research results: the first International Workshop on Expert Database Systems (Kerschberg 1986), and the First and Second International Conferences on Expert Database Systems (Kerschberg 1987, 1988).

Basically, an EDS supports applications that require "knowledge-directed processing of shared information" (Smith 1986). Thus, several "intelligent agents" can be envisaged as accessing a shared database, performing knowledge-based reasoning and suggesting (or taking) a series of actions or decisions.

The special appeal of EDSs is that they evoke a variety of ways in which knowledge and expertise can be incorporated into our system architectures. Several relevant scenarios can be envisaged:

(a) an expert system loosely coupled with a database system;

(b) a database management system (DBMS) enhanced with reasoning capabilities to perform knowledge-directed problem solving;

(c) a logic programming system, or an AI knowledge-representation system, enhanced with database access and manipulation primitives;

(d) a knowledge-based controller for query optimization, transaction processing or the management of knowledge/data environments; and

(e) an intelligent natural-language interface to a database system.

All the above architectures are meaningful and there indeed may be many others. The particular one chosen will depend on the application requirements and the availability of tools for their implementation.

1. The Need for Expert Database Systems

The motivations for EDS architectures can be explored in terms of different types of applications. Organizations are rapidly realizing that knowledge-based applications serve as a vehicle for competitive advantage by providing reasoned advice for decision making.

The knowledge required for the application can usually be found in-house, and is culled by means of a process called knowledge engineering. Often, this knowledge will process large amounts of data contained in databases that have been developed over many years.

This application type may best be met by loosely coupling a knowledge-based system and a database system (as in (a) above). An example of such an architecture is the KEE connection product from IntelliCorp, which interfaces the knowledge engineering environment (KEE) with relational DBMSs supporting the SQL query language.

The application domain and its performance requirements will be instrumental in determining the overall EDS architecture. For example, Smith (1986) provides two military applications that require a very tight coupling between multiple expert systems and a database system. The first is an automated map production system in which the DBMS maintains a time-varying model of the world's surface. Raw image data is relayed by satellites and this data must be analyzed by expert systems to extract significant features. Information regarding these features is used to update the map database. The performance bottleneck is in the feature analysis, while the map database may be updated at a later time. The database size is approximately 10^{13} Mbytes.

The second application is a system for naval tactical situation assessment for use on board ship. Static information consists of maps, charts, and ship and weapons characteristics. Dynamic data include contact reports on the position and actions of other ships and aircraft in the vicinity. The database must process hundreds of contact reports per second and alert expert systems which analyze potential threats.

These two applications provide certain requirements for an EDS:

(a) a query language and data model that can express the "semantics" of space and time,

(b) the batched reintegration of updated replicated information in a possibly distributed database,

(c) efficient processing of a large number of situation–action rules (triggers) over the database on the arrival of new information, and

(d) the optimization and processing of recursive logic rules over the database in response to query requests.

In subsequent sections the way in which the fields of DM, AI and LP are dealing with these and related requirements is discussed.

1.1 The Role of Database Management

Database management systems support the organizational concept that data is a corporate resource that must be managed, refined, protected and made available to multiple users who are authorized to use it. Thus, concurrent access to large shared databases is the *raison d'être* of DBMSs. The commercial success of DBMS supporting the relational model of data has enabled users to develop information systems that query and update large structured collections of data that are viewed as "flat files."

However, DBMSs are used in increasingly more complex environments, those in which entities are related in very complex ways and the rules governing their behavior in response to updates need to be made explicit, rather than be hidden in application programs. The above requirements indicate that DBMSs should also be enhanced with reasoning capabilities for performance reasons.

For example, there is a need to manage different types of data: text, graphics, images, computer-aided design (CAD) schemes, and so on. Also, DBMSs are being used to support complex environments such as software engineering environments (SEE), configuration management (CM), and so on. Traditional DBMSs are hard pressed to handle these new duties, and more robust systems—those supporting more semantically meaningful "data models" and new features such as extensibility and long transactions—are being proposed.

This new class of systems is called "object-oriented database systems" (O-ODB) (Dittrich and Dayal 1986, Zaniolo et al. 1986). The goal of O-ODB is to provide data models whose structures, operations and constraints can deal with complex objects *as they are*! This implies that the objects may be hierarchical and the operations on them need not be decomposed into simpler operations. The modelling paradigm for these systems is based on object-oriented programming as exemplified by the Smalltalk language (Goldberg and Robson 1983).

In O-ODB the complex objects are organized into typed classes of objects, and each class has associated with it a collection of permissible operations called methods. In order to perform an operation on an instance (read member) of a class, a message must be sent to the class requesting that the operation be performed. Thus object classes know what types of operations are admissible and they are responsible for the execution of those operations.

In addition, the object classes are organized into type hierarchies in the traditional AI sense with property inheritance. Thus, if an object class does not have the requested method associated with it, the method may be found by moving up the type hierarchy. Such hierarchies are very important for the organization of both data and knowledge; they provide a powerful mechanism for placing data attributes and knowledge predicates (rules, constraints, methods) at the appropriate hierarchy level and object class.

There are many important issues to be addressed when building O-ODB (Zaniolo et al. 1986). These are outlined below:

(a) *Data abstraction and encapsulation.* An object class has a set of operators similar to abstract data types. In terms of the implementation interface, there must be both a public and a private interface.

(b) *Object identity.* Every object has a unique identifier which is independent of the particular property values that the object may have.

(c) *Messages.* Objects communicate by sending messages to one another, each message consisting of a receiver object identifier, the message name and message arguments.

(d) *Property inheritance.* The class hierarchies provide a degree of economy of specification by allowing generic properties to be defined for higher-level object classes and more specialized properties to be associated with lower-level object classes.

(e) *Graphics.* Complex objects and their methods can best be understood and manipulated through object-oriented graphics interfaces.

(f) *Transaction management.* In many complex applications, transactions may run for long time periods, and effective methods are needed to handle consistency control, recovery, and so on.

(g) *Protection.* Objects must be protected at the instance level. This is particularly important when multiple users are collaborating on the design of these objects, so that version control is an important issue.

(h) *Access management.* Specialized access paths, storage structures and main memory management are essential for complex objects.

(i) *Methodologies for object-oriented database design.* The object-oriented paradigm requires new approaches to database design. It is important to be able to model not only data but also knowledge about objects.

Notable projects currently underway to construct the next generation object-oriented DBMSs are POSTGRES at UC-Berkeley (Stonebraker 1986), PROBE at Computer Corporation of America (Manola and Dayal 1986), EXODUS at the University of Wisconsin (Carey et al. 1986), GEMSTONE at the Oregon Graduate Center and Servio Logic Development Corp. (Maier and Stein 1986), and GENESIS at the University of Texas at Austin (Batory 1986).

1.2 The Role of Artificial Intelligence Research

Researchers in AI have become increasingly aware of the need and advantages of EDS architectures. From the AI view, there is a need to have knowledge-based applications access large databases. Smith (1984) has pointed out that the reasoning (inference) component of a knowledge-based system is but a small fraction (6%) of the total system code; real systems require the integration of diverse and possibly distributed data and knowledge sources.

As knowledge bases becomes larger, they pose serious system performance problems. The pattern-matching processes involved in determining which rules are candidates for "firing" are performance bottlenecks because the rules are not indexed with respect to their component predicates. Most expert systems rely on operating system virtual memory techniques (Deering and Faletti 1986), and overall performance degrades under heavy paging requirements. Thus secondary storage access mechanisms are desirable for AI systems. They can be used to index a rule base and to provide fast access to facts stored in database files. The management of a knowledge base is an area of open research, although some results have been obtained (Potter and Kerschberg 1986, Cholvy and Demolombe 1987).

Another important avenue of AI research that impacts EDS is work concerning the knowledge level, and the insights gained by asking modal questions regarding the knowledge base and knowledge derived through inference (Brachman and Levesque 1986, 1987). By taking a functional view of a knowledge base as a knowledge server, one can "Tell" and "Ask" the knowledge base what it knows. One fundamental result of this work is that AI knowledge-representation systems require complicated processing and interpretation of symbolic information and axioms associated with the "world" being modelled. The processing involved is quite complex, exceeding the capabilities of current database systems; however, it may be possible to characterize different types of knowledge "engines" that are amenable to support by expert database systems. For an excellent review of the International Conference on Expert Database Systems—especially the Keynote Address and the Panels—see van de Riet (1986).

1.3 The Role of Logic and Logic Programming

Logic and logic programming play an important role in expert database system architectures. Logic provides a formal basis for both relational databases and database theory. For example, logic may be used to extend the expressive power of query languages to include recursive queries that handle the transitive closure operation found in applications such as the inventory parts-explosion problem, CAD/CAM and routing problems. In addition logic and logic programming provide efficient mechanisms to integrate data, metadata (data about data or schema information), domain-specific knowledge and control knowledge.

Logic views databases from two points of view: (a) the model theoretic approach, and (b) the proof theoretic approach. In the model theoretic approach the database definition, or schema, is viewed as a time-variant definition, a theory, specified by means of data-structure definitions and integrity constraints. The database state (the collection of data instances) at any time is an interpretation of that theory. Integrity constraints are proper axioms that the database state must satisfy at all times. Queries on the database are expressed as well-formed formulae to be translated into relational operations. Traditional DBMSs such as relational systems adhere to this viewpoint.

With the proof theoretic (or deductive database) approach there is no separation of the schema and the data. The database is represented as a first-order theory with equality. Facts (data instances) are represented as ground well-formed formulae (wffs) of the first-order theory. The set of proper axioms provides the wffs for deduction and integrity constraints. The set of theorems constitutes the implicitly derivable information. Queries are considered theorems to be proved from the axioms.

Logic programming provides a computational language, Prolog, for the proof theoretic approach. Prolog processes horn clauses which are a subset of first-order predicate calculus. However, Prolog is not logic programming because it has several additional features not found in logic programming. Prolog has:

(a) built-in input–output predicates to read and write to and from terminals and databases;

(b) control of search through depth-first-search and backtracking;

(c) built-in predicates such as cut and fail which can control the inference process; and

(d) performance sensitivity to the order of predicates in the knowledge base, and the order of terms within predicates.

A well-known phenomenon is the "impedance mismatch" between Prolog and relational databases; Prolog evaluation is tuple-at-a-time owing to the unification process, while relational databases perform associative retrieval on large collections of data. This presents performance problems in a loosely coupled architecture with a Prolog-based knowledge system and a relational DBMS.

Several excellent articles on the logic programming view of expert database systems are found in Parker *et al.* (1986), Sciore and Warren (1986), Zaniolo (1986). Recent research in logic programming has focused on more tightly coupled Prolog-DBMS architectures (Ceri *et al.* 1987), which take advantage of the DBMS data dictionary information regarding file index and storage structures to control access to data, and to prefetch collections of data into Prolog's fact base for more efficient processing.

Logic is a natural way to specify complex queries to a DBMS, but systems using Prolog as the query language require the user to be aware of Prolog's inference strategy and the order of evaluation. This results in the user having to specify the order of query predicates so as to avoid performance problems. The logic-based data language (Tsur and Zaniolo 1986) alleviates the requirement that the user must specify predicate ordering and, in addition, it eliminates the "impedance mismatch" by compiling logic queries into an extended relational algebra.

2. Implications for Intelligent Information Systems

Expert database system architectures will have a major impact on the next generation of software and hardware systems that support knowledge-directed processing of large shared databases. The research and development goals and requirements of expert database systems affecting intelligent information systems are as follows.

(a) A unified and formal knowledge/data model that captures not only data semantics (i.e., objects, properties, associations) but also knowledge semantics (i.e., concepts, rules, heuristics, uncertainty, scripts, etc.) of an application.

(b) The EDS specification and manipulation languages should have modelling primitives to express and reason about causal, temporal and spatial relationships. It should also have facilities to allow for user-extensible, object-oriented views of the enterprise or application domain.

(c) The EDS architecture will merge pattern-directed search and inference, such as those found in production, rule and logic-based systems, with DB associative retrieval, and join processing to provide efficient knowledge-based query processing and semantic integrity maintenance, as well as constraint-directed reasoning and system control. This merging of tools and techniques will require a knowledge encyclopedia to manage internal system knowledge as well as domain-specific knowledge and data, and to "package" it for the various tools that will access the knowledge/data base.

(d) The EDS should provide facilities for inexact reasoning over large databases, and an explanation facility will justify the reasoning process to application developers and users.

The above-mentioned EDS features will profoundly influence the design and development of intelligent information systems. The traditional phased, linear, development life-cycle will be replaced by an iterative, interactive, fast prototyping mode. In addition, the knowledge-based approach will promote new classes of applications in which the knowledge engineer will work with an expert to elucidate strategic and domain-specific knowledge. These new applications represent a vertical extension of applications beyond the well-defined, predictable, transaction-oriented systems to those with knowledge-directed reasoning and interpretation under conditions of uncertainty.

Just as DBMSs are used to manage data as a corporate resource, EDS will manage knowledge as a corporate resource. The availability of a unified knowledge/data model will facilitate a specification-based approach for creating knowledge schemes that express the semantics of both knowledge and data. The knowledge encyclopedia will represent both system and application knowledge in an object-oriented view in which object behavior is specified by explicit constraints (Shepherd and Kerschberg 1984, 1986). These constraints will be made available to tools that will help to design and manage the knowledge base. In fact the knowledge encyclopedia will also be used to formulate user interfaces for knowledge acquisition, and to provide a metaexplanation facility that would access both system and domain-specific knowledge, and could document and explain system structure and dynamics to the knowledge administrator.

3. Conclusions

The integration of concepts, tools and techniques from DB, AI, LP—as embodied in expert database systems—will create new and revolutionary environments for the specification, design, prototyping and maintenance of intelligent information systems. Many researchers and practitioners are providing insights and prototypes that will lead to new architectures for the software and hardware systems of the 1990s and beyond.

Bibliography

Batory D 1986 GENESIS: A project to develop an extensible database management system. In: Dittrich and Dayal 1986

Brachman R J, Levesque H J 1986 What makes a knowledge base knowledge? A view of databases from the knowledge level. In: Kerschberg 1986

Brachman R J, Levesque H J 1987 Tales from the far side of KRYPTON. In: Kerschberg 1987

Carey M J, DeWitt D, Frank D, Graefe G, Richardson J, Shekita E, Muralikrishna M 1986 The architecture of the EXODUS extensible DBMS. In: Dittrich and Dayal 1986

Ceri S, Gottlob G, Wiederhold G 1987 Interfacing relational databases and Prolog efficiently. In: Kerschberg 1987

Cholvy L, Demolombe R 1987 Querying a rule base. In: Kerschberg 1987

Deering M, Faletti J 1986 Database support for storage of AI reasoning knowledge. In: Kerschberg 1986

Dittrich K, Dayal U (eds.) 1986 *Proc. 1986 Int. Workshop Object-Oriented Database Systems*, September 23–26. IEEE, Piscataway, New Jersey

Goldberg A, Robson D 1983 *Smalltalk-80: The Language and its Implementation*. Addison–Wesley, Reading, Massachusetts

Kerschberg L (ed.) 1986 *Proc. 1st Int. Workshop Expert Database Systems*. Benjamin–Cummings, Menlo Park, California

Kerschberg L (ed.) 1987 *Proc. 1st Int. Conf. Expert Database Systems*. Benjamin–Cummings, Menlo Park, California

Kerschberg L (ed.) 1988 *Proc. 2nd Int. Conf. Expert Database Systems*. Benjamin–Cummings, Menlo Park, California

Maier D, Stein J 1986 Indexing in an object-oriented DBMS. In: Dittrich and Dayal 1986

Manola F, Dayal U 1986 PDM: An object-oriented data model. In: Dittrich and Dayal 1986

Parker D S, Carey M, Golshani F, Jarke M, Sciore E, Walker A 1986 Logic programming and databases, Working Group Report. In: Kerschberg 1986

Potter W D, Kerschberg L 1986 The knowledge/data model: A unified approach to modeling knowledge and data. In: Meersman R, Sowa J (eds.) *Proc. IFIP DS-2 Working Conf. Knowledge and Data*, Albufeira, November. North-Holland, Amsterdam

Sciore E, Warren D S 1986 Towards an integrated database-prolog system. In: Kerschberg 1986

Shepherd A, Kerschberg L 1984 PRISM: A knowledge-based system for semantic integrity specification and enforcement in database systems. *Proc. ACM SIGMOD Int. Conf. Management of Data*. Boston, Massachusetts, pp. 307–15

Shepherd A, Kerschberg L 1986 Constraint management in expert database systems. In: Kerschberg 1986

Smith J M 1986 Expert database systems: A database perspective. In: Kerschberg 1986
Smith R 1984 On the development of commercial expert systems. *AI Mag.* **3**, 61–73
Stonebraker M 1986 Object management in POSTGRES using procedures. In: Dittrich and Dayal 1986
Tsur S, Zaniolo C 1986 LDL: A logic-based data language. *Proc. 12th Int. Conf. Very Large Data Bases.* Kyoto. Morgan–Kaufmann, Los Altos, California
van de Riet R P 1986 Expert database systems, Conference Report. *Future Generat. Comput. Syst.* **2**(3), 191–6
Zaniolo C 1986 Prolog: A database query language for all seasons. In: Kerschberg 1986
Zaniolo C, Ait-Kaci H, Beech D, Cammarata S, Kerschberg L, Maier D 1986 Object-oriented database systems and knowledge systems. In: Kerschberg 1986

L. Kerschberg
[George Mason University, Fairfax,
Virginia, USA]

Expert Systems

An expert system is an intelligent system that is able to use expert knowledge, stored in the form of inference procedures, to resolve complex problems. The goal of the designer of an expert system is to somehow capture the knowledge of a human expert relative to some specific domain and code this in a computer in such a way that the knowledge of the expert is available to a less experienced user.

The knowledge of an expert will consist, in part, of fact files and knowledge sources. A fact file will consist of data and information that is generally agreed upon by a number of experts to characterize the domain under consideration. For the most part, a fact file is capable of being represented in a database. Knowledge sources consist of a typically large number of skill- and rule-based forms of knowledge that an expert may be expected to bring to bear upon a particular familiar issue in a given domain with which the expert is conversant. There are many ways in which this knowledge can be represented because knowledge sources are, for the most part, heuristic in nature since they are based upon the wisdom accumulated through experience.

A control structure or system, also known as an inference or cognitive engine, organizes and directs the steps that are actually taken to resolve a problem. The principal task of the cognitive engine is to act as an intelligent interpreter in the selection of those portions of the knowledge base, consisting of fact files and knowledge sources, which are most applicable to the resolution of a given issue. Finally, there must be interfaces between the two principal components of an expert system, the knowledge base and the cognitive engine, and between these subsystems, the expert whose knowledge is captured in the system and the ultimate users of the system. In other words, knowledge can be said to consist of facts, beliefs and heuristics. The knowledge base, cognitive engine and interface are coupled together as shown conceptually in Fig. 1.

1. Introduction to, and Taxonomy of, Expert Systems

A decision support system is designed to aid managers in determining appropriate courses of actions in situations that are unstructured or semistructured. An expert system is designed to assist users who are generally not experts in exercising judgement in situations that are familiar to, and therefore capable of being structured by, experts in the domain under consideration. Thus, the uses of an expert system could be much the same as those for a decision support system. The principal difference between the two approaches is that there is necessarily assumed to be one or more experts available to construct the knowledge base and the cognitive inference engine of an expert system. Users of a decision support system generally utilize their own knowledge, with the system acting as a structuring and organizing tool, for issue evaluation and resolution. Users of an expert system generally utilize the knowledge of others to aid in issue evaluation and resolution. Generally, this knowledge is obtained in the form of heuristic rules or wholistic skills. The subjects of knowledge acquisition, representation and use are important subareas of expert systems.

An expert system is much more than just a computer program. The primary difference is that in an expert system there will generally be a clear distinction, or at least a very conscious effort to maintain a distinction, between the general knowledge about a specific problem domain that constitutes the knowledge base and the control structure which contains the rule interpreter that results in specific use of the knowledge base for a given application. In a conventional computer program, however, the general

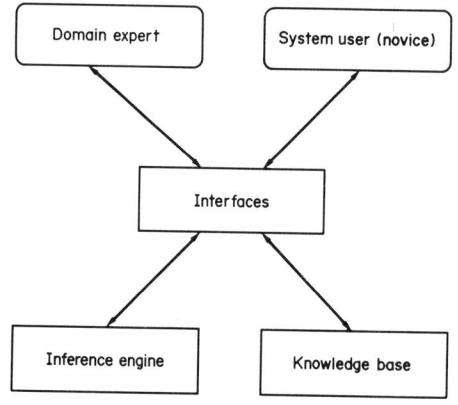

Figure 1
Generic structure of an expert system

knowledge that is relevant to a given problem and the methods for use of this knowledge are not separated. Typical expert systems attempt to maintain this distinction. This leads to a much greater scope of problems within a given knowledge domain to which an expert system might be applied.

Note that the knowledge base of an expert system is very analogous to the database management system of a decision support system, and the control structure or cognitive engine of an expert system has an analogous operational purpose to the model-base management system of a decision support system. The interfaces in an expert system are particularly important components, just as the dialog generation and management system is a particularly important component in a decision support system. Natural-language dialogue is a very important part of the interface portion of an expert system. Thus, while the generic block-diagram components of the two systems do have some similar-looking blocks and names, the theoretical and pragmatic function and purpose of the two types of knowledge support systems are really quite different.

2. Knowledge-Base Creation and Maintenance

It is possible, as has been noted in the introduction, to characterize the components of an expert system as belonging to the knowledge-base subsystem, the cognitive- (or inference) engine subsystem, or the interface subsystem which enables communication between the other two subsystems and users of the system. Most workers in expert systems share the belief that good design practice makes these subsystems as independent of one another as possible, as noted in Sect. 1. Complete independence is neither possible nor desirable, however. It is necessary to know the structural form of the knowledge base if proper use is to be made of the knowledge base by the cognitive engine. What is not desired, however, is that the operation of the cognitive-engine subsystem be dependent upon the specific domain-dependent knowledge that is contained in the knowledge base. This independence allows efficient and effective updating of the expert system as new knowledge is acquired.

2.1 Production Systems

There are a variety of generic approaches that may be used to represent knowledge in the knowledge-base subsystem. An important supplement to this article is the article *Knowledge Representation*. For purposes of simplicity, consideration is restricted to *production systems* in this article. Several motivating factors support this restriction and these are briefly discussed below. Production systems have been shown to be most useful when describing how people perform specific real-world tasks, such as those envisioned in the many ultimate applications of expert systems. Thus, production rules are natural expressions of "what to do" types of knowledge. They are modular in that individual production rules can be added, deleted or modified independently. Thus, they are easily able to accommodate the procedural human reactions to receiving new knowledge. This is very important in building a large knowledge base. Production systems form a *uniform* structural representation of knowledge. When coded to represent the specific area of application, a set of production rules can be manipulated with much the same ease as data in a relational database. The particular knowledge domain for many expert systems is one in which expert knowledge is diffuse and well suited to statement in the form of productions; this is in constrast to a formal subject area, such as electric circuit theory, in which there is a concise and unified theory.

If the knowledge in a particular domain were best expressed as an independent set of rules, and if expert knowledge could be easily separated from the manner in which it could be used, then a standard production-rule-based expert system would be ideal. This is unfortunately not the case in many intended applications as there are a number of dependent processes that chain together the production rules. Also, humans who have mastered a subject generally do not think exclusively, or perhaps even much of the time, in terms of rules. Script- and schema-based reasoning, or some form of analogous reasoning, is much more common. Doubtlessly there will also be instances where it will be desirable to consider knowledge representation and control as if they are merged. This reflects the context-dependent nature of activities involved in large integrated areas such as flexible manufacturing or command and control. Thus, there are disadvantages to rule-based production systems. Nevertheless, the advantages noted for production-rule systems generally offset the primary disadvantages of production rules. In other words, the disadvantages arising from the nonindependence of rules, and the integration of knowledge representation and control, will bring about inefficiency in program execution; a disadvantage which also results from the modularity and structural uniformity of the rules. Also, there are difficulties with the flow of control as the cognitive engine activates a production rule. These are aggravated by the context-dependent nature of knowledge representation and control. In this sense, production rules are opaque in that there is no easy visualization, such as would occur in a schema, semantic network or frame of direct paths between observations by the user of the expert system and recommended actions.

The basic production-rule-oriented expert system consists of three parts relating to the acquired productions: a *rule base* which is just a set of "if–then" statements; the *context*, which is the condition that must be present before the production can "fire" (i.e. the left-hand side of the production rule); and an *interpreter* which issues the judgement concerning what to do next. The behavior of a production-rule knowledge subsystem is typically cyclic. The rule interpreter of the control structure examines a variety of production rules to see which ones should become active or "fire." If more than a single production is found appropriate, there must be some higher-level interpretations made that ultimately enable a subset of the possible applicable productions to become active.

2.2 Knowledge Representation

The most appropriate techniques for representing knowledge are very much a function of the type of tasks to be undertaken, and the metaknowledge that is available concerning the tasks and the environment into which they are embedded.

There are a variety of knowledge representation techniques, including rules, formal logic, schema, semantic networks, frames, and scripts. Rule-based expert systems are undoubtedly the most common type of expert system. What is not as often recognized is the great multiplicity of roles that rules play in expert systems and in human judgement in general.

2.3 Problem Solving

There are a number of taxonomies of the ways in which humans, in an unaided fashion, approach problem-solving tasks. One particularly useful taxonomy conceptualizes three distinct types of problem-solving behavior or reasoning: formal knowledge-based behavior, rule-based behavior, and skill-based behavior. The choice of which type of reasoning to employ is made by the problem solver on the basis of experiential familiarity with the task at hand and the environment into which this task is embedded.

In an expert system, the need to cope with expert, and perhaps not so expert, judgement based on these three forms of reasoning also exists. Additional complexities arise, however, due to the fact that the (typical) expert system will have the capability of knowledge-base representation only in terms of rules. A simple example will illustrate the point. A typical knowledge-based production-rule system may have two rules that are directly applicable to a situation according to the if–then logic of the production rule. If only one rule can be applied at a time, and there does not exist an explicit rule indicating which of the two rules takes priority, then there must be some mechanism, again in the form of a production rule, that enables this prioritization. Thus, it can be seen that production rules are being used as surrogates for formal rule-based reasoning. To the efficient and effective achievement of such ends when there are a large number of rules and metarules is a much sought-after goal.

In a similar way, expert systems often attempt to use rule-based representations of skill-based knowledge. This knowledge may be expressed initially in any of several affective or intuitive forms that have been learned by the expert on the basis of much relevant experience. Although the expert may well have learned how to be an expert through formal means that require an absorbed and alert monitoring of the task components, experts may no longer be formally aware of all their monitoring actions, and may therefore give incomplete information concerning their activities. This simply reflects the view that expertise develops through perceptual learning and through the acquisition of a larger number of rules. Experts are not just faster and more accurate with their use of a larger number of rules, but can perceive situations, similarities and task objectives with considerable clarity. To attempt to represent this in the form of rules may well require an inordinately large number of rules. If this occurs, then the expert system may become very sluggish. This suggests the importance of a taxonomy of rule types. More importantly, it suggests the importance of methods to determine efficient and effective structural representations of production rules, so that the knowledge base may be managed in an effective and efficient manner.

Expert systems may be used in environments in which there is a requirement for advice before the expert system is able to conduct an exhaustive "search" of its knowledge base. In this case, it becomes especially important to be able to generate some reasonably good solution based on a limited search, perhaps eliminating dominated alternatives, and to then proceed in the time remaining to improve, to the extent possible, upon the initial recommendation. This is another requirement that must be satisfied to achieve the efficient and effective structuring and use of metaknowledge when designing expert systems.

Expertise comprises various kinds of knowledge, including facts about the specific domain of the intended user or users, and others to be aided by the expert system. There will be certain fixed rules and procedures that will always be valid. Problem situations will exist in which there is imprecision and uncertainty, where heuristic rules need to be applied with caution. Situations arise in which skill-based preceptions based on experiential familiarity with the task at hand are used. Finally, there will exist formal theories of the domain that need to be used when experiential familiarity with the task at hand and the environment into which it is embedded are insufficient to enable wise use of skill- and rule-based knowledge. Because of this great variety of knowledge, it is most likely that experts will be unable to present a complete and consistent set of fact files and knowledge relationships that would enable the construction of a "complete" knowledge-base subsystem. Thus the process of knowledge acquisition must often allow for iterative and incremental identification of knowledge as knowledge and experience with the domain of intended application grow.

The foregoing discussion highlights the three principal roles of the user of an expert system. The user may use the expert system in order to seek judgemental and problem-solving advice. From this, the user improves in terms of effectiveness and/or efficiency in dealing with problems. The user may also be a tutor to the system, so that the expert system increases or improves its knowledge and its ability to perform. Consequently, the process of knowledge acquisition cannot be totally separated from that of knowledge representation and knowledge utilization.

2.4 Knowledge Acquisition

In order to determine consistency and completeness of the knowledge base, it is necessary for the acquired knowledge to be subjected to appropriate tests. These will necessitate representation and use of the acquired knowledge, as it is on the basis of representation and use that such measures as consistency and completeness are determined. This requirement for an iterative and modular acquisition of knowledge is another motivating factor behind the selection of a production-system format for knowledge representation. Since each rule, and appropriate subsets of rules, represents a "natural" chunk of knowledge which can be easily augmented, modified or deleted, construction and interpretation of the knowledge base is simplified.

Thus, the process of knowledge acquisition is driven by the identification of existing deficiencies in the knowledge base. In so doing, the process of knowledge acquisition should become efficient and effective. Without the use of this form of metaknowledge to drive knowledge acquisition, the acquisition process is undirected and there is little that can be done to ensure the effectiveness of the knowledge base or efficiency in its acquisition. It is this preliminary interactive use of the knowledge base that enables an expert to detect errors in the performance of the expert system. These occur as reasoning or responses that the expert finds inappropriate. There must be some capability to work backwards through the system in order to detect the location of flaws and then allow for modification or augmentation of knowledge at that point.

Knowledge must be acquired from experts in the form of fact files, action and event knowledge, performance (knowledge about "how to do" things) and metaknowledge or knowledge about what is known and what is not known. One object of knowledge acquisition is to enlarge the knowledge base of the expert system with new productions expressed in terms of rules, contexts and interpretations. Inconsistency and incompleteness in the knowledge base are, generally, detected only through the application of concepts that are not yet known to the expert system. Thus, metaknowledge is essential to the construction of an expert system. This is at the heart of the TEIRESIAS model-based understanding process, which enables MYCIN to acquire new rules and otherwise complete the acquisition of its knowledge base. In TEIRESIAS, metalevel knowledge about the types of concepts and rules in the MYCIN database is used to build "expectations" in a model-based understanding process. These help in the transfer of English language responses into appropriate machine-internal representation as well as compensating for missing information.

Metalevel knowledge is, in many ways, equivalent to the knowledge of "values" common in decison support systems efforts. Thus, it can be used to prioritize the relevancy of rules in the database such that those rules most likely to be useful, given a current knowledge on the part of the expert system, are used first. Through the use of strategies such as this, acquisition of knowledge can be made effective and efficient.

3. Cognitive Engines or Control Structures

There are a variety of ways in which the rule interpreter of the control-structure subsystem portion of an expert system may organize and control the steps of problem solving. In the production-rule methods of knowledge representation, the if–then rules may be "chained" in order to form an appropriate method. When this chaining starts with an initial set of conditions and moves towards a set of conclusions, the approach is known as forward chaining, and is naturally related to causal and inductive reasoning. A potential difficulty with forward chaining is that all conclusions that may follow from an initial set of conditions may be obtained unless there is some appropriate method of pruning. Often this can be accomplished by (metalevel) heuristics. Backward chaining, or goal-directed reasoning, will start with final conditions or goals, and work backwards to initial conditions, or subgoals. Thus, backward chaining relates to deductive and diagnostic reasoning. Again this can result in an explosion of possible conjunctive subgoals or conditions that can lead to a given conclusion unless there are appropriate heuristics to guide the search. Determination of an appropriate reasoning method should be based upon three considerations: it would be desirable to move from a smaller set of states to a larger set to reduce the possible number of paths to be searched, movement from a node with a larger number of incoming branches to a node with a smaller number is also desirable, as is movement in a direction that is more like the natural direction of reasoning which a human would take in order to enhance the explicability of the path finally taken.

These are not the only methods of search. Often the natural nature of human reasoning will be the strongest component influencing the search method. When production rules are used for the knowledge base, forward reasoning will be most appropriate when data represents the natural starting point for problem solving. When goals and hypotheses are the natural starting points, as is often the case in diagnosis or planning, backward reasoning may be a natural method of choice. Of course these two approaches for rule interpretation by a control structure may be combined. When the problem-solving situation changes over time, an event-driven approach to reasoning may be most appropriate. This is an opportunistic approach, in which behavior of the rule interpreter is guided on the basis of new data or the discovery of a new situation or event. The knowledge source that is triggered is always the one that is most likely to lead to progress towards achieving system goals.

There are many other design philosophies that may be used to determine the cognitive engine or control-structure portion of an expert system. This has been one of the earliest areas of inquiry for artificial intelligence and is discussed in detail in texts on expert systems.

4. Interface and Expert-System Programming Language Shell Considerations

One of the major goals in expert-systems research is to enable experts and users of a system to communicate and interact with the system in a natural-language dialogue, without having to interact through a computer language. Major trends at this time result in the conceptualization of language as a knowledge-based system directed at communications. Consequently, research in cognition and language-understanding systems seeks to obtain an understanding of how linguistic knowledge and specific domain knowledge can be used to make the interfaces in an expert system more understandable and human-like. Systems that can cope with the totally unconstrained natural-language discourse of an expert and which also provides useful interpretations for the user concerning the obtained knowledge, perceptions and motivations of the system are hoped-for future goals.

The basic computer languages chosen for expert-system construction have been LISP and PROLOG; there are a large number of LISP variations. A major problem with both of these languages is that, especially in versions of these languages using interpreters, they are quite slow in execution. Many contemporary expert systems are now implemented using more efficient programming languages, such as C.

To simplify the construction of expert systems, a number of special very-high-level programming languages have been developed which are analogous to the program generators that have been developed for decision support system construction. Generally, these very-high-level languages are called expert-system shells. This is a more appropriate term in that the "shells" are usually quite well specified and allow structured approaches to knowledge acquisition, representation and use in which specific domain knowledge is missing initially. Adding this to the "shell" results in the operational expert system.

Available expert-system shells include: OPS5, an expert-system shell designed from LISP to enable relatively easy construction and use of production rules; EMYCIN a shell that enables the construction of production rules for the MYCIN environment; TEIRESIAS, a tool that enables interactive transfer of expertise from a human to an expert system using natural-language dialogue and which has been used as a metalevel tool with EMYCIN; and ROSIE, which generates INTERLISP statements from natural-language dialogue. R1 is an expert system that uses the OPS programming language that facilitated the use of production rules to configure VAX computer systems for purchasers. This existing system has reported major savings to the Digital Equipment Corporation. At the other end of the spectrum is AGE which is an expert-system shell as well as a very-high-level programming language that guides users in the incorporation of knowledge base and cognitive engines in an expert system. Two pre-designed configurations are assumed, a "blackboard" system and a "backchaining" system using production rules. ART, KEE and S1 are among the many other expert-shells for larger computers and special-purpose artificial-intelligence computers.

There are a large and growing number of expert-system shells that function on personal computers. Among these are the M1 shell from Tecknowledge, and Rulemaster from Radian Corporation. While the structural assumptions necessary to construct software shells and the speed of operation of the resulting systems may deter their use in actual applications, the notion of generating prototype expert systems using shells, and the recoding of the prototype in a high-level language for enhanced flexibility, effectiveness and ease of use is a very attractive one.

See also: Artificial Intelligence; Decision Support Systems; Human Information Processing; Knowledge Representation

Bibliography

Barr A, Feigenbaum E A (eds.) 1982, *The Handbook of Artificial Intelligence*, Vols. 1, 2. Kaufman, Los Altos, California

Buchanan B G, Duda R O 1983 Principles of rule-based expert systems. In: Yovits M (ed.) *Advances in Computers*, Vol. 22. Academic Press, New York

Buchanan B G, Shortliffe E H 1984 *Rule based expert systems*. Addison–Wesley, Reading, Massachusetts

Cohen P R, Feigenbaum E A (eds.) 1982 *The Handbook of Artificial Intelligence*, Vol. 3. Kaufman, Los Altos, California

Davis R, Lenat D B 1982 *Knowledge Based Systems in Artificial Intelligence*. McGraw-Hill, New York

Gevarter W B 1985 *Intelligent Machines: An Introductory Perspective of Artificial Intelligence and Robotics*. Prentice–Hall, Englewood Cliffs, New Jersey

Gevarter W B 1987 The nature and evaluation of commercial expert system building tools. *IEEE Comput.* **20**(5), 24–42

Hayes-Roth F, Waterman D A, Lenat D B 1983 *Building Expert Systems*. Addison–Wesley, Reading, Massachusetts

Lindsay R K, Buchanan B G, Feigenbaum E A, Lederberg J 1980 *Applications of Artificial Intelligence for Organic Chemistry: The DENDRAL Project*. McGraw–Hill, New York

Nilsson N J 1980 *Principles of Artificial Intelligence*. Tioga, Palo Alto, California

Rich E 1983 *Artificial Intelligence*. McGraw–Hill, New York

Richter M H 1986 An evaluation of expert system development tools. *Exp. Syst.* **3**(3), 166–83

Silverman B G (ed.) 1987 *Expert Systems for Business*. Addison–Wesley, Reading, Massachusetts

Stefik M, Alkins J, Balzer R, Benoit J, Birnbaum L, Hayes-Roth R, Sacerdoti E 1982 The organization of expert systems: A tutorial. *Artif. Intell.* **18**, 135–73

Tanimoto S L 1987 *The Elements of Artificial Intelligence*. Computer Science Press, Rockville, Maryland

Waterman D A 1986 *A Guide to Expert Systems*. Addison–Wesley, Reading, Massachusetts

A. P. Sage
[George Mason University, Fairfax, Virginia, USA]

Expert Systems for Managers: Design Issues

Since the 1960s computer-based systems have been developed to simulate the behavior of knowledgeable and experienced specialists in areas such as medicine, geology and engineering (Harmon and King 1985, Maney and Reid 1986, Waterman 1986, Silverman 1987). These systems, generally called expert systems, have been used to assist novices in performing specialized tasks and to understand more fully how experienced specialists perform these tasks. The tasks include diagnosing infectious diseases, exploring for mineral deposits and repairing faulty equipment. Although most of the early systems were experimental, many of the recent ones are being used in business and government.

The growing success of expert systems in technical areas such as medicine and engineering has stimulated the development of such systems to assist managers in making decisions and in performing analyses and making recommendations leading to a decision (Blanning 1984b, e, Dhar 1987). Examples of such decisions are in the areas of capital investment, new-product development and production planning. As with the early technical expert systems, many of the management expert systems now being developed are experimental systems, developed primarily at universities, so that the potential usefulness of these systems and the issues that will arise in their design and implementation can be determined. The purpose of this article is to examine some of these systems and issues.

1. Expert Systems for Managers

There are three principal areas of management in which expert systems have been developed. The first is resource allocation, which includes portfolio management and capital budgeting. The second is the diagnosis of impending or existing problems; for example, analyzing financial statements and auditing accounts receivable. The third is scheduling and assignment; for example, production scheduling and the scheduling of business meetings. There is also a fourth area, which is newer and more experimental: the management of causal decision models. This includes the construction, interpretation and integration of these models. This topic will be examined in Sect. 3.

1.1 Resource Allocation

Since managers must often allocate scarce resources (such as money, floor space, equipment and supplies) it is not surprising to find that expert systems have been developed to assist them. Two such systems are described here: one for portfolio management and one for capital budgeting.

The portfolio management system was the first expert system to be developed, although it was not called an expert system at the time (Clarkson 1962, 1963). The system simulated a bank trust officer preparing a portfolio of stocks for a client. The system contained information about the financial performance of industries and corporations and information about the US economy. It also contained rules for selecting stocks to meet client needs. The rules were obtained by observing a trust officer preparing portfolios and asking for a description of why certain tasks are being performed (i.e., why the client is being asked certain questions and why certain stocks are being selected and others rejected by the trust officer). This process is called protocol analysis.

The principal finding of the knowledge engineer (i.e., the person who designed the system) is that the trust officer performs two tasks. The first is to obtain information about the client, such as risk preference and tax status, and the second is to select appropriate stocks for that client. The rules also perform these tasks. The knowledge engineer validates the system by comparing it with the trust officer for four of the bank's new clients. The results are quite similar.

The capital budget system, called DECMAK, helps a manager to evaluate investment proposals for new equipment to be included in an equipment budget (Bohanek *et al.* 1983). The user enters information about the requirements for equipment performance (e.g., whether low cost is a requirement for acceptable performance) and then enters the characteristics of alternative equipment configurations for evaluation and comparison by DECMAK. DECMAK allows its users to enter certainty factors that indicate the degree of confidence they have in the data they are entering and the system then calculates certainty factors for its outputs.

Systems similar to the ones described above may be used to assist managers in making other resource allocation decisions. An example is the allocation of floor space in a factory, in which the positioning of machines and other equipment (e.g., parts bins) greatly affects the cost, throughput and timeliness of production. Another example is research and development (R&D) budgeting, in which proposed R&D projects must be analyzed for potential profitability and other benefits, and the individual proposals must be combined to produce an R&D budget.

1.2 Problem Diagnosis

Systems of this type help managers to anticipate or solve problems by analyzing information contained in periodic reports, such as financial and logistical reports. Two such systems are described here: one for auditing trade accounts receivable, and one for analyzing corporate financial statements.

The system for auditing trade accounts receivable is called AUDITOR (Dungan and Chandler 1985). AUDITOR recommends whether delinquent customer credit accounts should be reported as collectable in a company's financial statements. AUDITOR asks its user questions about the account (e.g., whether the customer is still an active customer) and allows the user to enter a number between −5 and +5 which expresses the degree to which the user believes that the statement is true. The knowledge base consists of 39 rules obtained from protocols taken from four auditors in a public accounting firm. The rules relate the user's input (i.e., his answers to the questions) to the collectability of the account. AUDITOR was validated by comparing its performance to that of human auditors who were not involved in the design of the system, and there was a 90% agreement. AUDITOR used a commercially available inference engine (i.e., a program for processing and managing the rules) called AL/X.

The system for analyzing financial statements estimates the financial condition of a company based on company and industry data (Bouwman 1983). Protocols were taken from financial analysts and students on a graduate-level course on financial analysis. The knowledge engineer found that financial analysts do not attempt to use all of the financial data available to them; rather, they look for patterns in the data. Examples are a consistent increase or decrease in an important variable over time (e.g., sales volume and profit) and a comparison of an important variable with the industry average. The output is a narrative description of the financial condition of the company being considered and the reasons for any problems. The system was compared with the narrative analyses of a financial analyst for several companies, and they were similar. The principal difference was that the system usually gave more detailed descriptions of the causes of financial problems.

Systems similar to these may be useful in diagnosing other types of problems. An example is the analysis of budget variance reports to determine the cause of cost or revenue overruns or underruns, and the degree to which any problems are temporary or are likely to persist. Another example is the analysis of production and maintenance reports to determine whether there are growing problems that should be addressed before they get out of hand.

1.3 Scheduling and Assignment

Another important task performed by managers is to schedule activities (e.g., production and distribution) and to assign certain entities (e.g., the production of products) to other entities (e.g., machines). Two expert systems in this area are described here: one for production scheduling and the other for scheduling business meetings.

The production scheduling system, ISIS, was developed for a turbine plant at Westinghouse (Fox and Smith 1984). The knowledge engineers discovered that production schedulers spend only 10–20% of their time scheduling production. The remainder of their time is devoted to communicating with other people about conflicting constraints that, if rigorously observed, would make scheduling impossible. (The constraints concern production requirements, cost limits, maintenance needs, requirements for schedule stability, etc.) That is, the constraints are collectively infeasible. ISIS contains information about the importance and relevance of these constraints and the relationships between them, and it relaxes them in an intelligent fashion so that they are collectively feasible. Thus, production is accomplished by converting an infeasible problem into a feasible one, and this is accomplished by intelligent constraint relaxation.

The system for scheduling business meetings, NUDGE, is similar to ISIS in that it attempts to convert an infeasible schedule into a feasible one by modifying some of the requirements imposed by the person using the system (Goldstein and Roberts 1982). For example, if a person is unavailable and another qualified person is available, NUDGE will attempt a substitution. The system can determine whether the other person is qualified because it can infer the purpose of the meeting and it knows the qualifications of the possible attendees.

Since there are many scheduling problems, especially in the area of logistics, and many assignment problems, especially in the areas of logistics and personnel, more systems of the type described above can be expected in the future. Possible application areas include distribution scheduling, the assignment of people to jobs or training programs and the assignment of tasks to machines.

2. System Construction and Validation

As with causal decision models, there are two important issues in the development of expert systems. The first concerns the construction of these systems (and especially the way in which knowledge is acquired from experts) and the way in which the knowledge bases of these systems are to be structured. The second is the validation of these systems once they have been designed.

2.1 System Construction

There are two issues in the construction of expert systems. The first is knowledge acquisition; that is, eliciting knowledge from experts and possibly other sources (such as training or procedure manuals). This is accomplished in the former case by protocol analysis, the recording of verbal comments made by experts as they perform a task. The second issue, which is a consequence of the first, is the selection of a structure for the knowledge base. One such structure is based on rules, but there are others.

(a) *Knowledge acquisition.* The principal way of acquiring knowledge is protocol analysis. Protocol analysis is typically acccomplished by asking an expert to comment verbally on what is being done as a task is being performed. This procedure was performed when designing the trust investment system and the system for analyzing financial statements described briefly in Sect. 1. Another approach is to ask experts to make comments as they read literature on their speciality area (e.g., articles, training manuals and case studies). This, as well as the first method, was used in designing the trust investment system. A third approach is to ask the expert to provide cues, items that the expert feels are important in performing a task, and to convert these into rules or other knowledge structures. This procedure was followed in the design of AUDITOR.

Another approach to knowledge acquisition is for the knowledge engineer to use written documentation (such as training manuals, repair manuals and policy statements) directly. However, this is best used as a starting point, and an expert should then be asked to comment on the results.

The protocols can be used to identify quantitative or qualitative measures. Quantitative measures are numerical parameters in the knowledge base. For example, after the rules in AUDITOR had been constructed, it was necessary to determine weights that indicated the degree of influence that the various rules should have in arriving at a judgement concerning collectability. This was done by asking several auditors to rate the relative importance of each rule, and the ratings were combined to determine the weights. Qualitative measures are patterns in the data. For example, the system for analyzing financial statements was based on simple patterns that appeared when the protocols were analyzed.

It may also be helpful in obtaining protocols to determine how experts allocate their time among different projects. In designing ISIS it was determined that production schedulers spend only a small fraction of their time scheduling production. This led to the question of what they do with most of their time. The answer (coordinating with others to reduce conflicts) determined the way in which ISIS was designed and the tasks it performed.

(b) *The structure of the knowledge base.* There are several possible structures for a knowledge base (Harmon and King 1985, Waterman 1986). The prevalent one is based on situation–action rules. This approach was used in AUDITOR. If the situation part of a rule is satisfied, then the action part of the rule is invoked. The latter may cause variables to be assigned values, values to be changed, programs to be executed, and so on. Various search strategies can be invoked to decide the sequence of rule firings and the conditions under which the search should stop.

Another type of knowledge structure is a frame-based structure. This was used in ISIS and NUDGE. A frame consists of an identifier (e.g., the name of a person, machine, concept) and one or more slots that represent its attributes (e.g., a height, weight, purpose, degree of validity). The power of frame-based systems results from the variety of possible slot types. A slot may contain a value, a default value, an expression, a program or a reference to another frame. In addition, a frame may inherit information from another frame. This knowledge structure is extremely flexible, a characteristic which makes it possible for frame-based systems to implement the constraint-relaxation approach used in ISIS and NUDGE.

The program that applies the knowledge base to a particular problem is called an inference engine, although on microcomputers it is often called an expert-system shell. The inference engine contains the procedures for searching the rules or frames (or other knowledge structures not described here) to arrive at a result. The result might be in the form of a qualitative or numerical value (as in AUDITOR) or a narrative description of a problem (as in the system for analyzing financial statements).

Inference engines are also used in constructing and maintaining knowledge bases. They facilitate the processes of adding, changing and deleting rules. Another type of software that may be useful in constructing knowledge bases is one that looks for anomalies in rules. An example is TIERESIAS, a software system that warns a knowledge engineer whenever a rule being entered appears to be at variance with other rules (Davis 1979).

2.2 System Validation

Validation of an expert system is accomplished by comparing the output of the system with that of a human expert for several test cases. The output may be qualitative, quantitative or narrative. For example, the output of the trust-investment system was qualitative (a list of stocks), the output of AUDITOR was quantitative (a probability that an account would not be collectable) and the output of the system that analyzed financial statements was in narrative form.

There are two principal issues that arise in the comparison of an expert system and an expert, and these are similar to two issues that have arisen in comparing causal decision models and the real-world processes that they are supposed to model. (The "real world" of an expert system is an expert.) The first is the criterion for "goodness" of agreement between the expert system and the expert. In validating the outputs of the systems described above, it was assumed that the expert system should mimic the expert as closely as possible for the same test case. However, there are instances in which this may not be true. An example is in the application of system dynamics to economic modelling, which makes use of both causal and subjective data (Forrester 1980a). It has been suggested that this is inappropriate because of the questionable nature of subjective data (Zellner 1980). The counterargument, advanced by proponents of system dynamics, is that subjective data are valid (Forrester 1980b). In addition they argue that system-dynamics models need not match the real world very closely as long as they capture certain characteristics (such as the presence or absence of trends or oscillations) of the real world. The same arguments may eventually be made with regard to certain expert systems.

The second issue is whether laboratory validation is itself valid or whether only field trials should be used. This issue has arisen in the context of decision calculus models which are used in marketing and have some of the characteristics of expert systems (Little 1970). It has been found that in laboratory studies these models are sometimes less reliable than unaided intuition (Chakravarti et al. 1981), but it has been argued that laboratory studies are not reliable sources of validation (Little and Lodish 1981). Similar arguments may arise in the context of expert systems.

3. Expert Model-Base Systems

Although some expert management systems will be stand-alone systems, increasingly they are being embedded (along with database systems, decision models, spreadsheet generators, statistical packages, etc.) in more comprehensive decision support systems (Blanning 1985, Holsapple and Whinston 1987, Turban 1988). This suggests an additional application of expert systems—to help managers to manage the causal decision models already at their disposal. It has recently been suggested that expert-systems technology be combined with database technology to produce a discipline called expert database systems (Kerschberg 1985). An expert database system has been defined as a "a system for developing applications requiring knowledge-based processing of shared information" (Smith 1984 p. K2). Implicit in this definition and its source (a workshop on expert database systems) is the assumption that the information of interest is stored data. In this section the case in which the information is contained in a network of management decision models is considered; here, a system for managing this type of information is called an expert model-base system.

There are three principal issues in expert model-base systems: the use of expert systems in constructing models, the use of expert systems in interpreting models, and the use of expert systems in integrating models (Blanning 1987a).

3.1 Model Construction

Since the construction of decision models requires knowledge and experience, it is not surprising that some preliminary investigations have been made into the possibility of using expert systems to help managers to construct models (Hwang 1985). Most of these investigations have resulted only in prototypes or partial prototypes, but they have also suggested that some of these systems may achieve more widespread and recognized application in the future.

There are three major types of models for which expert systems have been used to assist in model construction: statistical models, linear programming models and Monte Carlo simulations. An example of the first is REX, a system that helps users perform regression analyses (Gale and Pregibon 1985, Gale 1986). The user provides REX with observations of a dependent variable and one or more independent variables, and requests an ordinary least-squares regression. REX performs the regression, looks for anomalies in the result (e.g., departures from linearity, asymmetries in the residuals), and suggests transformations of the variables that will eliminate the anomalies. Another such system is ZEERA, which helps users select procedures for elementary statistical analysis (Marcoulides 1987).

The expert systems that help a user to construct linear-programming problems may be divided into three categories depending on the structures of their knowledge bases. The three different structures are rules, frames and semantic nets. One of the rule-based systems assumes that the system being modelled has a network structure, in which the network defines transformations in form (as in product mix models), time (as in dynamic models) and space (as in distribution models); this was implemented in PROLOG (Murphy and Stohr 1986). Another, more specialized, system helps to construct linear-programming models for production planning using EXSYS, a rule-based expert-system shell (Evans and Shafer 1987). The frame-based system, which is implemented in an object-oriented version of PROLOG, is more domain specific, the domain being production management

(Binbasioglu and Jarke 1986). The semantic-net system, which is still in the design stage, will contain templates of various types of similar linear-programming problems and attempt to recognize different problem types and construct the appropriate model (Evans and Camm 1987).

An expert system has been developed for translating a natural-language (i.e., English) description of a queuing problem into a GPSS program for execution (Heidorn 1975). The system reads the problem description and looks for various types of entities (e.g., trucks or loading docks) and actions (e.g., arrival of the truck at the dock or loading the truck), and attempts to construct a symbolic description of the problem. If the description is incomplete, it will request the missing information from the user and then construct the GPSS program.

3.2 Model Interpretation

Sometimes causal decision models will give anomalous results (e.g., a prediction that sales will increase but profits will decrease) and the user must interpret these results. It may be that the assumptions or data in the model are incorrect or that they are correct but interact in a way that is counterintuitive. Two expert systems have been developed for interpreting model results, one for linear-programming models and one for spreadsheet generators.

The system for interpreting the outputs of linear-programming models is called ANALYZE (Greenberg 1983, 1987) and it is based on a discipline called computer-assisted analysis (CAA) (Greenberg and Maybee 1981). CAA is based on the notion that most linear-programming models of network structures and that anomalies result from misspecification of network elements (i.e., errors) or counterintuitive interactions between network elements. ANALYZE uses this notion to interpret anomalies. One such anomaly is the lack of a feasible solution, which results from an overconstrained problem. ANALYZE looks for a single constraint or a small set of constraints that have caused this result. Another anomaly is an unbounded solution, which could result from the omission of a constraint involving a resource or an incorrect sign in the objective function. Yet another anomaly is the use of an expensive resource in a cost minimization problem, which can occur when the less expensive resources are capacitated.

The expert system for interpreting the output of spreadsheet generators, ERGO (King 1985, Kosy and Wise 1986), is based on work done at Carnegie-Mellon University, Pittsburgh, Pennsylvania (Kosy and Wise 1984, Wise and Kosy 1986). ERGO attempts to explain unexpected changes in a variable (e.g., net income) from one simulated year to the next, or between two different cases based on different assumptions. It assumes that any calculated variable is the root of a tree of calculations for which the inputs are the leaves. It proceeds down the tree attempting to find, for one or several nodes at each level, one or several nodes at the next lower level which account for a substantial part of the change in those nodes, and thus to explain the sequence of variable changes that account for most of the change in the root.

3.3 Model Integration

Expert systems can also be used to integrate models, that is, to assemble a set of models in a model bank and to execute them in a proper sequence in order to respond to a user query. The reason that a sequence is needed is that the inputs to some of the models in the set may be outputs of other models in the set. If the set is partially ordered (i.e., if there are no cycles in the set), then existing expert-systems techniques can be used to make the selection and sequencing decisions. Most of the literature on this subject is devoted to the acyclic case, and the more complex issue of cyclic model banks is mentioned only in passing. The discussion to follow will also be confined to acyclic model banks.

One approach is based on logic programming. The inputs and outputs of a model are described as facts (or axioms), the desired information is described as a goal to be attained (i.e., a theorem to be proven) and rules of inference for joining the models are formulated (Bonczek *et al.* 1981, Dutta and Basu 1984, Lee and Miller 1986). This idea has been extended to include connection graphs (Chen *et al.* 1982) for more efficient processing and it has been suggested that a PROLOG-like language be developed for model management (Blanning 1984a).

Other approaches have been proposed, based on other knowledge structuring and processing techniques. One is AND/OR graphs, in which the AND operation combines two or more models and the OR operation allows one model to be selected from a set of several models that can provide the same type of information (Bonczek *et al.* 1981). In addition, it has been suggested that frames (Dolk and Konsynski 1984), semantic nets (Elam *et al.* 1980) and situation–action rules (Blanning 1987b) be used for model-bank integration.

4. Is a Manager an Expert?

The reason for asking this question is that the answer may be helpful in identifying future applications of expert systems to management. That is, by studying the similarities and differences between managers and the other types of people for whom expert systems have been constructed, we may be able to identify potentially fruitful areas of expert-system development (Blanning 1984c, Hertz 1988).

In order to determine the similarities and differences we must first understand what managers do. There are three sources of information on how managers spend their time and what tasks they perform.

The first is general observations by executives (Barnard 1938), consultants (Drucker 1966) and academics (Simon 1957). The second is diary studies, in which managers fill out forms on what they are doing or have just completed doing (Carlson 1951, Mahoney et al. 1965, Stewart 1967). The third is direct observation by a researcher, similar to the "time and motion" studies that have been performed with factory workers (Mintzberg 1973, Kotter 1982).

The first conclusion of these studies is that managers perform certain tasks needed to accomplish the objectives of the organizations or organizational subunits for which they are responsible. These tasks include making decisions or recommendations (e.g., resource allocation and scheduling decisions), implementing the decisions (i.e., monitoring progress and making changes as necessary) and managing their human resources (organizing, staffing, recruiting, promoting, etc.). Lower-level managers devote more of their time to dealing with subordinates than do higher-level managers, who spend more of their time communicating with people outside of the units for which they are responsible.

The second conclusion is an extension of the latter point. Managers often establish a network of people, many of them outside of their organizations, with whom they exchange information and ideas. They seldom spend much time alone, and when alone they are often on the telephone. This is especially true of higher-level managers.

The third conclusion is that managers work in an unstructured and hectic environment in which they are forced to deal with a large number of brief activities, many of them unanticipated (i.e., crises or opportunities). It has been suggested that the economic view of management activities is inappropriate; managers must contend with cognitive limits to economically rational behavior that often leads them to seek satisfactory, rather than optimal, solutions to poorly understood problems (Simon 1957, 1972, Taylor 1975).

Since it takes knowledge and experience to do the types of activities just described, we may conclude that managers may properly be described as experts and ask how expert systems may help them to do their jobs more effectively. It may be useful in this regard to view managers as (a) decision makers and (b) communicators. The way in which expert systems help managers to make decisions by helping them to allocate resources, diagnose problems, etc., has already been described in Sect. 1. The question is whether they can help managers to communicate more effectively.

Although it is not clear whether expert systems will be useful in face-to-face or telephonic communication, they may be useful in more structured forms of communication, such as electronic mail. A system called information LENS has been developed to help users of an electronic-mail system to make more effective use of the system (Malone et al. 1987). The system allows the user to construct a rule base for finding important messages, filtering unwanted ones and sorting messages, along with message templates that assist in constructing messages. Systems of this type may help managers manage other types of information in the future.

5. Expert Systems as Competitive Weapons

As national markets are becoming regional and regional markets are becoming international, there is a growing interest in the subject of competitiveness; contained within this topic are the ways in which information-processing technology can help a company to be more competitive (by lowering cost, improving service, etc.). This article is concluded by asking whether expert systems can help a company to be more competitive.

It appears that they can (Barkocy and Blanning 1987). Expert systems that help managers to allocate resources, diagnose problems, and so on, can make managers more productive, when such systems are properly designed and implemented. It is not yet clear whether expert model-base systems and expert systems for communication will also be useful, but these appear to be potentially fruitful topics for research, and some research is already being done in these areas. Thus, it can be concluded that expert systems, like more traditional types of decision support systems, will make selected contributions to the productivity of managers and the competitiveness of their organizations.

See also: Decision Support Systems; Expert Database Systems; Expert Systems

Bibliography

Barkocy B E, Blanning R W 1987 Expert systems as competitive weapons. *Expert Systems in Business 1987 Proc.*, Learned Information, Medway, New Jersey, pp. 1–13

Barnard C I 1938 *The Functions of the Executive*. Harvard University Press, Cambridge, Massachusetts

Binbasioglu M, Jarke M 1986 Domain-specific DSS tools for knowledge-based model building. *Decis. Support Syst.* **2,** 213–23

Blanning R W 1984a A PROLOG-based framework for model management. *Proc. 1st Int. Workshop Expert Database Systems*. Benjamin–Cummings, Menlo Park, California, pp. 633–42

Blanning R W 1984b Expert systems for management: Possible application areas. In: Zmud R W (ed.) *DSS-84 Trans.* Institute for the Advancement of Decision Support Systems, pp 69–77

Blanning R W 1984c Issues in the design of expert systems for management. *Proc. National Computer Conf.* North-Holland, Amsterdam

Blanning R W 1984d Knowledge acquisition and system validation in expert systems for management. *Hum. Syst. Manage.* **4,** 280–85

Blanning R W 1984e Management applications of expert systems. *Inf. Manage.* **7,** 311–16

Blanning R W 1985 Expert systems for management: Research and applications. *J. Inf. Sci.* **9**, 153–62

Blanning R W 1987a A framework for expert modelbase systems. *Proc. National Computer Conf.* AFIPS, Reston, Virginia, pp. 13–17

Blanning R W 1987b The application of metaknowledge to information management. *Hum. Syst. Manage.* **7**, 49–57

Bohanek, M, Bratko I, Rajkovic V 1983 An expert system for decision making. In: Sol H G (ed.) *Processes and Tools for Decision Support.* North-Holland, Amsterdam, pp. 235–48

Bonczek R A, Holsapple C W, Whinston A B 1981 *Foundations of Decision Support Systems.* Academic Press, New York

Bouwman M J 1983 Human diagnostic reasoning by computer: An illustration from financial analysis. *Manage. Sci.* **29**, 653–72

Carlson S 1951 *Executive Behavior.* Stromberg, Stockholm

Chakravarti D, Mitchell A, Staelin R 1981 Judgement based marketing models: Problems and possible solutions. *J. Market.* **45**, 13–23

Chen M C, Fedorowicz J E, Henschen L J 1982 Deductive processes in databases and decision support systems. *Proc. North Central ACM 1982 Conf.* Association for Computing Machinery, New York, pp. 81–100

Clarkson G P E 1962 *Portfolio Selection: A Simulation of Trust Investment.* Prentice-Hall, Englewood Cliffs, New Jersey

Clarkson G P E 1963 A model of the trust investment process. In: Feigenbaum E A, Feldman H (eds.) *Computers and Thought.* McGraw-Hill, New York, pp. 347–71

Davis R 1979 Interactive transfer of expertise: Acquisition of new inference rules. *Artif. Intell.* **12**, 10–157

Dhar V 1987 On the plausibility and scope of expert systems in management. *J. Manage. Inf. Syst.* **4**, 25–41

Dolk D R, Konsynski B R 1984 Knowledge representation for model management systems. *IEEE Trans. Software Eng.* **10**, 619–28

Drucker P 1966 *The Effective Executive.* Harper & Row, New York

Dungan C W, Chandler J S 1985 AUDITOR: A microcomputer-based expert system to support auditors in the field. *Expert Syst.* **2**, 210–21

Dutta A, Basu A 1984 An artificial intelligence approach to model management in decision support systems. *IEEE Comput.* **17**, 89–97

Elam J J, Henderson J C, Miller L W 1980 Model management systems: An approach to decision support in complex organizations. *Proc. 1st Int. Conf. Information Systems* pp. 98–100

Evans J R, Camm J D 1987 Structuring the modeling process for linear programming. *Proc. 1987 Annual Meeting of the Decision Sciences Institute.* pp. 957–59

Evans J R, Shafer S M 1987 An expert modeling assistant for production planning optimization problems. *Proc. 1987 Annu. Meet. Decision Sciences Institute.* pp. 768–70

Forrester J W 1980a Information sources for modeling the national economy. *J. Am. Stat. Assoc.* **75**, 555–66

Forrester J W 1980b Rejoinder. *J. Am. Stat. Assoc.* **75**, 572–74

Fox M S, Smith S F 1984 ISIS—A knowledge-based system for factory scheduling. *Expert Syst.* **1**, 25–49

Gale W A 1986 *Artificial Intelligence and Statistics.* Addison–Wesley, Reading, Massachusetts

Gale W A, Pregibon D 1985 Artificial intelligence research in statistics. *AI Mag.* **5**, 72–75

Goldstein I P, Roberts B 1982 Using frames in scheduling. In: Winston P H, Brown R H (eds.) *Artificial Intelligence: An MIT Perspective.* MIT Press, Cambridge, Massachusetts, pp. 255–84

Greenberg H J 1983 A functional description of ANALYZE: A computer-assisted analysis system for linear programming models. *ACM Trans. Math. Software* **9**, 18–56

Greenberg H J 1987 A natural language discourse model to explain linear programming models and solutions. *Decis. Support Syst.* **3**, 333–42

Greenberg H J, Maybee J S 1981 *Computer-Assisted Analysis and Model Simplification.* Academic Press, New York

Harmon P, King D 1985 *Expert Systems: Artificial Intelligence in Business.* Wiley, New York

Heidorn G E 1975 Simulation programming through natural language dialogue. In: Geisler M A (ed.) *Logistics.* North-Holland, Amsterdam, pp. 71–83

Hertz D B 1988 *The Expert Executive.* Wiley, New York

Holsapple C W, Whinston A B 1987 *Business Expert Systems.* Irwin, Homewood, Illinois

Hwang S 1985 Automatic model building systems: A survey. In: Elam J J (ed.) *DSS-85 Trans.* The Institute for the Advancement of Decision Support Systems and the Institute of Management Sciences, College on Information Systems, pp. 22–32

Kerschberg L (ed.) 1985 *Proc. 1st Int. Conf. Expert Database Systems.* Benjamin–Cummings, Menlo Park, California

King D 1985 The ERGO project: A natural language query facility for explaining financial results. In: Fedorowicz J (ed.) *DSS-86 Trans.* The Institute of Management Sciences, College on Information Systems, pp. 131–50

Kosy D W, Wise B P 1984 Self-explanatory financial planning models. *Proc. National Conf. Artificial Intelligence.* pp. 176–81

Kosy D W, Wise B P 1986 Overview of ROME: A reason-oriented modeling environment. In: Pau L F (ed.) *Artifical Intelligence in Economics and Management.* North-Holland, Amsterdam, pp. 21–30

Kotter J P 1982 What effective managers really do. *Harv. Bus. Rev.* **60**, 156–67

Lee R M, Miller L W 1986 A logic programming framework for planning and simulation. *Decis. Support Syst.* **2**, 15–25

Little J D C 1970 Models and managers: The concept of a decision calculus. *Manage. Sci.* **16**, B466–85

Little J D C, Lodish L M 1981 Commentary on "judgement based marketing decision models." *J. Market.* **45**, 24–29

Mahoney T A, Jerdee T H, Carroll S J 1965 The job(s) of management. *Ind. Relat.* **4**, 97–110

Malone T W, Grant K R, Turbak F A, Brobst S A, Cohen M D 1987 Intelligent information-sharing systems. *Commun. ACM.* **30**, 390–402

Maney T, Reid I 1986 *A Management Guide to Artificial Intelligence.* Gower, Aldershot

Marcoulides G A 1987 An expert system for statistical consulting. *Proc. 1987 Annual Meeting of the Decision Sciences Institute.* pp. 1182–83

Mintzberg H 1973 *The Nature of Managerial Work.* Harper & Row, New York

Murphy F H, Stohr E A 1986 An intelligent system for formulating linear programs. *Decis. Support Sys.* **2**, 39–47

Silverman B (ed.) 1987 *Expert Systems for Business.* Addison–Wesley, Reading, Massachusetts

Simon H A 1957 *Administrative Behavior*, 2nd edn. Macmillan, New York

Simon H A 1972 Theories of bounded rationality. In: McGuire C B, Radner R *Decision and Organization*. North-Holland, Amsterdam

Smith J M 1984 Expert database systems: A database perspective. In: Kerschberg L (ed.) *Proc. 1st Int. Workshop on Expert Database Systems*. Benjamin–Cummings, Menlo Park, California, pp. K1–K22

Stewart R 1967 *Managers and Their Jobs*. Pan, London

Taylor R N 1975 Psychological determination of bounded rationality: Implications for decision-making strategies. *Decis. Sci.* **6**, 409–29

Turban E 1988 *Decision Support and Expert Systems*. Macmillan, New York

Waterman D A 1986 *A Guide to Expert Systems*. Addison–Wesley, Reading, Massachusetts

Wise B P, Kosy D W 1986 Model-based evaluation of long-range resource allocation plans. In: Pau L F (ed.) *Artificial Intelligence in Economics and Management*. North-Holland, Amsterdam, pp. 93–102

Zellner A 1980 Comment. *J. Am. Stat. Assoc.* **75**, 567–69

R. W. Blanning
[Vanderbilt University, Nashville, Tennessee, USA]

Fuzzy Reasoning Methods

In much of human reasoning, the form of reasoning is approximate rather than exact as in the statement:

> If a tomato is red then the tomato is ripe
> This tomato is more-or-less red
> ―――――――――――――――――――――――――――
> This tomato is more-or-less ripe

Such reasoning cannot be made sufficient by the inference rules of classical two-valued and many-valued logic.

To make such reasoning with fuzzy concepts, Zadeh (1975a,b) first suggested an inference rule called "the compositional rule of inference" and proposed translation rules for translating a fuzzy conditional proposition "If x is A then y is B" into a fuzzy relation. Since then several alternative approaches to that given by Zadeh for fuzzy reasoning have been presented by several researchers such as Baldwin (1979a,b), Tsukamoto (1979a,b), Yager (1980) and Mizumoto (1984, 1987) by introducing fuzzy logic with fuzzy truth values.

1. Zadeh's Fuzzy Reasoning Methods

We shall first discuss the following form of fuzzy reasoning in which a fuzzy conditional proposition "If ... then ..." is contained.

$$\begin{array}{l}\text{Ant. 1: If } x \text{ is } A \text{ then } y \text{ is } B \\ \text{Ant. 2: } x \text{ is } A' \\ \hline \text{Cons.: } y \text{ is } B' \end{array} \quad (1)$$

where x and y are the names of objects, and A, A', B and B' are fuzzy concepts represented by fuzzy sets in universes of discourse U, U, V and V, respectively. This form of fuzzy reasoning can be considered as fuzzy *modus ponens* which reduces to the classical *modus ponens* when $A' = A$ and $B' = B$.

The Ant. 1 of the form "If x is A then y is B" in (1) represents a certain relationship between A and B. From this point of view, Zadeh (1975a) proposed a translation rule for translating "If A then B" into a fuzzy relation $A \to B$ in $U \times V$. The consequence B' is deduced from Ant. 1 and Ant. 2 by taking the max–min composition ($\circ$) of the fuzzy set A' and the fuzzy relation $A \to B$ (the compositional rule of inference). Namely, we have

$$B' = A' \circ (A \to B) \quad (2)$$

$$\mu_{B'}(v) = \bigvee_u [\mu_{A'}(u) \wedge \mu_{A \to B}(u, v)] \quad (3)$$

As a rule for translating "If A then B" into a fuzzy relation $A \to B$, Zadeh proposed a translating rule called an "arithmetic rule" Ra.

Let A and B be fuzzy sets in U and V, respectively, then the arithmetic rule Ra is given as

$$Ra = A \to B = (\bar{A} \times V) \oplus (U \times B) \quad (4)$$

$$\mu_{Ra}(u, v) = \int_{U \times V} 1 \wedge [1 - \mu_A(u) + \mu_B(v)]/(u, v)$$

where $\oplus$ stands for bounded sum $x \oplus y = 1 \wedge (x + y)$. It is noted that the arithmetic rule Ra is based on the implication rule of Lukasiewicz's logic; i.e.,

$$a \to b = 1 \wedge (1 - a + b) \quad (5)$$

The consequence B' in (1) is given as follows.

$$B' = A' \circ Ra = A' \circ [(\bar{A} \times V) \oplus (U \times B)]$$

$$\mu_{B'}(v) = \bigvee_u \{\mu_{A'}(u) \wedge [1 \wedge (1 - \mu_A(u) + \mu_B(v))]\} \quad (6)$$

For example, when $A' = A$, the arithmetic rule Ra infers such a consequence as (see Mizumoto 1981, Mizumoto and Zimmermann 1982)

$$B' = \int_V \frac{1 + \mu_B(v)}{2} \bigg/ v \neq B \quad (7)$$

This inference result indicates that the arithmetic rule Ra does not satisfy the *modus ponens* which is quite a reasonable demand in fuzzy reasoning.

$$\begin{array}{l}\text{If } x \text{ is } A \text{ then } y \text{ is } B \\ x \text{ is } A \\ \hline y \text{ is } B\end{array} \quad (\text{modus ponens}) \quad (8)$$

In the case of Mamdani's method Rc (Mamdani 1974) which is often used in the discussion of fuzzy controls and is defined as the direct product $A \times B$ of fuzzy sets A and B which is based on the implication $a \to b = a \wedge b$, we have the consequence B' as

$$B' = A' \circ (A \to B) = A' \circ (A \times B) \quad (9)$$

When $A' = A$, the consequence B' is given as

$$B' A \circ Rc = A \circ (A \times B) = B \quad (10)$$

under the assumption that A is normal (maximal grade = 1). Therefore, Mamdani's method Rc satisfies the *modus ponens* of (8).

Although Zadeh's method Ra does not satisfy the *modus ponens* when using the max–min composition ($\circ$) as the compositional rule of inference, we shall next show that Ra satisfies the *modus ponens* if new compositions named as "max-$\odot$ composition" ($\square$) and max-$\wedge$ composition ($\blacktriangle$) are used in the compositional rule of inference. The operations $\odot$ and $\wedge$ are defined as:

Bounded product: $x \odot y = 0 \vee (x+y-1)$ (11)

Drastic product: $x \wedge y = \begin{cases} x \ldots y = 1 \\ y \ldots x = 1 \\ 0 \ldots x, y < 1 \end{cases}$ (12)

Max-$\odot$ composition $\square$ and max-$\wedge$ composition $\blacktriangle$ are obtained by replacing $\wedge$ by $\odot$ and $\wedge$ in Eqns. (3) or (6).

Using these new compositions, we have at $A' = A$:

$$B' = A \square Ra = B$$
$$B' = A \blacktriangle Ra = B$$

which indicates that Zadeh's method Ra satisfies the *modus ponens* of (8) under new compositions (Mizumoto 1979, 1982).

In addition to the methods Ra and Rc, it is possible to obtain a number of translating rules $A \rightarrow B$ by introducing implication rules $a \rightarrow b$ of many-valued logics as shown in the left of Table 1 (Mizumoto 1979, 1982, Mizumoto and Zimmermann 1982). Obviously, we can obtain $A \rightarrow B$ from $a \rightarrow b$ as follows.

$$\mu_{A \rightarrow B}(u, v) = \mu_A(u) \rightarrow \mu_B(v) \quad (13)$$

Table 1 shows inference results by various translating rules under ordinal max–min composition and new compositions discussed above. Moreover, this table contains inference results when A' is very A, more-or-less A and not A which are defined as

$$A' = \text{very } A = \int_U \mu_A(u)^2/u \quad (14)$$

$$A' = \text{more-or-less } A = \int_U [\mu_A(u)]^{1/2}/u \quad (15)$$

$$A' = \text{not } A = \int_U 1 - \mu_A(u)/u \quad (16)$$

It is found from this table that the inference results under new compositions of max-$\odot$ composition and max-$\wedge$ composition are more reasonable than those under max–min composition. In fact, all of the translating rules satisfy the *modus ponens* of (8) under new compositions and most of the translating rules provide intuitive inference results at $A' = $ very A, more-or-less A and not A.

We shall next consider the following form of fuzzy reasoning with fuzzy truth values τ_1 and τ_2.

Ant. 1: (If x is A then y is B) is τ_1
Ant. 2: (x is A') is τ_2

Cons.: y is B' (17)

A fuzzy truth value τ is a fuzzy set in the truth value space [0, 1]; some examples of fuzzy truth values are shown in Fig. 1. Fuzzy truth values *true* and *false* are defined as $\mu_{\text{true}}(t) = t$ and $\mu_{\text{false}}(t) = 1 - t$. Fuzzy truth values with very A, more-or-less A and not A are defined by using Eqns. (14)–(16).

Table 1
Inference results B' from A' and $A \rightarrow B$ ($A' = A$, very A, more-or-less A, or not A, as indicated)

$a \rightarrow b$	Max–min composition ($\circ$)				Max-$\odot$ composition ($\square$)				Max-$\wedge$ composition ($\blacktriangle$)			
	A	very A	more-or-less A	not A	A	very A	more-or-less A	not A	A	very A	more-or-less A	not A
$Ra: 1 \wedge (1-a+b)$	$\frac{1+\mu_B}{2}$	a	b	1	μ_B	μ_B	c	1	μ_B	μ_B	$(\mu_B)^{1/2}$	1
$Rm: (a \wedge b) \vee (1-a)$	$0.5 \vee \mu_B$	d	e	1	μ_B	μ_B	$0.25 \vee \mu_B$	1	μ_B	μ_B	μ_B	1
$Rc: a \wedge b$	μ_B	μ_B	μ_B	$0.5 \wedge \mu_B$	μ_B	μ_B	μ_B	0	μ_B	μ_B	μ_B	0
$Rs: \begin{cases} 1 \ldots a \leq b \\ 0 \ldots a > b \end{cases}$	μ_B	μ_{B^2}	$(\mu_B)^{1/2}$	1	μ_B	μ_{B^2}	$(\mu_B)^{1/2}$	1	μ_B	μ_{B^2}	$(\mu_B)^{1/2}$	1
$Rg: \begin{cases} 1 \ldots a \leq b \\ b \ldots a > b \end{cases}$	μ_B	μ_B	$(\mu_B)^{1/2}$	1	μ_B	μ_B	$(\mu_B)^{1/2}$	1	μ_B	μ_B	$(\mu_B)^{1/2}$	1
$Rb: (1-a) \vee b$	$0.5 \vee \mu_B$	d	e	1	μ_B	μ_B	$0.25 \vee \mu_B$	1	μ_B	μ_B	μ_B	1
$R\Delta: \begin{cases} 1 \ldots a \leq b \\ b/a \ldots a > b \end{cases}$	$(\mu_B)^{1/2}$	$(\mu_B)^{2/3}$	$(\mu_B)^{1/3}$	1	μ_B	μ_B	$(\mu_B)^{1/2}$	1	μ_B	μ_B	$(\mu_B)^{1/2}$	1

a $\frac{3+2\mu_B-(5+4\mu_B)^{1/2}}{2}$ b $\frac{(5+4\mu_B)^{1/2}-1}{2}$ c $\begin{cases} \mu_B+0.25 \ldots \mu_B \leq 0.25 \\ (\mu_B)^{1/2} \ldots \mu_B \geq 0.25 \end{cases}$ d $\frac{3-5^{1/2}}{2} \vee \mu_B$ e $\frac{5^{1/2}-1}{2} \vee \mu_B$

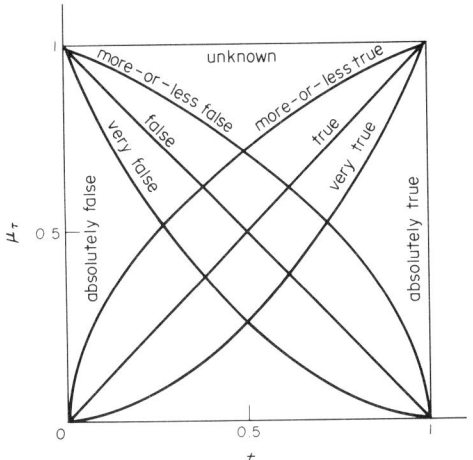

Figure 1
Various fuzzy truth values τ

We shall consider a fuzzy proposition "⌈ x is F ⌋" with a fuzzy truth value τ; that is, "⌈ (x is F) is τ ⌋" and obtain its equivalent fuzzy proposition "⌈ x is G ⌋."

$$(x \text{ is } F) \text{ is } \tau \Leftrightarrow x \text{ is } G \quad (18)$$

where F and G are fuzzy sets in the same universe U. G is obtained as follows (truth functional modification, Zadeh (1975b)).

$$\mu_G(u) = \mu_\tau[\mu_F(u)] \quad (19)$$

For example, if τ is true, very true, false, we have

$$(x \text{ is } F) \text{ is true} \Leftrightarrow x \text{ is } F \quad (20)$$
$$(x \text{ is } F) \text{ is very true} \Leftrightarrow x \text{ is very } F \quad (21)$$
$$(x \text{ is } F) \text{ is false} \Leftrightarrow x \text{ is not } F \quad (22)$$

Conversely, we derive a fuzzy truth value for a fuzzy proposition "⌈ x is F ⌋" when given a (reference) fuzzy proposition "⌈ x is G ⌋." The fuzzy truth value τ of "⌈ x is F ⌋" relative to "⌈ x is G ⌋" is defined by the following (inverse truth functional modification).

$$\tau = \text{truth } (x \text{ is } F/x \text{ is } G)$$
$$= \mu_G(u)/\mu_F(u) \quad (23)$$

A more explicit expression of τ is

$$\mu_\tau(t) = \bigvee_u \mu_G(u) \quad t \in [0, 1]$$

where u satisfies $\mu_F(u) = t$.

As a simple example, we obtain

$$\text{truth } (x \text{ is } F/x \text{ is } F) = \text{true} \quad (24)$$
$$\text{truth } (x \text{ is } F/x \text{ is not } F) = \text{false} \quad (25)$$
$$\text{truth } (x \text{ is } F/x \text{ is very } F) = \text{very true} \quad (26)$$

We shall next consider the form of fuzzy reasoning (17) with fuzzy truth values. Mizumoto (1987) shows the way of obtaining consequence B' by using Zadeh's method.

The consequence B' of (17) is obtained by the following.

(a) Using the truth functional modification of Eqn. (19), we obtain the new proposition "⌈ x is A'' ⌋" which is equivalent to "⌈ (x is A') is τ_2 ⌋" of Ant. 2 in (17). Namely,

$$x \text{ is } A'' \Leftrightarrow (x \text{ is } A') \text{ is } \tau_2$$

where

$$\mu_{A''}(u) = \mu_{\tau_2}[\mu_{A'}(u)]$$

(b) Using also the truth functional modification, a new fuzzy relation denoted as "$\tau_1(A \to B)$," is given as follows which is equivalent to "⌈ ($A \to B$) is τ_1 ⌋."

$$\mu_{\tau_1(A \to B)}(u, v) = \mu_{\tau_1}[\mu_{A \to B}(u, v)]$$

(c) The consequence B' is given by taking the max–min composition of A'' and $\tau_1(A \to B)$.

$$B' = A'' \circ \tau_1(A \to B)$$

$$\mu_{B'}(v) = \bigvee_u [\mu_{A''}(u) \wedge \mu_{\tau_1(A \to B)}(u, v)]$$

$$= \bigvee_u \{\mu_{\tau_2}[\mu_{A'}(u)] \wedge \mu_{\tau_1}[\mu_{A \to B}(u, v)]\}$$

EXAMPLE 1. *Let $A \to B = Ra$ of Eqn. (4), τ_1 = absolutely true (see Fig. 1), A' = more-or-less A, and τ_2 = very true in (17), then we have $A'' = A$ since*

$$(x \text{ is more-or-less } A) \text{ is very true} \Leftrightarrow x \text{ is } A$$

and $\tau_1(Ra)$ is

$$\mu_{\tau_1}\{1 \wedge [1 - \mu_A(u) + \mu_B(v)]\} = \begin{cases} 1 & \ldots \; \mu_A(u) \leqslant \mu_B(u) \\ 0 & \ldots \; \mu_A(u) > \mu_B(v) \end{cases}$$

which is equal to Rs in Table 1 which is based on the implication of standard sequence. Hence, the consequence B' is given as

$$B' = A'' \circ \tau_1(Ra) = A \circ Rs = B$$

2. Baldwin's Fuzzy Reasoning Methods

Baldwin (1979a,b) gives an alternative approach for fuzzy reasoning forms of (1) and (17) by using fuzzy truth values. At first, we shall begin with the form of fuzzy reasoning of (1) with no fuzzy truth values.

The consequence B' of (1) is obtained by the following.

(a) Using the inverse truth functional modification of Eqn. (23), we obtain a fuzzy truth value τ_A of "⌈ x is A ⌋" relative to "⌈ x is A' ⌋" in (1):

$$\tau_A = \text{truth } (x \text{ is } A/x \text{ is } A')$$

(b) The fuzzy truth values of "⌈x is A⌋" and "⌈y is B⌋" of (1) are considered as true from (20). Thus, a fuzzy conditional proposition "If true then true" can be translated into a fuzzy relation in $[0, 1] \times [0, 1]$ which is obtained by using, say, the arithmetic rule Ra of Eqn. (4).

$$\text{true} \to \text{true}$$
$$= (\text{not true}) \times [0, 1]) \oplus ([0, 1] \times \text{true})$$
$$= \int 1 \wedge [1 - \mu_{\text{true}}(t) + \mu_{\text{true}}(s)]/(t, s)$$
$$= \int 1 \wedge (1 - t + s)/(t, s)$$

(c) The truth value of "⌈y is B⌋" given "⌈y is A⌋" is obtained by taking the max–min composition ($\circ$) of τ_A and true → true. Namely,

$$\tau_B = \tau_A \circ (\text{true} \to \text{true})$$
$$\mu_{\tau_B}(s) = \bigvee_t \{\mu_{\tau_A}(t) \wedge [1 \wedge (1 - t + s)]\} \quad (27)$$

(d) Using the truth functional modification of (19), the consequence B' is obtained as

$$y \text{ is } B' \Leftrightarrow (y \text{ is } B) \text{ is } \tau_B$$

EXAMPLE 2. *We shall consider the case of $A' = A$ in (1). We derive*

$$\tau_A = \text{truth}(x \text{ is } A/x \text{ is } A) = \text{true}$$
$$\tau_B = \text{true} \circ (\text{true} \to \text{true}) = \int \frac{1 + s}{2} / s$$
$$\mu_{B'}(v) = \mu_{\tau_B}[\mu_B(v)] = \frac{1 + \mu_B(v)}{2}$$

Thus,

$$B' = \int \frac{1 + \mu_B(v)}{2} / v$$

This inference result B' at $A' = A$ is equal to Eqn. (7) by Zadeh's method Ra and hence Baldwin's method does not satisfy the *modus ponens* of (8). However, if new compositions of max-. composition and max-$\wedge$ composition are used in Eqn. (27), Baldwin's method can also get the consequence which satisfies the *modus ponens*.

When $A' = \text{very } A$, the consequence B' is as follows.

$$\tau_A = \text{truth}(x \text{ is } A/x \text{ is very } A) = \text{very true}$$
$$\tau_B = \text{very true} \circ (\text{true} \to \text{true})$$
$$= \int \frac{3 + 2s - (5 + 4s)^{1/2}}{2} / s$$
$$B' = \int_V \frac{3 + 2\mu_B(v) - [5 + 4\mu_B(v)]^{1/2}}{2} / v$$

which is also equal to the result by Zadeh's method at $A' = \text{very } A$ (see Table 1). The same holds for the cases of $A' = \text{more-or-less } A$ and not A. In fact, Tong and Festathiou (1982) point out that if the inverse of uA is a subjective mapping, Baldwin's method is equivalent to Zadeh's method and so Baldwin's method which is based on fuzzy truth values is inherently redundant and computationally inefficient.

As a generalization of the form of fuzzy reasoning of (1), Baldwin considers the fuzzy reasoning form (17) with fuzzy truth values.

The consequence B' of (17) is given as follows:

$$x \text{ is } A'' \Leftrightarrow (x \text{ is } A') \text{ is } \tau_2$$
$$\tau_A = \text{truth}(x \text{ is } A/x \text{ is } A'')$$
$$\tau_B = \tau_A \circ \tau_1 \text{ (true} \to \text{true)}$$
$$\mu_{\tau_B}(s) = \bigvee_t \{\mu_{\tau_A}(t) \wedge \mu_{\tau_1}[1 \wedge (1 - t + s)]\}$$

Hence,

$$\mu_{B'}(v) = \mu_{\tau_B}[\mu_B(v)]$$

3. Tsukamoto's Fuzzy Reasoning Method

Tsukamoto (1979a,b) introduced a different fuzzy reasoning method which is also based on a fuzzy logic with fuzzy truth values.

Let τ_A and τ_B be fuzzy truth values of fuzzy propositions "⌈x is A⌋" and "⌈y is B⌋," and let $a \to b$ be the implication rule of Lukasiewicz logic (5). Then the fuzzy truth value of $A \to B$ is given by

$$\tau_{A \to B} = 1 \wedge (1 - \tau_A + \tau_B) \quad (28)$$

where the operations $\wedge$, $-$ and $+$ are fuzzied ones which are defined by using the extension principle (Zadeh 1975b).

Introducing α-cuts of these fuzzy truth values, Eqn. (28) is rewritten as

$$\tau_{A \to B}^\alpha = 1 \wedge (1 - \tau_A^\alpha + \tau_B^\alpha) \quad (29)$$

where the α-cut of, say, τ_A is defined as

$$\tau_A^\alpha = \{t | \mu_{\tau_A}(t) \geq \alpha\}$$

When τ_A and $\tau_{A \to B}$ are given, τ_B is obtained by solving Eqn. (29). Let τ_A^α and $\tau_{A \to B}^\alpha$ be given as intervals in $[0, 1]$, say,

$$\tau_A^\alpha = [a_1, a_2], \qquad \tau_{A \to B}^\alpha = [c_1, c_2]$$

Then we can obtain from (29)

$$\tau_B^\alpha = \begin{cases} [0 \vee (a_1 + c_1 - 1), 1] & c_2 = 1 \\ [0 \vee (a_1 + c_1 - 1), a_2 + c_2 - 1] & a_2 + c_2 \geq 1, c_2 \neq 1 \\ \emptyset & 0 \leq a_2 + c_2 < 1 \end{cases}$$
(30)

As a simple case, let us assume that τ_A is normal and convex, and $\tau_{A \to B}$ is normal and its membership function is nondecreasing in its domain $[0, 1]$. Then we have

$\tau_A^\alpha = [a_1, a_2]$, $\tau_{A \to B}^\alpha = [c, 1]$. From this we can readily obtain τ_B^α as follows, by setting $c_2 = 1$ and $c_1 = c$ in Eqn. (30).

$$\tau_B^\alpha = [0 \vee (a_1 + c - 1), 1] \quad (31)$$

Now we shall apply Tsukamoto's method to the form of fuzzy reasoning of (17), The consequence B' is deduced by the following:

(a) We obtain the fuzzy truth value τ_A of "⌈x is A⌋" relative to "⌈(x is A') is τ_2⌋."

$$x \text{ is } A'' \Leftrightarrow (x \text{ is } A') \text{ is } \tau_2$$

$$\tau_A = \text{truth } (x \text{ is } A/x \text{ is } A'')$$

(b) From τ_A and $\tau_1 (= \tau_{A \to B})$, we calculate τ_B by using Eqn. (30) or (31).

(c) The consequence B' is obtained as

$$y \text{ is } B' \Leftrightarrow (y \text{ is } B) \text{ is } \tau_B$$

EXAMPLE 3. *We shall consider a simple case of $\tau_1 = \tau_2 = $ true in (17), which reduces to the form of fuzzy reasoning of (1) because of the property of (20).*
When $A' = A$, we have $A'' = A$ since $\tau_2 = $ true, and

$$\tau_A = \text{truth } (x \text{ is } A/x \text{ is } A) = \text{true}$$

is obtained. The α-cuts of τ_A ($=$ true) and $\tau_1 (= \tau_{A \to B})$ $=$ true are given as

$$\tau_A^\alpha = [\alpha, 1], \qquad \tau_{A \to B}^\alpha = [\alpha, 1]$$

We have from Eqn. (31)

$$\tau_B^\alpha = [0 \vee (\alpha + \alpha - 1), 1] = [0 \vee (2\alpha - 1), 1]$$

Thus,

$$\tau_B = \bigcup_\alpha \tau_A^\alpha = \int \frac{1+s}{2} \Big/ s$$

Hence the consequence B' is

$$B' = \int_V \frac{\mu_B(v) + 1}{2} \Big/ v$$

The consequence B' at $A' = A$ is equal to Eqn. (7) but not equal to B so that this method does not satisfy the *modus ponens* of (8).
When $A' = $ very A in (1), the consequence B' is

$$\tau_A = \text{truth } (x \text{ is } A/x \text{ is very } A) = \text{very true}$$

$$\tau_A^\alpha = [\alpha^{1/2}, 1], \tau_{A \to B}^\alpha = \text{true}^\alpha = [\alpha, 1]$$

$$\tau_B^\alpha = [0 \vee (\alpha^{1/2} + \alpha - 1), 1]$$

$$\tau_B = \int \frac{3 + 2s - (5 + 4s)^{1/2}}{2} \Big/ s$$

$$B' = \int_V \frac{3 + 2\mu_B(v) - [5 + 4\mu_B(v)]^{1/2}}{2} \Big/ v$$

which is equal to the inference result by Zadeh's method Ra (see Table 1) and Baldwin's method. In the same way, we can obtain inference results at $A' = $ more-or-less A and not A, which are all equal to the results by Zadeh's method Ra as in Table 1.

The above method is based on Lukasiewicz implication of Eqn. (5). It is possible to use other implication rules of Table 1. When we use implications $a \to b$ for Rg, Rb and $R\Delta$ in Table 1, the α-cut of τ_B of Eqn. (31) will be:

$$\tau_B^\alpha = [a_1 \wedge c, 1] \qquad \text{[case of } Rg\text{]} \quad (32)$$

$$\tau_B^\alpha = \begin{cases} [0, 1] & a_1 + c \leq 1 \\ [c, 1] & a_1 + c > 1 \end{cases} \qquad \text{[case of } Rb\text{]} \quad (33)$$

$$\tau_B^\alpha = [a_1 \times c, 1] \qquad \text{[case of } R\Delta\text{]} \quad (34)$$

For example, applying these methods to Example 3, we have the consequences B' at $A' = A$ as

$$\mu_{B'}(v) = \mu_B(v) \qquad \text{[case of (32)]}$$

$$\mu_{B'}(v) = 0.5 \vee \mu_B(v) \qquad \text{[case of (33)]}$$

$$\mu_{B'}(v) = [\mu_B(v)]^{1/2} \qquad \text{[case of (34)]}$$

It is found from these results that $B' = B$ is obtained from the method of (32) and thus the *modus ponens* of (8) is satisfied. Moreover, these consequences B' at $A' = A$ are the same as those by Rg, Rb and $R\Delta$ as shown in Table 1. It is interesting to note that the same holds for the cases of $A' = $ very A, more-or-less A and not A.

4. Yager's Fuzzy Reasoning Method

Yager's method (Yager 1980) is based on a similarity measure and a new implication rule. We shall be concerned with the fuzzy reasoning of (1).

The consequence B' is obtained as follows.

(a) Let S be a similarity measure of the fuzzy sets A and A' in (1), which indicates the degree to which "⌈x is A⌋" can be derived from "⌈x is A'⌋." In his method two similarity measures S_1 and S_2 are introduced:

$$S_1 = \frac{\bigvee_u [\mu_A(u) \wedge \mu_{A'}(u)]}{\bigvee_u \mu_A(u)} \quad (35)$$

$$S_2 = \int \mu_{A'}(u)/\mu_A(u) \quad (36)$$

The similarity measure S_1 has crisp numerical values in [0, 1]. The second measure S_2 is given as a fuzzy set in [0, 1] and is based on the compatibility of A and A' which has the same definition as Eqn. (23).

(b) In the fuzzy reasoning form of (1), it is natural to expect $B' \approx B$ at $A' \approx A$. Thus, the more similar A' is to A, the more similar B' is to B. Therefore, the larger the similarity is, the more important it is that "⌈y is B⌋" is satisfied. From this fact,

Yager suggests that the consequence B' is given as

$$B' = B^S \qquad (37)$$

which is based on a new implication rule:

$$a \to b = b^a \qquad (38)$$

When S is a numerical value, B^S is defined as

$$B^S = \int \mu_B(v)^S/v \qquad (39)$$

When S is a fuzzy set in $[0, 1]$, B^S is raised to a fuzzy set of type 2 whose grades are fuzzy sets in $[0, 1]$. Thus, the grade $\mu_B S(v)$ is defined as

$$\mu_{B^S}(v) = \int \mu_S(s)/\mu_B(v)^s \qquad s \in [0, 1] \qquad (40)$$

EXAMPLE 4. *We shall first consider the numerical similarity measure* S_1 *given in Eqn. (35). When* $A' = A$, *we have* $S_1 = 1$ *by Eqn. (35). Thus, from Eqn. (39) the consequence* B' *is obtained as*

$$B' = B^1 = B \ldots \text{ at } A' = A$$

which indicates the satisfaction of modus ponens of (8). *Similarly, at* $A' =$ *very* A, *we have* $S_1 = 1$. *Hence,*

$$B' = B^1 = B \ldots \text{ at } A' = \text{very } A$$

Furthermore, we have $B' = B$ *at* $A' =$ *more-or-less* A, *and* $B' =$ *more-or-less* B *at* $A' =$ *not* A, *since* $S_1 = 0.5$ *at* $A' =$ *not* A.

Next, we shall consider the fuzzy similarity measure S_2 *of Eqn. (36). When* $A' = A$, S_2 *is given from Eqn. (36) as*

$$S_2 = \int s/s \qquad s \in [0, 1]$$

The consequence B' *is inferred as* $B' = B^{S_2}$. *Namely, from Eqn. (40) the membership function of* B' *is given as*

$$\mu_{B'}(v) = \int \mu_{S_2}(s)/\mu_B(v)^s = \int s/\mu_B(v)^s$$

$$= \int \log_{\mu_B(v)} z/z \qquad z \in [\mu_B(v), 1]$$

which shows that the modus ponens is not satisfied.
Similarly, when $A' =$ *very* A, B' *is given as*

$$S_2 = \int s^2/s$$

$$\mu_{B'}(v) = \int s^2/\mu_B(v)^s = \int [\log_{\mu_B(v)} z]^2/z$$

It is possible in Yager's method to use other implication rules in (38). For example, the Lukasiewicz implication of (5) gives such a consequence B' as

$$\mu_{B'}(v) = 1 \wedge [1 - S + \mu_B(v)]$$

For example, when $A' = A$, $S_1 = 1$ and $S_2 = \int s/s$ are obtained and the consequences B' are as follows:

$$\mu_{B'}(v) = 1 \wedge [1 - 1 + \mu_B(v)]$$
$$= \mu_B(v) \ldots \text{ at } S_1 = 1$$

$$\mu_{B'}(v) = 1 \wedge [1 - S_2 + \mu_B(v)]$$
$$= \int 1 - z + \mu_B(v)/z$$
$$z \in [\mu_B(v), 1] \ldots \text{ at } S_2$$

5. Mizumoto's Fuzzy Reasoning Method

We shall give two fuzzy reasoning methods which also use fuzzy truth values (Mizumoto 1984, 1987).

The consequence B' of (1) by the first fuzzy reasoning method is given as follows.

(a) The truth value of "⌈ x is A ⌋" relative to "⌈ x is A' ⌋" is

$$\tau_A = \text{truth } (x \text{ is } A/x \text{ is } A')$$

(b) The fuzzy truth values of "⌈ x is A ⌋" and "⌈ y is B ⌋" in (1) are considered as true from (20). Thus, the truth value of the implication true → true is obtained as follows by the use of the extension principle (Zadeh 1975b).

$$\text{true} \to \text{true} = \int \mu_{\text{true}}(t) \wedge \mu_{\text{true}}(s)/t \to s \qquad (41)$$

(c) The truth value τ_B of "⌈ y is B ⌋" given "⌈ x is A ⌋" is

$$\tau_B = \tau_A \,\mathbb{\wedge}\, (\text{true} \to \text{true})$$

where $\mathbb{\wedge}$ stands for a fuzzified "min" defined by using the extension principle.

(d) The consequence B' is obtained as

$$y \text{ is } B' \Leftrightarrow (y \text{ is } B) \text{ is } \tau_B$$

EXAMPLE 5. *If we use Lukasiewicz implication of (5) as* $t \to s$ *in (41), the truth value of* true → true *is obtained as*

$$\text{true} \to \text{true} = \int \mu_{\text{true}}(t) \wedge \mu_{\text{true}}(s)/[1 \wedge (1 - t + s)]$$

$$= \int t \wedge s/[1 \wedge (1 - t + s)]$$

$$= 1 \wedge (1 - \text{true} + \text{true})$$

$$= \text{true}$$

When $A' = A$, τ_A *becomes* true *from Eqn. (23) and we have*

$$\tau_B = \text{true} \,\mathbb{\wedge}\, (\text{true} \to \text{true}) = \text{true} \,\mathbb{\wedge}\, \text{true} = \text{true}$$

Thus,

$$(y \text{ is } B) \text{ is true} \Leftrightarrow y \text{ is } B$$

Therefore, we have $B' = B$, which shows the satisfaction of modus ponens of (8).

In the same way, when $A' =$ very A, more-or-less A, and not A, the fuzzy truth values τ_A become very true, more-or-less true, and false ($=$ not true), respectively. Moreover, the fuzzy truth values τ_B are as follows:

$\tau_B =$ very true $\,\barwedge\,$ (true $\to$ true) $=$ very true $\,\barwedge\,$ true
$=$ true ... at $A' =$ very A

$\tau_B =$ more-or-less true $\,\barwedge\,$ true
$=$ more-or-less true ... at $A' =$ more-or-less A

$\tau_B =$ false $\,\barwedge\,$ true $=$ false ... at $A' =$ not A

Therefore, the consequences B' are:

$B' = B$ ... at $A' = A$

$B' = B$ ... at $A' =$ very A

$B' =$ more-or-less B ... at $A' =$ more-or-less A

$B' =$ not B ... at $A' =$ not A

Finally, we shall show another fuzzy reasoning method which also uses fuzzy truth values.

The consequence B' of (1) is obtained as:

(a) The fuzzy truth value of "⌈ x is A ⌋" relative to "⌈ x is A' ⌋" is given as

$$\tau = \text{truth } (x \text{ is } A/x \text{ is } A')$$

(b) Using the truth value τ, we have B' as

$$y \text{ is } B' \Leftrightarrow (y \text{ is } B) \text{ is } \tau$$

EXAMPLE 6. When $A' = A$ in (1), we have $\tau =$ true. Thus, the consequence B' is $B' = B$. Similarly, the truth values τ are very true, more-or-less true and false, respectively, when $A' =$ very A, more-or-less A and not A. Therefore, the consequences B' are as follows:

$B' = B$ ... at $A' = A$

$B' =$ very B ... at $A' =$ very A

$B' =$ more-or-less B ... at $A' =$ more-or-less A

$B' =$ not B ... at $A' =$ not A

Bibliography

Baldwin J F 1979a A new approach to approximate reasoning using a fuzzy logic. *Fuzzy Sets Syst.* **2**, 309–25

Baldwin J F 1979b Fuzzy logic and its application to fuzzy reasoning. In: Gupta M M, Ragade R K, Yager R R (eds.) *Advances in Fuzzy Set Theory and Applications*. North-Holland, Amsterdam, pp. 93–115

Mamdani E H 1974 Applications of fuzzy algorithms for control of a simple dynamic plant. *Proc. IEEE* **121**, 1585–88

Mizumoto M 1979 Fuzzy inference using max-$\wedge$ composition in the compositional rule of inference. In: Gupta M M, Ragade R K, Yager R R (eds.) *Advances in Fuzzy Set Theory and Applications*. North-Holland, Amsterdam, pp. 93–115

Mizumoto M 1981 Note on the arithmetic rule by Zadeh for fuzzy conditional inference. *Cybern. Syst.* **12**, 247–306

Mizumoto M 1982 Fuzzy conditional inference under max-$\odot$ composition. *Inf. Sci.* **27**, 183–209

Mizumoto M 1984 Fuzzy reasoning methods. *Syst. Control* **28**, 436–41 (in Japanese)

Mizumoto M 1987 Fuzzy logics and fuzzy reasoning. *Math. Sci.* **284**, 10–18 (in Japanese)

Mizumoto M, Zimmermann H J 1982 Comparison of fuzzy reasoning methods. *Fuzzy Sets Syst.* **8**, 253–84

Tong R M, Festathiou J 1982 A critical assessment of truth functional modification and its use in approximate reasoning. *Fuzzy Sets Syst.* **7**, 103–8

Tsukamoto Y 1979a An approach to fuzzy reasoning method. In: Gupta M M, Ragade R K, Yager R R (eds.) *Advances in Fuzzy Set Theory and Applications*. North-Holland, Amsterdam, pp. 137–49

Tsukamoto Y 1979b Fuzzy logic based on Lukasiewicz logic and its applications to diagnosis and control, Ph.D. thesis. Tokyo Institute of Technology, Tokyo, Japan

Yager R R 1980 An approach to inference in approximate reasoning. *J. Man-Mach. Stud.* **13**, 323–38

Zadeh L A 1975a Fuzzy logic and approximate reasoning. *Synthese* **30**, 407–28

Zadeh L A 1975b The concept of a linguistic variable and its application to approximate reasoning (I); (II); (III). *Inf. Sci.* **8**, 199–249; **8**, 301–57; **9**, 43–80

M. Mizumoto
[Osaka Electro-Communication University, Osaka, Japan]

G

Group Decision Making and Voting

Decisions often affect groups of people instead of isolated individuals. In such cases, managers, planners and decision makers are usually expected to consider the preferences of the individuals concerned. Approaches to the problem of amalgamating the individual preferences into a form which can be used to guide the decision maker are discussed in this article, with the emphasis on, voting, a very common form of group decision making.

In many presentations of the theory of decision making (Von Neumann and Morgenstern 1947, Raiffa 1968, Howard 1975, North 1968, Farris and Sage 1975), there is not necessarily a clear distinction between decision theory for individuals and decision theory for groups. This lack of distinction is not a liability of the theory because the theory prescribes maximization of the expected value of utility as a guide to rational behavior. It does not specify whether that utility must describe (a) a single attribute for a single individual, (b) multiple attributes for a single individual, (c) a single attribute for a group, or (d) multiple attributes for a group. The multiattribute utility aspects of preference, decision analysis and the organizational aspects of groups have been treated in other articles (see *Decision Analysis; Group Decision Support Systems*); here we concentrate on the voting and group aspects of preference and utility.

The utilities involved in a decision situation include attitudes toward risk. This makes interpersonal comparison of utilities, necessary for group judgement, very difficult. Preference and utility are each required for decision making. The preference structure is, in fact, the input to the utility determination process, and the resulting utilities are such that if A is preferred or indifferent to B, the utility of A is greater than or equal to that of B. In other words, the cardinal utility numbers possess the same ordinal relationships as the preferences they describe.

Some of the methods used in the past to determine social or group preference include dictatorship, widely encompassing sets of traditional rules or customs, market mechanisms and voting. With the possible exception of voting, it is reasonably clear that these methods do not necessarily use any "fair" scheme to determine group preferences for making decisions. As we shall indicate, voting is not nearly as perfect for determining group preferences as one might intuitively think. Thus we come to the question explored in this article: just how do we, or how should we, amalgamate individual preference structures into a group preference structure?

1. Notation

Before continuing our development, we must define some of the notation we will use. Preference must be determined among a set of alternatives $\{a, b, \ldots, x, y, z\}$. The preferences are to be considered for a society of n individuals denoted by $1, \ldots, i, \ldots, n$. If individual i prefers x to y, we write $x P_i y$, where the subscript indicates that this preference is true for individual i and not necessarily for any other individuals. If individual i is indifferent between x and y, we write $x I_i y$. If individual i does not prefer x to y, we write $x \tilde{P}_i y$. The statement $x \tilde{P}_i y$ is equivalent to stating either $y P_i x$ or $y I_i x$. We use the unsubscripted forms $x P y$, $x I y$, etc., to indicate preferences that are somehow ubiquitous across, or otherwise accepted by, the entire group. We also require that each individual be transitive in their preference structure. If $x P_i y$ and $y P_i z$, then we require that $x P_i z$. It might seem intuitively apparent that a group, consisting of individually transitive people, will be transitive. Unfortunately, this is not necessarily so and this fact causes great difficulties in determination of an appropriate voting system.

2. Voting Approaches

We assume that, by some means, a voting system is selected. Some of the most common voting rules, or systems, are the following.

(a) *Plurality*. Voters vote for one alternative and the candidate receiving the most votes wins.

(b) *Majority*. Voters vote for one alternative. A candidate alternative must receive more than 50% of the votes to win. If no alternative wins, run-off voting is held among alternatives who received the most votes and whose aggregate votes in the previous iteration constituted a plurality.

(c) *Weighted voting*. Voters assign weighted votes for the candidate alternatives according to their strength of preference for each one. The total weighted votes for each alternative are counted and the winner is the candidate with the largest total.

Borda voting is an example of a weighted voting method. Each voter gives $N-1$ votes for the most preferred alternative among N candidates, $N-2$ for the second preferred alternative, and so on. The total votes for each candidate are counted by the formula

183

Total votes:

$$(N-1)M_1 + (N-1)M_2 + \cdots + M_{N-1} + 0M_N$$

where M_1 is the number of voters having the candidate as first choice, M_2 is the number of voters having the candidate as second choice, etc., and M_N is the number of voters having that candidate as last choice.

There are many possible variations of weighted voting. One of these, that is receiving much current acclaim, is known as approval voting. In this system, which has been simultaneously discovered and advocated by several authors (Brams and Fishburn 1978, 1983), a person votes for, or approves of, as many candidates as desired. The winner is the candidate with the most votes. Approval voting collects much more information than does plurality voting in that a voter should vote for all acceptable candidates who are above a somehow-set threshold of acceptability. It is a form of weighted voting in which the weights for each candidate are either zero or one. If a person assigns a weight of one to a candidate, the voter "approves" of that candidate. If a weight of zero is assigned, the person making the assignment "disapproves" of that particular candidate. Less information is available than in Borda voting, but the voting scheme is also much less cumbersome to administer.

(d) *Binary comparison voting.* Votes are cast in a binary fashion for all possible paired alternative combinations. One such approach to binary comparison voting is the method of Condorcet voting. Here, the alternative or candidate that wins by a simple majority over all other alternatives in pairwise contests is the winner in the election.

Another variant of this type of voting is Copeland voting. Here, the score of each alternative is calculated by subtracting the number of its losses in pairwise contests with all other alternatives from the number of its wins. The alternative with the highest score is the winner.

In each and every voting system, the winner or winners are decided according to the rules of the voting system. If there is no winner, a decision is made either to start another round of voting or to choose winners by some other method. It is useful to examine several voting schemes.

3. Problems with Voting

We will illustrate some of the problems inherent in voting with two examples. The first example results in the well-known "paradox of voting." Suppose three individuals constitute a society, and they must establish a preference structure among three alternatives x, y and z. Furthermore, suppose that the individual transitive preference orderings are $x P_1 y P_1 z, y P_2 z P_2 x$ and $z P_3 x P_3 y$. If the society decides to use majority voting, we see that x is preferred to y on two out of three occasions, thus $x P y$. Similarly, y is preferred to z on two out of three occasions, thus $y P z$. If we require the social preference ordering to be transitive, we would have $x P z$. However, the majority rule for the aforementioned preference structures would yield $z P x$. Hence, we have a set of transitive individual preference orderings which leads to an intransitive group preference ordering. Intransitive behavior on the part of individuals or groups is usually deemed undesirable. A society which generated a preference structure like the one mentioned should question its validity, and must certainly question its usefulness. If valid, the preference structure is one which is likely to create considerable difficulties for the decision maker and for others. In this particular example, all ordinal preferences are known. In most voting systems, particularly plurality voting, nowhere near this much information is available. A candidate may be chosen as the winner, even if that candidate is not approved of as much as some other candidate by the majority of voters, and is strongly disapproved of by more voters than any other candidate. One can question the extent to which these possibilities are pathologic. Unfortunately, we do not know the real answer, as sufficiently complete information to make this determination is generally unavailable in most plurality-type elections.

Our second example considers the type of voting procedure used. Suppose a group of 60 individuals are voting for an office holder from a field of three candidates a, b and c. Suppose that among the individuals, 23 have preference order $a P c P b$, 19 have preference order $b P c P a$, 16 have preference order $c P b P a$, and 2 have preference order $c P a P b$. If a plurality is used to select the winner, a has 23 first place votes, b has 19 first place votes and c has 18 first place votes. Thus a is the winner.

It could be that a majority is required to select the winner. If so, there must be a runoff election between a and b. The preference orders remain unchanged, and $23 + 2 = 25$ voters express $a P b$ either directly or by transitivity. Similarly, $19 + 16 = 35$ voters express $b P a$. In this case, b is the winner.

One other method, the intensity method, is sometimes used to select a winner. In the intensity method, which is the Borda weighted voting system, a weight of 2 is given to the first place vote, a weight of 1 is given to the second place vote and the third place vote is not counted. Under this scheme, candidate a would receive $(23 \times 2) + (2 \times 1) = 48$ votes. Candidate b would receive $(19 \times 2) + (16 \times 1) = 54$ votes, while candidate c would receive $(23 \times 1) + (19 \times 1) + (16 \times 2) + (2 \times 2) = 78$ votes. Thus candidate c is the winner.

Let us examine the situation that exists when approval voting is used. We see immediately that we cannot really determine the result as we do not know the approval threshold that each voter will use, and each voter is free to adjust it differently. It makes no sense for a voter not to approve of at least one alternative unless, for some reason of principle, that voter wishes to throw their vote away. In a similar way, it is senseless to approve of all alternatives, as that has the same effect as voting for none. From the group of 23 people, we see that a will for sure receive 23 votes and b will receive 0 votes. Alternative c can receive anywhere from 0 votes to as many as 23 approval votes. In a similar way, the group of 19 voters will approve of b a total of 19 times and of a a total of 0 times. Alternative c can receive anywhere from 0 to as many as 19 approval votes from the group. Alternative c will receive a total of 16 votes from the group of 16 people with preference structure $cPbPa$ and alternative a will receive 0 votes. Alternative b will receive at least 0 votes and as many as 16 votes. Finally, the small group of two voters will provide 2 votes for alternative c and 0 votes for alternative b. The votes for a will be at least 0 and no more than 2. The final tallies for the various alternatives, using the approval voting scheme, will be

$$23 \leqslant \text{votes for } a \leqslant 25$$
$$19 \leqslant \text{votes for } b \leqslant 35$$
$$18 \leqslant \text{votes for } c \leqslant 60$$

and we see that any of the three candidates could be a winner! We do see that it is rather unlikely that a will be a winner unless the voters tend to approve of only one alternative. If, for example, half of the people in each group approve of their midranked alternative, then the approval votes will be 24 for a, 27 for b and 39 for c, and so c is the winner. On the other hand, if all voters approve of their two topmost choices, the final approval votes are 25 for a, 35 for b and 60 for c; we see that c wins by a "landslide." It is very interesting to note that c does not win when the plurality system is used; a does; nor does c win when the majority plurality system is used; b does, since candidate c is eliminated in the first round of elections. Figure 1 presents some interesting graphical results for this example.

Had we used Condorcet voting, where we simply count the total number of votes that each alternative obtains in all possible binary comparisons, we obtain 48 votes for a, 54 for b and 78 for c. When we use Copeland voting, we obtain the same number of "wins" as in Condorcet voting. The number of "losses" that we have are 72 for a, 66 for b and 42 for c. Thus the final scores for the various alternatives are -16 for a, -12 for b and $+36$ for c. Again, alternative c is the winner.

It is, of course, curious that such a fundamental subject as voting should be subject to present-day inquiry, yet it is. There are a number of questions which need to be posed relative to any voting scheme, such as those listed below.

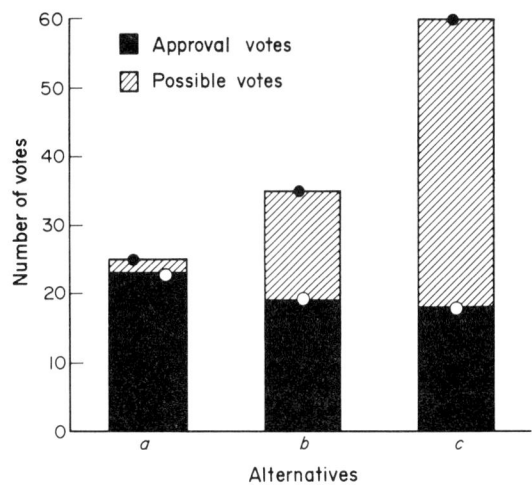

Figure 1
Approval voting possibilities and plurality voting results for a simple example: ●, maximum possible approval votes; ○, minimum possible approval votes and plurality votes

(a) Is the system subject to strategic voting possibilities in which a person can steer the outcome to one more to their liking by voting for preferences other than their own?

(b) Will the choice of voting system really make a difference? The classic example of a case where all ordinal voting schemes are equivalent is that of a two-person election to select a single winner. In three-or-more-person elections, most analomies are caused by one alternative or candidate being strongly favored by a minority, and where a second alternative is highly regarded by almost everyone, but not sufficiently well regarded to be the first choice for many people. In a case like this, which is the case in our last example, almost any winner can result, as a function of the voting system selected.

(c) Is a particular voting system feasible for implementation? If a particular system is too costly to implement, or too difficult to understand, then it is very unlikely to have much value.

Doubtless all voting systems based on ordinal preferences are vulnerable even if people correctly express their feelings. Even the cardinal schemes are vulnerable to strategic voting, as we will soon see.

All of this shows that any of the candidates in our simple election could be elected, depending on the method of voting that is employed. This is clearly an undesirable situation since every individual would prefer the method of voting which elects their candidate. The "social welfare function" is intended to alleviate this problem and provide an acceptable method for the amalgamation of individual preferences. In order to be acceptable, the social welfare function must satisfy some conditions, discussed in Sect. 5. It is necessary to distinguish between ordinal social welfare functions, which require measurements of weak preference orderings only, and cardinal social welfare functions, which require measurements of the interpersonal intensities of preference across individuals. Ordinal social welfare functions are discussed first. This is the type of social welfare function that we have tacitly assumed in all of our voting examples.

4. Ordinal Social Welfare Functions

A fairly precise definition of ordinal social welfare function can be given as follows. A society of n individuals desires to determine a preference structure among the alternatives in the set $\{a, b, \ldots, x, y, z\}$. The preference structure for each individual is transitive. Also, for any two alternatives x and y, exactly one of the following is true for individual i: $x P_i y, y P_i x$ or $x I_i y$. Arrow (1963) states the requirements for acceptability of the individual preference orderings and the resultant social ordering in the form of two axioms.

AXIOM 1. *For all x and y, either $x R y$ or $y R x$*

AXIOM 2. *For all x, y and z, $x R y$ and $y R z$ imply $x R z$.*

A relation which satisfies Axiom 1 is said to be connected, and a relation which satisfies Axiom 2 is said to be transitive.

The "paradox-of-voting" examples considered in Sect. 3 yielded intransitive social orderings from a set of transitive individual orderings. In these examples, Axiom 2 is not satisfied for the groups that are voting even though it is satisfied for every individual in the group. Thus, it turns out that ordinal voting could not yield an acceptable social ordering. Thus conventional voting may not be an acceptable social welfare function for these particular examples.

Together, these axioms imply that the alternatives form a linear order with respect to the relation R for group preferences. In general, R is a weak linear ordering, but if R is such that $x I y$ cannot exist for any x and y, then $x R y$ becomes $x P y$, and we denote such an occurrence a strong linear ordering.

Arrow's primary contribution to the problem of amalgamating individual preferences into a group preference structure is his definition of a set of five desirable conditions which it seems reasonable that an ordinal social welfare function should satisfy.

Part of the difficulty in determining a social welfare function stems from the diversity of preferences held by members of the society. At one extreme, we could have all individuals sharing the same preference structure. In such a case of unanimity, the task would be trivial, for the social welfare function would simply identify this single preference structure as the societal preference structure. Since unanimity is the exception rather than the rule, we must consider a broader class of admissible individual preference orderings. In particular, we consider all possible transitive individual orderings as admissible. To do less would deny the existence of certain preference orderings. If the group consisted of a single individual, we would again have a trivial problem, and the social preference structure would be simply the individual preference structure. Hence, we consider groups with at least two individuals. If there were only one alternative under consideration, the choice would be trivial. If there were two alternatives, the problem would be more complex but still fairly easily treated. Thus, we consider the case of at least three alternatives. Let us pose Arrow's axioms in a relatively simple form.

The preceding discussion is summarized as Condition 1.

CONDITION 1.

(a) *The number of alternatives is greater than or equal to three.*

(b) *The social welfare function is defined for all possible profiles of individual orderings*

(c) *There are at least two individuals.*

CONDITION 2. *If the social welfare function asserts that x is preferred to y for a given profile of individual preferences, it shall assert the same when the profile is modified as follows.*

(a) *The individual paired comparisons between alternatives other than x are not changed.*

(b) *Each individual paired comparison between x and any other alternative either remains unchanged or is modified in favor of x.*

To illustrate the requirements of Condition 3, suppose a rank-order method is used to vote among four candidates w, x, y and z. Let the method of voting require that the first place vote be given a rank of 4, the second place vote a rank of 3, the third place vote a rank of 2 and the fourth place vote a rank of 1. Suppose there are three individuals, and two of them express preferences $w P x P y P z$, while the third expresses their preferences as $y P z P w P x$. Under this system, w receives 10 votes, x receives 7 votes, y receives 8 votes and z receives 5 votes. Thus w is the winner. If we delete x from consideration, we would expect the same results, especially since w is preferred to x by all the voters. However, if we use the same voting scheme on the remaining candidates, w receives 10 votes, y receives 10 votes and z receives 7 votes. Here w and y are tied. The existence or nonexistence of x has made a difference in the social preference ordering. We refer to Condition 3 as the independence of irrelevant alternatives.

CONDITION 3. *Let H be a subset of alternatives from $\{a, b, \ldots, x, y, z\}$. If a profile of orderings is modified in such a way that the paired comparisons among the elements of H are unchanged, the social preference orderings resulting from the original and modified profiles should be identical for the elements in H.*

Now consider a social welfare function which asserts that xPy regardless of the preferences of any of the individuals in the society. Such an undesirable social welfare function is said to be imposed. To avoid imposed social preference orderings, we state Condition 4, which we call the condition of citizens' sovereignty.

CONDITION 4. *For each pair of alternatives x and y, there is some profile of individual orderings such that society prefers x to y.*

We do not want the social welfare function to be biased so that one individual's preference ordering necessarily controls the social preference ordering for the entire group. To avoid this kind of dominance, we define Condition 5, which is known as the condition of nondictatorship.

CONDITION 5. *There is no individual with the property that whenever they prefer x to y, for any x and y, society does likewise, regardless of the preferences of other individuals.*

THEOREM 1. (Possibility theorem for two alternatives, Arrow 1963). *If the total number of alternatives is two, the method of majority decision is a social welfare function which satisfies Conditions 1–5 and yields a social preference ordering of the two alternatives for every set of individual orderings.*

Theorem 1 supports the concept that majority rule is a desirable and "fair" social welfare function when there are only two alternatives. It could be viewed, somewhat simplistically perhaps, as the basis for the two-party political system.

THEOREM 2. Three or more alternatives—Arrow's impossibility theorem, Arrow 1963. *Unfortunately, for three or more alternatives, there does not exist a social welfare function which satisfies Conditions 1–5 by yielding a social ordering relation that is consistent with Axioms 1 and 2. As a result, we obtain Arrow's impossibility theorem.*

Before seeking ways to circumvent the implications of Arrow's impossibility theorem, we briefly examine two possible choices of social welfare functions and their drawbacks.

4.1 Majority Rule as a Social Welfare Function

The method of majority decision, or majority rule, satisfies Conditions 1–5 when there are only two alternatives. For more than two alternatives, intransitivities may result as shown in the "paradox-of-voting" example. In such a case, the relation induced on the set of alternatives by the social welfare function is not consistent with Axioms 1 and 2. Although this is a major drawback, it is almost the only one that majority rule has.

Arrow presents his proof of the possibility theorem for two alternatives (Arrow 1963) in such a way that Conditions 2, 4 and 5 are independent of the number of alternatives. He also shows that Condition 3 is satisfied by the method of majority decision. In doing so, he proves the following theorem.

THEOREM 3. *For any space of alternatives, the method of majority decision is a social welfare function satisfying Conditions 2–5.*

This theorem suggests that the method of circumventing the difficulties imposed by the impossibility theorem must involve the transitivity problem. Alternatively, we may abandon the hope of finding ordinal social welfare functions and seek a cardinal welfare function. A possibility theorem for cardinal welfare functions has been obtained by Keeney (1976). This necessarily involves interpersonal comparison of utilities, which is a very difficult task.

4.2 Unanimity as a Social Welfare Function

It is possible that a group could consist of individuals who all have the same preference orderings for the alternatives. This unanimity makes selection of a social welfare function trivial: the transitive social preference order is the same as the transitive individual preference orders. One might argue that this state of affairs permits a dictator in the group to establish their preference ordering. This is true, as we see from consideration of the definition of a dictator in Condition 5. In that case, everyone is a dictator, and the undesirability of a dictatorship becomes less important. While unanimous societies are the exception rather than the rule, unanimity is certainly an acceptable social welfare function in those few instances when it is applicable.

5. Modifications to Achieve a Social Welfare Function

Although Arrow's impossibility theorem ensures that we cannot find an ordinal social welfare function which satisfies Conditions 1–5, the problem of amalgamating individual preference orderings into some sort of social preference ordering still exists, and it must be dealt with. Decisions which affect groups must still be made, and responsible decision makers still seek ways of incorporating individual preferences into an overall preference structure which is acceptable to those concerned.

All of Arrow's conditions seem reasonable, and the logical method of attack seems to be to relax one or more of those conditions and find a social welfare function which satisfies the modified set of conditions.

5.1 Utility Combination Approaches

There have been a number of approaches that relax one or more of Arrow's conditions. Luce and Raiffa (1957) and Kirkwood (1972) identify Condition 3 as the most vulnerable of Arrow's conditions. They claim that the irrelevant alternatives may not be irrelevant at all, but that they can and should be used to indicate strengths of preferences. The following example, presented by Goodman and Markowitz (1952) illustrates this point. A host intends to serve refreshments to two guests. The host can serve them either coffee or tea, but not both. Guest 1 prefers coffee to tea and guest 2 prefers tea to coffee. Based on this information, one might conclude that the (ordinal) welfare function should indicate equal preference between tea and coffee. Suppose, however, that the host obtains additional information. It is discovered that guest 1 prefers coffee to tea, tea to cocoa, and cocoa to milk. On the other hand, guest 2 not only prefers tea to coffee, but also prefers cocoa to coffee, milk to coffee, and even water to coffee. With this additional information, it seems plausible to serve tea since it does not make "much difference" to guest 1 and it makes "a lot of difference" to guest 2. Although the (not truly considered) alternatives of cocoa and milk are irrelevant in the sense that they will not be served, they are relevant in indicating strength of preferences.

The preceding approach leads to consideration of the problem of interpersonal comparison of utilities. We have discussed the difference between utility and preference as measures of desire for an alternative. The work of Arrow concerned ways to combine preferences of individuals into a group preference structure. Utilities could have been used in that work, but the same results would have been obtained since the ordinal properties are the properties considered, and ordinal relationships for utilities and the preferences they describe are identical. We will return to preferences as the entity under investigation, but pause here to look briefly at some methods of combining individual utilities to obtain a group utility function.

Kirkwood (1972) presents several approaches aimed at determining a group utility function. All of them, in one way or another, require that the utility curves for each individual be assessed, and those individual utilities are combined by some appropriate mathematical function. Fleming (1952), Goodman and Markowitz (1952) and Harsanyi (1955) each present a set of conditions which, when satisfied, lead to a group utility function that is a weighted sum of the individual utilities. Nash (1950) presents a set of conditions which, when satisfied, lead to a group utility scheme wherein the alternative that the group should choose is the one that maximizes a product function of the individual utilities. All of these conditions involve symmetry properties among individual utilities and/or constants which must be evaluated and/or functions which must be determined. In every case, they are attempting to treat the problem of interpersonal comparison of utilities. Even if their conditions are satisfied, the constants and/or functions which must be determined limit the applicability of the approach.

5.2 Preference Structure Modification Approaches

If we leave Arrow's Condition 3 intact, the other likely candidate for modification is Condition 1. We can seek some way to modify the admissible preference orderings so that intransitivity will not occur. The "paradox-of-voting" example showed that the acceptable social welfare function for majority rule $W^{(n)}$ was mapped into a social preference ordering which was not contained in W, the set of alternatives.

Either of two modifications appear to be appropriate.

(a) we could leave $W^{(n)}$ unrestricted and require the mapping to yield a transitive social order contained in W; i.e., modify the range of the social welfare function.

(b) we could restrict the set of admissible profiles in $W^{(n)}$ such that the mapping yields a social preference order contained in W; i.e., modify the domain of the social welfare function.

We consider only the second of these approaches here.

5.3 Single-Peaked Preferences

Some of the preference profiles in $W^{(n)}$ yield a transitive social order when considered by the method of majority decision. If we restrict the set of admissible orderings to those selected profiles, the method of majority decision will satisfy Conditions 1–5 and serve as a social welfare function. One way to identify a set of admissible orderings is with the concept of single-peakedness developed by Black (1968).

Consider a set of alternatives $\{a, b, \ldots, x, y, z\}$ which have been ranked according to preference. Since the preference relation results in a linear order, we can represent it on a linear scale. As an example, consider the five alternatives v, w, x, y and z. Suppose individual i ranks them as $z P_i x P_i v P_i y I_i w$. This preference order may be indicated as shown in Fig. 2. The distances between elements on the scale do not indicate strengths of preferences; the ranking is purely an ordinal one.

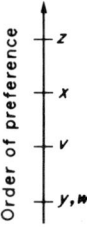

Figure 2
Linear-scale representation of preference

We may represent this preference order in another fashion. We may use a two-dimensional plot with the order-of-preference scale from Fig. 2 as the vertical scale, and some other ordering of the alternatives as the horizontal scale. For the preference order of Fig. 2, the plot in Fig. 3 results for one horizontal order. The only points of importance on the plot are the circled ones.

We may rearrange the order of the points on the horizontal axis to obtain a different plot of the same information. Two possible horizontal orders and their corresponding plots are shown in Fig. 4. The vertical scale is the same as that for Figs. 2 and 3. Both of the curves in Fig. 4 are said to be single-peaked. In Fig. 4 (b), the line segment from x to z is up-sloping, the line segment from z through v to y is down-sloping, and line segment from y to w is horizontal. We define a change of direction as a change in the curve from an up-sloping segment to a down-sloping segment (or vice versa) but not from an up-sloping or down-sloping segment to a horizontal segment. Thus Fig. 3 has three changes of direction, Fig. 4(a) has no changes of direction, and Fig. 4(b) has one change of direction. We formally define a single-peaked preference curve as a preference curve which has one change of direction.

An individual's preferences may always be ordered on the horizontal axis so that a single-peaked preference curve exists. Black (1968) has shown that when a horizontal ordering of the alternatives exists such that all members of the society have single-peaked preference curves, the method of majority decision results in a transitive social preference order. However, lack of single-peaked preference curves for all members of the society does not guarantee transitivity. Therefore, the existence of single-peaked preference curves for all individuals is a sufficient, but not necessary requirement for a transitive social ordering (Rothenberg 1961).

An example illustrates the determination of a social preference ordering when the members of the society have single-peaked preference curves. Suppose that a group with fifteen members is selecting a new president from a field of three candidates: x, y and z. Further

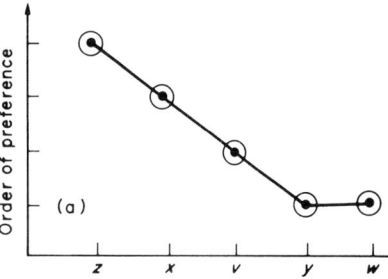

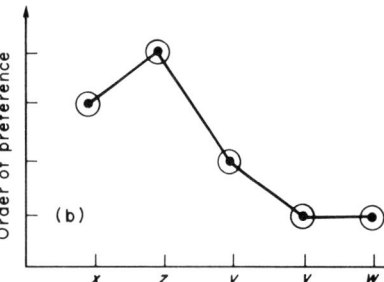

Figure 4
Alternative two-dimensional plots of preference

suppose that the following preference orders hold: five members rank $x P y P z$, four members rank $x P z P y$ and six members rank $y P x P z$. With three alternatives, there are $3! = 6$ possible rankings, but all six do not form a single-peaked group. These three rankings are single-peaked for the horizontal ordering z, x, y. According to Black, the median, or eighth preference curve, will contain the winner as its most preferred alternative. In this example, there are two distinct curves with peaks at x, but the median curve (counting from either direction) is one of the five solid-line curves shown in Fig. 5. Thus x is declared the winner. If knowledge of the second-place candidate is desired, x can be deleted from Fig. 5 and the resulting single-peaked curves considered again. Thus y is the second choice, and the overall preference structure is $x P y P z$. To verify this result, we may examine the preference orders on a pairwise basis. Candidate x wins over candidate y by a nine to six vote, and $x P y$. Candidate y wins over candidate z by an eleven to four vote, and $y P z$. If the order is transitive, the pairwise comparisons should indicate $x P z$. Indeed, candidate x wins over candidate z by a fifteen to zero vote. Again $x P y P z$.

Coombs (1950, 1954) observed similar behavior and indicated that such preference structures exist because of a "unidimensional, underlying continuum"; that is, the alternatives being ranked possess some attribute which determines, in large measure, the preferences of

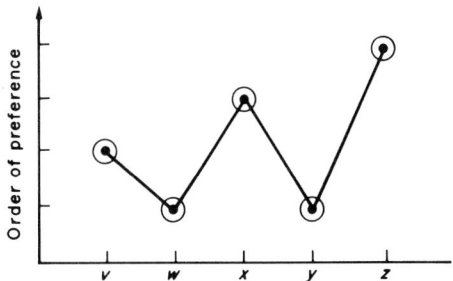

Figure 3
Two-dimensional plot of preference

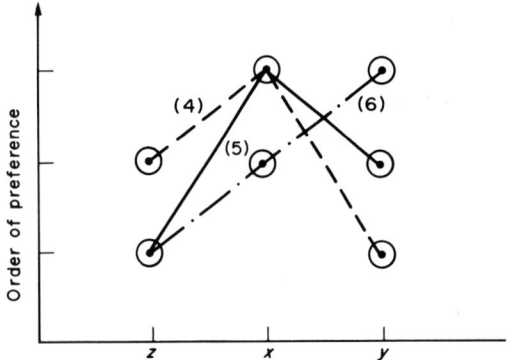

Figure 5
Single-peaked preference curve

the individuals. In the club-voting example, the continuum could be a conservatism–liberalism scale. On such a scale, each individual indicates the candidate which most nearly fits their "ideal" candidate, and preferences for other candidates decrease as their stand in the political spectrum departs from this "ideal."

This unidimensional underlying continuum is not always easily identifiable. However, it often exists and, when it does, it determines the individual's preferences. We must point out that existence of the unidimensional underlying continuum is not necessary for single-peaked preferences, but when it exists and is easily identified, one can reasonably expect to observe single-peaked preferences. One might expect to observe single-peaked preferences in a society which is homogeneous; that is, a society that shares very similar goals, attitudes and desires. An excellent example of such a society might be a closely knit religious group. In such a society, majority voting might be extremely successive in that intransitivities within a given denomination would, hopefully, be rare.

We have just considered determination of a preference order among a finite set of alternatives. Both the individual preference orders and the resulting social preference order deal with the same finite set of alternatives. Single-peaked preference curves contain a distinct alternative which is preferred above all the rest for each individual. The method of majority decision will yield one of those alternatives as society's most preferred choice. If the society wants the remainder of the preference order, it can be determined by the method of majority decision, and it will be transitive. Such a system is certainly acceptable when the alternatives possess this distinct nature; for example, candidates in an election or brands of consumer products.

Suppose that the society is asked to indicate its assessment of some quantity which is measured on a continuous numerical scale. For discussion purposes, suppose the quantity is the probability of the occurrence of some event. Each individual indicates their preferences as to what that probability is in the interval [0, 1]. Any probability which is different from an individual's assessment will be less preferred by that individual than their assessment. Furthermore, for two distinct probabilities which are both lower (or higher) than the individual's assessed value, the lowest (or highest) will be less preferred. Under these conditions, each individual's preference curve for assessment of the probability will be single-peaked, and the peak will be at the individual's assessed value. The horizontal order will be the interval. The set of individually assessed values (peaks) will be finite, and the method of majority decision will yield the social preference. In this case, however, the individually assessed peaks do not have the distinct nature that the candidates in an election have. In order for a particular value in the interval [0, 1] to be selected, it must be the particular assessment of one of the individuals. Since there are many other possible values in [0, 1], one might reasonably suggest that some "averaging" scheme be used instead.

To illustrate, suppose that 50 people assess 0.5 as the probability of the occurrence of an event, and that 51 people assess 0.7 as the probability of the event. Under majority rule, 0.7 would be selected. The 50 people who assessed 0.5 as the probability may feel that they have been treated unfairly, but they would be perfectly willing to settle for some compromise value of about 0.6 since 0.6 is also an alternative (though unsuggested). In this illustration we have used the mean as the function for determining preferences. It turns out that the mean is acceptable as a social welfare function for single-peaked, continuous preference curves.

Consider the problem of selecting a single numerical quantity from a continuous interval. Any member of the uncountable infinite set of numbers may be selected. Arrow's five conditions were stated for determination of preferences among a finite set of alternatives, but the concepts he identified are desirable for an infinite number of alternatives; and we examine the mean to determine whether it satisfies the intention of Arrow's conditions for social welfare functions. We note that this, in effect, assumes a quadratic social choice function and this will of course justify selection of the mean. In a sense this choice is totally arbitrary, and a great many functions may satisfy the Arrow conditions if assumed arbitrarily. However, there are many desirable features inherent in quadratic cost functions and this, at least in the past, justifies examination of the quadratic social choice function as one useful criterion reflecting strength of preference.

The mean value $\bar{x}$ of a set of numbers suggested by n individuals is defined as

$$\bar{x} = \frac{1}{n} \sum_{i=1}^{n} x_i$$

where x_i is the number suggested by individual i and x_i

is contained in the interval in question. We experience no loss in generality if we consider the interval [0, 1].

We must consider a modified version of Condition 1 wherein the set of admissible individual preference orders is continuous and single-peaked on the interval [0, 1]. Condition 1 requires that the relation induced on the alternative set by the social welfare function be connected and transitive. The purpose of the connected and transitive requirement is to ensure a rational approach and to reflect the individual preferences in the social preference ordering as accurately as possible. The mean does not generate an order on the uncountably infinite number of points $i \in [0, 1]$. Rather, it defines a single alternative which should represent the social preference for the quantity in [0, 1] being sought. Hence, the concepts of connectedness and transitivity lose meaning where the mean is the sought-after alternative. We can, however, indicate how accurately any choice identifies the social preference. We let c denote any choice selected as the social preference, and let

$$DI = \sum_{i=1}^{n} (x_i - c)^2$$

denote the "dissatisfaction index." Such an index is appropriate when the preference curves are single-peaked. It is easy to show that dissatisfaction is minimized when $c = \bar{x}$, where $\bar{x}$ is defined as the mean value. We conclude that the mean most accurately measures, in the sense defined, the social preference and therefore satisfies the intent of Condition 1.

Condition 2, positive association of social and individual values, is satisfied by the mean value. If individual i changes preference from x_i to x_i', where x_i' is a lesser value, the mean $\bar{x}$ also changes to a lesser value. Likewise, if i changes preference from x_i to x_i'', where x_i'' is a larger value, $\bar{x}$ also changes to a larger value, as required.

To verify satisfaction of Condition 3, which is the independence of irrelevant alternatives condition, we note that by asking for a numerical assessment from an interval, we automatically consider all values in the interval as relevant and all values outside the interval as irrelevant. If we prohibit consideration of those irrelevant alternatives, satisfaction of Condition 3 is trivial.

Clearly the social preference is determined by the individual preferences, and the mean satisfies Condition 4, the condition of citizen's sovereignty. Similarly, there is no single individual whose selection of a numerical quantity from [0, 1] will determine the mean, regardless of the preferences of other individuals. Thus there is no dictator and Condition 5 is satisfied.

With Conditions 1-5 satisfied, we have established that the mean is one appropriate social welfare function for determining group preference when the group must select a numerical quantity from a continuous interval and when the individuals' preference curves are single-peaked.

6. Cardinal Social Welfare Functions

There have been many studies of group decision making which show that, under a very mild set of realistic axioms, there is no assuredly successful and meaningful way in which ordinal preference functions of individuals may be combined into a preference function for the entire society. Conflicting values are the major culprit preventing this combination. This has a number of implications which suggest much caution in using ordinal preference voting systems, and any systemic approach based only on ordinal preferences among alternatives. Among other possible debilitating occurrences are agenda-dependent results which can, of course, be due to other effects. Several systemic methods have been proposed for forming and aggregating group opinions as described in the works of Hogarth (1978), Huber (1980), Hylland and Zeckhauser (1979), Rohrbaugh (1979), and Van de Ven and Delbecq (1974). An excellent survey of voting methods and associated paradoxes is presented by Fishburn (1974), Plott (1976) and Coombs et al. (1984).

Definitive studies of the interpersonal comparison of utilities have been conducted by Harsanyi (1976, 1977, 1979). He argues convincingly that we make interpersonal utility comparisons all the time whenever we make any allocation of resources to those to whom we feel the allocation will do the most good. The prescription against such comparisons is one of two key restrictions which lead to Arrow's impossibility theorem. By using cardinal utilities such that it becomes possible to determine preferences among utility differences (i.e., whether $u(a) - u(b) > u(b) - u(c)$), and interpersonal comparison of utilities, Harsanyi shows that Arrow's impossibility theorem becomes a possibility theorem. This is a major point in that it is generally not possible for a group to express meaningful transitive ordinal preferences for three or more alternatives, even though all individuals in the group have individually meaningful transitive ordinal preferences.

Harsanyi is concerned primarily with organizational design (Harsanyi 1979); that is, how to design social decision-making units to maximize the attainment of social objectives or value criteria. He shows that "rational morality" is based on maximization of the average (cardinal) utility level for all individuals in society. The utilitarian criterion is applied first to moral rules and then these moral rules are used to direct individual choices. Thus each utilitarian agent chooses a strategy to maximize social utility under the assumption that all other agents will follow the same strategy. Harsanyi recognizes a potential difficulty with this particular utilitarian theory of morality in that it is open to dangerous political abuses, as well as the numerous problems associated with information acquisition and analysis in a large centralized system. He posits a difference between moral rationality and game-theoretic rationality. He argues for the unavoidable use of interpersonal cardinal utility comparisons in moral rationality, and the inadmissibility of such comparisons in game theory. A great deal of Harsanyi's efforts concern game situations (Harsanyi 1977) in which outcomes depend on mutual interactions between morally rational individuals, each attempting to better their own interests.

Harsanyi's concept of utilitarianism has occasionally been criticized for making inadequate provision for equity, or equivalently for social group equality. John Rawls, a philosopher, has presented a theory of justice (Rawls 1971) which involves a difference principle in which decisions are made under uncertainty rather than under risk. This difference principle advocates selection of the alternative choice which is the best for the worst-off member of society and is, therefore, the direct social analog of the maximum principle for the problem of individual decisions under certainty. Rawls uses a "veil of ignorance" concept in which individuals must determine equitable distribution of societies' resources before they know their position in society. His argument is essentially that people will select a resource allocation rule that maximizes the utility of the worst-off member of society.

Other useful interpretations of cardinal utility and interpersonal utility comparisons have been made by Keeney and Kirkwood (1975) and Keeney (1976). Their axioms allow the development of a multiplicative group utility function in contrast to the additive utility function of Harsanyi. It is possible to deal more directly with equity considerations in a multiplicative group utility model than in an additive model. Papers by Bodily, Brock and Keeney in Kirkwood (1981) contain useful discussions concerning group and individual utilities of a multiattribute nature. Ulvila and Snider in Kirkwood (1981) illustrate the use of multiattribute utility models for group judgements in negotiations, while Raiffa (1982) takes a somewhat more general view.

See also: Collective Enquiry; Decision Analysis; Decision Support Systems; Group Decision Support Systems; Knowledge Representation

Bibliography

Arrow J 1963 *Social Choice and Individual Values*, 2nd edn. Yale University Press, New Haven, Connecticut
Black D 1968 *The Theory of Committees Elections*. Cambridge University Press, New York
Brams S J, Fishburn P C 1978 Approval voting. *Am. Polit. Sci. Rev.* **72,** 831–47
Brams S J, Fishburn P C 1983 *Approval Voting*. Birkhauser, Boston, Massachusetts
Coombs C H 1950 Psychological scaling without a unit of measurement. *Psychol. Rev.* **7**(3), 145–58
Coombs C H 1954 Social choice and strength of preference. In: Thrall R M, Coombs C H, Davis R L (eds.) *Decision Processes*. Wiley, New York
Coombs C H, Cohen J L, Chamberlain J 1984 An empirical study of some election schemes. *Am. Psychol.* **39,** 140–57
Farris D R, Sage A P 1975 Introduction and survey of group decision making with application to worth assessment. *IEEE Trans. Syst., Man Cybern.* **5**(3), 346–558
Fishburn P C 1974 Paradoxes of voting. *Am. Polit. Sci. Rev.* **68,** 537–46
Fleming M 1952 A cardinal concept of welfare. *Q. J. Econ.* **66**(3), 366–84
Goodman L A, Markowitz H 1952 Social welfare functions based on individual rankings. *Am. J. Sociol.* **58** (3), 257–62
Harsanyi J C 1955 Cardinal welfare, individualistic ethics, and interpersonal comparison of utility. *J. Polit. Econ.* **63**(4), 309–21
Harsanyi J C 1976 *Essays on Ethics, Social Behavior, and Scientific Explanation*. Reidel, Boston, Massachusetts
Harsanyi J C 1977 *Rational Behavior and Bargaining Equilibrium in Games and Social Situations*. Cambridge University Press, Cambridge
Harsanyi J C 1979 Bayesian decision theory, rule utilitarianism, and Arrow's impossibility theorem. *Theory Decis.* **11,** 289–317
Hogarth R M 1978 A note on aggregating opinions. *Organ. Behav. Hum. Perform.* **21,** 121–29
Howard R A 1975 Social decision analysis. *Proc. IEEE, Special Issue on Social Systems Engineering* **63,** 359–71
Huber G P 1980 *Managerial Decision Making*. Scott, Foresman, Glenview, Illinois
Hylland A, Zeckhauser R 1979 The impossibility of Bayesian group decision making with separate aggregation of beliefs and values. *Econometrica* **47**(6), 1321–36
Keeney R L 1976 A group preference axiomatization with cardinal utility. *Manage. Sci.* **23**(2), 140–45
Keeney R L, Kirkwood C W 1975 Group decision making using cardinal social welfare functions. *Manage. Sci.* **22**(4), 430–37
Kirkwood C W 1972 *Decision Analysis Incorporating Preferences of Groups*, Technical Report No. 74. Massachusetts Institute of Technology, Cambridge, Massachusetts
Kirkwood C W (ed.) 1981 *Operations Research*, Decision Analysis Special Issue **28**(1), 1–252
Luce R D, Raiffa H 1957 *Games and Decision*. Wiley, New York
Nash J F 1950 The bargaining problem. *Econometrica* **18**(2), 155–62
North D W 1968 A tutorial introduction to decision theory. *IEEE Trans. Syst., Man Cybern.* **4**(3), 200–10
Plott C R 1976 Axiomatic social choice theory: An overview and interpretation. *Am. J. Polit. Sci.* **20,** 511–96
Raiffa H 1968 *Decision Analysis—Introductory Lectures on Choices under Uncertainty*. Addison–Wesley, Reading, Massachusetts
Raiffa H 1982 *The Art and Science of Negotiation*. Harvard University Press, Cambridge, Massachusetts
Rawls J 1971 *A Theory of Justice*. Harvard University Press, Cambridge, Massachusetts
Rohrbaugh J 1979 Improving the quality of group judgment: Social judgment analysis and the Delphi technique. *Organ. Behav. Hum. Perform.* **24,** 73–92
Rothenberg J R 1961 *The Measurement of Social Welfare*. Prentice–Hall, Englewood Cliffs, New Jersey
Straffin P D Jr 1980 *Topics in the Theory of Voting*. Birkhauser, Boston, Massachusetts

Van de Ven A H, Delbecq A L 1974 The effectiveness of nominal, Delphi and interacting group decision making processes. *Acad. Manage. J.* **17**(4), 605–21

Von Neuman J, Morgenstern O 1947 *Theory of Games and Economic Behavior*, 2nd edn. Princeton University Press, Princeton, New Jersey

A. P. Sage
[George Mason University, Fairfax,
Virginia, USA]

Group Decision Support Systems

This article provides a very broad overview of group decision support systems that have the potential to support group and organizational decision-making functions. Rather than concentrate on one or two specific systems, a description is given of the many requirements that must be satisfied in order to produce an acceptable design for these systems.

There have been many definitions of an organization. A large number of them infer a group of individuals, established on a relatively continuous and stable basis, in an environment with changing characteristics. The organization contains relatively fixed boundaries, a normative order for management and authority, a communication system and a set of incentives that encourage engagement in activities that are in general pursuit of a common and accepted set of goals. From this definition it follows that there are four top-level attributes or success factors that are critical to the functionality of an organization. These are efficiency, effectiveness, adaptability to external environmental changes and job satisfaction. Each of these contributes to the primary goals of organizational management: to improve the products and services of the organization and to increase productivity in managing the organization. Four organizational needs and characteristics follow from these: complexity of tasks and the resulting specialization; centralization of authority into hierarchical levels; formalization and standardization of job duties; and a system with which to process organizational information. This article is primarily concerned with the development of information systems to support the decision-making functions by organizations and groups of individuals.

Management is vitally concerned with the processing (broadly defined to include acquisition, representation, transmission and use) of information in the organization. Information is generally recognized as a vital strategic resource. A simple three-step reasoning process leads to this conclusion: organizational success depends on management quality, management quality depends on decision quality, and decision quality depends on information quality. Of course, there are many other ingredients besides information quality that influence organizational success.

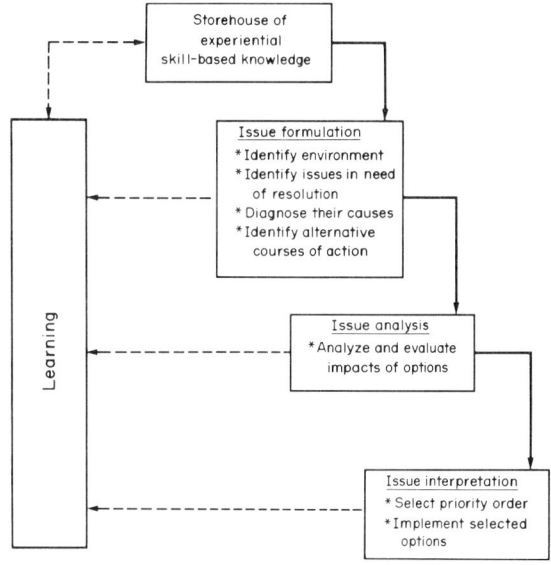

Figure 1
The three formal steps in problem solving and decision making

One of the major tasks of management is to minimize the equivocality or ambiguity of the information that results from the organization's interaction with the external environment. This is accomplished in order to enable the organization to understand its environment better, to detect or identify problems in need of resolution, to diagnose their causes, to identify alternative courses of action or policies to correct or resolve problems, to evaluate the potential efficacy of these policies, to select an appropriate priority order for problem resolution, to select appropriate policies for implementation and to augment existing knowledge with the new knowledge obtained in this implementation such that organizational learning occurs. Figure 1 illustrates the flow of these cognitive activities.

There is much research which shows that individuals and organizations use improperly simplified and often distorted models of the internal and external worlds that their environment comprises. The result of this is the utilization of flawed information-processing heuristics that lead to less than satisfactory judgement and choice. When this affects the learning process, poor results are an eventual, almost certain, possibility.

1. Information Needs for Group and Organizational Decision Making

Numerous disciplinary areas have contributed to the development of support systems that might potentially aid corporate management. These include computer science which provides the hardware and software tools necessary to implement support-system design constructs. The field of management science and operations research has provided the theoretical framework for modelling, optimization and decision analysis that is necessary to design useful and relevant normative approaches to choice making. The area of management information systems has provided the necessary database-design tools. The areas of organizational behavior and behavioral and cognitive science have provided rich sources of information on how humans and organizations process information and make judgements in a descriptive fashion.

There have been many attempts to classify different types of decisions. Among the classifications of particular interest here is the decision-type taxonomy, identified by Anthony (1965), in which four types of decisions are identified.

(a) *Strategic planning decisions*—decisions related to choosing highest-level policies and objectives, and associated resource allocations.

(b) *Control decisions*—decisions made for the purpose of assuring effectiveness in the acquisition and use of resources.

(c) *Operational control decisions*—decisions made for the purpose of assuring effectiveness in the performance of operations.

(d) *Operational performance decisions*—day-to-day decisions made while performing operations.

These decisions are not unrelated. Clearly, strategic planning decisions lead to management control decisions. These in turn lead to operational control decisions which, in turn, lead to operational performance decisions. There exists the opportunity for a decision support system at each of these hierarchical levels. Information flow is bilateral to and from each of these levels, and organizational learning occurs at each level, as suggested in Fig. 2.

The nature of the decisions, and the type of information that is required, differs across each of these four levels. Generally, operational activities occur much more frequently than strategic planning activities. Also, there is a difference in the degree to which the knowledge required for each of these levels is structured. Simon (1960) described decisions as structured or unstructured, depending on whether or not the decision-making process can be explicitly described prior to the time when it is necessary to make a decision. This taxonomy would seem to lead directly to that in which expert skills (wholistic reasoning), rules (heuristics) or formal reasoning (holistic evaluation) are normatively used for judgement. Generally, operational performance decisions are more likely than strategic planning decisions to be prestructured. As discussed later, expert systems are usually expected to be more appropriate for operational performance

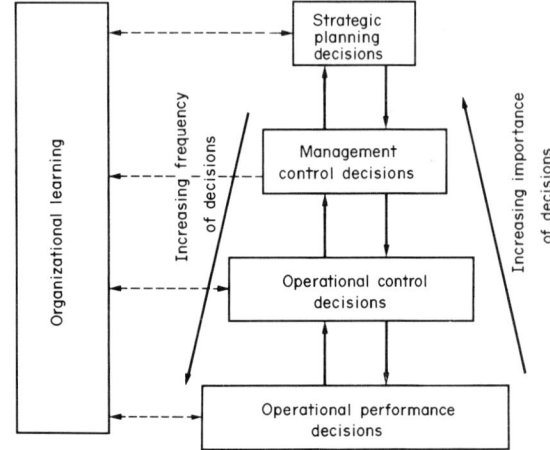

Figure 2
Organizational information and decision flows

and operational control decisions than they are for strategic planning and management planning decisions. In a similar way, decision support systems will often be more appropriate for strategic planning and management control than they are for operational control and operational performance.

There are a number of human abilities that a knowledge support system, which is a generic term that describes a computerized system that supports knowledge workers in performing cognitive tasks, should augment. It should support the decision maker in the formulation or framing of the decision situation in the sense of recognizing needs, identifying appropriate objectives by which to measure the successful resolution of an issue, and generating alternative courses of action that will resolve needs and satisfy objectives. It should also provide support in enhancing the abilities of the decision maker to obtain the possible impacts of the alternative courses of action. This analysis capability must be associated with provision of the capability to enhance the ability of the decision maker to provide an interpretation of these impacts in terms of objectives. This interpretation capability will lead to evaluation of the alternatives and selection of a preferred alternative option. Associated with all of these must be the ability to acquire, represent and utilize information or knowledge, and the ability to implement the chosen alternative course of action.

There are many variables that will affect the information that is, or should be, obtained relative to any given decision situation. These variables are very clearly task dependent. Included among them are the following.

(a) *Inherent and required accuracy of available*

information. Operational control and performance situations will often deal with information that is relatively accurate. The information in strategic planning and management control situations is often inaccurate.

(b) *Inherent precision of available information.* Generally, the information available for operational control and operational performance decisions is very imprecise.

(c) *Inherent relevancy of available information.* Operational control and performance situations will often deal with information that is relatively relevant to the task at hand because it has been prepared that way by management. The information in strategic planning and management control situations is often obtained from the external environment and may be irrelevant to the strategic tasks at hand, although it may not initially appear this way.

(d) *Inherent and required completeness of available information.* Operational control and performance situations will often deal with information that is relatively complete and sufficient for operational performance. The information in strategic planning and management control situations is often incomplete and insufficient to inspire great confidence in strategic planning and management control.

(e) *Inherent and required verifiability of available information.* Operational control and performance situations will often deal with information whose validity for the intended purpose is relatively verifiable. The information in strategic planning and management control situations is often unverifiable, or relatively so, and this gives rise to a potential lack of confidence in strategic planning and management control.

(f) *Inherent and required consistency and coherency of available information.* Operational control and performance situations will often deal with information that is relatively consistent and coherent. The information in strategic planning and management control situations is often inconsistent and perhaps even contradictory or incoherent, especially when it comes from multiple external sources.

(g) *Information scope.* Generally (but not always) operational decisions are made on the basis of narrow-scope information related to well-defined events that are internal to the organization. Strategic decisions are generally based upon broad-scope information and a wide range of factors that often cannot be fully anticipated prior to the need for the decision.

(h) *Information quantifiability.* In strategic planning, information is very likely to be highly qualitative, at least initially. For operational decisions, the available information is often highly quantified.

(i) *Information currency.* In strategic planning, information is often rather old, and it is often difficult to obtain current information about the external environment. For operational control decisions, current information is often present and needed.

(j) *Necessary level of detail.* Very detailed information is often needed for operational-type decisions. Highly aggregated information is often desired for strategic decisions. There are many difficulties associated with information summarization that need attention.

(k) *Time horizon for information needed.* Operational decisions are typically based on information over a short time horizon and the nature of the control may be changed very frequently. Strategic decisions are based on information and predictions with a long time horizon.

(l) *Frequency of use.* Strategic decisions are made infrequently, although they are perhaps refined fairly often. Operational decisions are made quite frequently, and are relatively easily changed.

(m) *Internal or external information source.* Operational decisions are often based on information that is available internal to the organization, whereas strategic decisions are much more likely to be dependent on information that can only be obtained external to the organization.

There are a number of human information-processing capabilities and limitations that interact with organizational arrangements and task requirements to strongly influence resource allocations for organizational problem solving. The concepts of information sharing and shared concept models then become especially important. There are many ingredients in these concepts, including the communication nodes and links that exist in electronic hardware, the perceptions that the different members of a group have regarding the internal and external environment, and the situation assessment and decision-making needs of the different members. A central need in such situations is that of the translation of thoughts and ideas into some more-or-less common language so they can be shared. Thus, questions of dialog generation and management, including information presentation, become especially important. Needs in this area have led to the development of group decision support systems (GDSSs). The purposes of these computerized aids in planning, problem solving and decision making include: removing a number of common communication barriers; providing techniques for structuring decisions; and systematically directing group discussion, and associated problem solving and decision making, in terms of the patterns, timing and content of the information that influences these actions.

Essentially the same maladies that affect individual decision-making and problem-solving behavior, as well as many others, can result from group and organizational limitations. There exists a considerable body of knowledge, generally qualitative, relating to organizational structure, effectiveness and decision making. The majority of these studies suggest that a bounded rationality or "satisficing" perspective, often heavily influenced by bureaucratic political considerations, will generally be the decision perspective adopted in actual decision-making practice in organizations (Sage 1981). To cope with this effectively requires the ability to deal concurrently with technological, organizational and cognitive structural concerns as they each, separately and collectively, motivate corporate problem-solving issues.

Satisficing, or bounded rationality, results from a complex decision situation, for either an individual or a group, in which it is not possible to identify all alternative courses of action in advance of the time when an alternative must be selected, and it is not possible to predict, with the needed degree of precision, all consequences of implementing a specified alternative. In situations like this, humans will typically attempt to satisfice; that is, pick a readily identifiable course of action that has been known to yield satisfactory performance in the past and perhaps make minor refinements to this alternative to render it more suitable for the given situation. Humans learn over time to adapt these past solutions to new problems more efficiently so that they are able to raise their aspiration levels. This bounded-rationality model of choice is roughly equivalent to the unconflicted adherence to an original course of action or unconflicted change to a new course of action in the stress-based model of judgement and choice due to Janis and Mann (1977) summarized in Fig. 3. In other words, they sublimate decision-making behavior to problem-solving behavior. The extent to which this is a desirable sublimation will be problem dependent.

Organizational ambiguity is a major reason why this bounded-rationality behavior is often cited as

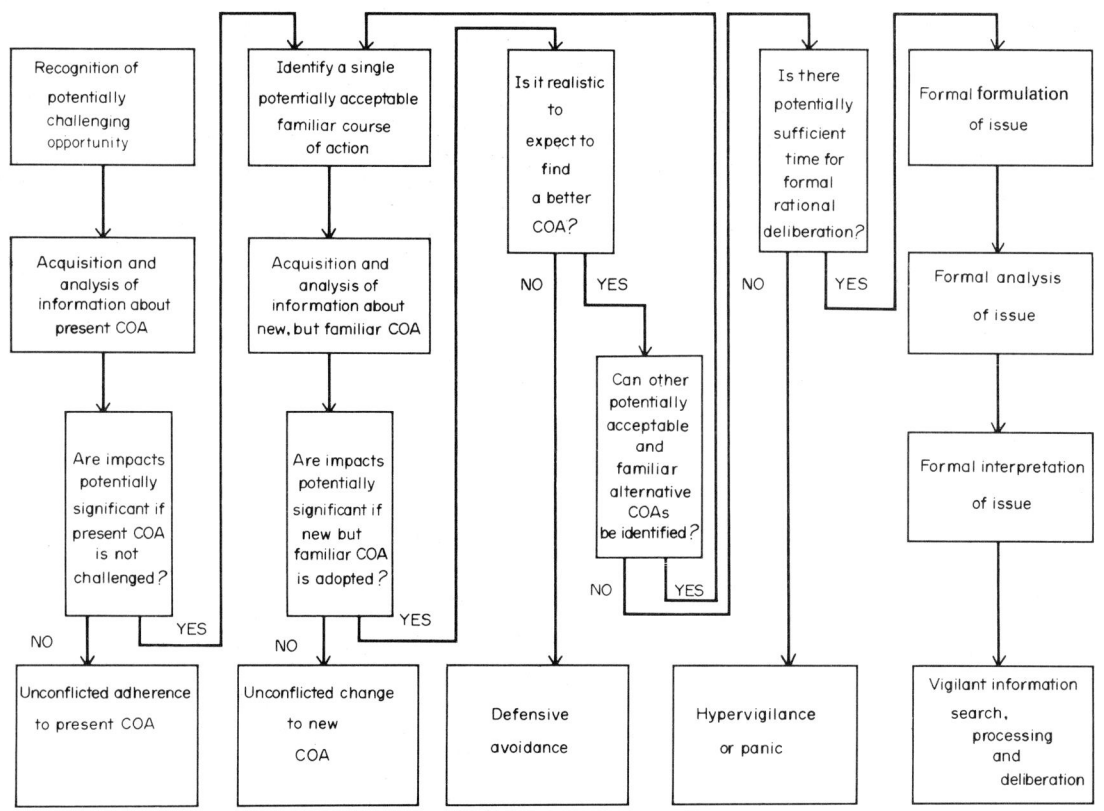

Figure 3
Contingency model of judgement and choice: COA = course of action

being so pervasive. There are at least four kinds of opaqueness or equivocality in organizations: ambiguity of intention, understanding, history and human participation. These four ambiguities relate to the structure, function and purpose of an organization, as well as to the perception of these decision-making agents in an organization. They influence the information that is communicated in an organization, and generally introduce one or more forms of information imperfection. The notions of organizational management and organizational information processing are, indeed, inseparable. In the context of human information processing, it would not be incorrect to define the central purpose of management as the development of a consensual grammar to ameliorate the effects of equivocality or ambiguity. This is the perspective taken by Weick (1979) in his noteworthy efforts concerning organizations.

2. Group Decision Support System Design Constructs

There have been a number of related definitions of decision support systems (DSSs) and group decision support systems (GDSSs). Simply stated, a DSS is an interactive computer-based system of hardware, software and interfaces that supports a decision-making process which involves the resolution of unstructured problems. A GDSS, then, is simply a DSS that supports a group of people or, more to the point, a group of decision makers.

It is important to note that the group of people may be centralized at one spot, or decentralized in space and/or time. Also, the decision considered by each individual in a decision-making group may or may not be the ultimate decision. The decision being considered may be sequential over time and may involve many component decisions. Alternatively, or in addition, many members in a decision-making group may be formulating and/or analyzing options, and preparing a short list of these for review by a person with greater authority. Figure 4 presents an illustration of a generic GDSS. Basically, Fig. 4 shows a collection of DSSs with some means of communications among the individuals that comprise the group.

A GDSS may influence the process of group decision making. A GDSS has the potential for changing the information-processing characteristics of individuals in the group. This may be accomplished at any or all of three levels. A GDSS provides a mechanism for group interaction. A GDSS may impose any of various structured processes on individuals in the group such as, for example, a particular voting scheme. A GDSS may impose any of several management control processes on the individuals in the group, such as that of imposing or removing the effects of a dominant personality. The design of the GDSS and the way in which it is used are the primary determinants of these.

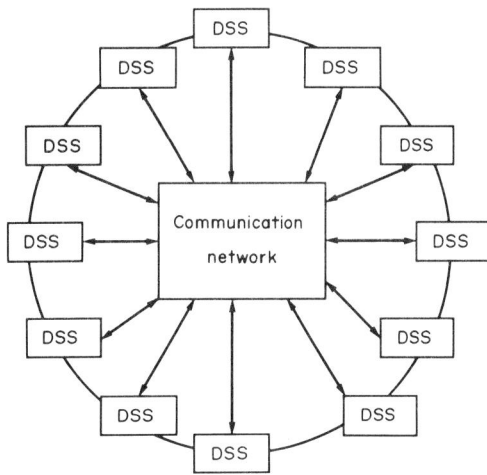

Figure 4
Generic GDSS as electronic communication among people

It is possible to develop a taxonomy of GDSSs based on the levels of support just discussed. From this perspective, a level I GDSS would simply be a medium for enhanced information interchange that might lead ultimately to a decision. Electronic mail, large videoscreen displays that can be viewed by a group, or a decision room that contains these features, could represent a level I GDSS. A level I GDSS provides only a mechanism for group interaction. Figure 5 could be regarded as representing a level I GDSS.

A level II GDSS (such as is represented in Fig. 6) would provide various decision structuring and other analytic tools that could act to reduce information imperfection. A decision room that contained software that could be used for problem solution would represent a level II GDSS. Thus, spreadsheets would primarily represent a level II DSS. To become a level II GDSS, there would also have to be some means of enabling group communication. Such a GDSS is simply a communications medium that has been augmented with some tools for problem structuring and solution with no prescribed management control of the use of these tools.

A Level III GDSS also includes the notion of management control of the decision process. Thus, there is a notion of facilitation of the process, either through the direct intervention of a human, or through some rule-based specifications of the management control process that is inherent in a level III GDSS. Clearly, there is no sharp transition line between one level and the next and it may not always be easy to identify at what level a GDSS is operating. The DSS generator, such as discussed above, would generally appear to produce a form of level III GDSS.

As noted by Huber (1984) and Huber and McDaniel (1986) and others, much of the concern in the design of group decision support systems should relate to the need for trade-offs between human decision-making needs for greater information sharing and the lack of time for, and other resistance to, attending a large number of group meetings. There is considerable contemporary interest in the subject of GDSS design. DeSanctis and Gallupe (1987), who initiated the notion of three levels of GDSSs just discussed, have provided a definitive overview of foundations for the study of GDSSs. The taxonomy of GDSS settings that DeSanctis and Gallupe identify includes group proximity (from face-to-face communication to dispersed communication) and group size (small groups to large groups.) Within this, they identify four recommended approaches: decision rooms for small group face-to-face meetings; legislative sessions for large group face-to-face meetings; local area decision networks for small dispersed groups; and computer-mediated conferencing for large groups which are dispersed. They discuss the design of facilities to enable this, as well as to enable techniques which may enhance the quality of efforts such as generation of ideas and actions, choosing from among alternative courses of action, and negotiating conflicts. On the basis of this, these authors recommend six areas as very promising for additional study: GDSS design methodologies; patterns of information exchange; mediation of the effects of participation; effects of (the presence or absence of) physical proximity, interpersonal attraction and group cohesion; effects on power and influence; and performance–satisfaction trade-offs.

Other relevant efforts and areas of interest involving GDSSs include group processes in computer-mediated communications, the computer support for collaboration and problem solving in the meetings study of Stefik et al. (1987), the organizational planning study of Appelgate et al. (1987) and the knowledge management and intelligent information-sharing systems study of Malone et al. (1987). Particularly interesting current issues surround the extent to which cognitive science and engineering studies that involve potential human information-processing flaws can be effectively dealt with, in the sense of design of debiasing aids, in GDSS design.

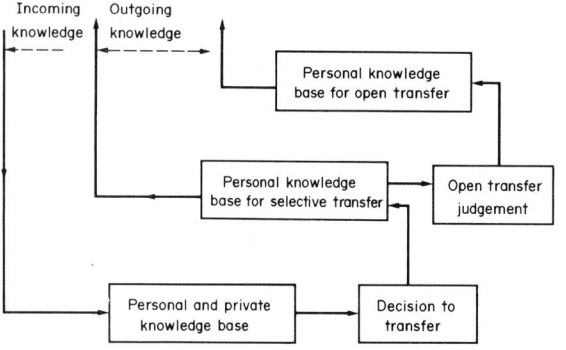

Figure 5
Conceptual model of three personal knowledge bases

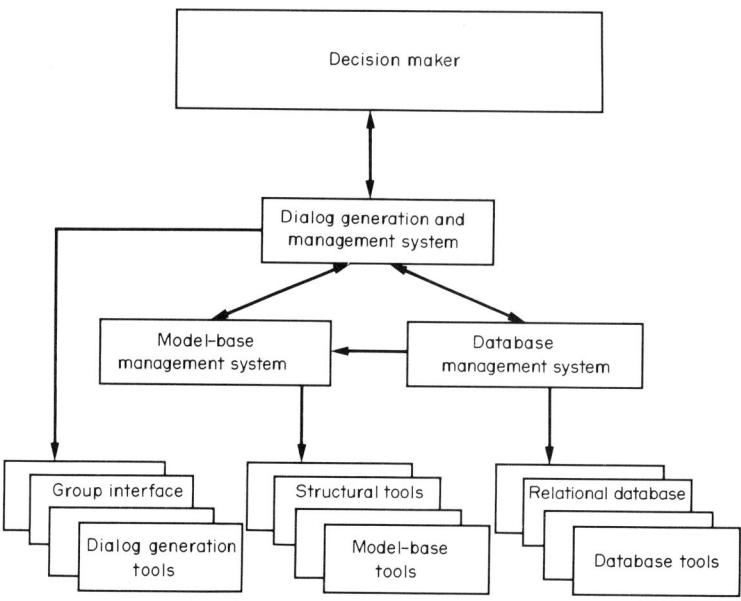

Figure 6
Generic level II GDSS

Especially interesting complications arise from group decision situations in which the objectives, perhaps due to different interpretations of information, are in partial conflict. Even this limited discussion makes it very clear that the role of the individual in a decentralized, distributed group effort may be much different from that traditionally assumed for an individual in a single-person centralized decision situation. In particular, it is essential that individuals in roles such as these be able to combine the tasks of information acquisition, representation, analysis and interpretation, and associated action planning and implementation. This is not an uncomplicated effort since each individual will have a partially different knowledge base which represents beliefs about others as well as beliefs about the environment and the intentions of others. Furthermore, activities selected for implementation will not necessarily be accomplished to full fruition: they may be brought to full fruition, or alternatively, they may be eliminated or modified due to the identification of new activities which have higher priority. These affect, to a considerable extent, the roles of the individual in a decentralized, distributed environment with respect to such activities as situation assessment, gathering information or sensing information distribution to others, potential plan identification or generation, evaluation of potential plans, resolution of conflicts with respect to information and activities, and execution of selected plans or action alternatives.

Knowledge representation is very important since the form and structure of knowledge exerts a very strong influence on the way in which it is used. Knowledge use includes the retrieval of information from the knowledge base, and aggregation of this knowledge with values to enable judgement formation. If a knowledge support system for a single individual is to be ultimately useful, it must allow for expansion and adaptation in such a way that the knowledge base is consistent and nonredundant. In a group decision support-agent situation, additional concerns emerge: data inputs from distributed sources and sharing of data now become requirements. These should be accomplished, from an efficiency viewpoint, such that only the necessary redundancy is obtained, only the necessary consistency is maintained, and integrated management of the composite knowledge base is possible. Data-independence concepts then become additional desirable requirements which will ensure efficiency in that modifications to a database can easily be accomplished. We should like to make the analogous statement concerning information and knowledge. That we cannot easily do this is indicative of the need for additional efforts that better enable us to consider information and knowledge as data. To accomplish this well is a central purpose of a model-base management subsystem in a GDSS.

Security of data, information and knowledge in terms of authentication, authorization and various protection mechanisms also becomes very important. The need for local and personal data and knowledge bases is easily established. A top-level manager may, for example, wish to test various hypotheses concerning particularly sensitive resource-deployment strategies. The impacts of various strategies will, after implementation, influence other items in the knowledge base. For a variety of reasons, a particular decision maker may not wish these impacts to become part of the shared data or knowledge base immediately. This illustrates the desirability of personal data and knowledge bases in a group decision support situation. In a similar way, the loss of a portion of the shared database may require the replacement of the now missing data with very subjective data, such as those contained in a personal database. Figure 5 illustrates the role of these various databases in a GDSS.

There are many important elements that need be considered relative to these three databases, and we have identified only some of them here. One very interesting concern is that a centralized knowledge base may represent codified group wisdom, doctrine or standard operating policies. Such centralized knowledge sources have strengths as well as weaknesses. They may well be quite poor in those cases where there is a fundamental change in the contingency task structure that was the basis for their creation. Thus, very poor results may come about from their use in situations where deception, surprise and the use of a new strategy are involved. This may exacerbate a potential crisis management situation. In such cases, use of a distributed information system may well yield results that are better than those that could be obtained from a centralized system. Thus, a very realistic question is: how do we deal with the three possible knowledge bases that may exist for a given decision situation? These are listed below.

(a) A personal and private knowledge base which the individual may not wish to transmit over the system to others. This is not sinister in any way, necessarily. We all have hypotheses which we desire to explore personally before telling others about them.

(b) A personal knowledge base which an individual wishes to transmit openly to everyone on the system.

(c) A personal knowledge base which the individual possessing it wishes to selectively transmit to others, for any of a variety of reasons.

Message summarization is an important need for decision makers in most decision situations. What one person will need in the form of summarized data may differ considerably from the needs of other organizational members due to differences both in task requirements and in experiential familiarity with task requirements. Thus, data and message summaries will represent important components of a personal data base. This suggests the investigation of various formats for message summaries and information-presentation protocols in local, remote and personal data and information bases. There are several ways in which the partially conflicting requirement for these three types of databases may be handled. One way is to allow for a personal copy of the data and knowledge that is shared, and for the personal modifications of these. This may, and in most cases will, produce partial inconsistency between the personal database and the shared database. The purpose of this is to allow the system users to explore potentially disconfirming information and, if it results in modifications to previously agreed judgements and choices, to encourage further exploration of resource allocations and strategies.

If there is a single purpose for a GDSS, it must be to enhance the value of information in judgement and decision-making tasks. Information-requirements analysis to facilitate the choice of information requirements is an important component of this. An auxiliary purpose of the chosen information-presentation framework should be to encourage the selection of effective and efficient information requirements. We see, therefore, that information-requirements determination, and information presentation and use, are not independent concepts. They relate strongly to the notion of value of information and the problem of making this determination, especially for normative and predictive purposes.

There have been many approaches suggested to the study of information value. These include empirical approaches, information-theoretic approaches, information-economics approaches and multiattribute utility theoretic approaches. The concept of the value of information is multifaceted. It implies much more than the information-theoretic notions concerning it might suggest. One of the fundamental reasons for this is that much of the information that people request is for surveillance purposes in an effort to uncover potentially embarrassing "surprises" and not strictly for the purposes of decision making. There are also a number of factors, such as interpersonal conflicts and power struggles, that encourage intentional and unintentional misrepresentation of information. This again indicates that information must be suspected of many potential forms of bias. Also, information is a symbol that suggests rationality and there are many incentives to displaying what looks like, but which may not be, this symbol. As a consequence, there will often be an expressed need for great quantities of information, but there may not be an equivalent desire to use appropriately the information that is requested. The information-presentation system should encourage parsimonious requests for that information which is truly used for, and which will be appropriately used in, resolving the decision situation.

Much of the discusson to be found in the judgement, choice and decision literature concentrates on what may be called formal reasoning and decision enactment efforts that involve the issue-resolution efforts that follow as part of the problem-solving efforts of issue formulation, analysis and interpretation discussed in a previous section. There are other decision-making activities as well. Very important among these are activities which allow perception, framing, editing and interpretation of the effects of actions upon the internal and external environments of a decision situation. These might be called information selection activities. There will also exist information retention activities that allow admission, rejection and modification of the set of selected information or knowledge so as to result in short-term learning through reduction of incongruities, and long-term learning through the acquisition of new schemata that reflect enhanced understanding. Although the basic GDSS design effort may well be concerned with the short-term effects of various problem-solving, decision-making and information-presentation formats, the actual knowledge that a person brings to bear on a given problem is a function of the accumulated experience that the person possesses, and thus long-term effects need to be considered, at least as a matter of secondary importance.

It was noted earlier that a major purpose of a GDSS is to enhance the value of information. Three attributes of information appear dominant in the discussion, as far as their value for problem-solving purposes and in the literature in general is concerned. These are the following.

(a) *Equivocality reduction.* It is generally accepted that high-quality information may reduce imperfection or equivocality. This equivocality generally takes the form of uncertainty, imprecision, inconsistency or incompleteness. It is very important to note that it is neither necessary nor desirable to obtain decision information that is unequivocal or totally "perfect." Information need be only sufficiently unequivocal or unambiguous for the task at hand.

(b) *Task relevance.* Of course, information must be relevant to the task at hand. It must allow the decision maker to know what needs to be known in order to make an effective and efficient decision. This is not as trivial a statement as might initially be suspected. Relevance varies considerably across individuals, as a function of the contingency task structure, and over time as well.

(c) *Representational appropriateness.* In addition to the need that information be relevant to the task at hand, it must be represented in a form that is appropriate for use by the person who needs the information.

Each of these top-level attributes may be decomposed into attributes at a lower level. They are needed as fundamental metrics for evaluation of information quality. We have just indicated that the components of equivocality or imperfection are uncertainty, imprecision, inconsistency and incompleteness. Some of the attributes of representational appropriateness are naturalness, transformability to naturalness, and conciseness. These attributes of information-presentation system effectiveness relate strongly to overall value-of-information concerns and should be measured as part of the information-systems evaluation effort even though any one of them may appear to be a secondary concern.

There are many ways in which we can characterize information. Among the attributes noted earlier and which we might use are accuracy, precision, completeness, sufficiency, understandability, relevancy, reliability, redundancy, verifiability, consistency, freedom from bias, frequency of use, age, timeliness and uncertainty. Our concerns with information involve at least the five desiderata below:

(a) information should be presented in very clear and very familiar ways to enable rapid comprehension;

(b) information should improve the precision of understanding of the task situation;

(c) information that contains an advice or decision recommendation component should contain an explication facility that enables the user to determine how and why results and advice are obtained;

(d) information needs should be based on identification of the information requirements for the particular situation; and

(e) information presentations and all other associated management-control aspects of the support process should be such that the decision maker, rather than a computerized support system, guides the process of judgement and choice.

It will generally be necessary to evaluate a GDSS to determine the extent to which these characteristics are present.

3. Evaluation Needs

There are a number of overall GDSS evaluation issues that need experimental evaluation efforts. In particular, it will be very important to evaluate the extent to which the overall concept accommodates and encourages heterarchical reasoning among group members in the decision situation. Trade-off relations that influence functionality and usability can be expected to be very important in information-systems engineering evaluation efforts. There are many interrelationships that affect organizational factors and system development and these also need to be considered in an evaluation.

The GDSS should be adaptive to user requirements. It should not force users into a particular mode of thought or force them into using a specific set of decision algorithms or paradigms, nor should it force them into a prescribed protocol or procedure. Above all, the process should yield results that are of value in and of themselves at the moment they are obtained, as contrasted with having to wait until the end of the process to obtain any useful results. This is potentially very important since realistic decision situations are such that there is no known fixed terminal time for the appearance of decision optimality, but a "rolling" often *a priori* unknown terminal time.

Many features of a GDSS should be user modifiable, or adaptive *to* the user, to accommodate the abilities and experiences of its users so as to enable them to be more efficient and effective. It must also be adaptive *from* the user in the sense of providing gentle encouragement to the user to modify the initially suggested user approach to the system to enable greater user effectiveness and efficiency. It is also important that these approaches be specifically designed to encourage users to avoid poor cognitive heuristics and biases in their expressions of knowledge. Many of these have been identified in the contemporary literature for the single-individual information-processing case. Little of this work has been extended to the group decision situation. It should be possible to consider specifically a number of these prototypical situations within an appropriate conceptual information-system design framework, and thereby to illustrate the extent to which poor cognitive heuristics and information-processing biases are encouraged or discouraged by the framework chosen. These represent some of the many points that should be addressed when developing evaluation metrics and when conducting an evaluation of existing systems.

See also: Decision Support Systems; Group Decision Support Systems: Software Architectures

Bibliography

Alter S L 1982 *Decision Support Systems: Current Practice and Continuing Challenges.* Addison–Wesley, Reading, Massachusetts

Andriole S J (ed.) 1985 *Corporate Crisis Management.* Petrocelli, Princeton, New Jersey

Andriole S J, Halpin S M (eds.) 1986 *IEEE Trans. Syst., Man. Cybern.*, Special issue on Information Technology for Command and Control **16**(6)

Anthony R N 1965 *Planning and Control Systems: A Framework for Analysis.* Harvard University Press, Cambridge, Massachusetts

Appelgate L M, Chen T T, Konsynski B R, Nunamaker J F 1987 Knowledge management in organizational planning. *J. Manage. Inf. Syst.* **3**(4), 20–38

DeSanctis G, Gallupe R B 1987 A foundation for the study of group decision support systems. *Manage. Sci.* **33**(5), 547–88

Dreyfus H L, Dreyfus S E 1986 *Mind Over Machine: The Power of Human Intuition and Expertise in the Age of the Computer*. Free Press, New York

Feldman M S, March J G 1981 Information in organizations as signal and symbol. *Adm. Sci. Q.* **26**, 171–86

Hakathorn R, Keen P 1981 Organizational strategies for personal computing in decision support systems. *MIS. Q.* **5**(3), 21–7

Huber G P 1984 Issues in the design of group decision support systems. *MIS Q.* **8**(3), 195–204

Huber G P, McDaniel R R 1986 The decision making paradigm of organizational design. *Manage. Sci.* **32**(5), 572–89

Janis I L, Mann L 1977 *Decision Making: A Psychological Analysis of Conflict, Choice and Commitment*. Free Press, New York

Kahneman D, Slovic P, Tversky A (eds.) 1982 *Judgements under Uncertainty: Heuristics and Biases*. Cambridge University Press, New York

Keen P G W, Scott Morton M S 1978 *Decision Support Systems: An Organizational Perspective*. Addison–Wesley, Reading, Massachusetts

Klein G A 1980 Automated aids for the proficient decision maker. *Proc. IEEE 1980 Conf. Systems, Man and Cybernetics*. IEEE Press, New York, pp. 301–4

Malone T W, Grant K R, Turbak F A, Brobst S A, Cohen M D 1987 Intelligent information sharing systems. *Commun. ACM* **30**(5), 390–402

Mintzberg H 1973 *The Nature of Managerial Work*. Harper and Row, New York

Mintzberg H 1983 *Structure in Fives: Designing Effective Organizations*. Prentice–Hall, Englewood Cliffs, New Jersey

Nickerson R S 1986 *Using Computers: Human Factors in Information Systems*. MIT Press, Cambridge, Massachusetts

Rasmussen J 1986 *Information Processing and Human–Machine Interaction: An Approach to Cognitive Engineering*. North-Holland, Amsterdam

Rockart J F, Bullen C V 1986 *The Rise of Managerial Computing*. Dow Jones Irwin, Homewood, Illinois

Sage A P 1981 Behavioral and organizational considerations in the design of information systems and processes for planning and decision support. *IEEE Trans. Syst., Man Cybern.* **11**(9), 640–78

Sage A P (ed.) 1987 *System Design for Human Interaction* IEEE Press, New York

Simon H A 1960 *The New Science of Management Decisions*. Harper, New York

Sprague R H, Carlson E D 1982 *Building Expert Systems*. Prentice–Hall, Englewood Cliffs, New Jersey

Sprague R H, McNurlin B C (eds.) 1986 *Information Systems Management in Practice*. Prentice–Hall, Englewood Cliffs, New Jersey

Stefik M, Foster G, Bobrow D G, Kahn K, Lanning S, Suchman L 1987 Beyond the chalkboard: Computer support for collaboration and problem solving in meetings. *Commun. ACM* **30**(1), 32–47

Weick K E 1979 *The Social Psychology of Organizing*. Addison–Wesley, Reading, Massachusetts

Weick K E 1985 Cosmos vs. chaos: Sense and nonsense in electronic contexts. *Organ. Dynamics* **14**, 50–64

Zmud R W 1983 *Information Systems in Organizations*. Scott Foresman, Glenview, Illinois

A. P. Sage
[George Mason University, Fairfax, Virginia, USA]

Group Decision Support Systems: Software Architecture

The development of software systems to support groups of people who are responsible for decision making represents an extension of supporting individual decision makers (such as business managers) through computer software. Spreadsheet software, word-processing and database packages that operate on the microcomputer have become a standard part of the modern office. As desktop computer systems are linked together to connect managers located throughout an office building or across the world, and as computers become increasingly used in the conference-room setting as well as the office, there is a corresponding interest in the development of software to support group work in organizations. Considerable commercial and research effort is being devoted to software systems that support collaborative work activities such as idea creation, message exchange, project planning, document preparation, mutual product creation and joint decision making. Particular attention is being given to the development of meeting software, or systems that aim to support dispersed and face-to-face meetings within organizations. Technical advances, such as the development of high-speed data communications networks and easy-to-use software interfaces, have contributed to the emergence of these systems.

Development of group decision support systems (GDSSs) typifies new technology developments in that a variety of approaches are being taken to software design, with little standardization. Lack of standardization is in part due to the early stage of knowledge regarding the appropriate design of shared office systems, including operating system configuration and data-management approaches. There is also, however, limited knowledge at present about the nature of collaborative work itself or work sharing in organizations. As a consequence, research in universities and corporate laboratories is proceeding along both of these fronts as software design in the GDSS area evolves.

This article reviews the status of GDSS design as it currently exists and identifies apparent software directions in the GDSS area. It must be appreciated, however, that this material will become dated as software development for group support matures; the technological frontier in this area is moving rapidly.

1. Components of Software Architectures

Group decision support systems combine computer, communication and decision technologies to support problem formulation and solution in group meetings. Computer technologies include, for example, multi-user operating systems, fourth-generation languages, databases and data-analysis facilities that cater to group discussion and joint problem solving. Communication technologies available within a GDSS include electronic messaging, local and wide-area networks, teleconferencing, and store and forward facilities. Decision-support technologies include agenda setting, decision modelling methods (decision trees, risk analysis, forecasting methods, multiattribute utility functions, etc.), structured group methods (e.g., the nominal group and Delphi techniques) and rules for directing group discussion.

In designing specific features for GDSSs the goal is to maintain or enhance the well-known strengths of group decision making, such as generation of a large number of alternatives, presentation of multiple perspectives on a problem, and promotion of synergy and commitment in the group. At the same time, GDSS features aim to diminish the common problems that occur in unsupported, or free-interacting, group meetings. These include, for example, the failure to develop a meeting strategy or plan, insufficient organization of ideas and preferences, reluctance by some people to participate in the discussion, inadequate attention by group members during the meeting and undue pressures to conform to the viewpoint of others.

The current capabilities of GDSSs can be identified in terms of the major facilities, or clusters of features, that they offer. These are the logical components that are available in GDSS software. Specific implementation of these components varies greatly across systems and not every system yet contains all of them:

(a) *Communication facilities.* These include the physical (hardware) linking together of users, as well as software facilities to support interpersonal communication. Message exchange, document exchange and other network-based communication facilities are examples. The use of a large common viewing screen or a "public" window at each group member's terminal is typical.

(b) *Meeting facilities.* These include calendar management for groups, shared notepads, electronic blackboards, electronic agenda support and software to support operation of audiovisual (AV) media (e.g., videodisks and slide shows). These features support the procedural aspects of the meeting and can be viewed as the computer-based extension of traditional meeting facilities such as blackboards, flipcharts and AV equipment.

(c) *Group-decision structuring.* Well-known group-decision approaches are frequently included in GDSS software so that members can adopt a systematic decision method and avoid a "muddling through" approach to their meetings. Techniques to guide the group through their meeting process are embedded within the computer system and include brainstorming techniques, such as the nominal group technique; strategic issues generation techniques, such as strategic assumptions surfacing and testing; and consensus forming methods, such as the Delphi technique. These approaches tend to encourage private work prior to public discussion and help the group to organize the ideas that are presented in the course of a meeting. A specific series of action steps for the meeting is provided to the group.

(d) *Decision modelling.* Decision trees, risk assessment, budget allocation models and multicriteria decision models have been incorporated into many GDSSs. These approaches encourage the group to express their preferences and choices in a quantitative manner. A mathematical model is then applied to support the group's choice of a strategy for action.

(e) *A language for user development of meeting rules.* Consistent with the trend in decision-support software to allow user-specification of decision methods or models, GDSSs increasingly provide the capability for users to define their own meeting procedures or rules for information exchange. These allow the users to customize the software to their own needs, rather than simply invoke "canned" or preset features. Rule-writing facilities may be implemented by so-called fourth-generation languages or within expert system software shells.

(f) *Expertise.* Some GDSSs include expert system capabilities that permit users to invoke a knowledge base and rule base during the course of their meeting. At the simplest level, the system asks the group to respond to a set of structured questions about the purpose of the meeting, the nature of the group, the available timeframe, etc., and then provides advice on how to conduct the meeting (e.g., which group structuring technique or decision model to use). More sophisticated systems allow the creation of a knowledge base and rule base over the course of many meetings that the group can then invoke when they address similar problem domains or issues in the future. The expert system provides a powerful "memory" for the group.

(g) *Integration with other information systems.* While most GDSS implementations are currently stand-alone systems, the trend is clearly to provide a link between the GDSS and other information systems in the organization. The starting point here is to interface the GDSS with the corporate database so that users have access to this information in the course of their meetings. A few systems allow GDSS users to bring data, programs or files from their office workstations or mainframe computer into the GDSS meeting environment. In the future it can be expected that GDSSs will become tightly linked to individual decision support system software, electronic mail systems and other commonly used information systems. Looking at this from the opposing perspective, it can be speculated that many information systems will take on a group orientation in the future. Systems that currently support the individual user at a private terminal session will evolve to provide a group mode in which multiple users can dynamically work together with the software.

2. Software Configurations

Two major types of GDSS implementations currently exist and these are characterized by the physical location of group participants as they meet or work together. First, there are computer conferencing systems that support groups whose members are dispersed, or working in their separate conference rooms, offices, homes or other locations. In addition, there are GDSSs that support face-to-face meetings that occur in one conference-room or boardroom setting. Both categories of systems support the decision making and related activities of working groups, and thus both are considered to be GDSSs. Systems of both types may also be referred to as "collaborative work systems" or "computer-aided meeting environments."

2.1 Dispersed Meeting Systems

A number of specific capabilities are considered important to successful dispersed GDSSs. These include: wide accessibility, or ability to access the system from work, home or while out of town; support for both private (participation by invitation only) and public (anyone can participate) meetings; a facility for a moderator to control meeting activity (such as membership, agenda or meeting content); archival storage of communication with search and retrieval of communications by content; and a user-friendly interface. Other characteristics may be important as well, but the general criterion is that use of the system should result in members' perception that "we had a good meeting."

There are two categories of GDSS for dispersed meetings as discussed below.

(a) Teleconferencing systems. This category supports audio and video conferencing between two physically distant meeting sites or conference rooms. These meetings have a synchronous quality in that all participants attend the meeting at the same time. In the past these systems relied exclusively on the sending of audio and video signals between the two sites for meeting support. Increasingly, these systems include software support as well, and in this sense are GDSSs. Typical software components would be some subset of facilities (*a*)–(*g*) listed in Sect. 1. In addition, specific software features might allow instant document exchange between the two meeting sites; simultaneous viewing of electronic blackboard space; data or text entry into a common modelling or other decision support program; and display of ideas, votes, data, graphs or tables to all groups members simultaneously.

(b) Computer-based communication systems. This category of GDSSs is designed to support collaborative work and decision making between group members who are individually isolated from one another for one reason or another. Meetings occur in an asynchronous mode, which means that all participants are not connected to the system at the same point in time. Electronic mail or bulletin-board systems might fall into this category if they are used to support decision making or related group activities. However, GDSSs typically involve more sophistication than simple message exchange. Dynamic document preparation, mutual problem formulation or group evaluation of alternative action steps occurs with the help of specialized software. Features such as (*a*)–(*g*) listed in Sect. 1 are implemented on a local or wide-area network. Group members can "drop in and out" of a meeting as they turn their desktop computers on and off and link into the network during the course of the working day.

2.2 Face-to-Face Meeting Systems

Interest in developing software for use in face-to-face meetings has come from three professional areas or traditions. First, AV specialists have been interested in extending the concept of the electronic boardroom to include GDSS software support. Electronic boardrooms typically include overhead projectors, high-quality graphics displays, videotape and disk players, digitizing cameras and so on. Electronic-boardroom design emphasizes remote control of devices and the importance of making the technology as unobtrusive as possible within the traditional meeting-room environment. In the past, computer support has been limited to providing electronic blackboards, terminal connections to a distant mainframe or software-based operation of AV devices. There is increasing interest in extending the electronic-boardroom concept to include GDSS software features, such as a common group scratchpad for recording ideas, agenda management facilities, decision structuring, decision modelling, and the ability to store and manage the notes of recurrent group meetings.

A second tradition from which current GDSS software to support face-to-face meetings is evolving is the area of organization development and consulting. Organizational development specialists often use face-to-face meetings as a mechanism for facilitating some sort of management change, such as structural reorganization, strategic planning or management-team building. In the past, consultants have relied heavily on group decision or collective inquiry techniques such as brainstorming, the nominal group technique or the Delphi method. Consultants generally make heavy use of flipcharts and dry marker boards as tools for recording the output of the group and providing feedback on group progress. Increasingly, these organizational change specialists are adding computer software to the set of tools that they bring to management meetings. The typical configuration is a microcomputer-based package that records and displays the ideas of participants on a large screen; the package includes a decision technique or mathematical model that operates on the preferences or votes of participants and displays the results in a graphical or tabular format. The outputs from the GDSS package are used by the consultant to structure meeting discussion and move the group toward consensus.

The third tradition from which face-to-face GDSS support is evolving is management information systems. Information system (IS) specialists have become interested in expanding the capabilities of existing communication and decision support systems to include features that support working group meetings. Whereas the systems that evolve out of the AV or consultant tradition are usually designed for operation by a single user (an AV technician, secretary, management consultant or perhaps a group leader) and include only one or two of the cluster of features (a)–(g) listed in Sect. 1, GDSSs designed by IS specialists tend to incorporate a more complex software architecture. The typical configuration developed in the IS tradition provides multiuser access to the GDSS (each group number is provided with a keyboard and cathode-ray tube (CRT) display) and includes three or more of the key software components.

Historically, electronic boardroom and consultant traditions have placed heavy emphasis on the arrangement of meeting surroundings, such as furnishings and equipment, and have only recently attended to software design issues. This can be characterized as an "outside–in" approach to GDSS design. The IS tradition, on the other hand, has taken an "inside–out" approach, attending first to issues of software design and only secondarily to meeting-room design. Although the GDSS concept arose from the IS field, and the software component of GDSSs may be the most critical to its implementation, the development of GDSSs requires that designers deal with matters of meeting surroundings, such as furnishings and AV equipment, as well as the specification of computer-based tools. In other words, the AV, organization development and IS traditions are merging with one another in the design of support systems for face-to-face meetings.

The term "decision room" is increasingly applied to GDSSs that support face-to-face meetings in conference room or boardroom settings. Section 3 further explores technologies for decision rooms and identifies various approaches that are currently being taken in the design of the software component of GDSSs.

3. Decision-Room Configurations

The components of a decision room include furnishings, AV equipment, computer hardware devices and computer software. The selection and arrangement of these varies tremendously across sites, yielding many configurations for GDSS design. Different approaches have been taken with regard to the room layout and placement of group members, computer terminals and AV devices. For example, some decision rooms have been arranged around a traditional conference-room-style table (oval or boat shaped) while others use a horseshoe-shaped table with a large common viewing screen at the front of the room. Some GDSS designers have embedded the computer terminals into the meeting-room table; others use laptop keypads for each group member; while others have placed the terminal stations on side tables adjacent to the conference table. For large-screen display some decision rooms rely on an electronic blackboard, while others use rear-screen projection systems or extremely large computer monitors. Some GDDSs use videodisk systems, high-speed workstations, mouses, hypercard and other new hardware devices, while others rely exclusively on more traditional IS technology, such as micro- or minicomputers, keyboards and CRT displays.

The arrangement of software features and the design of the GDSS interface varies nearly as much as the layouts of decision rooms. GDSSs for decision rooms have been implemented under many different operating systems and programming languages. Assuring efficient collection and exchange of information across group members' terminals or workstations, and between members' terminals and a public screen, creates a challenge to system designers. Special network software is usually developed for this purpose. Some systems display public information via shared windows on private terminals, while others rely only on the common viewing screen for the output of public information. Although some systems include only one group structuring approach or decision model for the group, decision-room systems increasingly include a variety of communication, decision structuring, modelling and general meeting facilities for the group. These are typically arranged in a shell design, or as a menu of choices from which specific features can be selected for use by the group.

One way in which to distinguish among available software configurations is to classify systems according to a series of criteria that are apparent to groups as they use GDSSs. These are characteristics of the system at its interface, and any one GDSS might vary on these criteria depending on how it is configured for a given meeting. Some example criteria are listed below.

(a) *Generic versus specialized.* Is the system designed to accomodate meetings in general and many different kinds of tasks, or are the features of the system customized to specific kinds of meetings or group decision tasks? Generic GDSSs are designed to accommodate creative tasks, choice tasks and scheduling problems, etc. Specialized GDSSs are designed for the needs of a specific task, group or organizational need. An example of a specialized GDSS is a decision room that is customized for computer programmers who meet to review coding and develop specifications for their programming activities.

(b) Facilitated versus user driven. Is the system designed to be operated by a technician, consultant or group leader, or can the system be operated by the group members themselves? Facilitated systems allow, or may even require, certain inputs or commands to be entered by a central terminal or workstation during the meeting. User-driven systems, on the other hand, do not designate any single terminal as determining the selection of features, their sequence, etc. Facilitated systems might be used in top-management strategic planning meetings, in collective bargaining sessions or in meetings where there is an extremely large number of participants. User-driven systems are typically used in small work groups that meet together on a repeated basis.

(c) Single-user versus multiuser. Is an interface provided only for the group as a whole, with one technician or group member serving as a system "chauffeur" for the group, or is every group member provided with a direct interface to the GDSS? Single-user systems typically provide one central processor into which the ideas of group members are input at a single keyboard, or perhaps via keypads. The software is designed so that the chauffeur provides all system inputs and decides the manner in which features are used. Outputs are displayed on a large screen for all group members to view. Multiuser systems provide every member with a keyboard, display device and processing power. Each group member can provide system inputs and view outputs at their terminal. Outputs intended for the group as a whole are displayed on a large screen or via windowing facilities at each terminal.

(d) "Low tech" versus "high tech". Is the system low or high tech in its interface? Low-tech systems may offer a limited number of system features and be simplistic in their design, but they are easy to use; familiarity with computers or group decision techniques or models is not required for their use. High-tech systems, on the other hand, utilize a wide range of hardware and software features, may be heavily graphics oriented and may require extensive user training for their operation. GDSS developers seem, at least at this point, to be deliberately choosing to configure their systems in a low- or high-tech fashion, depending on the sophistication of the intended user group.

A second, and perhaps more meaningful, way in which to classify decision-room configurations is according to their intended impact on the nature of group meetings. GDSS software, particularly in the decision-room setting, can be characterized by its degree of sophistication, or the degree to which it aims to intervene in the "natural" or unsupported group process.

(a) Level 1. Less sophisticated, or level 1, systems provide communication and meeting facilities to the group. A group scratchpad, support for agenda development, and public and private message exchange are examples of level 1 features. Idea recording, as well as rating, ranking or voting on ideas are also common capabilities in level 1 systems. Level 1 systems aim to help the group overcome common communication barriers in meetings, such as failure to follow an agenda or failure to capture the viewpoints of all group members.

(b) Level 2. These systems incorporate decision structuring and/or decision modelling in the GDSS software. The software provides a series of decision steps for the groups and guides the group through use of a decision technique such as brainstorming, or a decision model such as budget allocation. Level 2 systems aim to provide the group with a systematic decision path and encourage the development of meaningful rationales for choices.

(c) Level 3. These represent the most sophisticated GDSSs. Level 3 systems include a language for user development of meeting rules, provision of meeting advice and/or the development of a dynamic knowledge base that serves as the group memory. The goal of a level 3 GDSS is to provide the group with entirely new decision paths that would not be possible without the high degree of structure and rule specification that is provided by computer support.

Most systems do not yet include all three levels of sophistication at this point. Some systems allow a group leader, facilitator or other party to customize the set of GDSS features each time a meeting is held, thereby altering the degree of sophistication of the system across meetings. In this way a sophisticated GDSS offering a large menu of options can be reduced to a simple set of options for a particular meeting.

4. Critical Issues in the Advancement of GDSS Software

A number of important issues currently confront the developers and users of GDSS software as this technology continues to evolve. Some of these issues are technical, while others are more behavioral or managerial in nature. These are issues that must be addressed both for the successful design of GDSSs and for their effective use by organizational groups. These issues are relevant to GDSSs in both the dispersed and face-to-face settings.

4.1 Technical Issues

A number of technical issues must be resolved before standardization in GDSS architectures can be hoped for. One controversial area concerns appropriate operating systems for shared work environments. GDSSs are currently being implemented under a variety of operating-system environments, each of which dictates unique requirements for GDSS applications. Lack of standardization in network design and telecommunications protocols exacerbates this problem. As a result, current GDSSs tend to be operating-system dependent and, in some cases, hardware dependent as well.

A second, related concern is systems integration, or the ability to link GDSS hardware and software with other organizational information systems. Lack of linkages between GDSSs and other, more standard, office systems, as well as incompatibility in the architectures of these systems make nearly all GDSSs stand-alone systems at this time. Much design work is needed before users will be able to move readily between GDSS applications and electronic mail, mainframe applications and desktop software systems.

Other technical issues also face GDSS developers at this time. System developers must be continually aware of new technology developments that they can then adapt for use in GDSS contexts. For example, advances in the state-of-the-art of computer, telecommunications and AV systems put continual pressure on developers of GDSS software to update the internal architectures and interfaces of these systems. Also, it may be that graphical and image-based processing will become essential to the ultimate success and standardization of GDSSs. However, these technologies are still fairly new and not yet adapted to office applications such as GDSSs. Finally, there is much work yet to be done on knowledge representation in the GDSS environment. GDSS designers must work toward identifying effective approaches for representing group communication and decision making so that a group memory can be provided by the system and so that groups can use their own past meetings or those of other groups as a source of advice or counsel when conducting their meeting.

4.2 Behavioral Issues

The behavioral issues confronting GDSS development include: identifying the needs of groups in meetings and in other work settings; understanding the nature of collaboration, or what people actually do when they work together; identifying and addressing human factors interface considerations for group use of information systems; and developing methods for assessing the impacts of GDSSs on meetings and related group activities. Further advances in GDSS development efforts require greater understanding of the nature of group work in organizations. Only then is it possible to determine where the power of computing is best placed in group work settings and how software is best designed.

5. Conclusion

The success of an organizational meeting can be facilitated by a variety of technologies. Telecommunication systems, AV equipment and room furnishings are technologies that have long been used to support meetings, and a GDSS in some ways represents an extension of these as computer hardware and software become used to support meetings. While most efforts in the GDSS area to date have concentrated on the design of software for groups, there appears to be increasing interest among IS specialists in integrating other meeting technologies together with software so that effective group support can really be achieved. In other words, GDSS designers are moving away from simply providing software tools, or aids, for specific group needs, toward designing holistic environments which surround the group and in which the group can operate to meet its goals. The distinctions between computer software features, telecommunication systems, mechanical meeting devices and AV systems as they have been known in the past are becoming blurred. In this sense, the problem of architectures for GDSSs is becoming much more than a software issue. It is a complex web of technical and behavioral issues concerned with the nature of group work in organizations.

See also: Group Decision Support Systems

Bibliography

DeSanctis G, Gallupe R B 1987 A foundation for the study of group decision support systems. *Manage. Sci.* **33**(5), 589–609

Huber G P 1984 Issues in the design of group decision support systems. *MIS Q.* **8**(3), 195–204

Johansen R, Vallee J, Spangler K 1979 *Electronic Meetings: Technical Alternatives and Social Choices*. Addison-Wesley, Reading, Massachusetts

Kerr E B, Hiltz S R 1982 *Computer-Mediated Systems: Status and Evaluation*. Academic Press, New York

Steeb R, Johnston S C 1981 A computer-based interactive system for group decision making. *IEEE Trans. Syst., Man Cybern.* **11**(8), 544–52

Stefik M, Foster G, Bobrow D G, Kahn K, Lanning S, Suchman L 1987 Beyond the chalkboard: Computer support for collaboration and problem solving in meetings. *Commun. ACM* **30**(1), 32–47

Turoff M, Hiltz S R 1982 Computer support for group versus individual decisions. *IEEE Trans. Commun.* **30**(1), 82–90

G. DeSanctis
[University of Minnesota, Minneapolis, Minnesota, USA]

H

Human Factors Engineering

"Human factors engineering," or sometimes just "human factors," is the science and art of interfacing people with the machines they operate and interact with. One relevant type of interface is with the displays, controls and computer hardware which send, receive and process information. A second interface is the computer software and administrative procedures which determine how people allocate their effort, make decisions and take actions. A third relevant interface is between people and the seating, temperature, humidity, lighting, sound, radiation, vibration and other environmental factors which determine their ability to function. Finally, there is the selection and training of people for their machine interactive tasks.

Human factors engineering is generally synonymous with ergonomics, the former term being more popular in the USA, the latter in Europe. Where cybernetics is the science of communication and control with emphasis on analogies between animal and machine, and artificial intelligence is the science of performing human-like decision functions by machine alone, human factors engineering draws on both these disciplines together with experimental psychology and physiology, generally to design machines for human use. Because human factors engineering includes humans and machines in a common system (a human–machine system) it emphasizes system performance over and above the performance of either the person or the machine by itself.

It is common to consider the human operator in a control loop with a machine (Fig. 1). Salient signals from the machines go to mechanical or computer-based displays detected by the human senses. The central nervous system processes information, and the neuromuscular system, through the hands or feet, activates devices specially designed to communicate information back to the machine. This human–machine control loop was surely the first and most obvious example to the originators of control theory as we know it today. In fact, as formal control theory was being developed in the late 1930s and early 1940s, the human factors of hand controls and display devices for vehicles and other machines for industry and the military were already being considered. Later, control theory as well as information theory and decision theory, much of it borrowed from engineering, were applied to human–machine systems (Sheridan and Ferrell 1974) and finely tuned differential-equation models of the human operator of continuous control systems (flying aircraft in turbulence) emerged. Now human–computer interaction is the critical aspect of much human factors engineering activity.

1. Why Human Factors Engineering is Currently Important to Control Engineering

The history of control applications has been one of automating tasks previously performed by humans. Gradually, people have been removed from performing within the control loops where, if they cease to sense and act, the loop is opened and the system either stops or becomes unstable. Gradually people have been relegated to the task of supervisors of lower-level automatic systems (Fig. 2) where they select the mode of automation, turn the automation on and off, adjust its set points or trim its control parameters (Sheridan and Johannsen 1976, Sheridan 1987). In modern robotic systems it may be a matter of planning and programming or teaching the computer the initial conditions and constraints of the task, the goals and contingencies of what is wanted, and the objective function or criteria according to which of those goals are to be pursued. The human supervisor may then initiate and monitor automatic control, occasionally trim parameters as necessary, and intervene to take over control only in emergencies or when the automation has completed its assigned task or come

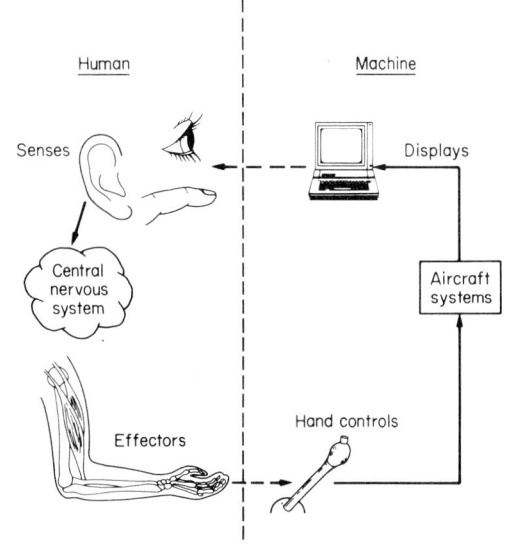

Figure 1
Pictorial representation of a human–machine system

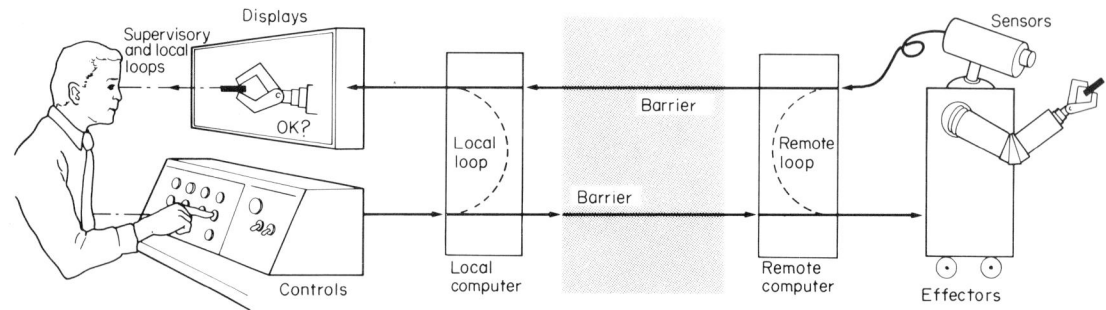

Figure 2
Supervisory control system

to a preprogrammed stopping point. Finally, the human supervisor is there to learn from experience and improve upon future automation.

Such semiautomated systems are becoming more complex; for example:

(a) air traffic control and aircraft landing;
(b) supertanker control near ports;
(c) process control in oil, chemical and nuclear-power plants;
(d) scheduling of robotic machinery in discrete parts manufacturing,
(e) remote control of "teleoperators" in deep ocean mines, space or other hazardous environments; and
(f) monitoring and control of gases and drugs administered to patients in operating rooms or intensive-care wards.

The concentration of capital and complexity of equipment are greater than in the older "manual" systems. The risk to human life, and therefore the costs of error, are increasing. The rationale, of course, is that the automation will result in greater performance, efficiency and reliability, although this is not always true.

The human supervisor is nevertheless called upon to perform increasingly sophisticated tasks, even though removed from the direct manual control loop. Most of the time, the automated system can function alone; that is, when everything is normal and the human operator can turn attention elsewhere (for seconds, minutes, hours or days, depending on the context). However, the demands on the operator, when they arise, may be more critical than before. Thus human factors engineering is likely to be at least as important after automation than it was before.

Many human factor problems remain, moreover, in conjunction with the more conventional control situations which are not computerized and/or which use the human operator within the loop, not in a supervisory fashion. Many simply powered and semiautomatic machines in agriculture, industry, the office or the home continue to fit into this category. In either case, we are far from "optimizing" the human–machine interface. Indeed, as new technology for display and control becomes available, as the human factors engineering appropriate to the old designs is no longer appropriate and as new science and art is developed to adapt the new technology, we may find ourselves further from the ideal in terms of human factors.

2. Design of Displays

The basic constraints of the human senses with respect to seeing and hearing (the senses of primary interest with respect to display of information from machines) are relatively well established. Somewhat less well understood are the senses of touch, taste and smell and the vestibular, kinesthetic (muscle) and other senses. For this reason, fewer system displays make use of these. These human sensory constraints are just as applicable to the design of computer-generated displays as to conventional displays.

What can be "just seen" (visually discriminated) is determined by factors mediating visual acuity. Primary among these are size, brightness and contrast. Figure 3 shows the trade-off between these variables and, if all three are adequate, humans can discriminate two spots separated by a minute of arc. For parallel lines, discrimination is roughly ten times better. For very brief exposures (a small fraction of a second), seeing improves with increasing exposure time. Naturally, color, vibration and other factors can also affect one's ability to see. What can be "just heard" is similarly determined by the energy intensity (loudness) and tonal frequency (pitch) relative to background sound (masking noise) (see McCormick and Sanders 1982).

Much of visual display design is an aggregation of trial-and-error design experience, together with the findings from applied research on such factors as

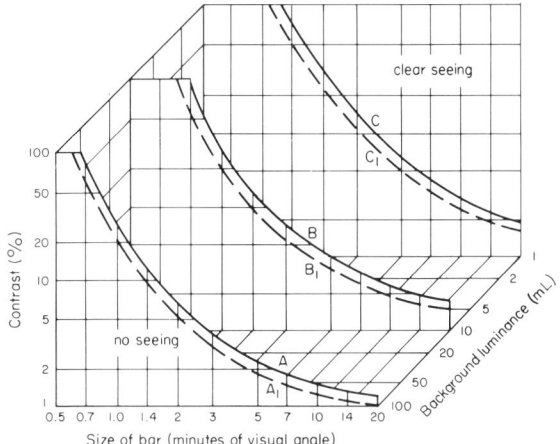

Figure 3
Conditions for clear seeing (after Cobb and Moss 1928)

letter proportion and shape, instrument scales, use of color, moving scales and fixed pointer versus moving pointer with fixed scale, linear versus circular indicators and self-illuminated versus display faces. Many design recommendations have a basis in common sense; for example, pointers should move up to the right for increase in the relevant variable (Bernotat and Gartner 1972). However, some surprising generalities have emerged from experimental research, such as the severe constraints on human short-term memory applied to simple sensory discriminations (Miller 1956).

Electronics has made radical changes in visual display technology in recent years. Earlier, conventional displays have been "dedicated" to particular variables, particular ranges (although sometimes the meaning of scales may be changed by factors of ten) and particular locations on the instrument panel. By contrast, electronic displays (cathode-ray tubes, plasma panels, light-emitting diode matrices, liquid-crystal displays) permit any display to be generated, subject to available resolution, color, gray-scale and update rate. Modern computer-generated displays permit millions of picture elements to be independently generated in a wide variety of colors and to be updated fast enough to appear continuous to the eye. This may drastically reduce the need for many separate display devices. However, such reduction may be at the cost of imposing the "keyhole effect," where the operator must actively "page" or request different displays in order to see them. The ability to move one's gaze to a remembered location and depend on seeing the corresponding display there is lost.

Grandjean (1987) reviews the desired human factor characteristics of video display terminal (VDT) workstations, including lighting, display and seating/viewing anthropometrics. In recent years there have been many complaints from individuals who work with VDTs for long periods. There is some supporting evidence regarding the difficulty of maintaining visual focus on characters of text which are refreshed at an insufficient rate or are inadequately stable for other reasons, and certainly sustained posture in one position can induce fatigue. The more common concern that VDTs emit dangerous radiation is unsupported by objective evidence.

An auditor display has the great advantage that it can attract attention without a person having to be looking at it. Conventional auditory displays have been bells, whistles and other tonal signals. The computer enables generation of speech that can convey a much greater variety of information much faster than before.

Tactile and force displays serve a relatively narrow set of problems, from Braille documents, maps and computer outputs for the blind, to currently-emerging displays of forces and texture patterns sensed by the mechanical hands of remotely controlled manipulators working in hazardous environments. Although these are among the most primitive of the human senses in a developmental sense, the exploitation of displays for these senses is relatively little developed.

3. *Design of the Human's Controller Devices*

Control signals from the human operator may be entered into the machine through switches, key pads, knobs, joysticks, trackballs or light-pens. Other computer-graphic data entry devices are touch-sensitive which are arrays of switches or are capacitively, inductively or resistively coupled to measure continuous positions of a stylus or the operator's finger, and manipulator devices which articulate in up to six degrees of freedom.

It is important to decide whether the operator's controls are to be analogic or symbolic, or in what mix. In analogic control, the motions of the device are geometrically isomorphic with the meaning of the variable being controlled. Examples are regulating some continuous variable with a knob or controlling a vehicle or some other system to move in a direction corresponding to joystick displacement. With analogic control it is also important that the display and control devices should be spatially contiguous and should correspond in their direction of movement. Whenever possible, common stereotypes should be observed (such as up or to the right for "increase" or "on"). In contrast to analogic control by the human operator is symbolic control, where inputs consist of characters, words or sentences actuated by a typewriter keyboard, special dedicated keys or mouse, or voice commands. The latter may involve selecting menu options on a computer-graphic screen or concatenating remembered symbols. Thus command languages and linguistic or software interfaces must be designed to be easily remembered and efficiently and reliably used. Williges *et al.* (1987) review such design considerations.

The movable cursor and the touch-sensitive transparent overlay for the video computer-graphic display enable the control panel to be instantly reconfigured in the same way that the display can be reconfigured. Not only option lists but the arrangement, color, size, shape, labels and symbols can be changed depending on the state of the system or the last input from the operator. Thus a single color-graphic display generator can become the equivalent of an infinitely large display and control console (Greenstein and Arnaut 1987).

The biomechanical aspects of human control actuation are well understood and documented. There now exist a number of computer-graphic design aids for aiding the human factors engineer in workplace design. These incorporate kinematic models of the body, as well as statistical properties of various key body measurements. Chaffin and Andersson (1984) give a good review.

Dynamic models of the human operator of control systems have also been highly developed, at least for relatively well-defined continuous tracking and regulating tasks. This work is reviewed by Hess (1987).

4. Design of Integrated Control Rooms and Workplaces

Various physical properties of the human operator constrain the physical configuration of the control panel. The operator's effective span of vision is roughly 30° for comparing variables on visual displays within the same visual field, although of course the gaze can be moved from one point to another arbitrarily. What can be reached manually and what force can be exerted on a control is limited by the body dimensions of the operator and whether the posture is to be seated or standing. Anthropometric tables of the the statistical distributions of various body dimensions and reaches of men and women are readily available in the literature, as are tables of the forces that can be exerted at various angles and distances off the floor. Figure 4 shows an example of such anthropometric data.

The horizontal extent of the control panel or control room and the configuration of furniture or other equipment within it determine how far the operator must walk to see or operate certain controls or to perform a particular sequence or procedure. Newer computer-based control rooms and consoles, because of the flexibility of their controls and displays, can be much smaller in size. However, some operators complain about the new system, alleging that they prefer to employ spatial location to aid pattern recognition; namely, looking to a certain place knowing that certain information will be found at that location.

Closely associated with the design of control panels or consoles is the area lighting. In most cases some mix of self-illumination (cathode-ray tube, plasma panel, gas-discharge tube, light-emitting diode) and reflection (conventional displays, liquid-crystal panel) is used. The room light must be dim enough to permit good contrast and not "wash out" the self-illuminated sources, but bright enough to see the pointers and read the scales and labels of the conventional or liquid-crystal displays. Usually there is no easy compromise. In addition, glare from room lights can be deleterious to reading any display with a glass screen, whether self-illuminated or conventional. Hoods and antiglare filters are used, but these impose other restrictions.

The heating and air conditioning of operator workplaces, whether they are control rooms or elsewhere, and whether indoors or out, have a great effect on performance. "Effective temperature," what is felt as comfortable, is a function of dry-bulb temperature, humidity, air movement, radiant heat sources, rate of calorie production by the worker, and the clothing worn. In the normal office or factory workstation, the first two factors are usually sufficient to determine effective temperature, but to an astronaut undergoing extravehicular activity all the factors are important. A review of such considerations is given by Rohles and Konz (1987).

The sound environment is usually very important in any control room or other workplace. For the operator to hear alarm signals or auditory messages spoken by other persons, the ambient noise (from machinery or background speech of other persons) must be limited. There are well-established empirical rules for determining what sounds will mask other sounds. Sound absorption and location of key sound sources (for example, by use of earphones) are ways to control this and prevent masking (Jones and Broadbent 1987).

In special operating environments such as agricultural machinery, aircraft, space, deep-ocean diving and nuclear power, other environmental factors are important to ensure the health and performance of the operator: vibration, g-loading, composition and pressure of ambient gas to breathe, and radiation.

5. Task Analysis and Procedures

As people are called upon to interact in more complex ways with machines and computers, it becomes increasingly important to analyze the task and/or be explicit about the procedures for doing the task (Edwards and Lees 1974). Many otherwise well-designed machines, from inexpensive assemble-it-yourself toys to expensive and complex instruments and systems, fail in use because the task was never properly analyzed from the user's perspective, or because clear and concise procedures were never drawn up and communicated.

Human Factors Engineering

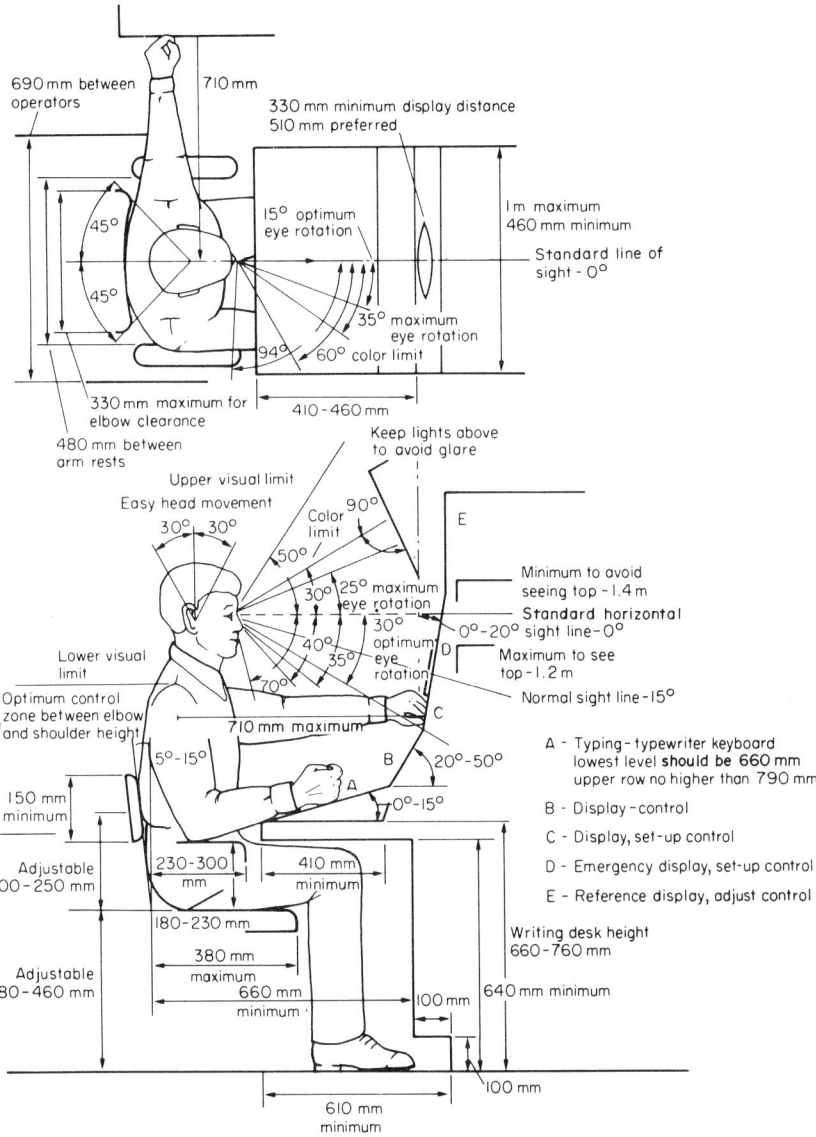

Figure 4
Anthropometric guidelines for the seated operator at a console (after Van Cott and Kinkade 1963)

Ideally, task analysis should be done at the time a machine or system is designed. It is usually a matter of a human factors professional working together with a "subject matter expert"—one who knows the operation and context, for example, of flying the aircraft, operating the nuclear-power plant or operating the computerized banking system. The activity to be performed is broken down into functional steps, typically hierarchically; that is, a small number of principal activities each of which consists of a series of secondary activities.

For each (major or minor) step the analysts try to identify:

(a) what displays or information sources a person should attend to;

(b) what decisions are to be made as a result of sensed information;

(c) what controls are operated in what way with what expected result;
(d) by what feedback one ensures that the system responds as intended; and
(e) what constitutes satisfactory completion, and what are the criteria by which human performance is judged for that step, including consequences of task omission or error.

The steps are usually displayed in the form of a flow chart, similar to that commonly used with computer programs, complete with conditional decision criteria for branching one way or another at each step (or not at all).

Such functional task analyses are sometimes augmented by geometric analyses of where and in what sequence the operator must move his gaze (to see the proper displays), move his hands (to manipulate controls) or move his body (to where he can see or manipulate). These analyses can take the form of trajectory graphs superimposed on photos or drawings of the control panel or control room.

Operator movement data for given experimental analysis can be represented by a series of nodes with arcs or arrows from each node to every other node, including remaining at the same node. Each arc is identified with a transition probability. Probabilities emanating from any one output must add up to unity.

When multiple persons interact in a task, the analyst may use a table or block diagram with a time line from top to bottom (or left to right) with each person's activity represented within one column (or row). If one or more computers are also making significant decisions, the computers' activities can be allocated their own columns. With arrows crossing from one column to another as they move down the page, diverging or converging on particular blocks, a "precedence graph" is achieved which indicates which steps must be taken by one person or computer before other steps are taken by another person or computer.

When a task has been sufficiently analyzed by such methods, procedural documents may be prepared. These can be concise; for example, instructions to teach new owners or operators how to assemble or start up a simple machine. They can be short checklist placards, as used by aircraft pilots as procedural reminders just before take-off or landing. Alternatively, they can be extensive documents, even small libraries, available for step-by-step reference in executing normal or emergency operations. The latter are found, for example, in nuclear-power plant control rooms, where procedures are specialized to many different functions (states to be achieved), both normal and emergency, as well as symptoms (what to do when a particular set of alarms occurs).

Procedures are human engineered in the form:

    (action verb) (controls, displays) and
    (action verb) (controls, displays) until (condition)
    otherwise (action verb) (controls, displays)

Clarity and conciseness in the language, readable text and absolute consistency in the use of terms are essential.

6. Design and Maintainability

Thus far we have been discussing people operating machines in the normal sense. Two other aspects of human factors engineering which are becoming more critical are design and maintainability. These are different activities, of course, but they are closely related insofar as they are usually off-line from the machine's operating activity, they are more self-paced, they are less well automated at present and require more creativity from the human operator, and the one is supported by the other (maintainability is "designed in").

For traditional design engineers attempting to perform the human factors themselves, human factors design has been carried out by use of design handbooks and guidebooks. These have tended to be published by various government agencies specializing in particular problems (e.g., nuclear-power plants, space) and contain specific recommendations for displays and controls, and so on. The danger in simply following such recommendations is that the circumstances under which the handbook writer intends the recommendations to be applied and the circumstances facing the designer about how to use those recommendations may be different. The designer needs to be circumspect, and must at least investigate the validity of the handbook data for the immediate problem.

There are new efforts to employ computer aids for the machine designer which query the designer on various aspects of the design problem and give human factors advice. Some of this might be based on tabulated data, and some on quantitative models, where the particular problem area is sufficiently well developed to support such models.

There have been numerous studies of human behavior in performing maintenance activities (Rouse 1978). Mostly, these are viewed as diagnosis and problem-solving tasks of a particular kind. The question of whether one can generalize about how humans perform such diagnoses and solve such problems is unresolved. It is obvious, however, that reliable design obviates maintenance and a simple design makes it easier when maintenance is necessary. Bond (1987) provides a good review of maintainability from a human factors perspective. An overall measure of maintainability performance relates mean time between failure (MTBF) to mean time to repair (MTTR), namely:

$$\frac{\text{MTBF}}{\text{MTBF} + \text{MTTR}}$$

7. Performance Measurement, Error and Workload

Generally it is agreed that when a human operator interacts closely with a machine, the performance of the human–machine system (combination) is what is important. A person may exert great effort or may accomplish feats of sensing, decision and control, but the performance of the system may be poor because of the interface or the ability of the machine to make use of information or energy. By contrast, a well-trained operator may perform easily and effortlessly, and because of good human–machine matching and machine capability, the system performance may excel.

As with any physical system, the common performance attributes of human–machine systems are:

(a) time (to complete tasks or subtasks),

(b) energy or other resources used, and

(c) accuracy (or precision).

The human operator's performance contributes, often but not always in a monotonic way, in terms of time, energy and accuracy. The human is always constrained to a trade-off between these factors. Indeed it has been shown that for simple positioning movements,

$$T \times \log(D/A) = \text{approximately constant}$$

where T is the time per movement, D is the distance moved and A is the accuracy (tolerance to within which the move must be completed). Fitts (1954) showed that this can be interpreted to mean that the human has a fixed limitation on transmitted bits per second in processing information.

In technical use, the term "error" typically means:

(a) a measure of performance in a continuously graded sense (for example, root-mean-squared or some other function of measurable variables which is continuous in time, geometry or some other extent); or

(b) the integral or average of a performance variable is outside some specified boundary; or

(c) an event or count of events of a performance variable is outside some specified boundary.

In psychological use, taxonomies of "error" distinguish errors of omission as against errors of commission, slips (intended actions which are not implemented) as against mistakes (actions intended by the actor which do not conform to some outside standard of intention), nonconformance with respect to sensing versus motor versus cognitive (memory, decision making) function, and so on. There is no consensus on error definition or taxonomy. In fact, at present, human error is meaningful only as defined in context. Therefore there is little or no science or engineering art for how to reduce or prevent human error in general.

Within specific applications (such as pilot error, typing error, nuclear-power plant operating error), however, there have been elaborate programs to analyze and reduce human error. In these cases, error is defined in terms of control states of vehicles or processes, the operator's adherence to specific procedures or other objective measures of performance.

One aspect of human behavior which is not the same as system performance but is alleged to be an important predictor of system performance is mental workload. Mental workload is an "intervening variable"; as with mental events in general, it is not directly measurable. Thus it is not like physical workload which can be measured by body-heat generation or by carbonization in respiratory gas exchange. Mental workload is commonly inferred by:

(a) direct subjective report of mental workload using category rating scales;

(b) secondary task performance, where presumably the better an imposed secondary task (such as arithmetic, reaction time, tracking) is performed, the less loaded the subject is assumed to be on the primary task;

(c) physiological indices, among which are heart-rate variability, galvanic skin response, pupillary diameter, spectral shifts of speech formats and special characteristics of the evoked potentials measured on the scalp in response to transient stimuli; and

(d) misestimation of elapsed time, and other psychological tests.

In spite of much recent research there is currently no consensus on either the definitions or measurements of mental workload. However, there are various means employed to prevent human error, whatever the cause:

(a) design to make correct operation obvious and easy;

(b) built-in feedback to call attention to incorrect operation in time to correct it;

(c) instructions and training;

(d) prevention of incorrect behavior by means of mechanical locks on controls or software; and

(e) warnings.

8. Simulation and Training

Simulation can entail any manipulation of physical objects or concepts which are representative of and therefore predictive of some other objects or concepts. The use of maps, drawings or three-dimensional models, applied mathematics and thinking itself are examples of simulation. In addition, of course, there are computer programs which represent physical or social events. Simulators are used because the real device or situation has not yet been built, is too costly to use or is otherwise unavailable.

The idea of having an actual person interact with a simulator (drawing, programmed text, three-dimensional mockup, computer terminal or "realistic" simulator) is not new. Flight simulators came into wide use during the 1940s for training purposes and have been continually refined; now they include not only accurate representation of vehicle dynamics, but very realistic "out-of-the-window" visual simulation of the runway during takeoff and landing as well as convincing representations of vibrations and sounds. Today, pilots learning to fly a new commercial aircraft may train in a simulator right up to the point where they take off for the first time in the actual aircraft with a full complement of passengers aboard.

Such simulators have been used to train astronauts as well as to engineer space vehicles and missions, although some properties of the actual environment, such as zero gravity, have been difficult to simulate. Similarly, simulators which imitate the whole bridge of a large ship, including ship dynamics and computer-driven representation of out-of-the-window views, are used to train crews to maneuver such ships through difficult straits and into harbors. The nuclear-power industry now utilizes a number of whole control rooms which are exact duplicates of those in actual plants, except that all the instruments and controls are interconnected to a large computer which simulates the complex dynamics of the plant. In such simulators, crews of operators learn and practice normal as well as emergency response procedures. The computers associated with these simulators can be programmed not only to provide the proper display feedback to imposed situations and individual operator responses, but also to provide the trainee with a comprehensive performance evaluation and analysis. Such techniques have been employed successfully with trainees in both aircraft and nuclear-power plant simulators.

While simulators nowadays can faithfully reproduce almost every aspect of reality, the aspect that is most difficulty to reproduce is the emotional stress sensed by the human operator in an actual emergency. In short, operators know when they are in a simulator and that the simulated crisis is not real. Therefore there remains the question of whether the experience is fully valid.

Engineers and managers faced with human factors design or training of operators for various technical tasks err by thinking too much in terms of high-fidelity simulation. Consequently, many critical human factors, such as those involving installation and maintenance of equipment, go unaided by simulation. Not only are high-fidelity simulators usually very expensive, they are certainly not necessary for the early stages of training or instrument-panel design. A whole range of simpler or "part-task" approaches is available, from static mockups to simple computer-interactive devices with randomly accessible video frames stored on disks which, being simpler, may be much better for training or for investigating a particular engineering question at an early stage.

Of course, instructional devices do not have to be built into simulators. The development of computer-aided instructional devices has been advancing for many years, and new technologies of video disks, semantic memories and reconfiguration of displays as a function of trainee performance are all important new tools.

Closely associated with training (really preceding it) is the selection of individuals for jobs. This has some objective basis; physical criteria such as size, strength, visual and hearing capabilities, and mental criteria such as linguistic, mathematical and general intellectual skills. All of these factors can be measured to help discriminate between qualifications of different individuals, the physical factors being more easily specified than the mental factors. However, the very process of discriminating among job applicants raises many questions of fairness and often becomes embroiled in government regulations and politics.

9. Current Human Factors Engineering Practice and Problems

Human factors, human factors engineering or ergonomics is gradually being recognized as a viable, independent professional discipline. Training of such professionals is usually a mix of engineering and psychology, with modest amounts of physiology, depending on the area of application. The practice of human factors places a heavy emphasis on design and statistical analysis of data from experiments with human subjects. Reports of scientific research and applications are found in special journals, such as *Human Factors* in the USA and *Ergonomics* in the UK, with counterpart professional societies in other countries. Most of the larger engineering societies have subspecialities of human factors engineering. A number of design handbooks have been published for the system designer to provide guidelines for the design of particular types of displays, control, seating, lighting and so on (Van Cott and Kinkade 1963, Bailey 1982, McCormick and Sanders 1982, Salvendy 1987). Certain government and private agencies (for example, military, nuclear power) have developed their own specialized versions.

Although there exists in the literature much research and engineering art on human factors of conventional (non-computer-based) displays and controls, the new partnership between the human and the computer has posed many new human factors engineering issues which are far from understood. As described earlier for such systems as aviation, fossil-fuel and nuclear power, chemical and oil processing, manufacturing, oil and gas extraction, operations in space and many military operations, the human operator has been replaced in many control and decision-making functions by computers together with mechanical automation. The same is true in many bank and business operations which are mostly computer information processing in place of routine human information processing. The operator has been relegated to a supervisory role, making use of computers to gather and refine information and to implement the objectives decided upon. Thus the software or computer linguistic interface becomes critically important, both at the conceptual level (what concepts must the operator use to get information and achieve objectives) and at the more superficial communication level (where the often-stated need is for the computer to be user friendly) (see Schneiderman (1980) for an outline of these problems).

In this regard there is much to be learned about how computer-based expert systems should be designed for efficiency of use by people, and how human experts can most effectively put their expertise into the computer in the first place (Harmon and King 1985). Another area where the need for human factors information far exceeds the availability is in communication and decision making by teams of operators or users, a combination of human–machine interaction and interpersonal behavior.

Ritter (1988) provides an international case-study analysis of the relevance of new technologies for ergonomics/human factors. In it he calls attention to the worldwide trend towards more complex systems, interest in cognitive aspects, demand for treating sociological factors, and desire to be more anticipatory in planning and design for human factors.

See also: Human Factors Engineering: Information-Processing Concerns; Human–System Interaction: Information-Presentation Requirements

Bibliography

Bailey R W 1982 *Human Performance Engineering: A Guide for Systems Designers.* Prentice–Hall, New York
Bernotat R K, Gartner K P (eds.) 1972 *Displays and Controls.* Swets and Zeitlinger, Amsterdam
Bond N A 1987 Maintainability. In: Salvendy 1987, pp. 1329–52
Chaffin D B, Andersson G 1984 *Occupational Biomechanics.* Wiley, New York
Cobb P W, Moss F I 1928 Four fundamental factors in vision. *Trans. Illum. Eng. Soc.* **23,** 496–506
Edwards E, Lees F P 1974 *The Human Operator in Process Control.* Taylor and Francis, London
Fitts P M 1954 The information capacity of the human motor system in controlling the amplitude of movement. *J. Exp. Psychol.* **47,** 381–91
Grandjean E 1987 Design of VDT workstations. In: Salvendy 1987, pp. 1359–97
Greenstein J S, Arnaut L Y 1987 Human factors aspects of manual computer input devices. In: Salvendy 1987, pp. 1451–86
Harmon P, King D 1985 *Expert Systems.* Wiley, New York
Hess R 1987 Feedback control models. In: Salvendy 1987, pp.1212–42
Jones D M, Broadbent D E 1987 Noise. In: Salvendy 1987, pp. 623–49
McCormick E J, Sanders M S 1982 *Human Factors in Engineering and Design.* McGraw–Hill, New York
Miller G A 1956 The magical number seven plus or minus two: Some limits on our capacity for processing information. *Psychol. Rev.* **63,** 81–97
Ritter A 1988 *Relevance of New Technologies for Ergonomics/Human Factor Science*, Results of an International Case Study. University of Kaiserslautern, Kaiserslautern
Rohles F H, Konz S A 1987 Climate. In: Salvendy 1987, pp. 697–707
Rouse W B 1978 A model of human decision making in a fault diagnosis task. *IEEE Trans. Syst., Man Cybern.* **8,** 357–61
Salvendy G (ed.) 1987 *Handbook of Human Factors.* Wiley, New York
Schneiderman B 1980 *Software Psychology.* Winthrop, Cambridge, Massachusetts
Sheridan T B 1987 Supervisory control. In: Salvendy 1987, pp. 1243–68
Sheridan T B, Ferrell W R 1974 *Man–Machine Systems: Information Control and Decision Models of Human Performance.* MIT Press, Cambridge, Massachusetts
Sheridan T B, Johannsen G (eds.) 1976 *Monitoring Behavior and Supervisory Control.* Plenum, New York
Van Cott H P, Kinkade R G (eds.) 1963 *Human Engineering Guide to Equipment Design.* McGraw–Hill, New York
Williges R C, Williges B H, Elkerton J 1987 Software Interface design. In: Salvendy 1987, pp. 1416–50

T. B. Sheridan
[Massachusetts Institute of Technology,
Cambridge, Massachusetts, USA]

Human Factors Engineering: Information-Processing Concerns

All living creatures process information. This activity is so vital that it may serve as a definition of life itself. The more advanced the creature, the more complex the physiological apparatus for information processing. The often-debated opinion that the human animal stands at the pinnacle of evolution is at least corroborated by the fact that the human central nervous system is the most complex structure in the known universe. Comprehending the manner in which this amazing structure processes sensory information in the pursuit of goals is of no small consequence in the successful design of systems intended for human use. The discipline most often associated with the design of such systems is that of human factors engineering. A review of some of the paradigms which researchers in this and related fields employ to facilitate understanding of human information processing is the subject of this article.

1. Overview of Human Information Processing

A rigorous definition of information can be provided by appealing to a branch of applied mathematics known as information theory. Here, the average information H_{av}, in bits, associated with a series of N events each occurring with a probability p_i is

$$H_{av} = \sum_{i=1}^{N} p_i \log_2\left(\frac{1}{p_i}\right)$$

While the information-theoretic approach to the study of human information processing has not proved as useful as was once hoped, it is not without its contributions. For example, it has yielded a fundamental law involving human choice reaction time, called the Hick–Hyman law. However, for the purposes of this exposition, information will be defined simply as "that which reduces uncertainty."

Almost any human goal-directed behavior can be described in terms of the information-processing activities involved. The detail in which these activities are described depends, of course, on how closely one views the structure of the human nervous system. Thus, one could begin a discussion of human information processing by describing the structure and activity of the most fundamental information-processing unit in the nervous system: the nerve cell or neuron. This "bottom-up" approach, while well-focused in terms of physiology, would not be of immediate interest or utility to the human factors engineer who is concerned with elements of macroscopic human behavior. From the perspective of this engineer, a more satisfactory approach is to view the nervous system in terms of function, and to do so in a "top-down" manner.

The top-down approach to a discussion of human information processing leads almost immediately to the subject of goal-directed behavior and to an emphasis of the human as an adaptive organism. The question now becomes: "How does the human obtain and process information about the environment in achieving desired goals, in a variety of different tasks?" It is of paramount importance to realize at the outset that the human is selective in acquiring information from the environment. This selectivity is the result of training or, more appropriately, of learning and is a necessary consequence of the temporal limitations of the human's information-processing system. In the parlance of a computer scientist, the human nervous system is quite limited in the number of serial operations per second that it can perform in processing information. However, the effects of these limitations are mitigated considerably by the fact that, in reality, the human operates as an "anticipatory" system (Rosen 1985).

Determining the specific information requirements to support successful human anticipatory behavior in goal-directed activity defines much of the job of the human factors engineer. Here, "successful" behavior is meant to imply that which allows the desired goals to be achieved while involving acceptable levels of workload for the human. There are many definitions of workload in the engineering psychology and human factors literature. At this juncture, workload implies a formal recognition of the limitations of the human information-processing system and the fact that information-processing activity appears to have a definite subjective "cost" as far as the human is concerned.

At the risk of oversimplification, human information processing can be associated with three systems defining specific functional activities within the nervous system:

(a) the perceptual system,

(b) the motor system, and

(c) the cognitive system.

The perceptual system transforms external signals arriving at the sensory organs into meaningful perceptual experiences; the motor system creates human output through the activation of voluntary muscles; and the cognitive system provides higher-level information processing associated with decision making and response selection. These activities are shown in Fig. 1. The caveat here is to realize that while this categorization of human information processing does have certain physiological isomorphisms, its appeal for the purpose of this discussion is primarily heuristic.

1.1 The Perceptual System

Table 1 briefly summarizes human sensory capabilities or sensory channels. Of course, a complete treatise could be devoted to any entry in this table; however, here the intention is merely to enumerate. Associated with any sensory capability or channel are what engineers might call "performance specifications." These specifications are of definite interest to the human factors engineer and typically specify the useful operating range and sensitivity of the sensory organ in question. They have been empirically determined and can be found in appropriate handbooks (e.g., Salvendy 1987).

The sensory organs referred to in Table 1 are essentially *transducers* or *receptors* which transform one type of energy (from the stimulus) into electrochemical energy (for transmission through the nervous system). This energy is the raw material for the information-processing hierarchy associated with human goal-directed behavior. A great deal of processing occurs in the sensory pathways leading to the highest level of the perceptual system in the cerebral cortex of the brain. As information from a particular sensory channel moves up the processing hierarchy, it becomes integrated with information from other channels. Finally, this complex dynamic process leads to the phenomenom of perception. What is often

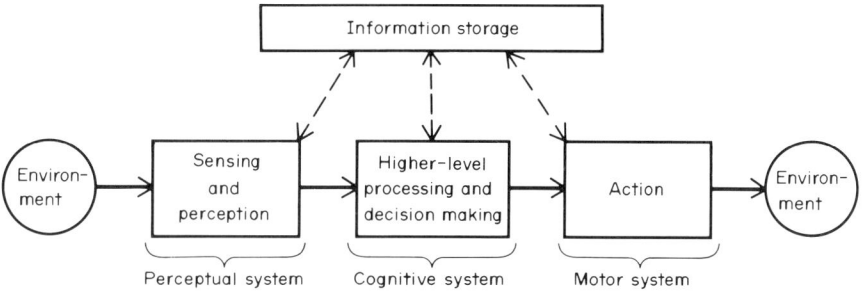

Figure 1
Elements of human information processing

Table 1
Human sensory capabilities or sensory channels

Sensation	Sensory organ	Stimulus
Sight	eye	light (electromagnetic energy)
Hearing	ear	pressure waves in surrounding medium
Linear and angular acceleration	vestibular system in inner ear	accelerations
Taste	specialized cells in tongue and mouth	chemical substances dissolved in saliva
Smell	specialized cells in nasal mucous membrane	chemical substances dissolved in air
Touch	specialized cells in skin	mechanical pressure
Temperature	free nerve endings in skin	temperature (molecular energy)

referred to as perceptual skill is that attribute which gives coherence to the data that is received by the sensory organs.

1.2 The Motor System
The human motor or neuromotor system generates physical forces. This force generation is a product of muscular activity which in turn results from the processing of sensory information in conjunction with goal-directed human behavior. Approximately 40% of the muscles in the human body are under conscious control, with the remaining 60% under involuntary control maintaining the functioning of the vital organs. Attempting to tabulate the "performance specifications" of the motor system as illustrated in Table 1 for the sensory system would be an exhausting task. The number and variety of muscles in the human body discourages such an undertaking.

The precision which is characteristic of human motor control is the result of the operation of a very complex physiological feedback mechanism. This feedback mechanism involves sensory organs not included in Table 1; in this table, entries were devoted to organs capable of sensing characteristics of the environment (external to the human). The one exception is the eye which can, of course, sense the position of the limbs. The sensory organs which are responsible for the feedback operation of the human motor system are referred to as proprioceptors. Examples are the muscle spindle and Golgi tendon organs which play pivotal roles in human motor control (McRuer 1980). Figure 2 is a very simplified representation of the feedback characteristics of the human arm from the perspective of a control system engineer. This block diagram representation emphasizes the role of the muscle spindles and Golgi tendon organs in the feedback process. As in the case of the perceptual system, what is often referred to as motor skill is that attribute which allows the smooth coordinated execution of complex movements without apparent conscious effort.

1.3 The Cognitive System
As Fig. 1 indicates, the cognitive system can be conceptualized as being located midway along the path of human information processing, between perception and action. The activities of the cognitive system include learning, remembering, problem solving, reasoning and creative thinking. Thus it might be accurate to consider the cognitive system as the highest point in

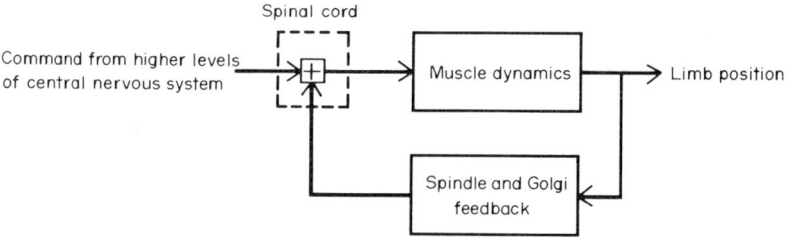

Figure 2
A simplified model of human neuromotor feedback characteristics

the hierarchy describing human information processing. Indeed, cognition, the act of knowing, is most often cited as the characteristic delineating man from the lower animals. As will be seen in Sect. 2, it is useful to envision the cognitive system as a dynamic internal model which the human calls into play in all goal-directed behavior.

It is interesting to note that it is the activity of the cognitive system which researchers in the field of artificial intelligence are trying to reproduce in machines such as computers (Newell and Simon 1972). Physiologically, the cognitive system is probably centered in the limbic lobe of the cerebral cortex, the latter representing the most recent area of the brain in evolutionary terms. What is referred to as intellectual skill is that attribute which allows the efficient linking of perception to an appropriate action based on reasoning, decision making or problem solving.

2. Models of Human Information Processing

A model is an abstract representation of a physical system or process. The most predominant models are mathematical in nature, although they can also be structural or even verbal. Mathematical models tend to be the most powerful in terms of predictive power, while structural and verbal models aid in understanding the fundamental nature of systems or processes being studied. Models are useful for human factors engineers as they can provide a framework within which pertinent aspects of human behavior can be interpreted. Three models of human information processing which have appeared in the human-machine literature are now presented and briefly discussed. These models will allow the natural introduction of pertinent topics in human information processing not covered in the brief discussion of Sect. 1.

2.1 Optimal Control and Decision Model

Figure 3 is a diagrammatic representation of a mathematical model of human information processing in manual control tasks (Kleinman et al. 1970). Strictly speaking, this is a human performance model in that it has been very successful in predicting human tracking performance in a variety of human–machine tasks. In addition to tracking performance studies, other information-processing issues have also been addressed with the model. For example, analytical studies aimed at determining the effects of display parameter and format variations in human–machine systems have been reported (e.g., Curry et al. 1977). The model given in Fig. 3 has also been referred to as an algorithmic human performance model since performance predictions are obtained through the algorithmic solution of a set of nonlinear differential equations which arise in the study of linear optimal feedback control problems.

The elements of the optimal control and decision model which correspond to the perceptual, cognitive and motor systems are reasonably easy to highlight. The perceptual aspects of the model are contained implicitly in the selection of displayed and perceived variables, and explicitly in the observation noise, the Kalman estimator and predictor. The neuromotor aspects are contained in the optimal feedback gains, motor noise and the neuromotor dynamics. The cognitive aspects of the model are implicitly contained in the procedure which yields an optimum estimation and control structure for any manual control task. This mathematical model has been extended to describe the discrete decision-making capabilities of the human operator (Pattipati et al. 1983). Decision making is clearly a cognitive-system activity, the most challenging of which typically exhibits three attributes:

(a) multiple possible choices,

(b) a time frame for the decision process which is long relative to human reaction time (which is of the order of 0.5 s), and

(c) a good deal of uncertainty as regards the "best" decision.

The optimal decision model assumes that the human makes decisions which are based on maximizing the subjective expected value of the decision. Obviously, effective decision making is highly dependent on efficient information processing and is particularly sensitive to problems related to memory.

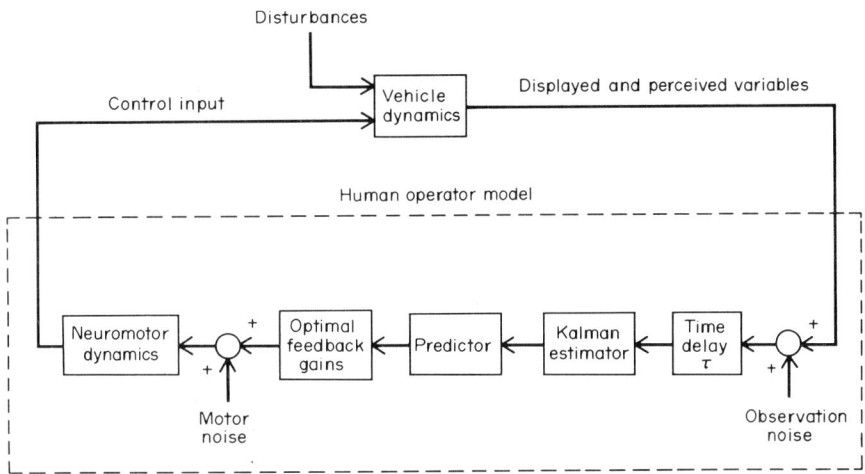

Figure 3
An optimal control and decision model of the human

2.2 Engineering Psychology Model

Figure 4 represents a model of human information processing which is not tied to any particular mathematical algorithm (Wickens 1984). It is essentially a structural model which explicitly labels the activities introduced in Sect. 1. Models like those of Fig. 4 are of interest to human factors engineers since this conceptualization provides a framework for examining potential limitations in performance. For example, a model very similar in form to that of Fig. 4 has been used successfully by Card *et al.* (1983) to quantify the performance of humans in a variety of discrete tasks involving fine-grained behavior which is representative of human–computer interaction. Their model treated the human as a set of memories and processors together with a set of principles of operation. These principles embodied many of the fundamental laws which form the basis of human factors engineering; for example, Fitts law, the power law of practice and the Hick–Hyman law mentioned in Sect. 1.

The perceptual, cognitive and motor aspects of this model are apparent in Fig. 4. Here, as in Fig. 1, reference is made to information storage in the form of blocks labelled "long-term memory" and "working memory." Working memory holds information under current consideration (i.e., intermediate products of the cognitive process and representations produced by the perceptual system), while long-term memory stores information for future use. This dichotomy in memory storage has been experimentally verified in the human. For example, destruction of part of the limbic system of the brain known as the hippocampus leads to loss of the ability to learn anything new. Old memories stored before the hippocampal damage, however, are not affected.

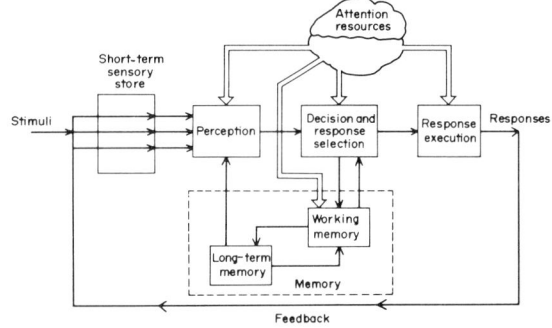

Figure 4
An engineering psychology model of human information processing (after Wickens 1984)

In order to be transmitted, interpreted and ultimately stored in sensory, working or long-term memory, information must be coded. It is common to distinguish between five different ways in which the human nervous system codes information. The codes, shown in Fig. 5 along with the associated sensory stimuli, are echoic, iconic, phonetic, visual and semantic. The echoic code represents the "echo" of a sound that persists after the physical stimulus has terminated. The iconic code is the visual counterpart of the echoic code and describes the briefly prolonged visual image evident in the human visual information-processing system. The phonetic code is similar to the echoic, but need not be preceded by an auditory stimulus. The visual code refers to information in the form of visual images. Finally, the semantic code implies information in the form of meaning.

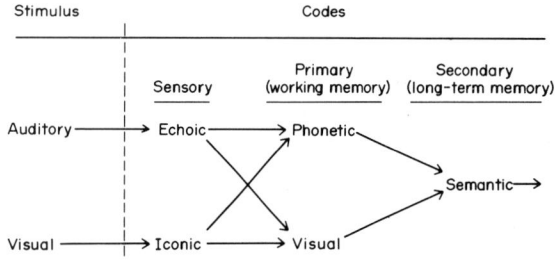

Figure 5
Coding in human memory (after Wickens 1984)

2.3 Qualitative Model

Figure 6 represents a model of human interaction with complex dynamic systems offered by Hess (1987). Like the model of Fig. 4, it is not tied to a particular mathematical algorithm. It is also the most qualitative of the three models considered in this article and emphasizes the hierarchical nature of human information processing referred to in Sect. 1. The model consists of a behavior generator, an internal model and a sensory information processor. All three elements are hierarchical in nature and the internal model serves as a link between the two elements responsible for sensing and action.

As in the case of the previous two models, the perceptual, cognitive and motor aspects of human information-processing activity can be delineated in the qualitative model by the sensory information processor, internal model and behavior generator, respectively. The loops connecting the internal model with the sensory information processor imply (a) expectations (EXP) about sensory inputs being supplied to the sensory information processor by the internal model, and (b) internal model states (SDM, etc.) being supplied to the internal model by the sensory information processor. The loops connecting the internal model with the behavior generator represent transformations (F(W) = D, etc.) in which successively more action-oriented internal model representations are created as one moves down the behavior-generating hierarchy.

The qualitative model of Fig. 6 may shed some light upon the important mechanisms behind skill development in the perceptual, cognitive and motor systems. The transformations F(W), Sc(D), T(L) and C(S) represent what Hess refers to as the selection of appropriate frames, scripts, tasks and controls in the human's interaction with complex dynamic systems. The rapidity with which these selections are made and their suitability to the achievement of the desired goal define human information-processing skill. While the perceptual, cognitive and motor systems have been informally associated with the three vertical structures apparent in the qualitative model of Fig. 6, skill

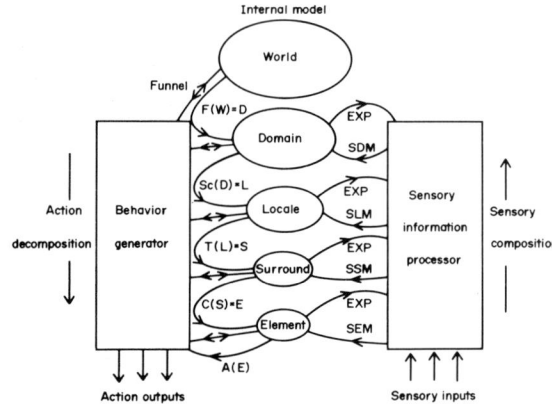

Figure 6
A qualitative model of human interaction with complex dynamic systems (Hess 1987)

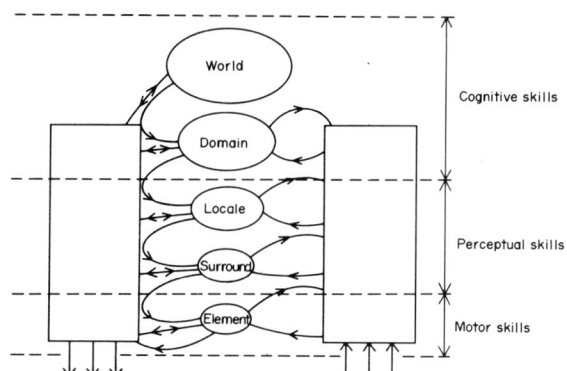

Figure 7
Interpreting human skill development in the model of Fig. 6

development is associated with activity across horizontal segments of the model, as indicated in Fig. 7. For example, motor skill can be identified with efficient operation at the level of the element submodel of the internal model, while perceptual and cognitive skills can be identified with efficient operation at the levels of the locale/surround and world/domain models, respectively. The role which training and experience (learning) play in skill development is that of honing the human's ability to rapidly select appropriate frames, scripts, tasks, controls and actions in a fluid manner which is characteristic of anticipatory behavior. It is this ability which can overcome the temporal limitations of the human information-processing system since these frames, scripts, etc., can be "hard-wired" in human memory.

3. Implications for Human Factors Engineering

The human factors engineer is typically concerned with those aspects of human behavior, capabilities and limitations which affect the design and operation of systems intended for human use. From this article it should be apparent that issues relating to human information processing are relevant to the design and operation of every such system. This is particularly true in the light of the number of systems currently in existence or being designed which involve human interaction with a computer. From microwave ovens through airliner cockpits to the word processor, human activity is increasingly being mediated by computers. Thus, it seems apparent that human behavior, capabilities and limitations in processing information will find a role of growing importance in human factors engineering.

See also: Human Factors Engineering; Human Information Processing

Bibliography

Card S K, Moran T P, Newell A 1983 *The Psychology of Human–Computer Interaction.* Erlbaum, Hillsdale, New Jersey

Curry R E, Kleinman D L, Hoffman W C 1977 A design procedure for control/display systems. *Hum. Factors* **19**(5), 421–36

Hess R A 1987 A qualitative model of human interaction with complex dynamic systems. *IEEE Trans. Syst., Man Cybern.* **17**(1), 33–51

Kleinman D L, Levison W H, Baron S 1970 An optimal control model of human response. *Automatica* **6**(3), 357–69

McRuer D T 1980 Human dynamics in man-machine systems. *Automatica.* **16**(3), 237–53

Newell A, Simon H A 1972 *Human Problem Solving.* Prentice–Hall, Englewood Cliffs, New Jersey

Pattipati K R, Kleinman D L, Ephrath A R 1983 A dynamic decision model of human task selection performance. *IEEE Trans. Syst., Man Cybern.* **13**(2), 145–66

Rosen R 1985 *Anticipatory Systems, Philosophical, Mathematical and Methodological Foundations,* Pergamon, New York

Salvendy G (ed.) 1987 *Handbook of Human Factors.* Wiley, New York

Wickens C D 1984 *Engineering Psychology and Human Performance.* Merrill, Columbus, Ohio

R. A. Hess
[University of California, Davis,
California, USA]

Human Information Processing

Problem solving, judgement and decision making imply both thought and action. Hence, decision making can be defined as the processes of thought and action involving an irrevocable allocation of resources that culminates in choice behavior. In making a decision, the human decision maker is dealing, more often than not, with environments that are characterized by risks, hazards, uncertainty, complexity, changes over time, and conflict. Furthermore, the quality of a decision depends on how well the decision maker is able to acquire, analyze, evaluate and interpret information so as to discriminate between relevant and irrelevant data. Decision quality also depends on how well the decision maker may arrive at a good problem solution, decision or judgement.

1. Introduction and Physiological Models of Information Processing

A number of studies, such as those by Barron and Person (1975), Bettman (1979), Chorba and New (1980), Delaney and Wallsten (1977), Feather (1981), Howell and Fleishman (1981), Montgomery and Svenson (1976), Moskowitz *et al.* (1976), Wallsten (1977, 1980), and Wright (1974), discuss the vital role of human information processing as a crucial task for effective decision making. Taken together, they state that the type of decision problem, the nature of the decision environment and the current state of the decision maker combine to determine decision style and decision strategy for a specific task.

An information-processing theory of problem solving, judgement and decision making is based on the assumption that individuals have an input mechanism for acquisition of information, an ouput mechanism for interpretation and choice making, internal processes for filtering and other analysis efforts associated with information, and memories for long- and short-term storage of information. There are a large number of ways of representing human information processing. Many of these are described in texts in cognitive psychology such as Anderson (1980) and Posner (1973), and in works in consumer choice such as Bettman (1979).

Figure 1 presents some aspects of an engineering framework for human information processing. There are doubtless a number of components missing from this model. It does not show, for example, the essentially iterative nature of the process. Nevertheless it provides a useful point of departure and a structure for the initial efforts in this article which describe a physiological model of human information processing. As shown in this figure, the key functions which determine how a specific problem or decision situation is cognized depend on an interaction of the memory and higher-order cognition of the problem solver with the environment. This occurs through what is denoted as the contingency task structure. The various information analysis and interpretation processes of thinking, task performance, objective identification, evaluation and decision rule identification, are called "higher-order" cognition. This is not

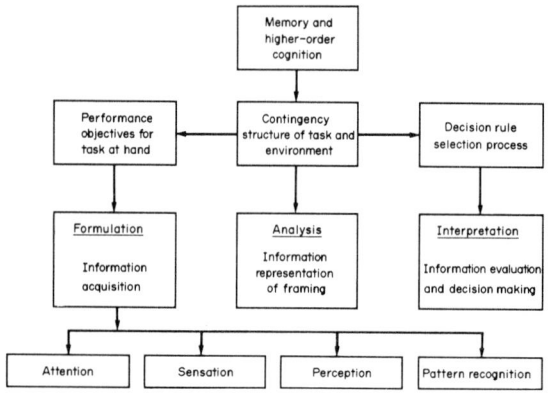

Figure 1
Model of human information processing

because they are somehow more important than the so-called "lower-order" cognition efforts of information acquisition that involve such formulation efforts as sensation, attention, perception and pattern recognition. They are called higher order because they occur later in time in the overall information-processing effort, after initial completion of the acquisition formulation efforts.

Information-processing and decision-making efforts intimately involve memory. Memory influences human judgement in a number of ways. It will influence the perception of the contingency task structure associated with an issue, as well as the decision rules used for evaluation of alternatives. Two characteristics of human memory are of special importance here. First, information will be encoded in more-or-less efficient and effective ways in terms of human abilities for recall. Furthermore, the coding process is dependent on the interpretation attached to information and this strongly influences event recall, perceptions and associated cognitive biases. The literature concerned with memory and its components, and their relations and interaction with human perceptual experience and behavior, is vast and speculative in nature. There have been many studies, both physiological and psychological, concerned with the identification of the memory engram, which is hypothesized to be the fundamental unit of memory. We need not be especially concerned here with the various related behavior therapies; however, the essentials will be reviewed briefly. Useful brief surveys of the literature on memory are presented in Michon *et al.* (1979) and Radcliff (1978).

Human memory has two major components: short-term memory and long-term memory. Short-term memory plays a key role in the immediate recall of actively rehearsed limited information. Unless conscious effort is put forth in recalling information from short-term memory, this cannot be done after a lapse of 30–60 s from the initial presentation. Models of a working short-term memory involve a number of mechanisms, such as an articulatory rehearsal loop that has the capacity to retain short verbal sequences. This is just one mechanism by which short-term retention is possible. There are a number of other sensory registers. It is important to note that short-term memory is an integrated network of many mechanisms and is associated in use with a number of skilled processes.

Shiffrin and Schneider (1977) incorporate concepts of attention, memory and perceptual learning in their theory of short-term retention. They hypothesize short-term storage that enables such functions as active control of thinking, reasoning and general memory processes. According to Shiffrin and Schneider, short-term storage is an activated subset of long-term storage. Transfer of information from short-term storage to long-term storage is dependent on attentional limitations, interference from strong external and internal stimuli, extent of analysis of information, and formation of associations in long-term storage. There have been many studies involving concepts such as retrieval processes, memory trace identification, encoding processes and recognition which are not discussed here as they appear to be of secondary importance to the goals of this particular effort. While five to seven unconnected items is believed to be the maximum amount of information that can be retained in short-term memory, long-term memory may contain a virtually limitless amount of information.

Thus we see an enormous difference between human abilities and computer abilities. Because of its large long-term memory and ability for quick search and recall, a human mind easily reasons wholistically. Wholistic reasoning, such as reasoning by analogy, is not at all easy for a computer. Significant unaided computational effort would be difficult for a human since computation must be done in short-term memory. There exists the possibility that information stored in long-term memory is flawed because of cognitive biases introduced by processing in short-term memory. Computers are quite agile at performing computational tasks. Thus we see the possibility of meaningful computer-based support to human information processing, as well as judgement and choice. A principal task of computer-aided support must be to augment human capabilities in need of augmentation, while not diminishing abilities in those areas in which human abilities exceed those of the computer.

This article is devoted to a description of the various processes which support information acquisition and analysis. Some of the cognitive biases that can result from "poor" information acquisition and analysis are also discussed. Information interpretation, which leads to alternative evaluation and decision making, is an important and somewhat distinct part of the overall information-processing model.

The types of operations involved in information acquisition are sensation, attention, perception and pattern recognition. Doubtless there are other valid ways of categorizing these operations but the taxonomy used here is sufficient for our purposes. In sensation, information is acquired through the five major sense modalities, which are environmentally activated, in response to a specific array of stimulus energies. In a specific decision-making situation, the decision maker filters out data believed to be irrelevant. The filtering process is based on task characteristics, experience and motivation, as well as other features and demands of the specific decision-making situation. If such a filtering mechanism did not exist, the decision maker would often encounter information overload which would generally result in a form of cognitive saturation and the inability to process sufficient information for the task at hand. Short-term and long-term memory components play key roles in the information-acquisition process as the decision maker proceeds with efforts that culminate in choice. A response system couples the memory system to the sensory system and the environment. Thus it controls or activates the sensory modalities on the basis of the actions taken. Through the response system we close the information-flow feedback loop. A model of the principal components of information flow might consist of the response system, the sensory system, the memory system and the central processor. The central processor coordinates memorizing, thinking, evaluation of information and final decision making.

Ultimately involved in retention processes is the notion of attention. In order for information to be transferred from short-term memory to long-term memory, constant conscious attention, in terms of rehearsal, is required. Information entering short-term memory that is not attended to through specific conscious processes is lost. Processing of information demands attention to relevant incoming data and the transfer of the data into long-term memory for future retrieval for making a decision. Interferences of various types may interrupt attention and thus hinder transfer and retention of relevant stimuli into long-term memory.

The process of pattern recognition is inherent in the processing of information acquisition. This process generally involves two phases: extraction and identification. A given stimulus is coded in terms of its features. These extracted features of the object or stimulus describe the stimulus. The term "features" implies such characteristics as angles, lines or edges. A stimulus may be received through any of the sense modalities. The meaning that a stimulus conveys to the decision maker, or the manner in which the decision maker perceives the stimulus, is dependent on the patterns extracted from the stimulus. In the identification phase, the sensory-perceptual system classifies the stimulus object. This is often assumed to occur by a weighted matching of the current feature list against a likely set of prototypes in long-term memory with the input being classified according to the name of the best-matching prototype. The quality or extent of the sensory information extracted determines the accuracy of identification. Thus, pattern recognition processes involve memory and the other three components of information acquisition: sensation, the initial experience of stimulation from the sensory modalities; attention, the concentration of cognitive effort on sensory stimuli; and perception, the use of higher-order cognition to interpret sensory stimuli.

We have just described what might be regarded as a component, or physiological, model of information processing. In such a stimulus–response approach, behavior is seen as being initiated by the onset of stimuli. A seeming deficiency in approaches of this sort is that there is little consideration of how information is aggregated to influence choice, and how the decision maker goes about the process of information formulation or acquisition, analysis and interpretation. These details are needed in studies of information processing in systems and organizations.

Within the uncertain and unpredictable environment in which decision makers operate, it appears both possible and desirable to conceptualize the decision-making process as fundamentally being one of knowledge acquisition, knowledge representation and knowledge use, rather than simply a physiological response to available information. To accomplish this, we should first look at knowledge perspectives for design in terms of potential ways in which we might represent human knowledge in the knowledge base of a support system, and then examine ways in which humans represent knowledge as a function of the contingency task structure. To do this well, we will doubtless need an appropriate integrated taxonomy of human leadership in organization and human information-processing functions. Concern here is with the latter.

Two distinct phases can be identified in the process of information and knowledge acquisition. The first state is a generative phase in which the need for knowledge acquisition is recognized and some requirements concerning the scope of this knowledge are identified. Next, there is a cognitive validation phase which is concerned with degrees of validity and confidence that should be attributed to the present knowledge and level of expertise of decision makers relative to tasks at hand. This leads, among other things, to an identification of the metalevel decision concerning how to decide, a judgement concerning objectives to be achieved for the task at hand, and information needs for the issue being addressed. The articles, *Human Judgement and Decision Rules*, *Knowledge Representation* and, in particular, *Cognitive Management and Models of Judgement and Choice Processes* are very relevant to the present discussion.

During the various stages of a judgement and choice or decision-making process, each of the generation and validation efforts may be repeated several times. Initially, a preliminary set of requirements concerning the scope of available information is identified. This set of requirements leads to an estimate of validity and confidence relative to the expertise associated with the task at hand. This in turn leads to the implicit identification of the decision perspective that will be used for selection of an alternative course of action. In some cases, the associated information-processing behavior is "open" in the sense that the decision maker actively searches for potentially disconfirming information. At times it will be "closed" in the sense that the decision maker will ignore information that is potentially disconfirming to beliefs already held. This open and closed information-processing behavior has been observed by several researchers. Kruglanski (1980), Kruglanski and Ajzen (1983) and Kruglanski and Freund (1983) conceptualize these tendencies as consequences of epistemic motivations and use the terms "freezing" and "unfreezing."

Examining conditions under which one of these information-processing behavior patterns is evoked should yield much insight into the variables that influence metalevel decisions concerning how to decide. In part, this might be accomplished by identifying classes of internal and external factors that influence various "freezing–unfreezing" tendencies. Three types of epistemic motivations which influence these tendencies have been suggested: fear of invalidity, sensed need for structure, and need for a desired conclusion. Several external or environmental factors that influence these may be identified: availability and saliency of information, time pressure, and group and organizational factors.

We will now examine the ways in which humans actually process information that is acquired. Some guidelines that potentially enable better information processing are then provided.

2. *Cognitive Information-Processing Biases*

A large number of contemporary studies in cognitive psychology indicate that the attempts of people, including experts, to apply various intuitive strategies in order to acquire and analyze information for purposes such as prediction, forecasting and planning, are often flawed. Many studies have been conducted to describe and explain the way information is acquired and analyzed and the results of faulty acquisition and analysis. Generally the descriptive behavior of subjects in tasks involving information acquisition and analysis is compared to the normative results that would prevail if people followed an "optimal" procedure. Most of these information-processing biases involve the processing of statistical information, and a Bayesian framework is usually assumed in order to obtain normative results. There have been a number of discussions, from several perspectives, of cognitive biases. The texts by Nisbett and Ross (1980) and Hogarth (1980) concerning strategies and biases associated with judgement and choice are especially noteworthy, as is the collection edited by Kahneman *et al.* (1982).

We will describe only a single bias in any detail here. It is known as the base-rate bias or base-rate fallacy. Suppose that it is known that 25% of the cards in a standard 52-card deck are clubs. A single card is drawn, face down, and we are asked the question: what is the probability that the card drawn is not a club? It turns out that almost everyone will say 0.75 or 75%. In almost all cases like this the base-rate information is used as representative information, and a particular sample is assumed to have the same statistical properties as the entire set of items.

Now suppose that we are allowed to ask the opinion of a spy. The spy says that it was a club. But spies have been known to be inaccurate. So a vision test is given the spy. The vision test is precise and it determines that the spy can correctly identify the suit of a card 80% of the time. This means that the probability that the card will be identified as a club given that it is a club is 0.80; that is, $P(SC|C) = 0.80$. The visual ability of the spy also means that the probability that the spy will say that it is not a club, given that it is not a club, is also 0.80; that is, $P(SNC|NC) = 0.80$. The other two conditional probabilities are, of course, $P(SNC|C) = 0.20$ and $P(SC|NC) = 0.20$. Often the last two sentences are not provided to the subject; in many cases they will be, and they would generally be provided if requested by the subject.

The question now posed is: given the uncertainty associated with the response of the spy, what is the probability that the card is a club, given that the spy says that it is a club? Most people will reason that, since the spy says it is a club and since the spy is accurate 80% of the time, the probability that the card drawn from the deck is actually a club is 0.80 or 80%. There is a significant problem associated with this answer as the subjects have ignored base rates. What we really wish to know is the probability of the event "card is a club, given that the spy says that it is a club." It is quite possible that the subjects misinterpret the conditional probabilities that are given, and perceive these as probabilities of the actual suit of the card given the claimed suit seen by the spy. The experimenter is generally very explicit in indicating to the subjects that this is not the case and that the spy is really telling what suit the spy believes was observed. The actual probability of the card being a club conditioned upon the observation by the spy that it was a club, may be obtained from Bayes' rule as $P(C|SC) = P(SC|C)P(C)/P(SC)$. We compute $P(SC) = P(SC|C)P(C) + P(SC|NC)P(NC)$ as $P(SC) = 0.8(0.25) + (0.2)(0.75) = 0.35$. Thus, we have $P(C|SC) = 0.8(0.25)/(0.35) = 4/7 = 0.571$. Rather than the spy being correct, in that the card is a club, with probability 0.8, the spy is only correct with probability 0.571. The difficulty here, generally unrecognized by those who do not do the calculation, is that the spy

226

has a lot of "false alarms"; that is to say he misdiagnoses a large percentage of nonclubs as clubs. However, it appears that not only do subjects not do calculations like this, they neglect base rates completely when they are given individuating information.

This is a prototypical illustration of the sort of information-processing bias that is observed. The many studies that have been made suggest that the errors that occur are systemic and not just random errors that might be due to factors such as guessing. Kahneman and Tversky (1979) indicate that there are three primary reasons for study of these systematic errors in inferential biases:

(a) they expose human intellectual limitations and suggest ways to improve the quality of human reasoning and information processing;
(b) they reveal the psychological processes that govern human inference and judgement; and
(c) they indicate those portions of statistical theory which are nonintuitive or counterintuitive.

In their definitive study of behavioral and normative decision analysis, von Winterfelt and Edwards (1986) refer to these information-processing biases as cognitive illusions. They indicate that there are four fundamental elements to every cognitive illusion:

(a) a formal operational rule that determines the correct solution to an intellectual question;
(b) an intellectual question that almost invariably includes all of the information required to obtain the correct answer through use of the formal rule;
(c) a human judgement, generally made without the use of these analytical tools, that is intended to answer the posed question; and
(d) a systematic and generally large and unforgivable discrepancy between the correct answer and the human judgement.

Illusions have been a subject of much study in psychology. Most of these are visual illusions, such as involved in determining which of the three parallel lines in Fig. 2(a) is the longest. In Fig. 2(a), modelled after the classic Müller–Lyer illusion, it would appear that the line closest to the bottom of the figure is the longest. When we frame the lines with a rectangle, as in Fig. 2(b), it is apparent that it is actually the line at the top that is the longest. In a similar way, what is argued is that the framing of cognitive issues is often improper, and this leads to cognitive illusions.

Among the cognitive biases that have been identified are several which affect information formulation or acquisition, analysis and interpretation. Among these biases, which are not independent, are the following.

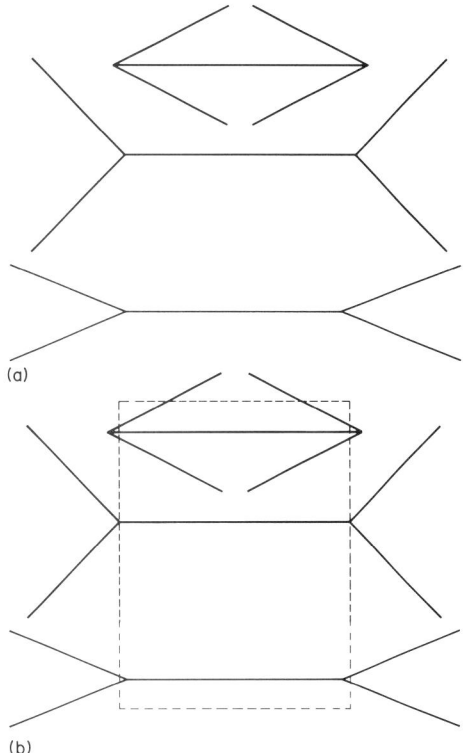

Figure 2
(a) Visual illusion based on the Müller–Lyer illusion; (b) the same illusion with framing to reveal the true line lengths

(1) *Adjustment and anchoring*. Often a person finds that difficulty in problem solving is due not to the lack of data and information, but rather to the existence of excess data and information. In such situations, the person often resorts to heuristics which may reduce the mental efforts required to arrive at a solution. In using the anchoring and adjustment heuristic when confronted with a large amount of data, the person selects a particular datum, such as the mean, as an initial or starting point, or anchor, and then adjusts that value improperly in order to incorporate the rest of the data so as to result in flawed information.

(2) *Availability*. The decision maker only uses easily available information and ignores sources of significant information not easily available. An event is believed to occur frequently (that is, with high probability) if it is easy to recall similar events.

(3) *Base rate*. The likelihood of occurrence of two events is often compared by contrasting the number of times the two events occur and ignoring the rate of occurrence of each event. This bias often occurs when the decision maker has concrete experience with one event but only statistical or abstract information on

the other. Generally, abstract information will be ignored at the expense of concrete information. A base rate determined primarily from concrete information may be called a causal base rate whereas that determined from abstract information is an incidental base rate. When information updates occur, this individuating information is often given much more weight than it deserves. It is much easier for individuating information to override incidental base rates than casual base rates.

(4) *Confirmation bias.* People are more prone to utilize information that is likely to validate currently held beliefs than information that might disconfirm or falsify these beliefs.

(5) *Conservatism.* The failure to revise estimates as much as they should be revised, based on the receipt of new significant information, is known as conservatism. This is related to data saturation and regression-effects biases.

(6) *Data presentation context.* The impact of summarized data, for example, may be much greater than that of the same data presented in detail, nonsummarized form. Also, different scales may be used to considerably change the impact of the same data.

(7) *Data saturation.* People often reach premature conclusions on the basis of too small a sample of information while ignoring the rest of the data that is received later on, or stopping acquisition of data prematurely.

(8) *Desire for self-fulfilling prophecies.* The decision maker values a certain outcome, interpretation or conclusion, and only acquires and analyzes the information that supports this conclusion. This is another form of selective perception.

(9) *Ease of recall.* Data which can easily be recalled or assessed will affect perception of the likelihood of similar events occurring again. People typically weigh easily recalled data more than data which cannot easily be recalled.

(10) *Expectations.* People often remember and attach higher validity to information which confirms their previously held beliefs and expectations than they do to disconfirming information. Thus the presence of large amounts of information makes it easier for one to selectively ignore disconfirming information so as to reach any conclusion and thereby prove anything that one desires to prove.

(11) *Fact-value confusion.* Strongly held values may often be regarded and presented as facts. Information is sought which confirms or lends credibility to one's views and values. Information which contradicts one's views or values is ignored. This is related to wishful thinking in that both are forms of selective perception.

(12) *Fundamental attribution error (success/failure error).* The decision maker associates success with inherent personal ability and associates failure with poor luck in chance events. This is related to availability and representativeness.

(13) *Gamblers fallacy.* The decision maker falsely assumes that the unexpected occurrence of a "run" of some events enhances the probability of occurrence of an event that has not occurred.

(14) *Habit.* Familiarity with a particular rule for solving a problem may result in reutilization of the same procedure and selection of the same alternative when confronted with a similar type of problem and similar information. We choose an alternative because it has previously been acceptable for a perceived similar purpose, or because of superstition.

(15) *Hindsight.* People are often unable to think objectively if they receive information that an outcome has occurred and they are told to ignore this information.

(16) *Illusion of control.* A good outcome in a chance situation may well have resulted from a poor decision. The decision maker may assume a feeling of control over events that is not reasonable.

(17) *Illusion of correlation.* A mistaken belief that two events covary when they do not covary is known as the illusion of correlation.

(18) *Law of small numbers.* People are insufficiently sensitive to quality of evidence. They often express greater confidence in predictions based on small samples of data with no disconfirming evidence than in much larger samples with minor disconfirming evidence. Sample size and reliability often have little influence on confidence.

(19) *Order effects.* The order in which information is presented affects information retention in memory. Typically, the first piece of information presented (primacy effect) and the last presented (recency effect) assume undue importance in the mind of the decision maker.

(20) *Outcome-irrelevant learning system.* Use of an inferior processing or decision rule can lead to poor results, and the decision maker can believe that these are good because of an inability to evaluate the impacts of the choices not selected and the hypotheses not tested.

(21) *Overconfidence.* People generally ascribe more credibility to data than is warranted and hence overestimate the probability of success merely due to the presence or an abundance of data. The greater the amount of data, the more confident the person is of the accuracy of the data.

(22) *Redundancy.* The more redundancy in the data, the more confidence people often have in their predic-

tions, although this confidence is usually unwarranted.

(23) *Reference effect.* People normally perceive and evaluate stimuli in accordance with their present and past experiential level for the stimuli. They sense a reference level in accordance with past experience. Thus reactions to stimuli, such as a comment from an associate, are interpreted favorably or unfavorably in accordance with previous expectations and experiences. A reference point defines an operating point in the space of outcomes. Changes in perceptions due to changes in the reference point are called reference effects. These changes may not be based upon proper, statistically relevant computations.

(24) *Regression effects.* The largest observed values of observations are used without regressing towards the mean to consider the effects of noisy measurements. In effect, this ignores uncertainties.

(25) *Representativeness.* When making inference from data, too much weight is given to results of small samples. As the sample size is increased, the results of small samples are taken to be representative of the larger population. The "laws" of representativeness differ considerably from the laws of probability and violations of the conjunction rule, $P(A/B) < P(A)$ are often observed.

(26) *Selective perceptions.* People often seek only information that confirms their views and values. They disregard or ignore disconfirming evidence. Issues are structured on the basis of personal experience and wishful thinking. There are many illustrations of selective perception. One is "reading between the lines" such as, for example, to deny antecedent statements and, as a consequence, accept "if you don't promote me, I won't perform well" as following inferentially from "I will perform well if you promote me."

(27) *Spurious cues.* Often cues appear only by occurrence of a low-probability event but they are accepted by the decision maker as commonly occurring.

(28) *Substitution of correlation for causation.* Often, we assume that because two events are correlated, that there must also be some causative relation between them. Causation must imply correlation. However, correlation does not infer any necessary causative relationships.

(29) *Wishful thinking.* The preference of the decision maker for particular outcomes and particular decisions can lead to the choice of an alternative that the decision maker would like to have associated with a desirable outcome. This implies a confounding of facts and values and is a form of selective perception.

Doubtless there are other information acquisition, analysis and interpretation biases not identified here. In reality, any categorization into acquisition, analysis and interpretation bias is somewhat arbitrary since iteration and feedback will often, in practice, not allow this separation. Also, many of the identified biases overlap in meaning and, therefore, are related to others.

A central goal of research in psychological decision theory appears to be debiasing, so that descriptive decision theory approaches normative decision theory to enable a more efficacious approach to prescriptive decision aiding. A number of authors have indicated the strong possibility that subjective assessments may almost always be biased and therefore misleading. Kahneman and Tversky (1979) have offered the following additional observations concerning human bias and intuitive prediction:

(a) there is often a highly consistent bias in setting confidence intervals and probability distributions;

(b) a surprise occurs if an estimate falls outside the confidence interval;

(c) if confidence reflects knowledge, then the true value should fall outside the k percent confidence interval on approximately $(1-k)$ percent of cases;

(d) people may be overconfident or underconfident, depending on how the percentage of surprises compares with that initially anticipated;

(e) the degree of overconfidence generally increases with ignorance;

(f) overconfidence does not generally occur when a person has considerable knowledge of conditional outcome distributions, probably due to repetitive situations and outcome feedback associated with this knowledge;

(g) sample size and information reliability do not significantly influence human confidence in judgements;

(h) insensitivity to evidence quality may explain overconfidence effects;

(i) oversensitivity to the consistency of available data is a second cause of overconfidence;

(j) in a search for coherence, people often see patterns where none exist, reinterpret data to increase consistency, and ignore evidence that does not fit their view, thereby overestimating the consistency of, and deriving too much confidence from, information.

Of particular interest are circumstances under which these biases occur; their effects on activities such as decision making, issue resolution, planning, and forecasting and assessment; and appropriate styles which might result in debiasing or amelioration of the effects of cognitive information-processing bias.

Many of the cognitive biases that are known to exist have been found in the unfamiliar surroundings of the experimental laboratory, and generalization of this work to real-world situations is a contemporary research area of much interest. However, most of the laboratory experiments have concerned very simple, if unfamiliar tasks. A number of studies have compared expert performance with simple quantitative models for decision making such as those by Brehmer (1980), Cohen (1979) and several authors in Wallsten (1980).

A particular cogent summary of those principles that encourage the use of proper information processing, particularly in the statistical settings in which many of the information-processing biases have been developed is contained in Nisbett *et al.* (1983). Three task variables are identified as being particularly important in influencing adults, capable of formal operational thought in the sense of Piaget, to reason correctly in a statistical sense. These include: the degree to which randomness in data-sensing devices is evident; experiential familiarity with analogous situations; and cultural disposition for statistical reasoning in the particular task being considered. The results of much of this work, although controversial, show that simple quantitative models perform better in human judgement and decision-making tasks, including information processing, than wholistic expert performance in similar tasks. This would appear to have major implications and cast major doubts on such processes as "expert forecasting." This caution is strongly emphasized in the works of Hogarth and Makridakis (1981); Makridakis and Wheelwright (1979) and Armstrong (1978, 1980). Beyth-Marom and Dekel (1985) and Einhorn and Hogarth (1987a,b) provide guidelines that should be useful in assisting people to improve the processing of statistical information. Klayman (1984) and Klayman and Ha (1987) are particularly concerned with the provision of appropriate feedback, so that humans can process information more correctly in stochastic environments. We will now briefly examine some of these approaches.

3. Debiasing

There are a number of prescriptions which might be given to encourage avoidance of possible cognitive biases and to debias those that do occur. Some suggestions to avoid cognitive bias are listed below.

(a) sample information from a broad database and be especially careful to include databases which might contain disconfirming information.

(b) include sample size, confidence intervals and other measures of information validity in addition to mean values.

(c) encourage the use of models and quantitative aids to improve information analysis through proper aggregation of acquired information.

(d) avoid the hindsight bias by providing access to information at critical past times.

(e) encourage decision makers to distinguish good and bad decisions from good and bad outcomes in order to avoid forms of selective perception such as, for example, the illusion of control.

(f) encourage effective learning from experience. Encourage understanding of the decision situation, and methods and rules used in practice to process information and make decisions, to avoid outcome-irrelevant learning systems.

(g) Use structured frameworks based on logical reasoning in order to avoid confusing facts and values and wishful thinking, and to assist in processing information updates.

(h) collect both qualitative and quantitative data, and be sure that all data is regarded with appropriate emphasis. None of the data should be overweighted or underweighted in accordance with personal views, beliefs or values alone.

(i) people should be reminded, from time to time, of the type or size of sample from which data are being gathered, so as to avoid the representativeness bias.

(j) Information should be presented in several orderings so as to avoid recency and primacy order effects, and the data-presentation context and data-saturation biases.

Kahneman and Tversky (1979) discuss a systematic procedure to enhance debiasing of information-processing activities. A five-step procedure, designed to produce properly regressive procedures by experts who are familiar with the subject area of the investigation, is proposed:

(a) select a proper reference class;

(b) make a statistical estimate of the distribution of the reference class;

(c) make an intuitive, generally nonregressive, estimate;

(d) assess probabilities; and

(e) correct the intuitive estimate.

A definitive discussion of debiasing methods for hindsight and overconfidence is presented by Fischoff in Kahneman *et al.* (1982). He suggests identifying faulty judges, faulty tasks, and mismatches between judges and tasks. Strategies for each of these situations are given.

4. Constrasting Views

Not everyone agrees with the conclusions reached about cognitive human information processing and inferential behavior. Several arguments have been advanced for a decidedly less pessimistic view of human inference and decision. In one of these, Cohen (1979, 1981) argues that all of this research is based on a conventional model for probabilistic reasoning, which he calls the "Pascalian" probability calculus. He expresses the view that human behavior does not appear biased at all when it is viewed in terms of other equally appropriate schemes for probabilistic reasoning, such as his own "inductive" probability system. Cohen states that human irrationality can never be demonstrated in laboratory experiments, especially experiments which are based upon the use of what he calls "probabilistic conundrums."

There are several current views about probability and inference that do not depend upon conventional Bayesian logic. Other articles in the Encyclopedia discuss many of these alternative schemes. Other concerns are based upon what are believed to be inadequacies of the studies upon which the conclusions are based. von Winterfeldt and Edwards (1986) and Phillips (1984) describe some of the ways in which subjects might have been put at a disadvantage in this research on cognitive heuristics and information-processing biases. Much of this centers around the fact that the subjects have little experiential familiarity with the tasks that they are asked to perform.

As inference tasks are decomposed and better structured, it is very likely that a large number of information-processing biases will disappear. Thus, concern should be expressed about the structuring of inference and decision problems and the learning that is reflected by revisions of problem structure in the light of new knowledge. The real task for the designer of an information system is to provide knowledge bases and ways for humans to interact with these to facilitate appropriate problems structuring.

In a sense, the results of this article are disturbing in that they tend to support the "intellectual cripple" hypothesis of Slovic, and to imply that humans may well be little more than masters of the art of self-deception. On the other hand, there is strong evidence that humans are very strongly motivated to understand, to cope with, and to improve themselves and the environment in which they function. While there are a number of fundamental limitations to systematic efforts to assist in bettering the quality of human judgement, choice and decision making, there are also a number of desirable activities. These can assist in increasing the relevance of systematic approaches such as those which result in information-processing support systems for policy analysis, forecasting, planning, and other judgement and decision tasks in which information acquisition, representation and use interpretation play a necessary and vital role.

See also: Collective Enquiry; Decision Support Systems; Information Requirements Determinatiion; Knowledge Representation

Bibliography

Anderson J R 1980 *Cognitive Psychology and its Implications.* Freeman, San Francisco, California
Anderson J R 1983 *The Architecture of Cognition.* Harvard University Press, Cambridge, Massachusetts
Arkes H R, Hammond K R (eds.) 1986 *Judgment and Decision Making.* Cambridge University Press, Cambridge
Armstrong J S 1978 *Long Range Planning: From Crystal Ball to Computer.* Wiley, New York
Armstrong J S 1980 The Seersucker theory: The value of experts in forecasting. *Technol. Rev.* **80**(June), 19–24
Barron F H, Person H B 1975 An information processing methodology of inquiring into decision processes. In: White D J, Bowen U C (eds.) *The Role of Effectiveness of Theories of Decision in Practice.* Crane Russak, New York, pp. 195–206
Bettman J R 1979 *An Information Processing Theory of Consumer Choice.* Addison–Wesley, Reading, Massachusetts
Beyth-Marom, Dekel S 1985 *An Elementary Approach to Thinking Under Uncertainty.* Erlbaum, Hillsdale, New Jersey
Brehmer N 1980 In one word: Not from experience. *Acta. Psychol.* **45**, 223–41
Brehmer B, Jungerman H, Lourens P, Sevon G (eds.) 1986 *New Directions in Research on Decision Making.* North-Holland, Amsterdam
Chorba R W, New J L 1980 Information support for decision-maker learning in a competitive environment: An experimental study. *Decis. Sci.* **22**(4), 603–15
Cohen L J 1979 In the psychology of prediction: Whose is the fallacy. *Cognition* **7**(4), 385–407
Cohen L J 1981 Can human irrationality be experimentally demonstrated? *Behav. Brain Sci.* **4**, 317–70
Covello V T, von Winterfeldt D, Slovic P 1986 Risk communication: A review of the literature. *Risk Abstr.* **3**(4), 171–81
Dawes R M 1975 The mind, the model, and the task. In: Restle F, Green T, Anderson J (eds.) *Cognitive Theory*, Vol. 1. Erlbaum, Hillsdale, New Jersey, pp. 571–82
Dawes R M 1979 The robust beauty of improper linear models in decision making. *Am. Psychol.* **34**, 571–82
Delaney H D, Wallsten T S 1977 Probabilistic information processing: Effects of a biased payoff matrix on choices and bids. *Organ. Behav. Hum. Perform.* **32**(2), 203–37
Einhorn H J, Hogarth R M 1986 Judging probable cause. *Psychol. Bull.* **99**(1), 3–19
Einhorn H J, Hogarth R M 1987a Decision making: Going forward in reverse. *Harv. Bus. Rev.* **65**(1), 66–70
Einhorn H J, Hogarth R M 1987b Decision making under ambiguity. In: Hogarth and Reder 1987, pp. 41–66
Estes W K 1975–1979 *Handbook of Learning and Cognitive Processes*, Vols 1–6. Erlbaum, Hillsdale, New Jersey
Feather N (ed.) 1981 *Expectancy, Incentive, and Action.* Erlbaum, Hillsdale, New Jersey
Feldman M P Broadhurst A (eds.) 1976 *Theoretical and Experimental Bases of Behavior Therapies.* Wiley, London
Fischhoff B, Beyth-Marom R 1983 Hypothesis evaluation from a Bayesian perspective. *Psychol. Rev.* **90**(3), 239–60
Frey B S, Foppa K 1986 Human Behavior: Possibilities explain action. *J. Econ. Psychol.* **7**, 137–60
Friedman L, Howell W C, Jensen C R 1985 Diagnostic judgment as a function of the preprocessing of evidence. *Hum. Factors* **27**(6), 665–73

Goldstein W M, Einhorn H J 1987 Expression theory and the preference reversal phenomena. *Psychol. Rev.* **94**(2), 236–54

Hammond K R, McClelland G H, Mumpower J 1980 *Human Judgement and Decision Making: Theories, Methods, and Procedures*. Hemisphere–Praeger, New York

Hogarth R M 1980 *Judgment and Choice: The Psychology of Decision*. Wiley, New York

Hogarth R M, Makridakis S 1981 Forecasting and planning: An evaluation. *Manage. Sci.* **27**(2), 115–38

Hogarth R M, Reder M W (eds.) 1987 *Rational Choice*. University of Chicago Press, Chicago, Illinois

Howell S C, Fleishman E A 1981 *Information Processing and Decision Making*. Erlbaum, Hillsdale, New Jersey

Kahneman D, Miller D T 1986 Norm theory: Comparing reality to its alternatives. *Psychol. Rev.* **93**(2), 136–53

Kahneman D, Slovic P, Tversky A (eds.) 1982 *Judgement Under Uncertainty: Heuristics and Biases*. Cambridge University Press, New York

Kahneman D, Tversky A 1979 Intuitive prediction, biases and corrective procedures. In: Makridakis and Wheelwright 1979, pp. 313–27

Kahneman D, Tversky A 1984 Choices, values, and frames. *Am. Psychol.* **39**, 341–50

Klayman J 1984 Learning from feedback in probabilistic environments. *Acta Psychol.* **56**, 81–92

Klayman J, Ha Y W 1987 Confirmation, disconfirmation, and information in hypothesis-testing. *Psychol. Rev.* **94**(2), 211–28

Kruglanski A W 1980 Lay-epistemic logic-process and content: Another look at attribution theory. *Psychol. Rev.* **87**, 70–87

Kruglanski A W, Ajzen I 1983 Bias and error in human judgment. *Eur. J. Soc. Psychol.* **13**, 1–44

Kruglanski A W, Freund T 1983 The freezing and unfreezing of lay-influences: Effects on impressionable primacy, ethnic stereotyping, and numerical anchoring. *J. Exp. Soc. Psychol.* **19**, 448–68

Makridakis S, Wheelwright S C (eds.) 1979 *Forecasting*. North-Holland, New York

Michon J A, Eljkman Eg G J, DeKlerk L F W 1979 *Handbook of Psychonomics*, Vols. I, II. North-Holland, New York

Montgomery H, Svenson O 1976 On decision rules and information processing strategies for choices among multiattribute alternatives. *Scand. J. Psychol.* **17**(4), 283–91

Moskowitz M, Schaefer R E, Borcherding K 1976 Irrationality of managerial judgements: Implications for information systems. *Omega* **4**(2), 125–40

Neale M A 1985 The effects of framing and negotiator overconfidence on bargaining behaviors and outcomes. *Acad. Manage. J.* **28**(1), 34–49

Newman D P 1980 Prospect theory: Implications for information evaluation. *Account. Organ. Soc.* **5**(2), 217–30

Nisbett R E, Krantz D H, Jepson C, Kunda Z 1983 The use of statistical heuristics in everyday reasoning. *Psychol. Rev.* **90**(4), 339–63

Nisbett R, Ross L 1980 *Human Inference: Strategies and Shortcomings of Social Judgment*. Prentice-Hall, Englewood Cliffs, New Jersey

Phillips L 1984 Theoretical perspectives on heuristics and biases in probabilistic thinking. In: Humphries P C, Svenson O, Vari O (eds.) *Analyzing and Aiding Decision Problems*. North-Holland, New York, pp. 29–48

Posner M I 1973 *Cognition: An Introduction*. Scott Foresman, Glenview, Illinois

Radcliff R A 1978 A theory of memory retrieval. *Psychol. Rev.* **85**, 59–108

Schneider W, Shiffrin R M 1977 Controlled and automatic human information processing: Detection search and attention. *Psychol. Rev.* **84**, 1–66

Shiffrin R M, Schneider W 1977 Controlled and automatic human information processing, I; Perceptual learning, automatic attending and a general theory. *Psychol. Rev.* **84**, 127–90

Sjoberg L, Tyszka T, Wise J A (eds.) 1983 *Human Decision Making*. Doxa, Bodafors, Sweden

Svenson O, Karlsson G 1986 Attractiveness of decision alternatives characterized by numerical and non-numerical information. *Scand. J. Psychol.* **27**, 74–84

Tversky A, Kahneman D 1986 Rational choice and the framing of decisions. *J. Bus.* **59**(4), 251–58

von Winterfeldt D, Edwards W 1986 *Decision Analysis and Behavioral Research*. Cambridge University Press, Cambridge

Wallsten T S 1977 Processing information for decisions. In: Castellan N J, Pisoni D B, Potts G (eds.) *Cognitive Theory*, Vol. 2. Erlbaum, Hillsdale, New Jersey, pp. 87–116

Wallsten T S (ed.) 1980 *Cognitive Processes in Choice and Decision Behavior*. Erlbaum, Hillsdale, New Jersey

Wright P 1974 The harassed decision maker: Time pressures, distractions and the use of evidence. *J. Appl. Psychol.* **59**(5), 555–61

A. P. Sage
[George Mason University, Fairfax, Virginia USA]

Human Judgement and Decision Rules

To select an alternative plan or course of action for ultimate implementation, a decision maker applies one or more decision rules which enable comparison, prioritization and, ultimately, selection of a single policy from a set of choice alternatives. The purpose of a decision rule is to specify the most preferred alternative; generally from a partial or total ordering, or a prioritization of alternatives. To use a decision rule, we must have a set of alternatives, a set of objectives to be accomplished by the alternatives, a knowledge of the impacts of the alternatives, evaluation of these impacts, and associated preference information. Decision rules may be explicit or implicit in terms of the way in which they are used in the decision process.

We can assume, without loss of generality, that each single policy alternative may represent a complex portfolio of individual alternatives and that the set of choice alternatives contains mutually exclusive components. This formulation can always be accomplished but may result in a very large set of policy alternatives since n individual alternatives can be combined into 2^n possible portfolios of alternatives. Failure to consider a combination of alternatives may result in significant errors in decision making unless each of the individual alternatives represents one component of a portfolio of all possible combinations of individual alternatives, or unless the individual alternatives are independent or mutually exclusive.

It is assumed, at the interpretation step of the decision process, that formulation and analysis have been accomplished such that there exists a decision situation structural model and the results of exercising that model. Thus objectives, relevant constraints, some bounds on the issue, possible policy alternatives, impacts of policy alternatives, and so on, are assumed to be known. The choice of a decision rule will depend, to a large measure, upon the decision situation structural model as reflected in the contingency task structure. In this article we will discuss a variety of models for human judgement and decision making.

1. Introduction

Individuals and decision environments vary so greatly that there are a great number of decision rules that will be needed to describe actual decision situations. Schoemaker (1980) is among a number of authors who have attempted classification schemes to allow categorization of various descriptive decision rule models. His first-level categorization separates decision rules into holistic and nonholistic categories. In a holistic decision rule, each alternative, or portfolio of alternatives, is evaluated and assigned a value or utility. After all alternatives have been evaluated, they are compared; alternative A is said to be preferred to alternative B if its evaluation has given it a greater utility such that $U(A) > U(B)$. In nonholistic decision rules, individual alternatives, or portfolios of alternatives, are generally compared with one another in a sequential elimination process. This comparison may be against some standard, across a few attributes within alternative pairs, or across alternatives, with alternative attributes being compared one at a time.

Each of these categories appears to imply disaggregation into components of the event outcomes likely to follow from decisions. A contingency task structure model may be discussed in the form of a dynamic evolving cognitive-style model which admits expert situational understanding that involves reasoning by analogy, intuitive effect, and other forms of nonverbal, almost unconscious, perception. We elect to call this type of reasoning wholistic and add this third category to the classification scheme of Schoemaker.

Thus, we envision three first-level general categories of decision rules: holistic, heuristic and wholistic. In a *holistic* decision rule, there is an attempt to consider all aspects of a decision situation in evaluating choices by means of disaggregation of various choice components. In a *heuristic* decision rule, detailed complicated comparisons are not used. Rather, simplified approximations to holistic decision rules are used. In a *wholistic* decision rule, the evaluation and choice of alternatives is based upon the use of previous experience, hopefully true expertise, with respect to similar decision situations. The selection of an alternative is based upon its perceived or presumed worth as a whole and without detailed conscious consideration of the individual aspects of each alternative. It is possible to define a number of decision rules and categorize them. The first-level categories we have defined are not mutually exclusive. A number of decision rules can doubtless be categorized into more than one of these first-level decision categories. Figure 1 illustrates a possible inclusion structure for the decision rules described here. The wholistic, heuristic and holistic decision rule taxonomy is essentially equivalent to the skill-based, rule-based and formal-reasoning-based taxonomy of knowledge in the definitive work of Rasmussen (1983).

2. Holistic Approaches to Judgement and Decision Making

2.1 Expected Utility Theory

Our first decision rule is based on expected utility theory and is doubtless the most familiar decision rule to engineers. This rule derives from a "rational-actor" decision model. The rational-actor model is a normative model. von Neumann and Morgenstern (1947), who introduced the axioms of this model, stated the purpose of their work as: "... to find mathematically complete principles which define 'rational behavior' ... a set of rules for each participant which tell him how to behave in every situation which may conceivably arise."

The idea of rationality originated in the economics literature where microeconomic models of the consumer and the firm assumed complete information and rationality. The rational person is assumed to have identified a set of well-defined objectives and goals and is assumed to be able to express preferences between different states of affairs according to the degree of satisfaction of attaining these objectives and goals. A rational person identifies available alternative courses of action and the possible consequences of each alternative. The rational person makes a consistent choice of alternative actions in order to maximize the expected degree of satisfaction associated with attaining identified objectives and goals.

A number of elements are assumed to exist in the rational-actor model:

(a) a set of policy alternatives A;

(b) the set of possible consequences of choice or future states of nature or decision outcomes, called S;

(c) a utility function $U(s)$ that is defined for all elements s of S;

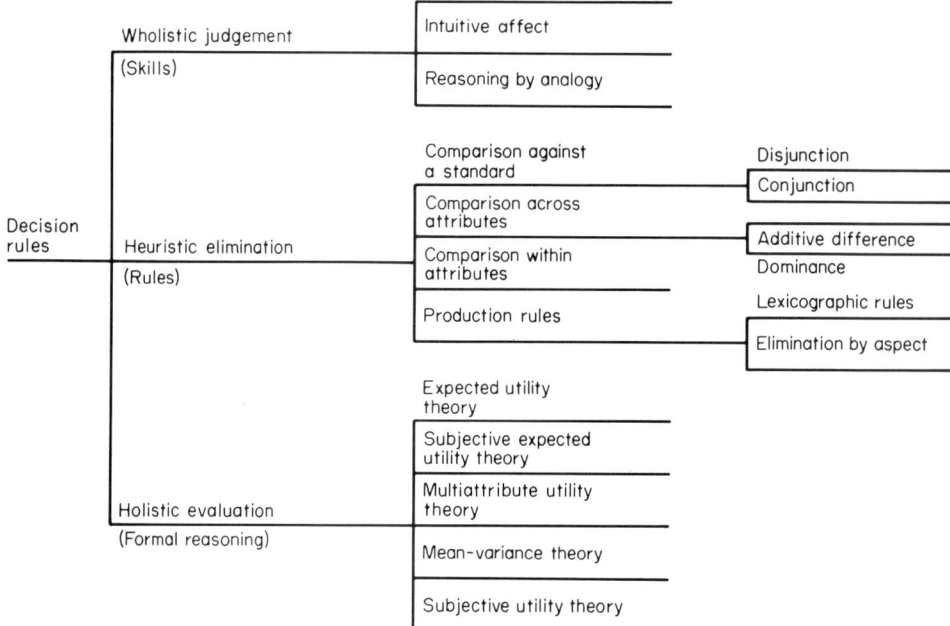

Figure 1
Hierarchical structure of decision rules

(d) information as to which outcomes will occur if a particular policy alternative a in A is chosen; and

(e) information as to the probability of occurrence of any particular outcome if an alternative $a \in A$ is chosen. $P_a(s)$ is the probability that $s \in S$ will occur if $a \in A$ is chosen.

There are a number of ways in which the axioms associated with the rational-actor model may be stated. Each statement of the axioms allows proof of the fact that cardinal utility functions will exist and be unique only up to positive linear transformations. Further, the evaluation of expected utility allows choice making and prioritization of alternatives in accordance with the expected utility of each alternative. There are a number of textbook accounts of expected utility theory which give alternative sets of axioms and detailed accounts of the use of expected utility theory (Raiffa 1968, Keeney and Raiffa 1976, Sage 1977). MacCrimmon and Larson (1979) interrelate the major axiom systems in expected utility theory in a noteworthy contribution to understanding the several systems that lead to (essentially) the same results for the rational-actor model (Allais and Hagen 1979).

The rational-actor model is often accepted as a normative model of how decisions should be made, at least in a substantive or "as if" fashion. It is often observed that the model is not an accurate description of either the substance or the process of actual unaided choice-making behavior. Some of these observers use empirical evidence of the deviation of actual decision makers from either substantive rationality or process rationality.

The rational-actor model is, however, invaluable in that it can often be used as a reference for comparison of actual behavior with ideal "aided" or normative behavior. Further, it provides a benchmark against which to compare simplified heuristics.

Simon and his colleagues introduced the concept of bounded rationality and developed a satisfactory model for individual choice making. It is worth noting that boundedly rational actors are basically rational subject to constraints on the formulation, analysis and interpretation of information, and the substitution of achievement of a target level of return, or aspiration level, for selection of the best alternative. Typically, people satisfice, that is, obtain an acceptable solution by adaptive adjustment of aspirations such that, in repetitive decision situations, optimizing behavior is approached (Park 1978).

There is absolutely nothing in the formulation of the rational-actor model which requires identification of all objectives, all possible alternatives or all possible impacts of alternatives. The rational-actor model is perfectly capable of being used to allow prioritization and selection of the best alternative, by evaluating some impacts and, with knowledge of some objectives, from among an incomplete set. In no sense does it necessarily require completeness in everything and the associated complexity that this would require. Actual decision-making behavior may not, however, even be boundedly rational, but may employ such poor heuristics as to result in inferior choice making even to the extent of selecting inferior choices from among those in a bounded set.

There have been a number of experimental studies and field studies of the appropriateness of the expected utility model as a descriptive model of substantive unaided behavior. Schoemaker (1980) provides a very readable brief survey of some of this literature. While the evidence is mixed, most studies indicate that the expected utility decision rule simply does not function well in a descriptive substantive sense.

In its simplest form, the expected utility of alternative a is computed from

$$E\{U(a_i)\} = \sum_{j=1}^{n} P[s_j(a_i)]U[s_j(a_i)] \qquad (1)$$

where $s_j(a_i), j=1, 2, \ldots, n$, are the states which may result from alternative a_i and the $P[s_j(a_i)]$ are the associated probabilities. In the expected utility formulation, the $P[s_j(a_i)] = P_j(a_i) = P_j$ are assumed to be objective probabilities and, of course, $\sum_{j=1}^{n} P_j = 1$. Generally these probabilities are not alternative invariant although notationally they are sometimes written as if they were independent of alternatives. The $U[s_j(a_i)]$ are the utilities, or values (Rokeach 1973), of the decision maker for the various outcome states. Johnson and Huber (1977) survey a number of procedures that can be used to elicit utility functions. Most of the textbooks cited earlier also contain a discussion of utility assessment procedures.

2.2 Subjective Expected Utility

Often it occurs that objective probabilities are, for any of a variety of reasons, unavailable in a given situation. The subjective expected utility model is obtained when subjective probabilities $f(P_j)$ are substituted for the P_j in Eqn. (1). The $f(P_j)$ are generally elicited such that $\sum_{j=1}^{n} f(P_j) = 1$ and so the subjective probabilities behave in a way consistent with the laws of probability. There are a number of discussions concerning probability elicitation (Morris 1974, Spetzler and Holstein 1975, Lindley et al. 1979) that present appropriate procedures to enable the determination of subjective probabilities from individuals and groups. Conventional approaches to elicitation of utility in expected utility theory may confound the strength of preference felt for alternative event outcomes and the attitude toward risk. Also, the elicitation procedure can become cumbersome. Recent research has formally separated these factors and shows much promise in enhancing understanding of attitudes towards risk. In this approach, the utility concept is devoid of risk. It takes on a meaning more like that in conventional microeconomics where it measures strength of preference for certain outcomes only. This research could provide additional linkages and understanding between the expected utility and subjective expected utility concepts by providing for incorporation of risk aversion effects in a relatively simple way.

Numerous studies have indicated that the relation between subjective and objective probabilities is nonlinear and situation dependent. It is usually indicated that people often underestimate high probabilities and overestimate low ones. More recent research has indicated that this appears true only for favorable outcomes. Just the opposite appears true when the outcome is unfavorable. This appears to be a form of wishful thinking for low probability events and "everything bad happens to me" for high probabilities. What we will call subjective utility theory attempts to incorporate situation-dependent nonlinearities that may exist between subjective and objective probabilities.

2.3 Multiattribute Outcomes

Often decision situations are sufficiently complex that it is difficult to evaluate, in a wholistic fashion, the utility of each outcome. Often it is possible to disaggregate the features on which utility is based into a number of components called attributes. An attribute tree is a hierarchical structure which, when quantified through elicitation of values of the outcomes on the lowest level attributes and relative weights of the attributes, can be used to determine the utility of event outcomes. The types of multiattribute utility models used have varied from very simple unit weight linear models to rather complex multiplicative models. Dawes (1979) documents the robust beauty of linear models of the form

$$U(s_i) = \sum_{j=1}^{m} h_j u_j(s_i), \quad \sum_{j=1}^{m} h_j = 1 \qquad (2)$$

where there are assumed to be m attributes, h_j is the weight of the jth attribute and $u_j(s_i)$ the value score on the jth attribute of outcome s_i. In much of the work in this area, decisions under certainty are considered such that there is a one-to-one correspondence between alternative a_i and outcome s_i. Under decision-under-certainty conditions we can let $s_i = a_i$ in Eqn. (2).

Multiattribute models have been used very successfully to predict decision behavior in field settings or many professional groups. Hammond and his colleagues (Hammond et al. 1977, 1980) have developed an approach known as social judgement theory in which the "policy" of the decision maker, equivalent in this circumstance to the weights h_j, is identified from wholistic prioritization of decision outcomes through use of regression analysis techniques. Edwards and his colleagues (Edwards 1977) have elicited weights from decision makers for the model of Eqn. (2) in a useful straightforward procedure called the simple multi-attribute ranking technique (SMART) that has seen a number of realistic applications. Results of the surveys of Fischer (1979), Slovic and Lichtenstein (1971), Slovic et al. (1977), Shanteau (1980) and others indicate that simple linear models are very potent predictors of reliable judgement, especially under conditions of certainty, in that one can replicate the substantive judgement of decision makers. This is the case even though the simple linear model may not do a very good job of modelling the decision process. "Boot strapping" is the name given to the task of substituting a decision rule for a decision maker. The studies in the cited references show that the elimination of human judgement error made possible by boot strapping enables it to be superior to unaided human judgement. One can even misspecify weights and ignore attribute dependencies and still find that weighted linear models do quite well (Dawes 1979).

The fact that the weighted linear rule may be so good is a rather mixed blessing. In circumstances in which there is no requirement for knowledge of the underlying decision process, the substantive predictive ability of the linear additive model may make it quite useful. Situations such as evaluating credit card applicants or applicants for admissions to colleges are repetitive judgement and decision situations which fit into this category. Use of a simple formal linear model may well, in situations such as these, lead to a more efficient as well as more effective and equitable selection process than one based on unaided human intuition (Dawes 1979, Shweder 1980). In unstructured or semistructured nonrepetitive decision situations, it is much less clear that a decision rule that is not guaranteed to be faithful to the underlying decision process will be nearly as valuable as one that is, in terms of enabling decision makers to make better decisions. A hoped-for achievement is a sensitivity-based analysis of deviations from optimality to determine, among other things, the role of experience in decision making and those components and principles of decision making which can be usefully and meaningfully learned from experience.

Multiattribute utility models are based on the expected utility theory of von Neumann and Morgenstern (1947) and are considerably more complex than those of behavioral decision theory. Often there are efforts to determine the existence of various attribute independence conditions so as to validate the use of a linear model of the form of Eqn. (2) or a multiplicative model of the form

$$1 + HU(s_i) = \prod_{j=1}^{m} [1 + h_i HU_j(s_i)], \quad \sum_{j=1}^{n} h_j = 1 \quad (3)$$

The foremost proponents of this approach are Keeney and Raiffa (1976). There are many contributions to this area and variations of the basic approach. It is proposed exclusively as a normative approach and has been successfully used for a variety of applications including proposal evaluation (Sarin et al. 1978), siting power plants, and budgeting and planning (Buehring et al. 1979).

2.4 Mean-Variance

There are a number of models and associated decision rules based upon mean-variance (EV) models. Markowitz's portfolio theory, which is well summarized in Libby and Fishburn (1977) and Baron (1979), is based in part on the assumption of a quadratic utility function

$$U(s) = \alpha + \beta s + \gamma s^2 \quad (4)$$

where the same states are assumed invariant over all alternatives such that we have a quadratic programming problem in prioritizing alternatives, where

$$\begin{aligned} E\{U(a_i)\} &= \sum_{j=1}^{n} p_j(a_i) U(s_j) \\ &= \alpha + \beta E\{a_i\} + \gamma E\{a_i^2\} \\ &= \alpha + \beta \mu_i + \gamma (\sigma_i^2 + \mu_i^2) \end{aligned}$$

Coombs (Coombs and Pruitt 1960, Coombs and Avrunin 1977) and Kahneman et al. (1982) have also been concerned with portfolio theory and assume an optimum risk level, in the form of a single-peaked risk preference function, for every expected value level. Gambles of equal expected value are judged on the basis of lower variance in the Markowitz portfolio theory, and on the basis of deviation from optimum risk level in Coombs' portfolio theory. Stochastic dominance concepts are especially useful in dealing with problems in the mean-variance models of portfolio theory. Unfortunately, the results from using mean-variance portfolio theory are not necessarily consistent with results obtained from expected utility theory. For example, if the outcomes of decision a_1 are $10 with probability 0.5 and $20 with probability 0.5, and the outcome of decision a_2 is $10 with probability 1.0, then the EV rule ($\mu_{a_1} = \$15$, $\sigma_{a_1} = \$5$) ($\mu_{a_2} = \$10$, $\sigma_{a_2} = 0$) is indeterminate in that there is no Pareto superior or dominance alternative in an EV sense. Yet any reasonable person would prefer alternative a_1 to alternative a_2.

Fishburn (1977) has considered a variation of the mean-variance model which involves concepts based on target level of return, aspiration level, or reference level, to define the risk of an alternative. The "risk" of alternative a is determined from the probability of receiving a return not to exceed x, denoted $F(x)$, by

$$R(a) = \int_{-\infty}^{t} (t-x)^{\alpha} \, dF(x) = \int_{-\infty}^{t} (t-x)^{\alpha} p(x) \, dx$$

where t is the target return and α is a nonnegative parameter that is used to indicate relative importance of deviations below target return. For $0 \leq \alpha < 1$ the decision maker's primary concern is failure to achieve the target with little regard to the size of the deviation. For $\alpha > 1$ the decision maker is very concerned with sizable deviations from target and relatively unconcerned with small deviations. In the former case, the decision maker is risk-seeking for losses and has a utility function that is convex for losses. In the latter case, the decision maker is risk-averse for losses and has a utility function that is concave for losses.

In this model, the mean return from an alternative and its risk are the two attributes determining preference. This model thus appears very similar to the standard EV model in that $a_1 \succ a_2$ iff $\mu(a_1) \geqslant \mu(a_2)$ and $R(a_1) \leqslant R(a_2)$ with at least one inequality being valid. In the example just considered, the mean values are as given previously and the risks are:

$$R(a_1) = \begin{cases} 0 & t \leqslant 10 \\ 0.5(t-10)^\alpha & 10 \leqslant t \leqslant 20 \\ 0.5(t-10)^\alpha + 0.5(t-20)^\alpha & 20 \leqslant t \end{cases}$$

$$R(a_2) = \begin{cases} 0 & t \leqslant 10 \\ (t-10)^\alpha & 10 \leqslant t \end{cases}$$

Thus we see that the risk is the same (that is, zero) if $t \leqslant 10$ and so we prefer a_1. The risk associated with a_1 is one half that associated with a_2 if the target return is between $10 and $20. The risk associated with a_1 is less than that associated with a_2 if $t \geqslant 20$. Hence, since $\mu(a_1) > \mu(a_2)$, we prefer a_1 regardless of the target return. Generally, as in this case, Fishburn's below-target model will resolve ambiguities associated with the standard mean-variance model. The decision maker is free to specify α and t. Thus this represents a rather useful dominance-type decision rule. Extensions of this rule to the case of multiattribute and multiobjective preferences would have considerable value.

2.5 Subjective Utility Theory

A number of researchers have proposed holistic decision rules based on the observation that people in unaided situations do not typically perceive (objective) probabilities such that the fundamental probability property $\Sigma_{j=1}^n p_j = 1$ is satisfied. There presently exist several decision situation models based on a subjective utility theory in which probabilities do not sum to one. Among these are certainty equivalence theory, due to Handa (1977); subjectively weighted utility theory, due to Karmarkar (1978, 1979); and prospect theory, due to Tversky and Kahneman (1979, 1981). There have been several additional studies involving prospect theory including those of Thaler (1980) and Hershey and Schoemaker (1980). Some of the foundations for these subjective utility theory efforts can be found in the early work of Allais (Allais and Hagen 1979), who was among the first to note that the normative expected utility approach of von Neumann and Morgenstern (1947) and the subjective expected utility modifications did not necessarily describe actual descriptive choice behavior. We believe that these studies are especially relevant to information system design and so summarize relevant features from these effects here.

In certainty equivalence theory, five axioms are assumed. We will use the term prospect or (s, P) to mean the opportunity to obtain outcome s with probability P. Simply stated, these are as follows.

(a) Preferences are governed only by utilities and outcomes. One is indifferent between a nonsimple prospect and an actuarially identical simple prospect with a single event node.

(b) Complete ordering of prospects is possible and transitivity of prospects exists.

(c) Continuity exists such that if $(s_1, P_1) \succeq (s_2, P_2) \succeq (s_3, P_3)$ then there exists an α such that $(s_2, P_2) \sim (\alpha s_1, P_1) + (s_3 - \alpha s_3, P_3)$.

(d) Independence exists such that if $(s_i, P_i) \sim (x_i, 1) \forall i$, then $(s, P) \sim (\Sigma x_i, 1)$ where s and P represent vectors of outcomes and probabilities s_i and P_i.

(e) Enhanced prospects are preferred iff a basic prospect is preferred. Thus $(\beta s_1, P_1) \succeq (\beta s, P_2) \forall \beta \geqslant 0$ iff $(s_1, P_1) \succeq (s_2, P_2)$.

These axioms are sufficient to ensure that the subjective utility function of alternative a_i, $CE(a_i) = CE[s(a_i), P(a_i)] = U(s^i, P^i)$, is linear in s_i and of the form

$$U(s^i, P^i) = \sum_{j=1}^n s_j^i w(P_j^i) = \mathbf{w}^T(P^i)s^i \quad (5)$$

Axioms (a), (d) and (e) incorporate the major changes from the von Neumann–Morgenstern axioms. It appears unduly restrictive to require the utility function to be linear in the outcome, and this is reason enough to warrant the development of a more robust theory.

Fishburn (1978), however, has shown that certainty equivalence theory must reduce to the expected value model, $U(s, P) = P^T s$, $\Sigma_{j=1}^n w(P_j) = 1$. This occurs because of the requirement that one must be indifferent between a nonsimple prospect and an actuarially equivalent simple prospect. To ensure this for the two-outcome case, for the general actuarially equivalent two-outcome prospects of Fig. 2 requires that $w(P) + w(1-P) = 1$. For the n-outcome case we would have $\Sigma_{j=1}^n w(P_j) = 1$ and we see that the only general $w(P_j)$ that will ensure this is $w(P_j) = P_j$. This certainty must be viewed as another limitation of this certainty equivalence theory and indicates the considerable care that must be exercised in modifying the basic utility theory axioms.

The subjective weighted utility (SWU) model yields for the SWU of alternative a_i

$$SWU(a_i) = \sum_{j=1}^n w[P_j(a_i)]U[s_j(a_i)] \quad (6)$$

where the subjective weighted probabilities are

$$w[P_j(a)] = \frac{f[P_j(a)]}{\sum_{j=1}^n f[P_j(a)]} \quad (7)$$

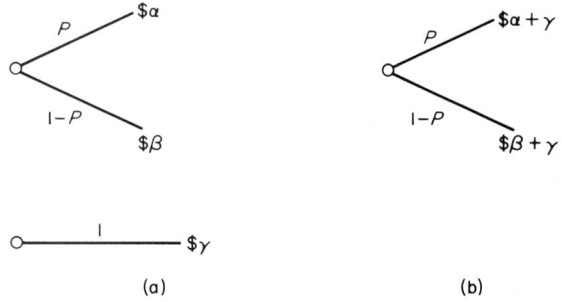

Figure 2
Two actually equivalent prospects

Although a variety of probability weighting functions are possible, Karmarker (1978, 1979) proposes use of a log normal function

$$\ln\left(\frac{f}{1-f}\right) = a \ln\left(\frac{P}{1-P}\right) \quad (8)$$

or

$$f(P) = \frac{P^\alpha}{P^\alpha + (1-P)^\alpha} \quad (9)$$

where $0 \leq \alpha \leq 1$. This transformation of probabilities is such that large probabilities are understated and small probabilities overstated. Karmarker emphasizes that the probability weighting function does not represent a probability perception phenomenon but represents a bias in the way in which (objective) probabilities are descriptively incorporated into the evaluation, prioritization and choice-making process. In this model, the final weighted probabilities do sum to one in accordance with the conventional subjective expected utility theory. However, the expression for any normalized weight $w[P_j(a)]$ is actually a function of the value of all other probabilities as seen in Eqn. (7). The effects of this confounding of influence remain to be investigated.

The considerably more sophisticated prospect theory of Tversky and Kahneman (1979, 1981) contains a number of modifications to expected utility theory. Prospect theory consists of an editing phase involving framing of contingencies, alternatives and outcomes, followed by an evaluation phase. These modify subjective expected utility theory so as to enhance unaided descriptive realism of the theory.

(a) In the editing phase, the decision situation is recast into a number of simpler situations to make the evaluation task simpler for the choice maker. The tasks in editing are very much dependent on the contingency situation at hand and offer possibilities for coding, combining, segregating, cancelling and detection of dominance.

(b) Value functions are devoid of risk attitude and are unique only up to positive ratio transformations.

(c) Outcomes are expressed as positive or negative deviations from a reference or nominal outcome which is assigned a value of zero. Thus, value changes represent changes in asset position. Positive and negative values are treated differently with the typical value function being an S-shaped curve that is convex below the reference point and concave above it. Displeasure with loss is typically greater than pleasure associated with the same gain.

(d) Probability weights, $w[P_j(a)]$, reflect an uncertain outcome contribution to the attractiveness of a prospect. As in subjective expected utility theory, high probabilities are underweighted and low ones overweighted. The following are among the properties of the probability weighting function:

  (i) true at extremes, $w(0) = 0$, $w(1) = 1$
  (ii) subadditive at low P, $w(\alpha P) > \alpha w(P)$, $0 < \alpha$
  (iii) overweighted for small P, $w(P) > P$, $P \ll 1$
  (iv) underweighted for large P, $w(P) < P$, $P \gg 0$
  (v) subcertain, $w(P) + w(1-P) < 1$
  (vi) subproportional

  $$\frac{w(\alpha P)}{w(P)} \leq \frac{w(\alpha \beta P)}{w(\beta P)} \quad 0 < \alpha, \beta \leq 1$$

(e) The value of a prospect $(s, P) = (s_1, P_1) + (s_2, P_2)$ is given by

$$V(s, P) = v(s_2) + w(P_1)[v(s_1) - v(s_2)] \quad (10)$$

for strictly positive prospects in which $P_1 + P_2 = 1$ and $s_1 > s_2 > 0$, or strictly negative prospects in which $P_1 + P_2 = 1$, $s_1 < s_2 < 0$;

$$V(s, P) = w(P_1)v(s_1) + w(P_2)v(s_2) \quad (11)$$

for regular prospects which are prospects that are neither strictly positive nor strictly negative in that either $P_1 + P_2 \neq 1$ and/or $v(s_1)$ and $v(s_2)$ are of opposite sign.

In no sense is prospect theory posed as a normative theory of how people should make decisions. The editing or framing of contingencies, alternative acts and outcomes is similar to the formulation step of the systems process. It is in this forming phase that the contingency task structure and decision situation model are, in effect, formed. For example, in a population of one million people where black lung disease might kill two thousand people, possible forms are the two below.

Form 1—alternative a_1 will save 500 people, whereas if alternative a_2 is adopted there is a 0.25 probability of saving two thousand people and a 0.75 probability of not saving anyone.

Form 2—alternative a_3 will result in death of 1500

people, whereas alternative a_4 will result in a 0.25 probability that no one will die and a 0.75 probability that 2000 people will die.

These two forms are really the same, yet many people will interpret them differently. The editing or forming phase of prospect theory allows different interpretations and thus makes provision for different evaluation of results in terms of alternative formulations of the same issue.

Prospect theory is especially able to cope with certainty effects, in which people overweigh outcomes considered certain compared with those considered only highly probable; reflection effects, in which preferences are reversed when two positively valued outcomes are replaced by two negatively valued outcomes; and isolation effects, in which people disregard common outcome components shared by outcomes and focus only on components that distinguish alternatives. Kahneman and Tversky (1979) have established an axiomatic basis for prospect theory for the two-outcome case.

In a study involving prospect theory, Hershey and Schoemaker (1980) question the generality of the reflection hypothesis of prospect theory which states that asymmetric preferences are found when comparing gain prospects with loss prospects. They introduce four types of reflectivity depending upon whether subjects choose positive prospect (s_1, P_1) or the noninferior prospect (s_2, P_2), and whether they choose negative prospect $(-s_1, P_1)$ or $(-s_2, P_2)$. Across-subject and within-subject reflectivity are examined in terms of whether subjects do or do not choose between, and do or do not switch from, safe to risky prospects. They conclude that predictions of prospect theory concerning reflectivity depend upon the size of probabilities. For P large enough to ensure underweighting of probabilities, it appears that the reflectivity hypothesis is quite valid. For smaller values of P, reflectivity is neither predicted nor excluded from the results of Hershey and Schoemaker.

In another study, Hershey and Schoemaker examine preferences for basic insurance-loss lotteries and show that risk taking is prevalent in the domain of losses. They suggest a utility function which is concave for low losses and convex for larger ones. They indicate a context effect in which various insurance formulations lead to more risk-averse behavior than for statistically equivalent gambling formulations. Their conclusion, that probabilities and outcomes may be of less guidance in influencing decision behavior as uncertainties concerning their magnitude increase, strengthens conjectures concerning the influence of context and perceptions of decision situation structural models upon decision results.

Thaler (1980) examines a number of the tenets of prospect theory with generally very positive confirming results. Additional comments concerning the seminal prospect theory appear in a survey by Sage and White (1980), including the observation that a number of the results of prospect theory, which are seemingly at variance with expected utility theory, can be accommodated successfully using multiattribute utility theory. Extensions of prospect theory to include multiattribute preferences, large numbers of outcomes, sequential multistage decision making, risk-aversion coefficients and subjective probability effects would do much to enable this significant development to be of even greater usefulness in explaining complex positive, or descriptive, decision behavior. This might well be of much normative use as well.

3. Heuristic Decision Rules

A number of decision rules do not involve comparisons in a true holistic fashion. Rather, they involve comparisons of one alternative with another, generally within a restricted alternative set and attribute set. Within the heuristic class of decision rules, we may distinguish those which compare alternatives against some standard by means of conjunctive or disjunctive comparisons, those which compare alternatives across attributes, and those which make comparisons within attributes. All of these rules can result, when improperly applied, in intransitive choices (Ranyard 1977). We will consider several rules from each subcategory. First we will discuss two noncompensatory rules that are often used when there is an overabundance of data present.

3.1 Disjunctive Decision Rule

A disjunctive decision rule is one in which the decision maker identifies minimally acceptable value standards for each relevant attribute. Alternatives which pass the critical standard on one or more attributes are retained. Alternatives which fall below the critical standards on all attributes are eliminated. A single alternative is accepted when the critical standards are set such that all but one alternative fail to exceed any of the critical standards on attributes. Unlike multiattribute utility theory rules, where poor performance on one attribute can be made up by good performance on other attributes such that the rule is compensatory, a disjunctive decision rule is noncompensatory. A compensatory approximation to a disjunctive decision rule for attributes s_i is

$$U = \sum_{i=1}^{m} \frac{1}{[1+(s_i/c_i)]^{n_i}} \quad (n_i \gg 1) \quad (12)$$

where m represents the number of attributes and c_i is the critical value on the ith attribute. If U is greater than one, the alternative in question is retained.

3.2 Conjunctive Decision Rule

A conjunctive decision rule is one in which minimally acceptable value standards for each relevant attribute are identified. Alternatives are acceptable if they exceed all minimum standards. They are rejected if they fail to exceed any minimum standard. The critical values for disjunctive and conjunctive rules are generally different. A compensatory approximation to the noncompensatory conjunctive decision rule is

$$U = \prod_{i=1}^{m} \frac{1}{[1+(c_i/s_i)]^{n_i}} \quad (n_i \gg 1) \qquad (13)$$

An alternative is retained if the corresponding utility U is above a threshold which is set just slightly below 1. These approximations for the disjunctive and conjunctive rules become noncompensatory as n_i approaches infinity.

By iterating through the conjunctive acceptance and disjunctive rejection rule several times with adjustable critical values or aspiration levels, these rules become, in effect, forms of satisficing rules.

Dominance models and additive difference models are two examples of models which lead to decision rules involving comparison across some, but not necessarily all, attributes. No minimum standard of performance on attributes, that is to say minimum aspects, are identified.

3.3 Dominance Decision Rule

A dominance decision rule is one which chooses alternative a_1 over a_2 if a_1 is better than a_2 on at least one aspect and not worse than a_2 on any other aspect. An aspect is the score of a specific attention on a specific attribute. There are a number of applications of dominance theory, including stochastic dominance, to decision-making situations.

3.4 Additive Difference Rule

In an additive difference rule, differences are considered between values for a_1 and a_2 on each relevant attribute. Differences of the form $U_i(a_1) - U_i(a_2)$ are computed. Each of the differences is weighted in proportion to the importance of the differences between alternatives on the various attributes. The resulting weight is $f_i[U_i(a_1) - U_i(a_2)]$. Alternative 1 is preferred to alternative 2 only if

$$\sum_{i=1}^{n} f_i[U_i(a_1) - U_i(a_2)] > 0$$

This is a compensatory rule and can be used to compare any number of alternatives merely by retaining the winner in each comparison (Payne 1976). Only if the functions f_i are linear will the additive difference rule necessarily lead to transitive choices.

A third important subcategorization involves comparison within attributes. There are a variety of lexicographic procedures (Fishburn 1977), and the elimination by aspects rule (Tversky 1972, 1973), which explicitly involve comparison of alternatives on one, or at most a few, attributes.

3.5 Lexicographic Decision Rule

This rule prescribes a choice of the alternative which is most attractive on the most important attribute. If two aspects on this attribute are equally attractive, the decision will be based upon the most attractive aspect on the attribute next in order of importance, and so on.

3.6 Minimum Difference Lexicographic Rule

This rule is much like the lexicographic rule, with the additional assumption that for each attribute there is a minimum acceptable difference Δ_i of alternative scores. Thus, only differences greater than Δ_i between the attractiveness values of two alternatives may determine a decision. If the difference on the most important attribute is less than Δ_i, then the attribute next in the lexicographic order is considered. The lexicographic semiorder rule is a special case of this decision rule where Δ_i is defined only for the most important attribute. For all other attributes $\Delta_i = 0$. This procedure may easily be extended to cases where the Δ_i are defined for the two most important aspects. This rule is often used in situations where information about attributes is missing as a result of imperfect discrimination among alternatives on a given attribute or of unreliability of available information. In general, this rule leads to intransitive choices when there are more than two alternatives. It may even lead to agenda-dependent results for the case where there are only three alternatives. One should be especially careful to examine relations used for ordering alternatives to attempt to detect use of heuristics such as this, especially if concepts such as transitivity are used, perhaps inferentially, to determine partial orderings. This suggests the need for special care when attempting to use transitivity concepts to infer ordinal preferences. The resulting failure to seek disconfirming information may well create structural preference illusions.

Einhorn (1980a,b) uses the term "outcome irrelevant learning structure" (OILS) to describe processes which use deficient heuristics, and which then reinforce poor choices through experiences involving feedback and lack of disconfirming evidence. These OILS may result either from unaided judgement processes, or from poorly conceived, or possibly well-conceived but improperly utilized, and therefore irrelevant, systemic methods or processes.

3.7 The Minimizing Number of Attributes in Greater Attractiveness Rule

This rule prescribes a choice of the alternative that has the greater number of favorable attributes. Specifically, the rule requires that the aspect of a decision alternative must be classified for each attribute as better, equal or worse than the attractiveness of the other alternative for that attribute. The preferred alternative will be that which has the greatest number of favorable classifications.

3.8 Elimination by Aspects

In this rule, attributes are assumed to have difference importance weights (Ranyard 1976). An attribute is selected with which to compare alternatives with a probability that is proportional to its weight. Alternatives which do not have attribute scores above some aspiration or critical level are eliminated. A second attribute is selected with probability proportional to its weight and evaluation by elimination continues. The elimination by aspects model is thus seen to be a lexicographic rule in which decision-forming attributes are picked according to a probabilistic mechanism.

4. Wholistic Decision Rules

It is not possible to provide anywhere near a complete listing or discussion of the many possible wholistic decision rules. Three of these wholistic judgement processes occur perhaps more frequently than others: standard operating procedures, intuitive affect and reasoning by analogy.

4.1 Standard Operating Procedures

Standard operating procedures may result from the application of holistic or heuristic procedures, or other wholistic judgement approaches. A standard operating procedure is essentially what the name implies, a set of experience-based guides to behavior which are typically used without resort to the underlying rationale which led to the procedure. Often, standard operating procedures are formulated by one person or group and then implemented by another person or group. Sometimes they involve habit or folk custom, such as "drink white wine with fish." Contemporary popular music contains a vast number of modern "standard operating procedure" proverbs, many of which are seemingly irrational (Protinski and Popp 1978).

Often user's guides and operating manuals are written in an attempt to standardize operating procedures for performance. The greatest value of these procedures is as a checklist, reminder or options profile of attributes to look for, judgements to make or activities to select or perform. A fundamental often-occurring difficulty is that an expert may be able to use a checklist or profile of options as a guide to performance based on the ability of the expert to recognize quickly the features inherent in the situation. Lack of training and experience will often make it not possible for the novice to utilize this capacity for task need recognition. Lyon and Slovic (1976) pose that the lack of training and experience inherent in the novice, the associated lack of ability to recognize contextual relations and analogous situations, and the inability of guides to be able to teach this ability are all fundamental impediments to the use of many standard operating procedure type guides to judgement and performance.

4.2 Intuitive Affect

A person who makes judgements based on intuitive affect typically takes in information by looking at the "whole" of a situation rather than by disaggregating the situation into its component parts and acquiring data on the parts. Valuation is typically based on an attempt to determine whether alternatives are pleasant or unpleasant, likeable or unlikeable, good or bad for individuals. It stresses the uniqueness of personalistic value judgements. Zajonc (1980) presents a very useful discussion of affect or feeling as postcognitive activity.

4.3 Reasoning by Analogy

Many philosophers of science claim that reasoning by analogy is the basis of hypothesis generation (Sternberg 1977). It is fundamentally different from deductive inference or inductive inference-based reasoning. In analogical reasoning we use analogies, prototypes or other paradigms with which we are familiar to guide us in new tasks. These exemplars encourage recognition in a present situation in terms of experientially based knowledge. The definitive work of Silverman (1983) contains an overview and interpretation of many contemporary works that discuss various aspects of reasoning by analogy.

Doubtless, analogical reasoning, as well as reaning by intuitive affect and standard operating procedures, are each heavily influenced by the contingency structure of the task at hand and the environment. These are the judgement processes used by many in reaching decisions.

5. Summary

In this article we have examined a number of decision-making paradigms or rules. We have discussed holistic, heuristic and wholistic rules. The holistic models or rules are generally substantive and not necessarily process models. They may be prescriptive or descriptive in intent and use. Initially most holistic models, such as the subjective utility and multiattribute utility theory models were normative or prescriptive. More recently, descriptive holistic models, such as prospect theory, have been proposed.

There is considerable current interest in these descriptive holistic models. Machina (1982, 1987a,b) notes that expected (and subjective expected) utility theory is based on three axioms: continuity, independence and ordering. If there are three possible outcomes at an event node, the utility of this outcome is given by

$$U(P_1, P_2, P_3) = P_1 U_1 + P_2 U_2 + P_3 U_3$$

but since $P_1 + P_2 + P_3 = 1$, it is clearly possible to write the utility function in terms of two probability variables as

$$U(P_1, P_3) = P_1 U_1 + (1 - P_1 - P_3) U_2 + P_3 U_3$$

The particularly interesting thing about this equation is that, in probability space, the slope dP_3/dP_1, with overall utility $U(P_1, P_3)$ held constant, is just $(U_2 - U_1)/(U_3 - U_2)$ and so we know that the indifference curves are positively sloped parallel lines. They must be parallel since the slope of the lines is independent of the fixed value of $U(P_1, P_3)$. There are many implications of this. One of them is that knowledge of a person's preferences in any local region of utility space makes it theoretically possible to determine them anywhere throughout space, up to a linear transformation. One of Machina's major observations is that the independence axiom is often not descriptively correct. To cope with this, he allows the gradient function dP_3/dP_1 to be based on other than just the utility difference ratio noted above. When the independence assumption or axiom is relaxed, many of the observed information-processing conundrums or biases, such as the often-cited Allais paradox, vanish (Allais and Hagen 1979).

Other recent approaches (Bell 1982, 1985, Loomes and Sugden 1982, Sage and White 1983) have re-examined the classic notions of regret theory and show that it is possible to explain many of the observed human information processing biases using this approach.

The heuristic and wholistic models are more process oriented than the holistic models. In unaided situations people generally do not have the cognitive stamina to utilize the holistic rules, or may not sense a need for them even if they could utilize them. A variety of contemporary research (Payne et al., 1978, 1980, Payne 1980) has presented the strongest evidence that the choice of decision rules is very task dependent and actual choices may vary appreciably across different interpretations of the same decision situations. Preference reversals have even been noted with translation of gambles and target return, reference point or aspiration level effects. Phenomena such as these have recently been studied and shown to be potentially explainable by a descriptive model of risky choice due to Fishburn (1977) and by prospect theory.

We note that people use different decision rules and models at different phases of a decision process as a function of a number of influencing variables such as education, experience, motivation, familiarity with the environment and, above all, stress. Etzioni (1967, 1968) has proposed a mixed scanning model of decision making that forms the basis for some current research in information systems for planning and decision support in Sage and White (1984). This provides for a dominance-based decision-making approach that combines some of the features of the heuristic and holistic paradigms. Norm theory (Kahneman and Miller 1986), and approaches which involve contingent weighting (Tversky et al. 1987), and explanation of descriptively observed phenomena with (normative-like) analytical models, provide paradigms for various information-processing and judgement strategies that are biased from the perspective of subjective expected utility theory. Hogarth and Reder (1987) contains a number of excellent papers that also deal, in part, with these issues.

See also: Decision Support Systems; Human Information Processing; Information Requirements Determination; Knowledge Representation

Bibliography

Allais M, Hagen O (eds.) 1979 *Expected Utility Hypotheses and the Allais Paradox*. Reidel, Boston, Massachusetts

Baron D P 1979 Investment policy, optimality and the mean-variance model. *J. Finance* **1**, 207–32

Bell D 1982 Regret in decision making under uncertainty. *Oper. Res.* **30**, 961–81

Bell D 1985 Disappointment in decision making under uncertainty. *Oper. Res.* **33**, 1–27

Brown R V, Lindley D V 1986 Plural analysis: Multiple approaches to quantitative research. *Theory Decis.* **20**, 133–54

Buehring W A, Fieli W K, Keeney R L 1979 Examining energy/environment policy using decision analysis. *Energy Syst. Policy* **2**(3), 341–67

Cohen B, Murphy G 1984 Models of concepts. *Cognit. Sci.* **8**, 27–58

Cohen M D, Axelrod R 1984 Coping with complexity: The adaptive value of changing utility. *Am. Econ. Rev.* **74**(1), 30–41

Coombs C H, Avrunin G S 1977 Single-peaked functions and the theory of preference. *Psychol. Rev.* **84**, 216–30

Coombs C H, Pruitt D G 1960 Components of risk in decision making: Probability and variance preferences. *J. Exp. Psychol.* **6**(5), 265–77

Covello V T, von Winterfeldt D, Slovic P 1986 Risk communication: A review of the literature. *Risk Abstr.* **3**(4), 171–81

Currim I S, Sarin R K 1989 Prospect versus utility: An empirical comparison. *Manage. Sci.* **35**(1)

Cyert R M, Simon H A 1983 The behavioral approach: With emphasis on economics. *Behav. Sci.* **28**, 95–108

Dawes R M 1979 The robust beauty of improper linear models in decision making. *Am. Psychol.* **34**(7), 571–82

Edwards W 1977 How to use multiattribute utility measurement for social decisionmaking. In: Sage A P (ed.) *Systems Engineering: Methodology & Applications*. Institute of Electrical and Electronics Engineers, New York

Einhorn H J 1980a Learning from experience and sub-optimal rules in decision making. In: Wallsten T S (ed.) *Cognitive Processes in Choice and Decision Behavior*. Erlbaum, Hillsdale, New Jersey, pp. 1–20

Einhorn H J 1980b Overconfidence in judgment. In: Shweder R A (ed.) *Fallible Judgment in Behavioral Research*. Jossey-Bass, San Francisco, California, pp. 1–16

Einhorn H J, Hogarth R M 1986 Judging probable cause. *Psychol. Bull.* **99**(1), 3–19

Einhorn H J, Hogarth R M 1987 Decision making: Going forward in reverse. *Harv. Bus. Rev.* **65**(1), 66–70

Etzioni A 1967 Mixed scanning, a 'third' approach to decision making. *Public Admin. Rev.* **27**, 385–92

Etzioni A 1968 *The Active Society*. Free Press, New York

Fischer G 1979 Utility models for multiple objective decisions: Do they accurately represent human preferences? *Decis. Sci.* **10**, 451–79

Fischhoff B, Beyth-Marom R 1983 Hypothesis evaluation from a Bayesian perspective. *Psychol. Rev.* **90**(3), 239–60

Fishburn P C 1977 Mean-risk analysis with risk associated with below target returns. *Am. Econ. Rev.* **67**, 116–26

Fishburn P C 1978 On Handa's 'New Theory of Cardinal Utility' and the maximization of expected return. *J. Polit. Econ.* **86**(2), 321–24

Fishburn P C 1986 Implicit mean value and certainty equivalence. *Econometrica* **54**(5), 1197–205

Fishburn P C 1987 Reconsiderations in the foundations of decision under uncertainty. *Econ. J.* **97**(388), 825–41

Fishburn P C, LaValle I H 1988 Transitivity is equivalent to independence for states-additive SSB utilities. *J. Econ. Theory* **44**(1), 202–8

Frey B S, Foppa K (1986) Human behavior: Possibilities explain action. *J. Econ. Psychol.* **7**, 137–60

Friedman L, Howell W C, Jensen C R 1985 Diagnostic judgment as a function of the preprocessing of evidence. *Hum. Factors* **27**(6), 665–73

Goldstein W M, Einhorn H J 1987 Expression theory and the preference reversal phenomena. *Psychol. Rev.* **94**(2), 236–54

Hammond K R, McClelland G H, Mumpower J 1980 *Human Judgment and Decision Making: Theories, Methods, and Procedures.* Hemisphere/Praeger, New York

Hammond K R, Mumpower J L, Smith T H 1977 Linking environmental modes with modes of human judgment: A symmetrical decision aid. *IEEE Trans.* **7**, 358–67

Handa J 1977 Risk, probabilities, and a new theory of cardinal utility. *J. Polit. Econ.* **85**(1), 97–122

Hershey J C, Schoemaker P J 1980 Prospect theory's reflection hypothesis: A critical examination. *Organ. Behav. Hum. Perform.* **25**, 395–418

Hogarth R M, Einhorn H J 1988 *Venture Theory: A Model of Decision Weights.* University of Chicago, Chicago, Illinois

Hogarth R M, Reder M W (eds.) 1987 *Rational Choice: The Contrast Between Economics and Psychology.* University of Chicago Press, Chicago, Illinois

Holt C A 1986 Preference reversals and the independence axiom. *Am. Econ. Rev.* **76**(3), 508–15

Johnson E M, Huber G P 1977 The technology of utility assessment. *IEEE Trans. Syst., Man Cybern.* **7**(5), 311–25

Jones E E 1986 Interpreting interpersonal behavior: The effects of expectancies. *Science* **234**, 41–6

Kahneman D, Miller D T 1986 Norm theory: Comparing reality to its alternatives. *Psychol. Rev.* **93**(2), 136–53

Kahneman D, Slovic P, Tversky A (eds.) 1982 *Judgment Under Uncertainty: Heuristics and Biases.* Cambridge University Press, New York

Kahneman D, Tversky A 1979 Prospect theory: An analysis of decisions under risk. *Econometrica* **47**(2), 263–391

Kahneman D, Tversky A 1984 Choices, values, and frames. *Am. Psychol.* 341–50

Karmarkar U S 1978 Subjectively weighted utility: A descriptive extension of the expected utility model. *Organ. Behav. Hum. Perform.* **21**(1), 61–72

Karmarkar U S 1979 Subjectively weighted utility and the Allais paradox. *Organ. Behav. Hum. Perform.* **24**, 67–72

Keeney R L, Raiffa H 1976 *Decisions with Multiple Objectives, Preferences and Value Tradeoffs.* Wiley, New York

Klayman J 1984 Learning from feedback in probabilistic environments. *Acta Psychol.* **56**, 81–92

Klayman J, Ha Y W 1987 Confirmation, disconfirmation, and information in hypothesis-testing. *Psychol. Rev.* **94**(2), 211–28

LaValle I H, Fishburn P C 1987 Equivalent decision trees and their associated strategy sets. *Theory Decis.* **23**, 37–63

Lewis M W, Anderson J R 1985 Discrimination of operator schemata in problem solving: Learning from examples. *Cognit. Psychol.* **17**, 26–65

Libby R, Fishburn P C 1977 Behavioral models of risk taking in business decisions: A survey and evaluation. *J. Account. Res.* **15**(3), 272–92

Lindley D V, Tversky A, Brown R 1979 On the reconciliation of probability assessments. *J. R. Stat. Soc., Ser. A* **142**(Pt. 2), 146–80

Loomes G, Sugden R 1982 Regret theory: An alternative theory of rational choice under uncertainty. *Econ. Theory* **92**, 805–24

Loomes G, Sugden R 1983 A rationale for preference reversal. *Am. Econ. Rev.* **73**(3), 428–32

Lyon D, Slovic P 1976 Dominance of accuracy information and neglect of base rates in probability estimation. *Acta Psychol.* **40**, 287–98

MacCrimmon K R, Larson S 1979 Utility theory: Axioms versus paradoxes. In: Allais M, Hagen O (eds.) *Expected Utility and the Allais Paradox.* Reidel, Dordrecht, pp. 333–409

Machina M J 1982 Expected utility analysis without the independence axiom. *Econometrica* **50**(2), 277–323

Machina M J 1987a Choice under uncertainty: Problems solved and unsolved. *Econ. Perspect.* **1**(1), 121–54

Machina M J 1987b Decision-making in the presence of risk. *Science* **236**, 537–43

Machina M J, Neilson W 1987 The Ross characterization of risk aversion: Strengthening and extension. *Econometrica* **55**(5), 1139–49

March J G 1979 Ambiguity and the engineering of choice. *Int. Stud. Manage. Organ.* **IX**(3), 9–39

March J G 1988 Variable risk preferences and adaptive aspitations. *J. Econ. Behav. Organ.* **9**, 5–24

Morris P A 1974 Decision analysis expert use. *Manage. Sci.* **20**(9), 1233–41

Narens L, Luce R D 1986 Measurement: The theory of numerical assignments. *Psychol. Bull.* **99**(2), 166–80

Neale M A 1985 The effects of framing and negotiator overconfidence on bargaining behaviors and outcomes. *Acad. Manage. J.* **28**(1), 34–49

Newman D P 1980 Prospect theory: Implications for information evaluation. *Account., Organ. Soc.* **5**(2), 217–30

Nisbett R E, Krantz D H 1983 The use of statistical heuristics in everyday inductive reasoning. *Psychol. Rev.* **90**(4), 330–63

Park C W 1978 A seven point scale and a decision maker's simplifying choice strategy: An operationalized satisficing plus model. *Organ. Behav. Hum. Perform.* **24**, 252–71

Payne J W 1976 Task complexity and contingent processing in decision making: An information search and protocol analysis. *Organ. Behav. Hum. Perform.* **16**, 366–87

Payne J W 1980 Information processing theory: Some concepts and methods applied to decision research. In: Wallsten T S (ed.) *Cognitive Processes in Choice and Decision Behavior.* Erlbaum, Hillsdale, New Jersey, pp. 95–116

Payne J W, Braunstein M L, Carroll J S 1978 Exploring predecisional behavior: An alternative approach to decision research. *Organ. Behav. Hum. Perform* **22**, 17–44

Payne J W, Laughhunn D J, Crum R 1980 Translation of gambler and aspiration level effects in risky choice behavior. *Manage. Sci.* **26**(10), 1039–60

Phillips L D 1984 A theory of requisite decision models. *Acta Psychol.* **56,** 29–48
Protinski H, Popp R 1978 Irrational philosophies in popular music. *Cognit. Ther. Res.* **2,** 71–74
Raiffa H 1968 *Decision Analysis.* Addison–Wesley, Reading, Massachusetts
Ranyard R H 1976 Elimination by aspects as a decision rule for risky choice. *Acta Psychol.* **40,** 299–310
Ranyard R H 1977 Risky decisions which violate transitivity and double cancellation. *Acta Psychol.* **41**(6), 449–59
Rasmussen J 1983 Skills, rules, and knowledge: Signals, signs and symbols; and other distinctions in human performance models. *IEEE Trans. Syst., Man Cybern.* **13**(3), 257–66
Rokeach M 1973 *The Nature of Human Values.* Free Press, New York
Sage A P 1977 *Systems Engineering: Methodologies and Application.* Wiley, New York
Sage A P (ed.) 1987 *Systems Design for Human Interaction.* IEEE Press, New York
Sage A P, White C C 1984 ARIADNE: A knowledge based interactive system for decision support. *IEEE Trans. Syst., Man Cybern.* **14**(1), 35–47
Sage A P, White E B 1980 Methodologies for risk and hazard assessment: A survey and status report. *IEEE Trans. Syst., Man Cybern.* **10,** 425–46
Sage A P, White E B 1983 Decision and information structures in regret models of judgment and choice. *IEEE Trans. Syst., Man Cybern.* **13**(2), 136–45
Sarin R K, Sicherman A, Nair K 1978 Evaluating proposals using decision analysis. *IEEE Trans. Syst., Man Cybern.* **8**(2), 128–31
Schoemaker P J 1980 *Experiments on Decisions Under Risk: The Expected Utility Hypothesis.* Nijhoff, Boston, Massachusetts
Schoemaker P J H 1988 *The Scenario Approach to Strategic Thinking: Methodological, Cognitive and Organizational Perspectives.* University of Chicago, Chicago, Illinois
Shafer G 1986 Savage revisited. *Stat. Sci.* **1**(4), 463–501
Shanteau J 1980 *The Concept of Weight in Judgment and Decision Making: A Review and Some Unifying Proposals,* Report No. 228. Center for Research on Judgment and Policy, University of Colorado, Boulder, Colorado
Shweder R A (ed.) 1980 *Fallible Judgment in Behavioral Research.* Jossey–Bass, San Francisco, California
Silverman B G 1983 Analogy in systems management: A theoretical inquiry. *IEEE Trans. Syst., Man Cybern.* **13**(6), 1049–75
Slovic P, Fischhoff B, Lichtenstein S 1977 Behavioral decision theory. *Annu. Rev. Psychol.* **28,** 1–39
Slovic P, Lichtenstein S 1971 Comparison of Bayesian and regression approaches to the study of information processing judgment. *Organ. Behav. Hum. Perform.* **6,** 649–744
Spetzler C S, Holstein C A von 1975 Probability encoding in decision analysis. *Manage. Sci.* **22**(3), 340–58
Sternberg R H 1977 Component processes in analogical reasoning. *Psychol. Rev.* **84**(4), 353–78
Sugden R 1986 New developments in the theory of choice under uncertainty. *Bull. Econ. Res.* **38**(1), 1–24
Svenson O, Karlsson G 1986 Attractiveness of decision alternatives characterized by numerical and non-numerical information. *Scand. J. Psychol.* **27,** 74–84
Thaler R 1980 Toward a positive theory of consumer choice. *Econ. Behav. Organ.* **1**(1), 39–60
Tversky A 1972 Elimination by aspects: A theory of choice. *Psychol. Rev.* **79**(4), 281–99
Tversky A 1973 Availability: A heuristic for judging frequency and probability. *Cognit. Psychol.* **5,** 207–32
Tversky A, Hutchinson J W 1986 Nearest neighbor analysis of psychological spaces. *Psychol. Rev.* **93**(1), 3–22
Tversky A, Kahneman D 1981 The framing of decisions and the psychology of choice. *Science* **211,** 453–58
Tversky A, Kahneman D 1986 Rational choice and the framing of decisions. *J. Bus.* **59**(4), 521–58
Tversky A, Sattath S, Slovic P 1987 *Contingency Weighting in Judgment and Choice.* Stanford University Report, Stanford University, Stanford, California
von Neumann J, Morgenstern O 1947 *Theory of Games and Economic Behavior.* Princeton University Press, Princeton, New Jersey
Zajonc R B 1980 Feeling and thinking-preferences need no inferences. *Am. Psychol.* **35**(2), 151–75

A. P. Sage
[George Mason University, Fairfax, Virginia, USA]

Human–System Interaction: Information-Presentation Requirements

Human factors research on the interactions between users and information systems suggests that dramatic improvements on current systems are possible. With careful attention to the human factors in information presentation on computers, it is possible to build lucid and powerful systems for both experts and novices. Changes in screen formats, data entry and display methods, menu structures and graphical interfaces based on a knowledge of the cognitive abilities of the user, can significantly improve the user–system interface. Developers of guidelines governing interface design for information storage, manipulation and retrieval can benefit from prior work with print technologies, but computerized databases present unique problems and opportunities for the user.

1. Interface Design

The structure of presented information can either aid or hinder the user's performance. Good human factors design reduces the likelihood of errors and increases user productivity. A coherent structured user–system interface design makes training on the system or application easier and more effective. Retention of training is also facilitated by good interface design. If the interface is easy to learn and the operations are transparent to the user, the user is less likely to be distracted from the task to be performed. Relative ease of learning, productivity, reliability and error-free performance also promotes user satisfaction with the system.

A poor interface design distracts the user from the task by requiring the user to focus attention on aspects of the interface rather than focusing on the task. The short-term, or working memory capacity of any person is demonstrably limited. If the user has to think about the system, cognitive capacity is taken away from the problem. Good interface design reduces cognitive workload. Thus, a screen design that decreases the need for a user to memorize and recall how to enter specific types of data would also decrease cognitive demands on the user. A naïve theory of cognitive effort suggests that making the interface counterintuitive, less structured and less predictable somehow forces the user to be more careful and do better work. However, the actual result of this naïve notion is to make the user's task more difficult. The goal should be to reduce the cognitive effort attributable to the interface so that the user may concentrate on the task.

1.1 Interface-Design Principles

Guidelines exist which offer detailed specifications for many different styles of interactions (Galitz 1985, Smith and Mosier 1986, Brown 1988). Two guiding principles of interface design can be applied regardless of the interaction style:

(a) *Consistency principle*. Be consistent in the format of information displayed on the screen and be consistent in the actions required of the user.

All aspects of the screen format and the interaction process should have an underlying uniformity and predictability. For example, the screen format should be the same for all screens within an application. If page numbering information is provided for each screen, then the page number should always appear in the same place for each screen. The interactions should also be predictable. If pressing a specific function key saves a file at one point in the application, this result should be attained by the same operation throughout the application. Changing the effects of the key press to mean deleting a file at another point in the application would guarantee errors and performance decrements.

The interface design should be consistent with the expectations of the user population. The conventions and expectations may differ across user populations. For example, if the users need to specify time on a 12-hour clock rather than a 24-hour clock, they should be able to enter 2.00 pm rather than 1400 hours. When there are no user conventions, then consistent pretested standards and formats need to be agreed upon and followed. The user population will develop expectations based on their experiences with the interface. If the anticipated users are novices rather than trained and highly practised experts, they may require more on-line help or on-screen assistance to perform their tasks. The presentation of information on the screen can be tailored to fit the user population.

Understanding the user population and analyzing the tasks are important steps in developing the interface. The interface design should reflect the needs of the users rather than the untested, and possibly unconscious, biases of the designers. User testing provides a check to see how well the interface works before the design is final.

(b) *User-testing principle*. Test the interface on the targeted user population.

Even when the designer has good intentions and follows recommended guidelines, the interface may still create unforeseen problems for the user since the designer may not fully understand the characteristics and expectations of the user. The same type of users who are expected to use the interface should participate in testing the interface. An iterative process where prospective interfaces are tested, redesigned and then retested shows the designer where the user makes errors or has difficulties with the interface. Thus, potential problems are corrected in the process of creating the interface.

2. Information Presentation

In addition to the two guiding principles of interface design, there are additional guidelines for particular styles of interaction. Four styles of information presentation are considered here, each of which has specific format recommendations. The first style, text presentation, focuses on users whose interactions with a computer involve reading or searching through files of text. The second, data entry and display, focuses on interactions where data are entered by users and displayed by computers, and how the screen format should be configured. The third, menus, focuses on menu design and techniques of selection. The fourth, graphics, focuses on the use of icons and direct manipulation interactions. These categories are not mutually exclusive. Strategies and techniques useful for one interaction style may also be useful for another. For example, recommendations for formatting a data display may be applied in designing a menu.

2.1 Text Presentation

The display of written text on computer screens poses some problems for the designer. There are trade-offs between screen readability and the efficient use of screen space. Screen size, font design and the users' tasks have an effect on how the text could be presented. The amount or density of information that is displayed on the screen affects screen readability. Uppercase and lowercase fonts for displaying text on computer screens continue to be developed. Since computers have not had the centuries of evolutionary development that print technologies have had in the design of letters, future development efforts are expected to increase both the legibility and readability of fonts to be used with computers. Computer screens are generally harder to read than paper, except for certain antialiased or grayscale fonts and high-resolution screens. Sometimes the user will want to print text that is presented on-line. Text should be displayed on the screen exactly as it would be printed so that what is seen corresponds to the printed output. Some on-line text, such as help manuals, are useful when also provided in printed form.

Mills and Weldon (1987) reviewed research on the readability of text on computer screens and concluded that the user's task is an important variable in determining how information should be displayed. The user may wish to browse through text; for example, reading about some topic of interest while in a museum or library setting. Alternatively, the user may want to read carefully, to understand technical or other complex information, such as reading articles in on-line manuals, journals or encyclopedias. Novice users are especially helped by formatting the text in ways that mimic books; for example, using page turning rather than vertical scrolling to traverse the text.

Research suggests that double-spaced text, rather than single-spaced, facilitates reading. Furthermore, reading performance is better with appropriate mixed-case text (uppercase and lowercase) rather than text which is all in uppercase letters. Text is more readable when presented in wide columns that use most of the full width of the standard screen, and can be generally read faster when there are more characters per line; that is, 80-character lines are easier to read than 40-character lines. With continuous-prose text, greater density seems to produce more efficient reading, with the exception that double-spaced text is easier to read than single-spaced text. When screen space is very limited, single spacing may be used. Readability improves when more than two lines of text are displayed at a time. When there is a very small display area, dynamic display of text can be used to present a few words at a time. Reading the dynamic text may be facilitated by segmenting and presenting the text according to aspects of its linguistic structure (Mills and Weldon 1987).

Disruption of the continuous flow of text should be avoided. The format for on-line text should eliminate or minimize hyphenation. Lines should be composed of whole words, and pages should be composed of complete sentences. For page-displayed text, the breaking of sentences across pages should be avoided. The displayed text should be left-justified with jagged right edges. Right-justification, with inconsistent spacing between words, appears to reduce reading efficiency.

Since the computer is not a book, the user does not have physical-location cues; there is no sense of how long an article is, or where the reader is, in the context of the article. A context should be supplied to prevent the user from getting lost. A scroll bar can give an analog sense of position or an area at the top of the screen can be reserved to display the title of the article being read and the number of the currently displayed page (e.g., Page 4 of 12). The user is less likely to become lost in navigating through the database when there are signposts to indicate location. A reserved area at the bottom of the screen can be used to display prompts or other messages or to allow the user to enter commands or selections. The reserved areas need to be clearly demarcated to avoid being confused with the displayed text.

When the task is different, the text-presentation requirements also change. If the user is searching the database for particular information rather than reading the text, then the designer may want to specify some words in upper case or in color. Although text in uppercase is more difficult to read, words that are in uppercase are easier to find when the user is scanning through text. Search tasks are also easier if a target item being searched for is in color. When color is available as an option, care must be taken to use it in a systematic, organized, moderate and consistent way. If a heading or category label for a particular topic is green, then it should be green throughout the application. Random application of color can be worse than having no color coding. If the item is green at some times and yellow at other times, then a visual search will be slowed rather than facilitated by the use of color. Furthermore, stereotypes or expectancies of the user population should not be violated when using color. If the expectation is that green indicates "go" or "execute," then using green as a warning or caution label will create problems for the user.

2.2 Data Entry and Display

A second category of information presentation is concerned with the task of data entry and the related task of data display. The format of the interactive screen should take into account the needs of the user. If the user is entering data from a printed form, then the screen display and the form should match. The user should enter the data into specified fields on the computer screen that reflect the corresponding format on the printed form. The user should not be made to translate data from one form to another; for example, if a name on the form is to be entered surname first into the computer, then the surname should be first on the form.

The data to be entered should also be organized such that entry proceeds from the top to the bottom of the screen in a systematic pattern that minimizes required cursor movement. The user requires feedback showing the data as they are entered. Fast computer-response time is preferred, but the user should control the timing of data entry. The cursor should quickly and accurately reflect the user's actions. The user may need to fill in successive data fields on a screen. Once the data are entered, feedback showing successful completion of the screen or processing of the data can be provided for the user.

The interface should allow the user to control the data entry by explicitly signalling when the data are to be entered or when they are to be deleted; entry should not be automatic. The user should be able to reverse or undo any action just completed. Reversible actions allow the user to make immediate corrections or changes. When the user is making major changes or deletions, a separate confirming action can be beneficial.

All necessary information should be available, visible and in a directly usable form. The user should not have to consult additional manuals to find special codes or other necessary information. Only the information that is necessary should be displayed to avoid screen clutter. The data entry and display screens should ideally contain all necessary information for a transaction or task on one screen. The user should not have to page back and forth between different screens to complete the task.

If entry is not made from a form but directly into the computer, then the focus for the user will be on screen format. The design of the elements in an on-screen fill-in form or data display should be based on an understanding of the user's tasks. The organization or grouping of screen elements is critical for data entry and display. Galitz (1985) and Smith and Mosier (1986) recommend grouping elements or items into categories. The structure may be meaningful, such as grouping items by function. Items with similar functions would be located together on the screen, or located in the same area on different screens. All items related to a given task or transaction would also share a common spatial location. Items that need to be acted upon in a particular temporal sequence could be grouped together. Alternatively, the screen structure or format might reflect frequency of use. The most frequent interaction would be at the top of the data-entry screen, followed by tasks in descending order of frequency. Similarly, data entry and display could reflect the importance of the items, with the most important item first.

The data fields should be labelled consistently, with the labels close to, but separate from, the data fields. A standard symbol, such as a colon followed by a space (:) should be used as a prompt for data entry. The field boundaries or lengths can be marked to indicate the range of values or length of the data string to be entered. If there are defaults for entries, they should be shown. The computer can also check the entered values automatically, to determine whether or not they are in the correct range.

Messages to and from the computer should occur in a reserved area at the bottom of the screen. When commands to the computer are entered, they are more likely to be correct if they occur in a standard location. If the computer transmits error messages, they should be informative and nondisruptive to other interactions. After an out-of-range entry, for example, the user could continue with other data-field entries on the screen until ready to respond to the message "months range from 1–12."

Another characteristic of efficient design for data entry that supports the user is to free the user from entering information that is already on the screen. It is easier for the user to select from displayed choices than it is to remember what the choices are. If items are not selectable, the user could copy or "cut and paste" the needed text, decreasing the likelihood of making data entry errors.

Data-display formats should be consistent with data-entry formats, with consistent labelling for similar data across the formats and consistent procedures for users to follow. Positioning and labelling of data rows and columns should be similar for similar types of data. Parallel procedures for data-entry and data-display formats decrease the user's learning requirements and search times. Springer (1987) showed that the search time that users needed to find an item in a display could be significantly decreased by changing the display format. The redundant screen information was reduced by listing a surname only once for directory-assistance telephone listing displays; this correspondingly decreased search time. The amount of information displayed at one time also impacts on search time. Springer found that items located in the top quarter of the screen took longer to find in a full screen of information than in partial screens, such as one half or one quarter of a screen display. More information on the screen increased search time. Tullis (1988) measured search times for a variety of formats and screen densities, and concluded that the number and size of groups of characters were the most important display parameters. Increases in either the number or size of data fields of characters result in increases in search time. The designer's task is to reduce the user's visual search time by providing consistency and structure in the display formats. Smith and Mosier (1986) suggest the technique of using spacing to present data in logical groups. The visual display components should be distinctive, and displays should be uncluttered. A crowded display can be made readable by presenting the data on more than one page. As with text, pages should be numbered, with related data on the same page.

Color may be used as an organizing display feature. However, it is important to make color redundant by using it with some other display characteristic, since some users' vision will be color deficient. The display should be well-designed with distinctive display elements, before the addition of color as an organizing feature. Color should be used cautiously and conservatively; the overuse or inconsistent use of color can make displays more difficult for the user.

In the dialog between the user and the computer there are differences between data-entry and data-display screens. Data entry of numbers in response to a prompt or a fill-in field should be entered directly after the prompt, such as, "age: 39" or "age: 8." The user generally should not be required to enter age as "08." In data display, however, with age as a heading and the numbers 39 and 8 in a corresponding column, the numbers should be displayed with the last digit right-justified. Similarly, numbers with decimal points should be aligned on the decimal point when displayed as a column, but the user generally should not be required to enter leading or trailing zeros.

2.3 Menus

The menu remains the prototypical form of information presentation for novice users of computers. Having choices presented as selectable items from a menu is especially helpful to users who are unfamiliar with the applications or with computer languages. The available choices are presented and the user selects from the list. Menu items should be selectable with minimal, simple actions. It should be easy for the user to make selections and to undo or change the item selected.

Brown (1988) notes that menus allow the user to recognize the correct choice rather than having to recall it from memory. Recognition of what choice to make is typically an easier task than recall. If the user's task is to get rid of a file, it may be simpler to choose "delete" from a menu containing a list of the choices "create, save, copy, delete, print" than to recall the appropriate command from memory. This advantage of menus is also apparent for users who may not be novices, but who are intermittent or infrequent users who may work with a variety of systems with incompatible commands, and may not immediately remember whether the command to get rid of a file in a particular context is "remove," "erase," "kill," "drop," or "delete."

Selecting items from menus eliminates the need to memorize computer languages and syntax. Nevertheless, expert users may prefer using command languages, which give them more power by enabling them to specify their operations more quickly when the computer has slow response times and a slow display (screen fill) rate. The design of the menu interface should include shortcuts for the expert user. Even with fast response times, experts using a menu-driven system might be more efficient if they are able to use a command language to complete their task or use type-ahead to specify a pathway through menus that would eliminate the need to display intermediate levels of menus.

In most cases, the users of a menu system will not be equally familiar with all choices and pathways in a given menu structure, such as a tree or hierarchical structure representation of the menu. They may not know which choices lead to other choices. The interface should minimize the chances of a user getting lost among the menu choices. It should be possible for the user to partially retrace a path back to where an incorrect decision was made, then to continue along the correct path. With keyboard entry used for menu selection, a single keystroke should be sufficient to return the user to the higher-level menu.

Menu structures vary from one application to another in the number of nodes or choices and the number of paths branching from each choice point. In general, user performance is better on menus with a broad, shallow structure than with a narrow, deep structure. A broad, shallow structure is one where there are more choices on fewer numbers of screens. The user needs fewer menus to arrive at the desired location. A narrow, deep structure has few choices per menu, with more menus to traverse to arrive at a given location. There is a greater likelihood for the user to become lost with a greater number of menus to traverse. Nevertheless, a narrow, deep structure can be better with slow computer display rates, since it is faster to display more menus with fewer choices than long menus with many choices.

The user should be provided with a global view of the menu hierarchy. An overview of the menu structure that can be referred to, perhaps as on-line help, will assist users having difficulties in finding the right path. A graphical overview, or system map, showing the interconnections between the major nodes provides location cues for users. Alternatively, the menu choices could be represented as items in a table of contents, with level of indentation indicating the depth in the menu hierarchy. The user's current position within the menu structure should be indicated.

The screen design should have a consistent format for all menus. Selectable items should be listed one per line. The names of items should be distinctive and categorically mutually exclusive and exhaustive. If the menus are revised, the names of items should be retained, not changed. As the user traverses the menu structure, the path should be indicated as feedback to the user. For example, at the top level of the menu hierarchy, there could be a selection of items from which to choose. If the top level is "Musical Works by Beethoven," which lists the types of musical works, including "The Nine Symphonies" as the user's choice, then when the next menu appears it should have as the menu title "The Nine Symphonies" rather than "Symphonic Works of the 18th and 19th Centuries." The label of the item that is selected should be identical to the title of the next menu. By having informative feedback, the user can be confident that the menu that appears is the one that was requested, the decisions that the user makes being confirmed by the menu titles. When there is sufficient space on the screen, the path that was taken might be indicated by an explicit listing of the titles for each selected level of the menu hierarchy.

The menu choices that are listed should be selectable. Cluttering the screen with nonvalid menu choices should be avoided. If menu choices are available at some times but not others, as is the case with some interfaces, then the nonvalid choices should be easily identifiable. Some menu choice or procedural option should always be available; the user should not be presented with a blank screen. Within a menu, the choices should be meaningfully organized, and within an application the menus themselves should be meaningfully ordered.

Different styles of menus should be tested to determine which are appropriate to the users' tasks. Shneiderman (1987) describes numerous menu structures and styles that have been developed. Menu styles include a static listing of choices, pull-down menus and pop-up menus. Nonstandard menu styles include pie or circular menus and embedded menus. Pie menus, used with graphical interfaces, incorporate directional motion as an added feature to cue the user. Embedded menus can include menu choices highlighted in continuous text rather than explicitly listed.

The top level of the menu hierarchy should always be easy for the user to return to, whatever the structure of the menu. One keystroke, or one selection, should enable the user to return to the top level. With a graphical interface that shows the menu structure, the labelled icons representing the selectable nodes could help the user to find a desired location within the menu hierarchy.

2.4 Graphics

The graphical interface is typically used either to conduct a dialog with a computer or to display data. A graphical user dialog with the computer can occur by the direct manipulation of icons. Foley and van Dam (1982) emphasize the need for attention to the human factors aspects of the graphical interface, by stating that the ease of use of the interface is as important as its functionality. The most important human factors consideration is to ensure continuous correct feedback to the user that reflects the actions being taken. The concept of direct manipulation, whether in a textual or graphic environment, emphasizes the visibility of objects and operations that may be pointed to directly and selected, rather than those occurring as a result of command language syntax entered by the user (Schneiderman 1987). With direct manipulation, actions are rapid, immediately visible and easily reversible.

Icons are symbols or pictorial representations that are analogous to physical objects or actions. The user manipulates the icons, causing actions to occur. The icons to be manipulated may be selected from a menu of icons representing items or actions available to the user. Icons should resemble the objects they represent. Pretesting the icons should be done to determine whether the users understand what the icons are supposed to represent. If there is ambiguity, the icons may need to be labelled. Additionally, a legend could be available to explain what the available icons represent. Once an icon is created to represent an object, it should exclusively represent that same object within a system. Icons should uniquely represent processes as well as objects. Thus, if an icon of a page represents a document then that icon must not be used to represent a document printer.

Pictorial symbols can be more informative than words or text as symbols in a graphical environment. Well-designed icons may replace blocks of text and save screen space. Icons can also be used to show relationships among objects. It is easier for the user to understand that icons representing documents may be moved into icons representing file folders than it is to realize that these actions could be done with movable strings of text. Similarly, it is easier for the user to visualize the layout of an office by manipulating icons of furniture or other items than by manipulating blocks of text, such as "chair," "desk" or "electrical outlet." There should be stimulus–response compatibility in the movements used in the graphical interface. For example, when using a mouse as an input device, if the user selects an icon and moves the mouse to the left, then the icon should also move left.

Continuous feedback shows the action as it occurs, such as moving or dragging a selected icon across the screen, and shows the result of actions, such as removing the file icon from the screen when the user has deleted the file. Users should be able to temporarily place icons over other icons without deleting or destroying the obscured icon, and the process of deleting icons should require a confirmation from the user. Highlighting an icon provides feedback to the user that the icon has been selected and direct manipulation also gives the user immediate feedback by showing the results of an action. Error messages are less necessary for direct manipulation; the user does not need to be told to correct an action because the screen will show the action that occurred. The interface design should allow the user to quickly and easily reverse any incorrect actions.

Various devices can be used to control the graphical interaction: keyboard, mouse, touchscreen, joystick, lightpen and trackball. The type of input device should be determined by the user's tasks. For the design interface to be most useful, the actions and objects should be easily understandable to the user. The results of actions can be seen or previewed by the user and changes can be implemented rapidly. More than one input device may be used for a single graphical interface, such as the common occurrence of a mouse used with a keyboard. If the user's task has a predominance of one type of input, such as mouse movements, then the user should have the option to use that same input device to control other processes. The interface should be designed so that the user can choose whether to use commands entered from the keyboard or selected by mouse from pull-down or pop-up menus.

A cursor for the graphical interface must be easily identifiable and rapidly responsive to the user's actions. The user needs to be able to position the cursor precisely and be able to distinguish it from the background. With some application interfaces, the user may require very precise positioning, which can be accomplished by providing a zoom-in and zoom-out function.

The graphical interface is useful for constructing two- or three-dimensional representations of objects.

The design interface for an application used for constructing three-dimensional objects should allow dynamic manipulation of the objects, such as rotation along the axes and varying the object size. The illustrations and animations that are possible with the use of a graphical interface have had a significant impact on computer-aided design and manufacture. The user should be provided with aids to manipulate graphical representations. If the user needs to draw lines, constraints should be provided to ensure that the lines being drawn are straight, vertical, horizontal, diagonal, curved or however else specified by the user. Rubber banding, where there is a fixed point and a user-controlled movable point, could also be provided. The user needs to be able to select, copy, move, join or disconnect parts of graphical objects.

The properties or attributes of graphical objects, such as line widths or borders for a drawing, can be displayed as menus for the user. The menu choices should show the attribute, rather than verbally label them, so that the user can see how the final graphic would appear. For example, the names of the font styles that could be chosen for alphabetical labelling could be shown in that font style: e.g., *italic*, **boldface**.

Graphics are used to display data to make complex variables and relationships apparent and understandable to the viewer. Display density can be reduced by replacing lists of numerical data with a graphical display of data points. Graphs make data comparison easier for the user. Graphical display of related data sets can show on a single screen what might take multiple screens if presented as rows and columns of data. The user can compare linear relationships of variables more directly with the graphical interface.

Graphics generated by the computer should be presented in ways that are under the user's control. The interface designer should provide options to aid the user, such as templates or other aids for plotting and drawing graphs. The computer could automatically plot data points for complex data on a graph rather than require the user to position each point. If the user chooses to enter points, then the interface should allow the user to zoom in on a particular section of the graph. An overview that shows the display can be maintained as an inset so the user can still see the relationship between the magnified zoom-in area and the overall display. It is important for the user to be able to maintain a sense of the context in which the task is being done. When a zoom function is used, the relative scale between the overall display and the zoom area should be apparent. With a continuously changing range of sizes during zooming, a changing scale or legend could be provided for the user.

Line graphs, bar charts and pie charts can be used to represent numerical data on the graphical interface in the same ways they are displayed on paper. Conventions for ordering axes or labelling graphs should be followed and standard intervals and consistent scaling should be used for the displayed data. Related sets of graphics should be meaningfully ordered, with legends to label or explain the variables for the user. The graphical interface has additional possibilities for data display beyond what is possible with paper. Graphs with dynamically changing values can be shown in real time on the displays; data that are changing can be monitored and displayed. Animation of icons or other pictorial symbols can also be added to the display.

Graphical displays should be presented with an uncluttered screen format. Since a primary advantage of graphics is that they can reduce display density, only necessary information should be displayed. Users should also be able to expand or contract the display, as needed to complete their tasks.

Table 1
Selected guidelines for information presentation

General principles:	Be consistent in screen format design and in the user interaction processes
	Perform user testing on prospective interface designs
Text presentation:	Readability of prose text is enhanced by double-spaced lines with an appropriate combination of uppercase and lowercase letters
	Searching in prose text is enhanced by presenting labels in uppercase letters
Data entry and display:	Data entry from printed forms is easier when the screen and printed formats match
	Data that are grouped for display in meaningful ways are easier to comprehend and use
Menus:	Menu selection is generally more accurate when designed to have fewer screens with more choices per screen
	User traversal of menus is more accurate when the user has access to a map of the menu structure
Graphics:	Direct manipulation of graphical objects requires continuous correct and rapid feedback showing the results of user actions
	Icons are generally more informative and easier to manipulate in a graphical environment than verbal labels for objects

3. Conclusions

New applications, new input devices and novel interfaces will continue to be developed. Guidelines for the information-presentation requirements for future interfaces may be similar to the guidelines for present interfaces. Table 1 summarizes selected guidelines for information presentation. As with any set of guidelines, exceptions are likely, depending on user characteristics, tasks, applications or available resources. The present guidelines should not be automatically assumed to be correct for future applications. Though the guidelines for human–system interactions may change with technological advances, the two principles of interface design (consistency and user testing) will remain as strategies for maximizing user performance. Guidelines, practical experience and research data are contributing to improving information presentation. Designers have a great opportunity to dramatically improve on current interfaces and more than ever there is the potential for invention and discovery of clear, error-free and enjoyable user interfaces.

See also: Human Factors Engineering; Human Factors Engineering: Information-Processing Concerns

Bibliography

Brown C M 1988 *Human–Computer Interface Design Guidelines.* Ablex, Norwood, New Jersey
Foley J D, van Dam A 1982 *Fundamentals of Interactive Computer Graphics.* Addison–Wesley, Reading, Massachusetts
Galitz W O 1985 *Handbook of Screen Format Design,* 2nd edn. QED Information Sciences, Wellesley, Massachusetts
Mills C B, Weldon L J 1987 Reading text from computer screens. *ACM Comput. Surv.* **19,** 329–58
Shneiderman B 1987 *Designing the User Interface.* Addison–Wesley, Reading, Massachusetts
Smith S L, Mosier J N 1986 *Guidelines for Designing User Interface Software,* NTIS Document AD A177 198. National Technical Information Service, Springfield, Virginia
Springer C J 1987 Retrieval of information from complex alphanumeric displays: Screen formatting variables' effects on target identification time. In: Salvendy G (ed.) *Cognitive Engineering in the Design of Human–Computer Interaction and Expert Systems.* Elsevier, Amsterdam, pp. 375–82
Tullis T S 1988 A system for evaluating screen formats: Research and application. In: Hartson H R, Hix D (eds.) *Advances in Human–Computer Interaction,* Vol. 2. Ablex, Norwood, New Jersey, pp. 214–86

L. J. Weldon
[Essex Community College, Baltimore, Maryland, USA]

Hypothesis Testing

The two major areas of statistical inference are the testing of hypotheses and the estimation of system states and parameters. The former area, hypothesis testing, is the subject of this article. We will develop some aspects of classical decision theory, and describe simple applications to communication and control sciences.

There are many situations in which hypothesis testing (often called detection theory in the communication theory literature) is applicable. A radar return is observed, and the presence or absence of a target is to be determined; from a smear of human tissue we attempt to determine whether a patient has cancer; from fluctuations in activity of a particular stock on one of the exchanges, we decide whether or not to buy some shares of the stock.

In each case we choose an answer yes or no, and we refer to these two choices (yes and no) as hypotheses $\mathcal{H}_0$ and $\mathcal{H}_1$. It is possible to have more than two hypotheses and to attempt to decide which one of N hypotheses to accept.

1. Purpose of Hypothesis Testing

In the analysis phase of the systems process, it is often desirable to assess the validity of various assumptions concerning systems operation. In any situation where hypotheses or assumptions are used, there is the possibility of accepting a false hypothesis or rejecting a true hypothesis. These two situations are called type I and type II errors. Figure 1 indicates type I and type II errors for a hypothetical situation. In the absence of a hypothesis testing method, the probability of a type I or type II error is unknown. Hypothesis testing provides measures that enable the determination of whether too much significance is attached to results which occur through pure chance. It is not generally possible to reduce the probability of a type I or type II error to zero. However, either but not both of these probabilities can be reduced to the extent that they are virtually eliminated. This process is known as establishing a level of significance.

Hypothesis testing is used when assumptions must be evaluated, and where it is not possible to study the entire "population" of values about which these assumptions have been made. In its simplest form, two hypotheses are defined: the null hypothesis $\mathcal{H}_0$ and the alternative hypothesis $\mathcal{H}_1$. Typically, the alternative hypothesis is developed first. It usually concerns the positive aspect of an issue and may come directly from the issue formulation elements. For example, the alternative hypothesis might be: "There *has been* a reduction in energy use in *London* over the past twelve months." It is important to note that the basis of the hypothesis testing method is the null hypothesis. Type I and type II errors are based on the rejection of, or the inability to reject, the null hypothesis. In other words,

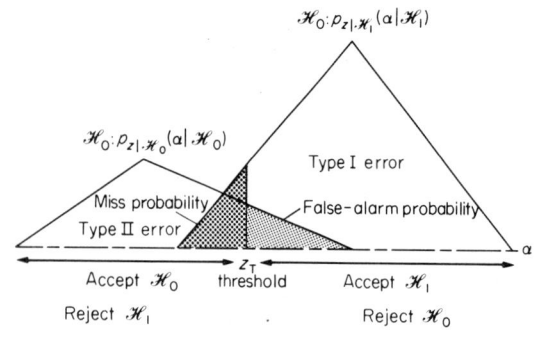

Figure 1
Probability densities for illustration of type I and type II errors. A single sample is made, and if the result is less than z_T, then $\mathcal{H}_0$ is accepted; otherwise $\mathcal{H}_1$ is accepted

Reality	Decision	
	Accept $\mathcal{H}_0$	Reject $\mathcal{H}_0$
$\mathcal{H}_0$ true	Correct decision	Type I error (probability α)
$\mathcal{H}_0$ false	Type II error (probability β)	Correct decision

the alternative hypothesis will only be accepted if the null hypothesis is rejected. If the null hypothesis cannot be rejected then no conclusion is possible concerning the alternative hypothesis. The null hypothesis and the alternative hypothesis must be selected so that data supporting the alternative hypothesis is such that it can potentially cause the null hypothesis to be rejected. $\mathcal{H}_1$ is designed so that it is more likely to be true if $\mathcal{H}_0$ is rejected. The following statement would be inappropriate as a null hypothesis to accompany the previous $\mathcal{H}_1$. "There *has not been* a reduction in energy use in the *UK* over the past twelve months." Results of a sample taken to determine the validity of this hypothesis would not provide meaningful information about $\mathcal{H}_1$. An appropriate null hypothesis is the negative of the alternative hypothesis. "There *has not been* a reduction in energy use in *London* over the past twelve months" is a good null hypothesis to use in conjunction with the $\mathcal{H}_1$ stated above.

Following the selection of the two hypotheses, specification of the level of significance is needed. The value of this level is arbitrary, and is specified in accordance with the decision maker's desires. The level of significance α is compared to a statistical analysis on the results of an experiment performed on a random sample of the population. This "population" is the same set of values for all tests. Statistical analysis of the test results yields the probability of finding the results of that test if $\mathcal{H}_0$ were actually true. If the statistical value is smaller than the present level of significance, it is concluded that $\mathcal{H}_0$ should be rejected and $\mathcal{H}_1$ accepted. If the statistical value, or likelihood, is greater than α it is concluded that the sample information does not provide sufficient evidence to reject $\mathcal{H}_0$. The deviation from data that support $\mathcal{H}_0$ found in the sample could be due solely to random factors. It is desired to reduce this possibility. Tests are generally designed to keep the possibility of making type I errors small. Since the null hypothesis usually states what is believed to be true in the absence of data, it is generally appropriate to structure the problem such that supporting data will tend to cause rejection of the null hypothesis and acceptance of the alternative hypothesis. Often it is more costly to make a type I error than a type II error of the same relative amount, and if this is the case we try to avoid making that type of error.

Selection of an appropriate test statistic is based on the population being studied. Normal distributions, chi-square, t or F distributions are typical choices and are picked as a function of the degrees of freedom or continuity of range in the possible outcomes. For example, the possible outcomes of the roll of a pair of dice has fewer degrees of freedom than the outcome of selecting a colored jellybean from a jar of 2000 beans of 20 different colors. Proper selection of the distribution is based on the statistical properties (mean, variance, etc.) of the population. However, if these are not known, sample results may be used to calculate these values. This complicates the computation of error probabilities considerably.

Design of the sample size is often a function of how much freedom the analyst has to choose the sample size. Statistical methods for computing the minimum sample size are available. The sample size is based on the minimum size necessary to guarantee that certain constraints will be met. The parameter α is the probability that a type I error will be made, and β the probability that a type II error will be made. Although β cannot be calculated unless $\mathcal{H}_1$ is an exact hypothesis, it is known that, for a specified α, the parameter β will decrease as the sample size increases. This means that the possibility of properly rejecting a false hypothesis increases as more information becomes available.

Extreme care must be taken to ensure that all samples are taken in a truly random fashion. The validity of the statistical outcome depends heavily on the randomness of the sample, and this indicates the considerable importance of randomness in the collection process.

Once the mean, variance and other relevant aspects of the test have been calculated, the value p must be calculated. Here p is the likelihood that a particular test result, given that $\mathcal{H}_0$ is true, is found in a random sample. It also represents the fraction of times that the test results achieved in the test can be expected among a very large number of similar tests, given that $\mathcal{H}_0$ is in fact true. The analyst compares the values of p to the preset α. If p is smaller than α, it is concluded that this particular test result is so unlikely if $\mathcal{H}_0$ is true that $\mathcal{H}_0$ must be rejected. If p is greater than α then it is concluded that the deviation in the test result from $\mathcal{H}_0$ could be accounted for by random chance. There is, in this case, not enough evidence to reject $\mathcal{H}_0$.

Hypothesis testing is useful in any situation where it is desirable that hypotheses be accepted or rejected on the basis of statistical information. It is not uncommon that the issue formulation and analysis steps of the systems process do not initially result in complete and precise information about one or more aspects of system operation. It is often useful to have a method to evaluate assumptions about the system, rather than basing an important decision merely on intuition. It is to these ends that hypothesis testing is most useful. Hypothesis testing can be valuable in the system implementation or operation when an action depends on a judgement about the actual state of a system, and where complete information about system operation is not attainable.

2. Elementary Mathematics for Hypothesis Testing

Each hypothesis in a given problem results from a source which generates one of the hypotheses as an output. Data to enable acceptance or rejection of the hypothesis is not observed directly, or there would be no decision problem. A probabilistic transition mechanism "separates" the hypothesis from our observations. This device knows which hypothesis is true and generates a point or points in observation space according to some probability law. We have access to the observation space, and form a decision on the basis of a decision rule as to which hypothesis to accept. This decision is based upon a knowledge of the *a priori* probability of the various hypotheses and of the conditional probabilities inherent in the probabilistic transition mechanism. If the (*a priori*) probability that $\mathcal{H}_0$ will occur is $P_{\mathcal{H}_0}$ and the probability of $\mathcal{H}_1$ is $P_{\mathcal{H}_1}$, then $P_{\mathcal{H}_0} + P_{\mathcal{H}_1} = 1$, since one of the hypotheses $\mathcal{H}_0$ or $\mathcal{H}_1$ must be true. We make a single observation z corrupted by noise (which may have different statistical characteristics, depending on which hypothesis was true), and attempt to make a decision from the hypotheses

$$\mathcal{H}_0: z = v_0$$
$$\mathcal{H}_1: z = 1 + v_1$$

Knowledge of the probabilistic transition mechanism is equivalent to a knowledge of the probability density functions associated with v_0 and v_1. In much of the work in systems and control v_0 and v_1 are called measurement noise. Figure 2 illustrates the elements of the binary hypothesis testing problem.

Two kinds of errors are possible in simple binary decision problems, as we have stated. We may accept $\mathcal{H}_0$ when it is false, or we may accept $\mathcal{H}_1$ when it is false. In the radar problem, where $\mathcal{H}_0$ corresponds to the absence of a target and $\mathcal{H}_1$ corresponds to the

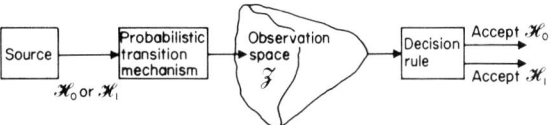

Figure 2
Elements of the binary hypothesis testing problem

presence of one, acceptance of $\mathcal{H}_0$ when it is false is called a "miss," and the probability of doing this is called the miss probability P_M. One minus the miss probability is called the detection probability, $P_D = 1 - P_M$. Accepting $\mathcal{H}_1$, deciding that a target is present when $\mathcal{H}_1$ is false and a target is not present is called a false alarm and the associated probability is the false-alarm probability P_F.

These ideas may be illustrated in a simple graphical fashion. An alternative statement of the problem is that under $\mathcal{H}_0$, we have $p_z(\alpha) = p_{z|\mathcal{H}}(\alpha|\mathcal{H}_0)$, and under $\mathcal{H}_1$ we have $p_z(\alpha) = p_{z|\mathcal{H}}(\alpha|\mathcal{H}_1)$. Thus the object of the hypothesis testing problem is to accept one of the two density functions $p_{z|\mathcal{H}_0}$ or $p_{z|\mathcal{H}_1}$ as being "most representative" of the density of a given population. These densities may appear as illustrated in Fig. 1. Assume a threshold at $\alpha = z_T$, so that if a single observation $z = \alpha_1$ is greater than z_T, we accept $\mathcal{H}_1$ and if it is less than z_T, we accept $\mathcal{H}_0$. In a more realistic situation the parameter α is defined as a sufficient statistic, and may be made up of several observations rather than obtained from a single observation. Here, we find it convenient to consider α as a scalar observation.

We determine false-alarm and miss probabilities for a simple single observation case. From Fig. 1 and the foregoing reasoning the miss probability is

$$P_M = \int_{-\infty}^{z_T} p_{z|\mathcal{H}}(\alpha|\mathcal{H}_1) \, d\alpha \tag{1}$$

while the false-alarm probability becomes

$$P_F = \int_{z_T}^{\infty} p_{z|\mathcal{H}}(\alpha|\mathcal{H}_0) \, d\alpha \tag{2}$$

The miss probability may be made as small as desired at the expense of the false-alarm probability. In a practical situation one of the probabilities, such as P_F, may be fixed, and a test is selected. This might be the threshold z_T selected, so that P_M is minimized. This criterion, known as a Neyman–Pearson criterion, is trivial in this particular situation, since fixing the false-alarm probability fixes the threshold, and hence the miss probability. In a more realistic situation there would be more than one observation, and thus ample opportunity to constrain the false-alarm probability by using Lagrange multipliers without simultaneously fixing the miss probability. Hence, we would obtain a minimum of

$$J_{NP} = P_M + \lambda [P_F - \gamma] \tag{3}$$

Hypothesis Testing

where λ is a Lagrange multiplier, and γ is the desired false-alarm probability. We set the derivative of J_{NP} with respect to z_T equal to zero to obtain, by using Eqns. (1) and (2) such that we have a likelihood-ratio test for an observation $z=\alpha$,

$$\frac{p_{z|\mathscr{H}}(\alpha|\mathscr{H}_1)}{p_{z|\mathscr{H}}(\alpha|\mathscr{H}_0)} \underset{\text{accept } \mathscr{H}_0}{\overset{\text{accept } \mathscr{H}_1}{\gtrless}} \lambda \quad (4)$$

which says that we accept $\mathscr{H}_1$ if the ratio is greater than λ and accept $\mathscr{H}_0$ if the ratio is less than λ when evaluated at $z=\alpha$. We adjust the variable λ, the Lagrange multiplier, so that $P_F = \lambda$.

If a false alarm is as serious as a miss, an appropriate criterion might be to minimize the miss probability plus false-alarm probability. Thus we minimize

$$P_{F+M} = P_M + P_F = \int_{-\infty}^{z_T} p_{z|\mathscr{H}}(\alpha|\mathscr{H}_1) d\alpha$$
$$+ \int_{z_T}^{\infty} p_{z|\mathscr{H}}(\alpha|\mathscr{H}_0) d\alpha \quad (5)$$

by a proper choice of z_T. We take the derivative of the foregoing expression with respect to z_T and set it equal to zero to obtain the threshold as the value for which the two densities are equal. If $z=\alpha$, then $p_{z|\mathscr{H}_1} > p_{z|\mathscr{H}_0}$, and we accept hypothesis $\mathscr{H}_1$. In this case we have a likelihood-ratio test such that, since λ is in effect equal to 1,

$$\frac{p_{z|\mathscr{H}}(\alpha|\mathscr{H}_1)}{p_{z|\mathscr{H}}(\alpha|\mathscr{H}_0)} \underset{\text{accept } \mathscr{H}_0}{\overset{\text{accept } \mathscr{H}_1}{\gtrless}} 1 \quad (6)$$

Hypothesis testing problems are generally much more complex than the simple scalar observation problem presented here. Often it is unrealistic to assume that false alarms and misses are equally serious. There may be different costs associated with these errors, and there may be costs associated with correct decisions. The Bayes' test, or Bayes' risk criterion, is used to treat problems of this type. We briefly examine this criterion here.

The four courses of action in testing hypotheses against single alternatives and their associated costs are

C_{00}: cost of accepting $\mathscr{H}_0$ when $\mathscr{H}_0$ is true
C_{01}: cost of accepting $\mathscr{H}_0$ when $\mathscr{H}_1$ is true
C_{10}: cost of accepting $\mathscr{H}_1$ when $\mathscr{H}_0$ is true
C_{11}: cost of accepting $\mathscr{H}_1$ when $\mathscr{H}_1$ is true

C_{00} and C_{11} represent costs associated with correct decisions, whereas C_{01} and C_{10} represent costs associated with incorrect decisions.

It is not unrealistic to associate "costs" with correct decisions. In an application of decision theory to investment, for example, the cost associated with not buying a stock, when the correct decision is *not* to buy a stock, is that the money which could be invested in the market for potentially large returns is not being invested, or is being invested at much lower rates of return. In a similar way, there is "cost" associated with purchasing a certain stock when the correct decision should be to buy that stock, since the money invested is now "risk capital," not safely invested in a bank. To identify and use these costs we need to know the *a priori* probabilities $P_{\mathscr{H}_0}$ and $P_{\mathscr{H}_1}$ associated with the two hypotheses. We will define Bayes' risk $\mathscr{B}$ as the expected value of the cost for the four alternatives, so that

$$\mathscr{B} = C_{00} P(\text{accept } \mathscr{H}_0, \mathscr{H}_0 \text{ true})$$
$$+ C_{01} P(\text{accept } \mathscr{H}_0, \mathscr{H}_1 \text{ true})$$
$$+ C_{10} P(\text{accept } \mathscr{H}_1, \mathscr{H}_0 \text{ true})$$
$$+ C_{11} P(\text{accept } \mathscr{H}_1, \mathscr{H}_1 \text{ true}) \quad (7)$$

In terms of conditional density functions for the transition mechanism and the *a priori* event probabilities for the two hypotheses, $\mathscr{B}$ may be rewritten by use of the conditional probability law $P(A,B) = P(A|B)P(B)$ as

$$\mathscr{B} = C_{00} P_{\mathscr{H}_0} P(\text{accept } \mathscr{H}_0 | \mathscr{H}_0 \text{ true})$$
$$+ C_{01} P_{\mathscr{H}_1} P(\text{accept } \mathscr{H}_0 | \mathscr{H}_1 \text{ true})$$
$$+ C_{10} P_{\mathscr{H}_0} P(\text{accept } \mathscr{H}_1 | \mathscr{H}_0 \text{ true})$$
$$+ C_{11} P_{\mathscr{H}_1} P(\text{accept } \mathscr{H}_1 | \mathscr{H}_1 \text{ true})$$

Now, if the decision rule is a simple threshold test in which we accept $\mathscr{H}_1$ if the observation α is greater than the threshold z_T and we accept $\mathscr{H}_0$ if $\alpha < z_T$, then $\mathscr{B}$ becomes

$$\mathscr{B} = C_{00} P_{\mathscr{H}_0} \int_{-\infty}^{z_T} p_{z|\mathscr{H}}(\alpha|\mathscr{H}_0) d\alpha$$
$$+ C_{01} P_{\mathscr{H}_1} \int_{-\infty}^{z_T} p_{z|\mathscr{H}}(\alpha|\mathscr{H}_1) d\alpha$$
$$+ C_{10} P_{\mathscr{H}_0} \int_{z_T}^{\infty} p_{z|\mathscr{H}}(\alpha|\mathscr{H}_0) d\alpha$$
$$+ C_{11} P_{\mathscr{H}_1} \int_{z_T}^{\infty} p_{z|\mathscr{H}}(\alpha|\mathscr{H}_1) d\alpha \quad (8)$$

We select the threshold, or decision region, to minimize the Bayes' risk in Eqn. (8). It is reasonable that the cost of an incorrect decision will be greater than that of a correct decision (often the correct decision cost will be zero) and that all costs will be nonnegative, so that $C_{00} < C_{10}$ and $C_{11} < C_{01}$. A way of specifying the decision is

$$\frac{p_{z|\mathscr{H}}(\alpha|\mathscr{H}_1)}{p_{z|\mathscr{H}}(\alpha|\mathscr{H}_0)} \underset{\text{accept } \mathscr{H}_0}{\overset{\text{accept } \mathscr{H}_1}{\gtrless}} \frac{(C_{10}-C_{00})P_{\mathscr{H}_0}}{(C_{01}-C_{11})P_{\mathscr{H}_1}} \quad (9)$$

The ratio of the two conditional densities is called the likelihood ratio

$$\mathscr{L}(\alpha) = \frac{p_{z|\mathscr{H}}(\alpha|\mathscr{H}_1)}{p_{z|\mathscr{H}}(\alpha|\mathscr{H}_0)} \quad (10)$$

The threshold of the test is defined as

$$\mathcal{T} = \frac{P_{\mathcal{H}_0}(C_{10} - C_{00})}{P_{\mathcal{H}_1}(C_{01} - C_{11})} \quad (11)$$

and thus the Bayes risk criterion has resulted in a likelihood-ratio test

$$\mathcal{L}(\alpha) \underset{\text{accept } \mathcal{H}_0}{\overset{\text{accept } \mathcal{H}_1}{\gtrless}} \mathcal{T} \quad (12)$$

to determine the best decision. Often, particularly when we deal with Gaussian densities, it is convenient to take the natural logarithm of Eqn. (12). In the analysis so far, it has been assumed that we know the information required to compute the threshold of the test $\mathcal{T}$. In practice, the costs and a priori probabilities may need to be adjusted or updated by using actual observations to obtain an adaptive decision system.

Sometimes the costs are known, but not the a priori probabilities $P_{\mathcal{H}_0}$ and $P_{\mathcal{H}_1}$. In this case, it is possible to use a minimax test and choose the Bayes' test which corresponds to the worst possible values of the prior probabilities. The minimax risk is obtained by minimizing the Bayes' risk by choice of a threshold at that value of $P_{\mathcal{H}_0}$ which maximizes the risk. There are advantages to the minimax criterion, but it must be realized that a very conservative decision rule is obtained.

In the vast majority of decision-theoretic problems, a single observation does not suffice to yield a minimum Bayes' risk low enough for practical application. This makes it necessary to take more than one observation. We consider a space of observations which we will find convenient to denote by the vector $\mathbf{z}^T = [z_1 z_2 \cdots z_k]$. The Bayes' risk criterion must now be extended to the case of a vector observation. This is easily accomplished, and we have the vector equivalent of Eqn. (8):

$$\mathcal{B} = C_{00} P_{\mathcal{H}_0} \int_{\mathcal{Z}_0} p_{\mathbf{z}|\mathcal{H}}(\alpha|\mathcal{H}_0) \, d\alpha$$
$$+ C_{01} P_{\mathcal{H}_1} \int_{\mathcal{Z}_0} p_{\mathbf{z}|\mathcal{H}}(\alpha|\mathcal{H}_1) \, d\alpha$$
$$+ C_{10} P_{\mathcal{H}_0} \int_{\mathcal{Z}_1} p_{\mathbf{z}|\mathcal{H}}(\alpha|\mathcal{H}_0) \, d\alpha$$
$$+ C_{11} P_{\mathcal{H}_1} \int_{\mathcal{Z}_1} p_{\mathbf{z}|\mathcal{H}}(\alpha|\mathcal{H}_1) \, d\alpha \quad (13)$$

where $\mathcal{Z}_0$ and $\mathcal{Z}_1$ are the decision regions such that, if the observation falls in $\mathcal{Z}_1$, hypothesis $\mathcal{H}_1$ is accepted, and if the observation falls in $\mathcal{Z}_0$, hypothesis $\mathcal{H}_0$ is accepted. The Bayes' risk test turns out to be

$$\mathcal{L}(\alpha) \underset{\text{accept } \mathcal{H}_0}{\overset{\text{accept } \mathcal{H}_1}{\gtrless}} \mathcal{T} \quad (14)$$

where $\mathcal{L}(\alpha)$ is the likelihood ratio

$$\mathcal{L}(\alpha) \triangleq \frac{p_{\mathbf{z}|\mathcal{H}}(\alpha|\mathcal{H}_1)}{p_{\mathbf{z}|\mathcal{H}}(\alpha|\mathcal{H}_0)} \quad (15)$$

and $\mathcal{T}$ is the threshold of the test

$$\mathcal{T} \triangleq \frac{(C_{10} - C_{00}) P_{\mathcal{H}_0}}{(C_{01} - C_{11}) P_{\mathcal{H}_1}} \quad (16)$$

The foregoing three relations for the case of a vector observation represent the generalization of the scalar results. For the binary hypothesis case, it is possible to obtain a scalar sufficient statistic $S(z)$, and therefore obtain a threshold for the sufficient statistic $\mathcal{T}_S(z)$. Roughly speaking, we may call a statistic sufficient if it contains all the necessary information to make a decision.

3. Measures of Success in Hypothesis Testing

The measures of success in a hypothesis testing process are as follows.

(a) *Is the likelihood that the conclusion is incorrect sufficiently small?* Although hypothesis testing cannot be used to prove anything beyond any doubt, it is possible to reduce the probability that an incorrect decision of a given type will be made.

(b) *Was the sampling process executed properly?* Statistical probabilities are the result of a large number of tests. In practice, only one test is used. It is, therefore, critical that the data gathered for analysis be truly representative of the population and be purely random in nature. There is a possibility that the test results will exceed the normal confidence interval. If possible, independent samples should be gathered to eliminate the possibility that a "bad" sample is used. If test results on the two samples are sufficiently different, it may be appropriate to gather a third sample, or reexamine the test statistic that has been used.

(c) *Does the outcome of the hypothesis test aid the decision maker?* The decision maker must be able to make a decision based on an analysis of the assumptions evaluated. If no conclusion can be made, due to an inability to reject $\mathcal{H}_0$, then it may be possible to gather more information in the form of a larger sample. It may be equally appropriate to review the sampling process, and to reexamine the statements and assumptions concerning $\mathcal{H}_1$ and $\mathcal{H}_0$. Another possibility is to adjust the values of α and β. For small α, the null hypothesis is favored. Often α values are much smaller than β values in realistic hypothesis testing. $\mathcal{H}_0$ will then be rejected only if there is strong evidence against it.

4. Example 1

One of the simplest problems we may consider is that of detection of a constant in the presence of an additive

Hypothesis Testing

zero-mean Gaussian disturbance. Under $\mathcal{H}_0$ there is no signal; under $\mathcal{H}_1$ there is a signal of amplitude $m > 0$. Thus,

$$\mathcal{H}_0: z = v$$
$$\mathcal{H}_1: z = m + v$$

where

$$p_v(\alpha) = \frac{1}{(2\pi)^{1/2}\sigma} \exp(-\alpha^2/2\sigma^2)$$

This formulation results naturally when we test whether the mean of a Gaussian population has one of two values, 0 or m. The required density functions for the likelihood-ratio test are

$$p_{z|\mathcal{H}}(\alpha|\mathcal{H}_0) = \frac{1}{(2\pi)^{1/2}\sigma} \exp(-\alpha^2/2\sigma^2)$$

$$p_{z|\mathcal{H}}(\alpha|\mathcal{H}_1) = \frac{1}{(2\pi)^{1/2}\sigma} \exp[-(\alpha-m)^2/2\sigma^2]$$

so that the logarithm of the likelihood ratio becomes

$$\ln \mathcal{L}(\alpha) = \frac{-(\alpha-m)^2 + (\alpha^2)}{2\sigma^2} = \frac{m(\alpha - m/2)}{\sigma^2}$$

Thus the likelihood-ratio test is (where the observation is the value α)

$$\frac{m(\alpha - m/2)}{\sigma^2} \underset{\text{accept } \mathcal{H}_0}{\overset{\text{accept } \mathcal{H}_1}{\gtreqless}} \ln \frac{P_{\mathcal{H}_0}(C_{10} - C_{00})}{P_{\mathcal{H}_1}(C_{01} - C_{11})}$$

or

$$\alpha \underset{\text{accept } \mathcal{H}_0}{\overset{\text{accept } \mathcal{H}_1}{\gtreqless}} \frac{m}{2} + \frac{\sigma^2}{m} \ln \frac{P_{\mathcal{H}_0}(C_{10} - C_{00})}{P_{\mathcal{H}_1}(C_{01} - C_{11})} = z_T$$

We compare the observation α versus the threshold z_T and make a decision.

If we consider the costs of correct decisions to be zero, $C_{11} = C_{00} = 0$, and the costs of the two types of errors being equal, the hypothesis test becomes

$$\alpha \underset{\text{accept } \mathcal{H}_0}{\overset{\text{accept } \mathcal{H}_1}{\gtreqless}} \frac{m}{2} + \frac{\sigma^2}{m} \ln \frac{P_{\mathcal{H}_0}}{P_{\mathcal{H}_1}}$$

If $P_{\mathcal{H}_1} > P_{\mathcal{H}_0}$, the threshold is less than $m/2$, because $\mathcal{H}_1$ occurs more often than $\mathcal{H}_0$. If $P_{\mathcal{H}_1} = P_{\mathcal{H}_0} = 0.5$, the threshold is just $m/2$, which is reasonable, since the a priori occurrences of $\mathcal{H}_1$ and $\mathcal{H}_0$ are equally likely.

The false-alarm and miss probabilities are given by

$$P_M = \int_{-\infty}^{(z_T - m)/\sigma} \frac{1}{(2\pi)^{1/2}} \exp(-\gamma^2/2) \, d\gamma$$

$$P_F = \int_{z_T/\sigma}^{\infty} \frac{1}{(2\pi)^{1/2}} \exp(-\gamma^2/2) \, d\gamma$$

The detection probability is defined as 1 minus the miss probability, so that

$$P_D = 1 - P_M = \int_{(z_T - m)/\sigma}^{\infty} \frac{1}{(2\pi)^{1/2}} \exp(-\gamma^2/2) \, d\gamma$$

We may now plot P_D vs P_F for different values of m, with z_T as the varying parameter. The resulting curves are often called receiver operating characteristic (ROC) curves. An interpretation similar to this is obtained in the more realistic case of multiple observations. The single observation of this example is simply replaced by a sufficient statistic in the more general case.

5. Example 2

At the last monthly division-meeting, a division manager expresses great interest in the fuel consumption figures for the division. The four group managers in the division have issued specific instructions that they do not expect to see the fuel consumption in any of their groups increase over time. Therefore conservation efforts should be implemented immediately. There exists a concern, however, as to whether group fuel use is increasing, decreasing or remaining constant. A procedure may be used to make a judgement about the trend in fuel use.

Last month's figures are available for study and the average consumption has been calculated. There are 3000 fuel-burning pieces of equipment in the group. The group manager desires that the probability of concluding that a decrease had occurred when in fact the consumption stayed the same or increased by less than 5% ($\alpha = 0.05$). This is the probability of a type I error.

The two hypotheses to be used in the test are

$\mathcal{H}_0$: There has been no decrease in the fuel consumption average in the group.

$\mathcal{H}_1$: There has been a decrease in the fuel consumption average in the group.

The average consumption calculated from last month's data is 300 gallons per piece of equipment with a standard deviation of 100 gallons. The analyst determined that the distribution was virtually normal (Gaussian) since 68% of the consumption figures fell within 102 gallons of the mean. The analyst, therefore, decides to use the normal distribution in conducting the hypothesis test.

The analyst decides to select randomly 100 units of fuel-burning equipment and calculate test statistics from them. The analyst determines that with a sample size of 100, the chance of failing to pick up a decrease of 10% is less than 0.1. The analyst feels that time is so limited that the sample size increase required to further reduce the chance of a type II error is neither feasible nor appropriate.

The relevant information is contained in last month's consolidated report concerning fuel usage and a random-number table. The first 100 random numbers in the table are selected. These are made to correspond to particular pieces of fuel-burning equipment. The fuel-consumption data on the selected items of equipment is then requested.

Calculating the average of this sample yields 280 gallons. The probability of finding this result (280) or any lower value in a 100 item sample given that $\mathscr{H}_0$ is true is only 0.022. Since 0.022 is smaller than 0.05 (α), the decision is made to reject $\mathscr{H}_0$ and conclude that the data supports acceptance of $\mathscr{H}_1$. In fact, the analyst would have rejected $\mathscr{H}_0$ had there been obtained any average consumption less than 283.3, as that is the value which yields a probability of 0.05 for the type I error.

It is important to note that there is a 0.022 probability that this conclusion is wrong. The hypothesis test cannot, however, quantify the decrease in fuel consumption. To conclude that the decrease in overall consumption was related to the decrease exhibited in the sample is not justified. A hypothesis concerning the decrease is certainly possible, of course. This is not the subject of this example and is a different issue which may well be worth examining.

The conclusion, in this case, to reject $\mathscr{H}_0$ was strongly influenced by the implicit imposition of $\beta = 0.1$. The sample size selected gives confidence in the statistical conclusion. Had a sample of 25 items been selected, it turns out that the probability of finding an average of 280 gallons is 0.1587. This number is much larger than $\alpha = 0.05$, and therefore no conclusion can be made as to the consumption trend. It is certainly false to try to decide either way on the basis of a 280 gallon sample mean in a sample of 25. Care should be taken to select a sample size which tends to provide reasonable probability of detecting a trend in favor of $\mathscr{H}_1$ when $\mathscr{H}_0$ is false. This may be done through use of minimum required sample size calculations, as found in any management statistics book. The minimum sample in this case is 92.

See also: Decision Analysis; Systems Methodology

Bibliography

Bishop Y M M, Fienberg S E, Holland P W 1975 *Discrete Multivariate Analysis: Theory and Practice.* MIT Press, Cambridge, Massachusetts

Fitz-Gibbon C T, Morris L L 1978 *How to Calculate Statistics.* Sage Publications, Beverly Hills, California

Henkel R E 1976 *Tests of Significance*, Sage University Series on Quantitative Applications in the Social Sciences. Sage Publications, Beverly Hills, California

Sage A P, Melsa J L 1971 *Estimation Theory with Applications to Communications and Control.* McGraw–Hill, New York

Winkler R L, Hays W L 1975 *Statistics: Probability, Inference, and Decision.* Holt, Rinehart and Winston, New York

A. P. Sage
[George Mason University, Fairfax, Virginia, USA]

Inference and Impact Analysis

This article presents an overview of contemporary efforts associated with impact assessment and forecasting. Here we are especially concerned with the use of cross-impact analysis and hierarchical inference analysis for the design of knowledge-based systems, typically based on Bayesian approaches that assist individuals and groups in the processing of inferential information of a causal or diagnostic nature.

I. Basic Mathematics for Cross-Impact Analysis

Consider two events e_i and e_j and denote the probability of occurrence of these events as $P(i)$ and $P(j)$. Considered together, these two events may be totally uncoupled, coupled or totally included, as indicated in Fig. 1. Totally uncoupled events are those events whose occurrence or nonoccurrence has no effect upon the occurrence or nonoccurrence of other events in the event set. Coupled events are those whose occurrence or nonoccurrence will affect the likelihood of occurrence or nonoccurrence of other events in the element set. A totally included event is one which is entirely contained in another event such that if one event occurs, then the totally included event must also occur. If an event does not occur, then a totally included event cannot occur. It is necessary to consider conditional probabilities and cross-impact analysis in order to deal with coupled events. Uncoupled and totally included events are somewhat easier to deal with and may not need to be subjected to cross-impact analysis. However, events of importance are rarely uncoupled or totally included with all other events.

Bayes' rule states that the probabilities of events e_i and e_j must be related by

$$P(i|j) = \frac{P(j|i)}{P(j)} P(i) \qquad (1)$$

We consider two types of connecting modes for impacting events: enhancing and inhibiting. If the probability of event i occurring conditioned upon the knowledge that event j has occurred or will occur is greater than the probability of event i occurring, we say that event e_j is enhancing to event e_i. If the probability of event i occurring conditioned upon the knowledge that event j has occurred or will occur is less than the probability of event i occurring, we say that event e_j is inhibiting to event e_i. Finally, if the probability of event e_i occurring is independent of the occurrence or nonoccurrence of event e_j, we say that

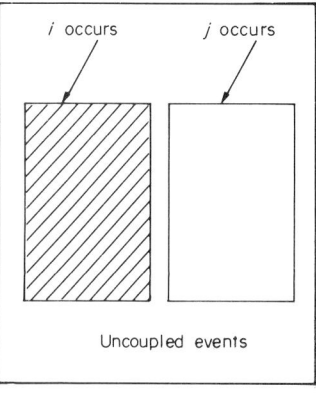

(a)

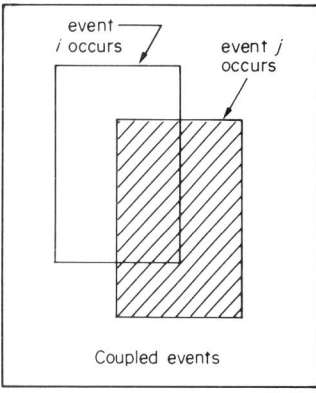

(b)

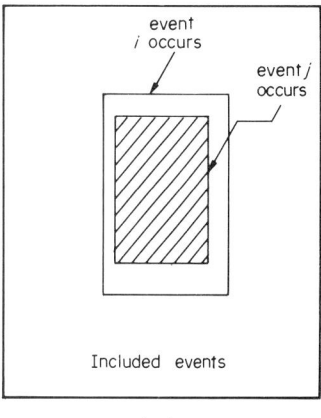

(c)

Figure 1
Possible event relationships

Inference and Impact Analysis

event e_i is independent of event e_j. In symbols,

if $P(i|j) > P(i)$, then e_j enhances e_i
if $P(i|j) < P(i)$, then e_j inhibits e_i
if $P(i|j) = P(i)$, then e_i is independent of e_j

Figure 1(a) represents the case where events i and j are uncoupled and nonindependent, and $P(j|i) = 0$. Thus event i is completely inhibiting to event j. Figure 1(c) represents the totally included and nonindependent case where $P(j|i) = 1$; event i is completely enhancing to event j. The much more interesting case is represented by Fig. 1(b). The relationship between events i and j may take any of the forms shown in Fig. 2. In this figure the probability of each of the various events is presumed equal to the fraction of the total area occupied by the event space. The three cases of Fig. 2 are:

(a) $\dfrac{P(j|i)}{P(j)} = 1$, independent events;

(b) $\dfrac{P(j|i)}{P(j)} > 1$, event i enhances event j;

(c) $\dfrac{P(j|i)}{P(j)} < 1$, event i inhibits event j.

It is of value to determine bounds on enhancement and inhibition of event j upon event i. From the laws of joint probability we have

$$P(i) = P(ij) + P(i\bar{j}) \qquad (2)$$

where $P(ij)$ is the probability of occurrence of events i and j and $P(i\bar{j})$ is the probability of occurrence of i and nonoccurrence of j. Using the conditional probability laws allows us to write this as

$$P(i) = P(j)P(i|j) + [1 - P(j)]P(i|\bar{j}) \qquad (3)$$

Now since $0 \leqslant P(j) \leqslant 1$ and $0 \leqslant P(i|\bar{j}) \leqslant 1$, the second term in the above must be positive, and so we have

$$P(i) \geqslant P(j)P(i|j) \qquad (4)$$

We see that an upper bound on the conditional or impacted probability $P(i|j)$ is

$$P(i|j) \leqslant \left[\dfrac{1}{P(j)}\right][P(i)] = aP(i) \qquad (5)$$

The number a must be positive and greater than 1. Thus this upper bound must appear in Fig. 3.

From the probability law for compound events, we have

$$P(i \cup j) = P(i) + P(j) - P(i|j)P(j) \qquad (6)$$

where $P(i \cup j)$ is the probability that event i or j or both will occur. We know that this probability must be greater than 0 and less than 1, and so we have

$$P(i|j) \geqslant \dfrac{P(i) + P(j) - 1}{P(j)} = \dfrac{P(i) - 1}{P(j)} + 1 \qquad (7)$$

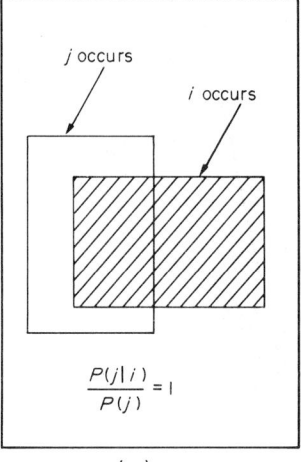
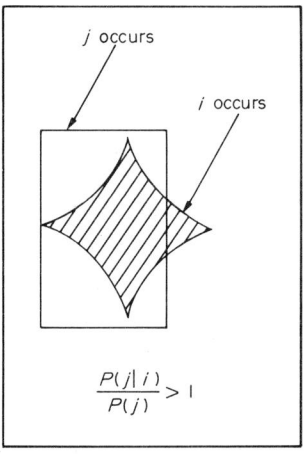
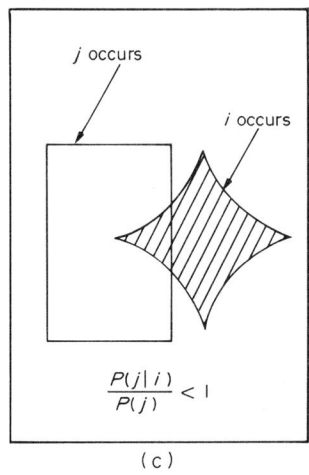

Figure 2
Independent, enhancing and inhibiting events

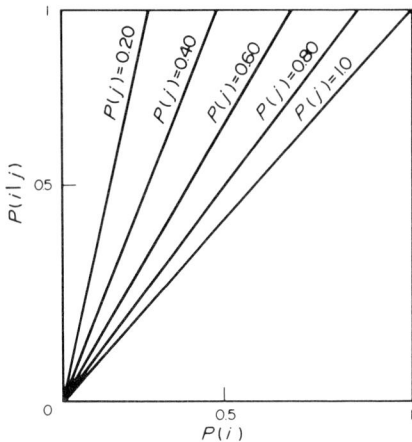

Figure 3
Upper bound for $P(i|j)$

and

$$P(i|j) \leqslant \frac{P(i)+P(j)}{P(j)} = 1 + \frac{1}{P(j)}P(i) \qquad (8)$$

Now the inequality of Eqn. (5) is stronger than that of Eqn. (8), so we do not need to consider Eqn. (8) any further. Equation (7) represents a lower bound on the impacted or conditional probability $P(i|j)$ in terms of the initial probability of the imported event $P(i)$ and this bound is illustrated in Fig. 3.

The event j will either be enhancing to, inhibiting to, or independent of event i. If event j enhances i, then $P(i|j)$ is greater than $P(i)$. The limiting case for enhancement occurs when we have independent events and $P(i|j) = P(i)$. The bound for enhancing event j is, therefore,

$$P(i) \leqslant P(i|j) \leqslant \left[\frac{1}{P(j)}\right]P(i), \quad j \text{ enhancing} \qquad (9)$$

For inhibiting event j we know that $P(i|j)$ is less than $P(i)$, with equality occurring when events i and j are independent. The bounds for inhibiting event j are determined from this inequality and Eqn. (7) as

$$1 + \frac{1}{P(j)}[P(i)-1] \leqslant P(i|j) \leqslant P(i), \quad j \text{ inhibiting} \qquad (10)$$

We can also consider probability bounds for non-occurrence of impacting events e_j. It is straightforward to show that these bounds are

$$P(i) \leqslant P(i|\bar{j}) \leqslant \frac{P(i)}{1-P(j)}, \quad j \text{ inhibiting} \qquad (11)$$

$$1 - \frac{1-P(i)}{1-P(j)} \leqslant P(i|\bar{j}) \leqslant P(i), \quad j \text{ enhancing} \qquad (12)$$

We must use these bounds to ensure consistency of probabilities. If we specify three of the four probabilities $P(i)$, $P(j)$, $P(j|i)$, then the other probability is immediately determined. Even if only two of these probabilities are specified, the third may not be chosen arbitrarily. The bounds just developed must be satisfied.

2. Use of Cross-Impact Analysis

Consider a set of events which may occur at specific times in the future. These events are denoted by $e_1, e_2, \ldots, e_n$ and have associated (marginal) probabilities of occurrence $P(1), P(2), \ldots, P(n)$. Suppose that $P(1) = 1$, so that event e_1 occurs with certainty. How does the known occurrence of e_1 affect the probabilities of occurrence of the other events? If there is a cross impact between events, the impacted probability of individual events will either increase or decrease with the occurrence or nonoccurrence of other elements. In the general case we wish to obtain conditional probability responses to the question: If event e_j occurs, what is the probability of event e_i, $P(i|j)$, for all i and j? Many people will find it difficult to respond to this query, and so instead the question may be reposed. If event e_j occurs, is the probability of event e_i occurring enhanced, inhibited or unaffected? By how much? A cross-impact matrix can be filled in from responses to the above. The responses and entries may vary from binary entries $+1, 0, -1$ to integer entries on a scale of 10, 100 or 10^{24}. For example, a cross-impact matrix might be as shown in Table 1, where $+10$ represents maximum enhancement and -10 represents maximum inhibition.

Gordon and Hayward (1968) categorize enhancing events as those which are enabling in the sense of necessitating that effort be expended to bring about the occurrence of other events. In a similar way, inhibiting events are those which are denigrating in the sense of making other events infeasible or impractical or antagonistic by necessitating that effort be expended to bring about the nonoccurrence of other events.

Early researchers in cross-impact analysis have assumed that the impacted probability is a quadratic function of the impacting event. Thus

$$P(i/j) = P(i) + A_{ij}P(i)[1-P(i)]$$

Table 1
A cross-impact matrix

| If this event occurs | then the probability of | | | |
	e_1	e_2	e_3	e_4
e_1		+3	−6	+10
e_2	+2		+3	0
e_3	−7	+1		0
e_4	+8	0	0	

The shilling fraction is used here to denote the most general impacted probability $P(i/j)$ such that if $P(i) = 0$, then $P(i/j) = 0$, and if $P(i) = 1$, then $P(i/j) = 1$. For $A_{ij} = 0$, we have independence between events i and j. For $A_{ij} > 0$, event j enhances event i, and for $A_{ij} < 0$, event j inhibits event i. Individuals participating in a cross-impact exercise would be asked to provide their estimates for the (marginal) probability $P(j)$ of event j as well as their estimate of impact factors which are transformed into a value of A_{ij}.

There are, however, several very uncomfortable features of this approach. First, there is no guarantee that Bayes' rule will be satisfied if a group picks all four terms $P(i)$, $P(j)$, A_{ij}, and A_{ji}. In fact, there is no guarantee that the appropriate inequalities obtained earlier will be satisfied. Thus we have used the symbol $P(i/j)$ rather than $P(i|j)$ in the foregoing and have refrained from calling $P(i/j)$ a conditional probability. There is no guarantee that it will even be a valid probability function.

Second, the relationship between $P(i/j)$ and $P(i)$ determined from the foregoing is not even symmetrical. We can show that, as a consequence, an enhancing event cannot make other than minor changes in a low-probability $P(i)$, and an inhibiting event cannot significantly change a high-probability $P(i)$. Enzer (1970) has proposed utilizing the expression

$$P(i/j) = \frac{r_{ij} P(i)}{1 + (r_{ij} - 1) P(i)}$$

where r_{ij} is a "likelihood ratio" of the impacted odds for event j impacting upon event i. For this expression the impacted probability contours are symmetrical for the required values of r_{ij}. Also, any positive value of r_{ij} may be used to completely span the space of impacted probabilities, whereas we must impose the restriction $-1 \leq A_{ij} \leq 1$ in order to avoid senseless impacted probabilities that are negative or greater than 1. This restriction makes it impossible to completely span all admissible $P(i/j)$. The use of the likelihood-ratio impacted-probability expression does resolve the problem of symmetry; however, neither the likelihood-ratio impacted-probability expression nor the quadratic impacted-probability expression will generally result in probabilities which are correct according to Bayesian probability theory.

Third, just as the occurrence of an event j influences, in general, the probability of occurrence of event i, so also will the known nonoccurrence of event j influence the probability of occurrence of event i. This must happen unless $P(i|j) = P(i)$, which would indicate that event i is independent of event j. This could, of course, occur, but there is certainly no reason why it must. The classical cross-impact method represented assumes that nonoccurrence of any event has no impact on any other event and this may be very unrealistic.

Fourth, time is an important variable, and events must generally be associated with time. It is quite a different matter to determine $P(i|j)$ when the time of occurrence of i is later than that of j than it is when the time of occurrence of j is later than that of i. It is vitally important to consider the time order of events when they are defined, and failure to do this can lead to crucial errors.

3. How to Use Cross-Impact Analysis

From a statement of appropriate probabilities of occurrence and nonoccurrence of events, a cross-impact analysis will provide a statement of probabilities of future events. Thus cross-impact analysis can be associated closely with a quantitative deterministic systems analysis model in a more complete simulation exercise to evolve time-dependent future predictions. We propose the following principal steps in conducting a cross-impact analysis.

(a) Use collective enquiry methods to generate a set of appropriate events, elements and relations for a particular problem.

(b) Use a structural modelling method to evolve a structure for the events under consideration.

(c) Develop a scale so that one may translate expert opinion and knowledge concerning the likelihood of occurrence of events into probabilities. This scale should be discussed, understood and approved by the group supplying the probability estimates.

(d) Obtain an initial set of probabilities of the type in which estimators have most confidence. Every effort should be made to obtain as many of the direct tree-related conditional probabilities as possible. For direct tree-related conditional probabilities not estimated, obtain sufficient marginal and lower-order conditional probabilities, and impact assessments, to bound the direct tree-related conditional probabilities. These upper and lower bounds are computed.

(e) Display the set of direct tree-related conditional probabilities or bounds computed on these probabilities if they are not directly estimated. Obtain final probabilities with which to determine future probabilities.

(f) Determine future event probabilities.

(g) Incorporate the results of the cross-impact analysis into a system simulation model of realities in which events are assumed to occur or not occur as predicted from the results of the cross-impact analysis. Inputs or policies connected with the events must be determined in order to accomplish this simulation. Iterate these simulation runs for other likely futures.

(h) Incorporate the results of the cross-impact analysis and system simulation exercise as the systems analysis phase of systems engineering activities for the particular problem under consideration.

4. Inference Updating and Impact Analysis

The cross-impact analysis approach may be viewed as inference updating and information aggregation. Gettys et al. (1973) are among many who demonstrate that humans are suboptimal in the way they aggregate various pieces of information to form revised probability estimates. When a chain of events relates data and hypotheses, there is a very strong tendency to ignore all but the most dominant, or salient, chain in the hierarchy. Gettys et al. report the results of two studies which substantiate the fact that inference is greatly improved by using a problem decomposition approach and associated hierarchical inference aggregation and processing. They also report results of a study in which lack of disconfirming or negative data represented a bias that led to errors in the construction of an inference tree. The adverse effects on inference tasks of failing to seek disconfirming information have been well documented.

Schum and Kelly (1973) have developed an adjusted likelihood-ratio approach which allows inclusion of the impact of information obtained from a finite collection of unreliable sources for the case of binomial event classes. This work was extended to multinomial event classes by Schum and Pfeiffer (1973). They emphasize the importance of the independence and conditional independence relations among events and reports for obtaining tractable results.

Kelly and Barclay (1973) present a normative model for the general hierarchical inference problem. The importance of simplifying conditional independence assumptions in the analysis of hierarchical inference processes is evident.

In another seminal paper, Schum (1977) explores the effects of prior evidence, both reliable and unreliable, on the inferential impact of new evidence. He found that the extent of the conditioning or contrast effect is dependent on six factors. These give rise to a combinatorially large number of cases. He extends Bayesian hierarchical inference to include the contrast effect for several special cases of interest. The six factors that affect the extent of conditioning are:

(a) the strength of the conditional nonindependence of current and prior events;

(b) the credibility of the sources of current and prior reports;

(c) the strength of the conditional nonindependence of current and prior reports;

(d) the strength of the conditional nonindependence of reports and events (current or prior);

(e) the extent to which current and/or prior source credibility is contingent upon the hypotheses being considered; and

(f) the rareness of the events being reported.

An interesting and important extension to the hierarchical inference concept has recently been reported by Pearl (1982a). The concept of distributed Bayesian processing is used to generalize the Bayes likelihood-ratio updating rule, thereby enabling consideration of the impact on belief of a hierarchical tree structure in which each event or observable has a single direct antecedent node. When new data are received, updating of the inference structure is accomplished by local communication between each node and its neighbors, rather than by a central processor. In most Bayesian updating schemes the desired diagnostic inferences (probability of the hypothesis given the data) are computed from causal inferences (probability of the data given the hypothesis) using Bayes' rule. In Pearl's scheme, each node in the network is characterized by two probability distributions, one representing the impact of the state (node) on descendants (nodes below it and directly connected to it) and the other representing the effect of antecedents (all higher nodes) on the state. It is assumed that the impact of all higher nodes is contained in the immediately antecedent node so that the probability associated with a state is conditionally independent of the past, given the single immediate antecedent.

When a new piece of information is obtained, its effect propagates up and down through the network causing the various adjusted likelihood ratios to be updated and thereby a new equilibrium to be established. Thus, the Bayesian updating principle can be used in a distributed local network where each node need only exchange information with its immediate neighbors to update inferences. In this way a distributed network of local, autonomous processors can be used rather than a central network processor that requires a large storage capacity. We recall that the conditional independence assumption is a key concept needed to realize the distributed structure. In this sense, Pearl's work is similar to many of the previously cited works on hierarchical inference, which also employ independence assumptions in order to obtain computationally manageable results. If the independence conditions are not met, Pearl's entire scheme would need to be reformulated. The updating scheme would undoubtedly become much more complex. In particular, it would still be possible to characterize the probability at each node by the product of two conditional probabilities, one involving only conditional descendants and one involving only conditional antecedents of the node in question; considerable complexities are, however, now introduced. More extensive communication among nodes would generally be needed to perform the required updating after the acquisition of each new piece of information.

5. Bayesian Updating of Probabilistic Inferences

In this section the basic formulation of the Bayesian algorithm for updating probabilistic inferences is presented. The simplest case of hierarchical inference involving a single unreliable observer is considered. Let $\{H_i\}$ be the set of mutually exclusive and exhaustive hypotheses, $i = 1, \ldots, n$; $\{D_j\}$ be the set of possible data states, $j = 1, \ldots, m$; and $E \in \{D_j\}$ be the reported data state. Under one of the hypotheses H_i a data state D_j results and the unreliable observer reports the occurrence of data state D_k (with k possibly unequal to j). Based on this unreliable report, we wish to determine the posterior probabilities $\{P(H_i|E)\}$ of each hypothesis. We further suppose that $P(H_i)$ is the prior probability that H_i is true, $P(D_j|H_i)$ is the conditional probability of data state D_j occurring when H_i is true, and $P(E = D_k|D_j)$ is the conditional probability that the observer reports D_k occurred, when in fact D_j occurred. Next, we use Bayes' rule to obtain

$$P(H_i|E) = \frac{P(E|H_i)P(H_i)}{P(E)} = \frac{P(E|H_i)P(H_i)}{\sum_{k=1}^{n} P(E|H_k)P(H_k)}$$

Since exactly one of the data states $\{D_j\}$ occurs, we have

$$P(E|H_i) = \sum_{j=1}^{m} P(E, D_j|H_i)$$

$$P(E, D_j|H_i) = P(E|D_j, H_i) \cdot P(D_j|H_i)$$

The usual assumption is that E is conditionally independent of H_i, given the data state. Thus, if the data state is known, knowledge of the true hypothesis is irrelevant for the determination of E; that is to say,

$$P(E|D_j, H_i) = P(E|D_j) \quad (13)$$

so that we have

$$P(H_i|E) = \frac{\sum_{j=1}^{m} P(E|D_j) \cdot P(D_j|H_i)P(H_i)}{\sum_{k=1}^{n} \sum_{j=1}^{m} P(E|D_j) \cdot P(D_j|H_k)P(H_k)} \quad (14)$$

Use of this rule requires knowledge of n prior probabilities, $\{P(H_i)\}$, and $mn + m^2$ conditional probabilities, $\{P(D_j|H_i)\}$ and $\{P(E|D_j)\}$. If there are just two hypotheses, H and $\bar{H}$, Eqn. (14) reduces to the more familiar likelihood-ratio form:

$$\frac{P(H|E)}{P(\bar{H}|E)} = \frac{\sum_{j=1}^{m} P(E|D_j) \cdot P(D_j|H) \cdot P(H)}{\sum_{j=1}^{m} P(E|D_j) \cdot P(D_j|\bar{H}) \cdot P(\bar{H})} \quad (15)$$

or

$$\frac{P(H|E)}{P(\bar{H}|E)} = \Lambda \cdot \frac{P(H)}{P(\bar{H})} \quad (16)$$

where

$$\Lambda = \frac{\sum_{j=1}^{m} P(E|D_j) \cdot P(D_j|H)}{\sum_{j=1}^{m} P(E|D_j) \cdot P(D_j|\bar{H})} \quad (17)$$

In the case of a perfect observer, we have

$$P(E = D_k|D_j) = \begin{cases} 1 & \text{if } k = j \\ 0 & \text{otherwise} \end{cases}$$

so that there results

$$\frac{P(H|E = D_k)}{P(\bar{H}|E = D_k)} = \frac{P(D_k|H)}{P(D_k|\bar{H})} \frac{P(H)}{P(\bar{H})} \quad (18)$$

which is just the familiar odds-likelihood form of updating, resulting from application of Bayes' rule.

The analysis above can be extended to more complex hierarchical inference structures involving multiple levels. From the simple case considered here, it can be appreciated that the analysis and the associated computer implementation quickly become rather cumbersome. Without making liberal use of conditional independence assumptions such as Eqn. (13), the results rapidly become unwieldy. Examination of Eqn. (14) also points out the common criticism of using the formal Bayesian analysis in that the data need may be very high. All of the prior conditional probabilities must be known; the number of these grows very rapidly as larger inference nets are considered, especially if the appropriate conditional independence assumptions do not apply. Some idea of the resulting complexity may be obtained by referring to Kelly and Barclay (1973). The problems here are twofold. Even if all of the relevant data are available, storing and processing it may be extraordinarily complex computationally. Even more importantly, the relevant data may not be known, or only known imprecisely. Let us now turn our attention to these concerns.

6. Hierarchical Inference and Extensions

Inferential activities based on imprecise, incomplete, inconsistent or otherwise imperfect knowledge are becoming more important in the design, implementation and operation of systems that support enhanced human information processing. Inference is concerned with the generation of theories and hypotheses beyond those originally given. In planning and decision-making activities the information that is usually available initially is limited to allow satisfactory performance of judgement and choice. Hence, inference is an essential activity for humans, as well as for systems intended to aid humans in information-processing activities.

Several approaches for making inferences from available information have been developed, ranging from strict probabilistic Bayesian reasoning to less mathematically rigorous approaches. Analysis of systems based on these methods reveals discrepancies in the results obtained due largely to the differences in the underlying assumptions on which they are based. Quinlan (1983) contrasts several of these approaches and classifies their dissimilarities in terms of the way in which the uncertain information about propositions is represented, the assumptions that form the basis for propagating information, the control structure used for this propagation, and the treatment of inconsistent information. Sage and Botta (1983) also present a summary of contemporary research involving inference mechanisms for information processing in systems, concentrating on the extent to which these mechanisms can be Bayesian.

On the topic of inference much research exists which uses probability theory as the standard for the representation, aggregation and interpretation of information. However, while such theories have the advantage of modelling the uncertainties and imprecision present in human discourse, their semantic correspondence to natural-language expressions is questionable on occasion. A large number of studies in cognitive psychology indicate that human judgements of probability values are often inconsistent with the simple axioms of probability. A comprehensive review of these efforts can be found in Sage (1981a,b). Often these errors are of considerable magnitude and not just small deviations usually expected from intuitive, subjective assessments. Failure to follow the rules of probability is generally attributed to errors of application and errors of comprehension of such rules. An error of application exists if there is evidence that people know and accept a rule that they did not apply. If people do not recognize the validity of the rule they violated, it is called an error of comprehension. Since both types of errors are described in terms of violations of the rules of probability, we could also claim that the errors are the result of a misrepresentation of human judgements about uncertainty. An error of representation refers to the semantic correspondence between the natural-language expression and the symbolic representation and rules of aggregation used for inference. Errors of representation may result in a set of inconsistent hypotheses; hence, an inferential inconsistency may indicate an error in representation but the contrary is not true (i.e., agreement does not necessarily reflect understanding of semantic principles). Consequently, questions arise concerning how to detect and avoid errors of representation and which framework to use in modelling uncertainty and imprecision.

Inferential activities based on logical interconnection of elements in a hierarchical net or tree are called hierarchical inference. Hierarchical inference usually entails a series of inversion, aggregation and cascading processes to compute the likelihood of underlying hypotheses and observable evidence based on their logical relations. Inversion involves reversing the logical relation among elements in the network in order to calculate the desired relation more easily. In a Bayesian model, the process of inversion is represented by Bayes' theorem. When a datum D is perceived to have an impact on the occurrence of an event H, the relation between D and H is given by

$$P(H|D) = \frac{P(H)}{P(D)} P(D|H) \qquad (19)$$

Hence, the perceived effect of the likelihood of H given D is expressed in terms of the perceived effect of the likelihood of D given H. Aggregation is the task of assessing the impact of a set of data on a given hypothesis based on the immediate logical relations between the data $\{D^1, D^2, \ldots\}$ and the hypothesis H. Symbolically we have $P(H|D^1, D^2, \ldots) = R[P(H|D^1), P(H|D^2), \ldots]$ where R is the function which aggregates the local relations $P(H|D^i)$ to form the global relation $P(H|D^1, D^2, \ldots)$. Cascading is the combination of a series of immediate relations on a chain of sequential impacts to assess a global relation. For example, if a datum D is perceived to have an effect on an event E and this in turn effects H ($D \rightarrow E \rightarrow H$), then the process of cascading consists of calculating $P(H|D)$ based on the local relations $P(H|E)$ and $P(E|D)$.

The general case of hierarchical inference involves a number of processes of inversion, aggregation and cascading. A node in the hierarchical inference net represents a finite partition of exclusive and exhaustive possible states. It may be a set of hypotheses, a set of observable or unobservable events, or more generally just data.

The impact of a given state D_i on a state A_j is given by Bayes' inversion theorem as

$$P(A_j|D_i) = \frac{P(A_j)}{P(D_i)} P(D_i|A_j) \qquad (20)$$

Conditioning on the states of the intermediate node B to calculate $P(D_i|A_j)$ and then inverting and cascading the result gives us

$$P(A_j|D_i) = \frac{P(A_j)}{P(D_i)} \sum_{k=1}^{b} P(D_i|A_j, B_k) P(B_k|A_j) \qquad (21)$$

In decomposition for cascading, it is usually assumed that the relation among the states of adjacent nodes is unaffected by the occurrence of states at other nodes. In this case, the likelihood of state D_i given that B_k occurred is independent of every state A_j so $P(D_i|A_j, B_k) = P(D_i|B_k)$ and Eqn. (21) becomes for the chain of nodes $A \rightarrow C \rightarrow E$

$$P(A_j|E_1) = P(A_j) \sum_{k=1}^{c} \frac{P(C_k|E_1) P(C_k|A_j)}{P(C_k)} \qquad (22)$$

Equation (22) is sometimes referred to as the modified Bayes' theorem (Gettys and Willke 1969) and has been used in a class of procedures called probabilistic information processing (Edwards et al. 1968) to help people overcome the suboptimum behavior they show when revising probabilities of interrelated events. Use of this equation requires the assessment of large amounts of data that may be very difficult to assess intuitively in complex hierarchical inference structures. For example, the meaning of the likelihood or probability of a new state given all previous information is difficult to understand when it comprises the conjunction of a large number of states. In addition, the complexity in the processing, storing and assessment steps increases rapidly with the number of nodes in the network. This has led to the common criticism of using a formal Bayesian framework for inference (Kelly and Barclay 1973). Recent work, especially that by Pearl (1982a,b, 1983) indicates that this criticism may not be fully justified.

An interesting, efficient scheme for the propagation of beliefs or evidence in hierarchically organized inference structures has been reported by Pearl (1982a, b). The scheme relies on decomposing an inference task into a series of simpler intuitive inferences linking each stage in the hierarchy to produce a global assessment. The computation of the global assessment is simplified by reformulating the general Bayesian procedure for the hierarchically organized inference structures discussed here. Data can be communicated among adjacent nodes and used to update the information at every node throughout the network. The decomposed Bayesian processing, characteristic of this scheme, allows updating to be performed by a series of local updating processes between each node and its neighbors, rather than by central processing as in the general Bayesian framework. The likelihood of the various states of a given node depends on the entire data observed. Hence, the impact of the entire data on a given node can be decomposed into two disjoint sets of data: that obtained from the network rooted at that node, and data from the network above the node. At node A let $D_d(A)$ stand for data obtained from the network rooted at A (i.e., nodes $B^1, \ldots, B^L$ and nodes in the networks rooted on these) and let $D^u(A)$ be data obtained from nodes in the network above A (i.e., B and nodes above it, $A^1, \ldots, A^M$ and nodes rooted on these). This decomposition prescribes how information obtained from above and below some node should be combined. A series of manipulations leads to

$$P(A_i) = ag(A_i)q(A_i) \qquad (23)$$

where $g(A_i) = P(D_d(A)|A_i)$ represents the probabilistic support attributed to A_i by the nodes below it; $q(A_i) = P(A_i|D^u(A))$ represents the probabilistic support received by A_i from the nodes above it; and a is a normalization constant defined as $a = P(D_d(A)|D^u(A))^{-1}$. The value $P(A_i)$ is in fact a conditional probability conditioned on the existing state of knowledge.

Updating the values of g and q at every node in the light of new information allows for the calculation of the probability or likelihood of the state of every node. The calculation of g at a node involves only data obtained from the network rooted at that node. The data obtained from the network rooted at A are equivalent to data obtained from each of the networks rooted at nodes adjacent to A. This says that g can be calculated at a node if the g values of the nodes immediately below it and the conditional probabilities quantifying the relations between these nodes are known.

The data above A, $D^u(A)$, required to calculate $q(A_i)$, can be decomposed into two disjoint sets: $D^u(B)$ and D_d (siblings of A). Following the same reasoning as just used, we obtain a result that enables us to compute $P(A_i)$ and $P(B_j)$ without requiring normalization. These results indicate that information needed to perform the local processing can be represented at each node by assessed conditional probabilities relating adjacent nodes in the hierarchy and computed values of g and $P(\cdot)$ at each node.

To initialize the inference net for propagation, we need the assessed conditional probabilities at each node. At an observational node every state is equally likely to occur in the absence of any information, hence $g(\cdot)$ is set to 1 at every observational node. From this, the value of g at every other node can be calculated. From the prior probability at the top node and the computed values of g, the probability of the states of each node can be calculated. Once the net is initialized, the occurrence of a particular state at an observational node will cause g to be updated. This information is then propagated up to update the g values of all other nodes and then down to update the likelihood of the states of each node.

In contrast with strict Bayesian procedures (Edwards et al. 1968, Gettys and Willke 1969), Pearl's scheme requires only the assessment of a piror probability for the node at the top of the hierarchy; that is, the last stage of the hierarchical inference structure usually representing the hypotheses being studied. The probabilities of all other stages in the structure are uniquely determined by the assessed conditional probabilities at each node, thus reducing somewhat the amount and complexity of prior information required. On the other hand, Pearl's work relies on stricter independence assumptions in order to obtain computationally tractable results, and also requires prior knowledge about the distribution of the underlying hypothesis being studied.

The "divide and conquer" philosophy pervades the entire Bayesian approach to information processing, including inference and impact analysis. The behavioral basis that potentially argues against this approach comprises the many observations stating that humans do not, in general, aggregate probabilistic information in anything like an optimal fashion. Burns and Pearl (1981) have succinctly put this notion into perspective. They observe that decision support technologies are based upon the conviction that synthetic inferences based upon holistic aggregation of many fragmentary judgements are superior to direct wholistic judgements. They point out that the following three major decision-aiding techniques involve building up inferences from component parts based upon causal relationships:

(a) cascading—chaining a sequence of cause–effect relationships to form a relation;

(b) aggregation—combining solutions to subsets of a problem to form the overall problem solution; and

(c) inversion—the use of causal linkages to arrive at desired diagnostic inferences (i.e., as in Bayes' rule).

These authors conducted an experiment to determine whether people are better at diagnostic or causal inference. Their results do not support the presumed superiority of causal inference over diagnostic inference. Neither approach seems uniquely better for encoding knowledge about common experiences. Burns and Pearl conclude that care should be used when applying the "divide and conquer" philosophy. They state that forced transformations from diagnostic to causal judgements, when they are performed at the expense of conceptual simplicity, may lead people to inferences of lower quality than those that would result from direct, wholistic, skill-based judgements.

It has often been remarked that Bayesian analysis makes no distinction between uncertain knowledge and imprecise knowledge, and that the same representational system is used to represent probability and possibility. A related major criticism of Bayesian approaches is the need to identify point values about the probability of events. Usually, a point-value assessment of the probability of an event is an overstatement about our actual knowledge of the likelihood of occurrence of that particular event. In response to the need to represent the imprecision of Bayesian probability values, Dempster (1967) utilized the concept of lower and upper probabilities to deal with the subjective imprecision of uncertainty measures. Shafer (1976, 1981) presents a comprehensive exposition of this novel idea as well as extensions to the theory of inference based on the concept of upper and lower probabilities. The basic idea of this concept is that instead of representing the probability of an event A by a point value $P(A)$, it may be bounded by a subinterval of $[0, 1]$; that is, the exact probability $P(A)$ may be unknown but bounded. This kind of representation has solid grounds in the Dempster–Shafer theory of basic probability and for that reason has received considerable recent attention. The article *Knowledge Support Systems: Uncertain Information Processing* discusses these alternative representational systems in some detail.

7. Logical Reasoning Models and Inference

In many ways, models for logical reasoning have much in common, particularly structurally, with inference analysis models. Of particular interest here is the work of Toulmin *et al.* (1979) in that they have constructed an explicit structured model of logical reasoning that is suited for analytical enquiry and computer implementation. The model is sufficiently general for it to be used to represent logical reasoning in a number of application areas.

Starting from the assumption that whenever we make a claim there must be some grounds on which to base our conclusion, Toulmin states that our thoughts are generally directed from the "grounds" to the "claim." The grounds and the claim are statements that express facts and values. As a means of stating observed patterns of stating a claim, there must be a reason that can be identified to connect the grounds and the claim. This connection is called the "warrant," and it is the warrant that gives the grounds–claim connection its logical validity.

We say that the grounds support the claim on the basis of the existence of a warrant that explains the connection between the grounds and the claim. It is easy to relate the structure of these basic elements with the process of inference, whether statistical, deductive or inductive. The warrants are the set of rules of inference, and the grounds and claim are the set of well-defined propositions or hypotheses. It will be only the sequence and procedures, which are used to come up with the three basic elements and their structure in a logical fashion, that will determine the type of inference that is used.

Sometimes, in the course of reasoning about an issue, it is not enough that the warrant will be the absolute reason to believe the claim on the basis of the grounds. For that, Toulmin allows for further "backing" which, in his representation, supports the warrant. It is the backing that provides the reliability, in terms of truth, associated with the use of the warrant. The relationship here is analogous to the way in which the grounds support the claim. An argument will be valid and will give the claim solid support only if the warrant is relied upon and is relevant to the particular case under examination. The concept of logical validity seems to imply that we can only make a claim when both the warrant and the grounds are certain. However, imprecision and uncertainty in the form of exceptions to the rules or a low degree of certainty in both the grounds and the warrant does not prevent us on occasions from making a "hedge" or a vague claim. Very commonly, we must arrive at conclusions on the basis of less than perfect evidence; we put those claims forward not with absolute and irrefutable truth but rather with some doubt or degree of speculation.

To allow for these cases, Toulmin adds "modal qualifiers" and "possible rebuttals" to his framework for logical reasoning. Modal qualifiers refer to the strength or weakness with which a claim is made. In essence every argument has a certain modality. Its place in the structure presented so far must reflect the generality of the warrant in connecting the grounds to the claim, and also with the condition of validity of the set of facts as grounds. Possible rebuttals, on the other hand, are exceptions to the rules. Although modal qualifiers serve the purpose of weakening or strengthening the validity of a claim, there may still be conditions that invalidate either the grounds or the warrants, and this will result in the deactivation of the link between the claim and the grounds. These cases are represented by the possible rebuttals.

The resulting structure of logical reasoning provides a very useful framework for the study of human information-processing activities (Sage 1981a). The order in which the six elements of logical reasoning have been presented serves only the purpose of illustrating their function and interdependence in the structure of an argument about a specific issue. It does not represent any normative pattern of argument formation. In fact, due to the dynamic nature of human reasoning, the concept formation and framing that results in a particular structure may occur in different ways. The six-element model of logical reasoning is shown in Fig. 4.

The effects of various forms of inquiry upon issues of representation and detection of judgemental errors in human information processing have been investigated (Lagomasino and Sage, 1985a, b, c) using this structure of rational argument. The frameworks for Bayesian inference just discussed require probability values as primary inputs. Since most events of interest are unique or little is known about their relative frequencies of occurrence, the assessment of probability values usually requires human judgement. Substantial psychological research has shown that people are unable to elicit probability values consistent with the rules of probabilities and that they are suboptimum in revising probability assessment when new information is obtained.

Kahneman and Tversky (1982) have shown that dominance of causal over diagnostic information exists in assessing conditional probabilities. They concluded, in a series of experiments, that if some information has both causal and diagnostic implications, then people, instead of weighting the causal and diagnostic impacts of the evidence, apparently assess conditional probabilities primarily in terms of the direct causal effect of the impacts. Thus, if A is perceived to be the cause of B, people will give higher probabilities to $P(B|A)$ than to $P(A|B)$. Burns and Pearl (1981) conducted a study to test the validity of judgements made by these two forms of reasoning. Thus, they investigated whether causal or diagnostic judgement is a more natural way of encoding knowledge about everyday experiences. Their results demonstrated that neither one was found to be more accurate than the other. In a similar study, Moskowitz and Sarin (1983) reported that individuals found it easier and showed more confidence in assessing $P(A|B)$ if B is causal to A.

This apparent contradiction of results may be explained by the difference in the contingency in which the experiments were performed, and suggests that the choice of which form of inference to invoke depends more on the level of familiarity of the observer with the task at hand and the cognitive style which determines the way in which the knowledge was originally perceived. Most structuring procedures for decision making rely on the "divide and conquer" approach under the assumption that judgement is improved when a complex, ill-defined problem is decomposed, analyzed and solved by a set of smaller, well-defined problems. The findings of these studies, aside from having implications on the validity of the "divide and conquer" approach, imply that the form of representation of judgements used should correspond with the meaning of the judgements assessed.

Falk and Bar-Hillel (1979) have recognized the importance of distinguishing between probabilistic and logical support. Probabilistic support refers to the increased in likelihood of the occurrence of an event A given that another event B has occurred. That is, A supports B if $P(B|A) > P(B)$. Logical support exhibits the relation of implication between two premises, denoted $A \to B$, that fails to hold only if the first is true and the second is false. Logical support is transitive; if $A \to B$ and $B \to C$, then $A \to C$. When $A \to B$, it is also true that $\tilde{B} \to \tilde{A}$. With these definitions, the distinctions between probabilistic and logical support should be apparent. Logical support does not imply conditions similar to those that follow from probabilistic support. $A \to B$ is logically equivalent to $\tilde{B} \to \tilde{A}$, but does not say anything about the truth of $\tilde{A} \to \tilde{B}$ or $B \to A$. Likewise, probabilistic support is not transitive and logical support must be transitive. A major point in this distinction that arises here is when to apply these two methods of representation in inferential activities. We are concerned with this issue because, as previous research has shown, the method used to represent human judgement may influence its validity and consistency. Suppes (1970) has provided an analysis of causality based on probabilistic support relations that finds difficulties in distinguishing spurious from genuine causes as well as direct from indirect causes. After an attempt to overcome these difficulties by making modifications to Suppes' theory, Ottes (1981) concludes that it is impossible to give a detailed

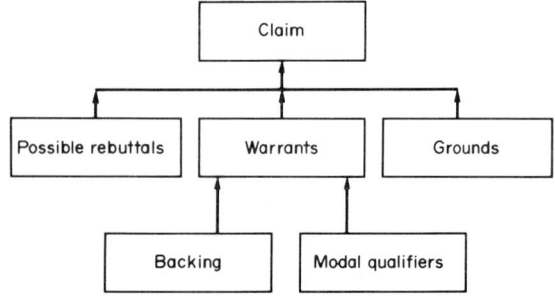

Figure 4
The Toulmin six-element model of logical reasoning

account of causation using only probabilistic relations. He points out that the belief that a positive cause raises the probability of its effect, fundamental to Suppes' theory, is flawed. He illustrates this point with examples in which an event A is clearly caused by another event B and yet most people believe that $P(A|B) < P(A)$.

It is especially important here to note that we can ascribe uncertainty to the truth of logical support by referring to the probability by which A implies B, $P(A \rightarrow B)$. The importance of this will concern us next in the development of a general framework for inference. Much research has been concerned with developing a framework of inference suitable for assessing and structuring complex problems that derives from the logic of reasoning of Toulmin and the calculus of probabilities to make inferences on the likelihood of the events or premises that comprise the inference structure. Assessments by the decision maker in the form of logical support relations among the events are used to structure the problem, and assessments in the form of set-inclusion inequalities among the events and their relations are combined using the probability calculus to draw inferences.

The framework and process for inference support developed here is applicable to a general class of networks of interrelated propositions. Specifically, it can be applied to finite connected networks where the number of propositions is finite and where every pair of distinct propositions is joined by at least one chain of relations. We have developed a procedure that describes the information-processing elements involved in the structuring and analysis of an issue within this framework. The information-processing functions associated with the use of the framework for inference described here involve four steps: initial problem framing, hypothesis generation, parameter value assessment, and hypothesis evaluation and situation assessment.

The intent of the first step is to capture those elements and relations that constitute an issue and to represent them in a form which is suitable for inference. The inference network developed here is not necessarily hierarchical as contrasted with the case of Bayesian inference. We are able to deal with structures that correspond to a very general type of inference network. Nodes in the network represent the propositions of interest in the particular issue. Inferential links between propositions are defined in terms of the set of consistency-relational equations, including the set of consistency relations and any other assessed relations between the propositions at each node. The probability value of the propositions at each node is underconstrained and acquisition of information about the relation between the nodes is the primary means of further constraining the probability values of the propositions at each node.

Given the assessed initial problem frame, the task of hypothesis generation involves the generation of reasonable hypotheses that are based on situational perception and information needed for the task at hand. In most cases this involves the specification of alternative hypotheses at each node. Ideally, the set of hypotheses under consideration at each node should be mutually exclusive and exhaustive. This task also involves the selection of the basic premises and possible rebuttals relevant for each inferential link.

The parameter value identification step provides for the continual assessment of the parameters of the inference model. This includes the assessment of probability values of the propositions at each node as well as the probability values representing the uncertain logical relations at each inferential link. These assessments can be related and represented imprecisely in the form of bounded intervals and/or linear inequalities on the set of parameters. Achieving the task of parameter value assessment with minimal imprecision will depend strongly on the quality of the information available and the person's perception and familiarity with the task at hand.

The hypothesis evaluation and situation assessment step involves probability categorization, over a set of alternative hypotheses, of the probable situations as captured by the information that is provided to the inference model. Given the set of consistency-relational equations for each link in the inference network, we can calculate the probability values for the propositions at each node. These probability values will usually be stated in the form of bounded intervals and linear inequalities. If information which is more precise is required, further assessments of the relations and propositions in the network must be performed. This suggests the generation of alternative hypotheses and the assessment of parameter values which are more precise. The information-processing tasks required in the use of the framework for inference based on logical reasoning describe an iterative process suitable for situations where knowledge is ill-defined or imperfectly described. The objective of this portion of the discussion has been to suggest various approaches for inference based on imprecise knowledge. We have discussed a new approach for inference based on logical support relations that differs considerably from Bayesian approaches which rely on probabilistic support relations. This approach has the interesting feature of being reasonably simple computationally, capable of working with a general class of inference networks, not relying on idealistic independence assumptions, and not having to make a clear distinction between hypothetical and evidential types of information.

8. Complications Affecting Inference and Impact Analysis

As noted in Sect. 6, there are a number of complications which, in practice, may significantly affect our ability to use unmodified Bayesian analysis algorithms. These concern such issues as unreliable observations, potential computational complexity of the Bayesian algorithms, human cognitive biases, imprecise knowledge or lack of knowledge (as opposed to uncertain knowledge) and the need to use causal as well as diagnostic inference rules.

Schum and Pfeiffer (1973) consider the problem of combining reports from a group of unreliable observers in order to decide which of several alternative hypotheses or states of nature is true. The observers are not allowed to collaborate; it is further assumed that the observer's reports are conditionally independent given the existing data state, which is itself probabilistically dependent on the underlying state of nature. The authors define a likelihood ratio that is influenced by sensor reliability and data impact, as well as by the pattern of sensor reports. A number of studies are cited, including those by Snapper and Fryback (1971) and Schum et al. (1973), which demonstrate that unaided humans typically fail to degrade the impact of evidence supplied by an observer by an amount consistent with the unreliability of the observer. Therefore, it may be necessary to use objective procedures to assess the impact of data, and associated uncertainty, before any procedure is used to aggregate the results of the individual observers. Otherwise, an algorithmic aggregation procedure, given the inflated impact of evidence reported by individuals, may result in unwarranted extreme inferences. It should be noted that the results in the Schum et al. paper depend very strongly on the conditional independence assumption for computational tractability. If this assumption does not hold, the approach is still valid, but results quickly become unwieldy.

There are many potential sources of incoherence in individual estimates of probabilities, or in the aggregation of individual estimates to form a group estimate. If we contemplate the use of Bayesian processing schemes, it is necessary that a set of mutually exclusive and exhaustive hypotheses be identified. Precision in the formulation or framing of hypotheses is necessary to accomplish the former. We can often use formal approaches to determine whether or not a set of hypotheses is mutually exclusive, but it will often not be possible to determine whether or not we have identified all reasonable hypotheses. Forecasts based on a presumed set of exhaustive hypotheses have context validity only within that set of hypotheses. It is always necessary to ensure that what has been omitted in issue framing and hypothesis generation is not more important than what has been included.

Even if hypotheses are coherently formulated, there may exist numerous difficulties associated with the estimation of probabilities and likelihood ratios. There are a number of information-processing biases to which humans are prone. Reprints of much of the seminal literature concerning cognitive heuristics and information-processing biases are presented in Kahneman et al. (1982). The article *Human Information Processing* discusses many of these biases. One particular difficulty, for example, which greatly affects information analysis, is the tendency of people to be concerned with the probability of obtaining some observed data conditioned upon some hypothesis, $P(D|H)$, but not to be concerned with whether or not the probability of obtaining the data under the null hypothesis, $P(D|\bar{H})$, might not be greater.

Another difficulty occurs in sequential multievent situations in which conditional probabilities are needed. Moskowitz and Sarin (1983) have shown that people are often not especially bothered by assessing conditional probabilities that violate the probability calculus, such as assuming that $P(A|B) > P(A)$ and $P(B|A) < P(B)$. They propose the use of a joint probability table as a judgemental aid to improving assessments of higher-order conditional probabilities. Approaches such as the one due to Moskowitz and Sarin (1983), and that of Brown and Lindley (1982), are potentially very useful in enhancing the ability of people to obtain coherence and consistency in their estimates and forecasts.

Often people will make a meta-inference concerning their own knowledge. The results of this meta-inference will suggest a lack of knowledge and a requirement to reason from this incomplete knowledge (Collins et al. 1975). Often, lack of knowledge relative to an assertion decreases a person's estimate of the likelihood that the assertion is true. The research of Gentner and Collins (1981) has shown that the more important an assertion and the more expert the person who lacks knowledge, the more pronounced the lack of knowledge will be, as indicated by a decrease in the estimated likelihood of the assertion.

There are many interesting and relevant issues to be explored in human inference analysis and the use of support procedures to aid this. A recent definitive work by Schum (1988) describes much of our presently available knowledge.

See also: Decision Analysis; Decision Support Systems; Evidentiary Reasoning and Human Information Processing; Human Information Processing

Bibliography

Brown R, Lindley D 1982 Improving judgment by reconciling incoherence. *Theory Decis.* **14**(2), 113–32
Burns M, Pearl J 1981 Causal and diagnostic inferences: A comparison of validity. *Organ. Behav. Hum. Perform.* **28**, 379–94
Collins A, Warnock E H, Aiello N, Miller M L 1975 Reasoning from incomplete knowledge. In: Bobrow D, Collins A (eds.) *Representation and Understanding.* Academic Press, New York, pp. 383–416
Dempster A P 1967 Upper and lower probabilities induced by a multivalued mapping. *Ann. Math. Stat.* **38**, 325–39
Dubois D, Prade H 1988 Default reasoning and possibility theory. *Artif. Intell.* **35**(2), 243–57
Duda R O, Hart P E, Nilsson N 1976 Subjective Bayesian

methods for rule-based inference systems. *Proc. National Computer Conf.*, Vol. 45. AFIPS, Arlington, Virginia, pp. 1075–82

Edwards W, Phillips L D, Hays W L, Goodman B C 1968 Probabilistic information processing systems: Design and evaluation. *IEEE Trans. Syst. Sci. Cybern.* **4**, 248–65

Enzer S 1970 A case study using forecasting as a decision-making aid. *Futures* **2**(4), 341–62

Falk R, Bar-Hillel M 1979 *Probabilistic Dependence Between Events*, Hebrew University of Jerusalem Report. Hebrew University of Jerusalem, Jerusalem

Gentner D, Collins A 1981 Studies of inference from lack of knowledge. *Mem. Cognit.* **9**(4), 343–43

Gettys C, Michel C, Steiger J, Kelly C, Peterson C 1973 Multiple-stage probabilistic information processing. *Organ. Behav. Hum. Perform.* **10**, 374–87

Gettys C, Willke T A 1969 The application of Bayes' theorem when the true data state is uncertain. *Organ. Behav. Hum. Perform.* **4**, 125–41

Gevarter W B 1984 *Artificial Intelligence, Expert Systems, Computer Vision and Natural Language Processing*. Noyes Data Corp., Park Ridge, New Jersey

Gordon T J, Hayward H 1968 Initial experiences with cross-impact matrix method of forecasting. *Futures* **1**(2), 100–16

Hogarth R M, Makridakis M 1981 Forecasting and planning: An evaluation. *Manage. Sci.* **27**(2), 115–38

Ishizuka M 1983 Inference methods based on extended Dempster–Shafer theory for problems with uncertainty/fuzziness. *New Generation Comput.* **1**, 159–68

Kahneman D, Slovic P, Tversky A (eds.) 1982 *Judgements Under Uncertainty: Heuristics and Biases*. Cambridge University Press, New York

Kahneman D, Tversky A 1982 Variants of uncertainty. *Cognition* **11**(2), 143–57

Kelly C W, Barclay S 1973 A general Bayesian model for heirarchical inference. *Organ. Behav. Hum. Perform.* **10**, 338–403

Lagomasino A, Sage A P 1985a An interactive inquiry system. *Large Scale Syst.* **9**, 231–44

Lagomasino A, Sage A P 1985b Imprecise knowledge representation in inferential activities. In: Gupta M M, Kandel A, Bandler W, Kiszka J B (eds.) *Approximate Reasoning in Expert Systems*. North-Holland, Amsterdam, pp. 473–97

Lagomasino A, Sage A P 1985c Representation and interpretation of information for decision support with imperfect knowledge. *Large Scale Syst.* **9**(2), 169–81

Moskowitz H, Sarin R K 1983 Improving the consistency of conditional probability assessments for forecasting and decision making. *Manage. Sci.* **29**(6), 735–49

Ottes R 1981 A critique of Suppes' theory of causality. *Synthese* **48**(2), 167–89

Pearl J 1982a *Distributed Bayesian Processing for Belief Maintenance in Heirarchical Inference Systems*, UCLA Cognitive Systems Laboratory Report UCLA-ENG-CSL-82-11. University of California, Los Angeles, California

Pearl J 1982b Reverend Bayes on inference engines: A distributed heirarchical approach. *Proc. AAAI Conf.* American Association for Artificial Intelligence, Menlo Park, California

Pearl J 1983 *Heuristics: Partially Informed Strategies for Computer Problem Solving*. Addison–Wesley, Reading, Massachusetts

Pearl J 1986 On evidential reasoning in a hierarchy of hypotheses. *Artif. Intell.* **28**, 9–15

Quinlan J R 1983 Inferno: A cautious approach to uncertain inference. *Comput. J.* **26**(3), 255–66

Rescher N, Manor R 1970 On inference from inconsistent premises. *Theory Decis.* **1**, 179–217

Sage A P 1977 *Methodology For Large Scale Systems*. McGraw–Hill, New York

Sage A P 1981a Behavioral and organizational considerations in the design of information systems and processes for planning and decision support. *IEEE Trans. Syst., Man Cybern.* **11**(9), 640–78

Sage A P 1981b Hierarchical inference in large scale systems. *Proc. IFAC World Congr.* Pergamon, Oxford, pp. 1–9

Sage A P 1987 *System Design for Human Interaction*. IEEE Press, New York

Sage A P, Botta R 1983 On human information processing and its enhancement using knowledge-based systems. *Large Scale Syst.* **5**, 208–23

Sage A P, Lagomasino A 1984 Knowledge representation and man machine dialogue. In: Rouse W B (ed.) *Advances in Man–Machine Systems Research*. JAI Press, Greenwich, Connecticut, pp. 223–60

Sage A P, White C C III 1984 ARIADNE: A knowledge-based interactive system for decision support. *IEEE Trans. Syst., Man Cybern.* **14**(1)

Schum D A 1977 Contrast effects in inference: On the conditioning of current evidence by prior evidence. *Organ. Behav. Hum. Perform.* **18**, 217–53

Schum D A 1988 *Evidence and Inference for the Intelligence Analysts*, Vols. 1 and 2. University Press of America, Lanham, Maryland

Schum D A, Du Charme W M, De Fitts K E 1973 Research on human multiphase probabilistic inference processes. *Organ. Behav. Hum. Perform.* **10**, 318–48

Schum D A, Kelly D W 1973 A problem in cascaded inference: Determining the inferential impact of confirming and conflicting reports from several unreliable sources. *Organ. Behav. Hum. Perform.* **10**, 404–23

Schum D A, Pfeiffer P E 1973 Observer reliability and human inference. *IEEE Trans. Reliab.* **22**, 170–76

Shafer G 1976 *A Mathematical Theory of Evidence*. Princeton University Press, Princeton, New Jersey

Shafer G 1981 Constructive probability. *Synthese* **48**, 1–60

Snapper K, Fryback D 1981 Inferences on unreliable reports. *J. Exp. Psychol.* **87**, 401–4

Suppes P 1970 *A Probabilistic Theory of Causality*. North-Holland, Amsterdam

Toulmin S, Reike R, Janik A 1979 *An Introduction to Reasoning*. MacMillan, New York

von Winterfeldt D, Edwards W 1986 *Decision Analysis and Behavioral Research*. Cambridge University Press, New York

Wolfenson M, Fine T L 1982 Bayes-like decision making with upper and lower probabilities. *J. Am. Stat. Assoc.*, Theory and Methods Section **77**, 80–88

A. P. Sage
[George Mason University, Fairfax, Virginia, USA]

Information Laws of Systems

Since the concepts of systems and of information are both very rich, it will be impossible to mention all that is noteworthy about their intersection in this article.

Information Laws of Systems

We will concentrate on systems understood abstractly as collections of interacting parts or variables, on information as understood in the context of mathematical information theory, and on information laws which can be expressed in a mathematical form.

1. Use of Information Theory in Systems Analysis

Shannon's information theory (Shannon and Weaver 1949) was originally created for the purpose of studying the communication of messages from one point to another; its focus is the question "How can the constraint between the two variables X (message sent) and Y (message received) be measured and maximized?" Shannon's theory as generalized to N dimensions (McGill 1954, Ashby 1965) is a powerful tool for the analysis of constraints and relations in multivariable systems. This comes about because in any system of several variables interacting in a lively way, some variables exert influences on others. These influences are reflected statistically as nonindependence of the variables involved; that is, as a constraint between them. To the extent that variables or subsystems are not independent, they are "in communication" with each other, and N-dimensional information theory (NDIT) can be used to analyze this nonindependence, and thereby to measure the degree of mutual constraint between the variables. The fluctuation of values taken by any variable can be viewed as a message it sends—a flow of information about itself to all other parts of the system which are "listening." This view of systems as networks of information flow leads to novel quantitative conclusions about system behavior.

NDIT is a good mathematical tool for investigating the structure of systems, and for this it has several advantages over other statistical techniques of systems analysis. It is applicable to a very wide class of systems, both linear and nonlinear, metric or nonmetric, discrete or continuous; the measures of NDIT possess additivity properties which allow the convenient decomposition of system constraints and which make possible a calculus of system structure; it is well suited to analysis of systems with many variables; and it allows measurements of rates of constraint (i.e., constraint per unit time between dynamic variables, with past history taken into account).

2. Notation

In order to present the information laws of systems in a mathematical form, it is necessary to introduce a system of notation and to briefly summarize the basic definitions of NDIT.

A system is commonly defined as a set of variables together with a relation holding over those variables. (The relation is discussed in Sect. 10.) We will represent a system simply as an ordered set of variables: $S = \{X_1, X_2, \ldots, X_n\}$. Because of context, no confusion results from failing to distinguish such a set from the list of its elements. Accordingly the symbols S and $X_1, X_2, \ldots, X_n$ will be used interchangeably, and an analogous convention will be followed for subsystems (i.e., ordered subsets of the variables of S).

In general, the system S affects and is affected by its environment E (variables which are relevant but are not in S). Those variables X in S which can be directly observed from its environment constitute output variables, denoted $S_o = X_1, X_2, \ldots, X_k$. The remaining X in S are internal variables, denoted $S_{int} = X_l, X_m, \ldots, X_n$. Thus, using "=" for equivalence and commas for set union and also for demarcation of list elements,

$$S = S_o, S_{int} = X_1, X_2, \ldots, X_k, X_l, X_m, \ldots, X_n$$

S can be partitioned into N disjoint subsystems S^i ($i = 1, 2, \ldots, N$). Each S^i receives input E^i from its environment (all variables not in S^i) and includes a set $S_o^i = X_1^i, X_2^i, \ldots, X_{k_i}^i$ of directly observable or output variables and a set $S_{int}^i = X_l^i, X_m^i, \ldots, X_{n_i}^i$ of internal variables. (Note that a system variable may be in S_o^i while not in S_o.) The subsystems can be partitioned similarly.

The S^i fall into two classes, those which contain one or more variables in S_o and those which do not, called, respectively, output subsystems, denoted $S_{out} = S^1, S^2, \ldots, S^K$, and internal subsystems, denoted $S_{int} = S^L, S^M, \ldots, S^N$. Thus $S = S_{int}, S_{out}$. Of course any of these sets may be empty.

3. N-Dimensional Information Theory

The basic informational quantity associated with a discrete variable X is its entropy $H(X)$, which is a function of the probability distribution on X as follows:

$$H(X) = -\sum_X p(x) \log_2 p(x)$$

where the summation is over all the values x taken by X. $H(X)$ measures the average unexpectedness of the values x, the average amount of uncertainty associated with X, or the average information one obtains when informed of the value taken by X on an arbitrary occasion. If X has a finite number m of values, $H(X)$ falls in the interval $[0, \log_2(m)]$, low values indicating that $p(x)$ is concentrated and high values that it is diffuse. The entropy is often called the "uncertainty" since the higher the value of $H(X)$ the more uncertain one is about the value which will be taken by X on a typical occasion. The generalization of the definition of entropy to cover sets of variables, such as S, is obvious:

$$H(S) = -\sum_S p(s) \log_2 p(s)$$

where the summation is over all possible (vector) values s of $S = X_1, X_2, \ldots, X_n$ and $p(s)$ is the distribution on the n-tuples s of S. $H(S)$ is the uncertainty of S when it is viewed as a single, vector-valued variable.

Conditional entropies may be defined through conditional probabilities but are more easily defined through (unconditional) entropies as follows:

$$H_{S^1}(S^2) = H(S^1, S^2) - H(S^1)$$

$H_{S^1}(S^2)$ measures the average uncertainty of S^2 which remains for one who knows S^1; i.e., the variability of S^2 which is independent of S^1. $H_{S^1}(S^2)$ falls in the interval $[0, H(S^2)]$, being zero if S^2 is determined by S^1 in the sense that $p(s^2|s^1) = 0$ or 1 for all values s^2 of S^2, and being maximum if S^2 is independent of S^1 in the sense that $p(s^2|s^1) = p(s^2)$ for all s^1.

All entropies and conditional entropies are non-negative. If the definition of conditional entropy is rearranged it illustrates the very important additivity property of the entropy function:

$$H(S^1, S^2) = H(S^1) + H_{s^1}(S^2)$$

which when applied recursively leads to a chain rule for entropy:

$$H(S) = H(X_1) + H_{X_1}(X_2) + \cdots + H_{X_1 X_2 \ldots X_{n-1}}(X_n)$$

which may be interpreted as partitioning the uncertainty of S into the uncertainty about X_1, the uncertainty about X_2 which remains after knowledge of $X_1, \ldots$, and the uncertainty of X_n which remains after knowledge of $X_1, \ldots, X_{n-1}$. It is a consequence of the chain rule and the nature of conditioning that $H_{S^i}(S^i, S^j) = H_{S^i}(S^j)$, a useful simplification. Of course the above chain rule may be applied to any subset S^i of S.

The amount by which two variables are related is measured by the transmission between them, denoted $T(X_i : X_j)$ and defined by

$$T(X_i : X_j) = H(X_i) + H(X_j) - H(X_i, X_j)$$
$$= H(X_i) - H_{X_j}(X_i)$$
$$= H(X_j) - H_{X_i}(X_j)$$

The transmission is symmetric and measures the amount by which the joint uncertainty $H(X_i, X_j)$ is smaller than it would be if X_i and X_j were independent (the first form), or the amount by which knowledge of one variable reduces uncertainty about the other (the last two forms). The transmission is a measure of relatedness, constraint or coordination between variables, which underlies its usefulness in systems science. $T(X_i : X_j)$ falls in the interval $[0, \min(H(X_i), H(X_j))]$, being zero if and only if X_i and X_j are statistically independent, and being maximum if and only if one variable determines the other. Generalizing the definition to n dimensions,

$$T(X_i : X_j : \ldots : X_n) = \sum_{i=1}^{n} H(X_i) - H(X_1, X_2, \ldots, X_n)$$

defines the transmission between n variables. This transmission, henceforth abbreviated $T(:S)$, measures the total amount of relatedness, constraint or mutual coordination in a system of n variables and is an upper bound on all NDIT measures of system structure. A chain rule for transmissions resembles the chain rule for entropies:

$$T(:S) = T(X_1 : X_2) + T(X_1, X_2 : X_3) + \cdots$$
$$\cdots + T(X_1, X_2, \ldots, X_{n-1} : X_n)$$

The generalization of this for sets of variables is:

$$T(S^1 : S^2 : \ldots : S^N) = T(S^1 : S^2)$$
$$+ T(S^1, S^2 : S^3) + \cdots + T(S^1, S^2, \ldots, S^{N-1} : S^N)$$

This transmission is a measure of the constraint between the subsystems of S considered as integral units. Another definition for the same quantity follows by an obvious generalization of the definition of $T(:S)$, as follows:

$$T(S^1 : S^2 : \ldots : S^N) = \sum_{i=1}^{N} H(S^i) - H(S^1, S^2, \ldots, S^N).$$

Conditional transmissions such as $T_{S^1}(S^2 : S^3 : S^4)$ are defined from similar unconditional transmissions, by conditioning all terms on the same variable or set of variables. For example,

$$T_{X_1, S^2}(X_2 : S^3) = H_{X_1, S^2}(X_2)$$
$$+ H_{X_1, S^2}(S^3) - H_{X_1, S^2}(X_2, S^3)$$

All transmissions and conditional transmissions are nonnegative.

A third quantity of NDIT, interaction (Q), is defined for three variables by

$$Q(X_1, X_2, X_3) = T_{X_1}(X_2, X_3) - T(X_2 : X_3)$$

(although some authors reverse the signs in this definition) and by two other forms which are symmetrical by rotation of subscripts. Although Q appears in the literature and was once thought to be useful for structural analysis, it has since been discredited (Krippendorff 1980) owing to difficulties in its interpretation arising from the fact that it is not nonnegative. It will not be further pursued here.

Any identity of NDIT also leads to another identity by uniformly conditioning (subscripting) every term in the identity on the same variable and where necessary deleting redundant (duplicate) subscripts. The converse operation (cancelling uniform subscripts) does not necessarily yield an identity. Identities of NDIT are useful because they correspond closely to hypotheses of system structure, as will be discussed below.

4. Rate Definitions for NDIT

If the variables X_i represent successive temporal samples of a dynamical variable X, then the entropy rate $H'(X)$, measuring the uncertainty of X per unit time or the amount of information conveyed by X per unit time, is defined as

$$H'(X) = \lim_{k \to \infty} H(X_1, X_2, \ldots, X_k)/k$$

Information Laws of Systems

Joint entropy rates are defined by replacing X_i by S^i, a set of dynamical variables. The transmission rate $T'(X_1:X_2:\ldots:X_n)$, abbreviated $T'(:S)$ henceforth, representing the dynamical constraint between n dynamical variables is

$$T'(:S) = \sum H'(X_i) - H'(S)$$

It is clearly of the same form as the definition for the mutual constraint $T(:S)$ given earlier. The definitions for rates of conditional entropy and transmission are likewise of the same forms given earlier. In rate definitions, as elsewhere, any X_i can be replaced by a set S^i of dynamical variables. Any identity of NDIT leads to a corresponding identity involving rates by simply interpreting the variables in it as dynamical variables and replacing H by H' and T by T'.

5. Channel Capacity and Constraint Capacity

To every physical system with dynamical input X_i and output X_j there corresponds a finite channel capacity (Shannon and Weaver 1949), which is an upper bound on the rate at which information can be passed through the system, called the transmission rate. This channel capacity is defined by max $T'(X_i:X_j)$, where the maximum is over all possible inputs X_i. This standard definition can be generalized by replacing variables X_i and X_j by sets S^i and S^j, or in NDIT by extending the dimensionality to define constraint capacity as max $T'(:S)$.

It is possible for the output entropy rate $H'(Y)$ of a system to exceed the transmission rate $T'(X:Y)$, where X is the input variable, but only if the system generates information internally, since

$$H'(Y) = T'(X:Y) + H'_X(Y)$$

and the last term, representing internally generated information, is zero for deterministic systems; i.e., those for which the output sequence is determined by the input sequence and the initial system state.

6. Information Laws of Finite State Machines

Any finite state machine (FSM) is a loser of information; that is, from knowledge of its output sequence it is impossible in general to deduce its input sequence. This can be expressed as follows:

$H'(\text{input}) = H'(\text{output})$
$\qquad + H'_{\text{output}}(\text{state}) + H'_{\text{output,state}}(\text{input})$

This formulation indicates that the information rate at the input equals the information rate at the output plus two nonnegative terms indicating information losses. Similarly, from knowledge of the state and output sequence it is impossible in general to deduce the input sequence

$$H'(\text{input}) = H'(\text{state, output}) + H'_{\text{state,output}}(\text{input})$$

where the third term represents the nonnegative loss.

Although FSMs lose information, all of the information in the output sequence can be used to reduce the uncertainty of the input sequence: T' (input:output) measures the rate of this reduction.

All of the above statements also apply to arbitrarily interconnected collection of FSMs. Such networks may be characterized by graph-theoretic means and the information flows within the network analyzed in terms of channel capacities (Elias et al. 1956).

An FSM with no input is also a loser of information in the sense that the state sequence cannot generally be deduced from the output sequence. In fact the information rate H'(output) for such a machine is zero.

The process of observing an FSM (or in fact of observing any variables in any system), since it is characterized by a mapping from "true" values to "observed" values, loses information in general about the FSM and its behavior because of convergence of the mapping (though it may introduce spurious information unrelated to the FSM if the observation process is "noisy"). Both the FSMs and the observational process itself can be regarded as channels in the sense of Shannon information theory and therefore can transmit only a finite amount of information per unit time.

7. Law of Constraint Loss

Less obvious is the fact that FSMs and the observational process lose information not only about their input processes but also about relations between their inputs, when there are several; if there is a constraint over the inputs to a family of FSMs, the image of this constraint in the outputs of the FSMs will be weaker, in general, than the input constraint. Similarly if a relation between variables is observed by means of a convergent mapping, the observed constraint between the variables will be weaker, in general, than the true constraint.

For the observational process this can be expressed as follows: let $Y_i = f_i(X_i)$ be the variables output from the observational process. Then $T(:S)$ is the constraint over the variables X_i, and $T(Y_1:Y_2:\ldots:Y_n)$ is the corresponding observed constraint. The law of constraint loss (Conant 1976) states that

$$T(Y_1:Y_2:\ldots:Y_n) \leqslant T(:S)$$

with equality if and only if all f_i are one-to-one (perfect observation). For example, if $n=2$ the loss of constraint is

$$\text{loss} = T(X_1:X_2) - T(Y_1:Y_2)$$
$$= T_{Y_2}(X_1:X_2) + T_{Y_1}(X_1:Y_2)$$

which is nonnegative since all conditional transmissions are nonnegative.

If $E^1, E^2, \ldots, E^m$ are the (possibly multivariable) inputs from the respective environments of n FSMs, and $S^1, S^2, \ldots, S^n$ their respective outputs, then another form of the law of constraint loss is:

$$T'(S^1:S^2:\ldots:S^m) \leqslant T'(E^1:E^2:\ldots:E^m)$$

that is, the dynamic constraint over the respective outputs is in general weaker than that over the inputs.

8. Laws of Requisite Variety and Requisite Transmission

One of the best known, simple and useful laws of information is Ashby's law of requisite variety (LRV) (Ashby 1958). To formulate this law we assume that R (a regulating system) and D (another system, of disturbances) each partially determine a sequence of outcomes Z, via a function $f: R \times D \to Z$, and that the objective of R is to choose behaviors or values appropriately matched to those of D so as to cause the outcomes to fall in a "desirable" subset G of Z. For example, R may be a thermostat plus furnace, D a fluctuating ambient temperature, Z the temperature of a room controlled by R, and G the desired temperature range, and the task of R is to add heat to a room when the disturbance attempts to cool it.

Suppose that for every value r of R the function f when restricted to that value maps D one-to-one onto Z, so that for every r in R, M different values of D necessarily result in M different values of Z. Then the LRV states that

variety of $Z \geqslant$ variety of D/variety of R

where variety means number of distinct values. If the objective of R is to reduce the variety of Z (i.e., to block disturbances from affecting the output) then the LRV can be interpreted as stating that "only variety (of R) can destroy variety (of Z)," since if the variety of D is taken as fixed, a decrease on the left side of the inequality requires an increase in the variety of R. An information-theoretic version of the LRV is:

$$H(Z) \geqslant H(D) - T(R:D) \geqslant H(D)$$

and since $T(R:D)$ represents constraint or coordination between the regulator and the system of disturbances, this version indicates that variability in Z can be reduced only to the extent that the behavior of R is appropriately coordinated with that of D. A rate version of the LRV is

$$H'(Z) \geqslant H'(D) - T'(R:D) \geqslant H'(D)$$

It can be shown that the output of an optimal regulator R is a deterministic function of D, and that such a regulator represents a noiseless channel with output $H'(R) = T'(R:D)$. The information-theoretic interpretation of regulation is that perfect regulation would result in a complete blockage of the information channel from D to Z: an observer of the outcomes Z would be completely unable to deduce anything at all about the disturbances, their effects having been completely blocked by the regulator.

The output information rate of a noiseless channel cannot exceed the input rate and consequently the rate version of the LRV states that the success of a regulator in preventing information in D from appearing in Z is bounded by the dynamic coordination between R and D, which is in turn bounded by the input information available to R. In other words, regulation is possible only when the regulator has access to sufficient relevant information and is able to make appropriate use of it. The LRV thus establishes a clear connection between information theory and control theory.

The law of requisite transmission (LRT) (Conant 1969) is a refinement of the LRV which withdraws the restrictive assumption that for every r in R the mapping f restricted to r is one-to-one from D onto Z. Generally when restricted to an arbitrary value of R, f is a many-to-one mapping from D onto Z, and k represents the maximum of this convergence factor of f; K is defined as $\log_2(k)$; and in the LRV, k is assumed to be 1. In the LRT, the amount of regulation V is defined as the decrease in $H(Z)$ attributable to the activity of R, beyond any minimum possible by simply fixing R permanently at an optimum value. The LRT is

$$V \leqslant T(R:D) - T(R:Z) + K$$

and a corollary, using the nonnegativity of transmissions, is

$$V \leqslant T(R:D) + K$$

Thus the amount of regulation is bounded by $T(R:D) + K$, with K being a parameter of the function f. It can be shown (Conant 1969) that

$$T(R:D) = 0 \Rightarrow V = 0$$

regardless of K, and thus the transfer of information is an essential component of the regulatory process.

The LRT, like the LRV, has an analogous interpretation using rates:

$$V' \leqslant T'(R:D) - T'(R:Z) + K$$

In the case of error-controlled feedback regulators in which Z corresponds to the feedback error of the system, it turns out that V is the difference between the redundancy in the sequence of D values and the redundancy in the sequence of error values; that regulation represents noiseless encoding of the D sequence into the error sequence; and that perfect regulation is theoretically impossible.

The importance of the LRV and LRT is in their demonstration that the process of regulation is limited by the information available to the regulator, by the channel capacity of the regulator and by the ability of the regulator to adopt behavior which is coordinated with the disturbances against which it is attempting to regulate. One interpretation of this coordination is that the regulator must "model" the disturbances.

9. Decomposition Laws for System Constraints

The total constraint $T(:S)$ in a system of variables can be partitioned in several ways, each corresponding to one law of decomposition for the constraint embodied in the system and therefore to one way of analyzing the structure of the system. In most decomposition rules $T(:S)$ is expressed as a sum of transmissions or conditional transmissions each of which is nonnegative, so that the rule amounts to a book-keeping calculus for system structure, and to a law of conservation of constraint. This led Broekstra (1981) to describe NDIT aptly as a "language of structure." We will mention just four of the many such identities (Ashby 1969, Conant 1976) in which any variable X may be replaced by a set of variables. All of the identities also hold when interpreted as rate identities.

The first is the chain rule for transmissions, sometimes called the sequential decomposition identity:

$$T(:S) = T(X_1 : X_2) + T(X_1 X_2 : X_3) + \cdots$$
$$\cdots + T(X_1 X_2 \cdots X_{n-2} X_{n-1} : X_n)$$

In this rule the total constraint is decomposed in a chain-like fashion into a sequence of binary relations involving one "new" variable in each term. It is useful when studying the incremental structural contribution made by each variable as it is added to a collection which, when complete, is the system S.

The second, which is convenient when one variable X_1 is of unique status, is the pyramidal decomposition identity:

$$T(:S) = \sum_{j=2}^{n} T(X_1 : X_j) + T_{X_1}(X_2 : X_3 : \ldots : X_n)$$

In this identity, $T(:S)$ is decomposed into the (unconditional) constraints between X_1 and the other variables, plus the conditional constraint between the others when X_1 is known or held constant. It is suggestive of a system structure in which X_1 represents the "boss" and $X_2, X_3, \ldots, X_n$ represent the "subordinates," with X_1 the apex of a pyramid and $X_2, \ldots, X_n$ the $n-1$ vertices of its base.

A third identity is the hierarchical decomposition identity:

$$T(:S) = \sum_{j=1}^{N} T(X_1^j : X_2^j : \ldots : X_n^j)$$
$$+ T(S^1 : S^2 : \ldots : S^N)$$
$$= \sum_{j=1}^{N} T(:S^j) + T(S^1 : S^2 : \ldots : S^N)$$

where $S^j = X_1^j, X_2^j, \ldots, X_n^j$. This identity decomposes $T(:S)$ into the N constraints representing coordination *within* the N disjoint subsystems, plus one constraint *between* the N subsystems viewed as integral units. It can be used to determine the relative strength of constraints within and between subsystems and therefore to estimate the degree to which a system is nearly decomposable. The constraints within the subsystems may be analyzed similarly, by applying the identity recursively to the $T(:S^j)$.

The identities above contain only nonnegative terms, so that the right-hand side of each identity contains terms which may be viewed as partitioning the total constraint on the left-hand side.

The fourth identity is the reconstructability identity (Broekstra 1981), so called because it is of central importance in NDIT versions of reconstructability analysis. Using the notation

$$C_j = \bigcup_{k<j} (S^k \cap S^j),$$

$$C'_j = \bigcup_{k<j} (S^k - S^j)$$

$$C''_j = S^j - \bigcup_{k<j} S^k,$$

(with $S^0 = \emptyset$) this identity is:

$$T(:S) = \sum_{j=1}^{k} T(:S^j) - \sum_{j=1}^{k} T(:C_j) + \sum_{j=1}^{k} T_{C_j}(C'_j : C''_j)$$

It is a generalization of the hierarchical decomposition identity for S, but in which the S^j are not necessarily disjoint. It is used to analyze the structure of S into the relations within and between the nondisjoint subsystems indicated by the sets C^j.

10. Detection of System Structure using NDIT

Reconstructability analysis (RA) (Klir 1985) and dependency analysis (DA) (Conant 1981) are recent tools of systems methodology which have as their aim understanding the structure of a system through analysis of system behavior. In this context the structure of a system is a function of the relation R holding over its variables, and RA and DA attempt to find the simplest possible decomposition of R into component subrelations which collectively contain enough information to reconstruct the original relation R. For example, if $R(X_1, X_2, X_3, X_4, X_5, X_6) = R_{123456}$ contains neither more nor less information than the collection of subrelations $\{R_{1234}, R_{135}, R_{46}\}$, then the system is said to be consistent with the structure hypotheses 1234/135/46, and in information-theoretic terms the collection of subrelations is a coded form of the original relation. The importance of this is that characterizing a high-order system in terms of a set of smaller subsystems, when possible, is usually of significant help both in understanding the system and in storing information about it. Thus RA and DA are methods of enlightened reductionism, methods for system decomposition in which one is guaranteed that the decomposition loses no information about the system, or at most a tolerable amount controlled by the investigator.

The structure of systems can be characterized in several ways according to the form of uncertainty employed in the analysis. The most highly developed form of RA and DA utilizes the probabilistic characterization of uncertainty and therefore identifies the relation R with the multidimensional probability distribution $p(S)$.

In the RA version, a search-and-test technique is used to explore successively simpler hypotheses about system structure until the simplest structure is found which is in agreement with $p(S)$, either exactly or within a preset error tolerance. The testing of structure hypotheses can employ Broekstra's reconstructability identity described in Sect. 9, since each possible structure hypothesis corresponds to a unique NDIT identity in which certain terms are assumed to be zero, usually the conditional transmission terms in the identity. By testing whether or not these terms are zero (or insignificant), the structure hypothesis can be confirmed or denied.

Alternatively, the DA version is based on finding, for each variable, those other variables with which it has a direct relation. This is done by finding, for each variable in the system, a set of variables which is maximally informative about the target variable, but which is minimal in size. NDIT is central to the method in the discovery of the direct relations. DA has been used successfully to discover the structure of systems having hundreds of variables (Conant 1988).

11. Partition Laws of Information Rates

The partition law of information rates (PLIR) (Conant 1976) is an identity partitioning $\Sigma H'(X_i)$ into four nonnegative components each with a particular interpretation given below. Since $H'(X)$ is the information rate associated with X and may be interpreted as the rate of information flow through that variable, the PLIR may be viewed as a conservation law of information flow in systems. The five terms of the law are:

total rate $\quad F_{tot} = \sum_{i=1}^{n} H'(X_i)$

throughput rate $\quad F_t = T'(E:S_o)$

blockage rate $\quad F_b = T'_{S_o}(E:S_{int})$

coordination rate $F_c = T'(:S)$

noise rate $\quad F_n = H'_E(S)$

and the PLIR can be expressed in the following way.

$$F_{tot} = F_t + F_b + F_c + F_n$$

For deterministic systems, three of the terms simplify as follows: $F_t = H'(S_o)$, $F_b = H'_{S_o}(S_{int})$ and $F_n = 0$. The PLIR thus simplified is called the deterministic PLIR.

The quantity F_t is the rate at which information flows through the system, and it is bounded by the conventional channel capacity of the system. Not all information which is input to S from its environment E has an effect on the output of S in general, since some of the information is irrelevant to the objective of the system but must be taken in and processed so that it can be recognized as irrelevant, and F_b is a measure of the rate at which such information is blocked. It is not widely appreciated that such blockage of irrelevant information does indeed place a burden on the computational or information-processing resources of the system, but this is apparent from the PLIR. F_c measures the internal coordination within S; whenever the parts of a system must cooperate and coordinate in order to accomplish a systemic objective, information resources are required to accomplish this dynamic coordination. Finally, F_n is a measure of the rate at which information is generated internally in the system.

The importance of the PLIR is in its indication of the fixed-sum relationship of the various information rates for a system. When F_{tot} is bounded, for example in a system containing a finite number of components each of a finite channel capacity (such as the human brain or a computer), then the PLIR makes it apparent that an increase in one type of demand upon the information-processing resources of the system must entail a corresponding decrease in the other types, or else an increase in the total rate for the system.

The PLIR also can be seen as implying design criteria for systems, since it makes it apparent that to minimize F_{tot} a system should minimize all terms, and thus should minimize F_t (avoid producing any unnecessary output), F_b (take in a minimum of irrelevant input), F_c (reduce internal coordination to the minimum required for the operation of the system; i.e., maximize the freedom of the components) and F_n (make the system fully deterministic). Moreover the minimization of F_{tot} implies that all components of a system should be operated at their channel capacities, by matching components to tasks (letting each component do what it does best, and working it at its maximum rate).

The PLIR may be applied, although perhaps not rigorously, to the understanding and even the design of organizations, where (loosely interpreted) it has obvious consequences.

12. Other Relations Between Information and Systems

There are many other profound relations between information and system which must be left unexplored in an article of this length. For example, the uncertainty principle of physics can be seen as an information law of systems to the effect that perfect information about any physical system is impossible to obtain. Bremermann's limit (Bremermann 1962) is a law which states that there is a physical limit, based on quantum mechanical considerations, on the rate at which matter can process information. Brillouin (1950) and others have explored the profound relation between thermodynamic entropy of a system and Shannon's measure of entropy used in NDIT. It is well known, for example by considerations involving Maxwell's demon, that gaining information about a system entails an expenditure of energy; Miller's analysis of living systems (Miller 1978), in which consideration of information processing plays a central role, provides an example of a rich source of observations about information and systems too voluminous to be explored here.

See also: Information Theory

Bibliography

Ashby W R 1958 Requisite variety and its implications for the control of complex systems. *Mechanisms of Intelligence*: *Ross Ashby's Writings on Cybernetics*. Intersystems, Seaside, California
Ashby W R 1965 Measuring the internal information exchange in a system. *Mechanisms of Intelligence*: *Ross Ashby's Writings on Cybernetics*. Intersystems, Seaside, California
Ashby W R 1969 Two tables of identities governing information flows within complex systems. *Mechanisms of Intelligence*: *Ross Ashby's Writings on Cybernetics*. Intersystems, Seaside, California
Bremermann H J 1962 Optimization through evolution and recombination. In: Yovits M C, Cameron S (eds.) *Self-Organizing Systems*. Spartan, Washington, DC
Brillouin L 1950 Thermodynamics and information theory. *Am. Sci.* **38**, 549
Broekstra G 1981 C-analysis of C-structures. *Int. J. Gen. Syst.* **7**, 33–61
Conant R C 1969 The information transfer required in regulatory processes. *IEEE Trans. Syst. Sci. Cybern.* **5**, 334–38
Conant R C 1974 Information flows in hierarchical systems. *Int. J. Gen. Syst.* **1**, 9–18
Conant R C 1976 Laws of information which govern systems. *IEEE Trans. Syst., Man Cybern.* **6**, 240–55
Conant R C 1981 Detection and analysis of dependancy structures. *Int. J. Gen. Syst.* **7**, 81–91
Conant R C 1988 Extended dependency analysis of large systems, Part I: Dynamic systems; Part II: Static systems. *Int. J. Gen. Syst.* **14**(2), 97–123
Elias P E, Feinstein A, Shannon C E 1956 A note on the maximum flow through a network. *IRE Trans. Inf. Theory* **2**, 117–19
Hartmanis J, Stearns R E 1966 *Algebraic Structure Theory of Sequential Machines*. Prentice–Hall, New York
Klir G J 1981 Special issue on reconstructability analysis. *Int. J. Gen. Syst.* **7**, 1–107
Klir G J 1985 *Architecture of Systems Problem Solving*. Plenum, New York
Krippendorff K 1980 An interpretation of the information theoretical Q measure. *Proc. 5th Int. Meeting Society Cybernetics and Systems Research*, Vienna
McGill W J 1954 Multivariate information transmission. *Psychometrika* **19**, 97–116
Miller J G 1978 *Living Systems*. McGraw–Hill, New York
Shannon C E, Weaver W 1949 *The Mathematical Theory of Communication*. University of Illinois Press, Urbana, Illinois

R. C. Conant
[University of Illinois, Chicago, Illinois, USA]

Information Requirements Determination

Judgements, or at least prudent judgements, are seldom made without information. It is only through information that one becomes aware of the need for judgement and choice activities and the result of these—a decision. Information is often defined as data which is of value in decision making. The activities of data acquisition, representation storage, distribution and use are generally involved in information processing. The task of information requirements determination is necessarily involved with all of these, although formally it is concerned with determination of what information is to be acquired. This cannot be done, however, without some perceptions concerning what will be done with information after acquisition to convert it to useful knowledge. The objectives of human information processing for decision making include acquiring the information which is most relevant to the task at hand, and obtaining a relatively full and complete interpretation of the information that is obtained.

This interpretation involves identification of the issues that are worthy of investigation, identification of potentially appropriate courses of action, identification of a recommended course of action, and monitoring to determine the extent to which the selected course of action is attaining the desired goals. Iteration and feedback are involved in this, as there should also be an indication of when it is better to switch to a new course of action. Therefore we see that information requirements determination involves all of the elemental considerations that are requisite for a systems study. Human and organizational concerns are critical in this, as in any systems study, as appropriate system design must be based on a satisfactory conceptual model of the decision situation and the problem space of the decision maker; that is, the "contingency task structure." Figure 1 represents one concepualization of all of this. It shows, in particular, the three fundamental problem-solving steps of formulation, analysis and interpretation. As indicated in the article *Systems Methodology*, these are to be found, formally or informally, in every phase of the life cycle of systems engineering efforts.

There are many ways in which we can characterize information. Among the attributes that have been used to characterize information are accuracy, precision, sufficiency, completeness, understandability, relevance, reliability, verifiability, consistency, freedom from bias, frequency of use, age and quantifiability. Alternatively, information can be

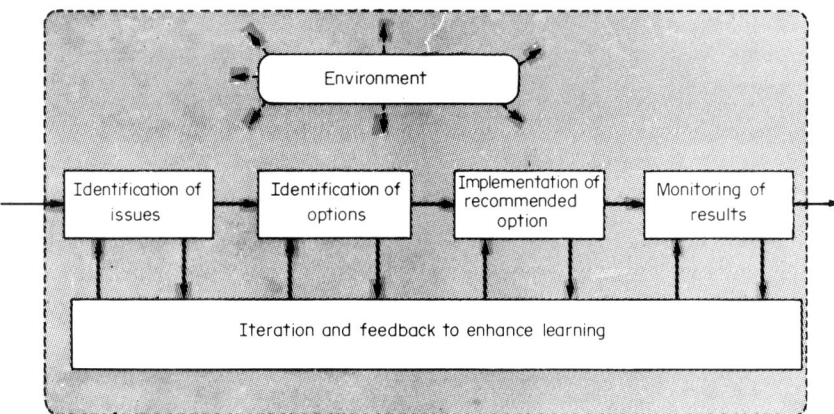

Figure 1
Activities involved in information requirements identification

characterized according to its intended use. This would include strategic, tactical and operational purposes, such as planning or design. Generally, it is much easier to structure information in operational settings than in strategic settings. Also there is generally a greater degree of certainty, precision and consistency inherent in available information in operational settings. Consequently, there is less need to utilize methods that allow for imprecision and uncertainty in these environments than in strategic environments.

It is possible to define information at several levels (Shannon and Weaver 1949). At the *technical* level, information and associated measures are concerned with the transmission quality of information over a channel. At the *semantic* level, concern is with the meaning and efficiency of various messages. At the *pragmatic* level, information is valued in terms of its effectiveness in accomplishing an intended purpose. Successful decision support system design must be based on considerations at all three levels. The following four requirements for a decision support system identified by Carlson (1977) and Sprague and Carlson (1982) are appropriate at each level:

(a) the ability to present information to a decision maker in ways that are very clear, familiar and permit rapid comprehension;

(b) ease of use in terms of operations and commands to enable information acquisition and presentation;

(c) explicability in terms of retention of results and how the results were obtained; and

(d) management control in terms of enabling the decision maker, rather than the decision support system, to guide the process of judgement and choice.

Although these four requirements are concerns at the implementation phase of systems design, lack of attention to them at the information requirements determination stage of the requirements specification phase of systems design is a cause of many ill-designed systems.

The technical-level approach to information is best exemplified by the seminal "information theory" work of Shannon and Weaver (1949). While these concepts are very appropriate for maximizing channel capacity or otherwise enabling the optimization of technology components for best transmission of the data that is in a given message, they do not directly concern whether the information that is transmitted is appropriate.

The now classic *value-of-information* concept, described in most texts on decision making (Sage 1977), does just this, but primarily from an efficiency perspective. From this perspective, information can have positive value only as long as it is "free," since the statistics that describe the information are assumed known, as is the structure of the decision situation. Various possible information-gathering activities that are possible are evaluated in terms of the (economic) benefit that will be expected to result from them. If the benefits from obtaining a particular item of information exceed the cost that must be paid to obtain it, then the information should be purchased according to the value-of-information concept. Cohen and Freeling (1981) provide a lengthy presentation of this important concept. The greatest impediments to using this approach exclusively to value information are that the requirements for a very detailed structural model of the decision situation are often not met in practice, that sensitivity analysis to determine the effects of imprecise parameters and knowledge is not at all easy to perform, and that concern is primarily with efficiency of information as contrasted with effectiveness. Also, it is difficult to interpret information sets that are structurally or parametrically inconsistent, in whole or in part, since the basis for derivation of the value-of-information concept assumes consistency and economic rationality. Nevertheless, the economic efficiency value of information is an important concept and is of much potential value in information system design.

Yovitz et al. (1981) have expanded on the classical value-of-information concept to encompass many measures of effectiveness as well as efficiency. They conceptualize a model for human information processing called a generalized information system. It is assumed that the decision maker will:

(a) choose a best course of action based on all available information, which necessarily includes a prediction of the outcomes likely to follow from implementation of the course of action;

(b) compare the actual results with those predicted;

(c) update the model of the decision situation based on this; and

(d) iterate the process repeatedly, selecting a new course of action until the information that is obtained from the decision process enables identification and implementation of a finally acceptable course of action.

Information and decision metrics are identified so that the amount of information available in any given decision state, information value and decision-maker effectiveness can be identified. Using these, it becomes possible to evaluate the amount of information available in a potential data set that might be acquired. This can be positive, which indicates information that enhances the decision maker's understanding of the situation. A negative amount of information indicates that the number of structural components in the decision situation, such as a previously unidentified course of action, is greater than it otherwise was thought to be. The value of a new item of information depends on the actual difference in decision-maker effectiveness before and after the information is received. This approach would appear to be of considerable potential value for both descriptive and normative purposes, especially if notions of fuzzyness and imprecision (Zadeh 1973, Freeling 1980, Gupta and Sanchez 1982a,b, Sage 1987a,b), and information-effectiveness-based growth of decision structural models (Rajala and Sage 1980a,b, Pearl et al. 1982) are incorporated into the metrics.

Taggart and Tharp (1977) have developed an approach called management information requirements analysis which is based on the realization that human communication needs and information complexity are important components of a decision support system design. The goal of this approach is to obtain a set of information elements through examination of pertinent reports and management responsibilities to determine the necessary information components. These elements are then translated into a set of information requirements. The approach is based on a careful definition of what the decision maker does, determining a set of elements from this, and examining them for verb and noun indicators of information needs. The approach appears to be based on examination of reports and discussions with managers to determine key decisions and the information needs to support them.

Rockart (1979) has developed an approach to information requirements determination which is based on critical success factors. To determine these key indicators requires identification of a set of factors important to the success of the organization. There are a number of contemporary management science applications that make use of critical success factors or success attributes (Rockart and Bullen 1986).

A number of other approaches have been described in the literature for determination of information needs in decision making which are based on examination of reports and discussions with people. Bandyopadhyay (1977), Munro and Davis (1977) and Taggart and Tharp (1977) describe much of this research. The information requirements determination methodology of Davis (1982) represents what appears to be the most thorough and definitive of these approaches. In many respects, it is a complete synthesis of the earlier research on this subject.

The process of constructing a support system for aiding the decision maker in the resolution of issues involves many competing concerns. Often, these may not be determined merely by asking people or by reading reports and examining actual systems to learn what an organization believes it does now and what it wishes to do. Sometimes an experimental approach is needed in which a trial system is constructed and installed in an operational environment to learn what the actual information requirements are. The approach of Davis (1982) combines all of these in the particular blend that appears to be most appropriate for the particular task at hand.

Davis has developed a framework for choosing one or more of four strategies for determining information requirements. According to him, two levels of information requirements are necessary for the design of an information support system. Organizational-level requirements specify the information system structure, portfolios of applications and boundaries for individual decisions. Application-level requirements determine specific information-processing needs to be implemented in a specific application. Although the uses of information at these two levels are different, the generic procedures for determining information requirements are the same for each level.

The specific procedures most useful at a given level will depend upon several factors, as will be seen.

On the basis of three human limitations—limited information-processing ability, bias in the selection and use of information, and limited knowledge of appropriate problem-solving behavior—Davis identified four strategies for determining their requirements. The first is simply to ask people for their requirements. The appropriateness and completeness of the information needs determined by this approach will be determined by the extent to which the people in question can define and structure their problem space and can compensate for their biases. This approach can be further subdivided into interacting-group and nominal-group approaches. There has been some research into questions concerning the best design of interacting-group and nominal-group approaches to issue formulation concerns, such as identification of information requirements. The article *Collective Enquiry* is relevant in this context.

The second strategy is to elicit information requirements from existing systems that are similar in nature and purpose to the one in question. Properly executed anchoring and adjustment strategies, or perhaps analogous-reasoning strategies, are useful here, since a starting point can be determined from the existing system and this can then be extrapolated. Examination of existing plans and reports represents one approach to identifying information requirements from an existing or conceptualized system.

The third strategy for determining information requirements identified by Davis consists of synthesizing information requirements from characteristics of the utilizing system. This permits an analytic structure for the problem space to be defined, from which information requirements can be determined. This strategy is appropriate when the system in question is in a state of change and thus cannot be compared with an existing system. Techniques applicable in this strategy include input–process–output analysis, decision analysis and critical success factors approaches.

The fourth strategy consists of discovering necessary items of information by experimentation. Additional information can be requested as the system is employed in an operational, or simulated operational, setting and problem areas are encountered. The initial set of requirements for the system provides an anchor point for the experimentation. This represents an expensive approach, but is often the only alternative when an experience base for using one of the other approaches does not exist.

Davis is concerned with enhancing the abilities of system users to specify requirements as well as the abilities of analysts to elicit and evaluate requirements. To this end, it is desirable to be able to select the best mix of these four strategies for information requirements determination at the two levels (specific-problem level and metaproblem level) identified by Davis. The method of selecting the most appropriate strategy is based primarily on determining the amount of uncertainty involved in the set of information requirements that result from the use of each strategy. Here, *uncertainty* is used in a very general context to imply general information imperfection. Five steps are potentially useful in selecting an appropriate information requirements determination strategy in terms of the amounts of uncertainty involved in a particular problem:

(a) identify characteristics of the utilizing system elements, information system elements, users and analysts that affect the system development process and that affect uncertainty of information requirements determination;

(b) evaluate the effect of the characteristics of these four elements on three types of information requirements determination uncertainties (availability of a set of requirements, ability of users to specify requirements, ability of systems analysts to elicit and specify requirements);

(c) evaluate the combined effect of the information requirements determination process uncertainties on overall requirements uncertainty;

(d) select a primary information requirements determination strategy;

(e) select a set of specific methods to implement the primary requirements determination strategy.

Figure 2 illustrates the use of these steps to identify an appropriate mix of information requirements identification strategies.

The requirements determination process uncertainty (that is, the amount of information imperfection that exists in the environment for the particular task) influences the selection from among the four basic strategies as indicated in Table 1. In terms of the organizational-level elements, the factors that primarily influence or effect information imperfection include: stability of the environment; stability of organizational management; experience with planning, design and use of information systems; and the extent to which the present information system is appropriate. Taken together, these enable the selection of a set of information requirements determination approaches which considers three essential contingency-dependent variables relating to uncertainties relative to information determination. These three variables include uncertainty with respect to (a) existence and stability of information requirements, (b) user ability to specify requirements, and (c) the abilities of systems analysts to identify information requirements and to evaluate their completeness and correctness.

Information requirements determination has also been a subject of much interest in software systems engineering (Miller 1964, Tiechroew 1972, Heninger 1980, Peters 1980, Thorngate 1980, Sommerville 1982, Mills 1983). Researchers in this area have come to

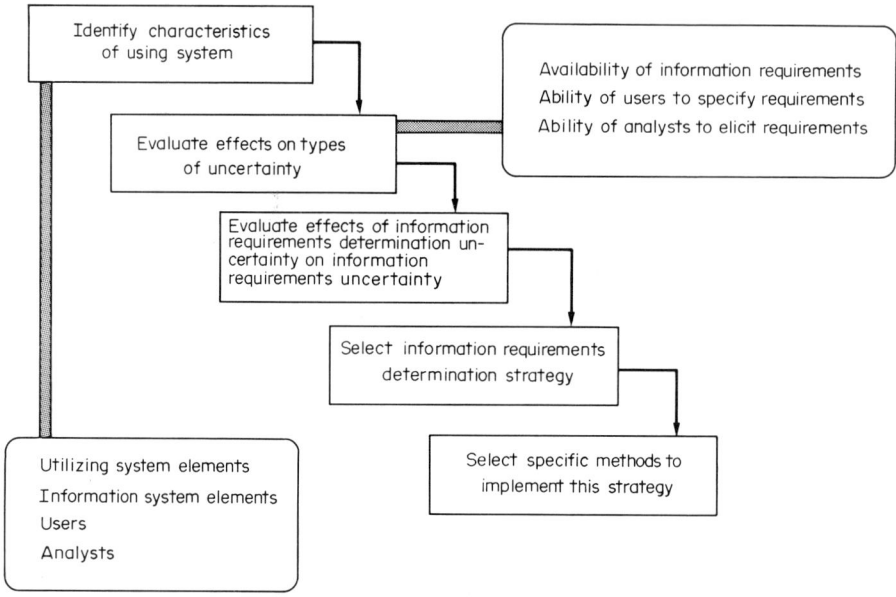

Figure 2
Identification of an information requirements determination strategy

Table 1
Strategies for primary requirements determination

Uncertainty	Strategy
Low	asking
Low–moderate	derivation from existing system
Moderate–high	synthesis from utilizing system
High	discovery by experiment

much the same conclusions as systems analysts that humans have great difficulty in specifying requirements in terms of verbal discourse or unstructured paragraphs of natural language. Many general design approaches in software systems engineering are much like those advocated in more general systems engineering contexts (Sage 1977, 1987a,b).

There has been some development of programming languages to assist in information requirements determination (Tiechroew 1972, Yadav 1983). The problem statement language/problem statement analyzer language of Tiechroew and Hershey (1977) is typical of several general-purpose languages for specifying requirements. These identified requirements are translated into system inputs which are stored in a database for later recall and possible updating. Software tools produce a report directly from the identified database. A top-down approach is used which allows development of criteria, and definition of system boundaries through examination of the internal and external problem environment. After this is accomplished, as many as 22 objects may be utilized to define the conceptual qualities of the proposed system. Relations between each of these objects are next identified. These are stored in a centralized database for later use in responding to queries.

A manual system can be developed to function in much the same manner as a computerized system for requirements determination. Heninger (1980) describes one such system used to describe the input, output and functional relationships relating output to input for a particular software system for aircraft. The system requirements were determined through analysis of the completed forms. The object of this was to develop a software requirements document which would serve as a reference tool and provide formal documentation of initial wisdom concerning the system's life cycle. One purpose for a document such as this, as well as for formal statements of information requirements, is that it then becomes possible to validate the requirements, at least in part, with respect to such important considerations as consistency, completeness, realism and responsiveness to the needs of the system user.

Knowledge requirements identification in artificial-intelligence-based expert systems has also been a subject area of recent interest, although primary efforts in this field have been more concerned with representation and utilization of information. Related to this is the identification of information requirements based on analogous reasoning. The research of Silverman (1983) is particularly important in this regard.

Huber (1983) and others have noted that the construction of support systems incorporating the "cognitive style" of decision makers has proved ineffectual. Although it may be possible to implant one particular decision maker's cognitive style for one particular task in a support system to some degree, it would not have the flexibility to support different decision makers or even a single decision maker whose cognitive style would be expected to vary as a function of experiental familiarity with the task at hand. The works of Dreyfus (1982), Dreyfus and Dreyfus (1986) and Klein (1980, 1982) are especially significant in providing cogent models for this change in cognitive style as a function of familiarity and expertise with respect to the demands of a particular task. It is highly desirable that an aid for information requirements determination be capable of assistance to people at various stages of expertise with respect to a given set of task requirements. This is a very demanding requirement for success in the design of decision support systems.

Bibliography

Bandyopadhyay R 1977 Information for organizational decisionmaking: A literature review. *IEEE Trans. Syst., Man Cybern.* **7**, 1–15
Carlson E D 1977 *Proc. Conf. Decision Support Systems, Data Base*
Cohen M, Freeling A 1981 *The Impact of Information on Decisions: Command and Control System Evaluation*, Technical Report 81-1. Decision Science Consortium
Davis G B 1982 Strategies for information requirements determination. *IBM Syst. J.* **21**, 4–30
Dreyfus S E 1982 Formal models vs human situational understanding: Inherent limitations in the modeling of business expertise. *Office Technol. People* **1**, 133–65
Dreyfus S E, Drefus H L 1986 *Mind Over Machine: The Power of Human Intuition and Expertise in the Era of the Computer*. Free Press, New York
Freeling A N S 1980 Fuzzy sets and decision analysis. *IEEE Trans. Syst., Man Cybern.* **10**, 341–54
Gupta M M, Sanchez M (eds.) 1982a *Approximate Reasoning in Decision Analysis*. North-Holland, Amsterdam
Gupta M M, Sanchez M (eds.) 1982b *Fuzzy Information and Decision Processes*. North-Holland, Amsterdam
Heninger K L 1980 Specifying software requirements for complex systems: New techniques and their applications. *IEEE Trans. Software Eng.* **6**, 2–13
Huber G P 1983 Cognitive style as a basis for designing MIS and DSS: Much ado about nothing? *Manage. Sci.* **29**, 567–79
Klein G A 1980 Automated aids for the proficient decision maker. *Proc. IEEE Systems, Man and Cybernetics Annual Conf.* IEEE, New York, pp. 301–4
Klein G A 1982 The use of comparison cases. *Proc. IEEE Systems, Man and Cybernetics, Annual Conf.* IEEE, New York, pp. 88–91
Miller J C 1964 Conceptual models for determining information requirements. *Proc. AFIPS Nat. Comput. Conf.* **25**, 609–20
Mills H D 1983 *Software Productivity*. Little, Brown, Boston, Massachusetts
Munro M C, Davis G B 1977 Determining management information needs: A comparison of methods. *MIS Q.* **12**, 55–67
Pearl J, Leal A, Saleh J 1982 GODDESS: A goal directed decision structuring system. *IEEE Trans. Patt. Anal. Mach. Recog.* **4**, 250–62
Peters L J 1980 Software representation and composition techniques. *Proc. IEEE* **68**, 1085–93
Rajala D W, Sage A P 1980a On decision situation structural models. *Policy Anal. Inf. Sci.* **4**, 53–81
Rajala D W, Sage A P 1980b On measures for decision model structuring. *Int. J. Syst. Sci.* **11**, 17–31
Rasmussen J 1980 Skills, rules, and knowledge: Signals, signs, and symbols; and other distinctions in human performance models. *IEEE Trans. Syst., Man Cybern.* **13**, 257–66
Rockart J F 1979 Chief executives define their own data needs: Critical success factors. *Harv. Bus. Rev.* **57**, 81–93
Rockart J F, Bullen C V (eds.) 1986 *The Rise of Managerial Computing*. Dow Jones Irwin, Homewood, Illinois
Sage A P 1977 *Methodology for Large Scale Systems*. McGraw–Hill, New York
Sage A P 1987a On the management of information imperfection in knowledge systems. In: Bouchon B, Yager R (eds.) *Uncertainty in Knowledge Based Systems*. Springer, Berlin
Sage A P 1987b *System Design for Human Interaction*. IEEE, New York
Sage A P, Galing B, Lagomasino A 1983 Methodologies for the determination of information requirements for decision support systems. *Large Scale Syst.* **5**(2), 131–67
Shannon C E, Weaver W 1949 *The Mathematical Theory of Communication*. University of Illinois Press, Urbana, Illinois
Silverman B G 1983 Analogy in systems management: A theoretical inquiry. *IEEE Trans. Syst., Man Cybern.* **13**(6)
Sommerville I 1982 *Software Engineering*. Addison–Wesley, Wokingham, UK
Sprague R H Jr, Carlson E D 1982 *Building Effective Decision Support Systems*. Prentice–Hall, Englewood Cliffs, New Jersey
Taggart W M, Tharp M O 1977 A survey of information requirements analysis techniques. *Comput. Surv.* **9**, 273–90
Thorngate W 1980 Efficient decision heuristics. *Behav. Sci.* **25**, 219–25
Tiechroew D 1972 A survey of languages for stating requirements for computer based information systems. *Proc. AFIPS Nat. Comput. Conf.* **41**, 1203–24
Tiechroew D, Hershey E A 1977 PSL/PSA: A computer aided technique for structured documentation and analysis of computer based information system. *IEEE Trans. Software Eng.* **3**, 41–48
Yadav B B 1983 Determining an organizations information requirements: A state of the art survey. *Database* Spring, 3–20
Yovitz M C, Foulk C R, Rose L L 1981 Information flow and analysis: Theory, simulation and experiments. *J. Am. Soc. Inf. Sci.* **32**, 187–202; 203–10; 243–48

Zadeh L A 1973 Outline of a new approach to the analysis of complex systems and decision process. *IEEE Trans. Syst., Man Cybern.* **3**, 28–44

A. P. Sage
[George Mason University, Fairfax, Virginia, USA]

Information Systems

In 1980 Alvin Toffler published his bestselling book *The Third Wave*, with his future-oriented conceptions, elucidating that the world is accelerating towards an information society. People, no matter where and who they are, have been increasingly feeling and witnessing the overwhelming impact of information activities. Information technology and its products have been incorporated into business machines, automobiles and home appliances. They are available for immediate use on the desktop, and are also transforming the ways in which people live, think, perceive, conduct business and communicate with one another. Our lives are being irrevocably changed.

The nucleus of the information society hinges on the easy acquisition, processing, production and dissemination of information. But, what *is* information? Basically, information is intellectual knowledge which is generally viewed differently from the definition of data. Data are the raw materials of information and are mostly unrelated bare facts, such as measurements or statistics, that are used as a basis for discussion, decision and calculation. When we start manipulating them to increase their value or utility, they become the sources of information. Thus, data generate information through manipulation. The system which performs this data-to-information process is called an information system. From a more technical perspective, an information system may be defined as an input–output structure which acquires, stores and processes data, and produces and/or disseminates information in an organized manner. A basic configuration of an information system is shown in Fig. 1.

The concept of an information system is not something pertaining only to the electronic computer or other modern machines. The human mind is one of the oldest information systems in nature. We are selective in extracting information from our surroundings. What we recall and think as we grow older is increasingly governed by what we have seen and remembered before. We are capable of storing and processing certain words, stories, rituals and history in our brains, preserving them so that they can be used repeatedly; we are even capable of speaking and writing in an organized manner within some prespecified format. All these capabilities are obviously identical to the operating procedure of a modern computer. Furthermore, with the development of the printing press, the library (or equivalent system) has become

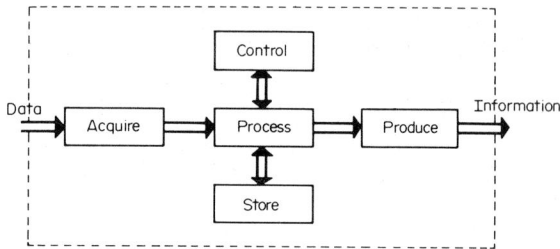

Figure 1
A basic configuration of an information system

firmly established as an information system which is not only able to store information indefinitely but is also able to transmit and distribute the information to anyone anywhere at a relatively low cost. Other examples of such systems are numerous and include banking systems, corporate planning systems and management decision-making systems.

With the knowledge explosion in the technological world, there has been a remarkable growth in awareness of the demand for automated tools and devices to generate, modify, store, retrieve, transmit and receive huge volumes of information. It has become the logical step to employ the modern digital computer and its related peripheral devices to achieve the goal of automated information systems. Computers, working with digits at electronic speed, can manipulate symbols according to set rules and simultaneously process and store massive amounts of information without human intervention. It is this type of computerized information system that is employed as the nucleus of current and future information systems. Hence, the description and interpretation of information systems in this article will be confined to computer-based information systems.

1. Organization of Information Systems

The input–output structure of an information system requires a series of planned actions and operations upon data to achieve a desired result. To achieve this result, the system configuration basically consists of five major components, as shown in Fig. 1, although the devices involved may vary over time as technology progresses. They are described below.

1.1 Data Acquisition Unit

Data acquisition units are essentially reading devices that convert human-readable data in alphanumeric and/or graphic voice types to machine-readable code and transmit them to the storage unit. Among the various devices available for inputs to computerized information systems are card readers, paper-tape readers, communication devices, console typewriters, keyboards, display terminals, touch-tone devices, optical-scanning equipment and devices that accept instructions from the human voice.

1.2 Storage or Memory

The processing of information requires that all program instructions must first be stored in the computer's main memory and the data to be processed must pass through it for further processing. The main memory must be able to hold a large program with many data fields and be able to send these data to the processing unit, and instructions to the control unit, with a minimum of delay. When information is retrieved or written out from certain locations in the memory, it must still remain intact at those locations for future use. Information in the memory may be destroyed, either by clearing memory locations or by storing other information at those locations. Instructions, data, intermediate results or reference tables may be stored in the memory in an organized structure. For all practical purposes, the memory is analogous to the way in which information is stored in a reference book. To recall information, it is necessary to tell the machine the location at which the information is stored in the memory.

Magnetic core has been used as the main memory for almost twenty years in the evolution of computer development. Since 1970, however, solid-state memories, such as those made by bipolar and metal oxide semiconductor (MOS) technology, have played a dominant role in modern information storage.

The storage facilities of an information system are not limited to the main storage only, but also include secondary and off-line storages. These storages include conventional magnetic recording devices such as magnetic-disk/drum units, tape/cassette/cartridge units and the recent mass storage units which are manufactured by using charge-coupled-device (CCD) and magnetic bubble technology. In terms of the cost of memory in US cents per bit and the speed of access time, these information storages are listed in the following descending order: bipolar, MOS, core, CCD, bubble, fixed-head disk/drum, moving-head disk and various tape units. Both main storage and secondary storage are available for on-line information processing while the off-line type is not under computer control.

1.3 Processing Unit

Information operations are performed by transmitting data from their storage locations to the processing unit and back into the storage. The processing unit is manipulated to perform the appropriate arithmetical and logical operations. It contains many registers such as adders, accumulators, complementors, comparators and flip-flop circuits. They can add, subtract, multiply, divide, compare, shift numbers and signs, and make logical decisions.

1.4 Control Unit

Information is read from the data acquisition devices into the memory, where it can be combined with stored information and manipulated through the processing unit. The results are then produced by output devices. These operations in themselves are not complete. A control unit is necessary to instruct the various components of the information system as to what is to be done and in what sequence. In essence, the control unit is the brain of the information system. It operates under the direction of program instructions stored in the memory.

1.5 Information-Producing Unit

Once the information has been processed, it is necessary to communicate this information to the user in the user-specified output form. The type of information output device employed depends on the information desired. Some of the data acquisition devices mentioned previously—magnetic-tape units, magnetic-disk units, communication devices, display terminals (character and/or graphic) and console typewriters—can be used to produce information output. In addition, card punches, paper-tape punches and various types of printers, plotters and audio response units also serve as output devices. Furthermore, information output can be in the form of electrical pulses that are used to direct other computers or instruments to perform other functions or for further processing.

2. Information Management

Data are the foundation of any information system. A programmer's, analyst's or user's knowledge of data organization and their alternative approaches to processing and managing data so it becomes useful, reliable and consistent information are critical to the success of an information system. Information management is concerned with the storage and retrieval of information entrusted in the system in much the same manner as that of a library. The following are the basic functions of information management (Madnick and Donovan 1974), which are manipulated mainly by software methods.

(a) keeping track of all information in the system.

(b) deciding policy to determine where and how information is stored and who gets access to the information.

(c) allocating the information resources.

(d) deallocating the resources.

These software methods were incorporated into packages called file systems in the early period of computer development. They encourage a close dependency between data and the programs using the data but reveal some limitations as the number of applications increases. It is the database management system (DBMS) that overcomes these limitations and its use has prevailed in recent times. The DBMS can manage a collection of interrelated data stored together in some structured ways (hierarchical, network or relational) with controlled redundancy to serve one or more applications in an optimal fashion. In addition, it can arrange the data independently of the given programs, add new data, and modify and retrieve the existing ones within the database by a common and controlled approach. A simplified DBMS allows user access to operate the programs without the need for knowing the actual details of the database structure. A DBMS package is not only able to correlate data within the database, but is also able to provide data security and query language capability.

A DBMS package is quite complicated; hence, most users do not develop their own packages. Computer manufacturers and software vendors have made DBMS software available in a variety of forms, from "bare-bones" models to sophisticated packages with many options and features for mainframes, minicomputers and even microcomputers.

With a DBMS in place, there are basically two ways to access the database—through application programs and through query languages, as shown in Fig. 2. Application programs can be used to call special access programs that are part of the DBMS. Instructions to access the database can be embedded in the high-level programming language that was conventionally used. Since query language is also a high-level language, users with no formal programming training can use it to specify their requirements without any difficulty. A user can be taught to use a query language with minimal instruction. In response to queries, the DBMS will search for the database information and return it to the user.

In the 1960s, almost all information systems usually kept their on-line databases in one centralized location. Centralization produced better control and the consolidation of equipment led to economies of scale. If data were stored in seperate locations, separate and unrelated computers were necessary to look after them. The complexities involved in scattering the data geographically were too enormous. Eventually, however, total centralization proved to be inconvenient. This limitation has been solved by the progress in network and data communication technology which makes decentralized or distributed information available.

The distributed information system can accommodate not only remote access but also remote processing. Processing is no longer done exclusively by the central computer. Rather, the processing and files are dispersed among several remote locations and can be handled by computers—usually mini- or microcomputers—all hooked up to the central host computer and sometimes to each other as well. The functional components of a distributed information system are the same as those of a centralized information system, but with additional components: the communication port, the network data directory and the network data management systems. Hence, the distributed approach of information systems gives rise to new problems and the need for new functions. The most important need is for a network-wide definition of the location and characteristics of all data in the system, including the method of partitioning or replication. It is more complex and usually more expensive than exclusively centralized information systems, but it provides many more benefits to users.

As previously mentioned, a centralized information system can have a hierarchical, network or relational data structure. The same structural alternatives can also be chosen for the data stored in a distributed system. Its data structure should be independent of the structure of the communication network.

The major advantages of a distributed system over a centralized system include (Martin 1976):

(a) multiple computers at multiple locations, which makes it more reliable;

(b) faster access and lower communication costs because data can be stored at locations where they are frequently used;

(c) variable system capacity to meet the changing needs more easily; and

(d) localized management control of the data.

There are various types of information systems that already exist including systems for corporate and business-management information (personnel, vendors, accounting, inventory), financial and banking information (customer, accounts, security position, investment analysis), government information (legislative actions, constituent opinion analysis, balloting history), legal information (applicable laws,

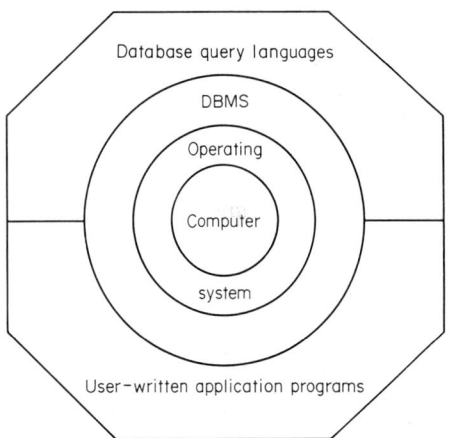

Figure 2
The structure of a database system

precedents) and medical information (diagnosis, treatment, medical history). As the hardware costs plummet and the data communication capabilities steadily improve, it is envisioned that distributed information systems will become a part of the day-to-day operations of human life and will eventually revolutionize the information processing being done today.

See also: Distributed Decision Making: Information Systems; Information Systems and Software Productivity; Information Systems Design in Industrial Practice

Bibliography

Madnick S E, Donovan J J 1974 *Operating Systems.* McGraw–Hill, New York
Martin J 1976 *Principles of Data-Base Management.* Prentice–Hall, Englewood Cliffs, New Jersey
Toffler A 1980 *The Third Wave.* Morrow, New York

L. R. Chow
[Tamkang University, Taipei, Taiwan]

Information Systems and Software Productivity

The efficient and effective development of information systems is greatly influenced by the approaches used to construct the software that forms the basis of the information system. As the name implies, information systems concern data that is organized and meaningful and has a purpose for the group using it. How information systems perform is often dependent on the methods and techniques used to develop the software that supports the system. Information systems may be developed using a variety of methods and approaches; each of these has its own attributes and deficiencies, some take longer to produce results, and the quality of software construction is definitively influenced by the approach. In this article we discuss information systems from the perspective of software development and examine the ways that software productivity affects the construction of information systems.

Of particular interest are the "micro" and "macro" approaches to enhancing software productivity for information systems construction; here, we provide an overview of both enhancement approaches. Micro-enhancement techniques include structured design approaches, use of computer-assisted software engineering (CASE) tools, fourth-generation language (4GL) generators and other methodologies aimed at programmer-productivity improvements. Macroenhancement techniques are those that address the overall production of the software product and include reusability, prototyping and the use of knowledge-based systems. The objective of the present effort is to provide a framework for the discussion of information systems and software productivity by defining it, followed by a review of the most prevalent approaches to the improvement of software productivity.

1. Definition of Software Productivity

In economic terms, productivity means the creation of economic value or the production of goods and services of economic value. Software productivity for the development or modification of information systems has been defined as the value of the output produced divided by the input cost (Boehm 1981). Output value for the delivered information system may be measured on the basis of user satisfaction, unit cost of the product, source lines of code delivered, complexity measures, or similar parameters. Output may be confined to the development process of the software product or it may cover the entire useful life of the information system. Input cost is determined by summing the costs of labor, capital, material and energy in relationship to the budgets, established for these factors, required to produce an information system product.

From this definition of software productivity we are able to explicitly indicate the goals of software productivity as follows (Palmer 1987).

> *The goals of software productivity* are to assure the production of a high quality information system that is delivered on time and within the original budgeted cost that fulfills user requirements, meets performance, reliability, availability, and maintainability specifications, and is capable of being modified throughout the useful life without significant restructuring of source code.

The ability to measure productivity, especially determination of metrics of output, is a difficult task. One measure is the source line of code (SLOC). It is hard to achieve a consensus as to what constitutes a SLOC because it is not a uniform metric, resists precise definition, fails to address the notion of software quality and does not correlate with the notion of value added (Boehm 1981). However, SLOC remains the primary parameter for a metric to determine output cost, because it represents virtually the only item which may be quantitatively measured that is related to output.

2. The Need for Software Productivity Improvement

Software productivity for development or modification of information systems is a topic of increasing interest and importance owing to the continuing crisis in software development, in which demand continues to increase much more rapidly than the ability to produce. Software-engineering responses to the crisis in software development have been to consider productivity improvements at the microenhancement level of tool support and to examine the effect of macroenhancements through the consideration of improvements of software development environments.

Efforts have been expended at all phases of the software development life cycle, especially in the area of automating code generation to improve software productivity. The major outcomes of these efforts are tools that have been developed to assist the programmer to accomplish the task of producing code more efficiently. Productivity improvement needs are compounded by the rapid improvements in hardware, the coming of age of very-large-scale integration (VLSI), parallel and distributed architectures and other technology advances.

3. Software Productivity Improvement from Microenhancement Techniques

Microenhancement aids to improve software productivity for information systems development are applied to one of the several phases of software development and generally tend to address improvement of that particular phase with little or no impact on other phases. A taxonomy of microenhancement methods that have been used at various times to improve software productivity is given in Table 1 (Beam et al. 1987).

3.1 Structured Design and Logical Processes for Productivity Improvement

The most effective way to provide for structured flow control is to apply a top-down, modular approach to both system and program development. In this approach, major functions or procedures are identified in solution algorithms that are broken into subfunctions or subprocedures in the solution hierarchy until all of the functional program modules required to solve the problem have been identified. The interfaces to each function must be defined; that is, the functional modules are independent of other modules in the system.

Several structured processes and procedures are given below:

(a) flow charts,

(b) data-flow diagrams (DFD),

(c) data dictionaries,

(d) process specifications,

(e) entity-relationship diagrams,

(f) technology for automated generation of systems,

(g) state-transition diagrams, and

(h) HIPO Charts.

Flow charts. Flow charts are the most widely used technique for the documentation of design specifications emanating from requirements analysis for the information system. Flow-chart symbols have been standardized and are defined in American National Standards X3.5-1970 *Flow Chart Symbols and their Usage in Information Processing* (ANSI 1970).

Data-flow diagrams (DFDs). These diagrams provide a graphic means of modelling the flow of data through any system, and may be implemented either manually, through automated processes, or by a mixture of each (Yourdon 1982). The basic elements of a DFD are sources or sinks of data, data flows, processes and data stores. A typical system requires several levels to depict an accurate and complete picture of the entire data-flow process. As information moves through a module or system it may be stored, transformed, processed or connected to some other portion of the system.

Data dictionaries. A data dictionary is a specialized database application that is concerned with the identification, standardization and use of all data elements and entities in the processing environment. It is produced with predefined schema and specialized programs for dictionary information. The data dictionary assists in information-resource management processes through the tasks of data-error reduction, program modification support, and maintenance of data items.

In a typical system, there are likely to be several thousand data definitions. These definitions enable the analyst to represent data in one of three ways: as a sequence of data, as a selection from among a set of data, or as a repeated grouping of data.

The data dictionary also contains logic notation that enables operations to be included as part of the information contained. For very large information-system designs, it is necessary that the data dictionary development process be automated. It is physically

Table 1
Microenhancement-based approaches

Improved programming technology

   Error prevention techniques
      structured programming
      composite design
      hierarchical design
      top-down design

   Error removal techniques
      design code inspection
      structured walkthrough
      design reviews

   Direct aids to productivity
      high-level programming languages
      on-line development tools
      preprogrammed modules

Nonprocedural techniques

   Query languages to update and model bases
   Report generators to format and produce results
   Graphic languages
   Very-high-level programming languages

impossible to manually maintain a dictionary of this size and retain consistency and unambiguous terms for each data element or composite of data elements. Therefore, any of the several automation tools currently available for development and maintenance of a data dictionary are utilized.

Data-structure-oriented methods. These approaches use data structure to assist the systems analyst in identifying entities and processes, to structure data in an hierarchical format, to formalize the data structure representation and to provide a systematic approach for developing program structure from the hierarchical data structure. Warnier (1981) has provided a graphical notation for representation of the information hierarchy that permits software structure to be developed directly from data structure; this has evolved into the data structured systems development (DSSD) methodology.

Warnier diagrams, DSSD. The hierarchical structure of data is utilized for the analysis of the information content of requirements and specifications at any level of detail. Each data item may be a sequence or collection of data items or an elementary item at the base level of the hierarchical data structure. DSSD notation calls for sequences of data entities, identification of repetitive data entities, and selection as used for data dictionary development. DSSD utilizes the entity diagram as a means of portraying the data structure and the hierarchy of information. DSSD also provides for hardware considerations as part of the analysis process. This includes parameters such as performance, reliability, system security, actual hardware required, and the necessary interfaces between databases, hardware and networks.

Entity relationship diagrams. These diagrams are used to identify and highlight the major objects or entities of stored data with which the information system must deal, and the relationships that exist between objects and support DSSD. These charts consist of a group of bubble charts with the particular system under consideration specified as the center bubble. Each interface between the system in the center bubble chart and any other system is indicated by an arrow or directed spoke from the center bubble chart. The data to be transferred over the interface is so labelled, with the direction of the arrow indicating the information flow.

Such a chart provides information as to what data entities are to be processed, where the information originates and the destination, and the context of the data entities, through various interfaces to other potential users. Interfaces are shown on the diagram between each of the application functions.

Jackson system development. Jackson system development (JSD) (Jackson 1983) associates information between domain analyses and various relationships among program development and system design. This approach is similar in many ways to DFD and DSSD, providing a logical approach to the organization of information and a model to develop the information flow, data entities and interface requirements.

JSD begins with a brief statement of the information-system problem in natural language. Entities are selected by reviewing all the nouns used in the description. Actions are determined through a review of the verbs contained in the statement. Action verbs serve as candidates for selection and, as in entity selection, must operate on the model of the information flow.

Entities and actions are selected and relationships between them are ordered through structure diagrams. First, a specification of the actual system is constructed with a system specification diagram (SSD), using special notation designed for this purpose. Following this, a data-stream connection (DSC) is constructed to show the flow of information and the various processes to which the data streams are subjected.

3.2 Direct Aids to Productivity Improvement

There are more than 400 commercial packages available that automate some portion of the software development life cycle for the design and development of information systems. Commonly available automated tools include those given below (Pressman 1987):

(a) DSSD (Orr & Associates),
(b) Design Aid (Nastec, Corp.),
(c) Execelerator (Index Technology, Inc.),
(d) Higher order software (HOS) (HOS, Inc.),
(e) Information engineering workbench (Knowledgeware, Inc.),
(f) JSD,
(g) Logical construction of systems (LOS),
(h) PSL/PSA (ISDOS, Inc.),
(i) Software requirements engineering methodology (SREM and SYREM),
(j) Structured analysis and technique (SADT) (Softech, Inc.),
(k) Structured analysis tools (Tektronix),
(l) Systems development methodology (SDM) (CAP Gemini), and
(m) Technology for automated generation of systems (TAGS) (Teledyne Brown, Inc.).

Many tool taxonomies have been developed to classify tools according to such activities as application, data element and functionality. The most well-known of these are CASE tools. CASE tool components have to fulfill the following requirements.

They must:

(a) provide front-end design and specification graphic support;

(b) provide design analysis, including tracking and reporting of basic design flaws and detection of design inconsistencies, in accordance with the rule-set implemented in the tool;

(c) provide code generation, including automatic translation of specifications developed earlier in the process;

(d) provide a data dictionary, including a metadictionary which holds comprehensive entity models or views of the system; and

(e) provide the capability of being installed on a PC (or similar commonly used processor) that is user friendly and has interfaces including windows and menus.

CASE tool sets bring together all of the traditional tools for software development including compilers and linkers, as well as more recently available capabilities such as project management software, graphical analysis tools and many additional contemporary assistance features besides those required to implement nonprocedural techniques, including report generators and graphic languages.

Much effort has been expended to develop CASE environments, available for personal computers and workstations, that migrate to minicomputers and mainframes. This integrated environment increases the productivity of the individual analyst and the entire development group through the introduction of automated processes to replace manual tasks, through consistency in the definition of terms, and through commonality of effort aimed at achieving a common goal.

Some other automated software development processes are described in the following.

The structural analysis and design technique (SADT), a product of Softech, Inc., is intended to provide assistance in the understanding of functions of complicated structures in order to accomplish information system definition, requirements analysis and software design (Ross 1977, 1985). SADT was originally developed as a manual system that guided the analyst in the decomposition of software into various functions as a set of graphic notations, modelling principles, review procedures and interviewing techniques. These are SADT actigrams and datagrams, and are graphical notations that provide relationships of information-to-function within software and project control guides for application. The goal of this procedure is to produce models of the system that may be examined by the software-development team. SADT is a very robust method for accomplishing the requirements analysis phase of the software development life cycle. It is capable of representing semantic information, possesses a good review process, but is weak in applications guidance.

Software requirements engineering methodology (SREM) is an automated tool that addresses the requirements analysis phase of the software development life cycle for the information system (Alford 1985). It uses the requirements statement language (RSL) for specifying requirements, and a set of automated techniques called requirements evaluation validation system (REVS).

SREM notation is used to describe elements, relationships, attributes and structures. RSL, together with an accompanying narrative, serves to provide the necessary information for a requirements specification. REVS is a combination report generator and computer graphics display used to review the flow of information, establish consistency throughout the system and examine the dynamic relationships that exist between and among elements. REVS interprets the language, performs consistency checks, carries out completeness and traceability analyses, develops simulators to exercise the requirements and provides for graphic support and documentation needs.

With the problem statement language/problem statement analyzer (PSL/PSA) (Teichroew and Hershey 1977) the analyst is able to describe information without regard to the application; create databases that contain descriptions of the information system; add, delete and modify descriptors; and produce formatted documentation and reports on the specifications. It is based on an entity-relationship model and is a nonprocedural language that is able to describe a system from several viewpoints.

Once the requirements are specified in PSL, the specification is processed by the PSA. The PSA produces reports about the requirements and builds a database of the requirements and system attributes, any modifications that have been made to the specification database, various reference reports, analysis reports and summary reports that may be used to evaluate the database.

Another direct aid to productivity improvement is known as the Petri net. The Petri net (Peterson 1981) format of graphical representation of state-space transitions is capable of supporting synchronization and parallel processing requirements of multievent, unordered activities. Such a model is the system-state model which is defined as follows: the state of a system at any time t_0 is the minimum of a set of numbers $x_1(t_0), x_2(t_0), \ldots, x_n(t_0)$ which, along with the input of the system for $t \geq t_0$, is sufficient to determine the behavior of the system for all $t \geq t_0$.

When we have simultaneous occurrence of several events we seek a representation schema that is able to handle parallel processing and accommodate concurrent processing systems and event synchronization. The state of a system represents the minimum amount of information that is required in order that the future behavior may be determined without reference prior to time t_0. It is possible to represent state transitions of complex systems of nth-order linear equations in state-variable form as n first-order differential equations and an output expression.

$$\dot{x}(t) = \mathbf{A}x(t) + \mathbf{B}u(t) \qquad (1)$$
$$y(t) = \mathbf{C}x(t) \qquad (2)$$

Where x is an n-dimensional state vector, u is an r-dimensional control vector, y is an m-dimensional output vector, $\mathbf{A}$ is an $n \times n$ system matrix, $\mathbf{B}$ is an $n \times r$ control matrix and $\mathbf{C}$ is an $m \times n$ output matrix.

$$f(\text{state } A_1, \text{event } 1) = \text{state } A_2 \qquad (3)$$

represents the transition from single state A_1 to a single state A_2 due to a single event 1.

An event table may also be used to depict the various states and events the give rise to specific actions. In a system in which several of these events must take place prior to a change of state, we have the situation of parallel events and the problem of event synchronization. A simple representation of this condition from the general equations of state is as follows:

$$f(\text{state } A, \text{event } 1, \text{event } 2, \ldots, \text{event } N) = \text{state } S \qquad (4)$$

Once the transition has begun, the system may move into several states in parallel. This is represented as

$$f(\text{state } A, \text{event } 1, \text{event } 2, \ldots, \text{event } N)$$
$$= (\text{state } 1, \text{state } 2, \ldots, \text{state } M) \qquad (5)$$

Another direct aid is the 4GL technique. To meet the generally accepted proviso to be classed as a 4GL, such a system must provide at least an order of magnitude (10:1) productivity increase over a higher-order language such as COBOL; however, there is no standard definition. The major attributes of a 4GL are that it is a processing environment that provides a single, integrated systems development tool embedded within a comprehensive development facility, has a DBMS with automatic database navigation with a logical view or relational processing, and an integrated active data dictionary/directory. It should possess a query facility with English-like language or a menu approach that supports Boolean selects, have a report generator, word processing and graphics, and be able to support procedural and nonprocedural languages while maintaining integrity, security and command structures.

3.3 Limitations to Microenhancement Productivity Improvement

Major improvements in productivity through removal of artificial barriers (Beam et al. 1987, Brooks 1987) will not prove to be much more efficacious than production of software would have been without these artificial barriers in the first place. The limits to improvement are constrained by the use of standardized approaches such as implementation of software development according to the waterfall life-cycle model. Other limits arise due to failure by applications specialists to use existing technology for structured approaches, the late stage in the software product life cycle at which the programming task occurs, and costly repairs and modifications in software products that are usually a consequence of poorly derived requirements/specifications or changing requirements and applications from the user. The elimination of some of the error-prone steps in software development due to conventional languages, and the use of new processes and technologies, will result in shorter time periods being required to develop and write software with concomitant lower costs, particularly when automated program construction techniques are applied.

Modifications that influence the effectiveness of the software product must be addressed earlier in the development cycle and iterated throughout the design process to assure minimal impact of changing requirements and applications. Generally, errors introduced by inadequate requirement specifications or design cannot be corrected by the application of structured methodologies at the programming phase of the development effort.

Orders-of-magnitude improvements in productivity are not feasible. For example, the percentage of the total time spent on coding of a program has been estimated to be of the order of 30%; the effort expended on maintenance and testing is of approximately the same value; and the time spent on requirements/specifications is only 15 to 20%. Thus, no matter what we achieve in developing automatic code generators and documentation capability, we simply cannot improve by more than the time actually allocated to the procedure in the first instance. Automating activities by individual phase of the software development life cycle offers little unless we modify the way in which we view the total life cycle.

A software components factory for the development of information systems has been built by the Toshiba Fuchu Software Works in Japan to overcome some of these limitations. In this factory, families of components are developed, selection of the appropriate component is based on measurable characteristics, and software synthesis is based on rational principles. Software factories in Japan are used to develop customized large-scale information systems, and are purported to achieve production rates of 3100 instructions per worker-month with error rates of two to three faults per 1000 source lines. These software factories utilize software development environments that support programming, assembling, compiling and debugging at the source code level, and support for tests, maintenance, program management and quality assurance. Methodologies supported in these environments include SADT, HIPO and various structured design constructs, and the approach taken uses the classical waterfall software development life cycle.

4. Software Productivity Improvement from Macroenhancement Techniques

Macroenhancement techniques to improve software productivity for the development and modification of information systems are those that address more than a single phase or activity within the software development life cycle. Considerations include examination of the cost of introducing improvements, the question of what happens to quality, how much time will be spent on techniques and production of software, and the role of reusability, prototyping and knowledge-based tools. Prototyping is by far the most mature technology, followed by reusability, with knowledge-based systems still being very much in the development stage.

4.1 Prototyping

Prototyping is a methodology for increasing productivity of software parts production through modelling of software at various stages of development throughout the software development life cycle. One of the more important uses is to increase user awareness of the software product that is being developed as the development is proceeding. Some uncertainties may be removed from requirements specifications by using prototypes to provide feedback between the software designer and the user.

Initial prototypes are those that show human–machine interactions and assist the user in understanding how the system will work. A working prototype demonstrates implementation of some portion of the system and is used for developmental review. An existing program that is reusable is a prototype to demonstrate a particular module of a design.

The greatest use of prototyping in contemporary systems development lies in the acquisition of feedback early in the development process. This feedback is important to sofware designers and management and to information-system users to identify issues and problems with the development process to that point. It is possible to save considerable amounts of time and resource prior to the commitment of effort in nonproductive activities.

The prototype software development model was created to overcome some of the disadvantages of the waterfall model. It is a functionally immature model of a proposed system, built to demonstrate feasibility, explore potential requirements or investigate alternatives (Church *et al.* 1986). Three examples of prototyping models are given below (Riddle and Williams 1986).

(a) *Exploratory prototyping*: this is used for the purpose of problem or solution formulation.

(b) *Experimental prototyping*: this is used for the investigation of alternative solution approaches.

(c) *Evolutionary prototyping*: this is used for the iterative creation and evolution of a system.

Another classification identifies the three categories of prototyping below (Carey and Mason 1983).

(a) *Scenario or simulation prototype*: this presents the user with a scenario of the user interface, but the eventual application logic is not developed. This user interface may be used in the actual production system, depending on the tool used to build the scenario.

(b) *Demonstration prototype*: this processes a limited range of user queries or data, using limited files. Frequently, some portion of the demonstration prototype is carried over to the production system. On the other hand, the entire demonstration prototype can be coded as a throwaway.

(c) *Version 0 prototype*: this is a functionally limited system that is released to the customer. Although it is specifically designed as a test release, it is expected to evolve into the final product.

Prototyping is primarily used to provide early feedback to developers and management, before money and time are spent on building a system based on misinterpreted requirements (Taylor and Standish 1982, Carey and Mason 1983, Mason and Carey 1983, Sharer 1983, Alavi 1984, Boehm *et al.* 1984, Gomaa 1984, Harrison 1985, Church *et al.* 1986). A prototype may form the basis of the final product (evolutionary or version 0 prototype) or be a throwaway prototype (Brooks 1975). The decision whether the prototype should be refined into the complete system or be thrown away is based on the costs and benefits of each alternative (Agresti 1986). Two such key factors are how much functionality is already present in the prototype; and will the design support a maintainable system (is the prototype worth the investment of more effort)?

Rapid prototyping, with its emphasis on resolving requirements deficiencies, has the most immediate effect on improving software productivity. Prototyping of all kinds supports macroenhancement of software productivity. If we take the long view of productivity to include the total useful life of the software product and software that meets the needs of the user, productivity improvement is substantial.

4.2 Reusability and Software Productivity

Reusability of software is defined as the ability to take already constructed software parts from other information systems and apply these in other software development projects (or different places in the same program). The most common form of reusability found at this time is the individual programmer or systems designer recalling a program that has been built which has a software part that may work in the present project, locating this part, modifying it and using it over again in the new effort. Efforts at reuse at this level clearly make significant contributions to software productivity and are utilized by any experienced systems designer or programmer. If it is possible to identify an entire program that will accomplish the user requirements, this becomes the ideal, least expensive and most productive way to construct software. Interchange of data between programs is also most beneficial to improved productivity.

The need to define the type and structure of software parts, together with classification and retrieval schema, is essential for successful reusablity. This means that future software should be constructed so that understanding, modification and component integration are feasible for maximum reusablity.

The development of a software part for reuse is initiated with an analysis of system components such as requirements, specifications, testing needs, data flow, control flow and output generation. Utilization of prototypes is extremely valuable and may result in a prototype system comprising reusable software parts.

4.3 Knowledge-Based Systems

This approach is in its infancy, yet with prototyping and reusability it shows great promise for increasing software productivity and assisting in resolving the software crisis in the development and modification of information systems. Beginning with requirements definitions, knowledge representation plays an essential and important role in the software development program. Currently available expert systems are of the rule-base form and have been used to address application areas such as configuration management and version control, project planning, data structure selection, and transformational schemes for small-scale programming.

The transformational paradigm is a knowledge-based model based upon a combination of the previously discussed models and the work done with artificial intelligence in the area of expert systems (Cheatham et al. 1981, Kant and Barstow 1981, Bauer 1982). It uses automated support to apply a series of transformations that change a specification into a concrete software system (Partsch and Steinbruggen 1983). The computer functions as an assistant in system development. Software engineering knowledge is separated from application knowledge, and this knowledge, along with the process paradigm, is captured in a database. Rules based on accepted software engineering techniques are encoded into expert systems. These software-engineering expert systems are used in conjunction with expert systems containing application knowledge rules to form a specific instance of a software system.

In practice, this automated paradigm has been applied to restricted application areas and at the level of individual programs (Balzer 1981, Partsch and Steinbruggen 1983, Wile 1983).

Three products emerge from the transformational paradigm. These are the formal specification, the delivered system and the formal development record. The main advantage of such a model is the potential for increasing software productivity. Theoretically, the model's descriptive power, generality and suitability for automation allow the construction of systems much larger than those being conceived today.

There are several expert systems currently available that purport to perform a variety of operations relative to the development of software products. Expert systems that aid in the automated development of software include KnowledgeBUILD, offered by Cullinet Software, Inc. KnowledgeBUILD provides an application generator that is stand-alone and operates in the VAX environment to provide nonprocedural application definition, generation of complete applications, and easy-to-use tools. The system supports interactive development of customized user interfaces, report layout and screen layout for use in COBOL, FORTRAN or BASIC applications.

Approaches to the use of knowledge-based systems for improvement in software productivity have shown their greatest effect to be in relatively narrowly defined application domains. If expert system technology is to show any real improvement in the area of software productivity, it must be able to operate in a variety of domains with equal effectiveness. These generic systems must support knowledge acquisition to be able to respond to changing domains of interest, evolving technology and changing user needs, and support a wide variety of techniques and methodologies for software development, while fitting well into a total software development environment. These applications are on the horizon and we should expect to see an increasing number of releases of CASE and other software development support tools in the near future. The general goal of these tools is to increase software productivity by allowing the computer to do the things best done by the computer and leaving the individual to perform the intellectual tasks best done by individuals; a best-of-both-worlds approach.

Expert systems may be considered as being in an immature stage for software development purposes. Some uses of expert systems have been marketed in the areas of specification development and as computer aids to detailed design. Many other areas are under investigation, and the introduction of expert systems is an important prospect for obtaining significant improvement in software productivity.

5. Summary

Information systems are affected by the approaches used in their construction in a variety of ways. For increases in productivity and, hence, timeliness of delivery of the system, it is essential that the methods utilized be productive, accurate and complete, or else we will have produced an information system that will not accomplish the task for which it was intended.

Many improvements have been made in recent years that address both the accuracy and completeness issues. These are represented by the microenhancement approaches to improve the productivity of software development for information systems. Some improvements in productivity have been realized by the use of these methods; however, the limitations to improvement of productivity are such that increases in productivity of 10 to 30% are anticipated.

The major opportunities for significant improvements in productivity for the development of information systems will come from macroenhancement techniques. We have seen that, of the approaches examined, prototyping is furthermost along in development, while expert systems and reusability constructs require much additional work before they can be translated into standard software development environments. The common thread running through macroenhancement approaches is the construction of advanced software development environments that support multiple views of the software, provide graphic representation, and take into account the cognitive aspects of interface design.

The development and modification of information systems is a complex and time-consuming activity. Prior to the introduction of techniques that have been described here as productivity aids, the production of an information system was a painful experience that included a lengthy and often nonproductive debugging stage before the information system could be put to work. With the methods and approaches given in this article, the development and modification of information systems is organized and produces software that is much less prone to errors. Much improvement is needed in the future, and research and development efforts are being carried on in many of the areas noted.

See also: Information Systems

Bibliography

Agresti W W 1986 Framework for a flexible development process. In: *New Paradigms of Software Development.* IEEE Press, New York, pp. 11–14

Alavi M 1984 An assessment of the prototyping approach to information systems development. *Commun. ACM* 27(6), 556–63

Alford M 1985 SERM at the age of eight: The distributed computing design system. *Computer* 18(4)

American National Standards Institute 1970 *Flow Chart Symbols and their Usage in Information Processing*, ANSI standard X3. 5-1970. ANSI, New York

Balzer R 1981 Transformational implementation: An example. *IEEE Trans. Software Eng.* 7(1), 3–14

Bauer F L 1982 From specifications to machine code: Program construction through formal reasoning. *Proc. 6th Int. Conf. Software Engineering.* IEEE Press, New York, pp. 84–91

Beam W R, Palmer J D, Sage A P 1987 Systems engineering for software productivity. *IEEE Trans. Syst., Man Cybern.* 17(2), 163–86

Boehm B W 1981 *Software Engineering Economics.* Prentice–Hall, Englewood Cliffs, New Jersey

Boehm B W, Gray T E, Seewaldt T 1984 Prototyping versus specifying: A multiproject experiment. *IEEE Trans. Software Eng.* 10(3), 290–302

Brooks F P Jr 1975 *The Mythical Man-Month.* Addison–Wesley, Reading, Massachusetts

Brooks F P Jr 1987 No silver bullet—Essence and accidents of software engineering. *IEEE Comput.* April

Carey T T, Mason R E A 1983 Information system prototyping: Techniques, tools and methodologies. *Can. J. Oper. Res. Inf. Process.* 21(3), 177–91

Cheatham T E Jr, Holloway G H, Townley G A 1981 A program refinement by transformation. *Proc. 5th Int. Conf. Software Eng.* IEEE Press, New York, pp. 430–37

Church V E, Card D N, Agresti W W, Jordan Q L 1986 An approach for assessing software prototypes. *ACM SIGSOFT Software Eng. Notes* 11(3), 1–12

Gomaa H 1984 A software design method for real time systems. *Commun. ACM* 27(9)

Harrison T S 1985 Techniques and issues in rapid prototyping. *J. Syst. Manage.* June, pp. 8–13

Jackson M A 1983 *System Development.* Prentice–Hall, London

Kant E, Barstow D R 1981 The refinement paradigm: The interaction of coding and efficiency knowledge in programming synthesis. *IEEE Trans. Software Eng.* 7(5), 458–71

Mason R E A, Carey T T 1983 Prototyping interactive information systems. *Commun. ACM* 26(5), 347–54

Palmer J D 1987 *Advanced Software Systems Engineering Environments.* AESOP, Baltimore, Maryland

Partsch H, Steinbruggen R 1983 Program transformation systems. *Comput. Surv.* 15(3), 199–236

Peterson J L 1981 *Petri-Net Theory and the Modeling of Systems.* Prentice–Hall, Englewood Cliffs, New Jersey

Pressman R S 1987 *Software Engineering: A Practitioner's Approach*, 2nd edn. McGraw–Hill, New York

Riddle W E, Williams L G 1986 Software environments workshop report. *ACM SIGSOFT Software Eng. Notes* 11(1), 73–102

Ross D 1977 Structured analysis (SA): A language for communicating ideas. *IEEE Trans. Software Eng.* 20(1)

Ross D 1985 Applications of SADT. *Computer* 18(4), 25–35

Scharer L 1983 The prototyping alternative. *ITT Programm.* 1(1), 34–43

Taylor T, Standish T A 1982 Initial thoughts on rapid prototyping techniques. *ACM SIGSOFT Software Eng. Notes* 7(5), 160–66

Teichroew K, Hershey D 1977 PSL/PSA: A computer aided technique for structured documentation and analysis of information processing systems. *IEEE Trans. Software Eng.* 3(1), 41–48

Warnier J D 1981 *Logical Construction of Systems.* Van Nostrand Reinhold, New York

Wile D S 1983 Program developments: Formal explanations of implementations. *Commun. ACM* 26(11), 902–11

Yourdon E 1982 *Managing the Systems Life Cycle: A Software Development Methodology Overview.* Yourdon Press, New York

J. D. Palmer
[George Mason University, Fairfax, Virginia, USA]

Information Systems Design in Industrial Practice

Although the development of large information systems has been a difficult, expensive and failure-prone adventure for many organizations, this experience is by no means universal. Large information systems are being developed successfully using strategies borrowed from architecture and other engineering disciplines.

No other ubiquitous large systems (e.g., buildings, highways and computers) are developed in the way that information systems have traditionally been developed. An information system project usually starts with the detailed specification of all the functions and features of the system—the "requirements." Only after this specification process is complete is a software design prepared. Imagine the outcome if a builder tried to detail every tenant's unique specifications before starting the design of an office building, or if an aerospace firm had to define every payload's specifications before designing a space vehicle! For such systems, a total system design is created early in the project that will satisfy the requirements of a whole class of intended users. For example, a commercial building is designed for a class of tenant—offices, light manufacturing or warehousing—but not for specific tenants. Common requirements for all prospective tenants are incorporated into the design. Tailoring the space to each tenant occurs later, perhaps even after the building is completed. This article describes how some organizations are applying a comparable strategy to successfully develop large information systems.

1. Information Systems

Information systems record data about the real world in a database and enable people to access the data in ways that turn it into useful information. This definition is perhaps more all-inclusive than the conventional usage of the term, which is usually associated with administrative and management systems such as accounting, payroll and inventory control. There is no clear distinction, however, between such "traditional" information systems and systems that support military command and control, satellite tracking and the like. That these nontraditional information systems include components that acquire data from sensors rather than people is not significant except in the technology required to develop and operate them. Information systems support two distinct classes of functions in an organization: operations, and planning and decision support.

Operations functions execute and control the ongoing activities of the organization. Information systems that support them record data about these activities and generate outputs that are used in their performance. For example, an operational system for inventory control records receipts and issues from inventory, and it may generate documents such as pick lists and reorder notices as well as reports of stock on hand, monthly activity by item code, and so on. A system supporting an operations function represents the system of record for the organization. To be effective, the system's database must be a current, accurate representation of the supported function. An inventory control system, for example, is only useful to the extent that it accurately reflects the current status of inventory. If the data in the system is two weeks out of date, it may be worthless.

Planning and decision support functions provide executive-level decisions to influence the future direction of the organization. Information systems that support them summarize historical data to identify patterns and trends and to forecast outcomes based on assumptions about the future. For example, a decision support system for inventory control may compute optimal reorder points based on historical usage data and assumptions about future demand. In contrast to the operational system, the decision support system is not the system of record. Its database must contain accurate historical data to support the planning and forecasting activities, but it need not reflect the current status of the organization. Indeed, it would be difficult at best to carry out modelling in an environment where the basis of the model is changing by the hour.

Both types of information systems comprise the same four types of components: a database, application programs, a user interface and a technical environment.

The database stores data about the real world. In an operational system, the database records the details about entities and events—called primitive data (Inmon and Loper 1988). It should not contain summary or statistical data—called derivative data—which is the proper domain of a decision support system. The database for a decision support system may include both derivative and primitive data, and it is refreshed periodically with data extracted from operational systems.

The application programs process input data and store it in the database, generate useful outputs such as paychecks and purchase orders, and generate information in the form of reports and interactive queries. Application programs may perform predefined, application-specific functions (custom programs) or they may perform general purpose functions (e.g., a modelling package or report generator). Both operational systems and decision support systems usually include both types of programs, though the proportion of custom software in a decision support system is usually much smaller than in an operational system.

The user interface permits users to communicate with the system to enter data, retrieve information and control its operation; the user interface includes security procedures and controls. There is no significant difference between the capabilities required for operational systems and decision support systems.

The technical environment consists of the hardware, telecommunications and system software supporting the database, application programs and user interface. Again there is no significant difference between the capabilities required for operational systems and decision support systems. However, performance considerations may influence the selection of specific components of the environment.

To develop an information system is to specify, design, construct and implement these components. Specification is the preparation of the logical model for the system, which defines the functions and features that the system is to provide. The logical model includes the contents of the database, the input transaction formats, the computational algorithms, the report formats, and so on. Design is the preparation of the physical model, which allocates the functions and features to physical components. The physical model includes the design of the database files, application programs, user manuals, procedures, and so on. Construction is the creation and testing of the physical components in conformance with the specifications and design. Implementation is the introduction of the system into routine operation in the technical environment, including installation, user and operator training, and conversion of existing data.

2. Why Large Information Systems Projects are so Difficult

Expressed this way, information system development sounds straightforward. It appears to be a linear progression from defining the functions and features to be provided, through the design of the physical components and the creation of the database, application programs and user interface, to implementation. For small systems, in fact, this process works well. Small information systems, comprising up to about 50 000 lines of delivered source instructions, are routinely developed by teams of up to 5–6 people in less than a year. Large systems are a different matter. The techniques that work for small systems have not been effective when applied to problems an order of magnitude or more larger in size and complexity. Projects to develop many such large systems have involved a hundred people or more, lasted for 5–10 years and cost tens of millions of dollars; yet in some cases they have been terminated without producing a working system. Even successful projects tend to be more difficult and costly than expected. Why don't the techniques that work for small systems also work for large ones?

Small systems comprise a relatively small number of components, perhaps up to 100 application programs and database tables. Because all of the members of the project team can participate in the specification and design of the entire system, they all have a reasonably consistent vision of how it will be built and used. Each member of the team can develop his or her components with an understanding of their context in the completed system. The project manager's role is one of functional and technical leadership, personally ensuring that each team member's work is consistent with the vision. This integrated team perspective is lost on large projects. The sheer volume of the functional specifications exceeds the intellectual capacity of any one individual. The project organization consists of multiple teams, each responsible for the specification, design, construction and implementation of a portion of the system. Instead of leading the development personally, the project manager must coordinate the efforts of the subsystem team leaders to ensure that the functional objectives of the total system are met, that the subsystems interface properly and that uniform development standards are enforced. Although the subsystems defined at the start of the project may seem to fit together seamlessly, the subsystems as developed often do not, as represented in Fig. 1. This is an almost inevitable consequence of having separate teams prepare functional specifications, and then physical subsystem designs, without an overall system design to guide them.

Large systems have to be addressed as a problem in system design rather than program design. Given a coherent and detailed specification for a program, most professional programmers are perfectly capable of producing a well-structured, working program. This is not the problem. The problem is how to ensure that the functions and features are allocated to components in a way that will result in a system with the desired characteristics. Stated another way, the problem is to ensure that the logical and physical models

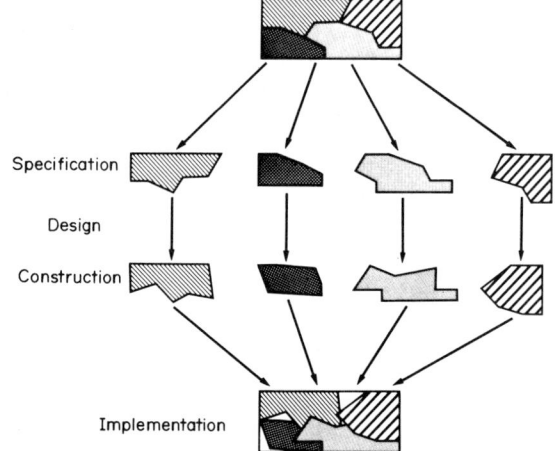

Figure 1
The problem with developing subsystems in a large project using the integrated team perspective

are congruent and optimal. Since the development of the very first information systems in the 1960s, however, most projects have used a development strategy that postpones the physical model until the logical model has been specified in detail. The development process usually comprises the following sequence of activities:

(a) defining functional requirements and specifications,
(b) designing software architecture and components,
(c) developing and testing components,
(d) integration and system testing, and
(e) implementation.

We will refer to this as the traditional life cycle.

The traditional life cycle begins with functional specialists defining what the system will do—the logical model. These people are familiar with the functional areas spanned by the new system. In order to develop the specifications in detail, they typically divide the project into subsystems and assign a team of people to work on each subsystem under the direction of the overall project manager. Each team independently specifies the functions and features of its subsystem, coordinating with the others to ensure compatible interfaces. After the functional specifications are complete, the subsystem teams add technically trained staff and proceed to design the database, application programs and other components—the physical model. In this phase of the life cycle, the technical specialists define how the system will accomplish its functional specifications. This is much too late, because the preparation of the logical model for a large system predetermines, in an unplanned way, the physical model; that is, the process of specifying the system's functions and features imposes a physical design to the exclusion of other, perhaps better, alternatives. Because specifications make up the detailed logical model of the system—inputs, outputs, algorithms, data stores, and so—it is easy to see that they can have this effect. On a project to develop a small system, this is not a problem because the team members can visualize the individual programs in the context of the completed system. Even if they follow a methodology that causes them to document the functional specifications in detail before preparing the physical model, they develop an early vision, perhaps intuitive, of a viable physical model. On a project to develop a large system, however, each team member sees too little of the total system to form this vision. The physical model of programs and database tables emerges in a piecemeal fashion as the logical modelling process identifies processes and data stores. Achieving uniformity in the user interface and in the internal technical design across the subsystems requires active coordination between the teams and is rarely completely successful. By the time that any fundamental deficiencies in the physical model are identified, such as poor performance or operational complexity, they are difficult and costly to correct.

If there is such a serious defect in the traditional life cycle, how did it originate and why has it persisted? It originated because the earliest application programmers developed their software without any formal specifications at all. They translated the guidance of the system sponsor into executable code without first documenting the specifications and the design. A flow chart of the program was considered good design practice. It became clear that the programmers and sponsor needed a mutually agreed definition of what the program would do. This was called the requirements document because it defined what the sponsor required of the software. The requirements document was always intended to leave the programmers the latitude to write the software as they saw fit. It was not supposed to constrain the structure or detailed logic of the programs. This process was satisfactory for small systems, but it broke down when applied to large ones. The requirements document for a large system was thick and difficult to comprehend, and development teams had difficulty translating it to software that met the objectives of the sponsor. The term "Victorian novel" was applied pejoratively to such documents.

In the late 1970s, a methodology was developed that promised to solve this problem. Called structured analysis, it enables a project team to decompose a system into a set of primitive processes and data flows by functional decomposition (DeMarco 1978). It uses a graphic representation called data flow diagrams to depict the sources and sinks of data, processes and data stores, and the flow of data among them. Following structured analysis, the project team iteratively decomposes each process in a data flow diagram into a lower-level diagram, eventually creating a hierarchically organized, complete depiction of the processes and data in the new system. Explicit in the methodology is the preparation of the logical model before the physical model. Only after the logical model is reviewed and approved is the physical model developed.

Structured analysis is the most widely used methodology for specifying information systems. It imposes a discipline on the functional specification process and it results in documentation from which programmers can write programs. These characteristics have caused many organizations to adopt structured analysis as the basis of their development methodologies. But structured analysis has not solved the problems associated with the development of large systems. Because it encourages the postponement of physical design issues, it does not address the need for congruence of the logical and physical models. It does not reduce the intellectual complexity of the functional specifications; it only provides a mechanism to manage the detail.

Large information systems are being developed successfully, however, using strategies that avoid the problems caused by the traditional functional decomposition approach. These strategies are borrowed from other engineering disciplines which have had to cope with the same fundamental problem—how to efficiently translate a complex set of objectives and constraints into a system that satisfies them.

3. A Systems Engineering Approach to Designing Information Systems

Systems engineering evolved in the 1950s from the need to develop ever larger and more complex engineering systems, such as weapons, aircraft and especially spacecraft. It introduced a new step at the start of the design process to permit the project team to formulate and evaluate alternative solutions and to create a high-level design. It synchronized the development of the logical and physical models. The high-level design defines the major components and their interfaces, and allocates functions and features to each. Each subsystem team then has a well-defined specification to work toward, one that will ensure a successfully integrated system if the high-level design was carried out correctly. The same approach is being applied successfully to the development of large information systems. The approach consists of the following major life-cycle steps:

(a) development of a system concept;
(b) design of software architecture;
(c) development of detailed functional specifications;
(d) design of components;
(e) development and testing of components;
(f) integration and system testing; and
(g) implementation.

The key difference from the traditional life cycle is the development of the high-level logical and physical models *before* preparing the detailed functional specifications. The project starts with a system concept phase to develop a complete understanding of the objectives and constraints of the system and to define an overall functional, design, construction and implementation approach. When the system concept is complete and has been approved, the next step is to develop the high-level software design for the system. Then, within the context of this design, detailed functional specifications are prepared.

The system concept provides a model of the as-built system. It allows a small project team to explore a variety of design approaches, evaluating them for feasibility, risks, schedule impacts, benefits and costs. It permits early consideration of such fundamental issues as: how to distribute data and processing among nodes in a network of computers; whether and how to convert data from systems that will be replaced; and how to interface the system with other existing systems. The system concept avoids one of the basic problems with the traditional approach—the postponement of physical design until the functional specifications are complete. Preparation of a system concept also provides the opportunity to neutralize the other major difficulty presented by large systems projects—the overwhelming volume of functional detail in the logical model. Hoare (1981) stated the following lesson that he learned from a failed software project early in his career.

> I conclude that there are two ways of constructing a software design . . . so simple that there are **obviously** no deficiencies, . . . so complicated that there are no **obvious** deficiencies.

Large systems developed by the traditional approach are almost always so complicated that their deficiencies are not apparent until too late in the development life cycle. To avoid the development of complicated systems, the intellectual complexity of the functional specifications has to be reduced to a manageable level. Jones suggests the solution: find the pattern in the problem (Jones 1980).

> . . . the main principle in dealing with complicated problems is to transform them into simple ones. This recoding, or restructuring, process depends upon the use of a pattern which brings crucial aspects to the fore.

He provides a graphic representation of this concept, shown in Fig. 2.

> The complicated pattern of the network on the left can be transformed into the simple pattern on the right by rearranging the nodes. This is analogous to the "change of set" which can enable one to solve a previously insoluble problem.

We have some excellent examples of software that exploit the patterns inherent in their problem domains. A ubiquitous example is the spreadsheet package, which allows the solution of problems that can be

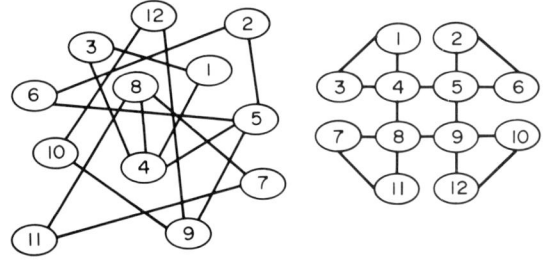

Figure 2
Graphic representation of problem solution by pattern finding (after Jones 1980. © Wiley, New York. Reproduced with permission)

represented as rows and columns of values, labels and formulas. Anyone who has used one of these products can appreciate what a large class of problems this is, and how much effort would be required to develop custom software to do what can be done in an hour on a personal computer.

Another example is the relational database model, which permits logical data models of arbitrary complexity to be represented as a set of normalized tables. The power of the relational model is not just in the vendor products that implement it. Even more, it has changed the way that we approach data modelling. By thinking of a data model as a set of normalized tables, we derive more general and complete database specifications. By recognizing the pattern in the problem, Codd freed us from the arbitrary complexities of the hierarchical and network data models (Codd 1970).

How does a project team find the pattern early in its work on a new system? Neither the functional sponsor for the system nor its intended users are likely to say during an interview, "I think that there's a pattern in this problem." As the team gathers information early in the project, the pattern is unlikely to emerge in a clear vision. More likely, it will be obscured by the myriad of details. The pattern can be identified by abstracting the details into higher-order constructs. As the project team works on the logical model of the new system, it has to actively formulate abstractions and test them against the details. The correct abstractions will restate the details in a unified manner. More valuably, they will disclose previously unrecognized functions and features. This translates directly into reduced maintenance costs later in the life cycle, because these unrecognized capabilities will not have to be added as enhancements.

Once identified, the pattern suggests a structure for the system. The system can be thought of as a mechanism for processing instances of the pattern. This leads naturally to a search for common functions that will be required to support the processing of these instances. Finding the pattern leads to an improved understanding of what the system must do and how it will do it. The system concept is the proper stage in the development life cycle to identify the pattern in the problem and to formulate a design based on the pattern.

4. *Developing the System Concept*

The activities involved in the development of a system concept can be loosely grouped into four major tasks:

(a) refining objectives and constraints, and defining scope;
(b) formulating a high-level functional model;
(c) formulating a design and implementation strategy; and
(d) reviewing and documenting the system concept.

A concept study should be completed in 3–6 months, even for a large system. The project team should consist of up to 6 or 7 senior people with relevant functional and technical skills and experience. The team includes functional specialists because defining the high-level functional model is an integral part of a concept study. It includes technical specialists to formulate and evaluate design approaches. Most importantly, the participants have to work as a single team: a system concept cannot be developed by the loosely coordinated efforts of separate teams.

The first major task in a concept study is to refine the objectives and constraints for the new system and to define its scope. Many information system projects have been undertaken with a scope that is either too narrow to meet the organization's real needs or too broad to be feasible. The scope should be broad enough to encompass related functions throughout the organization, but not so broad as to exceed the organization's ability to develop the system. In defining scope, it is essential to differentiate between operational and decision support systems. Operational systems should generally be developed to support a well-defined function or related group of functions within the organization. Decision support systems, on the other hand, are most useful when they support planning and analysis which cross functional boundaries. For example, the following scope would be too broad for an operational system: "The new system will provide automated support for manufacturing, marketing, personnel and accounting." This would be a perfectly reasonable scope for a decision support system if the wording were changed slightly, as follows: "The new system will provide consolidated manufacturing, marketing, personnel and accounting data on a weekly basis." It requires a great deal of judgement to properly set the scope of a new system.

The second major task is to formulate the high-level functional model, which consists of a high-level data model and process model. The data model identifies the entities and their relationships that will be represented in the database of the system. The process model identifies the events in the real world that the system will respond to, the types of decisions that it will support, key interfaces with other systems, essential features of the user interface, and so on. The development of the high-level functional model is the opportunity to identify the pattern in the problem. The concept team has to actively seek functional abstractions for both processes and data which can be exploited to simplify the specification and design of the system. As an example, consider a financial management system which records accounting events such as purchase orders, invoices, revenue receipts and journal vouchers. Each of these financial events can be represented as instances of a common pattern—a document consisting of a header and a repeating group of identically formatted detail lines. For each document type, of course, the specific data elements in the header and detail lines would be unique. For example, the header of a purchase order would contain data about the vendor and the date due, and its detail lines would contain data about the items being ordered. Exploiting this pattern, the system can be conceived as processing instances of the standard document format. Common functions required for all documents—such as interactive data entry, transaction suspense and audit trail creation—can be defined once and targeted for implementation in table-driven common software. Document-unique functions, such as editing the data elements and posting updates to the database, can be abstracted into standard processing logic and targeted for implementation within skeleton programs. As this example suggests, finding and exploiting the pattern in the problem can reduce the intellectual complexity of the functional specifications, suggest a software architecture, and provide a template for subsequent work on the detailed logical model.

The third major task is to formulate a design and implementation strategy. This phase of concept development is an iterative process of synthesis and analysis. The team has to synthesize potential strategies, analyze them for feasibility, risk, costs and benefits, and converge on a solution. Listed below are examples of issues that a concept team might address in this task:

(a) whether to develop a custom system, acquire a package and use it as is, or acquire a package and modify it;

(b) whether to implement the system at all locations at once, at a pilot location followed by all locations at once, or at one location at a time; and

(c) whether to retain archived documents on microfiche, hard copy, optical disk or a combination of these media.

The process of formulating and evaluating options exposes issues requiring detailed analysis. Each significant issue is analyzed and documented in a decision paper, which is then circulated to all members of the team for review, comment and resolution. Decision papers help to prevent difficult issues from delaying completion of the concept study.

After the functional model and the design and implementation strategy are complete, the final task is to prepare a draft concept document and conduct detailed reviews. Although a system concept document is usually quite comprehensible, it is insufficient simply to circulate it for comments. Detailed reviews are essential. To conduct the reviews, the team develops operational scenarios and "walks" through them with prospective users and operators of the new system. The scenarios represent business and technical situations, both typical and exceptional, that the system will encounter. The "walk throughs" enable the reviewers either to validate the concept or to identify additional issues that must be addressed.

At the conclusion of a system concept study, the organization has a clearly defined, documented model for the new system. The project is ready to proceed to the next step, designing the software architecture.

5. A Software Architecture for Information Systems

The designer's goal is to decompose the system into a set of software components and interfaces that is in some sense optimal. Traditionally, software has been designed by decomposing the logical model to a fine level of detail using structured analysis, then defining the programs and interfaces from the primitive functions in the logical model. This approach has a serious deficiency; if the programs and interfaces it defines prove not to be optimal, it is too late to correct the problem. A different strategy, again based on analogy with other engineering disciplines, has proven much more effective. This strategy views an information system as an assembly of standard component types plugged into a framework which provides common service functions. Consider the analogy with electronic equipment. Individual circuit boards are mounted in a chassis which provides power and cooling to all the boards and also provides the interconnections among them. In an information system, the circuit boards become the programs that perform functions unique to the application. Information systems consist of a small number of unique types of application components, as follows (examples are drawn from a financial system):

(a) process input transactions that record events (e.g., a purchase order);

(b) produce reports (e.g., budgeted versus actual expenditures by month);

(c) respond to interactive queries (e.g., whether an invoice has been paid);

(d) process scheduled jobs in response to the passage of time (e.g., month-end closing);

(e) extract data from the database to send to other systems (e.g., to a decision support system); and

(f) load data from other systems into the database (e.g., financial data from the payroll system).

The chassis becomes the software that performs common functions, for example:

(a) interactive dialog management—menus, security, help, data entry;

(b) transaction management—transaction suspense, error correction, audit trails; and

(c) scheduled job management—job-stream creation, job scheduling and control, operator communications.

Designing the software architecture early in the project permits the team to predefine the features that common software will perform. A uniform user interface can be specified for the entire system, for example, eliminating the need (or the possibility) for each subsystem team to define its own. The common software can be designed to invoke the standard types of application-unique components in a standard way, eliminating yet another source of effort and variability.

Organizations that are using this strategy for a software architecture are developing successful information systems on short time frames. They implement the common functions in reusable software, which eliminates the need to redefine and redevelop the common functions anew for each system. The architecture is at once a template for specifying a new system and reusable software for constructing it. As a template, the architecture supports (and enforces) a standard way of performing common functions. As reusable software, it eliminates the specification, design and development of a significant amount of code. The approach is applicable to problems in diverse functional areas. It is useful for developing both operational systems and decision support systems. Although the application-unique components of these two classes of systems are different in some cases, especially with regard to transaction processing, many of the common functions are applicable to both.

In addition to stimulating the use of reuseable common software, this architectural strategy also simplifies the specification, design and development of the application-unique programs. During the development of the detailed functional specifications, each function is decomposed into the standard set of application component types. In the financial system, for example, the revenue functions might decompose into eight input transactions, 17 reports, five queries, and so on for the other component types. If the project team has also succeeded in identifying a pattern in the problem (for example, the header/detail document model), then a standard structure can be defined for all programs that process instances of the pattern. Thus, if the financial system includes 40 different document types, all 40 document edit/update programs can share a common control structure. The benefits of such uniformity in a system are overwhelming—reduced effort to specify and develop the system, improved reliability, and reduced effort to maintain the system after implementation.

6. Conclusion

Organizations applying the systems engineering approach to information systems have been able to overcome the deficiencies in the traditional life cycle. Developing a system concept as the initial phase of a new project provides both a functional model and a design and implementation strategy before significant effort is devoted to detailed specifications. It provides an early opportunity to consider difficult and critical issues and to select solutions that increase the likelihood of a successful outcome.

The system concept provides the opportunity to identify abstractions in the problem domain that will reduce the intellectual complexity of the functional specifications. Because the specifications can be patterned on the abstraction, they are more likely to be complete and consistent, and to result in a system that is easy for users to learn and work with.

The software architecture defines a high-level system design that comprises instances of standard component types within a framework that performs common functions. The framework can be implemented in reusable software and applied to the development of systems in a variety of functional areas. The standard components impose a discipline on the development of the detailed functional specifications, helping the project team to decompose the system's functionality into primitives that correspond to these components.

If this strategy for designing information systems results in better systems at lower cost, why have more organizations not adopted it? The answers are several: most information system developers are not trained in systems engineering; the strategy has not been widely publicized; and there is a large body of literature advocating the traditional life cycle. As more organizations become aware that there are alternatives to the traditional life cycle, more information systems will be developed using these concepts.

See also: Information Systems

Bibliography

Codd E F 1970 A relational model of data for large shared data banks. *Commun. ACM* **13**, 377–87
DeMarco T 1978 *Structured Analysis and System Specification.* Yourdon, New York
Hoare C A R 1981 The Emperor's old clothes. *Comun. ACM* **24**, 75–83
Inmon W H, Loper M L 1988 A unified data architecture for systems integration. *Proc. US Army Technology Strategies Conf.*, pp. 169–78
Jones J C 1980 *Design Methods.* Wiley, Chichester

M. S. Hess
[American Management Systems, Inc., Arlington, Virginia, USA]

Information Theory

Information theory was first developed by Shannon (1948) as the mathematical theory of communication.

It combines various mathematical methods, including those of probability, statistics, analysis, functional equations, functional analysis, Fourier analysis and some parts of algebra. It now has applications far beyond communications theory; in engineering, mathematics, the sciences and even economics (Theil 1967, Aczél 1984).

1. Measures of Information, Properties and Characterizations (Aczél and Daróczy 1975)

Let $A_1, \ldots, A_n$ be events (messages, weather or market situations, possible results of an experiment, etc.; here in finite number, see Sect. 2 for a more general definition, in particular of entropies) with probabilities (frequencies) $p_k = P(A_k)$. The Shannon entropy

$$H(P(A_k)|_{k=1}^n) = H(p_1, \ldots, p_n) = -\sum p_k \log p_k$$

($0 \log 0 = 0$ by definition, $p_k \geq 0$, $\Sigma p_k = 1$) may be interpreted as the measure of uncertainty in (or of information expected from) the outcome of the experiment, because it has, among others, the following properties.

(a) $0 \leq H(p_1, \ldots, p_n) \leq H(1, \ldots, 1/n)$. The uncertainty is nonnegative and greatest when all events (outcomes) are equally probable.

(b) H is symmetric. The uncertainty does not depend upon the labelling of the events.

(c) $H(p_1, \ldots, p_n, 0) = H(p_1, \ldots, p_n)$. Addition of an event with zero probability does not change the uncertainty.

(d) $H(p_1(1-q), p_1 q, p_2, \ldots, p_n) = H(p_1, \ldots, p_n) + H(1-q, q)p_1$. This describes what happens when one event is split into two.

(e) $H(P(A_j \text{ and } B_k)|_{j=1, k=1}^{m, n}) \leq H(P(A_j)|_{j=1}^m) + H(P(B_k)|_{k=1}^n)$. The amount of information expected from two experiments is not greater than the sum of those expected from the individual experiments.

(f) There is equality in (e) when the two experiments are independent, i.e., $P(A_j \text{ and } B_k) = P(A_j)P(B_k)$ for all j, k.

A few of these characterize the Shannon entropy up to a multiplicative constant, for instance Daróczy and Katai proved (see Aczél and Daróczy 1975) that (d), (b) and (a) are sufficient. Furthermore, Diderrich (see Maksa 1980) has shown that (a) can be replaced by the boundedness of $H_2(1-q, q)$. However, (b), (c), (e) and (f) characterize (see Aczél and Daróczy 1975) the linear combinations, with nonnegative coefficients, of Shannon and of Hartley entropy (which is the logarithm of the number of events with nonzero probabilities). There are other entropies in use, e.g., those of degree $a > 1$: $(2^{1-a} - 1)^{-1}(\Sigma p_k^a - 1)$, which do not satisfy (f) and satisfy (d) with p_1^a at the end instead of p_1, and those of order $a > 0$ ($a \neq 1$—Rényi entropies): $(1-a)^{-1} \log \Sigma p_k^a$ which does not satisfy (d) and (e). The limit of both as $a \to 1$ is Shannon entropy and the limit of those of order a as $a \to 0$ is Hartley entropy.

Other important measures of information are the first-order redundancy $1 - H(p_1, \ldots, p_n)/\log n)$ (nonnegative, by (a)), the conditional entropy

$$H(P(A_j)|_{j=1}^m / P(B_k)|_{k=1}^n) = H(P(A_j \text{ and } B_k)|_{j=1, k=1}^{m, n}) - H(P(B_k)|_{k=1}^n)$$

(nonnegative and, by (e), not greater than $H(P(A_j)|_{j=1}^m)$: the conditional uncertainty is not greater than the unconditional one), and the mutual information

$$H(P(A_j)|_{j=1}^m) - H(P(A_j)|_{j=1}^m / P(B_k)|_{k=1}^n)$$

(nonnegative, by (e), also not greater than $H(P(A_j)|_{j=1}^m)$).

If $A_j|_{j=1}^m$ is the input and $B_k|_{k=1}^n$ the output of a channel, then the channel capacity is the maximum of the mutual information over all possible inputs. If more than one probability is assigned to the same system of events, then measures of comparison are used, such as the directed divergence $\Sigma P(A_k) \log(P(A_k)/Q(A_k))$ (Kullback 1959) (also nonnegative) and the information improvement $\Sigma P(A_k) \log(R(A_k)/Q(A_k))$ (Theil 1967). There are, again, similar measures of other degrees and orders. All these additional measures have natural properties and may be characterized by some of them.

A connection with forecasting theory is established by the task of "keeping the forecaster honest": the probabilities $P(A_k)|_{k=1}^n$ are estimated by the forecaster as $Q(A_k)|_{k=1}^n$. The forecaster is given a payoff $f(Q(A_k))$ if the event A_k happens. We want to choose the payoff function f so that the forecaster's expected gain is maximal when $Q(A_k) = P(A_k)$, that is,

$$\sum_{k=1}^n P(A_k) f(Q(A_k)) \leq \sum_{k=1}^n P(A_k) f(P(A_k))$$

If $n > 2$, then according to Aczél and Daróczy (1975) $f(t) = c \log t + b$ ($c \geq 0$), so the maximal expected gain is $c \Sigma P(A_k) \log P(A_k) + b$, which contains Shannon entropy. (The converse is a consequence of the nonnegativity of the directed divergence.)

2. Entropy and Dynamical Systems (Sinai 1970, Walters 1975)

A dynamical system is a quadruple $(X, \mathscr{F}, P, T)$ where $(X, \mathscr{F}, P)$ is a probability space and T (metric endomorphism) is a measurable transformation of X to itself that preserves the probability measure P; that is, for each $F \in \mathscr{F}: T^{-1}F \in \mathscr{F}$ and $P(T^{-1}F) = P(F)$. Let $\alpha = \{A_1, A_2, \ldots\}$ and $\beta = \{B_1, B_2, \ldots\}$ be two finite or countably infinite measurable partitions of X (experiments). That is, $A_i, B_h \in \mathscr{F}$ for all $i, h = 1, 2, \ldots$, $A_i \cap A_j = B_h \cap B_k = \emptyset$ for all (i, j) and (h, k) with

$i \neq j$, $h \neq k$ and, finally, $\bigcup_i A_i = X$, $\bigcup_h B_h = X$. The symbol $\alpha \vee \beta$ denotes the collection (measurable partition of X) of all sets of the form $A_i \cap B_h$. Consider an experiment α with finite Shannon entropy

$$H(\alpha) = -\sum_i P(A_i) \log P(A_i)$$

and the amount of uncertainty measured by Shannon's entropy

$$H_n(\alpha) = H\left(\bigvee_{j=0}^{n-1} T^{-j}\right)$$

which is associated with the experiment $\vee_{j=0}^{n-1} T^{-j}$. The fact (Sect. 1(a, e)) that $H_n \geq 0$ for all nonnegative integers n and the subadditivity of Shannon's entropy $(H(\alpha \vee \beta) \leq H(\alpha) + H(\beta))$ guarantee the existence of $\lim_{n \to \infty} (H_n/n)$. The quantity

$$h(T, \alpha) = \lim_{n \to \infty} (H_n/n)$$

has been called the rate of information about α generated by T or entropy of T given α. As conditional entropy, for each experiment α, $h(T, \alpha)$ cannot exceed the amount of uncertainty (entropy) associated with the transformation T. Thus, in a quite natural way, the entropy or Kolmogorov–Sinai invariant of the dynamical system $(X, \mathscr{F}, P, T)$ is defined by the equation

$$h(T) = \sup \{h(T, \alpha): \alpha \in \mathscr{E}\}$$

where $\mathscr{E}$ is the set of all finite measurable partitions of X (Sinai 1970, Walters 1975). In several cases $h(T)$ is actually attained by $h(T, \alpha)$, $\alpha \in \mathscr{E}$; that is, $h(T)$ is a maximum. This occurs for instance when the dynamical system has a generating partition. A partition η is a generating partition for $(X, \mathscr{F}, P, T)$ if $H(\eta)$ is finite and

$$\bigvee_{j=-\infty}^{\infty} T^{-j} = \varepsilon \pmod{0}$$

where ε is the set of all singletons (one-element subsets) of X. Indeed if $(X, \mathscr{F}, P, T)$ has a generating partition η then $h(T) = h(T, \eta)$.

Two dynamical systems $(X_1, \mathscr{F}_1, P_1, T_1)$ and $(X_2, \mathscr{F}_2, P_2, T_2)$ are isomorphic if there exists an invertible measure preserving transformation S of X_1 to X_2 such that $S(T_1 x) = T_2(Sx)$ for all x in X. If the two systems are isomorphic then $h(T_1) = h(T_2)$ (Sinai 1970, Walters 1975); that is, the entropy $h(T)$ is isomorphism invariant. For a special case of dynamical systems, the Bernoulli system, the converse of this statement is also true: if two Bernoulli systems have the same entropy h then they are isomorphic (Ornstein 1970, Keane and Smorodinski 1979). Let $A = 1, 2, \ldots, a$ be a finite alphabet ($a \geq 2$) and $p_1, p_2, \ldots, p_a$ a finite probability distribution on A. A Bernoulli system is the dynamical system $(X(A), \mathscr{F}, \mu, B)$ where $X(A) = A^z$ is the set of all doubly infinite sequences of letters from A, $\mathscr{F}$ is the product σ-algebra on $X(A)$, i.e., the σ-algebra generated by the cylinder sets C of $X(A)$, $\mu = p^z$ is the probability measure on $\mathscr{F}$ generated by the measure defined for the cylinder sets as product (independence) of probabilities p_i and B is the shift transformation $Bx = y$, $y_j = x_{j+1}$ for each integer j (Bernoulli shift).

A Bernoulli system has as generating partition the finite partition η of $X(A)$ into the elementary cylinders C_i^0, $i = 1, 2, \ldots$, where C_i^0 is the set of all sequences $\{\ldots, x_{-2}, x_{-1}, x_0, x_1, x_2, \ldots\}$ such that $x_0 = i$. Therefore the entropy $h(B)$ of a Bernoulli system is simply

$$h(B) = h(B, \eta) = H(\eta) = -\sum_{i=1}^{a} p_i \log p_i$$

3. Information Systems—The Source (Martin and England 1981)

In the standard representation of an information system (source → encoder → channel → decoder → destination) the source is a device that produces information in the form of a string of letters (message) in a given finite alphabet A (discrete source). These strings are supposed to be doubly infinite; they are the singletons of a set $X(A)$ and to each of them a probability is attached, that defines a probability measure P on the σ-algebra generated by these singletons. A discrete source is said to be stationary if the probability P is preserved by the shift transformation B; i.e., $P(B^{-1}F) = P(F)$ for all $F \in \mathscr{F}$. Hence for a discrete stationary source (and only in this case) the quadruple $(X(A), \mathscr{F}, P, B)$ is a dynamical system. The corresponding entropy $h(B)$ is called the source entropy of the information system and it is usually denoted by H_∞. A source is ergodic if the shift transformation B is ergodic; i.e., if $B^{-1}F = F$ (F invariant under B) implies $P(F) = 0$ or $P(F) = 1$. If the probability of each message is the product of the probabilities p_i, $i = 1, 2, \ldots, a$ of its letters, i.e., if no letter of the message depends on the others, then the source is said to be memoryless. In this case the dynamical system $(X(A), \mathscr{F}, P, B)$ is a Bernoulli system. More generally, a discrete source is a Bernoulli source if the dynamical system $(X(A), \mathscr{F}, P, B)$ that represents the source is isomorphic to a Bernoulli system.

4. Information Systems—The Channel (Gallager 1968, Wolfowitz 1978, Martin and England 1981)

The channel receives the messages produced by the source in an input alphabet A_1 from the encoder. The message is processed by the channel that produces an output in an output alphabet A_2. The channel is a discrete channel if both A_1 and A_2 are finite.

A channel $(X(A_1), X(A_2), P(\cdot/x))$ is determined by the sets $X(A_1)$ and $X(A_2)$ of all possible inputs x and outputs y and a conditional probability distribution $P(\cdot/x)$ on the σ-algebra $\mathscr{F}_{A_2}$ generated by the output strings y. For each $F \in \mathscr{F}_{A_2}$, $P(F/x)$ represents the probability that the output y is in the set F, given that the input was x.

If, for each $x \in X(A_1)$, there exists a $y \in X(A_2)$ such that $P(y/x) = 1$, the channel is said to be noiseless. Indeed the fact that the correspondence between input and output is not one-to-one but probabilistic is due to the presence of noise in the information system.

The channel is stationary if the probability distributions $P(\cdot/x)$ are invariant under the shift transformation B; that is, if $P(B^{-1}F/B^{-1}x) = P(F/x)$ for each $x \in X(A_1)$ and every $F \in \mathscr{F}_{A_2}$. If a channel is noiseless then it is just an (invertible) code from $X(A_1)$ to $X(A_2)$.

Finally, a discrete channel is memoryless if each letter of the output depends only upon the corresponding (simultaneous) input letter. In a discrete memoryless channel the mutual information (see Sect. 1) of the output about the input $I(A_1, A_2)$ represents also the so-called rate of information R about the source, processed by the channel. The maximum of $I(A_1, A_2)$ over all admissible inputs is the channel capacity (see Sect. 1). The following classical coding theorems describe the success of information theory in communication systems design.

THEOREM 1 (Shannon 1948). *Let* $(X(A_1), X(A_2), P(\cdot/x))$ *be a discrete, stationary, memoryless channel with capacity* C, *and let* $(X(A), \mathscr{F}, P, B)$ *be a discrete, stationary and ergodic source with entropy* H_∞ (*cf. Sects. 2, 3*), *then*

(a) *if* $H_\infty < C$, *for every* $\varepsilon > 0$ *one can find a code or measurable mapping* $X(A) \to X(A_1)$ *such that the rate of information R about this source, processed by the given channel, is greater than* $H_\infty - \varepsilon$;

(b) *if* $H_\infty > C$, *there exists no code with R arbitrarily close to* H_∞.

THEOREM 2 (Feinstein 1958). *Given a discrete, memoryless, stationary channel with positive capacity C, for every* $0 < \varepsilon < C$ *one can find a positive integer M such that, for each $m > M$, the set*

$$\overbrace{A_1 \times A_1 \times \cdots \times A_1}^{m} = A_1^m$$

of all strings (messages) of length m contains n strings $x_1, x_2, \ldots, x_n$ and, correspondingly,

$$\overbrace{A_1 \times A_2 \times \cdots \times A_2}^{m} = A_2^m$$

can be partitioned into n sets $B_1, B_2, \ldots, B_n$ so that

$$P(x = x_i / y \in B_i) > 1 - \varepsilon, \quad i = 1, 2, \ldots, n,$$
$$n > \exp(m(C - \varepsilon))$$

Theorems which provide lower bounds for the probability of an error in transmitting information over a noisy channel are called converses to coding theorem 1. For instance a (weak) converse theorem states that, if the rate of information R is greater than C, then the probability of an error (output different from the corresponding input) in a string of length n cannot tend to zero as n tends to infinity. Strong converses to the coding theorem actually give a positive lower bound for the probability of an error or even provide conditions for the probability to tend to 1 as n tends to infinity (Gallager 1968, Sinai 1970, Martin and England 1981).

5. Deriving Probability Distributions: The Maximum Entropy Principle (Levine and Tribus 1979, Aczél and Forte 1986, Forte and Hughes 1988)

Shannon's entropy and any other probabilistic entropy can be interpreted as the measure of the amount of uncertainty one has about the outcome of an experiment $\alpha = \{A_1, A_2, \ldots, A_n\}$ knowing the probability p_i of each possible outcome A_i and considering any other information (like the partition α itself) as irrelevant. It is natural to assume that neglecting information will not reduce the uncertainty and adding information will not increase the uncertainty. For instance, if one does not know the probability distribution $\{p_1, p_2, \ldots, p_n\}$ but only that it satisfies a certain given equation or system of equations

$$g(p_1, p_2, \ldots, p_n) = 0 \qquad (1)$$

then we expect the amount of unconditional uncertainty $I(\alpha)$ about the outcome of the experiment α to be such that $I(\alpha) \geqslant \sup H(\alpha)$, where the supremum is taken over all the probability distributions that verify Eqn. (1). $H(\alpha)$ here denotes Shannon entropy or any other probabilistic entropy as dictated by the particular application. The maximum entropy principle postulates that, if a unique probability distribution $p_1^*, p_2^*, \ldots, p_n^*$ exists that satisfies Eqn. (1) and $I(\alpha) = H(\alpha) \leqslant H(p_1^*, p_2^*, \ldots, p_n^*)$ ($H(\alpha)$ under the condition (1) has a maximum value at $\{p_1^*, p_2^*, \ldots, p_n^*\}$), then this probability distribution is the "true" one. The corresponding method for deriving probability distributions has proved to be both simple and successful in connection with several classical probability distributions like the Maxwell–Boltzmann distribution (Jaynes 1957), and Fermi–Dirac and Bose–Einstein distributions (Forte and Sempi 1976). The (controversial) principle of maximum entropy provides indeed a simple unified formalism for choosing one particular probability distribution in a class of probability distributions.

The above-mentioned probability distributions belong to the vast category of probability distributions that can be derived by maximizing Shannon entropy, given the mean values

$$\sum_{i=1}^{n} p_i a_i^{(j)} = \langle Y^{(j)} \rangle \quad (j = 1, 2, \ldots, m)$$

of a certain number m of random variables $Y^{(j)}$ over α. The simplest case is the Laplace–Gauss distribution that maximizes Shannon entropy

$$H(\alpha) = -\sum_{i=1}^{n} p_i \log p_i$$

given the mean value $\langle Y \rangle$ and the variance $\langle Y^2 \rangle$ of a random variable Y; i.e., under the conditions

$$g_1(p_1, p_2, \ldots, p_n) = p_1 + p_2 + \cdots + p_n = 1$$
$$g_2(p_1, p_2, \ldots, p_n) = a_1 p_1 + a_2 p_2 + \cdots + a_n p_n$$
$$= \langle Y \rangle$$
$$g_3(p_1, p_2, \ldots, p_n) = a_1^2 p_1 + a_2^2 p_2 + \cdots + a_n^2 p_n$$
$$= \langle Y^2 \rangle$$

The trivial case is of course when only the first condition $g_1 = 1$ is given, in which case the (unique) probability distribution that maximizes the Shannon entropy is the uniform distribution $p_1^* = p_2^* = \cdots = 1/n$ (see property (a) in Sect. 1). Less trivial is the case (that can be easily generalized) where the probability distributions $p_1, p_2, \ldots, p_m$ and $q_1, q_2, \ldots, q_n$ of the experiments $\alpha = \{A_1, A_2, \ldots, A_m\}$ and $\beta = \{B_1, B_2, \ldots, B_n\}$, respectively, are given, but one does not know the joint probability distribution π_{ij}, $i = 1, \ldots, m$, $j = 1, \ldots, n$ of the experiment $\alpha \vee \beta$. The (unique) probability distribution π_{ij}^*, $i = 1, \ldots, m$, $j = 1, \ldots, n$ that maximizes Shannon entropy under the conditions

$$\sum_{i,j} \pi_{ij} = 1$$

$$\sum_{j} \pi_{ij} = p_i \quad (i = 1, 2, \ldots, m)$$

$$\sum_{i} \pi_{ij} = q_j \quad (j = 1, 2, \ldots, n)$$

is the product probability distribution $\pi_{ij} = p_i q_j$, $i = 1, \ldots, m, j = 1, \ldots, n$ (see properties (e) and (f) in Sect. 1).

6. Questions and Questionnaires (Picard 1980)

A questionnaire is an alternating sequence of questions and answers. A questionnaire is mathematically represented by a finite directed graph (X, Γ), where X is a finite set of points (*vertices*), Γ maps X into $X \times X$, $\Gamma(X)$ being such that, if the arc $(i, j) \in \Gamma(X)$, then $(j, k) \notin \Gamma(X)$. In an arc (i, j) the vertex i is called the *origin* and j is called the *terminal vertex*. Furthermore those graphs (X, Γ) which represent questionnaires have the following properties: (a) they have no circuits (no closed path), (b) no vertex is the origin of just one arc in $\Gamma(X)$, and (c) there exists a mapping P of $\Gamma(X)$ into the interval $[0, 1]$ such that

$$\sum_{j \in \Gamma i} P(i, j) = \sum_{h \in \Gamma^{-1} i} P(h, j), \quad \sum_{e \in E} \sum_{h \in \Gamma^{-1} e} P(h, e) = 1$$

where Γi denotes, for each fixed i, the set of all terminal vertices j such that $(i, j) \in \Gamma(X)$, $\Gamma^{-1} i$ is the set of the origins of all arcs with the same terminal vertex i and E is the set of all vertices i (final answers to the questionnaire) such that $\Gamma i = \emptyset$. Thus the set X splits into two disjoint sets E and F; $X = E \cup F$, where F is the set of all *questions* (internal vertices of (X, Γ)). If $i \in F$, the set Γi is the set of all possible *answers* to the question i.

The valuation P defines a complete probability distribution p on E, the probability of each answer e in E being given by

$$p(e) = \sum_{h \in \Gamma^{-1} e} P(h, e)$$

A typical problem to which questionnaire theory may be applied can be formulated as follows: given each single question x, its possible answers y and their probabilities $p(y)$, design a questionnaire $Q = (X, \Gamma, P_\Gamma)$ (that is, find Γ and P_Γ) that exhibits certain properties of optimality. These properties of optimality require some functions of (X, Γ, P_Γ) to be maximal or minimal. The most common functions are the following.

(a) The routing length $L(Q)$. This is defined by the equation

$$L(Q) = \sum_{i \in F} \sum_{j \in \Gamma i} P(i, j) = \sum_{i \in F} p(i)$$

Minimizing the routing length leads to the Huffman questionnaires.

(b) The information transmitted by a questionnaire Q, which is the Shannon entropy

$$I(Q) = -\sum_{e \in E} p(e) \log p(e)$$

(c) The information processed by a question i, defined by

$$J(i) = \sum_{j \in \Gamma i} \frac{P(i,j)}{P(i)} \log \frac{P(i)}{P(i,j)}, \quad p(i) = \sum_{j \in \Gamma i} P(i,j)$$

(d) The information processed by a questionnaire. This is defined by

$$J(Q) = \sum_{i \in F} p(i) J(i)$$

Maximizing the processed information (J-optimality) leads to Shannon–Fano questionnaires (Picard 1980).

(e) The acquisition of a question i. This is the quantity

$$A(i) = \sum_{j \in \Gamma i} \frac{P(i,j)}{p(i)} \log_{a_i} \frac{P(i)}{P(i,j)}$$

where a_i (out-degree of the question i) is the total number of possible answers to the question i.

(f) The acquisition of a questionnaire Q. This is simply defined as

$$A(Q) = \sum_{i \in F} p(i) A(i)$$

A questionnaire is A-optimal if it maximizes the acquisition.

More sophisticated models of questionnaires have been considered for different applications. The quasi-questionnaires and the pseudoquestionnaires are worth mentioning (Picard 1980). Recently, interesting applications of information theory to image representation and pattern recognition have been found (Forte 1987).

See also: Information Laws of Systems

Bibliography

Aczél J 1984 Measuring information beyond communication theory—Some probably useful and some almost certainly useless generalizations. *Inf. Process. Manage.* **20,** 385–95
Aczél J, Daróczy Z 1975 *On Measures of Information and their Characterizations.* Academic Press, New York
Aczél J, Forte B 1986 Generalized entropies and the maximum entropy principle. In: Justice J H (ed.) *Bayesian Entropy and Bayesian Methods in Applied Statistics.* Cambridge University Press, Cambridge, pp. 95–100
Feinstein A 1958 *Foundations of Information Theory.* McGraw-Hill, New York
Forte B 1987 *Topics in Information Theory,* Lecture Notes. School for Advanced Studies in Industrial and Applied Mathematics, Tecnopolis, Bari, Italy
Forte B, Hughes W 1988 The maximum entropy principle: A tool to define new entropies. *Rep. Math. Phys.,* **26**(2), 71–79.
Forte B, Sempi C 1976 Maximizing conditional entropies: A derivation of quantal statistics. *Rend. Mat.* **6,** 551–66
Gallager R C 1968 *Information Theory and Reliable Communication.* Wiley, New York
Jaynes E T 1957 Information theory and statistical mechanics. *Phys. Rev.* **106,** 620–30; **108,** 171–90
Keane M, Smorodinsky M 1979 Bernoulli schemes of the same entropy are finitarily isomorphic. *Ann. Math.* **109,** 397–406
Kullback S 1959 *Information Theory and Statistics.* Wiley, New York
Levine R D, Tribus M 1979 *The Maximum Entropy Formalism.* MIT Press, Cambridge, Massachusetts
Maksa G 1980 Bounded symmetric information functions. *C. R. Math. Rep. Acad. Sci. Canada* **2,** 247–52
Martin N F G, England J W 1981 Mathematical theory of entropy. *Encyclopedia of Mathematics and its Applications,* Vol. 12. Addison–Wesley, Reading, Massachusetts
Ornstein D S 1970 Bernoulli shifts with the same entropy are isomorphic. *Adv. Math.* **4,** 337–52
Picard C F 1980 *Graphs and Questionnaires.* North-Holland, New York
Shannon C E 1948 A mathematical theory of communications, *Bell Syst. Tech. J.* **27,** 379–423; 623–56
Sinai J C 1970 *Theory of Dynamical Systems,* Lecture Notes Series No. 23. Matematisk Institut, Aarhus, Denmark
Theil H 1967 *Economics and Information Theory.* North-Holland, Amsterdam
Walters P 1975 *Ergodic Theory—Introductory Lectures,* Lecture Notes in Mathematics, Vol. 458. Springer, Berlin
Wolfowitz J 1978 *Coding Theorems of Information Theory,* Ergebn. Math. Grenzgeb. NF, Vol. 31. Springer, Berlin

J. Aczél and B. Forte
[University of Waterloo, Waterloo, Ontario, Canada]

Intuitive and Analytical Cognition: Information Models

Rapid advances in the electronic transfer of information have produced a massive industry and large-scale changes in society; however, our understanding of the cognitive processes that transform information into knowledge and action remains fragmentary and, therefore, the subject of considerable research by scientists from a wide variety of disciplines. Much of the research is directed toward understanding what appears to be two antithetical types of information processing—analytical and intuitive cognition.

The meaning of analytical cognition in ordinary language is clear; it signifies a step-by-step, conscious, logically defensible process of problem solving. The ordinary meaning of intuition signifies the opposite, a cognitive process that somehow permits the achievement of an answer, solution or idea without the use of a conscious, logically defensible, step-by-step process. Analysis has always had an advantage over intuition in clarity of meaning because its meaning could be exhausted in any given case by reference to a logical and/or mathematical argument or model; moreover, analytical cognition is the basis of rationality, and a rational argument calls for an overt, step-by-step, defensible process. Thus, analytical cognition and overt definition are part of the same system of thought. This is not the case with intuition; throughout its history it has acquired a mystique, an ineffable, undefinable character as well as a mixed reputation. As a result there are numerous models for analytical cognition to which information scientists may turn, but no fully worked-out models of intuitive cognition.

The word intuition is in frequent use, however, and we all seem to understand what we mean by it, so it is natural to appeal to a dictionary. As it turns out, *Webster's Third New International Dictionary* is instructive; it tells us that intuition means "coming to direct knowledge or certainty without reasoning or inferring: immediate cognizance or conviction without rational thought." There are two aspects of Webster's definition worth noting: (a) whatever intuitive cognition is, it happens *immediately*; and (b) it is the *absence* of something we are familiar with (that is, "without reasoning" (or inferring)) that forms the basis of the definition. Thus, Webster defines intuition negatively, in terms of qualities it does not possess.

Webster's negative approach apparently evolved from what philosophers and psychologists have had to say about intuition over the centuries. Rorty (1967) gives considerable attention to this important but elusive aspect of our cognitive activity; the description given is largely in terms of departures from analysis, and is therefore also negative in character. Psychologists hold views similar to philosophers: for example, von Winterfeldt and Edwards (1986) describe four different types of intuition, but their definitions are merely examples of what they have in mind; no model of intuition is put forward.

Such negative definitions are of more than academic significance to information scientists for at least two reasons. Information science does not end with the objective features of information display systems; subjective features—the cognitive system of the receiver, the person who reads (decodes) the display—must also be considered. Otherwise the definition of information—including surprise—cannot be fulfilled. Therefore, some theory about the nature of the receiving system must be included in a description of the display–receiver system. If a system is designed on the assumption that the display will be interpreted analytically, then it will be possible to test the efficacy of the system by running the data of the display through the appropriate analytical model of the receiver system. Because the analytical model will be specified *a priori*, the actual response of the receiver system can be evaluated against the correct response specified by the analytical model. However, if the receiver system consists of a person, as it frequently will, then there exists the possibility of a nonanalytical (that is, intuitive) cognitive system being applied to the displayed data. However, if our definitions of intuition are negative—if no model of intuitive cognition exists—then we are left with unexplained departures from the desired operation; we can only note departures from analysis, we cannot specify approaches to intuition because it is left undefined. Consequently, we cannot predict what the response to the displayed data will be, other than that it will not be analytically based.

A second reason why negative definitions are troublesome concerns action, the consequence of information, or more specifically, the justification of action based on information. If information is processed analytically, the subsequent action can be defended and justified by recourse to an explicit model. However, if the justification of action is based on an intuitive, and thus an inexpressible mode of processing information for which no model exists, then it can be charged that the action was literally unjustified.

Information scientists may find it incredible that any professional action would be based on inexpressible knowledge or unjustified beliefs. Yet psychologists (and others) will point out that intuition-based knowledge is in fact regularly accepted by engineers and scientists, not only in terms of the discovery, creation or production of an idea, rule or belief, but in terms of justifying the acceptance of these, and actions based on them. The judgement to launch the ill-fated *Challenger* Space Shuttle, for example, was certainly not based on a formal rational/analytic treatment of information, but on an inexpressible (and thus indefensible) inference that the chances of a disaster were small, an inference later shown by analytical work to be clearly wrong (Feynman 1986).

1. Empirical Basis for Negative Views of the Value of Intuitive Cognition

Psychological research has consistently found intuitive cognition to be fallacious: for example, a typical psychological experiment will show that the cognitive efforts of a group of subjects violated Bayes' rule or other normative criteria and, therefore, the subjects' intuitions were fallacious. One of the better known examples of this type of research comes from Tversky and Kahneman (1983) who show that most of their subjects violated the conjunction rule. This rule, based on the commonly accepted probability calculus, asserts that the product (conjunction) of two probabilities must be smaller than either probability alone. Yet most of their subjects, after stating the individual probabilities for two events, indicated that the probability of their joint occurrence was larger than either alone. As is customary, the departure from the normative rule is taken to demonstrate a fallacy produced by intuitive cognition. Most importantly, these and other researchers have concluded that such fallacies are common, that they are not easy to correct, and that even experts are not exempt from them. (For a striking example in medicine, see Eddy (1982).)

Despite the absence of clearly developed models of intuitive cognition, psychologists nevertheless frequently offer explanations of why people's intuitions often fail to follow normative rules. For example, Kahneman *et al.* (1982) present a coherent body of research that offers the explanation that people use intuitive heuristics when making judgements under uncertainty, and that these heuristics lead to biases and thus errors in judgement. Another coherent body of research can be found in the work of Wason and Johnson-Laird (1972) who demonstrate what they call a "confirmation bias," the tendency for people to seek only confirmatory evidence in the search for the truth or falsity of a hypothesis, when the most efficient procedure is to seek evidence that will disconfirm the hypothesis. The confirmation bias could lead to serious consequences in research and technical and scientific decision making.

One of the difficulties in interpreting research of this sort follows from the negative definition of intuition. Since the research only documents the departure from correct analytical solutions, we cannot be certain that it was not flawed analytical cognition (an incorrect logical model) that produced the incorrect answer. Nevertheless, empty definitions or not and empirical research aside, intuitive cognition has strong supporters.

2. The Positive View of Intuitive Cognition

Although psychological research since the 1960s has generally focused on the negative consequences of intuition, almost every other discipline finds it to be a positive and highly desirable aspect of cognition, not to be lightly given up. Consider the physicist Freeman Dyson's description of how the famous Nobel Prize winner Richard Feynman's departure from the rational/analytical mode of cognition made him an object of wonder among his colleagues (Dyson 1979 pp. 55–56):

> The reason Dick's physics was so hard for ordinary physicists to grasp was that he did not use equations. Since the time of Newton, the usual way of doing theoretical physics had been to begin by writing down some equations and then to work hard calculating solutions of the equations. This was the way Hans and Oppy and Julian Schwinger did physics. Dick just wrote down the solutions out of his head without ever writing down the equations. He had a physical picture of the way things happen, and the picture gave him the solutions directly, with a minimum of calculation. It was no wonder that people who had spent their lives solving equations were baffled by him. Their minds were analytical; his mind was pictorial.

The struggle between pictorial and mathematical/analytical representations of reality appears in Wechsler's discussion of arguments among physicists at the time of the introduction of quantum theory (Wechsler 1978 p. 72):

> Whereas Heisenberg's mode of thinking committed him to continue to work with a corpuscular-based theory lacking visualization, Bohr, Born, and Schrödinger believed otherwise; their need for the customary intuition linked with visualization was strong. Heisenberg's reply was that a new definition of intuition was necessary, linking it with the mathematical formalism of his new quantum mechanics. Visualization was regained through Bohr's personal aesthetic choice of the complementarity of wave and particle pictures, thereby linking physical theory with our experiences of the world of sensations.

A diagram in Charles Darwin's notes for his *Origin of Species* offers perhaps the most stunning example of intuitive, pictorial cognition existing side-by-side on the same page with an analytical exposition of the meaning of the diagram (Fig. 1). Examination of Darwin's visualization of his pictorial image of evolution (described by him as what "I think" in the upper left-hand corner of his diagram), together with his analytical–verbal deduction (indicated by the underlining of "requires" in the upper right-hand side) thus provides us with a museum piece for cognition: intui-

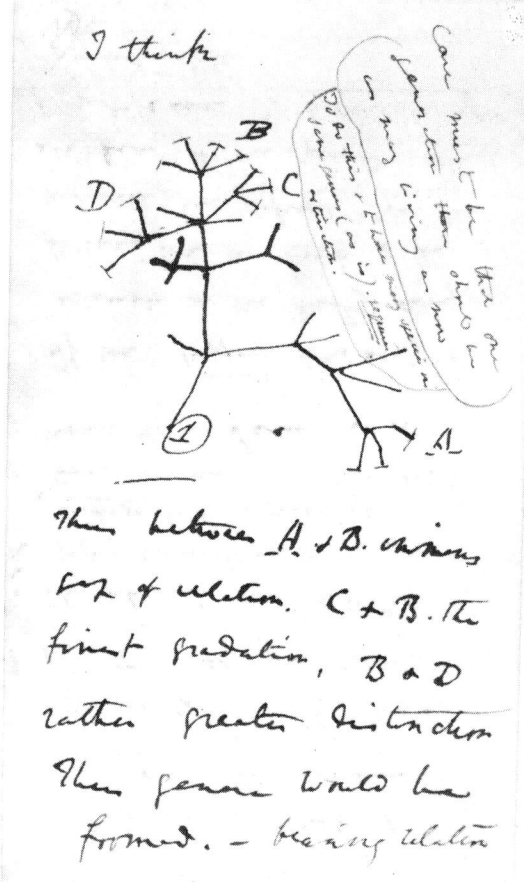

Figure 1
Darwin's third tree diagram, on page 36 of the first notebook. The text reads "I think," followed by the diagram. Then, "Thus between A & B immense gap of relation, C & B, the finest gradation, B & D rather greater distinction. Thus genera would be formed,—bearing relation (end of p. 36, beginning of p. 37) to ancient types." The marginal insertion alongside the tree diagram reads, "Case must be that one generation then should have as many living as now. To do this & to have many species in the same genus (as is), *requires* extinction." (From Gruber (1978). Courtesy of the Syndics of Cambridge University Library, Cambridge, Massachusetts. Reproduced with permission)

tion and analysis are joined on the same page in one of our greatest intellectual achievements.

These examples could be multiplied by the hundreds; experts in all professional fields, including medicine and engineering, are presumed to make good use of intuitive cognition, usually thought to be born out of extensive experience. Their scepticism regarding the findings of psychologists has been matched by psychologists' scepticism of the accuracy of the description. New conceptions of cognitive processes may yet reconcile these opposing views.

3. More Recent Conceptions of Cognitive Processes

Around the 1950s, two psychologists introduced a new idea that, roughly 30 years later, became well-known and to some extent put into practice: Egon Brunswik and Herbert Simon independently asserted that the most common form of cognition is not well represented by either intuition or analysis as those terms are commonly understood (Brunswik 1956, Simon 1957). Brunswik emphasized the role of "quasirationality"; Simon emphasized what he called "bounded rationality." Both meant to imply that although both intuition and analysis are indeed applied to certain problems, for the most part cognition was unlikely to be either purely intuitive or fully analytical.

Both these new concepts—quasirationality and bounded rationality—approximate the notion of "common sense"; that is, it is assumed that analysis goes as far as it can within the limits of time and analytical resources, and then resorts to something less when the problem remains unsolved. Thus the centuries-old dichotomy between intuition and analysis was broken by Brunswik and Simon into a tripartite scheme of (a) intuition, (b) quasirationality or bounded rationality, and (c) analysis.

There is, however, an important distinction to be drawn between Brunswik's quasirationality and Simon's bounded rationality, and it is a distinction that carries implications for information-processing models. Brunswik's quasirationality leads to a concept of cognitive processes that includes some components of analysis and some components of intuition. A judgement of the quality of a painting, for example, may rest partly on an inexpressible intuitive perception of its beauty, and partly on easily defended analytical arguments concerning the painting's balance, development of perspective, technical detail in drawing, and so on. Any judgement based on information may therefore be partly analytical and partly intuitive.

Simon's concept of bounded rationality is that cognition is all rationality; it is simply applied to a restricted area of the problem space. Thus: "The capacity of the human mind for formulating and solving complex problems is very small compared with the size of the problems whose solution is required for objectively rational behavior in the real world—or even for a reasonable approximation to such objective rationality" (Simon 1957 p. 198). The disparity between the small capacity of the human mind and the large size of the problem it faces means that decision makers and problem solvers must diminish the search space to a manageable size. Therefore, rather than seeking optimal solutions, they "satisfice"; that is, seek a satisfactory solution rather than attempt to search every nook and cranny of the problem space. Even the expert chess player, for example, does not pursue each and every alternative possibility at each choice point, but simply examines a number of possibilities that satisfy him/her that s/he is making the correct, or at least best, move.

What are the consequences of adapting either of these views of cognition that depart from the traditional dichotomous view? In the Brunswikian view, different task conditions evoke different relative amounts of intuition and analysis. If true, those who develop information displays should consider the type of cognition a given display will induce, a topic explored further below. Simon argues differently: "It is a fallacy to contrast "analytical" and "intuitive" styles of management. Intuition and judgement—at least good judgment—are simply analyses frozen into habit and into the capacity for rapid response through recognition" (Simon 1987 p. 63). The designer of display systems can, from this perspective, be confident that analytical cognition will always apply—unless good judgement fails!

The present author made explicit Brunswik's concept of a cognitive continuum that is anchored by pure intuition at one pole and pure analysis at the other. The anchoring properties of intuition and analysis are presented in Table 1. Specification of these properties makes it possible to recognize intuitive cognition. Thus, for example, if a person were to (a) exhibit low cognitive control (not make the same judgement in response to the same situation over several occasions), (b) rapidly reach a judgement, (c) demonstrate that s/he had little conscious awareness of the manner in which the judgement was reached (i.e., offer an "inexpressible" basis for the judgement), (d) use a simple method (e.g., weighted average or

Table 1
Properties of intuition and analysis

	Intuition	Analysis
Cognitive control	low	high
Rate of data processing	rapid	slow
Conscious awareness	low	high
Organizing principle	weighted average	task specific
Errors	normally distributed	few, but large
Confidence	high confidence in answer; low confidence in method	low confidence in answer; high confidence in method

summative procedure) to organize or aggregate the information into a judgement, (e) produce a set of judgements for which the errors were normally distributed, and (f) indicate that s/he had high confidence in his/her answer or judgement but low confidence in the method by which it was produced, then, according to cognitive continuum theory, this person would be employing intuitive cognition. The above set of attributes are put forward as a model for intuitive information processing. Their opposites provide the defining properties for analytical cognition (also presented in Table 1) and offer a model for analytical cognition that goes beyond the usual normative models. (An example of the application of the theory to expert highway engineers may be found in Hammond et al. (1987).)

Darwin's cognitive efforts depicted in Fig. 1 illustrate both polar types. His schematic diagram can be seen as an effort to express an idea that could not be expressed in any other way than by a picture that would carry meaning only for its creator. His written attempts at analysis, however, were intended to meet the criteria of explicitness and logic, and therefore contained the commonly accepted properties of analytical cognition. Thus, in his effort to create the concept of evolution he moved from one pole of the cognitive continuum to the other.

4. Circumstances Inducing Different Cognitive Activities

Up to this point we have discussed different aspects of cognitive activity regardless of the circumstances which evoke them and to which they are applied. However, such specification will be of great importance to information scientists who design systems for the display of information. Therefore we return to the objective features of information transfer. First, consider the problem of specifying the properties of information displays that induce (but do not compel) different cognitive activities. Hammond et al. (1987) attempt to do this in the following way: If (a) the displayed data present many redundant cues (attributes or features), (b) the cue values are continuous, (c) the cues are displayed simultaneously, (d) the cues are measured perceptually, and (e) the subject has available no explicit principle, scientific theory or method for organizing this information (cues) into a judgement, then intuitive cognition will be employed. Analytical cognition will be induced by the opposite set of conditions.

These specifications make it possible to quantify virtually any task with respect to its location on a "task continuum index" and the resulting cognitive activity on a "cognitive continuum index." The relationship between the two offers a rich opportunity for research. For example, the conceptual framework leads to the hypothesis that the cognitive activity induced by the task will be more effective than any other. The alternative to this hypothesis is that "bounded rationality" will be most effective. Another alternative is that the most analytical form of cognition will be more effective regardless of the form of the display.

5. Static versus Dynamic Tasks

The concept of a cognitive continuum may be useful in moving toward a positive definition of intuition as well as analysis within a framework of the psychology of judgement, but so far it has only been discussed in terms of static, but not dynamic cognition. Although roughly 100 years ago William James had emphasized the dynamic changing character of the world and the dynamic cognitive activity we engage in to cope with it, judgement and decision making in dynamic tasks has hardly been touched by researchers, despite its obvious importance.

Brehmer (1987a,b), one of the first psychologists to undertake empirical investigations of human performance and cognitive activity in dynamic tasks, has found that not only do his subjects perform poorly but they are poor learners. If found to be generally true, his findings carry considerable significance for the design of displays that require judgement and decision making under changing conditions.

Curiously, no one has described (and predicted) the change in cognition over time better than philosopher Stephen Pepper (Pepper 1948 pp. 22–23):

> This tension between common sense and expert knowledge, between cognition security without responsibility and cognitive responsibility without full security, is the interior dynamics of the knowledge situation. The indefiniteness of much detail in common sense, its contradictions, its lack of established grounds, drive thought to seek definiteness, consistency, and reasons. Thought finds these in the criticized and refined knowledge of mathematics, science, and philosophy, only to discover that these tend to thin out into arbitrary definitions, pointer readings, and tentative hypotheses. Astounded at the thinness and hollowness of these culminating achievements of conscientiously responsible cognition, thought seeks matter for its definitions, significance for its pointer readings, and support for its wobbling hypotheses. Responsible cognition finds itself insecure as a result of the very earnestness of its virtues. But where shall it turn? It does, in fact, turn back to common sense, that indefinite and irresponsible source which it so lately scorned. But it does so, generally, with a bad grace. After filling its empty definitions and pointer readings and hypotheses with meanings out of the rich confusion of common sense, it generally turns its head away, shuts its eyes to what it has been doing, and affirms dogmatically the self-evidence and certainty of the common-sense significance it has drawn into its concepts. Then it pretends to be securely based on self-evident principles or indubitable facts ... Thus the circle is completed. Common sense continually demands the responsible criticism of refined knowledge, and refined knowledge sooner or later requires the security of common-sense support.

Pepper's remarks serve an excellent purpose; they open a new topic—movement on the cognitive continuum—and that is a profound idea. What would induce such movement? Pepper clearly implies that failure induces movement. One pursues the answer to a problem analytically, in terms of responsible (read "analytical, justifiable") cognition insofar as one can maintain cognitive security (read "confidence"). However, when that security falls below the threshold one gives up cognitive responsibility in favor of security and turns back to what Pepper calls "common sense"; that is, toward the intuitive pole of the cognitive continuum. When irresponsible (unjustifiable) albeit secure (confident) intuitive cognition comes under attack, we return to seeking the responsibility of analysis, until it becomes insecure and cognition once more turns to analysis.

Although failure will cause cognitive activity to move on the cognitive continuum in static tasks, it is changing task conditions that induce movement in dynamic tasks. For example, an operator of a system may be reading a set of instruments in a sequential, analytically-justified fashion as s/he is trained to do, when an unexpected development produces a never before encountered situation in which the readings on several instruments change simultaneously and thus demand instant attention. The demand for reading several instruments simultaneously without the assistance of a preestablished principle for aggregating the information will drive cognitive activity from the analytical pole toward the intuitive pole of the cognitive continuum. The need for justification of one's actions, however, will drive cognition back to analysis, if this is possible. If it is not, the operator is forced to admit to action taken on the basis of inexpressible knowledge.

6. Summary

Despite the fact that the distinction between intuitive and analytical cognition was apparent to the ancient Greeks, our advance toward understanding this fascinating and important topic has been asymmetrical. Much has been learned about analysis and our models of it are clear and unambiguous, although disputes may still arise about which model is appropriate for which occasion. However, intuitive cognition remains mysterious and no models have as yet gained general confidence; no comprehensive models of intuitive cognition whose use could be empirically justified in information science currently exist. The model described here was presented for illustrative purposes; no claim is made for its general empirical validity.

Nevertheless, progress has definitely been made. Intuitive cognition has been brought under empirical experimental investigation since the 1930s, and intensively so since the 1960s. Hundreds of studies of intuitive cognition are now conducted every year by scientists in a wide variety of disciplines. The development of scientifically sound models of intuitive cognition may not be far off. As for the present, information scientists would do well to consider carefully the various means of information displays, the mode of cognition likely to be induced by them, and the consequences for judgement and decision making under benign as well as stressful conditions.

7. Acknowledgements

The author thanks Gary Bradshaw and Martha Neal for their assistance in the preparation of this article. Support for writing the article was provided by the Office of Basic Research, Army Research Institute Contract MDA903-86-C-0142. The views, opinions and findings contained therein are those of the author and should not be construed as an official Department of the Army position, policy or decision, unless so designated by other official documentation.

Bibliography

Brehmer B 1987a Models of diagnostic judgements. In: Rasmussen J, Duncan K, Leplat J (eds.) *New Technologies and Work: New Technology and Human Error*. Wiley, Chichester, pp. 87–95

Brehmer B 1987b Systems design and the psychology of complex systems. In: Rasmussen J, Zunde P (eds.) *Empirical Foundations of Information and Software Science III*. Plenum, New York, pp. 21–32

Brunswik E 1956 *Perception and the Representative Design of Psychological Experiments*, 2nd edn. University of California Press, Berkeley, California

Dyson F 1979 *Disturbing the Universe*. Harper and Row, New York

Eddy D 1982 Probabilistic reasoning in clinical medicine: Problems and opportunities. In: Kahneman D, Slovic P, Tversky A (eds.) *Judgment under Uncertainty: Heuristics and Biases*. Cambridge University Press, Cambridge, pp. 249–67

Feynman R P 1986 *Personal Observations on the Reliability of the Shuttle*, unpublished manuscript. California Institute of Technology, Pasadena, California

Gruber H E 1978 Darwin's "tree of nature" and other images of wide scope. In: Wechsler J (ed.) *On Aesthetics in Science*. MIT Press, Cambridge, Massachusetts

Hammond K R, Hamm R M, Grassia, J, Pearson, T 1987 Direct comparison of the efficacy of intuitive and analytical cognition in expert judgment. *IEEE Trans. Syst. Man, Cybern.* **17**(5), 753–70

Kahneman D, Slovic P, Tversky A (eds.) 1982 *Judgment under Uncertainty: Heuristics and Biases*. Cambridge University Press, Cambridge

Pepper S 1948 *World Hypotheses*. University of California Press, Berkeley, California

Rorty R 1967 Intuition. In: Edwards P (ed.) *The Encyclopedia of Philosophy*, Vol. 2. Macmillan, New York, pp. 204–12

Simon H A 1957 *Models of Man*. Wiley, New York

Simon H A 1987 Making management decisions: The role of intuition and emotion. *Acad. Manage. Exec.* **1**, 57–63

Tversky A, Kahneman D 1983 Extensional versus intuitive

reasoning: The conjunction fallacy in probability judgment. *Psychol. Rev.* **90**(4), 293–315

von Winterfeldt D, Edwards W 1986 *Decision Analysis and Behavioral Research*. Cambridge University Press, New York

Wason P C, Johnson-Laird P N 1972 *Psychology of Reasoning: Structure and Content*. Harvard University Press, Cambridge, Massachusetts

Wechsler J (ed.) 1978 *On Aesthetics in Science*. MIT Press, Cambridge, Massachusetts

K. R. Hammond
[University of Colorado, Boulder, Colorado, USA]

Knowledge Acquisition: Storyboarding and Computer-Based System Decision Research

Knowledge acquisition (known as requirements analysis in conventional computer-based systems engineering) is the critical bottleneck in the design and development process. Knowledge acquisition is typically tedious, time consuming and exceedingly difficult to do well; there are multiple techniques for extractng knowledge from domain experts, but none of them guarantees the acquisition of reliable, valid, comprehensive knowledge. The task is made more complex in the case of advanced cognitive computer-based problem-solving systems (such as the increasingly ubiquitous class of decision support systems, knowledge-based systems in artificial intelligence (AI), and the intelligent decision-support hybrids which are appearing with increasing frequency).

Several generalizations about knowledge acquisition for this general class of problem-solving/decision-aiding systems can be offered at the outset. First, there are multiple methods and tools available to the knowledge engineer (questionnaires, observation, experiments, interviews, and so forth). Second, all are fallible and yield "knowledge" about a domain which is almost invariably complex in nature and riddled with uncertainty. Third, the approach advocated in this article combines the relatively new technique of storyboarding with a suite of special methods taken from the decision, psychological, statistical and related sciences.

This generalized approach allows the knowledge engineer (or requirements analysis specialist) to elicit many kinds of information from users, show users reconstructed versions of the decision (or problem solving) process for the domain, and iterate on the reconstructed portrait until the user is satisfied that the real process has been captured adequately. The strategy for doing this entails an increasingly refined transition from generic decision-making process/task templates (Wohl 1981, Hopple 1986) to storyboarding (across several or multiple generations if necessary) and then system prototype design; the latter highlights the decision and analytical activities and processes involved.

1. Conventional Knowledge Acquisition

Traditionally, the knowledge acquisition process (as profiled in Waterman (1986) and other AI and knowledge-based system/expert system textbooks) relies on a series of intense and systematic interviews; the behavioral science literature on elite (and other forms of) interviewing is actually more pertinent to the knowledge engineer than arcane concepts from the field of AI. The process often takes many months, underlining the earlier point that knowledge acquisition is the bottleneck in system design and development.

As Waterman (1986) emphasizes, asking experts directly for the rules or methods used is rarely effective. Experts state their conclusions and revelant reasoning in general terms and make complex judgements rapidly. The paradox of expertise refers to the fact that the most competent experts in a domain are least capable of describing (reconstructing and articulating) the knowledge used to solve problems or make decisions. True expert knowledge is compiled, and thus collapsed to its minimum and efficient form and therefore is difficult to extract; "super" experts (such as a skilled physician as opposed to a medical school student, or a trained mechanic as opposed to a novice) simply cannot state their expertise very well.

Knowledge acquisition techniques include:

(a) the content analysis of textbooks in a domain (along with reports, briefing packages and other forms of "hard copy" or archived expertise);

(b) testing and experimentation;

(c) interviews (structured and/or unstructured);

(d) questionnaires;

(e) Delphi and other group-based elicitation processes;

(f) observation (or participant observation); and

(g) introspection or subjective inference of decision processes.

All seven techniques are used singly or in various combinations. None is perfect, all are expensive, and the weakest—introspection—tends to be used the most often. The barriers are exacerbated by the fact that knowledge (as opposed to data) tends to include opinions of experts (which are almost invariably biased) and is typically incomplete, idealized, fuzzy, incorrect, unreliable, uncertain and implausible.

Waterman (1986) profiles the actual techniques in terms of the dichotomous alternatives of observation (especially via the use of thinking-aloud protocols) and intuitive introspective "methods." He identifies seven techniques for the actual process of extracting knowledge:

(a) on-site observation (watching the expert solve real problems);

(b) problem discussion (explore the kinds of data, knowledge and procedures necessary to solve specific problems);

(c) problem description (the expert describes a prototypical problem for each category of answer in the domain);

(d) problem analysis (involving a series of realistic problems to be solved aloud);

(e) system refinement (where the expert provides a series of problems to solve via rules from interviews—done before the actual system is operational);

(f) system examination (the expert examines or critiques the rules and control structure of the prototype system); and

(g) system validation (involving the presentation of cases solved by the expert and the prototype system to outside experts).

This set of procedures can be used to develop a valid and reliable knowledge base. These approaches are actually conventional systems engineering and requirements analysis tools, not AI methods. Adelman (1987) provides one of the few sophisticated discussions of knowledge engineering or knowledge acquisition as a statistical-measurement problem in which analysis of variance can be used to attribute the quality of a knowledge base to the main (and interactive) effects of varying domain experts, knowledge engineers (for example, ones trained in different disciplines), methods for eliciting knowledge, and characteristics of the problem setting and structure.

2. Storyboarding

Andriole (1988) provides a useful survey of storyboarding, emphasizing the utility of storyboard prototyping for requirements verification. Storyboarding can be defined succinctly as a new prototyping technique that borrows from requirements analysis and simulation. Storyboards are interactive screen displays of system functions. They are typically designed and developed with off-the-shelf software. Andriole describes them as inexpensive "shells" of system performance (that is, they are not usually driven by working software but instead constitute screen displays of functions that will be programmed after sufficient validation has occurred).

Storyboards permit and facilitate the crucial system design and development task of system "sizing." Sizing involves the specification of the data and knowledge bases necessary to drive the candidate system, the specification of the analytical methods that could be incarnated in the system (for example, AI versus operations research versus engineering methods), and the development of alternative interface strategies. Sizing becomes particularly important (and problematic) when the system being designed is intended to focus on decision support or the actual making of decisions.

While storyboarding has not yet been validated in a definitive sense, the early data suggest that the approach is a viable alternative to conventional modelling and prototyping. It should also be noted that storyboarding is superior to simple paper screen displays of the envisioned system. Computer-generated (and animated) screen displays simulate human–computer interaction and allow the user to interact with, explore and "play with" the prototype system concept (an especially desirable option when decision processes are being represented, since the user can see if the system veridically captures the dynamics and structure of the decision being made). With the more recent animation packages on the market, it is now possible to animate the storyboard and thereby mimic sophisticated interactive graphics capabilities. Users of sophisticated decision support and knowledge-based systems clearly favor the use of graphics as a display medium (Hopple 1988).

3. Approaching the Decision Process

The approach for inferring and reconstructing (and then representing in a system) predecisional analytical activities (for example, the "intelligence" or situation assessment function so central to government and business) and actual stages of the decision process (such as option generation, option assessment, option selection, and so forth) combines three stages. First, the decision-making process (or the cognitive task to be performed or supported) must be profiled. Second, storyboarding must be used to generate prototype systems that users can look at and assess. Third, decision research for knowledge acquisition, a concept borrowed from Benbasat's stimulating essay on research methodologies for information and decision support systems (Benbasat 1984), must be conducted along with the task profiling and storyboarding iteration processes. This third module of the overall approach is the most difficult to perform successfully; there are off-the-shelf ways to do this, but none is easy or straightforward. Effective results often require the use of a melange of the methods and tools described below.

3.1 Generic Cognitive Task Templates

Hopple (1986) and Wohl (1981) provide useful summaries of the general area of cognitive problem-solving task taxonomies. Wohl's very succinct model involves the stages of stimulus identification and characterization, hypothesis generation, option generation, and response execution; a fifth task also generally ensues—assessment of the quality of the decision-making process (or decision aiding/support system). This phase is known in different domains as evaluation, postmortems, after-action reports, and so forth. It is often done haphazardly, with an emphasis on political considerations, or not at all.

Hopple (1986) discusses these notions in terms of two task typology contexts: decision situation (simple/complex, familiarity/frequency dimension, open and closed contexts, low or high uncertainty) and decision-making functions or tasks.

Three generic classes of decision situations can be identified. First, there are closed or routine situations; the simplest kind of decision can be automated through the use of an operations research or statistical technique. Open decision situations are inherently complex and pose serious challenges to the designer of decision support or knowledge-based systems. Crisis decision situations (where severe time stress or extreme temporal limitations and high uncertainty intersect) are the most problematic of the three classes and may not be aidable at all (suggesting that the emphasis on real-time and emergency management or warning support systems may not lead to very many useful and deployable aids).

Hopple (1986) reviews three of the major decision-process task conceptual schemes in detail. Decision making is central to most human activities and many researchers have attempted to characterize this process. Research (both published and unpublished) by Hopple and many other cognitive scientists demonstrates that the core decision task may be the intelligence, problem recognition/structuring, problem identification or stimulus function. This task is apparently much more important than option selection. Hypothesis and option generation are also crucial; few aids for these tasks have been developed. Some support systems focus on the intelligence or stimulus characterization task, but there is clearly a need for more basic research here.

Finally, Wohl notes that (Wohl 1981 pp. 623–24):

> The preponderance of work in decision theory has concentrated on techniques for option *selection* with little research on those portions of the process which are of greatest interest to military commanders, namely, the *creation, evaluation, and refinement* of both hypotheses (i.e., what is the situation) and options (i.e., what can be done about it).

This generalization holds well beyond the military sphere.

3.2 Use of Storyboarding to Generate Prototype Systems

The basics of storyboarding have already been presented. The technique can be joined with task templates and decision-research models and methods to form a useful analytical strategy for designing, developing and evaluating computer-based problem-solving systems. This can be a very expensive and time-consuming process; often, multiple generations of storyboarding must be developed for a single system to let the user examine the effectiveness with which the system represents the relevant decision process.

Increasingly sophisticated storyboarding software is available for the Apple Macintosh and IBM PC. Without any kind of programming, the system designer can use very sophisticated graphics and animation capabilities. Human–machine interface (HMI) simulation software is also now available off-the-shelf. The HMI (or user–system interface) dimension of decision support and knowledge-based systems is undoubtedly the key to system effectiveness for the user and his or her organization, reinforcing the importance of high-quality software for the HMI aspect of a system.

3.3 Decision Research and Knowledge Acquisition

Benbasat (1984) provides the only comprehensive treatment of decision research methods and models as a mechanism for acquiring knowledge for advanced problem-solving systems. The literature is voluminous for decision research and ranges across psychology, decision theory and many other fields.

A knowledge-based system (KBS) attempts to support, extend and amplify the analysis and decision processes of the decision maker. Therefore, a description of current decision processes must precede system design.

Two classes of tools can be used to reconstruct or infer decision processes: empirical research strategies from the behavioral sciences, and decision research models and methods.

Empirical research strategies fall into three general categories, according to Benbasat. There are studies conducted in natural behavior settings, the most "externally valid" area. These include case studies of decisions (in a single organization or by one person, with no experimental designs or controls). Case studies are quite useful for generating hypotheses. Field studies, in contrast, involve an experimental design but not the imposition of controls; such studies can be useful for testing hypotheses, describing the operation of a system, and developing hypotheses. Field experiments manipulate one or more independent variables and try to control other variables that might confound the experimental findings. The focus here is on genuine hypothesis testing.

Studies in contrived and created settings include laboratory experiments, with subjects assigned to control and treatment groups. The investigator manipulates one or more independent variables and tightly controls other relevant independent variables. This approach offers the advantage of replicability; the focus is on hypothesis testing. Included here are person–computer experiments and judgement tasks. The latter are used to capture information utilization and decision-making approaches via protocol analysis and/or regression analysis.

Finally, there is the setting-independent class of studies (sample surveys, interviews, questionnaires). There is no experimental manipulation of any independent variables; statistical controls on extraneous variables are imposed. The focus is the exploration of variables (and possibly their interrelationships) or hypothesis testing.

With empirical research strategies, it is clear that there is no best overall strategy. The system designer is advised to use a number of the strategies simultaneously to compensate for the limitations of each.

Decision research models and methods subsume a wide variety of tools. Overall, the focus is on the description of decision and information-use activities. These descriptions can provide the basis for storyboards of a system design concept; users can react to several versions of the storyboard, iterating until the information use or decision process is represented accurately. Decision research tools fall into two very broad classes: case and field study models, and laboratory experiment models.

The case and field study models in turn fall into three distinct categories. The belief/attitude model makes the assumption that the beliefs of the decision maker about and attitudes toward objects in the decision situation are key determinants of all facets of decision-making behavior. The interaction model uses structured observation to map the decision maker's interaction patterns with the organizational (internal) or external environment. The communication model examines the series of information exchanges between the decision maker and other sources of information in the decision situation. Communications networks (structure, loads, rates of message flow, the extent of message distortion) are central to this approach.

Laboratory-based models include the algebraic-regression representation model, where the decision maker is given data (cues) and judges or predicts the events. Weights are assigned and empirically estimated by regression analysis (where Y equals the dependent variable and the X values are the data provided or predictor variables).

A second family refers to predecision-behavior models, where two process-tracing approaches are employed to identify information use and decision processes. First, protocol analysis can be used to yield a transcript of the user's verbalized thoughts and actions. Second, there are techniques for the analysis of information acquisition (the subject's use of objective, external information).

There are limits to all of these tools (as is also true for empirical research strategy methods). A universal problem is the impact of time constraints. The different methods have different strengths and weaknesses. Decision research can be used productively for knowledge acquisition, but is difficult to do well.

See also: Decision Analysis; Decision-Problem Structuring; Decision Support Systems

Bibliography

Adelman L 1987 Toward considering psychological measurement issues when developing expert systems. *Proc. Annu. Meeting Syst., Man Cybern. Soc.*, Alexandria, Virginia

Andriole S J 1988 Storyboard prototyping for requirements verification. *Large Scale Syst.* (in press)

Benbasat I 1984 *The Information Systems Research Challenge: Proceedings.* Harvard Business School Press, Boston, Massachusetts

Hopple G W 1986 Decision aiding dangers: The law of the hammer and other maxims. *IEEE Trans. Syst., Man Cybern.* **16**(6)

Hopple G W 1988 *The State of the Art in Decision Support Systems.* QED Information Sciences, Wellesley, Massachusetts

Waterman D 1986 *A Guide to Expert Systems.* Addison–Wesley, Reading, Massachusetts

Wohl J 1981 Force management decision requirements for air force tactical command and control. *IEEE Trans. Syst., Man Cybern.* **11**(5)

G. W. Hopple
[George Mason University, Fairfax, Virginia, USA]

Knowledge-Based Simulation

Knowledge-based simulation (KBS) is a relatively new technology that permits the simulation of processes and systems in which there is a significant amount of noncausal knowledge that determines the behavior and performance of the system. Since it is a type of simulation, it facilitates the construction of models that endeavor to portray and delineate the behavior of an evolving process or system over time. It is the replication of process behavior over time that distinguishes KBS from other knowledge-based systems and expert systems. The latter have little or no relevance to the characterization of how processes perform and change over time. (If knowledge-based systems and expert systems incorporate dynamic models into their reasoning functions, at that point they become, by our definition, knowledge-based simulations.) Beyond the consideration of time that is common to all of simulation, KBS supports explicit representation of, and reasoning from, judgemental, declarative, associative and other forms of knowledge in addition to causal and procedural knowledge that have always been inherent within simulation. Conventional simulation models have always been concerned with the representation of causal and procedural knowledge and the extraction of useful information from that knowledge.

Potential advantages of KBS over conventional simulation are many and include improved intelligibility (increased descriptive power, explicit rules, assumptions), improved modifiability, improved credibility (greater explanation facilities) and rapid prototyping (capability to get a model up and running rapidly) according to Klahr and Faught (1980). Because KBS provides a representation and reasoning capability for additional knowledge forms beyond causal and procedural knowledge, it is possible to build within KBS systems intelligent facilities for aiding the user in formulation of KBS models and for interpretation of the results produced by such models, as suggested by O'Keefe (1986).

1. Development of KBS

Knowledge-based simulation grew out of the need for more features than conventional simulation languages provide. The term knowledge-based simulation first appeared in a description of Rand Corporation's simulation of a military air battle (Klahr and Faught 1980). The simulation was typical of advanced models in that it involved a hierarchy of components running in parallel and acting on the basis of rules. Conventional simulation languages could not easily model the communications and conditional responses required of these advanced models, nor could conventional languages provide explanations of the behavior of the simulation.

Klahr and Faught used the term knowledge-based simulation to describe ROSS, a new simulation system that incorporated objects, message passing, AI-like production rules and an ability to determine why the model behaved as it did. With ROSS, based on LISP, they were able to model the complex command and control scenarios of a modern air battlefield. T-PROLOG, obviously derived from PROLOG, was developed in Hungary to achieve similar modelling capabilities; that is, conditional responses, hierarchical interaction structures and behavior explanation (Futo and Szeredum 1982). These two languages were forerunners in the development of KBS languages and systems.

Reddy and Fox (1982) reported on a tool they developed and named "KBS," a knowledge-based simulation system. Their system, similar in some respects to ROSS, incorporated routines for automatic analysis of results. Graphics capabilities were included to improve the user's understanding of both the simulation model and the simulation results. "KBS" was developed as the kernel of a larger system with interfaces to support factory management. The system served as a test vehicle for several features found in current simulation systems.

KEE was introduced in 1983 by Intellicorp. The popularity of simulation models with KEE users was the impetus for the development of a simulation package for KEE in 1985; the package provided explicit support for simulation through inclusion of facilities for event control, statistics collection and reporting, generation of random variates and other features to simplify construction and execution of simulations in KEE.

Knowledge-based simulation systems distinguished themselves from other simulation systems by employing two additional concepts. The object-oriented paradigm (prominent in software engineering) of SIMULA was adopted to provide capabilities for attribute inheritance and hierarchical control. In addition to the objects, the object-oriented paradigm has provisions for message passing that are useful in a simulation context. Production rules from expert systems were incorporated to provide for more complex object behavior representation and explicit behavior description. These two concepts, the object-oriented paradigm and production rules, are complementary and provide the capability to construct more easily understood and more easily modified models of very complex situations. The object-oriented paradigm embedded within most knowledge-based simulations enables the noncausal knowledge to be partitioned on the basis of object ownership. This prevents the entire knowledge base from being processed each time there is a need to emulate the reasoning function of a particular object. Only that particular object's knowledge need be processed.

The appearance of commercially available LISP machines in 1982 added incentive for the development of KBS packages. Although these machines were developed and marketed to meet the demand arising from interest in expert systems and other AI applications, the larger address space of these machines (typically 64 times the size of laboratory computers) made implementation of complex simulation models feasible.

Concurrent with the rise of KBS was the improvement in computer graphics technology. The available technology was incorporated in the new LISP machines and provided the means to include interactive graphics in the KBS systems being developed. Graphical presentation of the dynamics of a model and graphical interpretation of the results significantly enhanced user confidence (Bell and O'Keefe 1987). During the same period and for the same reasons, graphics technology was also incorporated into conventional simulation packages.

In summary, knowledge-based simulation grew from the requirements of complex models. Beginning with publicly developed software and growing with the increasing capabilities of hardware, KBS has become a tool for the analysis of complex problems, as suggested in Sect. 2.

2. Applications of KBS

KBS is being used to model managerial processes in which there is much indigenous decision making inherent within the process that involves judgemental and other knowledge forms in addition to causal and procedural knowledge. Because of the hierarchical nature of managerial systems, examples of such systems abound. Illustrative of such systems is the two-tiered managerial system shown in Fig. 1. Hierarchical management structures are prevalent in both the private and public sectors. One such structure that has been extensively studied using KBS is the tactical battlefield where commander's decisions are specifically included within the model (Kameny et al. 1987).

KBS is also being used to model processes in which forms of knowledge other than causal knowledge

Knowledge-Based Simulation

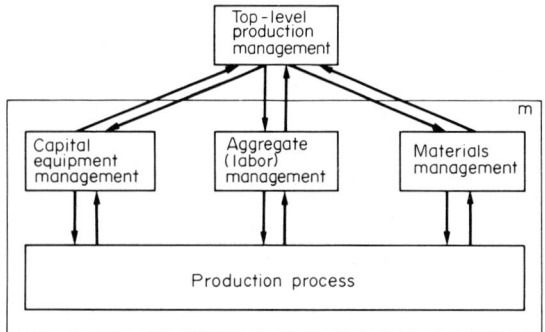

Figure 1
Managerial hierarchy required to control a process

strongly effect the behavior and performance of the process. For example, it can be used to model automated manufacturing systems (Nielsen 1986) in which the automation system must make decisions after the fashion of a human assembler who perceives the work environment in a certain state and reacts in a manner consistent with the needs of that environment. Such reactions are based on both perception and judgement. The explicit representation of judgement is one advantage afforded by KBS.

3. User Interface

Generally, KBS systems employ computer graphics in their user interface. The effectiveness of the graphics interface was recognized in the mid-1970s (Bell and O'Keefe 1987), and as the capabilities of engineering workstations supported high-resolution bit- or memory-mapped displays, graphics were incorporated into the KBS software.

Windows, menus and icons are common in the user interface for KBS systems (see Fig. 2). The windows may be either standard system windows which offer the user choices of options (a menu), or they may be user-defined windows in which the user specifies the contents using the inherent programming capabilities of the system. Windows typically follow a tree structure to provide access to categories of related basic functions. Horizontal and vertical scrolling are used to overcome limitations on window sizes.

Among the more useful features found among the various system interfaces is the library of iconic instruments (dials, meters, gauges, thermometers, etc.) for displaying simulation performance. These may be selected and associated with attribute values of various objects in the simulation and used to display continuously the value of an attribute as the simulation progresses. The library may contain built-in icons, user-defined icons or both, depending on the system.

When available, the combination of iconic instruments and horizontal and vertical scrolling allow the user to achieve a "fish eye" effect; that is, the user may focus on a specific segment of the model and observe its performance while excluding the rest of the model from view. This capability allows the user to validate the model by selectively monitoring critical (or questionable) portions to ensure the behavior mirrors the real world.

Preprogrammed function keys and a command syntax are common among user interfaces. These input features do not differ from conventional computer applications. The mouse is also found in some user interfaces. The mouse allows the user to navigate quickly through several levels of windows and menus and to select rapidly from the choices, using its "point and shoot" facilities.

The programming environment is improved over that provided by conventional simulation for several reasons. First, a full-screen editor may be interactive with the simulation during its execution. If an error is detected, the programmer is returned to the source code at the point where the execution error occurred. Formulation rules may facilitate the construction process, insisting on consistency and completeness. The entire environment is object-oriented. There is growing recognition and perception within the simulation community that there are distinct advantages to the use of the object-oriented paradigm within simulation technology; yet most conventional simulation environments do not support it.

4. KBS Architectures

There are several ways in which KBS systems can be configured. A simulation subsystem could be embedded within a knowledge engineering environment as depicted in Fig. 3(a). The knowledge engineering environment could be an expert-system shell that is programmable. In either case the required facilities for simulation are implemented in the host language (usually LISP) of the environment or shell. This is the most customary form of KBS architecture.

A second architecture for implementation of KBS is to employ two distinct systems (an expert system and a simulation system) and allow them to execute concurrently and to interact with each other in a UNIX environment, as suggested in Fig. 3(b). Judgemental, declarative and associative knowledge would be codified in the knowledge-based system (expert system) while causal and procedural knowledge would be codified within the simulation system. The knowledge-based system would perform necessary cognition and reasoning functions while the simulation system would portray the system behavior over time.

A third architecture would embed the knowledge subsystem within the simulation system environment, as shown in Fig. 3(c). The necessary knowledge system software would be written in the host language of the simulation environment.

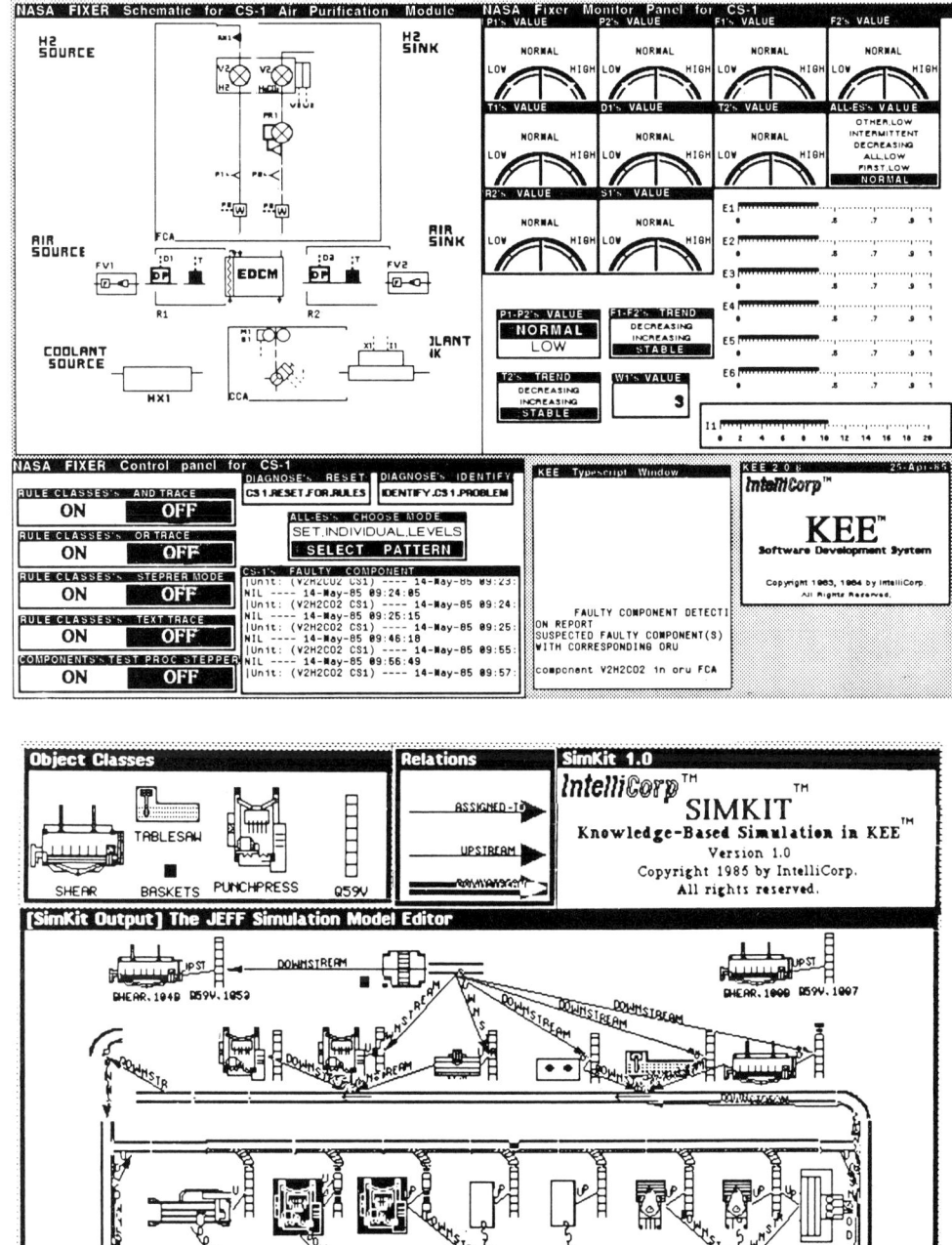

Figure 2
Examples of KBS user interfaces. (Taken from: Faught WS 1986 Applications of AI in engineering. *IEEE Comput*. **19**(7), 17–32. © IEEE, New York. Reproduced with permission)

Knowledge-Based Simulation

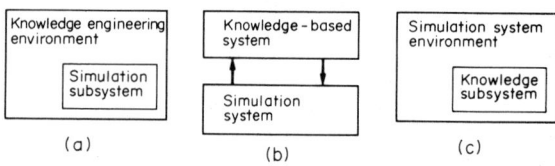

Figure 3
KBS architectures

The architecture shown in Fig. 3(a) is the most popular for several reasons. The knowledge-engineering environment provides superior facilities for model development (rapid prototyping and model modification) and model use (user interaction with the model during its execution and postprocessing analysis), as suggested by Nielsen (1986). Commercially available implementations of this architecture now provide prefabricated object libraries. To each such object is attached a graphics icon (see Fig. 2(b)) which can be used to construct a network simulation model. Specialized object libraries can be developed and used to assemble a simulation model in a particular problem domain. Graphics editors are used to construct icons for each newly formed object. Using these icons, a visual, schematic model of the system can be formulated. A corresponding logical representation of the model is developed automatically by the KBS system from the visual model. Multiple levels of representational detail are possible as a composite object may itself be composed of composites.

5. Mechanics of KBS

Methods for time advance within KBS could be either continuous, discrete or time-step. In a continuous simulation of the Forrester type, it would be possible to incorporate explicit reasoners within certain rates as shown in Fig. 4. Traditionally, rates have been the control mechanisms of a Forrester model. Conventionally, rates performed their tasks by use of a simple equation which mapped the inputs to the rate into a scalar output: the rate of flow. An "intelligent" rate might accept the same inputs but process them after the fashion of an expert, using a knowledge base and inferencing procedure.

Discrete-event KBSs are the most commonplace among KBS types. In discrete-event simulations, systems are represented as a sequence of activities engaged in by objects. Activities are tasks having definite starting times, ending times and time durations that, in general, are random. The starting and ending times of activities are instants in time called events. In KBS simulations, events are fundamentally of two types—physical and cognitive. They represent instants in time at which the modelled objects undergo a state change that is important to an understanding of the behavior of the process. No reasoning or cognition takes place

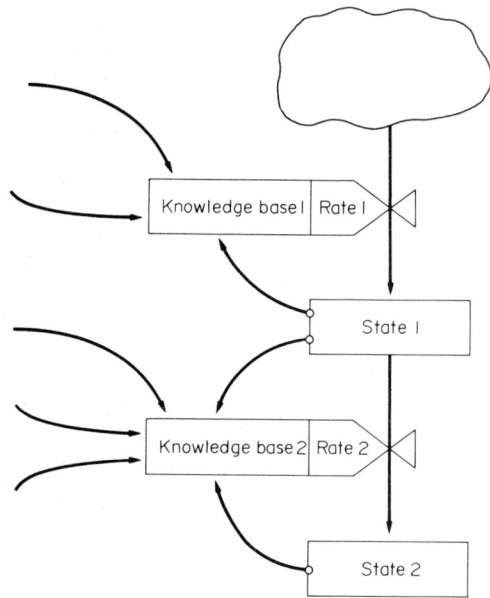

Figure 4
Incorporating KBS concepts within Forrester models

within physical events. Cognitive events, on the other hand, endeavor to represent reasoning and cognition explicitly. Objects may be mobile or fixed, passive or active (affecting other objects), cognitive or physical. In addition, objects may be representative of a real-world object or a system-supplied object required to support the simulation overhead (such as an event scheduler, a historian or a statistician).

6. State of the Technology of KBS

Of the extant commercial simulation packages, few provide the user with full support for KBSs. Those that do support KBS employ architecture (a) in Fig. 3, in which the simulation system is embedded in the knowledge system. Expert-system shells that do not have embedded simulation environments may allow simulation procedures to be coded as attributes of internal objects. These procedures (more properly called "methods") are placed within an attribute of an object and executed on demand within the simulation to represent a particular behavior of that object. Early simulations with KEE employed this method.

Alternatively, several expert-system shells have "hooks" that allow the execution of subroutines which could implement a simulation system. This type of system would conform to architecture (b) in Fig. 3. A user who has purchased an expert-system shell for other purposes and has substantial experience in programming simulations in general-purpose languages might find such an approach attractive; knowledge and knowledge processing would be done in the expert-system shell and event scheduling, random variate generation, queue management and so forth would be done in user-supplied routines written in a conventional programming language like C. If the hooks of the expert-system shells were compatible with a conventional simulation language such as GPSS or CSMP, architecture (b) in Fig. 3 might be chosen by a user with a library of conventional simulation models. Either method will pose a programming problem and may not provide the facile user interface found in implementations of architecture (a) in Fig. 3. There are no well-known conventional simulation languages which fully support the object-oriented paradigm and the explicit representation of noncausal knowledge; consequently, there are no known instances of architecture (c). However, addition of explicit knowledge-based simulation capabilities to SIMSCRIPT or SIMULA might be feasible and would certainly appeal to current users of these languages.

Adding all of the judgemental, declarative and associative knowledge detail within any simulation might be expected to slow execution times, and this is seen to be the case. Simulation has always been one of the most process-bound of computer software applications. Inclusion of facilities for representation of, and reasoning with, these other forms of knowledge makes it even more so. For this reason, many of the KBS models currently implemented are deterministic. The inclusion of Monte Carlo and stochastic detail may make the running times of the larger KBS models unacceptably slow. Fortunately, the future promises to provide significantly faster hardware that will support the extremely process-bound operation of KBS.

7. Formulation of KBS Models

In KBS, there is a stronger emphasis upon the software engineering aspects of model formulation than there is within simulation in general. This emphasis derives from the object-oriented approach incorporated in most of the KBS packages. The model formulation process begins with a formal analysis of needs and purposes; these are evolved into a detailed requirements analysis. The process proceeds from there to preliminary architectural design and ultimately to detailed design. Object-oriented design methods should be introduced by the time detailed design is begun. Flow analysis, functional analysis and state-change analysis have been recommended as approaches for the analysis of conventional simulations (Emshoff and Sisson 1970). Used singly, any one of these three may be inadequate due to the complexity of typical KBS models; a combination of all three may be needed to identify all the objects and their attributes, all of the operations on those objects, the commonality among objects, the interfaces among objects, appropriate superclasses, and inheritances from superclass to subclass. Identifying and specifying all of these draws on the whole of software engineering.

At the implementation level, it is first necessary to build a library of prototypes for each permanent object in the domain of interest. Where possible, a prototype should be defined as a subclass of an appropriate simulation library of objects (provided in the simulation system). Once the prototypes are built, it is necessary only to name each instance of each object in the simulation domain. Classes for the movable (transient, temporary) objects of the model are next to be entered in the domain library; these movable objects may be jobs in progress in a factory simulation, combat units in a battlefield simulation, supplies or material, parts, subassemblies and so forth. Defining movable object prototypes also involves describing the reactions of permanent objects to the movable objects and of the movable objects to each other. These behaviors will be described by methods that are defined within slots of the objects that possess such behaviors. In other cases these behaviors will be defined through inheritance. The final entries in the library are the interaction relations which specify the adjacency chains that are possible within a network over which the movable objects may travel. Domain-specific interaction relations are described for the domain library to supplement the standard interaction relations that may be provided in the simulation system.

Random inputs to the simulation are provided by standard random-variate generators. These are attached to objects that initiate instances of movable objects; in this role the random-variate generator governs the timing of inputted instance objects. At the time the generator is attached, statistical parameters are specified to achieve the desired input distribution. Random-variate generators are also used within event methods to generate a random activity time duration. User-supplied generators may be used should an unusual random-variate distribution be required. Of course, a user-developed random-variate generator should be written with reuse in mind and placed in a general library.

Lastly, the instrumentation for the model is selected from the array of monitor devices in the monitor objects library. These are attached to specified dynamic attributes of objects so as to record and/or present the information for user analysis. Again, user-developed monitors may be used and placed in the monitor objects library for reuse.

The level of detail contained in a KBS model may create difficulties for someone trained in a simulation methodology which obscures details with average values. As an example of this level of detail, Nielsen (1986) describes the communication system in a model as including prototype communication links, appropriate protocols for each type of link, methods for protocol checking and conversion for each communication link, and inheritance schemes for these attributes. The inheritance process of the object-oriented system makes this level of detail feasible because, once defined in a prototype, all instances are provided with the defined attributes.

After all the permanent and movable objects and their interaction relations have been defined in the domain library, implementation of a specific model is straightforward. Using the facilities of the simulation package, instances of objects are created, and a network is formed that is consistent with the interaction relations. Random-variate generators with appropriate distribution parameters are attached to certain objects to describe activity duration times of activities those objects can engage in and to characterize inter-arrival times. Monitors are then attached to dynamic attributes within certain objects and the simulation is executed.

A knowledge acquisition methodology is needed if substantial rule-based behavior is to be included in the model. It is conceivable that the knowledge acquisition task for a complex model will be greater than for the typical expert system, depending on the number of decision makers and the number of judgement domains included in the model.

In addition to modelling a human decision maker, rule-based knowledge may be used for situations in which the causal relationships are not known. In this case, historical records may allow preparation of rules with complex antecedents to simulate the outcome of a situation. A third use of rule-based processing would arise if complex policy decisions were to be tested in a model. Policy decisions would be included as rules influencing the behavior of the model. A model of a firm and the effect of new tax laws on that firm might be a situation for the use of a rule base. These examples demonstrate some of the potential requirements for knowledge acquisition in simulations.

The knowledge acquisition methodology employed may dictate the path of model development. A prototype may be needed to elicit from the expert all the expertise required in the simulation (Harmon and King 1985). Prototyping circumvents the traditional software engineering process in that coding is begun before all of the requirements are known and the user is active in directing the course of development. As it is refined, the prototype becomes the KBS. The need for a noncausal knowledge acquisition methodology distinguishes KBS from conventional simulation and from traditional software engineering.

With or without a prototype, the general steps of software engineering are adhered to in the development of any KBS. These steps consist of requirements analysis, architectural design, detailed design, coding and implementation. As with any other software system, each of these steps must be documented. The implementation phase focuses on correctness, modifiability and reuse, whether by traditional development or by prototyping. The goal is cost-effective decision support for management.

8. Summary and Conclusion

Conventional simulation models and systems have always been capable of representation and reasoning upon causal and procedural knowledge. KBS holds forth the promise for increased authenticity and improved validity through inclusion of additional knowledge detail previously overlooked within conventional simulation. The capability to represent and reason from not only causal knowledge but also judgemental knowledge, declarative knowledge and associative knowledge is compelling. Explicit and graphic representations of the components of the problem space and their interactions does not make KBS simulations advantageous over conventional simulations because conventional simulations support such dynamic graphical user interfaces as well. However, the explicit reasoning and cognition that can be incorporated into KBS allows the objects to behave and interact with each other in intelligent ways. In addition, most KBS models are developed and used in knowledge environments that support the formulation of such models as well as explanations of why the models behaved as they did.

See also: Expert Systems; Simulation Methodology and Model Manipulation

Bibliography

Bell P, O'Keefe R 1987 Visual interactive simulation—history, recent developments, and major issues. *Simulation* **49**(3), 109–16

Burns J, Morgeson J 1989 An object–oriented world-view for intelligent, discrete, next-event simulation. *Manage. Sci.* (in press)

Emshoff J, Sisson R 1970 *Design and Use of Computer Simulation Models.* Macmillan, New York

Futo I, Szeredum J 1982 A discrete simulation model based on artificial intelligence methods. *Proc. IMACS European Simulation Meeting.* North-Holland, Amsterdam

Harmon P, King D 1985 *Expert Systems: Artificial Intelligence in Business.* Wiley, New York

Kameny I, Cammarate S, Rothenberg J 1987 Concept for an integrated development environment for knowledge-based simulation. *Proc. IEEE Int. Conf. Systems, Man, and Cybernetics.* IEEE Press, Washington, DC

Klahr P, Faught W 1980 Knowledge-based simulation. *Proc. National Conf. Artificial Intelligence.* American Association for Artificial Intelligence, Stanford University, Stanford, California

Nielsen N 1986 Knowledge-based simulation programming. *Proc. National Computer Conf.* American Federation of Information Processing Societies, Las Vegas, Nevada

O'Keefe R 1986 Simulation and expert systems—A taxonomy and some examples. *Simulation* **46**(1), 10–16

Reddy Y, Fox M 1982 *KBS: An Artificial Intelligence Approach to Flexible Simulation.* Technical Report CMU-RI-TR-82-1. Carnegie-Mellon University, Pittsburgh, Pennsylvania

J. R. Burns and D. A. Haworth
[Texas Tech University, Lubbock, Texas, USA]

Knowledge Representation

The importance of information and knowledge in problem-solving tasks is certainly recognized. A meta-theory of knowledge is very important in enabling the development and use of knowledge-based decision support systems by people with diverse experiential familiarity with a particular task. This experiential familiarity will strongly influence the method of knowledge representation and cognitive operations on the knowledge base, as well as the memory, control and user–system interfaces that are most appropriate for a given task. This article presents a description and interpretation of several approaches for knowledge representation and knowledge aggregation that support holistic, heuristic and wholistic reasoning in systems and organizations.

1. Introduction

There are at least two major complementary viewpoints concerning how people represent knowledge and perform various problem-solving tasks. The distinction between the declarative and the procedural representations (Nilsson 1980) of knowledge has been an important subject for artificial intelligence and for cognitive science in general. The first of these perspectives emerges from the need to resolve specific issues or to accomplish specific tasks. This is the declarativist perspective which is typified by direct lines of inferential reasoning using very domain-specific heuristics. It is based on the assumption that knowledge consists primarily of "knowing facts," that is to say static, encyclopedic, database-type knowledge about specific events, objects and other elements and the relationships between them. From this viewpoint, the system designer addresses the problem of building machines or systems which exhibit intelligence and which are based on explicit knowledge of a specific, generally rather restricted subject area. The expert is, in effect, represented by a stored program or procedure, with knowledge represented by the explicit content or database that is embedded into these programs.

The top-level goal of system design, from this viewpoint, is to produce a system capable of assistance that would be regarded as intelligent if the same very specific assistance, based on knowledge of a very explicit set of "standard operating policy"-type facts, were obtained from a human. An advantage to declarativist approaches is the directness of the inference chains. This enables them to be especially suited for "concrete operational" mechanical tasks; intelligent robots and other forms of automation are generally based on these approaches. A disadvantage of this perspective is that judgements may be made concerning issues where the "expert" is not really expert, and this is not recognized due to the unquestioned use of the facts stored in the database, and the generally restricted formal reasoning ability that is incorporated into the knowledge-based system.

The second viewpoint is aimed at understanding intelligence from the perspective of knowing how to use knowledge. This is known as the proceduralist perspective (Winograd 1975). It is concerned with finding the most relevant facts from a broader set, and making inductive and deductive inferences from them. Thus it is concerned with formal knowledge that may be represented by rules concerning "how." Thus, procedural knowledge includes information that enables manipulation and selection, from a broad base of declarative knowledge, of those aspects deemed most relevant to a given situation or objective.

Some researchers will also include control knowledge as a third component of knowledge that enables coordination of a problem-solving task through a variety of processes, structures and strategies. From this view, performance is based on skills, which correspond to declarative performance, rules, which correspond to procedural performance, and knowledge, which corresponds to control performance (Rasmussen 1983). A somewhat analogous characterization of judgement uses the terms wholistic, heuristic and holistic (Sage 1981). Others will simply use the term "procedures," or "cognitive engine," to refer to both procedural and control aspects of problem solving.

Purely declarativist systems are not based on the belief that knowledge is inherently based on procedures for its use. Thus, a purely declarativist approach would seem to be closely related to wholistic or concrete-operational thought in which the response to a given stimulus arises instantaneously out of the experiential database of the problem solver without a conscious effort to follow rules (Sage 1981). This analogy is not exact, however, as the declarativist perspective is insufficient to describe such wholistic thought processes as intuitive affect and reasoning by analogy. Representation of wholistic thought processes such as these is a challenge for knowledge-based systems (Winston 1980, Carbonell 1983).

Proceduralist approaches are rather flexible and effective, since a single piece of data will typically be used for multiple purposes. Systems based on this perspective are understandable, and therefore explicable, since they allow for the explanation of judgements; they are thus useful as learning systems. Because of the formal thought process that they involve, adaptation and growth of knowledge over time is possible. Often, however, knowledge-based systems designed from this perspective alone will not be efficient or economic in terms of the time required to reach judgements, due to the time required to process a formal approach.

In practice, it would appear that the most successful knowledge-based systems will be those that use features of both the proceduralist and the declarativist approaches, or which blend concrete-operational thought process with formal-operational thought processes appropriate for the particular issue under consideration, and the experiential familiarity of the expert with the issue and the environment into which it is embedded. This is especially the case since it is difficult to conceive of situations in which a totally declarative or wholistic, or totally procedural or holistic perspective is most appropriate as the perspective from which judgement should arise. Rather, it would appear that expert intelligence and judgement will more often come from a general set of procedures for manipulating facts, and a typically large set of facts which describe the expert's knowledge about the issue under consideration, and related issues. An especially important related issue is the experiential familiarity with the environment and the task requirements in this environment. This determines the way in which a cognitive engine and knowledge base will be invoked so as to enable general procedures to be applied to specific data in order that inferences and deductions can be made.

Early efforts to construct intelligent systems concentrated primarily on various functional views of intelligence. The results of these efforts have been ad hoc systems that perform successfully in, and perhaps near, the domain for which they were initially constructed. Systems based on the more global information-processing view that incorporates proceduralist and declarativist perspectives have perhaps been less successful than systems based on the exclusively ad hoc or functional approach. A major difficulty in using a combined approach, however, is that little is known about how the components that comprise a cognitive system interact to enable contingency-based processing and use of information in problem-solving activities. There are a number of reasons for believing that systems created from this viewpoint are, to a much greater degree than functional systems, domain-independent and flexible. As a consequence of this, they should be capable of operation in a much greater variety of environments. Therefore, they should be able to outperform the exclusively functional or ad hoc systems.

Contemporary approaches to knowledge representation typically utilize an information-processing approach that allows consideration of the operational components which, at least substantively, make up an intelligent system (Newell and Simon 1972, Bossel 1977). These operational components typically include:

(a) *perceptors*—used to receive information;

(b) *effectors*—used to perform actions such as communications;

(c) *representation scheme*—used to interpret and identify information;

(d) *control*—used to monitor and regulate the actions to be performed;

(e) *decision-making*—used to allocate cognitive resources;

(f) *domain specific knowledge*—the facts that describe a situation;

(g) *metaknowledge*—information about knowledge representation (how we know what we know);

(h) *memory*—a physical embodiment of the knowledge base; and

(i) *world*—a model of the environment.

All of these components are essential for adequate intelligent interaction. No claim is made that this model is physiologically correct, but rather that each of these components is necessary for a substantive representation of intelligence.

There are a number of other models of human information processing and associated judgement. Wohl (1981), for example, has developed a model of human judgement processes that involves stimulus information processing, hypothesis generation and evaluation, option generation and evaluation, and execution response. This model, called the SHOR model, is very useful as a framework for structuring decision tasks. Janis and Mann (1977) and Janis (1983) have postulated a stress-based model that is very useful in describing how various contingencies lead people to decide how to decide. This model and related models are described in Sage (1981) and in the articles on *Human Judgement and Decision Rules* and *Systems Knowledge: Philosophical Perspectives*.

Several intelligent-systems-design complexities arise at the cognitive-process level of systems management. These relate to the forms, frames or perspectives associated with acquiring, integrating and applying vast amounts of knowledge. These forms range from the systemic framework of formulation, analysis and interpretation that is characteristic of formal-operational and holistic thought, to intuitive affect that is characteristic of concrete-operational and wholistic thought. The knowledge perspectives that are used for a given task depend on the task requirements, the experiential familiarity of the decision maker with the task, and the rationality perspectives that are used for task resolution (Sage 1981).

An appropriate framework in which knowledge could be organized and utilized efficiently and effectively is desired. This is especially necessary as studies have shown that the way in which a task is framed exerts a very strong influence upon the way in which task requirements and task resolution efforts are determined. This requires that we be able to address the modelling of knowledge-based decision support systems from several perspectives, especially as these relate to the different components of an intelligent system. Of particular interest will be those components at the interface between the cognitive-process level of systems management and the problem level, and at the knowledge metalevel which will enable effective modelling of the cognitive system itself. There seems little question but that this will involve an inquiry system (Churchman 1971), as suggested in the conceptual diagram of Fig. 1.

In this article, we expand these notions by discussing several approaches for the representation of knowledge in intelligent systems. Then we examine some metaknowledge considerations that are very important in the design of intelligent systems. Following this, we indicate some concerns relative to the veridicality of expert knowledge bases. We argue that there exists a major need for incorporation of approaches that enable questions of uncertainty and imprecision to be considered. Several approaches that may be useful towards this end are described.

2. Knowledge Representation Strategies

Approaches that will enable effective knowledge representation, and associated inference activities, in large knowledge bases have been the subject of investigation for many researchers. Although there are other representation schemes, the definitive *Handbook of Artificial Intelligence* (Barr et al. 1981 Vol. I) describes seven representation schemes: logic, procedural representations, semantic networks, production systems, direct (analogical) representations, semantic primitives, and frames and scripts. Each of these may be used to describe the four different types of factual knowledge elements that may be captured in a knowledge base: objects, events, performance and metaknowledge. These representations will also assist in identification of the values that need to be associated with facts in order to enable judgement and choice. Finally, they may be used to describe knowledge retrieval, reasoning, and acquisition of new knowledge and relating this new knowledge to already known knowledge. An ultimate goal of all this is knowledge-based program construction (Barstow 1979).

Newell (1982), in discussing the role of knowledge and its representation, has introduced the concept of a knowledge-level mechanism that is analogous to the concept of computer system levels, as well as to the information-processing view of intelligent systems. Knowledge at the knowledge level is perceived as the medium by which an agent fulfils its goals and/or explains its actions. Goals and actions are the essential components at the knowledge level. Finally, the behavioral law that controls this mechanism is the principle of rationality, which states that actions are selected to attain the agent's goals. This principle implies goal optimization or satisfaction in the attainment of target aspirations.

The main theme of Newell's research is that knowledge and its representation, although highly related, exist at two different levels. Knowledge exists as the *medium* at the knowledge level described above, and its representation lies at the *program* or *symbol* level in a computer system. This implies the existence of a knowledge base, a cognitive engine, and appropriate control and interface mechanisms to enable communication between these elements of the knowledge-based system and the system input and output.

This representation is not unlike the representation model for the problem space and associated problem-solving activities in traditional means–ends analysis (Newell and Simon 1972). In the means–ends representation of the problem space, there exists:

(a) a problem space;

(b) a set of all possible problem states within the problem space;

(c) one state which is known as the initial problem state;

(d) one, or possibly more than one, state which is known as the goal state;

(e) a set of conditional operators that will transform one problem state into another problem state, all within the problem space;

(f) an error comparator which computes the difference between two states, typically between the goal state and the present state;

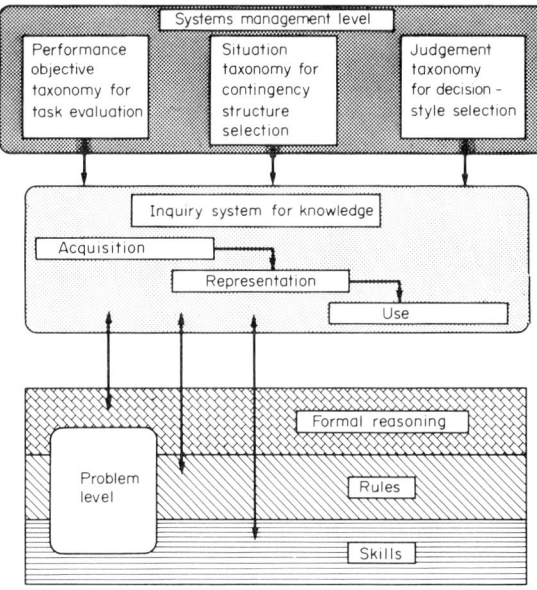

Figure 1
The inquiry system as an interface between systems management and problem solving

(g) a controller which applies a control that is a function of the error difference that is detected; and

(h) a set of path constraints that must be satisfied in order for a problem solution to be admissible.

Within this problem space, problem solving using means–ends analysis comprises four generic activities:

(a) comparison of the current state with the goal state;

(b) choice of a control that will reduce this difference;

(c) application of this control if it is admissible and, if it is not, determination of a suitable subproblem and application of means–ends analysis to the sub-problem; and

(d) resumption of effort on the original problem or task when the subproblem has been solved.

It is from this perspective that the issue of knowledge representation will be addressed in this article. Approaching knowledge representation from this perspective will also help in the understanding of some of the many metaknowledge concerns that are required to ensure acceptable human–machine interactions in systems engineering. Although we will not explore the point in any detail here, there is much present evidence to show that analogous reasoning (Silverman 1983) is not necessarily a totally wholistic process; but that at least some forms of analogous reasoning can be represented by holistic processes, such as means–ends analysis (Carbonell 1983). As we have noted, our concern here will be primarily with the information–processing representation of knowledge. The purpose of a particular knowledge representation is to enable the use of knowledge for retrieving factual information from the knowledge base that is judged relevant to the task at hand, reasoning about these facts in the search for a resolution of the task requirements, and acquiring more knowledge.

2.1 Production Systems

There are various mechanisms that can be used to represent the organization of declarative and procedural knowledge. The most common, and simplest, representation is that in which knowledge is structured as a set of facts, with each fact related to one or more facts in a causal type of inferential relationship. This modular cause–effect structuring of knowledge into the form of a production rule, which was first developed by Newell and Simon (1972), has seen many applications, including strategic planning, policy analysis, decision making and other areas. Many of these are in areas formally outside the artificial intelligence communities (Axelrod 1976, Roberts 1976, Eden *et al.* 1979, Mitroff and Mason 1982) and employ constructs that are more restrictive than those that are often found in production rule systems. A variety of approaches to knowledge representation and machine learning (Davis and Buchanan 1977, Davis and King 1977, Davis *et al.* 1977, Michalski *et al.* 1983) are of considerable contemporary interest in decision support system and expert system design and will be discussed later in this article.

The basic idea behind a production system is that there exists a set of productions, or rules, in the form of various condition–action pairs, generally in the form of "if–then" combinations. Initially these were exclusively explicit rules, although there is much current interest in incorporating fuzziness and imprecision into production rule concepts (Rouse 1983). Generally, production rules are heuristic in nature, and may be appropriate or inappropriate to the task at hand. The normative goal of an expert system is to use "good" heuristics, of course.

2.2 Semantic Networks

The problem of representing knowledge in terms of nodes that represent objects, concepts or events, and links between the nodes to represent their interrelations, is one of the forms of knowledge representation that has been of continuous interest in the field of artificial intelligence. Much of the initial research concerning semantic networks, as these representations are called, stems from the desire to model human associative memory. Current research (Winograd 1983) is very concerned with the representation of strings in natural language for story understanding (Norman *et al.* 1975, Schank and Abelson 1977, Findler 1979, Carbonell 1981).

The work on semantic network representation, such as described in the publications by Quillian (1968), Schank (1975, 1982), Rumelhart and Ortony (1977) and others, has been especially concerned with basic notions for representing human verbal knowledge in "understander" systems. Schank and his colleagues, for example, have been especially concerned with the use of semantic networks as aids in the teaching of reading. Semantic networks are usually described in terms of their purpose, such as the purpose of aiding reading or aiding the understanding of the belief structure of a person concerning some issue.

The basic concept of having nodes that represent elements in the universe and links that represent the contextual relations between these elements is very appealing. A semantic network is intended to represent concepts expressed by natural-language words and phrases as interconnected nodes, connected by a particular set of arcs called semantic relations. Concepts in this system of semantic networks are word-sense meanings. Semantic relations are those which the verb of a sentence has with its subject, object and prepositional phrase arguments, in addition to those that underlie common lexical, classificational and modificational relations. It would appear that the coding method of Wrightson in Axelrod's work on cognitive mapping (Axelrod 1976), which is based on Axelrod's earlier definitive structural modelling work and the theory of psycho-logic (Axelrod 1972), and Eden's cognitive mapping coding techniques (Eden *et al.* 1979) are based on these sentence characteristics.

A semantic network is a convenient computational representation, readily implementable on computers, in which to represent knowledge which is expressed in natural language. The extent to which this type of knowledge representation can be effectively utilized for inference processes depends on the existence, or lack thereof, of a well-structured and sophisticated set of rules. The antecedent–consequent type of rule is commonly used. Structurally the left-hand side of the rule, or antecedent, represents the set of assumptions or conditions appropriate for use of the rule. The right-hand or consequent side of the rule represents the set of ends results. Conjunctions, disjunctions and negations can occur on either side of the typical relational rule. This form of representation, although simple, has been powerful enough to support much of the early work in artificial intelligence. The contemporary frame and script concept, in which the structure and framework within which new information is interpreted is in terms of the concepts that have been acquired through previous experience, has evolved from semantic network concepts. Again we see the strong contextual dependency, or expectation-driven processing, of scripts and frames such that one looks for things based on the context that one believes exists.

Semantic networks are capable of representing both the physical descriptions of actions as well as the purposeful aspects of these actions. Thus a semantic network representational system must include the goals or objectives that can be obtained by actions, the scripts which describe scenarios in simple stereotyped situations, the plans which allow for flexible description of essentially appropriate action–impact pairs, and the themes which allow for such environmental descriptions as the occupations and aspirations of actors involved in the issue under consideration. In this way, a semantic network may be a descriptive as well as a prescriptive mechanism.

Unfortunately semantic networks do have a number of defects. Winston and Brown (1979) have cited three of these:

(a) they lack a way of smoothly creating aggregate concepts that can be manipulated as simply as they could be if they were elementary concepts;

(b) they lack a simple mechanism whereby one concept can acquire or otherwise inherit information from another concept, other than by those that have been explicitly stated in the inference rules; and

(c) they lack a structural representation that is internal to a given concept.

There are also bound to be difficulties when the size of the semantic network, in terms of the associated database, becomes sufficiently large that it can represent a nontrivial amount of knowledge. The computational difficulties in processing the network and the cognitive difficulties in coping with the associated complexity may be overwhelming. This leads to the need for network aggregation in order to obtain "summary" representations that are efficient and effective. These aggregate networks are called frames. Thus the concept of a frame, originally due to Minsky (1975), as a chunk of slots and their contents does eliminate many of the defects of semantic networks.

There are also other difficulties associated with the semantic network concept. There are, for example, difficulties associated with representing time, as structural models are basically static devices. There are difficulties associated with maintaining a distinction between "facts" and "values," and in incorporating concepts of uncertainty, fuzziness and imprecision. Situations often arise, for example, in which reasoning must be accomplished using incomplete, inconsistent and perhaps even contradictory data. These may arise when collecting data from information summaries, or from imperfect and/or distributed sources. Much research is being done in semantic networks to improve their usefulness as representational schemes for general knowledge. A collection of papers edited by Findler (1979) describes various applications, recent developments and extensions of semantic networks. Some applications illustrate the use of semantic networks in constructing the knowledge base of programs which exhibit some aspects of understanding—paraphrasing, abstracting and classifying a corpus of text, answering questions on the basis of common-sense reasoning, drawing deductive and inductive inferences, and obeying commands.

2.3 Cognitive Maps

A much simpler network-based representation is one in which knowledge is structured as a set of concepts, with each concept related to one or more facts by a single causal type of relationship. Necessary to accomplish a structural model of this sort is a theory of psycho-logic (Abelson and Rosenberg 1958, Axelrod 1972, Abelson 1973 or pulsed digraphs (Roberts 1976) in which relations may have enhancing ($+1$), inhibiting (-1) or neutral (0) causal influences on other relations. A number of applications of the resulting cognitive maps as these structural models are often called, have been reported by Axelrod (1976), Eden *et al.* (1979) and others. Very early uses of the term cognitive map described how animals cognized the spatial environment around them (Tolman 1948), and this particular restrictive use of the term is still common (Downs and Stea 1977). In its more general form, a cognitive map is the result of an attempt to capture an individual's view of the world with respect to a particular issue.

Unlike semantic networks, which are typically multirelational structures and as such require a sophisticated set of production rules or grammars for representation and interpretation, a cognitive map is based on a single specific contextual relation, such that any given element will have enhancing, inhibiting or neutral causal impacts on each other element in the cognitive map. Thus the representation and analysis of a cognitive map will usually be simpler than is the case for semantic networks. The simple contextuality of the cognitive map may make it difficult for such a map to replicate a complex belief structure. However, the elements which represent concepts in a cognitive map are variables that can take on different values. The linkage, or contextual relation, among concepts may represent causal assertions and perceptions concerning how one concept variable affects another concept variable.

Since the dynamics of the reasoning mechanism in a cognitive map is embedded in structural considerations, it is a simple matter to stimulate the reasoning process of a person if we can assume that the cognitive map has been faithfully constructed. Eden *et al.* (1980) have developed computer simulations of cognitive map constructs using graph-theoretic methods. These methods provide a convenient matrix technique for the representation and manipulation of concepts and their structural relationships (Harary *et al.* 1965, Sage 1977). Among the operations that may be better understood and communicated by means of a cognitive map are the formulation of alternative explanations of an event that has occurred or is anticipated to occur (diagnosis), the development of perceptions concerning the expected consequences of an event (prognosis), and the search for and ranking of relevant policy options (decision making). It is necessary, of course, to be aware of the considerable possibilities for flawed judgement in these activities (Sage and White 1983), and a major use for a cognitive map may well be to explore the possibilities for flawed information processing and judgement that may result from use of such a map.

2.4 Schema

The schema theory of judgement suggests that people have images or schemas that they use for comparison purposes. Some of these schemas describe individual goals or objectives, some describe an individual's view of the present and the future. It is these schemas, including their structure and interrelatedness, that determine the judgements that an individual will make. When choosing among alternatives, an individual views relevant schemas associated with the alternatives and their possible impacts, and accepts those alternatives whose schemas are congruent with desirable outcome schemas. Those incongruent with schemas or images of desirable impacts are rejected. If there is more than one alternative with congruent schemas, then any of several strategies for schema adjustment are made; perhaps some sort of adjustment that leads to a single "dominant" schema and the alternative associated with this is then selected.

Fundamentally, a schema is a data structure for representing generic concepts as stored in memory (Holland *et al.* 1987). Schemas represent knowledge about concepts. The purposeful definition of a schema is simply that it is a framework to enable comprehension and understanding of acquired information. Of course, the schemas that a person has in memory will, at least in part, determine the way they go about acquiring information. Schemas do exist in memory as the "things" that a person knows. Every schema is structurally organized about some theme. Schemas are said to contain slots that are filled by specific information about some concept.

There are perhaps four generically different types of schemas:

(a) a *self* schema which comprises the objectives and goals to which one aspires;

(b) a *normative trajectory* schema which comprises the images of the paths that an individual would like to be on;

(c) a *nominal trajectory* schema which comprises the images of the paths that will evolve if the current course of action is not changed; and

(d) an *action alternative* schema which comprises a set of alternative courses of action and the trajectory images that will follow if the action alternatives are implemented.

The schema-based theory of judgement suggests that an individual first compares the nominal trajectory schema with the normative trajectory schema. If the incongruence between these two schemas is below some critical threshold level, then unconflicted adherence to the original course of action, the nominal trajectory schema, results. When the incongruence between these two is above some threshold, an examination is made of the action alternative schemas to see if there is a single familiar schema that has a sufficiently high concordance or congruence with the normative trajectory schema such that unconflicted change to a new course of action is possible. We see that schemas are both knowledge sources and preprogrammed guides for routing operational judgements. They are closely related to two later-emerging concepts, frames and scripts, which are discussed in the following sections.

There also exist cases in which the nominal trajectory schema is unacceptable, and where none of the impacts of the readily identified action alternatives are acceptable in the sense of being congruent with the normative trajectory schema. This incongruence will lead to decidophobia when the stakes are small, and to hypervigilance or panic when they are large and where there does not appear to be sufficient time to identify potentially suitable alternatives.

When there is time for vigilant search and deliberation, when the stakes are sufficiently high, and where the nominal trajectory schemas and familiar action alternative schemas are unacceptable, then the individual will synthesize new action alternative schemas and attempt a more formal maximization of utility-type approaches to enable evaluation of the newly identified alternative courses of action. The switch from a satisficing or sufficiency paradigm of choice, in which expert judgement is the basis for action, to a maximizing-type paradigm based on formal reasoning is apparent. Both of these paradigms seem capable of being accommodated within the general understanding of schema theory.

Also seen in this is a multilayer approach to judgement. First an anticipative judgement is made with respect to whether there is a need for a change in the present course of action. This judgement is made on the basis of detection of incongruity between nominal trajectory schemas and normative trajectory schemas. If a change is to be made, an adoption decision is made relative to unconflicted change to a new course of action, for situations with which the decision maker has considerable experiential familiarity. When this familiarity is not present, decidophobia may result when the stakes are small. Formal knowledge-based judgement results when the stakes are high and there is sufficient time for thorough search and deliberation. This results in vigilant construction of new schemas. Hypervigilance results when this is not the case.

There are major questions of flexibility, and particularly of "imperfect" schemas, in all of the above. Often, schemas will contain uncertainties, incomplete information, imprecise information and (especially where there are groups involved) inconsistent information. There are several ways in which one could perform experiments to test this theory. One of these would be a simulation approach, in which an expert-system-like model would be used to construct the whole schema-based theory. This would force the identification of areas where empirical research might be most productive. For example, we do not know how the congruence and/or incongruence thresholds are set and it might be possible to obtain answers to questions such as these. There are a number of potentially useful questions that might be asked. While they are posed specifically for schema theory here, they could be rephrased for other forms of knowledge representation.

(a) can individuals describe the four types of schemas just identified in either (or both) a prospective or retrospective way?

(b) do individuals have "reasoning forward" or "reasoning backward" type schemas? What influences this, and can and should these influences be changed?

(c) how do individuals cope with "imperfect" schemas, especially when the imperfection leads to detectable inconsistencies or conflicts in one or more aspects of the resulting schemas?

(d) how do people go about identifying new alternative courses of action and describing them as alternative action schemas?

(e) why do some people identify different alternative action schemas? How do individuals continue to pursue new action alternatives, whereas others will reverse their initial judgements because of any of several decision conflicts?

(f) what support processes can be used to aid people in any of these tasks and how would this be evaluated?

(g) what are the implications of all of this for group and distributed decision making?

2.5 Frame Representation

Minsky (1975), in a paper on frame systems, presents a rather different approach to semantic networks that eliminates some of their defects. He advocates the use of local procedures within a "frame" in order to represent structured knowledge. A frame is, as we have noted, a chunk of knowledge for representing a stereotyped situation. Attached to each frame are several kinds of information. Some of this information concerns how to use the frame and some of the information may concern what can happen next. A frame can then be represented as a hierarchical network of nodes and relations. The top-level element in the frame will represent facts that are always assumed to be true about the generic situation at hand. The lower levels of the frame will have many terminal slots that must be filled by the specific context-dependent information about the frame and the situation at hand.

Although this frame-based theory attempts to address identification of a general system, whose purpose is to represent knowledge as a collection of separate and simple fragments, there seem to exist many technical gaps at present concerning how to design an operational system that makes best use of this theory of frames. Automated procedures to organize knowledge in such a hierarchically structured framework appear necessary to make this theory functional. The problem of efficient search involving a very large knowledge base is one of great concern both in terms of time and in terms of the possible combinatorial explosion of knowledge that can occur. Some researchers (Bobrow and Collins 1975, Bobrow and Winograd 1977, Hayes-Roth and Waterman 1978, Wilensky 1981, Davis and Lenat 1982) have subscribed to the idea of using metaknowledge to guide the search procedures in order to reduce the resulting knowledge-based system to a manageable size. Others have advocated parallel processing through networks of structural knowledge in order to reduce the search time in very large knowledge-based systems as much as possible (Fahlman 1977).

2.6 Scripts

The script concept is very closely related to those of frames and schemas. Each of these consists of organized structures of stereotypical knowledge about a general concept; each results from extraction and synthesis of common related elements in a series of events, situations or actions. There are three related notions:

(a) how an issue is represented in memory strongly influences understanding of the issue;

(b) how an issue is understood influences how alternatives are formulated and issues resolved; and

(c) previous experience with similar issues influences the frames, scripts or schema that are stored in memory and which strongly influence representation of new information.

Like schemas and frames, scripts are knowledge structures about a stereotypical sequence of frequently performed actions. They capture the action–event relations in situations so frequently encountered that the need for formal methods of problem solving seldom arises. They are self-contained knowledge chunks. As a consequence, it is difficult to transfer knowledge from one script to another. Also, scripts may lack understanding, or at least the intentionality of understanding. A person, according to the script representational construct, will follow the prescriptions of the script without necessarily understanding the reasons for this behavior. Clearly there are instances where such behavior is very appropriate, and also others where it may be very inappropriate. Schank and Abelson (1977) and Abelson (1981) provide much additional commentary concerning the script concept.

2.7 Analogous Representations

Analogies and analogous inference play a very important role in human judgement. Philosophers of science often claim that reasoning by analogy is the basis for hypothesis formation and identification in science. Often analogous reasoning (Sternberg 1977, 1982, Gick and Holyoak 1980, Winston 1980) is used when there exists uncertainty and imprecision associated with the judgement task at hand. We have alluded to learning as a process whereby we are able to do things more efficiently or effectively, or more efficiently and effectively the next time that we do them. Thus, learning can involve rote memory and direct implementation of instruction, to reasoning by analogy, and through discovery and observation, of a concrete or formal nature.

When there is a lack of explicit, certain and concrete knowledge about a specific issue, reasoning by analogy will often be used. In such cases one searches for similarities between the task situation extant and a previously experienced and familiar situation. When the situations are sufficiently analogous that one can see parallels between elements in one situation and elements in the other, then reasoning by analogy becomes possible.

Silverman (1983), in an extensive review of research concerning analogous inference in systems management, identifies a taxonomy that facilitates the development of procedures and protocols for the identification and correction of pitfalls in this form of reasoning. Sternberg (1977) presents a descriptive theory of analogous reasoning and experimentally identifies sources of errors that may occur during each of the operations that constitutes his paradigm for analogous reasoning. The basic operations in Sternberg's model are: encoding, inference, mapping, application and response. This research provides a great deal of descriptive information that has motivated the development of normative theories of concept formation and issue formulation. Carbonell (1983) has modelled analogous reasoning using means–ends analysis. He uses this model to integrate skill refinement with knowledge acquisition as an effective procedure for reliable and effective problem solution.

Nakamura and Iwai (1982) and Nakamura et al. (1983) have developed a questioning–answering system for information retrieval in which the system relates its own associative knowledge with the user's knowledge in an analogous fashion. The system's associative knowledge is represented as a semantic network and an information metric is introduced to measure topological distances that represent analogous reasoning similarities. The question–answer dialogue is such as to encourage user responses which enable identification of analogous situations through direction of the questioning to enable maximum similarity determination.

2.8 Summary

This section has been concerned with those aspects of knowledge representation that seem most relevant to the overall objectives of this article. By way of summary, a knowledge representation is a set of symbols used for illustration, a method for arranging them, and a reasoning mechanism for using the arranged symbols to hold and convey knowledge. Sound approaches to knowledge representation are needed as the foundation for much contemporary large systems efforts in the human–machine systems area, regardless of whether the application efforts involve fault diagnosis and repair, planning, language understanding, or any of a large number of areas.

There is no available theory comparing the different types of knowledge representation schemes that is capable of indicating which will be the most useful in any particular application. Nevertheless, several authors, including McCarthy and Hayes (1969) and Winston (1977), have suggested different and useful criteria that are very important in enabling selection from among the several knowledge representation schemes. These criteria include the following.

(a) Epistemological adequacy: sufficient knowledge should be present and capable of being captured by the knowledge representation scheme used such that the task requirements can, in principle, be met.

(b) Heuristic adequacy: a knowledge representation approach potentially expressing information helpful in solving problems should also offer ways of avoiding or greatly reducing search complexity.

(c) Extendability: the knowledge-based system should be designed so as to minimize the difficulty of associating and linking new information to existing information.

Finally, we might remark that it is especially necessary that the knowledge representation scheme be capable of coping with the types of expertise, and the reasoning perspectives, that can reasonably be expected to exist among the users of the knowledge-based system. In this way we will be much better able to accomplish needed activities that involve learning and discovery (Hayes-Roth 1983) such as the diagnosis of faulty theories, the proper assimilation of new knowledge, and useful frameworks in which to pose questions such that they are understandable and interpretable in the way in which the questioner (should have) intended. Clearly, all of this has major implications for subjects such as decision making in general and such important subareas as human detection and diagnosis of system failures (Rasmussen and Rouse 1981).

3. Some Metaknowledge Considerations in the Design of Intelligent Systems

Various assumptions about the nature and characteristics of the contingency task structural elements of task, environment, and human problem-solver familiarity with these, are considered essential in the design of inquiry systems to enable effective and efficient organization of knowledge about specific situation domains. Among these assumptions, the following are especially pertinent here:

(a) the world is basically orderly enough that, at least imperfect, observation of it is possible;

(b) identification of the task and the environment may generally not be performed in a value-free context; and

(c) some value judgements always precede the collection of any set of data, or the construction of any model.

There are two basic components that make up any nontrivial inquiry system such that a combination of information structures and appropriate interpretation procedures will lead to intelligent behavior: a knowledge base that will contain relevant facts concerning objects, events and performance, and will also contain a value system; and a cognitive engine that will enable aggregation of facts and values to enable judgements. Each of these is necessary in an inquiry system in order for it to be possible to use knowledge through the acts of information retrieval, reasoning using facts and values, and acquisition and aggregation of new knowledge which relates something that is new to that which is already known. There exist two diametrically opposed perspectives on learning, or acquisition of new knowledge and subsequent aggregation of new knowledge into an existing knowledge base. At this point we could make a distinction between the knowledge acts of learning and discovery and the manner in which these perspectives differ according to whether knowledge acquisition is through learning or discovery. This would involve concerns of passive knowledge acquisition versus active, or experiential, knowledge acquisition. The journey would be interesting, but unfortunately somewhat long, and not among the most important of concerns here. Sternberg's definitive work (Sternberg 1982) contains detailed discussions of concerns of this nature.

3.1 Knowledge Acquisition: Learning

The two perspectives referred to above concern how individuals go about (in a procedural manner) the retrieval of information, the use of information for reasoning, and the feedback process that enables acquisition of new knowledge. One perspective is that learning is performed by an elementary-to-complex process in which simple things are learned first and, from this, more advanced concepts are then learned. The other perspective is based on the belief that learning starts with complex statements about the description of a situation, and that through decomposition into simpler statements a system is able to increase its understanding of the specific situation domain.

As a means of illustrating the two perspectives on the knowledge acquisition process, it is useful to compare problem-solving activities and natural-language understanding in some detail with respect to these two perspectives.

The elementary-to-complex process of learning could be characterized by activities involved in understanding natural language. For example, natural-language statements are generally composed of actors, actions and a set of cases that are associated with particular actions. From this, the reader must infer why the action has occurred and what must have been present in order for the action to be possible. To aid understanding of a story, the reader searches for an explanation of the action or situation described in the story.

Formal efforts at problem solving, on the other hand, involve the construction of a plan to satisfy a set of goals. This generally involves a process of iterative use and reuse of understanding mechanisms. Often, especially when the problem solver does not recognize an inherent structure of the problem so that wholistic thought is possible, it involves a process of decomposition or disaggregation of task components in a manner that is typical of the complex-to-elementary mode of knowledge acquisition. The process of decomposing a problem into manageable subgoals is clearly an important aspect of planning and problem solving, at least for initially unstructured or semi-structured problems.

The analysis of Sacerdoti (1977) is concerned with this process. His top-down planning system NOAH is based on a knowledge structure that permits subgoals to be chosen and placed in an efficient sequence. This is accomplished through the use of a large number of small modular programs, each of which may contain specialized knowledge about actions and their impacts on the problem domain, which may be invoked at times that are appropriate to the goals that the actions will achieve.

At one extreme of the knowledge aggregation role, learning is represented by inputs of a set of facts and inference rules about a specific domain. The system has no control over this domain and cannot question the validity of judgements that result from the use of facts and inference rules in it. At the other extreme, judgements evolve from facts, values and an aggregation procedure for facts and inference rules that can be questioned and tested with respect to simplicity and truth, through use of the existing accumulated knowledge base. These processes may involve the identification of inconsistencies in the aggregated knowledge base and resolution, and associated efforts to correct these by means of some well structured human–machine dialog.

Most artificial intelligence systems in use today are based on the first perspective with respect to acquisition and aggregation of new knowledge; that is, they use the elementary-to-complex perspective, and also do not verify, validate or otherwise seek to determine the consistency of the resulting knowledge base. The resulting lack of control over questions of the validity of the resulting knowledge base is characteristic of an incomplete intelligent system. If this perspective of knowledge acquisition and aggregation is used exclusively, then some essential components of an intelligent cognitive system have been omitted, or the interaction between the knowledge base and the user has been inadequately modelled.

As previously noted, systems that operate at the other extreme of the knowledge acquisition spectrum, such that learning proceeds in a complex-to-elementary fashion, have been difficult to implement. In reality, both modes of learning are appropriate and both are used by the human problem solver. Although the knowledge-base component of decision support systems is generally small, the typical knowledge base of a management-oriented decision support system is often based on complex-to-elementary elicitation of subjective knowledge. Integration of the two approaches is clearly desirable. We briefly address this topic and the related topic of veridicality in knowledge-based systems in Sect. 4.

3.2 Information Seeking: Input

The representation of knowledge at the symbol level suggests the existence of some form of prior knowledge which enables the system to perform the function of acquisition and aggregation of the new knowledge with the existing knowledge. We have discussed in the previous section various approaches to knowledge representation in terms of their characteristics, functions and purposes. We will now describe a general knowledge-representation system in terms of some elementary *a priori* knowledge that is assumed common to any representational scheme. This *a priori* knowledge is characterized by the existence of an input component capable of labelling, chunking, structuring and storing data into the resulting knowledge base.

The input component is concerned with the processes by which information that is relevant to a situation is obtained from the environment. The three basic cognitive processes involved in this are perception, consciousness and memory. Together, these provide both a description and an explanation of the situation so as to enable generation of a set of beliefs or knowledge, organized into a representation, about the situation. It should be noted that what may be a belief to one person may be knowledge to another. Abelson (1979) presents a cogent discussion of this subjective interpretation of belief and knowledge. There must also be a generalization component or inference mechanism that is equipped with some form of basic logic to enable access to the knowledge base for formation of inferences and judgements. A fundamental question arises from this discussion concerning how *a priori* knowledge and the generalization component influence the operation of the complete knowledge-representation system.

In the context of devices to aid human information processing, there exist two design philosophies concerning the proper relationship between the input component and the generalizing sector. One advocates the view that these sectors should be considered as operating separately, with the input component in charge of knowledge acquisition and representation considered as if it was independent of the generalizing sector which is in charge of aggregation. This approach offers simplicity in system design, at the expense of effectiveness, as the mode of representation of information will influence the success or failure of the inquirer in arriving at a solution. This deficiency seems to be characteristic of most current information systems. They are passive systems and it is up to the user to recognize an information need and then seek out the required information.

The other approach considers that the two sectors are essentially inseparable and that each supports and enhances the functioning of the other; but this in turn complicates the system design, perhaps by a considerable amount. In this approach, the internal interactions of the input and generalizing sector are capable of generating user–system interaction. There are various ways in which a system can initiate a dialog with a user:

(a) identification of "gaps" in the knowledge base that prevent the system from making inferences or from adequately summarizing the information in a sector of the knowledge base;

(b) identification of an inconsistent set of information followed by detection of the inability of the system to resolve it; and

(c) inability of the system to satisfy the desired goals of the user.

Identification of these potential deficiencies and use of prompts based on them for purposes of computer–control dialog are needs in intelligent system design. The systems AM and TEIRESIAS described in Davis and Lenat (1982) are state-of-the-art programs that perform system-initiated dialog of the first type described above. AM, for example, is designed to reason about a set of existing elementary knowledge and to create new concepts and plausible hypotheses based on this knowledge base. The knowledge base that is used to test the veridicality of the system is a set of mathematical propositions and heuristics that are commonly used in mathematics, the subject domain for AM. In this process the system searches, by means of internal and external communications, for new concepts and/or plausible heuristics with which to identify, generate or discover new concepts. Lenat notes that AM has not discovered anything new to the body of mathematical knowledge, but has been able to provide interesting interpretations to well-known concepts in mathematics. Perhaps most importantly, it has demonstrated that a symbiotic human–machine combination is potentially able to produce better results than either might do alone.

TEIRESIAS is designed to allow interactive capture and transfer of expertise from a human expert to the knowledge base of a system, using dialog that is generated and initiated by the system. The system is capable of improving its knowledge base by identifying defects in the existing base, a debugging-acquisition phase, as well as explaining the why and the how of the conclusions that it reaches (an explanation phase). The similarity between these two systems is their capacity for reasoning and conducting inquiry on the basis of knowing about the system's own knowledge.

In at least one way, incomplete and inconsistent knowledge is valuable, as the recognition of this may encourage people, and knowledge-based systems, to initiate questioning as part of a search for potentially disconfirming information. Mitroff et al. (1983) describe a system that conducts an inquiry on the basis of defects such as these in the knowledge base. In their system, defects may arise in either of two ways: through improper aggregation of information from distributed, potentially conflicting, information sources; or through the internal generation of conflicting premises that lead to challenges to the system user concerning the veridicality and completeness of the existing knowledge base.

This last mode of system initiated and generated dialog involves a process that is the inverse of the sequence normally followed in means–ends analysis (Newell and Simon 1972). This is essentially an inverse optimal control problem (Sage and White 1977), or a problem for which the regression-analysis-based policy capture (Hammond et al. 1980) is appropriate. It is also related to the Hegelian inquirer perspective described by Churchman (1971) that serves as the basis for the dialectic-inquiry approach that is advocated by Mitroff et al. (1983). Approaches to directing an enquiry into the structure of decision situations (Sage and Rajala 1978, Rajala and Sage 1980a,b, Pearl et al. 1982) in terms of the response to queries to the decision maker are also related to this approach.

In the definitive goal-directed structuring system (GODDESS) of Pearl, for example, the inquiry process proceeds from the identification of desired goals to actions that might achieve the goals, and then conditions that must exist in order for these actions to be optimal in achieving the goals. In turn, these conditions generate more subgoals. It has been shown (Pearl et al. 1982) that the goal-directed dialog stimulates the generation of relevant ideas and provides for the structuring of initially ill-structured problems in a more effective and efficient manner than undirected questioning. External user–system interaction of the sort described here is a highly desirable feature for information systems. It should, in principle, strongly influence the integrated functioning and success of the input and generalizing sectors. Doubtless, future knowledge-based system designs will be much influenced by these considerations.

4. Summary

In this article, we have discussed forms of knowledge representation. The form or frame, of knowledge representation that a person uses is very much a function of the perspective that the person has with respect to the particular issue under consideration. This suggests a contingency task structural approach as being very important. For it is the particular task at hand, the environment into which this task is embedded, and the experiential familiarity of the decision maker with the task and environment that determines the information acquisition and analysis strategy that is adopted as a precursor to judgement and choice. Thus we need to be aware of a variety of knowledge representations, and the way in which metalevel knowledge leads to a knowledge representation in terms of the information requirements determined for a particular task, the method of analyzing the acquired information, and the way in which associated facts and values are aggregated to enable judgement formation. We have been especially concerned here with the fact that the information that is used for judgement and choice is typically not precise clerical and accounting data, but a mixture of this data and information of an imprecise, uncertain and otherwise imperfect nature. Needless to say, it is believed to be an important area for continued research, together with the many other activities that are associated with knowledge representation for information processing in systems and organizations, for enhanced understanding and improved decisions.

See also: Analogical Reasoning; Artificial Intelligence; Cognitive Management and Models of Judgement and Choice Processes; Decision Analysis; Decision Support Systems

Bibliography

Abelson R P 1973 The structure of belief systems. In: Schank and Colby 1973, pp. 287–339
Abelson R P 1979 Differences between belief and knowledge systems. *Cognit. Sci.* **3**, 355–66
Abelson R P 1981 The psychological status of the script concept. *Am. Psychol.* **36**, 715–29
Abelson R P, Rosenberg M J 1958 Symbolic psycho-logic: A model of attitudinal cognition. *Behav. Sci.* **3**, 1–13
Aitkenhead A M, Slack J M (eds.) 1985 *Issues in Cognitive Modeling.* Erlbaum, Hillsdale, New Jersey
Anderson J R (ed.) 1981 *Cognitive Skills and Their Acquisition.* Erlbaum, Hillsdale, New Jersey
Anderson J R 1983 *The Architecture of Cognition.* Harvard University Press, Cambridge, Massachusetts
Axelrod R M 1972 *Framework for a General Theory of Cognition and Choice.* University of California at Berkeley, Berkeley, California
Axelrod R M (ed.) 1976 *Structure of Decision: The Cognitive Maps of Political Elites.* Princeton University Press, Princeton, New Jersey
Barr A, Cohen P R, Feigenbaum E A (eds.) 1981–82 *Handbook of Artificial Intelligence*, Vols. I–III. Kaufman, Los Altos, California
Barstow D R 1979 *Knowledge-Based Program Construction.* Elsevier, New York
Bobrow D G, Collins A (eds.) 1975 *Representation and Understanding: Studies in Cognitive Science.* Academic Press, New York
Bobrow D G, Winograd T 1977 An overview of KRL, a knowledge representation language. *Cognit Sci.* **1**(1), 3–46
Bossel H (ed.) 1977 *Concepts and Tools of Computer Assisted Policy Analysis*, Vols. 1–3. Birkhauser, Cambridge, Massachusetts
Carbonell J G 1981 *Subjective Understanding: Computer Models of Belief Systems.* UMI Research Press, Ann Arbor, Michigan
Carbonell J G 1983 Learning by analogy: Formulating and generalizing plans from past experience. In: Michalski *et al.* 1983, pp. 137–62
Churchman C W 1971 *Design of Inquiring Systems.* Basic Books, New York
Davis R, Buchanan B G 1977 Meta-level knowledge: Overview and applications. *IJCAI* **5**, 920–27
Davis R, Buchanan B G, Shortliffe E H 1977 Production rules as a representation for a knowledge-based consultation system. *Artif. Intell.* **8**, 15–45
Davis R, King J J 1977 An overview of production systems. In: Elcock E, Michie D (eds.) *Machine Intelligence*, Vol. 8. Wiley, New York, pp. 300–32
Davis R, Lenat D B 1982 *Knowledge-Base Systems in Artificial Intelligence.* McGraw-Hill, New York
Downs R M, Stea D 1977 *Maps in Minds: Reflections in Cognitive Maps.* Harper and Row, New York
Eden C, Jones S, Sims D 1979 *Thinking in Organizations.* Macmillan, London
Eden C, Smithin T, Wiltshire J 1980 Cognition, simulation and learning. *Experiential Learning and Simulation* **2**, 131–43
Eysenck M W 1984 *A Handbook of Cognitive Psychology.* Erlbaum, Hillsdale, New Jersey
Fahlman S E 1979 *NETL: A System for Representing and Using Real-World Knowledge.* MIT Press, Cambridge, Massachusetts
Falmagne R J (ed.) 1975 *Reasoning: Representation and Process.* Erlbaum, Hillsdale, New Jersey
Findler N V 1979 *Associative Networks: The Representation and Use of Knowledge by Computers.* Academic Press, New York
Gick M L, Holyoak K J 1980 Analogical problem solving. *Cognit. Psychol.* **12**, 306–55
Goodstein L P, Anderson H B, Olsen S E (eds.) 1988 *Tasks, Errors and Mental Models.* Taylor and Francis, London
Hammond K R, McClelland G H, Mumpower J 1980 *Human Judgement and Decision Making.* Praeger, New York
Harary F, Norman R, Cartwright D 1965 *Structural Models: An Introduction to the Theory of Directed Graphs.* Wiley, New York
Harre R 1970 *The Principles of Scientific Thinking.* Chicago Publishing, Chicago, Illinois
Hayes-Roth F 1983 Using proofs and refutations to learn from experience. In: Michalski *et al. Machine Learning.* Tioga, Palo Alto, California, pp. 221–40
Hayes-Roth F, Waterman D 1978 Principles of pattern directed inference systems. In: Waterman D, Hayes-Roth F (eds.) *Pattern Directed Inference Systems.* Academic Press, New York
Holland J H, Holyoak K J, Nisbett R E, Thagard P R 1987 *Induction: Process of Inference, Learning and Discovery.* MIT Press, Cambridge, Massachusetts
Janis I L 1983 *Groupthink.* Free Press, New York

Janis I L, Mann L 1977 *Decision Making*. Free Press, New York

Johnson-Laird P N, Wason P C 1977 *Thinking: Readings in Cognitive Science*. Cambridge University Press, Cambridge

Kahneman D, Slovic P, Tversky A 1982 *Judgement Under Uncertainty: Heuristics and Biases*. Cambridge University Press, Cambridge

Klein G A 1980 Automated aids for the proficient decision maker. *Proc. Conf. Systems, Man and Cybernetics*. IEEE Press, New York, pp. 301–4

Klein G A 1982 The use of comparison cases. *Proc. Annual Conf. Systems, Man and Cybernetics*. IEEE Press, New York, pp. 88–91

Levi I 1980 *The Enterprise of Knowledge*. MIT Press, Cambridge, Massachusetts

McCarthy J, Hayes P J 1969 Some philosophical problems from the standpoint of artificial intelligence. In: Meltzer B, Michie D (eds.) *Machine Intelligence*, Vol. 1, Edinburgh University Press, Edinburgh

Mandler G 1985 *Cognitive Psychology*. Erlbaum, Hillsdale, New Jersey

Mayer R E 1983 *Thinking, Problem Solving, Cognition*. Freeman, San Francisco

Michalski R S, Carbonell J G, Mitchell T M 1983 *Machine Learning: An Artificial Intelligence Approach*. Tioga, Palo Alto, California

Minsky M 1975 A framework for representing knowledge. In: Winston P A (ed.) *The Psychology of Computer Vision*. McGraw–Hill, New York

Mitroff I, Mason R O 1982 Business policy and physics: Some philosophical considerations. *Acad. Manage.* **7**(3), 361–71

Mitroff I, Quinton H, Mason R O 1983 Beyond contradiction and consistency: A design for dialectical policy systems. *Theory Decis.* **15**, 107–20

Nakamura K, Iwai S 1982 Topological fuzzy sets as a quantitative description of analogical inference and its application to questioning-answering systems for information retrieval. *IEEE Trans. Syst., Man Cybern.* **12**(2), 193–204

Nakamura K, Sage A P, Iwai S 1983 An intelligent database interface using psychological similarity between data. *IEEE Trans. Syst., Man Cybern.* **13**, 558–68

Neisser U 1976 *Cognition and Reality*. Freeman, San Francisco

Newell A 1982 The knowledge level. *Artificial Intelligence*. **18**, 87–127

Newell A, Simon H A 1972 *Human Problem Solving*. Prentice–Hall, Englewood Cliffs, New Jersey

Nilsson N J 1980 *Principles of Artificial Intelligence*. Tioga Palo Alto, California

Norman D A, Rumelhart D E, LNR Research Group 1975 *Explorations in Cognition*. Freeman, San Francisco, California

Pearl J, Leal A, Saleh J 1982 GODDESS: A goal directing decision structuring system. *IEEE Trans. Pattern Anal. Mach. Recognition* **4**(3), 250–62

Quillian M R 1968 Semantic memory. In: Minsky M (ed.) *Semantic Information Processing*. MIT Press, Cambridge, Massachusetts

Rajala D W, Sage A P 1980a On decision situation structural models. *Policy Anal. Inf. Sci.* **4**(1), 53–81

Rajala D W, Sage A P 1980b On measures for decision model structuring. *Int. J. Syst. Sci.* **11**(1), 17–31

Rasmussen J 1983 Skills, rules and knowledge: Signals, signs and symbols; and other distinctions in human performance models. *IEEE Trans. Syst., Man Cybern.* **13**(3)

Rasmussen J, Rouse W B (eds.) 1981 *Human Detection and Diagnosis of System Failures*. Plenum, New York

Roberts F S 1976 *Discrete Mathematical Models: With Application to Social, Biological, and Environmental Problems*. Prentice–Hall, Englewood Cliffs, New Jersey

Rouse W B 1983 Models of human problem solving: Detection, diagnosis, and compensation for system failures. *Automatica* **19**, 613–25

Rumelhart D E, Ortony A 1977 The representation of knowledge in memory. In: Anderson R C, Spiro R, Montague W (eds.) *Schooling and the Acquisition of Knowledge*. Erlbaum, Hillsdale, New Jersey

Ruspini E H 1982 Possibility theory approaches for advanced information systems. *Computer* **15**(10), 83–91

Sacerdoti E D 1977 *A Structure for Plans and Behavior*. Elsevier, New York

Sage A P 1977 *Methodology for Large Scale Systems*. McGraw–Hill, New York

Sage A P 1981 Organizational and behavioral considerations in the design of information systems and processes for planning and decision support. *IEEE Trans. Syst., Man Cybern.* **11**(9), 640–78

Sage A P, Lagomasino A 1984 Knowledge representation and man machine dialog. In: Rouse W B (ed.) *Advances in Man Machine Systems Research*, Vol. 1, JAI Press, Greenwich, Connecticut, pp. 223–60

Sage A P, Rajala D W 1978 On the role of structure in policy analysis and decision making. In: Sutherland J W (ed.) *Management Handbook for Public Administration*. Van Nostrand Reinhold, New York

Sage A P, White C C 1977 *Optimum Systems Control*. Prentice–Hall, Englewood Cliffs, New Jersey

Sage A P, White E B 1983 Decision and information structures in regret models of judgement and choice. *IEEE Trans. Syst. Man Cybern.* **13**, 136–45

Schank R C 1975 *Conceptual Information Processing*. North-Holland, Amsterdam

Schank R C 1982 *Reading and Understanding*. Erlbaum, Hillsdale, New Jersey

Schank R C, Abelson R P 1977 *Scripts, Plans, Goals, and Understanding*. Erlbaum, Hillsdale, New Jersey

Schank R C, Colby K M (eds.) 1973 *Computer Models of Thought and Language*. Freeman, San Francisco, California

Shapiro S C (ed.) 1987 *Encyclopedia of Artificial Intelligence*. Wiley, New York

Silverman B G 1983 Analogy in systems management: An information processing view with implications for comparison guiding aids. *IEEE Trans. Syst., Man Cybern.* **13**(6)

Sternberg R J 1977 *Intelligence, Information Processing, and Analogical Reasoning: the Componential Analysis of Human Abilities*. Erlbaum, Hillsdale, New Jersey

Sternberg R J (ed.) 1982 *Handbook of Artificial Intelligence*. Cambridge University Press, Cambridge

Svenson I 1979 Process descriptions of decision making. *Organ. Behav. Hum. Perform.* **23**, 86–112

Tolman R C 1948 Cognitive maps in rats and men. *Psychol. Rev.* **55**, 189–208

Tweney R D, Doherty M E, Mynatt C R 1981 *On Scientific Thinking*. Columbia University Press, New York

Wason P C, Johnson-Laird P N 1972 *Psychology of Reasoning: Structure and Content*. Batsford, London

Wilensky R 1981 Meta-planning: Representing and using

knowledge about planning in problem solving and natural language understanding. *Cognit. Sci.* **5**, 197–233
Winograd T 1975 Frame representations and the declarative-procedural controversy. In: Bobrow and Collins 1975, pp. 185–210
Winograd T 1983 *Language as a Cognitive Process.* Addison–Wesley, Reading, Massachusetts
Winston P H 1977 *Artificial Intelligence.* Addison–Wesley, Reading, Massachusetts
Winston P H 1980 Learning and reasoning by analogy. *Commun. ACM* **23**(12), 689–703
Winston P H, Brown R H (eds.) 1979 *Artificial Intelligence: An MIT Perspective.* MIT Press, Cambridge, Massachusetts
Wohl J G 1981 Force management requirements for air force tactical command and control. *IEEE Trans. Syst., Man Cybern.* **11**(9), 618–39

A. P. Sage
[George Mason University, Fairfax, Virginia, USA]

Knowledge Support Systems: Uncertain Information Processing

Almost all information is subject to uncertainty. It may arise from inaccurate or incomplete data (e.g., how large are the current US petroleum reserves?), from linguistic imprecision (what exactly do we count as petroleum reserves?), from difficulties in prediction (what will the US annual petroleum consumption be in ten years?) and from disagreement between information sources. Even where in principle we have complete information, uncertainty may arise from unavoidable approximations required to render models computationally tractable. As well as being uncertain about what is the case in the external world, we may be uncertain about our preferences and about what actions to take; that is, about our decisions. Very possibly we may even be uncertain about our degree of uncertainty.

Various schemes have been developed to formalize the notion of uncertainty, to quantify degrees of belief and to mechanize reasoning under uncertainty. The best-known formalism is probability; however, apparent practical difficulties in applying probabilistic schemes to model complex bodies of uncertain knowledge have given rise to the development of a variety of alternatives. These include interval representations such as Dempster–Shafer belief functions, heuristic approximations to probability used in rule-based expert systems (such as certainty factors), fuzzy set theory designed to handle linguistic imprecision, and several nonnumerical approaches including nonmonotonic logic and default reasoning. There has been some controversy about the underlying assumptions, relative appropriateness and practicality of these various techniques. Meanwhile, recent developments in applied probability and decision analysis, notably belief nets and influence diagrams, have provided more flexible tools for encoding complex uncertain knowledge. These appear to resolve many of the earlier difficulties of the probabilistic approach.

Two critical issues for the acceptance of any scheme for uncertain information processing are the ease of encoding human expert knowledge into the scheme (a process known as knowledge engineering) and the comprehensibility of the scheme to users. The design of acceptable systems requires some understanding of the psychology of human reasoning under uncertainty.

1. Probability

The most commonly encountered view of probability at the introductory level is the frequentist (or classical) view. However, it is the personalist view (also known as subjective or Bayesian) that is generally most useful in knowledge support systems. Consequently, it is important to understand the distinction.

1.1 The Frequentist View

In the frequentist view, the probability of an event occurring in a particular trial is defined in terms of the frequency with which it occurs in a long sequence of similar trials. More precisely, the probability is the value to which the long-run frequency converges as the number of trials increases. In this view, the probability is actually a property of a theoretically infinite sequence of trials rather than of a single event. It is sometimes thought of as a property of the physical system that generates the events, such as the coin or dice. With an event such as the toss of a coin, it is easy to think of the sequence of trials of which it is a member, and natural to judge that each trial is typical of all trials (that is, it is exchangeable with other trials in the sequence.)

The problem is that, for many events of interest in real-world domains, it is not clear what the relevant population of trials of similar events should be. When estimating the probability that a particular chemical is carcinogenic, it is unclear what the relevant parent population is: is it the population of all known chemicals, only those tested for carcinogenicity, or only those chemicals with a similar molecular structure? Many important events are essentially unique, such as the probability that room-temperature superconductors will be identified before the year 2000.

1.2 The Personalist or Bayesian View

In the personalist view of probability (also known as the subjective or Bayesian view), the probability of an event is the degree of belief that a person has that it will occur, given all the relevant information currently known to that person. In this view, probabilities may be assigned to any well-defined event, whether unique or repeated. Thus this view is generally more useful for knowledge support systems.

A probability is a function not only of the event, but of the state of information. Thus it is a function of two arguments, denoted as $P(h|s)$, where h is the uncertain event, and s is the person's state of information on which it is conditioned. If additional evidence e becomes available to the person, his new probability is conditional on this, $P(h|e, s)$, where the comma denotes the conjunction of e and s. Since different people may have different information relevant to an event, and the same person may acquire new information as time progresses, there is strictly no such thing as "the" probability of an event. Different people at one time or one person at different times may legitimately assign different probabilities to the same event. In this view, probability is fundamentally unlike empirical properties such as mass or length in classical physics. It is akin to relativistic physics in that it depends in an essential way on the observer. Thus we should talk of "your" probability or "my" probability rather than "the" probability.

This personalist view does not imply that a person's probability assignments can be completely arbitrary. To be legitimate, probabilities must be consistent with the axioms of probability, whether they are frequentist or personalist. As a simple example, if you assign probability P to a hypothesis h, you should assign probability $1 - P$ to its complement, that h is false. This consistency criterion is termed coherence.

Suppose you believe that all trials in a sequence are uncertain (i.e., have a probability greater than 0 and less than 1) and are exchangeable with each other (as in all tosses of the same coin). Then, if you are coherent in updating your beliefs, your probability for the coin coming up heads will converge to the long-run frequency of heads as you observe more and more trials. Hence, where there is sufficient empirical data for the frequentist to estimate a probability, the personalist's assessment of "his" probability will converge to the frequentist's estimate of "the" probability of the event. In other words, they will tend to agree. The difference is that if there are no data, say in assessing the probability of heads for a newly bent coin, the personalist would still be able to assess a probability, while the frequentist would not.

1.3 Bayesian Inference

Coherence implies that updating of beliefs is carried out in accordance with Bayes' rule, which is a simple consequence of the axioms of probability. Bayes' rule gives your posterior probability $P(h|e, s)$; that is, your belief in a hypothesis h after seeing evidence e, as a function of your prior probability before seeing e, $P(h|s)$ and the likelihoods $P(e|h, s)$ and $P(e|\sim h, s)$ you assess of observing e given h is true or false:

$$P(h|e, s) = \frac{P(h|s) P(e|h, s)}{P(h|s) P(e|h, s) + [1 - P(h|s)] P(e|\sim h, s)}$$

The usefulness of Bayes' rule derives from the fact that it is often easier to assess the prior and the likelihoods and compute the posterior rather than assess the posterior directly. This is common when h is a possible cause of e; for example, if h is a disease and e is one of its symptoms. It is usually easier to assess the probability of a symptom conditional on a disease rather than the probability of the disease conditional on the symptom. Thus Bayes' rule offers a way to obtain inverse relationships expressed in the causal direction to provide diagnostic reasoning. See Shachter and Heckerman (1987) and Henrion (1987) for discussions.

Bayesian inference may be generalized to cases with multiple hypotheses and multiple pieces of evidence. Consider a medical example with n possible hypotheses, $h_1, h_2, \ldots h_n$, (diseases), and m pieces of evidence, $e_1, e_2, \ldots e_m$, (symptoms, lab findings, etc.). Since a patient may have zero, one or several diseases, the number of possible disease combinations is 2^n, and the complete prior requires specification of $2^n - 1$ parameters. Similarly, the general conditional distribution for each combination of evidence given each disease combination (the likelihoods) requires specification of $2^n(2^m - 1)$ parameters. Clearly this generality would be quite impractical for more than a very few diseases and pieces of evidence, and some simplification is essential.

1.4 Simplified Bayesian Diagnosis

A widely used approach makes two simplifying assumptions. First, it assumes that the hypotheses are mutually exclusive and exhaustive. Hence, only the n singleton hypotheses h_i need to be considered. Second, each piece of evidence e_j is conditionally independent of every other piece of evidence e_k, given any hypothesis h_i; i.e.,

$$P(e_j|h_i, s) = P(e_j|e_k, h_i, s) \quad \text{for all}$$
$$i, j, k, \text{ where } j \neq k$$

With these assumptions, less than nm probabilities are required. The simplicity of this approach has led to the epithet "Idiot's Bayes." It has been popular, particularly for systems to support medical diagnosis (Szolovits and Pauker 1984). While sometimes useful, the assumptions are often too restrictive; for example, multiple diseases are common in many areas of medicine. However, as explained below, it is a misconception to believe that the assumptions of mutual exclusiveness of hypotheses and conditional independence of evidence are essential to tractable Bayesian inference.

2. Heuristic Schemes and Rule-Based Systems

One response to the apparent dilemma between restrictive assumptions or intractability of coherent probabilistic schemes was the development of numerical representations of uncertainty, intended as more tractable approximations to probability. The best known of these, such as the certainty factors (CFs) of MYCIN (Shortliffe and Buchanan 1976) are combined with rule-based knowledge representations. In these, knowledge is represented as a collection of production rules of the form "If ⟨condition⟩ then ⟨conclusion⟩ with certainty ⟨c⟩." An example from the MYCIN expert system for diagnosis and therapy of bacterial infections is:

If: (1) the gram stain of the organism is gramnegative, and (2) the morphology of the organism is rod, and (3) the aerobicity of the organism is anaerobic

Then: there is suggestive evidence (CF = 0.6) that the identity of the organism is bacterioides

Each rule and each proposition, such as the three elements of the condition and the conclusion, has an associated CF in the range −1 to 1 representing the degree of disconfirmation or confirmation. −1 means "proved false," 0 means "no evidence" and 1 means "proved true." Certainty factors represent changes rather than absolute degrees of belief. The uncertain inference scheme provides methods for computing the CF for a Boolean combination of propositions in a condition, and for a conclusion based on the certainty of each rule and its condition. (See Shortliffe and Buchanan (1976) for details.) The CF scheme is available in several commercial shells (computer languages) for implementing rule-based expert systems and has been widely applied.

Another well-known rule-based scheme is that of Prospector, an expert system for identification of mineral deposits. This employs probabilities and a heuristic approximation to Bayes' rule for diagnostic reasoning. Other numerical schemes using heuristic approximations to probabilistic reasoning, developed by artificial intelligence researchers for medical applications, include Internist-1, PIP and Casnet (see Clancy and Shortliffe (1984), Szolovits and Pauker (1984), Horvitz et al. (1988) for reviews).

The production-rule representation was originally developed for logical reasoning without uncertainty. A major part of its appeal lies in its modularity; that is, individual rules may be added or removed without having to modify others to maintain consistency. Unfortunately it has become apparent that uncertain knowledge is intrinsically less modular than certain knowledge, and the assumption of modularity in rule-based schemes has certain restrictive implications. Analysis of these schemes in probabilistic terms demonstrates that they, too, unavoidably make various dependence assumptions which may not always be appropriate (Horvitz et al. 1988).

3. Uncertainty and Decision Making

3.1 Decision Theory

Ultimately, the purpose of a knowledge support system is not just better information and knowledge but better decisions. In medicine, the goal is not just better diagnosis but better choice of therapies; in financial investment, not just better forecasts of performance, but better choices of investment. To support decision making, a system needs to represent the goals, preferences and risk attitudes of the decision maker(s). Bayesian decision theory provides a framework which integrates the quantifying of uncertain beliefs as probabilities, preferences as utilities, and a criterion for optimal decision making, namely maximizing expected utility. It is based on a set of axioms which provide a theory of rational behavior. It is normative; that is, if you subscribe to its axioms, it prescribes what decisions are best consistent with your beliefs and preferences. It does not necessarily purport to be descriptive of how people actually behave.

3.2 Decision Analysis

Decision analysis comprises a set of practical techniques for applying decision theory to support decision making for real problems. It includes techniques for structuring problems as decision trees and influence diagrams, for eliciting uncertain beliefs from people to encode them as probabilities, for encoding preferences as utility functions, and for using this information to derive recommended decisions. An important part of the process is sensitivity analysis to examine the effect of uncertainties in the encoded numbers and to identify which assumptions are most critical, and where effort is likely to be most productively spent in obtaining better data or judgements, or in refining the model. The most useful results of effective decision analysis are generally improved insights into the problem rather than direct recommendations. See Raiffa (1968), Howard and Matheson (1984b) and the article *Decision Analysis* for descriptions of decision analysis. Many knowledge support systems are based on decision-analytic principles (e.g., Morgan and Henrion 1988).

3.3 Influence Diagrams and Belief Nets

Influence diagrams and belief nets are techniques for the graphical representation of the elements of a problem in decision making or probabilistic inference. Influence diagrams are widely used by decision analysts as an aid to knowledge engineering; that is, structuring and encoding the beliefs and preferences of experts and decision makers. They are also useful for communicating problem structures.

Figure 1 illustrates an influence diagram representing a decision problem involving a heart patient. The squares represent decisions under the direct control of the decision maker: whether to perform an angiogram test to determine the extent of coronary artery disease, and whether to undertake coronary bypass graft surgery. Single circles represent currently uncertain states of the world, such as whether the patient has coronary artery disease (CAD) and its possible consequences— chest pain, now and in the future—and myocardial infarction (MI) (heart attack). The double circle represents a state of the world—financial cost—which is

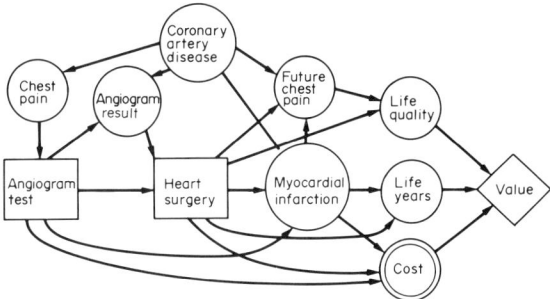

Figure 1
An influence diagram describing a decision problem involving a patient with heart disease. Squares represent decisions, circles represent possibly uncertain states of the world, and the diamond is the outcome value to the patient. Arrows represent influences (After Horvitz *et al.* 1988)

a certain function of its inputs. The diamond represents the total value (utility) of the eventual outcomes to the patient, including quality of life, years of survival and financial cost. Diagrams containing only state variables (circles) but no decisions or value nodes are often termed Bayesian nets or belief nets (Pearl 1988).

Arrows into decisions represent information from nodes whose values will be known at the time the decision is made; for example, that the result of the angiogram will be known before the decision is made on surgery. Arrows into uncertain state nodes represent uncertain influences. For example, life quality is influenced by future chest pain and heart surgery.

The presence or absence of arrows is a qualitative encoding of various dependence and independence relations. For example, the diagram shows that, before doing the angiogram test, the presence of chest pain is judged conditionally independent of the angiogram result given the CAD. This is because there are arrows from CAD to each finding, but no arrow between them. Similarly, life quality is conditionally independent of its indirect predecessors (e.g., CAD and MI) given its direct predecessors (future chest pain and heart surgery).

In this way the diagram offers a flexible and intuitively qualitative way to express an expert's opinion about dependencies and independencies without restrictive assumptions. Having drawn the diagram to express these relations at the qualitative level, the next stage is to quantify the influences. In general, these are expressed numerically in the form of the conditional probability distribution for each uncertain state variable for each combination of values of its predecessors (the variables which influence it). A variety of methods are available for eliciting numerical probabilities (Morgan and Henrion 1988). See Howard and Matheson (1984a) for an introduction to influence diagrams, and Pearl (1988) for an extensive presentation of belief nets.

4. Linguistic Imprecision

A noteworthy feature of human language is that we often use terms without precise definitions. We may find it useful to say that a river is "wide," that rain tomorrow is "likely," or refer to the "price of gasoline in ten years time," without bothering to explain exactly what we mean.

4.1 The Clarity Test

The standard approach in decision analysis is to seek to eliminate linguistic imprecision as a first step towards encoding uncertain knowledge. Even from the personalist view, an event or quantity must be well specified for a meaningful probability distribution to be assessable. The clarity test is a conceptual way to sharpen up the notion of well-specifiedness (Howard and Matheson 1984b): imagine a clairvoyant who could know all facts about the universe, past, present and future. Given the description of the event or quantity, could the clairvoyant say unambiguously whether the event will occur (or had occurred) or could he/she give the exact numerical value of the quantity? If so, then it is well-specified.

"The price of gasoline in ten years" would not pass the clarity test. The clairvoyant would want to know what kind of gasoline, sold where and exactly when, before he/she could give its exact value. A better specification of the quantity might be "the average retail price of regular unleaded gasoline in dollars per gallon observed at service stations in Pittsburgh on January 1, 1999." Without such precision, vagueness about what the quantity represents is liable to be confounded with uncertainty about its true value.

4.2 Fuzzy Set Theory

An alternative view is proposed by advocates of fuzzy set theory. Since imprecision is intrinsic in human language, they suggest that knowledge engineering and other aspects of human–computer interaction will be greatly eased if the imprecision is represented explicitly. Fuzzy sets are one way to do this. Fuzzy sets are sets that do not have a crisply defined membership, but rather allow elements to have degrees of membership between 0 and 1. For example, the linguistic variable "wide river" may be represented by a fuzzy set with a membership function that associates degrees of membership with different widths, as shown in Fig. 2. Thus, a river of width 10 m has membership 0 in "wide river," one with width 100 m membership 1, and intermediate widths have intermediate degrees of membership.

Fuzzy modifiers, such as "very" or "somewhat," may be used to modify the meaning of fuzzy sets; for example, obtaining a membership function for a "very wide" river from a "wide" river. Fuzzy set theory provides operators for deriving the membership of unions, intersections and complements of fuzzy sets. For example, the membership of an element in the

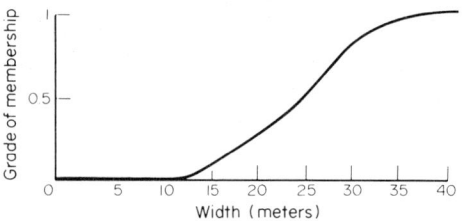

Figure 2
A membership function for the fuzzy set "wide rivers" in terms of their width in meters

union of two fuzzy sets is defined as the maximum of its memberships in each of the components. This also provides a basis for fuzzy logics with propositions having fuzzy truth values between 0 and 1. Fuzzy quantifiers, such as "most," "almost always" and "usually" allow fuzzy syllogistic reasoning intended to emulate commonsense reasoning. There exists a large literature on fuzzy set theory. See, Zadeh (1984) and *Fuzzy Reasoning Methods* for introductions. There has been a number of successful applications useful to process controllers employing fuzzy logic.

4.3 Verbal Probabilities

The grade of membership of an element of a fuzzy set is not a probability, but rather a measure of the compatibility between the element and the concept represented by the fuzzy set. However, it is possible to represent imprecision in a probability by fuzzy probabilities, using a membership function (sometimes referred to as a possibility distribution) over the range of numerical probabilities expressing the degree to which the numbers are compatible with the probability of an event. This approach has been used to interpret verbally expressed probabilities, such as "unlikely," "probable" and "almost certain." Certainly, most people seem more comfortable with such phrases than with the numbers.

Psychological research on the correspondence between numerical probabilities and probabilities expressed by verbal phrases shows that there is some consistency in the ordering of the terms between different people. Unfortunately, there is considerable variation in the way different people interpret the phrases. Moreover, even for one person, interpretation is very context-dependent. Saying that rain is "fairly likely" tomorrow means something quite different in England than in Arizona. Similarly, the quantitative implications of "Pat is tall" are greatly affected by knowledge of whether Pat is male or female, adult or child. There is still considerable room for research into developing more empirically based models of linguistic imprecision, but these examples suggest that context-free mappings between words and numbers will not be adequate.

5. Uncertainty about Probabilities

Probabilities expressed by verbal phrases produce one kind of uncertainty about probability, which is due to linguistic imprecision. But even if assessors are asked to express probabilities numerically, they will generally feel uncertain about exactly what number best expresses their degree of belief. A variety of approaches has been suggested to represent this, in addition to the fuzzy probabilities described above.

5.1 Probability Intervals

Perhaps the simplest approach conceptually is to represent degrees of belief by a range of probabilities, with numerical upper and lower bounds. More generally, uncertainty about a probability distribution over a set of alternative values for a variable may be represented by a convex set of probability distributions. Of course, this requires the assessor to provide more numbers than with simple point-valued probabilities, but the assessor may feel more comfortable with this looser range. In principle, it is straightforward to generalize all the techniques for probabilistic inference to deal with sets of probabilities, although in practice it can be computationally complex.

An important question is how to make decisions when uncertainty is represented as probability intervals and no single decision has maximum expected utility for all probability values. One response is simply to conclude that the decision is undetermined in such cases, and leave it at that. A second approach is to select the particular point-valued distribution from within the specified set that maximizes entropy, and use this for decision making. A third approach is to conduct a sensitivity analysis to discover which component probability assessment ranges contribute most to the uncertainty about which decision has the highest expected value. Then, further effort is devoted to obtaining a more precise assessment of these, and the procedure is iterated until one decision can be selected unambiguously.

5.2 Dempster–Shafer Belief Functions

Dempster–Shafer belief functions are a generalization of point-valued probabilities that has attracted particular interest. Consider an uncertain variable which has a set of, say, three mutually exclusive and exhaustive values $X = \{x_1, x_2, x_3\}$. Where a conventional probabilistic approach is to distribute the unit probability mass among each of these three possible values, the belief function, $Bel(X)$, allows mass to be distributed among all the subsets of X, including singletons, doublets and the entire set; that is,

$$\{\{x_1\}, \{x_2\}, \{x_3\}, \{x_1, x_2\}, \{x_1, x_3\}, \{x_2, x_3\}, \{x_1, x_2, x_3\}\}$$

This set is termed the frame of discernment. This approach provides more flexibility than simple probabilities. If you are unsure how to assign belief between, say, x_1 and x_2, you can leave it unspecified and simply assign the belief to their union $\{x_1, x_2\}$. The support, Sup(h), for a hypothesis h, which is any set of values in the frame, is defined as the sum of the masses assigned to h and all its subsets:

$$\text{Sup}(h) = \sum_{X \in h} \text{Bel}(X)$$

The plausibility, Pl(h), of a hypothesis is defined as the complement of the total support for all hypotheses incompatible with h; that is, all subsets of X that do not contain h:

$$\text{Pl}(h) = 1 - \text{Sup}(h^c)$$

If all the belief is assigned to the singleton hypotheses x_1, x_2 and x_3, then the belief function reduces to a conventional probability distribution, and the support and plausibility will be equal; otherwise, the support will be less than the plausibility. In the extreme case of total ignorance, all belief is assigned to the entire set, and for every proper subset, the support is 0 and the plausibility is 1. Dempster's rule is used for combining evidence from multiple sources. See Shafer (1976) for an introduction to this scheme.

Dempster (the originator of this approach) and others interpret the support and plausibility numbers as bounds on the probability. In this case, belief functions can be seen as a generalization of point-valued probabilities, but a special case of convex sets of probabilities. Dempster's rule for combination of evidence can be seen as a special case of Bayesian inference. However, Shafer, who has done much to develop and popularize the scheme, denies these probabilistic interpretations of the belief function.

5.3 Second-Order Probability Distributions

A more sophisticated approach to representing uncertainty about probabilities is to use a probability distribution over the probability distribution; that is, a second-order probability distribution. Questions have been raised as to what exactly this might mean, given that probabilities are only defined for well-specified quantities. Assigning a subjective probability distribution to a frequency (objective probability), such as the failure rate in a large population of similar components of a nuclear power plant, poses no theoretical problems. However, it does not appear that a subjective probability itself can pass the clarity test, since it is one person's opinion and not open to empirical measurement even in principle.

One useful interpretation of your probability distribution on a probability is as your current opinion on what your posterior probability would be after you have observed some relevant information. For example, suppose you currently assign a probability of 0.5 to "rain tomorrow." When you hear the weather forecast, you may change your probability. Before you hear it you may assess your predictive distribution of what your posterior probability of rain will be after

hearing it. In this case, the second-order distribution is relative to a particular information source, namely the weather forecast. The more informative the source, the greater the uncertainty of this distribution, since you are more likely to change your opinion.

If you are coherent, your current probability, 0.5, of rain must be the expected value of the second-order distribution. If you plan to make a decision influenced by the weather before hearing the forecast, then you only need the expected probability, 0.5. In this sense, second-order distributions make no difference and can be ignored. However, if you wish to decide whether it is worth paying some price for the information, or delaying the decision at some cost, then the second-order distribution may be useful. You may use it to calculate the expected value of the information. See Howard (1988) for discussion of these issues.

6. Psychology of Judgement under Uncertainty

One strategy in artificial intelligence research has been to attempt to emulate human cognitive processes. This has been an explicit motivation in the development of fuzzy set theory. Certainly, in some tasks, such as visual perception and sensory motor coordination, humans by far outperform current artificial systems and emulation is a worthy, if ambitious, goal. Unfortunately, cognitive scientists have so far made only modest progress in developing descriptive models of human reasoning. However, they have accumulated a large body of evidence suggesting that our intuitive reasoning under uncertainty is highly fallible and liable to systematic biases and inconsistencies, at least in tasks where it can be compared with normative models of rationality. As one example, it is easy to construct pairs of bets (e.g., lottery tickets) for which most subjects, if offered a free choice, would choose one, but if asked to bid for them, are willing to pay more for the other. This seems irreconcilable with principles of rationality. Experimental studies of this and many other deficiencies in human judgement are described in Kahneman et al. (1982).

These results suggest it may be wiser to base knowledge support systems on schemes with a normative basis, such as probabilities and decision theory, rather than attempting to emulate human reasoning. Indeed, these results provide a justification for developing such aids to support human decision making rather than relying on purely intuitive methods.

Whether or not a scheme is intended to emulate human reasoning, it must be possible to translate from the mental representation of human experts into the formal representation in knowledge engineering. Conversely, it must be possible to explain the reasoning process and results of the knowledge support system in terms compatible with the users' mental models. To do these satisfactorily requires at least some understanding of human reasoning under uncertainty. For example, decision analysts have developed a battery of techniques for obtaining probability assessments from experts which are designed to mitigate the effects of known cognitive biases (Kahneman *et al.* 1982, Morgan and Henrion 1988).

7. *Nonmonotonic and Default Reasoning*

Nonmonotonic and default reasoning schemes are a qualitative way of handling uncertainty without attempting to quantify degrees of belief numerically. Unlike commonsense reasoning, standard logic is monotonic; that is, the addition of a new assertion cannot render a previous assertion false. Nonmonotonic logics allow the possibility that new information may invalidate previous beliefs. The following is a good example.

Assertion: Tweety is a bird

Question: Does he fly? *Answer:* Yes

Assertion: Tweety is a penguin

Question: Does he fly? *Answer:* No

Here, the system is making a default assumption that, in the absence of information to the contrary, birds fly. However, it also knows that penguins do not fly, and the information that Tweety is a penguin overrides the previous default. A nonmonotonic reasoning system contains some assertions that it considers irrevocably true and some are revokable, being based on default assumptions, e.g., birds fly. Whenever a new fact is learned, any beliefs derived from revocable assumptions may be invalidated. Thus, a practical system must be able to keep track of the assumptions that underlie any inference, so that it can withdraw such inferences when necessary. Such systems are known as automatic truth maintenance systems (ATMS).

A major issue in nonmonotonic reasoning is what to do when assumptions conflict, and how to prioritize them. An example is given below.

Assumption: Republicans are hawks

Assumption: Quakers are doves

Assertion: Nixon is a Republican Quaker

Question: Is Nixon a dove?

A variety of solutions have been proposed to such problems (Ginsberg 1987). One view of default assumptions is that they are beliefs that are held with sufficient strength that they can be accepted as true for the moment. The justification is that it is computationally easier to handle such uncertain beliefs with qualitative logics than to carry around probabilities or other numeric measures with them. In this view, the logic is a more tractable approximation to, say, probabilistic reasoning, and the difficulties with conflicting assumptions may be resolved by recourse to an underlying probabilistic scheme (e.g., Pearl 1988). However, such interpretations remain controversial.

8. *Comparing Approaches*

There is much active research on all the approaches discussed and, as yet, there is little consensus about their relative merits and the tasks for which each is appropriate. In selecting a technique for a particular application it is important to consider several criteria. These include its theoretical rationale, computational tractability, performance, compatibility for encoding expert knowledge, and the comprehensibility of the representation. Future systems may combine several approaches in an integrated fashion, and select among representations and computational techniques as appropriate for the needs of specific tasks.

Coherent probabilistic schemes have the advantage of an axiomatically based theory for reasoning under uncertainty which, unlike other schemes, is integrated with a normative theory of decision making. Decision analysts have a record of successful applications of the approach to practical decision making. The key questions about probabilistic schemes are tractability for knowledge engineering and inference in large-scale systems. The use of influence diagrams and belief nets appears to greatly facilitate the encoding and explanation of probabilistic knowledge, and there is also progress towards more efficient algorithms. However, large-scale applications remain to be demonstrated.

Heuristic numeric schemes and rule-based representations have been most popular for large knowledge bases for expert systems. In the past there was a belief among artificial intelligence researchers that the details of the uncertainty calculus generally make little practical difference to system performance. However, recent experimental comparisons of heuristic approximations to coherent probabilistic schemes have found disturbing discrepancies (e.g., Wise and Henrion, 1986, Henrion 1987). The relative performance depends on the class of inference task, and the differences between techniques are most significant when evidence is weak or conflicting.

Explicit handling of linguistic imprecision and uncertainties about degrees of belief seems desirable for ease of communication between knowledge support systems and users, and to facilitate sensitivity analysis. So far, fuzzy set theory is the most developed approach, although interval probabilities, Dempster-Shafer belief functions and second-order probability distributions may also play a role. Computational tractability is currently an issue for all these approaches.

Bibliography

Clancy W J, Shortliffe E H 1984 *Readings in Medical Artificial Intelligence: The First Decade.* Addison–Wesley, Reading, Massachusetts

Ginsberg M L 1987 *Readings in Nonmonotonic Logic*. Morgan Kaufman, Los Altos, California

Henrion M 1987 Uncertainty in artificial intelligence: Is probability epistemologically and heuristically adequate? In: Mumpower J *et al.* (eds.) *Expert Judgment and Expert Systems*. Springer-Verlag, Berlin, pp. 105–30

Horvitz E J, Breese J S, Henrion M 1988 Decision theory in expert systems and artificial intelligence. *Int. J. Approx. Reasoning*

Howard R A 1988 Uncertainty about probability: A decision analysis perspective. *Risk Anal.* **8**(1), 91–98

Howard R A, Matheson J E 1984a Influence diagrams. In: Howard and Matheson 1984b, pp. 719–62

Howard R A, Matheson J E (eds) 1984b *Readings in the Principles and Applications of Decision Analysis*. Strategic Decisions Group, Menlo Park, California

Kahneman D, Slovic P, Tversky A 1982 *Judgment under Uncertainty: Heuristics and Biases*. Cambridge University Press, Cambridge

Kanal L N, Lemmer J (eds) 1986 *Uncertainty in Artificial Intelligence*, Machine Intelligence and Pattern Recognition, Vol. 4. Elsevier, Amsterdam

Morgan M G, Henrion M 1988 *Uncertainty: A Guide to the Treatment of Uncertainty in Quantitative Policy and Risk Analysis*. Cambridge University Press, Cambridge

Pearl J 1988 *Probabilistic Reasoning in Intelligent Systems: Networks of Plausible Inference*. Morgan Kaufman, Los Altos, California

Raiffa H 1968 *Decision Analysis: Introductory Lectures on Choice Under Uncertainty*. Addison–Wesley, Reading, Massachusetts

Shachter R D, Heckerman D 1987 Thinking backwards for knowledge acquisition. *Artif. Intell.* **8**, 55–62

Shafer G 1976 *A Mathematical Theory of Evidence*. Princeton University Press, Princeton, New Jersey

Shortliffe E H, Buchanan B G 1976 A model of inexact reasoning in medicine. *Math. Biosci.* **23**, 351–79

Szolovits P, Pauker S G 1984 Categorical and probabilistic reasoning in medical diagnois. In Clancy and Shortliffe 1984

Wise B P, Henrion M 1986 A framework for comparing uncertain inference systems to probability. In Kanal and Lemmer 1986, pp. 69–84

Zadeh L A 1984 The role of fuzzy logic in the management of uncertainty in expert systems. *Fuzzy Sets Syst.* **11**, 199–227

M. Henrion
[Carnegie Mellon University, Pittsburgh, Pennsylvania, USA]

M

Multiattribute Utility Theory

The purpose of decision support is to provide tools for improving human performance in the resolution of complex decision problems. One class of aiding techniques is decision analysis based on multiattribute utility theory (MAUT). One of the most useful features of the MAUT-based approach is that it provides guidelines and a framework for selecting relevant alternatives by means of the identification and analysis of many aspects of their outcomes and their probabilities. Decomposition is essential for the analysis of complex decision problems because of the multiple noncommensurate nature of the attributes of the outcomes that follow from alternative courses of action. The MAUT approach presumes that candidate alternatives can be studied in terms of different dimensions or attributes of value. By decomposing the decision space, and subsequently analyzing the relative preferences of the decision maker on each dimension and across the different dimensions, MAUT-based decision analysis offers a prescriptive procedure for alternative selection on the basis of normative behavior for rational choice.

While decision analysis is a creative medium for capturing and analyzing the value perceptions and knowledge of the decision maker concerning a complex decision problem, the organization of the decision process as expressed through the creation of a decision-situation structural model is a major determinant of the result of using the decision analysis process. In the existing formal decision analysis methodology, the analyst first develops a model based on the decision maker's supplied information about the problem. An analysis is then performed using this model and finally, a decision based on model-supplied information is recommended to the decision maker.

Information requirements for multiattribute analysis are primarily determined by the functional form of the decision-situation model used. Consequently, the coordination of the information assessment step would be a straightforward process once the decision-situation structural model has been identified. However, this is the case only if all the relevant information is precise and readily available. However, difficulties in obtaining consistent numerically scaled utility functions, even for a single-dimensional attribute or utility space, and related difficulties in the assessment of probabilities and risk attitude coefficients, often impose barriers to obtaining the precise, consistent and complete information that is needed for easy and direct use of the MAUT process.

This article reviews several operational and behavioral issues in the use of MAUT-based decision support models.

1. The MAUT Framework for Decision Analysis

In the decision analysis paradigm (Keeney and Raiffa 1976, Sage 1977), it is assumed that a set of feasible alternatives $A = (a_1, \ldots, a_m)$ and a set of attributes or evaluators of the alternatives $(X_1, \ldots, X_n)$ can be identified. Associated with each alternative a in A, there is a corresponding consequence $(X_1(a), X_2(a), \ldots, X_n(a))$ in the n-dimensional consequence space $X = X_1 \times X_2 \times \cdots \times X_n$.

The problem for the decision maker is to choose an alternative a in A so that the payoff $(X_1(a), \ldots, X_n(a))$ will be "satisfying" or perhaps even the largest possible value. It is always possible in principle to compare the values of each $X_i(a)$ for different alternatives, but in most situations, the magnitudes of $X_i(a)$ and $X_j(a)$ for $i \neq j$ cannot be meaningfully compared since they may be measured in totally different units. Thus, a scalar-valued utility function defined on the attributes $(X_1, \ldots, X_n)$ is sought that will allow comparison of the alternatives across the attributes. The existence of this scalar-valued function, as a mechanism for representation and selection of alternatives in a utility space, is based on the fundamental representation theorem of simple preferences (Krantz et al. 1971 p. 39, Roberts 1979 p. 109) which states that, under certain conditions of rational behavior, there exists a real-valued utility function u such that

$$a_1 \succsim a_2 \Leftrightarrow u(a_1) \geqslant u(a_2)$$

where the symbol $\succsim$ is a weak preference relation indicating that a_1 is at least as preferred as a_2. When a set A is ordered by a weak preference relation without any other structural assumption, measurement is unique up to monotonic transformations.

Another kind of preference judgement is the concept of strength of preference or preference intensity (Krantz et al. 1971, Roberts 1979). This is concerned with preference comparisons between pairs of alternatives and addresses the question: is your difference in preference between *these* two alternatives less than, equal to, or greater than your difference in preference between *those* two alternatives? This type of judgement is much more difficult to understand than simple preference judgements, and consequently presents operational difficulties which will be discussed later.

Denoting elements of A by a_1, a_2, a_3 and a_4, we denote pairs representing strength of preference in A

by a_1a_2, a_3a_4, and so on. A strength-of-preference relation in $A^* = A \times A$ denoted by $\succsim^*$ is defined, where $a_1a_2 \succsim^* a_3a_4$ is taken to mean that the strength of preference of a_1 over a_2 is as much or greater than the strength of preference of a_3 over a_4. When the relation $\succsim^*$ in A^* satisfies certain axiomatic principles, then a real-valued function u, reflecting strength-of-preference relations among pairs of alternatives in $A \times A$ into difference orders in the real line, exists such that

$$a_1a_2 \succsim^* a_3a_4 \Leftrightarrow u(a_1) - u(a_2) \geq u(a_3) - u(a_4)$$

In this representation, u is a different kind of utility function to that in the ordinal representation. It is often called a measurable real-valued utility function because it preserves preference difference comparisons and is unique up to positive linear transformations.

There are several alternative axiom systems for measurable utility functions. Some of these systems allow both positive and negative preference differences and are called algebraic difference structures. For example, the degree of preference of a_1 over a_2 would be negative if a_2 was preferred to a_1. Earlier sets of sufficient conditions for algebraic difference measurement were given by Suppes and Winet (1955), Debreu (1959) and Scott and Suppes (1958). The only known set of axioms that are both necessary and sufficient for difference measurement is due to Scott (1964), and requires the assumption that A be finite. More recently, Krantz et al. (1971) presented much refined versions of these axioms for difference measurement. One of these is based on algebraic difference structures; another assumes that negative differences are not allowed, and hence is called a positive difference structure.

A primary interest in the literature on MAUT is to structure and assess a utility function u of the form

$$u(X_1(a), \ldots, X_n(a)) = f[u_1(X_1(a)), \ldots, u_n(X_n(a)), k_1, \ldots, k_n]$$

where u_i is a utility function over the single attribute X_i, the k_j values are scaling constants, and f aggregates the values of the single-attribute utility functions such as to enable one to compute the scalar utility of the alternatives. The utility functions u and u_i are assumed to be monotonic and bounded. Usually, they are scaled by $u(x^*) = 1$, $u(x^0) = 0$, $u_i(x_i^*) = 1$ and $u_i(x_i^0) = 0$ for all i. Here $x^* = (x_1^*, x_2^*, \ldots, x_n^*)$ designates the most desirable consequence and $x^0 = (x_1^0, x_2^0, \ldots, x_n^0)$ designates the least desirable. The symbols x_i^* and x_i^0 refer to the best and worst consequences, respectively, for each attribute X_i; that is, $x_i^* = X_i(a_*)$ where a_* is the best alternative for attribute i, and $x_i^0 = X_i(a_0)$ where a_0 is the worst alternative for attribute i.

We have very briefly described the case where a known associated consequence follows with certainty from the implementation of each alternative. This is often called the "certain decision" case.

The foundations of principles for decision making under risk are provided by the work of von Neumann and Morgenstern (1964). The implications of this work are that probabilities and utilities can be used to calculate the expected utility of each alternative and that alternatives with higher expected utilities should be preferred by a decision maker who is "rational." All that can be truly claimed here is that the decision maker is rational in the sense of accepting the axioms, which surely do appear reasonable, on the basis of which the results are obtained.

2. Independence Concepts

Multiattribute utility theory provides representation theorems, based on various forms of independence across the attributes, that describe the functional form of the multiattribute utility u as an additive, multiplicative or multilinear function of the conditional single-attribute utility functions u_i (Fishburn 1964, 1970, Keeney and Raiffa 1976). Here, independence concepts and related implications for the case of certainty and for the case involving risk in a decision-making context are reviewed. The following two independence concepts concern simple preference judgements among alternatives. They imply invariance of simple preference orders with common changes in attribute levels.

2.1 Preferential Independence

Given a set of attributes $(X_1, X_2, \ldots, X_n)$, a subset of attributes Y is preferentially independent of the complementary set $\hat{Y}$ if and only if the preference order of consequences involving only changes in the levels in Y does not depend on the levels at which attributes in $\hat{Y}$ are held fixed. Symbolically, the attributes of Y are preferentially independent if and only if for any set of consequences Y', Y'', Y^+

$$[(Y', \hat{Y}^+) \succsim (Y'', \hat{Y}^+)] \Rightarrow$$
$$[(Y', \hat{Y}) \succsim (Y'', \hat{Y})] \quad \text{for all } \hat{Y}$$

We are mostly interested in the case where the subsets Y are the attributes X_i, $i = 1, \ldots, n$, the case where each attribute X_i is preferentially independent of its complement. This interest occurs because of the following reasons:

(a) it is the weakest form of independence possible in this case,

(b) it holds naturally in most decision situations, and

(c) it is relatively easy to check for independence in analytically and behaviorally relevant ways.

2.2 Mutual Preferential Independence

The attributes $X_1, X_2, \ldots, X_n$ are mutually preferentially independent if every subset Y of these attributes is preferentially independent of its complementary set $\hat{Y}$. Obviously, this is a much stronger condition than preferential independence, and one whose use is more difficult to justify. The following two concepts (Dyer and Sarin 1979) pertain to the strength-of-preference relations between pairs of alternatives.

2.3 Difference Consistency

The set of mutually preferentially independent attributes $X_1, X_2, \ldots, X_n$ is difference consistent if, for all $x_i', x_i'' \in X_i$

$$(x_i', \bar{x}_i) \gtrsim (x_i'', \bar{x}_i) \Leftrightarrow (x_i', \bar{x}_i)(x_i^0, \bar{x}_i)$$
$$\gtrsim^* (x_i'', \bar{x}_i)(x_i^0, \bar{x}_i) \quad \text{for all } i$$

Difference consistency provides a connection between the relations $\gtrsim$ in X and $\gtrsim^*$ in $X \times X$. For instance, if the strength of preference among identical alternatives is considered null, then the relation $a_1 \gtrsim a_2 \Leftrightarrow a_1 a_2 \gtrsim^* a_1 a_1$ is interpreted as meaning that a_1 is as good as a_2 if and only if the preference difference or the strength of preference of a_1 over a_2 is "positive." In a decision problem involving both simple preference and strength-of-preference judgements, the difference-consistence assumption must hold.

2.4 Difference Independence

Given a set of attributes $X_1, X_2, \ldots, X_n$, an attribute X_i is said to be difference independent of $\hat{X}_i$ if and only if the preference difference of consequences involving only changes in the levels of X_i is not affected by the levels at which attributes in $\hat{X}_i$ are held fixed. Symbolically, X_i is difference independent of $\hat{X}_i$ if and only if, for all $x_i', x_i'' \in X_i$

$$(x_i', \bar{x}_i^+) \gtrsim (x_i'', \bar{x}_i^+) \Rightarrow (x_i', \bar{x}_i^+)(x_i'', \bar{x}_i^+)$$
$$\gtrsim^* (x_i', \bar{x}_i)(x_i'', \bar{x}_i) \quad \text{for all } \bar{x}_i \in \hat{X}_i$$

Note that difference independence and difference consistence imply preferential independence. The converse is not necessarily true. From difference consistence we have that

$$(x_i', \bar{x}_i^+)(x_i'', \bar{x}_i^+) \gtrsim^* (x_i', \bar{x}_i^+)(x_i', \bar{x}_i^+)$$

By transitivity of $\gtrsim^*$ it follows that

$$(x_i', \bar{x}_i)(x_i'', \bar{x}_i) \gtrsim^* (x_i', \bar{x}_i^+)(x_i', \bar{x}_i^+)$$

or equivalently, by difference consistency, that $(x_i', \bar{x}_i) \gtrsim (x_i'', \bar{x}_i)$. Hence, we can write the statement defining difference independence as

$$(x_i', \bar{x}_i^+) \gtrsim (x_i'', \bar{x}_i^+) \Rightarrow (x_i', \bar{x}_i) \gtrsim (x_i'', \bar{x}_i) \quad \text{for all } \bar{x}_i$$

which is the same as the statement of preferential independence of X_i.

Some independence concepts which are relevant to decision situations involving risk are discussed below. These concepts describe the preference behavior of the decision maker involving lotteries instead of consequences that occur with certainty. By a lottery $\bar{x}$ we mean a set of possible consequences, each associated with a known probability value. Preference over lotteries reflects both strength of preference and risk-attitude behavior of the decision maker.

2.5 Utility Independence

A subset of attributes Y is utility independent of its complement $\hat{Y}$ if the conditional preference order for lotteries involving only changes in the levels of attributes in Y does not depend on the levels at which the attributes in $\hat{Y}$ are held fixed. Symbolically, Y is utility independent of $\hat{Y}$ if and only if for any lotteries $\bar{y}', \bar{y}''$ and consequence $\bar{y}^+$,

$$(\bar{y}', \bar{y}^+) \gtrsim (\bar{y}'', \bar{y}^+) \Rightarrow (\bar{y}', \bar{y}) \gtrsim (\bar{y}'', \bar{y}) \quad \text{for all } \bar{y} \in \hat{y}.$$

Similar to the certainty case, the case where the subsets Y are the attributes X_i, $i = 1, 2, \ldots, n$ (i.e., the case where each attribute is utility independent) is of significant importance in that it is the weakest form of independence for the case involving risk. Utility independence is a generalization of preferential independence for the certainty case. Some important definitions are as follows.

DEFINITION 1 (Mutual utility independence). *Attributes $X_1, X_2, \ldots, X_n$ are said to be mutually utility independent if every subset of $\{X_1, X_2, \ldots, X_n\}$ is utility independent of its complement.*

DEFINITION 2 (Additive independence). *Attributes $X_1, X_2, \ldots, X_n$ are additive independent if preferences over lotteries involving levels of $X_1, X_2, \ldots, X_n$ depend only on the marginal probability distribution of each attribute and not on their joint probability distribution.*

Additive independence is a very strong assumption, and it most likely does not hold, in any strict sense, in real decision problems. We might expect that preferences over lotteries involving consequences in $X_1, X_2, \ldots, X_n$ depend not only on the marginal probability of the respective attributes, but also on their joint probability distribution since in fact they occur conjointly. In addition, additive independence is often very difficult to test in practice. It is, however, a very desirable goal to identify, define and structure a set of attributes that are additively independent, or nearly so. This is especially helpful in view of the much simplified computational and logic structure that results.

3. Representation Theorems and Structural Implications

The main results of MAUT are representation theorems that specify the functional form of the utility function when certain independence properties concerning the decision maker's preferences are appropriate. In this section are reviewed some of the most widely used representations such as the multilinear, multiplicative and additive representations, and their underlying assumptions are related to the structural properties that these impose on the decision situation. Special attention is devoted to the additive representation because of its simplicity and wide usage.

More details on these representations can be found in the comprehensive works of Fishburn (1964, 1970), Krantz et al. (1971), and Keeney and Raiffa (1976). More recently, Tamura and Nakamura (1983) have introduced a more general concept of convex dependence and associated convex decompositions of multiattribute utility functions which include as special cases the additive and multiplicative representations.

3.1 Multilinear Representation

THEOREM 1 (Keeney and Raiffa 1976). *Given the set of attributes* $\{X_1, X_2, \ldots, X_n\}$ *with* $n \geq 2$, *if* X_i *is utility independent of* $\bar{X}_i$, $i = 1, \ldots, n$, *then*

$$u(x_1, \ldots, x_n)$$
$$= \sum_{i=1}^{n} k_i u_i(x_i) + \sum_{i=1}^{n-1} \sum_{j>i} k_{ij} u_i(x_i) u_j(x_j)$$
$$+ \sum_{i=1}^{n-2} \sum_{j>i} \sum_{l>j} k_{ijl} u_i(x_i) u_j(x_j) u_l(x_l)$$
$$+ \cdots + k_{12\ldots n} u_1(x_1) u_2(x_2) \ldots u_n(x_n)$$

where:

(a) u is normalized by $u(x_1^0, x_2^0, \ldots, x_n^0) = 0$ and $u(x_1^*, x_2^*, \ldots, x_n^*) = 1$;

(b) $u_i = u_i(X_i(a))$ is a single-attribute utility function normalized by $u_i(x_i^0) = 0$ and $u_i(x_i^*) = 1$; and

(c) The scaling constants (k) can be evaluated by the following formulas, where $\bar{x}_{ij\ldots l}^0$ designates that the levels of all attributes except $i, j, \ldots, l$ have been set equal to their worst score:

$$k_i = u(x_i^*, \bar{x}_i^0)$$
$$k_{ij} = u(x_i^*, x_j^*, \bar{x}_{ij}^0) - k_i - k_j$$
$$k_{ijl} = u(x_i^*, x_j^*, x_l^*, \bar{x}_{ijl}^0) - k_{ij} - k_{il} - k_{jl}$$
$$\qquad - k_i - k_j - k_l$$
$$\cdots$$
$$\cdots$$
$$k_{1,2,\ldots,n} = 1 - \sum_i k_{1\ldots(i-1)(i+1)\ldots n} \cdots$$
$$\qquad - \sum_{i,j>i} k_{ij} - \sum_i k_i$$

3.2 Multiplicative Representation

THEOREM 2 (Keeney 1974). *If attributes* $X_1, X_2, \ldots, X_n$ *are mutually utility independent, then*

$$u(x_1, \ldots, x_n)$$
$$= \sum_{i=1}^{n} k_i u_i(x_i) + k \sum_{\substack{i=1 \\ j>i}}^{n} k_i k_j u_i(x_i) u_j(x_j)$$

$$+ k^2 \sum_{\substack{i=1 \\ j>i \\ l>j}} k_i k_j k_l u_i(x_i) u_j(x_j) u_l(x_l) + \cdots$$
$$\cdots + k^{n-1} k_1 k_2 \cdots k_n u_1(x_1) u_2(x_2) \cdots u_n(x_n)$$

where

(a) u is normalized by $u(x_1^0, x_2^0, \ldots, x_n^0) = 0$ and $u(x_1^*, x_2^*, \ldots, x_n^*) = 1$;

(b) $u_i = u_i(X_i(a))$ is a conditional utility function on X_i normalized by $u_i(x_i^0) = 0$ and $u_i(x_i^*) = 1$, $i = 1, 2, \ldots, n$;

(c) $k_i = u(x_i^*, \bar{x}_i^0)$; and

(d) k is a scaling constant that is a solution to

$$1 + k = \prod_{i=1}^{n} (1 + kk_i)$$

3.3 Additive Representation

The simplicity of additive decision models has motivated the development of a wide variety of methods for solving complex multiattribute decision problems based on this very simple representation. It would be a simple task to use an additive representation if we could calculate the utility of the alternatives in A by merely calculating the utility on each attribute separately using preference information on these, and then adding them. This special case of the more general additive representation problem is usually referred to as the additive conjoint representation problem, taking the form

$$(x_1^1, \ldots, x_n^1) \succsim (x_1^2, \ldots, x_n^2) \Leftrightarrow \sum_{i=1}^{n} u_i(x_i^1) \geq \sum_{i=1}^{n} u_i(x_i^2)$$

Here we review some of the work concerned with finding conditions that are necessary and/or sufficient for the existence of an additive representation in decision models, and relate this to the structural conditions that it imposes on the problem.

The following theorem, relating mutual preferential independence and the existence of an additive representation, is presented in Keeney and Raiffa (1976).

THEOREM 3. *Given attributes* $X_1, X_2, \ldots, X_n$, $n \geq 3$, *an additive utility function*

$$u(x_1, \ldots, x_n) = \sum_{i=1}^{n} k_i u_i(x_i)$$

exists if and only if the attributes are mutually preferentially independent, where:

(a) u is normalized by $u(x_1^0, x_2^0, \ldots, x_n^0) = 0$ and $u(x_1^*, x_2^*, \ldots, x_n^*) = 1$;

(b) $u_i = u_i(X_i(a))$ is a single-attribute utility function normalized by $u_i(x_i^0) = 0$ and $u_i(x_i^*) = 1$; and

(c) $k_i = u(x_i^*, \bar{x}_i^0)$, $i = 1, 2, \ldots, n$.

This result seems to provide a feasible way to test conditions for the existence of an additive representation. However, the number of empirical tests required to determine if the attributes are mutually preferentially independent may grow very rapidly with increases in the number of alternatives m and the number of attributes n. For example, if $m=n=5$ we will have to make 375 tests of preference orders, while for $m=n=6$ the number is 1116. When X_i is continuous, a test can only be approximate.

A set of conditions necessary and sufficient for the existence of an additive representation in conjoint measurement is given by Scott (1964). Let X^m represent the m-fold Cartesian product of X with itself. That is, for $m=2$, X^2 contains pairs of alternatives in n attributes, X^3 contains triplets of alternatives, and so on. Let $(x^1, x^2, \ldots, x^m)$, $(y^1, y^2, \ldots, y^m)$ be elements in X^m; x^j, y^j are alternatives in X. The notation $(x^1 \cdots x^m) E_m(y^1 \cdots y^m)$, for $m>1$, indicates that for each attribute i, the set $(x_i^1 \cdots x_i^m)$ is a permutation of $(y_i^1 \cdots y_i^m)$.

THEOREM 4 (Scott 1964). *Suppose that $X = X_1 \times X_2 \times \cdots \times X_n$ is finite and $\succsim$ is a binary relation on X. Then:*

(a) *for all $x, y \in X$, $x \succsim y$ or $y \succsim x$; and*

(b) *for all $x^1, \ldots, x^m, y^1, \ldots, y^m \in X$ and $m = 2, 3, \ldots$,*

$$[(x^1 \cdots x^m) E_m(y^1 \cdots y^m), x^j \succsim y^j$$
$$\text{for } j = 1, \ldots, m-1] \Rightarrow y^m \succsim x^m$$

if and only if there are real-valued functions $u_1, \ldots, u_n$ on $X_1, \ldots, X_n$, respectively, such that for all $x, y \in X$

$$x \succsim y \Leftrightarrow \sum_{i=1}^{n} u_i(x_i) \geq \sum_{i=1}^{n} u_i(y_i)$$

Observe that (b) is an infinite bundle of conditions, one set of conditions for each m, and that there is no finite number m satisfying the existence of an additive representation. In practice, however, since X is finite, m must also be finite before we start repeating the same alternatives, adding no new information about preferences.

It is of interest to examine these two theorems with respect to conditions sufficient for justifying the use of representation (1). We will use an example to facilitate the analysis. Consider the case of three attributes $X_1 = \{x_1^1, x_1^2\}$, $X_2 = \{x_2^1, x_2^2\}$, $X_3 = \{x_3^1, x_3^2\}$. The set of possible alternatives in the product structure X is then

$$X = X_1 \times X_2 \times X_3$$
$$= \{(x_1^1, x_2^1, x_3^1), (x_1^1, x_2^1, x_3^2),$$
$$(x_1^1, x_2^2, x_3^1), (x_1^1, x_2^2, x_3^2),$$
$$(x_1^2, x_2^1, x_3^1), (x_1^2, x_2^1, x_3^2),$$
$$(x_1^2, x_2^2, x_3^1), (x_1^2, x_2^2, x_3^2)\}$$

Mutual preferential independence on the set of attributes is expressed equivalently in condition (b) of Theorem 4 for $m=2$. In the present example,

$$((x_1^2, x_2^2, x_3^1), (x_1^1, x_2^1, x_3^2)) E_2$$
$$((x_1^1, x_2^1, x_3^1), (x_1^2, x_2^2, x_3^2))$$

So, if $(x_1^2, x_2^2, x_3^1) \succsim (x_1^1, x_2^1, x_3^1)$ then $(x_1^2, x_2^2, x_3^2) \succsim (x_1^1, x_2^1, x_3^2)$ and this is one of the conditions for $\{X_1, X_2\}$ to be preferentially independent of X_3.

The existence of a value function u_i over each X_i in Theorem 3 requires that a transitive relation on X exists. This is represented in Theorem 4 in condition (b) for $m=3$. In our example,

$$((x_1^1, x_2^1, x_3^1), (x_1^1, x_2^1, x_3^1), (x_1^1, x_2^2, x_3^1))$$
$$E_3$$
$$((x_1^1, x_2^1, x_3^2), (x_1^1, x_2^2, x_3^1), (x_1^1, x_2^1, x_3^1))$$

So, if $(x_1^1, x_2^1, x_3^1) \succsim (x_1^1, x_2^1, x_3^2)$ and $(x_1^1, x_2^1, x_3^2) \succsim (x_1^1, x_2^2, x_3^1)$ then $(x_1^1, x_2^2, x_3^1) \succsim (x_1^1, x_2^1, x_3^1)$. However, there are conditions in (b) for $m=3$ that are not covered by either transitivity or mutual preferential independence in Theorem 3. One such case is

$$((x_1^1, x_2^1, x_3^1), (x_1^1, x_2^1, x_3^2), (x_1^1, x_2^2, x_3^2))$$
$$E_3$$
$$((x_1^1, x_2^1, x_3^2), (x_1^1, x_2^2, x_3^1), (x_1^1, x_2^1, x_3^1))$$

and if $(x_1^1, x_2^1, x_3^1) \succsim (x_1^1, x_2^1, x_3^2)$ and $(x_1^1, x_2^1, x_3^2) \succsim (x_1^1, x_2^2, x_3^1)$ then $(x_1^1, x_2^2, x_3^2) \succsim (x_1^1, x_2^1, x_3^1)$. It is easy to see that this property must hold if an additive representation exists. From the first two preferential conditions we obtain

$$(x_1^1, x_2^1, x_3^1) \succsim (x_1^1, x_2^1, x_3^2)$$
$$\Leftrightarrow$$
$$u_1(x_1^1) + u_2(x_2^1) + u_3(x_3^1) \geq u_1(x_1^1) + u_2(x_2^1) + u_3(x_3^2)$$

and

$$(x_1^1, x_2^1, x_3^2) \succsim (x_1^1, x_2^2, x_3^1)$$
$$\Leftrightarrow$$
$$u_1(x_1^1) + u_2(x_2^1) + u_3(x_3^2) \geq u_1(x_1^1) + u_2(x_2^2) + u_3(x_3^1)$$

Adding the consequences in both implications and eliminating the term $u_1(x_1^1) + u_2(x_2^1) + u_3(x_3^1)$, common to both expressions, we have

$$u_1(x_1^1) + u_2(x_2^2) + u_3(x_3^2) \geq u_1(x_1^1) + u_2(x_2^2) + u_3(x_3^2)$$

which is equivalent to $(x_1^1, x_2^2, x_3^2) \succsim (x_1^1, x_2^2, x_3^1)$. Similar cases for $m = 4, 5, \ldots$ could be cited that are not covered by transitivity or mutual preferential independence and yet are necessary for the existence of an additive representation. This suggests that mutual preferential independence in Theorem 3 is necessary but not sufficient for the existence of an additive representation.

Krantz et al. (1971) present a much refined version of the Luce and Tuckey theorem (Luce and Tuckey

1964) which gives sufficient conditions for an additive representation in conjoint measurement. It is based on the concept of an additive conjoint structure defined as follows.

DEFINITION 3 (Additive conjoint structure). *The relational system $(X, \gtrsim)$ is an n-component additive conjoint structure, $n \geq 3$, if and only if it satisfies the following conditions:*

(a) weak ordering,

(b) mutual preferential independence,

(c) restricted solvability,

(d) every strictly bounded standard sequence on each attribute is finite, and

(e) at least three components are essential.

THEOREM 5 (Krantz et al. 1971). *If $(X, \gtrsim)$ is an n-component additive conjoint structure, $n \geq 3$, then there exist real-valued functions u_i on X_i, $i = 1, \ldots, n$, such that for all $(x_1^1, \ldots, x_n^1), (x_1^2, \ldots, x_n^2) \in X$,*

$$(x_1^1, \ldots, x_n^1) \gtrsim (x_1^2, \ldots, x_n^2) \Leftrightarrow \sum_{i=1}^n u_i(x_i^1) \geq \sum_{i=1}^n u_i(x_i^2) \quad (1)$$

Moreover, the functions u_i are unique up to positive linear transformations with a common multiplier.

Conditions (a) and (b) in Definition 3 have been mentioned previously. Weak ordering is generally accepted as a condition of rational behavior in decision problems, while mutual preferential independence is often accepted if the decision problem is properly structured such that for each attribute more is better and the attributes are not complementary. In the following, the other conditions are discussed in order to interpret their implications about the structure of a general multiattribute decision-making problem.

Let m be the index set $\{1, 2, \ldots\}$. Then the sequence $\{x_i^j : x_i^j \in X_i, j \in m\}$ is a standard sequence (on the ith component) if there are $\bar{x}_i', \bar{x}_i'' \in \hat{X}_i$ such that $(\bar{x}_i' \sim \bar{x}_i'')$ does not hold for all j, $j + 1 \in m$:

$$(x_i^j, \bar{x}_i') \sim (x_i^{j+1}, \bar{x}_i'')$$

The standard sequence is strictly bounded if there are x_i^* and x_i^0 in X_i such that $x_i^* \gtrsim x_i^j$ and $x_i^j \gtrsim x_i^0$ for all $j \in m$. The idea of a standard sequence is that the preference difference between two successive elements is the same. In the context of a decision problem, this is equivalent to saying that the change in the level of satisfaction between adjacent alternatives in a simple preference order is the same. That is,

$$(x_i^j, \bar{x}_i') \sim (x_i^{j+1}, \bar{x}_i'') \Rightarrow u_i(x_i^j) + u_{\bar{i}}(\bar{x}_i')$$
$$= u_i(x_i^{j+1}) + u_{\bar{i}}(\bar{x}_i'')$$
$$\Rightarrow u_i(x_i^{j+1}) - u_i(x_i^j)$$
$$= u_{\bar{i}}(\bar{x}_i') - u_{\bar{i}}(\bar{x}_i'') \quad \text{for all } j \in m$$

The condition that every strictly bounded sequence is finite follows directly from the additive representation (1); hence it is necessary. By contradiction, suppose that the sequence $\{x_i^j\}$ is infinite in the ith component. We have from above that

$$u_i(x_i^{j+1}) - u_i(x_i^j) = u_i^-(\bar{x}_i') - u_i^-(\bar{x}_i'')$$

Thus, for $k > 0$, define $u_i(x_i^k)$ as

$$u_i(x_i^k) = u_i(x_i^0) - k[u_i^-(\bar{x}_i'') - u_i^-(\bar{x}_i')]$$

Since not $(\bar{x}_i' \sim \bar{x}_i'')$ we have $u_i^-(\bar{x}_i'') - u_i^-(\bar{x}_i') \neq 0$. If $u_i^-(\bar{x}_i'') - u_i^-(\bar{x}_i') > 0$, we fix any $x_i \in X_i$. By the Archimedean property of the reals, there is a positive integer k such that

$$u_i(x_i^0) - k[u_i^-(\bar{x}_i'') - u_i^-(\bar{x}_i')] < u_i(x_i)$$

so $x_i \gtrsim x_i^k$. Similarly, if $u_i^-(\bar{x}_i'') - u_i^-(\bar{x}_i') < 0$, there is for each $x_i \in X_i$ a positive integer k such that $x_i^k \gtrsim x_i$. Thus, the sequence $\{x_i^j\}$ is not strictly bounded. We have then shown that, under the additive representation, every strictly bounded sequence is finite.

The next two conditions are not necessary for the existence of an additive representation; that is, they do not follow from the representation. A binary relation $(X, \gtrsim)$ satisfies restricted solvability (on the ith component) if, whenever $x_i^j, x_i^*, x_i^0 \in X_i$ and $\bar{x}_i', \bar{x}_i'' \in \hat{X}_i$ and

$$(x_i^*, \bar{x}_i'') \gtrsim (x_i^j, \bar{x}_i') \gtrsim (x_i^0, \bar{x}_i'')$$

there exist $x_i \in X_i$ such that $(x_i, \bar{x}_i'') \sim (x_i^j, \bar{x}_i')$. We say that the ith attribute X_i is essential if there are $x_i', x_i'' \in X_i$ such that not $(x_i' \sim^i x_i'')$.

Having described the meaning of the five conditions of the additive conjoint structure, we proceed to interpret the special characteristics that a decision situation should satisfy in order to be precisely modelled by an additive representation.

3.4 Interpreting the Additive Conjoint Structure

By imposing the conditions of the additive conjoint structure to a general multiattribute decision-making problem, we discover very interesting implications about the nature of the problem in order for it to be representable by an additive model. We assume that a set of alternatives A can be represented in the product structure $X = X_1 \times X_2 \times \cdots \times X_n$ and that a weak preference relation $\gtrsim$ defined on X exists and is a weak ordering. Also, we define an indifference relation as usual, $x \sim y \equiv x \gtrsim y$ and $y \gtrsim x$. For our discussion here, we presume that all attributes are essential. This causes no loss in generality to our exposition because by the condition of mutual preferential independence it is easy to see that we could eliminate a nonessential attribute without affecting the final ordering of the alternatives. Assume that there are $x_i^*, x_i^j, x_i^0 \in X_i$ and $\bar{x}_i', \bar{x}_i'' \in \hat{X}_i$ such that

$$x_i^* \gtrsim x_i^j \gtrsim x_i^0 \quad \text{and} \quad \bar{x}_i' \gtrsim \bar{x}_i'' \quad (2)$$

These assumptions seem reasonable from the essentiality condition. Using the mutual preferential independence assumption, we must have that $(x_i^*, \bar{x}_i') \gtrsim (x_i^j, \bar{x}_i'')$ and $(x_i^*, \bar{x}_i') \gtrsim (x_i^0, \bar{x}_i')$. So, assuming $(x_i^j, \bar{x}_i'') \gtrsim (x_i^0, \bar{x}_i')$ we have

$$(x_i^*, \bar{x}_i') \gtrsim (x_i^j, \bar{x}_i'') \gtrsim (x_i^0, \bar{x}_i') \quad (3)$$

The restricted solvability condition indicates that there must be an x_i in X_i such that

$$(x_i, \bar{x}_i') \sim (x_i^j, \bar{x}_i'') \quad (4)$$

Since we have assumed that $\bar{x}_i' \gtrsim \bar{x}_i''$, then it must be true that not $(x_i \gtrsim x_i^j)$. Otherwise we violate mutual preferential independence. It must also be true that not $(x_i^0 > x_i)$ because, if $x_i^0 > x_i$, by mutual preferential independence $(x_i^0, \bar{x}_i') \gtrsim (x_i, \bar{x}_i')$, Eqn. (4) suggests $(x_i^0, \bar{x}_i') \gtrsim (x_i^j, \bar{x}_i'')$ which contradicts Eqn. (3). Figure 1 presents a pictorial interpretation of the argument here by showing the feasible region of $x_i \in X_i$ in a preference scale. That is, $x_i^j \gtrsim x_i$ and $x_i \gtrsim x_i^0$.

Assuming $(x_i^*, \bar{x}_i'') \gtrsim (x_i^j, \bar{x}_i')$ we obtain, by a similar argument, that the feasible region of $x_i \in X_i$ satisfying the restricted solvability condition is $x_i \gtrsim x_i^j$ and $x_i^* \gtrsim x_i$. This is shown in Fig. 2.

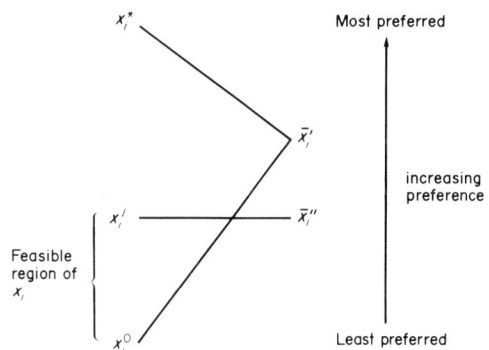

Figure 1
Feasible region of x_i

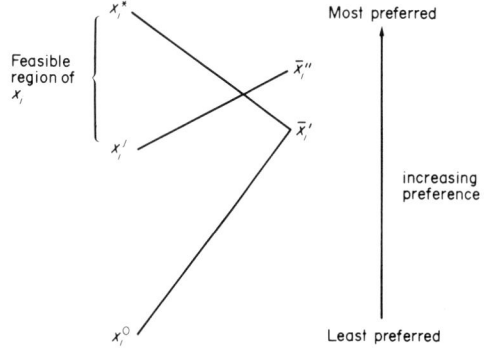

Figure 2
Feasible region of x_i

In either of the above cases, if $x_i \neq x_i^0$ and $x_i \neq x_i^*$ then we have a new triplet satisfying Eqn. (2) and again by restricted solvability a new x_i must exist. This process continues until the new x_i is equal to either x_i^* or x_i^0 in which case the sequence $\{x_i\}$ made of all the x_i obtained from the restricted solvability condition is a standard sequence. Hence, there is a standard sequence for each pair $\bar{x}_i', \bar{x}_i'' \in \hat{X}_i$ such that not $(\bar{x}_i' \sim \bar{x}_i'')$.

3.5. Implications of the Additive Conjoint Structure

There are two significant implications about the nature of a decision problem that follow from the assumption of it being an additive conjoint structure. First, the elements $x_i \in X_i$, for each i, form a standard sequence. In other words, the elements on each attribute are equally spaced in a preference scale. Second, a difference in preference (gain or loss) in one attribute must be compensable by (or indifferent to) a difference in preference (loss or gain) in the other complementary attributes. This situation is very unlikely to exist even for relatively simple alternative choice problems. It says, for example, that if, in terms of comfort, you prefer a Cadillac over a Chevrolet over a Volkswagen then: first, your degree of preference of a Cadillac over a Chevrolet must be the same as your degree of preference of a Chevrolet over a Volkswagen; second, there must be levels on the remaining attributes (say, economy and safety) whose difference in degree of preference is indifferent to that in comfort. If these conditions are satisfied together with weak order and mutual preferential independence of attributes, an additive utility model unique to positive linear transformations with a common scale unit can be justified.

All is not lost, however. When assumptions of continuity and boundedness are imposed on the single-attribute utilities u_i, then restricted solvability is satisfied and the above argument is irrelevant. More often than not, however, we are faced with decision problems that are inherently discrete, at least along some dimensions or attributes, in which case restricted solvability may imply the existence of alternatives that are not only infeasible or hypothetical but inconceivable—like, for example, trading half of a chimney for a certain improvement in the insulation factor of a house.

The argument presented here is often referred to as the compensatory nature of the additive representation. It is easy to see that at any level of utility given by an additive utility function $u(a) = \Sigma_i u_i(a)$ one should be able to accept reduced utility of an attribute in exchange for an increase in utility of another attribute. Even when the utility functions of each attribute are considered to be continuous, it is common practice to discretize the decision space in order to simplify the assessment of independence conditions and utility values. By our exposition here, such discretization cannot be arbitrarily made under the additivity assumptions.

THEOREM 6 (Dyer and Sarin 1979). *If the attributes $X_1, X_2, \ldots, X_n$, $n \geqslant 3$, are mutually preferentially independent and difference consistent, and X_1 is difference independent of $\hat{X}_1$, then there exist functions $u_i: X^i \to \text{Re}$, $i = 1, 2, \ldots, n$ such that for all $a_j = (x_1^j, x_2^j, \ldots, x_n^j) \in X$, $j = 1, 2, \ldots, m$,*

$$a_1 a_2 \succsim^* a_3 a_4 \Leftrightarrow \sum_{i=1}^{n} u_i(x_i^1) - \sum_{i=1}^{n} u_i(x_i^2)$$
$$\geqslant \sum_{i=1}^{n} u_i(x_i^3) - \sum_{i=1}^{n} u_i(x_i^4)$$

In addition the functions u_i are unique up to positive linear transformations with the same scale unit.

The importance of this result is that under the premises of the theorem the additive representation also provides difference measurement on X. In addition to the conditions explicitly stated in the theorem, assumptions such as conditions (c)–(e) of Definition 1 of the *n*-component additive conjoint structure are required. In essence, the above theorem states that an *n*-component additive conjoint structure also satisfying difference consistence and difference independence in one attribute allows for difference measurement with additive utilities on X. Similar to the interpretations given to the additive conjoint structure, this representation theorem imposes certain restrictions on the characteristics of the decision situation and on the behavior of the decision maker in judgement and choice.

Fishburn (1964, 1970) has done extensive work in additive utility theory. Among the various situations for which he has derived necessary and sufficient conditions for additive utility functions, the one concerning product structures is of particular interest here. For the case of *n* attributes, Fishburn's additive representation theorem is as follows.

THEOREM 7 (Fishburn 1970). *The n-attribute additive utility function*

$$u(x) = \sum_{i=1}^{n} k_i u_i(x_i)$$

is appropriate if and only if the additive independence condition holds among attributes $X_1, X_2, \ldots, X_n$ where

(a) *u is normalized by $u(x_1^0, x_2^0, \ldots, x_n^0) = 0$ and $u(x_1^*, x_2^*, \ldots, x_n^*) = 1$,*

(b) *$u_i = u_i(X_i(a))$ is a single-attribute utility function normalized by $u_i(x_i^0) = 0$ and $u_i(x_i^*) = 1$, and*

(c) *$k_i = u(x_i^*, \bar{x}_i^0)$ $i = 1, 2, \ldots, n$.*

This section has presented a detailed overview of representation theorems of multiattribute decision models, the purpose of which was to contrast the relation between the complexity of the functional form of the model and the restrictiveness of the required conditions. As might be expected, the simpler the functional form of the model, the more restrictive the assumptions that are necessary on the structure of the decision situation and on the decision maker's behavior in judgement and choice. No representation theorem exists that describes the form of u for the weakest independence condition in the certainty case, namely preferential independence. In the case involving risk, utility independence results in the multilinear representation and mutual utility independence in the multiplicative representation. While these independence conditions are relatively weak and may hold in a large number of cases, they result in rather complex functional representations.

The simplest representation, the additive model, requires the conditions of an additive conjoint structure in the certainty case and additive independence in the case involving risk. Additive independence, besides being very difficult to show, is intuitively unjustifiable. The conditions of the additive conjoint structure are very restrictive, at least in the context of multiattribute decision problems. Its implications suggest that the discretization of a multiattribute decision problem cannot be arbitrary if it is represented by an additive model; or, if the problem is naturally discrete, it must have the special characteristics implied by the additive conjoint structure.

4. Dominance and the Efficient Frontier

Various methods intended to screen candidate alternatives in decision-making activities are discussed below. Some of these are based on the concept of dominance defined as follows.

Let alternatives a_1, a_2 be represented in the consequence space as

$$a_1 = (X_1(a_1), \ldots, X_n(a_1))$$

and

$$a_2 = (X_1(a_2), \ldots, X_n(a_2))$$

We say that a_1 dominates a_2 whenever a_1 is at least as good as a_2 for every consequence $X_i, i = 1, \ldots, n$, and strictly better for at least one consequence. Symbolically,

$$a_1 > a_2 \Leftrightarrow \begin{cases} \text{(a)} & X_i(a_1) \succsim X_i(a_2) \text{ for all } i \\ \text{(b)} & X_i(a_1) > X_i(a_2) \text{ for some } i \end{cases} \quad (5)$$

Note that the notion of dominance requires knowledge of only the ordinal preference of the alternatives for each consequence and not any comparison or trade-off among consequences.

The notion of dominance is very often used to generate the set of nondominated alternatives and to discard those that are dominated since they presumably cannot be candidates for best. In Sect. 3.5 we showed that the concept of dominance as a criterion to generate the nondominated set of alternatives implies at least preferential independence across the attributes, a condition that does not always exist.

For any feasible alternative $a_i \in A$ there is a corresponding consequence $(X_1(a_i), \ldots, X_n(a_i))$ representing that alternative in the consequence space X. Let R be the set of consequences in X whose members are associated with alternatives in A; the set R is the so-called range set of the vector mapping defined on the domain A.

The set of consequences of R that are not dominated is called the efficient frontier of R or the Pareto optimal set. There is a considerable body of literature on optimization theory that is concerned with the mathematics of Pareto optimality.

5. Decision Analysis Methodology

The methodology of decision analysis, based in MAUT is generally decomposed in four major steps as indicated in the article *Decision Analysis* and in Fig. 3.

Step 1: Identify the decision problem. This includes the generation of alternatives and the specification of objectives and hence attributes to be used in the evaluation of alternatives.

Step 2: Assess the possible consequences for each alternative. In the case of certainty, this consists of specifying the unique known consequence that follows for certain from implementation of each alternative. When various possible consequences may occur, a probability distribution function over the set of attributes for each alternative must be determined.

Step 3: Determine the preferential information. The structure of the model is determined and the quantification of its parameters is made. This step requires relevant, precise and consistent information about value assessment, value trade-offs and risk attitude.

Step 4: Evaluate the alternatives and perform a sensitivity analysis. The information gathered is synthesized by use of the expected utility criterion. The alternative with the highest expected utility is the most desired. Finally, the sensitivity of the decision to a variety of changes is explored, in order to gain some confidence about the recommended decision.

6. Assessment Methods

In applying the decision analysis paradigm for the resolution of complex decision problems, assessment methods are needed to obtain precise utility values. The fundamental results for the representation of simple preference and degree of preference, and the classical results of von Neumann and Morgenstern (1964) when risk is involved, guarantee the existence of a real-valued utility function that quantifies the value judgement and risk attitude of the decision maker. These results give rise to the development of various assessment methods for quantifying the underlying utility functions precisely. The precise assessment of utility values is deemed necessary in order to operationalize these results in effective decision aids. In the following subsections, some of the most widely used methods for utility assessment are briefly reviewed. More detailed discussions of these and other assessment techniques can be found in von Winterfelt and Edwards (1986), Keeney and Raiffa (1976), Johnson and Huber (1977), and Krzysztofowicz and Duckstein (1980).

6.1 Direct Elicitation

The decision maker is asked to assign objects from a measurable set to the levels of a set of attributes indicating its relative utility for him or her. The assignment might be into preassigned categories (e.g., fair, good, excellent), each associated with a particular worth score. This technique is used extensively in psychometric studies and its application in decision analysis is a direct extension of existing procedures in that field. The assignments could also be into numerical values on a predefined scale. The range of the scale could be anchored, the most common anchor points used being 0–100, or could be left open, being normalized after the elicitation is completed. Direct methods can provide precise numerical scores and therefore are very attractive for their speed in application. However, providing precise, consistent and meaningful numerical values is a very difficult cognitive task.

6.2 Ranking Methods

In these methods the decision maker orders the levels of a specific set of attributes from most preferred to least preferred. The ordering may consist of levels of a single attribute, in the case of assessing single-attribute

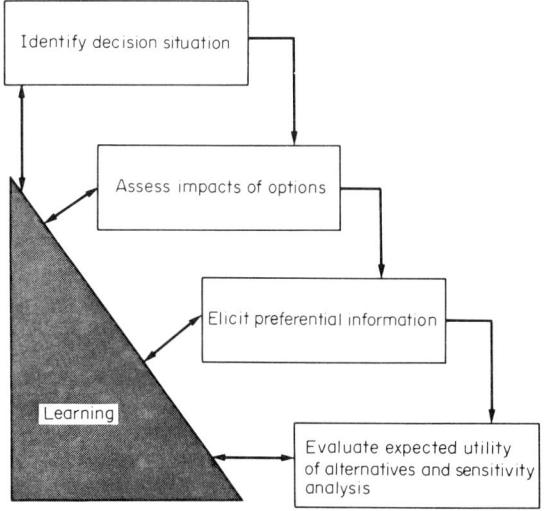

Figure 3
Steps in a multiattribute decision process

utility functions. Alternatively, it may involve combinations of the levels of two or more attributes, in the case of investigating value trade-offs, or when assessing the utility of nonindependent attributes. The larger the number of attributes in the combinations to be ordered, the more difficult the task for the decision maker and the more likely that the heuristic process utilized to simplify the complexity of the task will be inadequate. Ranking methods are also employed to order the intervals between the orders. This type of assessment measures the relative strength of preference of one preference relation with respect to another preference relation. While the ordering of levels of attribute combinations is a task which is very acceptable and easy to implement, the strength-of-preference concept presents serious operational problems.

The major challenge in implementing this type of assessment is to have the decision maker focus on the exchange and not on the final outcomes. Given two pairs of alternatives (a_i, a_j), (a_k, a_l) such that $a_i \gtrsim a_j$ and $a_k \gtrsim a_l$, we could ask the decision maker which exchange is perceived to be more favorable: a_i for a_j or a_k for a_l. If the former exchange is believed to be the favorable one, then the interval between a_i and a_j is larger than the interval between a_k and a_l. A common misinterpretation of this type of assessment is that instead of focusing on the exchange, the decision maker ranks the exchanges on the basis of the final outcomes a_i and a_k. For example, if the decision maker prefers an exchange of $1 000 000 for $1 000 001 to an exchange of $5 for $500, then emphasis is placed on the preference of $1 000 001 over $500 and not on the substitution of one outcome for another. Dyer and Sarin (1979) and Fishburn (1970) present more detailed discussions of this as well as other proposed methods and respective difficulties for assessing strength of preference relations. In summary, the analyst must be aware of this possible misinterpretation and caution the decision maker about this possibility.

6.3 Indifference Methods

These methods consist of identifying indifference points in a decision space. Indifference methods may involve the joint assessment of several possible combinations of levels of attributes and determining indifference among these combinations. In this case, it requires judgement of "trade-offs" between the utilities of various attribute level combinations. Strength-of-preference information is obtained exclusively when no risk or uncertainty is present.

When risk is involved, indifference methods rely on the ability of the decision maker to choose between a lottery involving uncertain outcomes with known probabilities and an alternative resulting in a sure outcome. In this case, we obtain what is called the certainty equivalent of a lottery; that is, the level of attributes for which the decision maker is indifferent to that lottery. Indifference judgements involving lotteries provide a combined assessment of strength of preference and risk attitude (Dyer and Sarin 1982).

Note that the indifference methods require the assumption of either continuity or restricted solvability on X. Furthermore, they also require prior knowledge of the functional form of the decision model.

In standard multiattribute decision analysis, ranking methods are often used prior to the use of indifference methods. They provide a rough and imprecise assessment of the possible values of the parameters of the model facilitating the coordination of the subsequent precise assessments by means of indifference methods.

6.4 Assessment Through Decision Observation

This approach consists of observing decision behavior in real-world or simulated real-world situations and inferring the parameters of a prespecified model from these observations. The work of Hammond et al. (1980) on social judgement theory makes use of this concept. Techniques based on this approach have been shown to be particularly useful in policy formulation and analysis and so they are usually called "policy capture" or "bootstrapping" techniques. Use of regression analysis is central to this observation approach. There are a number of studies that make use of regression analysis to determine the parameters of a decision model. A good example is presented by Dawes (1971) in which a regression model is used to screen applications for admission to a graduate program.

7. Summary

This article has provided a summary of the axiological basis for MAUT. It is important for the user of a tool to have an appropriate understanding of the strengths and limitations of the tool. While much of the discussion in this article may seem to be far removed from practice, there are indeed pitfalls associated with the use of an approach and an unknowing violation of some of the fundamental assumptions on which the approach is based.

See also: Decision Analysis; Decision Support Systems

Bibliography

Brown R, Kahr A, Peterson C 1974 *Decision Analysis for the Manager*. Holt, Reinhart and Winston, New York

Chankong V, Haimes Y Y 1984 *Multiobjective Decision Making: Theory and Methodology*. North-Holland, New York

Charnetski J R, Soland R M 1978 Multiattribute decision making with partial information. *Nav. Res. Logist. Q.* **25**(2), 279–88

Charnetski J R, Soland R M 1979 Multiattribute decision making with partial information: The expected value criterion. *Nav. Res. Logist. Q.* **26**(2), 249–56

Cohon J L 1978 *Multiobjective Programming and Planning*. Academic Press, New York

Dawes R M 1971 A case study of graduate admissions: Applications of three principles of human decision making. *Am. Psychol.* **26**, 180–88

Debreu G 1959 Topological methods in cardinal utility theory. In: Arrow K J, Karlin S, Suppes P (eds.) *Mathematical Methods in the Social Sciences*. Stanford University Press, Stanford, California, pp. 16–26

DeWispelare A, Sage A P 1981 On combined multiple objective optimization theory and multiple attribute utility theory for evaluation and choice making. *Large Scale Syst.* **2**(1), 1–19

Dyer D S, Sarin R K 1979 Measurable multiattribute value functions. *Oper. Res.* **27**(4), 810–22

Dyer D S, Sarin R K 1982 Relative risk aversion. *Manage. Sci.* **28**(8), 875–86

Edwards W 1977 How to use multiattribute utility measurement for social decisionmaking. *IEEE Trans. Syst., Man Cybern.* **7**, 326–40

Farris D, Sage A P 1975a Introduction and survey of group decision making with applications to worth assessment. *IEEE Trans. Syst., Man Cybern.* **5**(3), 346–58

Farris D, Sage A P 1975b On decision making and worth assessment. *Int. J. Syst. Sci.* **6**(6)

Fishburn P C 1964 *Decision and Value Theory*. Wiley, New York

Fishburn P C 1965 Analysis of decisions with incomplete knowledge of probabilities. *Oper. Res.* **13**(2), 217–37

Fishburn P 1968 Utility theory. *Manage. Sci.* **14**(5), 335–78

Fishburn P C 1970 *Utility Theory for Decision Making*. Wiley, New York

Freeling A N S 1981 Reconciliation of multiple probability assessments. *Organ. Behav. Hum. Perform.* **28**, 395–414

Hammond K R, McClelland G H, Mumpower J 1980 *Human Judgement and Decision Making: Theories Methods and Procedures*. Hemisphere/Praeger, New York

Holloway C A *Decision Making Under Uncertainty: Models and Choice*. Prentice–Hall, Englewood Cliffs, New Jersey

Howard R A 1968 The foundations of decision analysis. *IEEE Trans. Syst., Sci. Cybern.* **4**(3), 211–19

Howard R A 1975 Social decision analysis (Special issue on social systems engineering). *IEEE Proc.* **63**(3), 359–71

Howard R A 1980 An assessment of decision analysis. *Oper. Res.* **28**(1), 4–27

Johnson E M, Huber G P 1977 The technology of utility assessment. *IEEE Trans. Syst., Man Cybern.* **7**(5), 311–25

Keeney R L 1974 Multiplicative utility functions. *Oper. Res.* **22**, 22

Keeney R L 1982 Decision analysis: An overview. *Oper. Res.* **30**(5), 803–38

Keeney R L, Raiffa H 1976 *Decisions with Multiple Objectives: Preferences and Value Tradeoffs*. Wiley, New York

Kmietowicz Z W, Pearman A D 1981 *Decision Theory and Incomplete Knowledge*. Gower, Aldershot

Krantz D H, Luce R D, Suppes P, Tversky A 1971 *Foundations of Measurement*, Vol. I. Academic Press, New York, p. 39

Krzysztofowicz R 1983 Strength of preference and risk attitude in utility measurement. *Organ. Behav. Hum. Perform.* **31**(1), 88–113

Krzysztofowicz R, Duckstein L 1980 Assessment errors in multiattribute utility functions. *Organ. Behav. Hum. Perform.* **26**, 326–48

Lindley D V, Tversky A, Brown R V 1979 On the reconciliation of probability assessments. *J. R. Stat. Soc., Ser. A* **142**, 146–80

Luce R D, Tuckey J W 1964 Simultaneous conjoint measurement: A new type of fundamental measurement. *J. Math. Psychol.* **1**, 1–27

North D W 1968 A tutorial introduction to decision theory. *IEEE Trans. Syst., Sci. Cybern.* **4**(3), 200–10

Pratt J W 1964 Risk aversion in the small and in the large. *Econometrica* **32**(1–2), 122–36

Raiffa H 1968 *Decision Analysis—Introductory Lectures on Choices Under Certainty*. Addison–Wesley, Reading, Massachusetts

Rescher N, Manor R 1970 On inference from inconsistent premises. *Theory Decis.* **1**, 179–217

Roberts F S 1979 *Measurement Theory*. Addison–Wesley, Reading, Massachusetts, p. 109

Sage A P 1977 *Methodology for Large Scale Systems*. McGraw–Hill, New York

Sage A P 1981 Behavioral and organizational considerations in the design of information systems and processes for planning and decision support. *IEEE Trans. Syst., Man Cybern.* **11**(9), 640–78

Sage A P (ed.) 1987 *System Design for Human Interaction*. IEEE Press, New York

Sarin R K 1977 Screening of multiattribute alternatives. *Omega* **5**(4), 481–89

Scott D 1964 Measurement structures and linear inequalities. *J. Math. Psychol.* **1**(2), 233–47

Scott D, Suppes P 1958 Foundational aspects of theories of measurement. *J. Symb. Log.* **23**, 205–28

Spetzler C S, von Holstein C A 1975 Probability encoding in decision analysis. *Manage. Sci.* **22**(3), 340–58

Suppes P, Winet M 1955 An axiomatization of utility based on the notion of utility differences. *Manage. Sci.* **1**, 259–70

Tamura H, Nakamura Y 1983 Decompositions of multiattribute utility functions based on convex dependence. *Oper. Res.* **31**(3), 488–506

von Neumann J, Morgenstern O 1964 *Theory of Games and Economic Behavior*, 3rd edn. Wiley, New York

von Winterfeldt D, Edwards W 1986 *Decision Analysis and Behavioral Research*. Cambridge University Press, Cambridge

Whitmore G A, Findlay N C (eds.) 1978 *Stochastic Dominance*. Lexington Books, Lexington, Massachusetts

Zeleny M 1982 *Multiple Criteria Decision Making*. McGraw–Hill, New York

A. P. Sage
[George Mason University, Fairfax, Virginia, USA]

A. Lagomasino
[AT&T Bell Telephone Laboratories, Holmdel, New Jersey, USA]

Multicriteria Decision Problem

Decision problems involving multiple and conflicting objectives, goals or attributes are generally referred to as multicriteria decision problems. In the literature on the multicriteria decision problem, the terms objectives, goals and attributes are used to convey some distinct meanings, although they are often used interchangeably (see, for instance, Hwang and Masud

(1979) and Zeleny (1982)). An objective is a general statement about the direction of a desired state. A goal is a specific level of aspiration which the organization seeks to attain. Thus, goals are either achieved or not. For instance, while "maximizing the net profit" is an objective, "achieving the total sales of 10 000 units of the product next year" is a goal. An attribute is designed to indicate the degree to which alternatives meet the objective. Criteria are measures, rules and standards that guide decision making.

In many situations, it is useful to establish the hierarchy of objectives. For instance, an overall objective would be the broad and general statement about the desirable future state of the organization and is not often adequate for any operational purpose. The general statement is translated into more specific subobjectives. Subobjectives may be further broken down into lower-level objectives so as to identify attribute scales that can be objectively assessed. For further discussion on constructing the hierarchy of objectives see Keeney and Raiffa (1976).

Since the distinguishing feature of the multicriteria decision problem is the existence of conflicting and incommensurable objectives, there is no optimum solution which optimizes all the objectives simultaneously. The concept of the efficient solution, instead of optimality, is basic to the multicriteria decision problem. An efficient solution is a feasible one which is not dominated by any other solutions. It is also referred to as a Pareto optimum, a noninferior or a nondominated solution. The set of feasible solutions is reducible to the set of efficient solutions without any information about the preferences of the decision maker. To get the final solution which is a preferred or a best-compromise solution for the decision maker, it is required to identify the structure of the decision maker's preferences as well as the structure of the problem.

According to the structure of the problem, multicriteria decision problems are often classified into discrete problems (or multiattribute decision problems) and continuous problems. In the former, there is a limited number of predetermined alternatives characterized by multiple attributes. The primary concern is with choosing the best one for the decision maker, ranking them in order of importance or reducing the number of alternatives for final decision. In decisions under certainty, the multiattribute value function (also known as the ordinal utility function) is a popular model for the preferences of the decision maker. There are other approaches which admit the information of preferences including inconsistency; one is the (fuzzy) outranking relation model which does not require the assumption of transitivity nor the complete comparability in the underlying preference relation (Roy 1977, Goicoechea et al. 1982).

Another approach is the analytic hierarchy process (AHP) which establishes the priorities of objectives having a hierarchy structure based on the subjective judgements. The distinguishing feature of the AHP is that it admits the inconsistency in judgements and provides a measure for inconsistency at the same time.

The multiattribute utility theory (MAUT) in decision analysis deals with decision problems involving both risk and multiattribute outcomes. The distinguishing characteristics of MAUT are the abilities to incorporate the attitude of the decision maker toward risk as well as the value trade-offs among attributes. Evaluating alternatives involves calculating the expected utility of each of the alternatives.

In continuous problems, instead of predetermined alternatives, a set of constraints which specify the feasible solutions are given. We are primarily concerned with the efficient solutions or the preferred solution. Many methods exist according to how and when to extract information on the preferences of the decision maker to reconcile conflicting objectives. Some methods require *a priori* preferences, others require them progressively in the process of searching for the preferred solution. The former, among others, include goal programming and fuzzy multiobjective linear programming. They require *a priori* specified multigoals or aspiration levels. The latter include several interactive methods. *A priori* knowledge of the overall utility function is, in general, not necessary to obtain the preferred solution alone. Many human–machine interactive procedures require only the local information of the overall utility function, which is not known explicitly, at each trial solution in order to arrive at the preferred solution.

1. Multiattribute Utility Theory

Let $X = \{X_1, X_2, \ldots, X_p\}$ be the set of attributes. Consequences are designated by $x = (x_1, x_2, \ldots, x_p)$, where x_i designates a specific amount of X_i for $i = 1, 2, \ldots, p$. Let $u(x)$ be a cardinal (von Neumann–Morgenstern) utility function. There are various independence assumptions which allow us to decompose a multidimensional utility function $u(x)$ into a set of lower-dimensional, hopefully unidimensional, utility functions (Keeney and Raiffa 1976). The two basic assumptions used are the concepts of preferential- and utility-independence.

Attribute Z, where $Z \subset X$, is said to be preferentially-independent of its complement $\bar{Z}$ in X if the preference order of consequences involving only changes in the levels in Z does not depend on the levels at which the attributes in $\bar{Z}$ are held fixed. Attribute Z is utility-independent of its complement $\bar{Z}$ in X if the conditional preference order for lotteries involving only changes in the levels of attributes in Z does not depend on the levels at which the attributes in $\bar{Z}$ are held fixed (Keeney and Raiffa 1976).

The following decomposition theorem due to Keeney (1974) has been widely used since the assumptions are reasonable and operationally verifiable and the assessment of the resulting utility function is greatly simplified.

When $p \geq 3$, if, for some X_i, $\{X_i, X_j\}$ (denoted by X_{ij}) is preferentially-independent of $\bar{X}_{ij}$ for all $j \neq i$ and X_i is utility-independent of $\bar{X}_i$, then either the additive form

$$u(x) = \sum_{i=1}^{p} k_i u_i(x_i), \quad \sum_{i=1}^{p} k_i = 1$$

or the multiplicative form

$$1 + Ku(x) = \prod_{i=1}^{p} [1 + K k_i u_i(x_i)], \quad \sum_{i=1}^{p} k_i \neq 1$$

holds, where:

(a) $u(x^*) = 1$ and $u(x^0) = 0$, where x^* designates the most desirable and x^0 the least desirable consequence;

(b) $u_i(x_i)$ is a conditional utility function on X_i normalized by $u_i(x_i^0) = 0$ and $u_i(x_i^*) = 1$, $i = 1, 2, \ldots, p$;

(c) $k_i = u(x_1^0, x_2^0, \ldots, x_i^*, \ldots, x_p^0)$; and

(d) K is a scaling constant that is a solution of:

$$1 + K = \prod_{i=1}^{p} [1 + K k_i]$$

For $p = 2$, if X_1 is utility-independent of X_2, and X_2 is utility-independent of X_1, then the utility function $u(x_1, x_2)$ is either additive or multiplicative.

Multiattribute utility theory is discussed in detail in Keeney and Raiffa (1976) (see also *Multiattribute Utility Theory*).

2. Analytic Hierarchy Process

The analytic hierarchy process consists of four steps (Saaty 1988).

Step 1. Construct a hierarchy of objectives. The lowest level of the hierarchy consists of a set of alternatives.

Step 2. At each level $k = 2, 3, \ldots, h$ of the hierarchy, for any fixed objective in the immediate higher level $(k - 1)$, construct a reciprocal matrix.

Step 3. Elicit the relative weights (or priorities) from each reciprocal matrix which is obtained at step 2.

Step 4. Aggregate the relative weights to get the overall priorities of alternatives.

In step 2, at each level of the hierarchy, all pairwise comparisons of the objectives (or alternatives at the last level of the hierarchy) within the level are randomly presented to the decision maker. The decision maker is asked to respond, by weight ratios, as to which contributes more to achieving each objective in the immediate higher level. A table of the nine-semantic scale is provided to facilitate the answers of the decision maker (Table 1).

Table 1
The nine-semantic scale of judgement. 2, 4, 6 and 8 are intermediate values between the two adjacent judgements

Intensity of importance	Definition
1	equally important
3	weakly more important
5	strongly more important
7	demonstratably more important
9	absolutely more important

Assume that there are m objectives in level k. For any fixed objective, say X, of the immediate higher level $(k - 1)$, let a_{ij} be the weight ratio of importance of objective i over objective j in achieving X. The reciprocal value is then automatically entered for a_{ji}.

The matrix $\mathbf{A} = (a_{ij})$, with $a_{ji} = 1/a_{ij}$ for all i, j and $a_{ii} = 1$ for all i, is called a reciprocal matrix. The matrix is said to be consistent if it satisfies the cardinal consistency property $a_{ik} \times a_{kj} = a_{ij}$ for all i, j, k.

In step 3, the eigenvector method is proposed to elicit the relative weights from the reciprocal matrix. Let $\mathbf{w} = (w_1, w_2, \ldots, w_m)$ be the relative weights for m objectives with respect to the higher objective X. Then an estimate of $\mathbf{w}$ is obtained from $\mathbf{A}$ by solving the eigenvalue problem:

$$\mathbf{A}\hat{\mathbf{w}} = \lambda_{\max} \hat{\mathbf{w}}$$

where $\lambda_{\max}$ is the maximum eigenvalue of $\mathbf{A}$ and $\hat{\mathbf{w}}$ is the corresponding normalized eigenvector. It is known that $\lambda_{\max} \geq m$ with equality if and only if $\mathbf{A}$ is consistent.

$$\mathrm{CI} = (\lambda_{\max} - m)/(m - 1)$$

serves as a measure of consistency.

In step 4, the composite priority vector $\bar{\mathbf{w}}$ for the lowest level h of the hierarchy is calculated as follows. In the complete hierarchy for which all elements in one level contribute to all elements in the immediate higher level, let $\mathbf{B}_k$ be the matrix whose ith column vector is the relative weights vector at the kth level with respect to the ith element in the $(k-1)$th level. Then,

$$\bar{\mathbf{w}} = B_h \times B_{h-1} \times \cdots \times B_2$$

3. Vector Optimization Problem

Given a vector-valued objective function $f(x) = (f_1(x), f_2(x), \ldots, f_p(x))$ defined over $X \subset \mathbb{R}^n$ the vector maximization problem (VMP) is formally stated as V-max $f(x)$ subject to

$$x \in X = \{x \in \mathbb{R}^n | g_j(x) \leq 0 \quad j = 1, 2, \ldots, m\}$$

where V-max means that each objective $f_i(x)$, $i = 1, 2, \ldots, p$, is to be maximized over X.

The VMP is primarily concerned with efficient solutions. A feasible solution x^0 is efficient for VMP if there is no other feasible solution x such that $f(x) \geq f(x^0)$ where the vector notation $\geq$ means $\geqslant$ and $\neq$.

The duality theory of the vector optimization and properties of efficient solutions are discussed in, for example, Sawaragi et al. (1985), and Chankong and Haimes (1983).

The concept of nondominated solutions proposed by Yu (1974) is a more general solution concept including that of efficient solutions as a special case. The concept of domination structure then serves to explain how strong an assumption has been imposed in nondominated solutions.

An important special class of VMPs is the multiobjective linear programming (MOLP) problem. It is defined by

$$\text{V-max} f(x) = Cx$$

subject to

$$x \in X = \{x \in \mathbb{R}^n | Ax \leq b, x \geq 0\}$$

where C is a $p \times n$ matrix consisting of p row vectors c^i, $i=1, 2, \ldots, p$, so that $f_i(x) = c^i x$, A is an $m \times n$ matrix, and $b \in \mathbb{R}^m$.

Given $\lambda \in \mathbb{R}^p$ to the MOLP problem, let the problem P_λ be $\max_{x \in X} \lambda Cx$. The well-known result is that x^0 is an efficient solution for the MOLP problem if and only if x^0 is an optimum solution to the problem (P_λ) for some $\lambda > 0$. Using this result, multicriteria simplex method and various algorithms have been developed for locating all efficient solutions (Zeleny 1982, Yu 1985).

A multicriteria and multiconstraint-level simplex method has also been developed (Yu 1985).

4. Goal Programming and Fuzzy Multiobjective Programming

The goal programming formulation of VMP is, in general,

$$\text{L-min } z = (h_1(y_+, y_-), h_2(y_+, y_-), \ldots, h_k(y_+, y_-))$$

subject to

$$f_j(x) + y_j^- - y_j^+ = o_j \quad j=1, 2, \ldots, p$$

$$x \in X$$

$$y_j^-, y_j^+ \geqq 0 \quad j=1, 2, \ldots, p$$

where

(a) L-min designates minimizing lexicographically;

(b) o_j is the jth goal, which is classified into K priority levels;

(c) y_j^+, y_j^- denote positive and negative deviation variables, respectively;

(d) $h_k(y_+, y_-)$ is a function of the deviation variables associated with the goals in priority level k. In the kth priority level, in general, if it is desirable that the underachievement (overachievement) of the goal o_j is as small as possible, only y_j^- (y_j^+) is included in h_k and y_j^+ (y_j^-) does not appear in h_k. If it is desirable that both under- and overachievement of o_j is as small as possible, then $w_j^+ y_j^+ + w_j^- y_j^-$ is included in h_k, where w_j^+ and w_j^- are weights. (See, for instance, Lee (1972), Ignizio (1976).)

Fuzzy multiobjective linear programming is another approach under the assumption of predetermined aspiration levels (Zimmermann 1978). This approach makes no distinction between objective functions and constraints. They are represented by fuzzy sets and the solution set is defined as the intersection of all fuzzy sets. Thus a fuzzy approach to the MOLP problem is stated as

$$Cx \mathrel{\underset{\sim}{\leqslant}} z^0$$

$$Ax \mathrel{\underset{\sim}{\leqslant}} b$$

$$x \geq 0$$

where z^0 denotes the aspiration levels for the objective functions and $\mathrel{\underset{\sim}{\leqslant}}$ denotes "essentially smaller than or equal to."

Let the membership function be of the simplest type

$$\mu_i[Bx] = \begin{cases} 1 & \text{for } (B'x)_i \leqslant o_i \\ 1 - \dfrac{[(Bx)_i - o_i]}{d_i} & \text{for } o_i < (Bx)_i \leqslant o_i + d_i \\ 0 & \text{for } (Bx)_i > o_i + d_i \end{cases}$$

where B is the matrix A augmented by C, $o = (o_i)$ is the vector b augmented by z^0, $(Bx)_i$ is the ith element of Bx, and d_i is a subjectively chosen constant of admissible violation. Then the "maximizing" decision can be determined by

$$\max_{x \geq 0} \min_i \mu_i[Bx]$$

Rewriting this yields the equivalent problem: $\max \lambda$, subject to

$$\lambda \leqslant o_i' - (B'x)_i \quad x \geq 0$$

where $o_i' = o_i/d_i$ and $(B'x)_i = (Bx)_i/d_i$.

Although the above formulation does not involve fuzziness in the coefficients, an interactive multiobjective programming has also been developed for problems in which coefficients of the objective functions and the constraints are only fuzzily known (Seo and Sakawa 1987).

5. Interactive Approaches

Earlier interactive procedures include the step method (STEM) (Benayoun et al. 1971), the interactive Frank–Wolfe method (Geoffrion et al. 1972), the surrogate worth trade-off (SWT) method (Haimes et al. 1975) and the interactive multiobjective programming (Zionts and Wallenius 1976).

The STEM is an interactive procedure for the MOLP problem. The best compromise solution is reached after a certain number of cycles. Each cycle m consists of a calculation phase and a decision phase. A payoff table $T=(t_{ij})$ is constructed before the cycle. Let x^{i*} be an optimum solution of the problem:

$$\max f_i(x) = c^i x$$

subject to

$$Ax \leqslant b$$
$$x \geqslant 0$$

Let

$$M_i = f_i(x^{i*}), \quad t_{ij} = f_j(x^{i*})$$

For each cycle m, the calculation phase consists of the determination of the feasible solution x^m which is closest, in the minimax sense, to the ideal solution $Z=(M_1, M_2, \ldots, M_p)$. In the decision phase, the compromise solution x^m is proposed to the decision maker. If some of objectives are satisfactory and others are not, the decision maker must specify the amount by which the satisfactory objectives can be relaxed to allow an improvement of the unsatisfactory ones in the next cycle. Thus, for the next cycle the feasible region is modified.

The second procedure is the modified Frank–Wolfe method including the feature of the interaction with the decision maker. The problem is formally stated using the implicit utility function U, which is not known explicitly to the decision maker, as max $U[f(x)]$, subject to

$$x \in X = \{x \in \mathbb{R}^n | g_j(x) \leqq 0, \quad j=1, 2, \ldots, m\}$$

where $f(x) = (f_1(x), f_2(x), \ldots, f_p(x))$.

For convergence, it is assumed that the constraint set X is compact and convex and that $U[f(x)]$ is continuously differentiable and concave on X.

The "best direction" at each trial solution is, through interaction with the decision maker, approximated by assessing the marginal rates of substitution between each f_i, $i=1, 2, \ldots, p$, and the first or reference criterion f_1, and the step size problem is solved in a tabular or graphic way.

The third approach is based on the ε-constraint method which is a method for finding efficient solutions to the VMP.

The ε-constraint problem is max $f_i(x)$, subject to

$$f_j(x) \geqslant \varepsilon_i \quad i=2, \ldots, p$$
$$g_j(x) \leqslant 0 \quad j=1, 2, \ldots, m$$

where f_1 is a primary objective and ε_i is a lower bound on the ith objective.

The generalized Lagrangian to the above problem is:

$$L = f_1(x) + \sum \mu_j g_j(x) + \sum \lambda_{1i}(f_i(x) - \varepsilon_i)$$

where μ_j and λ_{1i} are generalized Lagrange multipliers. From the Kuhn–Tucker conditions, it follows that, for $\lambda_{1i} > 0$,

$$\lambda_{1i} = -\frac{\partial f_1}{\partial f_i} \quad i=2, \ldots, p$$

which is a trade-off between f_1 and f_i. The efficient solutions are those with nonzero Lagrange multipliers.

The SWT method consists of the following steps.

(a) Generate a representative subset of efficient solutions varying ε_i parametrically.

(b) For each efficient solution, obtain the trade-offs between a standing objective f_1 and each of the other objectives which are the values of λ_{1i} satisfying the Kuhn–Tucker conditions.

(c) At each efficient solution, the decision maker is asked to assign the surrogate worth w_{1i} (on an ordinal scale from -10 to $+10$ with 0 indicating indifference) to each λ_{1i}.

(d) An efficient solution whose surrogate worth functions are all zero is the preferred solution.

The fourth approach converts the original problem into the MOLP problem by linear approximations. The implicit utility function U is assumed to be a linear function, and more generally a concave function of the objective functions. First, an arbitrary set of weights $\lambda > 0$ is chosen and an efficient extreme solution is obtained by solving the P_λ problem. The reduced cost vector $(w_{1j}, w_{2j}, \ldots, w_{pj})$ of the nonbasic variable x_j in the multicriteria simplex tableau represents a marginal trade-off among the objectives; that is, w_{ij} represents the decrease in the ith objective due to the introduction of x_j into the basis. The decision maker is asked to evaluate the trade-off vector. For positive, negative and indifferent responses, we construct, respectively, constraints of the form

$$\sum w_{ij}\lambda_i \leqslant -\varepsilon$$
$$\sum w_{ij}\lambda_i \geqslant \varepsilon$$
$$\sum w_{ij}\lambda_i = \varepsilon$$

where ε is a sufficiently small positive number.

Using the responses of the decision maker to a number of such trade-offs, the constraints are added successively to restrict the choice of the weights λ to the problem P_λ for finding efficient solutions. The process is continued until an efficient solution is obtained at which no nonbasic variables are attractive to the decision maker.

See also: Decision Analysis; Multiattribute Utility Theory

Bibliography

Benayoun R, de Montgolfier J, Tergny J, Laritchev O 1971 Linear programming with multiple objective functions: Step method (STEM). *Math. Program.* **1**, 366–75.

Chankong V, Haimes Y Y 1983 *Multiobjective Decision Making: Theory and Methodology.* North–Holland, New York

Geoffrion A M, Dyer J S, Feinberg A 1972 An interactive approach for multi-criterion optimization, with an application to the operation of an academic department. *Manage. Sci.* **19,** 357–68

Goicoechea A, Hansen D R, Duckstein L 1982 *Multiobjective Decision Analysis with Engineering and Business Applications.* Wiley, New York

Haimes Y Y, Hall W A, Freedman H T 1975 *Multiobjective Optimization in Water Resources Systems; The Surrogate Worth Trade-Off Method.* Elsevier, New York

Hwang C L, Masud A S M 1979 *Multiple Objective Decision Making—Methods and Applications: A State-of-the-Art Survey.* Springer-Verlag, New York

Hwang C L, Yoon K 1981 *Multiple Attribute Decision Making—Methods and Applications: A State-of-the-Art Survey.* Springer-Verlag, New York

Ignizio J P 1976 *Goal Programming and Extensions.* Heath, Lexington, Massachusetts

Keeney R L 1974 Multiplicative utility functions. *Oper. Res.* **22,** 22–34

Keeney R L, Raiffa H 1976 *Decisions with Multiple Objectives: Preferences and Value Tradeoffs.* Wiley, New York

Lee S M 1972 *Goal Programming for Decision Analysis.* Auerbach, Philadelphia, Pennsylvania

Roy B 1977 Partial preference analysis and decision-aid: The fuzzy outranking relation concept. In: Bell D E, Keeney R L, Raiffa H (eds.) *Conflicting Objectives in Decisions.* Wiley, Chichester, pp. 40–75

Saaty T 1988 *Multicriteria Decision Making: The Analytic Hierarchy Process.* RWS Publications, Pittsburgh, Pennsylvania

Sawaragi Y, Nakayama H, Tanino T 1985 *Theory of Multiobjective Optimization.* Academic Press, Orlando, Florida

Seo F, Sakawa M 1987 *Multiple Criteria Decision Analysis in Regional Planning: Concepts, Methods and Applications.* Reidel, Dordrecht

Yu P L 1974 Cone convexity, cone extreme points and nondominated solutions in decision problems with multiobjectives. *J. Optim. Theory Appl.* **14,** 319–77

Yu P L 1985 *Multiple Criteria Decision Making: Concepts, Techniques and Extensions.* Plenum, New York

Zeleny M 1982 *Multiple Criteria Decision Making.* McGraw-Hill, New York

Zimmerman H-J 1978 Fuzzy programming and linear programming with several objective functions. *Fuzzy Sets Syst.* **1,** 45–56

Zimmermann H-J 1985 *Fuzzy Set Theory and its Applications.* Nijhoff, The Hague

Zionts S, Wallenius J 1976 An interactive programming method for solving the multiple criteria problem. *Manage. Sci.* **22,** 652–63

E. Takeda
[Ashiya University, Rokurokuso, Ashiya, Japan]

O

Office Automation

Office automation refers to the use of technology for improving the productivity of white-collar workers. The initial applications involved improving the routine typing tasks associated with secretarial work. The technology has since been applied during its development to all levels of office work, from the simple creation and dissemination of routine letters and memoranda to meetings among senior executives.

The automation of office work is the result of the merging of two technologies, the computer and communications, to create entirely new capabilities. In this article the following examples of office automation are discussed:

(a) word processing,
(b) electronic mail,
(c) voice mail,
(d) facsimile, graphical scanners and optical character readers;
(e) executive workstations,
(f) information-retrieval systems,
(g) natural-language software and expert systems,
(h) telecommuting,
(i) computer conferences,
(j) video conferences,
(k) decision rooms, and
(l) local area networks.

The human-factor considerations are also briefly discussed.

Office automation technologies are established in varying degrees; word processing is nearing universality, whereas telecommuting and video conferencing, for example, are in their infancy.

In the discussion that follows, the focus will be on the functions performed rather than the specific implementations. The range of features available with these technologies will be described; the availability of particular features depends on the system realization. Versions of many of the services discussed here are available on computers ranging in size from mainframes to microcomputers. The telecommunications technology ranges from hard-wiring within a building through the public telephone system, to satellite systems.

1. Word Processing

Word processing is a term introduced in the mid-1960s to refer to the use of on-line, computer-based text preparation systems. In such systems, a text file is entered into the computer and resides on a storage medium, typically disk. Conceptually, word processing works like audio or video tape in that revisions are made by retrieving the original text, making changes by deletions and insertions, and then storing the corrected version. In this way, the latest version is always available. Printed (often called "hard") copy is obtained by forwarding the text to a printer.

As the above implies, word processing is a software program for editing text. Such software is available on specialized word-processing computers, mainframes and microcomputers. In addition to allowing text to be changed, most word-processing software provides control over output format (margins, spacing, centering, page numbers, headers and footers, etc.), the ability to move text for "cut and paste," and global delete and replace (e.g., change "color" to "colour" everywhere). Specialized capabilities include the individualization of text (e.g., individualizing a form letter with the recipient's name referred to in the text), spellers to assist in locating and correcting typographical errors, automatic hyphenation, a thesaurus, the alphabetization of the lists, the creation of tables of contents and indexes, outlining, and the merging of address lists with standard text for mass mailings.

Word processors are used in firms both by individual secretaries and by specialized word-processing departments. In the latter case, the objective is to obtain economies of scale when preparing letters and documents, by centralization and by the sharing of resources such as printers. High-quality, computer-controlled printers are available (using a variety of technologies, including laser printing) that allow word-processing systems to create documents with a variety of type fonts and type sizes.

The principal economies achieved by word processing result from the ability to correct and change existing text, and the ability to save text on electronic media rather than in filing cabinets. Word-processing software is also available on home computers and on microcomputers in the office. As a result, many professional and office workers create their own text and do not require the use of typists for routine work.

At the most sophisticated levels of word-processing technology, text files created on one word processor can be sent to another word processor by a telecommunications link. This is one form of electronic mail. Software is also available that allows comments

361

to be placed in the text together with the name of the editor. These techniques lead to improved joint authoring of documents.

2. Electronic Mail

In electronic mail systems, the computer's memory is used as a message handler. As in standard mail systems, the originator creates a message, memo, letter or report, and addresses it. The text-editing and word-processing capabilities of the computer are used to produce the message. Mail can be sent to an individual or several addressees on a distribution list. The computer attaches the mail to each recipient's file and notifies them that they have new mail. In the best systems, notification is effectively on-line for people currently logged on. Others are notified when they next log on.

When displayed on a computer screen, the message typically shows the name of the sender and the time it was sent. The recipient can create printed copy, keep a copy in his personal file or delete the message. Most systems also provide reply and forwarding features; that is, the recipient can create an answer that is sent back to the originator and can also forward a copy of the message to other people in the organization (with or without a reply).

Electronic mail provides extremely rapid communication both within a site and between remote sites in an organization. This is particularly useful for project coordination, especially when projects are changing rapidly or facing severe deadlines. When used in conjunction with software that keeps track of calendars, electronic mail has been found to be an effective vehicle for meshing calendars to establish meetings. Its chief limitation is that only people tied to a particular computer or computer network (typically confined to a single firm) can be reached; however, various commercial and nonprofit electronic mail services are available that provide much greater connectivity. For example, BITNET connects people in universities worldwide. Furthermore, "gateways" allow different networks to communicate with one another. Thus, a person or a network can communicate with any person on any of the connected networks.

Electronic mail is effective when participants (or their assistants) either keep their terminal on-line or check regularly for messages. In commercial services, communications and connection costs are incurred whenever an inquiry is made, whether there is mail or not. The chief hazard of electronic mail is the ability to create and proliferate electronic junk mail within the organization. Administrative procedures are usually sufficient to control this problem.

3. Voice Mailboxes

Voice mailboxes are a form of electronic mail that transmit vocal rather than textual messages. They were developed by a number of communications firms as a solution to the "telephone tag" problem; that is, the problem that for people in large organizations a number of telephone calls (stretching over extensive periods of time) have to be placed before two people can talk to each other.

From the point of view of the caller, the computer acts like a versatile telephone-answering machine. A major advantage is that a message can be sent to many people as well as to a single person. The computer acts in a store-and-forward mode. It digitizes the voice message and forwards it to each addressee. When an individual dials the system, either to send or receive messages, they are told whether they have new messages and are able to listen to them if they so choose. As with electronic mail, replies can be sent and messages can be deleted, kept for future reference or forwarded to others. Hard copy is, of course, not available. Some systems also provide a "forced delivery" capability; that is, the recipient's phone is rung at regular intervals until the message is received. Experience with voice mailboxes indicates that there is an increase in efficiency due to reduced telephone tag and shorter messages; people tend to eliminate small talk and extraneous information when speaking to a machine.

Typical applications of voice mailboxes have included notifying groups of people of changes (e.g., part-timers, extras, flight crews), quick reactions in decision making, communications across time zones, and setting up meetings. Voice-mailbox systems provide a way of using a computer without typing and are preferred by people who operate principally in a verbal rather than a written mode. Their effectiveness depends on inculcating the habit of sending and retrieving messages so that the speed advantages are realized.

Voice mailboxes are basically a system for large organizations since they require investment in a special-purpose minicomputer and the extensive associated communications equipment. Some suppliers provide a public voice-mailbox service that can be used by small- and medium-sized organizations. In the USA, suppliers include major firms such as IBM and AT&T as well as firms that specialize in voice-mailbox systems.

4. Facsimile, Scanners and Optical Character Readers

A major cost in both time and money in word processing and electronic mail is keystroking to enter information. Voice mailboxes are one way of avoiding keystroking; facsimile, graphical scanners and optical character readers (OCRs) are another. In each case, images on a sheet of paper are read electronically and converted into digital form. The three units differ in purpose and use as shown below.

(a) Facsimile digitizes information to transmit it over ordinary telephone lines and reconstitutes it at the far end in its original form.

(b) Graphical scanners digitize the image and store it in the computer as a picture. Thus, they provide graphic output.

(c) OCRs scan text and convert them into a standard code such as ASCII.

Although these technologies have been available for many years, only recently have the costs been reduced and the technologies matured sufficiently to make their use routine in office-automation applications. Facsimile offers the opportunity to send hand-written messages and signatures without intermediaries. Scanners and OCRs allow the direct entry of document information into the computer without rekeying. Combining facsimile with a scanner permits entering typed text directly into a remote computer. As facsimile costs are reduced they can be expected to be a serious competitor to electronic mail, particularly for people at senior executive levels.

5. Executive Workstations

Just as word processing represents the augmentation of secretarial capabilities with computers, executive workstations are designed to assist middle and upper managers in firms by providing them with computer facilities for handling text and calculations. Executive workstations are essentially microcomputers with software and devices to aid the performance of managerial functions. Executive workstations are usually designed to require a minimum of typing when communicating with the computer. The rationale for this approach is that most executives do not know how to type well or prefer not to type. Two typical devices are the touch screen and the "mouse."

As its name implies, a touch screen allows the user to put his finger on the screen to select an item from the alternatives shown. Typical alternatives include choosing information, selecting a value to be assigned or an operating command such as NEXT SCREEN. Touch screens require careful preparation of alternatives, usually in menu form. Furthermore, the number of choices that can be made available is limited because there must be enough space between choices to accommodate people with thick fingers.

The mouse is an external device that is used to point to items on the screen. A mouse is a small box which is moved across a flat surface and has one or more push buttons. The motion of the mouse is tracked (e.g., by following the motion of a ball bearing on its bottom surface and converting the change of position electrically) by a pointer or indicator (i.e., cursor) on the screen. When the cursor is at the desired location, a button on the mouse is pressed to select the item at that location.

The mouse becomes particularly powerful when coupled with icons on the screen. An icon is a graphical representation of a file or function available on the computer (e.g., a document, a collection of files, a printer, a communications device, electronic "in box" or "out box"). When an icon is selected by using the mouse, it becomes available for manipulation. For example, if the icon represents a document, the document can be "opened" to make its text appear on the screen, copied, moved to another location, and so on. If a document is moved on top of an icon representing a printer, a sequence of steps leading to obtaining a printed copy is initiated. If the icon is moved on top of an item representing an out box, it can be mailed. A screen containing icons is, in effect, a desktop and the desktop metaphor has been used extensively in designing these systems. Commands such as OPEN, CLOSE, COPY or MOVE are available either as function keys on a keyboard or as menu items on screen.

Development of the mouse-and-icon concept began in the 1960s at Stanford Research Institute under Doug Engelbart. Commercial development of executive workstations began in the late 1970s. Among the initial workstations on the market using the mouse-and-icon concept was the STAR by Xerox, followed several years later by LISA and MACINTOSH from Apple Computer. These initial implementations of workstations, while quite sophisticated, tended to have slow response times and to be relatively expensive. Product improvement has increased speed and reduced cost. Executive workstations are available in both stand-alone and network configurations. Network configurations are designed to increase both effectiveness and efficiency within a firm by allowing workstations to communicate with one another and with other computer-based systems, to share computer storage and to access a common printer. The network interconnection is typically through a base-band system such as ETHERNET.

The design philosophy of the systems varies. The STAR, for example, excels at document retrieval and text manipulation whereas the LISA is more oriented toward computation. Both machines, however, provide an extensive graphics capability. For example, the LISA includes a CPM/PERT package that allows a manager to change a graphically presented planning-network diagram and obtain an updated network with new critical paths shown and expected times computed.

6. Information-Retrieval Systems

The ability of terminals in the office to communicate with remotely located computers has resulted in the establishment of services which provide access to large public databases. These databases provide both current information (e.g., current stock prices and news reports) and library information. Some of these services also provide the capability for ordering goods and performing various transactions such as bank transfers. The growth of the on-line transaction services has been relatively slow. Attempts to move these services into the home using television receivers (usually referred to as video text) have met with low success in the USA (where they are privately sponsored) but have proved popular in France, where they are offered by the PT&T.

Two emerging technologies in information retrieval are CD-ROM (compact-disk read-only memory) and WORM (write once, read many), which are both high-capacity storage devices. In the former, a compact disk is used to store large amounts of fixed data (e.g., an encyclopedia). In the latter, as its name implies, it is possible to write only once on the storage medium but to read it as often as desired.

7. *Software Innovations*

Innovative software packages allow office workers to perform relatively complex model-based calculations without knowledge of computer programming. These packages range from those that create fairly simple "spreadsheets" to full-service, fourth-generation computer languages that permit the expression of mathematical relations in nearly natural-language form. These packages are available both on mainframes and on stand-alone microcomputers, and are intended for on-line use. One of their main advantages is the ability to carry out "what if" calculations; that is, to alter one or more assumptions in the model and determine the effect of changes.

A spreadsheet is simply a two-dimensional matrix presentation of results, where each column typically represents one time period and each row represents the values of a variable. Intended primarily for financial calculations, the level of sophistication of spreadsheet packages has increased rapidly. Features available include various built-in mathematical, financial and statistical functions; communication between the spreadsheet package and company databases; graphical presentation of data including color graphics; and the ability to treat output as text so that the spreadsheet can be integrated with word processing.

In fourth-generation computer languages, it is possible to express mathematical relations in direct, full-word format; for example:

SALES = MARKET * MARKET SHARE

Some of these languages are nonprocedural; that is, it is not necessary to define a quantity before it is used as long as it is defined at some point in the program. The advantage of nonprocedural languages is that they are easier to use and can serve as a form of communication between the model builder and the user. Their disadvantage is that they require more memory and have slower execution speeds than conventional procedural languages. Nonprocedural languages typically produce spreadsheet outputs if no formatting instructions are given, but can be instructed to provide customized formatted reports. They contain extensive financial, statistical and mathematical functions. Many are provided with built-in fixed-time-interval simulation options that allow risk analyses to be performed. Their "what if" capabilities include sensitivity analysis and goal seeking. These languages also permit the consolidation of multiple reports into a single report.

8. *Natural-Language Software and Expert Systems*

As a spinoff from research in artificial intelligence, software is being developed that allows users to interact with the computer in nearly natural language; that is, in their ordinary way of speaking. The nonprocedural languages discussed above were early harbingers of such natural-language software. Although implementations are still relatively crude and restrict the user to relatively narrow vocabularies that the computer can understand, the quality of products directed toward natural-language input continues to improve.

Expert systems is a term referring to software that:

(a) contains an extensive set of information on a given subject (referred to as a knowledge base), and

(b) that can perform logical operations on the knowledge base interactively.

The knowledge base is obtained from experts in the subject. In a typical expert system, the software asks the user questions which are designed to reduce the set of possible answers and, using built-in "if–then–else" rules, recommends a course of action. Expert systems have proved to be most useful in diagnostic situations such as determining infections.

9. *Telecommuting*

For organizations which are highly computer-intensive (insurance, banking, finance, administrative units of manufacturing organizations, computer support groups such as programmers), the availability of communications allows the workers who interact with the computer and the computer itself to be in different places. Thus, it is possible to place a central computer in one place and to put offices in multiple locations either within a metropolitan area or across the country. Telecommuting (also called telework and flexiplace) is the concept of substituting communications for transportation by moving work to locations close to where workers live, rather than having the workers commute each day to the computer location. Telecommuting can involve either work at home or at an office located close to home.

The advantages of telecommuting to a company include a reduced need for erecting large office buildings in the expensive real estate of downtown areas, access to new labor markets where transportation is a problem, the ability to time-share jobs and equipment, greater employee morale, greater retention of staff, reduced staff training, and reduced wages in outlying areas compared to downtown locations. From an employee's point of view, the reduced need for commuting and the flexibility of hours are among the advantages. In a telecommuting environment, changing assignments involves changing the data set being used rather than changing the office location. The disadvantages of telecommuting include the physical separation of workers from their supervisors and the loss of an individual's visibility which could impede their vertical mobility in the organization. In a telecommuting environment, the supervisory function can be divided between local supervision for punctuality, work habits, supplies, and so on, and remote supervision (using the computer–communications link provided for telecommuting) for the technical content of the work.

Surveys of telecommuters working at home indicate that telecommuters have increased productivity, that remote supervision is adequate and that there is little feeling of loss of socialization. However, to be successful in the work-at-home mode, the telecommuter must have regular self-scheduled work habits.

10. Electronic Meetings

A typical conference is a meeting involving a group of people of nearly equal status in an organization for the purpose of exchanging information or reaching a decision. A conference is an intellectual activity, involving structured communication whose outputs lead to consensus and action. For conferences involving people whose normal work locations are geographically separate, conferencing methods include:

(a) face-to-face,

(b) speakerphone,

(c) computer-based, and

(d) video.

In a face-to-face conference, people travel to the same location and all participants are in the same room. The major problems in face-to-face conferences are scheduling and cost. Tangible costs include transportation, hotels, food and salaries. Opportunity and intangible costs result from being away from the office and from the catch-up required upon return. Research findings in the UK, Sweden and the USA indicate that remote communication can be substituted for face-to-face meetings to a large extent. Initial contacts should be made face-to-face so that people can obtain visual images and develop mutual trust and respect. There also appears to be a periodic need (every six to twelve months) to refresh face-to-face contact. In the interim, electronic meetings serve as a viable substitute.

In speakerphone conferences, people at each location gather in a conference room. A telephone connection is used, with a loudspeaker attachment to each phone. The advantage of speakerphone meetings is that communication costs are minimized because only telephone bandwidths are required. The difficulties with such a meeting are identifying who is speaking and developing protocols for determining who is to be recognized next. Although relatively successful for two locations, speakerphone conferences are much more difficult for multiple locations. As a graphics supplement to speakerphone conferences, electronic "blackboards" have been developed which allow drawings to be transmitted, as they are being made, over a telephone circuit. This technique involves using pressure-sensitive digitized pads. Speakerphone conferences are sometimes augmented with a personal computer and/or facsimile at each location. The computers, also operating over phone lines, provide the ability to send and display text and pictures as well as transmitting voices.

In a computer conference, participants are separated in both space and time rather than being present in the same place at the same time. The participants use terminals and telecommunications to interact. Commercially available computer-conference systems are usually implemented on large mainframes to store the central files and employ packet-switching networks for communications. Technically, computer conferences are an extension of electronic mail.

Although a computer conference can be on-line with all participants at terminals simultaneously, they are usually off-line and run over several days or weeks. The "conference" is really a file at the central computer containing the messages (also referred to as items) from participants. On a typical day, a participant reviews the items sent by other participants, responds to their items and adds ideas by creating new items. These messages can be "public" so that they can be accessed by all participants or "private" (e.g., electronic mail) in which case they are addressed to specific individuals. In addition to providing a record (including a printed record) of the meeting, computer conferences usually provide the ability to edit previous statements, to add responses directly at the end of the items, to vote on specific issues and to keep records on participants.

Computer conferences have been used to exchange information, reach consensus, write joint reports and scientific papers, and for consulting activities. Experience indicates that if a computer conference involving many people is to be successful, the following factors must be present:

(a) a strong moderator to ensure closure,

(b) persistence and involvement by the participants, and

(c) people willing to type at terminals.

Video conferences overcome the technical limitations of speakerphone conferences and the nonsimultaneity and typing requirements of computer conference. In video conferencing, people gather in instrumented conference rooms to obtain both sound and pictures. A variety of video-conferencing systems have been developed. These systems include:

(a) one-way video, one-way audio;

(b) compressed video; and

(c) two-way video.

In one-way video and one-way audio systems, the activities of the participants at a central location are televised over closed circuits to all other locations; however, the people at the remote locations are only able to reply over speakerphones. Such one-way systems are particularly useful for meetings whose purpose is to transmit information to a large number of people. These systems have been used within metropolitan areas by a number of universities to televise courses to people working in industry. They have been implemented commercially by hotel chains over large geographic areas, by using communications satellites for transmitting the video. One-way video systems have been used by companies for sales meetings and product introductions, and by politicians for fund raising.

The cost of full video transmission can be overcome somewhat by using compressed video. These systems are based on the idea that visual images in a meeting change slowly and hence only the changes in the picture need to be sent. These systems give reduced-quality images for rapid motion. However, they are usually adequate for meetings in which people are sitting around a table talking. Both one-way video and compressed-video systems are a compromise between speakerphone and full two-way video conferences.

In a video conference, participants gather at conference rooms with video transmission and receiving capabilities. A typical video-conference room contains several cameras, two screens (one to show the picture from the remote location and the other to show what is being transmitted), a conference table for the participants, and a spectator area. Some rooms contain voice-actuated microphones that allow the picture to follow the conversation, if desired. Controls are provided to the chairperson or their designee to select the picture to be transmitted. Visual aids (slides, flip charts, transparencies) are provided, as are facsimile and personal computers.

Experience with two-way video conferences indicates that they are successful when they involve fewer than 15 people, when the people know one another, and if the meeting is highly structured and lasts less than three hours. These meetings also tend to be more efficient because the participants are aware of the costs involved. Two-way video is not appropriate for initial contacts, delicate negotiations or personnel matters.

Two-way video-conferencing systems have been installed worldwide. Public studio systems in which participants come to studios located centrally within their city are provided by many telephone systems including those in Australia, Canada, France, the UK, Japan, the Netherlands, Sweden and the USA. Private systems are used by government agencies and large corporations.

In summary, electronic meetings have the following benefits.

(a) Improved communications. They add to existing communications, provide a faster response to problems and not only serve as substitutes for face-to-face meetings but also allow premeeting communications and trip follow-up.

(b) Organizational effectiveness. It becomes easier to reach an individual in an organization and to reach more people in the organization; as a result, more people know what is going on. Specialized skills can be brought into a meeting more easily and junior people can participate, thus enhancing their skills and knowledge.

(c) Economic benefits. In addition to net travel-cost savings, there are productivity gains from having people in the office rather than on trips. There is also reduction in losses, owing to the elimination of travel fatigue.

11. Decision Rooms

In both government and industry, decisions are usually taken only after establishing a consensus within the organization. A significant portion of the consensus development process occurs in conferences. However, in most organizations, conference rooms contain little office automation. Decision rooms are conference rooms containing office-automation technology to support the decision-making process. Specifically, executive workstations and video displays in a decision room make possible the retrieval of information from computers, the rapid evaluation of alternatives, the visual display of complex information in graphic form and the participation of people located remotely through teleconferencing.

Decision rooms are at an early stage of development. Experimental decision rooms have been built that make use of the full spectrum of technology. The key problems to be solved are how to use the available capabilities effectively in the decision process and how to train people to use these capabilities. Unresolved issues include such questions as whether the quality of decision making is improved, the best arrangement of equipment and people and the best way to display information.

Decision rooms can be characterized by sponsorship and purpose. They can either be located within a firm or can be made available as an outside service. In the latter case, the equipment can either be brought into the firm's premises or members of the firm can travel to the equipment. The decision room may be single purpose (i.e., used for only one type of decision) or multipurpose.

The most complex decision rooms in service have been built by governmental units—in particular, in the Office of the President of the USA and in the US Department of Defence. Several relatively simple decision rooms are in commercial service. As an example of an outside service, a consulting firm provides a conference room to which clients can come and go through a "decision analysis" process; a terminal providing access to the computer of the consulting firm is used to record information and to perform any necessary calculations. As another example, at least two firms provide equipment to aid in reaching consensus; this equipment is portable and is usually brought to the client's offices. Systems for experimental use, including some multipurpose decision rooms, have been built at several universities. Observations at these experimental facilities indicate that these facilities are better for large meetings (more than six or eight people) than small meetings (three or four people). In the case of small meetings, the technology adds little of value. In large meetings, a phenomenon usually referred to as "human parallel processing" takes place; that is, people are required to enter information into the meeting simultaneously through the computer, hence working in parallel rather than sequentially. Thus, for example, rather than each of ten people in an hour's meeting having an average of 6 min to speak, 15–20 min of computer input by all participants provides much richer results more efficiently.

12. Local Area Networks

Local area networks are communication networks that tie individual computers together and allow the sharing of programs and data among many workstations simultaneously. "Local" implies that these networks cover a small geographical area, such as a building or a contiguous work area for a group. These networks require both hardware and software. The hardware consists of cabling that interconnects the units, and electronic boards that provide the communications interfaces among the computers. Typically, one unit on the network acts as a "file server"; that is, a place where the programs and files to be shared are stored. Thus, servers usually have a large hard-disk storage capacity available. Servers also provide printing and external communications interfaces that connect the network to common printers, to other networks and/or mainframes. Networks may have anywhere from a few to hundreds of users connected to them. With a local network, the users can communicate with one another and with the file server.

The network software moves data between the user workstations and the file server, controls data access and file sharing, and manages security. It often includes electronic mail. Networks can be connected (in increasing order of speed and cost) with twisted pair wire, coaxial cable or fiber-optic cable. The interaction between the cabling method and the software determines the speed with which information can be moved across the network. The units in the network are connected in either a bus, a ring or a star configuration. In a bus configuration, a single cable runs past all the workstations. A ring is similar to a bus, except that the two ends of the cable are hooked together. In a star configuration, each workstation is connected directly to the server. A bus or ring requires less wiring (and hence less cost) than a star, whereas the star is easier to troubleshoot.

Applications that run on a network usually require special versions of the software to run successfully. The basic problem is that data sharing requires data integrity. The application has to be set up so that if one user is accessing data, another user cannot change it at the same time. Otherwise, chaos will result.

Local area networks make up one solution to the data-sharing problem. An alternative is the departmental computer. Here a time-sharing minicomputer is dedicated to a department for its own use. The choice between a departmental computer and a local area network involves a trade-off among costs and benefits. Local area networks can add costs of US$1000 or more per workstation. Personal computers are more expensive than terminals. On the other hand, the minicomputer and the associated software costs are also significant. For an organization with a considerable investment in stand-alone workstations, local area networking provides a reasonable upgrade to connectivity. For a new installation, a detailed cost–benefit analysis needs to be performed.

13. Human Factors and Social Considerations

Office automation changes the way people work. Not all of these changes are necessarily good or well-designed. Increasing attention is being given to good ergonomic design in screens, lighting, chairs and other elements of the automated office. Radiation hazards from screens are a matter of controversy and telecommuting has been characterized by some as the "new sweatshop." Working in a computer/communications world requires higher technical skills and hence more education. Concern exists that some groups, such as social minorities and the poor, will be even further disadvantaged in an office-automation world. Software developments in natural language and expert systems are, however, a countervailing trend.

In summary, increasing the technological content of office work necessitates taking human as well as technical factors into account.

See also: Collective Enquiry; Human Factors Engineering; Human–System Interaction: Information-Presentation Requirements

Bibliography

Mullins C, West T 1982 *Office Automation: Harnessing Information Technologies for Greater Productivity.* Prentice–Hall, Englewood Cliffs, New Jersey

P. Gray
[Claremont Graduate School, Claremont, California, USA]

Organizational Information Structures: Quantitative Models

Modern decision-making organizations process large amounts of information obtained from external sources (sensors) and from internal databases. The latter can be centralized or decentralized, depending on the architecture of the communications system that connects the members of the organization. The manner in which information is processed and distributed within an organization affects the process of decision making and consequently the organization's performance as measured by the accuracy and the timeliness of the output, whether a decision or an action.

Galbraith (1977) describes the various approaches to organization design as follows. In classical management theory, the key concept is that of division of labor. A modern counterpart of that approach is the functional decomposition of tasks and the subsequent allocation of those to the organization members so that some objective function is maximized. Parallel, hierarchical and mixed structures result. In contrast to this mechanistic approach is the human-relations approach in which the style of leadership determines the organizational form. Empirically based, it leads to the consideration of incentives, tangible and intangible, as the means to improve performance. The third approach, which is closest to the conceptual framework for the quantitative modelling of information structures, is based on the view of the organization as an information-processing and decision-making system. The cognitive limitations of humans (or the memory and information-processing limitations of machines) determine the organizational form. This approach admits the allocation of functions to both humans and machines.

1. Assumptions

In order to obtain quantitative models that can be used for design, a restricted class of organizations, teams, is considered. A team is defined as an organization in which the members have a common goal, have the same interests and same beliefs, and have activities that must be coordinated so as to achieve a higher effectiveness. This implies that the information structure is expected to enhance both the individual's and the organization's performance; there is no attempt to withhold information deliberately so that an individual's performance is degraded. A second assumption is that it should be possible to draw a boundary that defines what is included in the organization and what is excluded; that is, what resides in the external environment. The information-processing tasks that the organization must perform are generated in the environment by one or more sources which may or may not be synchronized. The organization acts upon these inputs and produces a response, including the null response, that is directed to the environment. Thus, the interface between the system and the environment is composed of the sensors and the effectors. Whether to include the sensors or the effectors or both as parts of the organization or as parts of the environment is a question that must be addressed in each particular case. This issue becomes relevant when alternative organizational designs are evaluated; the comparison must be done on the same basis.

The elements of the organization are human decision makers, databases, processors and communication systems. A decision aid is defined as any technique or procedure that restructures the methods by which problems are analyzed, alternatives developed and decisions taken. Decision support systems, a specific form of decision aids, do not automate a specific decision-making process, but must facilitate it (Keene and Scott Morton 1978). Decision support systems are considered here as higher-level components that may consist of processors, databases and communication systems.

Relationships are the links that tie these elements together. These relationships can be considered at three levels: they may describe the physical arrangement of the components, such as the geographical location of the organizational units, or the functional relationship between components, such as their relative position in a hierarchy, or the rules and protocols that govern the interactions, such as the conditions under which two units may share information. While this demarcation between relationships and components is often hard to justify, it is assumed that it can be done.

The Petri net formalism (Reisig 1985) has been found to be very convenient for describing the concurrent and asynchronous characteristics of the various interactions that characterize an organizational information structure. Furthermore, they lead to a mathematical description of the organizational structure that can then be investigated analytically; the algebraic representation of the nets and the calculus of invariants leads to a set of algorithms that are essential for the quantitative analysis of the net properties and for the design of information structures that are guaranteed to satisfy given requirements. For this reason, Sect. 2 provides a brief introduction to Petri nets; Sect. 3 introduces the basic model of the interactions that constitute the organizational information structure; and Sects. 4 and 5 provide two alternative approaches to quantitative modelling and design.

2. Overview of Petri Net Theory

A Petri net, denoted by PN, is a bipartite directed graph represented by a quadruple PN = (P, T, I, O), where P is a finite set of places, denoted by circles, and T is a finite set of transitions, denoted by bars. A node will refer to either a place or a transition of PN. The mappings I and O correspond to the set of directed arcs from places to transitions and to the set of directed arcs from transitions to places, respectively. When I and O take values in $\{0,1\}$, the resulting nets are called ordinary Petri nets.

A marking of a Petri net is a mapping M which assigns a nonnegative integer number of tokens to each place of the net. A marking can be represented by an n-dimensional integer vector, also denoted by M, whose components correspond to the places of the net.

A transition t is enabled by a given marking M if and only if for each input place p of t, $M(p) \geq I(p,t)$. When a transition is enabled it can fire. The new marking M' reached after the firing of t is defined as follows:

$$(\forall p \in P) \; M'(p) = M(p) - I(p,t) + O(t,p) \qquad (1)$$

A place p and a transition t are on a self-loop if p is both an input and an output place of t. A Petri net will be pure if it does not contain self-loops. Petri nets under consideration in this article will all be pure; this is a reasonable assumption for information structures.

Certain basic graph-theoretic definitions apply readily to Petri nets. A Petri net is connected if and only if there exists a path, not necessarily directed, from any node to any other node; it is strongly connected if and only if there exists a directed path from any node to any other node.

A directed circuit is a directed path from one node back to itself. A directed elementary circuit is a directed circuit in which no node appears more than once. Directed elementary circuits will play a key role in the theory of net invariants.

The topological structure of a pure Petri net can be represented by an integer matrix C called an incidence or flow matrix. C is an $n \times m$ matrix whose columns correspond to the m transitions and whose rows correspond to the n places of the net. C is defined as follows:

$$C_{ij} = O(t_j, p_i) - I(p_i, t_j) \quad \text{for } 1 \leq i \leq n \text{ and } 1 \leq j \leq m \qquad (2)$$

Note that the definition is restricted to pure Petri nets. There is actually a problem with nonpure Petri nets in the sense that self-loops cannot be represented in the incidence matrix: a 1 and a -1 cancel each other to yield a zero in the matrix, losing track of the existence of the self-loop.

The mappings O and I can be reconstructed from the matrix C in the following trivial way:

$$O(t_j, p_i) = \max\{C_{ij}, 0\} \qquad (3a)$$

$$I(p_i, t_j) = \min\{C_{ij}, 0\} \qquad (3b)$$

An initial marking M^0 is bounded if there exists a positive integer k such that for every reachable marking M the number of tokens in each place is bounded by k. If $k = 1$, the marking is said to be safe. A Petri net PN is structurally bounded if any initial marking of PN is bounded. A marking M^0 is live if for any transition t and for every reachable marking M there exists a firing sequence from M that includes t. In other words every transition of the net can fire an infinite number of times. A Petri net PN is structurally live if any initial marking of PN is live.

A marked graph is a strongly connected Petri net in which each place has exactly one input and one output transition. Pure marked graphs will be the class of Petri nets that is used to generate information structures. There is a useful relationship between the circuits of a marked graph and the S-invariants.

An S-invariant is an $n \times 1$ nonnegative integer vector element X of the kernel of the transpose of the incidence matrix C; i.e., X verifies the relation:

$$C' \cdot X = 0 \qquad (4)$$

Similarly, a T-invariant is an $m \times 1$ nonnegative integer vector element Y of the kernel of C; i.e., Y verifies the relation:

$$C \cdot Y = 0 \qquad (5)$$

The set of places (resp. transitions) whose corresponding components in X (resp. Y) are strictly positive is called the support of the invariant and is denoted $\langle X \rangle$ (resp. $\langle Y \rangle$). The support of an invariant is said to be minimal if and only if it does not contain the support of another invariant but itself and the empty set. Let X be an S-invariant of a Petri net PN and let $\langle X \rangle$ be its support. $\langle X \rangle$ is a set of places of PN; i.e., a subset of P. We call S-component associated with X, denoted $[X]$, the subnet of PN whose set of places is $\langle X \rangle$ and whose transitions are the input and output transitions of the places of $\langle X \rangle$ in PN. T-components are defined in a similar way.

Some useful properties of S- and T-invariants are listed without proof. The first property establishes the conservation of the number of tokens belonging to the support $\langle X \rangle$ of an S-invariant of a Petri net. X is an S-invariant of PN if and only if for any initial marking M^0 of PN and for any reachable marking M,

$$X' \cdot M = X' \cdot M^0 \qquad (6)$$

Marked graphs play a key role in the quantitative modelling of information structures. The following two results, due to Commoner and Holt (1971), are of primary importance. In a marked graph, the number of tokens in any elementary directed circuit—the token content of the circuit—remains invariant by transition firings. Furthermore, a marking of a marked graph is live if and only if the token content of every directed elementary circuit is strictly positive. Another result relates directed circuits and S-components of a marked graph. It gives an algebraic characterization of a topological concept and will be extensively used in the sequel: the minimal S-components of a marked graph are exactly its elementary directed circuits.

3. Information Structures

The key components of an organization are the information-processing and decision-making elements. These can be human decision makers or machines. The Petri net model of the human decision maker who interacts with other components and with the environment is shown in Fig. 1 (Levis 1984). The decision maker (DM) receives input signals x at the situation assessment (SA) stage from a variety of sources: from the environment, from a decision support system (DSS) or from the rest of the organization. The DM processes this input, with or without use of information stored in a database (memory), to obtain an estimate of x and of z, the "assessed situation," which may be shared with other DMs. Other information, z'', may also be received at this point from the rest of the organization. The DM combines this information with his own assessment in the information fusion (IF) stage, which contains a data fusion algorithm, to obtain the final assessment of the situation, labelled z'. The next step is the consideration of inputs v' from other DMs which could result in a restriction of the set of alternatives for generating the response to the given input. This is the command interpretation (CI) stage. The outcome of the CI stage is a signal v, which contains the data z' and the rule v', to be used in the response selection (RS) stage to select the procedure or algorithm for generating the output y. This is the response of the DM; it may be sent to the environment or to other DMs within the organization.

In the Petri net representation of the DM model, the transitions stand for the algorithms, the connectors for the precedence relations between these algorithms, and the tokens for their input and output. The tokens, in the simplest version of the model, are all indistinguishable. A token in a place means simply that an item of information is available to the output transition(s) of that place. It is also possible to associate attributes with the tokens. In this case, the source can be represented by a finite number of distinct tokens x, each one occurring with some probability $p(x)$. However, if the protocols ruling their processing do not vary from one set of attributes to the other, they can be considered as indistinguishable tokens.

Other organization components can be modelled using the same basic four-stage model, but eliminating one or more of the stages. For example, a processor that receives sensor data and converts it to an estimate of a vector variable can be modelled by a single SA transition, while a data fusion algorithm can be modelled by an IF transition. With this model of the organization member and its variants used to model other components, it is now possible to formulate the problem of designing distributed decision-making organizations.

It was shown in Fig. 1 that a DM can only receive inputs at the SA, IF and CI stages, and produce outputs at the SA and RS stages. These conditions lead to the set of admissible interactions between two DMs shown in Fig. 2. For clarity, only the connectors from DM^i to DM^j are shown; the interactions from DM^j to DM^i are identical.

The mathematical representation of the interactions between DMs is based on the connector labels e_i, s_i, F_{ij}, G_{ij}, H_{ij} and C_{ij} of Fig. 2; they are integer variables taking values in $\{0, 1\}$ where 1 indicates that the corresponding directed link is actually present in the organization, while 0 reflects the absence of the link. These variables can be aggregated into two vectors e and s, and four matrices F, G, H and C. The interaction structure of an n-decision-maker organization may be represented by the following six arrays: two $n \times 1$ vectors e and s, representing the interactions between the external environment and the organization:

$$e \equiv [e_i], \quad s \equiv [s_i] \quad \text{for } i = 1, 2, \ldots, n$$

and four $n \times n$ matrices F, G, H and C representing the interactions between decision makers inside the organization:

$$F \equiv [F_{ij}], \quad G \equiv [G_{ij}],$$
$$H \equiv [H_{ij}], \quad C \equiv [C_{ij}]$$
$$\text{for } i = 1, 2, \ldots, n \quad \text{and} \quad j = 1, 2, \ldots, n$$

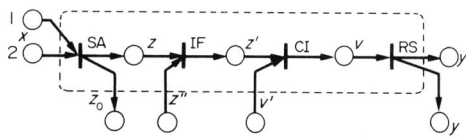

Figure 1
Four-stage model of a DM

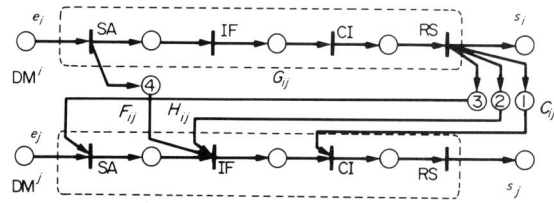

Figure 2
Allowable interactions between DMs

Since there are four possible links between any two different DMs, the maximum number of interconnecting links that an n-decision-maker organization can have is

$$k_{max} = 4n^2 - 2n \qquad (7)$$

Consequently, if no other considerations were taken into account, there could be $2^{k_{max}}$ alternative organizational forms. This is a very large number: 2^{90} for a five-person organization.

4. Generation of Architectures

The analytical description of the possible interactions between organization members forms the basis for an algorithm that generates all the architectures that meet some structural constraints as well as application-specific constraints that may be present. The set of structural constraints that has been introduced rules out a large number of architectures. The most important constraint addresses the connectivity of the organization—it eliminates information structures that do not represent a single integrated organization.

An algorithm has been developed (Remy and Levis 1988) that determines the maximal and minimal elements of the set of designs that satisfy all the constraints; the entire set can then be generated from its boundaries. The algorithm is based on the notion of a simple path—a directed path without loops from the source to the sink. Feasible architectures are obtained as unions of simple paths. Consequently, they constitute a partially ordered set.

The sextuple $\{e, s, F, G, H, C\}$ is called a well-defined net (WDN) of dimension n, where n is the number of components in the organization. The set of all well-defined nets of dimension n is denoted Ψ^n; its cardinality is given by $2^{k_{max}}$, where k_{max} is given by Eqn. (7). The notion of a subnet of a WDN can be defined as follows. Let $\Pi = \{e, s, F, G, H, C\}$ and $\Pi' = \{e', s', F', G', H', C'\}$ be two WDNs. The WDN Π is a subnet of Π' if and only if

$$e' \leqslant e; \qquad F' \leqslant F, \qquad G' \leqslant G$$
$$s' \leqslant s, \qquad H' \leqslant H, \qquad C' \leqslant C$$

where the inequality between arrays is interpreted element by element. In other words, Π' is a subnet of Π if any interaction in Π'; i.e., a 1 in any of the arrays e', s', F', G', H', C', is also an interaction in Π. The union of two subnets Π_1 and Π_2 of a WDN Π is a new net that contains all the interactions that appear in either Π_1 or Π_2 or in both.

A WDN can be represented in two different ways: (a) the matrix representation; i.e., the set of arrays $\{e, s, F, G, H C\}$; and (b) the Petri net representation, given by the graph or the incidence matrix of the net, with the associated labelling of the transitions. These two representations of a WDN are equivalent; i.e., a one-to-one correspondence exists between them.

Let the organizational structure be modelled as having a single source and a single sink place. Each internal place of a WDN has exactly one input and one output transition. The sink of a WDN has one input but no output transitions, while the opposite stands for the source. If source and sink are merged into one place, every place in the net will therefore have one input and one output transition. Since the net is strongly connected, it is a marked graph. Note that considering the source and the sink of a WDN as the same place has no bearing on the internal topology of the net. The assumption becomes important, however, when the dynamic behavior of a WDN is studied. The merging of source and sink limits the amount of information a given organization can process simultaneously. The initial marking of the place representing the external environment will define this bound. At this stage, a WDN may contain circuits.

While WDNs constitute the framework within which information structures will be designed, each WDN is not a valid organizational structure. Additional constraints to restrict the set of WDNs to useful information structures are needed. First, there are some WDNs corresponding to combinations of interactions between components that do not have a physical interpretation; e.g., DMS can exchange information—F_{ij} and F_{ji} can coexist—but commands are unilateral—either C_{ij} or C_{ji} or none, but not both. Those WDNs should be eliminated if realistic organizational forms are to be generated. The structural constraints define what kinds of combinations of interactions need to be ruled out. Second, any realistic design procedure should allow the designer to introduce specific structural characteristics appropriate to the particular design problem. User-defined constraints are introduced to address this issue. A set of four different structural constraints R_s is formulated that applies to all organizational structures being considered.

R_1 A directed path should exist from the source to every node of the structure and from every node to the sink.

R_2 The structure should have no loop; i.e., the organizational structures should be acyclical.

R_3 There can be at most one link from the RS stage of a DM to each one of the other DMs; i.e., for each i and j only one element of the triplet $\{G_{ij}, H_{ij}, C_{ij}\}$ can be nonzero.

R_4 Information fusion can take place only at the IF and CI stages. Consequently, the SA and RS stages of each DM can have only one input.

Constraint R_1 eliminates structures that do not represent a single integrated organization and ensures that the flow of information is continuous within an organization. Constraint R_2 allows acyclical organizations only. This restriction is made to avoid deadlock and circulation of messages within the organization. It also restricts the marked graphs to occurrence nets, which makes analysis much simpler. Particularly, liveness and safety are easily treated: if the source has initially exactly one token, then each transition fires exactly once and eventually the sink is marked. There is never more than one token in a place. Constraint R_3 states that the output of the RS stage of one DM or component can be transmitted to another DM or component only once: it does not make much sense to send the same information to the same decision maker at several different stages. Constraint R_4 prevents a decision maker from receiving more than one input at the SA stage. The rationale behind this limitation is that information cannot be merged at the SA stage; the IF stage has been specifically introduced to perform such a fusion.

To introduce constraints that will reflect the specific application the organization designer is considering, he can place the appropriate 0s and 1s in the arrays {e, s, F, G, H, C} defining a WDN. The other elements will remain unspecified and will constitute the degrees of freedom of the design. The set of user-defined constraints will be denoted R_u, while the complete set of constraints will be denoted R.

A feasible structure is a well-defined net that satisfies both the structural and the user-defined constraints. The design problem is to determine the set of all feasible structures corresponding to a specific set of constraints.

The notion of subnet introduced earlier defines an order (denoted $\leq$) on the set Ψ^n of all WDNs of dimension n. The concepts of maximal and minimal elements can therefore be defined. A maximal element of the set of all feasible structures is called a maximally connected organization (MAXO). Similarly, a minimal element is called a minimally connected organization (MINO). Maximally and minimally connected organizations can be interpreted as follows. A MAXO is a WDN such that it is not possible to add a single link without violating the set of constraints R. Similarly, a MINO is a WDN such that it is not possible to remove a single link without violating the set of constraints R. The following proposition is a direct consequence of the definition of maximal and minimal elements.

For any given feasible structure Π there is at least one MINO Π_{min} and one MAXO Π_{max} such that $\Pi_{min} \leq \Pi \leq \Pi_{max}$. Note that the net Π need not be a feasible. There is indeed no guarantee that a WDN located between a MAXO and a MINO will fulfill the constraints R, since such a net need not be connected. To address this problem, the concept of a simple path is used.

Let Π be a WDN that satisfies constraint R_1 and whose source and sink have been merged together into a single external place. A simple path of Π is a directed elementary circuit which includes the (merged) source and sink places. Since the Petri net representing Π is a marked graph, a simple path is a minimal support S-invariant of Π whose component corresponding to the external place is equal to 1. Note that if the latter property is not satisfied, the S-invariant is an internal loop of the net. The simple paths of a given WDN are themselves WDNs. We will denote by $Sp(R_u)$ the set of all simple paths of the WDN that satisfies the user constraints R_u:

$$Sp(R_u) = \{sp_1, \ldots, sp_r\} \qquad (8)$$

We will denote by $\bigcup Sp(R_u)$ the set of all possible unions of elements of $Sp(R_u)$, augmented with the null element φ of Ψ^n; i.e., the WDN with all elements identically equal to zero. The union of two elements of $\bigcup Sp(R_u)$ is the WDN composed of all the simple paths included in either one of the two considered elements. Every WDN, element of the set $\bigcup Sp(R_u)$, satisfies the connectivity constraint R_1; furthermore, a feasible structure that fulfills the constraint R_1 is an element of $\bigcup Sp(R_u)$.

The following proposition characterizes the set of all feasible organizations: Π is a feasible structure if and only if Π is a union of simple paths; i.e., $\Pi \in \bigcup Sp(R_u)$: and Π is bounded by at least one MINO and one MAXO. Note that in this approach, the incremental unit leading from a WDN to its immediate superordinate is a simple path and not an individual link. In generating organizational structures with simple paths, the connectivity constraint R_1 is automatically satisfied.

An algorithm has been developed (Remy et al. 1988) which generates, once the user-defined constraints are specified, the MINOs and the MAXOs which characterize the set of all organizational structures that satisfy the designer's requirements. The next step of the analysis consists of putting the MINOs and the MAXOs in their actual context, to give them a physical interpretation. If the organization designer is interested in a given pair of MINO and MAXO, because they contain interactions that are deemed desirable for the specific application, he can further investigate the intermediate nets by considering the chain of nets that are obtained by adding simple paths to the MINO until the MAXO is reached.

This methodology provides the designer of organizational information structures with a rational way to handle a problem whose combinatorial complexity is very large.

5. Data-Flow Structures

In an alternative approach to the generation of information structures, Andreadakis (1988) uses a five-stage information and decision-making process instead of the four-stage model of the decision maker. This approach has allowed the introduction of two additional design specifications: the degree of complexity of the organization and the degree of redundancy. The first measure addresses the complexity that results from transitions needing many different inputs to be enabled. The second reflects the number of output places associated with each transition.

The five generic stages of information processing are initial processing (IP), data fusion (DF), middle processing (MP), results fusion (RF) and final processing (FP). As data are received they are processed in the IP stage to obtain the situation assessment. Information (local or partial situation assessments) from several IP stages is fused in the DF stage to produce a global situation assessment. This is processed in the MP stage to generate options or alternative courses of action. These results are fused together in the RF stage to eliminate conflicting or infeasible options. Finally, a response is selected from the available options in the FP stage.

Not all stages need be present in an information structure. An information flow path with all five stages defines flow type 1 (Fig. 3).

Some MP transitions may generate the output of the organization (RF and FP stages null) as shown in flow type 2 while some IP transitions may provide results for fusion at an RF stage (DF and MP stages null) as in flow type 3. The data-flow structures (DFS) are classified according to the flow types of their information flow paths. If all the paths are of flow type 1, then the DFS belongs to class 1. If some paths are of flow type 1 and some of flow type 2, the DFS class is 12. The feasible classes are: 1, 2, 3, 12, 13 and 123. Class 23 is infeasible because flow type 2 and flow type 3 cannot exchange information: the flow type 2 information paths have data for fusion and DF transitions, while the flow type 3 information paths have results for fusion and RF transitions. A DFS with all three flow types (class 123) is shown in Fig. 4.

The grammar rules for the connectivity of the processing transitions are:

(a) exactly one MP node can receive data from a DF node;

(b) exactly one FP node can receive data from an RF node;

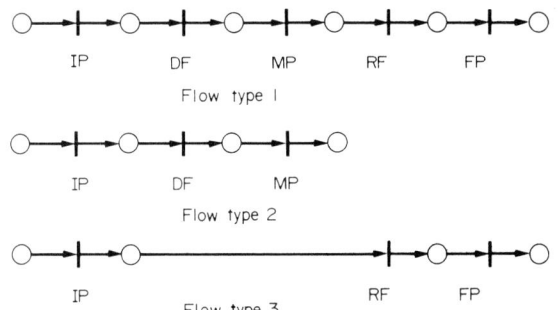

Figure 3
Basic flow types

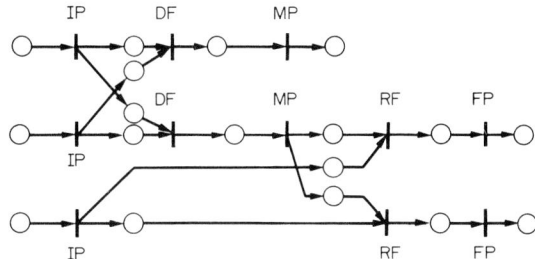

Figure 4
Data-flow structure with all three flow types

(c) one IP transition for each input to the organization; and

(d) one FP transition for each output of the organization.

The generation of data-flow structures takes into account the complexity and redundancy of information processing that is required by the task. The degree of complexity of a DF transition is defined as the number of transitions that feed data to the DF transition. The degree of complexity of the DF stage is defined as the maximum of the degrees of complexity of the DF transitions. The term complexity is justified by the observation that the more data that are fed to a fusion node, the more complex the processing that takes place.

The need for redundancy of information within the structure arises from survivability considerations and topological factors. The degree of redundancy of an IP transition is defined as the number of fusion stages that receive the output data of the IP transition. The degree of redundancy of the DF stage is defined as the maximum of the degrees of redundancy of the IP transitions. The term redundancy is justified by the fact that the same information is communicated to more than one fusion node and is therefore redundant in the data-flow structure.

The degree of complexity of an RF transition, the degree of redundancy of an MP transition, and the degrees of complexity and redundancy of the RF stage are similarly defined. A data-flow structure with degree of complexity $c_1 = 2$ and redundancy $r_1 = 2$ of the DF stage, and degree of complexity $c_2 = 3$ and redundancy $r_2 = 3$ of the RF stage is shown in Fig. 5.

The algorithm for the generation of data-flow structures is based on the grammar rules and is parametrized by the choice of flow types that should exist in the design. It produces the incidence matrix of the corresponding Petri net. In order to generate data-flow structures in a consistent, methodical way, the design parameters are varied between the minimum and maximum values they may obtain. The algorithm consists of seven steps.

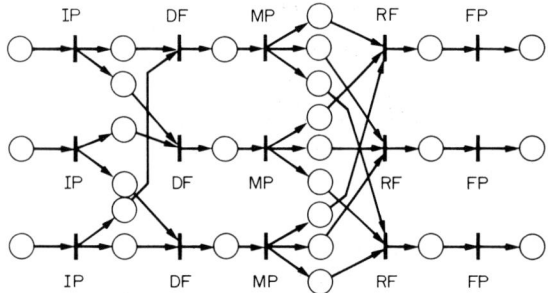

Figure 5
Data-flow structure: $c_1 = 2, r_1 = 2, c_2 = 3, r_2 = 3$

(a) *Step 1.* Select the class of the DFS on the basis of the requirements of the application.

(b) *Step 2.* Select the number n_1 of initial processing (IP) transitions that provide data for fusion (DF stage). Let n_2 be the number of initial processing (IP) transitions that provide results for fusion (RF stage). The total number n of IP transitions is

$$n = n_1 + n_2 \qquad (9)$$

(c) *Step 3.* Select the degree of complexity c_1 and the degree of redundancy r_1 of the DF stage. The number p of output places of IP transitions that belong to the set P_2 is

$$p = n_1 r_1 \qquad (10)$$

and the number k of data fusion transitions is

$$k = n_1 (r_1 / c_1) \qquad (11)$$

For the pair (r_1, c_1) to be feasible (i.e., for all transitions of the stage to have the same degree of complexity and degree of redundancy), the number k must be integer. Another constraint on k is that it be no larger than the number of available processing assets. Since each DF transition is connected to one middle processing (MP) transition, the number of MP transitions is also equal to k.

(d) *Step 4.* Since one IP transition is connected to each place that represents an input to the organization, and exactly one MP transition is connected to each output place of a DF transition, the corresponding elements of the incidence matrix can be assigned the values of 1 or 0.

(e) *Step 5.* Select the number k_2 of MP transitions that provide results for fusion (at the RF stage). Let k_1 be the number of middle processing transitions that produce outputs. The total number of MP transitions is

$$k = k_1 + k_2 \qquad (12)$$

(f) *Step 6.* Select the degree of complexity c_2 and the degree of redundancy r_2 of the RF stage. The number q of output places of IP transitions and MP transitions is

$$q = (n_2 + k_2) r_2 \qquad (13)$$

and the number of results fusion transitions, m, is

$$m = (n_2 + k_2)(r_2/c_2) \qquad (14)$$

For the pair (r_2, c_2) to be feasible (i.e., for all transitions of the stage to have the same degree of complexity and degree of redundancy) m must be integer. The second constraint on m is

$$m \leqslant a \qquad (15)$$

where a is the number of available information processing units. Since each RF transition is connected to one FP transition, the number of FP transitions is also equal to m.

(g) *Step 7.* Since each RF transition has exactly one output place, each FP transition has exactly one input place; exactly one place representing an output of the DFS is connected to an MP transition which produces a DFS output; and, finally, exactly one output place is connected to each FP transition, and the remaining entries of the incidence matrix are determined.

Several data-flow structures are generated by the algorithm. In order to select the feasible structures (i.e., those that are appropriate for the task) the designer must consider the suitability of the structure to the information processing required by the task. This is accomplished by analyzing the resulting structure and obtaining suitable measures of performance. Such measures include accuracy which is a measure of the quality of the information processing, another is response time, which is a measure of the timeliness of the response, another is throughput rate, and still others are information consistency, synchronization and coordination.

5. Conclusion

A framework for the quantitative modelling of organizational information structures has been presented; the formalism of Petri nets has been used to develop explicit graphical representations of the structures that are supported by algebraic representations. Two different algorithms for generating alternative structures that meet a variety of structural and application-specific constraints have been presented. The first one, the lattice algorithm, generates the complete set of partially ordered structures. The second one parametrizes the design with respect to the degree of complexity and the degree of redundancy required in the data-flow structure.

The mathematical framework and the algorithms characterize organizations that have fixed structures; i.e., the interconnections do not depend on the information processing task itself or on changes in the resources available to the organization. Current research is focused on the characterization of variable information structures using predicate transition nets, a form of higher-level nets.

Bibliography

Andreadakis S K 1988 Analysis and synthesis of decision-making organizations, Ph.D. thesis LIDS-TH-1740. Laboratory for Information and Decision Systems, MIT, Cambridge, Massachusetts
Commoner F, Holt A 1971 Marked directed graphs. *J. Comput. Syst. Sci.* **5**, 511–23
Galbraith J R 1977 *Organization Design*. Addison–Wesley, Reading, Massachusetts
Keene P G W, Scott Morton M S 1978 *Decision support systems: An organizational perspective*. Addison–Wesley, Reading, Massachusetts
Levis A H 1984 Information processing and decision-making organizations: A mathematical description. *Large Scale Syst.* **7**, 151–63
Reisig W 1985 *Petri Nets: An Introduction*. Springer-Verlag, Berlin
Remy P A, Levis A H 1988 On the generation of organizational architectures using Petri Nets. In: Rozenberg G (ed.) *Advances in Petri Nets*. Springer, Berlin
Remy P A, Levis A H, Jin V Y 1988 On the design of distributed organizational structures. *Automatica* **24**, 81–86

A. H. Levis
[Massachusetts Institute of Technology,
Cambridge, Massachusetts, USA]

Problem Formulation

Most models of planning and design, problem solving and decision making begin with a problem formulation phase. This phase, sometimes labelled problem definition, problem identification or problem diagnosis, is concerned with gathering information about the problem and classifying or describing the problem in sufficient detail so that the uncertainty and risk associated with subsequent action is reduced.

In recent years, researchers and practitioners have shown a special interest in the problem formulation phase. Because it is one of the first phases in a larger process, problem formulation can determine the direction of all succeeding phases. For example, if a problem is formulated as a technical problem when it would be better understood as a personnel problem, then this can lead to ineffective planning and loss of confidence in the planners or the process.

Determining which formulation of a problematic situation is the "correct" or preferable focus is not an easy task. It is unlikely that an individual can tell *a priori* from the syntax or semantics of a problem statement whether or not it will produce good solutions or ideas. For this reason, and because many complex problems require that multiple actions be taken to address multiple issues, a thorough exploration of the situation is often recommended.

This article is concerned with the problem formulation process, the factors that affect this process, and how problem formulation can be better managed to avoid committing a type III error (solving the "wrong" problem or a suboptimal problem). For simplification, the term "planning" will be used throughout this article to refer to planning and design, problem solving and decision making. While the focus of this article is on problems, many of the concepts expressed herein also apply to opportunities.

1. Definition and Description of a Problem

To understand the problem formulation process, we must first understand what a problem is. Most definitions of a problem focus on the difference between an existing (or anticipated) state and a desired state. A lack of clarity about the existing state, the desired state and/or how to get from the former to the latter is what makes the situation problematic. Whether or not a problem exists if no one is there to perceive it is open to debate.

Problem formulation is not so easily defined. In part, this is due to the fact that problem formulation is a process rather than a condition. To define a process one must understand and describe the essential steps in it. Because thinking is by nature a covert act, it has been difficult for researchers to observe the process. In addition, there has been a difference of opinion concerning when the formulation process begins. Regardless of whether or not an undetected problem is really a problem, no purposeful action will be taken until perception occurs. Some researchers have separated problem finding from problem formulation.

Problem finding involves recognizing that there is a discrepancy between actual and desired states. Recognition may occur immediately, but more likely it will depend on the nature of the discrepancy (its severity, variety, persistence, clarity) and other demands on the planner. A situation that is not defined as a problem may resurface as factors in the situation or demands on the planner change.

Problem formulation occurs once a situation is recognized as problematic. If the situation is familiar, the problem may be quickly defined. If the situation is not familiar (because the actual or desired state is unclear or unfamiliar), the process may be put on hold or a search initiated for more information. A search for more information will seek to determine what is part of the problem and what is not, how various parts of the problem are related to each other (e.g., causal, reciprocal, collateral) and whether or not more information is needed to accurately define or describe the problem. A situation may be difficult to formulate because information is simply not available (or is too costly to acquire) or because the problem is really many problems closely intertwined (i.e., a mess). Under these circumstances a planner might put the problem on hold, select a small part of the situation to address (moving incrementally) or try to gather more information (attacking the problem with a more sophisticated array of tools). These approaches suggest that a certain amount of cycling can occur within the formulation process, just as it does within and between the other phases of the planning process.

Given these descriptions of problem finding and problem formulation, problem finding might be defined as the process of recognizing that a problem exists. Problem formulation, then, is the process of understanding and defining the characteristics of a problem. These characteristics will relate to the current situation and the desired situation.

2. Factors Affecting Problem Formulation

There are three factors which can affect the formulation process. These are: the capabilities and experiences of the planners; the complexities of the problem; and the planning environment (Fig. 1).

Problem Formulation

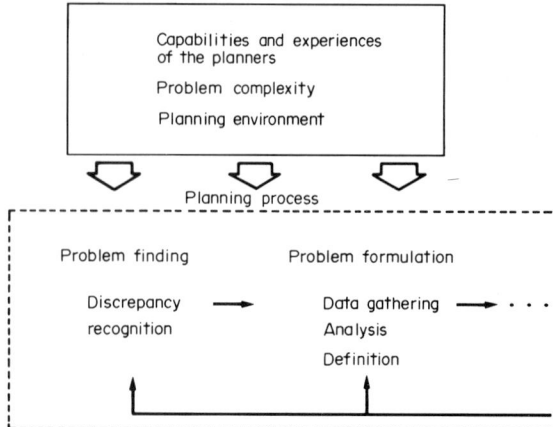

Figure 1
Factors affecting the problem formulation process

2.1 Capabilities and Experiences of the Planners

As suggested in Sect. 1, gathering and processing information is essential to the problem formulation process. Humans have several characteristics related to these activities which appear to be invariant across individuals and tasks. For example, there are five human senses used in gathering information. Although some people can see small, detailed objects better than others, and some people can see objects at a distance better than others, the limits of sight are fairly well defined. The same is true of the other sensory systems. Mechanical and electronic devices such as microscopes, telescopes and audio amplifiers are frequently used to augment these systems, but many problems emit certain cues prior to the use of these devices (e.g., a problem precipitated by negligence), and many cues are difficult to sense or measure at all (e.g., the mood of a department).

For storing information, humans have three types of memory: sensory stores, which exist for each sensory system and represent data in literal, unanalyzed form for very short periods of time; short-term memory, which is small but very fast; and long-term memory, which is very large with fast retrieval but slow storage times. While processing within these memories may operate in parallel (e.g., multiple processing of sensory stores and parallel processing of chunks of information in short-term memory), it appears that data passes between memory types sequentially. These characteristics limit the extent to which large quantities of data can be processed, since short-term memory is not large enough to hold all the elements of a problem and only information that has been used recently or frequently is likely to reside in long-term memory.

Limitations on gathering and processing information appear to affect how individuals draw inferences. A formulation is sometimes selected, for example, because it led to a satisfactory resolution in the past, even if the circumstances are now different. Information that is acquired early is often given more credence than information acquired later. In fact, a conscious attempt to discredit contradictory evidence may occur. On occasion, small samples of data are deemed representative of the population from which they are drawn and causal relationships are often ascribed to variables that are observed together when in reality they are being affected by another variable (e.g., sales-staff turnover and customer decline, which are being affected by increased competition).

In addition to physiological characteristics and limitations, recent studies of Jungian psychological types suggest that certain individuals may be predisposed to viewing different problems in the same way. According to this theory, there are four psychological types: sensation-thinking, intuition-thinking, sensation-feeling and intuition-feeling. The sensation and intuition orientations represent different ways of gathering information and can be thought of as extremes on a continuum. While sensation types dislike problems unless there are standard ways to solve them (and thus are inclined to narrow the scope of a problem quickly), intuitive types tend to keep the overall problem in mind, maintaining an openness to continually redefining the problem. The thinking and feeling orientations also represent opposite ends on a continuum, with thinking types more likely to emphasize a logical, systematic form of inquiry and feeling types more concerned with human interaction, feelings and emotions. Thus, it would appear that a person's psychological orientation would affect the amount of time devoted to formulation and where that attention is focused.

Finally, individual characteristics affect interpersonal communications. While it is not clear what internal language people use for processing information, natural language is generally used to communicate ideas to others. That is, all concepts and observations must be translated into English, Spanish, French, and so on. Some languages simply do not have words to describe certain concepts; and because of short-term and long-term memory limitations, the average person may have a working vocabulary of only a few thousand words. In the English language, the average working vocabulary for an adult is about 10 000 words, less than 2% of a complete vocabulary. Thus, a word or phrase used to communicate an aspect of a problem may be inadequate and/or interpreted in different ways by different people. While human memory capacity and processing power can be supplemented through chalk boards, flipcharts and computers, language is not so easily enhanced.

2.2 Problem Complexity

Complexity is a concept that is difficult to fully comprehend. The classic definition of complexity focuses on the number of elements in a system and their interactions. The greater the number of elements and interactions, the more complex the system.

While theoretically it is possible to talk about problem complexity in absolute terms, in reality what appears complex to one person may be straightforward to another. For example, a chaotic nonlinear system is perceived as complex if your frame of reference is forecasting, but it may be perceived as simple if your frame of reference is probability distributions. If you are not familiar with probability distributions, the problem may never appear simple. As this example illustrates, "experienced" complexity is a function of the capabilities and experiences of the planner(s). Familiarity with the problem, demands on attention, computational efficiency and interest in the problem mediate the extent to which a problem is perceived as simple or complex.

Human responses to inordinate complexity will vary. Sometimes people will continue to search for a model or heuristic that will bring clarity to the problem; other times people make simplifying assumptions. The risk of reducing a problem to manageable proportions, of course, is that important dimensions of the problem may be overlooked. Herein lies the importance of Ashby's law of requisite variety.

Ashby first wrote about the law of requisite variety as it pertains to control systems. According to Ashby, the complexity of a control system must match the system to be controlled. Too little control can lead to underdesign and system failure; too much control is inefficient and noisome. Applied to problem formulation, Ashby's law suggests that to address a problem adequately, the complexity of the formulation must match the complexity of the problem. If important dimensions of a problem are overlooked or taken for granted, solutions may be inefficient or the problem may resurface or manifest itself in other ways. Two recent events, one a success story and the other a tragedy, serve to illustrate this point.

In 1984, Bell Laboratories announced that Narenda Karmarkar had found a more efficient algorithm for solving linear programming problems. Rather than searching a multidimensional polytope from vertex to vertex, which is how the simplex method works, Karmarkar's approach begins in the interior of the polytope and uses projective geometry to find the best solution. By working from the interior, this approach recognizes another (spatial) dimension to the problem. To date, Karmarkar's approach has produced computations that are faster than the old method by a factor of ten or better.

The US space program, an extraordinary technological accomplishment, provides the second example. When the *Challenger* Space Shuttle disaster occurred, people naturally looked for a technical explanation. Failed O-rings, which were not designed to withstand the unusually cold weather experienced at launch time, were believed to be at fault. However, the O-rings were only part of the problem. Warnings from managers and technical specialists had gone unheeded right up to the launch. Not only had technical systems been taken for granted, but organizational systems as well.

Changing the scope of a problem statement (in particular, broadening the scope), often leads to the discovery of other dimensions of the problem. While one can only speculate on the effects that broadening the scope had or might have had for the above mentioned problems, the exercise is illustrative. For example, by recognizing that the reason for concern with O-rings is to ensure a successful mission, a larger array of issues and ideas is revealed (e.g., recommendations of technical experts, the health of the astronauts, public opinion, etc.).

2.3 Planning Environment

Every system is part of a larger or broader system which influences its behavior. Every organization, for example, resides within an operating environment (i.e., customers, competitors, suppliers) and a general environment (i.e., government regulations, economic conditions, social norms) which shape and limit organizational behavior. Since planning is conducted within an organizational context, it also is subject to these and other influences.

A number of factors in the immediate planning environment have been suggested in the literature. These include the number of groups involved (stakeholders), coalition development, time and money constraints, impact on organizational structure and resource allocations, and environmental stability. Each of these can potentially affect the formulation process as well.

The number of stakeholders is a factor that recently has been of special interest to researchers. Stakeholders are representatives of the operating and general environments of an organization that have a stake in the outcome. As the number of stakeholders increases arithmetically, the number of possible relationships between them increases geometrically. The more differentiated the belief structures of these stakeholders, the more difficult the formulation process becomes. In this sense, the number of stakeholders might be seen as a form of environmental complexity.

In a highly political process, where a large number of people are involved and a great deal appears to be at stake, problem statements may be offered for many different purposes. Besides the hope that a statement will lead to technically sound solutions, problem statements are used to keep people involved in the process, to minimize perceptual differences of the problem, to identify allies, to protect an agency's turf, to circumscribe the problem, to obscure or eliminate certain solutions, and to bring the process to a close, to name just a few. These purposes can be categorized according to who or what they promote: group outcome (e.g., to generate solutions), group process (e.g., to bring the process to a close) or self-interests (e.g., to protect an agency's turf). A statement that is offered for one purpose (e.g., to generate solutions) but interpreted as serving a different purpose (e.g., to obscure or eliminate certain solutions) can be dysfunctional for a group.

Time is another factor that can affect the formulation process. Perceived time pressures often cause people to curtail the formulation process or reduce a problem to a form that is familiar. Frequently, such an interpretation of the problem is very narrow in scope. While a narrow formulation of the problem can be efficient, it can also lead to a type III error if important dimensions of the problem are overlooked.

3. Managing the Formulation Process

Most formulation efforts begin with an exploration of the problematic (or opportunistic) situation. Through exploration, individuals develop cognitive maps which ultimately guide their choices and focus. At this early stage, it is important that all dimensions of the situation are identified, since this forms the basis for selecting the level (scope) at which to act and evaluate the final plan or design.

As suggested in Sect. 2, there are several factors which will affect the formulation process and choice of scope. In some case, these factors may promote an efficient formulation and resolution of the problem; in other cases the result might be a type III error.

Broadly speaking, planners can pursue two options to avoid solving the "wrong" problem. The first is to be aware of the circumstances that lead to premature narrowing of scope and premature closure. Familiarity with a solution and perceived time pressure are two factors which sometimes lead to this. Another more subtle factor occurs when the problem has been formulated by another party. For a variety of reasons, not the least of which is the anxiety most people feel from simply having a complex problem to solve, it is easy to accept someone else's formulation. If that person is in a position of responsibility or authority and appears to have invested some time in the formulation process, a person may be even more likely to accept the formulation without questioning its intent.

A similar result can occur when the situation is highly political and the number of stakeholders seems unmanageable. While limiting the number of stakeholders or the extent of their involvement is often appealing, the risk of simplification is that people who will be important in later stages of the planning process will be disenfranchised and the benefit of their insight during formulation will be lost (i.e., one or more dimensions of the problem will be missing).

The second option that can be pursued is to employ techniques and tools for examining the various dimensions of a problem (Table 1). The appropriateness of a technique can be determined in part by the factors outlined in Sect. 2. Very complex problems will have many dimensions and there will likely be a number of people with a stake in the outcome. Techniques such as brainstorming, brainwriting, nominal group technique (NGT) and Delphi can be used at various phases in the planning process, including the formulation phase. Each is capable of producing a list of problem statements for discussion. Nominal group technique and Delphi are particularly good for dealing with people who do not know each other well

Table 1
Techniques for managing problem dimensions. x, direct function, (x), indirect function

Technique	Reference	Function		
		Generating dimensions	Structuring dimensions	Evaluating dimensions
Brainstorming	Van Gundy (1981)	x		
Brainwriting	Van Gundy (1981)	x		
Nominal group technique	Delbecq et al. (1976)	x		x
Delphi	Delbecq et al. (1976)	x		x
Function expansion	Nadler (1981)		x	x
Interpretive structural modelling	Sage (1977)		x	(x)
Dialectical inquiry	Schwenk and Thomas (1983)	(x)	(x)	x
Devil's advocate	Schwenk and Thomas (1983)	(x)	(x)	x
Problem–purpose expansion	Volkema (1983)	x	x	(x)

or who do not get along. These two techniques are also designed to feed information back to the participants for review and evaluation.

Function expansion is a technique for taking the information that has been generated using NGT or Delphi and organizing the problem statements into a logical hierarchy. In this hierarchy, problem statements are arranged according to scope, from the statement with the narrowest scope to the statement with the broadest scope.

Another technique for organizing problem statements is interpretive structural modelling (ISM). While function expansion is primarily concerned with hierarchical relationships, ISM recognizes that influences and relationships can be cyclic. Therefore, ISM is a more generic technique for structuring problem statements. (There also are a number of quantitative techniques for structuring dimensions, including regression analysis.)

Each of the techniques uses some form of external memory (e.g., chalk board, newsprint) as a way of compensating for limitations in the human information-processing system. Computer programs that help with processing information (checklists, cognitive mapping, etc.) provide a similar function.

Even with these techniques and tools, however, there is no guarantee that critical dimensions of a problematic situation will be identified, and eventually a planning team is likely to narrow its focus to certain dimensions of the problem. This reduction may be based on assumptions (true or false) about the situation. Therefore, assumption testing should take place at key points throughout the planning process to check validity.

Two techniques have been suggested for testing assumptions: dialectical inquiry and devil's advocate. Dialectical inquiry involves the use of structured debate. Two opposing views of a situation are presented and argued, which in turn helps to define the assumptions associated with those views. The effect of the devil's advocate approach is similar. In this case, however, one individual is appointed resident critic.

Problem–purpose expansion provides a more systematic way of broadening the scope of a problem and implicitly challenging assumptions. The technique works by asking "What are we trying to accomplish by . . . ?" For example, one reason why city planners may want to "develop an urban rail system" is to "improve commuter transportation." This question can be repeated until no additional reformulations can be found. For example, one reason for wanting to improve commuter transportation might be to keep businesses in the city. The process reminds participants of higher-level objectives and opens up new dimensions of the problem (e.g., other forms of transportation, the importance of a tax base).

In most cases, however, each of these techniques is only as good as the people involved in the process. Since not all aspects of a problematic situation will be known to every participant, it is important that people with different bases of information representing as many dimensions of the problem as possible be selected to participate. It might also be appropriate to include people of differing psychological types.

4. Conclusion

Albert Einstein once wrote that the formulation of a problem is often more essential than its solution, which may be merely a matter of mathematical or experimental skill. Finding the correct formulation, however, is no easy task, particularly when the problem is complex.

Much of the difficulty with the formulation process is due to human physical limitations. The number and range of human senses and the size and processing speed of human memory affect our ability to see all the dimensions of a problem and how they interrelate. This is compounded by the psychological anxiety that many people feel when faced with a difficult problem, which often leads to moving through the formulation phase too quickly. Indeed, once an alternative is selected, the responsibility for implementation frequently shifts to someone else, thus absolving the formulator of anxiety (at least temporarily).

Mechanical and electronic devices are being developed and improved to augment human perception and processing capabilities. In addition to these tools, a number of techniques are available to assist with information gathering and analysis. These techniques are useful to the extent that they can help to identify the dimensions of a problem, to structure those dimensions and to evaluate them (for oversights and selection of scope). In identifying the dimensions of a problem, both the existing state and the desired state must be understood.

This may not occur immediately. Cycling often occurs within and between the phases of the planning process. In fact, it may not be until a course of action is selected and implementation begun that certain dimensions of a problem are discovered. At this point it becomes even more difficult to reformulate the problem, but nonetheless it is essential if solving the "wrong" problem is to be avoided and the discovery of opportunities to solve multiple problems is to be maximized.

See also: Decision-Problem Structuring; Human Information Processing

Bibliography

Ashby W R 1958 Requisite variety and its implications for the control of complex systems. *Cybernetica* **1**(2), 1–17
Carroll D W 1986 *The Psychology of Language*. Brooks/Cole, Monterey, California
Cowan D A 1986 Developing a process model of problem recognition. *Acad. Manage. Rev.* **11**(4), 763–76

Delbecq A L, Van de Ven A H, Gustafson D H 1976 *Group Techniques for Program Planning.* Scott Foresman, Glenview, Illinois

Hogarth R M 1987 *Judgement and Choice: The Psychology of Decision.* Wiley, New York

Nadler G 1981 *The Planning and Design Approach.* Wiley, New York

Sage A P 1977 *Methodology for Large-Scale Systems.* McGraw–Hill, New York

Schwenk C, Thomas H 1983 Formulating the mess: The role of decision aids in problem formulation. *Omega* **11**(3), 239–52

Van Gundy A 1981 *Techniques for Structured Problem Solving.* Wiley, New York

Volkema R 1983 Problem formulation in planning and design. *Manage. Sci.* **29**(6), 639–52

R. J. Volkema
[American University,
Washington, DC, USA]

Program Evaluation: A Systems and Model-Based Approach

Does the program work? Is it worth the cost? Can and should it be implemented elsewhere? It is the reputed purpose of evaluation to provide answers to these and related questions. Unfortunately, program evaluation has not lived up to expectations. The field of evaluation is littered with efforts which do not adequately address the important issues or objectives; which do not employ valid controls for comparison purposes; which rely on inadequate measures or include expensive collection of data on measures that are in fact never used in the evaluation; which rely on inappropriate measurement methods; or which employ inadequate analytic techniques. Most, if not all, of the above-cited problems could be mitigated by developing, at the beginning of an evaluation effort, a valid and comprehensive evaluation design.

Although there is no stock design that can be taken off-the-shelf and implemented without revision, there should be an approach or process by which such designs can be developed. Indeed, Tien (1987) outlines a systems approach—that is at once purposeful and systematic—for developing valid and comprehensive evaluation designs. The approach was first proposed by Tien (1979) and has since been successfully employed in a number of evaluation efforts (see, for example, Colton et al. (1982) and Tien and Cahn (1986)). While Tien (1987) summarizes, updates and extends his earlier work by emphasizing an approach that is not only systems-oriented in perspective but also model-based, the focus of this article is to highlight a practical application of the systems and model-based approach to program evaluation. In particular, the focus is on how the approach was applied to the evaluation of a national commercial security field-test (CSFT) program, including how the linear statistical model introduced in Tien (1987) was employed to support a "split-area" research design for the CSFT program evaluation. The remainder of this article is devoted to some background issues concerning the CSFT program, the evaluation design employed in the CSFT evaluation, the results of the evaluation conduct and some concluding remarks.

1. Program Background

Given the millions of dollars spent annually in the USA on security surveys and in the subsequent compliance with survey recommendations, the CSFT program (National Institute of Justice 1979) was undertaken to answer the question: Is the crime prevention approach of security surveys effective against commercial crimes? There were several reasons why previous studies (e.g., Chelimsky 1979, Bickman and Rosenbaum 1980) and evaluations (e.g., Lavrakas et al. 1978, Eversen 1979, Pearson 1980) of security survey programs could not provide an answer to this very important question. First, the programs were all parts of larger, more complex crime prevention efforts so that the resultant impacts could not have been attributed solely to the intervention of security surveys. Second, data regarding compliance with survey recommendations were conspicuously lacking; whatever evidence was presented suggested a low level of compliance, thus bringing into question whether the conduct of security surveys resulted in an actual "treatment" of the surveyed establishments. Third, the programs' research designs or selection schemes usually called for a dispersed (i.e., city-, county- or state-wide) focus for the conduct of security surveys, and a poorly controlled before-and-after (i.e., pretreatment and posttreatment) analysis of the crime impact measures. Fourth, the reported crime impacts were almost exclusively about burglary, largely because data on larceny were unavailable and data on robbery were too few.

The CSFT sought to overcome these problems. In particular, the program complexity problem was to be mitigated by the somewhat singular, security-survey-oriented focus of the CSFT; the low-compliance problem was explicitly dealt with by the CSFT, which called for the carrying out of compliance-enhancing activities; and the inadequate research design problem was likewise addressed by the CSFT's strong emphasis on evaluation. However, the inadequate crime-data problem pervading previous studies could not be overcome by the CSFT; again, extreme under-reporting of larcenies and low robbery rates, together with the fact that the resultant security survey recommendations were minimally focused on reducing the opportunities for larcenies and robberies, resulted in a CSFT program that was almost exclusively directed at the commercial crime of burglary.

Although the CSFT program grants were officially awarded by the National Institute of Justice (NIJ) to the

Denver Anti-Crime Council, the Long Beach Police Department and the St Louis Commission on Crime and Law Enforcement in April 1980, program-related activities had been ongoing for more than a year. In particular, and as is the custom in all NIJ-sponsored field tests, a CSFT Program Coordinating Team (PCT) was formed in the latter part of 1978. While identifying candidate cities in which to conduct the CSFT program, the PCT completed the test design (NIJ 1979) for the program in May 1979. This design document reviewed pertinent background material; articulated a set of program purposes, goals and objectives; defined an experimental selection scheme or research design; discussed a number of evaluation-related concerns; and suggested criteria for city selection as well as strategies for program implementation. By the time the evaluation grant was awarded to Public Systems Evaluation, Inc. (PSE) in October 1979, the list of candidate cities had, for all intents and purposes, been reduced to the final three candidates—Denver, Long Beach and St Louis.

Following the grant awards to the three cities in April 1980, the three grantees endeavored to meet the research design requirements of the test design (NIJ 1979) by identifying candidate pairs of commercial test areas (i.e., experimental and control) which had relatively high commercial crime rates as well as other specified characteristics. By October 1980 and following the PSE's review of the submitted site information, the PCT had randomly—by coin tosses—assigned them to experimental and control groups. Subsequently, security surveys were conducted in the experimental areas and several follow-up visits were made both to encourage compliance with survey recommendations and to determine the level of compliance. Finally, in April 1981, it was decided that the formal one-year test or evaluation period could begin. A year later, a final set of compliance checks was made in the experimental areas, while some security surveys were conducted in the control areas.

Because of input from the evaluator, the CSFT program that was eventually implemented in the three cities reflected a revised version of the program stipulated in the test design. First, while the test design called for 20-60 business establishments per test area, the grantees were encouraged for evaluation purposes to select test areas with a larger number of establishments. Second, the emphasis in the test design on establishing a close cooperative relationship between business and police could have resulted in a more complex program where other crime prevention activities (e.g., special police patrols assigned to the experimental areas) might have occurred, and therefore confounded the evaluation findings. Instead, the grantees were advised to cooperate with the businesspeople only to the extent of facilitating the conduct of the security surveys and enhancing compliance with survey recommendations. Third, pairwise-matching commercial areas on the basis of multiple criteria (i.e., crime rates, social demographics, traffic patterns, police community relations, etc.), as originally envisioned in the test design could not be accomplished. In fact, it was not possible to find even one matched pair among the ten pairs proposed by the grantees.

In response to the latter design difficulty, the evaluator developed and implemented an alternative, "split-area" research design in which the surveyed (i.e., experimental) areas were split into two groups according to whether the CSFT crime prevention staff categorized them as treated or untreated. Identifying an establishment as treated meant that it was judged to be less prone to burglary victimization as a result of compliance with the survey recommendations. This conceptual split was undertaken toward the end of the one-year test period by the same police officers and CSFT staff who were initially involved in the conduct of the security surveys; they categorized each surveyed establishment by reviewing from a risk-to-burglary perspective the establishment's compliance with the survey recommendations. Overall, 194 of the surveyed establishments were considered treated, while 236 were considered untreated. Actually, as expected, compliance—as defined by the percentage of recommended changes complied with—was a determining factor in whether an establishment was considered treated; the treated establishments had an average compliance level of 77.3%, as opposed to a 42.4% figure for the untreated establishments. Further, the sets of treated and untreated establishments were determined to be equivalent in terms of the types of business contained in each. In evaluation terms, this would have constituted an experimental design. However, because it was implemented retrospectively, the split-area research design was carried out in a quasi-experimental manner in regard to the CSFT evaluation.

2. Evaluation Design

As indicated earlier, the evaluation design for the CSFT effort was based on an explicit application of the dynamic roll-back approach advanced by Tien (1979, 1987). The roll-back aspect of the approach is reflected in the ordered sequence of interrogatories or steps that must be considered before an evaluation design can be developed: the sequence rolls back in time from (a) a projected look at the range of program characteristics (i.e., from its rationale through its operation and anticipated findings), to (b) a prospective consideration of the threats (i.e., problems and pitfalls) to the validity of the final evaluation, and to (c) a more immediate identification of the evaluation design elements. Thus, the anticipated program characteristics identify the possible threats to validity, which in turn point to the design elements that are necessary to mitigate, if not eliminate, these threats. The dynamic aspect of the approach refers to its nonstationary character; that is, the components of the process must be constantly updated throughout the entire development and implementation phases of the evaluation design. In this manner, the design elements can be adaptively refined if necessary, to account for any new threats to validity which may be caused by previously unidentified program characteristics. In sum, the dynamic roll-back approach is an adaptive process for developing purposeful and systematic evaluation designs.

It was the application of this dynamic roll-back approach that prompted the evaluators to recommend larger test areas, to advise against establishing a closer cooperation between the police and the businesspeople beyond facilitating the conduct of security surveys and enhancing compliance with survey recommendations, and to develop an alternative split-area research design. While details of the conduct of the CSFT evaluation can be found elsewhere (Tien and Cahn 1986), we focus in this section on the split-area research design.

Although splitting the establishments within an area provided a perfect control for neighborhood and other environmental factors (because of the colocation of both treated and untreated establishments in a test area), the retrospective implementation of the design raised a potentially severe regression artifact problem, as recognized by Campbell and Erlebacher (1975). More specifically, because the selection of treated and untreated establishments did not take into account the key measure of crime, the two groups of establishments were not equivalent in terms of this measure; as a result, a selection–regression artifact interaction threatened the validity of the observed impact on crime. In order to correct for this threat to validity, the simple linear model detailed in Tien (1987) was employed; further, the model was able to correct for another problem—a selection–intervention interaction threat to validity—that is typically also a consequence of a retrospectively configured research design. In sum, while the difficulties associated with a retrospectively implemented design would usually preclude it from being effective, it was felt in this case, since the evaluators had environmentally related comparability among the test units as well as a model that corrected for the two most significant statistically related difficulties, that it was justified to say that they had an effective design that yielded valid findings concerning the impact of security surveys on crime. The remainder of this section develops the above model.

Initially, the model assumptions are:

(a) a single selection measure X (i.e., pretreatment crime rate),
(b) a single impact measure Y (i.e., posttreatment crime rate),
(c) two groups: $j = t$ (treated), u (untreated),
(d) a treatment Z_j, where $Z_j = 0$ if $j = u$, and 1 if $j = t$,

(e) an error term e, which is uncorrelated with other measures and possesses an expected value of zero, and
(f) a linear causal relationship between Y_{ij} and X_{ij}; that is,

$$Y_{ij} = a + bZ_j + c_j(X_{ij} - \bar{X}_{..}) + e_{ij} \quad (1)$$

In Eqn. (1), Y_{ij} is the value of impact measure for test unit i in group j, X_{ij} is the value of selection measure for test unit i in group j, e_{ij} is the value of error associated with test unit i in group j, Z_j is the value (i.e., presence) of treatment in group j, and $\bar{X}_{..}$ is $\{X_{ij}\}$ averaged over both i and j (i.e., the "grand mean"). In the above expression, it should be noted that b reflects the (net) impact of the intervention; $c_j \neq 0$ reflects the presence of a selection–regression artifact interaction threat to validity; and $c_u \neq c_t$ reflects the presence of a selection–intervention threat to validity.

In deriving the impact b, let us first find

$$\begin{aligned}\bar{Y}_{.j} &= E[Y_{ij}|j=u] = a + bE[Z_u]\\ &\quad + c_u(\bar{X}_{.u} - \bar{X}_{..}) + E[e_{iu}]\\ &= a + c_u(\bar{X}_{.u} - \bar{X}_{..}) \quad (2)\end{aligned}$$

where E is the expectation value. Similarly,

$$\begin{aligned}\bar{Y}_{.t} &= E[Y_{ij}|j=t] = a + bE[Z_t]\\ &\quad + c_t(\bar{X}_{.t} - \bar{X}_{..}) + E[e_{it}]\\ &= a + b + c_t(\bar{X}_{.t} - \bar{X}_{..}) \quad (3)\end{aligned}$$

Subtracting Eqn. (2) from Eqn. (3) and solving for b, we have:

$$b = \bar{Y}^*_{.t} - \bar{Y}^*_{.u} \quad (4)$$

where

$$\bar{Y}^*_{.j} = \bar{Y}_{.j} - c_j(\bar{X}_{.j} - \bar{X}_{..}), \quad j = t, u \quad (5)$$

An alternative derivation for b is to compute the covariance of Y_{ij} and Z_j, compute the covariance of Y_{ij} and X_{ij}, and solve for b in terms of these covariances. Expressing b as a function of covariances has led to the recognition in the evaluation literature that a covariance adjustment is required when a linear causal relationship is assumed.

The above expressions can perhaps be best understood by reference to a graphical presentation such as Fig. 1. The b displayed in the figure is actually the impact of the intervention on a test unit with $\bar{X}_{..}$ as its selection measure. In general, for a test unit with a different selection measure—say X_a—we have

$$b|X_a = \bar{Y}^*_{.t}|X_a - \bar{Y}^*_{.u}|X_a \quad (6)$$

where

$$\bar{Y}^*_{.j}|X_a = \bar{Y}_{.j} - c_j(\bar{X}_{.j} - X_a), \quad j = t, u \quad (7)$$

It can also be seen from Fig. 1 that if $c_t = c_u$ (i.e., the regression lines are parallel), then $b|X_a = b|\bar{X}_{..} = b$; that is, the impact of the treatment is the same for all

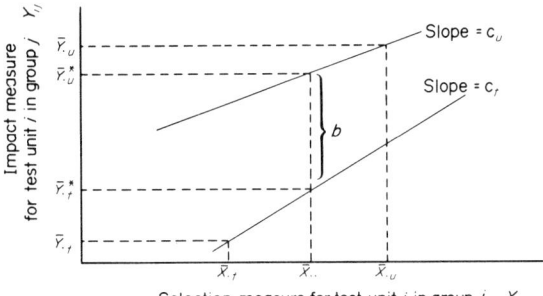

Figure 1
Split-area research design—impact of intervention: b, intervention impact

test units, even if they possess different selection measure values. Further, if $\bar{X}_{.t} = \bar{X}_{.u} = \bar{X}_{..}$ (i.e., the two groups are equivalent), then, as expected, b is simply equal to $(\bar{Y}_{.t} - \bar{Y}_{.u})$.

Finally, in order to determine if the impact b is statistically significant, we must conduct a t-test of the difference between two sample means with the null hypothesis being $b = \bar{Y}^*_{.t} - \bar{Y}^*_{.u} = 0$ and, if it is desirable for the impact to be negative (i.e., a decrease in crime rate), the alternative hypothesis being $b = (\bar{Y}^*_{.t} - \bar{Y}^*_{.u}) < 0$. More specifically, assuming T total treated units, U total untreated units, and a pooled sample standard deviation of $S(\bar{Y}^*_{it} - \bar{Y}^*_{iu})$, the t-statistic is given by

$$t\text{-statistic} = \frac{(\bar{Y}^*_{.t} - \bar{Y}^*_{.u})}{S(Y^*_{it} - Y^*_{iu})(1/T + 1/U)^{1/2}} \quad (8)$$

with $(T + U - 2)$ degrees of freedom. The pooled sample standard deviation is

$$S(Y^*_{it} - Y^*_{iu}) = \left[\frac{(T-1)S^2(Y^*_{it}) + (U-1)S^2(Y^*_{iu})}{T + U - 2}\right]^{1/2} \quad (9)$$

where

$$S^2(Y^*_{it}) = \sum_{i=1}^{T} \frac{(Y^*_{it} - \bar{Y}^*_{.t})^2}{(T-1)} \quad (10)$$

and

$$S^2(Y^*_{iu}) = \sum_{i=1}^{U} \frac{(Y^*_{iu} - \bar{Y}^*_{.u})^2}{(U-1)} \quad (11)$$

and, based on Eqn. (5),

$$Y^*_{ij} = Y_{ij} - c_j(X_{ij} - \bar{X}_{..}), \quad j = t, u \quad (12)$$

(It should of course be noted that, in the above computations, the Y_{ij} and the X_{ij} variables are measured, while all other variables are derived.) Now, assuming a type I error or level of significance of $a = 0.05$, then we would undertake a one-sided test and would "accept" or not reject the alternative hypothesis that $b < 0$ if the t-statistic value in Eqn. (8) is less than $(-t_{0.05})$ with $(T + U - 2)$ degrees of freedom. Obviously, if $(T + U - 2) > 30$ (which was typically the case in the CSFT effort), then the t-test becomes a z-test, which is based on the unit normal distribution. In the latter case, we would not reject the alternative hypothesis that $b < 0$, if the computed z—as computed by Eqn. (8)—is less than $-z_{0.05} = -1.64$.

Finally, it should be noted that the one-selection-measure model developed here can be extended. For example, for the general case of K selection measures (i.e., $X_k, k = 1, 2, \ldots, K$), Eqn. (5) becomes:

$$\bar{Y}^*_{.j} = \bar{Y}_{.j} - \sum_{k=1}^{K} c_{kj}(\bar{X}_{k.j} - \bar{X}_{k..}), \quad j = t, u \quad (13)$$

where c_{kj} is defined as the slope of the regression line of impact measure Y on the selection measure X_k within group j. Similarly, the model could be straightforwardly extended to include more than two groups and situations where the treatment variable is not just binary but also continuous (e.g., in vaccination studies where the dosage amount is critical).

3. Evaluation Conduct

The CSFT evaluation shed light on three critical issues: the impact of security surveys on commercial burglary, the impact of security surveys on fear, and the impact of business–police relations on the conduct of security surveys and the compliance with survey recommendations. In this article, we consider only the first issue as it relates to the split-area design; the other impacts are discussed in Tien and Cahn (1986).

A common, but not statistically sound, approach to considering the impact of a treatment is to compare the before (i.e., pretreatment) values or statistics of an impact measure with its after (i.e., posttreatment) statistics. Table 1 provides the burglary rate statistics (i.e., number of burglaries per establishment per year) in terms of treated and untreated establishments, which, as indicated earlier, were categorized from a risk-of-burglary perspective that was based on which survey recommendations had been complied with. In reviewing Table 1, note that although there are some impressive changes in burglary rate on a pretreatment-posttreatment basis, the changes are not statistically significant, as per a one-sided z-test of the difference between two sample means at a 0.05 level of significance. The reason for this apparent contradiction is, of course, the dispersed nature of the distribution of the burglary rate (as reflected in the relatively large standard deviation figures); in fact, if the coefficient of variation (i.e., ratio of the standard deviation of the burglary rate distribution to its average) is computed for each set of rate and standard deviation entries in Table 1, quite large coefficient of variation values are found, ranging between 2.37 and 4.13.

Careful scrutiny of Table 1 reveals two interesting trends: the treated establishments experienced a

Table 1
Commercial burglary statistics: pretreatment–posttreatment design analysis (pretreatment period, October 1, 1979–September 30, 1980; posttreatment period, April 1, 1981–March 31, 1982)

City	Number of establishments	Pretreatment period		Posttreatment period		Percent change in rate	z-statistic[a]
		Rate	Standard deviation	Rate	Standard deviation		
Denver							
treated	70	0.257	0.652	0.114	0.363	−55.6%	−1.60
untreated	76	0.184	0.687	0.237	0.709	+28.8%	0.47
total	146	0.219	0.670	0.178	0.572	−18.7%	−0.56
Long Beach							
treated	62	0.323	1.113	0.226	0.525	−30.0%	−0.62
untreated	63	0.079	0.326	0.095	0.390	+20.3%	0.25
total	125	0.200	0.823	0.160	0.465	−20.0%	−0.47
St Louis							
treated	62	0.210	0.792	0.290	0.687	+38.1%	0.60
untreated	97	0.247	0.693	0.278	0.800	+12.6%	0.29
total	159	0.233	0.731	0.283	0.756	+21.5%	0.60
All cities							
treated	194	0.263	0.863	0.206	0.538	−21.7%	−0.78
untreated	236	0.182	0.616	0.216	0.684	+18.7%	0.57
total	430	0.219	0.738	0.212	0.622	−3.2%	−0.15

[a] At a 0.05 level of significance, the z-statistic must be less than −1.64 for the change to be statistically significant: using this criterion, none of the reductions in commercial burglary rates listed above is statistically significant

decrease in burglary (except in the case of St Louis), while at the same time the untreated establishments experienced an increase. Again, although encouraging, these trends are not credible since they are based on a nonexperimental or weak pretreatment–posttreatment research design that cannot take into account a number of environmental factors that might have changed from the pretreatment period to the posttreatment period. In particular, it is important not only to consider the burglary statistics of the treated and untreated establishments separately, on a pretreatment–posttreatment basis, but also to compare both sets of statistics in a single statistical test, as is done in the split-area analysis. In this manner, any environmental changes—except for the treatment (i.e., security surveys with compliance)—which might affect the treated establishments would be taken into account by considering their effect on the untreated establishments (which are colocated in the same areas as the treated establishments).

Table 2 contains the results of applying the split-area model developed in Sect. 2 to the burglary statistics in Table 1. Overall, the net impact of security surveys (with a high level of compliance) was determined to be an 11.9% decrease in burglary rate. While not statistically significant, this result is still quite impressive and somewhat credible in that it is based on a quasiexperimental split-area design that, although retrospectively implemented, can take possible environmental changes into account. Of critical interest are the Denver results. On a 12-month basis, the net impact of the CSFT program in Denver was a statistically significant 64.8% reduction in burglary rate, while on an extended 21-month basis, the corresponding figure was an even more significant 74.2% reduction. (Since Denver maintained its crime statistics on a readily accessible computer, it was decided in the interest of research to obtain additional data from that city.) These statistically significant and credible results constitute strong evidence of the effectiveness of commercial security surveys—given that survey recommendations are complied with—as a strategy for reducing the incidence of commercial burglary. Furthermore, because the 21-month results represent an improvement over the 12-month results, there is some evidence that the effectiveness is lasting.

Several other comments should be made regarding Table 2. First, given Long Beach's quite favorable results when employing the pretreatment–posttreatment design (see Table 1), it is surprising to see in Table 2 that the net CSFT impact under the split-area design was a 63.0% increase. Actually, it should be noted that it was inappropriate to have applied the split-area design to the Long Beach burglary statistics; the reason being that the corresponding pretreatment burglary rates of the two groups (i.e., treated and untreated) of establishments were very different, as indicated in Table 1. This significant difference, in turn, implied that the two groups of establishments were not even closely comparable or equivalent with respect to burglary, so that no statistical model—including the split-area model—could have corrected for the difference. In sum, the net impact statistic for Long Beach in Table 2 is not valid. Second, as might have been expected given the results in Table 1, the net impact of a 9.9% increase in burglary rate for St Louis

Table 2
Commercial burglary statistics: split-area design analysis

Statistic	12-month evaluation periods				21-month evaluation periods in Denver
	Denver	Long Beach	St Louis	Total	
$\bar{X}_{..}$	0.219	0.200	0.233	0.219	0.163
$\bar{X}_{.t}$	0.257	0.323	0.210	0.263	0.171
$\bar{X}_{.u}$	0.184	0.079	0.247	0.182	0.156
$\bar{Y}_{.t}$	0.114	0.226	0.290	0.206	0.106
$\bar{Y}_{.u}$	0.237	0.095	0.278	0.216	0.218
c_t	0.173	0.124	0.381	0.157	0.322
c_u	0.382	−0.088	0.173	0.248	0.800
$\bar{Y}^*_{.t}$	0.108	0.211	0.299	0.199	0.103
$\bar{Y}^*_{.u}$	0.250	0.085	0.276	0.225	0.224
b	−0.142	0.126	0.023	−0.026	−0.121
$S(Y^*_{it})$	0.346	0.510	0.621	0.512	0.230
$S(Y^*_{iu})$	0.658	0.389	0.790	0.666	0.528
T	70	62	62	194	70
U	76	63	97	236	76
z-statistic[a]	−1.65	1.55	0.20	−0.46	−1.82
Net impact $[(b/\bar{X}_{..}) \times 100\%]$	−64.8%	+63.0%	+9.9%	−11.9%	−74.2%

[a] At a 0.05 level of significance, the z-statistic must be less than −1.64 for the change to be statistically significant: using this criterion, only the reductions in Denver's commercial burglary as listed above are statistically significant

is not surprising; however, interestingly enough, this figure seems less dramatic than the comparable pretreatment–posttreatment figures in Table 1. Third, despite integrating the invalid but large increase for St Louis, the net overall impact for the three cities is still a significant, though not statistically significant, reduction in the burglary rate of 11.9%; this result highlights the fact that the split-area model is not a simple additive model but a sophisticated statistical model. Fourth, if Long Beach were to be excluded from the split-area analysis, then the overall findings in Table 2 would be correspondingly and significantly improved.

In addition to the above-cited statistical reasons for the different findings in the three cities, there are other reasons. Most importantly, through on-site monitoring and subsequent analysis of the survey recommendations, the Denver staff arrived at their survey recommendations in a more rational manner than their counterparts in Long Beach and St Louis. For example, before conducting a security survey of a business establishment, the Denver staff reviewed the reports of all prior burglaries at the establishments; on the other hand, prior burglary reports were not available in Long Beach at the time security surveys were conducted, and only partially available in St Louis. Additionally, in analyzing the survey recommendations, it was noted that Denver had a wide range of recommendations, while Long Beach had similar recommendations for each establishment, and St Louis tended only to make inexpensive recommendations that stood a better chance of being implemented. Consequently, the lack of rationality in arriving at survey recommendations casts doubt on whether adequate treatments had been implemented in Long Beach and St Louis. Another possible reason for the poor findings in St Louis is the observation that the surveyed establishments were located in areas which were so depressed that they could not be "turned around"; indeed the burglary rate in each of the commercial test areas in St Louis increased significantly during the period of evaluation.

In sum, in response to the question of whether security surveys are effective against commercial burglary, the answer is "yes, only if the treatment is adequate"; that is, if the survey recommendations are rationally identified and complied with. Interestingly, this important finding suggests that the traditional manner of conducting security surveys—in which neither the rationality of the survey recommendations nor their compliance is emphasized—is totally inadequate. The importance of these two factors cannot be overstated. As discussed in Tien and Cahn (1986), the former factor can be dealt with simply by recognizing that each survey recommendation should be directed at decreasing an establishment's risk to a particular crime; that is, it should decrease the crime's likelihood (i.e., probability of it being attempted) and/or vulnerability (i.e., probability of it being successful, given an attempt) and/or cost (i.e., amount of loss, given a successful attempt). The latter factor is critical, and by implication it can be stated that the millions of dollars spent annually in the conduct of security surveys in the USA are wasted if the proprietors of the surveyed establishments choose not to comply with the survey recommendations. Certainly, the positive and significant findings of the CSFT evaluation effort should encourage proprietors to comply.

4. Conclusion

The following remarks should be made concerning the split-area research design. First, the design can, of course, be applied to other situations where treated and untreated units can be identified in an area or among a group of units. Of course, the design would have greater statistical power if it could be implemented prospectively (i.e., together with program implementation) and if the treated and untreated units could be randomly selected. Second, no research design, no matter how powerful, can be implemented in isolation; as emphasized by Tien (1979), the research design or selection scheme is but one component of an overall evaluation design. It is for this reason that we have discussed the development and application of the split-area research design within the context of the CSFT effort, including the identification of some complementary findings obtained through other evaluation activities (e.g., on-site monitoring). Third, although the split-area design was able to control for the environmental factors and the underlying model was able to correct for several statistical threats to validity in the CSFT evaluation, one threat or problem that remains bothersome is the issue of crime displacement. Since the treated and untreated establishments in the split-area design were obviously physically close to each other, there was naturally a potential for crime displacement. Further, as Reppetto (1976) indicates, geographical displacement is only one possibility; there could also be temporal, tactical, target and functional displacements of crime. Perhaps the only way to ascertain crime displacement is to undertake an extensive offender interview study, which remains a costly and controversial method of research.

In regard to the contents of this article, it should be noted that although the article focuses on program evaluation, the systems and model-based approach considered herein is, for the most part, applicable to any analysis effort. According to *Webster's Dictionary*, "to evaluate" means "to examine and judge"; thus, evaluation includes the step of analysis (i.e., examination) and can be thought of as a more judgement-oriented form of analysis.

Finally, the need for evaluation is growing in the USA, and it will continue to grow in the foreseeable future. Government at every level is increasingly being required to justify the value of its programs. On the other hand, increased federal deregulation, increased domestic and foreign competition and high interest rates have resulted in similar pressures on the leaders of private industry. Given a growing need for evaluation, it is critical and necessary that proper procedures exist for the design and conduct of evaluations which are valid and comprehensive. Certainly, the systems and model-based evaluation presented in this article reflects a real-world example in which such procedures were appropriately and effectively employed.

Bibliography

Bickman L, Rosenbaum D P 1980 *National Evaluation Program Phase I Assessment of Shoplifting and Employee Theft Programs*. Westinghouse Evaluation Institute, Evanston, Illinois

Campbell D T, Erlebacher A 1975 How regression artifacts in quasi-experimental evaluation can mistakenly make compensatory education look harmful. In: Struening E L, Guttentage M (eds.) *Handbook of Evaluation Research*, Vol. I. Sage Publications, Beverly Hills, California

Chelimsky E 1979 *Security and the Small Retailer*. Mitre Corporation, McLean, Virginia

Colton K W, Brandeau M L, Tien J M 1982 *A National Assessment of Police Command, Control, and Communications Systems*. National Institute of Justice, Washington, DC

Eversen T G 1979 *Greendale Crime Prevention Project*. Wisconsin Council on Criminal Justice, Madison, Wisconsin

Lavrakas P J, Maxfield M G, Henig J 1978 *Crime Prevention and Fear Reduction in the Commercial Environment*. Northwestern University Community Crime Prevention Workshop, Evanston, Illinois

National Institute of Justice 1979 *Commercial Security Test Design*. Law Enforcement Assistance Administration, US Department of Justice, Washington, DC

Pearson D A 1980 *Evaluation of Multnomah County's Commercial Burglary Prevention Program*. Oregon Law Enforcement Council, Evaluation and Research Unit, Salem, Oregon

Reppetto T A 1976 Crime prevention and the displacement phenomenon. *Crime and Delinquency*. April

Tien J M 1979 Toward a systematic approach to program evaluation design. *IEEE Trans. Syst., Man Cybern.* 9(9), 494–515

Tien J M 1987 Evaluation design: Systems and models approach. In: Singh M G (ed.) *Systems and Control Encyclopedia*. Pergamon, Oxford, pp. 1559–66

Tien J M, Cahn M F 1986 Commercial security field test program: A systematic evaluation of the impact of security surveys. In: Rosenbaum D P (ed.) *Preventing Crime in Residential and Commercial Areas*. Sage Publications, Beverly Hills, California

J. M. Tien
[Rensselaer Polytechnic Institute, Troy, New York, USA]

Prototyping as Information in Systems Design

Over the years, systems designers have discovered just how difficult it can be to capture user requirements. A variety of tools and techniques have been developed to assist systems analysts, but they have often proven inadequate, especially when requirements are complex and analytical. By and large, systems design and development life-cycle models fail to recognize the inherent requirements dilemma. Consequently, systems analysts have developed a new design perspective, one that assumes that requirements cannot be captured the first time through and that several iterations may be necessary to define requirements accurately. The new perspective is anchored in the value of prototyping. Prototyping "informs" the design process by leveraging increasingly specific and verifiable information in the requirements analysis process. The objective of prototyping is to demonstrate a system concept before expensive programming begins. Successful prototyping can be traced to iterative requirements analyses, user involvement and the use of one of several tools for converting requirements hypotheses into a tangible system concept (preferably in software). Prototypers usually build one of two kinds of demonstration systems: throwaway and evolutionary. Throwaway prototypes are developed when requirements are especially difficult to capture, which may be due to inarticulate users, a complex problem area or some combination of the two. As the label suggests, they are literally thrown away after each iteration until one prototype accurately represents requirements. This final prototype may then evolve into an evolutionary one, which can be incrementally enhanced over time. Prototypes are usually cost-effective additions to the systems design and development life cycle because they give designers an opportunity to "try before they buy."

1. Systems Design in Perspective

Not so many years ago computers were used mostly by scientists and engineers. As the field matured, computing was distributed to a larger set of professionals—accountants, budgeteers and some managers. The personal computer altered forever the way we think about computing. Initially the appeal of desktop power was mitigated by cost, but as soon as personal computers became affordable the revolution in personal computing began.

In the past, computers were used to perform calculations that were prohibitively expensive via any other means. Early interactive systems were barely so and engineers had to hack at them until they behaved. When general-purpose mainframes emerged, large organizations with huge databases expressed the most interest. It is safe to say that most early applications of general-purpose mainframe computers were database-oriented.

Today there are interactive decision support systems that can augment the decision-making power of human information processors. There are systems that help users to generate and evaluate options, and interpret the feedback received after they are implemented. There are systems that help users plan, create scenarios and diagnose diseases.

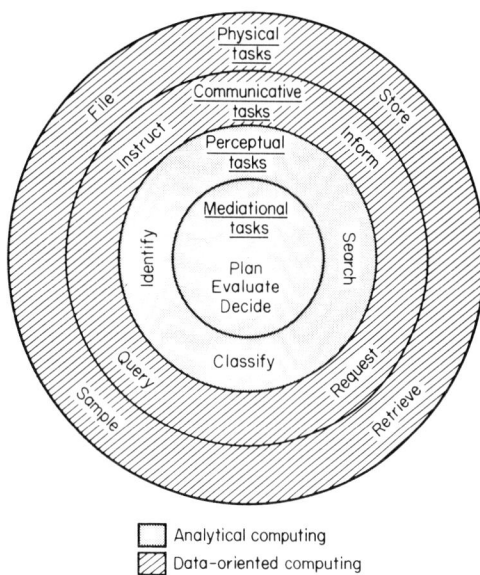

Figure 1
Analytical versus data-oriented computing

Figure 1 suggests where database-oriented and analytical computing begin and end (Andriole 1989). The differences are clear. Analytical problem solving assumes some degree of cognitive information processing. While all cognitive processing is anchored in data and knowledge that must be stored and manipulated, there are unique properties of cognitive information processing that call for unique requirements definitions. The difference between the collection and interpretation of diagnostic data illustrates database-oriented versus analytical problem solving (and, by implication, database-oriented versus analytical computing).

As computers become cheaper, smaller and faster, and as expectations about how they can be used rise, more and more instances of analytical computing will become necessary and eventually commonplace. The leverage lies in our ability to identify, define and validate complex requirements, hence the need for prototyping.

2. Conventional Design Methods and Models

There are a variety of conventional systems-design methods available to the software systems analyst and engineer. Royce (1970), Horowitz (1975), Hice *et al.* (1978), Andriole (1983), Dee (1984) and Pressman (1987), among many others, all propose some variation of the conventional software systems design and development process anchored in the waterfall method first introduced by Royce (1970) and Boehm (1976). As Fig. 2 suggests, all of them share some

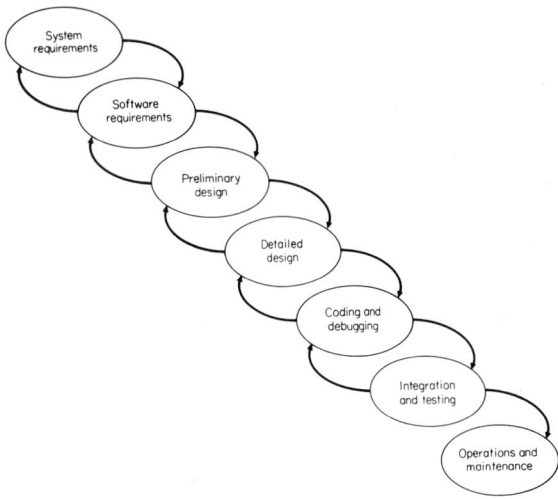

Figure 2
The waterfall life cycle

characteristics, such as a sequential nature, a single stage for identifying, defining and validating user requirements, and an orientation that seduces the designer into treating the process as manageable.

What is the problem here? First and foremost is the lack of emphasis upon user requirements. In the past it was assumed that requirements were easily defined. Since early computing requirements were often database intensive, the assumption was initially valid; as the need to fulfill analytical requirements grew, conventional life-cycle models failed to keep pace.

It is possible to conclude that conventional systems design models and methods ignore user requirements, and approaches to their modelling and verification, in favor of emphases that stress the importance of software engineering: program design and structure, coding, testing and debugging and the like.

This conclusion is supported by the vagueness with which conventional design methodologists treat the whole concept of user requirements. Requirements cannot be defined by simply asking users what they do or by watching them for a while. Even worse are requirements methods that rely upon handbooks, manuals or other written materials to define and refine user needs. They are worse because they disconnect the systems analyst from the user and presume that requirements can be identified in a vacuum.

In a sense the whole issue of conventional versus prototyping methods and models is a "strawman" unworthy of serious dispute because, as always, the problems the prospective system is intended to solve should determine life-cycle assumptions. Designers that begin *a priori* with a method will often fail, if only because they may end up matching the wrong life-cycle assumptions with the wrong problems.

Analytical problem-solving requirements cannot be captured through conventional systems design methods or models. Iteration is always the watchword in such cases. On the other hand, problems with an absence of analytical requirements might well be modelled via conventional methods.

3. The Prototyping Alternative

Modern systems design and development directs us to first look at the requirements that the system is intended to satisfy. It then suggests that some kind of modelling of the mock system can redefine our requirements which, in turn, will permit us to develop yet another functional description of the system, and so forth until the model accurately represents and satisfies requirements. Then, and only then, should we turn to software design and engineering; in turn, these steps should determine our hardware configuration. Bringing up the rear are packaging tasks, such as the preparation of users' manuals, and technology transfer tasks, such as the introduction of the system into the target environment.

There are debates about the way the first iteration of the system itself should be developed. Some hold that a thorough requirements analysis will assure the development of a responsive system, while others feel just as certain about the wisdom of some kind of prototyping strategy.

Applications prototyping (Boar 1984), the strategy that assumes that several iterations of an interactive system are necessary and desirable, has become very popular over the past few years. Among other advantages, prototyping supports modular software engineering, permits user participation in the design process and protects project resources from the jaws of tunnel programming. Most importantly, the applications prototyping strategy permits analysts to keep the requirements analysis process alive during the critical conversion process.

Prototyping assumes that the first version of the interactive system will be rejected and modified. It assumes that users and designers will have some difficulty identifying and defining critical system functions, and that a limited amount of money should be spent on each prototype until a durable system definition emerges. The money saved should be plowed back into requirements definition, tasks/methods matching and modelling.

Prototyping is as much a state of mind as it is a structured design methodology. Contrary to popular belief, prototyping is highly structured and extremely methodical in application. While some design theorists suggest that prototyping is loose and haphazard, successful prototyping requires adherence to a set of reasonably specific principles.

The primary assumption that prototypers make is that interactive systems cannot be developed easily, quickly or without input from prospective users. They assume that the system will have to be developed over and over again, but unlike conventional system developers, prototypers plan for iteration.

Figure 3 outlines the prototyping strategy. Note the many steps that precede programming, and the many decisions the requirements/systems analyst must make through the process. Iteration is inherent in the process, as are assumptions about flexibility. From a behavioral perspective, note that the process fails to recognize the possibility of accurately capturing or modelling requirements the first time through the process, and that those who need to do so will be disappointed whenever they engage users with complex analytical problems.

4. Prototyping Principles

There are essentially two ways to think about prototyping. One calls for the design and development of throwaway prototypes while the other calls for more evolutionary ones (Gomaa and Scott 1981, Bernstein 1985, Pressman 1987, Andriole 1989). Throwaway prototypes are as their name suggests, and should be developed when requirements are especially difficult to capture and model or when the target hardware/software configuration is unspecified (by design or by accident). Evolutionary prototypes are often developed when requirements are easier to identify and define, and when the hardware/software configuration is basically known to the system architect, analyst and prototyper.

These distinctions are not hard and fast, however. Sometimes, throwaway prototypes are developed to test an initial system concept and then, once the initial concept is validated, give way to a more evolutionary process. Furthermore, there are times when evolutionary prototypes yield too little insight into requirements and when assumptions about evolving requirements definitions cannot be justified. When this occurs, prudent prototypers switch from one perspective to the other until requirements have been well-enough defined to permit the use of evolutionary prototypes.

The appropriate perspective depends upon several factors, the most important of which is the recalcitrance of the requirements under investigation. If they can be identified and refined then it might be difficult to justify investments in a series of throwaways (some software might be useful when the project shifts to the software engineering phase). Other factors include the extent to which the hardware/software configuration has been predetermined, the extent to which hardware/software capabilities are known in advance, and the extent to which human expertise is available to implement a more evolutionary strategy.

There is debate about which perspective best serves the development team on another level as well. It may make more sense to have one team assist in requirements validation and another completely different team assume responsibility for programming. Proponents of the two-team approach argue that requirements should be refined and validated by those with no vested interest in their conversion into working software, that programmers sometimes force-fit requirements into programming conventions or procedural preferences that can distort requirements and undermine user involvement in the whole requirements analysis process. As always, such judgements must be made with reference to the capabilities and personalities of all those involved in the systems design and development team, although points about vested interests are usually well-taken.

There are organizational considerations as well. Not all software organizations support the notion of rapid (or nor not so rapid) prototyping. A surprising number of software houses define their life cycle not around what they might believe works, but around what their primary customers expect. This perspective assumes that regardless of what might be better, the best perspective is one that satisfies the customer. Perhaps overly pragmatic, the perspective is widely implemented.

Related to this is the perspective that regards any kind of prototyping as just too expensive. The notion that a goal can be realized faster through painful trial-and-error procedures is counterintuitive to many software project managers, in spite of the voluminous literature suggesting otherwise (Meister 1976, Schneiderman 1980, Galitz 1984, Brooks 1987, Pressman 1987). Many of the same managers worry about the expenditure of resources early in the life cycle and refuse to recognize the leverage almost always gained from a thorough front-end analysis.

According to Boar (1984), the following principles define the prototyping strategy:

Capture an initial set of needs and implement quickly those needs with the stated intent of iteratively expanding and refining them as mutual user/developer understanding of the problem grows;

Definition of the system occurs through gradual and evolutionary discovery as opposed to omniscient foresight; and

Project risk . . . is best controlled and minimized by using a technique that accepts gradual learning and incremental change as normal and desirable, and accommodates them efficiently by providing a technological 'play-dough/tinker toy' response . . . called prototyping.

Boar (1984) also suggests that prototyping involves the following specific steps:

Identification of Basic Needs. Determine the fundamental goals and objectives of the application, major . . . problems to be solved by the system, the data elements, record relationships, and functions to be performed;

Develop Working Model. Quickly build a working model that delivers the key items identified in the first step. Supplement the user's request with good system building

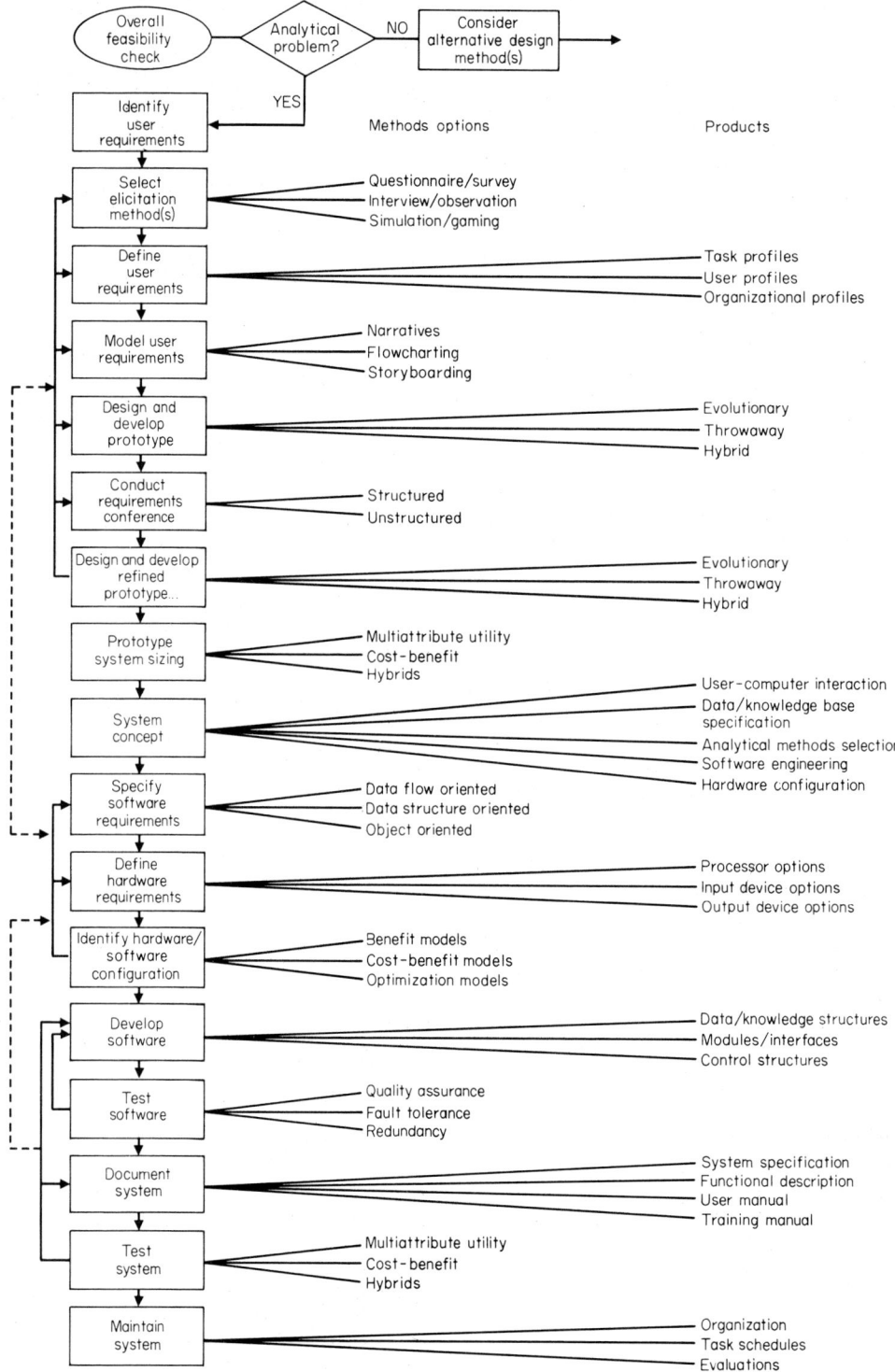

Figure 3
System design and development process using prototyping

practices. It is important to deliver the first model quickly to maintain user interest and confidence in the process;

Demonstrate in Context/Solicit Requirements and Extensions. Present the model to all interested parties, from data entry clerk to division manager and aggressively solicit additional requirements. Attempt to mimic performance of the ... [system] to discover shortcomings and desirable extensions. Walk through each component of the prototype explaining exactly what it does. Prompt the user by asking 'what if' questions; and

Prototype Done. Continue to iterate between demonstrating and revising until the functionality provided is satisfactory to and understood by all parties. Test the prototype ...

As Dee (1984) and Boar (1984) suggest—contrary to the recommendations of some design theorists—prototyping is a viable approach to large *and* small systems design and development.

Brooks (1987) offers some related principles:

The hardest single part of building a software system is deciding precisely what to build. No other part ... is as difficult as establishing the detailed technical requirements, including all the interfaces to people, to machines, and to other software systems. No other part of the work so cripples the resulting system if done wrong. No other part is more difficult to rectify later;

... the most important function that the software builder performs for the client is the iterative extraction and refinement of ... requirements;

A [good] prototype software system is one that simulates the important interfaces and performs the main functions of the intended system, while not necessarily being bound by the same hardware speed, size, or cost constraints;

Prototypes typically perform the mainline tasks of the application, but make no attempt to handle exceptional tasks, respond correctly to invalid inputs, or abort cleanly; and

The purpose of the prototype is to make real the conceptual structure specified, so that the client can test it for consistency and usability.

Perhaps the most important design principle comes from Brooks, who believes that software systems are "grown," not "written" or "built":

The building metaphor has outlived its usefulness ... the conceptual structures we construct today are too complicated to be specified accurately in advance, and too complex to be built faultlessly ... we must take a radically different approach ... let us turn to nature and study complexity in living things ... the secret is that [they] are grown, not built ... so it must be with our software systems ... the approach necessitates top-down design, for it is a top-down growing of the software. It allows easy backtracking. It lends itself to early prototypes. Each added function and new provision for more complex data or circumstances grows organically out of what is already there ...

Before prototypes can be built, requirements must be identified and defined. Evolutionary and throwaway prototypes are intended to help refine requirements, but there must be some strong sense of the tasks the system will perform, who the prospective users are and what demands the organization will make on the system and its organizational users.

5. Requirements Analysis Methods

There is no more important yet more neglected step in systems design than requirements analysis. As Meister (1976) and others have pointed out, without a clear set of requirements the system will satisfy the needs of the designers but not the intended users. Boar (1984) reports that 20–40% of all system problems can be traced to problems in the design process, while 60–80% can be traced to inaccurate requirements definitions. The message is clear: know thy user.

The prototyping strategy assumes that requirements cannot all be prespecified, that inherent communications gaps exist among design participants, and that "extensive iteration is necessary, inevitable, desirable, and to be encouraged" (Boar 1984).

The strategy also assumes that requirements do not stop once the tasks the system is supposed to support have been identified and defined. All good requirements definitions comprise user, task and organizational doctrinal requirements. In fact, the best possible requirements definition is a matrix linking all three dimensions together.

Requirements analysis also assumes feasibility. If you were to discover after a significant requirements investment that no one could define requirements, or that the ones that were defined were impossible to satisfy through computerization, or that in order to satisfy the requirements you had to spend ten times what any reasonable person would suggest the system should cost, then the problem can be said to have failed the feasibility test. Feasibility assessment is thus one outcome of requirements analysis; the others include task, user and organizational/doctrinal profiles, and the integrated tasks/users/ organizational–doctrinal matrix.

5.1 Task Requirements Analysis Methods

Task profiling consists of qualitative and, if possible, quantitative descriptions of the tasks that the system is intended to solve, automate, quasiautomate or ignore. Task profiles are important because the selection of the right analytical method depends upon how well the tasks have been defined. The tasks themselves should be arranged hierarchically all the way down to the lowest diagnostic subtask. While this is not to imply that each and every task and subtask be elaborately defined, it is to suggest that the task requirements process should be highly structured.

There are a variety of ways to structure task analyses. It is important to begin with some sense of how tasks differ generally. Over the years the psychological research community has developed a number of generic taxonomies that can be used as organizing frameworks for the subsequent development of problem-specific task taxonomies. Fleishman et al. (1984) present perhaps the most comprehensive review of this literature. They cite several approaches to task classification (and the development of task taxonomies) worth noting:

(a) behavior description approaches,

(b) behavior requirements approaches,

(c) ability requirements approaches, and

(d) task characteristics approaches.

Behavior description approaches include those that identify "categories of tasks . . . based upon observations and descriptions of what operators actually do while performing a task." Behavior requirements approaches emphasize the "cataloguing of behaviors that should be emitted or which are assumed to be required in order to achieve criterion levels of performance." Ability requirements approaches assume that "tasks are to be described, contrasted, and compared in terms of abilities that a given task requires of the individual performer or operator"; while task characteristics approaches are "predicated upon a definition that treats the task as a set of conditions that elicits performance" (Fleishman et al. 1984).

With the exception of task characteristics approaches, most approaches try to identify important processes, functions, behaviors or performance. The ideal task analysis would permit the systems designer to differentiate among the tasks and rank them according to their problem-solving importance.

It is important to note that the use of task taxonomies to profile user tasks occurs before, during and after the task-profiling process. Task taxonomies are used initially as organizing frameworks; they are used during the process as substantive and procedural compasses; and they emerge redefined as problem-specific taxonomies after the process. The latter is a key use: the purpose of applying an existing generic taxonomy (or developing a whole new one) is to help accelerate the development of the required problem-specific taxonomy. As soon as you begin your task requirements analysis you should reach for a generic task taxonomy to guide it.

There are a number of methods that have solid track records for developing task profiles. In fact, they all have weaknesses suggesting that the best approach to task profiling is eclectic, interdisciplinary and (as always) iterative. Experience with requirements analysis suggests that a single method never really captures the essence of the tasks we are trying to computerize. Successful task profiles were the result of having applied at least two task analysis methods.

The task requirements analysis methods discussed in this section fall into three broad categories: questionnaire and survey methods, interviews and field observation methods, and simulation and gaming methods.

As suggested, there are at least three ways to identify and define tasks. The first involves asking users what they do and how they do what they do, in questionnaires and surveys. The second involves asking them in person (in a variety of different settings), while the third suggests that the best way to profile tasks is through a simulation or gaming exercise.

Inherent in all of these methods is the belief that, given enough time and money, tasks can always be identified and defined. Nothing is further from the truth. There are many tasks that defy precise description; it is also naïve to assume that all users are articulate; hence the iterative prototyping strategy, which assumes that users are often unable to define their tasks and that some tasks are much more resistant to definition than others.

There are at least five ways to profile requirements through questionnaires and surveys (Ramsey and Atwood 1979):

(a) importance ratings questionnaires,

(b) time-estimate questionnaires,

(c) repertory grid techniques,

(d) Delphi techniques, and

(e) policy capture techniques.

The key to the successful use of questionnaire and survey methods lies in the ability to select users with unusually diagnostic understandings of what they do; users unable to introspect may only feed back perceptions of what they think they do, not accurate descriptions of what they actually do.

There are also obvious situations where questionnaires and/or surveys would be inappropriate. If your system is intended to serve a small but elite group of military analysts, then it is unlikely that any real insight could be gained from the results of a questionnaire. On the other hand, if your system is intended for use throughout the military or throughout a particular subset of the military (for example, the strategic intelligence community), and the user population is geographically dispersed, then mailed questionnaires may be the only feasible method.

Interview and field observation methods include unstructured and structured interviews, ad hoc working-group-based methods, critical incident techniques, and formal job analysis techniques.

In practice, the overwhelming majority of task requirements analyses consist of unstructured interviews and possibly an ad hoc working-group session or two. A series of questions are usually posed to one or more interviewees who tend to perceive requirements as anecdotes of their (usually limited) experiences. While these anecdotes are useful, they too often take the place of a structured requirements database.

The participatory approach to interactive systems design should be stressed again here. A few hours of a user's time is really quite worthless. If the system is to be responsive to real needs then a user's strike force must be established. As suggested earlier, users should be made members of the design team and given important design responsibilities.

It is also important to note that techniques such as formal job analysis are best suited for defining non-cognitive tasks, and that other methods, like structured interviews, working groups and protocol analyses are more likely to yield useful cognitive task definitions.

The application of simulation and gaming methods essentially calls for a scenario, some experts, and some techniques for documenting what happens when the experts are asked to address the scenario. Ramsey and Atwood (1979) and others (Carlisle 1973, Shubik 1975, Andriole 1983) suggest at least three kinds of simulations and games: paper simulations, protocol analysis, and interactive simulation or gaming.

Nearly all of the above requirements analysis methods can trace their origins to disciplines other than computer science or information systems. In fact, most of them can be traced to psychology and management science. This alone attests to the interdisciplinary aspect of requirements analysis, and the need to involve specialists from the behavioral, computer and management sciences in the requirements definition and validation process.

There are also aspects of the process that defy precise structuring. It is important to remember that requirements analysis is as much an art as it is a science. There is a "feel" to requirements analysis that comes after an analyst acquires a great deal of experience. Good requirements analysts also tend to learn a great deal about the target applications area; some of them become almost expert at the very tasks they are trying to define.

The use of generic task taxonomies is intended to guide the requirements analysis process, but the tasks in the taxonomies are not intended to replace those identified during the actual collection phase of the process. Figure 4 suggests how the taxonomies can be used to (a) guide the initial process and then (b) yield specific tasks and subtasks in a resource allocation scenario. Alternative requirements analysis methods are presented in the figure as intervening and iterative variables.

5.2 User Profiling Methods

Who will be using the system? Will the system be used by those relatively unsophisticated in the use of interactive systems, or is the user group experienced? These and similar questions are related to user profiling, the second critical dimension of the requirements definition.

There are a number of ways to classify users: by job function, by their level of experience with interactive computing, by their role in a larger problem-solving process, or by some combination of these and additional criteria. Ramsey and Atwood (1979) mix some criteria to produce at least three classes of users: naïve, managerial and scientific–technical. This classification of users according to their experience and job

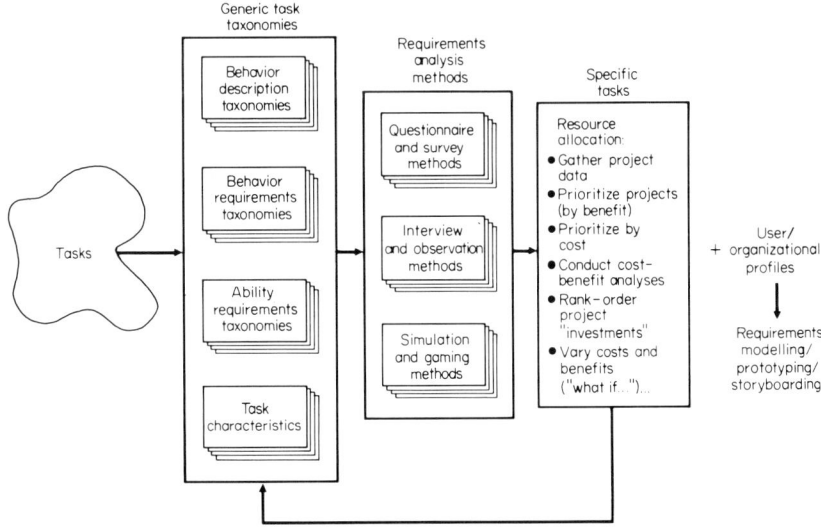

Figure 4
The task requirements analysis process

function can tell us a great deal about how the decision support system should be designed, but it also leaves out some important information. Will the system be used by frequent or infrequent users? Will it be used by users under situational pressure? Will the users be part of a larger organizational hierarchy, such as always occurs in the military?

User profiling, like task profiling, should begin with a look at some of the existing user taxonomies. However, it must be ensured that the taxonomies reflect the application and that they are based upon criteria meaningful to the community they are trying to help.

As a general rule, the following questions should be posed before, during and after the user profiling process.

(a) How experienced with interactive computing are the users?

(b) How experienced with analytical methodology are the users; are they inclined to think analytically or are they more passive users?

(c) How frequently will they use the decision support system?

(d) What cognitive styles will they bring to the system?

(e) To what extent is their behavior determined by their role or rank?

(f) How high are their expectations about what the system can do for them?

The answers to these questions (and others) will yield a user profile that will inform the systems design and development process; without the answers the designers will speculate about, or ignore altogether, the kind(s) of problem solvers that will operate the system.

Unfortunately, user requirements analysis methodology is not nearly as developed as task requirements analysis methodology. Methods for developing taxonomies based on experience and cognitive styles and requirements are thus not altogether different from task requirements methods, although the focus is very different.

There are several ways to gather information about how experienced the users are with interactive computing and analytical methodology. Note that the experience that should be measured includes experience with computing *and* analytical methods *and* analytical computing. These distinctions are important because many systems tend to be model oriented while much user experience with computing is data oriented. Users who feel very comfortable with a sophisticated database-management system cringe at the thought of interacting with a trivial analytical program. Conversely, users familiar with modelling software often find data retrieval and display programs completely useless.

Conventional requirements data collection methods, like interviews and field observation methods, can yield a good deal of insight into the users experience with analytical computing. But for these methods to be effective a great deal of front-end work must be done. The following questions can be used to structure an interview or interpret field observations.

(a) What is the nature of your prior experience with computing; has it been primarily data or model oriented?

(b) Are you a frequent (ten or more times a month) or infrequent (less than ten times a month) user; do you avoid computers whenever possible?

(c) Do you have any formal training in analytical methodology; if so, in what methods?

(d) What analytical programs have you used?

(e) What are your expectations about decision support?

These and similar questions can be used to profile users according to their general computing experience and their experience with analytical computing specifically. Scales can be developed to measure this experience, although they need only be very crude.

It is also possible to observe users in an analytical computing scenario where they must interact with a system that makes certain demands on their problem-solving skill.

There are two kinds of methods for profiling users' cognitive styles and capabilities. The first involves applying one or more generic descriptive cognitive taxonomies, while the second assumes that insight can be gained by applying a generic ability requirement taxonomy.

These taxonomies can be used to organize field- and scenario-based observation exercises. If there is time, and the circumstances are right, questionnaires can be administered to profile cognitive preferences and problem-solving styles. There are a variety of questionnaires available that purport to measure cognitive capabilities and styles, although few of them have been scientifically validated.

Cognitive profiling seeks to identify user perceptual and mediational processes. It is important to define these processes because they tell us a great deal about how the system should be designed and how it should interact with its users. Cognitive profiles can suggest, for example, that graphic output is inappropriate, that the interaction pace should be slow, and that the analytical method in the system should be highly visible. By and large, cognitive profiling informs the design of the human–machine interface and the system's behavioral characteristics. Figure 5 suggests how the user profiling process works.

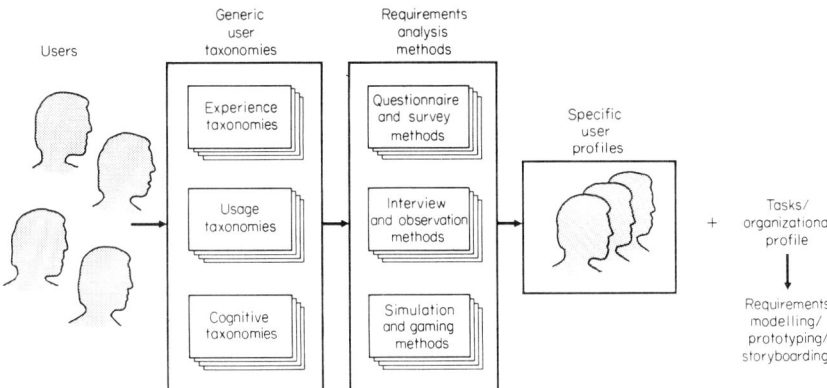

Figure 5
The user requirements analysis process

5.3 Organizational/Doctrinal Profiling Methods

Until recently very little attention was given to the impact that an analytical problem-solving system might have on an organization or bureaucracy. After countless systems were thrown out due largely to their incompatibility with established efficient problem-solving procedures, designers began to take note of the environment in which their systems were expected to perform. First, unless the mission explicitly calls for it, try to avoid creating the impression that the system will change the way things are now done. The most appropriate support image suggests that the system can help to organize and expedite problems that are otherwise tedious and time-consuming. Many early support systems were enthusiastically accepted when they helped to reduce information overload, to filter and route information, and to structure decision-option selection problems. However, resistance grew when they moved into the prescriptive provinces which were previously the exclusive preserve of humans. Worse still are the decision aids and support systems that not only try to change an organization's structure but try to do it with exotic analytical methodologies that require six months of "interactive training" before the system can be used.

Systems will fail if they are incompatible with the organizations they are intended to support, regardless of how well designed they are, just as mediocre systems will excel within organizations with which they are perfectly compatible. Designers must also understand doctrine and the requirements that it generates. If the focus here were on basic systems research then the issues would not be as important, but since the focus is on applied systems design and development the issue is unavoidable.

The least-developed requirements methodology is that available for organizational–doctrinal profiling. As suggested above, the interactive-systems design community has only recently recognized the importance of organizational context. Consequently, there are relatively few methods for profiling the organization and its doctrine that must be served by the system. The two general methods discussed here include critical activity profiling and compatibility testing methods.

It is essential that an organization's mission be fully understood before the system is functionally modelled. Here the reference is not to the individual tasks that make up the mission (and which are the focus of task requirements analysis), but rather to the higher-level function that the organization is supposed to perform. The relationships that the organization has with other organizations are also critical.

Critical activity profiling methods are primarily observation oriented. They are also fed by voluminous mission descriptions (also known as policies and procedures manuals). It is important to identify and define an organization's critical activities because, while a system may well help individuals to solve specific low-level problems, the solutions themselves may be incompatible with the organization's mission and modus operandi.

Compatibility testing methods provide insight into an organization's modus operandi and provide the means for averting major inconsistencies and incompatibilities between the system, the organization, and its doctrine. What are the organization's policies, procedures and protocols? How are problems solved within the organization? What is the hierarchical structure? Can the flow of information in the organization be modelled? Is it clear within this flow where the system will fit?

The methodology for profiling organizations comes from the organizational development community. In one study (Srinivasan and Kaiser 1987) an attempt was made to measure relationships between organizational factors and systems development. It was determined that the characteristics of an organization can positively or negatively affect systems design and development progress. Another study, by Baroudi et al. (1986), suggested that user involvement in the systems design process predicted levels of user satisfaction and usage. These and other studies suggest the likely relationship between organizational profiles and the extent to which systems support or hinder organizational performance.

It is safe to say that there is by no means an abundance of generic (or specific) organizational/doctrinal taxonomies targeted at interactive computer-based systems design and development. There are, however, a number of taxonomies that recognize organizational personalities and pathologies. Unfortunately, the relevant literature is of limited applied use. The best way to proceed is to develop a set of questions, identify a set of issues and analyze organizational manuals that shed light upon the organization's mission and modus operandi: gather some data via direct observation, supplement it with codified doctrine, and then develop a crude organizational profile as it pertains to the system you intend to grow.

Figure 6 suggests how organizations can be profiled.

5.4 The Task/User/Organizational–Doctrinal Matrix

A good requirements analysis will enable the construction of a problem-specific three dimensional matrix, as suggested in Fig. 7a; it will also permit the development of a prototype. But why go through all the trouble? Because numerous design issues can only be solved through the matrix. For example, user type(s) will determine the type of interactive dialogue to be used. Tasks will determine the analytical method selected to drive the system, while organizational–doctrinal considerations will determine the system's interface, input requirements, output, physical size and security characteristics. It is essential that user, task and organizational–doctrinal definitions be developed and integrated before the design process proceeds any further.

As Fig. 7 suggests, the requirements matrix leads directly to the prototype. Requirements define the hypothetical system concept embodied in the prototype.

The importance of requirements analysis cannot be overstated in the overall design and development process. The whole point of prototyping is to validate requirements by some tangible representation of the system concept. The extent to which requirements are accurately identified initially will determine the number of prototypes necessary to validate requirements.

6. Prototyping Methods

There are several ways to capture the essence of the system to be built. As soon as the requirements analysis is completed, the prototyping strategy requires the development of some kind of representation or model of how the system will operate.

It must be remembered that this prototype will be temporary; it is intended to introduce the system concept to the users. They will no doubt find it flawed, and so it must be adjusted until they are satisfied, knowing full well that they might never really be happy with the design (even as members of the design team). Such is the fate of the systems designer.

A good prototype or requirements model serves many purposes simultaneously. As suggested, it fosters discussion about what the system should and should not do; it also verifies the results of the requirements analysis. As members of the design team, users can inspect the integrated model and recommend changes. Finally, the model permits the design team to display something to its users early on in the design process; something that stimulates the design team, pleases management and convinces users that the team is dedicated to solving their problems.

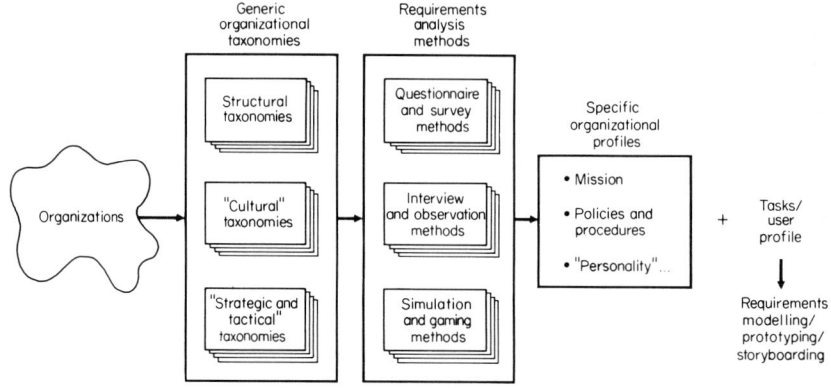

Figure 6
The organizational requirements analysis process

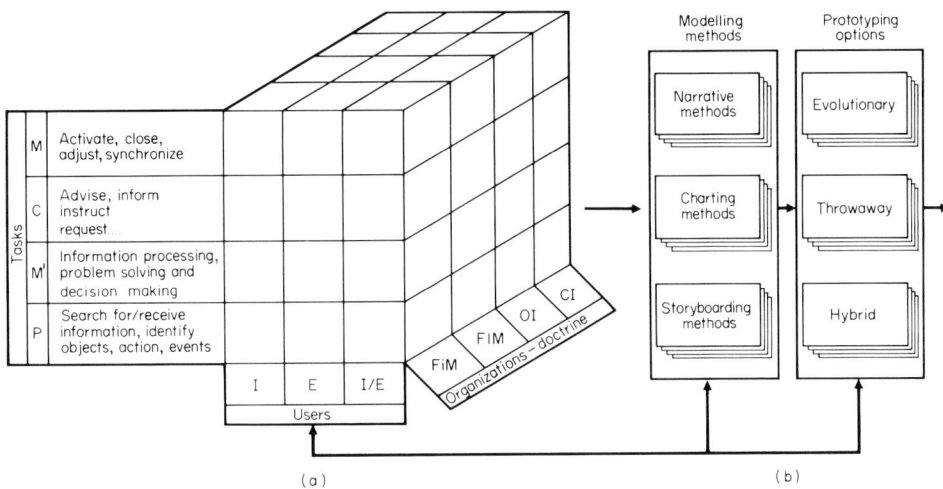

Figure 7
(a) The three-dimensional requirements matrix and (b) its relation to modelling methods and prototyping options. M, "motor"; C, communicative; M′, mediational; P, perceptual; I, inexperienced; E, experienced, I/E, infrequent (inexperienced or experienced); FiM, fixed military; FlM, flexible military, OI, open industry; CI, closed industry

There is very little agreement about which prototyping method(s) work best. Some believe that conventional flow charting is sufficient, while others demand a "live" demonstration of the system-to-be. There are at least four viable prototyping methods, including the development of narratives, the development of flow charts, methods based upon other information theories and methods, and those that yield storyboards.

6.1 Narrative Methods
Narratives remain powerful communication tools. When well done, they can accelerate the design process. Ideally they should describe what the system will do, indicate its input requirements, describe and illustrate its output and suggest a software/hardware configuration. At the same time, they should not be so long or verbose as to discourage study. Their prose should be terse and to the point, and should also be illustrated with simulated screen displays.

Narratives should only be used when the system is relatively uncomplicated, when the tasks to be performed are less than cognitive. They should also only be used when users will find them appropriate. Many military users, for example, may find narrative too tedious for serious study.

6.2 Flow-Charting Methods
We are all familiar with conventional (logic) flow charts. In the hands of an experienced systems analyst logic, flow charts are rich in information, but in the hands of a novice they are meaningless. There are other flow charts that can serve larger groups. Van Duyn (1982), for example, suggests that there are a variety of flow charts that can be used to develop prototype system models, which include the following.

(a) *Conceptual flow charts*: pictorial presentations of the flow of information.

(b) *General system flow charts*: top level visual presentations of the system intended for management inspection.

(c) *Functional flow charts*: visual presentations of the system, subsystem or program, showing the functions of data with no decision factors or other variables to distract the viewer.

(d) *Logic flow charts*: visual presentations of the flow of data through a subsystem and/or program, the location of decision processes, and the control of logic through switching or complicated decision processes. Logic flow charts are the conventional ones intended to reduce coding and debugging time.

(e) *Job-step flow charts*: visual presentations of a computer processing operation which often consists of one or more programs that process all input and generate all output.

(f) *Work flow charts*: visual presentations of the flow of paper or manual work.

6.3 Generic Model-Based Methods

Off-the-shelf modelling techniques can be used to represent a particular system. So long as the problem area fits the model (and vice versa) one or more of the models may work, but one must be very careful to match the right model with the right requirements definition. Some such models, as described by Ramsey and Atwood (1979) are discussed below.

(a) *Decision-theory models.* These models concern the decision-making behavior of the user. They require the specification of (i) a set of possible states of the world with their estimated probabilities and (ii) a set of possible decisions or courses of action which might be taken, together with their expected values and cost in the various possible states of the world. Considering the values and costs, together with the evidence of particular world states, a decision-theory model can select courses of action.

Decision-theory models can be used to suggest optimal decisions or to describe the observed decision-making behavior of users. In both modes, these models are frequently used in decision aids. If it is reasonable to describe user behavior in terms of such a model, these models can also be useful to the system designer by suggesting information required by the user.

(b) *Models of human information processing.* In general, these models involve a characterization of (i) the task environment, including the problem and means of solution available, (ii) the problem space employed by the subject to represent the problem and its evolving solution, and (iii) the procedure developed to achieve a solution. The method used to develop such models involves intensive analysis of the problem to be solved and of protocols obtained from problem solvers during solution.

Ideally, such efforts might lead to an integrative model of human information processing useful in a variety of design applications. However, existing models are either too task-specific for this use or are insufficiently detailed. Furthermore, relationships between task requirements and human performance capabilities and limitations are inadequately understood for human information processing tasks. There are many good models applicable to very specific tasks.

(c) *Computer system models.* These models attempt to describe the behavior of the computer component of an interactive system, but do not attempt to model user performance in detail. Some of the models do characterize user behavior in terms of the statistical properties of user commands for a particular application. The models usually attempt to predict such parameters as system response time, CPU and memory loads, and input–output requirements. These models tend to be relatively crude, but can be useful in determining whether or not user requirements with respect to response time and other gross system performance measures can be satisfied by a proposed system. They are of little assistance in determining what the user requirements are.

(d) *Network models.* These models treat user and system as equivalent elements in the overall process. The individual tasks performed by both the user and the system are described in terms of expected performance and in terms of logical predecessor–successor relationships. The relationships define a network of tasks which is used as a performance model of the user–computer system. Such models are usually used to predict either the probability of failure or success, or the completion time, of an aggregate set of tasks.

Network models allow performance data about users and computer systems to be integrated in a single model even though original data came from a variety of sources. However, performance data must be provided for each task, as must rules for combining performance data from each individual task to obtain aggregated performance predictions. This is often difficult because of questionable or lacking empirical data, and because performance interactions among tasks (especially cognitive tasks or tasks performed in parallel) may be very complex. Performance distributions are often assumed without data. In spite of these difficulties, the process of constructing such models is often a valuable source of understanding.

(e) *Control-theory models.* These models are based on control theory, statistical estimation and decision theory. The user is regarded as an element in a feedback control loop. Such models are usually used to predict overall performance of the user–computer system in continuous control and monitoring tasks.

Control-theory models are more quantitative than other performance models. They may address user–computer communication broadly, but ordinarily do not deal with details of the interface, such as display design. Therefore, their use as an aid to the interface system designer may be limited. Not much work has yet been done in applying these modelling techniques to situations in which the main user activities are monitoring and decision making, with infrequent control actions.

6.4 Screen Display and Storyboarding Methods

Perhaps the most useful prototype is one that displays to users precisely what they can expect the system to do, at least hypothetically. Paper copies of screen displays are extremely useful, since they permit users to inspect each part of the interactive sequence. Boar (1984) regards screen displays as acceptable hybrid prototypes.

While useful, paper screen displays pale against the impact of computer-generated (and animated) screen displays. Called storyboards, computer-generated displays simulate human–computer interaction. With new animation packages, it is now possible to animate the storyboard and thereby mimic sophisticated interactive graphics capabilities.

The animated storyboard and its paper equivalent provide users with the best of both worlds. The computer-generated storyboard permits them to actually experience the system, while the paper copy enables them to record their comments and suggestions. Each run through the storyboard becomes a documented experiment filled with information for the design team. The paper copies also create a permanent record of the iterative modelling process, an invaluable contribution to corporate or military institutional memories.

A typical storyboard will have over a hundred displays intended to communicate to users what the system will do, how it will do it, and how users will be expected to work with it. When strung together, these storyboards will communicate an interactive system concept to users, who are then free to comment upon and criticize the concept, thus triggering the development of the next prototype (or the enhancement of an evolutionary one), all as suggested in Fig. 3.

Bibliography

Andriole S J 1983 *Interactive Computer-Based Systems Design and Development*. Petrocelli, Princeton, New Jersey

Andriole S J 1989 *Storyboard Prototyping for Systems Design: A New Approach to User Requirements Validation and System Sizing*. QED Information Sciences, Wellesley, Massachusetts

Baroudi J J, Olson M H, Ives B 1986 An empirical study of the impact of user involvement on system usage and information satisfaction. *Commun. ACM* **29**(3)

Bernstein A 1985 Shortcut to systems design. *Bus. Comput. Syst.* **3**(6)

Boar B 1984 *Application Prototyping: A Requirements Definition Strategy for the 80s*. Wiley, New York

Boehm B W 1976 Software engineering. *IEEE Trans. Comput.* **25**(12)

Brooks F P 1987 No silver bullet: Essence and accidents of software engineering. *IEEE Comput.* **20**(4)

Carlisle J H 1973 *Comparing Behavior at Various Computer Display Consoles*. Rand, Santa Monica, California

Dee D 1984 Developing PC applications. *Datamation* **12**(4)

Fleischman E A, Quaintance M K, Broedling L A 1984 *Taxonomies of Human Performance*. Academic Press, New York

Galitz W O 1984 *Humanizing Office Automation*. QED Information Sciences, Wellesley, Massachusetts

Gomaa H, Scott D 1981 Prototyping as a tool in the specification of user requirements. *Proc. 5th Int. Conf. Software Eng.* IEEE, New York

Hice G F, Turner W S, Cashwell L F 1978 *System Development Methodology*. North-Holland, New York

Horowitz E 1975 *Practical Strategies for Developing Large Scale Software Systems*. Addison-Wesley, New York

Leslie R E 1986 *Systems Analysis and Design: Method and Invention*. Prentice-Hall, Englewood Cliffs, New Jersey

Meister D 1976 *Behavioral Foundations of System Development*. Wiley, New York

Pressman R S 1987 *Software Engineering: A Practitioner's Approach*. McGraw-Hill, New York

Ramsey H R, Atwood M E 1979 *Human Factors in Computer Systems: A Review of the Literature*. Science Applications, Boulder, Colorado

Royce W W 1970 *Managing and Development of Large Software Systems: Concepts and Techniques*, TRW Software Series. TRW, Redondo Beach, California

Schneiderman B 1980 *Software Psychology: Human Factors in Computer and Information Systems*. Winthrop, Cambridge, Massachusetts

Shubik M 1975 *Games for Society, Business and War*. Elsevier, New York

Srinivasan A, Kaiser K M 1987 Relationships between selected organizational factors and systems development. *Commun. ACM* **30**(6)

Van Duyn J 1982 *DP Professional's Guide to Writing Effective Technical Documentation*. Wiley, New York

S. J. Andriole
[George Mason University, Fairfax, Virginia, USA]

R

Real-Time Software Design: Information Concerns

Real-time software systems have several characteristics which distinguish them from other software systems. These are explained in the following paragraphs.

Such systems often have real-time constraints; that is, they must process events within a given time frame. Whereas in an interactive system, a human may be inconvenienced if the system response is delayed, in a real-time system a delay may be catastrophic. For example, inadequate response in an air traffic control system could result in a midair collision of two aircraft. The actual response time will vary by application, ranging from milliseconds in some cases to seconds in others.

A real-time system is often an embedded system; that is, the real-time software system is a component of a larger hardware–software system. An example of this is a robot controller which is a component of a robot system consisting of one or more mechanical arms, servomechanisms controlling axis motion, and sensors and actuators for interfacing to the external environment. A computerized automobile cruise-control system is embedded in an automobile in another such example.

A real-time system typically interacts with an external environment which is to a large extent non-human. For example, the real-time system may be controlling machines or manufacturing processes, or it may be monitoring chemical processes and reporting alarm conditions. This often necessitates a sensory interface for receiving data from the external environment and actuators for outputting data to, and controlling, the external environment.

A real-time system often involves real-time control; that is, the computer makes control decisions based on data received, without any human intervention. An automobile cruise-control system has to adjust the throttle based on measurements of current speed to ensure that the desired speed is maintained.

A real-time software system may indeed have non-real-time components. For example, real-time data collection necessitates gathering the data under real-time constraints, otherwise it will be lost. However, once collected, the data could be stored for subsequent non-real-time analysis.

A feature of all real-time systems is that of concurrent processing; that is, there are many events which are occurring simultaneously. Frequently the order of incoming events is unpredictable.

1. Concurrent Processing Concepts

As real-time systems deal with several events concurrently, it is highly desirable for a real-time software system to be structured into concurrent tasks (also known as concurrent processes). Thus, in a system with multiple input and output streams of data, each task can deal with one stream of data.

In this article, the concepts of concurrent processing (Dijkstra 1968, Brinch-Hansen 1973, Hoare 1974) are presented, with examples involving multiple robot systems and other industrial systems.

1.1 Concurrent Tasks

A software task (or process) is a program in execution; hence there is a one-to-one correspondence between a task and a program. Real-time systems typically consist of several concurrent tasks. Each task is sequential since it executes a program. Concurrency in the real-time software system is obtained by having multiple asynchronous tasks running at different speeds. From time to time, the tasks need to communicate and synchronize their operations with each other.

Consider the case of a robot system which controls up to four robot arms. Typically there is one robot program to control the operations of one robot arm. Thus, each executing robot program is considered a software task. For this to be possible, the robot system must be capable of supporting concurrent tasks.

Concurrent tasks may need to have their operations coordinated. Two examples of this are mutual exclusion and process synchronization.

1.2 Mutual Exclusion

Mutual exclusion is required when only one task at a time may enter a critical section. An application of this is robot entry into a "collision zone." Collision could occur if more than one robot is allowed to move into the collision zone at the same time. To prevent this, robot entry into the collision zone is made mutually exclusive. For example, there may be four robot tasks which are performing independent assembly operations. However, there is a collision zone where robot arms could potentially collide.

The mutual exclusion problem may be solved by using semaphores. Two operations are allowed on binary semaphores: $P(s)$ and $V(s)$, where s is the semaphore. The P operation is a potential wait operation. It is executed by a task when it wishes to enter the critical section. If the semaphore is set to 1 (meaning that no process is in the critical section), then it is decremented and the task is allowed to enter the critical section. If the semaphore is set to 0 when the *P* operation is executed by task A, this means that another task, say B, is in the critical section. Task A is suspended until task B signals that it is leaving the critical section by performing a *V* operation. This results in task A being allowed to enter the critical section.

An example of this follows for a robot task that wishes to enter the collision zone.

Perform operations outside collision zone

P(Collision_Zone_Semaphore)
Perform mutually exclusive operations in collision zone.
V(Collision_Zone_Semaphore)

Perform more operations outside collision zone

1.3 Synchronization of Tasks

Process synchronization is required when one task, typically a producer, wishes to signal another, the consumer. For example, the producer robot moves a part into position and then signals the event Part_Ready. The consumer robot, which is suspended waiting for the signal, is reactivated so that it can move to the part and pick it up.

Events may be used to synchronize the operations of two tasks. The producer task can perform a signal function as follows: Signal (E) which signals that an event E has taken place. The consumer task may perform a Wait (E) which suspends the task until the event has been signalled by the producer. If the event has already been signalled, then the task is not suspended.

An example of using events for synchronizing two robot systems is now given. A pick-and-place robot is to bring a part to a robot that is to drill four holes in it. On completion, the pick-and-place robot is to move the part away.

The pick-and-place robot A moves the part into position and then signals the event Part_Ready. The drilling robot B is activated, moves to the workplace and drills the holes. On completion, it signals a second event, Part_Completed, which is waited on by A. After being activated, Robot A removes the part. Each robot program is in a loop, as the robots will repetitively perform their tasks. The solution is as follows:

Robot A:

WHILE Work_Available DO

Pick up part
Move part to workplace
Release part
Move to safe position
Signal (Part_Ready)
Wait (Part_Completed)
Pick up part
Remove from workplace

END

Robot B:

WHILE Work_Available DO

Wait (Part_Ready)
Move to workplace
Drill four holes
Move to safe position
Signal (Part_Completed)

END

Next, consider the case where a producer robot hands over the part to a consumer robot. Once again, there is the potential problem of the two robots colliding with each other. However, this time we cannot prevent both robots being in the collision zone at the same time, since during the handover there is a time when both robots are holding the part.

The solution we adopt is that of allowing only one robot at a time to be in motion in the collision zone. First, one robot moves into the collision zone. It then signals to the other robot that it has reached the exchange position. The second robot now moves into the collision zone. An event signal Collision_Zone_Safe is used for this purpose. A second event signal Part_Ready is sent by the producer to notify the consumer that it is ready for the handover. Two more event signals are used during the handover, Part_Grasped and Part_Released.

Producer robot:

Pick up part
Move to edge of collision zone
Wait (Collision_Zone_Safe)
Move to exchange position
Signal (Part_Ready)
Wait (Part_Grasped)
Open Gripper to release part
Signal (Part_Released)
Wait (Collision_Zone_Safe)
Leave collision zone

Consumer robot:

Move to exchange position
Signal (Collision_Zone_Safe)
Wait (Part_Ready)
Close gripper to grasp part
Signal (Part_Grasped)
Wait (Part_Released)
Leave collision zone
Signal (Collision_Zone_Safe)

1.4 Message Communication

Concurrent tasks may communicate with each other using messages. Message communication is used when data needs to be passed between two tasks. Messages provide a general method of intertask communication. Thus Signal and Wait event commands may be packaged into messages.

The producer task P sends a message M to the consumer C. The consumer task C may request to receive a message from the producer. If a message is already available, the consumer will receive it and continue processing; otherwise it is suspended until the message arrives.

Two types of message communication are possible. With loosely coupled message communication (Fig. 1(a)), the producer sends the message to the consumer and then continues processing. In this case a message queue could build up between the producer and the consumer. With tightly coupled message communication (Fig. 1(b)), the producer sends the message and then waits for a reply. When the consumer receives the message, it will generate a reply and send it back to the producer. Both producer and consumer then continue processing. This type of communication is known in Ada as the rendezvous.

An example of message passing is that of data which needs to be passed between robots, or between a robot and another industrial system. For example, a vision system could pass part-location data to a robot task. As an example of message communication, consider the case where a vision system has to inform a robot of the type of part coming down a conveyor; e.g., whether a car body frame is a sedan or station wagon. The robot has a different program for each car body type. In addition, the vision system has to send the robot information about the location and orientation of a part on a conveyor. Usually this information is sent as an offset (i.e., relative position) from a point known to both systems. The part identification and offset information are sent in a message from the vision system to the robot. A sensor is used to indicate to the vision system that the car body frame has arrived. This is treated as an external event signal. The robot indicates that it has completed the welding operations it performs on the car by signalling the actuator Move_Car which results in the car being moved away by the conveyor

Vision system:

Wait (Car_Arrived)
Take picture of car body
Identify car body
Determine location and orientation of car body
Send message (car model identification, car body offset) to robot

Robot task:

Wait for message from vision system
Read message (car model identification, car body offset)
Select welding program for car model
Execute welding program using offset for car position
Signal (Move_Car)

2. Run-Time Support for Concurrent Tasks

Support for concurrent tasks can be provided either by a real-time executive or by a concurrent programming language.

2.1 Operating System Support for Concurrent Tasks

In the case where each task is written in a conventional sequential programming language such as Pascal, C or Fortran, intertask communication and synchronization is handled by calls to the real-time executive. A typical real-time executive (kernel of operating system) supports concurrent tasks by providing functions for priority preemption, task scheduling, intertask synchronization using events, mutual exclusion using semaphores, intertask communication using messages, and basic input–output support. Examples of such real-time executives are DEC's VAX/ELN and Hunter and Ready's VRTX. More details can be found in standard texts on operating systems (e.g., Peterson and Silberschatz 1985).

2.2 Language Support for Concurrent Tasks

Some languages provide support for concurrent tasks. Examples of such languages are Ada (Gehani 1984),

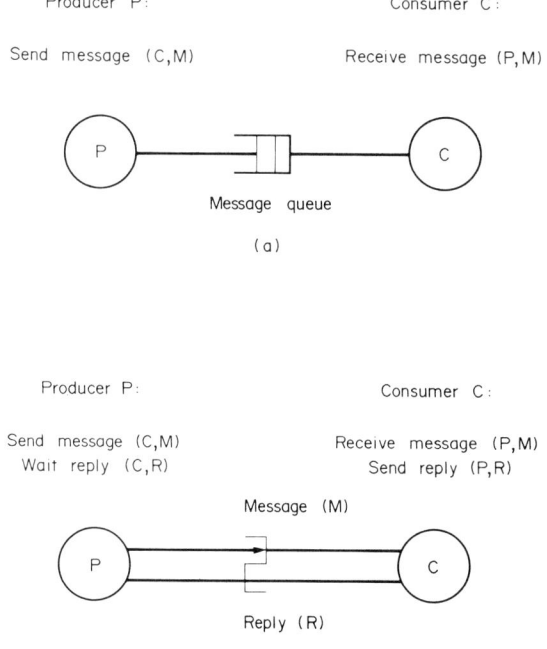

Figure 1
Message communication. (a) loosely coupled, (b) tightly coupled

Modula 2 and Concurrent Pascal. Typical features provided by the language are support for task creation and deletion, as well as support for intertask communication and synchronization. The run-time system would handle task scheduling and dispatching.

3. Analysis and Design of Real-Time Software Systems

Design methods for real-time systems need to take into account the special needs of these systems by supporting such concepts as concurrent tasks and state-transition diagrams, as well as more general design concepts such as information hiding (see Sect. 4.3 and Fig. 2). Analysis and design methods for real-time software systems include real-time structured analysis and design (Ward and Mellor 1985), the design approach for real-time systems (DARTS) (Gomaa 1984, 1986) and the US Naval Research Laboratory software cost reduction method (Parnas et al. 84).

To illustrate how a real-time software system may be designed, the DARTS design method is described, and an example of its use given, in the following section.

4. Design Approach for Real-Time Systems

DARTS is a design method for real-time systems. DARTS is a data-flow oriented design method. It may be considered an extension of the structured analysis (DeMarco 1978, Gane and Sarson 1979) and structured design methods (Yourdon and Constantine 1978). Page-Jones 1980), by providing an approach for structuring the system into tasks as well as a mechanism for defining the interfaces between tasks.

DARTS starts by developing a data-flow model of the system using the real-time extensions to structured analysis. The next stage involves transforming the data-flow model into a task structure model defining the concurrent tasks in the system and the interfaces between them. The emphasis of this transformation process is on concurrent processing and data abstraction. Next, each task, which represents a sequential program, is structured into modules using structured design.

4.1 Real-Time Extensions to Structured Analysis

Structured analysis has been extended to address the needs of real-time systems, as described in Ward and Mellor (1985). The steps involved are outlined briefly below.

(a) System context diagram. The system context diagram is developed, showing the interaction of the system to be developed with the external environment. The context diagram shows all inputs to the system and outputs from the system. The sources and sinks of data are shown explicitly on the diagram. The system to be developed is shown as one data transformation, which transforms the input data flows to output data flows. An example of a system context diagram is given in Fig. 3.

(b) Data-flow diagram decomposition. A hierarchical data-flow diagram decomposition is performed, in which the data transformation on the context diagram is decomposed into a data-flow diagram consisting of a number of data transformations (also known as processes or bubbles) connected by data flows and data stores, which are repositories of data. This decomposition may proceed to several levels, depending on the complexity of the system, and is typically based on functional decomposition. The contents of the data flows and stores are defined in a data dictionary. A data transformation which is not decomposed further has its function described, usually in structured English, in a minispecification. An example of a hierarchical data-flow diagram decomposition is given in Fig. 3 and 4, where the context diagram of Fig. 3 is hierarchically decomposed into the data-flow diagram shown in Fig. 4.

(c) State-transition diagrams. A feature of real-time structured analysis (RTSA) is the use of control transformations, which are defined by means of state-transition diagrams, in which they are depicted by a dashed circle. (A state-transition diagram describes the behavior pattern of a system or subsystem and is particularly important in systems where actions depend not only on input events but also on previous actions. This is a common feature of real-time systems.)

A state represents what is currently happening in the system, and so the system can be in only one state at a given time. In RTSA, states are depicted by rectangles and state transitions by arcs. The input event which causes the state transition is shown adjacent to the arc. Optionally, an action caused by the state transition may also be shown, either to the right of the event and separated by a / or underneath the event and separated by __. An example of a state-transition diagram is shown in Fig. 5, which defines the control transformation Validate Robot Command shown in Fig. 6.

(d) Event flows and control transformations. In addition to data flows, RTSA also supports event flows (indicated by dashed lines) to represent control flow. Three types of event flows are provided.

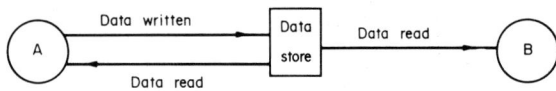

Figure 2
Information hiding module

Real-Time Software Design: Information Concerns

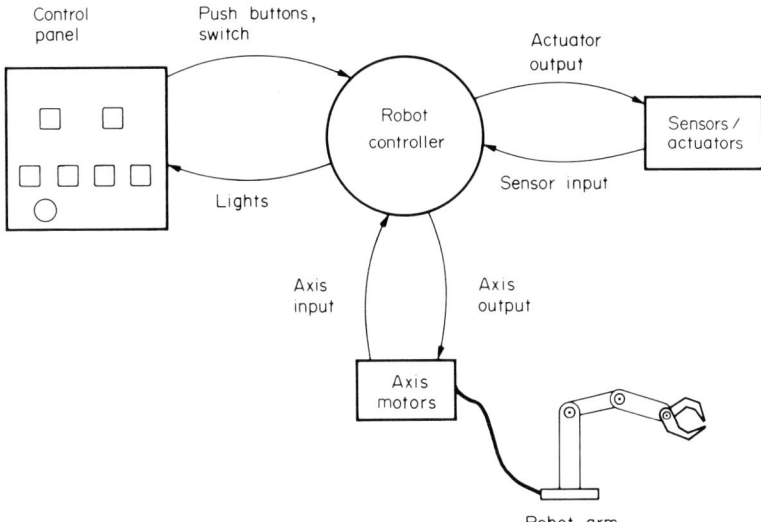

Figure 3
Robot controller system context diagram

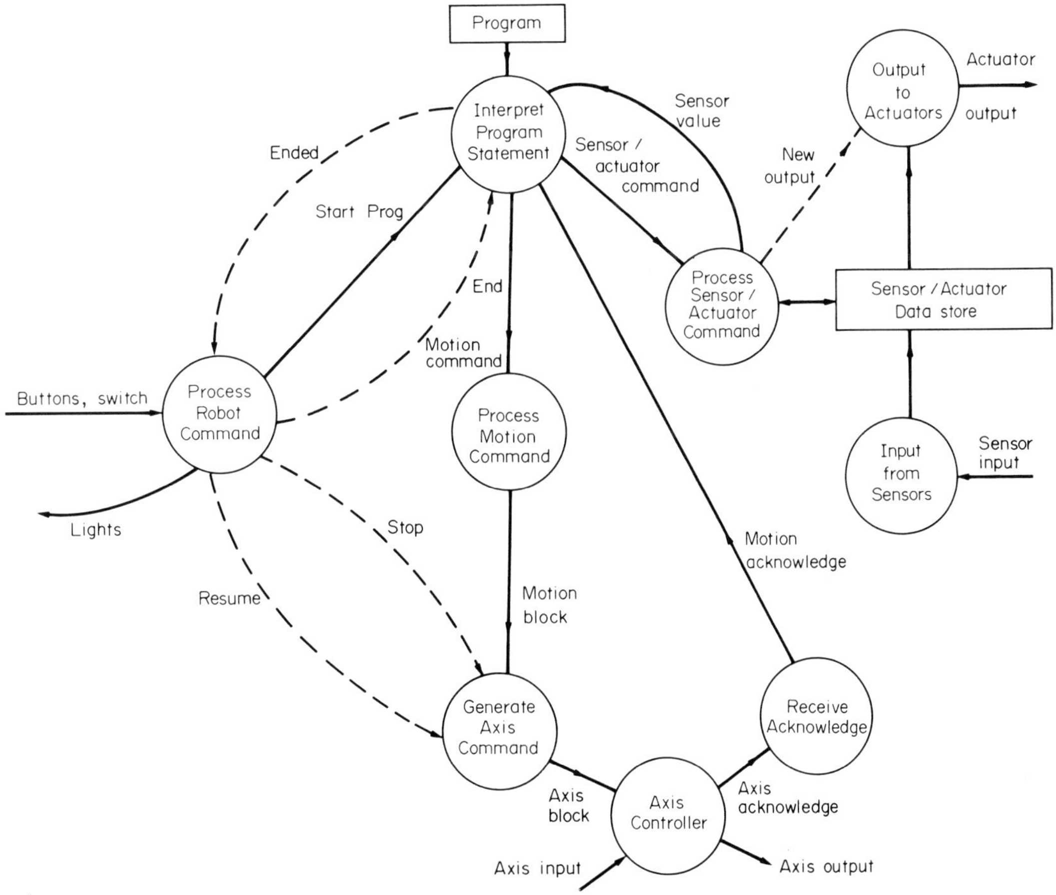

Figure 4
Overall robot controller data-flow diagram

407

Real-Time Software Design: Information Concerns

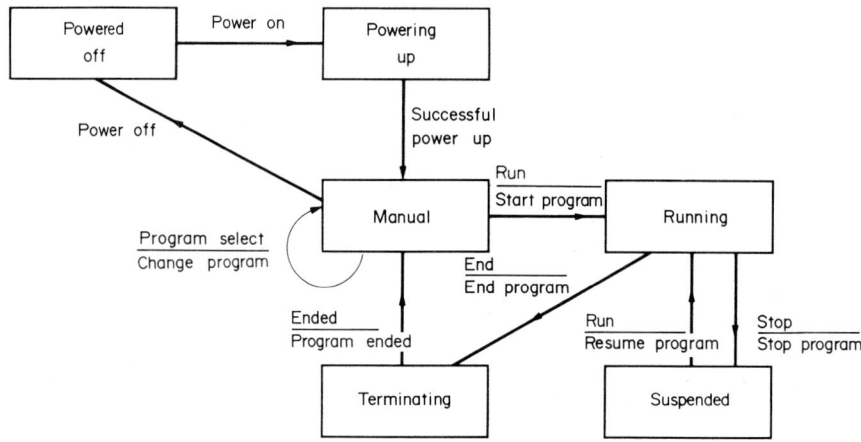

Figure 5
State-transition diagram. Instructions in capitals refer to Fig. 8

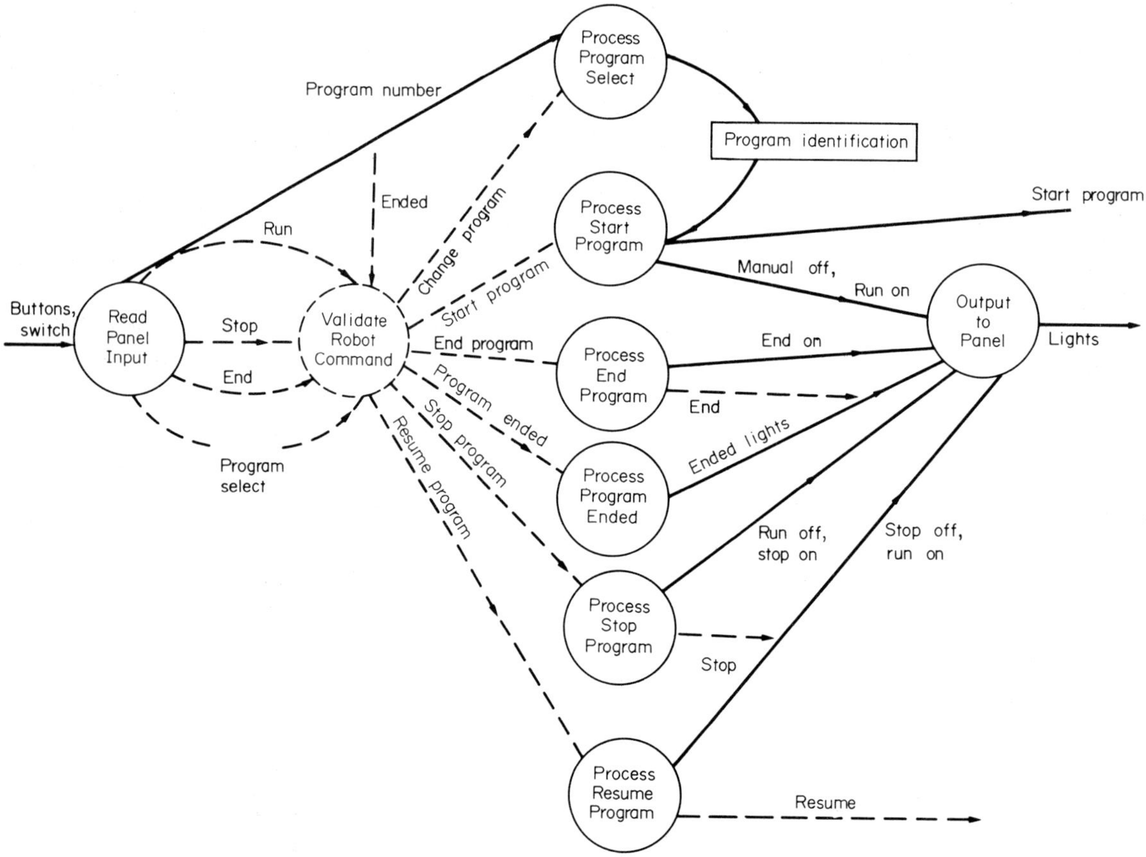

Figure 6
Data-flow diagram for Process Robot Command

(i) trigger, which signals an event occurrence thereby causing a data transformation to perform a specific action.

(ii) enable, which activates a data transformation. The transformation remains enabled until it is disabled by a subsequent event flow.

(iii) disable, which deactivates a previously enabled data transformation.

A control transformation may only receive trigger event flows as inputs. However it can generate any type of event flow as output.

4.2 Decomposition into Tasks

When all the functions in the system and the data flows between them have been defined, it is then possible to identify concurrency in the system. The next stage of the design method therefore involves considering how the concurrent tasks may be identified on the data-flow diagram (DFD).

The main consideration in decomposing a software system into concurrent tasks concerns the asynchronous nature of the functions within the system. The transforms in the DFD's (including control transformations) are analyzed to identify which of them may run concurrently and which need to be executed sequentially. By this means, the tasks in the system are identified. A task may encompass one or more transforms. Concurrent sets of transforms may be grouped into the same task.

The data diagrams are now redrawn showing the tasks and their interfaces. In doing this, a box is drawn around each transform or set of transforms which logically form a task. Each box then becomes a task. The criteria for deciding whether a transform should be a separate task or grouped with other transforms into a single task are given below.

(a) *Dependency on input–output.* A transform depending on input or output is often constrained to run at a speed dictated by the speed of the input–output device it is interacting with. In this case the transform needs to be a separate task.

(b) *Time-critical functions.* A time-critical function needs to run at a high priority and therefore can be structured as a separate high-priority task.

(c) *Computational requirements.* A computationally intensive function (or set of functions) may run as a lower priority task consuming spare CPU cycles.

(d) *Functional cohesion.* Certain transforms may be grouped into a task because they perform a set of closely related functions. The data traffic between these functions may be high, in which case having them as separate tasks could increase the system overhead. Instead, each function is implemented as a separate module within the same task. This ensures functional cohesion both at the module and task level.

(e) *Temporal cohesion.* Certain transforms may perform functions which are carried out at the same time. Consequently, these functions may be grouped into a task so that they are executed each time the task receives a stimulus. Each function should be implemented as a separate module to achieve functional cohesion at the module level. These modules are grouped into the task, thereby achieving temporal cohesion at the task level.

(f) *Periodic execution.* A transform that needs to be executed periodically may be structured as a separate task which is activated at regular intervals.

(g) *Server.* A server task may provide a service for other tasks in the system. It may maintain or manage a data store and respond to requests from other tasks to update or read data from the data store.

A control transformation may be structured as a separate time-critical task. Alternatively, it may be combined with other transforms that it interacts with into a task based on the temporal cohesion criterion.

4.3 Defining Task Interfaces

We now need to consider the interfaces between the tasks. On the data-flow diagrams, these interfaces are in the form of data flows, event flows or data stores. The next stage involves formalizing the task interfaces using the guidelines described below.

A *data flow* between two tasks is treated as one of the following:

(a) a loosely coupled message queue, if one task needs to pass information to the other and the two tasks may proceed at different speeds; or

(b) a tightly coupled message/reply, if information is passed from one task to the other but the first task cannot proceed until it has received a reply from the other.

Figure 1 shows the message communication mechanisms supported: the graphic notation for loosely coupled and tightly coupled message communication are shown.

A *data store* that needs to be accessed by two or more tasks is handled as an information hiding module (IHM) in which the data structure is defined, as well as the access routines to the data structure. The IHMs are based on the concepts of information hiding and data abstraction (Parnas 1972, 1979). Figure 2 shows the graphical notation used in DARTS for an IHM. The data store is shown as a box. In this example, there are two access procedures, shown by the transforms A and B. The access procedures actually execute within the task(s) which wish to access the data store. Since data in the store may be accessed by more than one task concurrently, it is necessary for the access procedures to provide the necessary synchronization of access to the data.

An *event flow* is treated in one of the following ways.

(a) an event signal, only if a notification of an event occurrence is required and no data transfer is required.

(b) If the destination task is on a separate processor, the event signal is implemented as a message containing the event notification.

(c) The event flow is also treated as a message if the destination task can receive several event signals and the order in which they are received is important. Having a FIFO message queue guarantees that event messages are received in the correct sequence.

The graphic notation used for task synchronization in DARTS is shown in Fig. 7.

Events are used for synchronization purposes between tasks where no actual information transfer is needed. A destination task may wait for an event occurrence. A source task may signal an event that activates the destination task. Furthermore, the synchronization mechanism is extended to allow one task to wait for any one of several events to be signalled. If any one event is signalled, the task is activated. A task may wait for events used for synchronization purposes only, as well as events associated with message queues.

4.4 Task Design

(*a*) *Structured design.* The next stage involves designing each individual task. Each task represents a sequential program. In this section we describe how the task could be designed using the structured design method (Yourdon and Constantine 1978, Page-Jones 1980). Depending on the nature of the task, either transform centered or transaction centered design is used.

We start by revisiting the data-flow diagrams developed in the first step of the design process. These earlier DFDs did not take concurrency into account, and we may find that what has now been identified as a task appeared as several transforms, connected by data flows and data stores, on an earlier diagram. In this case we extract and refine this group of transforms, as they form the basis of the design of this task. If the earlier decomposition has not been taken to this level of detail, then a new data-flow diagram is drawn for the task.

Next, the task is structured into modules using the structured design method. A structure chart is developed for each task, which identifies the modules in the task and the interfaces between them.

(*b*) *State dependency in transaction processing.* Of the two structured design strategies, transaction centered design has been found to be more useful than transform centered design for use in DARTS. However, a major limitation of transaction centered design is that the action taken on the incoming transaction depends only on the input data. In state-dependent real-time systems, the action to be taken depends not only on the incoming data but also on the current state of the system; that is, it depends on what has happened before.

The solution to this problem is to introduce a module called the state transition manager (STM). The STM maintains the current state of the system. It also maintains a state-transition table which defines all legal and illegal state transitions, as well as the actions to be performed. A control transformation is designed as an STM. The STM may be encapsulated within a task, in which case all communication with the task is via messages or event signals. Alternatively it is designed as a module which is called by more than one task.

The STM is called with the transaction as an input parameter. It then checks the state-transition tables to determine whether the input is legal, given the current state of the system. If it is legal, the STM changes the state of the system (if necessary) and returns a positive response to the calling task; otherwise it returns a negative response. Where appropriate, it also returns the valid action(s) to be performed by the task.

In DARTS, the STM is designed as an information hiding module which maintains a data structure, namely the state-transition table, which is hidden from the calling tasks. The module also contains the access procedures which check the validity of task requests, and performs the state transitions.

5. Example of Use of the DARTS Design Method

In this section, a case study is used to illustrate the DARTS design method. The case study consists of a robot controller which controls up to six axes of motion, as well as interacting with digital sensors and actuators. For the purposes of this article, the case study has been substantially simplified from the actual robot controller system design. However, it serves to illustrate the main concepts of the design method.

Control of the axes and the digital input–output is provided by executing a program which is initiated from a control panel. The control panel consists of a number of push buttons and a selector switch for program selection (Fig. 8). The state-transition diagram for the controller is shown in Fig. 5. For simplicity, error conditions have been ignored.

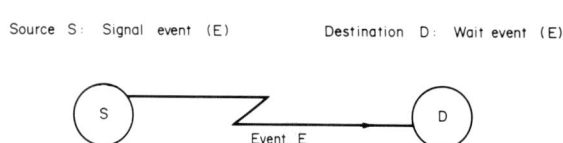

Figure 7
Task synchronization

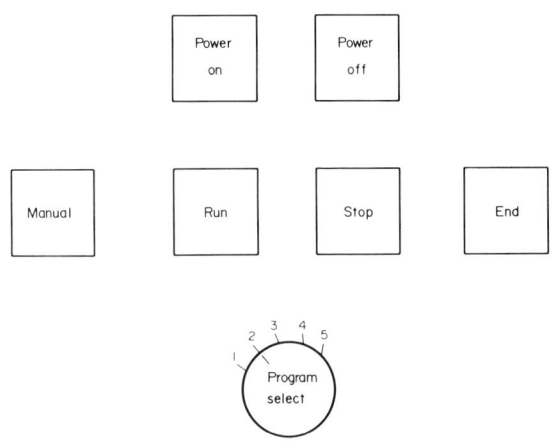

Figure 8
Robot control-panel layout

When the Power on button is pressed, the system enters the powering up state. On successful completion of the power-up sequence, the system enters Manual state. The operator may now select a program using the Program select rotary switch, which can be set to indicate the desired program number. Pressing Run initiates execution of the program currently selected. The system makes a transition into Running state. The operator may suspend execution of the program by pressing Stop. The system then transitions into Suspended state. The operator may then resume program execution by pressing Run. The system returns to Running state. To terminate the program, the operator presses End. The system now enters Terminating state. When the program terminates execution, the system returns to the Manual state.

5.1 Data-Flow Analysis
The system context diagram is shown in Fig. 3. The overall data-flow diagram for the controller is shown in Fig. 4. The decomposition of the Process Robot Command transform is shown in Fig. 6.

Each time a button is pressed, the control-panel input is read and validated by Process Robot Command. Since the validity of the inputs depends on the current state of the system, the controller state-transition table has to be checked. For simplicity, it is assumed that invalid user inputs are ignored. Valid robot commands are passed on to the appropriate transform, either Interpret Program Statement or Generate Axis Command. In addition Process Robot Command also· outputs the settings of the control-panel-status lights.

Process Robot Command passes the Start Program command to Interpret Program Statement which starts interpreting the program. It executes arithmetic and logical statements directly. Motion and sensor/actuator statements require further processing.

A motion command is passed on to Process Motion Command. Process Motion Command does some mathematical transformations on the data and passes a motion block to Generate Axis Command. Generate Axis Command converts the data to the required format for the Axis Controller and passes an axis block to the Axis Controller.

When Stop is pressed, Generate Axis Command stops feeding axis blocks to the Axis Controller. When Run is pressed, it resumes. When the axis motion associated with an axis block has been completed, an Axis acknowledgement is sent to Receive Acknowledge by the Axis Controller. This acknowledgement is processed and then passed back as a Motion acknowledgement to Interpret Program Statement.

In the case of a sensory/actuator input output statement, Interpret Program Statement sends a command to Process Sensor/Actuator Command. For a sensor command, Process Sensor/Actuator Command reads current sensor values from the sensor/actuator data store (placed there by Input from Sensors). For an actuator command, it updates the sensor/actuator data store and signals Output to Actuators to indicate that there is new output.

Figure 6 shows the data-flow diagram for Process Robot Command. Read Panel Input receives inputs from the control panel. The inputs are passed on to the control transformation Validate Robot Command, which implements the state-transition diagram shown in Fig. 5. Validate Robot Command checks that the input is valid given the current state of the system. Assuming the input is valid, the new state and desired action are determined from the state-transition table. The appropriate action transform is triggered to perform the action.

Consider the case when Run is pressed. Validate Robot Command looks up the state-transition table (Fig. 5) to determine what the next stage is and what the desired action is. Thus, a Run input identifies a Start program action if the system is in Manual state and a Resume program action if the system is in Suspended State. In both cases the system enters Running state. Assume the system is in Suspended state. In this case, the state-transition table indicates that the next state is Running and the action to be performed is Resume program.

Consequently, Validate Robot Command (Fig. 6) signals the transform Process Resume Program. This transform signals a Resume event, switches on the control-panel Run light and switches off the Stop light. Control-panel outputs are passed to the Output to Panel transform.

5.2 Structuring the System into Tasks
Having drawn the data-flow diagrams, we need to consider how the system may be structured into concurrent tasks. To determine this, we need to examine the transforms in Figs. 4 and 6 and apply the task

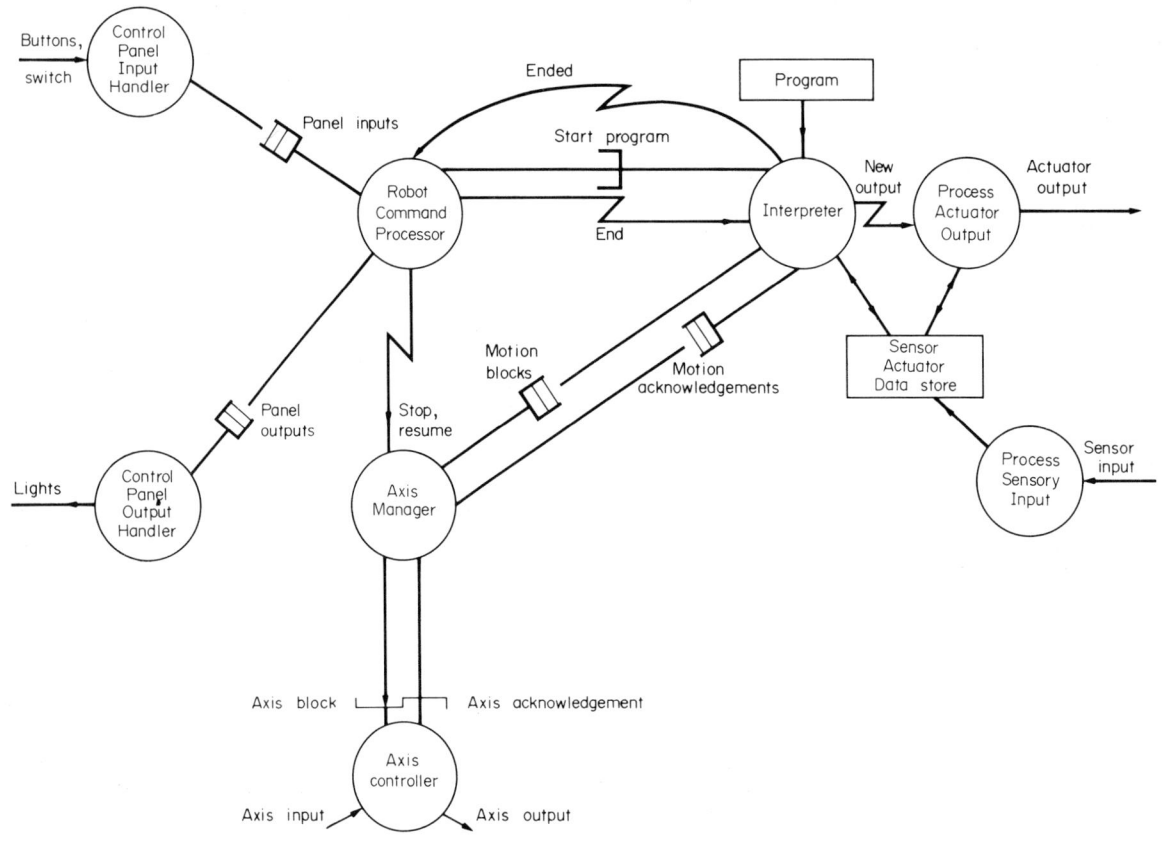

Figure 9
Task structure chart

decomposition criteria of Sect. 1.3. Fig. 9 shows the system structured into tasks.

Consider Fig. 6 first. As a first-task-structuring criterion, typically any function that interacts directly with an input–output device needs to be a separate task since its effective speed is governed by the speed of the device it is interacting with. Consequently the Read Panel Input transform needs to be a separate task, the Control Panel Input Handler, since it has to receive inputs from the control panel. Similarly, the Output to Panel transform needs to be a separate task, the Control Panel Output Handler.

The Validate Robot Command transform and all the transforms it signals may be grouped together into one task, the Robot Command Processor (RCP), according to the temporal-cohesion task-structuring criterion. Thus after each control-panel input is validated, the appropriate action is immediately processed.

Now consider Fig. 4. The transforms Interpret Program Statement, Process Motion Command and Process Sensor/Actuator Command represent the program Interpreter. These transforms are grouped together to form one task according to the functional-cohesion task-structuring criterion, as they represent a group of closely related functions.

The Generate Axis Command and Receive Acknowledge transforms are grouped together into one task, the Axis Manager, according to the temporal-cohesion task-structuring criterion. Each time Generate Axis Command outputs an axis block to the Axis Controller, Receive Acknowledge has to wait for an acknowledgement before Generate Axis Command can output the next block. Thus there is no advantage in concurrently executing the two transforms. In addition, the speed of these two transforms is dictated by the speed of the axes. Thus no other transforms can be combined with them into the Axis Manager task.

The Axis Controller is structured as a separate time-critical task. It runs on a separate processor as it interacts closely with the axes.

Sensor/Actuator requests from the Interpreter are processed by two tasks. The Output to Actuators transform is activated on demand whenever an output is required and so is structured as a separate input–output dependent task, Process Actuator Output. The Input from Sensors transform periodically scans the input sensors and so is structured as a separate periodic task, Process Sensory Input.

5.3 Defining Task Interfaces

Once the tasks have been identified (Fig. 9), the next step is to define the interfaces between the tasks using the guidelines given in Sect. 1.4.

Panel inputs are queued up for the Robot Command Processor by the Control Panel Input Handler. Thus the interface between the two tasks consists of a loosely coupled message queue. Similarly, panel outputs are queued for the Control Panel Output Handler by the RCP. The RCP sends a Start program message to the Interpreter identifying the program to be executed. The Interpreter generates motion blocks and places them in the motion-block queue. Since some motion blocks imply a long move while others are short, the queue between the Interpreter and the Axis Manager acts as a buffer. When the Interpreter reads a nonmotion statement (e.g., a sensor/actuator command), it needs to wait until axis motion has reached the desired position before executing the statement. Consequently the Interpreter waits for a Motion Acknowledgement message from the Axis Manager.

The main routine of the Interpreter consists of a Task Synchronization Module in which the Interpreter handles all synchronization conditions. Initially it waits for a Start program message from the RCP. After interpreting each line of the program, it checks whether an End event has been signalled. When interpreting has been temporarily suspended, it waits for either an End event or a Motion Acknowledgement message. When End is signalled, it completes program execution and then signals End to the RCP.

The Axis Manager receives motion blocks from the Interpreter in its message queue. The main routine of the Axis Manager is a Task Synchronization Module which handles all synchronization conditions. Each time the Axis Manager waits for a motion block from the Interpreter, it is suspended if one is not available. When it receives the block, it tests to see if a Stop event has been signalled. If so, it waits for a Resume signal. If there is no Stop condition or if Resume was

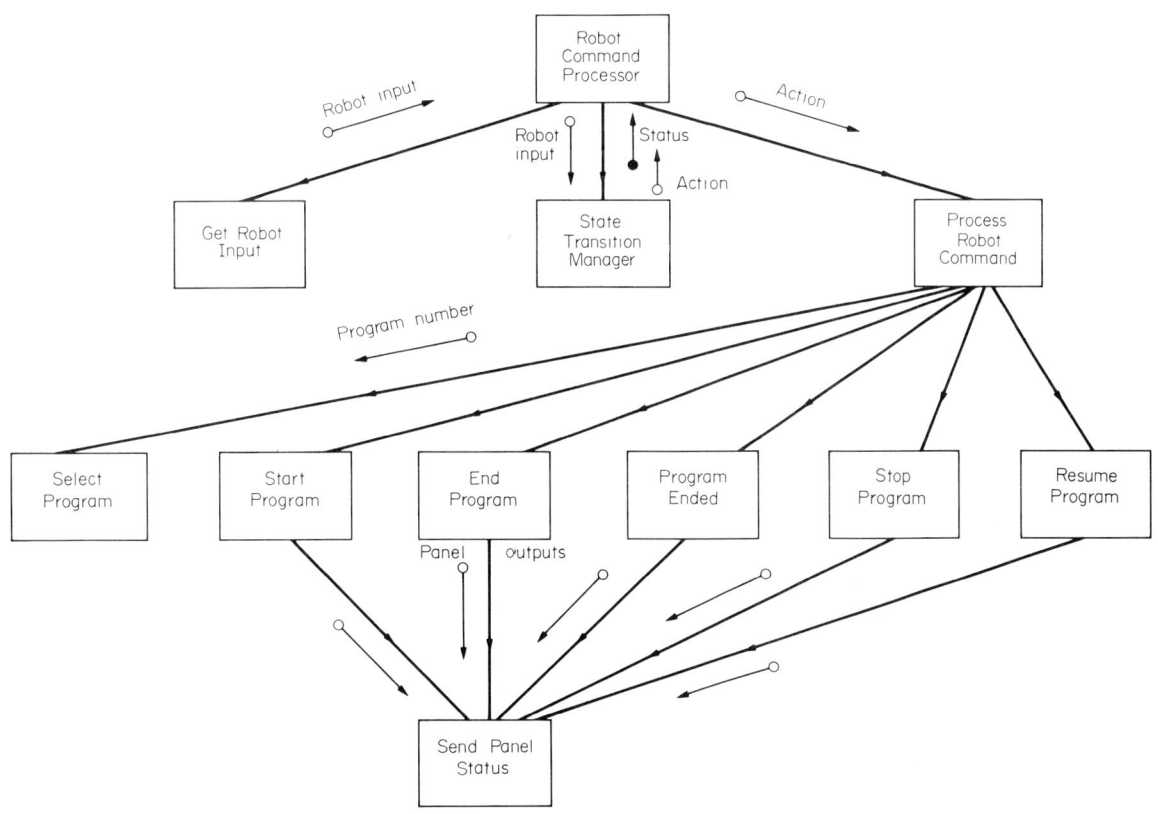

Figure 10
Structure chart for Robot Command Processor

signalled, the Axis Manager sends the axis block to the Axis Controller and waits for an axis acknowledgement of block completion. The communication between the Axis Manager and the Axis Controller is an example of tightly coupled message communication.

A Sensor Actuator Data Store (SADS) is used to store the current values of the sensors. If the interpreter processes an output command, it updates the SADS and signals the Process Actuator Output task that new output is available. The Process Sensory Input task periodically scans the input sensors and when a change takes place updates the SADS. If the interpreter processes a sensor command, it reads the SADS for the current value of the sensor. Since access is made to the SADS by three tasks, this access has to be synchronized by the access routines. The SADS and the access routines constitute an information hiding module.

5.4 Structuring Tasks Into Modules

After the interfaces between the tasks have been defined, the next step is to define the structure of each task. Each task is a sequential program. For each task, the data-flow diagram is drawn and from this the structure chart is derived using the structured design method. To illustrate this we consider one task, namely the Robot Command Processor. This is an example of transaction centered design supplemented by a state transition manager.

Figure 10 shows the structure chart for the Robot Command Processor. The main routine, also called the Robot Command Processor, is a task supervisory module. It calls Get Robot Input to receive a message or event. If one is not available, the task will be suspended. When the input message or event is received, the State Transition Manager (STM) is called with the robot input as a parameter. The STM returns a valid/invalid status and optionally an action to be performed. If the input is not valid for the current state (e.g. Stop is pressed while the system is in Manual state), an invalid status is returned by the STM. If the input is valid, the STM may return an action. The control module Process Robot Command is now called with the action as a parameter. Process Robot Command calls the appropriate action module to perform the action.

Bibliography

Brinch-Hansen P 1973 *Operating System Principles*. Prentice–Hall, Englewood Cliffs, New Jersey
DeMarco T 1978 *Structured Analysis and System Specification*. Yourdon Press, New York
Dijkstra E W 1968 Co-operating sequential processes. In: Genuys F (ed.) *Programming Languages*. Academic Press, New York, pp. 43–112
Gane C, Sarson T 1979 *Structured Systems Analysis*. Prentice–Hall, Englewood Cliffs, New Jersey
Gehani N 1984 *Ada: Concurrent Programming*. Prentice–Hall, Englewood Cliffs, New Jersey

Gomaa H 1984 A software design method for real time systems. *Commun. ACM* **27**(10)
Gomaa H 1986 Software development of real time systems. *Commun. ACM* **29**(7)
Hoare C A R 1974 Monitors: An operating system structuring concept. *Commun. ACM* **17**(10), 549–57
Page-Jones M 1980 *The Practical Guide to Structured Systems Design*. Yourdon Press, New York
Parnas D L 1972 On the criteria to be used in decomposing systems into modules. *Commun. ACM* **15**(12)
Parnas D L 1979 Designing software for ease of extension and contraction. *IEEE Trans. Software Eng.* March
Parnas D L, Clements P, Weiss D 1984 The module structure of complex systems. *Proc. 7th IEEE Int. Conf. Software Engineering*. IEEE Press, New York
Peterson J L, Silberschatz A 1985 *Operating System Concepts*, 2nd edn. Addison–Wesley, Reading, Massachusetts
Ward P, Mellor S 1985 *Structured Development for Real-Time Systems*, Vols. 1, 2. Yourdon Press, New York
Yourdon E, Constantine L 1978 *Structured Design*, 2nd edn. Yourdon Press, New York

H. Gomaa
[George Mason University, Fairfax, Virginia, USA]

Recognitional Decision Making: Information Requirements

Skilled personnel rely on recognitional decision making to handle naturalistic tasks such as commanding teams of urban firefighters, commanding crews that combat forest fires, leading tank platoons, playing high-level chess and performing battle management functions. People are likely to use recognitional approaches for tasks that are familiar, time pressured and dynamic. Decision support systems that are restricted to analytical forms of information may interfere with recognitional strategies and thereby degrade performance.

1. What is Recognitional Decision Making?

The concept of recognitional decision making states that proficient decision makers can generate and implement options by judging situations as familiar. This enables the decision maker to recognize the typical response to those situations. The process avoids the analytical strategy of generating a set of options and then evaluating them to select the best one. Under conditions such as time pressure, however, such analytical decision making may be impossible.

Recognitional decision making explains how people can function competently without performing analyses. A recognition-primed decision (RPD) model (Klein *et al.* 1986, Klein 1989) is presented in Fig. 1. The RPD model was derived from studies of urban fireground commanders. Faced with an incident, the experienced decision maker can judge it to be familiar

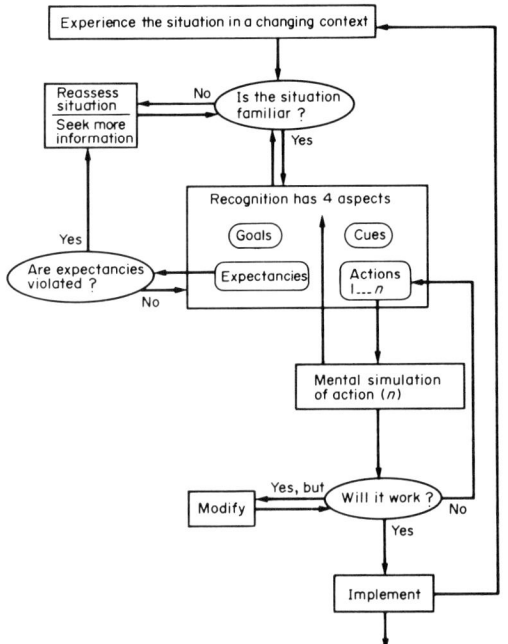

Figure 1
Recognition-primed decision (RPD) model

on the basis of prior incidents. If it is not, additional information is sought. With recognition of what is happening in the incident, the skilled decision maker receives an identification of plausible goals, an increased sensitivity to critical cues, a formulation of expectancies about the way the incident should develop, and an identification of a set of typical responses with the most usual response as the dominant item in the set.

How are options evaluated? Clearly it would be dangerous to carry out actions without checking whether they made sense in a new situation. The evaluation of options is done by imagining how they would be carried out within the context of the current incident. The decision maker thinks about whether any situational features might make an option unworkable. Finding serious problems, the decision maker may try to modify the option to implement it; otherwise it is rejected and a less typical option is considered. Thus the decision maker evaluates options one at a time, starting with the most typical, until an adequate one is found.

An example from the author's research may be useful. A fireground commander responded to a call on a Sunday night and found the front of a two-story brick building engulfed in flames. The building was identified as a molding company, and no one appeared to be inside. His first decision was to call for additional equipment. He then ordered his crews to begin an exterior attack using streams of water. He quickly judged that the water was not effective, suggesting that the streams were not hitting the seat of the fire. He sent a crew to the roof to open channels for heat and smoke to escape. They reported that the roof was "spongy" and hot, and that at the back there was an additional single-story section of the building that was invisible from the street. Fire was bursting out of each hole they punched in the roof, obviously under great pressure, so they suspected that plastics or hydrocarbons were burning. A new commander arrived with additional equipment and, after evaluating the situation, first ordered the crew to withdraw from the roof and then ordered an interior attack into the center of the building. After cutting through several padlocked fences and forcing open a garage door, the firefighters found themselves staring into what looked like the inside of a blast furnace. They later found that the building contained burning boxes of plastics, against which water is not greatly effective. The new commander quickly decided to abandon the interior attack and after 8–10 hours the firefighters were successful in containing the fire to the front part of the single-story area.

During this incident, the commanders made several decisions: calling for more equipment, starting an exterior attack in the front, sending a crew to the roof, withdrawing them when the roof appeared dangerous, initiating and then terminating an interior attack, and continuing with the exterior attack. Most of these decisions were made in less than a minute because once the situation was understood it was unnecessary to consider any alternatives. Therefore, decisions were being made without having to perform analyses such as generating and evaluating sets of alternative options to determine strengths and weaknesses in order to identify the best option.

One way to explain the RPD model is to contrast it with traditional models of decision making. Seven features distinguish the RPD model from analytical decision models.

(a) *situation assessment.* The RPD model views decisions in a changing context of how situations are perceived, in contrast to the analytical paradigm of studying relatively context-free decision making in static environments.

(b) *action recognition.* The RPD model asserts that when a situation is recognized the most typical response becomes obvious, in contrast to the analytical paradigm of randomly generating large sets of options to be sure of identifying a feasible action.

(c) *serial evaluation.* The decision maker evaluates the options one at a time rather than employing concurrent evaluation to assess relative strengths and weaknesses.

(d) *satisficing*. For most tasks the decision maker tries to find the first option that will work rather than optimizing by searching for the best option.

(e) *evaluation through imagination*. The decision maker evaluates the options by imagining how they will be carried out rather than by rating each option along weighted evaluation dimensions. The evaluation is context-bound because the examination of options is relative to the dynamics of the situation rather than being context-free and using general evaluation dimensions.

(f) *strengthening options*. The evaluation of options allows the decision maker to identify weaknesses that can be overcome by modifications to make them stronger, rather than forcing selection from an option set without trying to strengthen the options.

(g) *response availability*. If pressed to react quickly, the decision maker can select the current response being evaluated rather than having to wait until all analyses are completed to tabulate the results and identify the strongest options.

Under what task conditions do we expect to see recognitional decision making, as compared to analytical decision making? Time pressure clearly favors recognitional decision making. Zakay and Wooler (1984) showed that subjects trained to use multiattribute utility analyses (i.e., to evaluate each option on each evaluation dimension) showed no gains when the decision time was reduced to one minute. Task familiarity is relevant since the effective use of recognitional decision making depends on having acquired some familiarity with the task. Satisficing makes it more reasonable to use recognitional strategies, whereas optimizing requirements makes analytical decision making more likely. However, if the task requires justifying the choice there is a stronger tendency to use an analytical framework. This is especially marked when there are disputes between parties with different needs. Tasks involving abstract data are more likely to require analytical decision making than tasks involving concrete and perceptual data. Finally, tasks featuring computational complexity favor analytical methods.

2. Evidence for Recognitional Decision Making

Several of the key concepts of recognitional decision making were derived from studies of skilled performers. Simon (1955) observed business managers and administrators and described their performance in terms of satisficing. Simon found that the business environment rarely called for optimizing. More recently, Isenberg (1984) also reported that business executives rarely performed concurrent evaluation of several options to find the best one.

De Groot (1978) collected protocol data from highly skilled chess players and coined the term "progressive deepening" to describe how they conducted deep searches of interesting options rather than broad searches to include many options. In the RPD model, the concept of progressive deepening has evolved into the idea that proficient decision makers can evaluate single options by imagining how those options would be implemented.

Hammond *et al.* (1984) contrasted analytical and intuitive decision strategies as used by highway engineers to perform different aspects of their jobs and showed that each strategy works well with some subtasks but not with others. They postulated a cognitive continuum to describe the range of strategies possible, and they hypothesized that variables such as abstract/concrete cues and time pressure would affect the selection of a decision strategy.

Klein (1989) summarized a set of studies examining the frequency of use of different decision strategies. A modified critical incident technique was used to collect interview data about nonroutine decisions. Specific probes were used to obtain data about the types of cues judged relevant and the types of decision-making activities that were used. Several different subject populations were used: urban fireground commanders, wildfire incident commanders, tank platoon leaders, design engineers and battle managers. These studies were all characterized by the use of naturalistic tasks in contextually rich situations that were continually changing. Failure to accomplish the tasks had personal consequences. In addition, many of the studies used highly experienced decision makers and involved performance under a fair degree of time pressure. The urban fireground commanders (FGCs), for example, averaged 23 years of experience and reported that 85% of their decisions were made in less than one minute.

The results of these studies are presented in Table 1, which shows that even for nonroutine incidents the frequency of recognitional decision making was very high, ranging from 42 to 96%. It was also found that the studies including routine decisions as part of the critical incidents showed the highest rates of recognitional decision making.

Recently, several other researchers have presented evidence for recognitional decision strategies. Lipshitz (1987) obtained protocol data about actual decisions made by Israeli Defense Force personnel and showed that the decisions relied on recognitional rather than analytical strategies. Noble *et al.* (1987) also reported evidence favoring recognitional decision making in a task involving a Navy command-and-control scenario. Rasmussen (1985) has studied nuclear power plant operators and described a rule-based level of performance that is similar to the RPD model.

Much of this work is consistent with the phenomenological perspective presented by Dreyfus (Dreyfus 1979, Dreyfus and Dreyfus 1986). He claims that novices

Table 1
Proportion of decisions handled by RPD strategy

Study domain	Number of decisions	Percentage of decisions handled by RPD strategy
Urban FGC	156	80
Expert–novice FGC	110[a]	70
experts	61	70
novice	49	71
Wildland FGCs	110[a]	51
functional	79	56
organizational	31	39
Tank platoon leaders	55	42
Design engineers	51	60
Battle managers	27	96
Total	509	

[a] Total number of such FGCs

lack the experience base necessary to obtain recognitional matches of events and therefore have to rely on abstract rules of behavior. In contrast, experts can judge familiarity and recognize how to proceed without having to perform analyses of options. Therefore, skilled performance moves from the abstract to the concrete rather than vice versa.

3. Information Requirements

A key function of a descriptive model of naturalistic decision making is to provide guidance for designing decision support systems. These include human–computer interfaces, databases, communication networks and knowledge-based systems, as well as software specifically developed to improve the performance of perceptual and conceptual tasks.

The significance of a recognitional model of decision making is to suggest that analytical decision making occurs relatively infrequently and only under special conditions. Decision support systems that rely on analytical decision models may actually impede recognitional decision making. For example, some decision aids require the user to enter a set of alternatives, identify a set of evaluation dimensions, assign a weight to each dimension and rate each option along each evaluation dimension. These aids would make it difficult to use recognitional strategies. Other decision aids call upon the user to judge probabilities of events and utility values of problem states. These judgements may be incompatible with the performance of a context-bound evaluation of a single option.

One criterion for effective system design is that its use should not interfere with the skilled performance of operators who are proficient at their tasks. Another criterion is that the system should promote the development of skills in less-experienced operators.

A model of recognitional decision making suggests several system capabilities to help satisfy these criteria. These are described below.

3.1 Situation Assessment
It is important that the operators maintain a clear assessment of the situation at two levels: the external environment in which the operator is acting and the system environment with which the operator is interfacing.

3.2 Critical Cues
Operators need to understand how the external environment is changing and reacting to their responses. Systems should highlight critical cues, such as small changes that may signify the beginning of trends. Systems should also help the operator track expected changes and note when expectancies are violated. It is sometimes easier to notice unexpected changes that occur than it is to notice expected changes that fail to occur. To reduce the disorientation that results from shifting CRT displays, it may be useful to retain one overall situational display, open and close windows, and add and subtract detail within the context of this display.

3.3 Reliability Check
The operator needs to understand system functioning in sufficient detail to navigate easily through the possible system states and to quickly detect when the system is malfunctioning or becoming unreliable for a given task. Proficient commanders monitor subordinates, looking for nonverbal cues of exhaustion or confusion in order to know how much confidence to put in the subordinates' judgements. Similarly, proficient operators need to be able to monitor computer systems to detect signs of unreliability due perhaps to missing or contradictory data or to task conditions that the system is unable to handle effectively.

3.4 Typicality Flags
Intelligent systems can assist operators by suggesting typical goals and actions, thereby acting as a check on situation assessment.

3.5 Data Trends
Data formats should enable operators to rapidly identify trends and exceptions. Alphanumeric data are often harder to interpret than analog data. The additional precision afforded by using numerical data may be offset by the slower reactions to trends signified by these data.

3.6 Sensitivity
One of the limitations of digital systems relative to analog systems is the possibility of a slow response time. This is not an inherent problem, but sometimes designers build in a slow refresh rate in order to

conserve resources. The consequence is that extremely brief events such as system transients may be missed altogether. Also, the mapping of important trends may take too long, with operators staring at their CRTs waiting for the next point that will reveal the shape of the curve. It is important that designers identify critical cues and ensure that systems are designed to detect these cues, perhaps by changing refresh rates during significant task segments.

3.7 Visualization

Serial evaluation appears to depend on the ability of the decision maker to imagine the consequences of actions. Designers should try to support this process by making it easier to visualize different outcomes and to model these within the context of the system by allowing the operator to play out the scenario and to call up analytical support if it becomes too difficult to estimate certain variables or interactions.

3.8 External Memory

It may also be useful to let the operator tag each imagined scenario for later retrieval, review and elaboration. Operators also need help keeping track of plans and decisions.

3.9 Analog Retrieval

Another suggestion is that information in the system's memory be accessed in the form of analogs and prototypes. Memory systems organized on the basis of abstract features do not support recognitional decision making. Expertise seems to call for recognitional matches to prior events or to event prototypes, and this process can be mirrored through the use of systems such as case-based reasoning (Kolodner *et al.* 1985) that support analogical inferences. Such systems would enable operators to identify relevant cases, access the plans used in these cases, and adjust those plans to quickly arrive at a strategy for a new incident.

4. Conclusion

Proficient decision makers appear to rely on recognitional processes. If designers are sincere in their objective of enhancing operator capabilities, they will design systems that support recognitional decision making in the way those systems present information, store information and interact with operators.

Acknowledgement

The preparation of this article was supported by a Research Contract from the Army Research Institute for the Behavioral and Social Sciences, MDA903-85-C-0327. The views, opinions and findings contained here are those of the author and should not be construed as official Department of the Army position, policy or decision.

See also: Decision Making: Information Processing and Organizational Models; Knowledge Representation; Supervisory Control: Philosophical Considerations in Manufacturing Systems

Bibliography

de Groot A D 1978 *Thought and Choice in Chess*, 2nd ed. Mouton, New York
Dreyfus H L 1979 *What Computers Can't Do: The Limits of Artificial Intelligence*. Harper and Row, New York
Dreyfus H, Dreyfus S 1986 *Mind Over Machine: The Power of Human Intuitive Expertise in the Era of the Computer*. Free Press, New York
Hammond K R, Hamm R M, Grassia J, Pearson T 1984 *The Relative Efficacy of Intuitive and Analytical Cognition*. Center for Research on Judgment and Policy, Boulder, Colorado
Isenberg D J 1984 How senior managers think. *Harv. Bus. Rev.* **6**, 80–90
Klein G A 1989 Recognition-primed decisions. In: Rouse W R (ed.) *Advances in Man-Machine Systems Research*, 5. JAI Press, Greenwich, Connecticut
Klein G A, Calderwood R, Clinton-Cirocco A 1986 Rapid decision making on the fire ground. *Proc. Human Factors Soc. 30th Annual Meeting*. Human Factors Society, Dayton, Ohio, Vol. 1, pp. 576–80.
Kolodner J, Simpson R, Sycara-Cyranski K 1985 A process model of case-based reasoning in problem solving. In: Kaufmann M (ed.) *Proc. IJCAI–85*, pp. 284–90
Lipshitz R 1987 *Decision Making in the Real World: Developing Descriptions and Prescriptions from Decision Maker's Retrospective Accounts*, unpublished manuscript. Center for Applied Sciences, Boston University, Boston, Massachusetts
Noble D, Boehm-Davis D, Grosz C 1987 *Rules, Schema, and Decision Making*, Engineering Research Associates Work Unit No. NR 649-005. Office of Naval Research, Vienna, Virginia
Rasmussen J 1985 The role of hierarchical knowledge representation in decision making and system management. *IEEE Trans. Syst., Man Cybern.* **15**(2), 234–43
Simon H A 1955 A behavioral model of rational choice. *Q. J. Econ.* **69**, 99–118
Zakay D, Wooler S 1984 Time pressure, training, and decision effectiveness. *Ergonomics* **27**, 273–84

G. A. Klein
[Klein Associates, Yellow Springs, Ohio, USA]

S

Simulation Methodology and Model Manipulation

Modelling and simulation is an emerging field whose boundaries are not well defined. Model building can be traced back at least as far as the Newtonian era, but the tremendous impetus it received with the advent of the electronic computer is of course a relatively recent phenomenon. Moreover, there are at least two main sources of approach and technique—from physical science and operations research—which are still in the process of confluence and unification.

1. Origins of Computer Simulation

Physical scientists, especially in the applied and engineering branches, are faced with increasingly complex equations—combinations of general laws and empirical relations—for which analytic solutions are of limited use. In response, automatic solvers of differential equations were developed, whose operation was based on the integration capabilities of some particular natural medium. The early differential analyzers, developed in the 1920s by Bush and others, were based on mechanical motion. These were soon replaced by the faster and more reliable electronic analog computers, in which the integration is performed by capacitors and signals are normalized by high-gain amplifiers.

Analog computers saw heavy and significant use in the chemical and aerospace industries, among others, but limitations on problem size, stability and accuracy of computation led to harnessing of the emerging electronic digital computers to achieve equivalent capabilities. The latter perform integration numerically, using principles which originated with long-known manual approximation methods. However, what gave digital computers eventual primacy was their information-processing abilities: simulation programming languages could be designed which would provide for convenient specification, processing and manipulation of differential-equation models. Analog computation survives nowadays in the form of hybrid computers which couple analog integration with digital information processing and control.

The second source of approach and technique lay in operations research with its desire to ameliorate industrial processing networks plagued by congestion, unproductive delays and underutilization of resources. New concepts such as "event" and "activity" were developed which (in the beginning) had little to do with the classical modelling concepts. An associated development was the incorporation of direct experimentation subject to chance outcomes within the computation, originally known as Monte Carlo methods. The discrete modelling approach saw its tools being developed before there was adequate practical experience or theory to support them.

2. Definitions of Modelling and Simulation

As the field matures, the emphasis is shifting from simulation, as a set of computational techniques, to modelling, whether it be in a continuous or discrete form (or indeed, in forms which combine the two). Limitations are better appreciated, but so are the enormous potentials.

Definitions of modelling and simulation abound (Pritsker 1979), partly reflecting the many origins of the area. Perhaps the most representative is that of Shannon (1975):

> Simulation is the process of designing a model of a real system and conducting experiments with this model with the purpose of either understanding the behavior of the system or of evaluating various strategies (within the limits imposed by a criterion or set of criteria) for the operation of the system.

Shannon emphasizes the experimental orientation of simulation techniques but widens the term "simulation" to include modelling and design activities which are not necessarily simulation-related. Other definitions try to characterize simulation narrowly to distinguish it from other computational techniques. One such definition is that adopted by Pritsker (1979):

> Simulation modelling assumes that we can describe a system in terms acceptable to a computing system. In this regard, a key concept is the system state description. If a system can be characterized by a set of variables, with each combination of variable values representing a unique state or condition of the system, then manipulation of the variable values simulates movement of the system from state to state. This is precisely what simulation is: the representation of the dynamic behavior of the system by moving it from state to state in accordance with well defined operating rules.

It is characteristic of simulation tools that they facilitate a (hypothetical) description of the internal structure of a real system to the level of detail which the modeller perceives in reality. This power of representation distinguishes simulation from analytical techniques but also places a new burden on the modeller such as the choice of the level of detail compatible with the objectives of the modelling effort, the real-system data available and the computational and human resources at one's disposal. To write a detailed description of a system (i.e., a model) is one thing; to verify that it reflects one's intentions and then to validate it as a true description of the real system is another.

3. Activities Involved in Simulation Modelling

With the recognition that informal definitions can go only so far in conveying concepts and methods, a formal framework which founds a structure of definitions and theorems upon a set-theoretic basis has been developed (Zeigler 1976). A comprehensive structuring of the activities involved in good practice delineates the following categories (Ören 1982).

(a) Model generation or referencing: the generation of models (i.e., system descriptions) either by construction from scratch or by employing models retrieved from a model repository as components to be coupled together.

(b) Model processing: the manipulation of model texts (e.g., to produce documentation, to check consistency) and the generation of model behavior, of which simulation, restricted to mean computerized experimentation with models, is a predominant form.

(c) Behavior processing: the analysis and display of behavior in static (e.g., equilibrium), dynamic (i.e., concerning state trajectories) or structural (i.e., concerning changes in model structure) modes.

(d) Real-system experimentation: the gathering and organized storage of behavioral data from the real system or any of its components of interest.

(e) Model quality assurance: the verification of the simulation program or device as correctly implementing the intended model, the validation of the model as an adequate representation of the real system and the testing of other relations in which models participate.

This framework forms the basis for organization of articles on simulation methodology and model manipulation in Singh (1987).

4. Simulation and Artificial Intelligence

Although it has taken some time for it to become apparent, the natural synergy between the approaches of artificial intelligence (AI) and computer simulation are now being extensively exploited. In AI programming systems, an object is a conglomerate of data structures and associated operations, called methods. Objects are usually given generic descriptions so that classes of objects are defined and individual instances of such classes may be generated at will. Simulation languages have long employed such generic concepts. Not only have static entities been represented in such a fashion, but also dynamic entities such as events and processes. However, in conventional simulation, a distinct paradigm for decomposing problems into object classes and associated methods has not emerged. Conventional simulation languages offer no special support for such a programming style.

Furthermore, object-oriented programming bears a direct relation to the so-called frame-based knowledge representation schemes of AI. In such schemes, classes of objects form a taxonomical hierarchy in which they are arranged according to their degree of generality. Special kinds of objects have both attributes and methods that are unique, as well as those that are inherited from more general classes.

The incorporation of AI knowledge representation schemes within simulation models results in so-called knowledge-based simulation systems. Such schemes can be used to organize information, not only about the nature of the objects involved in the simulation, but also within the components themselves so as to model intelligent agents.

The application of AI techniques to modelling and simulation methodology has great potential. By extension, design and engineering activities may also be greatly enhanced, since they are increasingly dependent on simulation analysis. Expert systems, the spearhead of AI commercial application, are software systems that incorporate significant components of human knowledge and expertise in a limited problem domain. Since modelling and simulation is a difficult labor-intensive process, simulation researchers have been looking for areas where expert systems could be of assistance. Such systems could decrease the need for modellers to be experts in simulation programming, advise on selection of models or their components for specific purposes, interpret simulation results with expert statistical judgement, and so on.

While such potential is extremely attractive, expanding the user-friendliness and range of applicability of simulation, progress is not likely to be rapid. The fact is that the formalization of knowledge needed to conduct a meaningful simulation study is extremely difficult. Knowledge cannot be entered as a discrete set of independent units (rules) gleaned from observation of an expert solving a problem in a limited domain (the domain of modelling and simulation is vast and there are no experts in all its facets). Rather, knowledge must be encoded adhering to a coherent systematization derived from a sound conceptual framework (see *Simulation: Model-Base Organization and Utilization*).

5. Literature and Societies

Today, simulation methodology is employed in almost every field of science, engineering and decision making. Methodological and application studies are reported in many journals including *Simulation* and the *IMACS Journal*, organs of the two major societies devoted to the simulation profession: The Society for

Computer Simulation and the International Association for Mathematics and Computer Simulation, respectively. Among the major conferences are the Winter Simulation Conference, the Summer Computer Simulation Conference (both held in North America) and the triennial World Congress of IMACS.

See also: Simulation Methodology: Top-Down Approach; Simulation: Model-Base Organization and Utilization

Bibliography

Elzas M S, Ören T I, Zeigler B P 1987 *Modelling and Simulation Methodology in the Artificial Intelligence Era.* North-Holland, Amsterdam, pp. 195–210
Greenberg H J, Maybee J S 1981 *Computer-Assisted Model Analysis and Model Simplification.* Academic Press, New York
Ören T I 1982 Computer aided modelling systems. In: Cellier F E (ed.) *Progress in Modelling and Simulation.* Academic Press, London
Ören T I, Elzas M S, Zeigler B P 1983 *Simulation and Model-Based Methodologies: An Integrated View.* Springer-Verlag, New York
Pritsker A A B 1979 Compilation of definitions of simulation. *Simulation* **33**, 61–63
Shannon R E 1975 *Systems Simulation: The Art and the Science.* Prentice–Hall, Englewood Cliffs, New Jersey
Singh M G (ed.) 1987 *Systems and Control Encyclopedia.* Pergamon, Oxford
Vansteenkiste G C, Kerckhoffs E J H, Zeigler B P 1987 *Artificial Intelligence in Simulation.* SCS, San Diego, California
Vansteenkiste G C, Spriet J 1982 *Computer Aided Modelling and Simulation.* Academic Press, London
Zeigler B P 1976 *Theory of Modelling and Simulation.* Wiley, New York
Zeigler B P, Elzas M S, Klir G J, Ören T I 1979 *Methodology in Systems Modelling and Simulation.* North-Holland, Amsterdam

B. P. Zeigler
[University of Arizona, Tucson,
Arizona, USA]

Simulation Methodology: Top-Down Approach

Simulation is experimentation with dynamic models (Korn and Wait 1978). As shown in Fig. 1, a simulation study has basically three major components: (a) a description of the simulation study which in turn consists of the descriptions of a specific model and the experimental conditions, (b) behavior generation performed by a behavior generator which drives the model under the specified experimental conditions, to generate (c) model behavior, which can be either trajectory behavior, as is most often the case, or structural behavior to denote the structural changes of the model under the experimental conditions.

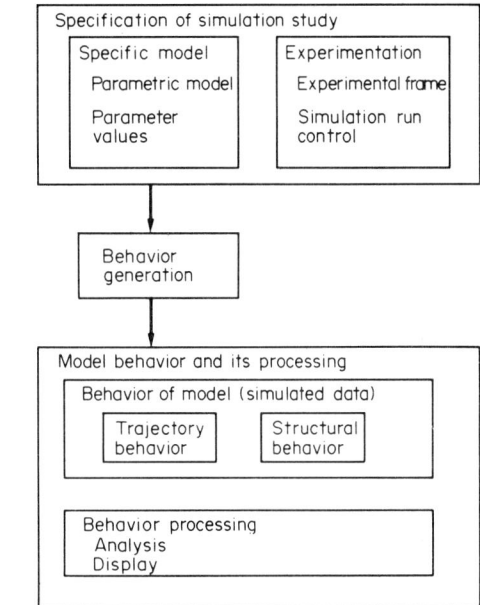

Figure 1
Elements of a simulation study

1. Model

There are several views on what a model is. Nalimov's view (Nalimov 1981 p. 77) is interesting from the point of view of fundamental research:

> A mathematical model, in the sense used here, is a question put by the researcher to nature ... Any question necessarily consists of two component parts: an assertive part which introduces some knowledge, thus making the question possible (this part can be regarded as a prerequisite of the question) and the interrogative part proper.

From the point of view of the relation of a model to reality and to an observer, an object A is a model of an object B if an observer C can use A to answer questions that interest him about B. This generic definition, due to Minsky (1965), is applicable to any type of model. Implicit the above definition is the goal of modelling. An object which can be considered to be a model of a real system for certain aspects of reality may not be considered as such for some other aspects. Therefore, the goal of the study should be explicitly stated for the acceptability assessment of models.

From another point of view, a model is a collection of variables (representing entities and/or their attributes) and relations among them. This point of view is used in both inductive system theories (Klir 1969) and deductive (axiomatic) system theories (Mesarovic et al. 1970, Ören 1974, Padulo and Arbib 1974, Wymore 1967).

In computerized simulation, the interest is concerned with computer-processable models which have behavior that can be indexed with time. Therefore, mathematical dynamic models are used (Zeigler 1976). However, in computer-aided experimentation, physical models (such as a scale model of an aircraft) can be used to observe the behavior of the model under some experimental conditions which can be partly or totally monitored by a computer that can also perform all data-collection activities. A model used in a simulation study consists of a parametric model and the associated set of parameter values (i.e., parameter set). A given parametric model can be associated with different parameter sets.

Furthermore, one can also conceive that every simulation model consists of a declarative part and a generative part. In the declarative part, the static structure of a model is given by specifying the names (and if necessary the range of acceptable values) of different types of descriptive variables of the model, such as input, state, output and auxiliary variables, constants, parameters, tabular functions and interpolated variables. In the generative part, the dynamic structure of a model is given by specifying how the state transitions occur to generate new values of state variables and how outputs are computed.

Further information on models is provided in Ören (1987c).

2. Experimental Conditions

Experimental conditions consist of two groups of information; namely, experimental frames and their application to (parametric model, model parameter set) pairs.

An experimental frame defines a limited set of circumstances under which a system or a model is to be observed or subjected to experimentation (Ören and Zeigler 1979). It consists basically of the following five components.

(a) Observational variables (i.e., the variables that we are interested in observing). They can be any descriptive variable and are not necessarily just the output variables of a model. Furthermore some or all output variables of a model may provide input(s) to itself (feedback coupling) or to another model and may not be directly observed at all.

(b) Admissible input segments (i.e., sequence of values of the input variable(s) acceptable by the model).

(c) Initial settings of the state variables.

(d) Termination conditions, which may be specified explicitly in terms of the simulated time or in terms of the descriptive variable(s) of the model.

(e) Specifications for collection, compression and display of simulated behavior.

Understanding the elements of an experimental frame is essential in externalizing questions posable to a model. Separation of models from the specification of experimental conditions was first recommended within the context of the simulation language GEST (Ören 1971). This concept is also an integral part of the theory of modelling and simulation (Zeigler 1976).

3. Behavior

As stated in the introduction, in a simulation study a behavior generator drives the model under the specified experimental conditions to generate the behavior of the model. Behavior can then be processed either for analysis or for display purposes (Ören 1987a).

4. Relation of Simulation to Other Model-Based Activities

Behavior generation is one aspect of model processing. There are other types of model-processing activities, called symbolic model processing, which are performed for reasons other than behavior generation (Ören 1987b).

Figure 2 shows a unified view of model-based activities. In Fig. 2, behavior generation and symbolic model processing are shown as special cases of model processing. Model-based simulation systems can benefit from the inclusion of symbolic model-processing activities.

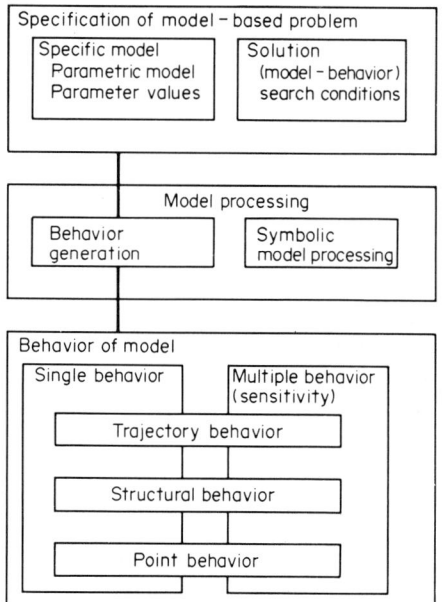

Figure 2
Unified view of model-based activities

In addition to trajectory and structural behavior, there is another type of behavior called point behavior (Ören 1987a). As shown in Fig. 2, by inclusion of point behavior in addition to trajectory and structural behavior, we are in a better position to conceive the common aspects of simulation and other model-based behavior generation techniques such as deductive or inductive inferencing, optimization or information retrieval. In an optimization study, for example, a mathematical model is "driven" by a behavior generator (analytical or a search technique) to find an "optimal solution" which has a point value in 1- or n-dimensional search space.

Figure 3 depicts a unified view of a model-based decision support system and the central position of simulation. Basically, such a system would have two parts: one dealing with reality and the other with model-based activities, which in turn are grouped in two parts: model referencing and model use.

Further information can be found in Ören (1984a, b), Ören *et al.* (1984), Zeigler (1979, 1980) and Zeigler *et al.* (1979).

5. Elements of a Model-Based Simulation Software System

The elements of a simulation system are highlighted in Fig. 4, where the elements of a model-based simulation software system are shown. Brief explanations of these elements and their functions are given here. The model-based simulation system executive is the module which interfaces the user and the software system. The model manager is responsible for the coordination of two basic tasks: modelling and model processing (use).

The modelling aspect involves two groups of activities computer-assisted modelling and model-base management. A computer-assisted modelling environment should provide guidance to the user in the specification of models, detect and explain errors, provide advice for any correction, and finally certify the acceptability of the model with respect to a set of explicitly stated semantic facts and rules. The semantic knowledge can be based on (a) modelling methodology used, (b) basic scientific fields such as physics, and (c) application-domain-specific knowledge such as ecology, population dynamics and engineering knowledge. Model-based management aims at keeping, in a model (i.e., model file), computer-processible models expressed in a model specification language (Ören 1982).

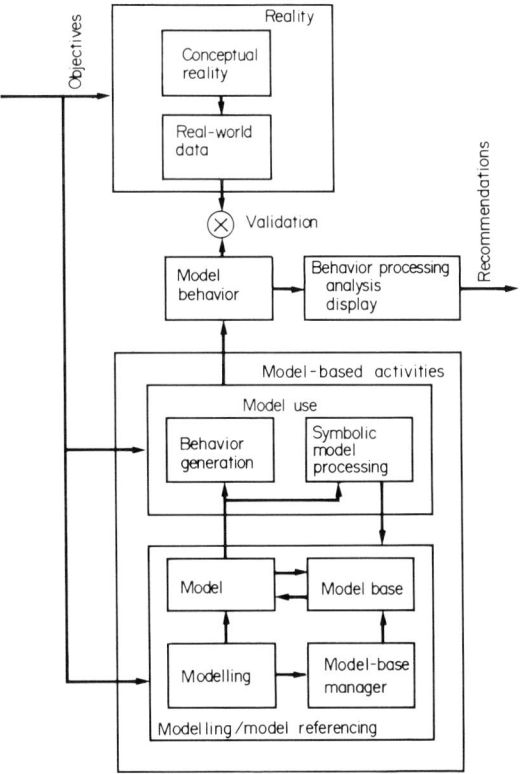

Figure 3
Unified view of a model-based decision support system and position of simulation

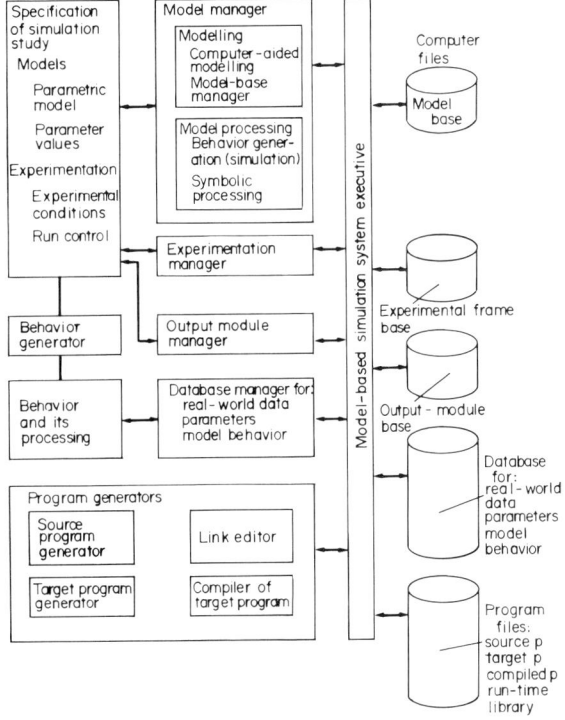

Figure 4
Elements of a model-based simulation system

Model processing (or model use) consists of two groups of activities: (a) symbolic model processing as explained by Ören (1987b), and (b) behavior generation (simulation) which is also explained by Ören (1987a).

The experimentation manager is responsible for

(a) computer-assisted experimental-frame specification;

(b) experimental-frame-base management;

(c) symbolic processing of specification of experimentation to check, for example, whether or not an experimental frame is applicable to a model or whether or not an experimental frame is contained within another one (in the latter case, for example, one could eliminate a simulation study and simply answer a query by processing the behavior obtained in the related simulation study); and

(d) simulation run-time monitoring.

The output-module manager is responsible for computer assistance in specifying the output modules and for their storage.

The database manager is responsible for storing, updating, searching and processing simulated data, real-world data and model parameters.

Specifically, a parameter manager is responsible for all or part of the following activities.

(a) Specification of parameter values:

   (i) parameter values are to be determined (computer-aided estimation of parameters): model identification, model fitting, model calibration;

   (ii) parameter values are already given (computer-assisted parameter specification).

(b) Parameter-base management.

(c) Symbolic processing of parameter values, which involves, for example, checking whether or not parameter values provided are acceptable for a model. If in a parametric model, ranges of acceptable values of parameters are specified by the modeller, it is possible to decide algorithmically whether or not a set of parameter values provided by a user is applicable for a model. Similar considerations are also applicable for tabular functions.

The following program generators and programs are needed: source program generator, target program generator, run-time program library and link editor. The source program generator accepts as input the specifications of the parametric model and corresponding parameter set, as well as specifications of the experimentation and output modules. After checking correctness, completeness and compatibility, it then links them into a source program expressed in a high-level model-based simulation language.

The target program generator translates the source program into a target program usually expressed in a high-level programming language which may be (but is not necessarily) a model-based language. Until the realization of compilers of model-based simulation languages, this translation step would satisfy a practical need. The system-generated target simulation program should be an interactive program; that is, it should allow a user to interactively update parameters and experimental conditions.

The run-time program library includes several types of utility programs needed during the execution of simulation program. It includes the following modules:

(a) simulation study monitor to control number and length of simulation runs, postrun and poststudy activities;

(b) model driver to activate different model modules at appropriate time instants;

(c) behavior generator to manage simulated time, to generate values of noninput descriptive variables or to monitor structural changes of a model; and

(d) other simulation utility programs for collection, storage, compression and display of data.

The link editor links the modules of compiled user programs and the necessary modules of the run-time library modules.

As shown in Fig. 4, the system would have the following computer files (or bases):

(a) model base to hold computer-processible models;

(b) experimental frame base;

(c) output module base; and

(d) databases for:

   (i) real-world data,
   (ii) parameter values,
   (iii) simulated behavior (trajectory behavior and structural behavior),
   (iv) programs (user programs and run-time library).

See also: Simulation Methodology and Model Manipulation

Bibliography

Director S W, Rohrer R A 1972 *Introduction to System Theory.* McGraw–Hill, New York

Elzas M S, Ören T, Zeigler B P (eds.) 1986 *Modelling and Simulation Methodology in the Artificial Intelligence Era.* North-Holland, Amsterdam

Klir G J 1969 *An Approach to General Systems Theory.* Van Nostrand Reinhold, New York

Korn G A, Wait J V 1978 *Digital Continuous-System Simulation*. Prentice–Hall, Englewood Cliffs, New Jersey

Mesarovic M C, Macko D, Takahara Y 1970 *Theory of Hierarchical, Multilevel Systems*. Academic Press, New York

Minsky M L 1965 Matter, mind and models. In: Kalenich W A (ed.) *Proc. IFIP Congr.*, Vol. 1. Spartan Books, Washington, DC, pp. 45–49

Nalimov V V 1981 *Faces of Science*. ISI Press, Philadelphia, Pennsylvania

Ören T I 1971 GEST: A combined digital simulation language for large scale systems. In: *Proc. Tokyo 1971 AICA Symp. on Simulation of Computer Systems*. Society of Analog Technique of Japan, Tokyo, pp. B1 1–4

Ören T I 1974 Deductive general systems theories and simulation of large scale systems. In: *Proc. 1974 Summer Computer Simulation Conf.* AFIPS Press, Montvale, New Jersey, pp. 13–16

Ören T I 1982 Computer-aided modelling systems (Keynote paper), SIMULATION '80 symposium. In: Cellier F E (ed.) *Progress in Modelling and Simulation*. Academic Press, London, pp. 189–203

Ören T I 1984a Model-based activities: A paradigm shift. In: Ören T I, Zeigler B P, Elzas M S (eds.) *Simulation and Model-Based Methodologies: An Integrative View*. Springer, Heidelberg, pp. 3–40

Ören T I 1984b Model-based information technology: Computer and system theoretic foundations. *Behav. Sci.* **29**(3), 179–85

Ören T I 1987a Model behavior: Types, taxonomy, generation and processing techniques. In: Singh 1987, pp. 3030–35

Ören T I 1987b Simulation models symbolic processing: Taxonomy. In: Singh 1987, pp. 4377–81

Ören T I 1987c Simulation models: Taxonomy. In: Singh 1987, pp. 4381–88

Ören T I, Aytaç K Z 1985 Architecture of magest: A knowledge-based modelling and simulation system. In: Jávor A (ed.) *Simulation in Research and Development*. North-Holland, Amsterdam, pp. 99–109

Ören T I, Zeigler B P 1979 Concepts for advanced simulation methodologies. *Simulation* **32**(3), 69–82

Ören T I, Zeigler B P 1986 From Stone tools to cognizant tools: The quest continues. In: Vansteenkiste G C, Kerckhoffs E J H, Dekker L, Zuidervaart J C (eds.) *Proc. 2nd European Simulation Congr.* SCS, San Diego, California, pp. 801–7

Ören T I, Zeigler B P 1987 Artificial intelligence in modelling and simulation: Directions to explore. *Simulation* **48**(4)

Ören T I, Zeigler B P, Elzas M E (eds.) 1984 *Simulation and Model-Based Methodologies: An Integrative View*. Springer, Heidelberg

Padulo L, Arbib M A 1974 *System Theory*. Saunders, Philadelphia, Pennsylvania

Singh M G (ed.) 1987 *Systems and Control Encyclopedia*. Pergamon, Oxford

Wymore A W W 1967 *A Mathematical Theory of Systems Engineering: The Elements*. Wiley, New York

Zeigler B P 1976 *Theory of Modelling and Simulation*. Wiley, New York

Zeigler B P 1979 Modelling and simulation methodology: State-of-the-art and promising directions. In: Dekker L, Savastano G, Vansteenkiste G C (eds.) *Proc. IMACS Simulation of Systems Conf.* North-Holland, Amsterdam, pp. 819–36

Zeigler B P 1980 Concepts and software for advanced simulation methodologies. In: Ören T I, Shub C M, Roth P F (eds.) *Proc. 1980 Winter Simulation Conf.* IEEE, New York, pp. 25–44

Zeigler B P, Elzas M S, Klir G J, Ören T I (eds.) 1979 *Methodology in Systems Modelling and Simulation*. North-Holland, Amsterdam

T. I. Ören
[University of Ottawa, Ottawa, Ontario, Canada]

Simulation: Model-Base Organization and Utilization

This article reviews the organization of models and data for storage and retrieval. Recognition of the importance of such repositories of information and knowledge in the modelling and simulation enterprise is relatively recent.

1. Modelling and Simulation as a Process

Figure 1 depicts the activities of modelling and simulation as a process (an integrated dynamic system) in which the model base figures centrally. The process is driven by objectives generated outside the system boundaries over time. As new objectives come in, they initiate model-synthesizing activity. The available knowledge for such activity comes from the model base and also from the database, which stores and organizes data gathered about the real system.

Model construction is followed by simulation (model experimentation) and validation phases. Validation leads to new experimentation on the real system and may require more modification or even rejection and reinitiation along different lines. In the process, new or more refined objectives may be formulated, as deficiencies in the current knowledge base (model, data) become more apparent. Ultimately, one or more models are produced to meet the external objectives. Besides being sent to the decision maker,

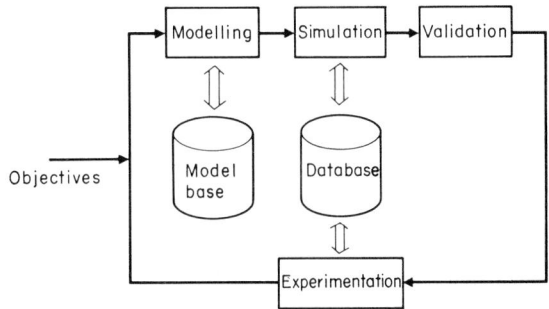

Figure 1
Modelling and simulation as a process

these models are also stored in the model base and so made available for further rounds of activity stimulated by new objectives.

Let us note some implications of the foregoing for management of the modelling and simulation process.

1.1 Continued and Indefinite Span of the Process

The process is viewed as an ongoing, never-ending set of activities, not as taking place only during a "modelling project." The classical view (which still governs funding allocation policies of government agencies, for example) is to initiate a modelling project with a set of objectives (more or less clearly stated), some funds and personnel and a delivery date. In this view, the process exists only between initiation and delivery dates; more precisely, an instance of the process exists between such initiation and delivery dates, each such instance being viewed as an independent start-from-scratch, one-shot sequence of activities. With no institutionalized integration and coordination of such instances, one may expect wasteful duplication, excessive cost and shortfall of objectives. Any cumulative growth in knowledge is only an accidental side product of modelling activity in the classical view.

1.2 Partial Data Availability and Partial Model Validity

At the initiation of modelling, there will usually be a lack of real system data for calibration and validation. Because experimentation during a project is limited, this will probably be true also at the project's termination. Thus, at the delivery date, the model will be in some state of partial validity. But if the model remains accessible in a model base, it can be tested against new relevant data whenever these are obtained, perhaps in connection with some other project. Moreover, the model is also being tested whenever it participates as a component in a composite model. Thus, while the integrated view recognizes the partialness of data and model validity, it also conceives of possibilities for efficient use of this available knowledge to sustain its continued growth.

1.3 Multiple Complementary and Competitive Representations in the Model Base

Models are competitive when they embody different, mutually exclusive hypotheses about how the real system works. They are complementary when they embody the same hypotheses but represent them in different ways. Both kinds of situations may exist in a model base. Because of the partial-validity problem, we may have to maintain competitive models (those achieving a certain confidence level, say) on which to base decision making. We should be able to test the sensitivity of management, control or design decisions to the model alternatives. Complementary models, on the other hand, represent the same hypotheses about the real system, but one representation may be better than another in a particular application. For example, even though time- and frequency-domain representations of a linear system embody the same information, the first is better for answering steady-state, the second for transient questions of behavior.

1.4 Models at Various Levels of Abstraction, Simplification and Aggregation

The modelling objectives should orient model construction and in particular determine the level of detail required. The advantage of minimizing detail is that the coarser a model is, the easier it is to construct, the less expensive it is in computer time and space, and the easier it is to calibrate, since it has fewer parameters. On the other hand, a more refined model is likely to represent the real system more accurately. A solution to this dilemma lies in constructing families of models at different complexity levels, which can be checked against each other (mutual consistency) and against the real system (validity).

Consider some goals for model-base systems. The user should be able to interact in the first instance, at the level at which he can formulate the questions about the system entities of interest to him. The support system should then produce models from a model base which can answer these questions or else should assist in synthesizing appropriate models using building-block components in the model base. More explicitly, the models retrieved or synthesized should be as computationally inexpensive as is permitted by the stated questions, so as to admit quick and extensive simulation experimentation. The user should be able to explore flexibly the subspace of models of interest by modifications of the questions and model descriptions rather than having to reprogram manually for each modification. The results of such exploration should be stored in a form which facilitates subsequent summary and analysis. The models in the model base should form a consistent whole so that calibration and assessment of new models is assisted by extant models rather than performed in isolation as is currently the case.

Examples of model-base systems are: the IAS (interactive system) developed by the Institute for Advanced Studies, Vienna; the SIM (system for interactive modelling) being developed at the Institute for System Studies, Moscow; and the MBS (model-base system) developed at the GMD, Bonn.

2. Structures for Model-Base Organization

Two key concepts for model base organization are the entity structure and the experimental frame. The entity structure is based on a treelike graph embodying the system boundaries and decompositions which have been conceived for the system. An entity signifies a conceptual part of the system which has been identified as a component in one or more decompositions.

Simulation: Model-Base Organization and Utilization

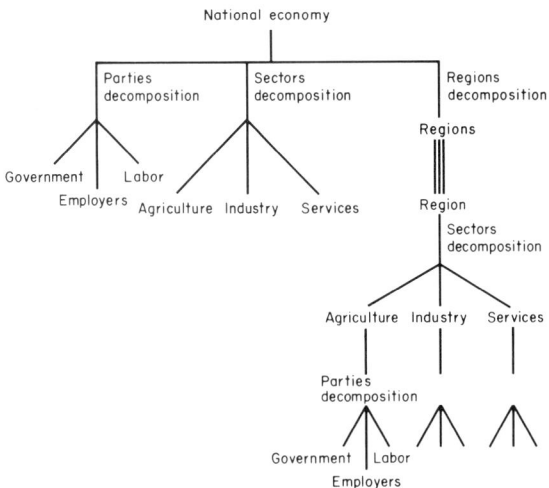

Figure 2
Entity structure for Elzas negotiation methodology

Figure 2 sketches an entity structure for modelling of the economy at national and regional levels. Note that the topmost entity is the national economy and thus the national border constitutes the widest system boundary of interest. A widened boundary which would allow explicit consideration of interaction with other countries would require extending the entity structure accordingly. Note that there are several ways of decomposing the national economy: into labor, business and government components; into economic sectors; and into regions such as states or provinces. Each such decomposition is called an aspect.

Actually, both entities and aspects are better thought of as types of components and decompositions, respectively, since (subject to constraints) they may appear more than once in the structure. In fact, anywhere it is placed, an entity (or aspect) carries with it the same decomposition substructure. For one thing this means that new refinements of decompositions may be specified by reapplying existing ones. For example, in Fig. 2 each region is further decomposed into economic sectors by attaching to it the same sectors aspect that has been attached to the national economy. More complex decompositions may be built up by successive reapplications of the same principle. Of course a naming convention must be adopted to distinguish multiple occurrences of the same entity (or aspect). For example, the agricultural sector of the national economy is to be distinguished from the agricultural sector of a particular region. But once this is done, we can see that the entity structure provides a compact means of displaying the components, and generating the various decompositions, that have been formulated for a given system.

The second important concept—the experimental frame—characterizes modelling objectives by specifying the form of the experimentation that is required in order to obtain answers to the questions of interest. At minimum, an experimental frame states the input and output variables that are of interest. Input variables are variables that are not under the control of the model (or counterpart real system) and hence must be determined by the experimenter (or the real system environment). Output variables are variables existing in the model (or measurable in the real system) which are determined in response to the input behavior. A frame thus sets up a space in which data may be collected in the form of pairs of input and associated output time series. It is by examining, aggregating and otherwise processing such data that answers to the motivating questions may be obtained.

One of the important functions of the entity structure is to organize all models and experimental frames of interest. The basic idea is to associate models and frames with the entities that they concern. Thus each entity represents a component of the real system and therefore ought to point to the experimental frames which characterize questions about it and the models which can be used to answer such questions.

3. Model-Base Utilization

We now discuss how the entity structure serves as a medium for model-base users to direct the construction of models to meet their objectives. As suggested above, the entity structure embodies the subsystems and decompositions that have been developed for a given modelling domain. More particularly, this means that the static structure of a model can be extracted from the entity structure in a process called pruning. Static structure here refers to the decomposition structure of the model; that is, a tree-like structure whose nodes signify model components, the variables attached to the nodes being those employed to describe the associated components.

Pruning starts at an entity and proceeds down the entity structure such that each time an entity is selected, a unique aspect is assigned to it. The variables attached to the nodes of the pruned entity structure are selected from those pertaining to the corresponding entities of the original entity structure. The following choices must be made:

(a) the entity at which pruning starts (the choice of system boundary and hence the system to be modelled);

(b) the aspect selected for each entity (the choice of decomposition of a component);

(c) the variables selected for each entity (the descriptive variables of a component); and

(d) the depth d (the maximum number of decompositions that will be undertaken).

The objectives that motivate the model construction should guide the making of these decisions.

The inverse process of pruning, called amalgamation, creates an entity stucture to represent the static structures for a set of models. The amalgamation of these static structures is the minimal entity structure from which they can each be extracted. It is the logical first stage required for model integration.

4. Computer Assistance and Model Construction Methodology

Adding a base of experimental frames can greatly augment the retrieval capability of a model-base system. The system must provide assistance in constructing an experimental frame to represent the data space of a set of objectives as well as assistance in locating this frame within the base of frames. The computer should be able to locate any models in the model base relevant to the new frames. Indeed there may already exist a model to which the frame is applicable; namely, a model capable of generating the kind of data demanded by the frame. If there is no model to which the frame applies, there should be assistance for constructing such a model either from scratch or by simplifying, modifying and coupling the relevant existing models to form a composite model.

The database should be organized according to the frames so that real system data elements belonging to a given frame can be conveniently stored and retrieved. The same is true for data elements of computationally expensive models. (The criterion for "computationally expensive" here is that it is cheaper to store simulation results rather than rerun the simulation.) The ability to access data by experimental frame keys would play a fundamental role in the validation process which involves comparison of data sets within the same experimental frame.

There should be assistance in simulation program construction and verification. There should be a model-specification segment and an experimental-frame segment. The latter specifies only the kind of experimentation to be done, not any particular experiment. Thus there must finally be an execution-control segment, which selects an input segment and an initial state setting to perform a particular experiment. Since the model and experimental frame could originate from their respective bases, there should be a test for applicability of the frame to the model before the segments are allowed to be combined.

The following summarizes the methodology for model construction just discussed.

(a) Operate on the entity structure:
  (i) identify the entity of interest (establish the boundaries of the system of interest);
  (ii) formulate an experimental frame E (specify the data space required to answer the questions of interest to the modelling objectives); and
  (iii) prune the entity structure to contain only those subentities, aspects and variables appearing in the experimental frame.

(b) Access the experimental frame and model bases:
  (i) discover frames and models relevant to E;
  (ii) simplify relevant models relative to E;
  (iii) expand the pruned entity structure to amalgamate the static structures of the simplified models; and
  (iv) add additional variables required for necessary model elaboration.

(c) Map the entity structure into a heirarchical model specification:
  (i) select input and output variables;
  (ii) designate state variables and parameters;
  (iii) specify coupling constraints; and
  (iv) assign component models and coupling schemes meeting the other constraints of (c) (using a top-down or bottom-up approach).

A more complete exposition of this methodology can be found in Zeigler (1984). Instances of model-base systems already exist and others are in the process of development. These systems can be viewed as subsystems of more comprehensive simulation and modelling support systems.

5. Model Bases and Knowledge Bases in System Design

Recently there has been much interest in merging artificial intelligence (AI) techniques with simulation. In particular, system design methodology should be supported by a knowledge base consisting of both simulation models and AI knowledge representations such as semantic nets, frames and rules. Such an approach encourages setting out: (a) the multiplicity of design objectives which, taken individually and in combination, must eventually be considered; (b) the elementary components and systems and their possible combinations that structure the space of design alternatives; and (c) the constraints that restrict the combinatorial explosion of alternatives to those plausible and permissible (Rozenblit and Zeigler 1987)

DEVS-scheme (Zeigler 1987) is a knowledge-based simulation environment for modelling and design which facilitates construction of families of models in a form easily reusable by retrieval from a model base. The environment supports construction of heirarchical discrete event models and is written in the PC-scheme language which runs on IBM compatible microcomputers and on the Texas Instruments Explorer. Model specification and retrieval in the DEVS-scheme simulation environment is mediated by a knowledge representation component designed using the system entity structuring concepts. The system entity structure incorporates decomposition, taxonomic and coupling knowledge concerning a system design domain (Sevinc and Zeigler 1988). A user prunes the entity structure according to the objectives of the modelling study, obtaining a reduced structure that specifies a heirarchical discrete-event model. The system then searches the model base for components specified in the pruned entity structure and synthesizes the desired model by coupling them together in a hierarchical manner. The result is a simulation model expressed in DEVS-scheme which is ready to be executed to perform simulation studies. A rule-based consultation system aids the pruning process.

See also: Simulation Methodology and Model Manipulation; Simulation Methodology: Top-Down Approach

Bibliography

Rozenblit J W, Zeigler B P 1987 Design and modelling concepts. In: Dorf R *Encyclopedia of Robotics.* Wiley, New York
Sevinc S, Zeigler B P 1988 Entity structure based design methodology: A LAN protocol example. *IEEE Trans. Software Eng.* **14**(3), 375–83
Zeigler B P 1979 Structuring principles for multifaceted system modelling. In: Zeigler B P, Elzas M S, Klir G J, Ören T I (eds.) *Methodology in Systems Modelling and Simulation.* North-Holland, Amsterdam
Zeigler B P 1984 *Multifaceted Modelling and Discrete Event Simulation.* Academic Press, London
Zeigler B P 1987 Heirarchical, modular discrete event modeling in an object oriented environment. *Simulation* **49**(5), 219–30

B. P. Zeigler
[University of Arizona, Tucson,
Arizona, USA]

Software Development: Human Information Processing

Software development is a human activity, and one would expect to find guidelines that direct the process. This is the goal of a design methodology. However, the human information processing aspect of software development is very complex. It involves a firm understanding of the application domain, such as banking for a banking application; knowledge of the technological domain, such as the computer system and programming languages; an ability to communicate and observe; and a talent for invention and integration.

Because software development requires many skills and varieties of knowledge, it is difficult to separate the cognitive activities that direct the problem solving from the other processes that affect designers and users during the development period. That is, the design methodology must be holistic; it must address the details of problem solving within the context of human information processing capabilities. As a result, all methods will be imperfect and subject to personal biases and environmental variations.

To comprehend how designers process information during the implementation of a software product, a foundation in two basic areas is required: how humans process information and how software is developed. Once this has been established, the cognitive aspects of development can be considered. The features of the development methodologies then can be classified with respect to how they approach the human information processing challenge.

It should be noted that this is not an article on software development for the human information processor; i.e., a treatise on human–machine interaction (details of this can be found in Norman and Draper (1986), Baecker and Buxton (1987), and Shneiderman (1987)). Instead, this is an article that explores how people design systems and what tools are of value for this activity. The topic is not well understood, and is in some cases controversial. The author has made every attempt to avoid inaccurate reporting, but the absence of error does not imply truth. What follows are the author's reasoned (but unproven) opinions; they are offered as a catalyst for further thought and investigation.

1. Human Information Processing

This section presents an overview of how the human mind processes information. The general study of this topic is called cognitive science, and it is a new discipline (Gardner 1985). Newell and Simon (1972) make the following observation.

> Within the last dozen years a general change in scientific outlook has occurred, consonant with the point of view represented here. One can date the change roughly from 1956: in psychology, by the appearance of Bruner, Goodnow, and Austin's *Study of Thinking* and George Miller's "The magic number seven"; in linguistics, by Noam Chomsky's "Three models of language"; and in computer science, by our own paper on the Logic Theory Machine.
>
> As these titles show, the common new emphasis was not the investigation of problem solving, but rather the exploration of complex processes and the acceptance of the need to be explicit about internal, symbolic systems.

Newell and Simon defined a model for information processing based upon the known constraints of the brain, that was also extensible to artificial processing environments; for example, the computer. This new cognitive perspective not only altered psychology but also impacted computer science (with the introduction of artificial intelligence) and philosophy (with the ontological issue of an inorganic intelligence). While a full discussion of these issues is beyond the scope of this article, a brief survey of the generally accepted findings follows.

Table 1 classifies human actions by the duration of the processing cycle. The smaller the processing cycle,

Table 1
Time scales of human action (adapted from Newell and Card 1985)

Time	Action	Theory
Decades	technology	social and organizational
Years	system	
Months	design	
Weeks	task	
Days	task (skill)	bounded rationality
Minutes	task (LTM)	
Tens of seconds	unit task (LTM)	psychological
Seconds	operator (STM)	
Tenths of seconds	cycle time (buffers)	
Centiseconds	signal	neural and biochemical
Milliseconds	pulse	

the easier it is to design a repeatable experiment to study the activity. Conversely, the longer the elapsed time, the greater the chance that uncontrolled stimuli will influence the outcome of an investigation. Consequently, we can be more precise about the neural and biochemical mechanisms than about the social and organizational processes.

Starting at the psychological level, there is a model of the human processor that provides a framework for understanding and evaluating human–computer interactions (Card *et al.* 1983). The model human processor consists of three systems: the perceptual processor receives visual and auditory inputs and enters them into a store, the motor processor takes commands and translates them into motor actions, and the cognitive processor operates upon working memory (including the visual and auditory image stores) and generates commands for the motor processor. The duration of most actions is a fraction of a second, and the major use of the model is in the analysis of short-term actions such as keystroke entry or the response to a visual alert. However, the model of the cognitive processor also provides insight into the action of longer-term activities.

There are two classes of memory. *Short-term memory* holds the information under current consideration; it is the working memory with which the cognitive processor interacts. There are a limited number of short-term memory (STM) registers (3–7) and, without rehearsal (reactivation), their contents have a half-life of 7–30 seconds. *Long-term memory* stores the knowledge for future use. Long-term memory (LTM) is considered to be nonerasable and unlimited in size. Retrieval from LTM is instantaneous, but the storage of new information with its associated links takes several seconds.

The units managed by memory are called chunks. A chunk is a symbolic entity (or pattern) that generally is expressed in terms of other chunks. Because STM is relatively small, the cognitive processor continuously activates chunks from LTM, which replace chunks in STM. The result is that there are bounds upon what can be retained in STM during a short period. For example, when one is asked to listen to and then repeat a string of random digits, the ceiling on a correct response is seven plus or minus two digits. This is not a function of intelligence; rather it is related to the number of STM chunks available and the time it takes to activate LTM. (This representation of STM, LTM and the information processor does not imply anything about the mechanism actually used by the brain. Rather, it is *an* explanation of the operation that is consistent with observations of human information processing.)

Of course, it is possible to repeat longer strings when the strings are expressed as chunks. For example, the string CBS IBM RCA USA is in reality four chunks: CBS IBM RCA USA. This provides a clue for a representation of LTM. It can be viewed as a network of related chunks that is accessed associatively from the contents of STM. The chunks contain facts, procedures, history, and so on. We retrieve chunks from LTM that are "closely related" to chunks in STM. We navigate through LTM by going from chunk to related chunk. For example, in one scenario CBS makes one think of a US television network, which makes one think of a TV set, which makes one think of the room in which the TV set is located, which makes one think of . . . . etc. This is a common association game for children. In actual problem solving, the chain of reasoning occurs quite rapidly, and it is very difficult to reconstruct the symbolic sequences applied.

Moving beyond psychology theory, Table 1 shows that LTM is used in the execution of tasks that extend from tens of seconds to minutes. Because the contents of STM are very perishable, the implication is that a task that requires minutes to perform will involve multiple retrievals from LTM. As already suggested, the chunks that can be activated from LTM will be restricted to the current context of STM; that is, the LTM chunks associated with chunks in STM. Because STM is small, the number of associative selections also will be limited. Thus, the information processor relies upon shallow reasoning; that is, once chunks are established in LTM, they may be used without reference to the events leading to their creation. For example, in computing the area of a rectangle, we use the formula $A = L \times W$ without reapplying the deeper reasoning process of deriving the formula. In fact, the ability to instantaneously retrieve chunks from a very large LTM without rejustification is what makes the information processor so powerful.

For actions that extend over hours or days, Table 1 uses the term skill. A skill is a learned activity that we can conduct in parallel with other learned activities. For example, we can drive an automobile, listen to the radio and read road signs concurrently because we are skilled in each activity and do not have to manage them consciously. However, the new driver is easily distracted, and the lost driver will concentrate on reading road signs. Once a skill is learned, it is difficult to manage it consciously; for example, one may stumble when trying to concentrate on how to walk up a flight of stairs. It is convenient to think of learned skills as patterns that help in LTM recall. They speed the processing of learned tasks and bypass conscious information processing.

Learning may be viewed as an increasing of the number of available patterns (chunks) in LTM. In experiments, chess masters were shown chess boards with legal situations and then asked to reconstruct them. Their ability to recall was significantly better than novice players. However, when shown random chess board setups, the masters' responses were no better than those of the novices. In the latter cases, there were no patterns that could be used to reduce the number of chunks. The same experiments have been repeated with programmers using real and scrambled programs; they produced similar results.

Learned skills and knowledge are stored in LTM in schemata (schemas) that provide the organization for retrieving and recognizing patterns. Studies of how students learn science, for example, show that learners look for meaning and will try to construct order even in the absence of complete information. That is, they seek to find a way to append the new information onto the existing schemata. The result is that naïve theories will always be formed as part of the learning process. Moreover, understanding will always rely upon relationships to established knowledge in the schemata. Information isolated from these structures will be lost or forgotten. Thus, all learning is carried out in the context of current perceptions.

Problem solving involves recall and selection from learned patterns. The chess-master experiments suggest that experience produces more stored patterns, which implies that there will be a higher probability that the "best" patterns will be recalled for a specific situation. Studies of how clinicians perform medical problem solving provide further insight into the process. This can be illustrated with the hypotheticodeductive model constructed by Elstein *et al.* (1978). It contains four steps.

(a) *Cue acquisition*. This includes taking a history, performing a physical examination, reviewing test results, and so on.

(b) *Hypothesis generation*. Retrieval from LTM of alternative hypotheses of the diagnosis.

(c) *Cue interpretation*. The data are considered in the context of the hypotheses previously generated.

(d) *Hypothesis evaluation*. The data are weighted and combined to determine which hypotheses are supported or ruled out.

The process is iterative. It may result in a decision that more data are required (i.e., that a test should be ordered), that a probable diagnosis (and associated therapy) is indicated, or both.

In analyzing this model, the researchers found that the generation of early hypotheses has considerable natural force; medical students generated early hypotheses even when asked to withhold judgement. The number of hypotheses is usually around four or five and appears to have an upper bound of six or seven. The generation of hypotheses was based more consistently on single salient cues rather than on combinations of cues. Very few cues seemed to be used, and hypothesis selection is biased by recent experience. It was also found that cue interpretation tended to use three measures: confirm, disconfirm and noncontributory; the use of a seven-point scale had no greater explanatory power. Finally, they noted that lack of thoroughness is not as important a cause of error in diagnosis as were problems in integrating and combining information.

Shneiderman (1987) adds another dimension to LTM by suggesting that (in the context of computer-user behavior) there are two types of knowledge: syntactic and semantic. Syntactic knowledge is varied, device dependent, and acquired by rote memorization; for example, the symbol used by a programming language as a statement terminator. Semantic knowledge, on the other hand, is structured, device independent, and acquired by meaningful learning; for example, the concept of a "do while." Syntactic knowledge is easily forgotten, but semantic knowledge is stable in memory. Consequently, tasks are best learned and retained when presented in a semantically meaningful way. Shneiderman uses the term direct manipulation for human–computer interaction tasks in which the action and its intent are directly linked; for example, word-processor use of the cursor and delete keys. One may think of these actions as being related to existing schemata and therefore natural.

This brief survey suggests the following model. The human information processor has a small working memory capacity. This working memory processes symbolic chunks. Its contents decay rapidly, and so it must be either rehearsed or activated from LTM. Activation is associative and is guided by the current context. The hypotheticodeductive model suggests that few cues are processed in combinations and that a three-point evaluation scale is satisfactory. This is consistent with the statement that the reasoning in STM is shallow; that is, it relies upon surface pattern matches and does not reason from first principles. The power of the human information processor lies in its vast store of LTM with its many links for recall. When learning new information, chunks are stored to match patterns already in the schemata. Where the existing schemata are incomplete, naïve theories are created to complete them. As experience grows, the schemata are reorganized, and more and better patterns become available for skilled activities and problem solving.

Naturally, the previous paragraph contains some gross simplifications. The main point, however, is that the human information processor can manage only a relatively small amount of information at one time; it is subject to information overload. Fortunately, processing continues in the subconscious (with an activity called incubation), and in many cases solutions to complex problems will emerge days after the initial problem was identified. In fact, much of the process of software design involves working out detailed problems using the conscious application of learned skills in parallel with the subconscious examination of deeper problems. The design methodologies provide tools for the former and rely upon human inspiration for the latter.

So far, this discussion has been limited to the information-processing mechanism. We have not considered issues of representation and the use of color or imagery. Modern brain research has shown that the two brain hemispheres support different functions (Springer and Deutch 1981). The left hemisphere is more adept at generating rapidly changing motor patterns, processing rapidly changing auditory patterns, and other forms of sequential processing. The right hemisphere, by contrast, is more effective in simultaneously processing the type of information required to perceive spatial patterns and relationships. Thus, knowledge is expressed analytically and holistically. The information processor must accommodate both representations.

Finally, we observe that the human information processor cannot be separated from the individual's physiological structure. Obviously we cannot ignore the individual, and this introduces another level of variation. Early studies in programming skills showed that there can be a 28:1 difference in the performance of programmers. These individual differences are both learned and inherent. There are suggestions that training can reduce some variations; nevertheless, differences will remain in personality type, intelligence and skill level. Mechanisms for managing the software development activity must be able to accommodate these differences.

2. The Software Process

The term software process is used to describe all activities related to the development of a software product from the initial concept formulation to the final retirement of the product. It begins with the identification of a need that can be met, in part, with the application of software. In this sense, the software process is a systems engineering process restricted to the software components of the target system. The software process can be characterized as a problem-solving activity that translates an informally stated need into a formal product that performs correctly and meets that need. The delivered products evolve over time, and this evolution is called maintenance. In general, the cost to maintain a software product over its lifetime will exceed its initial development cost.

The software process operates on two categories of information:

(a) *Subjective information*: this requires interpretation by the developers and users. The more experienced the team is in working together and with the users, the less detailed the documentation need be. However, no matter how detailed the documentation, there always will be room for interpretation.

(b) *Objective information*: this is independent of any interpretation by the developers or users. Examples are a formal database model for an application, the code for an algorithm, and a list of mandatory performance criteria. Although each may be subject to misinterpretation, each has a formal and unambiguous method for demonstrating that the information is correct.

Note that this is a rigid use of the terms objective and subjective. Subjective here does not mean imprecise; it implies that the statements are too incomplete to be verified in a mathematical sense. In most software life-cycle models, the initial specification is considered to be an objective document. In reality, however, this specification is subject to considerable interpretation.

Figure 1 presents an overview of the software process as a transition from the subjective to the objective. It shows the process beginning in the application domain and finishing in the implementation domain; that is, one starts with some needs and concludes with an implemented product that satisfies those needs. Naturally, the figure illustrates one iteration of a much more extended process. The key point that this figure makes is that the objectives of every product are determined by a cognitive activity. Using judgement, these objectives (the subjective model) are translated into a formal statement of what will be implemented. Once this objective representation exists, well-defined

Software Development: Human Information Processing

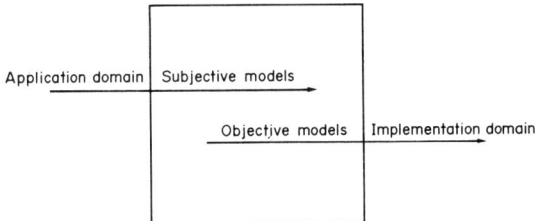

Figure 1
The software process transformation

methods can be used to ensure that the final product will be correct. One task of a design methodology is to guide the human information processer in the definition of that first formal model.

Figure 2 provides another view of this process and introduces the two quality activities. In this figure, the real-world needs are documented as a problem statement. The definition of this problem statement depends upon the experience, skill and judgement of the design team. It involves application-domain knowledge plus an understanding of how computer technology can be used to assist in the solution of the application problems. The next box involves the transformation of the problem statement into an implementation statement; that is, an operational product. The transformation is often depicted in the form of a waterfall chart that goes from requirements analysis, to function definition, to detailed design, to code and debug, and finally to test. Most of the preoperational software process is concerned with the production of the implementation statement, which can be translated automatically into executable program code. This code (with the supporting documentation and resources) becomes the system. The system is embedded in and alters the real world, and another iteration begins.

There are two quality attributes shown on the left of Fig. 2. Correspondence measures how well the delivered system meets its intended goals. Note that (at least in the case of information systems) correspondence must be subjective; human judgement is used to determine what is required and if the delivered product meets those needs effectively. Correctness, on the other hand, is objective. It measures whether a product is correct with respect to its parent specification. For example, compiled code is always correct with respect to the source code; one can demonstrate that a database is correct with respect to its conceptual data model.

Verification is the process of determining correctness. It can begin only after there is a formal specification that can be used as the basis for the proof. Correctness is objective and does not involve judgement. However, in real situations, the specifications are often informal and subject to interpretation. In this case, verification also will be subjective; that is, not really verification. Validation, on the other hand, is a continuing evaluation of design and implementation decisions to assure that the final product will correspond. It is a predictor of correspondence and, therefore, is always subjective. It can be stated thus: verification is concerned with getting the system right; validation is concerned with getting the right system.

Because the software process may extend over many years, it is essential that the quality processes be initiated as early as possible in the development cycle. For validation, this implies that the process begins as soon as there is some firm concept or document to be validated. That is, one cannot wait to validate until there is code. In the case of verification, on the other hand, the process must wait until there is a formal statement and a derived product that can be verified as correct with respect to that statement; for example, a module design specification and the program code for that module.

In general, the formal statement will be incomplete. (For example, a design specification will not name all the variables to be used in the program.) The formal specification prescribes only the essential behaviors of the product; one may add permissive details. Because verification tests the product with respect to the essential details, the effect of these permissive details is ignored. However, such details may introduce undesirable behaviors into the product. Thus, every verification should be followed by a validation obligation. Note that for every real-world problem, there are many acceptable problem statements, and for every formal (i.e., verifiable) problem statement there are many correct implementation statements. On the other hand, the translation of the final implementation statement (e.g., source code) into an implemen-

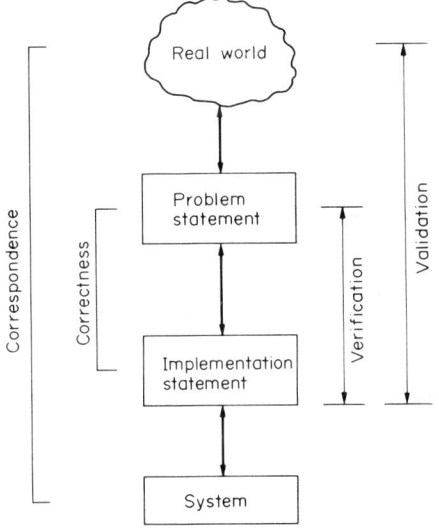

Figure 2
The software process with quality feedback

433

tation is automated and therefore requires no human judgement.

Lehman *et al.* (1984) use the term abstraction to describe the process of analyzing the application needs A to define the formal specification S of a system that meets those needs. The term reification describes the process of adding details to that specification to produce an implemented product P that is correct with respect to S. The definition of S cannot be formalized. (In the context of Fig. 1, it is the first point on the objective model line; there can be no formal derivation from a subjective model.) Because S is a formal specification, its detailed expansion, S_i, also will be a formal model. Thus, reification can be expressed as the sequence of transformations (detailing steps)

$$S \to S_1 \to S_2 \to \ldots \to S_n \to P$$

where each S_i is correct with respect to S_{i-1}.

This implies that, unlike abstraction, the process of reification must proceed in a serial sequence. If one begins work on S_i before S_{i-1} is complete, then there is no way to verify S_i (or S_j with $j > i$). That is, if we are to formalize the process objectively, then it must be done in a strict top-down fashion. Moreover, for $j > i$, S_j will introduce new behaviors beyond those already prescribed by S_i. That is, the reification process adds new details. As long as these behaviors are consistent with the intent of S, they are considered permissive. To confirm this, a validation obligation follows each reification step.

Figure 3 places the discussion of the software process in the context of human information processing. It expresses the process in two dimensions. On the left are the activities that transform the application need A into the first specification S, and on the right are the detailing activities that produce the finished product P. The top half of the figure involves the subjective processes that rely upon human understanding and insight; the objective processes that use formal methods are on the bottom. (The dotted lines indicate that a clear boundary does not exist.)

From the human perspective, the process may be summarized as follows.

(a) Human judgement is always used to determine what should be done. That is, there can be no objective method for establishing the system specification.

(b) For a given problem, there are many possible (and perhaps equally acceptable) solutions.

(c) Once a formal specification has been accepted, reification must follow a sequential flow if correctness is to be preserved.

(d) In general, each reification step adds to the volume of detail and introduces behaviors that were not explicitly specified but are considered permissible.

(e) Verification is a formal process; many different models may be equally correct with respect to given specification.

(f) Finally, all software development begins with an understanding of the application needs and, if successful, ends with the delivery of a product that corresponds to those needs.

Section 3 examines how the various design methodologies guide this process consistent with the strengths and limitations of the human information processor.

3. Software Development Methods and Tools

This section considers how methods and tools support human information processing in software development. A method is a systematic process for performing one or more phases (activities) in the software process. A tool is an (often automated) instrument that supports a task within a method. In general, no single method can support the entire software process, and the term methodology is used to represent an integrated collection of methods that cover many software process activities. An environment is an integrated collection of tools that supports a methodology. Thus, the methodology determines how the process will be conducted, and the environment and tools provide the mechanism for carrying out the process.

The problems that a methodology must address are numerous. We begin by cataloging the major information-processing difficulties inherent in the software process. The focus is on how the human information processor (HIP) must cope with the challenges of software development. In considering these issues, brief references are made to some of the more prominent design methodologies. Unfortunately, a more extensive examination of these methodologies is not

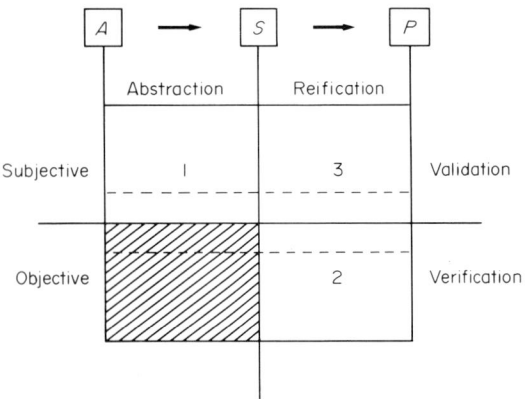

Figure 3
A static representation of the software process

possible here and the interested reader should consult one of the standard textbooks on software engineering for more information (Vick and Ramamoorthy 1984, Fairley 1985, Pressman 1987).

Brooks (1987) analyzed the essence of software and concluded that no "silver bullet" could be found that would have more than an accidental impact on the development process. The perspective of his paper was the software product, which he said inherently suffered from complexity, conformity (i.e., the product must be adapted to conform to the external requirements), changeability and invisibility. The perspective of this section is the development process. In what follows we establish some of the essential characteristics of that process and consider how each one impacts human information processing.

3.1 Complexity

Like the software product, the implementation of a software solution to a real-world problem is a complex process. The nature of the complexity, however, is different. The complexity of the program is at the level of bits, registers, control and timing. The complexity of the design process starts at a much higher level. To begin with, the process begins in the application domain with the recognition of a set of needs and some potential software solution. This implies that the designers must understand the application domain, the role that automation can play in that domain, and the tools that can be used to produce an implementation. This complexity contains the software complexity as a subset.

From the review of the HIP, it is seen that very little information can be maintained in active memory at any one time. Therefore, processing relies upon the use of symbolic chunks and their associations. Reasoning is relatively shallow and depends upon pattern matching from previous learning and experience. Stated another way, one may think of the chunks as abstractions that suppress unnecessary details. Because these abstractions are incomplete, there is a danger that they will imply conditions that are not valid for the context in which they are used. For example, an abstraction of an input processing flow may assume implicitly that some precondition has been met without explicitly associating that assertion with the abstraction.

All design methodologies provide tools for abstraction. (Here the term abstraction is used differently from the previous section, in which it represented the process of producing a specification from the application needs.) The abstractions are organized to represent a simplification, or view, of the system component being developed. Each methodology uses a limited number of views, and tools are provided to support the designer in elaborating these. Considerations foreign to a view are ignored, and it is assumed that most of the deferred factors ultimately will be resolved before the implementation is complete. Using an architect's analogy, one begins with a model that conveys external structure and function and then expands the design with a series of integrated views that describe load distribution, plumbing, electrical wiring, and so on. Each such view ignores information essential to other views, and all views must join the three-dimensional space of the building's realization.

In the case of software design, one begins with abstractions of what is desired and then adds details. As the details are added, the nature of the objects being abstracted changes, and further levels of abstractions are introduced. Because the HIP operates most efficiently at a shallow reasoning level, it requires considerable discipline to retain the confidence that every abstraction is consistent with the previous and overlapping abstractions. When there is a formal (mathematical) methodology, the user can have a high confidence in correctness. However, because all design must begin with subjective assumptions, there is always a concern that the abstractions leading to the formal solution will not have been derived from the initial abstractions. To reduce this risk, methodologies provide tools that maintain an audit trail of the decision process and thereby provide traceability.

3.2 Invisibility

The abstraction activity may be viewed as the modelling of nonvisualizable realities. One begins with the identification of needs and ultimately models a proposed solution. The solution model is formalized as a specification, and the reification process involves the production of increasingly detailed models until the final model, the program, exists. The different design methodologies offer various views to guide the modelling process, but none of these views has a physical realization that can be experimented with. Virtually all models are conceptual; they exist only in the HIP domain. Methodologies provide views that facilitate the abstraction and detailing, and they establish means for controlling the process.

There are two basic approaches to managing the details associated with the modelling activity. With decomposition one models the entire system by dividing it into partially independent components that, in turn, are modelled using decomposition. This is also called the top-down approach. The advantage of this approach is that it provides a clear derivation of each lower level of detail. The disadvantage is that the designers must make critical design decisions at the beginning of the design process, when they know the least about the problem to be solved.

An alternative method is composition in which one models first those aspects of the system that are well understood. Examples here include Jackson system design (JSD) and object-oriented design. In this case, the model concentrates on those real-world concepts that are best understood. With decomposition, there is always a model of the entire system, but it is incomplete. Conversely, with composition, there are models only of portions of the system, but each such model is complete. In actuality, the analysis process uses both techniques, but only one approach can be selected to manage the project.

In addition to structuring the sequence in which the components are defined, all design methodologies also restrict the objects used in their models. Structured analysis is primarily concerned with the flow of information, and the system is modelled as a network of information transformations described as data-flow diagrams. For example, the Jackson programming method (JSP) begins with models of the data and constructs the processes (i.e., programs) to conform to the data structures. In real-time applications, it is common to use Petri nets to model the interdependence among concurrent processes. Finally, knowledge-based paradigms model the knowledge separate from the processing control.

Many of the modelling techniques combine formal approaches with graphic representations. There are several reasons for this. The human brain processes both analytic and holistic information, and a pictorial approach affords a richer environment for expressing and communicating concepts. The diagram also introduces an additional dimension into a two-dimensional (paper) media. Each token (e.g., box or bubble) represents an abstraction. Thus a data-flow diagram depicts a relationship among abstractions. One disadvantage of a diagram is that it usually is subject to interpretation and does not map into a formal representation. Different viewers may have different interpretations, or key omissions may be obscured.

The previous paragraphs addressed techniques that design methodologies use to overcome the fact that the HIP has a narrow bandwidth; that is, is subject to overload if too much information is presented at one time. Each methodology provides both a mechanism for understanding small portions of the problem and a method for managing the many details of these smaller views. The general approach is to build a model and then expand it, small pieces at a time, until the implementable model is complete. Because the full model is too complex for the HIP to comprehend, submodels are defined. At each level the models are abstract (i.e., invisible), and it is the designers' responsibility to confirm that all submodels are consistent with their ancestors. Traceability is used to assure validity; automated tools, such as PSL/PSA and SREM, are used to check for consistency; and where formal models exist, verification procedures can be used to ascertain correctness.

3.3 Uncertainty

All projects begin in the application domain and rely upon subjective models. These models cannot be verified. In fact, one must wait until the finished product is delivered before it can be determined if the system corresponds to the environment's needs. Consequently, one of the goals of a design methodology is the early identification of uncertainty so that alternative solutions can be examined and risks constrained.

In some domains, it is possible to reduce uncertainty by referencing existing formal models. For example, in scientific applications, formulae are available. For more complex applications, simulations based upon those formulae can be built. In domains that cannot be supported effectively by formal models, prototypes can be built to gain a better understanding of the problem and its range of solutions. These techniques build up the experience base in order to limit the uncertainty and reduce risk. Other methods to accomplish the same ends include the decomposition of the product into builds that can be incrementally constructed, tested and delivered; the use of evolutionary development in which operational experience with limited functionality is used to establish the features of the next generation; and Boehm's spiral software development in which a sequence of risk-reducing prototype development/analysis steps precedes the requirements specification.

Every development activity designed to reduce the uncertainty, in the final analysis, must rest upon the judgement of the design team. Because the first models will be subjective, objective analysis can only identify mistakes; it cannot confirm validity. Thus, there is no alternative to the experience of the design team. From the HIP perspective, this experience is represented in the number and types of patterns stored and the schemata in which they are arranged. However, experience does not cross application domains. Schemata built during the design of many compilers will not necessarily have much depth in the domain of billing systems, and vice versa. In fact, the new information may be used to construct naïve theories. Thus, there is no substitute for experience, and that experience is always, to some degree, domain specific.

Current design methodologies provide little support in the area of experience building. To a limited extent, they provide a framework for the definition process so that the design team can work in a familiar environment and concentrate on learning about the problems that they are trying to solve. In this sense, they focus the activity and limit the distractions. Future environments may employ knowledge-based processing or software reuse to moderate the need for experience. However, in the short term, the major sources of experience are education, reading and on-the-job training.

Of course, once a formal specification exists, most of the uncertainty disappears; that is, there are formal methods to verify that each detailing step is correct with respect to its specification. The only area of uncertainty relates to the validity of the permissive behaviors. For this reason, many in the computer science community seek to establish tools that define a formal model early in the process. Naturally, any formal model must be derived from a subjective model based on understanding and experience. Creation of the objective model before the subjective model is complete is an invitation to produce an invalid system. (Recall that reification is a top-down activity, and all steps in the process assume the validity of the initial formal specification.) Consequently, the HIP must always deal with uncertainty; formal methods can be employed only after the uncertainty is minimized and when it is known what is wanted.

3.4 Change
Software development is not a static process. The cost to maintain a product exceeds the initial cost of implementation. The reason for this is that the needs are dynamic. They change for three reasons. First, the external environment alters the internal environment, thereby creating new needs. Second, as the designers and users improve their understanding, their evaluation of the needs will change. Finally, the installed system will introduce an element of change; it will require modifications, provide insight into new enhancements, or alter perceptions about the tasks being supported.

This need to support change creates an additional dimension to the complexity. Not only must the HIP manage a model of the entire system, but it must also manage that model temporally. The patterns and chunks used to describe the system model must be expanded to link decisons with temporal states and system versions. That is, not only must one be able to understand a problem solution, but one may also need to know the context at the time the decision was made. This is a very difficult problem, and few methodologies have support tools beyond those for identifying and managing the configuration items. The situation is most severe in the case of software maintenance where the maintainer was not part of the design team and has no easy access to the designers. In this situation, the maintainer must understand the problem to be solved and the product to be altered. The potential for naïve theories is great.

3.5 Volume
Volume refers to the bulk of the material to be managed. The HIP is subject to information overload. This is avoided by focusing only on limited portions of the problem and using abstractions to encapsulate the deeper assumptions. Abstraction reduces the volume, but the greater the volume, the greater the number of levels of abstraction that will be required. Without a formal separation and linking of the levels, volume introduces two problems. First, because the problem space is large, there is the danger that a local abstraction may not represent a valid assertion. For example, the abstraction "this process has already been initialized" may be incomplete, and the state at the beginning of the process being designed may not be as anticipated. The alternative to accepting this abstraction is to "reprove" it each time it is used, an activity that is very difficult for the HIP to perform without losing sight of the intended objective. (Strong data types and the explicit specification of calling sequences are designed to eliminate some of these kinds of errors.)

Second, as the volume increases, the system network grows, and no individual can be expected to understand the entire application. Each member of the development team, therefore, must deal with only a portion of the whole. To do this each individual must produce a model of the whole that establishes a framework for his segments. When this is done, there is a diffusion of understanding about the larger model. Subjective decisions are made in the context of each individual's local framework. Because all activities require some subjective decisions, it is essential that such decisions be examined in some detail. One tool used in the validation of decisions that extend beyond the formal specification is the review (also called a walkthrough or inspection). Here the objective is to express design decisions created in the context of one set of schemata so that they are examined by other individuals using different schemata. (The concept of the independent design team serves the same purpose; the designer and tester interpret the product from different perspectives.)

Reviews produce benefits during both their preparation and conduct. In the preparation, the material to be presented is examined from several viewpoints. Previously overlooked problems can be identified. Stated in terms of the HIP model, abstractions may be examined in more detail by exploring alternative associative paths. During the review process, there are group dynamics, additional experience and fresh perspectives. Both the preparation and conduct also provide a focus for the resolution of nagging problems by incubation. (Interestingly, a large number of the errors identified during a review entails missing information; the designer forgot or left something out.)

Some design methodologies offer tools that can reduce the volume. For example, with an application generator the formal (objective) representation is semantically close to the conceptual (subjective) model of what is desired. The detail below the level of the formal statement can be ignored. In this way, the volume and associated development effort are reduced. This reduction in volume also decreases the opportunity for introducing errors.

All methodologies provide mechanisms for managing the volume of details. In decomposition techniques, for example, the model is organized hierarchically and structured by type of object; e.g., data-flow diagrams, data dictionary, module specifications. In any case, a good methodology will allow its users to isolate their responsibilities from those of the other designers and, at the same time, observe how their units interconnect within the whole.

Conversely, a bad methodology will increase the volume by introducing overhead (or "housekeeping") that adds to the work but contributes little to the understanding. The difference between a good and bad methodology often rests with its local implementation. That is, the methodology is misapplied, and effort is diverted from problem solving to supporting the methodology. One characteristic of volume is that it can be quantified, and there is a temptation for managers to encourage the production of concrete objects. The HIP is very compliant; with the proper motivation it can convert a means into an end.

3.6 Multiple Domains

Software development cuts across many domains. The activity begins with an understanding of the application need. In many cases, the software is only one portion of a larger system solution. During the software design, well-organized external concepts become distributed among the implementation units. For example, the concept of an employee is decomposed into the views of employee as a wage earner, as a member of a project, and so on. These views are later examined in the context of processing time, storage allocation, potential concurrency conflicts, and so forth. Each set of concerns requires different domain knowledge to effect an efficient solution.

Because software development requires many different skills, few individuals will be skilled in all phases of the process. A skill is effective when it can be applied at a subconscious level. For example, the experienced programmer does not have to think about what symbols represent the programming language operations. The symbols are selected as the programmer works on the solution to a higher-level problem.

The concept of naïve theories also suggests that problems will be interpreted in the light of the skills available to create a solution. Where the necessary skills exist, a design methodology provides a tool for structuring and detailing the implementation. For new domains, there is a danger that an individual will be asked to do something for which he has inappropriate skills, or that he will interpret the assignment in the context of his current skills and interests. A corollary to this is that, as the process moves across problem-solving domains, members of the design team may lose sight of the larger objectives and optimize a solution based upon their skill strengths.

4. Conclusions

This article provides models of the HIP and the software process, and describes how various design methodologies respond to HIP needs. The discussion omits many human issues such as communications and management. The key observations can be summarized as follows:

(a) Software development is a complex cognitive activity. Many of the strengths of the HIP are not well-suited to this type of activity. Tools and methods are required to facilitate the process and reduce the risk.

(b) Much of the software process relies upon judgement and experience. Only a limited number of steps are subject to formal proof. The experience of the design team and the users is probably the most important factor in the success of a project.

(c) Because the software process involves the modelling of abstract concepts, feedback is essential. Prior to the existence of a testable product, this can be accomplished only by reviews. Because all lower levels build upon the assumptions of the previous levels, errors will multiply unless corrected early.

(d) While considerable discussion was devoted to tasks of under an hour in duration, most design decisions are the result of longer-term processes (incubation). This requires time and a relatively pressure-free environment. A constant focus on immediate problems will not leave the designer free to explore some essential aspects of system development. The result may be project failure.

In conclusion, the software process has presented the HIP with a major challenge. To date, most design methodologies have responded in an ad hoc, pragmatic manner. Unfortunately, there is no unifying theory for a more systematic approach to supporting the process. Perhaps, as we continue to learn, this may change.

5. Acknowledgement

This work was supported in part by the US Navy, Space and Naval Warfare Systems Command (SPAWAR) under contract N00039-87-C-5301, task ZMR with the Office of Naval Research (ONR).

See also: Human Factors Engineering: Information-Processing Concerns; Human Information Processing; Information Systems and Software Productivity

Bibliography

Baecker R M, Buxton W A S (eds.) 1987 *Readings in Human–Computer Interaction.* Morgan Kaufman, Los Altos, California

Brooks F P 1987 No şilver bullet. *IEEE Computer* **20**(4), 10–19

Card S K, Moran T P, Newell A 1983 *The Psychology of Human–Computer Interaction.* Erlbaum, Hillsdale, New Jersey

Elstein A S, Shulman L S, Sparafka S A 1978 *Medical Problem Solving.* Harvard University Press, Cambridge, Massachusetts

Fairley R 1985 *Software Engineering Concepts.* McGraw-Hill, New York

Gardner H 1985 *The Mind's New Science*. Basic Books, New York

Lehman M M, Stenning V, Turski W M 1984 Another look at software design methodology. *ACM SIGSOFT Software Eng. Notes* **9**(2), 38–53

Newell A, Card S K 1985 The prospect for psychological science in human–computer interaction. *Hum. Comput. Interact.* **1**, 209–42

Newell A, Simon H A 1972 *Human Problem Solving*. Prentice–Hall, Englewood Cliffs, New Jersey

Norman D A, Draper S W (eds) 1986 *User Centered System Design*. Erlbaum, Hillsdale, New Jersey

Pressman R S 1987 *Software Engineering, A Practitioner's Approach*, 2nd edn. McGraw–Hill, New York

Shneiderman B 1987 *Designing the User Interface: Strategies for Effective Human–Computer Interaction*. Addison–Wesley, Reading, Massachusetts

Springer S P, Deutch G 1981 *Left Brain, Right Brain*. Freeman, San Francisco

Vick C R, Ramamoorthy C V (eds.) 1984 *Handbook of Software Engineering*. Van Nostrand Reinhold, New York

B. I. Blum
[Johns Hopkins University, Laurel, Maryland, USA]

Supervisory Control: Philosophical Considerations in Manufacturing Systems

Most research into manufacturing automation in general, and flexible manufacturing system (FMS) scheduling and control in particular, focuses on the derivation of fully automated control and scheduling techniques; for example, optimal or heuristic analytic models or knowedge-based systems. An alternative and more realistic paradigm to "lights out" automation is presented in this article. The alternative paradigm—supervisory control of manufacturing processes—entails the design of control and scheduling systems that explicitly integrate human decision makers with the underlying automation. Supervisory control is a design philosophy that explicitly addresses the roles and functions of both human and automatic components of the control process. Supervisory control systems make use of capabilities and compensate for the limitations of both human decision makers and automatic components. More specifically, supervisory control designs the human–computer interaction in order to augment and extend the human's role and decision-making effectiveness. Neither the goal nor the unintended side-effects of supervisory control are to automate the human decision maker out of the system or to reduce the human's role to a set of undesirable or ineffective tasks.

This article describes some of the limitations of automated control systems in manufacturing, in particular why full automation is not possible. It also reviews some of the limitations in the typical use of emerging computer technology to provide decision support to the human decision maker. With this discussion as background, research in supervisory control of flexible manufacturing systems conducted with GT-FMS (Georgia Tech-flexible manufacturing system) is summarized. GT-FMS is a real-time, interactive simulator that can be configured to represent actual or planned multicell and multiworkstation FMS installations. GT-FMS research includes the design and evaluation of an operator function model for FMS cell-level supervisory control; design and evaluation of an "intelligent" operator workstation; and the evaluation of hierarchical versus heterarchical managerial structures to coordinate multiperson, multicell FMSs.

1. Background

The debate on US competitiveness and productivity has focused attention on manufacturing and manufacturing innovation (Scott and Lodge 1985, Jaikumar 1986, Krugman and Hatsopoulos 1987, Cohen and Zysman 1988). One interesting conclusion is that the difficulty in manufacturing arises from deficiencies not so much in machines and technology, but "... in organizations and the use of people in production" (Cohen and Zysman 1988 p. 1111). This article addresses one facet of the issue: the role of people in the control of increasingly automated manufacturing environments. It provides the background for understanding the choices in automated scheduling and control of a flexible manufacturing system (i.e., analytic versus knowledge-based), and offers an alternative view that proposes the use of experienced human operators to interact with the scheduling and control system and to fine-tune it as needed. The latter view, called supervisory control, explicitly addresses the utilization of people in the manufacturing process and identifies the human decision maker as a critical component in the planning and control process. Although supervisory control does not require additional or different machines or technologies, it does require the rethinking of the role of people in manufacturing systems. An understanding of the philosophy and meaning of supervisory control permits the utilization of expensive and valuable human resources and allows the definition of operator functions that complement existing automated functions. The definition and well-defined engineering specification of the human functions in system control provide a necessary context for the related information-processing issues, including types and mechanisms for decision support, design of operator workstations, and human factors and ergonomics of display screens and operator interaction. Although this article examines supervisory control issues in the context of scheduling and control of flexible manufacturing systems, many of the ideas and some of the research results have applicability to more general manufacturing control processes.

2. Limitations of "Full" Automation in Manufacturing Control

2.1 The "Lights Out Factory"

Although one oft-expressed intention of factory automation is the drastic reduction or total elimination of the human workforce on the shop floor, (e.g., the "lights out factory"), it is much more likely that increased implementation of automation will lead to changes in the numbers and skills of workers on the shop floor, rather than the elimination of people (Jaikumar 1986, Rasmussen 1986). Thus, the factory of the future will include human decision makers on the shop floor, but the roles and scopes of responsibilities of these individuals are likely to change drastically as the implementation of automation progresses (Young and Rossi 1988).

The reason why human decision makers must remain an integral part of the system is not hard to discover. Automation technologies often result in considerable system down time. Shaiken (1985a,b) explains this phenomenon concisely (Shaiken 1985a p. 18):

> Reducing human input often means instituting complex technologies that are prone to trouble. The drive to eliminate uncertainties arising from human influence only winds up creating mechanical and electronic uncertainties. Thus, despite the vision of total automation, workers must in the end play critical roles in operating as well as unjamming and repairing, computer-based production systems.

The necessity of integrating human decision makers into the manufacturing process is particularly important in process control. The size, costs and risks associated with malfunctions in control systems make reliable control a necessary condition for successful operation (Chambers and Nagel 1985, Rasmussen 1986). The complexity of the system and the resulting inability of software to cope with all possible future events imply that human decision makers provide an essential backup for the computer-based control system (e.g., Young and Rossi 1988).

It is unlikely that the limitations of full automation will be corrected in the near future. For example, scheduling and control systems based on analytic models of the process contain inherent limitations. The academic community involved in manufacturing, material handling and scheduling research has repeatedly found that sophisticated mathematical models of production and control require unrealistic assumptions about the manufacturing process and its parameters. Examples of such assumptions include deterministic processing and routing times, or workers who are assumed to perform at the same speed and possess the same skill levels (e.g., Johnson 1988). When implemented in actual systems, models based on assumptions that are not met in the application may fail to provide the mathematical optimality promised by the basic research. Such prominent researchers as Buzacott and Yao (1986) predict that mathematical models will never reflect the range of behaviors and uncertainties of real systems, and that the most that can be expected is that an analytical model can address a small, but hopefully important, subset of issues. Further clouding the prospects of analytic research in scheduling and control is concern that, because the real problems in manufacturing automation are so complex, academic research will address pseudoreal problems and pay only lip-service to real manufacturing applications (Ho 1987).

The use of artificial intelligence (AI) techniques in manufacturing automation has been proposed to remediate the gaps left by analytical models (e.g., Bourne and Fox 1984, Fox and Smith 1984, Miller 1985, Smith et al. 1986). In a case study of a turbine engine job shop, it was found that 80–90% of a scheduler's time is spent identifying constraints not typically reflected in analytic models. ISIS, an AI system using constraint-based reasoning to find satisfactory, as opposed to optimal, schedules, was developed as an attempt to cope with the range of analytic and informal constraints found in actual systems (Smith et al. 1986). Yet experimental AI systems have not provided the flexibility and adaptability initially expected (e.g., Smith et al. 1986, Young and Rossi 1988). Human decision makers remain an integral part of such systems (Wright and Bourne 1988, Young and Rossi 1988). The general consensus is that it will be a long time, if ever, before systems based on AI techniques can perform better than trained operators in unanticipated or novel situations (Chambers and Nagel 1985, Rasmussen 1986).

Most manufacturing control research acknowledges both the limitations of the predominant tools for automated control and the inevitable and intrinsic role of humans in the manufacturing process (Young and Rossi 1988, Cohen and Zysman 1988). Either implicitly or explicitly, an autonomous manufacturing system utilizing either an analytical model (e.g., Jones and Maxwell 1986, Jaikumar 1986) or AI techniques (e.g., Fox and Smith 1984, Miller 1985, Astrom 1985, Astrom et al. 1986, Smith et al. 1986) assumes the presence of human operators who monitor the automation and correct and fine-tune the process when necessary. While acknowledging the presence of human decision makers, few researchers in operations research or AI attempt to address explicitly the engineering and design of manufacturing control systems that integrate automation with the humans who are responsible for overseeing the effectiveness of system operation. The study of human–machine interaction in complex dynamic systems, a related area of engineering, addresses this issue directly.

2.2 Supervisory Control Systems

Systems in which humans primarily monitor automated control processes are called supervisory control systems (Sheridan and Johansen 1976). The role of humans in supervisory control systems is to compensate for the limitations of the automation and to provide flexible response in novel situations. Large scale systems whose control depends upon both autonomous and human subsystems are not unusual in the broader context of complex high-risk military, space and industrial systems (Rasmussen and Goodstein 1987). For example, it has long been acknowledged in the design of space system control, both on the ground and in space, that the human in such systems provides a necessary and integral part of successful system operation (Cohen and Erickson 1985). There is little reason to believe that manufacturing systems will be different. To the contrary, a number of researchers point out that there is one distinction between US and Japanese factories in the type of labor force. Although Japanese factories have fewer people, their skill levels and scopes of responsibility are often broader than those of their US counterparts (Shaiken 1985b, Jaikumar 1986, Cohen and Zysmann 1988).

It is insufficient, however, merely to make a commitment to a skilled workforce; effective systems and good engineering design require precise specification of the role of the human decision maker in automated manufacturing systems and integration of the human component into the overall system specification. Experience and research from existing supervisory control systems may provide some direction in manufacturing systems. Thus one objective of this article is to illustrate the principles of supervisory control in the context of manufacturing systems, specifically the control and scheduling of flexible manufacturing systems.

2.3 Supervisory Control Paradigm for FMS Control

As applied to manufacturing control, particularly to control and scheduling of a flexible manufacturing cell, supervisory control is proposed as a conceptual framework for organizing the design of the FMS (Ammons *et al.* 1988). An FMS is a network of versatile workstations connected by a flexible material handling system. The FMS workstations are capable of performing many different operations of an associated process; for example, machining, assembly or fabrication. There is minimum changeover time between operations, and the material handling system is capable of executing any desired job routing (Ammons *et al.* 1985). FMS is a philosophy of automation rather than a specific type of system design, and as such it is a good vehicle to illustrate the philosophy and concepts of supervisory control.

The supervisory control paradigm for FMS proposes a control system design that successfully integrates the resources of analytical models, AI and human supervisory controllers (Ammons *et al.* 1988). The integration utilizes the capabilities and compensates for the limitations of each component. Analytic models form the foundation of the automatic scheduling and control system. Given this level of background automation, knowledge-based systems are designed and implemented to compensate for the known limitations of the mathematical models (e.g., unrealistic model assumptions). Finally, an operator interface to the control system provides the human decison maker with information and controls with which to monitor and fine-tune the system in response to unanticipated or changing system conditions. This philosophy is depicted in Fig. 1.

There are three basic tenets of the supervisory control paradigm. The first is that FMS control systems should be designed and engineered with an explicit understanding of the position and role of the human operator responsible for the system. The second tenet is a corollary to the first: the design process should represent the human functions with as much precision and detail as the specification of system software and hardware. This representation requires the development of a detailed, dynamic model of operator functions, extending over the range of possible system states (Mitchell and Miller 1986, Mitchell 1987). Finally, given a model of operator functions, the supervisory control paradigm requires integration of the automatic parts of the control system into an integrated workstation through which the human supervisor can monitor the process, tune the parameters and compensate effectively for the deficiencies of the control automation.

The last point is important. It requires the designers of FMS control systems to design explicitly the human functions into the system and focuses the design process on enabling the system supervisor responsible for safe and effective operation to control the system effectively. A control system is supervisory only if the human supervisor has the information, decision tools and controls necessary to ensure effective and safe system operation when the limits of automated control are reached. An ineffective human operator, (e.g., someone who is bored, someone who has been given tasks that are not compatible with human capabilities, or someone who lacks the proper decision support information or tools), destroys the effectiveness of the

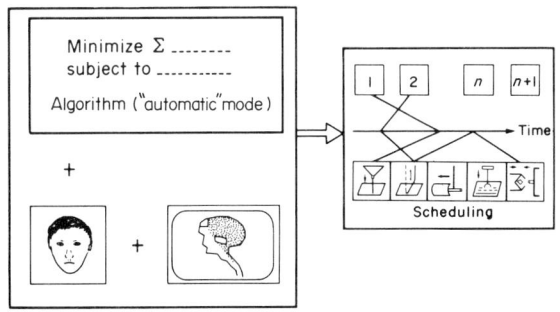

Figure 1
The supervisory control model

supervisory control design and reduces the system architecture to one of full automation plus a peripheral human who may occasionally interfere with the process.

The FMS supervisory control paradigm is a radical departure from the current emphasis in manufacturing automation design. Frequently, the human role in automated systems is defined as an afterthought. The human is included in the control process to compensate for the times or events that the automation handles inadequately or not at all. From an engineering perspective, the human's role is not designed, it is ad hoc, and often evolves over time as inadequacies arise in the automatic control system.

Similarly, human interfaces to such systems are also not designed. Typically, information displays provided to real-time decision makers are "data dumps" where a programmer unfamiliar with the domain or the operator's tasks designs information displays that show all data collected in the system at the level at which the data are collected—frequently the lowest level possible (Rasmussen 1986, Mitchell and Saisi 1987, Rasmussen and Goodstein 1987). It is the responsibility of the human supervisor to sift through the available data, aggregating and integrating as necessary. Likewise, user controls are often awkward; they are typically concatenations of low-level commands that sometimes leave the human supervisor in the position of tricking the system into performing the necessary functions.

Control system design explicitly incorporating the functions of the human supervisor requires not only an intention but also a rigorous specification of how humans are to be utilized in the system. Tools and techniques for effective supervisory control design are not widely available. Designers are often faced with a situation in which there is more user-interface technology than design knowledge about how to use the technology. Moreover, conventional wisdom and intuition do not necessarily result in useful applications. Section 3 reviews some of the problems associated with the design of operator workstations for complex systems, particularly the problems caused by the increasingly available automated decision aids. Given this background, GT-FMS (Georgia Tech-flexible manufacturing system) is described, as are several research programs using GT-FMS. The GT-FMS research program includes the design, implementation and empirical evaluation of supervisory control systems for FMS cell-level scheduling and control.

3. Use of Computers in Decision Support: Decision Making or Decision Aiding?

Advances in computer technology and AI provide new computational tools that greatly expand the potential to support decision making in the supervisory control of complex work environments (Woods 1986a). The most frequent use of this technology, however, is often inconsistent with human skills. ". . . the primary design focus is to use computational technology to produce a stand-alone machine expert that offers some form of problem solution . . . [Thus], the interface design process focuses on features to help the user *accept* the machine solution" (Woods 1986b p. 87). Woods notes that the primary issue in such systems is user acceptance of the proposed solution and that system designers will go so far as to suggest that the system should provide the user with placebo-like interaction (e.g., allow the user to report facts considered important, even though they are not used by the system) in order to facilitate user acceptance of the machine's recommendations.

Woods (1986b) identifies three problems with such systems. First, when the machine gives only its solution to a problem, the decision maker may not have the authority to override machine output in practice as well as in theory. Since the only practical options are to accept or reject system output, there is a great danger of what Woods calls the responsibility/authority double-bind in which the user always either rejects or accepts the machine solution. The former discards the enhancements that intelligent decision support may add to overall system effectiveness; the latter abrogates the responsibility and purpose of the human decision maker in the system. The second problem is that it is not clear whether people are skilled at discriminating correct from incorrect machine solutions. The effectiveness of human decision makers in system control may depend on intimate involvement in the decision process rather than simply on evaluation of the decision product. Research in other supervisory control domains shows that there is an optimum level of control system automation beyond which a human cannot effectively make the transition from the role of a relatively passive monitor to that of an active system controller (Bergeron 1981). Woods identifies the potential loss of cognitive skill as the third problem. Humans are retained in systems to compensate for the limitations of automation. A user who depends almost exclusively on the recommendations of the machine expert may be ill-prepared for the occasions when the machine expert fails and his/her skill is essential to safe and effective system operation.

Recent research provides experimental data which demonstrate problems with "decision making" decision support. In a series of experiments at Georgia Tech, advice-giving systems consistently failed to improve overall system performance (Knaueper and Morris 1984, Zinser 1986, Resnick *et al.* 1987, Zinser and Henneman 1988). The primary reason for the failure of these systems to enhance performance is that system users either did not ask for or did not take the advice. In one instance in which the machine-based system automatically recommended the next operator procedure, a pilot study showed that in order to dispel user animosity, the aid had to be "toned down" (Knaueper and Morris 1984). In the other two studies, although advice was free, subjects rarely asked for it; neither system had an implicit or explicit penalty for requesting advice.

These results raise interesting questions about the efficacy and style of decision support. In all three experiments, the aid explicitly gave advice, provided reminders and generally gave the impression that it was omniscient with regard to the task. Yet the human–computer interaction and related system performance did not suggest that advice-giving enhanced system effectiveness.

There is other research suggesting that decision support may not always be fruitless. Another Georgia Tech experiment used a computer to provide dynamically adapted system-status information. Information content and form was based on a domain-specific model of the human–machine interaction that tailored and grouped displayed information based on the current system state and current operator functions. This resulted in improved system performance across a variety of measures and did not have any user acceptance problems (Mitchell and Saisi 1987).

The differences between these sets of experiments provide insight into the more general issue of aiding. The experiment in which decision support had a positive effect used the computer to aid the user's decision-making process. The model of human–machine interaction was embedded into the workstation and provided system information at various levels of abstraction, with both type and level of abstraction estimated using a model of operator function and information about current system state. The workstation provided an initial view into the controlled system based on a "best guess" about the user's needs. Additional information, however, was always available at the user's request and the decision process always remained under the user's control.

Decision support systems that aid the user in the process of reaching a decision, rather than making or recommending a solution, are proposed as an alternative to the typical decision-aiding paradigm (Woods 1986b, Mitchell and Saisi 1987, Rasmussen and Goodstein 1987, Vicente 1987, Rubin et al. 1988). The basic principle that underlies a decision-aiding design is that automation and machine intelligence should enhance or extend human decision-making capabilities, not replace the decision maker (Woods 1986b).

In a recent article on decision support in the supervisory control of high-risk industrial systems, Rasmussen and Goodstein summarize this position succinctly (Rasmussen and Goodstein 1987 p. 663).

> Rather than continuing their efforts to make the preplanning (i.e., automation) of responses and countermeasures more and more complete and thus restrict the operator's own initiative, designers should take advantage of modern information technology to make available to operators their own conceptual model and their processing resources so as to allow the operators to function as their extended arm in coping with the plant. Such an interactive decision-making activity would thus benefit from this simultaneous availability of the design basis, up-to-date knowledge of the plant status, and accumulated operational experience.

Current research programs attempting to develop electronic or computer-based associates explicitly address the design of decision-aiding systems. The pilot's associate project is a research effort that addresses the operational issues of decision support in real-time decision-making environments (Chambers and Nagel 1985). The intent of this program is to produce a support system architecture that enhances human abilities, overcomes human limitations and complements individual human preferences.

A similar effort for a space satellite control-room application, OFMspert (Rubin et al. 1988), uses a blackboard architecture to infer operator intentions based on a normative model of operator function. Although OFMspert has been quite successful at inferring operator intentions for a laboratory task (Jones 1988), the next step in the development of an operator's associate—determination of the style and substance of interaction—is very difficult. Given a representation of operator intentions, OFMspert must interact with the user, providing information and/or assistance. The implementation and evaluation of such systems are essential (Bushman 1988).

Human–computer interaction, levels of automation and control of system initiative are unresolved research questions in manufacturing. In many ways manufacturing is a more difficult domain than typical supervisory control systems. In other system, (e.g., airplane cockpits), the system already exists and automation can be incrementally implemented in conjuction with existing pilot functions. In many manufacturing applications, such as FMS scheduling, there is not an "operator's job" to automate. The "factory of the future" and FMS are concepts waiting for system design specification to make them realities.

The Georgia Tech research program is one attempt to explore the essential features of this problem. GT-FMS was built as a domain in which to explore design possibilities for supervisory control of FMS scheduling. GT-FMS is a simulator that can be configured to represent many FMS systems. It is designed to be interactive and to facilitate the exploration of human–machine interaction issues in FMS control such as level of automation, supervisory control architecture and decision support system strategies. Section 4 summarizes the main features of GT-FMS together with recent and ongoing research conducted within the GT-FMS domain.

4. GT-FMS: *A Domain for Research in Supervisory Control of FMS Scheduling*

GT-FMS is a domain created to examine a range of research issues related to human–computer interaction and decision support in scheduling and control of FMSs. GT-FMS is an interactive, real-time simulator of a potentially multicell, multiworkstation FMS. GT-FMS is a real-time rather than a discrete-event simulation. Time flows proportionally to real time and a human decision maker can interact with GT-FMS in a manner similar to that of a scheduler or expediter on the shop floor. GT-FMS was designed to provide a workbench or laboratory in which human interaction with FMS scheduling and control can be observed, controlled and empirically evaluated given proposed decision aids and definitions of human functions.

GT-FMS is written in C and runs in the Unix operating system environment. The basic simulator consists of more than 10 000 lines of source code. Increasingly sophisticated operator workstations add to this core system. A single-cell version also runs on a PC AT. The simulator has been configured with data from several real manufacturing systems and with both machining and electronics assembly data. Details about GT-FMS and research performed with it are given in the following subsections.

4.1 *Structure of GT-FMS*

Although flexible in configuration, GT-FMS makes several assumptions about system configuration and limitations. GT-FMS can have several cells, each with its own WIP and workstations. Workstations are uniquely configurable, each workstation with its own set of manufacturing operations. For example, in GT-FMS it is possible for two or more workstations to do the same task but at different levels of efficiency. Cell WIPs have a finite capacity; default is twenty. There is a flexible material handling system that can carry out any desired routing within and between cells. Workstations have the capacity to hold two parts, one in progress and one in a single item buffer. Parts automatically return to the WIP between visits to workstations. Work cells share a common input buffer. Parts arrive at the input buffer with a due date; part type designates the set and sequence of operations that must be completed before the due date.

Currently, there are three versions of GT-FMS based on actual data. One version uses data supplied by Motoren und Turbinen Union GmbH (MTU), a West German diesel engine manufacturer. The MTU version configures GT-FMS as a one-cell system with four identical machining centers and two load/unload stations. The MTU GT-FMS also includes two batch processes that require parts of one type to accumulate for processes performed outside the FMS cell (Dunkler 1986, Dunkler *et al.* 1988).

Another version of GT-FMS is based on data supplied by Lockheed–Georgia. It too is a machining operation with identical workstations and load/unload positions. This version is being used to examine the effectiveness of weighted operations priority due date scheduling.

The third version of GT-FMS uses IBM electronics assembly data. This version is again one cell; it has eight machines, two single in-line package (SIP) inserters, three dual in-line package (DIP) inserters and three robots whose primary job is to insert modules but which have the capability to insert SIPs and DIPs, although with less efficiency than the dedicated SIP or DIP insertion machines (Krosner *et al.* 1987).

There is also a multicell version of GT-FMS. Although not based on actual data, this version is constructed to examine multicell, multioperator interaction in FMS scheduling and control. The hierarchical version of the multicell GT-FMS consists of two cells (each with an operator) and a supervisor that coordinates the cells to meet overall system goals. The heterarchical version consists of three cells, each cell containing fewer machines than the two-cell system, with a cell operator for each cell and no decision maker who is designated as the supervisor (Armstrong and Mitchell 1986). Empirical research examines the effectiveness of the hierarchical and heterarchical team structures for different levels of system load and communication delays (Armstrong 1988).

Research with GT-FMS is both theoretical and empirical. Several of the completed and ongoing studies are summarized below.

4.2 *Operator Function Model for GT-FMS*

One of the original pieces of research with GT-FMS was the development of a model of proposed operator functions for FMS cell-level scheduling and control. The model defined two major operator functions. First, the operator monitors item movement within the cell to ensure that parts within the cell are processed in a timely manner; that is, on or before the due date. Furthermore, if an item looks as if it will not finish on time, the operator intervenes to minimize the amount of time by which a part is late. The second operator responsibility is to carefully monitor the relationship between the input buffer and the FMS cell. The operator monitors both current cell and input buffer contents with two goals in mind: cell contents are closely watched to ensure that inventory carrying costs are within reasonable bounds; input buffer contents are monitored to ensure that parts pulled into the cell by the automatic scheduling and control system are those that require immediate processing and whose processes can be performed within the cell, given current cell status (e.g., the status of workstations that can perform the required operations).

These two operator functions may be called schedule management and inventory management depicted in Figs. 2 and 3, respectively. (Events in cell schedule management include machine failures, WIP arrivals, due-date changes for parts contained in the

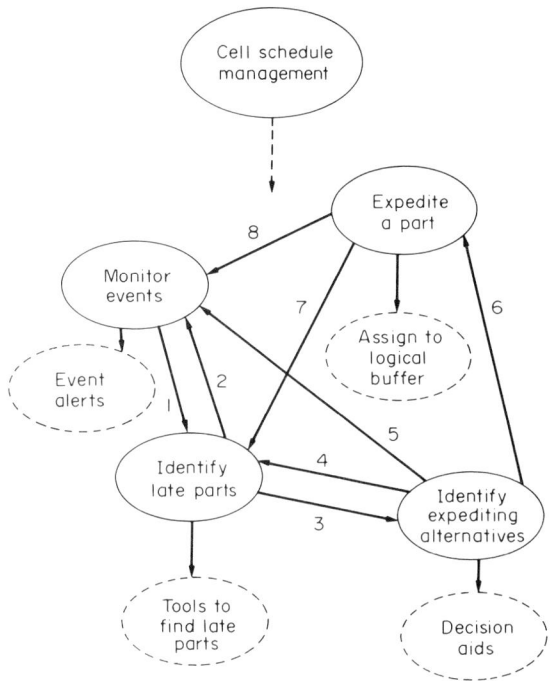

Figure 2
Operator function model for cell schedule management: 1, critical event occurs; 2, no late parts currently contained in cell; 3, one or more late parts found; 4, decision not to expedite late part with more late parts to consider; 5, decision not to expedite late part with no other late parts to consider; 6, decision to expedite a late part; 7, completion of expediting action; 8, end of task

cell, and schedule preemption by operator.) An operator function model was used to describe these functions more fully in the context of a dynamic manufacturing environment (Ammons et al. 1988). The plausibility of the model, together with an implementation of a specific set of operator interfaces and controls, was developed and empirically tested with the MTU version of GT-FMS. The experiment is described in the following subsections.

4.3 Supervisory Control of a Flexible Machining Center

As indicated above, this research used the GT-FMS version configured with MTU diesel engine data. Operator scheduling and control commands were based on the proposed model of FMS operator function. Operator commands included "expedite a part," "move a part" and "alter WIP setpoint." The "expedite" command was defined to allow the human operator to carry out both the inventory and cell schedule management subfunctions. Using the "expedite" command, the human supervisor preempts the automatic scheduling system and logically routes a part to a specified destination. The destination is either one of the six machines if the expedited part is currently in the WIP, or to the WIP if the expedited part is currently in either the arrival buffer or another temporary system buffer. If a part is expedited to a machine, it will be the next part processed, preempting the part currently waiting in the machine's buffer. If a part is expedited from one of the buffers to the WIP, the part is immediately transported to the WIP. The "free" command is available to cancel a pending "expedite" command for a machining center. This notion of expediting as a limited-horizon schedule preemption is one result of the formal modelling process. Expediting may be implemented in many ways; typically it is performed in an ad hoc manner that creates two permanent classes of parts—those that are expedited and those that are not. The latter interpretation of expediting may have adverse impacts on underlying optimization routines. The operator expedite command with a more limited horizon provides operator control in the context of a local problem.

The human supervisor can move a part from a broken machine back to the WIP using the "move" command. This command returns the part to the WIP and places it back within the control of the automatic scheduling system.

The "alter WIP" command allows the operator to alter the WIP setpoint from a default value of fourteen to some other level between zero and twenty. Thus, this command serves as an inventory management command.

The operator workstation consists of a single CRT where system status information can be obtained. The primary means of decision support in this system is a decision aid displaying a rank-ordered list of parts most likely, given current system state, to finish processing late. Called the Rush page, this display page, together with a cell-status page, provides the primary information about the system.

An experimental evaluation showed that the supervisory controller of this FMS cell consistently controlled the FMS cell more effectively than either the "first come first served" or "shortest processing time" dispatch rules operating in a fully automatic manner. Data summarizing these experimental results are given in Fig. 4. Detailed results can be found in Dunkler (1986) and Dunkler et al. (1988).

4.4 Workstation Enhancement

The GT-FMS using MTU data was augmented with an operator workstation that uses menu commands and windows to access system data (Tipton 1987). It was thought that a more user-friendly workstation would enhance system performance (Krosner et al. 1987, Tipton 1987). Recently collected experimental data showed no improvement, however.

In parallel with the human factors enhancements to the workstation, a more sophisticated, model-based

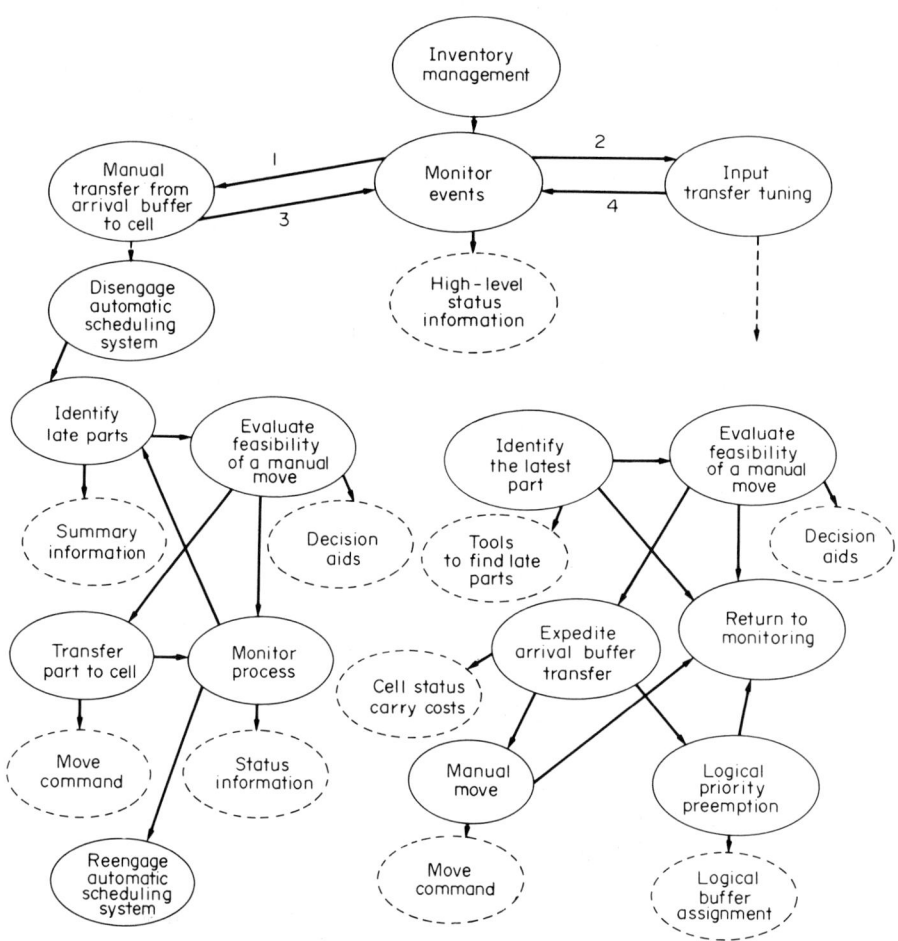

Figure 3
Operator function model for inventory management subfunction: 1, events including workstation failures or a large number of late parts contained in arrival buffer; 2, events including WIP departures, part completions and arrival buffer arrivals; 3, operator reengages automatic scheduling and controlling system and manual transfer subfunction is completed; 4, input transfer tuning is completed when the operator either physically moves, logically prioritizes a part in the arrival buffer or decides that preempting the automated schedule is not feasible

workstation is being designed for the electronics assembly version of GT-FMS. The intent of this project is to develop a model of human decision making that can provide the supervisory controller of the FMS with the correct information, at the appropriate level of abstraction, and in a timely manner. This model uses the operator function model (Mitchell 1987, Ammons et al. 1988) to structure information and Rasmussen's abstraction hierarchy (Rasmussen 1986) to guide the semantic representation of the information. When completed, the effectiveness of this workstation will be evaluated empirically.

4.5 Multioperator, Multicell Systems

The multicell, multioperator GT-FMS examines the effectiveness of two organizational structures: a hierarchical structure with two subordinates and a supervisor, and a heterarchical structure with three relatively autonomous cell controllers who coordinate voluntarily to achieve system goals. The multicell GT-FMS was enhanced to include the notion of batches; that is, a collection of parts due out of the system at the same time. Communication and coordination must occur among individual operators in order to meet not only part-due date at the cell level but also batch-due date at the overall system level. Figs. 5 and 6 shows the two organizational structures for this multicell, multioperator GT-FMS configuration.

Experiments are being conducted with the two- and three-cell systems in order to construct models of the command, control and communication processes for the two structures (Armstrong 1988). These models

Supervisory Control: Philosophical Considerations in Manufacturing Systems

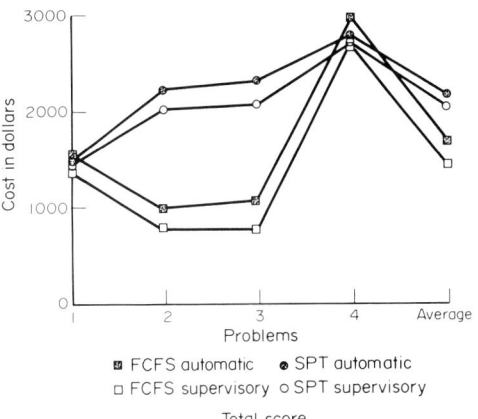

Figure 4
Results of supervisory control experiments

will give some insight into the multioperator decision process. Such models are a necessary prerequisite to understanding team performance and coordination and will provide insight for the design of teams that include both human and computer-based decision makers.

5. Summary

This article proposes supervisory control as an alternative to the goal of full automation in manufacturing

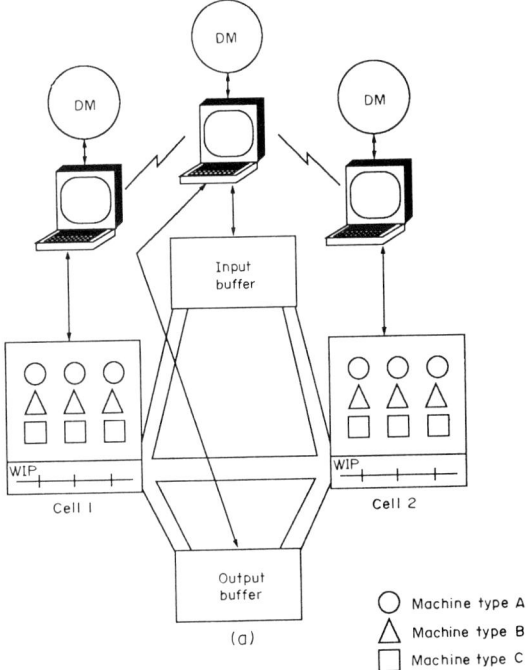

Figure 5
The hierarchical "team." DM, decision maker

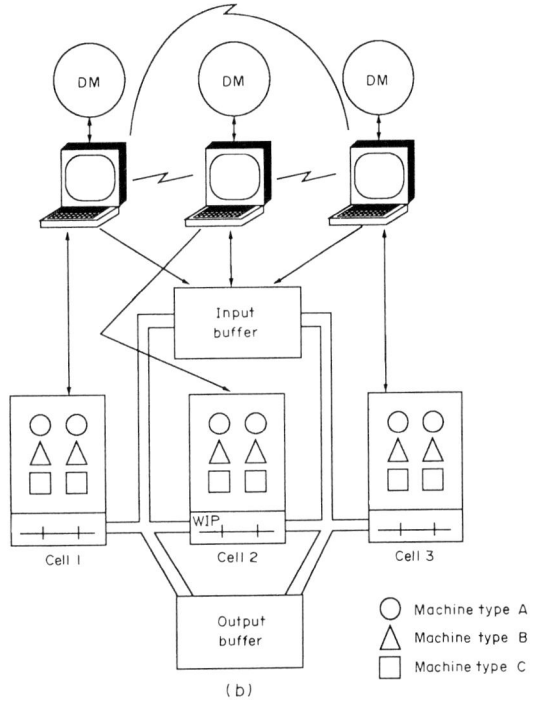

Figure 5
The heterarchical "team." DM, decision maker

processes. With supervisory control, the goal is to design into the control process human override functions that utilize human skills and enhance human effectiveness and overall system performance. A problem, however, in the design of human–machine interaction in complex, highly automated systems is the issue of decision support; in particular, it is important to distinguish between decision making and decision aiding. It is suggested here that decision support in the form of aiding the decision process is much more effective.

Bibliography

Ammons J C, Govindaraj T, Mitchell C M 1988 A supervisory control paradigm for real time control of flexible manufacturing systems. *Ann. OR* **15**, 313–35

Ammons J C, Lofgren C B, McGinnis L F 1985 A large scale loading problem. *Ann. OR* **2**, 319–32

Armstrong J 1988 Evaluation and model of effects of heterarchical versus hierarchical organizational structures in team comand-and-control, Ph.D. Thesis. School of Industrial and Systems Engineering, Georgia Institute of Technology, Atlanta, Georgia

Armstrong J M, Mitchell C M 1986 Organizational performance in supervisory control of a flexible manufacturing system. *Proc. 1986 IEEE Int. Conf. Systems Man and Cybernetics.* IEEE Press, New York, pp. 1437–41

Astrom K J 1985 Process control—Past, present and future. *IEEE Control Syst. Mag.* August, 3–10

Astrom K J, Anton J J, Arzen K E 1986 Expert control. *Automatica* **22**(3), 227–86

Bergeron H P 1981 Single pilot IFR autopilot complexity/benefit tradeoff study. *J. Aircraft* **18**(9)

Bourne D A, Fox M S 1984 Autonomous manufacturing: Automating the job-shop. *IEEE Comput.* **17**(9), 76–86

Bushman J B 1988 Identification of an operator's associate's model for cooperative supervisory control situations, Ph.D. Thesis. School of Industrial and Systems Engineering, Georgia Institute of Technology, Atlanta, Georgia

Buzacott J A, Yao D D 1986 Flexible manufacturing systems: A review of analytic models. *Manage. Sci.* **32**(7), 890–905

Chambers A B, Nagel D C 1985 Pilots of the future: Human or computer. *Commun. ACM* **28**(11), 1187–99

Cohen A, Erickson J D 1985 Future uses of machine intelligence and robotics for the space station and the implication for the U.S. economy. *IEEE J. Robot. Automat.* **1**, 117–23

Cohen S S, Zysman J 1988 Manufacturing innovation and American industrial competitiveness. *Science* **239**, 1110–15

Dunkler O 1986 *Human supervised scheduling and control in flexible manufacturing systems*, M.Sc. Thesis. School of Industrial and Systems Engineering, Georgia Institute of Technology, Atlanta, Georgia

Dunkler O, Mitchell C M, Govindaraj T, Ammons J C 1988 The effectiveness of supervisory control strategies in scheduling flexible manufacturing systems. *IEEE Trans. Syst., Man, Cybern.* **18**(2), 323–37

Fox M S, Smith S F 1984 ISIS: A knowledge-based system for factory scheduling. *Expert Syst.* **1**(1), 25–49

Ho Y C 1987 Basic research, manufacturing automation, and putting the cart before the horse. *IEEE Trans. Automatic Control* **32**(12), 1043

Jaikumar R 1986 Postindustrial manufacturing. *Harv. Bus. Rev.* **64**(Nov–Dec), 69–76

Johnson R V 1988 Optimally balancing large assembly lines with 'FABLE'. *Manage. Sci.* **34**(2), 240–53

Jones C V, Maxwell W L 1986 A system for manufacturing scheduling with interactive computer graphics. *IEEE Trans.* **18**(3), 298–303

Jones P M 1988 Constructing and validating a model-based operator's associate for supervisory control, M.Sc. Thesis. Center for Human–Machine Systems Research, CHMSR 88-1, Georgia Institute of Technology, Atlanta, Georgia

Knaeuper A, Morris N M 1984 A model-based approach for online aiding and training in process control. *Proc. IEEE Int. Conf. Cybernetics and Society*. IEEE Press, New York, pp. 173–77

Krosner S P, Mitchell C M, Tipton B C 1987 The role of the human operator in control of an FMS with random operation times. *Proc. IEEE Int. Conf. Systems, Man and Cybernetics*. IEEE Press, New York, pp. 671–74

Krugman P, Hatsopoulos G 1987 The problem of U.S. competitiveness in manufacturing. *N. Engl. Econ. Rev.* January/February, 18

Miller R K 1985 Artificial intelligence: A tool for manufacturing. *Manuf. Eng.* April, 56–62

Mitchell C M 1987 GT-MSOCC: A domain for research on human–computer interaction and decision aiding making in supervisory control systems. *IEEE Trans. Syst., Man Cybern.* **17**(4), 553–72

Mitchell C M, Miller R A 1986 A discrete control model of operator function: A methodology for information display design. *IEEE Trans. Syst., Man Cybern.* **16**(3), 343–57

Mitchell C M, Saisi D S 1987 Use of model-based qualitative icons and adaptive windows in workstations for supervisory control. *IEEE Trans. Syst., Man Cybern.* **16**(4), 573–93

Rasmussen J 1986 *Information Processing and Human–Machine Interaction*. North-Holland, New York

Rasmussen J, Goodstein L P 1987 Decision support in supervisory control of high risk industrial systems. *Automatica* **23**(5), 663–67

Resnick D E, Mitchell C M, Govindaraj T 1987 An embedded computer-based training system for rhino robot operators. *IEEE Control Syst. Mag.* **7**(3), 3–8

Rubin K S, Jones P J, Mitchell C M 1988 OFMspert: Inference of operator intentions in supervisory control using a blackboard architecture. *IEEE Trans. Syst., Man Cybern.* **18**(4), 618–37

Scott B R, Lodge G (eds.) 1985 *U.S. Competitiveness in the World Economy*. Harvard Business School Press, Boston, Massachusetts

Shaiken H 1985a The automated factory: The view from the shop floor. *Technol. Rev.* **88**(1), 16–24

Shaiken H 1985b *Work Transformed: Automation and Labor in the Computer Age*. Holt Rinehart, New York

Sheridan T B, Johansen G (eds.) 1976 *Monitoring Behavior and Supervisory Control*. Plenum, New York

Smith S F, Fox M S, Ow P S 1986 Constructing and maintaining detailed production plans: Investigations into the development of the knowledge-based factory scheduling system. *AI Mag.* **7**(4), 45–61

Tipton B C 1987 *The Importance of Human–Computer Interfaces used in Human Supervisory Control of Flexible Manufacturing Systems*, CIMS Project and Center for Man–Machine Systems Technical Report, Georgia Institute of Technology, Atlanta, Georgia

Vicente K J 1987 *The Role of Information Technology in Emergency Management: Expert System or Cognitive Instrument?* Riso National Laboratory, Roskilde, Denmark

Woods D D 1986a Cognitive technologies: The design of joint human–machine cognitive systems. *AI Mag.* **3**, 86–92

Woods D D 1986b Paradigms for intelligent decision support. In: Hollnagel E, Mancini G, Woods D (eds.) *Intelligent Decision Support in Process Environments*. Springer–Verlag, New York, pp. 153–74

Wright P K, Bourne D A 1988 *Manufacturing Intelligence*. Addison–Wesley, New York

Young R E, Rossi M A 1988 Toward knowledge-based control of flexible manufacturing systems. *IEEE Trans.* **20**(1), 36–43

Zinser K 1986 *Modeling and Aiding Human Decision Making in Operating and Supervising Dynamic Systems*, Center for Man–Machine Systems Technical Report 86-4. School of Industrial and Systems Engineering, Georgia Institute of Technology, Atlanta, Georgia

Zinser K, Henneman R L 1988 Development and evaluation of a model of human performance in a large-scale system. *IEEE Trans. Syst., Man Cybern.* (in press)

C. M. Mitchell
[Georgia Institute of Technology, Atlanta, Georgia, USA]

Support-System Design: Behavioral Concerns

The goal of most support systems is to enhance human information processing and decision behavior; however, many support systems do not effectively meet this goal. One of the reasons for this is that support-system designers often utilize decision-theoretic models and statistical principles that are inconsistent with how humans formulate problems, process information and make choices. This article provides an overview of two areas of research which demonstrate the inconsistency of unaided decision behavior with such models and principles. A conceptual framework is then presented in Sect. 3 for simultaneously representing the task and both the support-system user and designer. The short-term goal of this article is to help designers appreciate better how human decision behavior is guided through the application of mental representations and processing heuristics that help people understand and deal efficiently with a complex world taking into account that there are significant limitations in information-processing power. However, there is still ample room for improvement. Hence, the long-term goal is to facilitate the development of support systems that effectively combine human and computer strengths and thereby improve human decision behavior.

1. Bounded Rationality

The concept of bounded rationality is attributed to the Nobel laureate Herbert Simon (see Simon (1955, 1979), March (1978) and Hogarth (1987) for a general discussion), who argued that humans lack both the knowledge and computational skill required to make decisions in a manner which is compatible with economic notions of rational behavior. In order to deal with human and task limitations or bounds, Simon argued that humans simplify decision problems so that they can be addressed in a "reasonable" if not economically "rational" manner. In particular, Simon's approach was to specify what the rational economic model required humans to know and do, and then to ask how they could cope with the task given their limited knowledge, memory and processing capabilities. With regard to the former specification, the requirements of the rational model can be illustrated by the concept of a payoff matrix, an example of which is presented in Table 1. The rows of the matrix represent all of the different alternatives available to the decision maker for solving a particular decision problem. The columns represent all of the different states of the world, as defined by future events, that could affect the attractiveness of the alternatives. The $p_1 \ldots p_k$ values represent the probabilities for each state of the world. The cell entries in the matrix indicate the value (or utility) of the outcome (or payoff) for each combination of alternatives

Table 1
The decision making requirements of the rational economic model as represented in a payoff matrix

Alternatives	States of nature			
	$(p_1)S_1$	$(p_2)S_2$	$\ldots$	$(p_k)S_k$
A	a_1	a_2	$\ldots$	a_k
B	b_1	b_2	$\ldots$	b_k
.	.	.	$\ldots$	.
.	.	.	$\ldots$	.
.	.	.	$\ldots$	.
N	n_1	n_2	$\ldots$	n_k

and states of the world. Each outcome is presumed to represent a cumulative payoff comprising perceived advantages and disadvantages on multiple criteria of varying importance to the decision maker. Finally, the rational decision maker is required to select the alternative that maximizes expected utility. The latter is calculated for each alternative by multiplying the values for the outcomes and the probabilities for the states of nature, and then summing the products.

The rational economic model clearly assumes that the decision maker has extensive knowledge and impressive unaided computational power. In addition to Simon's research, substantial psychological research (Slovic *et al.* 1977, Einhorn and Hogarth 1981) indicates the inadequacy of these (and other) assumptions of the model. Therefore, how do we cope with the cognitive demands represented in the decision matrix? How does unaided human decision behavior remain purposeful and "reasonable" given the dynamic nature of the environment and our inherent information acquisition and processing limitations?

Simon suggested that people simplify the decision problem can be simplified by three strategies: first, by only considering a small number of alternatives and states of nature at a time; second, by setting aspiration (or acceptability) levels on the outcomes; and, third, by choosing the first alternative that satisfies the aspiration level. In other words, people do not optimize (i.e., choose the best of all possible alternatives), but "satisfice" (i.e., choose the first satisfactory alternative). In this way, a purposeful and reasonable manner can still be adopted while, information acquisition and processing demands are being reduced.

The strategies in Simon's theory of bounded rationality are not, however, without their costs. First, as Hogarth (1987) has pointed out, research on creativity suggests that one of the biggest deficiencies in human decision behavior is the failure to imagine sufficiently the complete range of alternatives and the various events that could occur in the future. Second, aspiration levels may be unrealistically high or low.

449

The former could well result in not only the elimination of potentially good alternatives early in the decision process, but also in the acceptance of a relatively inferior alternative later in the process, because subsequent events have caused the aspiration levels to be lowered. In contrast, unrealistically low aspiration levels and the "satisficing" strategy may well result in the acceptance of relatively poor alternatives early in the decision process.

It is important to emphasize that bounded rationality represents a descriptive theory of human decision behavior. It does not specify how people should make decisions but, rather, presents a theoretical perspective on how people do make decisions given a complex dynamic environment and limited information acquisition and processing capabilities. Moreover, subsequent research indicates that people are quite capable of using other, in some cases more complex, strategies than the three proposed by Simon. In contrast, the rational economic model is now typically seen as a prescriptive and not a descriptive theory of decision making. It is typically referred to as decision theory (or expected-utility theory or subjective expective-utility theory), and it provides an axiomatic basis for specifying how decisions should be made, as represented in the decision matrix given in Table 1, given that certain logically defined principles of behavior are accepted. Moreover, analytical procedures (called decision analysis) and various support systems have been developed to help implement decision theory. Although there are many books on decision theory and decision analysis, the texts by Brown *et al.* (1974) and Watson and Buede (1987) represent good introductions.

2. Heuristics and Biases

Simon used the rational economic model as a normative standard for comparing descriptive with prescriptive decision behavior. Numerous other researchers have used this normative standard and, more recently, probability and statistical theory to learn about human decision behavior. An overwhelming finding with considerable implications for support-system design is that human decision behavior systematically deviates from (or is biased when compared to) a normative model that is assumed to be the optimal way to make the decision under investigation. To quote Hogarth (1987 p. 5), "People do not possess intuitive 'calculators' that allow them to make what one might call 'optimal' calculations. Rather, they use fairly simple procedures, rules or 'tricks' (sometimes called 'heuristics') in order to reduce mental effort." Moreover, these heuristics are largely determined by the judgemental task facing the person. (See Sage (1981) for a review of this and other areas of decision research from the perspective of support-system design.)

Judgemental heuristics, and the biases they often spawn, are the results of human effort to understand and master our environment given limited information acquisition, retention and processing capacities. Specifically, research has demonstrated that the perception of information is not comprehensive but selective. As Hogarth (1987) points out, it has been estimated that, for example, only about one seventieth of what is present in the visual field can be perceived at one time. How do we know what to select? The answer is that we anticipate information on the basis of our causal model of the environment. Similarly, memory is limited; only a small part of the information we initially acquire is recalled. Moreover, current theories support the view that memory does not access information in its original form, but rather works by a process of associations that reconstruct past events and fragments of information that are typically consistent with our causal model of the environment. Finally, research indicates that considerable mental activity involves processing information that is both acquired from the environment and recalled from memory to make judgements of probable cause. There are, however, significant differences between causal and statistical (or normative) reasoning.

Kahneman *et al.* (1982) have compiled an anthology of research studies demonstrating that, when compared to the tenets of probability and statistical theory, humans have limited appreciation of the concepts of randomness, statistical independence, sampling variability, data reliability, regression effects and so on, when making probabilistic judgements. Einhorn and Hogarth (1986) and Hogarth (1987) have further advanced this research by focusing on three critical aspects of causal reasoning and contrasting them with the logic of probability theory. With regard to the former, their research indicates that people make judgements of probable cause on the basis of a "causal field" which is basically analogous to a perceptual field. Judgemental processes, like perceptual processes, are attuned to differences; therefore, the relevance of potential causes depends on whether they are considered as differences in the problem context. Second, various imperfect indicators of causal relations called "cues to causality" are used. These cues include, for example, temporal order, covariation, contiguity in time and space, and similarity of cause and effect. Third, the confidence that is placed in a causal explanation is affected by the extent to which plausible scenarios can be imagined for both it and alternative explanations. As Hogarth (1987 p. 161) points out in his discussion of creativity in problem solving, "... use of both causal fields and the cues-to-causality help the mind establish order out of the mass of information with which it is confronted. On the other hand, this order is bought at the cost of being able to perceive alternative problem formulations (i.e., causal fields) and potential causal candidates."

Meaning is attributed to information in order to make causal sense. Probability theory, however, does not necessarily do so, for the theory is merely a set of rules that permit one to infer the relationship between probabilistic events if certain assumptions are met. In fact, Einhorn and Hogarth have argued that the nature of causal reasoning not only differs in important respects from the dictates of probability theory, but that certain aspects of probability theory are antithetical to causal reasoning. As they point out, for example, causal reasoning is generally unidirectional (e.g., X causes Y). On the other hand, in statistical logic the relation between two events can be, and often is, discussed in either or both directions. For example, in order to use Bayes' theorem to calculate the posterior probability of a hypothesis (H) given new data or information (D) (i.e., $P(H|D)$), one needs to assess the likelihood of the data given the hypothesis (i.e, $P(D|H)$). Furthermore, whereas statistical theory is based on the logical structure of information, causal reasoning is responsive to both structure and content in terms of the causal field, cues to causality, and the plausibility of alternative scenarios and causal explanations. In sum, although it may not be normatively correct when compared to probability and statistical theory, heuristics are used that weight information on the basis of its perceived causal meaning and not its statistical diagnosticity.

The heuristics that humans use to attach meaning to information makes us susceptible to "biases" when compared to some normative (or presumed "optimal") standard. Substantial psychological research has been performed which attempts to identify the nature, cause and implications of these biases. In an effort to synthesize this research, Hogarth (1987) has catalogued cognitive biases according to the following four information processing stages: acquisition, processing, output and feedback. First, the acquisition of information from both the environment and memory can be biased depending on its saliency. For example, concrete information that is either based on experience or is well-publicized dominates abstract information (e.g., statistical base rates and summaries), even though the latter typically has greater predictive validity. Second, the manner in which information is processed can be biased if the individual uses an "inappropriate" heuristic. For example, the likelihood of an event is often judged by estimating its degree of similarity (or representativeness) to the class of events of which it is supposed to be an exemplar. This often results in stereotyping. Third, the manner in which one is required to respond can induce bias. For example, the relative preference for gambles can be reversed when people are asked to express choices in different ways. Lastly, feedback concerning the outcomes of a judgement can also induce bias. This bias might occur as a result of how either the outcomes or the nature of the environment are interpreted. With regard to the former, there is a tendency to erroneously atribute success to skill and failure to chance. Regarding the latter, outcomes often yield inaccurate or incomplete information concerning predictive relations. In a personnel selection setting, for example, we can seldom (if ever) learn how good our judgement is in a correlational sense because, although the success rate for the applicants that are selected is available, there is no information on the success rate of the applicants that are rejected.

The word "bias" has a negative connotation. Indeed, the research on cognitive biases has often been presented as a cataloguing of human fallibilities. However, the cognitive heuristics that spawn these biases have both strengths and weaknesses. On the positive side, they permit humans with limited information acquisition, retention and processing capabilities not only to establish order and meaning out of the mass of information with which they are confronted, but also to develop new and creative ways of improving (and hopefully never destroying) the environment. On the negative side, cognitive heuristics expose limitations in reasoning when compared with normative models of decision behavior. These normative models are not esoteric notions; they can be and have been used to improve unaided human decision behavior. The long-term goal is the design of support systems that will effectively combine human and computer strengths and thereby improve human decision behavior.

3. Social Judgement Theory

Social judgement theory (SJT) was formulated by Kenneth R. Hammond and his colleagues and students, and extends the theory of probabilistic functionalism developed by Egon Brunswik, a perception psychologist, to the realm of judgement and decision behavior. (For an overview, see Hammond *et al.* (1975) and Brehmer and Joyce (1989)). Figure 1 represents the

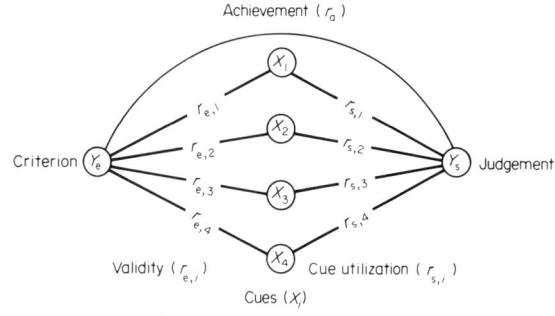

Figure 1
The lens model representing the decision task and decision maker

extension of Brunswik's lens model to the case of intuitive prediction. The goal of human judgement (Y_s) is to accurately predict environmental criteria (Y_e). These criteria may be causes of observed effects or future states of the world. Information or cues (X_i) are used to make these judgements. The cues may be acquired from the environment or human memory and are processed (i.e., utilized) by the person according to decision heuristics to produce the judgement (or "output" in Hogarth's terminology). In an effort to be accurate, the cues ($r_{s,i}$) are used in a manner that matches their environmental validity ($r_{e,i}$). It is, however, extremely difficult to do so for many tasks for the following reasons: the relationship between individual cues and the environmental criterion is typically probabilistic; the functional relations between individual cues and the criterion may assume a variety of forms (e.g., linear to curvilinear); the relations between the cues and the criterion may be organized (or combined) according to a variety of principles (e.g., additively or according to some pattern); and finally, overall task predictability is seldom perfect when using all the cues. In short, human judgement is not only difficult because of our limited information processing capabilities, but also because of the nature of the task itself.

Learning complex judgement tasks has been a major focus of research in SJT. The typical judgement task consists of presenting a person with a number of cases representing the judgement problem. Each case (or profile) for consideration consists of a mix of values of the several cues (X_i) being used to make predictions (Y_s) of the environmental criterion (Y_e). The cues have complex probabilistic relations with the criterion; consequently, their validity, and therefore utility, in predicting the criterion varies. Moreover, the overall predictability of the task using all the cues is typically less than perfect to represent uncertainty in the environment. This representation matches many repetitive real-world judgement problems such as personnel selection, medical diagnosis and securities forecasting.

The lens model equation (LME) presented in Eqn. 1 quantifies the relations between the environmental and cognitive systems represented in Fig. 1 for the above task.

$$r_a = G R_s R_e \qquad (1)$$

Since linear models, such as multiple regression and analysis of variance, have been routinely used in SJT research, they will be assumed in the description of the LME parameters although, as will become clear, the parameters represent more general concepts. Specifically, r_a is the correlation between the person's judgements (Y_s) and the environmental criterion (Y_e) over the cases; it represents the person's accuracy in predicting the criterion. G represents the correlations between the "best-fitting" linear model predicting the person's judgements (using a least-squares procedure) and the best-fitting linear model predicting the environment criterion. Conceptually, G represents the level of correspondence (or match) between the task and the person, and is considered a measure of knowledge. R_s is the correlation between the person's judgements and the predicted values of the judgements based on the (linear) model of the person. It is typically considered to be the overall consistency or "cognitive control" exhibited by the person when making a judgement. Finally, R_e is the correlation between the criterion and the predicted values of the criterion based on the (linear) environmental model; consequently, it represents the overall predictability of the environmental system.

The parameters of the LME provide important insights into the nature of many types of judgement tasks and people's ability to learn and perform them well, both in and outside of the laboratory. First, G (i.e., knowledge) and R_s (i.e., cognitive control) are statistically independent. Consequently, it is possible to perform quite poorly when one knows what to do but cannot do it consistently. Second, R_e sets an upper bound on achievement even if knowledge and cognitive control are perfect. In other words, task predictability is as important a determinant of judgement performance as our information processing capability and/or the support systems that are developed to improve it.

Considerable SJT research has focused on interpersonal learning where two or more persons work together to perform a task. Figure 2 presents the "triple system case" where one system is the task, one system is the user (e.g., a decision maker) for whom a support system is being developed and the third system is the support-system designer. It is important to keep four concepts in mind when considering the figure. First, learning how to predict another person's judgements is often a difficult judgement task. For

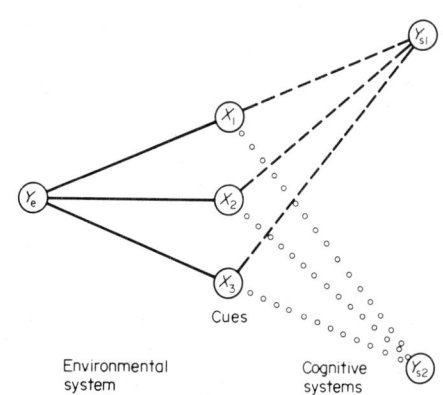

Figure 2
The lens model representing the decision task and the support-system designer and user

example, consider requirements analysis using the LME parameters. First, it is typically difficult for the designer to learn how the user performs cognitive tasks; that is, to maximize G in terms of the LME. SJT research on interpersonal learning, knowledge engineering efforts to develop expert systems, and the systems-development literature on requirements analysis all agree that, on the whole, users have very poor insight into how they process information to perform cognitive tasks. Second, users are inconsistent in their descriptions; that is, they have low task predictability (R_e) from the designer's perspective. Salient events in their environment or memory are usually those they bring to the designer's attention. These events are typically subject to processing biases owing to the inadequacy of the feedback available to the users from the environment. Moreover, the responses that users give to the designer are typically biased by the questions the designer asks, unless the latter uses multiple methods to overcome response biases. Finally, requirements analysis is compounded by the fact that designers themselves are not perfectly consistent; that is, R_s does not equal to 1.0.

The second concept is that, although they may interact extensively with the user, designers develop their own conceptualization of how to best solve the task. According to SJT, the support-system designer and the user must be considered as two interacting yet separate sytems trying to maximize achievement. Moreover, these two cognitive systems do not always agree. This point can be illustrated by assuming that the designer selects probability and statistical theory as the system's approach for processing the cue information to make predictions of probable cause. As discussed above, this normative approach does not match how humans intuitively make these judgements. Consequently, there will be substantial disagreement in principle (G) between the designer and user in the example given. Moreover, agreement in fact (r_a) will be further reduced to the extent that there are inconsistencies in their positions.

Although there have been substantial advances in the development of design tools over the last decade, the designer is basically an intuitive decision maker when designing a support system. That is, the designer has to deal with a complex task environment using limited information acquisition, retention and processing capabilities. Consequently, the concepts described above with respect to bounded rationality and judgement heuristics (and biases) apply to system designers as well as to system users. With regard to bounded rationality, both designers and users simplify the problem by reducing the range of alternatives and states of nature that are considered. Both parties set aspiration levels for what they consider to be a good product, and both "satisfice" in the form of making trade-offs between the perceived value of alternative system designs and dollar costs. With regard to heuristics, both designers and users make use of mental representations to bring order and meaning to the mass of available information. These representations are typically based on very different educational and professional experiences and, as Adelman *et al.* (1985) empirically demonstrated, users and designers evaluate system utility differently.

The third concept from SJT is that the achievement level of the system depends, in part, on how well it matches the performance requirements of the decision task (i.e., G). It is important to note that, in the example presented above, both the designer's "normative" model and the user's "descriptive" model are abstractions and hence simplifications of reality. As Hogarth points out (1987 p. 223), ". . . since a model is a simplification, it must—by necessity—fail to be a complete representation of the task. In this sense, therefore, outputs of optimal models must be 'wrong' to some degree. The critical question, therefore, is 'how wrong'." Furthermore, it could be asked how they could be improved when designing support systems.

The answer according to SJT is clearly to focus on all three systems. In so doing, the goal is to synthesize the typically normative perspective of the designer with the intuitive decision behavior of the user in order to increase the probability that the cue utilizations of the support system (and user) better match the task validities (i.e., G). Lehner and Zirk (1987) demonstrated the viability of this goal in a series of experiments in which they showed that naïve users could significantly improve their performance in a task requiring the pooling of the user's and an expert system's knowledge if the user was given a brief general description of how the expert system used an inference network to combine information when making a prediction. Moreover, their findings are consistent with those of SJT researchers in other settings who have empirically demonstrated the superiority of cognitive feedback (i.e., system properties) to outcome feedback (i.e., the correct answer). Unfortunately, outcome feedback is the predominant way in which people learn how to use support systems.

This brings us to the final concept, which is that achievement is also determined by cognitive control and task predictability. With regard to the former, it is important to remember that knowledge (G) and cognitive control (R_s) are independent constructs. In other words, if knowledge and task predictability are held constant, achievement will be a positive function of cognitive control. Consequently, support systems should be designed to permit users to implement their decision strategy in as consistent a fashion as possible. Furthermore, with regard to the latter, overall task predictability (R_e) represents an asymptote for system performance. This statement is not meant to imply that we should not attempt to improve our understanding of the environment or further the development of systems to improve our ability to deal with it. It is, however, meant to imply that perfection is not

453

an appropriate criterion for evaluating human decision behavior, either with or without system support, in many decision tasks. The quality of human decision behavior is determined by both task and human characteristics. Both designers and users need to keep this point in mind when developing and subsequently evaluating support systems.

See also: Decision Support Systems

Bibliography

Adelman L, Rook F W, Lehner P E 1985 User and R&D specialist evaluation of decision support systems: Development of a questionnaire and empirical results. *IEEE Trans. Syst., Man Cybern.* **15**, 334–42
Brehmer B, Joyce C R B (eds.) 1989 *Human Judgment: The SJT Approach.* North-Holland, Amsterdam
Brown R V, Kahr A S, Peterson C R 1974 *Decision Analysis for the Manager.* Holt Rinehart, New York
Einhorn H J, Hogarth R M 1981 Behavioral decision theory: Processes of judgment and choice. *Annu. Rev. Psychol.* **32**, 53–88
Einhorn H J, Hogarth R M 1986 Judging probable cause. *Psychol. Bull.* **99**, 3–19
Hammond K R, Stewart T R, Brehmer B, Steinmann D O 1975 Social judgment theory. In: Kaplan M F, Schwartz S (eds.) *Human Judgment and Decision Processes.* Academic Press, New York, pp. 271–312
Hogarth R M 1987 *Judgment and Choice*, 2nd edn. Wiley, New York
Kahneman D, Slovic P, Tversky A (eds.) 1982 *Judgment under Uncertainty: Heuristics and Biases.* Cambridge University Press, New York
Lehner P E, Zirk D A 1987 Cognitive factors in user/expert-system interaction. *Hum. Factors* **29**, 97–109
March J G 1978 Bounded rationality, ambiguity, and the engineering of choice. *Bell J. Econ.* **9**, 587–608
Sage A P 1981 Behavioral and organizational considerations in the design of information systems and processes for planning and decision support. *IEEE Trans. Syst., Man Cybern.* **11**, 640–78
Simon H A 1955 A behavioral model of rational choice. *Q. J. Econ.* **69**, 99–118
Simon H A 1979 Rational decision making in business organizations. *Am. Econ. Rev.* **69**, 493–513
Slovic P, Fischhoff B, Lichtenstein S 1977 Behavioral decision theory. *Annu. Rev. Psychol.* **28**, 1–39
Watson S, Buede D M 1987 *Decision Synthesis: The Principles and Practice of Decision Analysis.* Cambridge University Press, Cambridge

L. Adelman
[George Mason University, Fairfax,
Virginia, USA]

System Acquisition and Procurement

The overall process of specifying the requirements for a major system (through its design, development, production, and subsequent deployment and support) is known as the system acquisition process; the process generating the paperwork binding the buyer and the seller of this new system is called the procurement process. The implementation of these combined processes involves system engineers, component design engineers, procurement professionals, project (or program) managers, financial analysts, schedule and cost controllers, production experts and lawyers.

The development and production of a complex new system (whether it be an aircraft or a nuclear power plant), is essentially a problem of multivariable, constrained optimization. However, the problem is normally split into various functions, such as cost analysis, scheduling, system and subsystem design, production planning, risk analysis and subcontract management, each function being separately analyzed as part of some overall system's acquisition and procurement master plan.

To see how the overall acquisition process fits together, it is best to visualize it in terms of the major phases through which a new system evolves. While there is no standard categorization, most representations tend to fit into the following four categories:

(a) *phase zero*—definition,
(b) *phase one*—demonstration,
(c) *phase two*—full-scale development, and
(d) *phase three*—production and deployment.

1. Phase Zero: Concept Definition

The first issue is that of getting the activity off the ground. This comes from two unique (but often interacting) directions: either from a market analysis (or mission need) which establishes a requirement for this new system, or as a result of a new technological opportunity (where the potential development and/or demonstration of a new technology can be converted into some new system application). In general, these two directions have been found to make approximately equal contributions. However, those products arising from the requirements direction tend to be *quantitatively* different from previous products (for example, faster or harder) and are usually a result of evolutionary changes. Those products arising from the new technology direction frequently tend to be *qualitatively* different (showing changes of "type") and thus could only have been conceived of when the appropriate technology presented itself.

This initial phase of the program, the concept definition phase, combines the projected technical capability of a system with the projected market (or mission) need; in both cases forecasting years into the future to the time when the system is expected to be operational. (In some complex systems, this may be more than ten years ahead.)

At this early stage, it is important to clearly define the minimum acceptable system performance that is being aimed for and approximately how many units are planned, how much each one should cost and what technology (or technologies) are likely to be utilized. This allows the initial cost-effectiveness analyses to be performed on the proposed system. One of the most commonly made mistakes in the evolution of a new major system is to assume that it is too early to begin worrying about a system's production cost until after one has gone through phase one, or perhaps even phase two, and fully demonstrated the technology (and/or design) of the overall system. The problem is that, while the largest share of the projected program's total cost is not spent until a system is in full development and, mostly, in production, this money is nevertheless largely committed (in terms of having been designed into the system) at the time that the initial system concept is formulated. For example, if a new aircraft is the system under consideration, then whether it has one, two or four engines will have a major impact on the overall cost of the system, and is inherent in the basic concept of the system. Similarly, whether the product is planned to be produced in extremely large quantities or in very limited quantities will not only affect the production costs, but also may very well affect the whole approach taken to design and acquisition of the product. Since this phase is mostly confined to "paper studies," the cost of such analysis is very small; but the multiplier gained from this preliminary work, in terms of potential savings, is enormous.

Two key aspects of the acquisition process must be emphasized. First, there must be recognition that this is an incremental process in which key decisions are made as the system evolves through the stages of the process. For example, the next phase is that of the demonstration and validation of the concept defined during the preliminary activity. If only existing technologies are used, it may be possible to skip this phase entirely; however, if major new technologies are being considered, then this demonstration phase represents perhaps the most critical stage in the evolution of a new system. Second, it must be recognized that whenever significant risks are presented in the development of a new system, the development of alternatives must be considered. These may take the form of different industrial firms pursuing the same technology or they may take the form of the development of different technologies in parallel (to see which of these technologies proves superior). The cost of these multiple paths, particularly in the early phase of the acquisition process, is very small and the benefits are again usually quite significant.

2. Phase One: Demonstration

During the demonstration and validation phase, it is important to bear in mind that not only must new technologies be demonstrated at the system integration level, but also that critical technologies must be demonstrated at the component and subsystem level. (Numerous studies have shown that since about the early 1970s there has been a declining emphasis on, and funding for, technologies at the "lower tiers," and this deficiency is bound to have a cumulative impact over time.)

Perhaps the most difficult decision (from a management perspective) during the demonstration and validation phase is the question of whether or not a full system prototype should be developed and tested (as opposed to simply demonstrating critical parts of the system). There is, of course, no general answer to this question (or others associated with an acquisition plan), since it depends so totally upon the particular circumstances associated with the unique product. One of the most important things to remember, in terms of the development of an acquisition strategy for a new system, is that there are no general rules and that "each case is a special case." Naturally, if a prototype system is built (or competitive prototype systems are built), the risk associated with the subsequent development and production of the new system will be greatly reduced. However, this will also significantly increase the development time and somewhat increase the development costs. Usually, this choice is controlled by the degree of technological change being introduced into the new system.

3. Phase Two: Development

Once the system critical technologies and/or prototype have been demonstrated and the requirement for the system revalidated (through a more extensive market analysis, and/or detailed cost–benefit studies), it is possible to make a commitment to the subsequent full-scale development and production of the system. Notice that it is not until the initiation of this phase that substantial finance is required for the acquisition of the new system. Also, by this point, the basic design of the system has been largely completed and thus (as previously noted) the inherent costs in terms of major design elements are basically fixed. Nonetheless, there is a possibility for very significant "value engineering" work to be done (in analyzing lower-cost design options within the basic system characteristics and technology). As with the previous phase, it is possible to eliminate this phase totally, should, for example, a prototype have been built in the previous phase which proved so successful that the system might be ready to initiate production. Alternatively, by this point the developer may feel that the risk has been sufficiently reduced to allow commitment to a single phase that combines full-scale development and production initiation (the distinction here being in terms of the type of production tooling considered for the engineering model, the degree of detailed production methods developed during the engineering phase and so on).

One of the most important decisions to be made in this phase is that of the choice of developing alternatives to a single product by a single producer, during the full-scale development phase. Numerous studies have clearly shown that it is the presence of competition in some form during this phase of a major system acquisition that has the greatest impact on the subsequent production cost and performance of the system, as well as on the control of the R&D cost during the development phase. Therefore, the purchaser of the system (for example, a government buying it from industry) should ensure, whenever economically practical, the existence of two development sources. On the other hand, when a single firm is developing th system, the purchaser should ensure that alternative sources for critical elements of the system exist.

During any phase of the acquisition process, but particularly during full-scale development, it is necessary to have a detailed knowledge of, and control over, the critical areas of risk on the program. Analytic techniques have been developed which highlight the expected areas and levels of risk and provide indications to the project manager of both the likely schedule and cost impacts associated with problems during the development, as well as those problems for which management financial reserves should be established. Additionally, techniques have been developed (initially by contractors building military equipment for the US Government) which allow a relatively good overview of, and fair control over, program costs and schedules; for example, program evaluation and review techniques (PERT) of cost analysis. However, the best form of control will always be some form of continuous competition.

Naturally, the major effort during full-scale development is concentrated on the extremely large number of engineering details associated with the final design and subsequent production of the new system. However, of almost equal importance but frequently not sufficiently stressed, is the system's cost—as an engineering-design discipline. (This deficiency is particularly noticeable in systems designed for government use, such as military systems.) Cost must not be treated as an after-the-fact issue by engineers that is, one in which engineers design the system, and non-engineers price it and try to find the lowest bidder), but rather as an area in which the engineer continuously searches for lower-cost approaches, through advanced technology application, compatibility with advanced manufacturing techniques and/or through simplicity of design. Here, the engineer is in a position to make trade-offs between the ultimate in a system's performance and the cost of such performance. For example, it is often the case that achieving the last 5% of a system's performance will double the cost.

It must be noted that in recent years there has been an enormous improvement in the ability of engineers to perform cost analysis. Tools and techniques have been developed which provide good parametric estimates (such as cost per unit weight for different technologies), and other techniques are available which allow the achievement of good independent cost estimates of various system design approaches, thus making it feasible to trade-off cost and performance during the system's design evolution.

Another important lesson often overlooked by engineers in the development of a new system is the interrelationship between the time it takes to do a job and the cost of doing it. It is important to realistically schedule and budget a program, and then to stick to that schedule; otherwise, it is likely that there will be a significant cost overrun in the development of the system.

Finally, the last and perhaps most critical part of the full-scale development activities is that associated with the testing of the system. It must be realized that testing occurs throughout the development; a planned, coordinated, overall test program (ranging from component tests through subsystem and system tests) is critically important to the success of a system. Nonetheless, it is essential that the designer recognize that some final testing of the system must be performed in an environment as closely approximating that of its ultimate use as possible, including the operating and maintaining of the system by people with skill levels comparable to those who will be the ultimate users. The designer's ability to operate and maintain the system clearly has little relation to the user's ability to do this, unless the latter has been carefully considered in both the design and test phases.

4. Phase Three: Production and Deployment

When the development phase is successfully completed, as demonstrated by user testing, the production and deployment phase may begin. However, if the developer waits until this point to begin any consideration of such activities, it is far too late; it is essential that production and deployment planning starts early. The equipment should be designed to be producible in volume for low cost, and on existing or obtainable production equipment. Such facilities should have been ordered well in advance and their associated costs should have been calculated in the overall development decision process. Similarly, the field support of the system (for use after deployment) should be planned early, through the proper design and planning associated with field test equipment, maintenance concepts, warranties and so on.

The most important considerations in the production phase are those associated with maintaining an economically efficient production rate and a stable production program. Thus, design changes must be minimized in order to maintain a cost-effective production program. However, if changes are required, they must be introduced in "block changes," so that they do not continually disrupt the production process. The most common failing in production programs is the lack of recognition of the enormous costs that changes to a program cause, either in terms of engineering changes introduced into the product or in terms of schedule or rate changes introduced into the production plan.

The best way to control costs and schedules in a production program is through the use of some form of continuous competition (for varying shares of the business). The added start-up costs associated with setting up a second contractor to produce the equipment are usually more than paid for by the presence of competition in improving quality and driving down system costs during the duration of the program. The net overall benefit of production competition is a saving of, on average, the order of 25–30%.

Throughout the whole acquisition process, it must be recognized that for most major systems more than half of the total cost of the system is associated with subcontractors, purchased parts and materials. Thus, the issue of "make versus buy" (that is, whether the system contractor should produce an item or have a specialist make it) and the issue of managing the extremely large number of lower-tier suppliers (often in the thousands) are of major importance. It is not simply a question of placing an order and then assuming delivery. These lower-tier suppliers go through exactly the same acquisition process as that described for the system contractor, and the higher-risk technologies are frequently developed at the component or subsystem level. Thus it is an engineering problem, as well as an extreme management challenge, to integrate the large numbers of suppliers of high-technology products on any major system acquisition.

As noted above, this whole acquisition process is paralleled by a procurement process which contractually ties the buyer and the supplier together (whether it be between the system's contractor and its supplier or between the buyer, such as a government, and its suppliers). In the case of major systems being procured by, say, US Federal Government departments, the whole set of Government requirements are also involved: these range from detailed procurement specifications associated with how the process is to be executed and how "fairness" is to be maintained, to ensuring that all of the various legislative requirements, such as minority employment or small business preferences, are satisfied. There are formal processes for defining the steps by which the competition for the selection of a supplier is to be carried out, and exactly how the selection itself is to be accomplished. Additionally, such a government procurement has the added complexity that comes from the requirement for an annual budgetary cycle, thus introducing inherent tendencies for "instability" in a program; this is extremely disruptive and expensive.

Finally, whether a program is a government or an industrial procurement there is the problem of how to create proper incentives, in a contractual way, to ensure that the buyer's desires are satisfied at the lowest cost and in the fastest way possible. Frequently, these incentives take the form of an added profit (or penalty) associated with the realized cost, delivery or performance. Again, however, the best incentive is that associated with competition and the threat of losing the business to someone else unless the customer's desired objectives are achieved.

In summary, the overall acquisition and procurement process is an extremely complex technical and management issue, which can make as much difference to the success or failure of a major, high-technology system's development and production as can good engineering design.

See also: System-Acquisition Information: Knowledge-Based Representation; Technological Forecasting

Bibliography

Fox J R 1974 *Arming America—How the U.S. Buys Weapons*. Harvard University Press, Cambridge, Massachusetts
Gansler J S 1980 *The Defense Industry*. MIT Press, Cambridge, Massachusetts

J. S. Gansler
[Analytic Sciences Corporation, Arlington, Virginia, USA]

System-Acquisition Information: Knowledge-Based Representation

System engineering is concerned with the synthesis of discrete elements or components into an organized entity to satisfy some specified purpose. For example, to system-engineer a satellite for remote-sensing missions is to specify an organization of components, subsystems and interfaces that accomplishes the intended purpose of the satellite. The focus of system engineering is on what is to be built.

The term system acquisition generally refers to large-scale, complex, high-technology development projects that require extended periods of the order of several years to develop and place into operation. During the extended period, laws and regulations may be revised, new technological solutions may present themselves and the initially perceived system requirements may undergo change. Nuclear power facilities, petrochemical plants and advanced weapon systems are examples of such projects.

System acquisition management is concerned with the business strategy by which a system is built or otherwise acquired for use. Its focus is on how a system is to be acquired. The information needed to make informed business decisions relative to acquiring complex systems and technologies is referred to as system acquisition information; it comprises the following classes of information.

(a) System objectives—the high-level technical, performance, cost and delivery (time) parameters that characterize a system.

(b) Resources—the amount of time and money actually or potentially available for the acquisition of the system.

(c) Acquisition methods—the set of techniques or business practices for acquiring desired systems or technologies (e.g., off-the-shelf procurement, competitive prototyping, technical data packages).

The system acquisition problem can be viewed as one of searching for the set of acquisition methods that best achieve the system objectives within the resource constraints. On the surface, system acquisition appears to be a straightforward resource-allocation problem; however, in practice, the system objectives and resource constraints are seldom considered fixed. For the acquisition manager, the problem is to strike a balance between system objectives and resources in a business and technological environment that evolves over a usually extended time horizon.

System acquisition is concerned with high-level business strategy. In particular, its main focus is not with the administrative and legal details of preparing procurement documents, selecting a contract type, monitoring and evaluating contractor performance, or generally any of the multitude of tactical details that are necessary in any organization to execute the business plan. Rather, the fundamental purpose of systems acquisition is to produce the business plan itself. This activity is an example of design problem solving; design itself has been categorized as problem solving involving object synthesis through constraint satisfaction, and it is this paradigm that underlies the discussion in this article, which is organized as follows. First, we elaborate on the kind of objectives that are typical in large-scale systems acquisition and the sorts of acquisition methods that have been proposed to address these objectives. Next, we define object synthesis abstractly and then discuss a general model called a constraint satisfaction problem (CSP) formulation for representing this problem-solving activity. Next, we present a CSP representation of a system-acquisition problem. Finally, a discussion of other approaches to system-acquisition modelling is provided to place the CSP approach in perspective.

1. System-Acquisition Objectives

Typical objectives in acquiring large-scale systems incorporating complex technology include reduction of design risk, achieving or improving upon scheduled delivery, and achieving or improving upon target cost. Particularly, though not exclusively from the perspective of a government program manager, the following objective may also exist: expansion of the industrial base capability and capacity to ensure long-term sources of supply and industry competition. It is apparent that these objectives may often be competing. For example, reducing design risk by pursuing multiple alternative design approaches will frustrate a cost minimization objective. Moreover, any objective function over these attributes must capture the typically mathematically ill-behaved nature of the value (or utility) function for any single attribute. For example, there may be no intrinsic value in beginning a production run prior to a notional date. A hypothetical value function for production start, as well as two other typical value functions, are illustrated in Fig. 1.

The trade-offs among objectives must be dealt with explicitly. If the problem is stated as an ordered set of goals to be achieved sequentially, then goal programming may be suitable for formulating the problem. Alternatively, there may be an agreed-upon set of weights that could be incorporated into a multi-attribute utility function and standard optimization techniques applied. However, when weights are not specified precisely, it may be possible to express real-valued intervals over which the weights are likely to

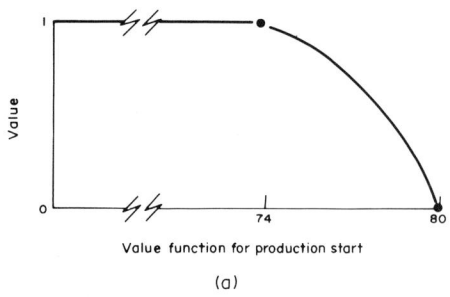
(a)
Value function for production start

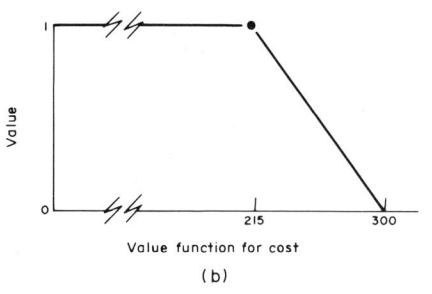
(b)
Value function for cost

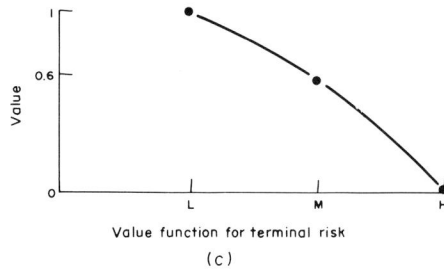
(c)
Value function for terminal risk

Figure 1
Typical value functions in acquisition strategy design

range, and these in turn can be used to induce a preference ordering on acquisition alternatives and identify nondominated alternatives (see White et al. (1984) and Sykes and White (1987) for discussions of this technique called imprecisely specified multiattribute utility theory—ISMAUT).

Another important feature of acquisition objectives is that a given set of them may conflict to the point where no solution exists at all. This situation requires a higher-order decision process whereby one or more objectives must be relaxed or eliminated altogether, or additional resources must be made available. Brown et al. (1987) propose a metalevel design process involving two levels of design abstraction. There is an "outer loop" design process that first produces a top-level design specification based on system requirements. An "inner-loop" design process then successively refines an initial design proposal in an attempt to satisfy the outer-loop design specification. If this inner design process fails, then there is no alternative but to produce a new design specification. This model aptly describes acquisition strategy development as well as other types of design problem solving.

2. Acquisition Methods

The set of methods or techniques for acquiring a system are typically multiple and varied, depending on the nature of the industry, the end item to be acquired and the state of technology. In the case of nondevelopment items, where little or no new design activity is required, the focus tends to be on methods that will satisfy delivery schedule and result in cost savings. Procurement of off-the-shelf hardware, software and consumable items fits this category, but these items are not generally the subject of this article. Development items, on the other hand, require acquisition methods that balance design uncertainty and risk with resource constraints on time and funds. These items require more sophisticated management and several general approaches have been proposed including:

(a) maintaining parallel design and development activities at the system level;
(b) maintaining parallel design and development activities at the subsystem level;
(c) prototyping systems and competitive prototyping;
(d) maintaining competitive forces by ensuring multiple sources of supply (e.g., by splitting the procurement quantity among multiple suppliers or subsystem breakout);
(e) incentivizing contractors through various reward schemes; and
(f) penalizing contractors for quality, cost or schedule delays.

Each of these techniques (and there are many variations on these themes) can be viewed as a heuristic for improving the outcome on one or more of the acquisition objectives. The overall effect of any one technique on the system to be acquired must be determined by modelling the interaction of the technique and the various attributes that capture the individual acquisition objectives.

3. System-Acquisition Planning as Object Synthesis

Object synthesis is the process of configuring or designing an object by selecting and organizing components to satisfy a set of specifications (Chandrasekaran 1985). The object to be synthesized may be a physical entity such as a computer configuration or circuit board, or more abstractly a strategic business plan, computer code, or maneuver plan for a robot or autonomous vehicle. The components to be synthesized may be, respectively, microprocessors, circuitry, marketing strategies, software subroutines, and subplans and plan actions. In a typical system-acquisition plan, the object to be synthesized is a plan, which represents a set of decisions that contribute collectively to an overall assessment of the degree to which the system objectives have been satisfied. The components in this plan are the individual acquisition methods, and the design problem is to synthesize a set of methods that optimizes system objectives.

3.1 Object Synthesis Through Constraint Satisfaction

A convenient way to model object synthesis is as a constraint satisfaction problem (CSP). CSPs have been studied extensively in artificial intelligence (Mackworth 1977, Dechter and Pearl 1985) and have found application in circuit design, scene interpretation (Montanari 1974) and belief (truth) maintenance systems (Dechter 1987). A CSP involves the simultaneous assignment of values to a set of variables, subject to a set of constraints existing among the variables. The representational structure used to capture a CSP is called a constraint network (CN). A CN consists of a set of n variables $(X_1, \ldots, X_n)$ with associated domains $(R_1, \ldots, R_n)$, and a set of constraints formed from subsets of the Cartesian product $R_1 \times \cdots \times R_n$. The tuples of a constraint specify all the simultaneous assignments of values to the variables that are permitted. A solution to a CSP is an assignment of variable values such that all constraints are satisfied. In general, we are interested in obtaining either one or all consistent assignments, depending on the application. However, in decision problems, we may impose an additional requirement on the computational procedure to find the "best" solution, defined as the solution that maximizes some explicit utility or value-function.

3.2 CSP Representation of a System-Acquisition Problem

Figure 2 presents a constraint network for a hypothetical system acquisition. We have in mind an advanced tactical missile but the discussion applies more generally to other systems and technologies. Simplistically, the development process is to allocate a certain level of resources (funds and time) to design and develop a system prototype. Following the expenditures of these resources, we will have a prototype system that has a certain residual design risk associated with it; that is, there are still likely to be some "bugs" in the design that inhibit its producibility, and one product of the design process is this "terminal" risk level. The decision maker must make the following decisions:

(a) when to start production (variable X_1 in Fig. 2);

(b) what level of funds to commit to the design—this affects the number of design alternatives (one or two) that can be pursued (variable X_2);

(c) how to time-phase development and production (variable X_6); and

(d) with what level of terminal risk to be satisfied (variable X_8).

As the constraint network indicates, terminal risk (variable X_8) is a function of the number of design alternatives pursued (variable X_7) and the phasing of the development and production phases of the acquisition (variable X_6), both of which are influenced by the level of technical challenge (variable X_5). The phasing of the acquisition can be incremental (I) (i.e., production starts *after* all development is completed), or concurrent (C) (i.e., production begins *before* all development is completed and design modifications are either retrofitted or multiple configurations of the produced system are permitted). For this hypothetical system, the technical challenge itself is an intervening variable, being a function of the packaging density (variable X_3) and the producibility (variable X_4), which are two key issues in the acquisition of tactical missiles. In other types of systems, different factors would determine the technical challenge. The technical challenge variable is a qualitative expression of going-in uncertainty and expressed as high (H), medium (M) or low (L). We also assume that if a single design is pursued, the estimated cost is US$215 million; if two designs are pursued, the cost is US$300 million. If the development and production phases run concurrently, the estimated time to production start is 74 months; otherwise it is 80 months.

Table 1 presents the domain of each variable in the constraint graph depicted in Fig. 2, and Table 2 presents the tuples satisfying the set of constraints in the problem. For example, if the variable value for technical challenge is high (X_5=H), then the only permitted value for phasing is incremental (X_6=I), expressing the notion that the development and production phases should not be overlapped in the presence of a high technical challenge.

In our problem, we are interested in finding not just any solution, but in the special sense described below, an optimal one. The solution procedure we use for this example problem is based on an algorithm presented in Dechter *et al.* (1987) which finds an optimal solution

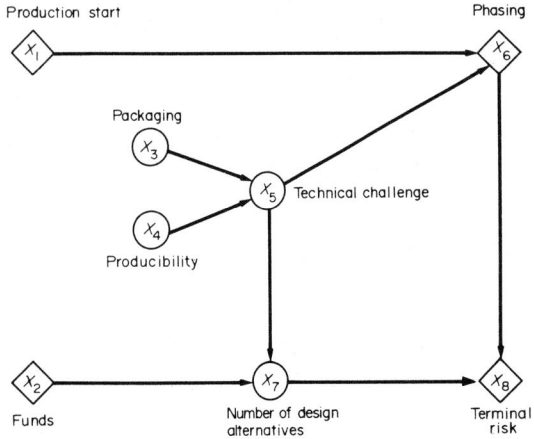

Figure 2
Constraint network for hypothetical system acquisition

Table 1
Variable domains

Variable	Domains
X_1	production start: {74 months, 80 months}
X_2	funds: {US$215 million, US$300 million}
X_3	packaging: {dense (D), not dense (N)}
X_4	producibility: {significant issues (S), no significant issues (N)}
X_5	technical challenge {high (H), medium (M), low (L)}
X_6	phasing: {concurrent (C), incremental (I)}
X_7	number of design alternatives: {1, 2}
X_8	terminal risk: {high (H), medium (M), low (L)}

Table 2
Constraints

Constraint	Satisfying tuples
X_1, X_6	(74, C) (80, I)
X_2, X_7	(215, 1) (300, 2)
X_3, X_5	(D, H) (N, M) (N, L)
X_4, X_5	(S, H) (S, M) (N, L)
X_5, X_6	(H, I) (M, I) (M, C) (L, I) (L, C)
X_5, X_7	(H, 2) (M, 2) (M, 1) (L, 1)
X_6, X_8	(I, M) (I, L) (C, H) (C, M) (C, L)
X_7, X_8	(1, H) (1, M) (2, M) (2, L)

to a CSP given a utility function over the problem variables. The optimal solution is the consistent assignment of variables that maximizes a simple additive utility function of the form:

$$U = \sum_{i=1}^{n} w_i V_i (X_i) \quad (1)$$

where U is the weighted sum of the individual value functions V_i and w_i are weights in the open interval (0, 1) that collectively sum to one. To use this algorithm, it must be possible to adequately express the acquisition objectives as functions of the problem variables; in general, this does not present a modelling problem. However, this algorithm does not produce the kind of results that would be possible using an approach such as goal programming, where the intent is to successively achieve an ordered set of goals.

The decision variables are denoted in Fig. 2 as diamonds. We assume the decision maker has formulated the following system-acquisition objectives: start production as soon as practicable, minimize design risk and minimize development cost. We also assume for our hypothetical system that the packaging requirement is not dense, but there are significant producibility issues; i.e., $X_3 = N$ and $X_4 = S$.

As pointed out in Sect. 1, since there may be no value in starting production prior to a nominal production-start date, the value function for production start might appear as shown in Fig. 1(a), where penalties accrue only if the nominal start date is exceeded. A value function for development cost is shown in Fig. 1(b); like production start, there may be no value in underspending the estimated budget, but a great disincentive to exceeding it. Finally, a typical value function for terminal risk is shown in Fig. 1(c) which reflects increasing aversion to terminal risk.

The heart of the algorithm for finding the optimal solution depends on the following property: for every CSP formulation represented as a primal-constraint graph, there exists an equivalent formulation of the problem, called the dual-constraint graph, with properties that can be more easily exploited to find an optimal solution. (See Dechter et al. 1987 for details.) A top-level description of the algorithm is presented in Table 3. (Note that the treatment of a variable in the constraint network by the solution procedure does not depend on whether it represents a decision or state variable.) Steps 1–3 transform the original problem into a representation that can be exploited to find the optimal solution in step 4. The primal-constraint graph, or primal, is simply the graph of the original problem formulation shown in Fig. 2. The dual-constraint graph, or dual, shown in Fig. 3, is constructed as follows.

(a) Generate subgraphs from the primal. A subgraph comprises a subset of arcs and nodes of the primal graph, chosen such that any two subgraphs F and G share at least one variable. In general, multiple subgraphs can be created from a single primal. The intent is that all instantiations of variables in F and G can be made independently, except those variables shared by F and G.

(b) Represent each subgraph generated by the previous step as a single node.

(c) Connect the two subgraphs F and G with an arc and label the arc with the set of common variables.

A join-tree, the output of step 2, is created from the dual by removing redundant arcs such that the resulting graph is connected and acyclic. A redundant arc is one in which every variable contained in its label is shared with another arc in some common cycle. A join-tree for this example is shown in Fig. 4(a). Note that a join-tree is not necessarily unique. In this example, there are two choices of arcs labelled X_6 and two labelled X_7, hence four join-trees are possible. A directed join-tree is created in step 3. A node of the join-tree is chosen as a root node, called node C. All nodes connected to C become its children $C_1, \ldots, C_k$. A child node C_i becomes a parent node if subtrees exist; i.e., C_i has children. This process is iterated for all subtrees until no more child nodes can be created. The directed join-tree for this example is shown in Fig. 4(b).

Step 4 finds feasible solutions and applies the utility function over the solution variables to produce the optimal solution. It employs the algorithm in Table 4. The initial set of variables to be instantiated is that

Table 3
CSP utility maximizing algorithm

Step	Description
0	given a primal-constraint graph
1	create the dual-constraint graph from the primal
2	create a join-tree for the dual
3	create a directed join-tree from the join-tree
4	find the utility for all subtrees recursively

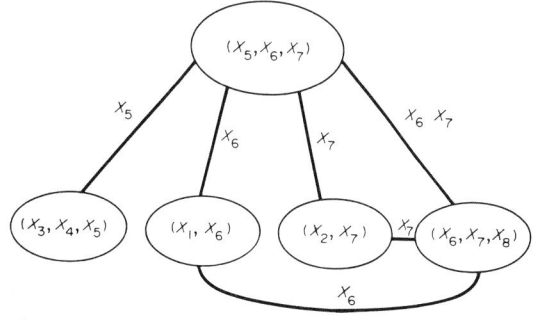

Figure 3
Dual-constraint graph

System-Acquisition Information: Knowledge-Based Representation

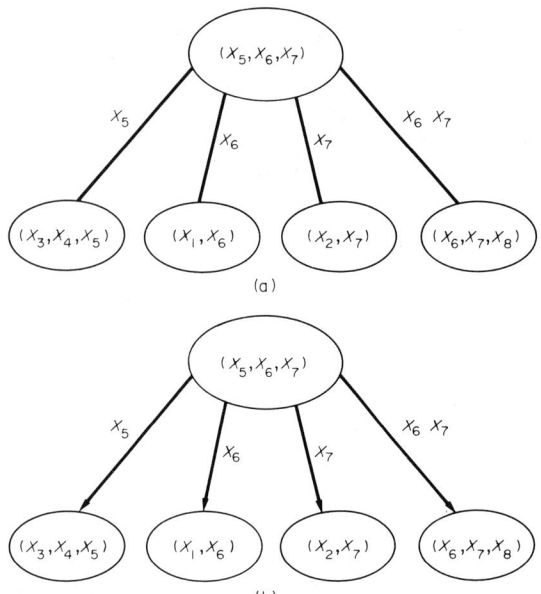

Figure 4
(a) Join-tree and (b) directed join-tree

Table 4
Variable instantiation algorithm

Step	Description
0	instantiate the variables in the root node C consistent with arc constraints
1	holding the instantiated variables in C constant, instantiate variables in child nodes C_i that do not violate any arc constraints
2	compute and sum the utilities for each solution, saving the solution with the greatest utility
3	repeat steps 1–3, exhausting all combinations consistent with arc constraints
4	stop

contained in the root node; i.e., that node containing the set of nodes (X_5, X_6, X_7). One possible instantiation, shown in Fig. 5, is $X_5 = M$; $X_6 = I$; $X_7 = 2$.

Suppose the utility function for this example is given as:

$$U = 0.6V(X_1) + 0.2V(X_2) + 0.2V(X_8) \qquad (2)$$

The computation of the values associated with the root node are shown in Fig. 5. This node, instantiated with (M, I, 2), is consistent with only one instantiation of node (X_3, X_4, X_5) (i.e., (N, S, M)), one instantiation of (X_1, X_6) (i.e., (80, I)), one instantiation of (X_2, X_7) (i.e., (300, 2)), and with two instantiations of $(X_6, X_7,$

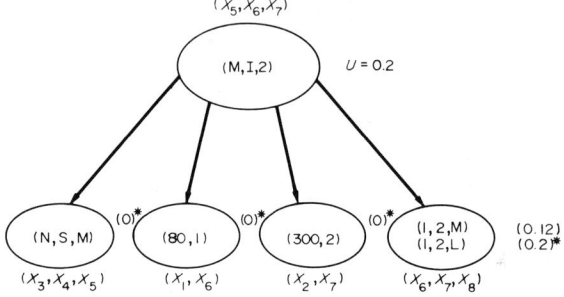

Figure 5
Variable instantiation in a directed join-tree

$X_8)$ (i.e., (I, 2, M) and (I, 2, L)). The values of the leaf tuples are their utility values, computed using Eqn. 2, and the highest value in each node is shown by an asterisk.

A local solution (i.e., complete variable assignment for each directed join-tree) is composed of the subtuples with the highest values. In the example join-tree of Fig. 5, the solution is:

$$X_1 = 80 \text{ months}$$
$$X_2 = \$300 \text{ million}$$
$$X_3 = \text{none}$$
$$X_4 = \text{significant}$$
$$X_5 = \text{medium}$$
$$X_6 = \text{incremental}$$
$$X_7 = 2$$
$$X_8 = \text{low}$$

This solution has a utility of 0.2.

The root node is evaluated for each consistent assignment, and the associated utility composted. The optimal assignment for this example (shown in Fig. 6) is achieved for the tuple (M, C, 1), yielding a utility of 0.92. The sensitivity of the solution to the emphasis on alternative objectives is illustrated by solving the same

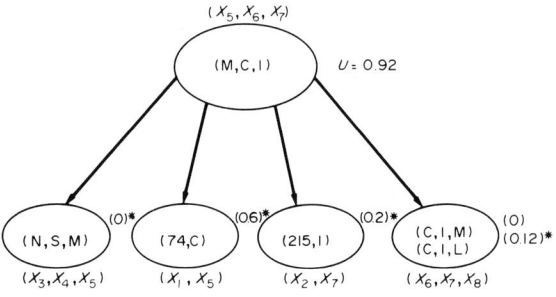

Figure 6
Optimal solution for example acquisition problem. $X_1 = 74$ months, $X_2 = \text{US\$215 million}$, $X_3 = \text{none}$, X_4 is significant, X_5 is medium, X_6 is concurrent, $X_7 = 1$, X_8 is medium

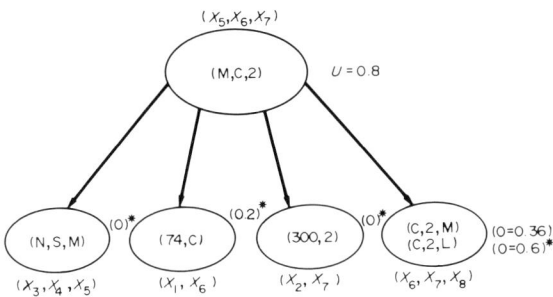

Figure 7
Optimal solution to example with new utility function.
$X_1 = 74$ months, $X_2 = $ US$300 million, $X_3 = $ none, X_4 is significant, X_5 is medium, X_6 is concurrent, $X_7 = 2$, X_8 is low

problem with a utility function reflecting different priorities. For example, consider the following utility function:

$$U = 0.2V(X_1) + 0.2V(X_2) + 0.6V(X_8) \quad (3)$$

where the priorities on reducing terminal risk (X_8) and starting production sooner (X_1) are reversed. The directed join-tree will be identical to the previous example as will the instantiation of variables; however, substitution into Eqn. 3 demonstrates that the optimal solution is now achieved by instantiating the root node to (M, C, 2) giving a utility of 0.8; the corresponding solution is shown in Fig. 7.

Dechter et al. (1987) have demonstrated that the complexity of the algorithm is linear in the tree size (i.e., number of nodes) and identical to the computational complexity of finding any solution. Some computational effort can also be saved through the observation that not all elements in the domains of certain variables need be evaluated. For example, in our problem, because the values for packaging (X_3) and producibility (X_4) were set at the beginning of the problem (being direct functions of the system to be built), inspection of the constraints among (X_3, X_5) and (X_4, X_5) reveals that $X_5 = $ L need not be considered in the solution procedure because it cannot appear in any solution where $X_4 = $ S.

4. Comparison of Constraint-Based Representation of System-Acquisition Information with Other Work

4.1 Comparison with Classical AI Planning and Design

Design problems can be contrasted with typical generative planning in artificial intelligence (AI) (see, for example, Sussman (1973), Waldinger (1975), Stefik (1981), Chapman (1987), Nilsson (1980)) principally by the lack of a clear and unambiguous goal state. In classical AI planning, the goal state is characterized by some declarative description of the world that is being modelled. For example, in planning for the movement of a robot to some room, the goal state may be represented in the predicate calculus as (LOCATED-IN robot room-1). Planning amounts to finding a sequence of operators (i.e., actions) that when executed will produce the desired goal state. In a design problem, these unambiguous goal-state descriptions can only be provided when design constraints are considered hard and fixed. Unfortunately, they seldom are (or only a few of them are) so the decision maker, in order to follow the classical planning paradigm, must decide what system objectives to treat as hard constraints—these become the goals for the planner. Thus, there is a kind of metadecision problem here that is essential just to pose a well-formed design problem, and in this regard, classical AI planning will not help. This requires the sort of metalevel design process that was discussed in Sect. 1.

4.2 Comparison with Decision Analytic Approaches

There has been relatively little effort to develop quantitative models of top-level system-acquisition strategy. Cox and Hullander (1981) identified the major factors influencing the design of an acquisition strategy for major weapon systems and conceptualized a strategy selection model that is based on the decision analysis paradigm. This concept, implemented first as the acquisition strategy comparison model (ASCM), was later refined by Clark and Bohn (1985) and renamed the procurement strategy model (PSM). The PSM defines an acquisition strategy as a four-tuple, where each element in the tuple represents the specific strategy option taken in each of the four phases that comprise the acquisition cycle. Table 5 illustrates the acquisition options available in each of the four phases.

The PSM accepts as input numerical measures of subsystem technical risk, the procurement quantity, schedule constraints, and relative measures of production cost indexed to a database of weapon systems. It calculates for every acquisition strategy (i.e., all possible tuples) except those specifically excluded by the model user, its associated cost, schedule and residual technical risk. Essentially, each strategy is plotted as a point in 3-space, producing a few dominating strategies which the user heuristically prunes to arrive at one or a small number of strategies that are most preferred. No attempt is made in PSM to weight the three attributes in order to produce an overall figure of merit for each strategy.

4.3 Comparison with Rule-Based Approaches

The PSM maps each acquisition strategy into a set of three attributes and thus amounts to a surface representation of how strategy is related to acquisition outcomes. However, this representation does not provide any insight into why a particular strategy affects the outcome in a particular way and another does not.

Table 5
Procurement phase alternatives (Clark and Bohn 1985)

Concept exploration (CE)	Demonstration and validation (D&V)	Full-scale engineering development (FSED)	Production and deployment (P&D)

Directed concept	Waive	Incremental development (no concurrency)
		  by single source
		  by multiple sources
			Single source
			  annual contract
			  with options for follow-on buys
			  multiyear contract

Concept performed
  by government activities
  by industrial firms
  jointly by government and industry
	Contract definition
	  by government activities
	  by single industrial firm
	  by multiple industrial firms
		Partial concurrency
		  by single source
		  by multiple sources
			Multiple sources
			  leader/follower
			  licensing
			  second sourcing using technical data package

	Subsystem/component development
	  by government activities
	  by single industrial firm
	  by multiple industrial firms
		Full (extreme) concurrency
		  by single source	

	System prototype
	  by government activities
	  by single industrial firm
	  by multiple industrial firms		

A deep-knowledge representation is required to represent this type of information explicitly; this motivated the development of the acquisition expert system (AES) (Hatfield 1985, Hatfield et al. 1987).

AES consists of a set of production rules and frames as data structures that capture some of the knowledge involved in determining the acquisition strategy for the full-scale engineering and development (FSED) phase of a tactical missile. It views acquisition strategy in a manner conceptually similar to and compatible with the PSM. However, it emphasizes the interaction of qualitative features of the weapon systems, the acquisition environment and resource constraints to produce recommendations about how to structure the FSED phase. Table 6 lists the principal frames in AES and the type of knowledge they contain. Table 7 illustrates the contents of the SYSTEM frame. Three example AES rules and their explanations are given below.

(RULE G00009
  (IF (INDUST-BASE NUMBER-SOURCES SINGLE-US)
    (SYSTEM CONCEPT ESTABLISHED)
    (PROD-PHASE OBJECTIVE MIN-PROD-COST))
  (THEN (PROD-PHASE ACCEPT-ALTS MULTIYEAR)))

Explanation: When no other production source exists to provide cost competition, cost may be reduced by negotiating a multiyear contract. There is incentive for the producer to offer a lower price based on economies of scale (e.g., large lot material purchases) and a longer, more stable production period.

(RULE G00106
  (IF (SYS-DEVELOP PRODUCIBILITY NO-SIGNIF-ISSUES)

Table 6
Acquisition expert system frames (Hatfield et al. 1987)

Frame	Description of contents
PROGRAM	program characteristics (e.g., production start date)
SYSTEM	basic system characteristics (e.g., system type, operational concept, system users and degree of technical challenge)
SUBSYS-DEVELOP	information pertaining to the amount of development work required on the various subsystems
SYS-DEVELOP	information pertaining to the current development status of the system as a whole (e.g., prototype, trade studies), and packaging and producibility issues
INDUST-BASE	information pertaining to the industrial base (e.g., the number of qualified sources and industry experience)
POLIT-ENVIRON	information pertaining to the political environment that might influence acquisition strategy development
FSED-PHASE	programmatic, funding, schedule and strategy information pertaining to the FSED phase
PROD-PHASE	programmatic, funding, schedule and strategy information pertaining to the production phase
COMPUTE-RISK	used by the system to heuristically generate a numerical risk estimate

Table 7
Example AES frame

Frame	System
Slot:	Type
Possible values:	Missiles
Explanation:	This slot contains information as to the type of weapon system to be developed and produced. The current knowledge base only contains information on tactical missiles
Slot:	New-or-mod
Possible values:	New, Mod
Explanation:	Enter MOD if the system is a modification to an earlier system; otherwise, enter NEW. The default value is NEW
Slot:	Concept
Possible values:	Established, Not-Firm
Explanation:	This slot contains information on how well the operational concept has been defined and accepted by the Service, OSD, the Congress and other factions
Slot:	Tech-challenge
Possible values:	(Derived by the system) High, Moderate, Low
Explanation:	This slot is normally filled by the program based on slots in the SYS-DEVELOP frame
Slot:	Numerical-risk
Possible values:	(Derived by the system) Value applies to last inferencing run
Explanation:	The value in this slot is computed on the basis of the development work required in each of the subsystems (as entered by the user in the SUBSYS-DEVELOP frame) and a series of rules that map the qualitative description of required subsystem development into a risk index ranging from 1 to 9. A system with a numerical risk greater than 5 probably should not enter FSED and one greater than 3 should not enter production
Slot:	Developers
Possible values:	US-firm, Foreign-firm
Explanation:	Enter here the nationality of the developing firm—foreign or US
Slot:	Users
Possible values:	US-forces, For-forces, US-and-for
Explanation:	This slot contains information on the services, both US and foreign, that use the system

```
(SYS-DEVELOP STATUS FULL-SYS-PROTO))
(THEN (SYSTEM TECH-CHALLENGE LOW)))
```

Explanation: When production technology has already been developed and full system prototyping has been accomplished (i.e., packaging issues have been solved), the bulk of the technical challenge has been eliminated.

```
(RULE G00111
    (IF (FSED-PHASE SOURCES-DESIRED SINGLE)
        (SYSTEM TECH-CHALLENGE HIGH))
    (THEN (PROD-PHASE ACCEPT-ALTS LEADER-FOLLOWER)))
```

Explanation: If only one source is desired (or mandated) through FSED and the technical challenge is high, but competition in production is desired, a leader-follower arrangement may be acceptable if the production quantity is sufficiently high.

The user supplies AES with the program acquisition objectives, system characteristics and resource constraints. AES applies rules to the entered data to map qualitative features of the system to a numerical risk index. This index drives traditional statistical cost- and schedule-estimating models to produce rough estimates of full-scale development phase cost and time. AES then forward-chains through the rule set, instantiating rule consequents whenever the antecedents are matched by a fact in the database. (AES also has a backward-chaining mode.)

AES is limited in that it does not perform any kind of consistency check to ensure that no conflict exists among elements of the strategy it designs. For example, if the user enters a low estimate of available funds, the system will recommend a *single* development source due to funding constraints. However, if the risk implied by the development status of the system as a whole is sufficiently great, AES will simultaneously recommend *multiple* sources in order to mitigate design risk. While AES does not resolve this conflict, the output of the system highlights these inconsistencies by instantiating a variable with multiple values. Recognition of this limitation motivated the development of the constraint-based approach to acquisition strategy design presented in Sect. 3.

See also: System Acquisition and Procurement

Bibliography

Brown D E, Sykes E A, White C C 1987 *Intelligent Design Aiding Systems*, Working Paper. Department of Systems Engineering, University of Virginia, Charlottesville, Virginia

Chandrasekaran B 1985 Generic tasks in knowledge-based reasoning: Characterizing and designing expert systems at the "right" level of abstraction. *Proc. IEEE Computer Society Int. Conf. AI.* IEEE, New York

Chapman D 1987 Planning for conjunctive goals. *Artif. Intell.* **32**, 333–77

Clark P G, Bohn M 1985 *Procurement Strategy Model*, Technical Report TR-4856-2. The Analytic Sciences Corp., Arlington, Virginia

Cox L W, Hullander R A 1981 *Feasibility and Development Study for a System Acquisition Strategy Model*, Technical Report TR-1375. The Analytic Sciences Corp., Arlington, Virginia

Dechter R 1987 *A Constraint Network Approach to Truth Maintenance*, Technical Report R-80. Cognitive Systems Laboratory, University of California, Los Angeles, California

Dechter R, Dechter A, Pearl J 1987 *Optimization in Constraint Networks*, Working Paper. Cognitive Systems Laboratory, University of California, Los Angeles, California

Dechter R, Pearl J 1985 The anatomy of easy problems: A constraint satisfaction formulation. *Proc. 9th Int. Conf. AI.* Morgan Kaufman, San Mateo, California

Hatfield F 1985 *Acquisition Expert System (AES) Tutorial*, Technical Report TR-5031-1. The Analytic Sciences Corp., Arlington, Virginia

Hatfield F, Varley T C, Madalon D A 1987 Knowledge-based representation of system acquisition knowledge. In: Silverman B G (ed.) *Expert Systems for Business*. Addison–Wesley, Reading, Massachusetts, pp. 140–60

Howard R A, Matheson J E 1981 Influence diagrams. In: Howard R A, Matheson J E (eds) *The Principles and Applications of Decision Analysis*, Vol. 2. Strategic Decisions Group, Menlo Park, California

Mackworth A K 1977 Consistency in networks of relations. *Artif. Intell.* **8**, 99–118

Montanari U 1974 Networks of constraints: Fundamental properties and applications to picture processing. *Inf. Sci.* **7**, 95–132

Nilsson N J 1980 *Principles of Artificial Intelligence*. Tioga, Palo Alto, California

Stefik M 1981 Planning and meta-planning. *Artif. Intell.* **16**, 141–70

Sussman G J 1973 A computational model of skill acquisition, Ph.D. thesis. Massachusetts Institute of Technology, Cambridge, Massachusetts

Sykes E A, White C C 1987 *Multiobjective Intelligent Computer-Aided Design*, Working Paper. Department of Systems Engineering, University of Virginia, Charlottesville, Virginia

Waldinger R 1975 *Achieving Several Goals Simultaneously*, Technical Note 107. Artificial Intelligence Center, SRI International, Menlo Park, California

White C C, Sage A P, Dozono S 1984 A model of multi-attribute decision making and trade-off weight determination under uncertainty. *IEEE Trans. Syst., Man Cybern.* **14**, 223–29

F. Hatfield
[Advanced Decision Systems, Arlington, Virginia, USA]

D. Madalon
[Booz, Allen and Hamilton, Bethesda, Maryland, USA]

System-Integration Fundamentals

Integration ensures that all "pieces" of the system will work together to realize system goals. These pieces include the hardware, software, people and procedures needed to support system operation. Successful integration implies that compatibility and effective operation have been achieved in both a technical and organizational sense. While it is appropriate to address system-integration concerns irrespective of the specific application being analyzed, the primary focus here is on information-processing systems.

1. Information System Engineering

The likelihood of successfully integrating a system, within the cost and schedule constraints imposed upon a project, is enhanced by using a disciplined approach such as the process shown in Fig. 1. This process includes all of the necessary activities and disciplines that encompass the system life cycle. These activities commence with the definition and analysis of user needs. User needs are sometimes also referred to as operational requirements. The process continues through several stages (e.g., system definition, functional allocation to hardware and software, hardware and software design, test and evaluation) prior to reaching the system-integration phase. Proof of successful system integration is exemplified in the user's view by the completion of successful acceptance testing, which usually involves participation by user personnel. The ultimate evidence of effective system integration is successful long-term operation of the system.

The steps leading to system integration are not necessarily sequential but are often iterative as changes and improvements occur in the development process. However, from the standpoint of developing an effective system in a timely and cost-effective manner, it is essential that these iterations have a relatively minor impact on the development cycle. This means that the activity in each of the areas identified in Fig. 1. must be well conceived and coordinated, and properly executed to minimize development disruptions.

System integration is supported by the requisite analysis and design activities which hypothesize, evaluate and select from alternative approaches to establish a preferred system configuration. Inherent in these activities is the feedback necessary to ensure covergence on the selected design.

Early development of the interface definition is essential to successful system integration. Interfaces are initially defined through the use of functional block diagrams and functional interface input–output charts which define the data flow in the system. These tools are developed during the functional definition effort discussed in Sect. 4.

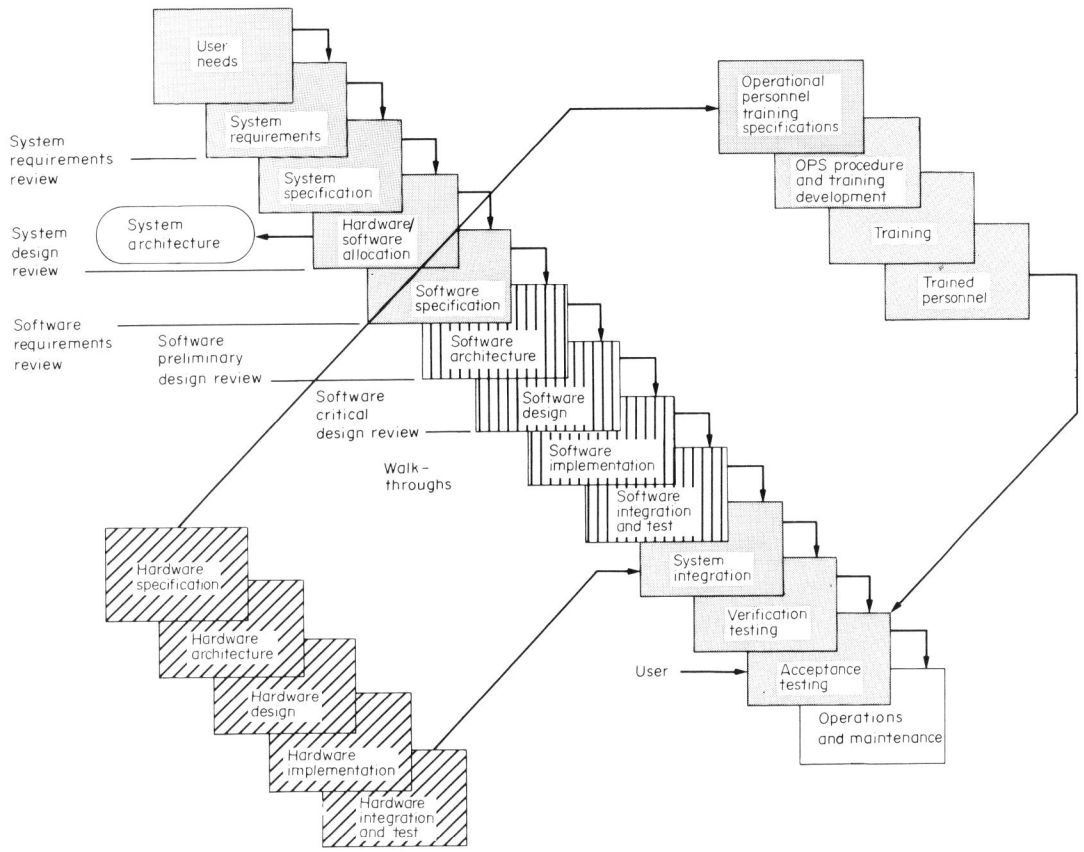

Figure 1
The information system engineering process

2. Defining User Requirements

This activity is not as straightforward as it might appear. In fact, "correct" information is often difficult to obtain because of the complexity of interactions and interfaces between system users and the inherent limitations on human information processing and problem solving.

There are four basic strategies for eliciting user needs. These strategies, along with the situations where each would be most appropriately used, are shown in Table 1. Success of the interviewing strategy presumes that system users and managers can overcome their biases or that system developers can make appropriate judgements concerning issues requiring resolution. User requirements may also be derived from an existing system, either the immediate precursor to the new system or a similar system used in another setting. Either approach permits the similarity in requirements to be exploited.

If there is no "model" of an existing system that can be used, user needs will need to be synthesized from the projected characteristics of the new system. This approach tends to work well only if the system developers have extensive experience in this type of activity.

Under conditions where the user requirements (especially those for decision support and management

Table 1
User-needs elicitation strategies: H, high; M, moderate; L, low

Strategy	Requisite skill/knowledge level	
	User	Developer
Interviewing	L/M	H
Derivation from existing system	M	M
Synthesis from new system characteristics	H	L/M
Experiment with an evolving system	L	L

support) are evolving, or where there is no well-defined information requirements model, or both system users and system developers do not have sufficient relevant experience, an evolutionary requirements-definition approach is used. This approach permits the risk associated with developing a system based on uncertain user needs to be alleviated since the system is developed in increments starting with a core set of operational requirements. Because one of the prime risk areas in information system development is the potential mismatch between system capabilities and operational requirements, the evolutionary development strategy is gaining in popularity.

3. Nature of Operational Requirements

The operational requirements for a prospective system should identify elements such as:

(a) functions/mission to be executed;

(b) deployment (sites/location of elements of the system);

(c) speed, accuracy, capacity, throughput needs;

(d) anticipated system lifetime (from initial operation to expected phase out);

(e) anticipated system utilization cycles (e.g., on/off cycles, hours per day of use);

(f) environmental conditions under which the system must operate; and

(g) key effectiveness measures which affect the system design (e.g. operational availability, maintenance downtime, operator skill levels, etc.)

Alternative design approaches are developed and system synthesis efforts are executed in accordance with the functional definition activities discussed below.

4. Functional Definition

After the operational requirements are formulated and agreed to by the system user and system developer, the basic capabilities needed to satisfy these requirements are established. These capabilities provide the necessary system functionality as well as the requisite system performance.

A traditional systems engineering methodology, functional analysis, is often used to support the definition of the necessary operational capabilities. A function includes the specific or discrete capabilities required to achieve a given objective or user need. These requisite capabilities may be accomplished during operation of the system by hardware, software, personnel or an appropriate combination thereof.

After the necessary functions are identified, functional flow diagrams are developed to illustrate series–parallel relationships, the hierarchy of system functions, and functional interfaces. Functional flow diagrams have significant value since they capture and display the functional decomposition process which is so vital to successful system analysis. The use of functional flow diagrams supports the logical and systematic approach needed to ensure effective system integration, since the proper sequences and functional interrelationships are explicitly established. Furthermore, external and internal interfaces, which constitute one of the most critical issues in system development, are clearly identified at an early stage in the development life cycle.

Functional flows also support the allocation of top-level requirements (such as operational availability) to lower levels of the system. This is important to ensure consistency and maintain top-down control over the design of the system. In the absence of this approach, each designer, working independently on specific aspects of the design, is liable to formulate performance requirements for individual subsystems or smaller system elements. However, when these independently derived independent requirements are appropriately combined, the top-level requirement may not be satisfied. Despite this, the use of functional flows supports the necessary consistency and traceability of system functional and performance characteristics.

5. Technical Integration Issues

Successful system integration requires that a broad range of factors be properly addressed throughout the system life cycle. Some of the most significant factors are discussed below.

5.1 Facilities Interface

The system development and facilities development efforts must be closely coordinated irrespective of whether an existing or new facility will house the system. The use of an existing facility usually presents more constraints than the broader latitude available if a new facility is being provided.

When an existing facility is to be used, the information system developer must be aware of the following detailed information about the facility:

(a) existing facility drawings,

(b) existing building support structures,

(c) special flooring, and

(d) other relevant facilities characteristics.

This will enable the system developer to appropriately establish the operational area layouts for equipment to be provided in the system. For either new or existing facilities, the system developer has responsibility for defining the following:

(a) detailed equipment specifications including size, weight, power and heat generated;

(b) major power-cable routes;

(c) special lighting requirements;
(d) the need for special rooms (e.g., with glass walls, large displays); and
(e) special equipment needs (e.g., water cooling, uninterruptible power supply).

These characteristics and requirements must be sufficiently understood as early as possible to permit the structural and environmental characteristics of the facility to be defined. Only in this way can the required facility modifications or construction be carried out in a timely way to accommodate the system development schedule.

In addition to the physical system characteristics alluded to above, the facility design may also be affected by institutional constraints, e.g., local government building-code regulations or federal government health and safety rules, which affect the placement of personnel and their associated equipment, alarm systems and other related items. Appropriate consideration must be given to these constraints to ensure that an acceptable system and facility are provided.

5.2 Computer-System Selection Considerations

The nature of the application being supported by the information system significantly affects the selection of computer equipment. Analysis of the operational requirements associated with the application provides insight into the system design requirements; for example, reliability, processing speed, main memory size, disk storage capacity and data transfer rates. Since the selection of computer systems is based on a comparative evaluation of commercially available systems or systems projected to be available in time for the initial implementation of the total information system, the characteristics just identified are used as points of departure for the initial screening of possible computer-system candidates.

After selecting viable computer systems for further evaluation, this evaluation is conducted, based on assessing the characteristics of each candidate with respect to:

(a) number of input–output channels supported;
(b) access control/security characteristics;
(c) number of terminals that can be supported;
(d) data communications protocols supported;
(e) software supported (e.g., compilers, operating systems, database management systems); and
(f) upward expandability of the computer system without hardware or software reconfiguration.

The ultimate selection of the appropriate computer system for the information system under development is based on a formal trade-off of the characteristics of each of the candidate computer systems against the ideal set of characteristics for the specific application. Usually, compromises with respect to system selection and/or relaxation of requirements are required during trade-off process. The ultimate objective is to select the preferred configuration based on an appropriately weighted set of technical and economic factors.

5.3 Reliability and Maintainability

To achieve operational feasibility, the appropriate incorporation of design-related specialties, such as reliability and maintainability, must be achieved. Reliability requirements are defined as part of the initial formulation of operational requirements. For example, these requirements might be expressed in terms of a maximum allowable failure rate or mean time between failure.

The integration of reliability and maintainability requirements with other operational requirements is accomplished through the implementation of a reliability planning effort. This effort is conducted to:

(a) ensure compatibility between the overall operational requirements, maintenance requirements and the reliability requirements;
(b) apportion reliability requirements to subsystem levels and below (this activity makes use of the functional flow diagrams discussed earlier);
(c) perform a failure modes and effects analysis (FMEA) including a criticality assessment of failure modes and the appropriate corrective action to be taken, in areas of special operational concern;
(d) develop reliability predictions and assessments of selected system elements and configurations;
(e) perform reliability tests and evaluations to confirm the predictions and assessments; and
(f) collect and analyze reliability data and initiate appropriate corrective actions as needed.

The FMEA is an especially important part of the reliability program; it identifies each significant system element that may fail, and is developed as a result of functional analysis activities described earlier. For each potential failure shown in the FMEA, the following characterization is provided.

(a) Mode of failure.
(b) Cause and effect of failure.
(c) Probability of occurrence.
(d) Criticality of failure in the context of the specific system configuration.
(e) Corrective action or preventative measures that may be used to mitigate the undesirable impact of the most critical problems (e.g., selective use of redundancy or increased level of maintenance).

The FMEA plays an important role in the integration of an appropriate system. The results of the FMEA highlight areas where redundancies or other alternative paths need to be provided to overcome prospective critical design difficulties which may preclude important operational requirements from being satisfied. The FMEA is also used to help establish the minimum system configuration (i.e., the number of hardware elements of each type and their interconnections), which will permit the system to operate properly despite failures in other parts of the system. If the minimum system configuration is operational, system reliability is assured.

Reliability, maintainability and availability (RMA) represent an intrinsically coupled systems-engineering discipline which supports system-integration activities. System availability represents a quantitative measure of reliability and maintainability. Availability values may be estimated based on knowledge of the constituents of the system or as a result of a test program.

The estimation of system availability requires knowledge of the mean time between maintenance actions and the typical time required to conduct necessary maintenance. Basically, availability represents the ratio of system "uptime" to the sum of system "uptime" and "downtime." The system is considered to be "up" when the minimum system configuration is operational and "down" when the minimum system configuration is not operational. However, there are three definitions of availability, each of which computes downtime in a different way.

Inherent availability A_i and achieved availability A_a each reflect the probability that a system will operate satisfactorily at any particular time. However, A_i considers only corrective maintenance in computing downtime while A_a considers both corrective and preventive maintenance. Both A_i and A_a assume an "ideal" support environment (i.e., readily available tools, spare parts, maintenance personnel, etc.). Operational availability (A_o) is the probability that a system will operate satisfactorily when needed in an actual operational environment. Therefore, A_o considers logistic and administrative delay times, in addition to the corrective and preventive maintenance factors, in computing system downtime. A_o appears to be the preferred figure of merit to employ. However, A_i and A_a are often used because the system developer usually has no control over the operational environment in which the system is to function, and cannot be held responsible for administrative shortcomings. Therefore, A_a or A_i would be appropriate figures of merit against which to assess the integrated system. Indeed, the system specification often contains a reliability/maintainability requirement expressed as a specific value of A_a or A_i.

Maintainability (like reliability), an inherent design characteristic of a system, pertains to the ease, accuracy, safety and economy of performing maintenance actions. The maintainability analysis conducted as part of the system-integration effort involves the ongoing evaluation of possible design and support alternatives to establish the preferred configuration.

The maintainability analysis is associated with the comparative evaluation of alternative system configurations and their associated repair policies, logistic support plans, and so on. Potential areas of concern involve a trade-off evaluation of reliability and maintainability and the "repair vs discard" evaluation where the former includes a detailed level of repair analysis.

Maintainability prediction involves an early assessment of the maintainability characteristics of the system design including estimation of maintenance elapsed-time factors, maintenance frequency factors and maintenance cost factors. An important aspect of the maintainability evaluation is the prediction of maintenance-resource requirements including personnel, training, test and support equipment, space and handling requirements. The most widely used technique in maintainability prediction is the logistic support analysis (Blanchard and Fabrycky 1981).

5.4 Software Development

In recent years, the software component of total information system cost has significantly increased. This may be attributed to the fact that most systems use commerical off-the-shelf (COTS) hardware, which has been dropping in price in relation to performance capabilities, and that software development problems have become increasingly significant and costly as systems have grown in size. To circumvent these problems as much as possible, the focus in software development activities should be on achieving a successful software product through the mechanism of a systematic and organized software development and maintenance process.

Viewing software as a product means that it should be correctly and precisely specified (complete, consistent and testable). Furthermore, the software produced should be easy to use, efficient and "tunable." A successful product results from the appropriate utilization of a development process involving planning, organizing, staffing, directing and controlling available personnel and resources to meet schedule and budgetary constraints. An integral part of a successful software development process is the validation and verification (V&V) of requirements, design, coding and implementation of the software product. The V&V activity is carried out internally by the software development team as well as by other test and evaluation personnel who are not part of the software development team. An effective software-development process includes allowance for, and careful assessment of, prospective maintenance (i.e., corrections and enhancements) of the implemented system, preparation of clear and complete documentation, and configuration control. The latter enables a definitive version of the software product (and its associated documentation) to be obtained at any time during the project implementation phase and after the system has been fielded.

One approach that can limit the cost, schedule and technical risk associated with large software-development projects is to evaluate the feasibility of reusing software already developed for other projects. While this approach can indeed produce cost and labor savings and lower one of the highest-risk aspects of system integration, a prospective pitfall surrounding the reuse of software is application incompatibility. Even if it appears that available software can potentially satisfy a new need, this apparent compatibility must be examined in detail to evaluate built-in assumptions about user capabilities, organizational operational philosophy and functionality.

Direct software reusability is not ordinarily feasible. Issues of customizing, integration with other necessary software, maintenance and documentation must be addressed. While reusability is a worthwhile objective and has inherent built-in advantages due to cost savings and more timely implementation, the system integrator must thoroughly understand the consequences of committing to the reuse of already developed software.

5.5 Data Communications

Data communications (i.e., the movement of encoded information in digital form between various elements of the information system) requires careful attention in the system-integration process. A data-communications system is defined to include equipment and software at two or more locations which are sending and receiving data processed by one or more computers through a connecting medium.

One of the important aspects of system integration deals with ensuring that there is a consistent protocol (i.e., fixed rules for handling data exchange) throughout the system. These rules include transmission sequence, location identification, error checking and control, handling of interruptions, and so on. The system-integration activity must not only ensure that a consistent protocol is used, but that data transmission speed, character codes and physical data transmission media are compatible.

Since information systems are likely to contain equipment from different manufacturers, there is a significant potential for inherent incompatibility. To assist in this process, data-communications standards have been developed. However, not all manufacturers adhere to the same set of standards. Some prefer to follow a self-established standard which they feel will provide them with a competitive advantage.

Therefore, two types of data communications networks can be defined:

(a) *proprietary networks*, which are designed for products of a specific manufacturer; and

(b) *open networks*, which are designed to accommodate products of various manufacturers who have adhered to the same standards.

The data-communications marketplace is showing an increase in the number of products that can be readily incorporated into open networks. This is primarily due to the impetus provided by the US Government in requiring the use of transmission control protocol/internet protocol (TCP/IP) in large data-system procurements. TCP/IP is very similar to the open system interconnection (OSI) model which has been proposed as a standard by the International Standards Organization. At present, it appears that there is a tendency toward eventual agreement on OSI (or a model which closely resembles it) despite the reluctance of some major computer system manufacturers to modify their commercially entrenched standards.

5.6 Technical Performance Measurement

Where large, costly information systems are being implemented, a technical performance measurement (TPM) effort is applied. Use of TPM ensures that potential operational and performance deficiencies are identified before their correction results in significant cost or schedule impact. TPM also supports risk-abatement activities by allowing time to pursue alternative solutions to problems when necessary. TPM represents a design assessment that predicts, through analyses or test measurements, the values of essential system level performance parameters. TPM represents an ongoing activity from the design phase through the system test and evaluation activity. It provides the primary focus for ensuring that the functional and performance characteristics of the information system are satisfied thereby reflecting successful system integration.

In implementing TPM, a set of measurement values is established.

(a) *Planned value*. This represents the anticipated value of a parameter at specific points in the development cycle.

(b) *Demonstrated value*. This represents the value estimated or measured in a particular analysis or test.

(c) *Specification value*. This represents the ultimate value of a parameter that must be attained prior to implementation.

(d) *Current value*. This represents the value of a parameter predicted to occur at implementation.

(e) *Demonstrated technical variance*. This represents the difference between the planned value and demonstrated value.

(f) *Predicted technical variance*. This represents the difference between the specified requirement and current value estimate for the parameter.

Variances associated with the critical technical parameters are carefully monitored and analyzed to determine the impact on the overall system. Cost, schedule and technical considerations are carefully assessed to determine if the aggregate set of variances will adversely affect the total system. Necessary corrective actions are then developed based on the determined impact.

Bibliography

Billington R, Allan R 1983 *Reliability Evaluation of Engineering Systems.* Plenum, New York

Blanchard B 1986 *Logistics Engineering and Management.* Prentice–Hall, Englewood Cliffs, New Jersey

Blanchard B, Fabrycky W 1981 *Systems Engineering and Analysis.* Prentice–Hall, Englewood Cliffs, New Jersey

Boehm B 1981 *Software Engineering Economics.* Prentice–Hall, Englewood Cliffs, New Jersey

Chase W 1985 *Management of Systems Engineering.* Krieger, Melbourne, Florida

Eisner H 1988 *Computer Aided Systems Engineering.* Prentice–Hall, Englewood Cliffs, New Jersey

Martin J 1981 *Computer Networks and Distributed Processing: Software Techniques and Architecture.* Prentice–Hall, Englewood Cliffs, New Jersey

O'Connor P 1985 *Practical Reliability Engineering.* Wiley, New York

Stuck B, Arthurs E 1985 *A Computer and Communications Network Performance Analysis Primer.* Prentice–Hall, Englewood Cliffs, New Jersey

T. R. Kornreich
[SAIC, McLean, Virginia, USA]

Systems Analysis and Modelling: Time Series

There are numerous occasions when humans wish to make a forecast of possible future states and events. There are several methods that might be used to accomplish this. Some of these are very crude and some are sophisticated. Some are based upon the information that constitutes the expert judgement of an individual or group; others are based upon mathematical approaches and formal reasoning. Here, we are concerned with quantitative forecasting approaches based on ordered time series of observations.

Many issues that involve information processing in humans and organizations can be associated with the analysis of change over time based on ordered sequences of observations. By definition, these constitute what is called a time series. Many time series are not at all well-behaved, and any persistent regularities and variances are hidden from all except perhaps the most experienced observer. Often these provide early clues to some impending crisis and their detection is consequently very important. Many techniques are useful for the analysis of change over time. Regression analysis techniques are some of the most commonly employed and useful techniques. In the design of a system to support human information processing, one important ingredient is a library of software tools that will support the user in determining how important variables are likely to behave in the future based upon their behavior in the past and the assumption of a model structure to relate system inputs and outputs.

Representation of real-world phenomena in terms of time series is a very practical and useful approach for understanding and predicting system behavior. A time-series analysis takes into account the nature of an observed process as it evolves through time. A time series is constructed to reflect the way a system behaves over time due to changes in input to the system. Usually, time-series analysis is considered to be an area of statistics or statistical estimation theory. It is rich in the choice of models potentially offered to the user, and for this reason modelling is a particularly important component of a realistic time-series analysis. It is important that an information system provides several ways of encoding dynamic behavior. There are at least five approaches to modelling observed phenomena:

(a) pictorial or graphical representation;

(b) verbal representation;

(c) flow diagram or graphic representation;

(d) control-theoretic modelling in the form of differential equations, perhaps with unspecified parameters that are to be determined as part of the modelling and analysis effort; and

(e) finite-state modelling, in which there exists a limited number of states or events, which can be used to characterize each of the state variables of a system.

(a) and (b) relate primarily to artificial intelligence and expert-system-based approaches where various forms of knowledge representation may be used: production rules, scripts, cognitive maps and schema being among them. The last of these relates to discrete-event and queuing representations. Methods (c) and (d) are representations appropriate for the use of time-series analysis.

There are at least three ways of representing a time series of an observed variable. If we choose serial dependencies in discrete time as the way of representing observations, we obtain what is called an autoregressive model and what are called input–output transfer functions. This is the common method used in time-series analysis and control theory and is the approach emphasized in this article. The major problem with this representation is that there is no general way in which we can become familiar with anything other than the input–output behavior of a system through the use of input–output data spaced at regular time intervals only. When it is necessary to know various internal and structural aspects of system behavior, a state-space model representation is more appropriate. This approach is more powerful than the input-output analysis approach but will often require more complex mathematics and a more detailed knowledge of the structure and interactions of the system being modelled.

1. Statistical Procedures

Statistical procedures can vary from the drawing and assessment of a few simple graphs with "eyeball" estimations of fit and average values, to very complex mathematical analysis accomplished through the use of sophisticated computers. In any area that is appropriate for statistical analysis, there is an essential random nature to the observations that are taken. In fact, "statistics" may be defined as the collection and analysis of data from random observations. Probability theory, which provides the mathematical basis for the models which describe random phenomena, is a necessary ingredient in any statistical analysis. Many statistical methods are designed to use data to identify a parameter within a system or perhaps even the underlying probability functions that are responsible for some random phenomenon. Problems in this area are known as system identification problems.

One purpose of a statistical analysis is the summarization, or standardized representation in terms of various norms, of data or information. There is a variety of ways in which this might be done. An idea of the "central value" of a random phenomenon, such as a time series, can be obtained by using the average value of the observations. It turns out that there are a variety of measures of average such as mean, median and mode of the observation. Another very important average measure of an observation concerns the variation of one piece of data from others. An often-used measure of this spread is known as the variance; by definition, this is the ensemble or time average of the squared difference between the values of the observations and the average value. The average of the square of the observations is known as the mean-square value. It can be shown that the variance of an observation is the mean-square value of the observation minus the square of the mean of the observation. The square root of the variance is commonly known as the standard deviation. This is often a very useful measure of spread in a set of observations. It is sometimes useful to describe a probability function by a mathematical relation that contains a few unknown parameters. Various approaches can be used to identify these parameters.

The most commonly used form of probability density function is the normal or Gaussian density function which (in the single variable case) depends on two parameters only, the mean and the variance. In the multivariable case, it is necessary also to use variance, correlation and covariance terms to describe a Gaussian process. While the variance of a set of observations is a measure of their spread or dispersion, the covariance is a statistical measure of the association between the variables. The covariance of two variables x and y is the average of the product of the deviations of corresponding x and y values from their respective means; thus it is seen that a variance function is a particular case of a covariance function. The correlation function is also often used; this is just the average of the product of the values of the variables x and y themselves. In most of the applications of interest here, we will be concerned with processes that evolve over time. In such cases the definition of the autocorrelation function of a variable $x(t)$ is

$$\phi_x(t_1, t_2) = E\{x(t_1)x(t_2)\}$$

where the symbol E denotes expectation. Often it is necessary to compute the cross-correlation function of two time variables $x(t)$ and $y(t)$. This is defined as

$$\phi_{xy}(t_1, t_2) = E\{x(t_1)y(t_2)\}$$

In general this expectation must be taken over an ensemble of records such that only a probabilistic definition and interpretation of this relation can be given. Many physical processes are stationary in the sense that the time average of the product of two random processes is a function only of the time difference in the age variable of the two processes. A stronger condition than stationarity is ergodicity. An ergodic process is one for which the time-average moments and ensemble-average moments of the process are the same. An ergodic process is always stationary. The converse is not necessarily true, however. When random processes are ergodic, then the expectation operator in the foregoing two relations can be replaced by a time average over a sufficiently long period of time. Measurement error is associated with a noninfinite time interval and there exists a large body of knowledge concerning measurement of correlation functions. For an ergodic random process, we have

$$\phi_{xy}(t_1 - t_2) = \phi_{xy}(t_1, t_2) = E\{x(t_1)y(t_2)\}$$

The time difference variable $t_1 - t_2$ is generally replaced by a single variable T. An ergodic autocorrelation function is symmetrical in T, and is therefore an even function. The variance function is always nonnegative. Generally, it will have a smaller value for a random variable x whose observations are always close to the mean value. The covariance may have any numerical value. It is positive when increases in x are generally associated with increases in y. The auto- and cross-correlation functions may take on any value, positive or negative. Essentially the only restriction is that the autocorrelation function must be nonnegative for zero difference in the age variable. At zero age variable, the autocorrelation function is simply the variance plus the square of the mean. The statistical technique known as analysis of variance is generally concerned with disaggregation of the components of variance, covariance and correlation functions into components which arise from specific causes.

2. Hypothesis Testing

Hypothesis testing is a common statistical method used to determine which of several possible explanations for an observed phenomenon is most likely to be correct. The usual approach in hypothesis testing is first to set up a null hypothesis. Observations are taken and, if an analysis of these suggests that the null hypothesis is implausible, then it is rejected. The amount by which an observed average value needs to be greater or less than a specified value in the null hypothesis in order to reject this null hypothesis depends on the statistical significance that is required of the test. This is equivalent to the probability of incorrectly rejecting the null hypothesis. This value may be chosen by the decision maker and/or analyst. Often a probability in the range 0.01–0.05 is used. It turns out that any effort to make this probability very small, such that it becomes very unlikely that we will reject the null hypothesis when it is true, is always associated with an increase in the probability that we will accept the non-null hypothesis when it is false. The first of these errors is generally called a false alarm and the second is called a miss. There have been many developments in statistical hypothesis testing, and a more extensive coverage of them is given in the article *Hypothesis Testing*.

3. Inference

Hypothesis testing can be considered as a portion of the subject of statistical inference. In general, inference is the process of using information from observed phenomena to derive conclusions about the underlying statistics, in particular the probability distribution, of the observations. A simple example will illustrate some of the basic concepts. Suppose that it is known that a coin has some unknown probability p of laying head-side up when it is tossed. We assume that the coin is somehow biased such that p is not equal to one half. The two prototypical problems of statistical inference are (a) to decide whether the coin is biased and (b) to estimate p. The first question can be answered using the method of hypothesis testing. In this case, the null hypothesis is that a coin which is not biased is being tested. The second question, concerning estimation of the probability p, can be answered using the methods of statistical estimation theory. The response to this question is not just a simple yes or no, but rather consists of obtaining an estimate of a parameter of interest. Usually, a measure of the precision of the estimate is also desired. Instead of giving a point estimate and the associated error variance, there are ways of obtaining a confidence interval for the estimate. Typically this confidence interval will be stated in terms of the probability that the true value occurs in some specified interval. The article *Inference and Impact Analysis* provides additional commentary on this subject.

4. Regression Analysis and Estimation Theory

Regression techniques are used to obtain a mathematical model that specifies the relations within a set of variables. The input to the model is data that represents observations of those variables. Generally, a regression analysis equation describes the value of one variable, the dependent variable, as a function of other independent variables. Regression analysis equations may be helpful for interpolation or extrapolation, or forecasting of events of interest. Alternatively they may be used as part of a more complicated mathematical description of some problem. The result of a regression analysis may also be useful as evidence to support or reject hypothetical theories about the existence of relations between variables in a system.

Estimation theory, which is closely related to regression analysis, is concerned with the determination of parameter values in a given equation such that use of the equation results in the best possible fit to observed data. Regression analysis and estimation theory also include the search for an appropriate structural equation or, alternatively, an input–output model that best replicates observed data. This aspect of regression analysis is often not emphasized to the extent appropriate for identification of useful models.

The following activities are associated with the solution of a typical regression problem.

Determination of candidate variables and data collection. The dependent variables that need to be described as a function of other variables are defined. This is usually guided by intuition and existing theory and knowledge. It should then be ascertained that a sufficient number of joint observations of the values of all the variables considered is available. Usually the number of data points should not be smaller than 10 times the number of variables. Often it is not possible to directly observe the values of variables and, because of this, noise-corrupted observations must be made.

Postulation of a mathematical model or structure. The form of the postulated equation may be linear, multiplicative, logarithmic, exponential, and so on. An initial postulate is made and, when possible, transformations are performed so that a linear relationship between the transformed variables results. If for example the assumed model structure has the form

$$y = ax^b z^c \tag{1}$$

then the logarithm is taken on both sides to yield

$$Y = \ln(y) = \ln(a) + b\ln(x) + c\ln(z) \tag{2}$$

or
$$Y = A + bX + CZ \qquad (3)$$

where $A = \ln(a)$, $X = \ln(x)$ and $Z = \ln(z)$. It is important to note here that while the resulting Eqn. (3) is linear in the transformed variables X, Y and Z, it is not linear in the original variables x, y and z. It should be noted that even though the logarithm of all data is taken so that the postulated relationship between the transformed data becomes linear, the values of a, b and c which best fit Eqn. (1) are not generally the values which best fit Eqns. (2) or (3).

Choice of estimation and selection method. The most widely used estimation method is generally referred to as "least squares," to indicate that it determines those coefficient values that will yield the smallest possible value for the sum of the squares of the differences between observed values of the dependent variable and values computed from the estimated relationship. In mathematical notation, if the function $f(x)$ is to be determined so as to best express y as a function of the set of state variables $x = (x_1, x_2, \ldots, x_n)$, and we have N observed values of $y = (y_1, y_2, \ldots, y_N)$, then we determine the unspecified coefficients in $f(x)$ such that the sum from $i=1$ to $i=N$ of the squared error expression $e_i^2 = (y_i - f(x))^2$ is minimal. There are a number of generalizations on the basic least-squares estimation criterion, used to include the dynamic evolution of observations over time and the notion of weights. These extensions make regression analysis and estimation theory problems virtually indistinguishable.

In regression analysis and estimation theory, one needs to determine which of the candidate independent variables needs to be taken into account in order to obtain a good description of variations in the dependent variable. One approach to this calls for first taking all of the candidate variables into account and then estimating the associated coefficient values and their uncertainty. Then, through use of hypothesis-testing techniques, it is determined which of the coefficients is most likely to represent no relation at all between the dependent and independent variables. The state variable corresponding to this is then dropped from further consideration in the analysis, and the process is repeated until the likelihood that any of the remaining coefficients actually represents no relation at all is smaller than some preset value or level of significance. The end result is the appropriate regression equation.

Another approach is based on a procedure which is inverse to the one just described. After all state variables to be considered have been included in the proposed regression equation, a ranking of the levels of significance of the respective coefficients in the regression equation is determined; an equation is then estimated using the most significant variables only. One state variable at a time is added to this regression equation, in decreasing order of initial significance, until it is observed that the addition of one more additional state variable does not lead to an appreciable improvement in the goodness of fit of the resulting regression equation.

Clearly, there are many variations of these basic approaches that are possible and potentially desirable for many applications. For example, it is possible to add more than one state variable at a time. As noted earlier, these structural aspects of regression analysis, and systems engineering in general, are underexplored relative to areas more conducive to completely analytical exploration. The success of a modelling effort is critically dependent, in most cases, upon success in choosing an appropriate structural model.

Determination of the regression curve. This step involves obtaining the necessary data, and the use of a subportion of the regression-analysis program in which algorithms for parameter estimation have been encoded.

Iteration and sensitivity analysis. Depending on the criticality of obtaining a good regression equation, various iterative and sensitivity forms of testing should be performed in which, for example, other structural models or different selection procedures are used.

Figure 1 illustrates the flow of these steps in regression analysis.

The following are conditions under which the use of regression analysis and estimation theory techniques may be appropriate.

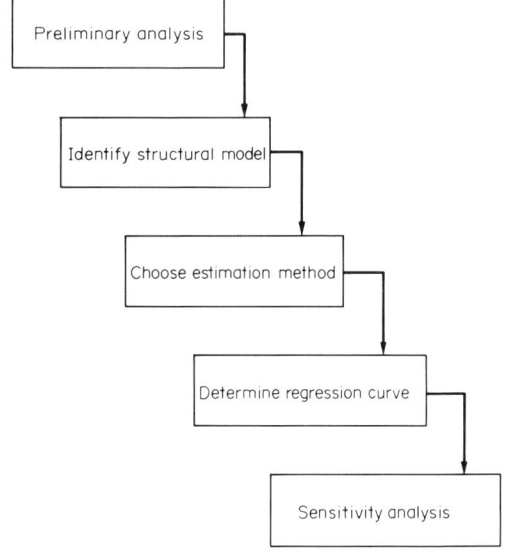

Figure 1
Steps in regression and estimation theory

(a) Data and theory need to be combined in order to determine an equation which best expresses the relations among a set of observed variables.

(b) A mathematical model of observed phenomena is desired and there exists no established theory to explain variations in a variable and, as a consequence, the determined model must be primarily databased rather than theory based.

(c) Data need to be critically examined to test the validity of a postulated hypothetical theory or assumption.

(d) It is desired to use data as a basis for suggesting theoretical relations between variables.

(e) Extrapolation of historical data into the future, or an interpolation of likely values occurring between data points, is needed.

(f) Parameter values for an assumed structural model need to be determined on the basis of empirical evidence.

(g) Data are corrupted by observation noise, and it is desired to "filter" this observed data in order to best separate data from noise.

Regression analysis and estimation theory are very often used in conjunction with other forms of mathematical modelling in order to attain extrapolations of likely futures or trends. Hypothesis testing is generally used as part of the regression-analysis process. The methods of regression analysis and estimation theory are closely related methodologically to optimization methods since, in each case, parameters are determined so as to lead to extreme values of a performance index.

In order to determine the completeness and usefulness of a regression analysis, it is important that the answers to the following questions be "yes."

(a) Have all the important explanatory variables been taken into account?

(b) Do the obtained results make sense, and can this assertion be validated in some manner?

(c) Are the results of the analysis useful in clarifying the structure of the problem and in leading to enhanced wisdom about its resolution?

The user of regression analysis and estimation theory techniques should be concerned with several observations which affect model validity.

(a) The results of regression analysis and estimation theory will be unreliable if they are based on an insufficient number of observations.

(b) Results that are obtained through use of these approaches in situations in which there exists little theoretical knowledge should be examined very carefully, as there is no guarantee that a regression relation which displays an excellent fit to observed data will really have any predictive power at all. Causation is required here and a good fit obtained using regression approaches only assures high correlation. In practice, this caveat seems to be often overlooked!

(c) In a similar way, the results of a regression analysis do not necessarily provide evidence or proof of causal relations among events.

(d) Poor data quality may make even the optimum fit a very poor one. There is no automatic assurance that the "best" is necessarily very good.

(e) The criteria for inclusion or exclusion of variables in an estimation or regression algorithm must be strongly dependent upon the purpose for which the resulting model is ultimately to be used.

5. Trend Extrapolation and Time-Series Forecasting

Trend extrapolation and time-series forecasting, which are very closely related to estimation and regression theory, are widely used as the basis for projection of the future in terms of a series of historical observations of one or more observed variables over time. The essential difference between time-series forecasting and regression analysis is that time is considered as the independent variable in the former case, but not necessarily in the latter. In this sense, time-series forecasting is a subset of regression analysis. However, there is a great wealth of research in this area and the subject doubtlessly deserves a separate treatment.

As in regression analysis, the basic ideas in time series forecasting are:

(a) to identify a mathematical structural relation that might potentially explain observed phenomena;

(b) to best identify unspecified parameters within this structure, such that some statistical error measure is minimized; and then

(c) to best estimate a parameter within the time interval of observation; and/or

(d) to use the determined relation in order to extend the observed data into the future based on the assumption that past trends will continue.

The typical results or final product of a time-series analysis include a projection or forecast of one or more future values of one or more variables that are of interest; an identified mathematical function or structural model, describing past observations, which is potentially useful as an aid to forecasting; and evidence that can be used to support or reject assumptions or theories about the mechanisms that govern the past behavior of one or more variables of interest.

In the use of time-series analysis algorithms, it is generally assumed that a time series of observations of sufficient length and quality is available. This length and quality depends upon the purpose of the forecast, in particular the time length of the extrapolation into the future that is needed and the dynamics of the process being modelled. The time interval over which observations are available should be long enough to allow detection of trends of potential interest, and the time interval between observations sufficiently small to enable isolation of phenomena of interest.

The following steps provide an elementary description of the process of time-series analysis.

Preliminary review of observed data and the environment in which the process evolves. A rough sketch of all, or a portion of, the observed data as it evolves over time is an initial and very helpful approach leading to the identification of readily apparent characteristics of a time series. Often cyclic components, general trends and random fluctuations can, at least in a preliminary way, be identified. This may be very helpful in the selection of appropriate structural forms or characteristics for an initial time-series model. Information on the physical process and the environment into which it is embedded may be of much assistance in enabling the selection of an appropriate mathematical model for the time-series representation.

Identification of a structural model for the time series. There is no general systemic approach for finding the appropriate structural model to use to represent a time series. When only a very crude analysis is contemplated, parameters for a linear differential equation of low order may be identified in order to provide a best fit to observed data. Both the functional form and order of the structural model and the criterion used to best fit the data to the model output are subject to change. The general form of a time series model is

$$Y_t = f(Y_{t-1}, Y_{t-2}, Y_{t-3}, \ldots, Y_{t-n}) + W_t$$

where Y_t indicates the, potentially transformed, observation of the time series at time t. The expression W_t represents a white-noise driving term. Other statistical analysis methods are used to characterize the error term associated with this. Once a tentative structural model has been identified, the undetermined coefficients or parameters of this model are estimated in order to make the output of the data best fit the observed data. These statistical tests are conducted to judge the adequacy of an assumed time-series model. Another candidate structural model is subjected to experimentation if the one under test is shown to be inadequate.

Verification and validation of an assumed model. Often, a time-series model that is based on part of the available data is obtained. The remaining portion of the data is then used to verify the model. For example, a model might be identified based on 30 days' worth of data, and then the model used to predict behavior for the next 5 days where data is available but where the data has not been used to identify the model. After the model has been verified in the way described, the data not previously used to identify model parameters may be used to refine these parameters.

Actual forecasting. The appropriate time-series model is used to forecast values of variables of interest. Often this is accompanied by an error analysis in which statistical uncertainties of the random functions are taken into account to enable computation of moments, perhaps even probability density functions, of appropriate variables such as forecast values. It is possible to obtain adaptive estimation and adaptive time-series analysis algorithms in which these estimated values are used to tune the parameters of the estimation or time-series analysis algorithms.

Examination of Fig. 1 indicates that the time-series analysis process is essentially the same, generically, as the regression-analysis process.

The presence of the following conditions makes the use of time-series analysis appropriate:

(a) there is a need for forecasting future values of critical variables;

(b) there exists sufficient past data about these variables;

(c) it is neither necessary nor possible to fully specify an appropriate model on the basis of accepted theories about the causes of change in important variables; or

(d) it is reasonable to assume that the information contained in historical data is the best and most reliable source of future predictions.

As has been noted before, there is much commonality among the approaches of regression analysis, estimation theory, curve fitting, hypothesis testing and time-series analysis. For almost all intents and purposes, all of these describe essentially similar processes which are used for essentially similar purposes. Earlier comments concerning validity cautions regarding the use of regression analysis and estimation theory are applicable here as well. With each of these, it should also be noted that:

(a) the environment may change over the forecasting time interval and, unless this is accommodated, poor results will often occur;

(b) it may be difficult to cope with information that is not easily quantified, and a consequence of this may be to ignore such information to the detriment of the analysis; and

(c) time series and regression models may not be fully useful for predicting the effect of options that were in effect over the time period for which data is obtained, especially if implementation of these options changes the structure of the model used for prediction and this change is not recognized.

It would be impossible to provide details of all the methods appropriate for time-series forecasting here. There are three basic types of models used for time-series forecasting: autoregressive models, moving average models and autoregressive moving-average models (which represent a hybrid approach). There are also variations of these. Simply stated, an autoregressive (AR) model is one represented by the first-order difference equation

$$x_t = a_1 x_{t-1} + w_t$$

where w_t is a zero-mean white-noise forcing function. The process x_t generated by this model is known as a first-order autoregressive process, and is also a Markov process which evoles from the model

$$x_t = a_1 x_{t-1} + a_2 x_{t-2} + \cdots + a_N x_{t-N} + w_t$$

A first-order moving average (MA) process is one which evolves over time from the model

$$x_t = w_t + b_1 w_{t-1}$$

where w_t is zero-mean white noise. For an Nth-order MA process, we have the model

$$x_t = w_t + b_1 w_{t-1} + b_2 w_{t-2} + \cdots + b_N w_{t-N}$$

The autoregressive moving average (ARMA) is just a combination of the AR and the MA process and can be written as

$$x_t = a_1 x_{t-1} + a_2 x_{t-2} + \cdots + a_N x_{t-N}$$
$$+ w_t + b_1 w_{t-1} + b_2 w_{t-2} + \cdots + b_N w_{t-N}$$

The tools useful for implementation of approaches to time-series analysis are simply computer implementations of algorithms associated with the methods discussed here; that is, least-squares curve fitting, regression analysis, estimation theory, hypothesis testing, system identification, and MA, AR and ARMA time-series analysis. The models to be used are the assumed models for the physical or organizational process being represented. Generally, these will be difference or differential equations of appropriate order. Generically, they will appear in the form

$$\frac{dx(t)}{dt} = \mathbf{A}(t)x(t) + \mathbf{B}(t)w(t)$$

$$z(t) = \mathbf{C}(t)x(t) + v(t)$$

for the differential equation case. Here $w(t)$ and $v(t)$ are zero-mean white-noise vector terms that are uncorrelated with one another. Prior statistics are associated with the initial mean and variance of the error in estimation of $x(t)$

$$e(t) = x(t) - \hat{x}(t)$$

and these are that the initial average error is zero $E\{e(t_0)\} = 0$, and that the error variance

$$P(t) = \text{var}\{e(t)\} = E\{[x(t) - \hat{x}(t)]^2\}$$

is known as $P(t_0) = P_0$. We have commented at length about the need for adequate modelling and the considerable effort that this involves. It may be the case that some of the parameters in the matrices $\mathbf{A}(t)$, $\mathbf{B}(t)$ and $\mathbf{C}(t)$ are unknown and need to be estimated or identified.

For the model just enumerated, it is possible to show that the estimation theory or time-series analysis algorithms which minimize the error covariance $P(t)$ are given by:

$$\frac{d\hat{x}(t)}{dt} = \mathbf{A}(t)\hat{x}(t) + K(t)[z(t) - \hat{x}(t)]$$

where the "gain" $K(t)$ is given by

$$K(t) = P(t)\mathbf{C}^T(t)R^{-1}(t)$$

and where the error covariance term propagates according to

$$\frac{dP(t)}{dt} = \mathbf{A}(t)P(t) + P(t)\mathbf{A}^T(t)$$
$$+ P(t)\mathbf{C}^T(t)R^{-1}(t)\mathbf{C}(t)P(t) - \mathbf{B}(t)Q(t)\mathbf{B}^T(t)$$

These filter or estimator algorithms are propagated with $\hat{x}(t_0) = 0$ and $P(t_0) = P_0$. There are many subtleties associated with solution of equations of this type. The references in the Bibliography present many of these.

6. System Identification

The general problem with constructing a mathematical representation of observed phenomena, which is fundamental to system identification, is the process of constructing a model which describes observed system behavior. This also describes the subject of statistical estimation theory and regression analysis. Although observed descriptive behavior is generally used as the basis for identification of a system, it is very important to note that the uses for system identification are primarily normative. That is to say that we need to identify or estimate the characteristics of systems at some future time in order to evolve optimal policies for these systems over this future time horizon. The purpose of the optimal policy is to accomplish some meaningful goal. The ultimate goal of systems control is to provide a certain function, product or service within reasonable cost so as to enable the fulfillment of some desired performance goals. These overall performance goals or objectives are typically translated, through the use of the systems engineering process, into a set of expected values of performance, reliability and safety. On the basis of this, it is the task of the system planner attempting conceptual specification of system architecture, the system designer attempting concept realization in the form of operational system specifications, as well as that of a human–machine intelligent system, to examine future issues in such a way as to be able to:

(a) identify task requirements, such as to be able to determine subissues to be examined further and those not to be considered further;

(b) identify a set of hypotheses or alternative courses of action which may resolve the identified issues that are to be resolved;

(c) identify the impacts of the alternative courses of action;

(d) interpret the impacts in terms of the objectives for the task at hand;

(e) select an alternative for implementation and implement the resulting control or policy; and

(f) monitor performance to enable determination of how well the integrated system is functioning.

These are just the fundamental formulation, analysis and interpretation steps of systems methodology and the article *Systems Methodology* provides considerably more detail concerning the role of analysis techniques, including time series and system identification.

Many of the above six activities involve system-identification needs. The identification of task requirements involves an effort to determine what is often called the contingency task structure—that is, the specific task at hand and the general objectives for the system, the environment into which the task is embedded, and the experiential familiarity of the problem solver with the task and the environment. Identification of the impacts of alternative courses of action can only be accomplished through use of some model of system operation. If that model has unspecified parameters associated with it, then there is a fundamental requirement for what is generally called system (parameter) identification or generalized system estimation.

The vast majority of effort in systems identification to date has been concerned with this particular aspect of system identification. The final systems engineering activity of performance monitoring enables determination of the online operating characteristics of intelligent machines and human supervisory controllers, and the operating environment for the overall system. This information enables the design of support systems that are appropriate blends of expert systems and decision support systems and that act as higher-level controllers to enhance overall system operation.

There are many modelling issues that arise in the use of time-series algorithms and related approaches in systems identification. Among them are the following.

(a) *Nature of the input–output relations involved.* In this characterization it is determined whether the system being dealt with is causal or noncausal, dynamic or static, finite state or infinite state, discrete or continuous event, etc.

(b) *Nature of the process involved.* In this characterization, the basic process involved in the form of a set of structural laws that are assumed correct is determined, together with a set of behavioral structural assumptions, the parameters of which require estimation or identification.

(c) *Information imprecision and uncertainties involved.* In this characterization, the nature of the uncertainties involved and the degree of precision and completeness that is associated with the process are determined.

Representation of time-series analysis and system-identification problems in terms of the nature of the input–output relations involved is usually not a conceptually difficult task, although it may be very tedious to accomplish, once the nature of the process that is involved has been characterized. There are a number of potential ways that may be used for process characterization, and the choice of one of these depends upon the method chosen to represent uncertainty and imprecision.

There appear to be three fundamental activities associated with any given time-series analysis and system identification effort: characterization of the generic type of effort involved; determination of the structure of the specific system to be identified; and identification of parameters within this structure. These three activities are related. The results of the first activity clearly influence the second, which in turn influences the third activity. In a similar way, what is presently available in terms of software implementation for structural representation and parameter determination influences the types of estimation and identification-issue characterization that is used. This suggests that future information systems for these purposes will involve carefully integrated software that "blends" characteristics of several approaches that have been carefully integrated together into a computer-aided specific system design package that acts as a program generator to produce operational, or nearly operational, software.

Bibliography

Armstrong J S 1978 *Long Range Forecasting: From Crystal Ball to Computer.* Wiley, New York

Box G E P 1970 *Time Series Analysis, Forecasting and Control.* Holden–Day, San Francisco, California

Granger C W J, Newbold P 1977 *Forecasting Economic Time Series.* Academic Press, New York

Kotz S, Johnson N L (eds) 1983 *Encyclopedia of Statistical Sciences.* Wiley, New York

Melsa J L, Sage A P 1973 *An Introduction to Probability and Stochastic Processes.* Prentice–Hall, Englewood Cliffs, New Jersey

Mood A M Graybill F A, Boes D C 1974 *Introduction to the*

Theory of Statistics, 3rd edn. Prentice–Hall, Englewood Cliffs, New Jersey

Sage A P, Melsa J L 1971a *Estimation Theory: With Application to Communication and Control*. McGraw–Hill, New York

Sage A P, Melsa J L 1971b *System Identification*. Academic Press, New York

Sage A P, White C C 1977 *Optimum Systems Control*, 2nd edn. Prentice–Hall, Englewood Cliffs, New Jersey

Wheelwright S C, Makridakis S 1980 *Forecasting Methods for Management*. Wiley, New York

A. P. Sage
[George Mason University, Fairfax,
Virginia, USA]

Systems Concepts: History

The historical features of the systems concept are various and not easy to pin down precisely. In a sense the systems approach goes back to holistic views in philosophy, but in practical terms it is represented by artificial intelligence, automation, cybernetics, mechanization, operational research and overall by the general systems perspective which encompasses all these disciplines. This in turn explicitly includes scientific method and its application to almost any system whatever. Today we increasingly associate all these matters with information science and information technology.

We will start from scientific method, since it can be applied to anything. However, here we need to limit it to a system to embody the notion of the systems approach. A system can be regarded as a well-defined group of related elements organized to satisfy some purpose—in mathematics a set of interacting particles, in astronomy a galaxy, and so on.

An approach to problems in a holistic manner to provide dynamic models, usually with feedback and adaptation, is therefore a recipe for the systems approach, where a system has to be identified by distinguishing its boundaries, however arbitrarily, to be aware of its purpose, and to define the level of abstraction at which the analysis is to be carried out. Systems may contain recognizable subsystems, sub-subsystems and so on; such arrangements are sometimes depicted and investigated as hierarchies. Their investigation can, as a result, also involve tree-searching procedures.

One of the discoveries made by the systems approach, a point made explicitly by Beer (1966), is the extent to which attempts to improve the performance of a subsystem by its own criteria may actually be detrimental to the total system and may even defeat its objectives. So we can say that an optimal set of subsystems does not necessarily imply an optimal system. A very simple example of such a system would be an aircraft for which enormously powerful engines were built which would be too strong for the airframe and would destroy the aircraft. The engines are optimal in themselves but make the whole system suboptimal.

1. Scientific Method

The basic processes, which are assumed to operate iteratively, involved in the hypotheticodeductive method are the following:

(a) hypotheses, laws, assumptions or generalizations;

(b) deduction, including both formal and informal (practical) logic;

(c) observation, confirmation, experiment; and

(d) induction and abduction (leading back to generalizations).

This process may "start" at (a) or (c) and proceed contextually (with any degree of detail necessary to a particular inquiry) without obvious termination. There is no point at which we can know when all the laws of "nature" (laws are simply hypotheses in which we have great confidence) are known, although all the laws of a particular system might well be known.

If we adopt the model–theory distinction (Braithwaite 1953), which is also context-dependent, we can regard the process of going from model to theory as interpretation and from theory to model as formalization. To formalize the steps (a)–(d) above, we could read the sequence in terms of

(a) axioms, postulates;

(b) rules of inference;

(c) confirmation (verification, degrees of factual support); and

(d) induction and abduction (uncertainty, probabilistic methods, statistics, Bayes' rule, for example).

The formalized version of the hypotheticodeductive method will often lead to the replacement of ordinary language (in part or whole) by mathematics, statistics and probabilities, as well as such axiomatic systems as occur, for example, in logistic systems.

The wider context of scientific method may involve epistemological, ontological and other isssues which will certainly involve syntax, semantics and pragmatics and will also involve the basic notions of meaning and truth. These concepts are all in some measure interlocked and apply not only to the hypotheticodeductive method but to a particular person rationally investigating any system, or indeed any rational (commonsense) human behavior, such as a business executive doing business in a business system. This is why scientific method is a kind of abstracted account of rational human behavior, which we are to use as a unifying principle for all humans operating (rationally) in all types of systems, such as a business house, a government or, perhaps first historically, a military organization.

We then introduce the notion of explanation, which is also contextual and refers to causal and definitional descriptions and is essentially derived from the hypotheticodeductive method but need not depend upon the detection of repetitive patterns.

Many of these activities have been a source of much debate, but there is a sufficient consensus for our immediate purpose, which is to provide unifying principles for the analysis of any system where people wish to predict (forecast), understand and control (take decisions and make plans), and this is what the system approach is about. Science provides the necessary steps of prediction, understanding and control most of all by way of periodicity in nature; this makes nature ideally deterministic but at least capable of statistical or probabilistic descriptions. If none of these applies, then science in the narrow sense is not possible. This should in no way, however, obscure the possibility of explaining a "one-off" event.

It will be noted that step (c) (observation) implies perception (including recognition), and the whole hypotheticodeductive cycle is involved with learning and thinking and the range of cognitive acts.

The process (a)–(d) of the scientific-method cycle can be given a variety of interpretations. Initially we have indicated how it operates in the context of scientific method. An explanation is essentially what occurs at step (a) having gone through (a)–(d). Meaning is concerned with the language used in the description of the cycle (semantics), while confirmation, at step (c), establishes the probable truth of the statements (especially at (a)) in the cycle.

It should be remembered that no empirical (synthetic) statement is indubitable, while logical (analytic) statements are not involved in step (d) at all and depend at step (c) only on the consistency of a formal, as opposed to factual, system such as symbolic logic or mathematics.

2. Systems Analysis

Historically, the systems concept as viewed above came to function in practical terms with the development of operational research. This occurred precisely when scientists from various disciplines were brought together in World War II to deal with problems of the optimum location of antiaircraft guns and the optimum search procedures (for submarines, etc.); this demanded direct application to problems involving military systems. After the war, in the McNamara era in the USA, still in the military context, we find the development of systems analysis.

Systems analysis is an organizing activity which existed before computers were invented and it is in the general method that our interest lies. The art of analyzing methods of doing things and designing and implementing new and better methods has been applied ever since humanity became organized into social groups (systems). Out of this organizing activity have developed the modern sciences of organization and methods, work study, systems engineering and other such methods. Systems analysis is the name given to the technique of determining how best to organize activities in the same way.

The main functions of systems analysis are:

(a) definition of the problem, including the goal;

(b) investigation of the working of existing systems;

(c) analysis of the results of the investigation so as to help determine the requirements of a new system;

(d) design of a new system that is practical and efficient and makes the best use of available hardware and software;

(e) communication of the new system to all parties concerned; and

(f) assistance in implementing the new system and its maintenance thereafter.

Each of these functions will form part of the analysis of any particular system; however, the relative importance of each step and the responsibility for undertaking it may vary considerably from system to system.

The systems approach involves analysis of procedures leading to goals but also involves the analysis of risk, so that decision taking involves consideration of the likely outcome of a decision in the light of possible opposition, as in the case of military commanders. They have the job in the field, while integrating their actions with military headquarters which may be thousands of miles away, to relate local knowledge (which the commanders have) to the overall picture (which headquarters have). This involves a major problem in communication and is the reason why semantic issues are so important to the systems approaches (see *Command and Control Information Systems*).

3. Cybernetics and Artificial Intelligence

Since we have suggested the systems approach is concerned with dynamic models which involve feedback and adaptation, it is natural that the science of cybernetics should be involved; this had its official birth in 1942. Cybernetics is the study of control and communication systems, both in hardware and theory. The basic question it attempts to answer is "could machines (artificially constructed systems) be made to think?" to which, depending on the precise meaning of "machine" and "think" at the very least, the answer is "yes." The term cybernetics itself was first suggested by Wiener (1948) as the name for the new science of control and communication in animals, humans and machines. It involves a study of the problems common to control and communication, which had their original background in many sciences but for our present purpose it could be nearly identified with the general systems approach. In spite of its complex origins, the various background sciences were all thought by Wiener to have some common features, and it is these which we refer to collectively as cybernetics; therefore, the associated problems we shall call cybernetic problems.

Cybernetics includes the concept of (negative) feedback and also feedforward as central themes, and it is from these concepts that the notions of adaptive systems and selectively reinforced systems arise. These are systems that modify their behavior in the light of a changing environment and it is from these features that both our simulation and our synthesis of organismic behavior are derived. Such behavior which is modified as a result of experience we call "adaptive." This includes simple adaptation from negative feedback and more complex adaptation through learning, which is an extension of, and depends upon, negative feedback. Learning itself, in the more advanced sense, depends directly on "selective reinforcement." This is the process of positively reinforcing satisfying and successful acts, and negatively reinforcing unsatisfying or unsuccessful acts; more simply, it is a matter of collecting knowledge for future use and, when the correct circumstances arise, using it. If we are right in an action, we must know we are right, and if we are wrong we must know we are wrong; in each case it is preferable to know why we were right or wrong, but to have knowledge of results is itself essential to selective reinforcement.

Cybernetics also involves the search for precision. Precision may be achieved in part by introducing mathematics or logic into a subject, especially by formalization. The application of cybernetics leads directly into artificial intelligence and automation.

Artificial intelligence (see *Artificial Intelligence*) and cybernetics are much the same, and certainly cover similar ground, although either discipline can be (and often is) interpreted in various ways. Whatever name is used, the science in question is concerned with manufacturing, in theory or in practice, artificially intelligent systems, and their application is essentially automation. Although the bulk of automation (applied cybernetics) had its origin in the field of servosystems and control engineering, there are two main motives for this work and they are different in their purpose. The first is to provide models of the human being which, even if they are not yet made of the same fabric, are intended to achieve the same ends by the same means: this we call simulation. The second motive is to achieve "intelligent" behavior by any means whatever, and this we call synthesis. Automation is concerned only with synthesis. There is a demand not for a general-purpose intelligence like that of a human being, but for machines capable of a series of special-purpose activities, which can be computerized. In some cases, special machinery—often mobile and autonomous—could also be built, but these implementations will not be dealt with here; the principles involved in the manufacture and the manner of operation of the systems and their integration become, as a whole, more nearly general-purpose. The emphasis is on adaptive- ("learning-") type systems and considers the information processing, omitting all discussion of the detail of the motor processes.

4. Expert Systems

A new system that has recently emerged is called an expert system. It has been based directly on work in artificial intelligence, and is used on a computer. Generally, it is utilized for problem-solving activities such as medical diagnosis, locating geological mineral sites or fault-finding on a computer. There are also expert system building programs which take in general information on the relevant subject and produce an expert system to deal with it (for example, MYCIN is an expert system which can be built by EMYCIN, an expert system builder).

It is important to represent knowledge suitably and then have logical procedures (deductive, abductive and inductive) to devise a suitable plan of action from the network of the expert system. A check can be made by looking at the explanation of the system, which is simply a description of the inference-making procedure it has gone through. Feedback of results leads, where necessary, to a modification of the model from which the plan of action emerges in the form of production rules.

Expert systems of a more complex character are presently being built which could be used to aid almost any kind of activity.

5. Automation of Factory and Office Systems

As a system, a factory is to be thought of as having a production line with sets of machines related to each other, by (possibly complicated) varying routes. Each machine performs some activity, such as bending or cutting metal or welding two components together. The input is either raw material or components, or both, and the output is finished articles (at least from the factory's point of view). To make all this possible there are stores both for input and for output. The need is for machine operations and maintenance, and also all the organizational paperwork which is entailed.

We can start with the classic operational research (linear programming) problem of stockholding. This can now be carried out by adaptive means. There is a production process which requires so much "X-stock," say. The demand for the product decides how much X-stock is needed, subject to two constraints, that the factory never runs out (or is very unlikely to) and that no capital is frozen that could be used for earning money. This calls for the classical type of linear program. This is replaced by a system which keeps a constant eye on the stock level and on the demand level, and balances one against the other automatically; as demand decreases, so safety stock limits go down.

Now this could be said to be an example of learning, and is even more obviously so if there is a control system anticipating change rather than reacting to it. To make this possible, the minicomputer (as it now in all probability turns out to be) collects trends by exponential smoothing or by some other trend analysis or forecasting method and anticipates the change in demand; all this can be computerized by ordering or depleting stock.

The monitoring of actual stock, as opposed to the records, is something that demands, in effect (assuming a human being is not used), an artificial eye. So this is a step towards synthesizing the sensation process. There are a number of devices used that can sense physical objects (sight and touch have been used) and they can, in mobile form (robots), be sent out like a maze-running machine to search out the actual contents of each store location and identify and count the numbers of components. The historical prototypes of such robots are the Craik maze runner and the Grey Walter tortoise. Since those early days, a whole range of feedback mechanisms have been developed, with sensory devices such as selenium discs, optical reading devices and the like which are used to do the actual sensing, with the storage of materials and components automated. Thus the factory system, starting at the time of the Industrial Revolution as a mechanized system, can now, in principle, be fully automated. According to Diebold (1952), the first automated factory was in operation in the nineteenth century in the USA.

Next we consider production control. For this purpose, there is a need to understand heuristic programming. An ordinary computer program is called algorithmic, by which we mean that the language (machine code) which ultimately controls what the computer does is wholly precise and unambiguous. For instance, an algorithmic process could determine how many "F-components" are in stock. To answer this question, we simply count them and provide a completely definite answer. By comparison, a heuristic program is a higher-level program which has its algorithmic equivalent between it and the computer. If the number of F-components is needed, but they are tiny and there are several millions of them, a random sampling count and an approximation will be satisfactory. The algorithmic program counts the numbers in two or three samples and from that the heuristic program makes an estimate of the whole number.

Heuritics are often necessary in production control in, say, finding an optimization for the processing of a particular set of orders. With a fairly complicated production system, having many different possible routes and involving many different machine states, the cost of changing routes and states may be very great. At the same time an attempt must be made to meet each order.

Next comes the output stock and transportation problem, and there is another program for this. Given that there are stockholding centers (depots) spread perhaps all over the world, we can write another set of adaptive programs which allow optimum allocation to each truck, van or barge, which is then linked adaptively to a route by air, sea or land to the various depots. An optimization procedure is needed for allocation, both in terms of van space and packing, and routing requires yet another procedure. In fact, routing to the depots provides a similar scheduling problem to that used in production control.

At this point we can automate (or cybernate) everything to do with handling of the factory processes, and we already know how to computerize all the paperwork. The accounts department can also provide a completely computerized payroll (one of the first problems ever tackled, many years ago). So we have come close to a cybernetic factory. With the increasing use of word processors to integrate all the clerical work, a natural development would be to use speech synthesizers and speech recognition systems, which already exist in various forms. Such systems make possible the passing of information and commands by computer-controlled human-like voices. So a human being can be told what to do by the computer speaking aloud and the person is able to speak back and be understood. An artificial voice is obviously not needed to talk to another computer's speech recognition system unless, of course, a human also has to be able to hear the message.

The most common system of all is perhaps the office. An approach to office automation was, in the factory, through "mechanization" of different office activities on a piecemeal basis. The office has emerged as one of the most important areas of application for microelectronic technology (see *Office Automation*). It is a vast set of systems presenting enormous opportunities for implementing computer-based automation, where the three main functions performed in any office are:

(a) originating, editing and updating text (in the form of letters, reports, memos, etc.);

(b) storing, cataloguing and retrieving data (filing); and

(c) disseminating information (by letters, telephone calls, in meetings).

In all these areas, automated tools based on microprocessors and other new technologies are now readily available.

These tools are at present mostly concentrated in the area of text processing. This emphasis is largely because of the development of word processors. Word processors offer immediate and measurable improvements in typist productivity for almost every kind of work and they can be installed instead of typewriters with the minimum of office reorganization. Over a period of several years, word processors have developed into powerful text manipulation systems. The facilities offered when combined with computers, and the frequent integration with a factory and through transportation facilities (another field for scientific analysis) make a sort of hierarchy of systems.

The history of the systems concept, in one form or another, goes back a very long time, but with the work of Forrester (1971) and the Club of Rome, work on operational research, computers, cybernetics and automation—work on systems—while still in some measure fragmented, has blossomed since World War II and especially since the 1960s.

See also: Artificial Intelligence

Bibliography

Beer S 1966 *Decision and Control.* Wiley, New York
Braithwaite R B 1953 *Scientific Explanation.* Cambridge University Press, Cambridge
Diebold J 1952 *Automation: The Advent of the Automatic Factory.* Van Nostrand Reinhold, New York
Forrester J W 1971 *World Dynamics.* Wright–Allen, New York
Johnson L, Keravnon E T 1985 *Expert Systems Technology: A Guide.* Abacus, Tunbridge Wells
Walter W G 1953 *The Living Brain.* Duckworth, London
Wiener N 1948 *Cybernetics or Control and Communication in the Animal and the Machine.* Wiley, New York

F. H. George
[Bureau of Information Science,
Beaconsfield, UK]

Systems Knowledge: Philosophical Perspectives

There are several ways that might be used to describe how individuals and groups acquire, represent and use information to portray their perceptions of the world and issues that are of importance. This article discusses perspectives on knowledge since they are of considerable importance to the subject of information processing in systems and organizations

1. Churchman's Concept

Churchman (1971) has described several inquiry systems which portray the various modes of inquiry that may be used by an individual. These inquiry systems are based on the teachings of various philosophers, translated into a modern systems-theory format. A brief description of the various inquirers and their applicability to information requirements determination is therefore of interest.

1.1 Leibnitzian Inquirer

This is a formal, symbolic inquiry system which takes an issue and constructs a mathematical representation of it. Information is then derived from the model by mathematical proof. The Leibnitzian inquirer begins with a set of "truths" which are the basic laws of science and nature. From these truths an ever-expanding and increasingly general and formal propositional truth structure is built. To become relevant information, data must adhere to this structure. The "guarantor" of this inquirer is the precise specification of what counts as proof of a derived theorem or proposition. The guarantor can also be internal consistency, completeness or comprehensiveness of the model. The final information content of the inquirer is its symbolic content (mathematical symbols, etc.). This type of inquirer is best suited to problems which are well-structured and for which an analytic solution exists.

1.2 Lockean Inquirer

This is a consensual, empirically based system. Examples of Lockean inquirers are traditional databanks and accounting systems, statistics and the Delphi procedure. In this inquirer, a model is known and represented by the *a priori* relationships of required data. Data is said to be relevant when there is high correlation between data received and the assumed *a priori* relationships which led to the search for the data. The guarantor of this inquirer is human agreement by experts. The final information content in this inquirer is its empirical content. Typical uses of this inquirer are for problems which are well-structured and for which there is a consensus of opinion on the nature of the problem.

1.3 Kantian Inquirer

This is a multimodel, synthetic system. At least two alternative representations are constructed for each problem or task. These are partly Leibnitzian and partly Lockean in nature. As such, there is a strong relationship between scientific theory (the Leibnitzian inquirer) and raw empirical data (the Lockean inquirer). This inquirer attempts to form a number of alternative representations of the problem, viewed from the various perspectives or frameworks seen by the problem solver. In so doing it gives many explicit views of the problem, thereby aiding in the search for relevant information. The guarantor of this inquirer is the degree of match between the underlying theory (Leibnitzian) and the data collected (Lockean). Final information content is a function of the theory and the data. This inquirer is best suited for problems which are moderately ill-structured.

1.4 Hegelian Inquirer

This inquiry system determines relevant information for an issue by presenting two or more conflicting opinions. These conflicting opinions can be preexisting ones, or they can be created if necessary. The opposing opinions are each Leibnitzian models combined with a set of Lockean data. This combination is performed in an attempt to illustrate the underlying theoretical assumptions of the Leibnitzian models. What eventuates is that both opinions can be argued and supported from the same set of data. If one considers the conflict of the opposing opinions to be a story, then according to Hegel, it is the drama more than the accuracy of the story that is important. The drama of the story potentially allows each event to partially contradict each subsequent event. Consequently, no story is necessarily ever completely consistent. The claim is that this allows for a freer exchange of ideas and generation of alternatives than might otherwise be possible. It is further claimed that this type of inquiry process can be quite useful when there is a myriad of potentially contradictory and inconsistent information confronting an individual. The guarantor of this inquirer is intense conflict. The intense conflict and confrontation of opinions is intended to enable the decision maker to gain a better perspective of the problem. This inquirer is appropriate for very ill-structured problems.

1.5 Singerian Inquirer

This inquirer has the property of continual learning and adaptation through feedback It has the capability to transform structured problems into ill-structured problems and vice versa. Hence, it appears applicable to any form of problem and can use, as appropriate, any of the aforementioned inquiry systems. One use of this inquiry system would be to study in a conceptual way the other inquiry systems so that the one best suited to a given problem can be selected.

1.6 Discussion of Inquiry Systems

Mitroff and his colleagues (Mitroff 1971, Mason and Mitroff 1973, Mitroff and Emshoff 1979, Mitroff and Mason 1982, Mitroff et al. 1983) express the belief that existing implementations of inquiry systems, in general, have not queried the user enough and/or are insensitive to the dangers of information misinterpretation. According to Mitroff, inquiry systems need to be able to determine whether what the decision maker perceives as information is actually information that is relevant to the task at hand. They appear not to have done this; as a result, inquirers have not assisted humans in determining whether their underlying view of the task at hand, issue or problem is reasonable. The unstated and unconscious assumptions of the decision maker need to be examined by these inquirers. This seems to imply that not only should inquirers seek out relevant information or encourage the problem solver to seek out this information, but that they should also compare this information and a variety of possibly related frames, scripts, schemas or other forms of knowledge representation to the specific cognitive interpretation that has been chosen by the decision maker. This implies that the inquiring system should be capable of recognizing the goals of the decision maker, determining what information is relevant to the task at hand and what is irrelevant, and summarizing this information in a form that is appropriate for the decision maker and various contingency-related elements of the task, such as time available for judgement and choice. Such an inquiry system might be useful in understanding the reasons why a decision maker disregards what should be viewed as decision-relevant information. Thus, for example, there exists the potential to build an aid for information requirements determination on the basis of the somewhat philosophical concepts of inquiry systems.

A dialectical inquiry system (Mitroff 1971) has been proposed as representing the solution to many of the aforementioned deficiencies of inquiry systems. A dialectical inquirer is basically an "intelligent" management information system which presents alternative, or pro–con arguments concerning specific items of importance to the decision maker. Data alone are unintelligible until joined to a person's image of reality or frame of the decision situation. It is at this point that data becomes information and knowledge. Thus, again we see the heavily context-dependent nature of information-processing tasks that involve judgement and choice. Until we are able to place measurements or observed data in some context that is presumed to be relevant and meaningful to the task at hand, then the data have little, if any, meaning. Input data change in character, interpretation and meaning when joined with a decision maker's own theories and hypotheses.

The dialectical inquirer presents the strongest possible debate and/or disagreement over problems. The disagreement is not over the data but rather about the underlying views on what the data represent. Two experts having opposing and diverging opinions on any issue can always be found (or created). After witnessing the debate by the two experts, one should, according to the prescriptions of the dialectical inquirer, be in a better position to understand the issue in question and the relation of relevant information to the issue. There is an implied assumption in this that out of two fundamentally different, opposing and perhaps artificially exaggerated positions, an observer will be able to understand the "truth" as lying somewhere between the two extremes. There has been a number of interesting applications of dialectic inquiry systems (Mason and Mitroff 1981).

2.1 Rationality Concepts

Human information seeking and decision behavior can be described in terms of the type of rationality that a person employs to guide this search and evaluation. In general terms, a person may be said to be rational if he or she acts in a way that is sensible in terms of the existing environment, the task requirements and the experiential familiarity or state of knowledge of the person with respect to these. According to this very informal definition, rationality is an instrumental way of thinking and a person may be said to be rational if they choose those activities which are most likely to lead to achievement of their goals. We immediately see that this is a multidimensional or multiobjective problem, and that there will be no simple unique determination of what is rational that is independent of the contingencies of the particular decision situation, especially since the dimensions involved include technical, economic, organizational, social and political considerations. Consequently, there is much more to rationality that can be achieved by a means–ends or input–output analysis and optimization to extremize a single scalar objective function.

The presentations of Diesing (1962), Steinbrunner (1974) and many others, such as those contained in several chapters of the *Handbook of Organizational Design* (Nystrom and Starbuck 1981), have discussed rationality as it pertains to human information processing and other judgement and choice activities. The various forms of rationality are very helpful in providing at least a partial explanation of why people seek the information they do. An understanding of these reasons will help to enable support systems to be designed so as to result in more effective ways to determine information needs. A variety of rationality forms may be defined; the following are the ones defined by Diesing and are the most common.

2.1 Technical Rationality

The activities of an individual are determined in such a way as to maximize the return, or benefit, to the individual from the investment cost of that activity. Technical rationality of an organization can be defined in a similar way. All activities within an organization are formed in a manner so as to reach the goals set by the organization. Most traditional engineering and organizational analysis has presumed technical rationality, at least implicitly. Systems are presumed to be designed to achieve optimal attainment of objectives. As we have noted, the presence of multidimensional and noncommensurate objectives often prevents this sort of optimization from being fully meaningful. The need for coordination and communication among people in modern decentralized organizations also makes technical rationality very difficult to attain. There are also a number of other reasons.

2.2 Economic Rationality

Maximum goal achievement with respect to technical production of a single product, subject to a production-cost constraint, is the typical desired end of the technical rationality. Economic rationality extends this concept to a number of products. It seeks to maximize the overall worth, in an economic sense, of a number of investments (Sage 1983). This is possible if desired goals are well-defined and measurable, the techniques employed to attain these goals are not limited in scope or hindered in application, supply and demand operates in a stable manner, and the interrelationships of supply and demand are known and available to all. In other words, the requirements for a perfectly competitive economy are satisfied.

Using this model of rationality, it is possible to maximize goal achievement, should there be any constraints placed on the above requirements. Some goals can typically be achieved, and this results in enhanced economic progress. Achievement of some goals becomes the means towards the achievement of other socially desirable goals. This process continues and the continuation of economic progress itself becomes the top-level goal to be achieved. In the long term, these decisions will be acceptable only as long as they do not adversely affect society as a whole. From an economic rationality perspective, those items of information which do not provide a basis for increasing profit, productivity or other goals of an organization are to be avoided. Thus it is a very useful but incomplete form of rationality.

2.3 Social Rationality

Society functions as a unit seeking betterment for itself. All its energy is directed towards the realization of this goal. The social system is cohesive in that all its activities reinforce achievement of the desired goal. Present decisions are related to those of the past and are projected into the future. While these actions and decisions are usually not efficient and sometimes not even effective, the cohesiveness of society provides continuity for the system. The roles and structure of society are reinforced by previous results, both good and bad, lending credence to the fact that a social system is rather intractable. It maintains a conservative appearance and avoids risk. That it ought to be adaptive to change can perhaps be shown by sudden changes in the morality or consciousness of the members of the society through a violent opposition to the status quo, such as opposition to or blatant disregard of the law by leaders of the society.

2.4 Political Rationality

The decision-making structure is assumed to be influenced by embedded beliefs, values and interpersonal relationships, the interaction of which defines roles on which actions and decisions are based. The three characteristics of this rationality are that all actors remain independent regardless of the pressures to be dependent on one another, the workload is distributed among all members so as to balance and moderate the actions of the group, and future decisions are chosen in such a way that the impacts of these decisions will act to bind the group together to a greater degree and increase participation.

2.5 Legal Rationality

A system exhibiting this form of rationality operates on the basis of rules which are complex, consistent, precise and detailed. As a result, no ambiguous conflict can occur. It is effective in preventing disputes even though the rules of this system to some extent apply differently to each person. The prevention of disputes is accomplished through a "legal" framework which provides a means for settlement of disputes that do result and which sets precedents to guide members of society.

There are other approaches that we could use to characterize rationality. Simon (1978a,b, 1983) has developed a two-element categorization of rationality as a function of whether an act is rational from an input–output perspective, or whether the internal components of the process used are rational. This leads to a description of substantive and procedural rationality.

2.6 Substantive Rationality

This is the classic, input–output or means–ends rationality of economics. This form of rationality is outcome-oriented in that behavior is considered to be acceptable when given goals are achieved. Given a set of goals, rational behavior is determined by the characteristics of the environment in which it takes place. For example, use of the methods of optimum systems control will result in a system that achieves a goal (minimum cost, perhaps) while satisfying a set of constraint equations that governs the behavior of the physical system concerned. That there are several possible mathematical representations of a given input–output behavior is immaterial. Substantive rationality is not concerned with this.

2.7 Procedural Rationality

This is the prevalent rationality of descriptive decision making in which any decision-making process must necessarily correspond to the capabilities of the user. It must allow a person to make use of knowledge components which make the maximum use of that person's abilities (reasoning ability, managerial ability, etc.) and minimize the use of those concerning areas in which the decision maker is not able to perform effectively. Behavior is rational, in a procedural sense, when a person effectively uses existing cognitive powers to choose actions to alleviate some issues. It is the process of selecting procedures for resolution of issues that is the basis for and the justification of rationality, rather than the outcome of the decision. Procedural rationality is, therefore, the method of searching for information for solutions to problems.

2.8 Discussion

The rationalities covered by Sects. 2.1–2.5 describe the environment within which one acts; these rationalities are interrelated, and are also related to the two types discussed in Sects. 2.6 and 2.7. For example, technical rationality is necessary for, and is also a part of, economic rationality. Social and political rationality are each concerned with internal processes and procedures. Generally, substantive rationality would be exhibited in an environment of technical or economic rationality. In the environments of social or political rationality we would expect procedural rationality to be the dominant form. Legal rationality would typically be a hybrid of the two, in that the initial development of codes would be based on procedural concerns but the actual functioning of an established code is substantive.

We could also attempt to categorize the inquiry systems in terms of the types of rationality employed. The Lockean inquirer appears to be primarily substance-oriented, the Leibnitzian inquirer appears to be more process-oriented and the remaining three use both substantive and process rationality. Rather than making a detailed comparison along these lines, it appears more relevant to examine actual decision-making paradigms that result from these rationality perspectives and then examine the information requirements for these decision-making models.

3. Linstone's Concept

The rationality concepts and the inquiry system models are fundamental perspectives from which a decision situation may be viewed. Linstone (1981, 1984) has proposed several perspectives which extend these concepts by providing a more pragmatic view of how people may view issues of concern to them. Based on a study of the literature, Linstone has chosen to define three perspectives: technical, organizational and personal.

3.1 Technical Perspective

The effects of alternatives that are proposed for implementation, including the effects they have on the environment in which they are to be utilized, are determined in detail using the technologies of systems engineering. Cost–benefit analyses are determined, statistics are used, computer models are constructed and other systems science and operations research methods are employed to ascertain the effects and results of a particular alternative that is being considered for implementation. This perspective is shown to be very important by the extensive use of polls and statistics by virtually all organizations. Of course, there are dangers in this. Often the quantity that is being measured is not a quantity that is fundamentally of interest, but a surrogate. A danger with overuse and improper use of the technological perspective is that sublimation of objectives measures for the objectives themselves may easily occur. For example, the objective "to obtain a high-school education that is a stepping stone to college and an appropriate career" may be replaced by the instrumental objective "to obtain a high score on the Scholastic Achievement Test." There is ample evidence that this sublimation does occur.

3.2 Personal Perspective

The concern here is with a person's cognitive and physiological properties. The personal dynamics of an individual can be such as to suggest capable leadership, the making of skill-based intuitive judgements when appropriate, or to illustrate selfishness and infinitely more other traits which each person brings to bear in one way or another on any decision. Also, one must be concerned with those persons on whom the decision maker relies for advice and judgement and their personal perspectives. The characteristics of these individuals may be such that they desire control from an inconspicuous position or seek in some other way to modify information and decisions. The quality of leadership may be the most important aspect of all that is a function of personal perspective. With it comes the ability to focus attention on a problem or set of problems while motivating people towards the accomplishment of a goal. Productivity can be enhanced and happy, contented workers generally produce more ideas of merit than would otherwise be the case. One must be cautious of "leadership" in this regard. Not only does it have the ability to produce "desired" events but it also has the ability to produce disastrous events.

3.3 Organizational Perspective

In this perspective, problems are looked at from the viewpoint of the organization as a whole. Rules and procedures are formulated within the organization and for the benefit of the organization. They may be explicitly stated and formally evolved and announced, or they may be ingrained as a matter of course and developed as a matter of tradition within the organization. Typically, an organizational perspective is such that future problems and decisions are discounted in favor of near-term issues and decisions. In theory, each member of the organization is aware of the organization's priorities and interests. Therefore, efforts to alter or change these directions will be resisted. New technology which is perceived to harm the organization will be resisted. Changes in the mode and manner of conducting business come slowly and are often permanently resisted. The organizational perspective also tends to alter individual behavior. A person may find a particular decision personally objectionable, yet may implement the decision nonetheless, as it is what is perceived as good or desired by the organization.

3.4 Discussion

Linstone does not suggest that any of these perspectives is inherently better than others. He suggests that the technical perspective encourages use of Leibnitzian (model-based), Lockean (data-based) or Kantian (multimodel-based) approach to inquiry. The organizational perspective will encourage the use of a Hegelian inquiry system, or a modification of this, to obtain a negotiated reality. The personal perspective is generally skill-based with judgements resulting from experientially based modes of judgement, such as intuition, rather than a formal inquiry system. He indicates that a blend of the three perspectives will result in a Singerian inquiring system—pragmatic yet meta-inquiring, wholistic yet analytical. In terms of information transmission, the technical report would be the preferred mode from a technical perspective, summaries and transcripts would be preferred from an organizational perspective, and oral communication from a personal perspective. An individual may prefer one perspective to another depending on personal experiences and the nature of the task. This suggests that information should be available from all three perspectives if it is to be truly useful in a group setting. This hybrid perspective would appear to combine features of the Kantian and Hegelian inquirers.

4. Models of Organizational Choice

We continue further in our journey from the philosophical to the pragmatic in our discussions of knowledge perspectives in systems and control engineering. We have examined the inquiry systems efforts initiated by Churchman and the development of dialectic inquiry as a realization of one of these. We have also examined the rationality perspectives of Diesing and Simon. Several researchers have attempted to examine actual decision situations from these perspectives. Models or decision frameworks for these situations have been developed and there have been attempts to determine the extent to which the various frameworks account for actual decision behavior. Although the literature concerning this is quite large, the works of Allison (1971), Argyris (1982), Argyris and Schon (1978), Axelrod (1972, 1976), Carbonnell (1981, 1983), Connolly (1977), Eden et al. (1979, 1980), March and Olsen (1979), Simon (1983), Steinbrunner (1974), Svenson (1979), Tweney et al. (1981) and Vroom and Yetton (1973) are of particular importance here.

Among the decision frameworks that have been identified are the following.

4.1 Rational-Actor Model

The decision maker becomes aware of a problem, structures the problem space, gathers information, identifies the impacts of alternatives and implements the best alternative based on a set of (objective and subjective) values. Since a complete identification of all needs, alterables, objectives and so on is not usually possible, one cannot be completely rational in the purest unconstrained sense. This observation and the more important observation that, in a descriptive sense, humans often do not attempt to follow the prescriptions of the rational-actor model (because of cognitive limitations) led Simon to develop the satisficing or bounded rationality framework.

4.2 Satisficing or Bounded-Rationality Model

Decisions are implemented on the basis of a minimum set of requirements to provide a degree of acceptable achievement in the short term. The decision maker does not attempt to extremize an objective function, not even in a substantive way, but rather attempts to achieve some aspiration level. The aspiration level may possibly change, owing to the difficulty in searching for a solution. It may be lowered if this is the case, or raised if the goal or aspiration level is too easily achieved.

4.3 Bureaucratic Politics, Incrementalism or "Muddling Through" Model

Bold changes to existing policies are avoided and decisions are based on a rather limited set of alternatives which are basically minor perturbations of existing policies. Long-range side effects are not dealt with, but rather are left to future decision makers who ameliorate these sides with other incremental policies.

4.4 Organizational Processes Model

In its purest form, everyone in the organization is aware of how it functions as it is based on a well-communicated set of standard operating procedures. Decisions to be made are structured around, and evaluated in terms of these procedures. Information needs are determined through discovery of how these standard operating policies or rules affected previous problems.

4.5 Garbage-Can Model

This model represents decision making as an iterative mix of ingredients. Decision making results from four variables: problems, solutions, choice opportunities and people. The interaction of these variables provides the opportunity for decision making. Generally this interaction is not controlled, but rather occurs in an almost random fashion.

4.6 Discussion

There are a number of frameworks that have been proposed from which to view decision situations. Steinbrunner (1974), for example, uses three situation models—analytic, cybernetic and cognitive—in his study of political actions. The analytic model is similar to the rational-actor model, and the cognitive model is much like the bounded-rationality framework. The cybernetic model appears to be a blend of the rational-actor model and the organizational processes model. It is a dynamic feedback-oriented model in which both energy and information flow into the system from outside. Learning occurs through the error control and feedback mechanisms. In a similar way, a social framework or model could be defined. Doubtless this decision framework would have much in common with the garbage-can framework.

In the many studies that have been performed, models other than the rational-actor model are generally selected as the decision frameworks actually used. A study of the Cuban missile crisis (Allison 1971) evaluated the rational actor, organizational processes and bureaucratic politics frameworks as best candidates for explaining the events surrounding this crisis. The bureaucratic politics model provided the best fit. The studies by Cohen *et al.* (1972), March and Olsen (1979) and March and Weissinger-Baylon (1984) show that the garbage-can model, which is a hybrid of the organizational processes, bureaucratic politics and bounded-rationality models was the decision situation framework that often matched the actual decision process. The articles *Distributed Decision Making: Information Systems* and *Distributed Information and Organizational Decision-Making Models* provide additional commentary on the garbage-can model, and other models of information processing in systems and organizations.

In a sense, the advocate of pure rationality can rejoice in that a large number of the decisions studied in these cases were often ones where very flawed results occurred. They might, therefore, speculate that much better decisions could have resulted had an economic-rationality-based approach been used. This might well be the case. However, the fact that the prescriptions of this framework were not used cannot be a cause for rejoicing, but a clear indication of the need to study human information processing as a prescriptive and as a descriptive effort. It is an effort that is especially needed for the design of decision support and knowledge-based systems, as well as any area in which there are interactions between human cognition and physical tasks.

See also: Decision Analysis; Decision Support Systems; Human Information Processing; Human Judgement and Decision Rules; Information Requirements Determination.

Bibliography

Allison G 1971 *Essence of Decision*. Little Brown, Boston, Massachusetts

Argyris C 1982 *Reasoning, Learning and Action*. Jossey–Bass, San Francisco, California

Argyris C, Schon D A 1978 *Organizational Learning: A Theory of Action Perspective*. Addison–Wesley, Reading, Massachusetts

Axelrod R M 1972 *Framework for a General Theory of Cognition and Choice*. University of California Press, Berkeley, California

Axelrod R M (ed.) 1976 *Structure of Decision: The Cognitive*

Maps of Political Elites. Princeton University Press, Princeton, New Jersey

Carbonell J G 1981 *Subjective Understanding: Computer Models of Belief Systems.* UMI Research Press, Ann Arbor, Michigan

Carbonell J G 1983 Learning by analogy: Formulating and generalizing plans from past experience. In: Michalski R S, Carbonell J G, Mitchell T M (eds.) *Machine Learning: An Artificial Intelligence Approach.* Tioga, Palo Alto, California, pp. 137–62

Churchman C W 1971 *Design of Inquiring Systems.* Basic Books, New York

Cohen M D, March J G, Olson J P 1972 A garbage can model of organizational choice. *Admin. Sci. Q.* **17,** 1–25

Connolly T 1977 Information processing and decision making in organizations. In: Staw B M, Salanic G R (eds.) *New Directions in Organizational Behavior.* St. Clair Press, Saint Paul, Minnesota, pp. 205–35

Diesing P 1962 *Reason in Society.* University of Illinois Press, Urbana, Illinois

Eden C, Jones S, Sims D 1979 *Thinking in Organizations.* Macmillan, New York

Eden C, Smithin T, Wiltshire J 1980 Cognition, simulation and learning. *J. Exper. Learn. Simul.* **2,** 131–43

Linstone H A 1981 The multiple perspective concept *Technol. Forcast. Soc. Change* **20,** 275–325

Linstone H A 1984 *Multiple Perspectives for Decision Making.* North-Holland, Amsterdam

March J G, Olsen J 1979 *Ambiguity and Choice in Organization.* Universitetsforlaget, New York

March J G, Weissinger-Baylon R 1984 *Ambiguity and Command.* Pitman, London

Mason R O, Mitroff I I 1973 A program for research on management information systems. *Manage. Sci.* **19,** 475–87

Mason R O, Mitroff I I 1981 *Challenging Strategic Planning Assumptions.* Wiley, New York

Mitroff I I 1971 A communication model of dialectical inquiring systems—A strategy for strategic planning. *Manage. Sci.* **17,** 634–48

Mitroff I I, Emshoff J R 1979 On strategic assumption making: A dialectical approach to policy and planning. *Acad. Manage. Rev.* **4,** 1–12

Mitroff I I, Mason R O 1982 Business policy and metaphysics: Some philosophical considerations. *Acad. Manage. Rev.* **7,** 361–71

Mitroff I I, Quinton H, Mason R O 1983 Beyond contradiction and consistency: A design for dialectical policy systems. *Theory Decis.* **15,** 107–20

Nystrom P C, Starbuck W H (eds.) 1981 *Handbook of Organizational Design.* Oxford University Press, Oxford

Sage A P 1983 *Economic Systems Analysis.* North-Holland, Amsterdam

Simon H A 1978a On how to decide what to do. *Bell J. Econ.* **10,** 479–507

Simon H A 1978b Rationality as process and as product of thought. *Am. Econ. Rev.* **68**(2), 1–16

Simon H A 1983 *Research in Human Affairs.* Stanford University Press, Stanford, California

Steinbrunner J D 1974 *The Cybernetic Theory of Decision.* Princeton University Press, Princeton, New Jersey

Svenson O 1979 Process descriptions of decision making. *Organ. Behav. Hum. Perform.* **23,** 86–112

Tweney R D, Doherty M E, Mynatt C R 1981 *On Scientific Thinking.* Columbia University Press, New York

Vroom V H, Yetton P W 1973 *Leadership and Decision Making.* University of Pittsburgh Press, Pittsburgh, Pennsylvania

A. P. Sage
[George Mason University, Fairfax, Virginia, USA]

Systems Management: Conflict Analysis

The conflict analysis methodology of Fraser and Hipel (1979, 1984) is a comprehensive and flexible procedure which can be employed to study real-world conflict. The systematic examination of a conflict consists of the two main stages of modelling and analysis. First, the particular conflict being studied is modelled by putting the available information about the dispute into proper perspective and logically structuring the problem. Second, at the analysis stage the conflict model is employed to predict possible compromise resolutions to the dispute. By appropriately varying the parameters in the conflict model, sensitivity analyses can be used to ascertain how robust or sensitive the predictions are to meaningful changes in the model. Based on the results of a conflict study, a given decision maker can behave in an optimal manner within the social and political constraints of the conflict.

There are many distinct advantages for employing conflict analysis in systems management. First, conflict analysis can handle general multiple-participant decision-making problems in which each participant can have multiple objectives. Second, documented applications for both current and historical disputes confirm that conflict analysis produces realistic and useful results. For example, the international business conflict studied by Stokes and Hipel (1983) was in fact analyzed while the conflict was in progress and the conflict analysis correctly predicted what eventually happened. References to other published applications of conflict analysis to environmental, military, energy, water resources, peace treaty and other kinds of disputes, are provided by Fraser and Hipel (1984, 1988) and Kilgour et al. (1987). A third attribute is that even though the theory underlying the sociological aspects of conflict analysis is firmly founded upon mathematical concepts from set theory and logic, it is not necessary for the practitioner to understand the underlying theory in order to apply the method to an actual dispute. Fourth, for each decision maker, at most it is only necessary that ordinal preference information be available so that the feasible scenarios or outcomes can be ranked from most to least preferred. If equally preferred outcomes are present or there are intransitive preferences where a participant prefers outcome x to y, y to z but z to x, these kinds of preference information can also be handled. Fifth, if there are misunderstandings among players to form what is called a hypergame (Bennett 1980, Wang et al. 1988), conflict analysis can be used to analyze the hypergame situation. A sixth benefit of conflict analysis is that it has been extended for use in bargaining and negotiation (Fraser and Hipel 1984 Chaps. 8, 9, Dagnino et al. 1987), including the situation where misperceptions abound (Hipel et al. 1988). A seventh asset of conflict analysis is that in games where there are at least three players, the technique can be used for modelling coalitions which are formed by groups of two or more players electing to join forces (Kuhn et al. 1983). Eighth, to model the dynamics of a conflict as it evolves over time, the state transition model, which is based upon the static conflict analysis model, can be employed (Fraser and Hipel 1984 Chaps. 6, 14). Finally, in order to allow systems managers to use conflict analysis in practice conveniently, a flexible decision support system for conflict analysis has been developed (Fraser and Hipel 1988).

After presenting some basic definitions the Cuban missile crisis of 1962 is used to demonstrate how to model and analyze an actual dispute using conflict analysis. This application is also utilized for explaining how conflict analysis can handle misperceptions within the hypergame structure. Volume 26 of the *Journal of Environmental Management* (1988) contains a special issue devoted to demonstrating how many of the latest developments in conflict analysis can be used to solve important environmental conflicts.

1. Definitions

Conflict analysis (Fraser and Hipel 1979, 1984) is a reformulation and extension of metagame analysis (Howard 1971), which in turn has some connections with classical game theory (von Neumann and Morgenstern 1953). Kilgour et al. (1984) show the exact mathematical relations between important game-theory methods and clearly indicate the many inherent theoretical advantages of conflict analysis.

In a conflict or game, two or more participants are in dispute over some resource or issue. Each participant in a conflict model is called a player and is considered to be an entity who can perform actions which have significance to other players in the conflict. The possible actions of each player are called options. Any set of options that can be taken by a player is called a strategy, and the situation where each player selects a strategy is called an outcome. Each player has their own preference ordering of all the outcomes in the conflict.

A game or conflict model consists of the players, their options and their preferences among the possible feasible outcomes. The analysis of the game is carried out by determining the stability of each outcome for every player. If an outcome is stable for a given player, it does not benefit the player to move unilaterally to any other outcome by changing his or her own strategy. An outcome that is stable for all players in the game model is an equilibrium and constitutes a possible resolution to the conflict. These definitions are clarified in Sects. 2 and 3.

2. Modelling the Cuban Missile Crisis

Following the conflict study carried out by Fraser and Hipel (1984 Chap. 1), the Cuban missile crisis of 1962 is modelled in this section and analyzed in Sect. 3. In this conflict, the USSR secretly installed offensive missiles in Cuba, 145 km from the US mainland. On 14 October 1962, US aerial reconnaissance discovered evidence of Russian offensive missiles in Cuba. Firm US reaction to this serious military threat led to the verge of nuclear war.

The first step in designing a conflict model is to select a point in time. For the Cuban missile crisis, the courses of action available to the USA and USSR became apparent around 17 October 1962, so this date is chosen as the appropriate point in time for constructing the conflict model. Next, the players and options in the dispute must be decided upon. Because Cuba had no relevant independent action that it could take, the only two players are the USA and the USSR. Although the Cuban conflict is only a two-player game, it should be emphasized that conflict analysis can readily handle a game with any finite number of players and options.

As shown by the option or binary form of the game (Howard 1971) in Table 1, each of the players has two options. The options available to the USA at this time are performing a "surgical" air strike on Cuba to destroy the missile sites (referred to as air strike in Table 1) and invoking a quarantine (blockade) of Cuba. The USA could select either option or both. The USSR could either dismantle and remove the missiles (withdraw), react with renewed aggression (escalate) or maintain the missiles in Cuba (indicated by selecting neither of these options). In Table 1, the

Table 1

Players, options and outcomes for the Cuban missile crisis

	Outcomes											
USA												
air strike	0	1	0	1	0	1	0	1	0	1	0	1
blockade	0	0	1	1	0	0	1	1	0	0	1	1
USSR												
withdraw	0	0	0	0	1	1	1	1	0	0	0	0
escalate	0	0	0	0	0	0	0	0	1	1	1	1
Decimalized outcomes	0	1	2	3	4	5	6	7	8	9	10	11

selection of an option by a given player is indicated by placing 1 opposite the option, while 0 means that the option is not taken. When either 1 or 0 is written opposite all of the options for a given player, this constitutes a strategy for the player. An outcome is formed by all of the players choosing a strategy, so in Table 1 each column of 1's and 0's constitutes an outcome for the Cuban missile crisis. For example, the seventh column from the left in Table 1 is outcome (0110). The 0 opposite the first option for the USA indicates that there is no US air strike, while the 1 opposite the second option means there is a US blockade of Cuba. Thus, the USA has selected the strategy (01). By withdrawing the missiles from Cuba and not escalating the dispute, the USSR has chosen the strategy (10), which combines with the US strategy (01) to form the outcome (0110).

Each option can be either chosen or not chosen by a player; hence a conflict with k options has 2^k outcomes. Thus, the four options in the model of the Cuban crisis mean that there are $2^4 = 16$ possible outcomes in this game. However, in general not all outcomes are possible or likely to occur in a game. In the Cuban crisis it is not considered possible for the USSR both to withdraw from Cuba and to escalate at the same time. Consequently, the four outcomes (0011), (1011), (0111) and (1111) are infeasible and should therefore be removed from the model. This leaves the twelve feasible outcomes shown in Table 1. When there are a large number of options in a game, techniques are available for efficiently removing infeasible outcomes by hand (Fraser and Hipel 1984) or using a microcomputer (Fraser and Hipel 1988). In practice, after the removal of infeasible outcomes there are usually no more than 50 feasible outcomes remaining, even in very complex games.

The binary outcome notation using 1's and 0's in Table 1 is designed for conveniently interpreting what each outcome means. In order to manipulate outcomes easily, it is necessary to use a short form notation to represent each outcome. By considering a column of 1's and 0's as a binary number, where the entry in the top position corresponds to 2^0, the entry in the second position to 2^1, and so on, the equivalent decimalized number can be determined. For example, the outcome in the seventh position from the left in Table 1 is written in binary form as (0110) and as a decimalized number as:

$$(0 \times 2^0) + (1 \times 2^1) + (1 \times 2^2) + (0 \times 2^3) = 6$$

The decimalized value corresponding to each outcome is listed at the bottom of Table 1.

The final step of the modelling process is to order the outcomes in Table 1 to reflect the preferences of the players. A preference vector (PV) is formed for each player by ordering outcomes from most preferred on the left to least preferred on the right. The PVs, labelled V_a for the USA and V_s for the USSR, are displayed in Table 2. Each PV embodies a great deal of

Table 2
Preference vectors

	Preference vector										
V_a	4	6	5	7	2	1	3	0	11	9	10	8
V_s	0	4	6	2	5	1	7	3	11	9	10	8

information about the given player's viewpoint regarding the conflict. The US PV given by V_a in Table 2 is based on the overriding concern that the conflict does not escalate into nuclear war and that the USSR withdraws the missiles. Thus, all outcomes in which the USSR withdraws its missiles appear on the left, whereas outcomes involving Russian escalation are on the right. The most preferred outcome for the USA is outcome 4 in the decimalized form or (0010) in binary form (see Table 1), where the USSR withdraws the missiles without any overt US action. As shown by V_s in Table 2, the USSR also wishes to avoid escalating the conflict into nuclear war. If the USSR were to escalate, it would prefer to do this in conjunction with aggressive action on the part of the USA. Consequently, outcome 8 or (0001) is its least preferred outcome. Without escalation, the USSR would prefer that the USA not strike Cuba and not impose a blockade. In the event of either or both of these aggressive actions, the USSR would prefer to withdraw its missiles. Without such US aggression, the USSR would prefer to leave them in Cuba. Accordingly, the most preferred outcome for the USSR is outcome 0.

3. Stability Analysis of the Cuban Missile Crisis

The entire stability analysis for the Cuban missile crisis is displayed in Table 3. Beneath some of the outcomes in the PVs are numbers labelled UI (unilateral improvement). A UI is an outcome to which particular players can unilaterally move by changing his strategy, assuming that the other player's strategy remains the same. Unilateral improvements from any given outcome are preferred by the player under consideration and appear to the left of the outcome in his PV. For example, consider outcome 5 for the USA. From the binary interpretation in Table 1, it can be seen that in this outcome the USSR has selected the strategy (10) where it withdraws its missiles. If the USSR maintains this strategy and the USA changes its strategy from (10) in outcome 5 to (00) or (01), the USA unilaterally improves to outcome (0010), which is 4 in decimalized form, or to outcome (0110) which is 6, respectively. From the V_a in Tables 2 and 3, it can be seen that outcome 4 is preferred to outcome 6 and both are preferred to outcome 5. Consequently, under outcome 5 in V_a (Table 3), outcome 4 is written above outcome 6. In a similar manner, all UIs for each player

Table 3
Stability analysis tableau for the Cuban missile crisis

USA												
E	E	X	X	X	X	X	X	X	X	X	X	overall stability
r	s	u	u	r	u	u	u	r	u	u	u	player stability
4	6	5	7	2	1	3	0	11	9	10	8	V_a
	4	4	4		2	2	2		11	11	11	⎫
		6	6			1	1			9	9	⎬ UIs
			5				3				10	⎭

USSR												
r	s	r	u	r	u	r	u	u	u	u	u	player stability
0	4	6	2	5	1	7	3	11	9	10	8	V_s
	0		6		5		7	7	5	6	0	⎫ UIs
								3	1	2	4	⎭

are listed under the appropriate outcomes in the player's PV in Table 3.

For any given feasible outcome there are four types of stability that can be determined for a game with n players in which each player can have any number of options at its disposal (Fraser and Hipel 1979, 1984). For a game with two players, these four kinds of stability are defined as follows for a given outcome from a particular player's point of view:

(a) Rational. An outcome is rational for a player if the player has no UI from the outcome. This type of stable outcome is indicated in Table 3 using the letter r.

(b) Sequentially stable. An outcome is sequentially stable for a player if the player has one or more UIs he can take to reach a more preferred outcome, but for each of his UIs, there is a UI that the other player can sequentially take to improve his individual position and also put the particular player in a less preferred position. A sequentially stable outcome is indicated by s.

(c) Unstable. An outcome is unstable for a player if the player can improve his position unilaterally with no credible deterrent available to the other player. An unstable outcome is denoted by the letter u.

(d) Simultaneous sanctioning. This occurs only rarely: as this type of stability does not occur in the Cuban missile crisis, it is not considered here. For a detailed description of simultaneous sanctioning, see Fraser and Hipel (1984).

For the Cuban missile crisis in Table 3, the type of individual stability for each outcome for a given player is written above each outcome in the player's PV. Each rational outcome can be located by looking for the outcomes which have no UIs below them. Consequently, an r is placed above outcomes 4, 2 and 11 in V_a, and above 0, 6, 5 and 7 in V_s. The outcomes having UIs below them are subsequently evaluated to see if the UIs can be sequentially blocked. Consider, for example, outcome 6 for the USA in V_a. The USA has a UI from outcome 6 or (0110) to 4 or (0010) by unilaterally changing its strategy from blockading to doing nothing. By examining V_s, however, it can be seen that the USSR has a subsequent improvement from outcome 4 or (0010) to 0 or (0000), that puts the USA in a less preferred position than the original outcome 6. The USA is therefore deterred from improving from outcome 6 because of the possibility that outcome 0 could come about. Because the USSR could improve its position by unilaterally improving from outcome 4 to 0, the sanction is credible. Consequently, outcome 6 is sequentially stable for the USA, and an s is written above outcome 6 in V_a.

At outcome 5, the USA has two UIs to outcomes 4 and 6. Although the first UI (outcome 4) is sequentially sanctioned by the USSR, the USA is undeterred in taking an improvement from outcome 5 to 6 from which the USSR has no UI. Therefore, a u is written above outcome 5 in V_a to indicate that it is unstable for the USA. Similarly, all the outcomes in V_a and those in V_s are labelled as s or u for the USA and the USSR, respectively.

If an outcome possesses some type of stability for all the players in a game, it is called an equilibrium and constitutes a possible resolution to the conflict. For example, outcome 4 is rational for the USA and is stable by simultaneous sanctioning for the USSR. This means that if the model represents the real-world situation correctly, the scenario in which the USSR withdraw their missiles while the USA performs no aggressive actions would be likely to persist, should it come about. Outcome 6, where the USA imposes a blockade and the USSR withdraws the missiles, is also an equilibrium, while all the other outcomes are unstable for at least one of the players. Equilibria are indicated by an E placed above the appropriate outcome for the topmost player in the stability analysis tableau. When an outcome is unstable for at least one player it is marked with an X above the appropriate outcome for the topmost player, to indicate that it cannot possibly form an equilibrium or resolution to the conflict.

The results in Table 3 provide significant insight into the Cuban missile crisis. For example, a resolution to the conflict will clearly be one of the equilibria so the USSR is expected to withdraw its missiles from Cuba. To determine which of the two equilibria one would expect to be the resolution, a valuable approach is to examine the current situation or status quo. The status quo on 17 October 1962, was no aggressive action by the USA, and neither withdrawal nor escalation by the USSR. This corresponds to outcome 0. Note that outcome 0 is rational for the USSR but that the USA has a UI that it would be expected to take to outcome 2, which is rational for it. Outcome 2 is unstable for the USSR, however, and the UI from 2 leads to outcome 6. Outcome 6 is an equilibrium, so this would be the expected resolution to the conflict. The actions that correspond to this sequence of outcome changes are that the USA imposes a blockade (0 to 2), after which the USSR withdraws its missiles (2 to 6). Outcome 6 is what happened historically.

4. Misperceptions

Some historians believe that Khrushchev expected a weak response from the USA to the placement of Russian missiles in Cuba. In other words, the Russian government had misperceived the true preferences of the USA. Let V_{as} denote the PV of the USA as perceived by the USSR. By comparing V_{as} in Table 4 to the true US PV given by V_a in Tables 2 and 3, it can be seen how this misunderstanding could have arisen. Notice, for example, in V_{as} in Table 4 the USSR thinks that outcome 0, the status quo, is more preferred by the USA to outcomes 6, 5, 7, 2, 1 and 3, in which the USA takes some type of coercive action against the USSR. As a matter of fact, in the true PV, V_a, of the USA in Tables 2 and 3, outcome 0 is less preferred than all of these coercive outcomes.

A conflict in which one or more players have misunderstandings about the dispute can be modelled as a hypergame. The mathematical structure which describes the way in which each player perceives a conflict is called the hypergame whereas the application of a stability analysis procedure to the hypergame model is referred to as hypergame analysis (Bennett 1980, Wang et al. 1988). A player in a hypergame may have a false understanding of the preferences of other players, an incorrect comprehension of the options available to other players, a false conception about which players are actually taking part in the dispute, or any combination of the above and other faulty interpretations.

In addition to modelling different kinds of misunderstandings, a hypergame can describe levels of expectation. These levels are caused by one player having misperceptions based upon other players' faulty interpretations of the dispute. Wang et al. (1988) provide comprehensive theoretical definitions for describing any type of hypergame and present a flexible and practical procedure for providing a hypergame stability analysis.

The basic idea behind modelling a given hypergame is to model the conflict as envisioned by each of the players, even if a player has misperceptions. To carry out a hypergame analysis the following general procedure is adhered to:

(a) Individual stability analyses: For each player's perceptual game, use the stability analysis algorithm described in Sect. 3 to determine the stable outcomes and equilibria perceived by that player.

(b) Overall hypergame stability analysis: Ascertain the overall equilibria to the hypergame based upon each player's expected behavior determined in step (a).

Owing to misperceptions, a player may be confronted by an overall equilibrium which was not expected. Depending on the particular application, the conflict may stop at this equilibrium, develop into another type of hypergame if misperceptions still exist or break down into a simple game where all the players now understand what is happening.

Consider, once again, the Cuban missile crisis to explain how hypergames can be modelled and analyzed. As shown by V_{as} in Table 4, the USSR had misperceptions about the US preferences. If the USA were unaware of the Russian misunderstandings, the level of expectation of the hypergame would be one. However, if it were assumed that the USA were aware of the Russians' faulty interpretation of the US preferences, the dispute could be modelled as a second-level hypergame. Fraser and Hipel (1984 Chap. 3) present both first- and second-level hypergame models of the Cuban crisis which can be analyzed using the algorithm of Wang et al. (1988).

To demonstrate how a hypergame analysis is carried out in practice, the results for the analysis of the first-level hypergame model of the Cuban conflict are presented. The individual stability analysis for each of the two players must first be separately calculated. When analyzing the conflict from the US viewpoint, the PVs given by V_a and V_s in Tables 2 and 3 are utilized, since the USA correctly perceives what is happening. The game, G_a, as envisioned by the USA is exactly the same as the one shown in Table 3 and the stability results are identical. Because the USSR

Table 4
The USA preference vector V_{as} as misperceived by the USSR

V_{as}	4	0	6	2	5	1	7	3	11	9	10	8

Table 5
Individual stability analysis of the Russian game G_s in the first-level hypergame

USA

r	r	u	u	u	u	u	u	r	u	u	u	player stability
4	0	6	2	5	1	7	3	11	9	10	8	V_{as}
		4	0	4	0	4	0		11	11	11	⎫
				6	2	6	2			9	9	⎬ UIS
						5	1				10	⎭

USSR

E	X	X	X	X	X	X	X	X	X	X	X	overall stability
r	u	r	u	r	u	r	u	u	u	u	u	player stability
0	4	6	2	5	1	7	3	11	9	10	8	V_s
		0		6		5		7	7	5	6	0 ⎱
								3	1	2	4	UIS ⎰

has misperceptions about the US preferences, the PVs given by V_s and V_{as} in Tables 2 and 4, respectively, are employed in their individual stability analysis to calculate the equilibrium that the USSR expects to occur. The individual stability analysis of G_s for the Russian game is presented in Table 5.

The individual stability analyses produce the perceptual equilibrium sets for each player. From Table 3, the USA perceives outcomes 4 and 6 as resolutions if the USSR withdraws its missiles from Cuba. However, the USA will not stay at these equilibria (or keep these strategy selections) if the USSR does not respond as expected. Because the USA believes that both the USSR and the USA prefer equilibrium 4 to 6, the USA is going to take the strategy of doing nothing, which is related to the equilibrium 4. However, as interpreted by the USSR in G_s in Table 5, the status quo position given by the outcome 0 is the only equilibrium in the game. Even outcome 4 is not an equilibrium because the USSR believes that the USA is not willing to use any of its aggressive options if the USSR maintains its missiles in Cuba.

The overall equilibria to the first-level hypergame analysis of the Cuban conflict can be determined by calculating how the strategies of the players in their perceptual equilibria can be combined. When the US strategies in outcomes 4 and 6 are joined with the single Russian strategy in outcome 0, the two overall equilibria are outcomes 0 and 2. Outcome 0 is more likely to happen because it is known from the individual stability analyses that the USA is taking the strategy of "do nothing" which is related to equilibrium 4 in Table 3, while the USSR is going to maintain its missiles which is connected to equilibrium 0 in Table 5.

The actual overall equilibrium is not expected by the USA. After the stable strategies are invoked, the USA realizes the mistakes in its perception, and it is willing to do anything possible to remedy the situation. Because the Cuban missile crisis is not the situation where the resolution to the conflict can be determined after both players make their decisions by selecting their initial strategies, outcome 0 is only a transitory equilibrium. The result gives the USA more information about this conflict because it now realizes its misinterpretation of the USSR. The USA now thinks not only about what is the PV of the USSR, but also about how the USSR interprets the US PV. In this new situation, a second-level hypergame must be used. When the second-level hypergame analyses are executed, the results clearly explain how the conflict eventually ends up at outcome 6. The explanation of the dynamics of the evolution of the conflict is more accurate and insightful using the hypergame approach than that provided by the stability analysis of the simple game in Table 3.

See also: Decision Analysis; Human Judgement and Decision Rules

Bibliography

Bennett P G 1980 Hypergames: Developing a model of conflict. *Futures* **8**, 489–507

Dagnino A, Hipel K W, Fraser N M 1987 Game theory analysis of a ground water contamination dispute. *J. Geol. Soc. India* **29**(1), 6–22

Fraser N M, Hipel K W 1979 Solving complex conflicts. *IEEE Trans. Syst., Man Cybern.* **9**(12), 805–16

Fraser N M, Hipel K W 1984 *Conflict Analysis: Models and Resolutions*. North-Holland, New York

Fraser N M, Hipel K W 1988 Decision support systems for conflict analysis. In: Singh M G, Salassa D, Hindi K S (eds.) *Proc. IMACS/IFOR 1st Int. Coll. Managerial Decision Support Systems and Knowledge-Based Systems*. North-Holland, New York

Hipel K W, Dagnino A, Fraser N M 1988 A hypergame algorithm for modeling misperceptions in bargaining. *J. Environ. Manage.* **26**

Howard N 1971 *Paradoxes of Rationality, Theory of Metagames and Political Behavior*. MIT Press, Cambridge, Massachusetts

Kilgour D M, Hipel K W, Fang L 1987 The graph model for conflict. *Automatica* **23**(1), 41–55

Kilgour D M, Hipel K W, Fraser N M 1984 Solution concepts in non-cooperative games. *Large Scale Syst.* **6**, 49–71

Kuhn J R D, Hipel K W, Fraser N M 1983 A coalition analysis algorithm with application to the Zimbabwe conflict. *IEEE Trans. Syst. Man Cybern* 13(3), 338–52

Stokes N W, Hipel K W 1983 Conflict analysis of an export credit trade dispute. *Omega* 11(4), 365-76

von Neumann J, Morgenstern O 1953 *Theory of Games and Economic Behavior*, 3rd edn. Princeton University Press, Princeton, New Jersey

Wang M, Hipel K W, Fraser N M 1988 Modeling misperceptions in games. *Behav. Sci.* 33

K. W. Hipel and N. M. Fraser
[University of Waterloo, Waterloo, Ontario, Canada]

Systems Methodology

Issues need to be resolved, policies formulated and decisions made and implemented every day at the individual, group, local, state, national and international levels—in private, corporate and public settings. In this article we discuss systems methodology and the associated selection of appropriate systematic approaches to assist policy and decision makers in the resolution of complicated issues. These methods are equally appropriate in the public and the private sectors, since complicated issue resolution in all these areas displays many common characteristics. While systems methodology may be ubiquitous across these areas, the specific methods that are most appropriate for a given task will generally be very task-dependent and dependent on the experiential familiarity of the problem solver with the task and the environment.

Typically, the identification of alternatives and the subsequent acts of judgement and choice that lead to selection of an alternative for implementation involve considerations of many affected individuals, groups or institutions, who often have conflicting or competitive desires. Resources are generally scarce, in that resource availability is insufficient to satisfy the needs of everyone. Trade-offs have to be made, generally between incommensurate attributes of proposed policies. Various special-interest groups often attempt to exert pressure on those responsible for making the trade-offs and resource allocations. At the same time, the impacts to be traded off are often poorly known. There are usually large uncertainties with respect to the future impacts of policies or decisions, as many future developments are beyond the control of the decision maker. Moreover, the values or needs to be satisfied may change in an often unpredictable way before a policy comes into effect. Institutional and organizational factors play an important and sometimes even crucial part in the realization of policies, controls or decisions. Those responsible for decisions, whether they act as individuals or as groups, have to consider all relevant aspects if they wish to identify and implement effective alternative courses of action.

Experts in a relevant field are often consulted to utilize their experience with an issue and obtain their views on the feasibility and impacts of policy alternatives. They may contribute much of their knowledge to the establishment of the database, or knowledge base, that is fundamental to decisions and resource allocations, even though these decisions may be made by, or may be the responsibility of, someone else.

A function of the system analyst or systems engineer is to assist the client in organizing knowledge so that the latter is better able to deal with the complex features of large scale and scope that surround significant judgement and choice issues. Analysts can provide assistance to clients in the problem-solving tasks of: identifying relevant aspects of an issue in terms of needs, constraints, alterables and objectives; identifying information needs and structuring the information related to an issue; generating alternative courses of action; investigating the impacts of these alternatives; and aiding in the evaluation and interpretation of alternative policies so as to enhance the selection of action alternatives for implementation that are consistent with the client's values or preferences. Systems engineers also play the role of information brokers and of facilitators who provide a framework for information exchange and informed discussion between various groups that have interests in the tasks at hand.

There will typically be different experts and analysts with various technical capabilities offering forms of knowledge-based support to decision makers. Many of these are experts on particular technologies or on the application of a small number of systematic methods for issue analysis and resolution. In the prevailing competitive environment they will claim that their particular technology is best. The analysts will also be likely to claim that their preferred method will yield results which are of better quality or more effective than approaches proposed by others. The person responsible for the decision is often not sufficiently familiar with the various analysis methods to be able to judge which approach would be most appropriate for a particular issue. As a result, the choice of approach is often determined not by the issue needs but rather by the salesmanship of the competing analysts and perhaps by prior experiences of the decision maker with analytical assistance. Precisely because there is often a mismatch between problem and method, and because many analysts are likely to overstate the potential power of their approach and raise higher expectations than are justified, many of these prior experiences are characterized by frustration. Often, different analysts have obtained different, sometimes even conflictng, conclusions on the same issue. This has added to the feeling that analysis results can be manipulated and has generated mistrust among managers and decision makers of the objectivity of analysts and the utility of analytical methods.

The problems resulting from anything less than the most cost-effective use of systems analysis are potentially very expensive—far more expensive than the cost of the systems study. Among the consequences is the expenditure of large sums of money to support studies, research and sometimes ultimate development of technologies and systems that do not lead to the best results—results that could be obtained for the same price or even at considerably lower cost in many cases.

1. Systems Engineering

Systems engineering involves the application of a general set of guidelines and methods useful for assisting clients in the resolution of issues and problems which are often of large scale and scope. Three fundamental steps may be distinguished:

(a) problem or issue formulation;

(b) problem or issue analysis; and

(c) interpretation of analysis results, including evaluation and selection of alternatives, and implementation of the chosen alternatives.

These steps are conducted at a number of phases throughout a system's life cycle. This life cycle begins with determination of requirements for a system through system design, development and installation, and ultimate system maintenance and replacement.

The systems engineering paradigm calls for processes that involve a study of issues in relation to their environment, with due consideration of causal or symptomatic, institutional or organizational norms or values and aspects of the problem. The necessity for a systematic, rational and purposeful course of action is emphasized in formal systems engineering approaches. Systems engineers make eclectic use of methods, theory and data based on a variety of disciplines such as behavioral and cognitive psychology, computer science, operations research, economics and systems and control theory. A serious attempt is made to consider as many relevant aspects of an issue as possible. These aspects typically cut across various fields of knowledge, institutions and traditional disciplinary boundaries. For example, an issue that initially might appear to be purely economic in nature might on closer inspection be found to be interwoven with technological, social, political and environmental problems. A systems engineer will attempt to take all these related fields into consideration when assisting the client in organizing knowledge, so that the client is better able to formulate, analyze and interpret the options available. The emphasis in this article is clearly the role of the systems engineer as a support person.

There are other ways in which we might characterize systems methodology. We might examine the three

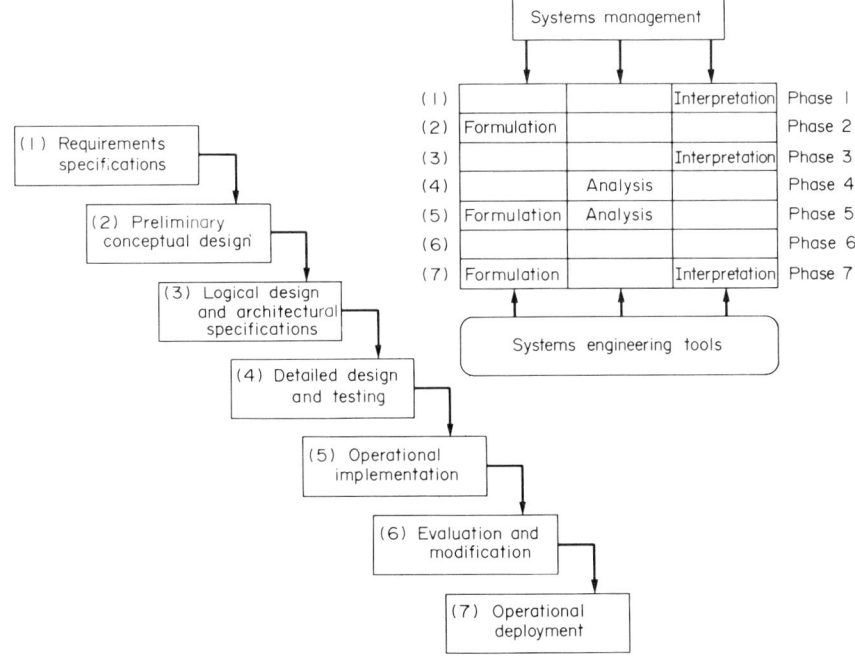

Figure 1
The systems engineering life cycle and the resulting methodological framework

fundamental steps of formulation, analysis and interpretation at each phase in the system life cycle. A typical life cycle is shown in Fig. 1. Alternatively, we might view systems methodology as the connecting link between the methods-and-tools dimension and a systems-management dimension, as shown in Fig. 2. In this article, our primary focus is on a methodology as an open set of procedures for problem solving. We are concerned with a methodological framework that enables the selection of appropriate methods with which to accomplish problem resolution.

The characteristics of the systems engineering approach make it particularly appropriate for ameliorating or resolving many contemporary large-scale problems. This is generally less costly and time-consuming in the long run than application of superficial, temporary and incremental solutions to recurring problems. Use of an appropriate systems engineering framework, and of the systemic methods useful within the framework, leads to efficient and effective use of available methods for dealing with complexity. It leads to a more efficient and effective use of the time allocated to issue resolution, and also to more efficient, effective, equitable and explicable resolution of issues. Adoption of the systems approach potentially leads to a better match of problems and techniques. Hence it makes the problem-solving process more effective and efficient, in that it results in better solutions at perhaps even lower costs than would otherwise be possible.

The systems engineering process aims at separation of facts and opinions from values, and separation of means from ends, as part of the systematic divide-and-conquer approach. This separation encourages more informed discourse about contemporary issues, especially those in which there are questions of risks, hazards and imprecise and uncertain knowledge.

In this article, a systems engineering framework involving the three steps of formulation, analysis and interpretation is chosen as the underlying structure

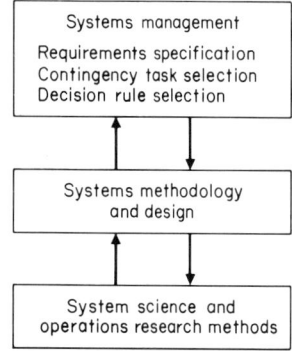

Figure 2
Model of the systems engineering process

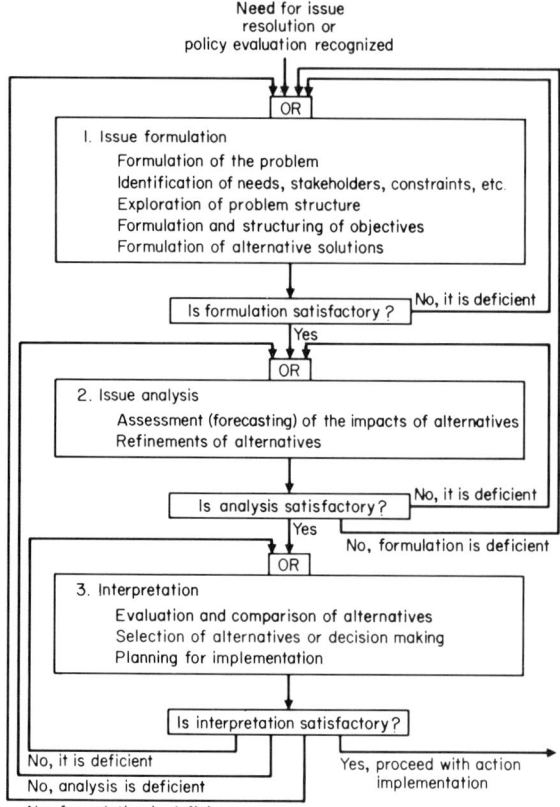

Figure 3
Flow chart of three-step systems engineering framework

ordering the methods to be discussed. We briefly elaborate on each of the three systems engineering steps and give particular attention to the methods appropriate for assistance in each step. Figure 3 illustrates these three steps. Supporting this are various methods or approaches from systems science and operations research. A systemic process is composed of human judgement and a methodology, and is strongly affected by the operational environment for systemic issue resolution. The systems process involves the interaction of systems methodology, as supported by systems science and operations research methods, with human judgement.

2. Systems Science and Operations Research Methods

In this section we briefly describe a number of methods which can be used as part of the systems engineering framework of Fig. 2, which indicates how the cognitive systems management structure influences the requirements specification and decision mode selection. Decision mode selection, which is in effect the decision on how to decide, "directs" the methodology to the use of specific methods for issue formulation, analysis and interpretation. This conceptual model of the problem-solving process has prescriptive and descriptive uses. We emphasize the prescriptive uses here.

2.1 Issue or Problem Formulation

The first part of a systems effort at problem resolution is typically concerned with problem or issue formulation and with identification of problem elements and characteristics such as, the groups affected by the issue and/or proposed solutions, their needs, relevant institutions, fields of knowledge, constraints, alterables, goals for the effort, policy instruments and actors involved. Subsequently a structuring or partitioning effort is often undertaken to facilitate understanding and perception and communication of the problem structure and the relations between the elements.

The first step in issue formulation is generally that of defining the problem or issue to be resolved. Problem definition, regardless of whether we are discussing program planning or any of the other phases of a systems engineering problem, is generally an "outscoping" activity, as it enlarges the scope of what was originally thought to be the problem. Problem or issue definition is ordinarily a group activity involving those familiar with or impacted by the issue or the problem, systems engineers and government and management specialists. It seeks to determine the needs, constraints, alterables and society sectors affecting a particular problem and relations between these elements.

Of particular importance are the identification and structuring of objectives for the policy or alternative to be chosen. This is often referred to as value system design. To be able to do this effectively, it is necessary to distinguish ends from means, or objectives from activities. This is effectively accomplished by the systems process. The objectives identified in value system design are effectively prioritized; this occurs as part of the issue evaluation and interpretation step. The analysis step determines the impacts of proposed alternatives on objectives. Thus the valuation of an alternative is determined in an objective a fashion as possible through the systemic divide-and-conquer process which separates means and ends.

Value is a relative term. We are primarily concerned with the relative value of an alternative policy, which denotes the degree to which we prefer it to other alternative policies. The term *value system* will be used to refer to the set of interacting elements which provides an ultimate basis for decision making. Value design is therefore construed to be the transformation of the properties of a thing into a format amenable to instrumental or extrinsic valuation. Allocation of resources represents and results from a value judgement. If we can characterize the value judgement in a manner that relates to human capabilities and human needs, then the judgement is amenable to reasoned analysis and criticism. The conclusion of the process of value judgement is an evaluation of alternatives and the decision to select one or more of them for implementation. Decision is the expression of preference for a particular option from a class of options. If a value judgement is an expression of preference, a proposed judgement which offers only one option must therefore be considered improper and incomplete, since preference implies comparison and this requires two or more class members. The do-nothing-at-all alternative is of course one option in most issues. Also, there is an important notion of timing and experiential familiarity which must be considered. Often a person very familiar with a situation will identify a single familiar course of action to resolve a given issue and adopt it. If the person is indeed experientially familiar with the issue at hand, then previous attempts at problem solution have enabled the identification of a number of alternatives and selection from among these. So, a judgement mode such as unconflicted change to a new course of action will generally be based upon past successful problem-solving experiences and will not necessarily represent irrational problem-solving behavior, in any sense.

It is very helpful to relate the objectives to the problem definition linkages of needs, alterables, constraints and society sectors. After some self- and cross-interaction matrices have been determined as in Figs. 4 and 5 which show interrelation among various issue-formulation elements, others can be generated mathematically by (Boolean) multiplication. This reduces the chances of producing inconsistencies in the cross-interaction matrices. Alternatively, all matrices may be determined first, and matrix multiplication

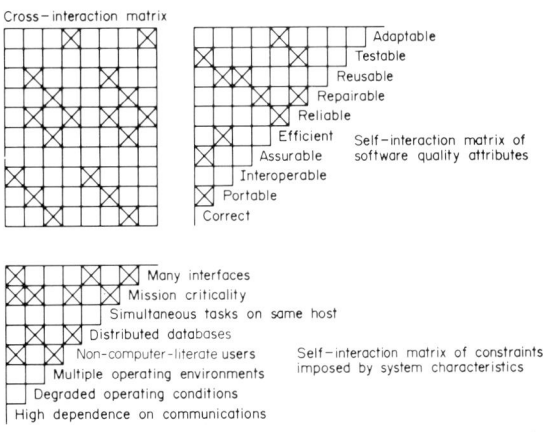

Figure 4
Self- and cross-interaction matrices for software development constraints and necessary quality attributes

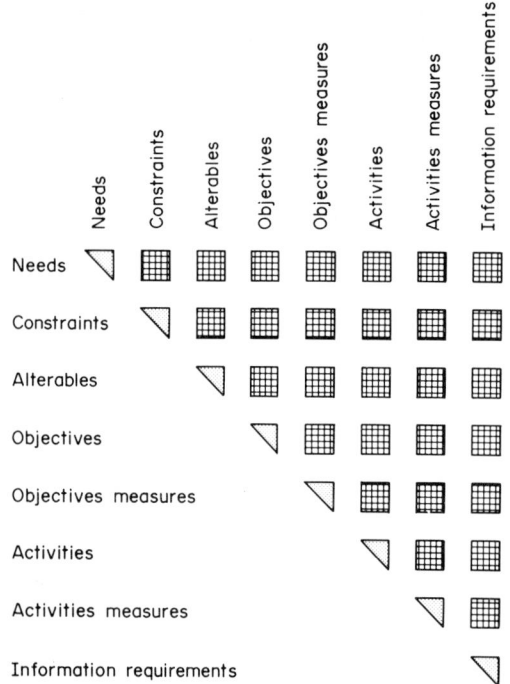

Figure 5
Self- and cross-interaction matrices for issue formulation

may then be used to check for inconsistencies in reasoning.

Essential also is the identification of alternatives, controls or policies potentially capable of resolving needs. The activity may range from a simple listing of the actions or policies currently available to influence the system, to a comprehensive design effort to conceive systems structures or organizations that are potentially responsive to the identified need so as to achieve the identified objectives. It is often not a simple task to generate meaningful and innovative alternatives. Option generation is a very important and often neglected area of problem solving and design effort.

This system or alternative synthesis step of issue formulation is concerned primarily with the answers to the following three questions. What are the alternative approaches for attaining objectives? How is each alternative approach described? How do we measure attainment of each alternative approach? The answers lead to a series of alternative activities or policies and a set of activities measures.

Several of the methods that are particularly helpful in the identification of issue formulation elements are based on principles of collective enquiry. This means that a group of interested and motivated people is brought together in the hope that they will stimulate each other's creativity in generating elements. We may distinguish two groups of collective inquiry methods here, depending on whether or not the group is physically present at the same physical location.

(a) Brainwashing, brainstorming, synectics and nominal group technique. These approaches typically require a few hours of time, a group of knowledgeable people gathered in one place and a group leader or facilitator. Brainwriting is typically better than brainstorming in reducing the influence of dominant individuals. Both methods can be very productive: 50–150 ideas or elements might be generated in less than an hour. Synectics, based on problem analogies, might be very appropriate if there is a need for truly unconventional, innovative ideas. Considerable experience with the method is a requirement, however, particularly for the group leader. The nominal group technique is based on a sequence of idea generation, discussion and prioritization. It can be very useful when initial screening of a large number of ideas or elements is needed. Synectics and brainstorming are directly interactive group methods, whereas brainwriting and nominal group efforts are "nominally" interactive, in that the members of the group do not directly communicate.

(b) Questionnaires, surveys and Delphi. These three methods of collective enquiry do not require the group of participants to gather at one place and time, but they typically take more time to achieve results than the methods in (*a*). In questionnaires and surveys, usually a large number of participants are asked individually for ideas or opinions, which are then processed to achieve an overall result. There is no interaction between participants. Delphi usually provides for written anonymous interaction between participants in several rounds. Results of previous rounds are fed back to participants, and they are asked to comment, revise their views as desired, and so on. A Delphi procedure can be very instructive but usually takes several weeks or months to complete.

Use of some of the many structuring methods to be discussed, in addition to leading to greater clarity of the problem formulation elements, typically leads also to identification of new elements and revision of element definitions. Most structuring methods contain an analytical component and they may therefore be more properly labelled as analysis methods. The following element structuring aids are among the many modelling aids available.

(c) Interaction matrices. These may be useful to identify clusters of closely related elements in a large set, in which case we have a self-interaction matrix; or to structure and identify the couplings between elements of different sets, for example objectives and alternatives. In this case we produce cross-interaction matrices. Interaction matrices are useful for initial, comprehensive exploration of sets of elements. Learning

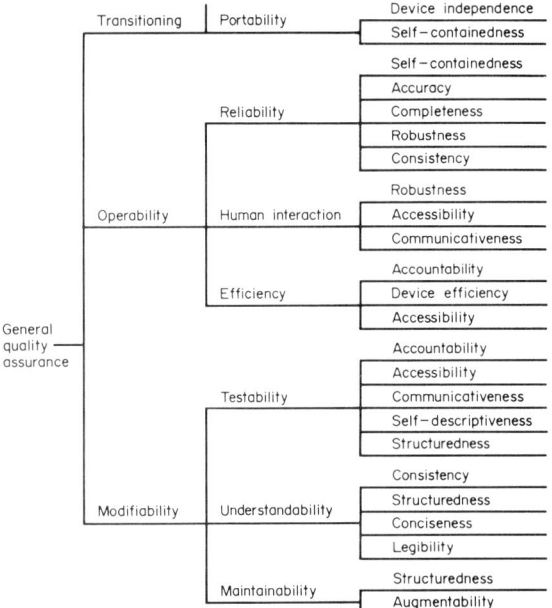

Figure 6
Tree structure of attributes for software quality assurance

about problem interrelations during the process of constructing an interaction matrix is a major result of the use of these matrices. Figures 4 and 5 present some prototypical self- and cross-interaction matrices as unidirected graphs.

(*d*) *Trees*. Trees are graphical aids particularly useful for portraying hierarchical or branching structures. They are excellent for communication, illustration and clarification. Figure 6 represents a simple tree structure. Trees may be useful in all steps and phases of a systems effort.

(*e*) *Structural modelling*. Structural modelling (or structured modelling) methods are computer-assisted methods designed for individual and group use in structuring a large set of elements. The computer is programmed to perform the more straightforward bookkeeping tasks, thus allowing the user group to concentrate on the elements and their relations. These approaches are particularly useful in assisting an individual or group of people in their effort to create clarity of perceptions of a set of elements, and to structure their discussion about the relations in the set. Among the many structural modelling approaches are cognitive mapping, interpretive structural modelling, semantic networks and frames.

(*f*) *Causal loop diagrams*. Causal loop diagrams, or influence diagrams, represent graphical pictures of causal interactions between sets of variables. They are particularly helpful in making explicit one's perception of the causes of change in a system, and can serve very well as communication aids.

Two other descriptive methods are potentially useful for issue formulation.

(*g*) *System definition matrix*. The system definition matrix checklist or options profile provides a framework for specification of the essential aspects, options or characteristics of an issue, a plan, a policy or a proposed or existing system. It can be helpful in the design and specification of alternative policies or other options. It is a simple table of elements and has been given a number of names. It may be a very useful aid.

(*h*) *Scenario writing*. This method is based on narrative, across-the-board descriptions of existing or possible situations or developments. Scenario descriptions can be very helpful for clarification and communication of ideas and obtaining feedback on those ideas. Scenarios may also be helpful in conjunction with various analysis and forecasting methods, where they may represent alternative or opposing views.

All of these approaches assume that "asking" will be predominant approach used to obtain issue formulation elements. Asking is often the simplest approach, but often valuable information can be obtained from observation of an existing and evolving system, or from a study of plans and other prescriptive documents. When these three approaches fail, it may be necessary to construct a "trial" system and determine issue formulation elements through experimentation and iteration with the trial system. These four methods (asking, study of an existing system, study of a normative system, experimentation with a prototype system) are each very useful for information requirements determination for systems design (see *Information Requirements Determination*).

2.2 Analysis

The analysis portion of a system effort typically consists of two steps. First, the options or alternatives defined in issue formulation are analyzed to assess the expected impacts of their implementation. This is often called impact assessment. Second, a refinement or optimization effort is often desirable. This is directed towards refinement or fine tuning of a viable alternative through adjustment of the parameters within it so as to obtain maximum performance in terms of needs satisfaction, subject to the given constraints.

Forecasting is an essential ingredient of impact assessment. There are many complications associated with forecasting in large-scale systems. Among these are uncertainty about important future events, about institutional changes and about values and changes in values. Numerous approaches have been designed and used for forecasting. There are two general classes

501

of methods: expert opinion methods and modelling and/or simulation methods.

Expert opinion methods are based on the assumption that knowledgeable people will be capable of saying sensible things about the impacts of alternative policies, on the basis of their experience with or insight into the issue or problem area. These methods are generally useful and are particularly appropriate when there are no established theories or data on system operation, thereby precluding the use of more precise analytical tools. As described more fully elsewhere (see *Human Information Processing*), there are a number of concerns relating to the fidelity of expert judgement that need to be given serious concern in the design of expert-opinion forecasting approaches. Among the most prominent expert-opinion-based forecasting methods are surveys and Delphi, mentioned in Sect. 2.1. There are of course many other ways of asking experts for their opinion, for example hearings, meetings or conferences. A particular problem with expert opinion models is, as we have noted, that cognitive bias is widespread; incorporation of bias into these models often results in inconsistent and self-contradictory results.

Simulation and modelling methods are based on the conceptualization and use of an abstraction or model which hopefully behaves in a similar way to the real system. Impacts of policy alternatives are studied through use of the model—something which often cannot easily be done through experimentation with the real system. Models are, of necessity, dependent on the value system and the purpose behind their utilization. We want to be able to determine the correctness of predictions based on the use of a model and thus to be able to validate the model. Given the definition of a problem, a value system and a set of proposed alternative courses of action, we wish to be able to design a model consisting of relevant elements of these three sets and to determine the results of implementing proposed policies.

There are three essential steps in constructing a model:

(a) determination of those issue formulation elements which are most relevant to a particular problem;

(b) determination of the structural relations between these elements; and

(c) determination of parametric coefficients within the structure.

We should interpret the word *model* here as an abstract generalization of an object or system. Any set of rules and relations that describes something is a model of that thing. When we model systems, we enhance our ability to comprehend their nuances and to understand their interrelations and our relation to them. The engineering sciences have made contributions toward the improvement of clarity in modelling. A typical result of a systems engineering model is the opportunity to see a system from several viewpoints and perspectives such as economic, technical, political or environmental. A system model may be viewed as a physical arrangement, as a causal flow diagram and/or as a set of actions and consequences that can be shown graphically over time, perhaps in a decision tree structure, as a simplified picture of reality. Developments and improvements in the methodology of modelling have become more important as systems have become more complex. Usually resource and other socioeconomic systems evolve as an aggregate of subsystems interacting with one another to create an interdependent whole. Thus models often contain submodels.

Gaming is a modelling method in which the real system is simulated by people taking on the roles of real-world actors. The approach is very appropriate for studying situations in which people's reactions to each other's actions are of great importance, such as competition between individuals or groups for limited resources. It is also a very appropriate learning method.

Most simulation and modelling methods employ the power of mathematical formulations and computers to keep track of many pieces of information at the same time. Two methods in which the power of computers is combined with subjective expert judgements are cross-impact analysis and workshop dynamic models. Cross-impact analysis is useful when there is a need to take the interactions in a set of future events into account to separate the more likely outcomes from the less likely. Typically, experts provide subjective estimates of event probabilities and event interactions. These are processed by a computer to explore their consequences and fed back to the analysts and thereafter to the experts for further study. Workshop dynamic modelling is a procedure in which a group of knowledgeable people interacts, through an analyst, with a computer to determine their perception of the basic mechanisms of change in a system. The computer derives the resulting behavior over time, giving rise to renewed discussion and revision of assumptions. This process can be very helpful as a group learning tool in a situation where causal interactions over time are of importance.

Expert judgement is virtually always involved in the use of any modelling method. Scenario writing can be an expert opinion modelling method, but typically this is a less direct and explicit way than in the expert opinion methods. As a result of this, internal inconsistency problems are reduced by using the methods based on mathematical modelling. Of course this only ensures consistency: a mathematical modelling approach *can* yield consistently wrong results. The following other forecasting methods, based on mathematical modelling and simulation, are among those available. In these methods, a structural model is generally formed on the basis of a combination of expert opinion and physical or behavioral relations. Information is then processed and various system identification methods are used to determine parameters within the structure.

(a) *Trend extrapolation/time-series forecasting.* This method is particularly useful when sufficient data about past and present developments are available but there is little theory about underlying mechanisms causing change. The method is based on the identification of a mathematical description or structure that will be capable of reproducing the data. This description is then used to extend the data series into the future, typically in the short to medium term. The primary concern is with input-output matching of observed data and results from using the model. Little attention is generally devoted to ensuring process realism.

(b) *Continuous-time dynamic simulation.* This is a method based on postulation and qualification of a causal structure underlying change over time. A computer is used to explore long-range behavior as it follows from the postulated causal structure. The method can be very useful as a learning and qualitative forecasting device, but its application may be rather costly and time-consuming.

(c) *Input–output analysis.* This has been especially designed for study of equilibrium situations and requirements in economic systems in which many industries are interdependent. Many economic data formats are directly suited for the method, which is mathematically relatively simple and can handle many details.

(d) *Econometrics.* This is another method primarily applied to economic description and forecasting problems. It is based on both theory and data. Emphasis is placed on the specifications of structural relations based on economic theory and the identification of unknown parameters, using available data, in the behavioral equations. The method requires expertise in economics, statistics and computer use. It can be quite expensive and time-consuming. It has been widely used for short- to medium-term economic analysis and forecasting. Figure 7 presents one view of the efforts needed to build an econometric model. With minor changes, this figure is applicable to modelling in general.

(e) *Microeconomic models.* These represent an application of economic theories of firms and consumers. The behavior of economic agents in a free-market economy is described as that set of actions which will maximize total benefits or utility for the agent. Microeconomic models are used to study and forecast economic quantities. Closely related to microeconomic models are welfare economics models, which incorporate equity concepts into microeconomic models.

(f) *Welfare (or normative) economic models.* These are concerned with equity considerations in economic systems models based on microeconomic theory. In particular, the fundamental concern of welfare economics is to examine the question: "What is the distribution of economic goods that will lead to maximum overall economic welfare?" For application of economic models, the utility or satisfaction derived by

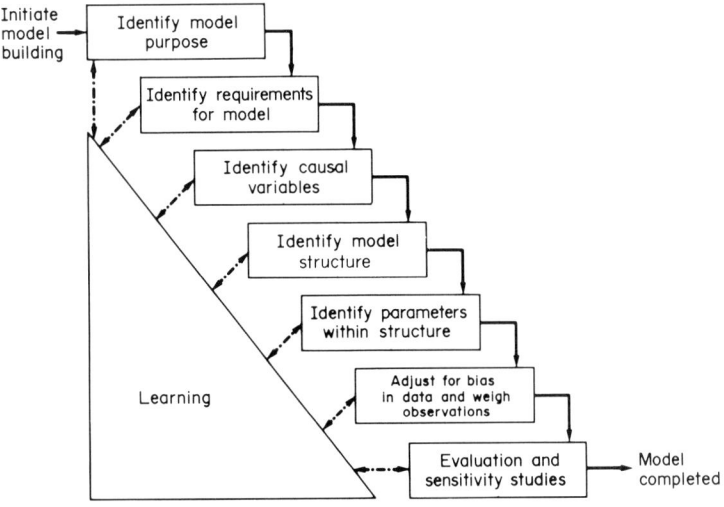

Figure 7
The systems modelling process

each economic agent from possession of certain economic goods must be expressed mathematically. Equity is a goal of welfare or normative economic modelling.

(g) Queuing theory and discrete-event simulation. These have been developed to study, analyze and forecast the behavior of systems in which queuing phenomena, such as waiting lines, are of importance. Queuing theory is a mathematical, pencil and paper approach, while discrete-event simulation is based on computer simulation of models of the queuing theory type. The two methods are used widely in the analysis and design of systems such as toll booths, service facilities or shipping terminals.

There are at least three uses to which models may normally be put. Model categories corresponding to these three uses are descriptive models, predictive or forecasting models and policy or planning models. Representation and replication of important features of a given problem are the object of a descriptive model. Good descriptive models are of considerable value in that they reveal much about the structure of a complex issue and demonstrate how the issue formation elements impact and interact with one other. An accurate descriptive model must be structurally and parametrically valid. One of the primary purposes behind constructing a descriptive model is to learn about the impacts of various policy alternatives.

In building a predictive or forecasting model, we must be especially concerned with determination of proper cause and effect, or input–output relations. If the future is to be predicted with integrity, we must have a method with which to determine exogenous or independent "given" variables accurately, the model structure must be valid and parameters within the structure must be accurately identified. Often it will not be possible to predict accurately all exogenous variables; in that case, conditional predictions can be made from scenarios. Consequently, predictive or forecasting models are often used to generate a variety of future scenarios, each a conditional prediction of the future.

Policy or planning models are much more than predictive or forecasting models, although any policy or planning model is also a predictive or forecasting model. The outcome from a policy or planning model must ultimately be evaluated in terms of a value system. Policy or planning efforts must not only predict outcomes from implementing alternative policies, they must also present these outcomes in terms of the value system in a form useful and suitable for the alternative ranking, evaluation and decision making that take place in the interpretation step of systems engineering.

Verification of a model is necessary to ensure that the model behaves in a fashion, and for the purpose, intended by the model builder and consequently the client. If we can determine that the structure of the model corresponds to the structure of the elements obtained in the issue formulation steps, then the model is verified with respect to behaving in a gross fashion as intended. Even if a model is verified, there is still no assurance that it is valid in the sense that predictions made from the model will occur. Since the results of alternative policies not implemented are generally not available, there is usually no way of completely validating a model used for other than descriptive purposes. Nevertheless there are several efforts which can be undertaken to validate a model with respect to those policies that have been implemented. These include a reasonableness test in which we attempt to determine from knowledgeable people that the overall model, as well as model subsystems, responds to inputs in a reasonable way. The model should also be valid according to statistical time series used to determine or estimate parameters and variables within it. Finally, the model should be epistemologically valid in the sense that the policy interpretations of the various model parameters, structure and recommendations are consistent with the ethical, professional and moral standards of the group affected by the model.

There are many areas for which particular types of simulation models have been developed; for example, demography, ecology, energy, economics, land use, transportation, industrial production and water resource management. The principles of these models are very similar to those described here. There are also many combinations of different models and modelling methods, for example input–output analysis and econometrics, or continuous-time dynamic models and time-series extrapolation and forecasting models.

There are also a number of specific aids in the quantification of models. Two of these are hypothesis testing, and regression analysis and estimation theory. Hypothesis testing provides a widely accepted set of rules for deriving conclusions on the basis of samples of information rather than full information. The approach is used widely in social science, engineering and quality control and in conjunction with regression analysis. Regression analysis and estimation theory are very useful methods for the identification of mathematical relations and parameter values in these relations from sets of data or measurements. Regression and estimation methods are used frequently in conjunction with mathematical modelling, in particular with trend extrapolation and time-series forecasting, and with econometrics. These methods are often also used to validate models. Often these approaches are called system identification approaches when the goal is to identify the parameters of a system, within an assumed structure, to minimize a function of the error between observed data and the model response.

There are a number of methods for fine tuning, refinement or optimization of specific alternative policies or systems. These are useful in determining the best (in terms of needs satisfaction) control settings or rules of operation in a well-defined quantitatively describable system. A single scalar indicator of performance or desirability is typically needed. However, there are approaches to multiple objective optimization which are based on optimization concepts of the welfare economic type.

Mathematical programming is used extensively in operations research, systems analysis and management science practice for resource allocation under constraints, resolution of planning or scheduling problems and similar applications. It is particularly useful when the best equilibrium or one-time setting has to be determined for a given policy or system.

Optimum systems control addresses the problem of determining the best controls or actions when the system, the controls or actions, the constraints or the performance index may change over time. A mathematical description of system change is necessary. Optimum systems control is particularly suitable for refining controls or parameters in systems in which trade-offs over time play an important part.

Markov decision models have been designed to assist in determining the best overall strategy in a system in which future change over time can be described as a succession of unpredictable events. Applications have been reported in the fields of maintenance strategies and inventory management.

Application of the various refinement or optimization methods like those briefly described here typically requires significant training and experience on the part of the analyst.

3. Interpretation

The third step in a systems effort starts with evaluation and comparison of alternatives, using the information gained by analysis. Subsequently, one or more alternatives are selected and a plan for their implementation is designed.

The evaluation of alternative actions must typically be accomplished, and implementation decisions made, in an atmosphere of uncertainty. The outcome from any proposed policy is seldom known with certainty. One of the purposes of efforts in the analysis step is to reduce as far as possible the uncertainties associated with the outcomes of proposed policies. Decision making, policy analysis and planning often involve a large number of decision makers who act according to their varied preferences. Often these decision makers will have diverse and conflicting data available to them and the resulting decision situation will be quite fragmented. Further, outcomes resulting from actions can often be adequately characterized only by a large number of incommensurable attributes. Comparison among and across these attributes in an evaluation and choice process is typically most difficult. Also, inadvertent biases, such as those due to a nonconscious ideology or any of several forms of selective perception, are systematic and prevalent in most unaided cognitive activities. Unaided evaluations, decisions and judgements are influenced by many heuristic procedures which may lead in some cases to selection of a very poor rule for the aggregation of facts, and to very inferior results. It is often quite difficult to disaggregate the valuation associated with policy outcomes from the causal and uncertain relations and events which determine these outcomes. This confounding of values with facts can lead to extreme difficulties in communication as well as in choice making.

It is important to note that there is a clear and distinct difference between the refinement of individual alternatives, or optimization step of analysis, and the evaluation of sets of refined alternatives. In some cases refinement or optimization of individual alternative policies not needed in the analysis step. But evaluation of alternatives is always needed, for if there is only a single policy alternative, there is really no alternative at all. It is especially important to avoid a large number of cognitive biases in evaluation and decision making. Clearly, the efforts involved in the interpretation step of evaluation and choice interact most strongly with the efforts in the other steps of the systems process.

There are a number of important methods for evaluation and choice, including the following.

(a) *Decision analysis*. This is a very general approach to option evaluation and selection (see *Decision Analysis*). It involves identification of action alternatives and possible consequences, identification of the probabilities of these consequences, identification of the valuation placed by the decision maker on these consequences, computation of the expected value of the consequences, and aggregation or summarization of these values for all consequences of each action. In doing this we obtain an evaluation of each alternative act: the one with the highest value is the most preferred action or option.

(b) *Multiattribute utility theory*. This has been designed to facilitate comparison and ranking of alternatives with many attributes or characteristics (see *Multiattribute Utility Theory*). The relevant attributes are identified and structured and a weight or relative utility is assigned by the decision maker to each basic attribute. The attribute measurements for each alternative are used to compute an overall worth or utility for each attribute. Multiattribute utility theory allows for various types of worth structures and for the explicit recognition and incorporation of the decision maker's attitude towards risk in the utility computation.

(c) *Policy capture (or social judgement theory)*. This has also been designed to assist decision makers in making values explicit and their decisions consistent with their values. In policy capture, the decision maker is asked to rank a set of alternatives. Then, alternative attributes and their attribute measures or scores are determined by elicitation from the decision maker for each alternative. A mathematical procedure involving regression analysis is used to determine that relative importance or weight of each attribute which will lead to a ranking as specified by the decision maker. The result is fed back to the decision maker who typically will express the view that some of his or her values, in terms of the weights associated with the attributes, are different. In an iterative learning process, preference weights and/or overall rankings are modified until the decision maker is satisfied with both the weights and the overall alternative ranking.

Two well-known heuristic methods of selection of alternatives are often used in practice to evaluate or prioritize alternatives.

(*d*) *Elimination by aspects*. This is a simple selection aid in which alternatives not fulfilling certain minimum requirements on every aspect or attribute are eliminated from further consideration. Alternatively, only alternatives which exceed a minimum aspiration level on each attribute may be retained. This is an extensively used heuristic. It is used in many areas as a screening method to select only those options for further consideration which meet a number of minimum requirements. It is very appropriate for this purpose. When used, as it often is in practice, to select a single "best" alternative, it can be very flawed.

(*e*) *Voting*. This is a well-known and widely used method of group decision making (see *Group Decision Making and Voting*). Different methods of voting may, and often will, lead to different results. Voting is subject to a number of theoretical difficulties, the principal one being intransitivity.

After the selection of an alternative action or policy has been made, implementation for action plans is determined. There are many methods and tools for implementation for action planning. Two very prominent ones are worth mentioning here.

(*f*) *Gantt charts*. These consist of a graphical representation of different activities in a project or plan, and the time during which they are (planned to be) carried out. Gantt charts are very useful for communication and for monitoring progress during implementation of a plan.

(*g*) *Network planning methods*. These include a wide variety of more specialized tools for planning complicated projects consisting of many activities, some of which must preceed others in order to be meaningful. The method is used extensively in the management of engineering projects and has also received widespread acclaim in other areas. It is of great help in scheduling different activities, determining the expected duration of a project, estimating the costs of reducing the project duration, identifying the latest possible or necessary completion times of certain project tasks on scheduling activities to reduce overload.

A systems effort is generally always conducted in an iterative rather than a sequenced manner. Typically, after some analysis has been accomplished, certain elements of issue formulation might be reconsidered and a first preliminary evaluation and selection of alternatives may be made. Only viable alternatives that pass this initial screening will then be subjected to more detailed analysis, including exploration of possible implementation plans, before further evaluation and selection are made.

4. Considerations in the Choice of Systemic Methods

Selection of an appropriate set of methods to attack a specific issue may be determined using a systemic approach similar to that used to resolve actual problems themselves. First the needs and constraints of the problem situation are assessed. Then we identify or design candidate approaches. Finally we study and compare the candidate approaches, select a subset and use them in the systems engineering process.

Some general guidelines concerning the identification of candidate methods for resolution of specific issues are appropriate and useful. These guidelines should be used with an awareness of their limitations, as must the systems engineering process itself. The methods most appropriate for a given situation depend very much on the characteristics of the task and the operational environment and on the experiential familiarity of the problem solver with these.

In the issue formulation step, a formulation is obtained and various elements relevant to the problem are identified. Study of the relevant literature is one approach towards elements identification. This will typically be supported and augmented by use of systemic methods for idea or element generation by experts and knowledgeable people. Should asking not be sufficient, we can study an evolving system, study a nominal system (or plans) or construct a prototype system and attempt to formulate the problem by determining the interactions of people with the prototype system.

The choice of method will primarily be determined by contingency task structural concerns governing the choice of performance objectives for the systemic process, such as:

(a) the location, number and the experiential familiarity of prospective participants with the task at hand and the operational environment in which it is embedded;

(b) the time and funds available to carry out the issue formulation elements for idea generation.

When there is little time available and relatively limited finance, brainwriting, brainstorming, synectics or the nominal group technique might be appropriate. The personal characteristics of participants might determine the further choice; brainwriting and the nominal group technique are better in reducing the influence of dominant individuals than the other two methods. Telephone polls or conferences could replace these when participants are widespread geographically. When the number of participants is large and they are geographically widespread, and if there is sufficient time and financial support, surveys, questionnaires and Delphi might be appropriate approaches.

After a set of elements representing descriptions of the problem, objectives to be realized by a solution and possible alternative solutions have been identified, we begin the analysis step. In this step we desire to obtain the impacts of proposed alternatives on the problem and measure these in terms of values and objectives. Often we also wish to adjust or refine various policy parameters so that individual policies are "best possible" in some defined sense.

The initial effort in analysis involves structuring the elements determined in the formulation step. After this, various parametric terms are associated with this structure. Generally it is difficult to determine a precise endpoint for the formulation step and corresponding starting point for the analysis step. In part this is due to the iterative nature of the systems process. Since visualization of structural realities among issue formulation elements may greatly assist in identification of additional elements and refinement of initial elements, it is certainly not unrealistic to involve element structuring as a terminal part of the issue formulation step.

In the element structuring effort, the purpose of the effort, the type of relation used for structuring and the type of effort are major determinants in the choice of a method. When a collective enquiry effort is preferred—that is, performed by a group of interacting people—cognitive mapping and interaction matrices might be useful. When the contextual relation used is direct and causal, causal loop diagrams are worth consideration. When the contextual relation is transitive (i.e. when if element A relates to element B, and element B relates to element C, then element A also relates to element C, when the elements are all positively related to one another), interpretive structural modelling is a very appropriate method. When it is desired to use more general types of relations, which may be negatively transitive for example, cognitive mapping would be an appropriate approach. For more general types of relations, and for identification of subsets of variables or other characteristic patterns, semantic network or frame-based approaches from artificial intelligence may be very appropriate.

Availability of data and theory and the time horizon or type of forecast desired are, along with available time and funds, the prime determinants in the choice of an impact assessment or analysis method.

When little or no data or theory are available, methods based on expert opinion and feedback (such as Delphi and scenario writing) or on "real life" simulation (such as gaming) are the prime learning, forecasting and impact assessment tools for various kinds of time horizons and forecasting needs. Workshop dynamic models are often useful for long-range exploration of interacting trends. Typically, the data needed in this approach are provided by experts and the method allows inclusion of both measurable as well as unmeasureable concepts or data.

When some theory about the system structure but little data are available, workshop dynamic models and dynamic simulation models are useful for long-range exploration. Workshop dynamic modelling is generally the simpler, faster, cheaper and less accurate method of the two. When data are abundant but theory that might assist in determining an appropriate structure is generally lacking, trend extrapolation or time-series forecasting can be very useful, particularly for short-to-medium-term forecasting.

A great many modelling methods have been developed for situations in which both theory and data are available. There are a number of important economic impact assessment modelling methods. Input–output analysis is appropriate for detailed analysis of productive systems. Econometrics is typically used for analysis of aggregate economics or macroeconomic variables. Microeconomic models are designed for description and study of specific economic sectors at a more detailed level. Welfare economic models incorporate equity concepts into microeconomics. Queuing theory and discrete-event simulation are especially appropriate for analysis and impact assessment in issues where phenomena such as probabilistic switching between a finite number of discrete states, and delays and waiting lines, are important.

The methods for refinement or optimization of individual alternative policies are useful when there exists a reliable mathematical description of relevant aspects of the issue formulation elements. The nature of the relevant mathematical description will determine the choice of method. When a best one-time or equilibrium setting has to be determined, mathematical programming can be used. This includes linear programming, a method widely used for resource allocation under constraints and for operational optimization of existing systems. When the system and controls vary over time according to known principles, optimum systems control is an appropriate method. When systems evolution can be described by unpredictable transitions from one state to another, with known probabilities, Markov decision models might be appropriate. These optimization-based approaches can become quite complicated if there is more than a single scalar performance index.

In the third systems engineering step, user, analyst and others evaluate and compare alternatives, choose one or more of these and prepare a plan for implementation of the selected alternative or decision.

Cost–benefit analysis provides a framework for systematic discussion of the advantages and disadvantages of alternatives, with emphasis on economic aspects. When advantages or disadvantages occur at different points in time, economic discounting concepts will be very helpful. Cost-effectiveness analysis is a term given to a modified form of cost–benefit analysis in which other than economic considerations form the basis for resource allocations. These and the results of other modelling and optimization analysis approaches provide very useful information input to the interpretation step.

It is often difficult to make trade-offs between the particular advantages and disadvantages of various alternatives in a given issue. Several related methods have been developed to assist decision makers in this task. The choice of a particular set of decision analysis approaches is typically determined by the nature of the alternatives, such as whether there exists uncertainty about the outcome states. The accuracy of available information and the user's willingness to spend time and money and to make values and preferences explicit also influence the particular decision analysis approaches selected. When uncertainty is present and when there are a number of attributes associated with outcome states, and user and analyst feel these should explicitly be taken into account, multiattribute utility is appropriate. When the decision maker wishes to express preferences over alternatives and to learn the impact on the importance weights for attributes, policy capture may be appropriate. The choice depends on whether the users prefer to make values explicit first and then apply them to the decision problem (multiattribute utility theory) or to rank alternatives and use this information to look into their implications in terms of attribute weights (policy capture).

While each individual modelling and analysis method may be very useful, it will often be more appropriate to use a combination of several methods for issue resolution and resource allocation efforts. But not all combinations of issue formulation, analysis and interpretation methods yield acceptable or viable overall approaches. There are several ways in which different systemic methods might be used together. Use of one method might yield results useful as input or starting information for another method. For example, element or idea generation methods produce lists of elements which serve as inputs to element structuring methods. Also use of one method might be required as an essential part of another one, such as the use of regression and estimation methods in the construction of time series and econometrics models. Combination of two approaches might yield a more powerful overall approach, for example by taking both future events and trends into account in a computer simulation model.

There are many possible combinations of methods that might be specially tailored to a specific problem. Thorough knowledge of what each method can accomplish under different conditions is a requirement for proper selection of a combination of modelling methods for a specific issue. Therefore, support of a knowledgeable systems analyst is very crucial in designing an overall issue resolution approach. In this regard it is especially critical that the contingency task structure of the decision maker be given full consideration in the development of an appropriate methodology or combination of procedures for problem resolution. Without this consideration it is very possible that the resulting systemic process may be so ill-matched to the real needs of the decision maker and the client group that very inferior results will be obtained. Perhaps even very unacceptable results may occur as a consequence of using the process. This caveat suggests a design approach for systemic processes which contains an operational evaluation component as an essential feature.

See also: Collective Enquiry; Decision Analysis; Decision Support Systems; Group Decision Making and Voting; Human Judgement and Decision Rules; Systems Analysis and Modelling: Time Series; Systems Management: Conflict Analysis

Bibliography

Andriole S J 1983 *The Handbook of Problem Solving.* Petrocelli, Princeton, New Jersey

Geoffrion A M 1987 An introduction to structured modelling. *Manage. Sci.* **33** (5)**,** 547–88

Green T B, Less S M, Newsom W B 1978 *The Decision Science Process.* Petrocelli, Princeton, New Jersey

Hammond K R, Stewart T R, Brehmer B, Steinmann D O 1975 Social judgement theory. In: Kaplan M F, Schwartz S (eds.) *Human Judgement and Decision Processes.* Academic Press, New York

Janis I L, Mann L 1977 *Decision Making: A Psychological Analysis of Conflict, Choice, and Commitment.* Free Press, New York

McGrath J E 1984 *Groups: Interaction and Performance.* Prentice–Hall, Englewood Cliffs, New Jersey

Majone G, Quade E S 1980 *Pitfalls of Analysis.* Wiley, New York

Nadler G 1985 Systems methodology and design. *IEEE Trans. Syst., Man Cybern.* **15** (6), 685–97

Newell A, Simon H A 1972 *Human Problem Solving.* Prentice–Hall, Englewood Cliffs, New Jersey

Rouse W B 1983 Models of human problem solving: Detection, diagnosis, and compensation for system failures. *Automatica* December 1983**,** 613–26

Sage A P 1977a *Methodology for Large Scale Systems.* McGraw–Hill, New York

Sage A P 1977b *Systems Engineering: Methodology and Applications.* IEEE–Wiley, New York

Sage A P 1982 Methodological considerations in the design of large scale systems engineering processes. In: Haimes Y (ed.) *Large Scale Systems.* North-Holland, Amsterdam, pp. 99–141

Sage A P 1986 Systems engineering: Analysis and design. In: Kutz M P (ed.) *Mechanical Engineers' Handbook*. Wiley, New York, Chap. 37, pp. 1051–87

Sage A P 1987a Knowledge, skills, and information requirements for systems design. In: Rouse W B, Boff K (eds.) *The Psychology of System Design*. Elsevier, New York

Sage A P (ed.) 1987b *System Design for Human Interaction*. IEEE Press, New York

Sage A P, Galing B, Lagomasino A 1983 Methodologies for the determination of information requirements for decision support systems. *Large Scale Syst.* **5** (2), 131–67

Sage A P, Rouse W B 1986 Aiding the human decision maker through the knowledge-based sciences. *IEEE Trans. Syst., Man Cybern*, **16**(4)

Warfield J N 1976 *Societal Systems: Planning, Policy, and Complexity*. Wiley, New York

Weiss J J, Zwahlen G W 1982 The structured decision conference: A case study. *Hospital and Health Services Adm.* **27**, 90–105

A. P. Sage
[George Mason University, Fairfax, Virginia, USA]

Technological Forecasting

A forecast predicts likely future states by a systematic and reproducible method. A technological forecast (TF) predicts the timing, degree or nature of change of specific technical parameters, or developments, of concern.

A TF is based on the observation that the processes of technological innovation are sufficiently orderly at some level of aggregation to allow a meaningful projection into the future. Innovation involves socioeconomic processes as well as technological development; therefore the developmental context must be well understood to make a viable technological forecast. Effective management of technology depends on awareness of likely changes, and it also entails consideration of the impacts of technology. Thus an effective forecast should be accompanied by a reasonable assessment of the full range of impacts of new technology (technology assessment) to help manage the development process. In an era of rapidly changing technology, industry, the military and civilian government require technological forecasting and assessment to "look before you leap."

The track record of technological forecasting parallels that of management science in one important respect: highly mathematical, sophisticated analyses may arouse admiration from professional peers but to date have failed to deliver significant usable results. The present article therefore emphasizes the simpler approaches that have proved to be effective.

1. Forecasting Principles: The Ten Commandments

Table 1 presents ten guiding principles to conduct a TF. These prescriptions involve a range of considerations which are addressed below.

(a) *Watch what you forecast.* TF contributes to organizational strategic planning. It aims, in particular

Table 1
Principles for technological forecasting

Watch what you forecast
Get the technology right
Get the context right
Beware core assumption drag
Take the middle way
Keep the time horizon short
Do it simply
Multiple approaches are best
Perform sensitivity analyses
Pray

instances, to identify new opportunities or emerging threats. Exactly who the users are and what their information needs are must be kept clearly in mind. For example, one common forecast tracks the continuing development of computer memory capacity. If one's organization is affected by memory capacity, that would be a viable parameter to forecast. On the other hand, if that organization cares primarily about the point of emergence of a specific memory technology, such a forecast would not be on target. The emergence of a specific technological innovation is inherently more difficult to predict than general progress along some technical parameter. For instance, an oscilloscope including superconducting electronics hit the market in 1987 with 5 ps speed and 50 MV sensitivity (Fitzgerald 1988); predicting the introduction of this instrument would have been more difficult than predicting a pattern of increasing speed and sensitivity for such instrumentation. A forecast building on a stream of small improvements is much more reliable. Furthermore, it is easier to predict the emergence of technical capabilities than it is to predict the attendant "innovation," that is, success in some economic market. For instance, the Hypres PSP-1000 oscilloscope mentioned above sells at almost five times the price of its closest rival—will its superior performance overcome this price differential to make for commercial success?

Selection of the precise parameters to study is a critical function of data availability, salience and understanding of the technological and socioeconomic systems involved. For instance, electric utilities after World War II were concerned about the cost of electricity from coal-fired plants. Had trends in coal prices, been extrapolated, the conclusion would have been that power costs would rise sharply. On the other hand, if the increasing efficiency of such plants during this period had been noted, the initial increase in electricity cost, followed by a steep decrease, could have been properly anticipated. The key to an effective forecast was to recognize that both fuel cost and plant efficiency affected electricity production cost. Performance of a system is a key in selecting parameters—for example, Knight (1985) addresses computer systems in terms of which technological changes affect system structure (e.g., memory processes, control schemes) and function (e.g., computing power, reliability).

Prediction may entail probable courses of future events or, merely, possible future occurrences. Contingent forecasts may be quite useful. Suppose one accepts a very high uncertainty in the prospects of commercial use of superconductivity. It could still be very useful for strategic planning to identify likely "what if ..." technological developments contingent on successful superconductivity development (or its absence).

(b) Get the technology right. This implies two major points. First, one must have an accurate description of the current state of the art along with the leverage points critical to its future development. Second, it is particularly important to consider the relation between the technology in question and other contributing or competing technologies, new or old. A prototypical example of a key contributing (or complementary) technology is the electric starter motor, which allowed the internal combustion engine to become sufficiently attractive to obliterate the steam engine in the automotive market. Prospects for converging developments may necessitate reconceptualization of the technology. Thinking out alternative configurations can drastically alter forecasts and their accuracy. For instance, a current US Air Force project, the "Designer's Associate," seeks to apply intelligent information technologies to aid cockpit design. Over the first 18 months of this project, the conceptualization of this system has been altered significantly by the emergence of relatively low cost, high capacity CD-ROM and "hypertext" systems.

(c) Get the context right. This is vital to any attempt to forecast innovation (but less critical to forecasting technical capabilities). One needs to identify the important institutions, critical decision points and socioeconomic influences on the technology, not only for the present but also for the whole time period covered by the TF.

The notion of the technological delivery system (TDS) of Wenk and Kuehn (1977) has been found to be most useful in mapping the relevant socioeconomic system. The TDS maps the institutions and processes involved in the development of a technological innovation. The "push" of scientific discovery and technological capability must link with the "pull" of societal and economic demand. Sometimes new technology drives the innovation process, leading to creation of new markets (e.g., the transistor). Some observers of US industry feel that it relies too much on this approach, rather than a market-driven one in which the pull of anxious markets orients carefully targeted R&D efforts (e.g., the Japanese adaptation of VCR technology for a home consumer market). The TDS model focuses on the delivery system per se—the "technological enterprise" that combines organization, capital, technology, skilled personnel and raw materials to produce the products (or services) in question. Institutional or economic shortcomings in the technological enterprise impede successful innovation—consider the difficulties in translating US National Laboratory R&D into commercial successes. In addition, the TDS seeks to identify critical outside factors likely to affect the innovation in question. These may include powerful lobbies (e.g., antinuclear), vested interests, governmental institutions (potentially supportive, e.g., development grants, and/or restrictive, e.g., OSHA requirements). The success or failure of many technologies depends as much on these socioeconomic factors as on technological viability per se.

(d) Beware core assumption drag. Forecasters with a modicum of success may miss changes in technology or in context. Ideologists may deny readily observable points that disagree with their theories (consider Chinese communist egalitarianism carried to the extreme during the Cultural Revolution, denying the need for technical expertise to run industries). For an example closer to home, electric utilities continued to forecast high demand growth during the 1970s, extrapolating past patterns, oblivious to constricting demand. The resulting overcapacity, combined with socially driven resistance to nuclear plants, has been economically catastrophic to some utilities.

(e) Take the middle way. Extreme forecasts are apt to miss the mark. Far-out forecasts are usually predicated on so many probabilistic presumptions that they have little chance of occurring. On the other hand, conservative forecasts often fail from lack of nerve. Scientific committees have a particularly poor record in this regard. An interesting case to note is a recent US National Academy Panel report foreseeing no serious unemployment problems from the industrial-era-to-information-age transition taking place (Cyert and Mowery 1987). Porter (1986) predicts staggering excess labor capacity requiring dramatic response, including abandonment of the "work ethic." The "middle way" suggests that somewhere in between is the sound forecast.

(f) Keep the time horizon short. This seeming platitude is very important in the successful conduct of technological forecasting. Ascher (1978) has compiled data showing that a short horizon is the strongest correlate of accuracy. Armstrong (1978) combines this observation with another that good data are hard to find, to offer a sensible rule of thumb:

$$d = 4(h)^{1/2}$$

where h is the forecast horizon (in future time periods) and d are the historical data desirable (in past time periods). Bright (1978) warns to beware of extrapolation beyond 20 years, because the assumptions of continuous technological development and a stationary context become too tenuous.

A practical implication of this principle is that one should favor "quick and dirty," but recent, forecasts over more elaborate, but older, ones. A $10 000 000 study of CAD/CAM/CAE development prospects prepared five years ago is worth less than a current $1000 scan of a bit of recent literature and phone calls to a few well-chosen experts.

(g) *Do it simply.* This means that methodological sophistication is rarely worth its cost. Ascher (1978) found no one method generally superior. One must assess the relative uncertainties in a forecast and invest the forecasting resources to reduce the most critical uncertainties. Rarely, if ever, are these uncertainties addressed by sophisticated mathematical models. Such models require simplification of the issues and often demand data that are expensive to obtain, or unavailable. A particularly baleful consequence may be exclusion of critical yet qualitative factors in favor of available quantitative measures. The implication is that one is better off putting resources into understanding the TDS and getting the basic principles of the technology right, than with elaborate mathematical manipulation.

(h) *Multiple approaches are best.* Given that no one method is generally superior and that technological forecasting is a high-uncertainty venture, it follows that convergence of results attained by diverse approaches is a great contributor to confidence. The more the methods used complement each other in relative strengths and weaknesses the better. This implies it would be better to carry out a modest survey of expert opinion and a modest trend extrapolation than to carry out a more thorough effort in only one or the other. Even in cases where trend data support modelling, a TF is well-served by including some expert opinion. At the least this can help assure that some convergent or competitive technology "breakthrough" or critical socioeconomic consideration is not missed.

(i) *Perform sensitivity analyses.* Various goals drive a TF. These may entail identification of alternative courses of action, strategic opportunities or potential threats. In general, it is the direction and rough magnitude of such changes that is of concern in extrapolative forecasts. In normative forecasts, more akin to planning per se, one identifies desirable future states to help clarify goals and develop present courses of action. In neither of these does the payoff from a TF depend substantially on forecast precision (unlike, say, quarterly economic forecasts). Rather, uncertainty reduction is a general aim. Robustness under varied assumptions, tested through sensitivity analyses, adds greatly to forecast confidence. Sensitivity analyses may be either qualitative or quantitative as appropriate. Scenarios and most models are designed to allow variation in the values of key parameters and/or functional relations in order to observe the results of these changes. Trend extrapolations and summaries of expert opinion are most useful when they provide not only singular measures of central tendency but also indications of the degree of uncertainty.

(j) *Pray.* This may or may not be taken literally. Unlike short-term econometric forecasting, longer-range technological forecasting must accept that many uncertainties exist and are likely to become compounded through their interaction over time. Intrinsic uncertainties in human choices and natural events will act upon the forecast. Indeed, a successful TF that highlights a threat should stimulate actions that counter the threat, ideally causing the forecast not to come true.

2. Forecasting Techniques

The three intellectual pillars of forecasting are theory, data and technique. We lack high-quality predictive theory with respect to sociotechnical change. Social change theories tend to be extremely "macro" in orientation (e.g., Marxism) and empirically untested, if not untestable. Technical change theories amount to little more than observation of the S-shape growth curves typical in many natural and technological processes.

Gathering data on technical processes often proves difficult. Rapid technological change in areas of interest makes lengthy time series irrelevant and inappropriate. Recent advances may be poorly documented or proprietary. Social change data upon which to base understanding and forecasting of the context of technological development are gathered without relation to social change theory. Recent efforts to gather social indicators data have been promising but sporadic. A framework for selection and organization is lacking. Often such data will not be at the level of aggregation that the forecaster needs.

Forecasting techniques are used to make up for deficiencies in theory and data. These techniques allow the use and integration of available information from disparate sources. At their best they facilitate human judgement in the forecasting process.

Well over 100 forecasting techniques have been identified. Many seem to have been developed primarily to impress others with their sophistication. Little evaluation of the effectiveness of different forecasting techniques has been performed; however, work such as that by Ascher (1978) finds little to warrant complicated and sophisticated approaches. Since most techniques are variations on a few basic approaches, five families of forecasting techniques (Table 2) are most useful, based on experience. The following presentation describes the techniques with their strengths and

Table 2
Five families of forecasting techniques

Monitoring
Expert opinion
Trend extrapolation
Modelling
Scenario construction

weaknesses and outlines potential uses; it does not explain how to perform the techniques in any detail.

(a) Monitoring. This is without doubt the simplest forecasting technique and the most fruitful. Monitoring entails scanning the environment for information pertinent to the topic of the forecast. One needs a systematic method to gather important information and filter out unessential items. Variations abound: one may establish a clippings file (or employ a clipping service), go a step beyond to prepare a monitoring journal with abstracts of items and key phrases highlighted, or move into computerized search and abstracting of various databases. The advent of computerized databases with personal computer access and Boolean search capabilities enhances monitoring tremendously. One no longer needs to generate the primary information base and search keywords can be varied at will. Application of "hypertext" systems (such as "Hypercards" for the Apple Macintosh) offer further potential to develop highly adaptable monitoring systems.

Monitoring assumes that the environment contains information useful for a forecast and that systematic observation can help to chart the course of future developments. Its strengths include collecting vast amounts of information from a wide range of sources at relatively low cost. Conversely, its outstanding weakness is the danger of accumulating large amounts of information lacking selectivity or structure and hence useless for forecasting. Human judgement plays the critical role in picking up signals of change and synthesizing them. Monitoring develops an information base that can generate forecasts directly or support the use of techniques such as expert opinion (e.g., one contacts experts identified by monitoring, after familiarizing oneself with issues raised in the literature monitored) or modelling (e.g., monitoring helps identify key parameters to model).

Whirlpool Corporation offers a nice example of successful monitoring. In the 1960s they tracked developments in the chemical and textile industries (not their business domains), identifying the introduction of permanent-press fabrics prior to commercialization. They took this information and generated the first washer and dryer permanent-press cycles, beating their competition to market by about a year, and substantially increasing their market share. Some firms, such as Whirlpool, locate monitoring activity within a corporate strategic planning group. Others disperse the activity. For instance, one food products company first identified the major areas in which new technology could impact either their production processes or their products per se. They then assigned each of some 20 engineers one or more areas to monitor. Upon detection of a prospective technological change, the engineer was to instigate investigation. In addition, they were to report regularly (e.g., every six months) on activity in their areas.

(b) Expert opinion. This technique involves obtaining and analyzing the opinions of experts in a particular area. Several types of technique can be identified. Forecasting by panel necessitates assembling a group of experts and having them interact to reach consensus. Such committee work tends to be expensive and time-consuming, but it may have the advantage of credibility if groups such as the US National Academy of Sciences back such committees. Variants of straightforward committee meetings have been advocated, especially to enhance creativity (e.g., brainstorming, nominal group technique). The survey technique entails posing questions to a sample of experts and analyzing their responses using statistical techniques. Delphi is a variant of the survey technique in which a questionnaire is administered to a sample of experts repeatedly (Linstone and Turoff 1975, Riggs 1983). Initial results are analyzed and provided to the respondents (e.g., as statistical distributions). Participants are then requested to answer the questions again in the light of the group's responses. Those who give extreme answers may be asked to offer reasons for them, to be shared anonymously. This process may be iterated until responses are stable (not necessarily in a consensus) or until the resources and patience of the experts are exhausted. A typical extent is three rounds (Linstone and Turoff 1975). Combinations of methods are also possible; for instance, the EFTE approach consists of estimation, feedback, talk and estimate, yielding a blend of the structured feedback of Delphi and the discussion of a panel (Nelms and Porter 1985). DELPAC, a mainframe program, supports administration of Delphi through computer networking; it can also be used to facilitate questionnaire generation, response analysis, feedback and further data manipulation (e.g., cross-impact) (Cundiff 1985).

Expert opinion methods assume that there exist individuals who know significantly more about certain matters than do others. They further assume that the forecaster can tap this expertise. In general it is desirable to use some form of expert opinion to complement other forecasting techniques in a study. Experts can provide an immeasurably useful check on the pertinence of gathered facts and trends, missed parameters and otherwise unavailable information by applying their "implicit models."

Several weaknesses must be pointed out. It is often difficult to identify experts—samples "of convenience" are not satisfactory. Criteria such as professional degrees, professional memberships, work experience, publications, patents, scientific insight or the perspective of a user are often problematic in identifying experts. It may be difficult to obtain experts willing to cooperate who do not have personal stakes in an issue which may bias their observations. A classic example is the US National Academy of Sciences study on the dangers of asbestos, in which most experts were found to be employed by the asbestos industry. Survey and

Delphi preparation and administration are subject to all the concerns of good social science survey practice. Care should be taken in questionnaire design, sample selection and analysis of results so that the process is procedurally competent.

Where sound data are unavailable or where modelling is difficult, expert opinion is likely to be the main forecasting technique. In other cases it will be an important auxiliary method contributing complementary information.

(c) *Trend extrapolation.* This set of techniques involves the use of graphical and/or statistical techniques to extend time-series data into the future. Trend extrapolation does not demand an understanding of the causal influences that result in the observed trend. It does require the assumption of stationarity; that is, whatever influences have resulted in past states of affairs will continue into the future. This assumption is more tenable with a complex mix of moderate influences than with major discontinuities, political choices or go/no-go decisions. The evolution of technical capabilities in the short term is most likely to meet these conditions. In trend extrapolation one must accept a basic trend form, whether an S-curve, exponential growth or linear growth. During the critical early stages of a particular trend, expert judgement is needed to determine which of these or other forms best depicts the trend. Trend extrapolation, of course, requires that suitable data be available.

Trend extrapolation first requires identification of the proper parameters: for instance, one must decide whether simple (e.g., aircraft speed) or compound (e.g., aircraft seat miles/gallon of fuel) parameters are suitable. One must then gather data and construct appropriate indicators. Establishing the trend can involve various actions (Makridakis *et al.* 1983, Martino 1983 Chaps. 4, 5) listed below.

(i) Eyeball fit of a future projection line from historical data.

(ii) Transformation of data before projection (e.g., log transformation is useful for exponential growth patterns in limited periods).

(iii) Mathematical curve fit, ranging from least-squares fit for linear functions (possibly after transformation) to S-shaped curves, such as the Gompertz or logistic curves; and smoothing, filtering, decomposition and other techniques taking into account autocorrelation (e.g., Box–Jenkins approaches and spectral analyses; however, TF data rarely warrant such treatment).

(iv) Identification of leading indicators (e.g., fighter plane speed as a leading indicator of commercial plane speed) may be effective. This reflects quantification of the approach of forecasting by analogy that can also use qualitative development parallels, as between VCR and CD-ROM adoption.

(v) Substitution theory may work where a new technology is taking over the market held by an old technology (e.g., diesel for steam-powered locomotives); other forms, such as the technological progress function, may work well in specific instances. (Note: (i, ii and iii) analyze some single technology parameter over time; (iv and v) incorporate multiple technologies.)

(vi) Results, however extrapolated, should be challenged with use of appropriate sensitivity analyses to establish confidence bands.

(vii) Trend results should be interpreted to aid the user by placing them in appropriate context with nonquantifiable parameters; identification of factors likely to alter the extrapolation increases credibility.

Trend extrapolation addresses two quite different processes: first, the evolution of technical capability (e.g., functions/volume of a semiconductor chip) and second, the manner of economic diffusion (e.g., sales of a particular generation of chips). Growth functions, reflected by an S-shaped curve, often characterize both of these processes well—slow initial growth, an exponential-like period of rapid expansion followed by a slowing, asymptotic approach to some limit. Figure 1 depicts such a diffusion profile for the extent to which industrial R&D professionals routinely use computers.

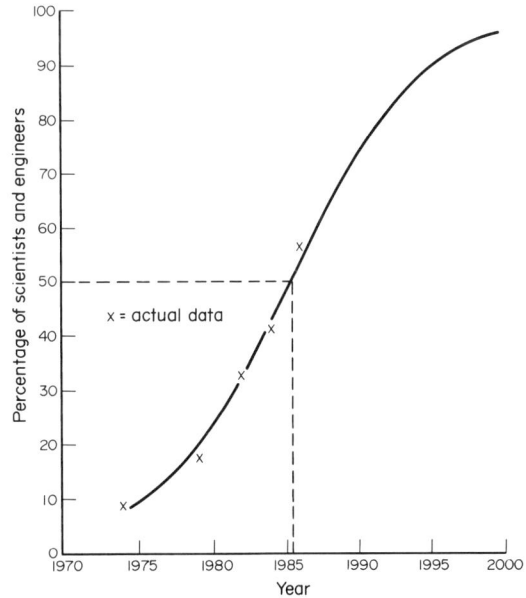

Figure 1
Percentage of R&D scientists and engineers who use computers regularly as a function of time (from Rossini *et al.* 1987)

Various models yield S-shaped curves with somewhat different characteristics (Lee and Lu 1987). The Fisher–Pry model (1971) has been most popular in describing the takeover of a market by one technology from another (e.g., 16-bit from 8-bit microprocessors). TechOverPLUS is an attractive (but not cheap) personal computer-based software package that allows one to fit various growth models, including Fisher–Pry, and perform analyses.

(d) *Modelling.* This represents a broad family of techniques. A model is a simplified representation of a part of the world that incorporates both structure and dynamics. Model dynamics may be used to forecast the future behavior of a system. Models are particularly useful in addressing the interaction of multiparameters. Ayres (1966) categorized models in a hierarchy ranging from conjecture and analogy to empirical and analytical. One can also note physical simulations and interactive gaming models. TF models range widely: simple conceptualizations at the level of boxes and arrows; occasional physical simulations; gaming; and, most importantly, various types of computerized simulation.

The strength of models lies in their ability to incorporate basic structure and processes of real events in appropriately simplified representations. Through such simplifications, models can also provide a framework to incorporate human judgement on the essential aspects of a system. Conversely, their greatest hazards lie in poor choice of parameters and faulty assumptions about structural interactions that may not be noticed in the face of stylized graphics and detailed analyses. Sometimes models are inappropriately forced toward quantifiable data, to the exclusion of important, but nonquantifiable, parameters. In general, simulation models of high credibility have been constructed for certain specific systems (for instance, Los Angeles Basin air pollution), whereas more general simulation efforts require real caution (for example, systems dynamics models of world population growth and its consequences).

Cross-effect models (Sage 1977 Chap. 5, Porter *et al.* 1980 Chap. 9), in particular those concerning cross impact, explicitly address the interaction between technological or other factors and their consequences. These may be particularly important in anticipating sociopolitical concerns that can markedly affect technological development. Some cross-impact procedures examine the interplay among trends over time; others consider the likelihood of specific events taking place affecting either the probabilities of other events or the shape of trends. Portland State University's systems science program has accumulated an interesting set of alternative cross-impact programs. Enzer (1986) markets an especially nice program for personal computers, XimpacT.

In fact, a major gain from cross-impact models may be the insights gained by the team that works to construct them (more than any specific forecasted results). Gaming takes human interaction even further to set up situations demanding strategic interactions among parties at interest (themselves or role-played). Simulating future military encounters or social policies in a game context can illuminate system deficiencies and superior alternatives. Various computerized games have been created, typically with specific substantive foci.

(c) *Scenarios.* These can take the form of "snapshots" of a possible future, incorporating a constellation of possible values of parameters of interest. Alternatively, "future histories" present development paths, step by step, plausibly linking the present to the future. A set of scenarios encompasses the plausible range of selected variables (e.g., maximum plausible rate of adoption of voice recognition technology in one scenario vs minimal adoption of that technology in an alternative scenario). Scenarios (Martino 1983 Chap. 10) attempt to capture the richness of future contexts, incorporating both quantifiable and nonquantifiable phenomena in an internally consistent manner. Scenario writing demands imaginative description to capture the interest of the user. (Science fiction, at its best, illustrates effective use of scenarios.) Scenarios can key on alternative profiles of technological development or on societal choices. Scenarios can effectively integrate technical and contextual information and communicate this to nontechnical audiences.

Systematic scenario construction (Becker 1983) requires several steps:

(i) identify the focal issue and strategic choices;

(ii) create a checklist of the relevant development, context and decision factors, and set out critical influences among them and probabilistic relationships (e.g., if A occurs, what does this do to the chances of B occurring?);

(iii) determine how many scenarios to have;

(iv) outline, possibly using a table format, the essential differences among the family of scenarios—which trend levels or event occurrences drive the different scenarios;

(v) construct the scenario narratives; and

(vi) evaluate and interpret the implications of the scenarios (possibly iterating the set if appropriate).

Huss and Honton (1986) offer a good framework to develop scenarios by making use of different computer packages such as INTERAX (the mainframe parent of XimpacT) and BASICS (Batelle scenario inputs to corporate strategies). They point out potential uses of scenarios to enhance strategic planning by integrating diverse kinds of information about the future, communicating key issues in a contextually meaningful way and forcing decision makers to address alternatives.

3. Evaluating Technological Forecasts

A number of questions can be raised to help to determine the adequacy of a technological forecast. The first issue concerns internal forecast validity, and asks the following questions.

(a) Are the most appropriate available data and parameters used?
(b) Are the appropriate techniques used in a sound manner?
(c) Do projections conform with actual developments where known and do they cover the appropriate time frame?
(d) Is the system appropriately modelled with cause-and-effect understanding?

To be truly useful, a forecast must go beyond validity issues to satisfy such concerns as the following.

(a) Are the variables of concern forecast?
(b) Are results interpreted for the target users?
(c) Is the forecast credible to the intended users, in terms of who the forecasters are and what techniques they use?
(d) Over what time period does the study retain its usefulness, and can it be updated?
(e) Does the study appropriately balance sophistication, available resources and timeliness of results?

Technological forecasting merits continued development. It would be particularly useful to track the accuracy of prior forecasts against eventual developments. Of course, this must be couched against the extent of system understanding at the time of the forecast and even the possibility that a forecast altered the future states or events. We close on a time-series note—historians claim that we can understand the present from the past; futurologists maintain that we can understand the present from the future. Managing from the perspective of the future allows us to be part of it.

See also: Collective Enquiry; Decision Support Systems; Hypothesis Testing

Bibliography

Armstrong J S 1978 *Long-Range Forecasting: From Crystal Ball to Computer*. Wiley-Interscience, New York
Ascher W 1978 *Forecasting: An Appraisal for Policy Makers and Planners*. Johns Hopkins University Press, Baltimore, Maryland
Ayres R U 1966 *On Technological Forecasting*. Hudson Institute, Croton-on-Hudson, New York
Ayres R U 1969 *Technological Forecasting and Long-Range Planning*. McGraw-Hill, New York
Becker H S 1983 Scenarios: A tool of growing importance to policy analysts in government and industry. *Technol. Forecast. Soc. Change* **23**, 95–119
Bright J R 1978 *Practical Technology Forecasting*. Industrial Management Center, Austin, Texas
Cundiff W E 1985 Interactive software for the capture, management and analysis of data in Delphi inquiries. *Technol. Forecast. Soc. Change* **28**, 173–85
Cyert R M, Mowery D C 1987 (eds.) *Technology and Employment*. National Academy Press, Washington, DC
Enzer S 1986 Building up the longer-term context for project and program appraisal: Dynamic strategic analysis. *Project Appraisal* **1**, 189–200
Fisher J, Pry R 1971 A simple substitution model of technological change. *Technol. Forecast. Soc. Change* **3**, 290–307
Fitzgerald K 1988 Instrumentation. *IEEE Spectrum* **25**(1), 47–49
Huss W R, Honton E J 1986 *Alternative Methods for Developing Business Scenarios*, Battelle Economics and Policy Analysis Occasional Paper No. 55. Battelle, Columbus, Ohio
Jones H, Twiss B C 1978 *Forecasting Technology for Planning Decisions*. Petrocelli, New York
Knight K E 1985 A functional and structural measurement of technology. *Technol. Forecast. Soc. Change* **28**, 107–27
Lee J C, Lu K W 1987 On a family of data-based transformed models useful in forecasting technological substitutions. *Technol. Forecast. Soc. Change* **31**, 61–78
Linstone H A, Turoff M (eds.) 1975 *The Delphi Method: Techniques and Applications*. Addison–Wesley, Reading, Massachusetts
Makridakis S, Wheelwright S C, McGee V E 1983 *Forecasting: Methods and Applications*, 2nd edn. Wiley, New York
Martino J P 1983 *Technological Forecasting for Decision Making*, 2nd edn. North-Holland, New York
Nelms K R, Porter A L 1985 EFTE: An interactive Delphi method. *Technol. Forecast. Soc. Change* **28**, 43–61
Porter A L 1986 Work in the new information age. *The Futurist* **20**(5), 9–14
Porter A L, Rossini F A, Carpenter S R, Roper A T 1980 *A Guidebook for Technology Assessment and Impact Analysis*. North-Holland, New York
Riggs W E 1983 The Delphi technique. *Technol. Forecast. Soc. Change* **23**, 89–94
Rossini F A, Porter A L, Jacobs C C 1987 *Computer Use in Industrial Research and Development: 1986 Data and Twelve Year Trends*. Industrial Research Institute, New York
Sage A P 1977 *Methodology for Large Scale Systems*. McGraw–Hill, New York
Wenk E Jr, Kuehn T J 1977 Interinstitutional networks in technological delivery systems. In: Haberer J (ed.) *Science and Technology Policy*. Lexington Books, Lexington, Massachusetts, pp. 153–75

A. L. Porter and F. A. Rossini
[Georgia Institute of Technology, Atlanta, Georgia, USA]

LIST OF CONTRIBUTORS

Contributors are listed in alphabetical order, together with their addresses. Titles of articles which they have authored follow in alphabetical order. Where articles are co-authored, this has been indicated by an asterisk preceding the article title.

Aczél, J.
Department of Applied Mathematics
University of Waterloo
Waterloo, Ontario N2L 3G1
CANADA
Information Theory

Adelman, L.
Department of Information Systems & Systems
 Engineering
George Mason University
4400 University Drive
Fairfax, VA 22030
USA
Support-System Design: Behavioral Concerns

Ames, T.
Goddard Space Flight Center
Greenbelt, MD 20771
USA
*Analogical Reasoning

Andriole, S. J.
Chair, Department of Information Systems &
 Systems Engineering
George Mason University
4400 University Drive
Fairfax, VA 22030
USA
Prototyping as Information in Systems Design

Blanning, R. W.
Owen Graduate School of Management
Vanderbilt University
Nashville, TN 37203
USA
Expert Systems for Managers: Design Issues

Blum, B. I.
Applied Physics Laboratory
Johns Hopkins University
Laurel, MD 20707
USA
Software Development: Human Information Processing

Brehmer, B.
Department of Psychology
University of Uppsala
PO Box 227
S-751 04 Uppsala
SWEDEN
Dynamic Decision Making

Burns, J. R.
College of Business Administration
Texas Tech University
P O Box 4320
Lubbock, TX 79409-4320
USA
*Knowledge-Based Simulation

Carley, K.
Department of Social and Decision Sciences
Carnegie-Mellon University
Pittsburgh, PA 15213
USA
*Distributed Information and Organizational Decision-
 Making Models*

Chow, L. R.
Vice President
Tamkang University
5199 Lane Kinghua Street
Taipei 106
Taiwan
REPUBLIC OF CHINA
Information Systems

Conant, R. C.
1108 Science & Engineering Office Building
Department of Electrical Engineering and
 Computer Science
University of Illinois at Chicago
Box 4348
Chicago, IL 60680
USA
Information Laws of Systems

DeSanctis, G.
Carlson School of Management
University of Minnesota
271 19th Avenue South
Minneapolis, MN 55455
USA
*Group Decision Support Systems: Software
 Architecture*

Dominy, R.
Goddard Space Flight Center
Greenbelt, MD 20771
USA
Analogical Reasoning

Donnell, M. L.
Donnell & Associates Inc.
PO Box 10161
McLean, VA 22102-8161
USA
Cognitive Science, Human Information Processing and Artificial Intelligence

Eisner, H.
10837 Deborah Drive
Potomac, MD 20854
USA
Computer-Aided Systems Engineering

Fletcher, J. D.
Institute for Defense Analyses
1801 N Beauregard Street
Alexandria, VA 22311
USA
Computer-Based Instruction: Costs and Effectiveness

Forte, B.
Department of Applied Mathematics
University of Waterloo
Waterloo, Ontario N2L 3G1
CANADA
Information Theory

Fraser, N. M.
Department of Systems Design Engineering
University of Waterloo
Waterloo, Ontario N2L 3G1
CANADA
Systems Management: Conflict Analysis

Gansler, J. S.
The Analytical Sciences Corporation
Suite 1220
1700 North Moore Street
Arlington, VA 22209
USA
System Acquisition and Procurement

George, F. H.
Clifton Cottage
Rawlings Lane
Seer Green
Beaconsfield
Buckinghamshire HP6 2RO
UK
Systems Concepts: History

Gomaa, H
Department of Information Systems & Systems Engineering
George Mason University
4400 University Drive
Fairfax, VA 22030
USA
Real-Time Software Design: Information Concerns

Gray, P.
Management Information Systems
Claremont Graduate School
Claremont, CA 91711-6190
USA
Office Automation

Hammond, K. R.
Center for Research on Judgment & Policy
University of Colorado
Campus Box 485
Boulder, CO 80309
USA
Intuitive and Analytical Cognition: Information Models

Hatfield, F.
Advanced Decision Systems
1500 Wilson Boulevard
Suite 512
Arlington, VA 22209-2401
USA
System-Acquisition Information: Knowledge-Based Representation

Haworth, D. A.
Texas Tech University
Lubbock, TX 79409
USA
Knowledge-Based Simulation

Henrion, M.
Department of Engineering & Public Policy
Carnegie Mellon University
Pittsburgh, PA 15213
USA
Knowledge Support Systems: Uncertain Information Processing

Hess, M. S.
American Management Systems, Inc.
1777 North Kent Street
Arlington, VA 22209
USA
Information Systems Design in Industrial Practice

Hess, R. A.
Department of Mechanical Engineering
University of California

Davis, CA 95616
USA
*Human Factors Engineering: Information-
   Processing Concerns*

Hipel, K. W.
Department of Systems Design Engineering
University of Waterloo
Waterloo, Ontario N2L 3G1
CANADA
*Systems Management: Conflict Analysis

Ho, J. L.
Graduate School of Management
University of California
Irvine, CA 92717
USA
*Decision-Problem Structuring

Hopple, G. W.
Department of Information Systems
   & Systems Engineering
George Mason University
4400 University Drive
Fairfax, VA 22030
USA
*Knowledge Acquisition: Storyboarding and
   Computer-Based System Decision Research*

Keller, L. R.
Graduate School of Management
University of California
Irvine, CA 92717
USA
*Decision-Problem Structuring

Kerschberg, L.
Department of Information Systems & Systems
   Engineering
George Mason University
4400 University Drive
Fairfax, VA 22030
USA
Expert Database Systems

Klein, G. A.
Klein Associates Inc.
PO Box 264
Yellow Springs, OH 45387
USA
*Recognitional Decision Making: Information
   Requirements*

Kornreich, T. R.
Science Applications International Corporation
1710 Goodridge Drive
PO Box 1303
McLean, VA 22102
USA
System-Integration Fundamentals

Lagomasino, A.
AT&T Bell Telephone Laboratories
Room 1A-605
Holmdel, NJ 07733
USA
*Multiattribute Utility Theory

Lehner, P. E.
Department of Information Systems
   & Systems Engineering
George Mason University
4400 University Drive
Fairfax, VA 22030
USA
Automated Planning

Levis, A. H.
Laboratory for Information & Decision Systems
Massachusetts Institute of Technology
Cambridge, MA 02139
USA
*Organizational Information Structures:
   Quantitative Models*

Madalon, D.
The Analytic Sciences Corporation
1700 North Moore
Suite 1800
Arlington, VA 22209
USA
**System-Acquisition Information: Knowledge-Based
   Representation*

Mitchell, C. M.
Center for Human-Machine Systems Research
School of Industrial and Systems Engineering
Georgia Institute of Technology
Atlanta, GA 30332-0205
USA
*Supervisory Control: Philosophical Considerations
   in Manufacturing Systems*

Mizumoto, M.
Osaka Electro-Communication University
Neyagawa
Osaka 572
JAPAN
Fuzzy Reasoning Methods

Ören, T. I.
Department of Computer Science
University of Ottawa
Ottawa, Ontario
CANADA
Simulation Methodology: Top-Down Approach

Palmer, J. D.
School of Information Technology & Engineering
George Mason University
4400 University Drive
Fairfax, VA 22030
USA
Information Systems and Software Productivity

Pimental, S.
Intellitek, Inc
Suite 208
5640 Nicholson Lane
Rockville, MD 20852
USA
*Analogical Reasoning

Porter, A. L.
School of Industrial & Systems Engineering
Georgia Institute of Technology
Atlanta, GA 30332
USA
*Technological Forecasting

Rada, R.
Department of Computer Science
University of Liverpool
PO Box 147
Liverpool L69 3BX
UK
Artificial Intelligence

Rossini, F. A.
School of Industrial & Systems Engineering
Georgia Institute of Technology
Atlanta, GA 30332
USA
*Technological Forecasting

Sage, A. P.
School of Information Technology & Engineering
George Mason University
4400 University Drive
Fairfax, VA 22030
USA
Cognitive Management and Models of Judgement and Choice Processes
Collective Enquiry
Decision Analysis
Decision Making: Information Processing and Organizational Models
Decision Support Systems
Design and Evaluation of Systems
Distributed Decision Making: Information Systems
Expert Systems
Group Decision Making and Voting
Group Decision Support Systems
Human Information Processing
Human Judgement and Decision Rules
Hypothesis Testing
Inference and Impact Analysis
Information Requirements Determination
Knowledge Representation
Multiattribute Utility Theory
Systems Analysis and Modelling: Time Series
Systems Knowledge: Philosophical Perspectives
Systems Methodology

Schum, D. A.
Department of Operations Research & Applied Statistics
School of Information Technology and Engineering
George Mason University
4400 University Drive
Fairfax, VA 22030
USA
Evidentiary Reasoning and Human Information Processing

Sheridan, T. B.
Department of Mechanical Engineering
Massachusetts Institute of Technology
Cambridge, MA 02139
USA
Automation: Social Effects
Human Factors Engineering

Silverman, B. G.
Institute for Artificial Intelligence
The George Washington University
Washington, DC 20052
USA
*Analogical Reasoning

Takeda, E.
Department of Industrial Education
Ashiya University
Rokurokuso
Ashiya 659
JAPAN
Multicriteria Decision Problem

Tien, J. M.
Department of Decision Sciences & Engineering Systems
Rensselaer Polytechnic Institute
Troy, NY 12180-3590
USA
Program Evaluation: A Systems and Model-Based Approach

Truszkowski, W.
Goddard Space Flight Center
Greenbelt, MD 20771
USA
*Analogical Reasoning

Volkema, R. J.
Kogod College of Business Administration
The American University
440 Massachusetts Avenue, NW
Washington, DC 20016
USA
Problem Formulation

Weldon, L. J.
Essex Community College
Baltimore, MD 21237
Human–System Interaction: Information-Presentation Requirements

Wohl, J. G.
Senior Vice President
Alphatech Inc.
2 Burlington Executive Center
111 Middlesex Turnpike
Burlington, MA 01803
USA
Command and Control Information Systems

Zeigler, B. P.
Department of Industrial & Systems Engineering
University of Arizona
Tucson, AZ 85721
USA
Simulation Methodology and Model Manipulation
Simulation: Model-Base Organization and Utilization

SUBJECT INDEX

The Subject Index has been compiled to assist the reader in locating all references to a particular topic in the Encyclopedia. Entries may have up to three levels of heading. Where there is a substantive discussion of the topic, the page numbers appear in ***bold italic*** type. As a further aid to the reader, cross-references have also been given to terms of related interest. These can be found at the bottom of the entry for the first-level term to which they apply. Every effort has been made to make the index as comprehensive as possible and to standardize the terms used.

Abstraction
   analogical reasoning 132
   automated planning 17
   organization decision making 132
   planning 52
   software development 435
   systems acquisition 459
ABSTRIPS 52
Adaptive control
   learning systems 48
Adaptive systems
   history 482
AGE 166
Air conditioning
   human factors engineering 212
Air traffic control
   human factors engineering 210
Algorithms
   chaining 11
   genetic algorithms 5
   learning algorithms 49
      analogical reasoning 7
   systems design engineering 119
AM 49, 333
Analogical reasoning *1*, 128
   abstraction 132
   connectionist models 5
   expert systems 163
   information requirements determination 282
   knowledge representation 330
   recognitional decision making 418
   wholistic decision rules 241
Analysis
   systems methodology *501*
Anticipatory systems
   human information processing 218
ARIEL 1
Artificial intelligence *9*, *42*, 222
   analogical reasoning *1*
   associative memory 1
   automated planning *15*, 51
   automatic deduction 46
   cognitive science *42*
   command and communication systems 32
   computer-assisted instruction 82
   constraint satisfaction problem 459
   data 10
   distributed decision making 142
   expert database systems *159*
   expert systems 13, *162*
   history *481*
   human factors engineering 209
   human information processing *42*, 429
   industrial vision systems *12*
   information requirements determination 282
   information systems *14*
      expert database systems 160
   knowledge acquisition *313*, 332
   knowledge-based simulation 317
   knowledge engineering 13
   knowledge levels 159
   knowledge representation *10*, 323
      semantic networks 6
   learning *11*
   learning systems *48*
   manufacturing computer control 440
   meta-level knowledge 331
   modelling 472
   natural-language processing *12*
   office automation 364
   organizational decision making 142
   planning 463
   probabilistic reasoning 155
   programme languages 10
   reasoning *10*
   robotics 13
   semantic networks 327
   simulation *420*, 428
   Turing test 9
   uncertainty 341
Assessment
   impact analysis 259
   probabilistic risk assessment 22
   technology assessment 22
Associative memory and retrieval *1*, 326, 330
   human associative memory 44
   recognitional decision making 418
Attributes
   heuristic decision rules 240
   independence 346
   multiattribute utility theory 345
   multicriteria decision making 356
   option evaluation *109*
   option generation *103*

ranking 353
Audiovisual media
  group decision support systems 203
Automatic strategic planning 20
Automation
  history *482*
  human factors engineering 209
  inventory control 482
  knowledge-based simulation 318
  limitations 440
  office automation *361*
  planning *15*
  social effects *21*
    office automation 367
  supervisory control *439*
  see also Office automation
Babbage 9
Bacon, F 154
Banking and finance
  expert systems 167
  information systems 284, 299
Bayes methods 336
  belief nets 339
  cognitive bias 226, 451
  cross-impact analysis *259*
  diagnostic problem solving 11
  evidentiary reasoning 152
    parallel semantic networks 6
  hierarchical inference 265
  hypothesis testing 254, 451
  inference updating 263, 337
  intuitive cognition 307
  probabilistic reasoning 263, 451
  scientific method 480
  simplified Bayes rule 337
Behavioral studies
  action theories 101
  behaviorism 43
  cognitive bias 227
  cognitive psychology 44
  collective enquiry *54*
  decision support systems 110
  human information processing *155*
  information systems design *127*
  knowledge acquisition 313, 315
  organizational decision making *96*, 206
  rationality 156
  support system design *449*
  theory of the firm
    organizational decision making 100
Beliefs 46
  a priori knowledge 332
  belief nets 338
  constraint satisfaction problem 459
  default reasoning 342
  Dempster–Schafer rule 340
  nonmonotonic reasoning 342
  philosophy 484

Bias 130, 505
  collective enquiry 55
  group decision support systems 198
  human information processing *226*, *450*
    long-term memory 224
  information requirements determination 281
  knowledge acquisition 313
  probability approaches 226
  psychological decision theory 229
  uncertainty 341
Blackboards
  associative memory and retrieval 4
  automated planning 19
  planning 53
Boole, G 9
Bottom-up methods
  information systems design 135
  planning 53
Brainstorming 57, 500, 514
  decision-problem structuring 107
  group decision support systems 206
  problem formulation 380
  technology assessment 22
Brainwriting 55, 500
  problem formulation 380
C 166
C3I systems *see* Military systems, Organizations
CAD
  expert database systems 158
  graphics 250
  human factors engineering 214
  systems design methodology 120
Cartography
  real-time cartography
    expert database systems 158
CASE *70*, 120
  decision support systems 113
  information systems 287
  information systems design 289
  software productivity 287
Causal inference *see* Causality, Induction, Inference
CD-ROM *see* Information retrieval
Certainty
  decision analysis 87
Chaining 11
  expert systems 165
Channel capacity *see* Information theory
Character recognition *see* Optical character recognition
Choice *see* Judgement (discernment)
Chomsky, N 429
CMDRS 3
Cognitive engines *see* Inference
Cognitive maps *see* Cognitive science, Psychological studies
Cognitive science *42*
  a priori knowledge 332
  analytical cognition *306*
  artificial intelligence *42*

bias 34, 130, *226*, 341, *450*, 505
   knowledge acquisition 313
bounded rationality *309*, *449*
cognition models *45*
cognitive maps
   knowledge representation *327*
cognitive networks 104
cues 431
decision support systems 110, 283
dynamic cognition 310
group decision support systems 198
human factors engineering 217
human information processing 130, 219, *429*
   modelling 220, 223, 306
   problem formulation 378
hypotheses 431
induction 47
information theory 44
intellectual development 30
intuition 488
   recognitional decision making 416
intuitive cognition *306*
judgement models *29*, 324
   intuitive cognition 309
learning 47
misperception
   conflict analysis 494
organizational decision making 142
philosophy of systems 488
Piaget's genetic epistemology 30
planning 51
requirements analysis 396
uncertainty 341
Collective enquiry *54*, 134
   brainstorming 57
   brainwriting 55
   computer-aided meetings environments 204, 365
   cross-impact analysis 262
   Delphi method 58
   dialectical enquiry 381
   forecasting methods 514
   human parallel processing 367
   information requirements determination 281
   knowledge acquisition 313
   nominal group technique 57
   problem formulation 380
   see also Group activity
Command and control systems *see* Military systems, Organizations
Committees *see* Collective enquiry
Communication
   distributed information systems 131
   systems integration 471
Communication theory *see* Information theory
Complex systems
   hierarchical decision making 146
Complexity
   dynamic decision tasks 14, 144, 147

human factors engineering 217
information requirements determination 280
information systems 296
knowledge-based simulation 317
multiattribute utility theory 345
problem formulation 378
software development 435
Computational linguistics 13
Computer-aided systems engineering *see* CASE
Computer architectures
   associative memory 1
      blackboards 4
   group decision support systems *202*
   information systems 298, 300
   knowledge-based simulation *318*
   systems integration 467
Computer pronunciation *see* Pronunciation
Computer software
   group decision support systems *202*
   information systems 287
   real-time software *403*
   systems integration 467
   user interface design 244
Computer–user interfaces *see* Human–system interaction, Interactive terminals
Computer vision *see* Industrial vision systems
Computers
   analog simulation 419
   data communications 471
   data entry devices 211, 246
      office automation 363
   display design 246
      office automation 363
   graphics 249
      knowledge-based simulation *317*
      prototyping 401
      storyboards 314
   icons 249
      knowledge-based simulation 318
      office automation 363
   information-processing psychology 44
   information systems 284
   instruction 81
   local area networks 367
   manufacturing computer control 442
   office automation *361*
   simulation methodology 419, 422, 428
   social effects of automation 26
   software development *429*
   systems design 389
   systems integration 469
   user interface design 244
Concurrency
   data processing 403
   programming languages 405
Configuration management 71
   expert database systems 158
   software development 470

software productivity 293
Conflict analysis 87, **490**
   judgement models 35
   organizational learning 101
Connection machine 3
Connectionism
   analogical reasoning **5**
   learning systems 11, 49
Constraints 500
   constraint satisfaction problem 459
      systems acquisition 460
   information theory 274
CONSTRUCT 142
Control systems
   cybernetics history 482
   data entry devices 211
   dynamic decision making 144
   expert systems 165
   human factors engineering 209
   supervisory control 209
Control theory
   C3I systems 69
   CASE 75
   human information processing models 220
   hypothesis testing 255
   law of requisite variety 275
   optimal control 505
   time series 472
Cost–benefit analysis 77, 508
   systems engineering 487
Cost-effectiveness analysis 77, 508
   computer-based instruction **76**
   systems acquisition 455
Costs
   computer-based instruction 77, 82
   hypothesis testing 254
   modelling 78
   opportunity cost 78
   systems acquisition 456
Creativity
   decision-problem structuring 107
   systems design 118
Crime prevention
   program evaluation 382
Crises
   organizational decision making 140, 142
Criteria
   multicriteria decision making 356
Cross-impact analysis *see* Impact analysis
Cybernetics
   decision-making models 489
   history **481**
   human factors engineering 209
   information-processing psychology 45
DAI *see* Distributed artificial intelligence
Darwin, C 308
Data abstraction
   model-base management systems 114

object-oriented database systems 159
Data acquisition
   information systems 284
Data-flow diagrams *see* Directed graphs
Data processing
   concurrent processing 403
Data security *see* Security of data
Database management systems
   CASE 70
   decision analysis 94
   decision support systems **114**
   expert database systems **158**, 170
   fourth-generation languages 291
   group decision support systems 198
   information systems 285
   logic programming 160
   query languages 286, 291
   simulation 424, 428
Databases
   computer literacy 81
   data dictionaries 288
   data entry 246
   data models 114
   distributed information systems 286
   expert database systems 158
   group decision support systems 202
   information presentation 246
   information requirements
      recognitional decision making 417
   information systems 286, 295
   knowledge representation 323
   object-oriented systems 159
   office automation 363
   relational databases 114, 160
      group decision support systems 198
   simulation 428
Decentralized systems
   dynamic decision making 145
   group decision support systems 197
Decision making
   aggregation 267
   analytic hierarchy process 357
   boot strapping 236, 354
   cascading 267
   cognitive bias 34, 227, 450
   cognitive maps 328
   collective enquiry **54**
   conflict analysis **490**
   conflict model 35
   decision analysis **87**
   decision-making units 137
   decision-problem structuring **103**, 315
      group decision support systems 131
   decision rules **232**
   decision support systems **110**
   distributed decision making **127**, **137**, 197
   dominance 352
   dynamic decision making **144**

intuitive cognition 310
  recognitional decision making 414
enquiry systems 484
expert systems 111
expert systems for management 172
group decision making 96, 115, *183*
  information requirements 193
  social welfare functions 186
group decision support systems *193*
heuristics 239, 450
hierarchical inference 264
hierarchical systems 146
human information processing 223
hypothesis testing 252
inference 129
information requirements determination *278*
inversion 267
knowledge acquisition *314*
learning 129
management control 110, 194
military systems *65*
  garbage-can models 133
  SHOR paradigm 66, 324
modelling 29, *96*, *137*, 203, 220, *233*, 324, 488
  cognitive models 142
  data-flow structures 372
  garbage-can models 98, 132, 138, 489
  incrementalism 99
  knowledge-based simulation 317, 322
  lens model 451
  Markov models 505
  mean-variance models 236
  multiattribute models 235
  organizational-process model 100
  parallel-processing models 140
  Petri net models 370
  prototyping 400
  rational-actor model 98, 233, 449, 488
  rationality 487
  recognition-primed models 414
  satisficing 99, 131, 234, 489
  structural models 279
  structure-based models 138
  supervisory control 446
  utility theory 233
multiattribute utility theory *345*, *356*
multicriteria decision making *355*
operational control and performance 110, 194
organizational decision making *96*, 131, *137*, 196, 488
  information requirements 193
  information structures 368
philosophy 484
Piaget's genetic epistemology 30
political decision making 100
problem formulation *377*
prospect theory 238
rationality *485*

recognitional decision making *414*
schema 328
sequential decision making 144
similarity 32
strategic planning 110, 194
stress 35, 131, 196, 324
supervisory control 439
systems design methodology 122
uncertainty *338*
see also Judgement (discernment)
Decision rooms 205, 366
Decision support systems *110*, 162, 295, 299
  automated planning 20
  behavioral aspects *449*
  C3I systems *64*
  CASE 70
  cognitive style 283
  command and communication systems 32
  conflict analysis 491
  design 37
  design frameworks 113
  distributed decision making 127
  effectiveness 129
  evaluation *115*
  expert systems for management *167*, 170
  group decision support systems 130, *193*
    design frameworks *197*
    evaluations 201
    organizational decision making 96
    software architectures *202*
  human–system interaction 115
  information requirements 279
    recognitional decision making 417
  information structures 368
  knowledge acquisition 313, 332
  knowledge-based simulation 322
  knowledge representation 323
  military systems *64*
  organizational decision making 96
  recognitional decision making 414
  requirements analysis 393
  simulation 423
  supervisory control *442*
  user requirements 467
  see also Knowledge support systems, Management information systems
Decision theory and analysis *87*, 505
  belief nets 338
  cognitive bias 227
  conflict analysis *490*
  decision trees 88
  decision-problem structuring *103*
  elementary decision analysis *87*
  evaluation 95
  group decision making *183*
  hypothesis testing *251*
  influence diagrams 338
  information requirements determination 121

knowledge acquisition 315
lotteries 88
multiattribute decision analysis 92
   decision support systems 115
multiattribute utility theory 91, 235, *345*, *356*
multicriteria decision making *355*
multiobjective optimization 94
preference 89
probability 88
psychological decision theory
   debiasing 229
rational-actor model 449
screening 93
sequential decision theory 146
SMART 91, 235
statistical decision theory 146
subjective utility *237*
systems acquisition 461
uncertainty 338
utility theory 91
Declarative knowledge *see* Knowledge representation
DECMAK 167
Decomposition
   data-flow diagrams
      real-time software design 406
   hierarchical inference 266
   information theory 276
   model-base systems 427
   multiattribute utility theory 345
   software development 435
Deduction 151, 165
   artificial intelligence 46
   learning systems 12
   scientific method 480
   simulation modelling 421
Delphi method 58, 500, 514
   decision-problem structuring 109
   DELPAC system 514
   group decision support systems 203
   knowledge acquisition 313
   philosophy 484
   problem formulation 380
   requirements analysis 396
   technology assessment 22
Dempster–Schafer rule
   belief functions 340
   evidentiary reasoning 153
      parallel semantic networks 6
DENDRAL 13
Design
   decision support systems 113
   displays 210, 246
   environments 121
   human factors engineering 214
   information systems *295*
      behavioral aspects *449*
      distributed decision making *127*
      human–system interaction 244

software tools 289
program evaluation methods 383
prototyping *388*
systems acquisition 454, 459, 461
systems design engineering *116*, 389, 466
   design environments 121
Detection theory *see* Hypotheses, Information theory
Diagnostic inference *see* Deduction, Goals, Inference
Diagrams
   information presentation 129
Dialog generation and management systems
   decision support systems *115*
   group decision support systems 198
   information sharing 128
   information systems 300
   see also Human–system interaction
Differential equations
   simulation 419
Directed graphs
   causal flow diagrams 502
   causal loop diagrams 501
   constraint satisfaction problem 461
   data-flow diagrams
      information structures 372
      information systems development 288, 297
      real-time software design 406
      software development 436
      tasks 409
   functional-flow diagrams 468
   information theory 305
   modelling 472
   operator function models 445
   Petri nets 369
   semantic networks 6
   state-transition diagrams
      real-time software design 406
Displays 210
   design 246
   graphics 249
      knowledge-based simulation 318
   icons 249, 363
      knowledge-based simulation 318
   intuitive cognition 307
   office automation 363
   prototyping 400
   storyboards 314
   text presentation 245
Distributed artificial intelligence
   analogical reasoning 1
   distributed agent architecture 4
Distributed processing
   analogical reasoning 1
   connectionism 7
Distributed systems
   information sharing 128
   information systems *286*
      design *127*, *137*, 199
Document retrieval *see* Information retrieval, Text

retrieval
Documentation
  group decision support systems 204
  information systems 297
  prototyping 399
  software development 470
  system design engineering 125
  systems engineering 74
  task analysis 214
DSSD 289
Dynamic decision making *144*
  intuitive cognition 310
  recognitional decision making 414
Dynamic programming
  CASE 75
  decision analysis 90
Dynamical systems
  entropy 302
Economics
  cost–benefit analysis 77
  cost-effectiveness analysis 77
  opportunity cost 78
  rational-actor model 98, 233, 449, 488
  rationality 486
  resource allocation
    computer-based instruction 76
  systems analysis methods 503
  theory of the firm
    organizational decision making 100
  value of information 134, 200
Education
  computer-assisted instruction 81
  computer-based instruction *76*
Educational computing *76*, 216
Effectiveness
  computer-based instruction 78, 83
  decision support systems 129
  systems design engineering 117, 121
  see also Efficiency, Evaluation
Efficiency
  organizational structure modelling 140
  systems design engineering 117, 121
  see also Effectiveness
Electronic mail *362*
  computer conferences 365
  computer literacy 81
  expert systems for management 172
  group decision support systems 197, 204
  voice mailboxes 362
Employment
  social effects of automation 23
EMYCIN 166
Encoding
  human information processing 221
  information theory 304
Entropy 272, *302*
  dynamical systems 302
  maximum entropy principle 304
  probability intervals 340
  see also Information theory
Ergonomics *see* Human factors engineering
Errors
  boot strapping 236
  cognitive bias 227, 268
  conflict analysis 494
  human factors engineering 215
  hypothesis testing 251
  organizational learning 101
  problem formulation 377
Estimation theory 251, *474*, 504
  C3I systems 69
  human information processing models 220
  system identification 478
  trend extrapolation 476
Evaluation
  computer-based instruction 80
  decision analysis 92, 95
  decision-problem structuring 103, 314
  decision support systems *115*
  design 383
  distributed information systems 135
  forecasting 517
  group decision support systems 201
  hypothesis testing 254
    information systems engineering 466
  knowledge representation 331
  logical reasoning 269
  model-based approach *382*
  modelling 80
  multiattribute utility theory 353
  options *109*
  recognitional decision making 416
  systems-based approach *382*
  systems design methodology 119
  systems engineering *125*
  technical performance measurement 471
  see also Effectiveness
Evidentiary reasoning 130, *151*, 263
  parallel semantic networks 6
Experiment
  simulation methodology 422, 425, 427
Expert database systems *157*, 170
Expert systems 13, *162*
  belief systems 46
  CASE 293
  decision making 111
  expert database systems *157*, 170
  financial computing 167
  group decision support systems 203
  history *482*
  human information processing 156
  human–system interaction 166, 217
  information requirements determination 282
  knowledge acquisition 165, 313, 332
  knowledge-based simulation 316, 318
  knowledge bases 163

knowledge representation 164, 169, 323
learning systems 49
management decision making *167*
medical diagnostic computing
    Quack 3
model-base management systems 114
model-base systems 170
modelling *170*, 472
network analysis 171
office automation 364
probabilistic reasoning 155
problem solving 164
production systems 163
programming languages 166
rule-based systems 30
shells 166, 170
simulation 420
software engineering 293
systems acquisition methods 464
taxonomy 162
validation 169
Explanation
  hypotheses 431
  knowledge-based systems 333
  learning systems 12
EXSYS 170
Facsimile machines 362
Failure *see* System failure and recovery
Feature analysis
  real-time cartography
    expert database systems 158
Feedback
  dynamic decision making 14, 145, 147
  human factors engineering 209
  human neuromotor system 219
Feynman, R 308
Filtering and prediction theory 476
Financial computing 284
  auditing 168
  expert systems 167
  information systems 299
  portfolio management 167
Finite-state machines
  information theory 274
First-order predicate calculus 10
  automated planning 18
  automatic deduction 47
Flexible manufacturing systems 441
  supervisory control *439*
Flight plans 17
  military systems 65
Flight simulation *see* Simulators
Flow charts
  prototyping 399
  software productivity 288
Forecasting 501, 504
  cognitive bias 229
  decision-problem structuring 109

Delphi method 514
estimation theory 474
group decision support systems 203
impact analysis 259
modelling 472, 516
monitoring 514
principles 511
regression analysis 474
scenarios 516
scientific method 481
statistical analysis 473
systems acquisition 454
technological forecasting 22, *511*
time series *472*, 503, 515
see also Planning, Strategies
Formal logic
  expert database systems 160
  first-order predicate calculus 10
    automated planning 18
    knowledge representation 10
  fuzzy logic 175
  fuzzy reasoning 155
  knowledge representation 164, 325
  logical reasoning 267
  Lukasiewicz logic 175
  multiagent reasoning 19
  nonmonotonic logic 19
  psycho-logic 327
  scientific method 480
  situation calculus
    automated planning 18
  temporal logics 20
  uncertainty 338
Fourier analysis
  information theory 302
Fourth-generation languages
  group decision support systems 203
  office automation 364
  software productivity 287, 291
  see also Very-high-level languages
Frames
  human information processing models 222
  knowledge representation 164, 325, *329*
    expert systems for management 169
  semantic networks 327
  structural modelling 501
Functional analysis
  functional-flow diagrams 468
  information theory 302
  knowledge-based simulation 321
  systems integration 468
Fuzzy reasoning 155, *175*
  production systems 326
  technology assessment 22
Fuzzy systems
  decision analysis 95
  expert database systems 157
  fuzzy multiobjective programming 358

uncertainty *339*
value of information 280
Game theory 87
   conflict analysis 491
   forecasting models 516
   group decision making 192
   hypergames 494
   metagames 491
Gantt charts 506
GARCORG 139
Genetic algorithms
   analogical reasoning 5
Goals
   goal programming 358
   human information processing 218
   multicriteria decision making 356
   rationality 486
GODDESS 333
GPS 43
   automated planning 16, 52
Graphics *see* Computers, Displays
Graphs
   belief nets 338
   cognitive maps 328
   computer graphics 250
   data flow diagrams
      information structures 372
      information systems development 288, 297
   influence diagrams 338
   modelling 472
   Petri nets 369
   preference curves 189
Group activity 115
   collective enquiry *54*
   decision making 115, *183*
      information requirements 193
   distributed decision making *127, 137*
   group decision support systems 130, *193*
      software architectures *202*
   groupthink 97
   organizational decision making *96, 137*
   problem solving 30
   social judgement theory 128, 451
   task analysis 214
   voting *183*, 506
   see also Collective enquiry
Heating systems
   human factors engineering 212
Hegel, G. W. F. 485
Heterarchical systems
   information systems design 135
   supervisory control 446
Heuristics 11, 37, 337
   decision analysis 93
   decision rules *239*
   decision support systems 115
   evaluation 506
   human information processing *450*

intuitive cognition 307
knowledge representation 323
organizational decision making 143
Hierarchical systems
   associative memory and retrieval 2
   automated planning 17
   data structured systems 289
   databases 114
   distributed decision making 137
   dynamic decision making 145
   frames 329
   inference *263*
   knowledge-based simulation 317
   menus 248
   model-base systems 426
   object-oriented database systems 159
   organizational decision making 194
   planning 51
   structured analysis 297
   supervisory control 446
Holistic methods
   decision rules *233*
   history 480
   knowledge representation 323
   software development 429, 436
Human factors engineering *209*
   decision rooms 205
   group decision support systems 206
   information presentation *244*
   information processing *217*
   office automation 367
   task analysis 212
Human information processing *42, 128, 218, 223,* 284, *429*
   analytical cognition *306*
   artificial intelligence *42*
   behavioral studies *155*
   bias *226, 450*
      regret theory 242
   bounded rationality 309, 430
   cognitive maps 328
   debiasing 230
   decision support systems 110
   distributed decision making 142
   encoding 221
   evidentiary reasoning *151*
   filtering 225
   group decision making 97, 142
   group decision support systems 194
   heuristics 450
   hierarchical inference 264
   human factors engineering *217*
   information requirements determination 278
   information structures 370
   information systems design 37
   information theory 218
   intuitive cognition *306*
   knowledge acquisition 332

law of requisite variety 379
learning 47, 431
limitations 121, 130, 378, **449**
   bias **226**
   dynamic decision making 144, 310
   information requirements determination 281
   information structures 368
logical reasoning 268
memory-based reasoning 3
modelling **29**, **220**, 324
   intuitive cognition 307
   physiological models **223**
   prototyping 400
neuromotor system 219
organization decision making 142
philosophy 484
physiological studies 432
Piaget's genetic epistemology 39
planning 51
problem formulation 378
rationality **485**
sensory perception 218
software development **429**
stress 35, 131, 196, 324
supervisory control 442
time scales 430
uncertainty 341
Human–system interaction **209**
automation 25
computer-assisted instruction 81, 216
computer language interface 217
decision rooms 205, 366
decision support systems 115
expert database systems 161
expert systems 166, 217
fuzzy set theory 339
group decision support systems 206
information presentation **244**
information processing **217**
information systems 129, 295, 333
interface design 244
intuitive cognition 307
knowledge acquisition 314
knowledge-based simulation 318
knowledge representation 330
office automation 362, 367
recognitional decision making 417
software development 429
supervisory control 439
user profiling 395
Hypotheses
  analogical reasoning 241, 330
  decision-problem structuring 108, 315
  generation 431
  intuitive cognition 307
  learning 50
  logical reasoning 269
  medical diagnostic computing 3

military decision making **67**
probabilistic reasoning 154, 264, 337
scientific method 480
systems design methodology 118
testing **251**, 315, 431, 474, 504
Icons *see* Computers, Displays
Ideawriting *see* Brainwriting
Identification
  system identification **478**
  time series modelling 477
Image processing *see* Picture processing
Impact analysis **259**, 501
  cross-impact analysis
    decision-problem structuring 109
  Delphi method 514
  forecasting models 516
Indifference *see* Utility theory
Induction 47, 151, 165
  Baconian probability 154
  Bayes' rule 152
  learning systems 12
  scientific method 480
  simulation modelling 421
Industrial robots
  automated planning 20
Industrial vision systems
  artificial intelligence **12**
Inference
  abductive reasoning 151
  aggregation 267
  analogical reasoning **1**, 128
    information requirements determination 282
    knowledge representation 330
    recognitional decision making 418
    wholistic decision rules 241
  analytical cognition 306
  Bayes' rule 152, 263, 337
  cascading 267
  causal inference 267
  causal reasoning 165
  chaining 165
  cognitive engine 165
  compositional rule 175
  decomposition 266
  default reasoning 342
  Dempster–Schafer rule 153, 267
  diagnostic inference 267
  evidentiary reasoning 130, **151**, 263
    parallel semantic networks 6,
  expert systems **165**
  expert systems for management 167
  forecasting 474
  fuzzy reasoning 155, **175**
  goal-directed reasoning 165
  hierarchical inference **263**
  human information processing 47, 128, **155**
  hypothesis testing 474
  impact analysis **259**

intuitive cognition 306
inversion 267
logical reasoning 267
memory-based reasoning 3
multiagent reasoning 19
nonmonotonic reasoning 47, 342
   automated planning 19
possibilistic reasoning 151
probabilistic reasoning 11, 152, 263, 337, 450
   Baconian probability 154
   human information processing 231
problem solving 51
scientific method 480
simulation modelling 423
uncertainty *341*
updating 263
see also Problem solving
Information presentation *244*
Information processing *217*, 284
   hierarchical inference 265
   human factors engineering *217*
   information requirements determination 278
   knowledge representation 324
   organizational information structures *368*
   probabilistic information processing 265
   uncertainty *336*
   see also Human information processing, Organizations
Information requirements *278*, 500
   application-level requirements 280
   decision support systems 279, 417
   group decision support systems *193*, 201
   inquiry systems 485
   knowledge acquisition 313
   organizational decision making 193
   organizational-level requirements 280
   programming languages 282
   recognitional decision making *417*
   software engineering 282
   systems design methodology *120*
   value of information 134, 279
   see also Requirements analysis
Information retrieval 285
   analogical reasoning 1
   artificial intelligence 331
   associative retrieval 2
   CD-ROM 364
   expert database systems 157
   group decision support systems 199
   model-base systems *425*
   office automation 363
   text retrieval 363
      CMDRS 3
   see also Text retrieval
Information systems *284*, *295*
   artificial intelligence *14*
      expert database systems 160
   C3I systems *64*

computers 469
configuration 284
data communications 471
data structured systems 289
database management systems 285
decision analysis 93
decision support systems *110*
design 36, *295*
   behavioral aspects *449*
   distributed decision making 127
   human–system interaction 244
   meta-level knowledge 331
   requirements analysis *393*
   software tools 289
   systems engineering approaches 298
distributed decision making *127*, 199
distributed systems *286*
documentation 297
human information processing 284
human–system interaction *244*
information management 285
information sharing 128, 198
information theory 303
inquiry systems 485
integration 203, 206, 207, *466*
intuitive cognition 307
judgement models 32
knowledge representation 324
life cycles 297
office automation 363
operational systems 295, 299
programming languages 286
prototyping 292
requirements analysis 295
software architecture 298, 300
software productivity *287*
structured analysis 289, 297
systems engineering 298, 466
technical performance measurement 47
text presentation 245, 285
uncertainty *336*
see also Decision support systems, Management information systems
Information theory *271*, 279, *301*
   CASE 75
   channel capacity 274
   channels 303
   cognitive science 44
   detection theory 251, 276
   dynamical systems 302
   entropy 302
   human information processing 121, 151, 218
   law of requisite variety 275
      problem formulation 379
   maximum entropy principle 304
   N-dimensional information theory 272, 302
   partition law of information rates 277
   probability intervals 340

535

questionnaires 305
sources 303
systems analysis *272*
value of information 134, 200, 279
see also Entropy
Inheritance
object-oriented database systems 159
semantic networks 6, 10
Input–output analysis 472, 504
information requirements determination 121
substantive rationality 487
system identification 479
systems analysis methods 503
Instruction *see* Education, Training
Integration of systems *see* Systems integration
Intelligence 9
Piaget's genetic epistemology 30
Intelligent information systems *see* Artificial intelligence, Information systems
Interactive terminals
CASE 75
data-entry devices 211, 246
office automation 363
display design 211, 246
group decision support systems 203
information systems 284
knowledge acquisition 314
menus 248
mouse 249, 363
office automation *363*
Interfaces *see* Human–system interaction, Interactive terminals
Interpretation
systems methodology *505*
Intuition *see* Cognitive science
Inventory control
automation history 482
supervisory control 444
Issue formulation *499*
collective enquiry 54
decision analysis 87, 92
decision support systems 111
evaluation 125
group decision support systems 203
hypothesis testing 251
knowledge acquisition 314
logical reasoning 269
problem formulation *377*
systems design methodology 120
JSD 289, 435
Judgement (discernment) *232*
analogical reasoning 330
behavioral studies 156
cognitive bias 450
cognitive maps 328
collective enquiry 55
conflict analysis 490
decision analysis 91

decision support systems 110
evidentiary reasoning 151
group decision making 97
heuristics 239, 450
hierarchical inference 264
holistic methods 233
human information processing 128, 223
information requirements determination 278
intuitive cognition 306
modelling *29*, 324
bias 226
decision rule models *232*
intuitive cognition 309
lens model 451
SHOR paradigm 66, 324
stress-based models 35, 131, 196
rationality 486
schema 328
social judgement theory 128, *451*, 505
uncertainty *341*
value judgement 499
wholistic methods 241
see also Decision making
Jurisprudence
evidentiary reasoning 152
legal rationality 487
social welfare functions 192
Kant, I. 484
KBS *see* Simulation
KEE 158, 166, 317, 320
Knowledge acquisition *313*, *331*
collective enquiry *54*
decision making *314*
expert systems 165
expert systems for management 167
human information processing 225
information systems design
distributed decision making 127
knowledge-based simulation 322
learning systems 49
prototyping *393*
storyboards 314
task profiling 393
validation 225
value of information 134
see also Requirements analysis
Knowledge bases *9*, 325
associative memory and retrieval 1
expert database systems 159
expert systems *163*
expert systems for management 167
group decision support systems 199, 206
information requirements
recognitional decision making 417
information systems design 134
knowledge acquisition 314, 332
knowledge-based simulation *316*
knowledge levels 159

learning systems 49
meta-level knowledge 165
problem solving 30
simulation 420, 428
software productivity 293
supervisory control 439
systems acquisition information *457*
systems design engineering 118
Knowledge engineering 13, 313
expert database systems 158
knowledge-based simulation 318
protocol analysis 167
simulation 318
systems design engineering 117
uncertainty 341
see also Artificial intelligence, Expert systems
Knowledge representation *10*, *323*
a priori knowledge 332
analogical reasoning 1, 330
associative memory and retrieval 1, 326
cognitive maps 327
decision making
organizational decision making 142
decision support systems 115
declarative knowledge 10, 316, *323*
evaluation 331
expert systems 164
first-order predicate calculus 10
frames 329
group decision support systems 199
information systems design
distributed decision making 127
knowledge acquisition 331
learning 331
modelling 472
procedural knowledge 10, 316, *323*
production systems 326
schema 328
scripts 330
semantic networks 6, 10, 326
software productivity 293
value of information 134
Knowledge support systems 194
behavioral aspects *449*
uncertain information processing *336*
see also Decision support systems, Information systems, Management information systems
Language (natural)
artificial intelligence *12*
conceptual dependency diagrams 10
expert systems 171
fuzzy set theory 339
human–system interaction
expert systems 166
imprecision *339*
learning 331
memory models 46
planning 53

programming languages
office automation 364
semantic networks 326
Large-scale systems
information systems 296
systems engineering 73
Law of requisite variety *see* Information theory
Learning 37, *331*
decision making 129
organizational decision making 142
decision-making models 489
dialectic learning 101
double-loop learning 101
errors 101
human information processing *47*, 431
modelling 222
induction 50
instructional effectiveness 78
organizational learning *100*, 193
group decision support systems 194
problem solving 29
single-loop learning 101
skill 49
social judgement theory 452
Learning systems 9, *11*
algorithms 49
analogical reasoning 7
artificial intelligence 47
connectionism 11, 49
genetic algorithms 5
history 482
inventory control 483
knowledge bases 49
memory-based reasoning 3
self-organizing systems 48
Least-squares methods 475
Leibnitz, G W von 484
LEX 49
Life cycles 497
costing 71
information systems development *297*
systems design engineering 116, 123, 389
systems engineering 73, 466
software productivity 291
Likelihood ratios
cross-impact analysis 262
hypothesis testing 254
Linear programming
CASE 75
decision support systems 115
expert systems for modelling 170
inventory control 482
judgement theories 128
Karmarkar's algorithm 379
multiattribute decision analysis 93
multiobjective linear programming 358
LISP 10, 166
knowledge-based simulation 317

Local area networks
  group decision support systems 203
  office automation *367*
  systems integration 471
Locke, J. 484
Logic (formal) *see* Formal logic
Logic programming
  expert database systems *160*
  expert systems for modelling 171
Logistics
  expert systems for management 168
Lotteries *see* Decision theory and analysis, Utility theory
LT 47
Lukasiewicz logic
  fuzzy reasoning 175
Machine learning *see* Learning systems
Machine pronunciation *see* Pronunciation
Machine reasoning *10*, 43
  see also Inference
Machine translation *see* Translation
MACSYMA 13
Maintenance
  automation history 482
  human factors engineering 214
  software development 432
  systems acquisition 456
  systems engineering 126
  systems integration 469
Man–machine systems *see* Human–system interaction
Management *171*
  decision making 110
  expert systems *167*
  hypothesis testing 256
  information requirements determination 280
  judgement models 29
  knowledge-based simulation 317
  organizational information structures 368
  organizational management 97, 142, 193
  resource allocation 167
  social effects of automation 25
  systems acquisition 454
Management information systems *112*, 284, 295
  decision support systems *110*
  dialectical inquirer 485
  expert systems *167*
  group decision support systems 193
    software architecture 202
  organizational decision making 96
  predictive systems 112
  user requirements 467
  see also Decision support systems, Information systems, Knowledge support systems
Management science
  decision support systems 110
  requirements analysis 395
  systems design methodology 120
Manufacturing computer control

  flexible manufacturing systems 441
  history *482*
  supervisory control *439*
Markov methods 505
Marx, K. 515
Matching 11
  analogical reasoning 1
  associative memory and retrieval 2
  recognitional decision making 418
Materials handling
  supervisory control 444
Mathematical programming 505
  multiattribute decision analysis 94
Matrix methods
  interaction matrices 500
  organizational information structures 371
Maximum entropy principle 304
MBR *see* Memory-based reasoning
MBRtalk 3
Means–ends analysis 43
  analogical reasoning 330
  automated planning 16
  knowledge representation 325
  planning 52
  problem solving 325
  substantive rationality 487
Medical diagnostic computing
  memory-based reasoning
    Quack 3
  MYCIN 13
  NEOMYCIN 13
  ONCOCIN 13
Meetings
  collective enquiry 54
  computer-aided meetings environments *204*
  decision rooms 205, 366
  group decision support systems 198
  office automation *365*
  scheduling
    expert systems for management 168
  teleconferencing 204, 365
Memory (computers)
  active memory 4
  associative memory *1*
    recognitional decision making 418
  expert database systems 159
  group decision support systems 206
  information systems *285*
  knowledge representation 324
  WORM 364
Memory (physiological) 103
  associative memory 44
  display design 211
  encoding 221
  human information processing *224*, 378, *430*
    modelling 221
  modelling 45, 224
  semantic memory 45

Memory-based reasoning 3
Menus
  human–system interaction 115, *248*
  knowledge-based simulation 318
Meta-level knowledge 129, 165, 324
  intelligent systems design *331*
  systems design engineering 117
Microcomputers
  CASE 75
  distributed information systems 286
  expert systems 166
  group decision support systems 202
  local area networks 367
  office automation 361
Military systems
  automated planning 20
  automation 26
  C3I systems *64*
  command and communication systems 32
  command and control 65, 295
  decision making *65*
    garbage-can models 133, 138
    recognitional decision making 416
  distributed information systems 131
  hierarchical decision making 146
  knowledge-based simulation 317
  prototyping 399
  systems acquisition 456
  systems analysis
    history 481
Mill, J S 154
Minicomputers
  CASE 75
Model-base management systems
  decision analysis 94
  decision support systems *114*
  group decision support systems 198
Model-base systems
  expert systems for management 170
  knowledge-based simulation 316
  simulation 423, *425*
  systems design engineering 118
Modelling *419*, *421*, 425
  ARMA models 478
  artificial intelligence 472
  autoregressive models 478
  cognition 45
  conflict analysis 490
  costs 78
  data flow diagrams
    information structures 372
    information systems development 288, 297
  data models 114
  decision making 132, 324
    dynamic decision making 145
    lens model 451
    Petri net models 370
    rationality 487

  recognition-primed models 414
  supervisory control 446
  decision-problem structuring 109
  decision rules *232*
  differential equations 472
  discrete-event modelling 472
  dynamic decision making 145
  estimation theory 474
  evaluation 80
  expert systems *170*
  finite-state models 472
  forecasting 472, 516
  human factors engineering 212
  human information processing 29, *220*
  information structures *368*
  information systems design 299
  intuitive cognition *306*
  judgement 29, *232*, 324
    knowledge-based simulation 317
  knowledge-based simulation *316*
  memory *45*, 224
  military decision making 67
  model integration
    expert systems 171
  Monte Carlo methods 419
  moving-average models 478
  organizational decision making *96*, 132, *137*, 488
  organizational information structures *368*
  philosophy 484
  program evaluation *382*
  prototyping 400
    software engineering 292
  queuing 472
  regression analysis 474
  scientific method 480
  software development 433, 435
  systems analysis methods *502*
  time series *472*
  see also Simulation, Structural modelling
Modus ponens
  fuzzy reasoning 175
MOLGEN 52
Monitoring
  forecasting 514
Monte Carlo methods 419
  expert systems for modelling 170
  knowledge-based simulation 321
Mouse
  human–system interaction 249
    office automation 363
  knowledge-based simulation 318
Multi-user computer systems
  CASE 75
  group decision support systems 203
  local area networks 367
Multiattribute utility theory 91, *92*, 103, *345*, *356*, 505
  CASE 75
  decision analysis 345, 353

decision-making models 235
group decision support systems 203
indifference methods 354
recognitional decision making 416
systems acquisition 458
technology assessment 22
value of information 134, 200
Multicriteria decision making *355*
   analytic hierarchy process 357
   conflict analysis ***490***
   fuzzy multiobjective programming 358
   goal programming 358
   multiattribute utility theory ***345***, 356
   vector optimization problem 357
Multiobjective optimization
   decision analysis 94
MYCIN 13, 51, 155, 165, 166, 337, 482
Natural language *see* Language (natural)
NEOMYCIN 13
NETL 6
Network analysis
   expert systems 171
Network methods
   analogical reasoning 1
   belief nets 338
   connectionism ***6***
   constraint networks 459
   data models 114
   distributed information systems 286
   frames 329
   modelling
      prototyping 400
   organizational information structures 369
   planning 506
   see also Petri nets
Networks (computers) *see* Computers
Neural networks
   simulation
      learning systems 11
Newton, I 308
NGT *see* Nominal group technique
Nominal group technique 57, 500, 514
   group decision support systems 203
   information requirements determination 121
   problem formulation 380
Nonlinear programming
   CASE 75
Nuclear power stations
   automation 26
   simulators for training 216
Object-oriented systems 435
   expert database systems 159
   expert systems for modelling 170
   knowledge-based simulation 317, 318, 321
   programming for simulation 420
Object synthesis
   systems acquisition ***459***
Objectives 500

multicriteria decision making 356
systems acquisition 458
OCR *see* Optical character recognition
Office automation *361*
   decision rooms 205, 366
   group decision support systems 202
   history ***482***
   telecommuting 364
Operations research ***498***
   automated planning 15
   CASE 75
   decision support systems 110
   expert systems for management 168
   inventory control 482
   mathematical programming 505
   simulation and modelling 419
   systems design methodology 120
OPS5 166
Optical character recognition
   office automation 362
Optimal control 505
   C3I systems 69
   human information processing models 220
   knowledge acquisition 333
Optimization
   CASE 75
   constraint satisfaction problem 459
   fuzzy multiobjective programming 358
   goal programming 358
   inventory control 483
   multiobjective linear programming 358
   Pareto optimality 353, 356
   recognitional decision making 416
   surrogate worth trade-off method 358
   systems acquisition 458
   systems analysis methods 504
   systems design engineering 117
   technical rationality 486
   vector optimization problem 357
Options 500
   evaluation attributes ***109***
   generating methods ***103***, 315
   military decision making 67
   organization 488
   organizational decision making 98
   schema 328
   systems design methodology 118
   see also Alternatives
Organizations ***96***, 132, 137, 193, 197
   activity profiling 397
   C3 systems 137
   command and control 137
   compatibility testing 397
   decision making 96, 130, 131
      cardinal social welfare functions 191
      hierarchical decision making 146
      information requirements 193
      modelling 98, ***137***, 138, ***488***

distributed decision making
   information systems design *131*
   group decision support systems 194, 202
   information processing *96*, 137
      decision support systems 110
   information requirements
        determination 280
   information structures *368*
   management 97, 193
   philosophy of systems 488
   planning environments 379
   scientific method 480
   social judgement theory 128, 451
   stakeholders 379
   technical rationality 486
Parallel processing
   active memory 4
   analogical reasoning 1
   associative memory and retrieval *3*
   connection machine 3
   connectionism 6
   genetic algorithms 5
   human parallel processing 367
   learning systems 11
   organizational decision making 140
   semantic networks 6
   software productivity 288
      Petri nets 290
Parameter estimation *see* Estimation theory,
      Identification
Pareto optimality 353, 356
PASCAL 10
Pattern matching *see* Matching
Pattern recognition
   human information processing 225
   information theory 306
   learning systems 48
PCs *see* Microcomputers
Perception (sensory) *see* Physiological studies
Performance indices 71
   C3I systems 70
   human factors engineering 215
   technical performance measurement 471
Personal computers *see* Microcomputers
PERT
   systems acquisition 456
Petri nets *369*
   C3I systems simulation 70
   organizational decision-making models 140
   organizational information structures 369
   software development 436
   software productivity 290
Philosophy
   scientific method 480
   systems concepts 480, *484*
Physics
   intuitive cognition 308
Physiological studies

human factors engineering 209
human information processing
   modelling *224*
   problem formulation 378
   memory 432
   neuromotor system 219
   sensory perception 210, 218, 225
Picture processing
   artificial intelligence 12
Pierce, C S 151
Planning *51*, 122, 504
   artificial intelligence 463
   automated planning *15*, 52
      decision support systems 20
      multiagent planning 19
      single-agent planning 16
   cognitive bias 229
   decision support systems 295
   Gantt charts 506
   hierarchical inference 264
   hierarchical planning 52
   mathematical programming 505
   military systems 65
   network methods 506
   opportunistic planning 45, 53,
   organizational decision making 142
   organizational environments 379
   problem formulation *377*
   production systems 326
   scheduling
      expert systems for management 168
   strategic planning
      computer-aided meetings environments 204
      decision support systems 110
      group decision support systems 194
      monitoring 514
   supervisory control 439
   systems acquisition 455
      object synthesis *459*
   systems design methodology 120
   systems engineering 74
   see also Forecasting, Scheduling
Policy capture *see* Social judgement theory
Politics
   decision making 100
   muddling through models 489
   rationality 486
   voting 183
Possibility theory
   inference 151
Pragmatics
   scientific method 480
Preference
   conflict analysis 491
   decision analysis 89
   group decision making 183, 188
   independence 346
   multiattribute utility theory 345

ranking 353
see also Ranking
Probability
   Baconian system 154
   Bayes' rule 152, 336
   CASE 75
   cognitive bias 226
   cross-impact analysis *259*
   decision analysis 88
   decision-problem structuring 107
   Dempster–Schafer rule 153, 267, 340
   evidentiary reasoning 152
   forecasting 473
   fuzzy probabilities 155
   human information processing 231, 450
   hypothesis testing *252*, 474
   inference 152, 263, 337
   information processing 265
   information theory 272, 302
   intervals 340
   intuitive cognition 307
   maximum entropy principle 304
   Neyman–Pearson criterion 253
   problem solving 11
   risk assessment 22
   scientific method 480
   second-order probability distributions 341
   subjective utility 238
   uncertainty *336*, 340
   see also Bayes methods
Problem solving *51*, 129
   analogical reasoning *1*
   analysis 278
   assumption testing 381
   automatic deduction 46
   brainstorming 57, 107, 380
   brainwriting 55, 380
   chaining 11
   cognition models 45
   cognitive bias 227, 450
   collective enquiry *54*
   complexity 378
   decision making 130
   decision-problem structuring *103*, 315
   Delphi method 58, 380
   diagnosis
      expert systems for management 168
   distributed decision making 127, 138
   formulation 278
   generate-and-test approach 11
   group decision support systems 130, *193*
   human information processing 223, 431
      problem formulation 378
   interpretation 278
   interpretive structural modelling 381
   knowledge acquisition 313, 332
   knowledge-based behavior 30
   knowledge representation 323, 324

   learning 29
   matching 11
   means–ends analysis 325
   modelling *29*
   multiattribute utility theory *345*, *356*
   multicriteria decision making *355*
   nominal group technique 57, 380
   opportunistic processing 45
   organizational problem solving 397
   philosophy 484
   probabilistic reasoning 11
   problem formulation *377*
   problem–solution pairs 4
   rule-based behavior 30
   searching 10
   skill-based behavior 30
   software development 432
   synectics 107
   systems design methodology 120
   systems engineering 499
   see also Inference
Procedural knowledge *see* Knowledge representation
Process control
   dynamic decision making 144, 147
   human factors engineering 210
   supervisory control *439*
Procurement *see* Systems procurement
Production control
   expert systems for management 168
Production rules
   decision support systems design 113
Production systems
   expert systems 163
   knowledge representation 325, *326*
   systems design methodology 119
   uncertainty 338
   see also Rules
Program evaluation and review technique *see* PERT
Programming
   CASE 75
   cognitive science 42
   computer literacy 81
   environments 75, 288
      knowledge-based simulation 318
   flow charts 288
   human information processing *429*
   information systems 287, 296
   object-oriented programming 420
   prototyping 390
   real-time software *403*
   software productivity 288
Programming languages
   artificial intelligence 10
   concurrent languages 405
   decision support systems 113
   expert systems *166*
   fourth-generation languages
      office automation 364

group decision support systems 203
information requirements determination 282
information systems 286, 287
knowledge-based simulation 317
natural-language software
  office automation 364
simulation languages 420
very-high-level languages 166
see also Fourth-generation languages, Very-high-level languages
PROLOG 10, 170, 317
  expert database systems *160*
  expert systems 166
Pronunciation
  computer pronunciation
    MBRtalk 3
Protocol analysis 167, 169
  knowledge acquisition 315
  knowledge-based simulation 321
  requirements analysis 395
Prototypes
  systems design methodology 119
Prototyping *388*
  flow charts 399
  information systems 292
  knowledge-based simulation 321
  modelling 400
  recognitional decision making 418
  requirements analysis 393
  software development 436
  software productivity 292
  storyboards *314*, 400
  systems acquisition 455, 458
  systems design methodology 390
Psychological studies
  cognitive maps
    knowledge representation *327*
  cognitive psychology 44
    bias 226, 451
  decision theory and analysis
    debiasing 229
  errors 215
  human factors engineering 209
  human information processing 429
    modelling 221, 223
    problem formulation 378
  illusions 227
  information-processing psychology *43*
  intuitive cognition *307*
  learning 50, 431
  perception 147
  psycho-logic 327
  requirements analysis 395
  sensory perception 147
  social judgement theory 451
  stress 35, 131, 196
    decision rules 242
  uncertainty *341*

workload 215, 218
Quack 3
Qualitative analysis
  artificial intelligence 14
Questionnaires 500
  Delphi method 59
  forecasting methods 514
  information theory 305
  knowledge acquisition 313
  requirements analysis 395
Queuing
  CASE 75
  modelling 472
  systems analysis methods 504
Ranking 353
  social judgement theory 505
  see also Preference
Rationality *485*
  bounded rationality 99, 131, 140, 196, 234, *309*, 430, *449*, 489
  conflict analysis 493
  decision-making models 98, 131, 140, 196, 233, 489
  human information processing 156
  intuitive cognition 309
  knowledge representation 325
  multiattribute utility theory 345
  quasirationality 309
  uncertainty 341
Real-time systems
  DARTS 406
  dynamic decision making 146
  software design *403*
Reasoning see Inference
Recognitional decision making *414*
Reconstructability analysis 276
Redundancy
  distributed information systems 128
  systems reliability 470
Regression analysis *474*, 504
  CASE 75
  decision-making models 354
  expert systems for modelling 170
  hypothesis testing 476
  knowledge acquisition 315, 333
  problem formulation 381
  social judgement theory 128
  system identification 478
  time series 476
  trend extrapolation 476
Relational databases see Databases
Reliability
  automation 26
  human factors engineering 214
  systems engineering 71
  systems integration 469
Requirements analysis 71, *313*, *393*, *499*
  group decision support systems 193

information presentation
  human–system interaction **244**
information systems design 295
organization profiling 397
software requirements engineering 290
storyboards 314, 400
systems acquisition 454
systems design methodology **120**, **122**, 390, **393**
systems integration 467
task profiling 393
user profiling 395
value of information 134, 279
see also Information requirements, Knowledge acquisition
Requirements determination
  information requirements **278**
Resource allocation
  computer-based instruction 76
  expert systems for management 167
  information systems 285
  mathematical programming 505
  military decision making 66
  organizational decision making 98
  systems acquisition 458
REX 170
Risk 71
  decision analysis 87
  decision modelling 203
  group decision making 183
  hypothesis testing 254
  probabilistic risk assessment
    technology forecasting 22
  problem formulation 377
  prospect theory 239
  systems acquisition 455, 460
  utility theory 90
Robotics 13
  automated planning 15, 19
  concurrent processing 403
  data flow diagrams 406, 411
  flexible manufacturing systems
    supervisory control **444**
  history 483
  human factors engineering 209
  real-time software **403**
  task analysis 411
  task synchronization 413
ROSIE 166
Rule-based systems 13
  expert systems 162, 169
  group decision support systems 197
  recognitional decision making 416
  simulation 429
  systems acquisition 463
  uncertainty 337
Rules 10, 472
  decision rules **232**
  heuristics 450

knowledge representation 164, **326**
problem solving 30
production rules 163
scientific method 480
simulation 419
uncertainty 338
see also Production systems
SADT 290
Satisficing **309**, 449
  bounded rationality **449**
  decision-making models 99, 131, 196, 234, 488
  recognitional decision making 416
Schafer's rule see Dempster–Schafer rule
Scenarios 501
  decision-problem structuring 109
  forecasting 516
  prototyping
    software engineering 292
  requirements analysis 395
Scheduling
  CASE 70
  expert systems for management 168
  information systems design 301
  network planning methods 506
  supervisory control 439
  systems acquisition 456
  see also Planning
Schema 472
  knowledge representation **328**
Scientific method **480**, 484
Scripts **330**, 472
  human information processing models 222
  knowledge representation 164, 325
  planning 53
Searching
  artificial intelligence 10
  CASE 75
  expert systems 164
  problem solving
    organizational decision making 100
  text retrieval 4
Security of data
  group decision support systems 199
Self-organizing systems see Learning systems
Semantic networks **10**
  associative memory and retrieval 6, 326
  conceptual dependency diagrams 10
  expert systems for modelling 171
  inheritance 6, 10
  knowledge representation 164, 325, **326**
  learning systems 49
  memory models 45
  structural modelling 501
Semantics
  encoding 221
  memory models 46, 431
  natural-language processing 12
  scientific method 480

Sensitivity analysis 81
  decision analysis 92
  probability intervals 340
  regression analysis 475
  trend extrapolation 515
  uncertainty 338
Sensory perception *see* Physiological studies
Serial processing
  associative memory and retrieval 2
Shells
  expert systems 166, 170
    group decision support systems 203
    knowledge-based simulation 318
    storyboards 314
Similarity
  associative memory and retrieval 2
  decision making 32
  learning systems 12
SIMSCRIPT 321
SIMULA 321
Simulation *419*, *421*, 425
  artificial intelligence *420*, 428
  CASE 70
  cognitive maps 328
  computer-assisted instruction 82
  cross-impact analysis 262
  decision-problem structuring 109
  discrete-event simulation 320
  expert systems 170, 420
  forecasting 516
  Forrester models 320
  history 482
  human factors engineering 215
  knowledge-based simulation *316*
  military decision making 69
  model generation 420, 421
  model manipulation 420
  model-base systems 423, *425*
  neural networks
    learning systems 11
  organizational decision making 138
  Petri nets
    C3I systems 70
  programming environments 318
  random-variate generation 321
  requirements analysis 395
  systems analysis methods *504*
  top-down methods *421*
  tutorial simulation 82
  see also Modelling
Simulation languages 422
  artificial intelligence 420
  knowledge-based simulation 317
  model-base systems 424
Simulators 216
Situation calculus
  automated planning 18
Skill

learning 49, 431
  philosophy of systems 488
  problem solving 30
  social effects of automation 24
  software development 438
Slots
  knowledge representation 169
SMALLTALK 159
Sociological studies
  automation *21*
    office automation 367
  conflict analysis 490
  human factors engineering 217
  organizations 97, 132, 197
  rationality 486
  social judgement theory 128, *451*
  social welfare functions 186
Software engineering
  CASE *70*
    information systems design 289
  configuration management 470
  data structured systems 289
  decision support systems 113
  expert database systems 158
  expert systems 293
  human information processing *429*
  information requirements determination 281
  knowledge-based simulation 317, 321
  modelling 435
  Petri nets 290
  prototyping 292, 322, 390
  real-time software *403*
  reusability 471
  software process *432*
  software productivity *287*
  systems integration 470
  systems design methodology 390
  validation 433
  verification 433
Software process *see* Software engineering
Space vehicles
  automated planning 20
Spreadsheets
  CASE 70
  computer literacy 81
  decision support systems 115
  expert systems for modelling 171
  group decision support systems 197, 202
  information systems design 298
  office automation 364
SQL 158
SREM 290
Stability
  conflict analysis 492
States of nature
  decision analysis 87
    generating methods 107
    option generation 105

Statistical analysis
   C3I systems 69
   CASE 72, 75
   expert systems for modelling 170
   forecasting *473*
   hypothesis testing *252*, 474
   information theory 302
   philosophy 484
   program evaluation 383
   scientific method 480
Statistics
   information theory 304
Stock control *see* Inventory control
Storyboards *see* Prototyping
Strategies
   automated strategic planning 20
   conflict analysis 491
   military systems 65
   multiattribute decision analysis 93
   planning decisions 110, 194
   systems acquisition 463
Stress (psychological) *see* Psychological studies
STRIPS 16, 52
Structural modelling 501
   decision making 279
   organizational information structures *368*
   Petri nets 369
   regression analysis 475
Structured analysis
   information systems 289, 297
   see also Systems analysis
Supervisory control *439*
Symbolic processing 44
Synetics 500
   decision-problem structuring 107
Syntax
   memory models 46, 431
   natural-language processing 12
   scientific method 480
System acquisition 74
System analysis
   C3I systems 70
   functional analysis 468
   time series *472*
System failure and recovery 469
System identification *see* Identification
System synthesis
   C3I systems 70
   CASE 72
   collective enquiry 63
   functional analysis 468
Systems acquisition *454*
   constraint satisfaction 459
   decision analytic methods 463
   knowledge-based methods *457*
Systems analysis
   cross-impact analysis 262
   decision analysis 87

   dependency analysis 276
   history *481*
   information systems
      software productivity 290
   information theory *271*, 302
   instructional systems 78
   military systems 481
   prototyping *388*
   real-time software 406
   reconstructability analysis 276
   requirements analysis 393
   structural methods 276
   structured analysis
      real-time software design 406
Systems concepts
   history *480*
   philosophy *484*
Systems design *see* Design, System analysis, System synthesis
Systems engineering *71*, *73*, *497*
   architectures 73
   availability 470
   C3I systems 64
   CASE *70*
      information systems design 289
   collective enquiry 63
   cross-impact analysis 262
   decision analysis 90
   decision support systems 111
   design *116*, 389
      environments 121
      information systems 128
   dialectic learning 101
   evaluation *125*
   functional analysis
      systems integration 468
   history 481
   human factors engineering 214
   human information processing 36
   hypothesis testing 253
   information requirements determination 278
   information systems design 289, *298*
   information systems integration 466
   integration 466
   life cycles 73
   maintenance 470
   reliability 469
   requirements analysis 313
   software development 432, 434, 470
   systems acquisition 454, 457
   technical issues 487
Systems integration *466*
   data communications 471
   human factors engineering 212
   information systems 203, 206
Systems management 39, 74, 116, 498
   conflict analysis *490*
   knowledge representation 324

Systems methodology **496**
  analysis 501
  information requirements determination 278
  information theory 271
  issue formulation 499
  program evaluation **382**
  simulation 419
  software development 434
Systems procurement 454, 457, 458
  decision analysis 463
Systems science **498**
  dynamic decision making 144
Systems synthesis
  history 482
Tactics
  automated tactical planning 20
  military systems 65
TAGS 289
Tasks
  data flow diagrams 409
  human factors engineering 212
  real-time software design **409**
  requirements analysis **393**
Teaching *see* Education
Technology
  assessment 22
  forecasting 22
TEIRESIAS 165, 166, 333
Telecommunications
  office automation **362**
  social effects of automation 26
  telecommuting **364**
Teleconferencing 204, 365
  videoconferencing 366
Text presentation 245
Text retrieval
  artificial intelligence 14
  CMDRS 3
  office automation 363
  see also Information retrieval
Thermodynamics
  information theory 277
Thought *see* Cognitive science
Time series
  forecasting **472**, 503, 515
  modelling 477
Tools (software) *see* Software engineering
Top-down methods
  human factors engineering 218
  information requirements determination 282
  information systems design 135
  planning 53
  simulation **421**
  software development 435
  software productivity 288
  systems engineering 72
Trade-offs *see* Utility theory
Training
  cost-effectiveness analysis 79
  human factors engineering 215
  see also Education
Transactions
  object-oriented database systems 159
  task synchronization 410
Translation
  expert systems 171
Trees (mathematics)
  constraint satisfaction problem 461
  decision trees 88
    group decision support systems 203
  fault trees 107
  hierarchical inference 265
  issue formulation 501
  model-base systems 426
  value trees 105
Trends
  extrapolation **476**, 503, 515
Turing, A 9
Turing test 9
Uncertainty
  Bayes' rule 336
  decision analysis 87
  decision making **338**
  Dempster–Schafer rule 340
  fuzzy set theory 339
  Heisenberg's uncertainty principle 277
  heuristics 337
  information processing **336**
  information requirements determination 281
  information theory 272, 303
  linguistic imprecision 339
  military decision making 68
  organizational decision making 100
  probability **336**, 340
  problem formulation 377
  psychological studies 341
  scientific method 480
  semantic networks 327
  software development 436
Utility theory
  CASE 75
  decision analysis **88**, **90**, 103
  decision rules 233
  group decision making 183, 188
  independence 347
  indifference methods 354
  lotteries 90
  mean-variance 236
  multiattribute utility theory **345**, **356**
  multiplicative group utility 192
  ranking 353
  subjective expected utility 235, 450
  subjective utility **237**
  systems acquisition 458
  trade-offs 354
  see also Multiattribute utility theory

Validation 504
    expert systems for management 169
    forecasting 517
    knowledge acquisition 314
    simulation models 420, 425
    software development 433, 470
    systems acquisition 455
    time series modelling 477
Value of information 279
    distributed decision making 134
    group decision support systems 200
Values 499
Verification 504
    simulation models 420
    software development 433, 470
    time series modelling 477
Very-high-level languages
    expert systems 166
    see also Fourth-generation languages
VHLLs *see* Very-high-level languages
Video for electronic meetings 366

Vision analysis *see* Picture processing
von Neumann, J 9
Voting *183*, 506
    Arrow's social choice theory 134, *186*
    group decision support systems 206
    paradox 134, *184*
    social welfare functions 186
Wholistic methods
    decision rules *241*
    knowledge representation 323
Wide-area networks
    group decision support systems 203
Word processing *361*
    computer literacy 81
    group decision support systems 202
    history 484
Workload
    human factors engineering 215, 218
    social effects of automation 24
Workstations *see* Interactive terminals
Worth assessment 91